Lecture Notes in Computer Science 4022

Commenced Publication in 1973
Founding and Former Series Editors:
Gerhard Goos, Juris Hartmanis, and Jan van Leeuwen

Carol Peters   Fredric C. Gey
Julio Gonzalo   Henning Müller
Gareth J.F. Jones   Michael Kluck
Bernardo Magnini   Maarten de Rijke (Eds.)

Accessing Multilingual Information Repositories

6th Workshop of the Cross-Language Evalution Forum, CLEF 2005
Vienna, Austria, 21-23 September, 2005
Revised Selected Papers

Springer

Volume Editors

Carol Peters, Istituto di Scienza e Tecnologie dell'Informazione, 56124 Pisa, Italy
E-mail: carol.peters@isti.cnr.it

Fredric C. Gey, University of California, Berkeley CA, USA
E-mail: gey@berkeley.edu

Julio Gonzalo, Universidad Nacional de Educación a Distancia, 28040 Madrid, Spain
E-mail: julio@lsi.uned.es

Henning Müller, University and Hospitals of Geneva, 1211 Geneva 4, Switzerland
E-mail: Henning.Mueller@sim.hcuge.ch

Gareth J.F. Jones, Dublin City University, Ireland
E-mail: gareth@computing.dcu.ie

Michael Kluck, Stiftung für Wissenschaft und Politk, 10719 Berlin, Germany
E-mail: Michael.Kluck@swp-berlin.org

Bernardo Magnini, Centro Ricerca Scientifica e Tecnologica, 38050 Povo, Italy
E-mail: magnini@itc.it

Maarten de Rijke, University of Amsterdam, Amsterdam, The Netherlands
E-mail: mdr@science.uva.nl

Managing Editor
Danilo Giampiccolo, CELCT, Trento, Italy
E-mail: giampiccolo@celct.it

Library of Congress Control Number: 200692799

CR Subject Classification (1998): H.3, I.2, H.4

LNCS Sublibrary: SL 3 – Information Systems and Application, incl. Internet/Web and HCI

ISSN 0302-9743
ISBN-10 3-540-45697-X Springer Berlin Heidelberg New York
ISBN-13 978-3-540-45697-1 Springer Berlin Heidelberg New York

Springer is a part of Springer Science+Business Media

springer.com

Printed in Germany

Typesetting: Camera-ready by author, data conversion by Scientific Publishing Services, Chennai, India
Printed on acid-free paper SPIN: 11878773 06/3142 5 4 3 2 1 0

Preface

The sixth campaign of the Cross Language Evaluation Forum (CLEF) for European languages was held from January to September 2005. CLEF is by now an established international evaluation initiative and 74 groups from all over the world submitted results for one or more of the different evaluation tracks in 2005, compared with 54 groups in 2004. There were eight distinct evaluation tracks, designed to test the performance of a wide range of systems for multilingual information access. Full details regarding the design of the tracks, the methodologies used for evaluation, and the results obtained by the participants can be found in the different sections of these proceedings.

As always the results of the campaign were reported and discussed at the annual workshop held in Vienna, Austria, September 21-23, immediately following the ninth European Conference on Digital Libraries. The workshop was attended by approximately 110 academic and industrial researchers and system developers. In addition to presentations by participants in the campaign, Noriko Kando from the National Institute of Informatics, Tokyo, gave an invited talk on the activities of the NTCIR evaluation initiative for Asian languages. Breakout sessions gave participants a chance to discuss ideas and results in detail. The final session was dedicated to proposals for activities for CLEF 2006. The presentations given at the workshop can be found on the CLEF Web site at: www.clef-campaign.org. We should like to thank the other members of the CLEF Steering Committee for their assistance in the coordination of this event.

These post-campaign proceedings represent extended and revised versions of the initial working notes presented at the workshop. All papers were subjected to a reviewing procedure. The final volume was prepared with the assistance of the Center for the Evaluation of Language and Communication Technologies (CELCT), Trento, Italy, under the coordination of Danilo Giampiccolo. The support of CELCT is gratefully acknowledged. We should also like to thank all our reviewers for their careful refereeing.

CLEF 2005 was an activity of the DELOS Network of Excellence for Digital Libraries, within the framework of the Information Society Technologies programme of the European Commission.

May 2006

Carol Peters
Fredric C. Gey
Julio Gonzalo
Gareth J.F. Jones
Michael Kluck
Bernardo Magnini
Henning Müller
Maarten de Rijke

Organization

Reviewers

The Editors express their gratitude to the colleagues listed below for their assistance in reviewing the papers in this volume:

- Mirna Adriani, Faculty of Computer Science, University of Indonesia, Indonesia
- Javier Artiles, Departamento de Lenguajes y Sistemas Informáticos, UNED, Madrid, Spain
- Paul Clough, Dept. of Information Studies, University of Sheffield, UK
- Thomas Deselaers, Lehrstuhl für Informatik 6, Aachen University of Technology (RWTH), Germany
- Giorgio Di Nunzio, Dept. of Information Engineering, University of Padua, Italy
- Nicola Ferro, Dept. of Information Engineering, University of Padua, Italy
- Carlos Figuerola, REINA Research Group, University of Salamanca, Spain
- Cam Fordyce, CELCT, Centre for Evaluation of Language and Communication Technologies, Trento, Italy
- Pamela Forner, CELCT, Centre for Evaluation of Language and Communication Technologies, Trento, Italy
- Danilo Giampiccolo, CELCT, Centre for Evaluation of Language and Communication Technologies, Trento, Italy
- Michael Grubinger, School of Computer Science and Mathematics, Victoria University, Melbourne, Australia
- Errol Haymann, CELCT, Centre for Evaluation of Language and Communication Technologies, Trento, Italy
- William Hersh, Dept. of Medical Informatics and Clinical Epidemiology, Oregon Health and Science University, Portland, USA
- Jeffery Jensen, Dept. of Medical Informatics and Clinical Epidemiology, Oregon Health and Science University, Portland, USA
- Jaap Kamps, Archive and Documentation Studies, University of Amsterdam, The Netherlands
- Thomas M. Lehmann, Dept. of Medical Informatics, Aachen University of Technology (RWTH), Germany
- Craig Macdonald, Dept. of Computing Science, University of Glasgow, UK
- Bernardo Magnini, Centro per la Ricerca Scientifica e Tecnologica, ITC-irst, Trento, Italy
- Thomas Mandl, Information Science, University of Hildesheim, Germany
- Trinitario Martínez, Dept. of Software and Computing Systems, University of Alicante, Spain
- Angel Martínez-Gonzales, Universidad Politécnica de Madrid, Spain
- David Pinto, Faculty of Computer Science, BUAP, Mexico
- Börkur Sigurbjörnsson, Informatics Institute, University of Amsterdam, The Netherlands
- Stephen Tomlinson, Hummingbird, USA

CLEF 2005 Coordination

CLEF is coordinated by the Istituto di Scienza e Tecnologie dell'Informazione, Consiglio Nazionale delle Ricerche, Pisa.

The following institutions contributed to the organization of the different tracks of the CLEF 2005 campaign:

- Centre for the Evaluation of Human Language and Multimodal Communication Technologies (CELCT), Trento, Italy
- Centro per la Ricerca Scientifica e Tecnologica, Istituto Trentino di Cultura, Trento, Italy
- College of Information Studies and Institute for Advanced Computer Studies, University of Maryland, USA
- Department of Computer Science, University of Helsinki, Finland
- Department of Computer Science and Information Systems, University of Limerick, Ireland
- Department of Information Engineering, University of Padua, Italy
- Department of Information Studies, University of Sheffield, UK
- Evaluations and Language Resources Distribution Agency (ELDA), Paris, France
- German Research Centre for Artificial Intelligence, DFKI, Saarbrücken, Germany
- Information and Language Processing Systems, University of Amsterdam, Netherlands
- Informationszentrum Sozialwissenschaften, Bonn, Germany
- IRMA group, Aachen University of Technology (RWTH), Germany
- Lenguajes y Sistemás Informáticos, Universidad Nacional de Educación a Distancia, Madrid, Spain
- Linguateca, Sintef, Oslo, Norway
- Linguistic Modelling Laboratory, Bulgarian Academy of Sciences, Bulgaria
- National Institute of Standards and Technology, Gaithersburg MD, USA
- Oregon Health and Science University, USA
- Research Computing Center of Moscow State University, Russia
- Research Institute for Linguistics, Hungarian Academy of Sciences, Hungary
- School of Computing, Dublin City University, Ireland
- School of Computer Science and Mathematics, Victoria University, Australia
- UC Data Archive and School of Information Management and Systems, UC Berkeley, USA
- University and University Hospitals of Geneva, Switzerland

CLEF 2005 Steering Committee

- Maristella Agosti, University of Padua, Italy
- Martin Braschler, Zurich University of Applied Sciences Winterthur, Switzerland
- Amedeo Cappelli, ISTI-CNR & CELCT, Italy
- Hsin-Hsi Chen, National Taiwan University, Taipei, Taiwan
- Khalid Choukri, Evaluations and Language Resources Distribution Agency, Paris, France
- Paul Clough, University of Sheffield, UK
- David A. Evans, Clairvoyance Corporation, USA
- Marcello Federico, ITC-irst, Trento, Italy
- Christian Fluhr, CEA-LIST, Fontenay-aux-Roses, France
- Norbert Fuhr, University of Duisburg, Germany
- Frederic C. Gey, U.C. Berkeley, USA
- Julio Gonzalo, LSI-UNED, Madrid, Spain
- Donna Harman, National Institute of Standards and Technology, USA
- Gareth Jones, Dublin City University, Ireland
- Franciska de Jong, University of Twente, Netherlands
- Noriko Kando, National Institute of Informatics, Tokyo, Japan
- Jussi Karlgren, Swedish Institute of Computer Science, Sweden
- Michael Kluck, Informationszentrum Sozialwissenschaften Bonn, Germany
- Natalia Loukachevitch, Moscow State University, Russia
- Bernardo Magnini, ITC-irst, Trento, Italy
- Paul McNamee, Johns Hopkins University, USA
- Henning Müller, University and Hospitals of Geneva, Switzerland
- Douglas W. Oard, University of Maryland, USA
- Maarten de Rijke, University of Amsterdam, Netherlands
- Diana Santos, Linguateca, Sintef, Oslo, Norway
- Jacques Savoy, University of Neuchatel, Switzerland
- Peter Schäuble, Eurospider Information Technologies, Switzerland
- Max Stempfhuber, Informationszentrum Sozialwissenschaften Bonn, Germany
- Richard Sutcliffe, University of Limerick, Ireland
- Hans Uszkoreit, German Research Center for Artificial Intelligence (DFKI), Germany
- Felisa Verdejo, LSI-UNED, Madrid, Spain
- José Luis Vicedo, University of Alicante, Spain
- Ellen Voorhees, National Institute of Standards and Technology, USA
- Christa Womser-Hacker, University of Hildesheim, Germany

Table of Contents

Monolingual Experiments

Part II. Domain-Specific Information Retrieval (Domain-Specific)

Part III. Interactive Cross-Language Information Retrieval (iCLEF)

Part IV. Multiple Language Question Answering (QA@CLEF)

Part V. Cross-Language Retrieval In Image Collections (ImageCLEF)

Part VIII. Cross-Language Geographical Retrieval (GeoCLEF)

Evaluation Issues

What Happened in CLEF 2005

Carol Peters

Istituto di Scienza e Tecnologie dell'Informazione (ISTI-CNR), Pisa, Italy
carol.peters@isti.cnr.it

Abstract. The organization of the CLEF 2005 evaluation campaign is described and details are provided concerning the tracks, test collections, evaluation infrastructure and participation.

1 Introduction

This volume reports the results of the sixth in a series of annual system evaluation campaigns organised by the Cross-Language Evaluation Forum (CLEF)[1]. The main objectives of CLEF are (i) to provide an infrastructure that facilitates testing of all kinds of multilingual information access systems – from monolingual retrieval for multiple languages to the implementation of complete multilingual multimedia search services, and (ii) to construct test-suites of reusable data that can be used for benchmarking purposes. These objectives are achieved through the organisation of evaluation campaigns that culminate each year in a workshop in which the groups that participated in the campaign can report and discuss their experiments. An additional aim of CLEF is to encourage contacts between the R&D and the application communities and promote the industrial take-up of research results.

The main features of the 2005 campaign are briefly outlined below in order to provide the necessary background to the experiments reported in these post-campaign proceedings.

2 Tracks and Tasks in CLEF 2005

Over the years CLEF has gradually increased the number of different tracks and tasks offered in order to facilitate experimentation with all kinds of multilingual information access. CLEF 2005 offered eight tracks designed to evaluate the performance of systems for:

- mono-, bi- and multilingual textual retrieval on news collections (Ad Hoc)
- mono- and cross-language retrieval on structured scientific data (Domain-Specific)
- interactive cross-language retrieval (iCLEF)

[1] CLEF 2005 was included in the activities of the DELOS Network of Excellence on Digital Libraries, funded by the Sixth Framework Programme of the European Commission. For information on DELOS, see www.delos.info.

C. Peters et al. (Eds.): CLEF 2005, LNCS 4022, pp. 1 – 10, 2006.

- multiple language question answering (QA@CLEF)
- cross-language retrieval in image collections (ImageCLEF)
- cross-language spoken document retrieval (CL-SR)
- multilingual retrieval of Web documents (WebCLEF)
- cross-language geographic retrieval (GeoCLEF)

Cross-Language Text Retrieval (Ad Hoc): As in past years, the CLEF 2005 ad hoc track was structured in three tasks, testing systems for monolingual (querying and finding documents in one language), bilingual (querying in one language and finding documents in another language) and multilingual (querying in one language and finding documents in multiple languages) retrieval. The monolingual and bilingual tasks were principally offered for Bulgarian, French, Hungarian and Portuguese target collections. Additionally, in the bilingual task only, newcomers (i.e. groups that had not previously participated in a CLEF cross-language task) or groups using a "new-to-CLEF" query language could choose to search the English document collection. The Multilingual task was based on the CLEF 2003 multilingual-8 test collection which contained news documents in eight languages: Dutch, English, French, German, Italian, Russian, Spanish, and Swedish. There were two subtasks: a traditional multilingual retrieval task requiring participants to carry out retrieval and merging (Multi-8 Two-Years-On), and a new task focussing only on the multilingual results merging problem using standard sets of ranked retrieval output (Multi-8 Merging Only).

Cross-Language Scientific Data Retrieval (Domain-Specific): This track studied retrieval in a domain-specific context using the GIRT-4 German/English social science database and the Russian Social Science Corpus (RSSC). Multilingual controlled vocabularies (German-English, English-German, German-Russian, English-Russian) were available. Monolingual and cross-language tasks were offered. Topics were prepared in English, German and Russian. Participants could make use of the indexing terms inside the documents and/or the Social Science Thesaurus provided, not only as translation means, but also for tuning relevance decisions of their system.

Interactive CLIR (iCLEF): This year, iCLEF focused on problems of cross-language question answering and image retrieval from a user-inclusive perspective. Participating groups were to adapt a shared user study design to test a hypothesis of their choice, comparing reference and contrastive systems.

Multilingual Question Answering (QA@CLEF): Monolingual (non-English) and cross-language QA systems were tested. Combinations between nine target collections (Bulgarian, Dutch, English, Finnish, French, German, Italian, Portuguese and Spanish) and questions in ten languages (the target languages plus Indonesian) were explored. Both factoid and definition questions were provided as input; a subset of the factoid questions was temporally restricted. New evaluation measures were introduced in order to build more challenging test sets and to explore the self-scoring ability of systems.

Cross-Language Retrieval in Image Collections (ImageCLEF): The aim of this track was to explore the use of both text and content-based retrieval methods for cross-language image retrieval. Three main tasks were offered: ad-hoc retrieval from a historic photographic collection, ad-hoc retrieval from a medical collection, and an automatic image annotation task on medical data.

Cross-Language Speech Retrieval (CL-SR): The focus this year was on searching spontaneous speech from oral history interviews rather than news broadcasts. The test collection created for the track in 2005 was an English subset of a large archive of videotaped oral histories from survivors, liberators, rescuers and witnesses of the Holocaust created by the Survivors of the Shoah Visual History Foundation (VHF). Topics were translated from English into Czech, French, German and Spanish to facilitate cross-language experimentation.

The final two tracks were introduced for the first time in CLEF 2005 as trial pilot tracks.

Multilingual Web Retrieval (WebCLEF): The aim of this track was to evaluate systems that address multilingual information needs on the web. Three tasks were organized: mixed monolingual, multilingual, and bilingual English to Spanish, with homepage and named page finding queries.

Cross-Language Geographical Retrieval (GeoCLEF): The aim of GeoCLEF was to provide the necessary framework in which to evaluate geographic IR systems for search tasks involving both spatial and multilingual aspects. Participants were offered an ad hoc style retrieval task based on existing CLEF collections but with a geographic orientation.

Details on the technical infrastructure, organisation and results of these tracks can be found in the track overview reports in this volume, collocated at the beginning of each section.

3 Document Collections

Seven different document collections were used in CLEF 2005 to build the test collections:

- CLEF multilingual comparable corpus of more than 2 million news docs in 12 languages (see Table 1)
- The GIRT-4 social science database in English and German and the Russian Social Science Corpus
- St Andrews historical photographic archive
- CasImage radiological medical database with case notes in French and English
- IRMA collection in English and German for automatic medical image annotation
- Malach collection of spontaneous conversational speech derived from the Shoah archives
- EuroGOV, a multilingual collection of about 2M webpages crawled from European governmental sites.

Two new collections – Bulgarian and Hungarian newspapers for 2002 - were added to the multilingual corpus this year. Moreover, the Portuguese collection was expanded

Table 1. Sources and dimensions of the main CLEF 2005 multilingual document collection

Collection	Added in	Size (MB)	No. of Docs	Median Size Docs. (Bytes)	Median Size Docs. (Tokens)[2]	Median Size of Docs (Features)
Bulgarian: Sega 2002	2005	120	33,356	NA	NA	NA
Bulgarian: Standart 2002	2005	93	35,839	NA	NA	NA
Dutch: Algemeen Dagblad 94/95	2001	241	106483	1282	166	112
Dutch: NRC Handelsblad 94/95	2001	299	84121	2153	354	203
English: LA Times 94	2000	425	113005	2204	421	246
English: Glasgow Herald 95	2003	154	56472	2219	343	202
Finnish: Aamulehti 94/95	2002	137	55344	1712	217	150
French: Le Monde 94	2000	158	44013	1994	361	213
French: ATS 94	2001	86	43178	1683	227	137
French: ATS 95	2003	88	42615	1715	234	140
German: Frankfurter Rundschau94	2000	320	139715	1598	225	161
German: Der Spiegel 94/95	2000	63	13979	1324	213	160
German: SDA 94	2001	144	71677	1672	186	131
German: SDA 95	2003	144	69438	1693	188	132
Hungarian: Magyar Hirlap'02	2005	105	49,530	NA	NA	NA
Italian: La Stampa 94	2000	193	58051	1915	435	268
Italian: AGZ 94	2001	86	50527	1454	187	129
Italian: AGZ 95	2003	85	48980	1474	192	132
Portuguese: Público 94	2004	164	51751	NA	NA	NA
Portuguese: Público 95	2004	176	55070	NA	NA	NA
Portuguese: Folha 94	2005	108	51,875	NA	NA	NA
Portuguese: Folha 94	2005	116	52,038	NA	NA	NA
Russian: Izvestia 95	2003	68	16761	NA	NA	NA
Spanish: EFE 94	2001	511	215738	2172	290	171
Spanish: EFE 95	2003	577	238307	2221	299	175
Swedish: TT 94/95	2002	352	142819	2171	183	121

SDA/ATS/AGZ = Schweizerische Depeschenagentur (Swiss News Agency); EFE = Agencia EFE S.A (Spanish News Agency); TT = Tidningarnas Telegrambyrå (Swedish newspaper)

NA = Not Available at this moment

[2] The number of tokens and features given in this table are approximations and may differ from actual implemented systems.

with the addition of a Brazilian newspaper: Folha. The multilingual corpus thus now contains approximately 2 million news documents in twelve languages, for 1994-1995: Dutch, English, Finnish, French, German, Italian, Portuguese, Russian, Spanish and Swedish, and for 2002: Bulgarian and Hungarian. Table 1 gives the main details.

Parts of this collection were used by the Ad Hoc (all languages except Finnish), Question Answering (all languages except Hungarian, Russian and Swedish), Interactive (English and French collections only) and GeoCLEF (English and German collections) tracks in CLEF 2005.

The domain-specific track used two collections: the GIRT-4 collection derived from the GIRT (German Indexing and Retrieval Test) social science database and RSSC (the Russian Social Science Corpus). GIRT-4 consists of over 150,000 documents and includes a pseudo-parallel English/German corpus. Controlled vocabularies in German-English and German-Russian were also made available to the participants. RSSC contains approximately 95,000 Russian social science documents.

The ImageCLEF track used three main collections: a collection of approximately 28,000 historic photographs with associated textual captions and metadata provided by St Andrews University, Scotland; a collection of about 9,000 medical images with French/English case notes made available by the University Hospitals, Geneva., and the IRMA database of 10,000 medical images made available by the IRMA group, Aachen University of Technology (RWTH).

The speech retrieval track used the MALACH collection extracted from the Shoah archives. The sub-collection used in CLEF 2005 contained 8,104 manually identified segments from 272 English interviews (589 hours). Automatic Speech Recognition (ASR) transcripts and both automatically assigned and manually assigned thesaurus terms were available as part of the collection.

The WebCLEF track used a collection crawled from European governmental sites, called EuroGOV. This collection consists of more than 3.35 million pages from 27 primary domains. The most frequent languages are Finnish (20%), German (18%), Hungarian (13%), English (10%), and Latvian (9%).

Each track was responsible for preparing its own topic/query statements and for performing relevance assessments of the results submitted by participating groups. The number of different topic languages differed from track to track from a minimum of three in the domain-specific track to more than twenty in the cross-language image retrieval track. Details and descriptions are given in the track overviews.

4 Evaluation Infrastructure

The CLEF technical evaluation infrastructure, currently used to manage the test data plus results submission and analyses for the ad hoc, question answering and geographic tracks, has been redesigned this year. The objective is to facilitate data management tasks but also to support the production and maintenance of the scientific data for subsequent in-depth evaluation studies. The technical infrastructure is thus now responsible for:

- the management of submission of experiments;
- the collection of metadata about experiments, and their validation;
- the creation of document pools and the management of relevance assessments;

- the provision of common statistical analysis tools for both organizers and participants in order to allow the comparison of experiments;
- the provision of common tools for summarizing, producing reports and graphs on the performances measured and analyses conducted.

The technical infrastructure is managed by the DIRECT system, developed at Padua University[3]

5 Participation

A total of 74 groups submitted runs in CLEF 2005, as opposed to 54 groups in CLEF 2004: 43(37) from Europe, 19(12) from North America; 10(5) from Asia and 1 each from South America and Australia. Last year's figures are given between brackets. Many groups participated in more than one track. The breakdown of participation of groups per track is as follows: Ad Hoc 23; Domain-Specific 8; iCLEF 5; QAatCLEF 24; ImageCLEF 24; CL-SR 7; WebCLEF 11; GeoCLEF 12. As in previous years,

Table 2. CLEF 2005 Participating Groups

Budapest U. Tech.&Econ. (HU)	Nat.Chiao-Tung U. (TW) *	U.Groningen (NL)
Bulgarian TreeBank (BG)*	Nat. Inst.Informatics (JP) *	U.Hagen (DE) **
California State U. (US)	Nat.Dong Hwa U. (TW) *	U.Helsinki (FI) *
CEA-LIST / LIC2M (FR)**	Nat.Taiwan U. (TW) ****	U.Hildesheim (DE) ***
Chinese U. of Hong Kong (CN)	Nat.U. Singapore (SG)	U.Indonesia (ID)
CLIPS-Grenoble (FR) **	Oregon Health & Sci. U. (US) *	U.Jaen (ES) ****
Carnegie Mellon U. (US)**	Priberam Informatica (PT)	U.Liege (BE)
Daedalus & Madrid Univs. (ES) **	RWTH Aaachen-CS (DE)*	U.Limerick (IE)**
	RWTH Aachen -Med.Inf. (DE)*	U.Lisbon (PT) *
DFKI (DE)**	SUNY Buffalo (US) **	U.Maryland (US) *****
Dublin City U.(IE) *	Swedish Inst.CS (SV) ****	U.Melbourne (AU)
ENSM - St Etienne (FR)	SYNAPSE Développement (FR)	U.Montreal (CA) *****
Hummingbird (CA) ****	Thomson Legal (US) ****	U. Nantes (FR)
Inst.Infocomm Research (SG)	U. Hospitals Geneva (CH) *	U.Neuchatel (CH) ****
IPAL-CNRS (IR2) (FR/SG)**	U.Alicante (ES) ****	U.Ottawa (CA)U.Pittsburgh (US)
IRIT/SIG,Toulouse (FR) ***	U.Amsterdam –Informatics1 (NL) ****	U.Politecnica Catalunya (ES)
ITC-irst Trento (IT) *****		U.Politecnica Valencia (ES)
Ist.Nac.Astrofisica, Optica, Electronica (MX)	U.Amsterdam –Informatics2 (NL)	U.Salamanca (ES)***
		U.Sheffield (UK) *****
Johns Hopkins U (US) *****	U.Autonomous Puebla (MX)	U.Stockholm (SV) *
LIMSI-CNRS (FR) **	U.Comahue (AR)	U.Surugadai (JP) **
Linguateca-Sintef (NO) *	U.Concordia (CA)	U.Waterloo (CA)
Linguit GmbH (DE)	U.Evora (PT)*	UC Berkeley -IM&S1(US)*****
Metacarta Inc (US)	U.Geneva (CH)	UC Berkeley-IM&S-2 (US) *
Moscow State U.(RU)	U.Glasgow (UK) *	UNED-LSI, (ES)****
Mount Holyoke College (US)	U.Granada (ES)	

[3] For more information, see G. Di Nunzio & N. Ferro, DIRECT: a System for Evaluating Information Access Components of Digital Libraries. In ECDL 2005 Proceedings, LNCS 3652, Springer, pp 483-484.

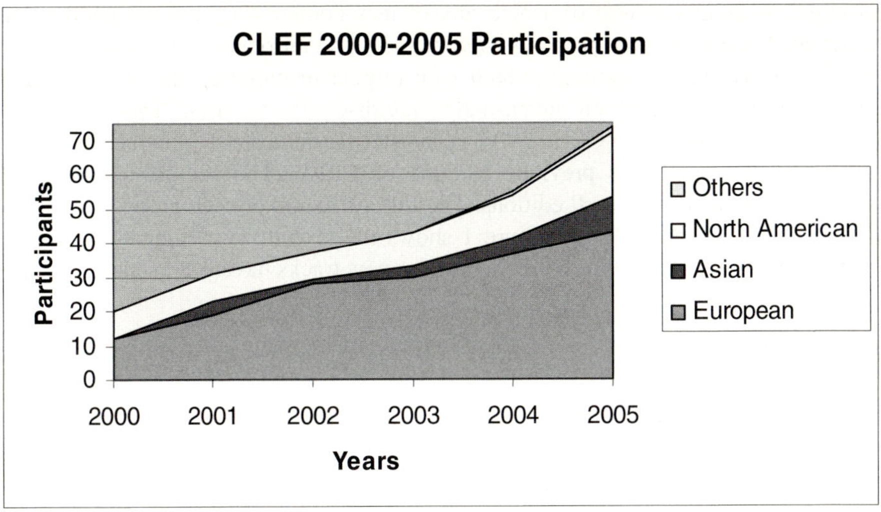

Fig. 1. CLEF 2000 – 2005 growth in participation

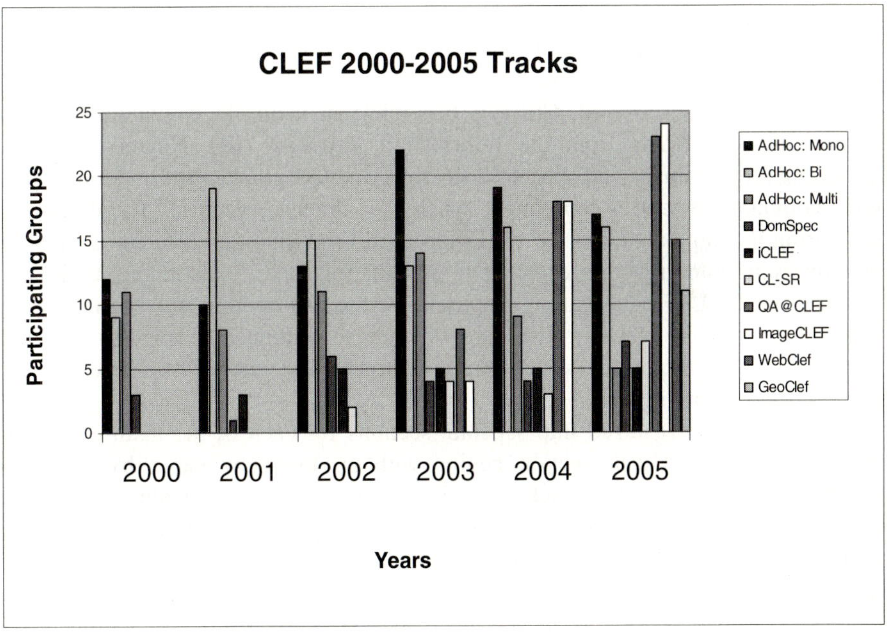

The mono-, bi-, and multilingual ad hoc tasks are listed separately; in 2002 the GIRT track also included the Amaryllis database.

Fig. 2. CLEF 2000 – 2005 - numbers of participants per track

participating groups consist of a nice mix of new-comers (26) and groups that had participated in one or more previous editions (48). The introduction of new tracks this year has clearly had a big impact both with respect to numbers and also regarding expertise – making CLEF an increasingly multidisciplinary forum. Table 2 lists the groups that participated in CLEF 2005 – the asterisks indicate the number of times a group has participated in previous editions of CLEF. The six groups with five asterisks have taken part in all editions. The full affiliation of each group can be seen in their papers in this volume. Figure 1 shows the growth in participation over the years and Figure 2 shows the shift in activity as new tracks have been added.

6 Main Results

CLEF 2005 saw a clear change in focus of interest from textual document retrieval to information extraction and multimedia retrieval over languages. This was evidenced, in particular, by the great success and consolidation of the tracks for cross-language question answering and cross-language retrieval in image collections (both introduced as pilots in 2003) and by the interest shown in the two new pilot tasks: WebCLEF and GeoCLEF. Research work was stimulated in many areas by the design of appropriate tasks within the tracks. In many cases, the problems studied were "new" (in the sense that this was the first time that an objective setting had been provided for testing, evaluation and comparison of the effectiveness of diverse approaches for a given problem).

As new areas are covered, CLEF is becoming an increasingly multidisciplinary forum with participants from the Information Retrieval (IR), Natural Language Processing (NLP), image and speech processing, and Geographic Information System (GIS) communities, and a consequent synergy of diverse expertise. The discussion lists during the campaign and the workshop at the end give the different groups the opportunity to come together exchanging and sharing ideas, experiences, tools and methodologies. CLEF puts a strong emphasis on resource building and sharing. Many groups that originally met at a CLEF workshop have continued to work together and collaborate. The result is a strong, well-connected and enthusiastic research and development community.

This volume is organized into separate sections for each of the main evaluation tracks listed above. Each section begins with an overview paper by the track coordinators describing the track objectives, setup, tasks and main results. The majority of the papers are thoroughly revised and expanded versions of the reports presented at the Workshop held in Vienna, Austria, September 2005. Many also include descriptions of additional experiments and results, as groups often further optimise their systems or try out new ideas as a consequence of discussions at the workshop. The final paper by Santos and Rocha reflects on the challenges that have to be addressed when adding language in CLEF evaluation activities. The individual results for all official ad hoc experiments in CLEF 2005 are given in the Appendix at the end of the Working Notes prepared for the 2005 Workshop. These are available online on the CLEF website at: http://www.clef-campaign.org/

Acknowledgements

It would be impossible to run the CLEF evaluation initiative and organize the annual workshops without considerable assistance from many groups. CLEF is organized on a distributed basis, with different research groups being responsible for the running of the various tracks. My gratitude goes to all those who have been involved in the coordination of the 2005 campaigns. A list of the main institutions involved is given at the beginning of this volume. Here below, let me thank those responsible for the coordination of the different tracks:

- Giorgio Di Nunzio, Nicola Ferro and Gareth Jones for the Ad Hoc Track
- Michael Kluck and Natalia Loukachevitch for the Domain-Specific track
- Julio Gonzalo, Paul Clough and Alessandro Vallin for iCLEF
- Bernardo Magnini, Alessandro Vallin, Danilo Giampiccolo, Lili Aunimo, Christelle Ayache, Petya Osenova, Anselmo Peñas, Maarten de Rijke, Bogdan Sacaleanu, Diana Santos and Richard Sutcliffe for QA@CLEF
- Paul Clough, Henning Müller, Thomas Deselaers , Michael Grubinger, Thomas Lehmann, Jeffery Jensen, and William Hersh for ImageCLEF
- Ryen W. White, Douglas W. Oard, Gareth J. F. Jones, Dagobert Soergel, Xiaoli Huang for CL-SR
- Börkur Sigurbjörnsson, Jaap Kamps, Maarten de Rijke for Web-CLEF
- Fredric Gey, Ray Larson, Mark Sanderson, Hideo Joho and Paul Clough for GeoCLEF

In addition, I must express my appreciation to Diana Santos and her colleagues at Linguateca in Norway and Portugal, for all their efforts aimed at supporting the inclusion of Portuguese in CLEF activities. I also thank all those colleagues who have helped us by preparing topic sets in different languages and in particular the NLP Lab., Dept. of Computer Science and Information Engineering of the National Taiwan University for their work on Chinese.

I should also like to thank the members of the CLEF Steering Committee who have assisted me with their advice and suggestions throughout this campaign.

Furthermore, I gratefully acknowledge the support of all the data providers and copyright holders, and in particular:

- The Los Angeles Times, for the American-English data collection
- SMG Newspapers (The Herald) for the British-English data collection
- Le Monde S.A. and ELDA: Evaluations and Language resources Distribution Agency, for the French data
- Frankfurter Rundschau, Druck und Verlagshaus Frankfurt am Main; Der Spiegel, Spiegel Verlag, Hamburg, for the German newspaper collections
- InformationsZentrum Sozialwissen-schaften, Bonn, for the GIRT database
- SocioNet system for the Russian Social Science Corpora
- Hypersystems Srl, Torino and La Stampa, for the Italian data
- Agencia EFE S.A. for the Spanish data

- NRC Handelsblad, Algemeen Dagblad and PCM Landelijke dagbladen/Het Parool for the Dutch newspaper data
- Aamulehti Oyj and Sanoma Osakeyhtiö for the Finnish newspaper data
- Russika-Izvestia for the Russian newspaper data
- Público, Portugal, and Linguateca for the Portuguese (PT) newspaper collection
- Folha, Brazil, and Linguateca for the Portuguese (BR) newspaper collection
- Tidningarnas Telegrambyrå (TT) SE-105 12 Stockholm, Sweden for the Swedish newspaper data
- Schweizerische Depeschenagentur, Switzerland, for the French, German and Italian Swiss news agency data
- Ringier Kiadoi Rt. [Ringier Publishing Inc.].and the Research Institute for Linguistics, Hungarian Acad. Sci. for the Hungarian newspaper documents
- Sega AD, Sofia; Standart Nyuz AD, Sofia, and the BulTreeBank Project, Linguistic Modelling Laboratory, IPP, Bulgarian Acad. Sci, for the Bulgarian newspaper documents
- St Andrews University Library for the historic photographic archive
- University and University Hospitals, Geneva, Switzerland and Oregon Health and Science University for the ImageCLEFmed Radiological Medical Database
- Aachen University of Technology (RWTH), Germany for the IRMA database of annotated medical images
- The Survivors of the Shoah Visual History Foundation, and IBM for the Malach spoken document collection

Without their contribution, this evaluation activity would be impossible.

Last and not least, I should like to express our gratitude to both Francesca Borri and Valeria Quochi at CNR in Pisa and Andreas Rauber and Rudolf Mayer, Technical University Vienna, for their assistance in the organisation of the CLEF 2005 Workshop.

CLEF 2005: Ad Hoc Track Overview

Giorgio M. Di Nunzio[1], Nicola Ferro[1], Gareth J.F. Jones[2], and Carol Peters[3]

[1] Department of Information Engineering, University of Padua, Italy
{dinunzio, ferro}@dei.unipd.it
[2] School of Computing, Dublin City University, Ireland
gjones@computing.dcu.ie
[3] ISTI-CNR, Area di Ricerca – 56124 Pisa – Italy
carol.peters@isti.cnr.it

Abstract. We describe the objectives and organization of the CLEF 2005 ad hoc track and discuss the main characteristics of the tasks offered to test monolingual, bilingual, and multilingual textual document retrieval. The performance achieved for each task is presented and a statistical analysis of results is given. The mono- and bilingual tasks followed the pattern of previous years but included target collections for two new-to-CLEF languages: Bulgarian and Hungarian. The multilingual tasks concentrated on exploring the reuse of existing test collections from an earlier CLEF campaign. The objectives were to attempt to measure progress in multilingual information retrieval by comparing the results for CLEF 2005 submissions with those of participants in earlier workshops, and also to encourage participants to explore multilingual list merging techniques.

1 Introduction

The ad hoc retrieval track is generally considered to be the core track in the *Cross-Language Evaluation Forum (CLEF)*. The aim of this track is to promote the development of monolingual and cross-language textual document retrieval systems. As in past years, the CLEF 2005 ad hoc track was structured in three tasks, testing systems for monolingual (querying and finding documents in one language), bilingual (querying in one language and finding documents in another language) and multilingual (querying in one language and finding documents in multiple languages) retrieval, thus helping groups to make the progression from simple to more complex tasks. The document collections used were taken from the CLEF multilingual comparable corpus of news documents.

The **Monolingual** and **Bilingual** tasks were principally offered for Bulgarian, French, Hungarian and Portuguese target collections. Additionally, in the bilingual task only, newcomers (i.e. groups that had not previously participated in a CLEF cross-language task) or groups using a "new-to-CLEF" query language could choose to search the English document collection. The aim in all cases was to retrieve relevant documents from the chosen target collection and submit the results in a ranked list.

C. Peters et al. (Eds.): CLEF 2005, LNCS 4022, pp. 11–36, 2006.

The **Multilingual** task was based on the CLEF 2003 multilingual-8 test collection which contained news documents in eight languages: Dutch, English, French, German, Italian, Russian, Spanish, and Swedish. There were two subtasks: a traditional multilingual retrieval task (Multi-8 Two-Years-On), and a new task focusing only on the multilingual results merging problem using standard sets of ranked retrieval output (Multi-8 Merging Only). One of the goals for the first task was to see whether it is possible to measure progress over time in multilingual system performance at CLEF by reusing a test collection created in a previous campaign. In running the merging only task our aim was to encourage participation by researchers interested in exploring the multilingual merging problem without the need to build retrieval systems for the document languages.

In this paper we describe the track setup, the evaluation methodology and the participation in the different tasks (Section 2) and present the main characteristics of the experiments and show the results (Sections 3 - 5). The final section provides a brief summing up. For information on the various approaches and resources used by the groups participating in this track and the issues they focused on, we refer the reader to the other papers in this section of the proceedings.

2 Track Setup

The ad hoc track in CLEF adopts a corpus-based, automatic scoring method for the assessment of system performance, based on ideas first introduced in the Cranfield experiments [1] in the late 1960s. The test collection used consists of a set of "topics" describing information needs and a collection of documents to be searched to find those documents that satisfy these information needs. Evaluation of system performance is then done by judging the documents retrieved in response to a topic with respect to their relevance, and computing the recall and precision measures. The distinguishing feature of CLEF is that it applies this evaluation paradigm in a multilingual setting. This means that the criteria normally adopted to create a test collection, consisting of suitable documents, sample queries and relevance assessments, have been adapted to satisfy the particular requirements of the multilingual context. All language dependent tasks such as topic creation and relevance judgment are performed in a distributed setting by native speakers. Rules are established and a tight central coordination is maintained in order to ensure consistency and coherency of topic and relevance judgment sets over the different collections, languages and tracks.

2.1 Test Collection

This year, for the first time, separate test collections were used in the ad hoc track: the monolingual and bilingual tasks were based on document collections in Bulgarian, English, French, Hungarian and Portuguese with new topics and relevance assessments, whereas the two multilingual tasks reused a test collection - documents, topics and relevance assessments - created in CLEF 2003.

Documents. The document collections used for the CLEF 2005 ad hoc tasks are part of the CLEF multilingual corpus of news documents described in the Introduction to these Proceedings.

In the monolingual and bilingual tasks, the English, French and Portuguese collections consisted of national newspapers and news agencies for the period 1994 and 1995. Different variants were used for each language. Thus, for English we had both US and British newspapers, for French we had a national newspaper of France plus Swiss French news agencies, and for Portuguese we had national newspapers from both Portugal and Brazil. This meant that, for each language, there were significant differences in orthography and lexicon over the sub-collections. This is a real world situation and system components, i.e. stemmers, translation resources, etc., should be sufficiently robust to handle such variants. The Bulgarian and Hungarian collections used in these tasks were new in CLEF 2005 and consisted of national newspapers for the year 2002[1]. This meant that the collections we used in the ad hoc mono- and bilingual tasks this year were not all for the same time period. This had important consequences on topic creation. For the multilingual tasks we reused the CLEF 2003 multilingual document collection. This consisted of news documents for 1994-95 in the eight languages listed above.

Topics. Topics in CLEF are structured statements representing information needs; the systems use the topics to derive their queries. Each topic consists of three parts: a brief "title" statement; a one-sentence "description"; a more complex "narrative" specifying the relevance assessment criteria.

Sets of 50 topics were created for the CLEF 2005 ad hoc mono- and bilingual tasks. One of the decisions taken early on in the organization of the CLEF ad hoc tracks was that the same set of topics would be used to query all collections, whatever the task. There are a number of reasons for this: it makes it easier to compare results over different collections, it means that there is a single master set that is rendered in all query languages, and a single set of relevance assessments for each language is sufficient for all tasks. However, the fact that the collections used in the CLEF 2005 ad hoc mono- and bilingual tasks were from two different time periods (1994-1995 and 2002) made topic creation particularly difficult. It was not possible to create time-dependent topics that referred to particular date-specific events as all topics had to refer to events that could have been reported in any of the collections, regardless of the dates. This meant that the CLEF 2005 topic set is somewhat different from the sets of previous years as the topics tend to be of broad coverage. However, it was difficult to construct topics that would find a limited number of relevant documents in each collection, and a - probably excessive - number of topics used for the 2005 mono- and bilingual tasks have a very large number of relevant documents. Although we have not analyzed in-depth the possible impact of this fact on results calculation, we suspect that it has meant that the 2005 ad hoc test collection is less

[1] It proved impossible to find national newspapers in electronic form for 1994 and/or 1995 in these languages.

effective in "discriminating" between the performance of different systems. For this reason, we subsequently decided to create separate test collections for the two different time-periods for the CLEF 2006 ad hoc mono- and bilingual tasks.

For the multilingual task, the CLEF 2003 topic sets of 60 topics were used. For CLEF 2005 these were divided into two sets: 20 topics for training and 40 for testing. Topics were potentially available in all the original languages for the CLEF 2003 tasks. For CLEF 2005 participants variously chose to use English, Dutch and Spanish language topics.

Below we give an example of the English version of a typical CLEF topic:

```
<top> <num> C254 </num>
<EN-title> Earthquake Damage </EN-title>
<EN-desc> Find documents describing damage to property or persons caused
by an earthquake and specifying the area affected.</EN-desc>
<EN-narr> Relevant documents will provide details on damage to buildings
and material goods or injuries to people as a result of an earthquake.
The geographical location (e.g. country, region, city) affected by the
earthquake must also be mentioned.</EN-narr>
</top>
```

2.2 Participation Guidelines

To carry out the retrieval tasks of the CLEF campaign, systems have to build supporting data structures. Allowable data structures include any new structures built automatically (such as inverted files, thesauri, conceptual networks, etc.) or manually (such as thesauri, synonym lists, knowledge bases, rules, etc.) from the documents. They may not, however, be modified in response to the topics, e.g. by adding topic words that are not already in the dictionaries used by their systems in order to extend coverage.

Some CLEF data collections contain manually assigned, controlled or uncontrolled index terms. The use of such terms has been limited to specific experiments that have to be declared as "manual" runs.

Topics can be converted into queries that a system can execute in many different ways. CLEF strongly encourages groups to determine what constitutes a base run for their experiments and to include these runs (officially or unofficially) to allow useful interpretations of the results. Unofficial runs are those not submitted to CLEF but evaluated using the trec_eval package. This year we have used the new package written by Chris Buckley for the *Text REtrieval Conference (TREC)* (trec_eval 7.3) and available from the TREC website.

As a consequence of limited evaluation resources, a maximum of 4 runs for each multilingual task and a maximum of 12 runs overall for the bilingual tasks, including all language combinations, was accepted. The number of runs for the monolingual task was limited to 12 runs. No more than 4 runs were allowed for any individual language combination. Overall, participants were allowed to submit at most 32 runs in total for the multilingual, bilingual and monolingual tasks.

2.3 Relevance Assessment

The number of documents in large test collections such as CLEF makes it impractical to judge every document for relevance. Instead approximate recall values are calculated using pooling techniques. The results submitted by the groups participating in the ad hoc tasks are used to form a pool of documents for each topic and language by collecting the highly ranked documents from all submissions. This pool is then used for subsequent relevance judgments. The stability of pools constructed in this way and their reliability for post-campaign experiments is discussed in [2] with respect to the CLEF 2003 pools. After calculating the effectiveness measures, the results are analyzed and run statistics produced and distributed. New pools were formed in CLEF 2005 for the runs submitted for the mono- and bilingual tasks and the relevance assessments were performed by native speakers. The multilingual tasks used the original pools and relevance assessments from CLEF 2003.

The individual results for all official ad hoc experiments in CLEF 2005 are given in the Appendix at the end of the on-line Working Notes prepared for the Workshop [3]. They are discussed below in Sections 3, 4 and 5, for the mono-, bi-, and multilingual tasks, respectively.

2.4 Result Calculation

Evaluation campaigns such as TREC and CLEF are based on the belief that the effectiveness of *Information Retrieval Systems (IRSs)* can be objectively evaluated by an analysis of a representative set of sample search results. For this, effectiveness measures are calculated based on the results submitted by the participant and the relevance assessments. Popular measures usually adopted for exercises of this type are Recall and Precision. Details on how they are calculated for CLEF are given in [4].

2.5 Participants and Experiments

As shown in Table 1, a total of 23 groups from 15 different countries submitted results for one or more of the ad hoc tasks - a slight decrease on the 26 participants of last year. A total of 254 experiments were submitted, nearly the same as the 250 experiments of 2004. Thus, there is a slight increase in the average number of submitted runs per participant: from 9.6 runs/participant of 2004 to 11 runs/participant of this year.

Participants were required to submit at least one title+description ("TD") run per task in order to increase comparability between experiments. The large majority of runs (188 out of 254, 74.02%) used this combination of topic fields, 54 (21.27%) used all fields, 10 (3.94%) used the title field, and only 2 (0.79%) used the description field. The majority of experiments were conducted using automatic query construction. A breakdown into the separate tasks is shown in Table 2(a).

Thirteen different topic languages were used in the ad hoc experiments - the Dutch run was in the multilingual tasks and used the CLEF 2003 topics.

Table 1. CLEF 2005 ad hoc participants – new groups are indicated by*

Part.icipant	Institution	Country
alicante	U. Alicante - Comp.Sci	Spain
buffalo	SUNY at Buffalo - Informatics	USA
clips	CLIPS-IMAG Grenoble	France
cmu	Carnegie Mellon U.- Lang.Tec.	USA
cocri	ENSM St. Etienne	France*
dcu	Dublin City U. - Comp.Sci.	Ireland
depok	U.Indonesia - Comp.Sci	Indonesia*
dsv-stockholm	U.Stockholm, NLP	Sweden
hildesheim	U.Hildesheim - Inf.Sci	Germany
hummingbird	Hummingbird Core Tech.	Canada
ilps	U.Amsterdam - Informatics	The Netherlands
isi-unige	U.Geneva - Inf.Systems	Switzerland*
jaen	U.Jaen - Intell.Systems	Spain
JHU/apl	Johns Hopkins U.- App.Physics	USA
miracle	Daedalus & Madrid Univs	Spain
msu-nivc	Moscow State U.- Computing	Russia*
sics	Swedish Inst. for Comp.Sci	Sweden
tlr	Thomson Legal Regulatory	USA
u.budapest	Budapest U. Tech. & Econom	Hungary*
u.glasgow	U.Glasgow - IR	UK
u.surugadai	U.Surugadai - Cultural Inf.	Japan
unine	U.Neuchatel - Informatics	Switzerland
xldb	U.Lisbon - Informatics	Portugal

As always, the most popular language for queries was English, and French was second. Note that Bulgarian and Hungarian, the new collections added this year, were quite popular as new monolingual tasks - Hungarian was also used in one case as a topic language in a bilingual run. The number of runs per topic language is shown in Table 2(b).

3 Monolingual Experiments

Monolingual retrieval was offered for Bulgarian, French, Hungarian, and Portuguese. As can be seen from Table 2(a), the number of participants and runs for each language was quite similar, with the exception of Bulgarian, which had a slightly smaller participation. This year just 5 groups out of 16 (31.25%) submitted monolingual runs only (down from ten groups last year), and just one of these groups was a first time participant in CLEF. This is in contrast with previous years where many new groups only participated in monolingual experiments. This year, most of the groups submitting monolingual runs were doing this as part of their bilingual or multilingual system testing activity.

Table 3 shows the top five groups for each target collection, ordered by mean average precision. The table reports: the short name of the participating group; the mean average precision achieved by the run; the run identifier, specifying

Table 2. Breakdown of experiments into tracks and topic languages

(a) Number of experiments per track, participant.

Track	# Part.	# Runs
AH-2-years-on	4	21
AH-Merging	3	20
AH-Bilingual-X2BG	4	12
AH-Bilingual-X2FR	9	31
AH-Bilingual-X2HU	3	7
AH-Bilingual-X2PT	8	28
AH-Bilingual-X2EN	4	13
AH-Monolingual-BG	7	20
AH-Monolingual-FR	12	38
AH-Monolingual-HU	10	32
AH-Monolingual-PT	9	32
Total		**254**

(b) List of experiments by topic language.

Topic Lang.		# Runs
EN	English	118
FR	French	42
HU	Hungarian	33
PT	Portuguese	33
BG	Bulgarian	32
ES	Spanish	20
ID	Indonesian	18
DE	German	15
AM	Amharic	8
GR	Greek	4
IT	Italian	3
RU	Russian	3
NL	Dutch	1
Total		**254**

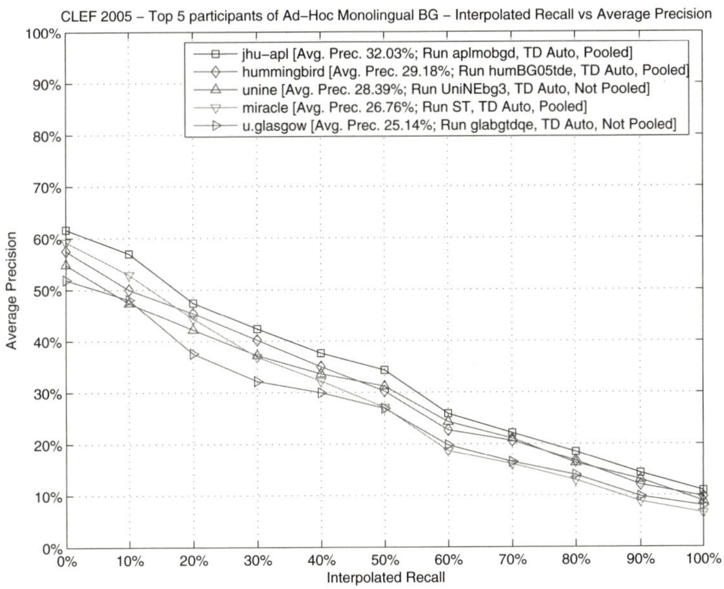

Fig. 1. Monolingual Bulgarian

whether the run has participated in the pool or not, and the page in Appendix A of the Working Notes [3] containing all figures and graphs for this run; and the performance difference between the first and the last participant. The pages of Appendix A containing the overview graphs are indicated under the name

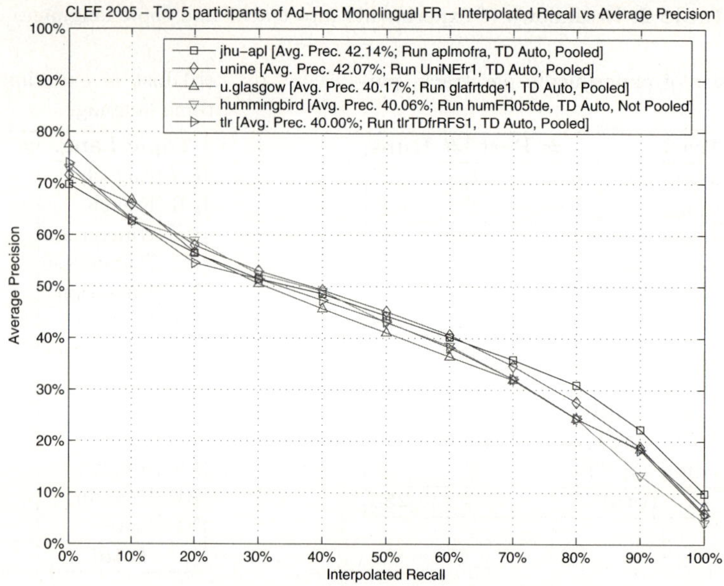

Fig. 2. Monolingual French

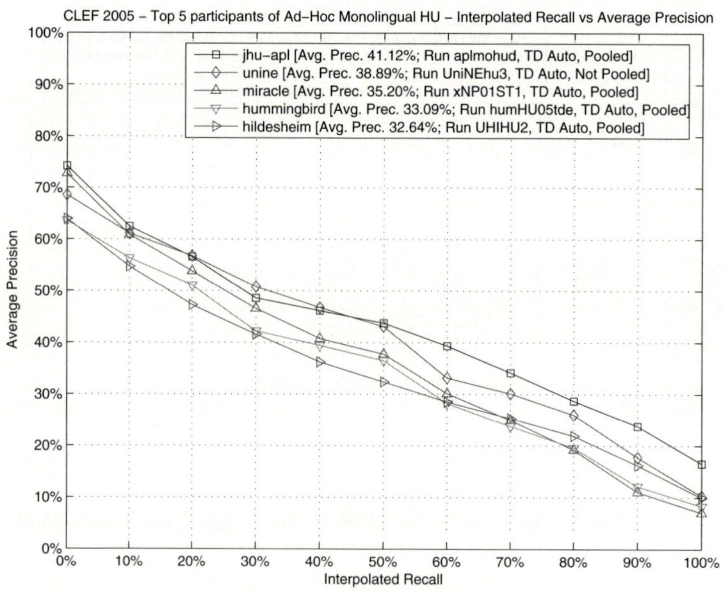

Fig. 3. Monolingual Hungarian

of the sub-task. Table 3 regards runs using title + description fields only (the mandatory run).

All the groups in the top five had participated in previous editions of CLEF. Both pooled and not pooled runs are included in the best entries for each track.

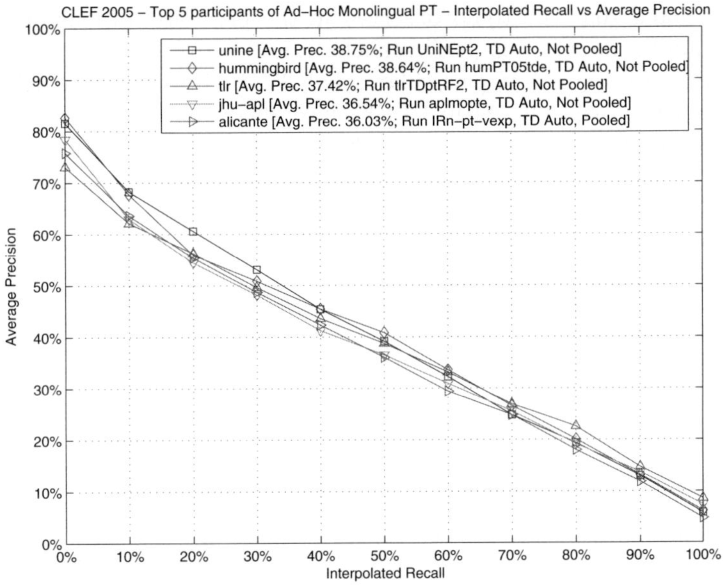

Fig. 4. Monolingual Portuguese

Table 3. Best entries for the monolingual track

Track	Participant Rank					Diff.
	1st	2nd	3rd	4th	5th	
Bulgarian (A.45–A.46)	jhu/apl 32.03% aplmobgd pooled (A.232)	hummingbird 29.18% humBG05tde pooled (A.230)	unine 28.39% UniNEbg3 not pooled (A.242)	miracle 26.76% ST pooled (A.235)	u.glasgow 25.14% glabgtdqe not pooled (A.239)	1st vs 5th 27.41%
French (A.49–A.50)	jhu/apl 42.14% aplmofra pooled (A.261)	unine 42.07% UniNEfr1 pooled (A.278)	u.glasgow 40.17% glafrtdqe1 pooled (A.275)	hummingbird 40.06% humFR05tde not pooled (A.260)	tlr 40.00% tlrTDfrRFS1 pooled (A.273)	1st vs 5th 5.35%
Hungarian (A.53–A.54)	jhu/apl 41.12% aplmohud pooled (A.294)	unine 38.89% UniNEhu3 not pooled (A.312)	miracle 35.20% xNP01ST1 pooled (A.297)	hummingbird 33.09% humHU05tde pooled (A.288)	hildesheim 32.64% UHIHU2 pooled (A.285)	1st vs 5th 25.98%
Portuguese (A.57–A.58)	unine 38.75% UniNEpt2 pooled (A.338)	hummingbird 38.64% humPT05tde not pooled (A.322)	tlr 37.42% tlrTDptRF2 not pooled (A.332)	jhu-apl 36.54% aplmopte not pooled (A.326)	alicante 36.03% IRn?pt?vexp pooled (A.314)	1st vs 5th 7.55%

It can be noted that the trend observed in the previous editions of CLEF is confirmed: differences for top performers for tracks with languages introduced in past campaigns are small: in particular only 5.35% in the case of French (French monolingual has been offered in CLEF since 2000) and 7.55% in the case of Portuguese, which was introduced in 2004. However, for the new languages, Bulgarian and Hungarian, the differences are much greater, in the order of 25%, showing that there should be room for improvement if these languages are offered in future campaigns.

A main focus in the monolingual tasks was the development of new or the adaptation of existing stemmers and/or morphological analysers for the "new" CLEF languages.

Figures from 1 to 4 compare the performances of the top participants of the Monolingual Bulgarian, French, Hungarian, Portuguese tasks.

4 Bilingual Experiments

The bilingual task was structured in four subtasks (X → BG, FR, HU or PT target collection) plus, as usual, an additional subtask with English as a target language restricted to newcomers to a CLEF cross-language task or to groups using unusual or new topic languages (Amharic, Greek, Indonesian, and Hungarian).

Table 4 shows the best results for this task for runs using the title+description topic fields. The performance difference between the best and the last (up to 5) placed groups is given (in terms of average precision. Again both pooled and non pooled runs are included in the best entries for each track, with the exception of Bilingual X → EN.

For bilingual retrieval evaluation, a common method is to compare results against monolingual baselines. We have the following results for CLEF 2005:

- X → FR: 85% of best monolingual French IR system;
- X → PT: 88% of best monolingual Portuguese IR system;
- X → BG: 74% of best monolingual Bulgarian IR system;
- X → HU: 73% of best monolingual Hungarian IR system.

Similarly to monolingual, this is an interesting result. Whereas, the figures for French and Portuguese reflect those of recent literature [5], for the new languages where there has been little *Cross Language Information Retrieval (CLIR)* system experience and testing so far it can be seen that, there is much room for improvement. It is interesting to note that when CLIR system evaluation began in 1997 at TREC-6 the best CLIR systems had the following results:

- EN → FR: 49% of best monolingual French IR system;
- EN → DE: 64% of best monolingual German IR system.

Figures 5 to 9 compare the performances of the top participants of the Bilingual tasks with the following target languages: Bulgarian, French, Hungarian,

Table 4. Best entries for the bilingual task

Track	Participant Rank					
	1st	2nd	3rd	4th	5th	Diff.
Bulgarian (A.25–A.26)	miracle 23.55% ENXST pooled (A.135)	unine 13.99% UniNEbibg3 not pooled (A.143)	u.glasgow 12.04% glaenbgtd pooled (A.136)	jhu/apl 9.59% aplbienbge pooled (A.133)		1st vs 4th 145.57%
French (A.33–A.34)	alicante 35.90% IRn-enfr-vexp not pooled	unine 34.67% UniNEbifr2 not pooled	hildesheim 34.65% UHIENFR2 not pooled	jhu/apl 34.42% aplbienfrc pooled	miracle 30.76% ENSST not pooled	1st vs 5th 16.71%
Hungarian (A.37–A.38)	miracle 30.16% ENMST not pooled	unine 28.82% UniNEbihu3 not pooled	jhu/apl 24.58% aplbienhue not pooled			1st vs 3rd 22.70%
Portuguese (A.41–A.42)	unine 34.04% UniNEbipt1 pooled (A.216)	jhu/apl 31.85% aplbiesptb not pooled (A.204)	miracle 31.06% ESAST not pooled (A.209)	alicante 29.18% IRn-enpt-vexp not pooled (A.197)	tlr 23.58% tlrTDfr2ptRFS1 pooled (A.212)	1st vs 5th 44.36%
English (A.29–A.30)	jhu/apl 33.13% aplbiidena pooled (A.152)	u.glasgow 29.35% glagrentdqe pooled (A.156)	depok 12.85% UI-TD10 pooled (A.146)			1st vs 3rd 157.82%

Portuguese, and English. Although, as usual, English was by far the most popular language for queries, some less common and interesting query to target language pairs were tried, e.g. Amharic, Spanish and German to French, and French to Portuguese.

From the reports of the groups that participated in the bilingual ad hoc tasks, it appears that the CLEF 2005 experiments provide a good overview of most of the traditional approaches to CLIR when matching between query and target collection, including n-gram indexing, machine translation, machine-readable bilingual dictionaries, multilingual ontologies, pivot languages, query and document translation - perhaps corpus-based approaches were less used than in previous years continuing a trend first noticed in CLEF 2004. Veteran groups were mainly concerned with fine tuning and optimizing strategies already tried in previous years. The issues examined were the usual ones: word-sense disambiguation, out-of-dictionary vocabulary, ways to apply relevance feedback, results merging, etc.

5 Multilingual Experiments

Table 5 shows results for the best entries for the multilingual tasks. The table reports: the short name of the participating group; the mean average precision achieved by the run; the run identifier; the page in Appendix A of the Working Notes [3] containing all figures and graphs for this run; the performance difference

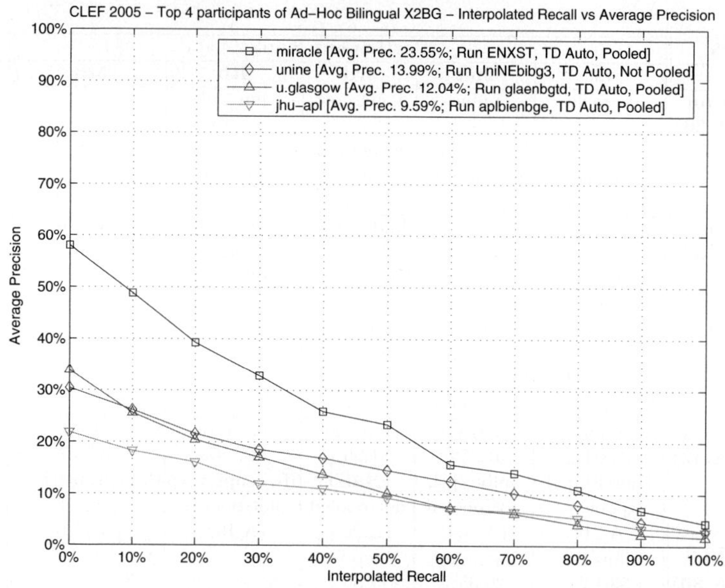

Fig. 5. Bilingual Bulgarian

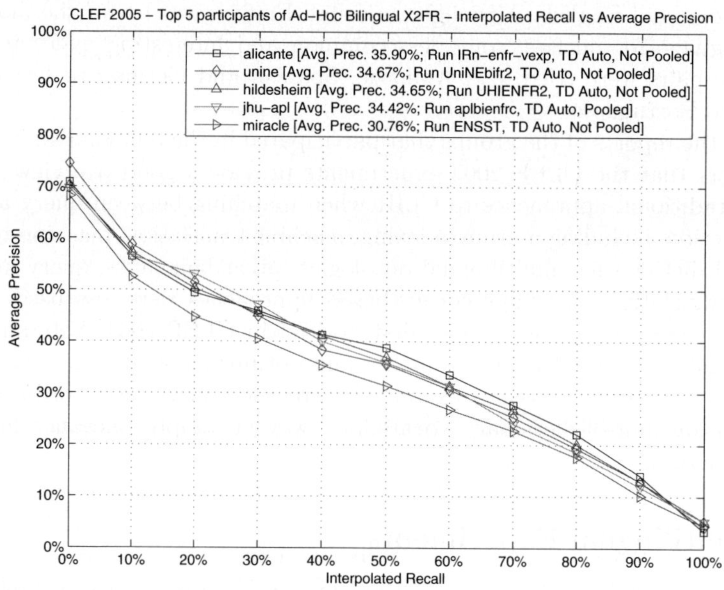

Fig. 6. Bilingual French

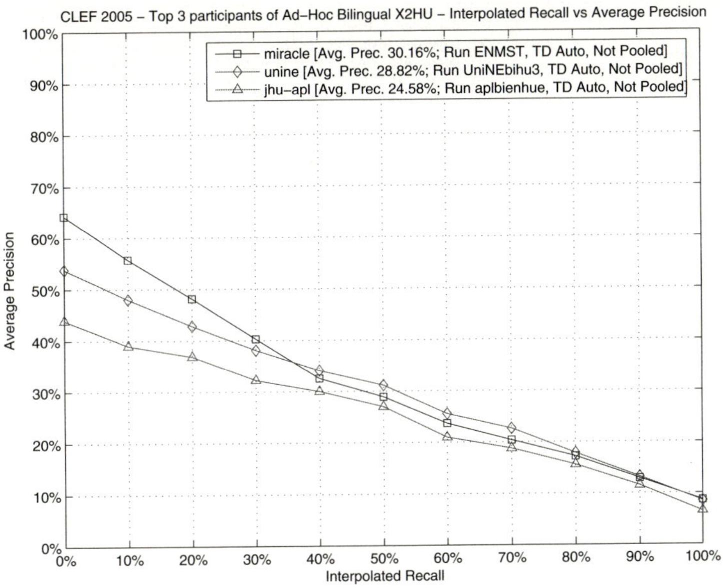

Fig. 7. Bilingual Hungarian

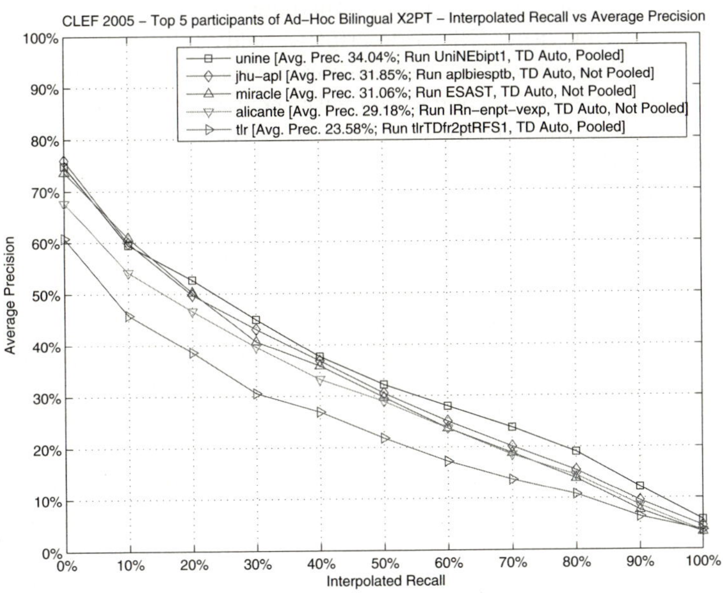

Fig. 8. Bilingual Portuguese

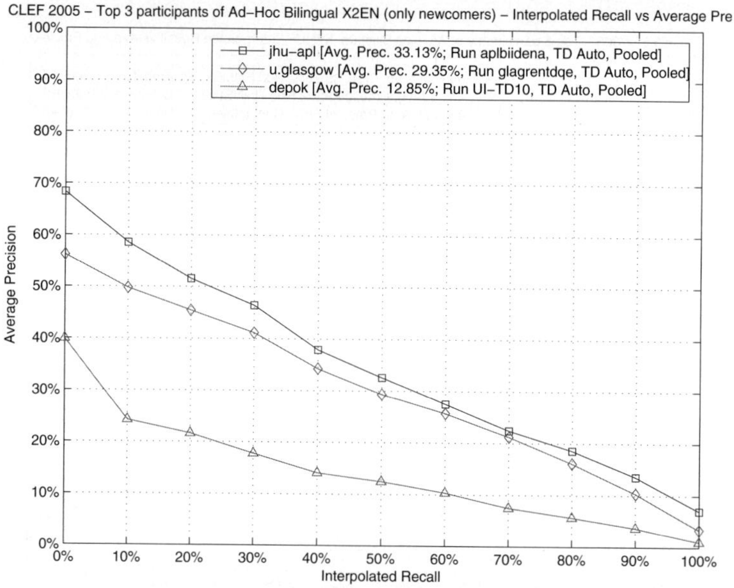

Fig. 9. Bilingual English

between the first and the last participant. The pages of Appendix A containing the overview graphs are indicated under the name of the sub-task.

Table 5 shows runs using title + description fields only (the mandatory run). The first row of the table shows the results of the top 5 group submissions of the CLEF 2003 Multi-8 task for comparison with the 2-Years-On and Merging tasks of this year. Additional rows for each task show the difference in the MAP for this run compared to the best performing run at this rank in the original CLEF 2003 Multi-8 task.

Since the CLEF 2005 multilingual tasks used only 40 topics of the original 60 topics of the 2003 as the test set (topics 161 to 200), while the first 20 topics (topics 141 to 160) were used as a training set, the average precision of the original 2003 runs was recomputed for the 40 test topics used this year. These revised MAP figures are reported in Table 5. These figures are thus slightly different from the original results which appear in the CLEF 2003 proceedings [2] which were calculated for the original set of 60 topics., although the ranking of these runs remains unchanged.

It can be seen from Table 5 that the performance difference between the first and the last participant for the 2-Years-On track is much greater (nearly 3 times) than the corresponding difference in 2003, even if the task performed in these two tracks is the same. On the other hand, the performance difference for the Merging track is nearly one third of the corresponding difference in 2003: it seems that merging the results of the run reduces the gap between the best and the last performer, even though there is still a considerable difference (35.63%), if compared to the small differences between the results for the most popular

Table 5. Best entries for the multilingual task

Track	Participant Rank					
	1st	2nd	3rd	4th	5th	Diff.
CLEF 2003	UC Berkeley 38.77% bkmul8en3 pooled	U. Neuchatel 35.69% UniNEml1 not pooled	U. Amsterdam 29.62% UAmsC03EnM8SS4G not pooled	jhu/apl 25.29% aplmuen8b not pooled	U. Tampere 18.95% UTAmul1 pooled	1st vs 5th 104.59%
2 Years On **(A.17–A.18)**	Cmu 44.93% adhocM5Trntes not pooled (A.93) +15.89%	jaen 29.57% UJAPRFRSV2RR not pooled (A.101) -17.34%	miracle 26.06% esml9XstiSTp not pooled (A.110) -12.02%	isi-unige 10.33% AUTOEN not pooled (A.96) -59.15%		1st vs 4th 334.95%
Merging **(A.21–A.22)**	Cmu 41.19% UNET150w05test – (A.118) +6.24%	dcu 32.86% dcu.Prositqgm2 – (A.121) -7.93%	Jaen 30.37% UJAMENEDFRR – (A.129) +2.53%			1st vs 3rd 35.63%

monolingual languages, e.g. 5.35% of monolingual French. We can note that the top participant of the 2-Years-On task achieves a 15.89% performance improvement with respect to the top participant of CLEF 2003 Multi-8. On the other hand, the fourth participant of the 2-Years-On task has a 59.15% decrease in performance with respect to the fourth participant of CLEF 2003 Multi-8. Similarly, we can note that the top participant of the Merging track achieves a 6.24% performance improvement with respect to the top participant of 2003.

In general, we can note that for the 2-Years-On task there is a performance improvement only for the top participant, while the performances deteriorate quickly for the other participants with respect to 2003. On the other hand, for the Merging task the performance improvement of the top participant with respect to 2003 is less than in the case of the 2-Years-On task. There is also less variation between the submissions for the Merging task than seen in the earlier 2003 runs. This is probably due to the fact that the participants were using the same ranked lists, and that the variation in performance arises only from the merging strategies adopted.

Figure 10 compares the performances in terms of the precision at different document cut-off values of the top participants of the 2-Years-On task with respect to the top and the fifth performer of CLEF 2003 Multilingual-8. Figure 11 shows corresponding results for the Multilingual Merging task. Trends in these figures are similar to those seen in Table 5. The top performing submissions for the Multilingual 2-Years-On and Merging tasks are both clearly higher than the best submission to the CLEF 2003 task. The variation between submissions for 2-Years-On is also greater than that observed for the Merging only task.

The multilingual tasks at CLEF 2005 were intended to assess whether re-use of the CLEF 2003 Multi-8 task data could give an indication of progress in multilingual information retrieval and to provide common sets of ranked lists to enable specific exploration of merging strategies for multilingual information retrieval. The submissions to these tasks show that multilingual performance can indeed be improved beyond that reported at CLEF 2003 both when performing

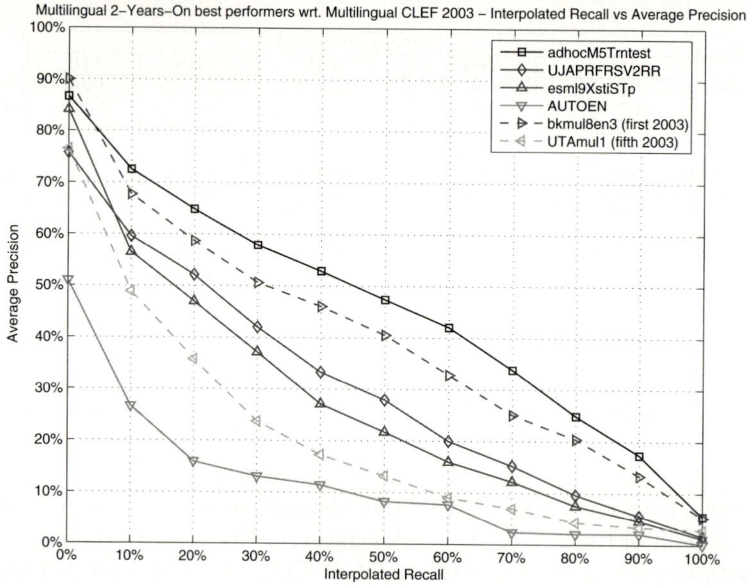

Fig. 10. Interpolated Recall vs Average Precision. Comparison between Multilingual 2-Years-On and CLEF 2003 Multilingual-8.

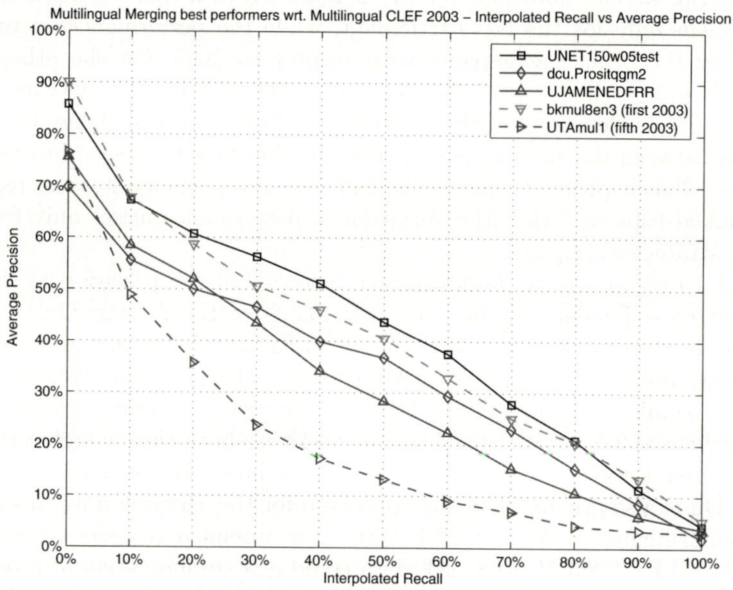

Fig. 11. Interpolated Recall vs Average Precision. Comparison between Multilingual Merging and CLEF 2003 Multilingual-8.

Table 6. Lilliefors test for each track with (LL) and without Tague-Sutcliffe arcsin transformation (LL & TS). Jarque-Bera test for each track with (JB) and without Tague-Sutcliffe arcsin transformation (JB & TS).

Track	LL	LL & TS	JB	JB & TS
2 Years On	8/21	17/21	13/21	19/21
Merging	8/20	15/20	13/20	18/20
Bilingual Bulgarian	0/12	1/12	0/12	5/12
Bilingual English	12/31	24/31	21/31	25/31
Bilingual French	6/31	19/31	19/31	22/31
Bilingual Hungarian	0/7	5/7	1/7	5/7
Bilingual Portuguese	9/28	19/28	10/28	19/28
Monolingual Bulgarian	4/20	17/20	14/20	19/20
Monolingual French	12/28	38/38	30/28	38/38
Monolingual Hungarian	2/32	17/32	12/32	26/32
Monolingual Portuguese	24/32	30/32	27/32	28/32

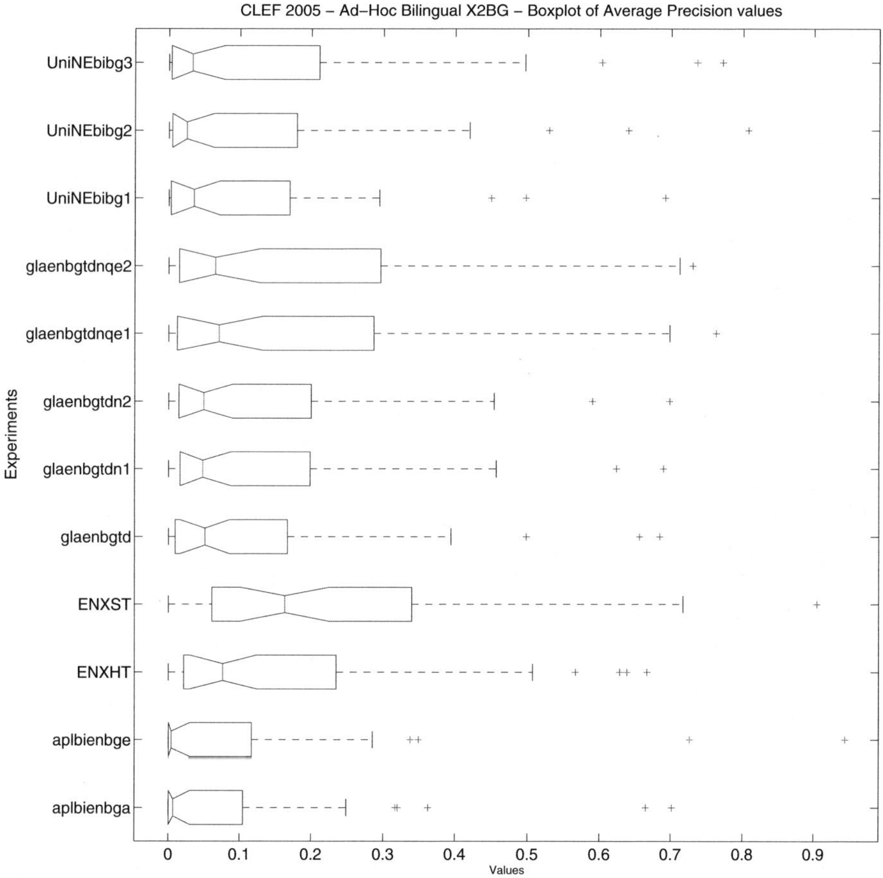

Fig. 12. Boxplot analysis of the bilingual task with Bulgarian target collection

Table 7. Monolingual Bulgarian. The table shows the Tukey T Test. The table reports the results of statistical analysis (two-way ANOVA) on the experiments.

Arcsin-transformed avg. prec. values	Run ID	Groups				
0.5687	aplmobgd	X				
0.5568	aplmobgc	X				
0.5343	humBG05tde	X	X			
0.5206	UniNEbg3	X	X	X		
0.5191	aplmobge	X	X	X		
0.5172	UniNEbg1	X	X	X		
0.5120	ST	X	X	X	X	
0.5120	humBG05td	X	X	X	X	
0.4937	UniNEbg2	X	X	X	X	X
0.4874	humBG05t	X	X	X	X	X
0.4742	glabgtdqe	X	X	X	X	X
0.4619	glabgtdnqe	X	X	X	X	X
0.4275	glabgtdn		X	X	X	X
0.4154	r1SR		X	X	X	X
0.4091	UHIBG2			X	X	X
0.3974	UHIBG1				X	X
0.3939	BGHT				X	X
0.3844	IRn-bu-vnexp					X
0.3775	IRn-bu-fexp					X
0.3755	IRn-bu-vexp					X

the complete retrieval process and when merging ranked result lists generated by other groups. The initial running of this task suggests that there is scope for further improvement in multilingual information retrieval from exploiting ongoing improvements in information retrieval methods, but also from focused exploration of merging techniques.

6 Statistical Testing

For reasons of practicality, the CLEF 2005 multilingual track used a limited number of queries (40), which are intended to represent a more or less appropriate sample of all possible queries that users would want to ask from the collection. When the goal is to validate how well results can be expected to hold beyond this particular set of queries, statistical testing can help to determine what differences between runs appear to be real as opposed to differences that are due to sampling issues. We aim to identify runs with results that are significantly different from the results of other runs. "Significantly different" in this context means that the difference between the performance scores for the runs in question appears greater than what might be expected by pure chance. As with all statistical testing, conclusions will be qualified by an error probability, which was chosen to be 0.05 in the following. We have designed our analysis to follow closely the methodology used by similar analyses carried out for TREC [6].

We used the MATLAB Statistics Toolbox 5.0.1 this year, which provides the necessary functionality plus some additional functions and utilities. We use the *ANalysis Of VAriance (ANOVA)* test. ANOVA makes some assumptions concerning the data be checked. Hull [6] provides details of these; in particular,

Table 8. Monolingual French. The table shows the Tukey T Test. The table reports the results of statistical analysis (two-way ANOVA) on the experiments.

Arcsin-transformed avg. prec. values	Run ID	Groups								
0.6821	UniNEfr1	X								
0.6779	aplmofra	X	X							
0.6691	aplmofrb	X	X	X						
0.6686	UniNEfr3	X	X	X						
0.6648	UniNEfr2	X	X	X						
0.6609	tlrTDfrRFS1	X	X	X						
0.6598	humFR05tde	X	X	X						
0.6581	glafrtdqe1	X	X	X						
0.6459	aHRSR	X	X	X	X					
0.6444	SrgdMono01	X	X	X	X					
0.6359	UHIFR2	X	X	X	X					
0.6328	UHIFR1	X	X	X	X					
0.6315	tlrTDfr3	X	X	X	X					
0.6279	aplmofre	X	X	X	X					
0.6276	aHRSRxNP01HR1	X	X	X	X					
0.6271	aplmofrc	X	X	X	X					
0.6265	humFR05td	X	X	X	X					
0.6251	aHTST	X	X	X	X					
0.6240	glafrtdqe2	X	X	X	X					
0.6002	IRn-fr-vexp	X	X	X	X	X				
0.5862	IRn-fr-fexp	X	X	X	X	X	X			
0.5779	sics-fr-k	X	X	X	X	X	X	X		
0.5672	sics-fr-b		X	X	X	X	X	X		
0.5653	glafrtdn		X	X	X	X	X	X		
0.5640	sics-fr-van			X	X	X	X	X		
0.5421	IRn-fr-vnexp				X	X	X	X	X	
0.5418	humFR05t				X	X	X	X	X	
0.4991	UHIFR4					X	X	X	X	
0.4929	UHIFR3					X	X	X	X	
0.4872	xNP01r1SR1					X	X	X	X	
0.4754	RIMfuzzLemme080					X	X	X	X	
0.4704	RIMfuzzLemme050					X	X	X	X	
0.4685	RIMfuzzTD050						X	X	X	
0.4313	CLIPS05FR0							X	X	X
0.4056	RIMfuzzET050							X	X	X
0.4054	RIMfuzzET020								X	X
0.3413	CLIPS05FR1									X
0.3209	CLIPS05FR2									X

the scores in question should be approximately normally distributed and their variance has to be approximately the same for all runs. Two tests for goodness of fit to a normal distribution were chosen using the MATLAB statistical toolbox: the Lilliefors test [7] and the Jarque-Bera test [8]. In the case of the CLEF tasks under analysis, both tests indicate that the assumption of normality is violated for most of the data samples (in this case the runs for each participant).

In such cases, a transformation of data should be performed. The transformation for measures that range from 0 to 1 is the arcsin-root transformation:

$$\arcsin\left(\sqrt{x}\right)$$

which Tague-Sutcliffe [9] recommends for use with precision/recall measures.

Table 6 shows the results of the Lilliefors test before and after applying the Tague-Sutcliffe transformation. After the transformation the analysis of the normality of samples distribution improves significantly, with the exception of the

Table 9. Monolingual Hungarian. The table shows the Tukey T Test. The table reports the results of statistical analysis (two-way ANOVA) on the experiments.

Arcsin-transformed avg. prec. values	Run ID	Groups								
0.6853	aplmohud	X								
0.6844	aplmohuc	X								
0.6834	aplmohue	X								
0.6571	UniNEhu3	X	X							
0.6284	UniNEhu1	X	X	X						
0.6103	xNP01ST1	X	X	X						
0.6012	aHTSTxNP01ST1	X	X	X						
0.5974	UniNEhu2	X	X	X						
0.5896	humHU05tde	X	X	X	X					
0.5786	UHIHU2	X	X	X	X	X				
0.5721	IRn-hu-vexp	X	X	X	X	X	X			
0.5659	qfstfs	X	X	X	X	X	X			
0.5634	qfirststemtall	X	X	X	X	X	X			
0.5606	IRn-hu-vnexp	X	X	X	X	X	X	X		
0.5587	humHU05td	X	X	X	X	X	X	X	X	
0.5575	IRn-hu-fexp	X	X	X	X	X	X	X	X	
0.5514	UHIHU1		X	X	X	X	X	X	X	
0.5361	tlrTDhuSC		X	X	X	X	X	X	X	
0.5321	tlrTDhuE		X	X	X	X	X	X	X	
0.5200	UAmsMoHu1AnH			X	X	X	X	X	X	
0.5193	HUHT			X	X	X	X	X	X	
0.5180	qalltall			X	X	X	X	X	X	
0.5179	UAmsMoHu3AnL			X	X	X	X	X	X	
0.5027	humHU05t			X	X	X	X	X	X	
0.4670	UAmsMoHu2AnG				X	X	X	X	X	
0.4423	qnostemtfirsstem					X	X	X	X	
0.4395	UAmsMoHu4AnV						X	X	X	
0.4289	qnostemtnostem							X	X	
0.4282	qnostemtall								X	
0.2685	glahutdnqe									X
0.2685	glahutdqe									X
0.2592	glahutdn									X

bilingual Bulgarian. Each entry shows the number of experiments whose performance distribution can be considered drawn from a Gaussian distribution, with respect to the total number of experiment of the track. The value of alpha for this test was set to 5%. The same table shows also the same analysis with respect to the Jarque-Bera test. The value of alpha for this test was set to 5%. The difficulty to transform the data into normally distributed samples derives from the original distribution of run performances which tend towards zero within the interval [0,1].

Figure 12 presents a boxplot graph providing a more detailed analysis of the above mentioned phenomenon for the bilingual task with Bulgarian target collection. As can be seen, the distribution of the average precision for the different experiments is skewed, and this helps to explain the deviation from the normality. Moreover, the data distribution tends towards low performances, which confirms the difficulty of dealing with new languages.

The following tables, from Table 7 to Table 17, summarize the results of this test. All experiments, regardless the topic language or topic fields, are included. Results are therefore only valid for comparison of individual pairs of runs, and not in terms of absolute performance. Each table shows the overall results where all the runs that are included in the same group do not have a significantly different

Table 10. Monolingual Portuguese. The table shows the Tukey T Test. The table reports the results of statistical analysis (two-way ANOVA) on the experiments.

Arcsin-transformed avg. prec. values	Run ID	Groups						
0.6573	humPT05tde	X						
0.6562	UniNEpt2	X						
0.6483	UniNEpt1	X	X					
0.6453	tlrTDptRF2	X	X					
0.6413	SR	X	X					
0.6336	xNP01SR1	X	X	X				
0.6323	aplmopte	X	X	X				
0.6289	humPT05td	X	X	X				
0.6269	IRn-pt-vexp	X	X	X				
0.6261	aplmoptc	X	X	X				
0.6257	UniNEpt3	X	X	X				
0.6257	tlrTDptRFS1	X	X	X				
0.6202	tlrTDpt3	X	X	X				
0.6165	ST	X	X	X				
0.6090	IRn-pt-fexp	X	X	X				
0.5983	IRn-pt-vnexp	X	X	X				
0.5816	UBmono-pt-rf2	X	X	X	X			
0.5792	UBmono-pt-rf1	X	X	X	X			
0.5788	UBmono-pt-comb1	X	X	X	X			
0.5777	UBmono-pt-rf3	X	X	X	X			
0.5770	aplmoptd	X	X	X	X			
0.5614	aplmopta	X	X	X	X			
0.5556	humPT05t	X	X	X	X			
0.5394	XLDBTumba01		X	X	X	X		
0.5217	aSRr1SR			X	X	X	X	
0.4860	glapttdqe				X	X	X	X
0.4832	XLDBTumba05				X	X	X	X
0.4826	glapttdnqe				X	X	X	X
0.4427	glapttdn					X	X	X
0.4127	XLDBTumba02						X	X
0.4071	XLDBTumba09							X
0.3942	XLDBTumba06							X

Table 11. Bilingual target Bulgarian. The table shows the Tukey T Test. The table reports the results of statistical analysis (two-way ANOVA) on the experiments.

Arcsin-transformed avg. prec. values	Run ID	Groups		
0.4608	ENXST	X		
0.3618	glaenbgtdnqe1	X	X	
0.3548	ENXHT	X	X	
0.3470	glaenbgtdnqe2	X	X	
0.3077	glaenbgtdn1		X	X
0.3000	glaenbgtdn2		X	X
0.2944	UniNEbibg3		X	X
0.2846	glaenbgtd		X	X
0.2711	UniNEbibg2		X	X
0.2598	UniNEbibg1		X	X
0.2111	aplbienbge			X
0.1951	aplbienbga			X

performance. All runs scoring below a certain group perform significantly worse than at least the top entry of the group. Likewise all the runs scoring above a certain group perform significantly better than at least the bottom entry in that group.

Table 12. Bilingual target French. The table shows the Tukey T Test. The table reports the results of statistical analysis (two-way ANOVA) on the experiments.

Arcsin-transformed avg. prec. values	Run ID	Groups					
0.6002	IRn-enfr-vexp	X					
0.5961	UniNEbifr2	X					
0.5958	UHIENFR2	X					
0.5950	UniNEbifr3	X					
0.5857	UniNEbifr1	X					
0.5804	aplbienfrc	X	X				
0.5789	UHIENFR1	X	X				
0.5543	ENSxNP01SR1	X	X				
0.5537	ESSxNP01SR1	X	X				
0.5448	ENSST	X	X	X			
0.5319	IRn-enfr-vnexp	X	X	X			
0.5256	ESSST	X	X	X			
0.5249	IRn-enfr-fexp	X	X	X			
0.5048	ESSxNP01HR1	X	X	X			
0.5011	glaitfrtdnqe	X	X	X			
0.5007	ENSxNP01HR1	X	X	X			
0.4847	UHIRUFR1	X	X	X			
0.4758	SrgdMgE03	X	X	X			
0.4731	SrgdQT04	X	X	X			
0.4644	SrgdMgG02	X	X	X			
0.4362	glaitfrtdn		X	X	X		
0.4078	glaitfrtd			X	X		
0.3065	SrgdDT05				X	X	
0.1693	CLIPS05DEFR0					X	X
0.1341	CLIPS05ESFR0						X
0.1337	CLIPS05DEFR						X
0.1257	CLIPS05EFR						X
0.1226	ds-am-fr-da-s						X
0.1224	ds-am-fr-nonda-s						X
0.1004	ds-am-fr-nonda-l						X
0.0898	ds-am-fr-da-l						X

Table 13. Bilingual target Hungarian. The table shows the Tukey T Test. The table reports the results of statistical analysis (two-way ANOVA) on the experiments.

Arcsin-transformed avg. prec. values	Run ID	Groups	
0.5448	aplbienhua	X	
0.5377	aplbienhue	X	
0.5097	UniNEbihu2	X	X
0.5004	UniNEbihu1	X	X
0.4385	UniNEbihu3	X	X
0.4346	ENMxNP01ST1	X	X
0.4098	ENMST		X

It is well-known that it is fairly difficult to detect statistically significant differences between retrieval results based on 40 queries [9,10]. While 40 queries remains a good choice based on practicality for doing relevance assessments, statistical testing would be one of the areas to benefit most from having additional topics. This fact is addressed by the measures taken to ensure stability of at least part of the document collection across different campaigns, which allows participants to run their system on aggregate sets of queries for post-hoc experiments.

Table 14. Bilingual target Portuguese. The table shows the Tukey T Test. The table reports the results of statistical analysis (two-way ANOVA) on the experiments.

Arcsin-transformed avg. prec. values	**Run ID**	**Groups**										
0.5943	UniNEbipt1	X										
0.5927	ESASR	X										
0.5828	ESAxNP01SR1	X	X									
0.5808	aplbiesptb	X	X									
0.5714	ESAST	X	X	X								
0.5632	UniNEbipt2	X	X	X								
0.5630	UniNEbipt3	X	X	X								
0.5567	aplbienptb	X	X	X								
0.5366	IRn-enpt-vexp	X	X	X								
0.5334	IRn-enpt-fexp	X	X	X	X							
0.5078	IRn-enpt-fexpfl	X	X	X	X	X						
0.4943	IRn-enpt-vnexp	X	X	X	X	X						
0.4640	tlrTDfr2ptRFS1		X	X	X	X	X					
0.4514	tlrTDfr2pt3			X	X	X	X	X				
0.4132	ENSSR				X	X	X	X				
0.4109	ENSxNP01SR1					X	X	X	X			
0.4024	ENSST					X	X	X	X			
0.3751	UBbi-en-pt-t2						X	X	X			
0.3741	UBbi-en-pt-comb2						X	X	X			
0.3740	UBbi-en-pt-t1						X	X	X			
0.3449	UBbi-en-pt-comb1							X	X	X		
0.3073	glaespttdnqe								X	X	X	
0.2448	glaespttdn									X	X	X
0.2202	glaespttd										X	X
0.1389	XLDBTumba03											X
0.1373	XLDBTumba04											X
0.1344	XLDBTumba08											X
0.1239	XLDBTumba07											X

Table 15. Bilingual target English. The table shows the Tukey T Test. The table reports the results of statistical analysis (two-way ANOVA) on the experiments.

Arcsin-transformed avg. prec. values	**Run ID**	**Groups**								
0.6952	IRn-en-vexp	X								
0.6844	IRn-en-fexp	X								
0.6757	IRn-en-vnexp	X								
0.6755	UBmono-en-3	X								
0.6673	prise2	X								
0.6668	UAmsC05EnEnStmLM	X								
0.6606	UAmsC05EnEnStm	X								
0.6548	UBmono-en-2	X								
0.6475	UBmono-en-1	X	X							
0.6310	aplbiidend	X	X							
0.6183	UAmsC05EnEn4Gr	X	X							
0.6016	UAmsC05EnEnWrdLM	X	X							
0.5972	prise4	X	X							
0.5736	aplbiidena	X	X	X						
0.5689	prise1	X	X	X						
0.5574	prise3	X	X	X						
0.5095	glagrentdqe		X	X	X					
0.4526	cirGHLAru2en			X	X	X				
0.4498	aplbigrena			X	X	X				
0.4457	glagrentdn			X	X	X				
0.4076	cirGHLAen2en100				X	X	X			
0.3973	cirGHLAen2en110				X	X	X	X		
0.3874	cirGHLAen2en150				X	X	X	X	X	
0.3777	aplbihuena				X	X	X	X	X	
0.3337	cirGHLAen2en152					X	X	X	X	X
0.2973	UI-TD10						X	X	X	X
0.2738	UI-TD20						X	X	X	X
0.2683	UI-TITLE20							X	X	X
0.2541	UI-TITLE10								X	X
0.2324	UI-DESC10									X
0.2275	UI-DESC20									X

Table 16. Multilingual Merging. The table shows the Tukey T Test. The table reports the results of statistical analysis (two-way ANOVA) on the experiments.

Arcsin-transformed avg. prec. values	**Run ID**	**Groups**							
0.6786	UNET150w05test	X							
0.6615	UNET15w05test	X	X						
0.6549	UNEC150test	X	X	X					
0.6448	UNEC1000test	X	X	X	X				
0.5996	HBC1000test	X	X	X	X	X			
0.5687	dcu.Prositqgm2		X	X	X	X	X		
0.5641	dcu.Prositqgm1		X	X	X	X	X		
0.5604	dcu.Prositqgt		X	X	X	X	X		
0.5512	UJAMENEDFRR			X	X	X	X		
0.5501	HBC150test				X	X	X		
0.5495	dcu.Prositqgp				X	X	X		
0.5446	HBT150w05test				X	X	X		
0.5397	UJAMENEDF					X	X		
0.5326	UJAMENEOK					X	X		
0.5326	UJAMENEOKRR					X	X		
0.4882	HBT15w05test						X	X	
0.4277	dcu.hump							X	X
0.4147	dcu.humm1							X	X
0.3985	dcu.humm2							X	X
0.3764	dcu.humt								X

Table 17. Multilingual 2 Years On. The table shows the Tukey T Test. The table reports the results of statistical analysis (two-way ANOVA) on the experiments.

Arcsin-transformed avg. prec. values	**Run ID**	**Groups**							
0.7247	adhocM3Trntest	X							
0.7184	adhocM4Trntest	X	X						
0.7046	adhocM5Trntest	X	X						
0.6992	adhocM5w1test	X	X						
0.5834	frml9XntfSRp		X	X					
0.5576	enml0XSRpHL			X	X				
0.5391	UJAPRFRSV2RR			X	X				
0.5357	UJAUARSV2RR			X	X				
0.5356	UJARSV2RR			X	X				
0.5310	UJARSV2			X	X				
0.5258	esml9XnteSRp			X	X				
0.4975	esml9XstiSTp			X	X	X			
0.4946	enmlXSRpA			X	X	X			
0.4841	enmlSTpHL			X	X	X			
0.4469	enmlSTpH			X	X	X	X		
0.4224	FEEDBCKEN				X	X	X	X	
0.3626	ADJUSTEN					X	X	X	X
0.3225	ADJUSTSP						X	X	X
0.3137	ADJUSTFR						X	X	X
0.3073	ADJUSTDU							X	X
0.2617	AUTOEN								X

7 Conclusions

We have reported the results of the ad hoc cross-language text document retrieval track at CLEF 2005. This track is considered to be central to CLEF as for many groups it is the first track in which they participate and provides them with them an opportunity to test their systems and compare performance between monolingual and cross-language runs, before perhaps moving on to more complex system development and subsequent evaluation. However, the track is certainly not just aimed at beginners. It also gives groups the possibility to measure advances in system performance over time. In addition, each year, we also include a task aimed at examining particular aspects of cross-language text retrieval. This year, the focus was on multilingual retrieval with our Multi-8 2-years-on and Multi-8 merging tasks.

The ad hoc track in CLEF 2006 offers the same target languages for the main mono- and bilingual tasks as in 2005 but has two additional focuses. Groups are encouraged to use non-European languages as topic languages in the bilingual task. Among others, we are offering Amharic, Hindi, Indonesian, Oromo, and Telugu. In addition, we have set up the "robust task" with the objective of providing the more expert groups with the chance to do in-depth failure analysis. At the time of writing, participation in these two particular tasks is encouraging. For more information, see our website[2].

Finally, it should be remembered that, although over the years we vary the topic and target languages offered in the track, all participating groups also have the possibility of accessing and using the test collections that have been created in previous years for all of the twelve languages included in the CLEF multilingual test collection. This test collection should soon be made publicly available on the *Evaluations and Language resources Distribution Agency (ELDA)* catalog[3].

References

1. Cleverdon, C.W.: The Cranfield Tests on Index Languages Devices. In Spack Jones, K., Willett, P., eds.: Readings in Information Retrieval, Morgan Kaufmann Publisher, Inc., San Francisco, California, USA (1997) 47–60
2. Braschler, M.: CLEF 2003 - Overview of results. In Peters, C., Braschler, M., Gonzalo, J., Kluck, M., eds.: Comparative Evaluation of Multilingual Information Access Systems: Fourth Workshop of the Cross–Language Evaluation Forum (CLEF 2003) Revised Selected Papers, Lecture Notes in Computer Science (LNCS) 3237, Springer, Heidelberg, Germany (2004) 44–63
3. Di Nunzio, G.M., Ferro, N.: Appendix A. Results of the Core Tracks and Domain-Specific Tracks. In Peters, C., Quochi, V., eds.: Working Notes for the CLEF 2005 Workshop, `http://www.clefcampaign.org/2005/working_notes/workingnotes2005/appendix_a.pdf` [last visited 2006, February 28] (2005)
4. Braschler, M., Peters, C.: CLEF 2003 Methodology and Metrics. In Peters, C., Braschler, M., Gonzalo, J., Kluck, M., eds.: Comparative Evaluation of Multilingual Information Access Systems: Fourth Workshop of the Cross–Language Evaluation Forum (CLEF 2003) Revised Selected Papers, Lecture Notes in Computer Science (LNCS) 3237, Springer, Heidelberg, Germany (2004) 7–20
5. Gonzalo, J., Peters, C.: The Impact of Evaluation on Multilingual Text Retrieval. In Baeza-Yates, R., Ziviani, N., Marchionini, G., Moffat, A., Tait, J., eds.: Proc. 28th Annual International ACM SIGIR Conference on Research and Development in Information Retrieval (SIGIR 2005), ACM Press, New York, USA (2005) 603–604

[2] `http://www.clef-campaign.org/`

[3] `http://www.elda.org/`

6. Hull, D.: Using Statistical Testing in the Evaluation of Retrieval Experiments. In Korfhage, R., Rasmussen, E., Willett, P., eds.: Proc. 16th Annual International ACM SIGIR Conference on Research and Development in Information Retrieval (SIGIR 1993), ACM Press, New York, USA (1993) 329–338
7. Conover, W.J.: Practical Nonparametric Statistics. 1st edn. John Wiley and Sons, New York, USA (1971)
8. Judge, G.G., Hill, R.C., Griffiths, W.E., Lütkepohl, H., Lee, T.C.: Introduction to the Theory and Practice of Econometrics. 2nd edn. John Wiley and Sons, New York, USA (1988)
9. Tague-Sutcliffe, J.: The Pragmatics of Information Retrieval Experimentation, Revisited. In Spack Jones, K., Willett, P., eds.: Readings in Information Retrieval, Morgan Kaufmann Publisher, Inc., San Francisco, California, USA (1997) 205–216
10. Voorhees, E.M., Buckley, C.: The Effect of Topic Set Size on Retrieval Experiment Error. In Croft, W.B., Moffat, A., van Rijsbergen, C.J., Wilkinson, R., Zobel, J., eds.: Proc. 21st Annual International ACM SIGIR Conference on Research and Development in Information Retrieval (SIGIR 1998), ACM Press, New York, USA (1998) 307–314

Ad-Hoc Mono- and Bilingual Retrieval Experiments at the University of Hildesheim

René Hackl, Thomas Mandl, and Christa Womser-Hacker

University of Hildesheim, Information Science
Marienburger Platz 22, D-31141 Hildesheim, Germany
mandl@uni-hildesheim.de

Abstract. This paper reports information retrieval experiments carried out within the CLEF 2005 ad-hoc multi-lingual track. The experiments focus on the two new languages Bulgarian and Hungarian. No relevance assessments are available for these collections yet. Optimization was mainly based on French data from CLEF 2004. Based on experience from last year, one of our main objectives was to improve and refine the n-gram-based indexing and retrieval algorithms within our system.

1 Introduction

In the CLEF 2004 campaign [1], we tested an adaptive fusion system based on the MIMOR model [4, 7] in the multi-lingual ad-hoc track [3]. In 2005, we applied our system based on Lucene[1] to the new multi-lingual collection: We focused on Bulgarian, French and Hungarian.

2 CLEF Retrieval Experiments with the MIMOR Approach

The optimization of the retrieval system parameters was based on the French corpus of last year. The tools employed this year include Lucene and Java™-based snowball[2] analyzers as well as the Egothor stemmer[3]. In previous CLEF results, it has been pointed out, that a tri-gram index does not produce good results for French [5]. A four-gram or five-gram indexing approach seems more promising. Consequently, we conducted some test runs experimenting with the following parameters:

- Document fields: only officially permitted document fields were indexed. These were indexed as they were as well as in an extra Field FULLTEXT enclosing all the contents from the other fields.
- Origin of query terms: query terms could come from either *title* or *description* fields or both.
- Phrase queries of ngram terms: length of phrases, Boolean operators for concatenating terms

[1] Lucene: http://lucene.apache.org
[2] Snowball: http://jakarta.apache.org/lucene/docs/lucene-sandbox/snowball/
[3] Egothor: http://www.egothor.org/

C. Peters et al. (Eds.): CLEF 2005, LNCS 4022, pp. 37 – 43, 2006.

- Rigidity of phrase queries: non-exact phrase queries
- Blind relevance feedback (BRF): relevant documents/expansion term configuration (with Robertson Selection Value as term weighting scheme) and origin of expansion terms [3].
- Weighting for all parameters mentioned above

The search field FULLTEXT provided best performance overall. Searching on the other fields by themselves or in combination and with weighting did not yield as good results as the simple full-text approach. The document field employed for BRF mattered much more. Here, best results were obtained with the TEXT field. For all runs, we used the stopword lists made available by the University of Neuchâtel and made a few minor changes.

2.1 Query Construction for N-Gram Indexing

For phrase queries, the approach that worked best was one that constructed queries as follows: Given a query with 3 grams NG1, NG2, NG3 build the query so that q = "NG1" OR "NG2" OR "NG3" OR "NG1 NG2" OR "NG2 NG3" OR "NG1 NG2 NG3". Of course, such a query is likely to retrieve a lot of documents. Effectively, in almost all cases the system retrieved between 80% and 95% of all documents in the database. This is comparable to a quorum search in an extended Boolean model. As Table 1 shows, these results can greatly be improved by applying a more sophisticated configuration on top of the depicted query construction. One means is to allow phrases to be non-exact match phrases, i.e. allow WITHIN or NEAR-like operations, denoted by *slop* in the table. Here, the best setting was five, values started getting visibly worse from 10 up.

Table 3 gives optimized boost values for the n-gram retrieval experiments. The ratio of these figures has been determined experimentally. It can be seen that title terms are more important than *description* terms. Moreover, longer phrases are better than short ones, limited by the fact that starting with phrases of length four, performance began to drop.

Table 1. Effect of NEAR n term operation for boosting singles

NEAR n terms (slop)	4-gram		5-gram	
	Recall, max=915	**Avg. prec.**	**Recall, max=915**	**Avg. prec.**
1	688	0.277	698	0.272
2	687	0.278	698	0.272
3	684	0.277	698	0.276
4	687	0.277	701	0.277
5	691	0.272	703	0.276
6	691	0.271	702	0.274
7	689	0.271	699	0.273
8	689	0.274	697	0.272
9	688	0.274	696	0.270
10	686	0.278	694	0.270

Table 2. Result overview boosting singles, slop 5

BRF		4-gram		5-gram	
Documents	**Terms**	**Recall, max=915**	**Avg. prec.**	**Recall, max=915**	**Avg. prec.**
5	10	685	0.264	706	0.275
5	20	689	0.269	707	0.280
5	30	694	0.270	711	0.282
5	40	691	0.264	710	0.283
10	10	645	0.218	670	0.222
10	20	649	0.221	675	0.230
10	30	646	0.227	677	0.234
10	40	641	0.233	676	0.232

Table 3. Boost values for n-gram-based retrieval experiments

	Boosts according to origin	
# of terms in phrase	Origin: title	Origin: description
1	3, if short: 10	1, if short: 8
2	4	2
3	5	2
4	5	2

The single most important issue though are short terms. Phrase queries with only one term are of course just plain term queries. If, however, such a term query contains a term that has a smaller word length than the gram size, and taking into account that stopwords are eliminated, there is strong evidence that that term is highly important. In fact, most of these terms were acronyms or foreign words, e.g. in 2004 topics “g7“, “sida“ (French acronym for AIDS), “mir“ (Russian space station), “lady“ (Diana).

Blind relevance feedback had little impact on n-gram retrieval performance. For some queries, good short terms like those mentioned above were added to the query. However, terms selected by the algorithm received no special weight, i.e. they received a weight of one. Higher weights worsened the retrieval results. Furthermore, considering more than the top five documents for blind relevance feedback did not improve performance. Table 4 summarizes the results the best configurations achieved.

Table 4. Recall and average precision figures for n-gram-based retrieval experiments

Indexing-Method	Optimization	Blind relevance feedback	Recall, max=915	Avg. prec.
4-gram	base run	none	507	0.126
4-gram	with single term phrases	none	551	0.178
4-gram	boosting single term phrases	none	684	0.26
4-gram,	boosting singles, slop 5	none	691	0.272
4-gram,	boosting, slop 5	5 docs, 30 terms	694	0.27
5-gram	boosting, slop 5	5 docs, 30 terms	711	0.282
5-gram	boosting	5 docs, 30 terms	707	0.275

2.2 Boosting Document Fields for Stemming Approaches

Subsequently, stemming replaced the n-gram indexing procedure in another test series. Three different stemmers were used: Egothor, Snowball[4] and Lucene´s internal stemmer. Table 5 shows the results of the base runs.

Table 5. Base runs with stemming algorithms

	Recall, max=915	**Avg. prec.**
Lucene Stemmer, base run	817	0.356
Snowball Stemmer, base run	821	0.344
Egothor Stemmer, base run	817	0.346

Table 6. Results with Lucene stemmer

Boost Values			**BRF**		**Results**	
Title	**Description**	**BRF**	**Docs.**	**Terms**	**Recall, max=915**	**Avg. prec.**
9	3	1	5	10	856	0.379
9	3	1	5	20	857	0.388
9	3	1	5	30	863	0.405
9	3	1	5	40	857	0.402
9	3	2	5	10	855	0.379
9	3	2	5	20	854	0.390
9	3	2	5	30	857	0.403
9	3	2	5	40	855	0.392
9	3	3	5	10	855	0.379
9	3	3	5	20	857	0.385
9	3	3	5	30	861	0.394
9	3	3	5	40	858	0.388
base run					817	0.356

Table 7. Results with Snowball stemmer

Boost Values			**BRF**		**Results**	
Title	**Description**	**BRF**	**Docs.**	**Terms**	**Recall, max=915**	**Avg. prec.**
9	3	1	5	10	850	0.362
9	3	1	5	20	855	0.387
9	3	1	5	30	856	0.400
9	3	1	5	40	854	0.396
9	3	2	5	10	851	0.359
9	3	2	5	20	853	0.376
9	3	2	5	30	855	0.391
9	3	2	5	40	854	0.385
9	3	3	5	10	851	0.362
9	3	3	5	20	852	0.377
9	3	3	5	30	856	0.385
9	3	3	5	40	853	0.382
base run					821	0.344

[4] Snowball: http://jakarta.apache.org/lucene/docs/lucene-sandbox/snowball/

Table 8. Results with Egothor stemmer

Boost Values			BRF		Results	
Title	**Description**	**BRF**	**Docs.**	**Terms**	**Recall, max=915**	**Avg. prec.**
9	3	1	5	10	849	0.359
9	3	1	5	20	850	0.376
9	3	1	5	30	852	0.389
9	3	1	5	40	848	0.388
9	3	2	5	10	852	0.354
9	3	2	5	20	850	0.385
9	3	2	5	30	851	0.390
9	3	2	5	40	837	0.389
9	3	3	5	10	855	0.351
9	3	3	5	20	849	0.382
9	3	3	5	30	843	0.389
9	3	3	5	40	831	0.386
base run					817	0.346

Table 9. Best runs of stemmer-based retrieval experiments

Stemmer	Run Type	Recall, max = 915	Avg. Prec.
Egothor	brf 5 10, boost 9 3 3	855	0.351
Egothor	brf 5 60, boost 9 3 1	843	0.394
Lucene	brf 5 30, boost 9 3 1	863	0.405
Snowball	brf 5 30, boost 9 3 1	856	0.400

Queries that contained terms from both *title* and *description* fields from the topic files performed better than those that were based on only one source. The weighting of these terms, however, was a major impact factor. Several experiments with different boost values and blind relevance feedback parameters were carried out for each stemmer. The following tables 6, 7 and 8 show the results for the three stemmers.

Yet again, searching on structured document parts instead of the full text was worse. More importantly, even the baseline run with an Egothor-based stemmer was better than any n-gram run. Table 9 summarizes the settings for the best runs. Boost values were applied to title, description and terms from blind relevance feedback in this order.

3 Results of Submitted Runs

The parameters settings optimized with the French collection of CLEF 2004 were applied to the multi lingual collection in 2005. We submitted monolingual runs for Bulgarian, French, Hungarian and domain specific (GIRT), bilingual runs for French and GIRT. For Bulgarian and Hungarian we employed the setting outlined above for two runs each – 4-gram and 5-gram: searching on full text representations, boosting single terms which were shorter than the grams length, using BRF (5 docs, 30 terms), and a slop of 5.

For French, we used the Lucene-stemmer and the settings derived above. Additionally, we carried out a 5-gram based run as a comparison to Bulgarian and Hungarian. Both of these monolingual were then reshaped by adding terms tentatively derived from the multilingual European terminology database Eurodicautom5. We extracted additional terms from the top three hits from the database, if they were available. At least one of the query terms had to be present in the resulting term list, no special subject domain was chosen. These terms were assigned a weight of one. The results of these runs are shown in table 10.

Table 10. Results from the CLEF 2005 Workshop. EDA = Euradicautom.

	RunID	Languages	Run Type	retrieved	Relevant docs.	Avg. Prec.
Monolingual	UHIBG1	Bulgarian	5-gram	587	778	0.189
	UHIBG2	Bulgarian	4-gram	597	778	0.195
	UHIHU1	Hungarian	5-gram	733	939	0.310
	UHIHU2	Hungarian	4-gram	776	939	0.326
	UHIFR1	French	Lucene stemmer	2346	2537	0.385
	UHIFR2	French	Lucene stemmer, EDA	2364	2537	0.382
	UHIFR3	French	5-gram	1816	2537	0.340
	UHIFR4	French	5-gram, EDA	1851	2537	0.274
bi-ling-ual	UHIENFR1	English -> French	ImTranslator	2269	2537	0.337
	UHIENFR2	English -> French	EDA	2307	2537	0.347
	UHIRUFR1	Russsian -> French	ImTranslator	1974	2537	0.269

In the ad-hoc task, we submitted two English-to-French runs, one of which was enhanced by additional Eurodicautom terms, and one Russian-to-French run, all translated by ImTranslator6. The settings were the same as for the monolingual runs.

Considering the lack of experience with the new languages, the results are satisfying. However, more work with n-gram as well as stemming approaches are necessary for these languages.

4 Outlook

For the participation in CLEF 2005, we could stabilize the n-gram indexing and search. The performance remains worse than for stemming based runs. We compared three stemmers with different parameter settings. For future participations in ad-hoc tasks, we intend to apply the RECOIN (REtrieval COmponent INtegrator)[7] framework [6]. RECOIN is an object oriented JAVA framework for information retrieval

[5] http://europa.eu.int/eurodicautom/Controller

[6] http://freetranslation.paralink.com/

[7] http://recoin.sourceforge.net

experiments. It allows the integration of heterogeneous components into an experimentation system where many experiments may be carried out.

Acknowledgements

We would like to thank Nina Kummer and Sarah Risse, both graduate students at the University of Hildesheim, for including the Egothor stemmer into our system.

References

1. Braschler, M.; Peters, C.: Cross-Language Evaluation Forum: Objectives, Results, Achievements. In: Information Retrieval 7 (1/2) (2004) 7-31
2. Carpineto, C.; de Mori, R.; Romano, G.; Bigi, B.: An Information-Theoretic Approach to Automatic Query Expansion. In: ACM Transactions on Information Systems. 19 (1) (2001) 1-27
3. Hackl, R.; Mandl, T.; Womser-Hacker, C. (2005): Mono- and Cross-lingual Retrieval Experiments at the University of Hildesheim. In: Clough, P. D.; Gonzalo, J.; Jones, G. J. F.; Kluck, M. ; Magnini, B.; Peters, C. (eds.): Multilingual Information Access for Text, Speech and Images. 5th Workshop of the Cross-Language Evaluation Forum. Lecture Notes in Computer Science, Vol. 3491. Springer-Verlag, Berlin Heidelberg New York (2005) 165-169
4. Mandl, T.; Womser-Hacker, C.: A Framework for long-term Learning of Topical User Preferences in Information Retrieval. In: New Library World 105 (5/6) (2004) 184-195
5. McNamee, P.; Mayfield, J.: Character N-Gram Tokenization for European Language Text Retrieval. In: Information Retrieval 7 (1/2) (2004) 73-98
6. Scheufen, J.-H.. (2006): RECOIN: Modell offener Schnittstellen für Information Retrieval Systeme und Komponenten. In: Mandl, T.; Womser-Hacker, C. (eds.): Effektive Information Retrieval Verfahren in der Praxis. Proceedings Vierter Hildesheimer Evaluierungs- und Retrievalworkshop (HIER 2005), Hildesheim, 20. Juli 2005. Schriften zur Informationswissenschaft, Vol. 45. UVK, Konstanz (2006) to appear
7. Womser-Hacker, C.: Das MIMOR-Modell. Mehrfachindexierung zur dynamischen Methoden-Objekt-Relationierung im Information Retrieval. Habilitationsschrift. Universität Regensburg, Informationswissenschaft (1997)

MIRACLE at Ad-Hoc CLEF 2005: Merging and Combining Without Using a Single Approach

José M. Goñi-Menoyo[1], José C. González-Cristóbal[1,3], and Julio Villena-Román[2,3]

[1] Universidad Politécnica de Madrid
[2] Universidad Carlos III de Madrid
[3] DAEDALUS - Data, Decisions and Language, S.A.
josemiguel.goni@upm.es, jgonzalez@dit.upm.es, julio.villena@uc3m.es

Abstract. This paper presents the 2005 Miracle's team approach to the Ad-Hoc Information Retrieval tasks. The goal for the experiments this year was twofold: to continue testing the effect of combination approaches on information retrieval tasks, and improving our basic processing and indexing tools, adapting them to new languages with strange encoding schemes. The starting point was a set of basic components: stemming, transforming, filtering, proper nouns extraction, paragraph extraction, and pseudo-relevance feedback. Some of these basic components were used in different combinations and order of application for document indexing and for query processing. Second-order combinations were also tested, by averaging or selective combination of the documents retrieved by different approaches for a particular query. In the multilingual track, we concentrated our work on the merging process of the results of monolingual runs to get the overall multilingual result, relying on available translations. In both cross-lingual tracks, we have used available translation resources, and in some cases we have used a combination approach.

1 Introduction

The MIRACLE team is made up of three university research groups located in Madrid (UPM, UC3M and UAM) along with DAEDALUS, a company founded in 1998 as a spin-off of two of these groups. DAEDALUS is a leading company in linguistic technologies in Spain and is the coordinator of the MIRACLE team. This is our third participation in CLEF, after 2003 and 2004. As well as bilingual, monolingual and cross lingual tasks, the team has participated this year in the ImageCLEF, Q&A, WebCLEF and GeoCLEF tracks.

The starting point was a set of basic components: stemming, transformation (transliteration, elimination of diacritics and conversion to lowercase), filtering (elimination of stop and frequent words), extracting proper nouns, extracting paragraphs, and pseudo-relevance feedback. Some of these basic components are used in different combinations and order of application for document indexing and for query processing. Second order combinations were also tested, mainly by averaging or by selective combination of the documents retrieved by different approaches for a particular query. When evidence is found of better precision of one system at one extreme of the recall level (i.e. 1), complemented by the better precision of another system at the

C. Peters et al. (Eds.): CLEF 2005, LNCS 4022, pp. 44 – 53, 2006.

other recall end (i.e. 0), then both are combined to benefit from their complementary results.

Additionally, during the last year our group has been improving an indexing system based on the trie data structure, which was reported last year. Tries [1] have been successfully used by the MIRACLE team for years, as an efficient technique for the storage and retrieval of huge lexical resources, combined with a continuation-based approach to morphological treatment [4]. However, the adaptation of these structures to manage document indexing and retrieval for IR applications efficiently has been a hard task, mainly in the issues concerning the performance of the construction of the index. Thus, this year we have used only our trie-based indexing system, and so, the Xapian [12] indexing system used in the previous CLEF editions was no longer needed. In fact, we have been able to carry out more experiments than the previous year, since we have had more computing time available because of this improvement in indexing efficiency.

For the 2005 bilingual track, runs were submitted for the following language pairs: English to Bulgarian, French, Hungarian and Portuguese; and Spanish to French and Portuguese. For the multilingual track, runs were submitted using as source language English, French, and Spanish. Finally, in the monolingual case runs were submitted for Bulgarian, French, Hungarian, and Portuguese.

2 Description of the MIRACLE Toolbox

Document collections were pre-processed before indexing, using different combinations of elementary processes, each one oriented towards a particular experiment. For each of these, topic queries were also processed using the same combination of processes. (Although some variants have been used, as will be described later.)

The baseline approach to document and topic query processing is made up of a combination of the following steps:

- **Extraction:** The raw text from different document collections or topic files is extracted with ad-hoc scripts that selected the contents of the desired XML elements. All those permitted for automatic runs were used. (Depending on the collection, all of the existing TEXT, TITLE, LEAD1, TX, LD, TI, or ST for document collections, and the contents of the TITLE, DESC, and NARR for topic queries.) The contents of these tags were concatenated, without further distinction to feed subsequent processing steps. This extraction treatment has a special filter for extracting topic queries in the case of the use of the narrative field: some patterns that were obtained from the topics of the past campaigns are eliminated, since they are recurrent and misleading in the retrieval process; for example, for English, "*... are not relevant.*", or "*...are to be excluded.*". All the sentences that contain these patterns are filtered out.
- **Paragraphs extraction:** In some experiments, we indexed paragraphs[1] instead of documents. Thus, the subsequent retrieval process returned document paragraphs, so we needed to combine the relevance measures from all paragraphs retrieved for

[1] Paragraphs are either marked by the <P> tag in the original XML document, or are separated from each other by two carriage returns, so they are easily detected.

the same document. We tested several approaches for this combination, for example counting the number of paragraphs, adding relevance measures or using the maximum of the relevance figures of the paragraphs retrieved. Experimentally, we got best results using the following formula for document relevance:

$$rel_N = rel_{mN} + \xi \cdot \frac{1}{n} \cdot \sum_{j \neq m} rel_{jN}$$

where n is the number of paragraphs retrieved for document N, rel_{jN} is the relevance measure obtained for the j-th paragraph of document N, and m refers to the paragraph with maximum relevance. The coefficient ξ was adjusted experimentally to 0.75. The idea behind this formula is to give paramount importance to the maximum paragraph relevance, but taking into account the rest of the relevant paragraphs to a lesser extent. Paragraph extraction was not used for topic processing.

- **Tokenization:** This process extracts basic text components, detecting and isolating punctuation symbols. Some basic entities are also treated, such as numbers, initials, abbreviations, and years. For now, we do not treat compounds, proper nouns, acronyms or other entities. The outcomes of this process are only single words and years that appear as numbers in the text (e.g. 1995, 2004, etc.).
- **Filtering:** All words recognized as *stopwords* are filtered out. *Stopwords* in the target languages were initially obtained from [11], but were extended using several other sources and our own knowledge and resources. We also used other lists of words to exclude from the indexing and querying processes, which were obtained from the topics of past CLEF editions. We consider that such words have no semantics in the type of queries used in CLEF; for example, in the English list: *appear, relevant, document, report,* etc.
- **Transformation:** The items that resulted from tokenization were normalized by converting all uppercase letters to lowercase and eliminating accents. This process is usually carried out after stemming, although it can be done before, but the resulting lexemes are different. We ought to do it before stemming in the case of the Bulgarian and Hungarian languages, since these stemmers did not work well with uppercase letters. Note that the accent removal process is not applicable for Bulgarian.
- **Stemming:** This process is applied to each one of the words to be indexed or used for retrieval. We used standard stemmers from Porter [8] for most languages, except for Hungarian, where we used a stemmer from Neuchatel [11].
- **Proper noun extraction:** In some experiments, we try to detect and extract proper nouns in the text. The detection was very simple: Any chunk that results from the tokenization process is considered a proper noun provided that its first letter is uppercase, unless this word is included in the *stopwords* list or in a specifically built list of words that are not suitable to be proper nouns (mainly verbs and adverbs). We opted for this simple strategy[2] since we did not have available huge lists of proper nouns. In the experiments that used this process, only the proper nouns extracted from the topics fed a query to an index of documents of *normal* words, where neither proper nouns were extracted nor stemming was carried out.
- **Linguistic processing:** In the Multi-8 track, and only in the case of Spanish as topic language, we tested an approach consisting in pre-processing the topics with

[2] Note that multi-word proper nouns cannot be treated this way.

a high quality morphologic analysis tool. This tool is STILUS[3]. STILUS not only recognizes closed words, but also expressions (prepositional, adverbial, etc.). In this case, STILUS is simply used to discard closed words and expressions from the topics and to obtain the main form of their component words (in most cases, singular masculine or feminine for nouns and adjectives and infinitive for verbs). The queries are so transformed to a simple list of words that are passed to the automatic translators (one word per line).

- **Translation:** For cross-lingual tracks, popular on-line translation or available dictionary resources were used to translate topic queries to target languages: ATRANS was used for the pairs EsFr and EsPt; Bultra and Webtrance for EnBg[4]; MoBiCAT for EnHu; and SYSTRAN was used for the language pairs EnFr, EsFr, and EnPt. However, for multilingual runs having English as topic language, we avoided working on the translation problem for some runs. In this case, we have used the provided translations for topic queries [2], testing Savoy's [10] approach to translation concatenations. Two cases were considered: all available translations are concatenated, and selected translations are concatenated. Table 1 shows the translations used for both cases.

  In the Multi-8 track we also used automatic translation systems: for Spanish and French as topic languages, ATRANS was used for the pairs EsFr and EsPt; WorldLingo for EsDe, EsIt, and EsNl; InterTrans for EsFi, EsSv, FrFi, and FrSv; and SYSTRAN was used for all the other language pairs. Only one translator was used for each pair.
- **Final use**
  - **Indexing:** When all the documents processed through a combination of the former steps are ready for indexing, they are fed into our indexing *trie* engine to build the document collection index.
  - **Retrieval:** When all the documents processed by a combination of the aforementioned steps are topic queries, they are fed to an ad-hoc front-end of the retrieval *trie* engine to search the previously built document collection index. In the 2005 experiments, only OR combinations of the search terms were used. The retrieval model used is the well-known Robertson's Okapi BM-25 [9] formula for the probabilistic retrieval model, without relevance feedback.

After retrieval, some other special processes were used to define additional experiments:

Pseudo-relevance feedback: We used this technique in some experiments. After a first retrieval step, we processed the first retrieved document to get their indexing terms that, after a standard processing[5] (see below) are fed back to a second retrieval step, whose result is used.

---

[3] STILUS® is a trademark of DAEDALUS-Data, Decisions and Language, S.A. It is the core of the Spanish-processing tools of the company, that include spell, grammar and style checkers, fuzzy search engines, semantic processing, etc.

[4] In the case of Bulgarian, an average combination of the results from the translations with the Webtrance and Bultra systems from English to Bulgarian has also been used.

[5] Both retrieval processes can be independent of each other: we could have used two different treatments for the queries and documents, so using different indexes for each of the retrievals. In our case, only standard treatments were used for both retrieval steps.

Table 1. Available automatic translations used for concatenating

	Topic language							
Translation	DE	EN	ES	FI	FR	IT	NL	SV
ALT					A			
BA1	AH		AH	AH	AH	AH	AH	AH
BA2	A		A	A	A	A	A	A
BA3	A		A	A		A	A	A
FRE	AH		AH		AH	AH	AH	
GOO	AH		AH		AH	AH		
INT	A		A	AH	A	A	A	AH
LIN					A			
REV	AH		AH		AH			
SYS	AH		A		A	A		

ALT for Babelfish Altavista, BA1, BA2, and BA3[6] for Babylon, FRE for FreeTranslation, GOO for Google Language Tools, INT for InterTrans, LIN for WordLingo, REV for Reverso, and SYS for Systran. The entries in the table contain A (for ALL) if a translation is available for English to the topic language shown in the heading row of a column, and it is used for the concatenation of all available translations; and H if a translation is used for the selected concatenation of translations.

– **Combination:** The results from some basic experiments were combined in different ways. The underlying hypothesis is that, to some extent, the documents with a good score in almost all experiments are more likely to be relevant than other documents that have a good score in one experiment, but a bad one in others. Two strategies were followed for combining experiments:

  • **Average:** The relevance figures obtained using the probabilistic retrieval in all the experiments to be combined for a particular document in a given query are added. This approach combines the relevance figures of the experiments without highlighting a particular experiment.
  • **Asymmetric WDX combination:** In this particular type of combination, two experiments are combined in the following way: The relevance of the first D documents for each query of the first experiment is preserved for the resulting combined relevance, whereas the relevance for the remaining documents in both experiments are combined using weights W and X. We have only run experiments labeled "011", that is, the ones that get the most relevant documents from the first basic experiment and all the remaining documents retrieved from the second basic experiment, re-sorting all the results using the original relevance measure value.

– **Merging:** In the multilingual case, the approach used requires that the monolingual results list for each one of the target languages have to be merged. The results obtained are very sensitive to the merging approach for the relevance measures. The

[6] The digit after BA shows how many words are used from the translation of a word, provided that it returns more than one.

probabilistic BM25 [9] formula used for monolingual retrieval gives relevance measures that depend heavily on parameters that are too dependent on the monolingual collection, so it is not very good for this type of multilingual merging, since relevance measures are not comparable between collections. In spite of this, we carried out merging experiments using the relevance figures obtained from each monolingual retrieval process, considering three cases:[7]

- Using original relevance measures for each document as obtained from the monolingual retrieval process. The results are made up of the documents with greater relevance measures.
- Normalizing relevance measures with respect to the maximum relevance measure obtained for each topic query *i* (*standard normalization*):

  $$rel_{i\,norm} = \frac{rel_i}{rel_{i\max}}$$

  Then, the results are made up of the documents with greater normalized relevance measures.
- Normalizing relevance measures with respect to the maximum and minimum relevance measure obtained for each topic query *i (alternate normalization)*:

  $$rel_{i\,alt} = \frac{rel_i - rel_{i\min}}{rel_{i\max} - rel_{i\min}}$$

  Then, the results are made up of the documents with greater alternate normalized relevance measures.

In addition to all this, we tried a different approach to merging: Considering that the more relevant documents for each of the topics are usually the first ones in the results list, we will select from each monolingual results file a variable number of documents, proportional to the average relevance number of the first N documents. Thus, if we need 1,000 documents for a given topic query, we will get more documents from languages where the average relevance of the first N relevant documents is greater. We did all this both from non-normalized runs, but normalized after the merging process is carried out (with *standard* and *alternate* normalization); and from runs normalized with *alternate* normalization. We tested several cases using results from baseline runs, using several values for N: 1, 10, 50, 125, 250, and 1,000.

3 Description of the Experiments

For this campaign we have designed several experiments in which the documents for indexing and the topic queries for retrieval are processed using a particular combination of some of the steps described in the previous section. A detailed inventory of the experiments, the processes used for each one, and their encoding in the name of the experiment can be found in the papers submitted to the CLEF 2005 Workshop ([3], [5]). Details of the documents collections and the tasks can be found in the introduction [8] and track overview [6] papers.

---

[7] Round-robin merging for results of each monolingual collection has not been used.

Several hundreds of experiments were run, and the criterion for choosing the ones to be submitted was the runs that obtained best results using topic queries and *qrels* sets from the 2004 campaign. Except for Portuguese, the best results obtained came from runs that were not submitted. We think that this behavior can be explained since the results depend to a great extent on the different topics selected each year. It is worth noting that we obtained the best results using the narrative field of the topic queries in all cases, as well as the standard processing approach.

We expected to have had better results using combinations of proper noun indexing with standard runs, as it seemed to follow from the results from 2004 campaign, but it has not been the case. It is clear that the quality of the tokenization step is of paramount importance for precise document processing. We still think that a high-quality entity recognition (proper nouns or acronyms for people, companies, countries, locations, and so on) could improve the precision and recall figures of the overall retrieval, as well as a correct recognition and normalization of dates, times, numbers, etc. Pseudo-relevance feedback has not performed quite well, but we ran quite few experiments of this type to extract general conclusions. On the other hand, these runs had a lot of querying terms, which made them very slow.

Regarding the basic experiments, the general conclusions were known in advance: retrieval performance can be improved by using stemming, filtering of frequent words and appropriate weighting.

Regarding cross-lingual experiments, the MIRACLE team has worked on their merging and combining aspects, departing from the translation ones. Combining approaches seems to improve results in some cases. For example, the average combining approach allows us to obtain better results when combining the results from translations for Bulgarian than the Bultra or Webtrance systems alone. In multilingual experiments, combining (concatenating) translations permits better results, as was reported previously [10], when good translations are available. Regarding the merging aspects, our approach did not obtain better results than standard merging, whether normalized or not. Alternate normalizations seem to behave better than the standard normalization, whereas the latter behaves better than no normalization. This occurs too when normalization is used in our own approach to merging.

Regarding the approach consisting of preprocessing queries in the source topic language with high quality tools for extracting content words before translation, the results have been good when used in the case of Spanish (with our tool STILUS). This approach achieved the best precision figures at 0 and at 1 recall extremes, although worse average precision than other runs.

In the appendix we have included two figures that summarize these results. Figure 1 shows a comparison of the results obtained in the best runs in the monolingual experiments for each target language. The best results are obtained for French and Portuguese, and the worst for Bulgarian. Figure 2 shows the results obtained in the best runs in the cross-lingual experiments for bilingual and multilingual runs, considering all source languages used.

4 Conclusions and Future Work

Future work of the MIRACLE team in these tasks will be directed to several lines of research: (a) Tuning our indexing and retrieval *trie*-based engine in order to get even better performance in the indexing and retrieval phases, and (b) improving the tokenization step; in our opinion, this is one of the most critical processing ones and can improve the overall results of the IR process. Good entity recognition and normalization is still missing from our processing scheme for these tasks. We need better performance of the retrieval system to drive runs that are efficient when the query has some hundred terms, as occurs when using pseudo-relevance feedback. We also need to explore further the combination schemes with these enhancements of the basic processes.

Regarding cross-lingual tasks, future work will be centered on the merging aspects of the monolingual results. The translation aspects of this process are of no interest to us, since our research interests depart from all this: we will only use translation resources available, and we will try to combine them to get better results.

On the other hand, the process of merging the monolingual results is very sensitive in the way it is done; there are some techniques to be explored. In addition to that, perhaps a different way of measuring relevance is needed for monolingual retrieval when multilingual merging has to be carried out. Such a measure should be independent of the collection, so monolingual relevance measures would be comparable.

Acknowledgements

This work has been partially supported by the Spanish R+D National Plan, by means of the project RIMMEL (Multilingual and Multimedia Information Retrieval, and its Evaluation), TIN2004-07588-C03-01.

Special mention to our colleagues of the MIRACLE team should be done (in alphabetical order): Ana María García-Serrano, Ana González-Ledesma, José Mª Guirao-Miras, Sara Lana-Serrano, José Luis Martínez-Fernández, Paloma Martínez-Fernández, Ángel Martínez-González, Antonio Moreno-Sandoval and César de Pablo-Sánchez.

References

1. Aoe, J.-I., Morimoto, K., and Sato, T.: An Efficient Implementation of Trie Structures. Software Practice and Experience 22(9): 695-721 (1992)
2. CLEF 2005 Multilingual Information Retrieval resources page. On line http://www.computing.dcu.ie/~gjones/CLEF2005/Multi-8/ [Visited 11/08/2005].
3. González, J.C., Goñi-Menoyo, J.M., and Villena-Román, J.: MIRACLE's 2005 Approach to Cross-lingual Information Retrieval. Working Notes for the CLEF 2005 Workshop. Vienna, Austria (2005) Online http://clef.isti.cnr.it/2005/working_notes/workingnotes2005/gonzalez05.pdf [Visited 05/11/2005].
4. Goñi-Menoyo, J. M., González-Cristóbal, J. C., and Fombella-Mourelle, J.: An optimised trie index for natural language processing lexicons. MIRACLE Technical Report. Universidad Politécnica de Madrid (2004)

5. Goñi-Menoyo, J. M., González, J. C., and Villena-Román, J.: MIRACLE's 2005 Approach to Monolingual Information Retrieval. Working Notes for the CLEF 2005 Workshop. Vienna,Austria (2005) On line http://clef.isti.cnr.it/2005/working_notes/workingnotes2005/menoyo05.pdf [Visited 05/11/2005].
6. Di Nunzio, G. M., Ferro, N., and Jones, G. J. F.: CLEF 2005: Ad Hoc Multilingual Track Overview. Proceedings of the Cross Language Evaluation Forum 2005, Springer Lecture Notes in Computer science, 2006 (in this volume).
7. Peters, C.: What happened in CLEF 2005. Proceedings of the Cross Language Evaluation Forum 2005, Springer Lecture Notes in Computer science, 2006 (in this volume).
8. Porter, M.: Snowball stemmers and resources page. On line http://www.snowball.tartarus.org [Visited 13/07/2005].
9. Robertson, S.E. et al.: Okapi at TREC-3. In Overview of the Third Text REtrieval Conference (TREC-3). D.K. Harman (Ed.). Gaithersburg, MD: NIST (1995)
10. Savoy, J.: Report on CLEF-2003 Multilingual Tracks. Comparative Evaluation of Multilingual Information Access Systems (Peters, C; Gonzalo, J.; Brascher, M.; and Kluck, M., Eds.). Lecture Notes in Computer Science, vol. 3237, pp. 64-73. Springer. (2004)
11. University of Neuchatel. Page of resources for CLEF (Stopwords, transliteration, stemmers…) On line http://www.unine.ch/info/clef [Visited 13/07/2005].
12. Xapian: an Open Source Probabilistic Information Retrieval library. On line http://www.xapian.org [Visited 13/07/2005].

Appendix

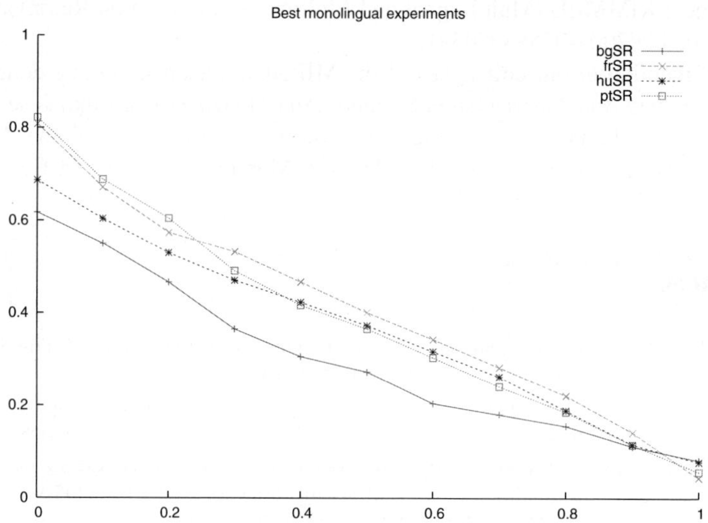

Fig. 1. Comparison of results from the best monolingual experiments

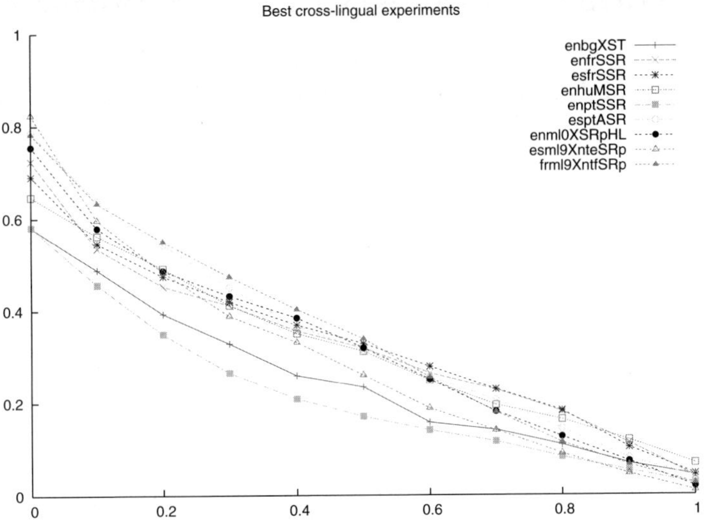

Fig. 2. Comparison of results from the best cross-lingual experiments

The XLDB Group at the CLEF 2005 Ad-Hoc Task

Nuno Cardoso[1], Leonardo Andrade[1], Alberto Simões[2], and Mário J. Silva[1]

[1] Grupo XLDB - Departamento de Informática
Faculdade de Ciências da Universidade de Lisboa
[2] Departamento de Informática, Universidade do Minho
{ncardoso, leonardo, mjs}@xldb.di.fc.ul.pt, ambs@di.uminho.pt

Abstract. This paper presents the participation of the XLDB Group in the CLEF 2005 ad-hoc monolingual and bilingual subtasks for Portuguese. We participated with an improved and extended configuration of the tumba! search engine software. We detail the new features and evaluate their performance.

1 Introduction

In 2004, the XLDB Group made its debut participation in CLEF, on the monolingual ad-hoc Portuguese retrieval task [1]. The main goals were to obtain hands-on experience in joint evaluations of information retrieval (IR) and evaluate tumba!, our web search engine [2] on this task. We learned that we had to come up with new approaches and methods, as the strategy for searching and indexing large web collections is different than when querying the kind of document collections used in the CLEF ad-hoc task.

This year, we embraced the ad-hoc task with the objective of evaluating new methods and algorithms for the task:

- Implementation of new logic operators on query strings to support expanded queries
- Development of new methods for using all the topic information provided and merging the combined result sets.
- Topic translation for submission of English to Portuguese bilingual runs.

This paper is organized as follows: Section 2 describes our system and enumerates the main changes from last year's configuration. In Section 3, we present our evaluation goals and submitted runs. Section 4 presents the results obtained. Section 5 summarises our conclusions.

2 Improvements

One of the main lessons learned from last year's CLEF ad-hoc task participation was that IR in large web collections is quite different from IR on small text collections. Simple adjustments to a web search engine aren't sufficient if we want to use all the information provided for each topic instead of just a few terms to query the CLEF ad-hoc collection. This motivated the development of a set of new software, to handle the task properly.

C. Peters et al. (Eds.): CLEF 2005, LNCS 4022, pp. 54–60, 2006.

We developed a new query expansion module that generates alternative queries from the descriptions given. This module, called QuerCol (Queries Collator) is external to the core tumba! search engine, but has an essential role in the production of the runs we submitted to CLEF in 2005.

We also improved tumba! in its capability to properly rank poorly linked and tagged documents. We developed an algorithm based on TF $\times$ IDF weighting to rank the results for CLEF 2005, added support for the 'OR' operator in query strings, and implemented new result set merging algorithms.

With these new modules, our group is now taking the first steps to include the basic set of components required for serious participation on in this kind of IR task – robust stemming, weighting scheme and blind feedback [3].

In the remainder of this section, we detail the design of QuerCol, the newly developed query expansion module, and the improvements made to the query processing sub-system of tumba!.

2.1 Query Expansion

The main conclusion of our CLEF 2004 participation was that, in order to achieve higher recall values, we need to expand the title terms into alternative variants, as collections include many documents relevant to the query topic without all the topic terms [1]. So, this year we created multiple queries for each topic, based on synonyms, morphological and lexical expansion of the title terms, and a selection of other terms from the topic description.

Query strings can now include the 'OR' (disjunction) operator, which wasn't supported by the query server that we had in 2004. This enabled us to make extensive use of synonyms and morphological variations of the title terms. Other systems and former CLEF participants, like Nateau et al, experimented query expansion modules based on the 'OR' operator [4], and that inspired us to start QuerCol.

QuerCol generates queries from a given topic using the following approach:

1. *Eliminate common stop-words and CLEF-related stop-words.* The latter include terms like 'document' and 'relevant', which are frequent in topic descriptions. We obtain these by selecting the top 5 most frequent terms from all topics.
2. *Obtain title concepts.* After stop-word elimination, we assume that all remaining title words are root-terms of Boolean expressions in the disjunctive normal form, each representing a **concept**, which must be present in all query strings derived from the topic. We used *jspell* to expand morphologically the title concepts [5,6]. *Jspell* is a morphological analyser based on derivation: words are created applying a set of rules over a root term. This way, it is easy to check the root term and apply rules to create word derivations for each title concept. From these, we only pick those having a frequency of at least 5 in the collection.
3. *Obtain expanded concepts.* For each topic title, we take the terms as a conjunction query, which is submitted to the tumba! instance indexing the CLEF ad-hoc collection. Then, we measure the TF $\times$ IDF value for each term in the topic's set of words, for each document in the obtained result set. We rank the top 8 terms and discard those with a document frequency lower than 5 in the collection. The selected terms are called **expanded concepts**.

4. *Compute the similarity between the title concepts and the expanded concepts*. For instance, if the title concepts are *shark* and *attack*, and the term *strike* is selected as an expanded concept, we want to relate it to the *attack* concept, to create a query like *shark attack OR shark strike*. We used a database of term co-occurrences of Portuguese terms developed by the Porto node of Linguateca, built from two Portuguese corpora, CETEMPublico [7] and WPT 03 [8]. In the example above, we queried the database for the top-20 terms that co-occur after the term *shark*. If *strike* is in the result, we can say that the two terms belong to the same concept, and we add *strike* to the *attack* concept term list.

   If an expanded concept isn't associated to a concept, it is later added to the query string as a disjunction. This means that expanded concepts don't influence the result set lists, but contribute to weighting the documents containing them.
5. *Query string generation*. In the end, each title concept is defined as a list of terms, selected both from the expanded concepts and from the morphological expansions of the initial title terms. With all the lists of concepts for each topic, we compute all term combinations as a $m \times n$ matrix of m concepts $\times n$ term list size for each concept, and finally we merge them with disjunction operators to generate a single query string.

For the English to Portuguese ad-hoc bilingual subtask, we devised the two following approaches:

1. Using the Babelfish web translation tool (`http://babelfish.altavista.com`). The topic strings were extracted and sent one at a time to the translator and the translations replaced the original topic strings.
2. Using Example Based Machine Translation (EBMT) methods in parallel corpora [9]. The translations were made from a translation memory built from multilingual thesauri freely available on the Internet (EuroVoc, Unesco thesaurus and others). The thesauri have not only simple term entries but also multi-word entries that help in the translation of some word sequences. The translation memory was then used to translate word sequences of the topics file. Words without a corresponding entry in the translation memory were individually translated using Babelfish.

2.2 Weighting and Ranking

Sidra is the indexing and ranking system used in the tumba! web search engine [10]. Sidra provides support for "all the terms" searches, exact phrase queries and field searches that restrict result sets to a specific subdomain or document format. Sidra was primarily designed to rank web documents, as its original ranking function relied mainly on metadata such as links' anchor text, URL strings and page titles. However, it performs poorly when handling document collections with scarce metadata, such as the CLEF ad-hoc collection. Sidra does not perform term stemming; the index terms are all the single words, indexed as a full inverted file.

To improve the performance of Sidra on CLEF, we made two major enhancements:

1. Implement a weighting algorithm based on TF $\times$ IDF. This enables us to tackle the absence of meta-data, and to have a baseline for a future implementation of a full Okapi BM 25 schema [11].

2. Develop support for disjunction of terms. Query strings submitted to Sidra may now include the 'OR' and 'AND' logic operators, as long as the query respects the Disjunctive Normal Form.

As Sidra query servers handle each conjunction as a simple query, support for the 'OR' operator consisted in devising strategies for merging the result sets of ranked documents obtained in each sub-query. We used two simple approaches:

Weight Merge: The final result set is obtained by sorting the weights of each result on the combined result set. The final weight of a document present in more than one result set is the sum of the weights of the document in each result set.

Round-Robin Merge: The final result set is generated by sorting the result sets by the weight of the top ranked document in the result set. Then, documents are picked from each result set using a round-robin rule. Documents already picked to the merged result set are ignored.

3 Runs

For the ad-hoc task, we submitted 5 runs for the Portuguese ad-hoc monolingual subtask (4 regular runs plus one mandatory run) and 4 for the English to Portuguese ad-hoc bilingual ad-hoc subtask. As we were testing implementations of the 'OR' operator on tumba!, we selected the result set merging methods as a parameter to measure which produced better results. Hence, we applied the Weight Merge algorithm to half the runs plus the mandatory run, and Round Robin Merge to the other half (see Table 1).

Table 1. Runs submitted to the ad-hoc task

Monolingual				
Query	Manual		Automatic	
Fusion	Weight	Round Robin	Weight	Round Robin
Run	XLDBTumba01	XLDBTumba05	XLDBTumba02 XLDBTumba09	XLDBTumba06

Bilingual				
Query	EBMT translation		Babelfish Translation	
Fusion	Weight	Round Robin	Weight	Round Robin
Run	XLDBTumba03	XLDBTumba07	XLDBTumba04	XLDBTumba08

In the monolingual subtask, we created runs XLDBTumba01 and XLDBTumba05 by manually adding all kinds of synonyms and morphological expansions that seem reasonable to the queries. We used it as a baseline for evaluation against other submitted runs. For runs XLDBTumba02 and XLDBTumba06, QuerCol automatically generated the queries. We aimed at obtaining result sets of the same level of quality as for manually created runs, as QuerCol used the same query creation approach. XLDBTumba09 is a mandatory run, with query strings automatically generated from the topics' title and description fields only.

On the bilingual subtask, the goal of our participation was to have a preliminary evaluation of the EBMT systems being developed at the Braga node of Linguateca.

4 Results

Figure 1 and Table 2 show the obtained results. One of our main goals was to compare the two result sets merging strategies, and in the end the Weight merge method outperformed the Round-Robin method. A deeper analysis on the results will provide valuable hints on the result set merging mechanism to implement for disjunctive queries.

Manual query creation (runs 01 and 05) performed better than automatic query creation (runs 02 and 06). Further analysis on the obtained results will also provide good hints for improving QuerCol to narrow the difference.

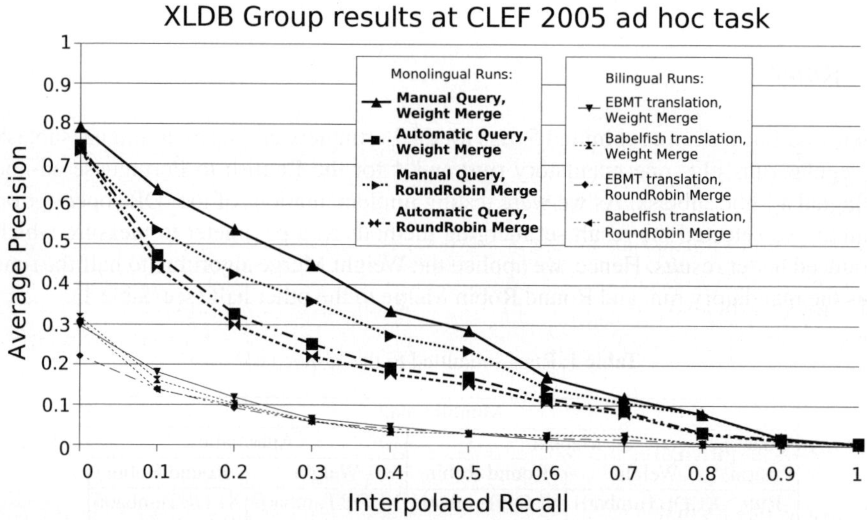

Fig. 1. Results of the XLDB Group on ad-hoc monolingual (thick lines) and bilingual subtasks (thin lines)

Table 2. Overall results on all runs

Run label	Retrieved	Relevant	Ret_rel	Avg. Prec.	R-Prec.	Overall Prec.	Overall Recall
XLDBTumba01	12595	2904	1675	29.0%	34.3%	13.3%	57.7%
XLDBTumba02	5546	2904	986	19.7%	23.2%	17.8%	34.0%
XLDBTumba05	12595	2904	1666	24.0 %	30.6%	13.2%	57.4%
XLDBTumba06	5546	2904	985	18.1%	22.5%	17.8%	34.0%
XLDBTumba03	4875	1991	605	5.8%	8.0%	12.4%	30.4%
XLDBTumba04	6774	2156	299	5.5%	7.4%	4.4%	13.9%
XLDBTumba07	4875	1991	617	4.7%	7.2%	12.6%	31.0%
XLDBTumba08	6774	2156	301	5.3%	7.4%	4.4%	14.0%
XLDBTumba09	6521	2904	989	19.4%	22.9%	15.2%	34.0%

The results of the monolingual runs are much better than the bilingual. This is likely to be a consequence of some poor translations. We concluded that we were using thesauri with less quality than expected. As we have overlaps (alternative translations coming from different thesauri), some of the used translations came from the wrong thesaurus and were the source of the bad translation results. Table 2 shows that the runs using EMBT translation obtained more relevant results with less retrieved documents, which is an encouraging result.

The relative performance of the best of our runs compared to other groups' submissions is close to the median. There are a few queries where our performance is much worse than the median for reasons that we have yet to find. However, given that in 2005 our weighting algorithm was very simple, we believe that an improvement here would likely raise the performance level of our software in future evaluations.

5 Conclusion

The results we obtained this year show a major improvement over last year. This comes as a direct consequence of the changes made to our IR system. Some of the developments for this CLEF task will be incorporated in the next version of tumba!

We have also identified further improvements, like extending QuerCol with a Portuguese stemmer. This would create better term expansions and improve the 'clustering' of terms from the same concept. QuerCol's generated queries also revealed some flaws that we need to amend, as there are concepts with more than one term that shouldn't be handled separately (for instance, *Bill Clinton*). Some morphological expansions of title terms might also produce misleading variations. Finally, we could also incorporate the software developed for our participation in GeoCLEF 2005 to expand geographic names in queries [12].

Acknowledgements

We would like to thank Daniel Gomes, who managed the tumba! repository instance created to support our participation in this joint evaluation. Thanks also to the developers of the tumba! search engine and the Portuguese language tools used to assemble the runs. Our participation was partly financed by the Portuguese Fundação para a Ciência e Tecnologia through grants POSI / PLP / 43931 / 2001 (Linguateca) and POSI / SRI / 40193 / 2001 (GREASE).

References

1. Cardoso, N., Silva, M.J., Costa, M.: The XLDB Group at CLEF 2004. In Peters, C., ed.: Working Notes for the CLEF 2004 Workshop, Bath, UK (2004)
2. Silva, M.J.: The Case for a Portuguese Web Search Engine. In: Proceedings of ICWI-03, the 2003 IADIS International Conference on WWW/Internet, Algarve, Portugal, IADIS (2003) 411–418
3. Braschler, M., Peters, C.: 1-2. In: Cross-Language Evaluation Forum: Objectives, Results, Achievements. Volume 7. Kluwer Academic Publishers (2004) 7–31

4. Nateau, D., Jarmasz, M., Barrière, C., Foster, G., St-Jacques, C.: Using COTS Search Engine and Custom Query Strategies at CLEF. In C.Peters, ed.: Working Notes for the CLEF 2004 Workshop, Bath, UK (2004)
5. Almeida, J.J., Pinto, U.: Jspell – a Module for Generic Natural Language Lexical Analysis. In: Actas do X Encontro da Associação Portuguesa de Linguística, Évora (1994) 1–15 in Portuguese. http://www.di.uminho.pt/~jj/pln/jspell1.ps.gz.
6. Simões, A.M., Almeida, J.J.: Jspell.pm – a Morphological Analysis Module for Natural Language Processing. In: Actas do XVII Encontro da Associação Portuguesa de Linguística, Lisbon (2001) 485–495 In Portuguese.
7. Rocha, P., Santos, D.: CETEMPúblico: Um corpus de grandes dimensões de linguagem jornalística portuguesa. In: Actas do V Encontro para o processamento computacional da língua portuguesa escrita e falada (PROPOR'2000), ("Atibaia, São Paulo, Brasil)
8. Martins, B., Silva, M.J.: A Statistical Study of the WPT 03 Corpus. Technical Report DI/FCUL TR-04-1, Departamento de Informática da Faculdade de Ciências da Universidade de Lisboa (2004)
9. Somers, H.: Review article: Example based machine translation. Machine Translation **14** (1999) 113–157
10. Costa, M.: Sidra: a flexible web search system. Master's thesis, Faculdade de Ciências da Universidade de Lisboa (2004)
11. Robertson, S.E., Walker, S., Jones, S., Hancock-Beaulieu, M.M.: Okapi at TREC-3. In Harman, D.K., ed.: IST Special Publication 500-225: Overview of the Third Text REtrieval Conference (TREC 3), Gaithersburg, MD, USA, Department of Commerce, National Institute of Standards and Technology (1995) 109–126
12. Cardoso, N., Martins, B., Chaves, M., Andrade, L., Silva, M.J.: The XLDB Group at GeoCLEF 2005. In Peters, C., ed.: Working Notes for the CLEF 2005 Workshop, Wien, Austria (2005)

Thomson Legal and Regulatory Experiments at CLEF-2005

Isabelle Moulinier and Ken Williams

Thomson Legal and Regulatory
610 Opperman Drive
Eagan, MN 55123, USA
{Isabelle.Moulinier, Ken.Williams}@thomson.com

Abstract. For the 2005 Cross-Language Evaluation Forum, Thomson Legal and Regulatory participated in the Hungarian, French, and Portuguese monolingual search tasks as well as French-to-Portuguese bilingual retrieval. Our Hungarian participation focused on comparing the effectiveness of different approaches toward morphological stemming. Our French and Portuguese monolingual efforts focused on different approaches to Pseudo-Relevance Feedback (PRF), in particular the evaluation of a scheme for selectively applying PRF only in the cases most likely to produce positive results. Our French-to-Portuguese bilingual effort applies our previous work in query translation to a new pair of languages and uses corpus-based language modeling to support term-by-term translation. We compare our approach to an off-the-self machine translation system that translates the query as a whole and find the latter approach to be more performant. All experiments were performed using our proprietary search engine. We remain encouraged by the overall success of our efforts, with our main submissions for each of the four tasks performing above the overall CLEF median. However, none of the specific enhancement techniques we attempted in this year's forum showed significant improvements over our initial result.

1 Introduction

Thomson Legal and Regulatory participated in the Hungarian, French, and Portuguese monolingual search tasks as well as French-to-Portuguese bilingual retrieval.

Our Hungarian participation further evaluates the configuration developed in prior participations for compounding languages such as German or Finnish. We rely on morphological stemming to normalize derivations and factor compound terms. As morphological stemming may generate multiple stems for a given term, we compare the effectiveness of selecting a single stem with selecting all stems.

In our CLEF 2004 participation, we applied pseudo-relevance feedback blindly to all queries, even though this approach can be detrimental to some query results. In our CLEF-2005 participation, we take a first step toward selectively applying pseudo-relevance feedback. We apply our simple approach to our French and Portuguese runs.

C. Peters et al. (Eds.): CLEF 2005, LNCS 4022, pp. 61–68, 2006.

Finally, our bilingual runs extend our previous work to two more languages. Our approach relies on query translation, where queries are translated term by term using translation resources built from parallel corpora. We compare our approach with off-the-shelf machine translation using Babelfish [1].

We describe our experimental framework in Section 2, and present our monolingual and bilingual runs in Sections 3 and 4, respectively.

2 Experimental Framework

The cornerstone of our experimental framework is our proprietary search engine which supports Boolean and Natural language search. Natural language search is based on an inference network retrieval model similar to INQUERY [2] and has been shown effective when compared to Boolean search on legal content [3]. For our CLEF experiments, we extended the search experience by incorporating the pseudo-relevance feedback functionality described in Section 2.3.

2.1 Indexing

Our indexing unit for European languages is a word. We identify words in sequences of characters using localized tokenization rules (for example, apostrophes are handled differently for French or Italian).

Each word is normalized for morphological variations. This includes identifying compounds if needed. We use the Inxight morphological stemmer [4] to perform such normalization which, in addition, can be configured to handle missing case and diacritic information.

Morphological stemming can produce multiple stems for a given term. We have introduced the option of selecting a single stem or keeping all stems. If candidate stems include compound terms, we select the stem with the fewest compound parts. If candidate stems are simple terms, we select the first one.

We do not remove stopwords from indices, as indexing supports both full-text search and natural language search. Stopwords are handled during search.

2.2 Search

Once documents are indexed, they can be searched. Given a query, we apply two steps: query formulation and document scoring.

Query formulation identifies "concepts" from natural language text by removing stopwords and other noise phrases, and imposes a Bayesian belief structure on these concepts. In many cases, each term in the natural language text represents a concept, and a flat structure gives the same weight to all concepts. However, phrases, compounds or misspellings can introduce more complex concepts, using operators such as "natural phrase," "compound," or "synonym." The structure is then used to score documents.

Scoring takes evidence from each document as a whole, as well as from the best portion which is computed dynamically, for each document, based on proximal concept occurrences. Each concept contributes a belief to the document (and portion) score. We use a standard *tf-idf* scheme for computing term beliefs in all our runs. The belief of a single concept is given by:

$$bel_{term}(Q) = 0.4 + 0.6 \cdot tf_{norm} \cdot idf_{norm}$$

where

$$tf_{norm} = \frac{\log(tf + 0.5)}{\log(tf_{max} + 1.0)} \quad \text{and} \quad idf_{norm} = \frac{log(C + 0.5) - log(df)}{log(C + 1.0)}$$

tf is the number of occurrences of the term within the document, tf_{max} is the maximum number of occurrences of any term within the document, *df* is the number of documents containing the term and C the total number of documents in the collection. The various constants in the formulae have been determined by prior testing on manually-labeled data. tf_{max} is a weak indicator of document length.

2.3 Pseudo-relevance Feedback

We have incorporated a pseudo-relevance feedback module into our search system. We follow the approach outlined by Haines and Croft [5].

We select terms for query expansion using a Rocchio-like formula and add the selected terms to the query. The added terms are weighted either using a fixed weight or a frequency-based weight.

$$sw = \alpha \cdot qf \cdot idf_{norm} + \frac{\beta}{|R|} \sum_{d \in R} (tf_{norm} \cdot idf_{norm}) - \frac{\gamma}{|\overline{R}|} \sum_{d \in \overline{R}} (tf_{norm} \cdot idf_{norm}) \quad (1)$$

where qf is the query weight, R is the set of documents considered relevant, $\overline{R}$ the set of documents considered not relevant, and $|X|$ denotes the cardinality of set X. The α, β and γ weights are set experimentally. The sets of documents R and $\overline{R}$ are extracted from the document list returned by the original search: R correspond to the top n documents and $\overline{R}$ to the bottom m, where n and m are determined through experiments on training data.

3 Monolingual Experiments

Our monolingual participation focuses on normalization for Hungarian and pseudo-relevance feedback for French and Portuguese.

3.1 Hungarian Experiments

As mentioned in Section 2.1, we use a morphological stemmer to identify compounds and normalize terms. The stemmer can be configured to allow for missing case and diacritic information. In addition, we can select to use one stem, or all stems.

Table 1. Comparison between two stemming choices for our official Hungarian runs

Run	MAP (Above/Equal/Below Median)	R-Prec	Reciprocal Rank
tlrTDhuE	0.2952 (27/0/23)	0.3210	0.5872
tlrTDhuSC	0.2964 (30/0/20)	0.2999	0.6070

At search time, compounds are treated as "natural phrases," i.e. as words within a proximity of 3. In addition, multiple stems are grouped under a single operator so that terms with multiple stems do not contribute more weight than terms with one single stem. Finally, we used the Hungarian stopword list developed by the Université de Neuchâtel [6].

We submitted two runs, each with its own indexing scheme:

- Run tlrTDhuE keeps all stems and allows for missing case and diacritic information.
- Run tlrTDhuSC keeps a single stem per term and does not correct missing information.

As illustrated by Table 1, there is no overall significant difference between the two runs, still we observe marked differences on a per-query basis: tlrTDhuSC outperforms tlrTDhuE on 25 queries and underperforms on 20 queries (differences range from a few percent to over 50%). This, we believe, is due to two factors: concepts in queries differ depending on the stemming approach; so do terms in the indices.

3.2 Pseudo-relevance Feedback Experiments

Pseudo-relevance feedback (PRF) is known to be useful on average but can be detrimental to the performance of individual queries. This year, we took a first step towards predicting whether or not PRF would aid individual queries.

We followed the following methodology: we selected our parameters for PRF using training data from previous CLEF participations for both French and Portuguese. We then manually derived a simple prediction rule that identifies those queries where PRF was very detrimental. Our decision rule is composed of two components: the score of the top ranked document and the maximum score any document can achieve for a given query, computed by setting the tf_{norm} factor in belief scores to 1. Our prediction rule is of the form:

```
if maxscore >= Min_MS_Value
   and (maxscore <  MS_Threshold or bestscore >= Min_TD_Value)
 Apply PRF
else
 Don't apply PRF
```

Using training data, we searched for the best parameters in this three-dimensional space (`Min_MS_Value`, `MS_Threshold`, and `Min_TD_Value`).

Our French and Portuguese results, reported in Table 2, show that PRF applied to all queries improved performance (although the difference is not always

Table 2. Official runs for French and Portuguese. Runs ending in 3 correspond to the base run without PRF. Runs ending in 2 are the PRF runs using the following configuration: add 5 terms from the top 10 documents; terms are selected with $\alpha = \beta = 1$ and $\gamma = 0$; expansion uses a fixed weight of 0.5 for each added term. Runs ending in 1 are PRF runs using the prediction rule. † indicates a statistically significant difference using the Wilcoxon signed-rank test and a p-value of 0.05.

Run	MAP (Above/Equal/Below Median)	R-Prec	Reciprocal Rank	Recall
tlrTDfr3	0.3735 (23/2/25)	0.3879	0.7014	0.8912
tlrTDfrRF2	0.4039† (35/0/15)	0.4012	0.6806	0.9141
tlrTDfrRFS1	0.4† (33/1/16)	0.3990	0.6806	0.9119
tlrTfr3	0.2925	0.3027	0.6163	0.7789
tlrTfrRF2	0.3073	0.3313	0.5729	0.8232
tlrTfrRFS1	0.3046	0.3278	0.5729	0.8215
tlrTDpt3	0.3501 (30/0/20)	0.3734	0.7542	0.8729
tlrTDptRF2	0.3742 (31/3/16)	0.3904	0.6704	0.9016
tlrTDptRFS1	0.3584 (31/3/16)	0.3805	0.6718	0.8939
tlrTpt3	0.2712	0.3141	0.6816	0.7358
tlrTptRF2	0.2844†	0.3215	0.6682	0.7544
tlrTptRFS1	0.2830	0.3208	0.6515	0.7544

Table 3. Comparison between base runs and PRF runs using the MAP measure

Compared Runs	# queries degraded	No change	# queries improved
tlrTDfr3 vs. tlrTDfrRF2	11	0	39
tlrTDfr3 vs. tlrTDfrRFS1	11	5	34
tlrTfr3 vs. tlrTfrRF2	23	2	25
tlrTfr3 vs. tlrTfrRFS1	23	3	24
tlrTDpt3 vs. tlrTDptRF2	21	0	29
tlrTDpt3 vs. tlrTDptRFS1	18	9	23
tlrTpt3 vs. tlrTptRF2	17	2	31
tlrTpt3 vs. tlrTptRFS1	17	3	30

statistically significant) but that PRF applied to selected queries did not provide additional improvement.

It is interesting to note that PRF, selective or not, degrades the Reciprocal Rank measure, i.e. the average rank of the first relevant document. This indicates that our PRF setting decreases precision in the top-ranked documents, although it increases recall overall. A comparative summary is provided in Table 3.

Although it performed reasonably well on our initial training data, our PRF selection rule often applied PRF when it was detrimental, and failed to apply it when it would have helped. Table 4 gives more details on the prediction effectiveness or lack thereof. The number of queries for which PRF degraded performance is not unexpected as we did not intend to cover all cases with our heuristic. What is surprising is the low number of cases where our prediction

Table 4. Effectiveness of our prediction rule. Correct corresponds to cases when the prediction rule correctly avoided applying PRF. Misses corresponds to cases when PRF would have helped but was not applied. Errors corresponds to cases when the rule applied PRF and the performance degraded.

Compared runs	Correct	Misses	Errors
tlrTDfr3 vs. tlrTDfrRFS1	0	5	11
tlrTfr3 vs. tlrTfrRFS1	0	1	23
tlrTDpt3 vs. tlrTDptRFS1	3	6	18
tlrTpt3 vs. tlrTptRFS1	0	1	17

rule prevented PRF from helping performance. We believe that the parameters we selected over-fitted the training data. Retrospectively, this is not all that surprising as we use raw values rather than proportions or normalized values.

4 French to Portuguese Bilingual Experiments

Our 2005 bilingual experiments follow the approach we established during our CLEF 2004 participation. We performed bilingual search by translating query terms. Translation resources were trained from parallel corpora using the GIZA++ statistical machine translation package [7].

We created a bilingual lexicon by training the IBM Model 3 on the Europarl parallel corpus [8] as we found Model 3 to provide better translations than Model 1. We selected at most three translations per term, excluding translations with probabilities smaller than 0.1. During query formulation, translations were grouped under a *SUM[1] operator so that concepts are given the same importance regardless of the number of translations. In addition, translations were weighted by their probabilities.

Table 5 summarizes our bilingual runs. We submitted runs with and without pseudo-relevance feedback. The PRF runs show a behavior similar to our monolingual runs as reciprocal rank degrades but recall improves. Five times out of 6, the prediction rule predicted correctly that PRF should not be applied. However the number of cases when PRF was applied and performance dropped was also high (around 20).

The bilingual runs achieved between 60 and 65% of the average precision of monolingual runs. This performance is comparable to our results with German to French search, but not as promising as our training runs, which reached 80%.

We then compared our approach with using an off-the-shelf machine translation system through Babelfish [1]. Using Babelfish, we translated the whole query at once rather than individually translating its terms. The translated query was then handled as a Portuguese query by the rest of our process.

Table 6 shows that, on average, translating the whole query yields better retrieval performance. However, there were 20 queries where our approach resulted in higher retrieval accuracy. We identified ambiguity as a major factor.

[1] A *SUM node averages the beliefs of its children.

Table 5. Official runs for French to Portuguese search. Runs ending in 3 correspond to the base run without PRF. Runs ending in 2 are the PRF runs use the following configuration: add 5 terms from the top 10 documents; terms are selected with $\alpha = \beta = 1$ and $\gamma = 0$; expansion uses a fixed weight of 0.5 for each added term. Runs ending in 1 use the prediction rule prior to applying PRF.

Run	MAP (Above/Equal/Below Median)	R-Prec	Reciprocal Rank	Recall
tlrTDfr2pt3	0.2209 (26/0/24)	0.2525	0.7147	0.7063
tlrTDfr2ptRF2	0.2318 (28/0/22)	0.2614	0.5442	0.7401
tlrTDfr2ptRFS1	0.2358 (29/0/21)	0.2689	0.5566	0.7415
tlrTfr2pt3	0.1741	0.2080	0.4807	0.6332
tlrTfr2ptRF2	0.1799	0.2056	0.3993	0.6563
tlrTfr2ptRFS1	0.1778	0.2045	0.4456	0.6582

Table 6. Comparison between off-the-shelf and corpus-based translation. Runs correspond to base runs without pseudo-relevance feedback. † indicates a statistically significant difference using a paired t-test and a p-value of 0.05.

Run	MAP	R-Prec	Reciprocal Rank	Recall
tlrTDfr2pt3	0.2209 (26/0/24)	0.2525	0.7147	0.7063
TDfr2pt3-Babelfish	0.2801†	0.3067	0.6326	0.7370
tlrTfr2pt3	0.1741	0.2080	0.4807	0.6332
Tfr2pt3-Babelfish	0.2166†	0.2529	0.5429	0.6271

For example, our approach picked up the two translations *reforma* and *pensões* for the French term *retraite* while Babelfish only produced the term *reforma*. On the other hand, multiple translations can harm our approach, for example when translating the French term *Etat* in query 271. This example outlines the dependence of our approach on the parallel corpus. For example, the term *Etat* is translated into *Estado-membro* among other translations as the phrase is commonly used in the Europarl corpus.

5 Conclusion

We remain encouraged by the overall success of our efforts, with our main submissions for each of the four tasks performing above the overall CLEF median. However, none of the specific enhancement techniques we attempted in this year's forum showed significant improvements over our initial results.

For monolingual retrieval in Hungarian, a highly morphological language, we explored two techniques for morphological stemming in order to identify compound terms and normalize them, but were unable to find significant differences between the results.

For monolingual retrieval in French and Portuguese, where we have previously shown pseudo-relevance feedback (PRF) to increase overall performance, we attempted to find a heuristic to identify specific queries for which PRF would be helpful. So far we have been unable to achieve this to a significant degree. In the future, we intend to explore additional techniques such as the use of machine learning including feature engineering as in [9] and methods for using normalized values rather than raw values to prevent over-fitting.

For bilingual retrieval from French to Portuguese, we achieve good performance relative to other submissions, but perhaps like other forum participants, we remain disappointed in the bilingual performance relative to the same queries performed in a monolingual setting.

Our unofficial runs using off-the-shelf machine translation exhibit a clear improvement over our corpus-based method, leading us to reconsider how to handle multiple translations. In particular, we plan to investigate the usefulness of translation disambiguation and context-sensitive translation methods.

References

1. (http://babelfish.altavista.com)
2. Croft, W.B., Callan, J., Broglio, J.: The INQUERY retrieval system. In: Proceedings of the 3rd International Conference on Database and Expert Systems Applications, Spain (1992)
3. Turtle, H.: Natural language vs. boolean query evaluation: a comparison of retrieval performance. In: Proceedings of the 17th Annual International ACM SIGIR Conference on Research and Development in Information Retrieval, Dublin, Ireland (1994) 212–220
4. (http://www.inxight.com/products/oem/linguistx)
5. Haines, D., Croft, W.: Relevance feedback and inference networks. In: Proceedings of the Sixteenth Annual International ACM SIGIR Conference on Research and Development in Information Retrieval. (1993) 2–11
6. (http://www.unine.ch/info/clef/)
7. Och, F.J., Ney, H.: A systematic comparison of various statistical alignment models. Computational Linguistics **29**(1) (2003) 19–51
8. Koehn, P.: Europarl: A multilingual corpus for evaluation of machine translation. Draft (2002)
9. Yom-Tov, E., Fine, S., Carmel, D., Darlow, A., Amitay, E.: Juru at trec 2004: Experiments with prediction of query difficulty. In Voorhees, E.M., Buckland, L.P., eds.: The Thirteenth Text Retrieval Conference (TREC 2004), NIST Special Publication: SP 500-261 (2004)

Using the X-IOTA System in Mono- and Bilingual Experiments at CLEF 2005

Loïc Maisonnasse[1], Gilles Sérasset[1], and Jean-Pierre Chevallet[2]

[1] Laboratoire CLIPS-IMAG, Grenoble France
loic.maisonnasse@imag.fr, gilles.serasset@imag.fr
[2] IPAL-CNRS, I2R A*STAR, National University of Singapore
viscjp@i2r.a-star.edu.sg

Abstract. This document describes the CLIPS experiments in the CLEF 2005 campaign. We used a surface-syntactic parser in order to extract new indexing terms. These terms are considered syntactic dependencies. Our goal was to evaluate their relevance for an information retrieval task. We used them in different forms in different information retrieval models, in particular in a language model. For the bilingual task, we tried two simple tests of Spanish and German to French retrieval; for the translation we used a lemmatizer and a dictionary.

1 Introduction

In the previous participation of the CLIPS laboratory in CLEF [1], we tested the use of surface-syntactic parsers in order to extract indexing terms. Last year, we only extracted simple indexing terms; this year we have tried to exploit the structure produced by the parser. We perforemd two separate evaluations; in the first one, we divided the structure into "complex descriptors", which contain part of the global structure. In the second one, we used a structure produced by the shallow parser, in a language model.

2 Sub-structure Training in the Monolingual Task

The shallow parser produces a structure, using only lemmas; we only use a part of the information produced . This year, we evaluated the relevance of the structural information produced by the parser. Two main types of parser are available; the dependency and the constituent. In our experiments we used a dependency parser; this kind of parser seems to be more appropriate for the information retrieval task [2] since it makes it possible to capture some sentence variation.

Different studies have already been made on the use of syntactic dependency structures. Some of these studies use dependency structure in order to extract phrases. For example, in [3], a closed structure is produced from a dependency tree for all sentences in a document. Some patterns are then applied on the structure for phrase extraction, and some selected phrases are then added to

C. Peters et al. (Eds.): CLEF 2005, LNCS 4022, pp. 69–78, 2006.

other descriptors in the document index. Finally, the tf-idf weighting schema is adjusted in order to give a higher idf for the extracted phrase. In this way, a 20% gain over average precision is obtained. However, this gain cannot be directly linked to the use of a dependency structure since the structure is only used to detect the phrase.

On the presumption that converting the structures to phrases leads to the loss of information, other papers have tried to use the syntactic dependency structure directly. In [4], a dependency tree is extracted from Japanese sentences, mainly document titles. Matching between a query and documents is provided by a projection of the query tree onto the document trees. In addition, to provide a better matching, some pruning can be made on the tree. In [5], the COP parser (Constituent Object Parser) is used to extract dependency trees. In the query, the user has to select important terms and indicate dependencies between them. The query is then compared to the documents using different types of matching. The two papers cited provided just one unambiguous structure per sentence; [6] incorporates syntactic ambiguity into the extracted structure. The model proposed is applied to phrases; the similarity is provided by tree matching but the IR results are lower than the results obtained when only considering the phrases represented in the tree.

In our experiments, we consider an intermediary representation level. For this purpose, we use sub-structures composed of one dependency relation. With this representation, a sentence is considered as a set of sub-structures that we call dependencies. In our formalism, the sentence "the cat eats the mouse" is represented by the set: DET(the, cat), DET(the, mouse), SUBJ(cat, eat), VMOD(mouse, eat). Where "the" is the determiner of "cat", "cat" is the subject of "eat", etc.

2.1 Experimental Schema

For this experiment, we only used the French corpus. We experimented the use of dependency descriptors on this corpus. For this purpose, we use an experimental sequence, described in Figure 1.

First, the different documents of the collection are analysed with the French parser XIP (Xerox Incremental Parser) [7]. Two descriptors are extracted from these documents: the dependencies and the lemmas. In a first experiment, we considered these descriptors separately and created two indexes. One contains lemmas and the other dependencies. We queried these two indexes separately with dependencies and lemmas extracted from queries by the same parser. We compared the results obtained with the two descriptors for different weighting schemes. In a second experiment, we regrouped the two descriptors into a unique index and we evaluated results for different weighting schemes.

For training, we used the French corpus of CLEF 2003. In this corpus, there are 3 sets of documents. For each set, we selected the following fields: TITLE and TEXT for "le monde 94", TI KW LD TX ST for "sda 94" and "sda 95". For the queries, we selected the fields FR-title FR-descr Fr-narr.

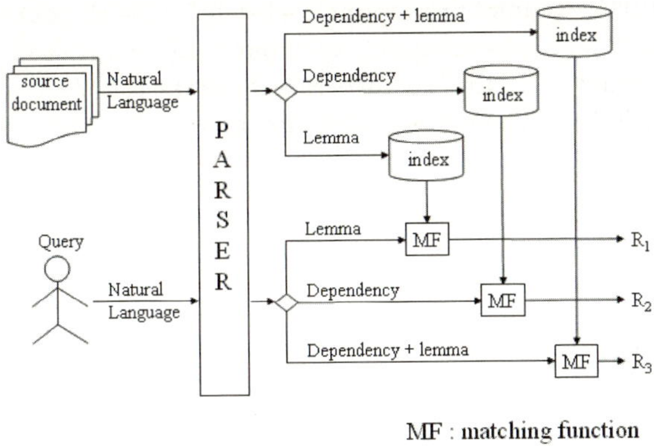

Fig. 1. Experimental procedure

2.2 Dependencies Versus Lemmas

We first compared results obtained using dependencies to results obtained with lemmas. In these experiments lemmas were used as the baseline as they have already shown their value in last year's CLIPS experiments [1]. After parsing the documents with XIP, we transformed the output into a common XML simplified format (shown below). From this XML format, on the one side we extracted the lemmas: for these descriptors, we only filtered nouns, proper nouns, verbs, adjectives and numbers.

XML simplified format for the sentence : "les manifestations contre le transport de déchets radioactifs par conteneurs." (Demonstrations against the transport of radioactive waste by containers)

```
<LUNIT>
<NODE num="2" tag="DET" lemma="le" ...>les</NODE>
<NODE num="3" tag="NOUN" lemma="manifestation" ... >
    manifestations</NODE>
<NODE num="5" tag="PREP" lemma="contre" ... >contre</NODE>
<NODE num="7" tag="DET" lemma="le" ... >le</NODE>
<NODE num="8" tag="NOUN" lemma="transport" ... >transport</NODE>
<NODE num="10" tag="PREP" lemma="de" ... >de</NODE>
<NODE num="12" tag="NOUN" lemma="dechet" ... >dchets</NODE>
<NODE num="14" tag="ADJ" lemma="radioactif" ... >
radioactifs</NODE>
<NODE num="16" tag="PREP" lemma="par" ... >par</NODE>
<NODE num="18" tag="NOUN" lemma="conteneur" ... >
conteneurs</NODE>
<NODE num="23" tag="SENT" lemma="." ... >.</NODE>
<DEP name="NMOD" ... w0="dechet" w1="radioactif"/>
<DEP name="NMOD" ...
w0="manifestation" w1="contre" w2="transport"/>
```

```
<DEP name="NMOD" ... w0="transport" w1="de" w2="d\'echet"/>
<DEP name="NMOD" ... w0="dechet" w1="par" w2="conteneur"/>
<DEP name="DETERM" ... w0="le" w1="manifestation"/>
<DEP name="DETERM" ... w0="le" w1="transport"/>
</LUNIT>
```

Table 1. Descriptor selected for the sentence: “les manifestations contre le transport de déchets radioactifs par conteneurs”

Selected lemmas	Selected Dependencies
manifestation	NMOD(déchet,radioactif)
transport	NMOD(manifestation,contre,transport)
déchet	NMOD(transport,de,déchet)
radioactif	NMOD(déchet,par,conteneur)
conteneur	DETERM(le,manifestation)
Allemagne	DETERM(le,transport)

On the other side, we extracted the dependencies (Table 1). As the number of dependencies can be very high, we queried each document set separately and then merged the results. We compared the IR results obtained with these two descriptors for different weighting schemes. We used the following weighting schemes on the document and on the query descriptors:

For the documents
nnn: Only the term frequency is used.
lnc: Use a log on term frequency and the cosine as the final normalization.
ltc: The classical tf*idf with a log on the term frequency.
nRn: Divergence from randomness

For the queries
nnn: Only the term frequency is used.
bnn: The binary model, 1 if terms are present, and 0 otherwise.
lnn: A log is used on the term frequency.
npn: Idf variant used by okapi.
ntn: classical idf.

For more details, see [1]. We first evaluated the c coefficient for the divergence from randomness weighting (nRn) on the document and with an nnn weighting on the queries. Results for the two descriptors are shown in Table 2 and 3. We then evaluated other weighting methods. The results are presented in Table 4.

Over all weighting schemes, dependency descriptors perform better than lemmas only for the nnn weighting. The divergence from randomness performs better than the other document's weighting for the two descriptors and the results are stable considering query weighting.

Table 2. Variation of c for nRn nnn (dependencies alone)

c	Average precision
2	25.53
3	25.50
4	25.83
4.25	25.93
4.5	26.01
4.75	26.00
5	25.88
5.5	25.84
6	25.84

Table 3. Variation of c for nRn nnn (lemmas alone)

c	Average precision
0	0.0152
0,5	0.4362
1	0.4647
1,75	0.4700
1,5	0.4703
2	0.4687
2,25	0.4728
2,5	0.4709
3	0.4577

Table 4. Lemmas or dependencies average precision

Document Weighting	Query Weighting									
	lemmas					dependencies				
	nnn	bnn	lnn	npn	ntn	nnn	bnn	lnn	npn	ntn
nnn	1,82	0,81	1,57	21,43	16,43	9,01	5,56	8,16	18,21	17,96
lnc	35,02	31,27	36,22	34,30	37,46	18,92	17,46	19,17	21,93	21,94
ltc	33,13	33,93	35,94	32,86	33,79	21,14	18,94	20,86	21,66	21,66
nRn	47,28	38,34	45,55	45,23	48,35	26,01	22,56	25,90	24,95	24,94

2.3 Lemmas and Dependencies

In our first experiment, we used dependencies and lemmas separately. In this second experiment we merged the two descriptors in one unique index and evaluated different weighting schemes for this index. Similarly to the previous experiment, we first evaluate divergence from randomness (Table 5) and the different weighting methods (Table 6).

The results obtained in this evaluation are better than those obtained with dependencies alone but they are lower than those obtain with lemmas. The reason is that the dependencies and the lemmas are considered as equivalent, whereas these two descriptors are clearly on two different levels as dependencies contain

Table 5. Variation of c for nRn nnn (lemmas and dependencies)

c	Average precision
0	0,0207
1	0,3798
1,5	0,3941
2	0,3947
2,25	0,3947
2,5	0,3934
3	0,3922

Table 6. Lemmas and dependencies average precision

Document Weighting	Query Weighting				
	nnn	bnn	lnn	npn	ntn
nnn	2.30	1.24	1.95	23.37	19.22
lnc	29.84	28.70	30.31	31.04	32.11
ltc	30.76	29.63	31.56	30.21	30.25
nRn	39.47	30.54	37.20	41.22	41.49

lemmas. This particular aspect was not taken into account in this experiment. Nevertheless, as we wanted to evaluate the use of dependencies, we submitted an official CLEF run with nRn nnn weighting with both dependencies and lemmas for the monolingual run and with the coefficient c at 2.25.

3 Language Models

In a second experiment, we integrated the syntactic structure in a language model. Some studies have already been made on the use of dependencies between terms in a language model in [8] [9]. These studies use statistical based methods in order to obtain a tree representation of a sentence; here we use a linguistically produced structure. In order to use a language model based on dependencies, from the previous XML simplified format, we have filtered only nouns, proper nouns, verbs, adjectives and numbers and the dependency that connects only these descriptors. For each sentence, we obtained a graph where the nodes are the significant elements of the sentence linked by dependencies (Figure 2). We used these graphs to apply a language model.

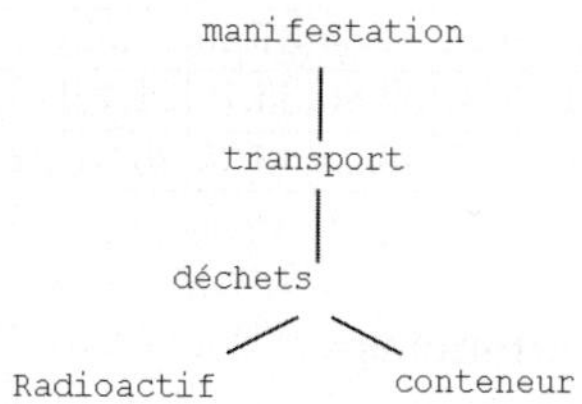

Fig. 2. Graph used by the langue model for the sentence: "les manifestations contre le transport de déchets radioactifs par conteneurs en Allemagne"

3.1 Our Language Model

The language model we used is a simplified version of the model proposed in [8]. This model assumes that the dependency structure on a sentence forms a undirected graph of term L and that the query generation is formulated as a two-stage process. At first a graph L is generated from a document following $P(L|D)$. The query is then generated following $P(Q|L,D)$; query terms are generated at this stage according to terms linked in L. Thus, in this model, the probability of the query $P(Q|D)$ over all possible graphs Ls is :

$$P(Q|D) = \sum_{L_s} P(Q,L|D) = \sum_{L_s} P(L|D)\,P(Q|L,D) \ . \qquad (1)$$

We assumed that the sum $\sum_{L_s} P(Q,L|D)$ over all the possible graphs L_S is dominated by a single graph L, which is the most probable graph. Here we consider that the most probable graph L is that extracted by our parser. We finally obtained:

$$P(Q|D) = log(P(L|D) + \sum_{i=1..m} P(q_i|D) + \sum_{(i,j)\in L} MI(q_i, q_j|L, D) \quad . \qquad (2)$$

where: $MI(q_i, q_j|L, D) = log\left(\frac{P((q_i,q_j|L,D)}{P(q_i|D)P(q_j|D)}\right)$

***P*((*L*|*D*).** We estimate $P((L|D)$ as the probability that two terms are linked if they appear in the same sentences in the document. For this estimation, we made an interpolation of the document probability with the collection probability.

$$P(L|D) = \prod_{l\in L} P(L|D) \propto \prod_{(i,j)\in L} (1-\lambda_d)\frac{D_R(q_i,q_j)}{D(q_i,q_j)} + \lambda_d\frac{C_R(q_i,q_j)}{C(q_i,q_j)} \quad . \qquad (3)$$

where l denotes a dependency between two terms

$D_R(q_i, q_j)$ denotes the number of time that q_i and q_j are linked in a sentence of the document

$D(q_i, q_j)$ denotes the number of time that q_i and q_j appear in the same sentence.

$C_R(q_i, q_j)$, $C(q_i, q_j)$ denotes the equivalent number but evaluated on the whole collection.

***P*(*qi*|*D*).** We estimate $P(qi|D)$ as the probability that a term appears in a document, and we made an interpolation on the collection.

$$P(q_i|D) = (1-\lambda_l) P(q_i|D) + \lambda_l P(q_i|C) \quad . \qquad (4)$$

In the two last estimations, if a lemma or a dependency does not appear in the collection the probability is set to zero, consequently the whole probability will be set to zero. To avoid this, in the query we consider only the dependencies and the lemmas found in the whole collection.

***MI*(*qi*, *qj*|*L*, *D*).** We use the same estimation as the one used in [8].

3.2 Training

We applied this model on the CLEF 2003 collection. The results obtained are presented in Table 7 where we evaluate variations of the coefficients λ_l and λ_d.

We see that the results are better when the coefficient λ_l is around 0.3 and when the coefficient λ_d is high. Thus the results are better when the dependencies in the query are not taken into account. This may come from the use of simple estimations; better estimations of the probability may give better results. We submitted a run for this language model with the coefficient λ_l at 0.3 and the coefficient λ_d at 0.9999; the same experimental conditions were used.

Table 7. Average precision on variation of λ_l l and λ_d

λ_d λ_l	0.1	0.2	0.3	0.4	0.5	0.6
0.5	0.2749	0.2724	0.2697	0.2536	0.2495	0.2428
0.9999	0.2778	0.2951	0.2890	-	-	-

4 Bilingual

For the cross-language training, we performed two simple runs from German and Spanish to French. For these two runs, we used the three query fields : XX-title, XX-descr, XX-narr. In this training, query words are lemmatized and then translated using the web dictionary interglot[1].

For the lemmatization, we used TreeTagger[2] for the German queries and we used agme lemmatizer [10] for the Spanish queries. If there is an ambiguity with these lemmatizers, we keep all possible forms. We translate the lemmas with the dictionary and we keep all the translations found. Finally, we query the index of French lemmas with the divergence from randomness weighting.

For the CLEF 2003 test suite, we obtained an average precision of 0.0902 for the German queries and an average precision of 0.0799 for the Spanish queries.

5 Results

5.1 Monolingual

For this evaluation, we submitted three different runs. Two of these runs were based on dependencies with lemmas index with a weighting schema "nRn nnn" with the coefficient c at 2.25. The first FR0 used the fields FR-title FR-desc of the queries, the second FR1 used all the fields. The third run FR2 used the language model described in Section 3.1. We can see that as FR1 used the field FR-narr for the query the results are lower than the run FR0 which did not use this field. This may result from the fact that we did not use a program that processes the topics in order to remove irrelevant phrases as "Les documents pertinents doivent expliquer" (relevant documents must explain). We observe that the results obtained in CLEF 2005 are lower than those obtained for CLEF 2003, especially when we used the three query fields. In this case, the results for CLEF 2005 are more than two times lower than the results for CLEF 2003. This result may come from the fact that the narrative part of the queries seems to be shorter in CLEF 2005. Another difference could be that noticed between FR1 and FR2 as these two runs show a difference of about 10 points of precision for CLEF 2003 but are very close in CLEF 2005.

5.2 Bilingual

In this experiment, we submitted two runs for each source language. One of these two runs used the topic fields XX-title and XX-desc. The second also used the field XX-narr. The results obtained were lower that those obtained in training, they follow a decrease proportional to the monolingual. Thus this decrease appears to result from the low monolingual results.

[1] http://interglot.com/

[2] http://www.ims.uni-stuttgart.de/projekte/corplex/TreeTagger/DecisionTreeTagger.html

Table 8. Monolingual results

	FR0	FR1	FR2
Average precision	21.56	14.11	13.07
Precision at 5 docs	38	36.40	30.40

Table 9. Bilingual results

	de-fr		es-fr	
	title +desc	title +desc +narr	title +desc	title +desc +narr
average precision	6.88	4.98	4.23	3.69
precision at 5 docs	17.20	12.80	10.80	11.60

6 Conclusion

For our participation in CLEF 2005 we evaluated the use of syntactic dependency structures extracted by a parser in an information retrieval task. In our first experiment, we tried to exploit the structure using descriptors that capture a part of the structure. In our second experiment, we directly exploited the structure extracted by the parser in a language model. The two experiments show that the structure is exploitable, but the results are still lower than those obtained using only lemmas with appropriate weightings.

As the syntactic structure has shown to be exploitable in IR, some improvements could be applied on this model. We used the XIP parser here, but this parser does not give information on the quality of the structure. Integrating this kind of information on the dependencies extracted could improve the IR results. Using a parser that extracts deeper syntactic dependencies may also give better results for the information retrieval task. Finally, our language model uses simple estimations, better estimations may improve the results.

Our conviction is that detailed syntactic information, which is already available using existing parsers, will improve results (especially, precision) in information retrieval tasks. However, such detailed information has to be combined with classical descriptors as, taken alone, it does not improve results. Obviously, we still have to find ways to combine the advantages of classical, raw descriptors with the added value of fine grain syntactic information in a single model. Independently of the task, we see that using the narrative part of the queries lowers our results. For our next participation, in order to improve our results, we will have to use a module that only selects the important part of the topic.

References

1. Chevallet, J.P., Sérasset, G.: Using surface-syntactic parser and deviation from randomness. In Peters, C., Clough, P., Gonzalo, J., Jones, G.J.F., Kluck, M., Magnini, B., eds.: CLEF. Volume 3491 of Lecture Notes in Computer Science., Springer (2004) 38–49
2. Koster, C.H.A.: Head/modifier frames for information retrieval. In Gelbukh, A.F., ed.: CICLing. Volume 2945 of Lecture Notes in Computer Science., Springer (2004) 420–432

3. Strzalkowski, T., Stein, G.C., Wise, G.B., Carballo, J.P., Tapanainen, P., Jarvinen, T., Voutilainen, A., Karlgren, J.: Natural language information retrieval: TREC-7 report. In: Text REtrieval Conference. (1998) 164–173
4. Matsumura, A., Takasu, A., Adachi, J.: The effect of information retrieval method using dependency relationship between words. In: Proceedings of the RIAO 2000 Conference. (2000) 1043–1058
5. Metzler, D.P., Haas, S.W.: The constituent object parser: syntactic structure matching for information retrieval. ACM Trans. Inf. Syst. **7**(3) (1989) 292–316
6. Smeaton, A.F.: Using NLP or NLP resources for information retrieval tasks. In Strzalkowski, T., ed.: Natural language information retrieval. Kluwer Academic Publishers, Dordrecht, NL (1999) 99–111
7. A¿it-Mokhtar, S., Chanod, J.P., Roux, C.: Robustness beyond shallowness: incremental deep parsing. Nat. Lang. Eng. **8**(3) (2002) 121–144
8. Gao, J., Nie, J.Y., Wu, G., Cao, G.: Dependence language model for information retrieval. In: SIGIR '04: Proceedings of the 27th annual international ACM SIGIR, New York, NY, USA, ACM Press (2004) 170–177
9. Nallapati, R., Allan, J.: Capturing term dependencies using a language model based on sentence trees. In: CIKM '02: Proceedings of the eleventh international conference on Information and knowledge management, New York, NY, USA, ACM Press (2002) 383–390
10. Gelbukh, A.F., Sidorov, G.: Approach to construction of automatic morphological analysis systems for inflective languages with little effort. In Gelbukh, A.F., ed.: CICLing. Volume 2588 of Lecture Notes in Computer Science., Springer (2003) 215–220

Bilingual and Multilingual Experiments with the IR-n System

Elisa Noguera[1], Fernando Llopis[1], Rafael Muñoz[1], Rafael M. Terol[1], Miguel A. García-Cumbreras[2], Fernando Martínez-Santiago[2], and Arturo Montejo-Raez[2]

[1] Grupo de investigación en Procesamiento del Lenguaje Natural y Sistemas de Información
Departamento de Lenguajes y Sistemas Informáticos
University of Alicante, Spain
{elisa, llopis, rafael, rafaelmt}@dlsi.ua.es

[2] Department of Computer Science. University of Jaen, Jaen, Spain
{magc, dofer, montejo}@ujaen.es

Abstract. Our paper describes the participation of the IR-n system at CLEF-2005. This year, we participated in the bilingual task (English-French and English-Portuguese) and the multilingual task (English, French, Italian, German, Dutch, Finish and Swedish). We introduced the method of combined passages for the bilingual task. Futhermore we have applied the method of logic forms in the same task. For the multilingual task we had a joint participation with the University of Alicante and University of Jaén. We want to emphasize the good score achieved in the bilingual task improving around 45% in terms of average precision.

1 Introduction

Information Retrieval (IR) systems [2] try to find the relevant documents given a user query from a document collection. We can find different types of IR systems in the literature. On the one hand, if the document collection and the user query are written in the same language then the IR system can be defined as a monolingual IR system. On the other hand, if the document collection and the user query are written in different languages then the IR system can be defined as a bilingual (two different languages) or multilingual (more than two languages) IR system. Obviously, the document collection for multilingual systems is written in at least two different languages. The IR-n system [3] can work with collections and queries in any language.

Passage Retrieval (PR) systems [1] are information retrieval systems that determine the similarity of a document with regard to a user query according to the similarity of fragments of the document (passages) with regard to the same query.

C. Peters et al. (Eds.): CLEF 2005, LNCS 4022, pp. 79–82, 2006.

2 Bilingual Task

2.1 Method 1: Machine Translation

We use different translators in order to obtain an automatic translation of queries. Three of them were used for all languages: FreeTranslation, Babel Fish and InterTran. Moreover, we have used one more method merging all translations. This is performed by merging several translations from the on-line translators. This strategy is based on the idea than the words which appear in multiple translations have more relevancy than those that only appear in one translation.

The method of combined passages was developed in the monolingual task [4], for this reason it has been also used in the bilingual task. In the training test, the best input configuration has been used for French and Portuguese. Best scores were achieved using the merge of translations in English-Portuguese and FreeTranslation in English-French.

2.2 Method 2: Logic Forms

The last release of our IR-n system introduced a set of features that are based on the application of logic forms to topics and in the incrementing of the weight of terms according to a set of syntactic rules. The reason for this is that IR-n system includes a new module that increments the weight of terms, applying a set of rules based on the representation of the topics in the way of logic forms [7].

3 Multilingual Task

This year we made a combination between the fusion algorithm 2-step RSV [6], developed by the University of Jaén, and the passage retrieval system IR-n, developed by the University of Alicante. A full detailed description of the experiments is available in this volume.

IR-n has been used as IR system in order to make some experiments in Multi-8 Two-years-on task. Thus, it has been applied over eight languages: English, Spanish, French, Italian, German, Dutch, Finnish and Swedish.

An in depth description of the training test is available in [6]. Firstly, each monolingual collection is preprocessed as usual (token extraction, stopwords are eliminated and stemming is applied to the rest of words). In addition, compound words are decompounded as possible for German, Swedish, Finnish and Dutch. We use the decompounding algorithm depicted in [5]. The preprocessed collections have been indexed using the passage retrieval system IR-n and the document retrieval system ZPrise. The IR-n system has been modified in order to return a list of the retrieved and relevant documents, the documents that contain the relevant passages. Finally, given a query and its translations into the other languages, each query is searched in the corresponding monolingual collection.

When the monolingual lists of relevant documents are returned, we apply the 2-step RSV fusion algorithm. This algorithm deals with the translations whose terms are known (aligned terms) in a different way that those words whose translation is unknown (non-aligned words) by giving two scores for each document. The first one is calculated taking into account aligned words, and the second one only uses non-aligned terms. Thus, both scores are combined into a only RSV per document and query by using some formulae:

1. Combining the RSV value of the aligned words and not aligned words with the formula:

$$0.6 < RSVAlignedDoc > +0.4 < RSVNotAligned >$$

2. By using Logistic Regression. The formula:

$$e^{\alpha \cdot <RSVAlignedDoc> + \beta \cdot <RSVNotAligned>}$$

3. The last one also uses Logistic Regression but include a new component, the ranking of the doc. It applies the formula:

$$e^{\alpha \cdot <RSVAlignedDoc> + \beta \cdot <RSVNotAligned> + \gamma \cdot <RankingDoc>}$$

4 Results at CLEF-2005

The IR-n system used the best configuration obtained in the training process. Three different runs have been submitted for each task. The first run IRn-xx-vexp uses the method of combined passages with query expansion. The second run IRn-xx-fexp only uses query expansion. The third run IRn-xx-vnexp uses the method of combined passages without query expansion. Furthermore, a fourth run IRn-xx-fexpfl has been submitted for English-Portuguese task. It uses the method of logic forms. Table 1 shows the scores achieved for each run.

Table 1 shows the official results for "Multi-8 Two-years on task. IR-n performs better than ZPrise except for Finnish results, the differences of average precision between both multilingual experiments is very small. The reason is that the merging algorithm is independent of the initial selection of relevant documents. This feature has been briefly discussed above and in more detail in [6].

5 Conclusions and Future Work

In the bilingual task the IR-n system has obtained better results merging translations than using single translations. On the other hand, the method of combined passages improves the scores in the bilingual task compared to the method of fixed passages, as it happens in the monolingual task.

Thus, in the multilingual task we conclude that IR-n is a good information retrieval system for CLIR systems. It improves on document-based systems such as OKAPI-ZPrise in bilingual experiments. In addition, the integration of this system with complex merging algorithms such as 2-step RSV is straightforward.

Possibly, if an IR-n like system were implemented for the creation of a dynamic index the multilingual results would be improved in the same way that the monolingual results are.

Table 1. CLEF 2005 official results. Bilingual and Multilingual tasks.

BILINGUAL TASK			
Language	**Run**	**AvgP**	**Dif**
English - Portuguese	CLEF Average	21.71	
	IRn-enpt-vexp	29.18	+34.4%
	IRn-enpt-fexp	28.94	
	IRn-enpt-vnexp	25.22	
	IRn-enpt-fexpfl	27.27	
English - French	CLEF Average	24.76	
	IRn-fr-vexp	35.90	+45.3%
	IRn-fr-fexp	29.12	
	IRn-fr-vnexp	29.13	

MULTILINGUAL TASK			
IR system	**Formula 1**	**Formula 2**	**Formula 3**
ZPrise+OKAPI	28.78	29.01	29.12
IR-n	28.85	29.09	29.18

Acknowledgements

This research has been partially funded by the Spanish Government under project CICyT number TIC2003-07158-C04-01 and by the Valencian Government under project numbers GV04B-276 and GV04B-268.

References

1. M. Kaskziel and J. Zobel: Passage Retrieval Revisited. In *Proceedings of the 20th annual ACM SIGIR Conference on Research and Development in Information Retrieval (SIGIR 97)*, Philadelphia, pages 178–185, 1997.
2. F. W. Lancaster: *Information Retrieval Systems: Characteristics, Testing and Eval.*, John Wiley and Sons, New York, 1979.
3. F. Llopis: *IR-n: Un Sistema de Recuperación de Información Basado en pasajes.* PhD thesis. University of Alicante, 2003.
4. F. Llopis and E. Noguera: Combining Passages in Monolingual Experiments with IR-n System. In *Workshop of Cross-Language Evaluation Forum (CLEF 2005)*, Vienna, In this volume.
5. F. Martínez-Santiago, M. García-Cumbreras and L. A. Ureña: SINAI at CLEF 2004: Using Machine Translation Resources with Mixed 2-Step RSV Merging Algorithm. *Multilingual Information Access for Text, Speech and Images: 5th Workshop of the Cross-Language Evaluation Forum*, Bath, page 156-164, 2005.
6. F. Martínez-Santiago, L. A. Ureña, and M. Martín: A Merging Strategy Proposal: Two Step Retrieval Status Value Method. *Information Retrieval*, 9(1):95–109, 2006.
7. R. M. Terol: The University of Alicante at CL-SR Track. In *Workshop of Cross-Language Evaluation Forum (CLEF 2005)*, Vienna, In this volume.

Dictionary-Based Amharic-French Information Retrieval

Atelach Alemu Argaw[1], Lars Asker[1], Rickard Cöster[2],
Jussi Karlgren[2], and Magnus Sahlgren[2]

[1] Department of Computer and Systems Sciences, Stockholm University/KTH
{atelach, asker}@dsv.su.se
[2] Swedish Institute of Computer Science (SICS)
{rick, jussi, mange}@sics.se

Abstract. We present four approaches to the Amharic - French bilingual track at CLEF 2005. All experiments use a dictionary based approach to translate the Amharic queries into French Bags-of-words, but while one approach uses word sense discrimination on the translated side of the queries, the other one includes all senses of a translated word in the query for searching. We used two search engines: The SICS experimental engine and Lucene, hence four runs with the two approaches. Non-content bearing words were removed both before and after the dictionary lookup. TF/IDF values supplemented by a heuristic function was used to remove the stop words from the Amharic queries and two French stopwords lists were used to remove them from the French translations. In our experiments, we found that the SICS search engine performs better than Lucene and that using the word sense discriminated keywords produce a slightly better result than the full set of non discriminated keywords.

1 Background

Amharic is an Afro-Asiatic language belonging to the Southwest Semitic group. It uses its own unique alphabet and is spoken mainly in Ethiopia but also to a limited extent in Egypt and Israel [10]. Amharic is the official government language of Ethiopia and is spoken by a substantial segment of the population. In the 1998 census, 17.4 million people claimed Amharic as their first language and 5.1 as their second language. Ethiopia is a multi lingual country with over 80 distinct languages [3], and with a population of more than 59.9 million as authorities estimated on the basis of the 1998 census. Owing to political and social conditions and the multiplicity of the languages, Amharic has gained ground through out the country. Amharic is used in business, government, and education. Newspapers are printed in Amharic as are numerous books on all subjects [5].

In this paper we describe our experiments at the CLEF 2005 Amharic - French bilingual track. It consists of four fully automatic approaches that differ in terms of how word sense discrimination is done and in terms of what search engine is used. We have experimented with two different search engines - Lucene [11],

C. Peters et al. (Eds.): CLEF 2005, LNCS 4022, pp. 83–92, 2006.

```
1. Amharic topic set
     |
     |   1a. Transliteration
     |
2. Transliterated Amharic topic set
     |
     |   2a. Trigram and Bigram dictionary lookup -----|
     |                                                 |
3. Remaining (non matched) Amharic topic set           |
     |                                                 |
     |   3a. Stemming                                  |
     |                                                 |
4. Stemmed Amharic topic set                           |
     |                                                 |
     |   4a. IDF-based stop word removal               |
     |                                                 |
5. Reduced Amharic topic set                           |
     |                                                 |
     |   5a. Dictionary lookup                         |
     |                                                 |
6. Topic set (in French) including all possible translations
     |                                       |
     |   6a. Word sense discrimination       |
     |                                       |
7. Reduced set of French terms               |
     |                                       |
     |   7a. Retrieval (Indexing, keyword search, ranking)
     |
8. Retrieved Documents
```

Fig. 1. Generalised flow chart for the four Amh-Fr runs

an open source search toolbox, and *Searcher*, an experimental search engine developed at SICS[1]. Two runs were submitted per search engine, one using all content bearing, expanded query terms without any word sense discrimination, and the other using a smaller 'disambiguated' set of content bearing query terms.

For the dictionary lookup we used one Amharic - French machine readable dictionary (MRD) containing 12.000 Amharic entries with corresponding 36,000 French entries [1]. We also used an Amharic - English machine readable dictionary with approximately 15.000 Amharic entries [2] as a complement for the cases when the Amharic terms where not found in the Amharic - French MRD.

2 Method

Figure 1 above, gives a brief overview of the different steps involved in the retrieval task. Each of these will be described in more detail in the following sections.

[1] The Swedish Institute of Computer Science.

2.1 Translation and Transliteration

The English topic set was initially translated into Amharic by human translators. Amharic uses its own and unique alphabet (Fidel) and there exist a number of fonts for this, but to date there is no standard for the language. The Amharic topic set was originally represented using an Ethiopic font but for ease of use and compatibility reasons we transliterated it into an ASCII representation using SERA[2]. The transliterated Amharic topic set was then used as the input to the following steps.

2.2 Bigram and Trigram Matching

Before any stemming was done on the Amharic topic set, the sentences from each topic was used to generate all possible trigrams and bigrams. These trigrams and bigrams where then matched against the entries in the two dictionaries. First the full (unstemmed) trigrams where matched against the Amharic - French and then the Amharic - English dictionaries. Secondly, prefixes were removed from the first word of each trigram and suffixes were removed from the last word of the same trigram and then what remained was matched against the two dictionaries. In this way, one trigram was matched and translated for the full Amharic topic set, using the Amharic - French dictionary.

Next, all bigrams where matched against the Amharic - French and the Amharic - English dictionaries. Including the prefix suffix removal, this resulted in the match and translation of 15 unique bigrams. Six were found only in the Amharic - French dictionary, another six were found in both dictionaries, and three were found only in the Amharic - English dictionary. For the six bigrams that were found in both dictionaries, the French translation was used.

2.3 Stop Word Removal

In these experiments, stop words were removed both before and after the dictionary lookup. First the number of Amharic words in the queries was reduced by using a stopword list that had been generated from a 2 million word Amharic news corpus using IDF measures. After the dictionary lookup further stop words removal was conducted on the French side separately for the two sets of experiments using the SICS engine and Lucene. For the SICS engine, this was done by using a separete French stop words list. For the Lucene experiments, we used the French Analyszer from the Apache Lucene Sandbox which supplements the query analyzer with its own list of French stop words and removes them before searching for a specific keywords list.

2.4 Amharic Stemming and Dictionary Lookup

The remaining Amharic words where then stemmed and matched against the entries in the two dictionaries. The Amharic - French dictionary was always preferred over the Amharic - English one. Only in cases when a term had not been

[2] SERA stands for System for Ethiopic Representation in ASCII, http://www.abyssiniacybergateway.net/fidel/sera-faq.html

matched in the French dictionary was it matched against the English one. In a similar way, trigrams were matched before bigrams, bigrams before unigrams, unstemmed terms before stemmed terms, unchanged root forms were matched before modified root forms, longer matches in the dictionary were preferred before shorter etc.

The terms for which matches were found only in the Amharic-English MRD where first translated into English and then further translated from English into French using an online electronic dictionary from WordReference [12].

2.5 Selecting Terms for Approximate Matching

Some words and phrases that where not found in any of the dictionaries (mostly proper names or inherited words) were instead handled by an edit-distance based similarity matching algorithm (Lucene) or a phonetic matching algorithm (Searcher). Frequency counts in a 2.4 million words Amharic news corpus was used to determine whether an out of dictionary word would qualify as a candidate for these approximate matching algorithms or not. The assumption here is that if a word that is not included in any dictionary appears quite often in an Amharic text collection, then it is likely that the word is a term in the language although not found in the dictionary. On the other hand, if a term rarely occurs in the news corpus (in our case we used a threshold of nine times or less, but this of course depends on the size of the corpus), the word has a higher probability of being a proper name or an inherited word. Although this is a crude assumption and inherited words may occur frequently in a language, those words tend to be mostly domain specific. In a news corpus such as the one we used, the occurrence of almost all inherited words which could not be matched in the MRDs was very limited.

2.6 Phonetic Matching

Words that were not found in the translation lexicon and selected for phonetic matching were matched through a flexible phonetic spelling algorithm to identify cognates: primarily names, technical terms, and some modern loan words. Some of these terms are too recent to have been entered into the lexicon; some loan words and trade marks have unstable transcription rules and are realized in different ways in the topics and in the lexicon.

The task is to match the unknown Amharic query terms – numbering 64, about one per topic, in all – to the most likely French index term.

Phonematic Normalization. The Amharic words were all represented in a reasonably standard phonematic notation. The French orthography, on the other hand, contains a number of historically motivated redundancies but is easy to normalize phonetically through a set of simple rewrite rules: examples include accent deletion, normalization of *c*, *q*, *ph*, removal of final *e* etc. Some of these rules are binding: all *c*s before front vowels are transcribed to *s*; whereas others are optional: words with final *e*s are kept in the index as they are and entered as a new record without the *e*.

The VOCNET **Algorithm.** Once index terms are normalized using rewrite rules, Amharic and French terms are matched using the Vocnet flexible string matching algorithm. The Vocnet algorithm is an extension of the classic Levenshtein edit distance, which is a measure of the similarity between two strings calculated as the number of deletions, insertions, or substitutions required to transform the source string into the target string [6]. Numerous implementations of Levenshtein edit distance calculation can be found for download on the net. The Vocnet string matching algorithm weights the edit operations differentially depending on an estimate of the phonotactic acceptability of the resulting string. First, base data are acquired through bigram extraction from a text corpus in the language under consideration. These data are used to compute weights for insertion and deletion of each candidate grapheme.

Replacement of a grapheme by another is calculated by an assessed phonetic and articulatory similarity weighting: vowels are all similar to each other; voiced plosives (b,g,d) form a similarity class, unvoiced (p,t,k) another, both classes similar to each other; d, n, and t are all somewhat similar owing to locus of articulation.

The results matched about half of unknown words with the most reasonable match from the index, when such a match existed – an overview of results is shown in Table 1. Post hoc error analysis gives reason to count on room for improvement both in the French normalization rules and the Amharic-French matching weights.

2.7 Word Sense Discrimination

For the word sense discrimination we made use of two MRDs to get all the different senses of a term (word or phrase) - as given by the MRD, and a statistical collocation measure of mutual information using the target language corpus to assign each term to the appropriate sense.

In our experiments we used the bag of words approach where context is considered as words in some window surrounding the target word, regarded as a group without consideration for their relationships to the target in terms of distance, grammatical relations, etc. There is a big difference between the two languages under consideration (Amharic and French) in terms of word ordering, morphology, syntax etc, and hence limiting the context to a few number of words surrounding the target word was intuitively undesirable. A sentence could have been taken as a context window, but following the "one sense per discourse" constraint [4] in discriminating amongst word senses, a context window of a whole article was implemented. This constraint states that the sense of a word is highly consistent within any given document, in our case a French news article. The words to be sense discriminated are the query keywords, which are mostly composed of nouns rather than verbs, or adjectives. Noun sense discrimination is reported to be aided by word collocations that have a context window of hundreds of words, while verb and adjective senses tend to fall off rapidly with distance from the target word. After going through the list of translated content bearing keywords, we noticed that the majority of these words are nouns, and hence the selection of the document context window.

Table 1. Match statistics

Successful matches		20
ripublik	republic	
vaklav hevel	vaclav havel	
radovan karadzik	radovan karadzic	
Semi-successful matches		**5**
golden	ex-golden	
konsert	ateliers-concert	
Normalization mismatch		**6**
maykrosoft	$ay- > i$	
maykerosoft	$ay- > i, e- > \epsilon$	
Vocabulary mismatch		**23**
swizerland	(French use “Suisse”)	
fokland	Malouines	
Tuning mismatch		**10**
nukuliyer	(Did not match nucleaire)	
kominist	(Did not match communiste)	

In these experiments the Mutual Information between word pairs in the target language text collection is used to discriminate word senses. (Pointwise) mutual information compares the probability of observing two events x and y together (the joint probability) with the probabilities of observing x and y independently (chance). If two (words), x and y, have probabilities P(x) and P(y), then their mutual information, I(x,y), is defined to be:

$$I(x, y) = log_2 \frac{P(x,y)}{P(x)*P(y)} = log_2 \frac{P(x/y)}{P(x)}$$

If there is a genuine association between x and y, P(x,y) will be much larger than chance P(x)* P(y), thus I(x,y) will be greater than 0. If there is no interesting relationship between x and y, P(x,y) will be approximately equal to P(x)* P(y), and thus, I(x,y) will be close to 0. And if x and y are in complementary distribution, P(x,y) will be much less than P(x)* P(y), and I(x,y) will be less than 0.

Although very widely used by researchers for different applications, MI has also been criticized by many as to its ability to capture the similarity between two events especially when there is data scarcity [7]. Since we had access to a large amount of text collection in the target language, and because of its wide implementation, we chose to use MI.

The translated French query terms were put in a bag of words, and the mutual information for each of the possible word pairs was calculated. When we put the expanded words we treat both synonyms and translations with a distinct sense as given in the MRD equally. Another way of handling this situation is to group synonyms before the discrimination. We chose the first approach with two assumptions: one is that even though words may be synonymous, it doesn't necessarily mean that they are all equally used in a certain context, and the other being even though a word may have distinct senses defined in the MRD, those distinctions may not necessarily be applicable in the context the term is currently used. This approach is believed to ensure that words with inappropriate senses and synonyms with less contextual usage will be removed while at the same time the query is being expanded with appropriate terms.

We used a subset of the CLEF French document collection consisting of 14,000 news articles with 4.5 million words in calculating the MI values. Both the French keywords and the document collection were lemmatized in order to cater for the different forms of each word under consideration.

Following the idea that ambiguous words can be used in a variety of contexts but collectively they indicate a single context and particular meanings, we relied on the number of association as given by MI values that a certain word has in order to determine whether the word should be removed from the query or not. Given the bag of words for each query, we calculated the mutual information for each unique pair. The next step was to see for each unique word how many positive associations it has with the rest of the words in the bag. We experimented with different levels of combining precision and recall values depending on which one of these two measures we want to give more importance to. To contrast the approach of using the maximum recall of words (no discrimination) we decided that precision should be given much more priority over recall (beta value of 0.15), and we set an empirical threshold value of 0.4. i.e. a word is kept in the query if it shows positive associations with 40% of the words in the list, otherwise it is removed. Here, note that the mutual information values are converted to a binary 0, and 1. 0 being assigned to words that have less than or equal to 0 MI values (independent term pairs), and 1 to those with positive MI values (dependent term pairs). We are simply taking all positive MI values as indicators of association without any consideration as to how strong the association is. This is done to input as much association between all the words in the query as possible rather than putting the focus on individual pairwise association values. Results of the experiments are given in the next section.

The amount of words in each query differed substantially from one query to another. After the dictionary lookup and stop word removal, there were queries with French words that ranged from 2 to 71. This is due to a large difference in the number of words and in the number of stop words in each query as well as the number of senses and synonyms that are given in the dictionary for each word.

When there were less than or equal to 8 words in the expanded query, there was no word sense discrimination done for those queries. This is an arbitrary number, and the idea here is that if the number of terms is as small as that, then it is much better to keep all words. We believe that erroneously removing appropriate words in short queries has a lot more disadvantage than keeping one with an inappropriate sense.

2.8 Retrieval

Retrieval Using Lucene. Apache Lucene is an open source high-performance, full-featured text search engine library written in Java [11]. It is a technology deemed suitable for applications that require full-text search, especially in a cross-platform.

Retrieval Using Searcher. The text retrieval engine used for these experiments is based on a standard retrieval system being developed at SICS. The system does not perform any lemmatization or other linguistic preprocessing of the queries or documents, as this is performed by other applications beforehand. A more detailed description of the system is provided in the CLEF paper from 2002 [8].

In retrieval, query terms are weighted by a combination of standard tf-idf metrics with pivoted document length normalization [9] and a boosting procedure where documents containing several of the query terms are boosted higher than documents with the equivalent number of occurrences. In effect, the more query terms that are matched in a document, the higher the boosting weight, but the final weight for that document is not neccessarily higher than for a document that has fewer matching terms.

3 Results

We have submitted four parallel Amharic-French runs at the CLEF 2005 ad-hoc bilingual track. We have used two search engines - Lucene [11], an open source search toolbox, and an experimental search engine developed at SICS (Searcher). The aim of using these two search engines is to compare the performance of the systems as well as to investigate the impact of performing word sense discrimination. Two runs were submitted that use the same search engine, with one of them searching for all content bearing, expanded query terms without any word

Table 2. Recall-Precision tables for the four runs

Recall	am-fr-da-l	am-fr-nonda-l	am-fr-da-s	am-fr-nonda-s
0.00	16.71	18.67	24.55	23.84
0.10	6.20	6.93	9.12	9.18
0.20	4.23	4.70	5.13	4.71
0.30	2.34	3.76	3.75	3.36
0.40	1.43	1.76	2.83	2.71
0.50	1.13	0.79	2.02	1.85
0.60	0.87	0.57	1.36	1.45
0.70	0.29	0.32	0.76	0.60
0.80	0.15	0.08	0.57	0.37
0.90	0.05	0.04	0.39	0.23
1.00	0.05	0.04	0.27	0.17

sense discrimination while the other one searches for the 'disambiguated' set of content bearing query terms. The four runs are:

1. Lucene with word sense discrimination (am-fr-da-l)
2. Lucene without word sense discrimination (am-fr-nonda-l)
3. Searcher with word sense discrimination (am-fr-da-s)
4. Searcher without word sense discrimination (am-fr-nonda-s)

Table 2 lists the precision at various levels of recall for the four runs.

A summary of the results obtained from all runs is reported in Table 3. The number of relevant documents, the retrieved relevant documents, the non-interpolated average precision as well as the precision after R (=num_rel) documents retrieved (R-Precision) are summarized in the table.

Table 3. Summary of results for the four runs

	Relevant-tot	*Relevant-retrieved*	*Avg Precision*	*R-Precision*
am-fr-da-l	2,537	479	2.22	3.84
am-fr-nonda-l	2,537	558	2.51	4.38
am-fr-da-s	2,537	535	3.43	5.16
am-fr-nonda-s	2,537	579	3.31	4.88

4 Conclusions

We have demonstrated the feasability of doing cross language information retrieval between Amharic and French. Although there is still much room for improvement of the results, we are pleased to have been able to use a fully automatic approach. The work on this project and the performed experiments have highlighted some of the more crucial steps on the road to better information access and retrieval between the two languages. The lack of electronic resources such as morphological analysers and large machine readable dictionaries have forced us to spend considerable time on getting access to, or developing these resources ourselves. We also believe that, in the absense of larger electronic dictionaries, one of the more important obstacles on this road is how to handle out-of-dictionary words. The approaches that we tested in our experiments, to use fuzzy string matching or phonetic matching in the retrieval step, seem to be only partially successful, mainly due to the large differences between the two languages. We have also been able to compare the performance between different search engines and to test different approaches to word sense discrimination.

Acknowledgements

The copyright to the two volumes of the French-Amharic and Amharic-French dictionary ("Dictionnaire Francais-Amharique" and "Dictionnaire Amharique-Francais") by Dr Berhanou Abebe and loi Fiquet is owned by the French Ministry of Foreign Affairs. We would like to thank the authors and the French embassy in Addis Ababafor allowing us to use the dictionary in this research.

The content of the "English - Amharic Dictionary" is the intellectual property of Dr Amsalu Aklilu. We would like to thank Dr Amsalu as well as Daniel Yacob of the Geez frontier foundation for making it possible for us to use the dictionary and other resources in this work.

Thanks to Timo Järvinen and Connexor Oy (http://www.connexor.com) for morphological analysis of the data.

References

1. Berhanou Abebe. *Dictionnaire Amharique-Francais.*
2. Amsalu Aklilu. *Amharic English Dictionary.*
3. M. L. Bender, S. W. Head, and R. Cowley. The ethiopian writing system.
4. William Gale, Kenneth Church, and David Yarowsky. One sense per discourse. In *the 4th DARPA Speech and Language Workshop*, 1992.
5. W. Leslau. *Amharic Textbook.* Berkeley University, Berkeley, California, 1968.
6. V.I. Levenshtein. Binary codes capable of correcting deletions, insertions, and reversals. In *Cybernetics and Control Theory 10*, pages 707–710, 1966.
7. Christopher D. Manning and Hinrich Schütze. *Foundations of Statistical Natural Language Processing.* MIT Press, Cambridge, MA, 1999.
8. M. Sahlgren, J. Karlgren, R. Cöster, and T. Järvinen. SICS at CLEF 2002: Automatic query expansion using random indexing. In *The CLEF 2002 Workshop*, September 19-20 2002.
9. A. Singhal, C. Buckley, and M. Mitra. Pivoted document length normalization. In *Proceedings of the 19th annual international ACM SIGIR conference on Research and Development in Information Retrieval*, pages 21–29, 1996.
10. URL. http://www.ethnologue.org/, 2004.
11. URL. http://lucene.apache.org/java/docs/index.html, 2005.
12. URL. http://www.wordreference.com/, 2005.

A Hybrid Approach to Query and Document Translation Using a Pivot Language for Cross-Language Information Retrieval

Kazuaki Kishida[1] and Noriko Kando[2]

[1] Surugadai University, 698 Azu, Hanno, Saitama 357-8555, Japan
kishida@surugadai.ac.jp
[2] National Institute of Informatics (NII), Tokyo 101-8430, Japan
kando@nii.ac.jp

Abstract. This paper reports experimental results for cross-language information retrieval (CLIR) from German to French, in which a hybrid approach to query and document translation was attempted, i.e., combining the results of query translation (German to French) and of document translation (French to German). In order to reduce the complexity of computation when translating a large amount of texts, we performed pseudo-translation, i.e., a simple replacement of terms by a bilingual dictionary (for query translation, a machine translation system was used). In particular, since English was used as an intermediary language for both translation directions between German and French, English translations at the middle stage were employed as document representations in order to reduce the number of translation steps. By omitting a translation step (English to German), the performance was improved. Unfortunately, our hybrid approach did not show better performance than a simple query translation. This may be due to the low performance of document translation, which was carried out by a simple replacement of terms using a bilingual dictionary with no term disambiguation.

1 Introduction

This paper describes our experiment of cross-language IR (CLIR) from German to French in the CLEF 2005 campaign. Our focus in this experiment is the search performance of a hybrid approach combining query translation and document translation, in which English is employed as an intermediary language for translation.

Some researchers have already attempted to merge the two results of query and of document translation to enhance the effectiveness of CLIR. One objective of combining them is to increase the possibility of successfully matching subject representations of the query with those of each document. One problem with this approach is that the document translation is usually a cost-intensive task, but we can alleviate it by using simpler translation techniques, e.g., "pseudo translation" [1] in which each term is simply replaced with its corresponding translations by a bilingual dictionary. We felt that it was worthwhile investigating the performance of the hybrid approach using this simpler, more practical document translation technique.

C. Peters et al. (Eds.): CLEF 2005, LNCS 4022, pp. 93 – 101, 2006.

This paper is organized as follows. In Section 2, the hybrid approach combining the two results of query and of document translation is discussed. Section 3 describes our system used in the CLEF 2005 experiment. The results are reported in Section 4.

2 A Hybrid Approach to Query and Document Translation

2.1 Combination of Query and Document Translation

In order to perform CLIR, we have to match representations between a query and the documents in the collection by translating either the query or the documents. In general, queries tend to be translated [2]. This may be due to ease of implementation, i.e., no special device is needed for CLIR other than a tool for translating the query text. In contrast, document translation has rarely been adopted as the strategy for CLIR partly because a very large amount of processing is needed to translate all documents in the whole database.

However, some researchers have reported that a hybrid approach of query and document translation improves the search performance in CLIR. For example, McCarley [3] attempted to use an average of two document scores which were computed from query translation and document translation respectively in order to rank documents for output. Fujii and Ishikawa [4] translated documents that were searched based on query translation, and tried to re-rank them according to the results of the document translation. In NTCIR-4, Kang et al. [1] tried to perform Korean to Chinese and Korean to Japanese bilingual retrieval using the hybrid approach.

An advantage of the hybrid approach is that it increases the possibility of correctly identifying documents having the same subject content as the query. Suppose that a term A is included in a given search query and its corresponding term in the language of documents is B. If a tool for translation from the query language to the document language can not translate A into B correctly, the system will fail to find documents containing term B by this query translation. However, if another tool for translation in the reverse direction, i.e., the document language into the query language, can identify term A from term B, matching between the query and documents including term B becomes successful.

To implement the hybrid approach, it is important to find an answer to the fact that that document translation is a cost-intensive task. For example, it may take too long to translate all the documents using commercial software for machine translation (MT). McCarley [3] applied a statistical translation technique to alleviate this problem. In contrast, Kang et al.[1] employed a "pseudo" translation technique, in which each term in documents is simply replaced with its translations by using a bilingual dictionary. Although the replacement is not exactly equal to MT, it is very fast and produces translations of a large amount of documents within a reasonable time.

2.2 Hybrid Approach with a Pivot Language

In our hybrid approach, queries in German are translated into French by a commercial MT system, and each term included in the French documents is replaced with its corresponding German word using bilingual dictionaries. After the translation, two

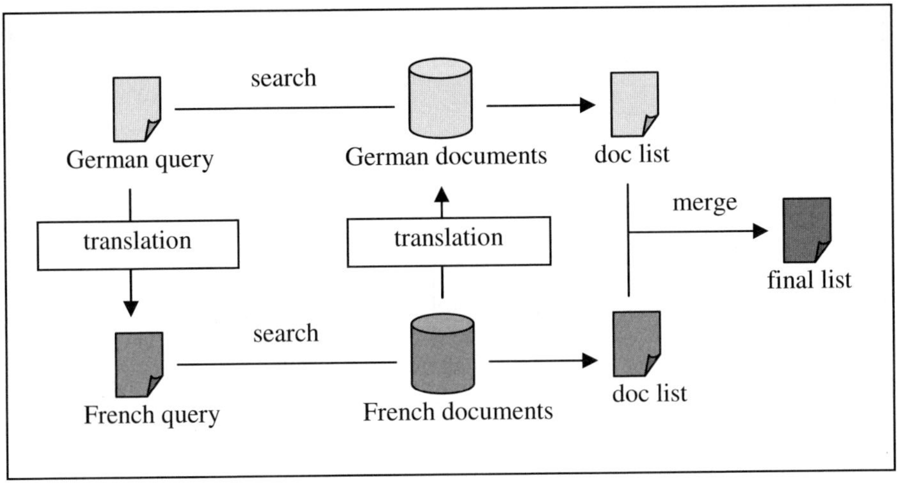

Fig. 1. Hybrid Approach Procedure (1)

scores are computed for each document from the results of query and document translation respectively. Finally, we calculate a final score for ranking the documents by using a simple linear formula such as

$$z = wx + (1 - w)y, \tag{1}$$

where x is a score computed from the results of query translation, y is the score from document translation, and w is a weight (in this paper, we always set $w = 0.7$). This procedure is shown in Figure 1.

Both the translation methods employed in this experiment, i.e., MT and dictionary-based method, make use of a pivot language. The MT software translates German sentences into English ones, and translates the results into French sentences. Similarly, each term in French documents is replaced with corresponding English translations by a French to English dictionary, and these English translations are replaced with German terms by an English to German dictionary. An appropriate translation resource is not always available for a pair of languages that actual users require. But in such cases, it is possible to find translation tools between English and these languages since English is an international language. Therefore, the pivot language approach via English is useful in real situations, although the two steps of translation in this approach often yield many irrelevant translations, particularly in the case of dictionary-based transitive translation, because all final translations obtained from an irrelevant English term in the middle stage are usually irrelevant [5]

One solution to this problem may be to limit the dictionary-based translation to only conversion of French terms into English ones. In order to compute document scores from documents translated into English, German queries have to be translated into English. In the case of the pivot language approach, an English version of the

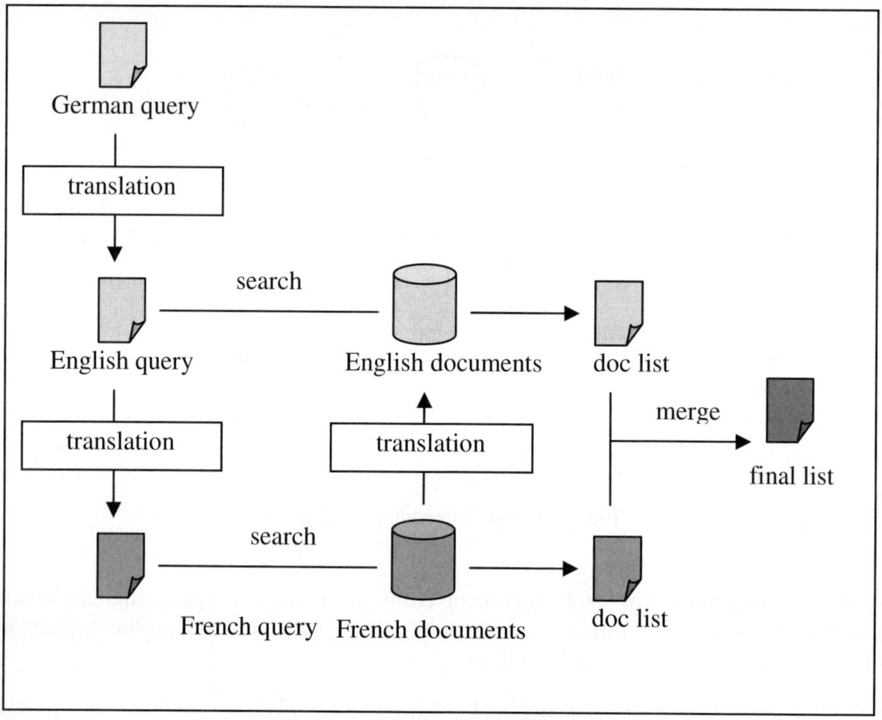

Fig. 2. Hybrid Approach Procedure (2)

query is automatically obtained in the middle stage of translation from German to French (see Figure 2). In this case, the number of translation operations is just three as shown in Figure 2. In contrast, the standard hybrid approach in Figure 1 using a pivot language needs four translation operations, i.e., (1) German query to English query, (2) English query to French query, (3) French documents to English documents and (4) English documents to German documents. Removing one operation, the dictionary-based translation, may help reduce erroneous translations and improve the search performance.

3 System Description

3.1 Text Processing

Both German and French texts (in documents and queries) were basically processed by the following steps: (1) identifying tokens, (2) removing stopwords, (3) lemmatization, and (4) stemming. In addition, for German text, decomposition of compound words was attempted based on a simple algorithm of longest matching with headwords included in the German to English dictionary in machine-readable form. For example, the German word, "Briefbombe," is broken down into two headwords listed in the German to English dictionary, "Brief" and "Bombe," according to the rule that the longest headwords included in the original compound word are extracted from it. If a substring of "Brief" or "Bombe" is also listed in the dictionary, the substring is not used as a separate word.

We downloaded free dictionaries (German to English and English to French) from the Internet[1]. Stemmer and stopword lists for German and French were also available through the Snowball project[2]. Stemming for English was conducted by the original Porter's algorithm [6].

3.2 Translation Procedure

We used a commercial MT system produced by a Japanese company[3] for query translation, and the French or English sentences output were processed according to the procedures described above. In the case of document translation, each German sentence was processed, and its words and decomposed elements of compound words were simply replaced with corresponding English terms using a German to English dictionary with no term disambiguation. If no corresponding headword was included in the dictionary for a German term, it was entered into the set of English terms with no change as an unknown term. Moreover, in order to obtain French translations, a set of the English translations was converted using an English to French dictionary by the same procedure as that for obtaining English translations. It should be noted that all terms included in these dictionaries were normalized through stemming and lemmatization processes with the same procedure applied to texts of documents and queries. Therefore, by the dictionary-based translation, a set of normalized English or French terms was obtained.

3.3 Search Algorithm

The standard Okapi BM25 [7] was used for all search runs, and for pseudo-relevance feedback we employed a term weighting formula,

$$w_t = r_t \times \log \frac{(r_t + 0.5)(N - R - n_t + r_t + 0.5)}{(N - n_t + 0.5)(R - r_t + 0.5)}, \qquad (2)$$

where N is the total number of documents, R is the number of top-ranked documents that are assumed to be relevant, n_t is the number of documents including term t, and r_t is the number of documents including term t in the top-ranked R documents. In this experiment, we always set $R = 30$ and ten terms were selected based on their weights in Eq. (2). Let y_t be the frequency of a given term in the query. If a newly selected term was already included in the set of search terms, the term frequency in the query y_t was changed to $1.5 \times y_t$. If not, the term frequency was set to 0.5 (i.e., $y_t = 0.5$). The pseudo-relevance feedback (PRF) procedure was carried out for all search runs in this experiment.

---

[1] http://www.freelang.net/

[2] http://snowball.tartarus.org/

[3] http://www.crosslanguage.co.jp/english/

3.4 Merging of Document Lists

To merge two document lists generated by different strategies (i.e., query and document translation), we used Eq.(1). More precisely, the procedure is as follows.

(a) Using the result of query translation, document scores are computed, and documents up to the 10,000th position in the ranked list are selected at maximum.

(b) Similarly, using the result of document translation, document scores are computed again, and documents up to the 10,000th position in the ranked list are selected at maximum.

(c) Final scores for documents selected in (a) and (b) are computed based on Eq.(1) and all documents are re-ranked (if a document was not included in either of the lists in (a) or (b), its score is set to zero in the list).

3.5 Type of Search Runs

We executed five runs in which the <TITLE> and <DESCRIPTION> fields in each search topic were used, and submitted the results to the organizers of CLEF 2005. All runs were executed on the information retrieval system ADOMAS (Advanced Document Management System) developed at Surugadai University in Japan. The five runs are as follows.

- **Hybrid-1:** merging two results of French translations for query and of German translation for documents
- **Hybrid-2:** merging two results of French translations for query and of English translation for documents as shown in Figure 1
- **Query translation:** using only query translation from German to Italian with no document translation as shown in Figure 2
- **Document translation:** using only document translation from French to German with no query translation
- **Monolingual:** searching the French document collection for the French topics (not translation)

In order to compare the performance of our hybrid approach, search runs using only query translation and only document translation were attempted. In addition, to check the effectiveness of these CLIR runs, a monolingual search was also executed.

4 Experimental Results

4.1 Basic Statistics

The target French collection includes 177,452 documents in total. The average document length is 232.65 words. When we translated the document collection into English using our dictionary substitution method, the average document length in the English collection amounted to 663.49 words and that in the German collection translated from the original French one was 1799.74. Since we did not incorporate any translation disambiguation into our process as mentioned above, each translated document became very long.

Table 1. Average precision and R-precision (average over all 50 topics)

Run	ID	Average Precision	R-Precision
French Monolingual	SrgdMono01	.3910	.3998
Hybrid-1: German doc translation	SrgdMgG02	.2492	.2579
Hybrid-2: English doc translation	SrgdMgE03	.2605	.2669
Query translation	SrgdQT04	.2658	.2642
Document translation	SrgdDT05	.1494	.1605

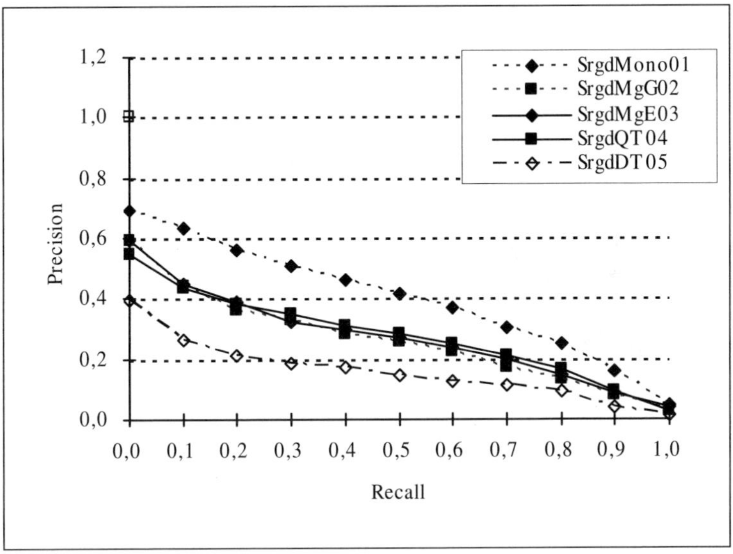

Fig. 3. Recall-precision curves

4.2 Results

Scores of average precision and R-precision are shown in Table 1, and the recall-precision curves of these runs are presented in Figure 3. Note that each value in Table 1 and Figure 3 is calculated for all 50 topics that were prepared for evaluating search runs.

As shown in Table 1, the hybrid approach using English documents translated from the original collection (hybrid-2, SrgdMgE03) outperforms another hybrid approach using German documents (hybrid-1, SrgdMgG02), i.e., the scores of mean average precision (MAP) are 0.2605 for hybrid-2 and 0.2492 for hybrid-1. Although the degree of difference is not large, the dominance of the hyper-2 approach is consistent with our logical expectation.

Unfortunately, the hybrid approach did not show better performance than a simple query translation approach (SrgdQT04), i.e., its MAP score was 0.2658, which is slightly greater than that of SrgdMgE03. This may be due to the low performance of the document translation approach, e.g., the MAP score of document translation from

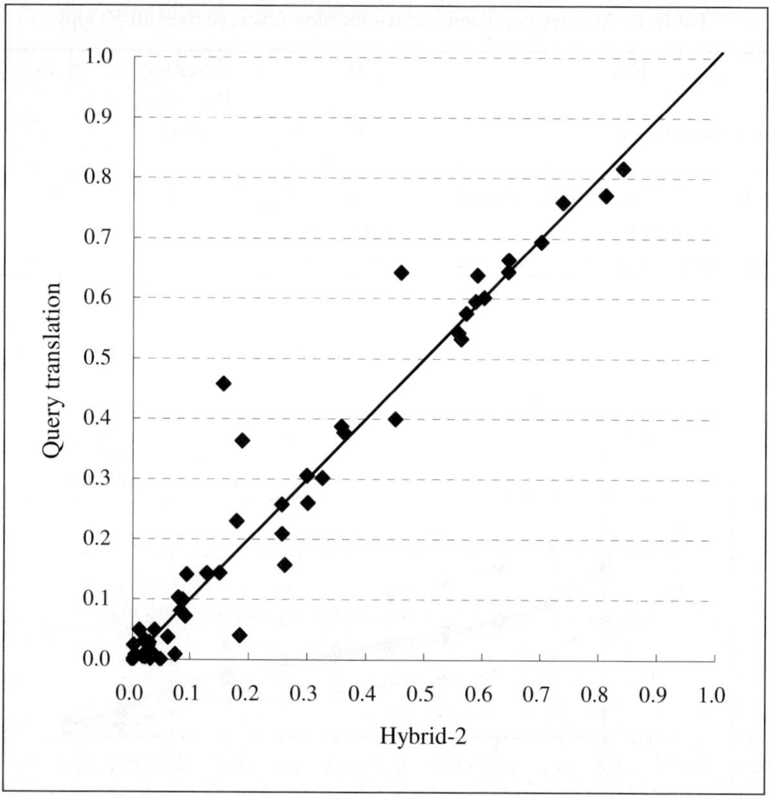

Fig. 4. Topic-by-topic analysis (average precision score)

French to German (SrgdDT05) was only 0.1494. That is, by combining results from document translation with those from query translation, ranking of relevant documents in the list generated by the query translation approach became lower forsome topics. Of course, in other topics, the performance was improved as shown in Figure 3, which is a topic-by-topic plot of the two scores of average precision for hyper-2 and the query translation approach. However, we should consider that our hybrid approach did not show better effectiveness due to the low performance of the document translation approach. The reason for the low performance may be (1) the quality of free dictionaries downloaded from the Internet and (2) the omission of translation disambiguation. We have to solve these problems in order to improve the performance of our hybrid approach.

5 Concluding Remarks

This paper reported the results of our experiment on German to French bilingual retrieval, for which a hybrid approach combining results of query translation and document translation was used. To reduce the complexity of computation for translating a large amount of documents in the database, we applied pseudo-translation, i.e., a simple replacement of terms by using a bilingual dictionary. In contrast, machine translation software was used for the translation of queries, which are usually short.

Since a pivot language approach was applied in the translation process by both the MT system and bilingual dictionaries, we attempted to reduce the number of translation steps by employing English translations from the original French collection as a result of document translation. It is empirically shown that this approach slightly outperforms the standard hybrid approach using German translations as representations of documents. Unfortunately, our hybrid approach did not show better effectiveness than a simple query translation approach partly because the performance of document translation was poor. We have to develop techniques to enhance the effectiveness of the document translation approach.

References

1. Kang, I. S., Na, S. H. Na , Lee, J. H.: POSTECH at NTCIR-4: CJKE Monolingual and Korean-related Cross-Language Retrieval Experiments. In NTCIR Workshop 4 Meeting Working Notes, 2004, p.89-95
2. Kishida, K.: Technical issues of cross-language information retrieval: a review. Information Processing & Management, 41 (2005), 433-455
3. Scott McCarley, J.: Should we translate the documents or the queries in cross-language information retrieval? In Proceedings of the 37th conference on Association for Computational Linguistics (1999) 208-214
4. Fujii, A, Ishikawa, T. Japanese-English cross-language information retrieval integrating query and document translation methods. The Transactions of the Institute of Electronics, Information and Communication Engineers. J84-D-II (2001) 362-369 (*In Japanese*)
5. Kishida, K., Kando, N.: Two-Stage refinement of query translation in a pivot language approach to cross-lingual information retrieval: an experiment at CLEF 2003. In C. Peters, J. Gonzalo, M. Braschler and M. Kluck (Eds), Comparative Evaluation of Multilingual Information Access Systems. LNCS 3237, Springer Verlag, pp.253-262.
6. Porter, M.F.: An algorithm for suffix stripping. Program. 14 (1980) 130-137
7. Robertson, S.E., Walker, S., Jones, S., Hancock-Beaulieu, M.M., Gatford, M.: Okapi at TREC-3. In Proceedings of TREC-3. National Institute of Standards and Technology, Gaithersburg (1995) http://trec.nist.gov/pubs/

Conceptual Indexing for Multilingual Information Retrieval

Jacques Guyot, Saïd Radhouani, and Gilles Falquet

Centre Universitaire d'Informatique. University of Geneva
24, rue Général-Dufour, CH-1211 Genève 4, Switzerland
{Said.Radhouani, Gilles.Falquet}@cui.unige.ch,
Jacques.Guyot@rolex.com

Abstract. We present a translation-free technique for multilingual information retrieval. This technique is based on an ontological representation of documents and queries. For each language, we use a dictionary (set of lexical reference for concepts) to map a term to its corresponding concept. The same mapping is applied to each document and each query. Then, we use a classic vector space model based on concept for indexing and querying the document corpus. The main advantages of our approach are: no merging phase is required; no dependency on automatic translators between all pairs of languages; and adding a new language only requires a new mapping dictionary to be added into the multilingual ontology. Experimental results on the CLEF 2005 multi8 collection show that this approach is efficient, even with relatively small and low fidelity dictionaries and without word sense disambiguation.

1 Introduction

The rapid spread of communication technologies, such as the Web, has enabled people to access previously unavailable information. With these advances, however, it has become increasingly clear that there is a growing need for access to information in many languages. The aim of Multilingual Information Retrieval (MIR) is to locate information when the language of the user query is different from the languages of the document corpus. With a MIR system, a user can formulate queries in his own language and the system will find relevant documents written in other languages. This task is motivated by the fact that it is generally easier to judge the relevance of a document in a foreign language than to formulate an effective query in such a language. It is thus suitable to be able to formulate queries on a multilingual corpus in one's mother tongue.

The existing MIR approaches use either translation of all documents into a common language, or automatic translation of the queries, or a combination of both query and document translations [2]. In all cases, these approaches need at least one automatic translator to or from each document and query languages supported by the system between all pairs of languages.

Translating all the documents and queries to a common language introduces ambiguities due to the polysemy of the common language. These ambiguities have of course a negative impact on the retrieval performance. In principle, this approach could sometimes suppress some ambiguities of the source document if the translator

C. Peters et al. (Eds.): CLEF 2005, LNCS 4022, pp. 102 – 112, 2006.

were able to do word sense disambiguation. However, current automatic translators have poor disambiguation performance.

If the system translates queries to all the corpus languages, then a sophisticated merging procedure is necessary to provide a unique ranked result list from the result lists obtained for each language. Moreover, adding a new language for queries (or documents) requires a new automatic translator between the new language and all the corpus (query) languages.

The approach we propose "dissolves" these problems by using of a multilingual ontology for representing documents and queries as sets of concepts. We have developed a MIR system that uses this ontological representation, and we used it to conduct a range of experiments involving multilingual test-collection. These experiments include retrieving documents written in Dutch, English, Finnish, French, German, Italian, Spanish and Swedish, independently of the query language.

In the remainder of this paper, we first present the baseline text indexing. We present our multilingual ontology in section 3. We introduce the conceptual indexing and the query module in sections 4 and 5 respectively. For the evaluation (cf. section 6), we have investigated the CLEF 2005 multi8 collection. Finally, we conclude and present our future work (cf. section 7).

2 Baseline Text Indexing

For the present work, we have used the vector space model (VSM) for text document representation [7]. Let *tf(d,t)* be the absolute frequency of term $t \in T$ in document $d \in D$, where D is the set of documents and $T = \{t1, \dots tn\}$ is the set of all different terms occurring in D. Let *df(t)* be the document frequency of term $t \in T$ that counts in how many documents term t appears. The *tf*idf* (term frequency – inverted document frequency) weights the frequency of a term in a document with a factor that discounts importance when it appears in almost all documents. The *tf*idf (d,t)* of term t in document d is defined by:

$$tf \cdot idf(d,t) := \log(tf(d,t)+1) \cdot \log(\frac{|D|}{df(t)}) \quad (1)$$

Finally, we denote by $\vec{d}$:= (tf*idf(d,t1),…, tf*idf(d,tn)) the term vector of the document d.

We will see in Section 4 that our approach consists of using the same vector computation on the concepts instead of the terms, so as to obtain a conceptual vector of the document instead of a term vector.

3 Multilingual Ontology

The knowledge we have exploited is given through a multilingual ontology. We first define it and describe its structure, and then we describe the ontology that we have used and its integration into the baseline text document representation.

Definition1. An ontology is a formal, explicit specification of a shared conceptualization [4].

'Conceptualisation' refers to an abstract model of some phenomenon in the world that identifies the relevant concepts of that phenomenon. 'Explicit' means that the type of concepts used and the constraints on their use are explicitly defined. 'Formal' refers to the fact that the ontology should be machine readable. 'Shared' refers to the fact that a particular community shares the ontology of a common domain. This helps both people and machines to communicate concisely, supporting the exchange of semantics and not only syntax.

Concepts are the basic building block for ontologies. They are typically hierarchically organized in a concept hierarchy. These concepts can have properties, which establish named relations to other concepts [1].

Based on [1], we present the formal model for ontologies as follow.

Definition2. A core ontology is a tuple $O_{di} := (C, \leq_C, R)$ *consisting of a set C whose elements are called concept identifiers, and a partial order* $\leq_C$ *on C, called concept hierarchy or taxonomy, and a set R whose elements are binary relations on C.*

Often we will call concept identifiers just concepts, for the sake of simplicity.

Definition3. A lexicon for an ontology O is a structure $Lex := (S, Ref)$ *consisting of a set S whose elements are called signs for concepts, and a relation* $Ref \subseteq S \times C$ *called lexical reference for concepts, where* $(c,c) \in Ref$ *holds for all* $c \in C \cap S$.

Based on *Ref*, we define, *for* $s \in S$, $Ref(s) := \{c \in C \mid (s,c) \in Ref\}$ and, for $c \in C$, $Ref^{1}(c) := \{s \in S \mid (s,c) \in Ref\}$.

Thus, an ontology with lexicon is a pair *(O, Lex)* where *O* is a core ontology and *Lex* is a lexicon for *O*.

Definition4. A multilingual ontology MO is a structure $MO := \{O, \{Lex_L\}\}$ consisting of one ontology *O*, and a set of multilingual lexicon $\{Lex_L\}$ where Lex_L is the lexicon for the ontology *O* in the language *L*. Based on *definition3*, a lexicon in a language *L* is a structure $Lex_L := (S_L, Ref_L)$ where S_L is the set of *signs for concepts* in the language *L*, and Ref_L is the *lexical reference for concepts* ($Ref_L \subseteq S_L \times C$),

Thus, a multilingual ontology with multilingual lexicons is a pair $\{O, \{Lex_L\}\}$ where *O* is an ontology and Lex_L is a lexicon for *O* in the language *L*.

For the purpose of actual evaluation of conceptual indexing, we have constructed our multilingual ontology based on UNL [9]. UNL Universal Words (UWs) compose the core ontology, and UNL dictionaries compose the Lexicons. For the sake of simplicity, we will call UWs just *concepts*.

For the purpose of actual evaluation of conceptual indexing, we have complemented our multilingual ontology with Esperanto dictionaries found on the Web (principally from Ergane [3]). Our ontology consists of 50100 concepts and 197000 lexical entries (terms) (13000 for French, 53000 for English, 20000 for German, 81000 for Dutch, 4500 for Italian, 19000 for Spanish, and 6500 for Swedish). We have also used automatic translations to complement all of them. Here, we present two examples of concepts extracted from our ontology:

- *Inch(icl>length unit): a unit of length (in United States and Britain) equal to one twelfth of a foot*
- *Thumb(icl>finger): the thick short innermost digit of the forelimb.*

In our multilingual ontology, the function Ref_L relates terms (e.g., s_1 ="thumb" and s_2 = "pouce") with their corresponding concepts (e.g., c_1 = "*Thumb(icl>finger)*" and c_2 = "*Inch(icl>length unit)*"). Thus, for the French term "pouce" appearing in a document *d*, Ref_{FR} allows for retrieving its corresponding concepts: $Ref_{FR}(pouce)$ *:= { Inch(icl>length unit), Thumb(icl>finger)}*. And for the concept "*Thumb(icl>finger)*", Ref_{EN}^{-1} allows for retrieving its corresponding terms in English: Ref_{EN}^{-1} *(Thumb(icl>finger)) := {thumb}.*

Fig.1 shows a screen shot containing an example of concept definition in UNL.

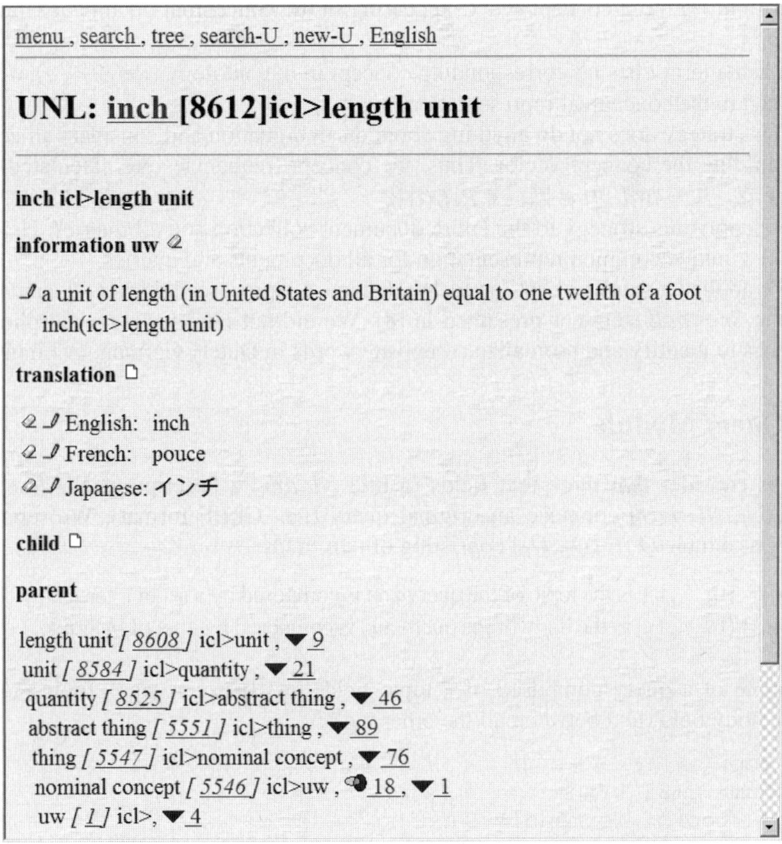

Fig. 1. Example of concepts defintion in UNL [10]

4 Conceptual Indexing

In order to have a common and unique document/query representation for all languages, we have investigated a simple strategy consisting of conceptual indexing. The principle is to replace the document terms by concepts from the core ontology. This has two benefits. First, we do not need any automatic translator. Second, we do not need any merging procedure during the query process.

Let us first consider a document $d_L \in D_L$ to be a set of terms $t \in T_L$, where D_L is the set of documents in the language L and $T_L = \{t_1,..., t_n\}$ is the set of all different terms occurring in D_L. For each document d_L, we build a new vector representation $\overrightarrow{d_c}$ composed of concepts instead of terms. In order to construct $\overrightarrow{d_c}$, we have modified each document representation by replacing terms by their corresponding concepts. For a document d_L, initially composed by a set of terms t, we apply the reference function Ref_L to all its terms. Thus, we obtain a conceptual representation $d_c := \{c \in C \mid c \in Ref_L(t)\}$. Hence, we obtain the concept vector $\overrightarrow{d_c}:= (cf{*}idf(d_L,c_1),...,cf{*}idf(d_L,c_m))$, with $m = |C|$ and $cf{*}idf(d_L,c)$ is calculated by applying the formula *(1)* to a concept $c \in C$ appearing in the conceptual document representation d_c.

When a term t has no corresponding concept in the ontology ($Ref_L(t)= \varnothing$), it will be retained in the conceptual representation.

This strategy does not do anything about disambiguation and considers all concepts for building the concept vector. Thus, the concept frequencies are calculated as follow: $cf(d_L,c) := tf(d_L, \{t \in T_L \mid c \in Ref_L(t)\})$.

We apply this strategy to the entire document collection and all queries. Hence, we obtain a unique common representation for all documents and queries.

We applied a stopword list for each language, andprocessed our text documents using the *Snowball* stemmer presented in [8]. We did not introduce any morphological analysis to identify and normalize composite words in Dutch, German, or Finnish.

5 Query Module

Let us consider that three text fields (a title *NL-title*, a description *NL-desc*, and a narrative *NL-narr*) compose an original query (i.e., CLEF format). We represent a query as a tuple $Q := (Q_T, Q_B)$ consisting of two fields:

- $Q_T := \{t_1, \ldots, t_n\}$ is the topic of the query and is composed by a set of n terms,
- $Q_B := \{t_1, \ldots, t_m\}$ is the body of the query and is composed by a set of m terms.

Example of a query composed of a topic field (text between tags <topic></topic>) and a body field (text between all the other tags).

```
<top>
<num> C182 </num>
   <topic> Normandië Landing </topic>
   <NL-title> 50e Herdenkingsdag van de Landing in Nor-
mandië </NL-title>
   <NL-desc> Zoek verslagen over de dropping van veter-
anen boven Sainte-Mère-Église tijdens de viering van de
50e herdenkingsdag van de landing in Normandië. </NL-
desc>
   <NL-narr> Ongeveer veertig veteranen sprongen
tijdens de viering van de 50e herdenkingsdag van de
```

landing in Normandië met een parachute boven Sainte-Mère-Église, net zoals ze vijftig jaar eerder op D-day hadden gedaan. Alle informatie over het programma of over de gebeurtenis zelf worden als relevant beschouwd.
</NL-narr>
</top>Once Q_T and Q_B are defined, we generate their conceptual representations as described in the previous section.

In the next section, we present how we use Q_T and Q_B during the matching process.

5.1 Matching Process

The relevance of a document with respect to a query Q is given by a combination of two techniques:

Filtering determines documents that contain the query topic Q_T concepts.

Ranking measures the importance of the obtained documents to the initial query and ranks them.

We present in the next section these two techniques. Figure 2 shows the conceptual indexing and querying process.

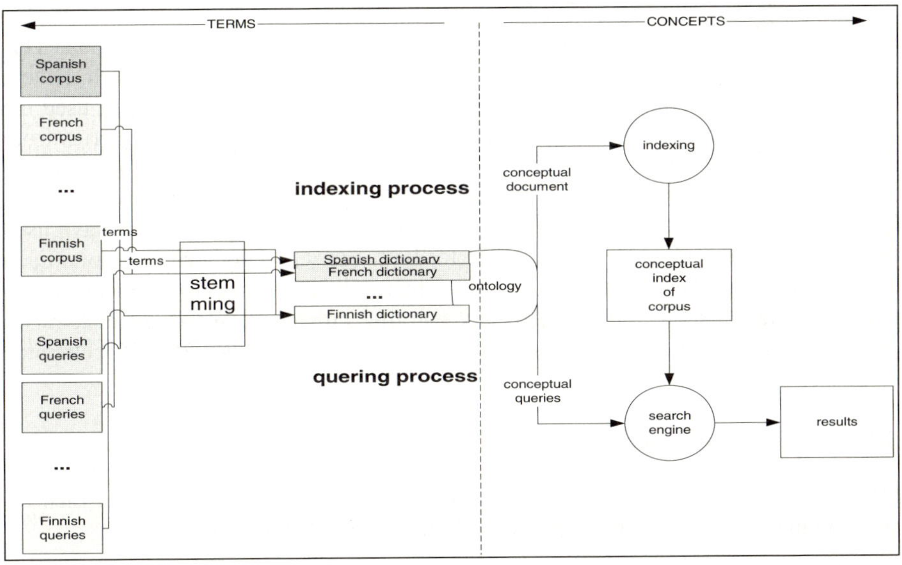

Fig. 2. Conceptual indexing and querying process

5.1.1 Filtering Technique

The filtering checks in which document the query topic concepts occur. Thus, we build a Boolean query topic by the conjunction of all its concepts. Then, we query the entire document collection. The result is a subset D_T of the collection where each document $d \in D_T$ contains all concepts of the query topic Q_T. After this filtering, the obtained subset D_T is still not ranked. In order to return, for each query, one ranked document list, we use the second technique that we describe in the next section.

5.1.2 Ranking Technique

In order to rank the document set D_T with respect to the query Q, we propose to query it using the query body Q_B using the VSM. This querying is based on the similarity value between the query body Q_B and each document d belonging to the set D_T. This similarity value is measured by the cosine of the angle between the vectors $\vec{d}$ and $\vec{q}$ representing respectively the document d and the query text field Q_B:

$$\cos(\prec(\vec{q},\vec{d})) := \frac{|\vec{q}| \cdot |\vec{d}|}{\|\vec{q}\| \cdot \|\vec{d}\|} \tag{2}$$

Finally, we have the subset D_Q that represents a ranked list of document obtained as answer for the query Q.

Another way to apply these two techniques using VSM querying can be to set up the filtering after the vector querying (post filtering). Applying the methods this way gives the same final result. The ordering used here reduces the number of documents to deal with for the final ranking.

6 Experiments

In order to evaluate our approach, we use the CLEF 2005 multi8 collection. This collection contains 1.500.000 documents in eight languages (English, French, Dutch, German, Italian, Swedish, Finnish, and Spanish). For the indexing, we have used the VLI experimental system [6]. As described in section 4, all documents/queries from all languages followthe same conceptual indexing process. It means that we have only one set for all the eight languages. We obtain a conceptual vector for each document. Hence, all documents in any language are merged in the same index. We have used the same indexing scheme with the VSM for both query and document vectors. Each query vector is applied to the unique index. The result is a unique list of documents in many languages. So we do not need any merging procedure. We evaluate retrieval performance in terms of uninterpolated Mean Average Precision (MAP) computed using trec_eval.

6.1 Experimental Results

Here, we first present results obtained when submitting queries in English, then results obtained when submitting queries in four different languages.

6.1.1 Submitting English Queries

For the filtering process, we have tested two strategies to construct the query topic field:

- AUTO: the topic field is composed by the terms of the title of the original query.
- ADJUST: the topic field is composed by the modified title by adding and/or removing terms. The added terms are extracted from the original query text.

For the ranking process, we have tested two strategies used to construct the query body:

- ORIGIN: the query body is composed of the description and narrative fields of the original query.

- FEEDBCK: the query body is composed of the description and narrative fields of the original query, and the first relevant document (if it exists) selected manually after a relevance feedback process.

We present here three runs set up using combinations of the presented strategies:

- AUTO-EN: *AUTO* and *ORIGIN*
- ADJUST-EN: *ADJUST* and *ORIGIN.*
- FEEDBCK-EN: *ADJUST* and *FEEDBCK.* The first relevant document (if it exists) is selected from the first 30 documents found after *ADJUST*.

Table 1 shows the result of each run. We obtained a MAP of 5.49% when we do not use any filtering with the topic (SANS-TOPIC). Using the filtering technique (AUTO-EN), we obtain a MAP of 10.33% which represents an improvement about 88.16%. We notice that it is difficult to have a good result for the AUTO-EN run while the topic contains all the concepts occurring to the query title field (10.33% of MAP). Using the adjusted topic, we obtain a MAP of 16.85% which represents an

Table 1. Results obtained using different strategies and different languages

Run	MAP (%)
SANS-TOPIC	5.49
AUTO-EN	10.33
ADJUST-EN	16.85
FEEDBC-EN	**21.02**
ADJSUT-DU	13.90
ADJSUT-FR	13.47
ADJSUT-SP	13.80

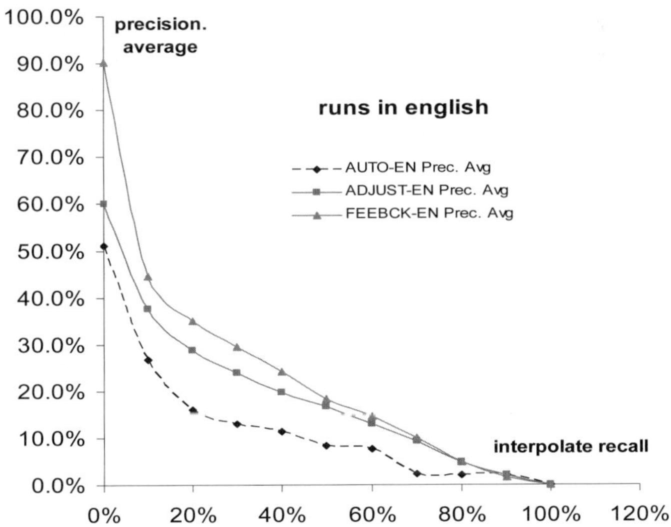

Fig. 3. Comparison of the system result using three strategies

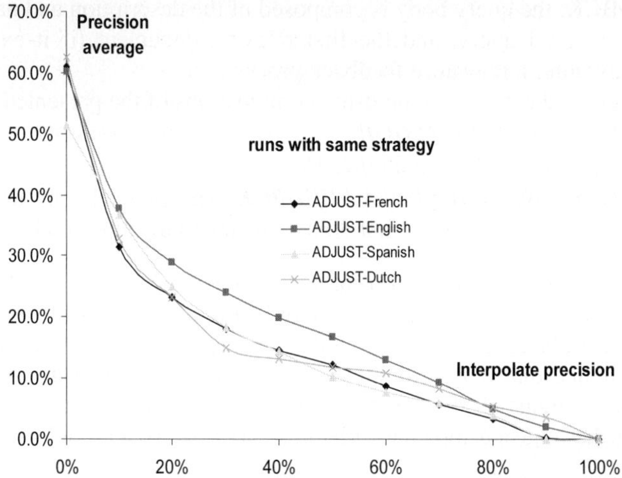

Fig. 4. Comparison of the system result using four languages

improvement about 63.11%. We succeeded in improving this result about 24.74% using relevance feedback (21.02%).

6.1.2 Submitting Different Query Languages

In order to compare the system results using different languages when submitting queries, we carried out three more runs: ADJUST-DU, ADJUST-FR, and ADJUST-SP. For each run, we use respectively Dutch, French, and Spanish when submitting queries. In these runs, topic field is composed of adjusted title as in ADJUST-EN (cf. 5.2.1) and the body field is composed of the original query text. For all the four runs, we obtain almost the same MAP: 13.90% for ADJUST-DU, 13.47% for ADJUST-FR, 13.80% for ADJUST-SP and 16.85 % for ADJSUT-EN. Results show that our system is not dependent of the query language. It gives nearly the same results when submitting queries in four different languages.

6.2 System Interface

We have also developed an interactive interface. Fig. 5 shows an example screen shot where Arabic is the query language (dinosaur egg), and the selected document is in Italian. This interface allows us to query the system using ten languages (Dutch, English, Finnish, French, German, Italian, Spanish, Swedish, Russian, and Arabic).

7 Conclusion and Future Works

In this paper, we evaluated a multilingual ontology-based approach for multilingual information retrieval. We did not use any translation either for documents or for queries. We carried out a common document/query conceptual representation based on a multilingual ontology. Then, we used the vector space model for indexing and querying. Compared with the existing approaches, our approach has several advantages. There is no dependency on automatic translators between all pairs of languages. When we add a new language, we only add, in the ontology, a new mapping dictionary. Also, we do not need any merging technique to rank the list of retrieved documents.

We have also used the same approach in the bi-text alignment field. We have used other languages such as Chinese, Arabic and Russian [5].

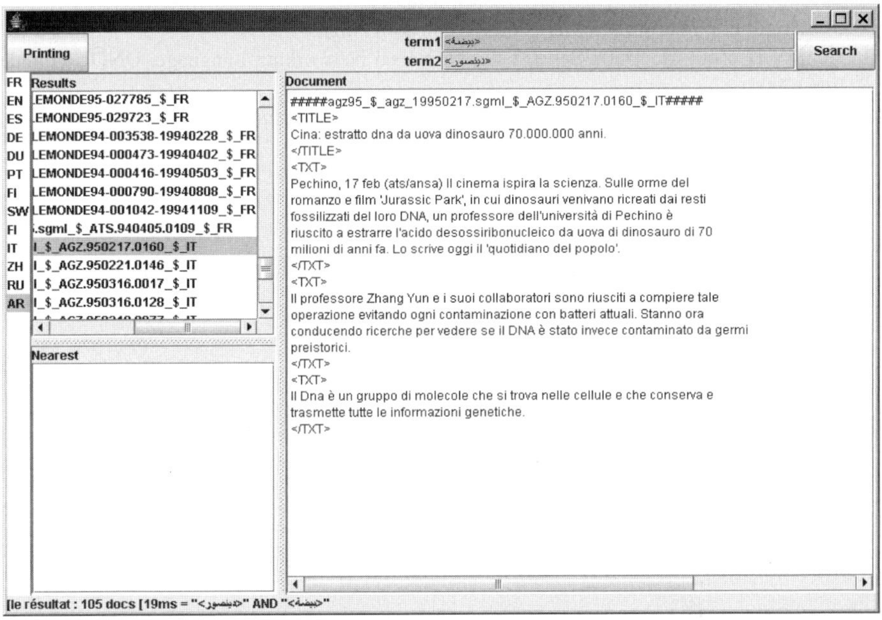

Fig. 5. System interface

In this preliminary work, we tried only to prove the feasibility of our approach. We tried also to prove that our system is independent of the query language. We still have some limits in our system because we did not introduce any morphological analysis to identify and normalize composite words in Dutch, German, or Finnish. Moreover, our ontology lexicons were incomplete and dirty (we have imported many errors with automatic translation). Currently, we are cleaning and checking them to improve the performance.

References

1. Bozsak, E. et al.: KAON – Towards a large scale Semantic Web. In Proceedings of EC-Web. Lecture Notes in Computer Science, Vol. 2455 Springer. Aix-en-Provence, France (2002) 304–313
2. Chen, A. and Gey, F. Combining query translation and document translation in cross-language retrieval. *In proceedings CLEF-2003*, pp. 39.48. Trondheim, (2005)

3. Ergane: http//download.travlang.com/, see also http://www.majstro.com/. [visited on August 2005]
4. Gruber, T.R..: A translation Approach to Portable Ontology Specifications, Knowledge Acquisition, 5: 199–220 (1993)
5. Guyot. J. : yaaa: yet another alignment algorithm - Alignement ontologique bi-texte pour un corpus multilingue. Cahier du CUI – Université de Genève (2005)
6. Guyot, J., Falquet, G.: Construire un moteur d'indexation. Cahier du CUI - Université de Genève (2005)
7. Salton, G.: Automatic Text Processing : The Transformation, Analysis and Retrieval of Information by Computer. Addison-Wesley (1989)
8. SnowBall: http://snowball.tartarus.org/ [visited on August 2005]
9. Uchida, H, Zhu, M., Della Senta T.G.: Universal Networking Language. UNDL Foundation (2005)
10. UNL: Universal Networking Language. http://cui.unige.ch/isi/unl

SINAI at CLEF 2005: Multi-8 Two-Years-on and Multi-8 Merging-Only Tasks

Fernando Martínez-Santiago, Miguel A. García-Cumbreras, and L.A. Ureña-López

Dpto. Computer Science. University of Jaén.Spain
{dofer, magc, laurena}@ujaen.es

Abstract. This year, we participated in *multilingual two years on* and *Multi-8 merging-only* CLEF tasks. Our main interest has been to test several standard CLIR techniques and investigate how they affect the final performance of the multilingual system. Specifically, we have evaluated the information retrieval (IR) model used to obtain each monolingual result, the merging algorithm, the translation approach and the application of query expansion techniques. The obtained results show that by means of improving merging algorithms and translation resources we reach better results than improving other CLIR modules such as IR engines or the expansion of queries.

1 Introduction

In order to evaluate the relevance of several standard CLIR modules, we have made a combination between the collection fusion algorithm 2-step RSV and several IR systems. The 2-step RSV collection fusion algorithm is described in detail in [4,?]; we outline this algorithm below.

1.1 The Merging Algorithm

Briefly, the basic 2-step RSV idea is straightforward: given a query term and its translations into the other languages, its document frequencies are grouped together. Therefore, the method requires recalculating the document score by changing the document frequency of each query term. Given a query term, the new document frequency will be calculated by means of the sum of the monolingual retrieved document frequency of the term and their translations. In a first step the query is translated and searched on each monolingual collection. This phase produces a T_0 vocabulary made up by "concepts". A concept consists of each term together with its corresponding translations. Moreover, we obtain a single multilingual collection D_0 of preselected documents as a result of the union of the first 1000 retrieved documents for each language. The second step consists of creating a dynamic index by re-indexing the multilingual collection D_0, but considering solely the T_0 vocabulary. Finally, a new query formed by concepts in T_0 is generated and this query is carried out against this dynamic index.

C. Peters et al. (Eds.): CLEF 2005, LNCS 4022, pp. 113–120, 2006.

Thus, the first step of 2-step RSV consists of retrieving relevant documents for each language, and the alignment of the query and its translations.

This year we tested the performance of the algorithm using several information retrieval engines for each monolingual collection, and then applying the second step of the merging algorithm over the retrieved documents.

The relevant documents lists for the first step are retrieved by:

1. The ZPrise IR system with the OKAPI weighting function [6]
2. The IRn passage retrieval system [2]
3. Several relevant document lists available from the Multi-8 Merging-only task

2 Experimentation Framework

In the first step each monolingual collection is preprocessed as usual (token extraction, stopper, stemmer). In addition, compound words for German, Swedish, Finnish and Dutch are decompounded wheb possible. We use the decompounding algorithm depicted in [3]. The preprocessed collections were indexed by using the passage retrieval system IRn and ZPrise. The IRn system was modified in order to return a list of relevant documents, the documents that contain relevant passages. Then, given a query and its translations, all of them are searched in the corresponding monolingual collection.

Since we have used machine translation (MT) for several languages (MT translates the whole of the phrase better than word-by-word) and because 2-step RSV requires us to group together the document frequency for each term and its own translations, our merging algorithm is not directly feasible with MT (given a word of the original query, its translation to the rest of languages must be known). Thus, we propose in [3] a straightforward and effective algorithm in order to align the original query and its translations at term level. It aligns about 80-85% of non-empty words (Table 1).

The proposed alignment algorithm works fine, even though it does not obtain fully aligned queries. In order to improve the system performance when some terms of the query are not aligned, we make two subqueries. The first one is made up only by the aligned terms and the other is formed with the non-aligned terms.

Table 1. Percent of aligned non-empty words (CLEF2005 query set, Title+Description fields,)

Language	Translation resource	Alignment percent
Dutch	Prompt (MT)	85.4%
Finnish	FinnPlace (MDR)	100 %
French	Reverso (MT)	85.6%
German	Prompt (MT)	82.9 %
Italian	FreeTrans (MT)	83.8 %
Spanish	Reverso (MT)	81.5 %
Swedish	Babylon (MDR)	100 %

Thus, for each query every retrieved document obtains two scores. The first score is obtained with 2-step RSV merging algorithm over the first subquery. On the other hand, the second subquery is used in a traditional monolingual system with the respective monolingual list of documents.

Therefore, we have two scores for each query, the first one is calculated by using the dynamic and global index created by 2-step RSV for all languages, and the other one is calculated locally for each language. Thus, we have integrated both values. As a way to deal with partially aligned queries (i.e. queries with some terms not aligned), we implemented several ways to combine the aligned and non-aligned score in a single score for each query and retrieved document:

1. *Raw mixed 2-step RSV.* Combining the RSV value of the aligned words and non aligned words with the formula:

$$0.6 < RSVAlignedDoc > +0.4 < RSVNotAligned >$$

2. *Mixed 2-step RSV by using Logistic Regression.* The formula:

$$e^{\alpha \cdot <RSVAlignedDoc> + \beta \cdot <RSVNotAligned>}$$

3. *Mixed 2-step RSV by using Logistic Regression and local score.* The last one also uses Logistic Regression, but includes a new component the ranking of the document. It applies the formula:

$$e^{\alpha \cdot <RSVAlignedDoc> + \beta \cdot <RSVNotAligned> + \gamma \cdot <RankingDoc>}$$

4. *Mixed 2-step RSV by using Bayesian Logistic Regression and local score.* The last one is very similar to the previous approach, but is based on bayesian logistic regression instead of logistic regression.

Methods two, three and four required a training set (topics and their relevance assessments), which must be available for each monolingual collection.

We used the CLEF queries (140-160) and the relevance assessments available this year for training purposes. Therefore, twenty queries were used for training and the other forty were used for evaluation.

3 Expanding the Queries

Some experiments based on ZPrise used the pseudo-relevance feedback technique. We have adopted Robertson-Croft's approach [1], where the system expands the original query generally by 10-15 search keywords, extracted from the 10-best ranked documents. We chose this configuration because empirically it obtained better results than other configurations available with the ZPrise system.

The second step of the merging method does not make use of automatic query expansion techniques such as relevance feedback (RF) or pseudo-relevance feedback (PRF) applied to monolingual queries. Since RF and PRF extend every

Table 2. Percent of aligned non-empty words (CLEF2005 query set+PRF, Title+Description fields)

Language	Alignment percent
Dutch	45.02 %
Finnish	59.97 %
French	48.11 %
German	42.23 %
Italian	44.69 %
Spanish	45.11 %
Swedish	51.2 %

monolingual query with collection-dependent words, the reindexing process (second step of 2-step RSV) will not take into account of all these words.

Because such words are not the same for each monolingual collection, and the translation to the other languages is unknown, our merging method ignores these new terms for the second step.

However, overall the performance will improve since PRF and RF improve on monolingual experiments and usually some extended terms are similar with terms of the original query, and such terms will be aligned. The rest of the expanded terms are integrated as non-aligned terms, by using the approaches depicted in section 2 for mixed 2-step RSV. Of course, the percentage of non-aligned words increases because of the application of PRF. Table 2 shows the percentage of aligned words for expanded queries by using PRF and Machine Translation.

4 Experiments and Results

Tables 3, 4, 5 show our official results. In order to evaluate the translation approach effect in the multilingual result, we recovered some old experiments from CLEF 2003 for 161-200 CLEF queries (experiment ujarsv2_2003). These experiments were based on Machine Dictionary Readable resources, and we compare them with the results of this year (experiment UJARSV2), based on Machine Translation. In order to evaluate the effect of query expansion we developed experiments ujaprfrsv2 and UJAPRFRSV2RR. Finally, experiments UJARSV2RR, UJAUARSV2RR, UJAMENEOKRR or UJAMENEDERR use several IR systems and models to obtain the lists of retrieved documents.

This table shows some interesting results:

- Note that the improvement for this year is considerable if compared to 2003, mainly because of a better translation strategy.
- In spite of the very different performance of the bilingual experiments (Table 6), final multilingual average precision is very similar independent of the selected documents for each IR system.
- Since the simultaneous application of PRF and Machine Translation dramatically decreases the percentage of aligned words, the application of PRF very slightly improves the final result.

Table 3. Multilingual experiments (I). Experiments with capital letters are official. The "main feature" is some particularity of each experiment in respect of the case base experiment. The name of the experiments: UJA[UA][PRF]RSV2[RR][_2003] means Univ. of Jaén[IRn system from Univ. of Alicante used][PRF used]2-step RSV merging algorithm[logistic regression used][CLEF 2003 results].

Experiment	Main feature	AvgP
UJARSV2	Case Base (OKAPI ZPrise IR, no PRF, MT, raw mixed 2-Step RSV)	28.78
ujaprfrsv2	UJARSV2+PRF	29.01
UJARSV2RR	different merging algorithm (see Table 4)	29.19
UJAPRFRSV2RR	UJARSV2RR+PRF	29.57
ujarsv2_2003	it uses MDR instead of MT	24.18
ujauarsv2	it uses IRn IR engine	28.81
UJAUARSV2RR	it uses IRn IR engine and a different merging algorithm	29.18

Table 4. Merging approaches. Experiments with capital letters are official.

Experiment	2-step RSV approach
UJARSV2	Raw mixed 2-step RSV
ujaprfrsv2	Raw mixed 2-step RSV
UJARSV2RR	Mixed 2-step RSV by using Logistic Regression and local score
UJAPRFRSV2RR	Mixed 2-step RSV by using Logistic Regression and local score
ujarsv2_2003	2-step RSV
ujauarsv2	Raw mixed 2-step RSV
UJAUARSV2RR	Mixed 2-step RSV by using Logistic Regression and local score

Table 5. Multi-8 merging-only experiments. Experiments with capital letters are official. "Documents" are several sets of relevant documents available for the task from Neuchatel Bilingual Runs from CLEF 2003 .

Experiment	Documents	Merging algorithm	AvgP
ujamenepr	Prosit	Raw mixed 2-step RSV	28.40
ujameprrr	Prosit	Mixed 2-step RSV by using Logistic Regression and local score	28.34
UJAMENEOK	Okapi	Raw mixed 2-step RSV	28.87
UJAMENEOKRR	Okapi	Mixed 2-step RSV by using Logistic Regression and local score	28.87
UJAMENEDF	DataFusion	Raw mixed 2-step RSV	29.42
UJAMENEDFRR	DataFusion	Mixed 2-step RSV by using Logistic Regression and local score	30.37

Table 6. Some bilingual results (except English which is a monolingual experiment)

Language	UJARSV2	ujaprfrsv2	UJAUARSV2RR	UJAMENEOKRR	UJAMENEDFRR
Dutch	30.94	38.71	34.03	35.15	44.94
English	52.06	50.73	50.96	50.29	55.71
Finnish	34.11	31.01	33.47	14.27	22.26
French	42.14	39.90	42.84	50.26	55.29
German	33.01	37.03	33.99	41.09	52.89
Italian	33.38	34.98	34.82	44.87	53.53
Spanish	37.35	40.63	39.68	43.73	51.07
Swedish	23.29	24.99	25.23	31.29	47.28

- Good performance of the raw-mixed 2-step RSV, obtaining a result very near to the result reached by means of logistic regression and neural networks. This result is counterintuitive since the method adds two values which are not directly comparable: the score obtained by both aligned and non-aligned terms. Some of the reasons for this good result are:
  - α parameter limits the weight of the unaligned factor.
  - Not all the terms to be added to the original query are new terms since some terms obtained by means of pseudo-relevance feedback are in the initial query. Thus, these terms are aligned terms. In the same way this explains the good performance of the original 2-step RSV method with expanded queries.
  - Only 20 queries were available for training.
  - The CLEF document collections are highly comparable (news stories from the same period). The results might be different if the collections have vastly different sizes and/or topics.

Thus, the 2-step RSV reaches the same precision in spite of using different IR systems. This is a drawback if the IR system used for the first step implements an IR model more sophisticated than the IR model implemented for the second step of the algorithm. In such a situation, the improvement is not fully exploited by the 2-step RSV merging algorithm because the 2-step RSV creates a dynamic index based on classic document retrieval models (more precisely the dynamic index is created by using a document-based OKAPI weighting scheme). So, what should we do to improve these results?. Since the second step is basically an OKAPI IR engine, we could improve such engine by using better IR models, and improving the translation and alignment processes.

5 Conclusions

In this work, we have tested the merging algorithm 2-step RSV in several ways. We have compared the CLEF 2003 and CLEF 2005 Multi-8 results, by using CLEF 160-200 queries. This year we obtained better results than in the 2003 edition. The main reason is a better translation approach and a more refined version of the merging algorithm.

The results obtained show that the improvement of merging algorithms and translation resources are higher than the improvement obtained by expanding the query by means of pseudo-relevance feedback.

In the same way, the improvement in the monolingual IR System used to retrieve each monolingual list of documents obtains very slightly better results in the final multilingual system. In order to evaluate the impact of the monolingual IR system, we have evaluated several lists of retrieved documents by using two IR systems and some of the retrieved documents available for the Multi-8 Merging-only task, but holding the same translation approach and merging algorithm. Results show that the precision is very similar independent of the monolingual IR engine. We conclude that improvements in the selection of documents by using some monolingual IR engine is not fully exploited by the 2-step RSV merging algorithm since this algorithm creates a dynamic index based on classic document retrieval models.

When pseudo-relevance feedback and machine translation is applied in the same experiment, the percentage of aligned words is too low to optimally apply some mixed variant of 2-step RSV. Thus, a more effective word alignment algorithm must be developed, especially for the new terms added to the query by means of PRF.

Finally, we think that the overall performance of the CLIR system will be improved if we develop better translation strategies and we improve the IR model used for the creation of the dynamic index for the second step of the algorithm.

Acknowledgments

Thank you very much to Fernando Llopis and Elisa Noguera from University of Alicante for their support with the IRn package.

Thank you very much to Jacques Savoy and Gareth Jones for supplying the results of several bilingual experiments for the Multi-8 Merging-only task and the administration of the web site.

This work has been supported by Spanish Government (MCYT) with grant TIC2003-07158-C04-04.

References

1. D. K. Harman: Relevance Feedback Revisited. In N. J. Belkin, P. Ingwersen, and A. M. Pejtersen, editors, *Proceedings of the 15th International ACM SIGIR Conference on Research and Development in Information Retrieval (SIGIR-92)*, pages 1–10. ACM, 1992.
2. F. LLopis: University of Alicante at CLEF 2002. In C. Peters, M. Braschler, J. Gonzalo, and M. Kluck, editors, *Advances in Cross-Language Information Retrieval, Third Workshop of the Cross-Language Evaluation Forum (CLEF 2002)*, Rome, pages 103–110, 2003.

3. F. Martínez-Santiago, M. García-Cumbreras and L. A. Ureña: SINAI at CLEF 2004: Using Machine Translation Resources with Mixed 2-Step RSV Merging Algorithm. *Multilingual Information Access for Text, Speech and Images: 5th Workshop of the Cross-Language Evaluation Forum*, Bath, page 156-164, 2005.
4. F. Martínez-Santiago, M. Martín, and L.A. Ureña: SINAI at CLEF 2002: Experiments with Merging Strategies. In C. Peters, M. Braschler, J. Gonzalo, and M. Kluck, editors, *Advances in Cross-Language Information Retrieval, Third Workshop of the Cross-Language Evaluation Forum (CLEF 2002)*, Rome, pages 103–110, 2003.
5. F. Martínez-Santiago, L. A. Ureña, and M. Martín: A Merging Strategy Proposal: Two Step Retrieval Status Value Method. *Information Retrieval*, 9(1):95–109, 2006.
6. S. E. Robertson and S. Walker. Okapi-Keenbow at TREC-8. In *Proceedings of the 8th Text Retrieval Conference TREC-8, NIST Special Publication 500-246*, pages 151–162, 1999.

CLEF 2005: Multilingual Retrieval by Combining Multiple Multilingual Ranked Lists

Luo Si and Jamie Callan

Language Technology Institute, School of Computer Science
Carnegie Mellon University, Pittsburgh, Pennsylvania, USA
{lsi, callan}@cs.cmu.edu

Abstract: We participated in two tasks: Multi-8 two-years-on retrieval and Multi-8 results merging. For the multi-8 two-years-on retrieval work, algorithms are proposed to combine simple multilingual ranked lists into a more accurate ranked list. Empirical study shows that the approach of combining multilingual retrieval results can substantially improve the accuracies over single multilingual ranked lists. The Multi-8 results merging task is viewed as similar to the results merging task of federated search. Query-specific and language-specific models are proposed to calculate comparable document scores for a small amount of documents and estimate logistic models by using information of these documents. The logistic models are used to estimate comparable scores for all documents and thus the documents can be sorted into a final ranked list. Experimental results demonstrate the advantage of the query-specific and language-specific models against several other alternatives.

1 Introduction

Multi-8 two-years-on task searches documents in eight languages with queries in a single language (e.g., English). Most previous methods first generate accurate bilingual retrieval results and then merge the bilingual retrieval results together. Previous research [3,10] has demonstrated how to do many instances of bilingual retrieval by tuning the methods of translating the query into a target language and then generate an accurate bilingual run. However, it is not easy to merge the bilingual retrieval results because the ranges and distributions of document scores within these bilingual lists can be very different as quite different retrieval methods have been tuned to generate accurate bilingual results of different languages separately [10]. An alternative approach generates simple bilingual runs by using the same type of retrieval algorithm with the same configuration, and then merges the bilingual results into a simple multilingual ranked list [3]. Many simple multilingual results can be obtained by applying different retrieval algorithms with different retrieval configurations. Finally, those simple multilingual ranked lists can be combined into a more accurate ranked list. In this work, we have proposed several methods to combine multilingual retrieval results. Empirical studies show that the approach of combining multilingual retrieval results can substantially improve the retrieval accuracy.

The second task is the Multi-8 results merging task, this required participants to merge provided sets of ranked lists of eight different languages into a single final list.

C. Peters et al. (Eds.): CLEF 2005, LNCS 4022, pp. 121 – 130, 2006.

It is viewed in this work as the results merging task in federated environment [11], which merges multiple ranked lists from different web resources into a single list. Previous research in [10] has proposed to build logistic models to estimate probabilities of relevance for all documents in bilingual ranked lists. This method is studied in this paper and a new variant of this method is proposed to improve the merging accuracy. These methods are language-specific methods as they build different models for different languages to estimate the probabilities of relevance. However, for different queries, they apply the same model for documents from a specific language, which may be problematic as documents from this language may contribute different values for different queries.

Based on this observation, we propose query-specific and language-specific results merging algorithms similar to those of federated search. For each query and each language, a few top ranked documents from each resource are downloaded, indexed and translated into English. Language-independent document scores are calculated for those downloaded documents and a logistic model is built for mapping all document scores in this ranked list to comparable language-independent document scores. Finally, all documents are ranked according to their comparable document scores. Experiments have been conducted to show that query-specific and language-specific merging algorithms outperform several other results merging algorithms.

2 Multilingual Retrieval System

This section first describes multilingual retrieval algorithms based on query translation and document translation; then it proposes methods to combine the results from multiple multilingual retrieval algorithms. Finally it shows the experimental results.

2.1 Multilingual Retrieval Via Query Translation or Document Translation

Before discussing the retrieval method, we introduce some basic text preprocessing methods: i) Stopword Lists: The Inquery stopword list [1] is used in this work for English documents. Stopword lists of Finnish, French, German, Italian, Spanish and Swedish are acquired from[1], while the snowball stopword[2] list is used for Dutch; ii) Stemming: Porter stemmer is used for English words. Dutch stemming algorithm is acquired from[2] and stemming algorithms from[1] are used for the other six languages; iii) Decompounding: Dutch, Finnish, German and Swedish are compound rich languages. We follow the same set of decompounding procedures described in previous research [4]; and iv) Word translation: The translation process in this work is mainly accomplished word-by-word using translation matrices generated using a parallel corpus. Specifically, the parallel corpus of the European Parliament proceedings 1996-2001[3] is used to build seven pairs of models between English and the other seven languages. The GIZA++ tool[4] is utilized to build the mappings of translating English words into words of the other languages or translating words in other

[1] http://www.unine.ch/info/clef/

[2] http://www.snowball.tartarus.org/

[3] http://people.csail.mit.edu/koehn/publications/europarl/

[4] http://www-i6.informatik.rwth-aachen.de/Colleagues/och/software/GIZA++.html

languages into English words. The online software Systran[5] is also utilized to translate query terms.

For retrieval via query translation, each English query word is first translated into top three candidates in the translation matrices of the other languages. All the three translated words of an English word are associated with normalized weights (i.e., the sum of the weights is 1.0) according to the weights in translation matrices. As the vocabulary of the parallel corpus is limited, we also utilize word-by-word translation results from online machine translation software Systran as a complement. A weight of 0.2 is assigned to the Systran translation and a weight of 0.8 is assigned to the translation with parallel corpus. The translated queries are used to search indexes built for each language. The okapi [8] retrieval algorithm is applied to accomplish this and each query term is weighted by its weight in the translation representation. As the same retrieval algorithm is applied on a corpus of different languages with original/translated queries of the same lengths, the raw scores in the ranked lists are somewhat comparable. Therefore, these ranked lists are merged together by their resource-specific scores into a final ranked list. The multilingual retrieval algorithm based on query translation via query expansion by pseudo relevance feedback is also applied by adding the 10 most common query terms within top 10 ranked documents of the initial retrieval result for each language and then doing the search and merging again.

An alternative multilingual retrieval method is to translate all documents in other languages into English and apply the original English queries. This method can provide complementary information for retrieval method via query translation [3]. The document translation process is conducted using translation matrices built from the parallel corpus. For each word in a language other than English, its top three English translations are considered. Five word slots are allocated to the three candidates with proportion to their normalized translation probabilities. All the translated documents as well as the original English documents are collected into a single database and indexed. Furthermore, the Okapi retrieval algorithm is applied on the single indexed database with original English queries to retrieve documents. The Okapi retrieval algorithm without query expansion as well as Okapi retrieval algorithm with query expansion by pseudo relevance feedback (i.e., 10 additional query terms from top 10 ranked documents) is used in this work.

2.2 Combine Multilingual Ranked Lists

One simple combination algorithm is proposed to favor documents retrieved by more retrieval methods as well as high ranking documents retrieved by single types of retrieval methods. Let drs_{k_mj} denote the resource-specific raw document score for the jth document retrieved from the mth ranked list for kth query, $drs_{k\_m\_max}$ and $drs_{k\_m\_min}$ represent the maximum and minimum document scores in this ranked list respectively. Then, the normalized score of the jth document is calculated as:

$$d_{s_{k\_mj}} = \frac{(d_{rs_{k\_mj}} - d_{rs_{k\_m\_min}})}{(d_{rs_{k\_m\_max}} - d_{rs_{k\_m\_min}})} \quad (1)$$

[5] http://www.systransoft.com/index.html

where ds_{k_mj} is the normalized document score. After the normalization step, the document scores among all ranked lists are summed up for a specific document and all documents can be ranked accordingly. Note that this method can be seen as a variant of the well-known CombSUM [5] algorithm for Meta information retrieval. This method is called equal weight combination method in this work. One particular issue about the proposed simple combination method is that it uses the linear method to normalize document scores and it treats the votes from multiple systems with equal weights. One more sophisticated idea is to learn a better score normalization method and the weights of systems with the help of training data. Formally, for M ranked lists to combine, the final combined document scores for a specific document d is calculated as:

$$score_{final}(d)=\frac{1}{M}\sum_{m=1}^{M} w_m score_m(d)^{r_m} \tag{2}$$

where $score_{final}(d)$ is the final combined document score and $score_m(d)$ (which is zero if the document is not in the mth ranked list) represents the normalized score for this document from the mth ranked list. $\vec{w}=\{w_1,...,w_M\}$ and $\vec{r}=\{r_1,...,r_M\}$ are the model parameters, where the pair of (w_m , r_m) represents the weight of the vote and the exponential normalization factor for the mth ranked list respectively. In this work, the mean average precision (MAP) criterion is used to optimize the accuracy for K training queries as:

$$\frac{1}{K}\sum_{k}\sum_{j\in D_k^+}\frac{rank_k^+(j)}{j} \tag{3}$$

where D_k^+ is the set of the ranks of relevant documents in the final ranked list for kth training query, and $rank_k^+(j)$ is the corresponding rank only among relevant documents. To avoid the overfitting problem of model parameter estimation, two regularization items are introduced for $\vec{w}$ and $\vec{r}$ respectively. The training optimization problem is represented as follows:

$$(\vec{w},\vec{r})^* = \underset{\vec{w},\vec{r}}{\operatorname{argmax}} (\log\left(\frac{1}{K}\sum_{k}\sum_{j\in D_k^+}\frac{rank_k^+(j)}{j}\right)-\sum_{m=1}^{M}\frac{(w_m-1)^2}{2*a}-\sum_{m=1}^{M}\frac{(r_m-1)^2}{2*b}) \tag{4}$$

where $(\vec{w},\vec{r})^*$ is the estimated model parameters and (a,b) are two regularization factors that are set to 4 in this work. This problem is not a convex optimization problem and multiple local maximal values exist. A common solution is to search with multiple initial points. Finally, the desired parameters are applied to combine ranked lists of test queries. This method is called learning combination method in this work.

2.3 Experimental Results: Multilingual Retrieval

Table 1 shows the results of five multilingual retrieval algorithms on training queries (first 20 queries), test queries (next 40 queries) and the overall accuracy. It can be seen that these methods produce results of similar accuracy, while the retrieval method based on document expansion that does not use query expansion has a small advantage. The results using the multilingual retrieval system from [10] (merged by the trained logistic transformation model by maximizing MAP as described in Section 4.1) are also shown in Table 1 as it is considered in this work for multilingual result combination. Two combination methods as equal weight combination method and learning combination method are applied in this work. The combination results are shown in Table 2. It can be seen that the accuracies of combined multilingual result lists are substantially higher than the accuracies of results from single types of multilingual retrieval algorithms. This demonstrates the power to combine multilingual retrieval results. Detailed analysis shows that the training combination method is consistently a little bit better than the equal weight combination method for the same configurations.

Table 1. Mean average precision of multilingual retrieval methods. Qry means by query translation. Doc means by document translation, nofb means no pseudo relevance feedback, fb means pseudo relevant back.

Methods	**Train**	**Test**	**All**
Qry_fb	0.317	0.353	0.341
Doc_nofb	0.346	0.360	0.356
Qry_nofb	0.312	0.335	0.327
Doc_fb	0.327	0.332	0.330
UniNe	0.322	0.330	0.327

Table 2. Mean average precision of merged multilingual list of different methods. M_X means to combine X results in the order of: 1). query translation with feedback, 2). document translation without feedback, 3). query translation without query expansion, 4). document translation with query expansion and 5). UniNE system. W1: combine with equal weight, Trn: combine with trained weights.

Methods	**Train**	**Test**	**All**
M2_W1	0.384	0.431	0.416
M2_Trn	0.389	0.434	0.419
M3_W1	0.373	0.423	0.406
M3_Trn	0.383	0.431	0.415
M4_W1	0.382	0.432	0.415
M4_Trn	0.389	0.434	0.419
M5_W1	0.401	0.446	0.431
M5_Trn	0.421	0.449	0.440

3 Results Merge for Multilingual Retrieval

For the multilingual results merging task, two sets of ranked lists across eight different languages are provided to be merged together. In our work, it is viewed as a task in multilingual federated search environment and we don't have direct access to the contents of all the documents. This section first describes an approach to learning a query-independent and language-specific logistic transformation merging model and a new extension of this model by maximizing mean average precision is proposed; then we propose the new approach to learning a query-specific and language-specific result merging algorithm; and finally show experimental results.

3.1 Learn Query-Independent and Language-Specific Merging Model Via Relevance Training Data

To make the retrieved results from different ranked lists comparable, one natural idea is to map all the document scores into the probabilities of relevance and rank all documents accordingly. Logistic transformation model has been successfully utilized in a previous study [10] and has been shown to be more effective than several alternatives. Let us assume that there are altogether I ranked lists from different languages to be merged, each of them provides J documents for each query and there are altogether K training queries with human relevance judgment. Particularly, d_{k_ij} represents the jth document from the ith language of training query k. The pair (r_{k_ij}, ds_{k_ij}) represents the rank of this document and the document score (normalized by Equation 1) respectively. The estimated probability of relevance of the document is calculated as:

$$P(rel|d_{k\_ij})=\frac{1}{1+\exp(a_i r_{k\_ij}+b_i ds_{k\_ij}+c_i)} \tag{5}$$

where ai ,bi and ci are the parameters of language-specific model that transforms all document scores of different queries from the ith language into the corresponding probabilities of relevance. The optimal parameter values are acquired generally by maximizing the log-likelihood (MLE) of training data [10]. This method equally treats each relevant document. However, this may not be a desired criterion in real world application. For example, a relevant document out of a total of 2 relevant documents for a query is generally more important to users than a relevant document out of total 100 relevant documents for another query. Therefore, the mean average precision (MAP) criterion is used in this work to treat individual queries equally instead of individual relevant documents. This is formally represented by the mean average precision (MAP) criterion as described in Equation 3. Particularly, different sets of model parameters $\{a_i, b_i \text{ and } c_i, 1<=i<=I\}$ generate different sets of relevant documents as $\{D_k^+, 1<=k<=K\}$ and thus achieve different MAP values. The training procedure of maximizing MAP searches for a set of model parameters that generates the highest MAP value. The new algorithm of training logistic model for mean average precision is called logistic model with MAP goal in this paper.

3.2 Learn Query-Specific and Language-Specific Merging Model

The query-independent and language-specific logistic transform model applies the same model on results of different queries for each language. This is problematic when result lists of different queries have similar score distributions but have different distributions of probability of relevance. This suggests that a query-specific model should be studied for high merging accuracy of multilingual retrieval. Previous research has proposed query-specific merging method that uses the two step Retrieval Status Values (RSV) [6,9] to index top ranked documents of different languages at the retrieval time and compute comparable document scores. However, this method is associated with a large amount of computation costs of translating and indexing many documents.

In a multilingual federated search environment, the cost of processing retrieved documents is even higher as the contents of all documents to translate are not directly accessible and they must be downloaded from corresponding servers. Also the corpus statistics (e.g., corpus inverse document frequencies) are generally not available and can only be simulated by collecting statistics from sampled documents. The query-based sampling method is utilized in this work to learn corpus statistics from each resource with a particular language [2]. Specifically, random one-term queries are sent to each resource and retrieve about 4 documents for each query to get total 3,000 documents for each resource. The corpus statistics are estimated from these documents.

In the online phase, for a user's query, the comparable document scores can be calculated based on query translation and document translation method. In a federated environment, retrieved documents need to be downloaded and indexed, and then the same retrieval algorithm applied on the downloaded documents to calculate comparable scores. Particularly, the retrieved documents are downloaded and an Okapi retrieval algorithm is applied on these documents with corpus statistics from the centralized sample database of the corresponding resource. Comparable document scores based on document translation are acquired by applying a single Okapi retrieval method on all retrieved English documents and all the translated documents from resources with other languages. Two sets of comparable document scores based on retrieval methods of query translation and document translation are merged together into a single set with the method described in Section 2. This results merging method downloads (also indexes and translates) all documents in the given ranked lists, it is called the complete downloading method.

The complete download method is associated with large communication and computation costs especially in the online manner. The key idea is to more efficiently calculate comparable document scores to only calculate scores for a small set of representative documents. Particularly, L top ranked documents from each resource are selected; the above procedure of downloading and calculating new scores based on query translation and document translation is applied on this set of documents. These documents that have both language-specific scores and calculated comparable scores serve as training data for learning a logistic model, which estimates the comparable document scores for other documents that have not been downloaded and indexed. Let the pair ($dc_{k'\_il}$, $ds_{k'\_il}$) denote the normalized comparable document score and normalized language-specific score for the lth downloaded document of the ith resource for k' the query. Let the pair ($a_{k'\_i}$, $b_{k'\_i}$) denote the parameters of the corresponding query-specific and language-specific model. These parameters are learned by solving the following optimization problem to minimize the mean squared error between exact normalized comparable scores and the estimated comparable scores as:

$$\left(a^*_{k'\_i}, b^*_{k'\_i}\right) = \underset{(a,b)}{\operatorname{argmin}} \sum_{d_{k'\_il} \in D_L \cup D_{NL}} \left(d_{C_{k'\_il}} - \frac{1}{1+\exp(a^* d_{S_{k'\_il}} + b^* 1)}\right)^2 \tag{6}$$

where D_L is the downloaded L documents from the resource and D_{NL} is a pseudo set of L documents with pseudo normalized comparable scores zero and pseudo normalized language-specific scores zero. This set of pseudo documents is introduced in order to make sure that the learned model ranks documents in the correct way (i.e., documents with higher language-specific scores are ranked higher in the ranked list with comparable scores than documents with lower language-specific scores). Finally, logistic models can be learned for all resources in the same way. They are applied to

Table 3. Language-specific retrieval accuracy in mean average precision of retrieval results from UniNE system (UnieNE) and HummingBird system (Hum)

Language	Dutch	English	Finnish	French	German	Italian	Spanish	Swedish
UniNE (MAP)	0.431	0.536	0.192	0.491	0.513	0.486	0.483	0.435
Hum (MAP)	0.236	0.514	0.163	0.350	0.263	0.325	0.298	0.269

all retrieved documents from all resources and the documents can then be ranked according to their estimated comparable scores. Note that exact comparable document scores are available for the documents that have been downloaded and processed. One method to take advantage of these scores is to combine them with the estimated scores. In this work, they are combined together with equal weights (i.e., 0.5).

3.3 Experimental Results: Results Merge

The language-specific retrieval accuracies of ranked lists of UniNE and HummingBird systems are shown in Table 3. The merging accuracy of two query-independent and language-specific results merging algorithms by optimizing the maximum likelihood criterion (MLE) and the mean average precision (MAP) criterion respectively are shown in Table 4 and Table 5. Note that the merging accuracies of learning algorithms on UniNE system are similar to those reported in [10]. Furthermore, it can be seen from both Tables 4 and 5 that the learning algorithm optimized for MAP is always more accurate than that optimized for MLE. This demonstrates the power to directly optimize for mean average precision accuracy as treating different queries equally against the strategy of optimizing for maximum likelihood that does not directly evaluate mean average precision.

To improve the merging accuracy, query-specific and language-specific algorithms are proposed as complete downloading method (C_X) and the method of only downloading top ranked documents and calculating their comparable documents to build logistic models. These models generate estimated comparable document scores and finally combine the estimated scores with acquired exact comparable scores wherever they are available (Top_X_C05). The experimental results of different variants of these algorithms on UniNE system and HummingBird system are shown in Tables 6 and 7 respectively. Note that both these two algorithms do not require human relevance judgment for training data. Therefore, the results on the training query set and the test query set are obtained separately without using any relevance judgment data.

It can be seen from Tables 6 and 7 that query-specific and language-specific merging algorithms substantially outperform query-independent and language-specific algorithms. The accuracies of the two query-specific methods (i.e., C_X and Top_X_C05) are close on the UniNE system. It is interesting that the Top_150_C05 method outperforms all C_X runs on the UniNE system. One possible explanation is that the estimated document scores can be seen as combination results from not only the two retrieval methods that are based on query translation and document translation but also the retrieval method of the UniNE system. Therefore, the combined results that are related with three retrieval systems may be better than those of exact comparable scores from two retrieval systems. It is encouraging to see that with a very limited amount of downloaded documents, the Top_10_C05 method still has

Table 4. Mean average precision of merged multilingual lists of different methods on UniNE result lists. TrainLog_MLE means trained logistic transformation model by maximizing MLE. TrainLog_MAP means trained logistic transformation model by maximizing MAP.

Methods	**Train**	**Test**	**All**
TrainLog_MLE	0.301	0.301	0.301
TrainLog_MAP	0.322	0.330	0.327

Table 5. Mean average precision of merged multilingual lists of different methods on HummingBird result lists. TrainLog_MLE means trained logistic transformation model by maximizing MLE. TrainLog_MAP means trained logistic transformation model by maximizing MAP.

Methods	**Train**	**Test**	**All**
TrainLog_MLE	0.186	0.171	0.176
TrainLog_MAP	0.210	0.192	0.198

Table 6. Mean average precision of merged multilingual lists of different methods on UniNE result lists. Top_x: x top documents are downloaded to generate logistic transformation model; C05: both scores from logistic transformation model and centralized document scores are utilized when they are available and they are combined with a linear weight as 0.5. C_X: merge top X documents for each language by their centralized doc scores.

Methods	**Train**	**Test**	**All**
Top_150_C05	0.360	0.412	0.395
Top_30_C05	0.357	0.399	0.385
Top_15_C05	0.346	0.402	0.383
Top_10_C05	0.330	0.393	0.372
Top_5_C05	0.296	0.372	0.347
C_1000	0.356	0.382	0.373
C_500	0.356	0.384	0.374
C_150	0.352	0.391	0.378

Table 7. Mean average precision of merged multilingual lists of different methods on HummingBird result lists. Top_x: x top documents are downloaded to generate logistic transformation model; C05: both scores from logistic transformation model and centralized document scores are utilized when they are available and they are combined with a linear weight as 0.5. C_X: merge top X documents for each language by their centralized doc scores.

Methods	**Train**	**Test**	**All**
Top_150_C05	0.278	0.297	0.291
Top_30_C05	0.260	0.268	0.265
Top_15_C05	0.235	0.253	0.247
Top_10_C05	0.222	0.248	0.239
Top_5_C05	0.210	0.234	0.226
C_1000	0.324	0.343	0.337
C_500	0.315	0.333	0.326
C_150	0.290	0.302	0.298

more than 10 percent advantage over the query-independent algorithms. Table 7 shows that the advantage of query-specific over query-independent is even larger for the results on HummingBird system than those on UniNE system. However, the Top_X_C05 runs are not as effective as C_X runs on HummingBird System because the ranked lists of HummingBird system are not as accurate as those of UniNE systems.

4 Conclusion

This paper describes the algorithms we have studied and proposed for the CLEF 2005 evaluation tasks as: Multi-8 two-years-on retrieval task and Multi-8 results merging task. For multi-8 two-years-on retrieval task, our focus is to generate and combine multilingual retrieval results that are built from simple bilingual (or monolingual) ranked lists. Several combination methods have been proposed and empirical studies have demonstrated that the combination of multilingual retrieval results can substantially improve the accuracies over single multilingual ranked lists. For the task of Multi-8 results merging task, we have proposed to apply results merging algorithm of federated search task for this problem. Top ranked documents within each ranked list are indexed and translated to compute comparable document scores. Query-specific and language-specific logistic models are built based on comparable document scores of these documents and also the scores of these documents in language-specific ranked lists. These logistic models have been built to estimate comparable document scores for all documents in ranked lists of different languages, and finally all documents are sorted accordingly. Experiments have shown that the new proposed methods outperform previous research and they only need to process (i.e., download, index and translate) a very small amount of documents (e.g., 10 per <query, language> pair) to acquire accurate results.

Acknowledgement

This work is supported in part by an ARDA grant under Phase II of the AQUAINT program. Any opinions, findings, conclusions, or recommendations expressed in this paper are the authors', and do not necessarily reflect those of the sponsor.

*A longer version of this paper can be found at:
http://www.clef-campaign.org/2005/working_notes/workingnotes2005/si05.pdf

References

[1]. Callan, J., Croft W. B. and Broglio, J. TREC and TIPSTER experiments with INQUERY. Information Processing and Management, 31(3) (1995).

[2]. Callan, J. and Connell, M. Query-based sampling of text databases. ACM Transactions on Information Systems, 19(2), (2001) 97-130.

[3]. Chen, A. and F. C. Gey. Cross-language Retrieval Experiments at CLEF-2003. In C. Peters(Ed.), Results of the CLEF2002 cross-language evaluation forum (2003).

[4]. Kamps, J., Monz, C., Rijke, Maarten de. and Sigurbjörnsson, Börkur. The University of Amsterdam at CLEF 2003. In C. Peters(Ed.), Results of the CLEF2003 (2003).

[5]. Lee. J. H. Analyses of multiple evidence combination. In Proceedings of the 20th Annual Int'l ACM SIGIR Conference (1997).

[6]. Martinez-Santiago, Martin M. and Urena, A. SINAI on CLEF 2002: Experiments with merging strategies. In C. Peters(Ed.), Results of the CLEF2002 (2002).

[7]. Ogilvie, P and Callan, J. Experiments using the Lemur toolkit. In Proceedings of the Tenth Text Retrieval Conference (TREC-10) (2001).

[8]. Robertson S. and Walker. S. Some simple effective approximations to the 2-poisson model for probabilistic weighted retrieval. In Proceedings of the 17th Annual International ACM SIGIR Conference (1994).

[9]. Rogati. M. and Yang Y. M. CONTROL: CLEF-2003 with Open, Transparent Resources Off-Line. Experiments with merging strategies. In C. Peters(Ed.), Results of the CLEF2003 (2003).

[10]. Savoy, J. Report on CLEF-2003 Experiments. In C. Peters(Ed.), Results of the CLEF2003 cross-language evaluation forum (2003).

[11]. Si, L. and Callan, J. "A Semi-Supervised Learning Method to Merge Search Engine Results" In ACM Transactions on Information Systems, 24(4). (2003) 457-491.

Monolingual, Bilingual, and GIRT Information Retrieval at CLEF-2005

Jacques Savoy and Pierre-Yves Berger

Institut interfacultaire d'informatique, Université de Neuchâtel,
Pierre-à-Mazel 7, 2001 Neuchâtel, Switzerland
Jacques.Savoy@unine.ch, Pierre-Yves.Berger@unine.ch

Abstract. For our fifth participation in the CLEF evaluation campaigns, our first objective was to propose an effective and general stopword list as well as a light stemming procedure for the Hungarian, Bulgarian and Portuguese (Brazilian) languages. Our second objective was to obtain a better picture of the relative merit of various search engines when processing documents in those languages. To do so we evaluated our scheme using two probabilistic models and five vector-processing approaches. In the bilingual track, we evaluated both the machine translation and bilingual dictionary approaches applied to automatically translate a query submitted in English into various target languages. Finally, using the GIRT corpora (available in English, German and Russian), we investigated the variations in retrieval effectiveness that resulted when we included or excluded manually assigned keywords attached to the bibliographic records (mainly comprising a title and an abstract).

1 Introduction

Since 2001, our research group has been investigating effective information retrieval (IR) techniques capable of handling a variety of natural languages [1], [2], in order to improve both monolingual and bilingual searches. Along this same stream, and based on our assumption that nouns and adjectives reveal the most about semantic content of documents (or requests), we designed a set of stopword lists and light stemming procedures for certain European languages. We then designed linguistic tools that would automatically remove inflectional suffixes attached to nouns and adjectives used to denote the gender (masculine, feminine, neural), the number (singular or plural) and the case (nominative, dative, ablative, etc.). Needless to say we have also investigated other linguistic phenomena, such as compound constructions.

The rest of this paper is organized as follows: Section 2 outlines the main aspects of our stopword lists and light stemming procedures. Section 3 explains the principal features of different indexing and search strategies, and then evaluates them using the available corpora. The data fusion approaches used in our experiments and our official results are exposed in Section 4. Our bilingual experiments are presented and evaluated in Section 5, and Section 6 describes our experiments involving the domain-specific GIRT corpus.

C. Peters et al. (Eds.): CLEF 2005, LNCS 4022, pp. 131–140, 2006.

2 Stopword Lists and Stemming Procedures

In order to define general stopword lists, we first created a list of the top 200 most frequently occurring words, and then removed some words from this list (e.g., police, minister, president, Magyar). To this list we then added articles, pronouns, prepositions, conjunctions or very frequently occurring verb forms (e.g., to be, is, has, etc.). As a result of this procedure, we compiled a new stopword list for the Bulgarian and Hungarian languages (available at `www.unine.ch/info/clef/`). Thus, our final stopword list contained 463 words for the French language, 737 (761 in a previous version) for Hungarian, 258 (418 in a previous version) for Bulgarian, and 400 for Portuguese-Brazilian (we added eight Brazilian words to our Portuguese stopword list. These eight words are usually variants with or without accents, such as "vezes" in Portuguese and "vêzes" in Brazilian).

Once high-frequency words had been removed, our indexing procedure generally applied a stemming algorithm in order to conflate word variants into the same stem or root. Our first step in developing this procedure was to remove inflectional suffixes. For the Bulgarian language, we encountered some additional morphological difficulties. In this language, the definite article is usually represented by a suffix; for example, "mope" (sea) becomes "mopeto" (the sea) while "mopeta" (seas) becomes "mopetata" (the seas). For nouns, the general pattern is as follows: <stem><plural><article>. Contrary to other Slavic languages (such as Russian), Bulgarian does not add a suffix to indicate grammatical cases.

The Hungarian language shares certain similarities with the Finnish language (although these languages do not strictly belong to the same family, they can be viewed as cousins). Like Finnish, Hungarian has several number cases (usually 18) and each case has its own unambiguous form. For example, the noun "house" ("hàz") may appear as "hàzat" (accusative case, as in "(I see) the house"), "hàzakat" (accusative plural case, as in "(I see) the houses"), "hàzamat" ("... my house") or "hàzamait" ("... my houses"). In this language, the general construction used for nouns is as follows: <stem><plural><possessive marker><case>. For example, for <hàz>a <m>a <t>in which the letter "a" is introduced to facilitate better pronunciation ("hàzmt" would be difficult to pronounce). From the IR point of view, some of Hungarian's linguistic features are viewed as good news. For example, a gender distinction is not attached to each noun (like in English) and adjectives are invariable, as in "... a szép hàzat" ("a beautiful house") or "... a szép hàzamat" ("my beautiful house"). Our suggested stemming procedures for these languages can be found at `www.unine.ch/info/clef/`.

Diacritic characters are usually not present in English collections (with certain exceptions, such as "résumé" or "cliché"). For the Hungarian, and Portuguese languages, we replaced these characters with their corresponding non-accentuated letters, even though the removal of accents from the Hungarian language can lead to some semantic ambiguity (e.g., between "kor" ("age") and "kór" ("illness"), or "ver" ("hurt") and "vér" ("blood")).

Finally, most European languages manifest other morphological characteristics, with compound word constructions being only one example (e.g., handgun, worldwide). In some experiments on Hungarian and German retrieval within the

GIRT corpus (Section 6), we used our own decompounding algorithm [3], leaving both the compound words and their component parts in the documents and queries.

3 Indexing and Searching Strategies

In order to obtain a broader view of the relative merit of various retrieval models, we first adopted the classical $tf \cdot idf$ weighting scheme (with cosine normalization, retrieval model denoted "doc=ntc, query=ntc" or "ntc-ntc"). To measure the similarity between documents and requests, we computed the inner product. Various other indexing weighting schemes have been suggested, as for example, the IR model denoted by "doc=Lnu" [4], "doc=dtu" [5].

In addition to these IR models based on the vector-space paradigm, we also considered probabilistic approaches such as the Okapi model [6]. As a second probabilistic approach, we implemented the Prosit model, one of a family of models suggested by Amati & Rijsbergen [7]. The exact specification of these IR models is given in [2].

To measure the retrieval performance, we adopted non-interpolated mean average precision (MAP). Then, to statistically determine whether or not a given search strategy would be better than another, we applied the bootstrap methodology [8]. Thus, in the tables in this paper we have underlined statistically significant differences resulting from the use of a two-sided non-parametric bootstrap test (significance level fixed at 5%).

We indexed the various collections using words as indexing units. The evaluations of our two probabilistic models and five vector-space schemes are listed in Table 1. In this table, the best performance under the given conditions is shown in bold type and it is used as a baseline for our statistical testing. The underlined results therefore indicate that the difference in mean average precision can be viewed as statistically significant when compared to the best system value. As can be seen in the top part of Table 1, the Okapi model was usually the best IR model for the French and Portuguese collections. For these two corpora however, the MAP differences between the various IR models are not always statistically significant. The Prosit model performs best result for the Bulgarian collection, while for the Hungarian corpus, the Okapi probabilistic approach was the solution that performed best (bottom part of Table 1). For this same language, statistics for five IR models revealed similar performance levels (Okapi, Prosit, "Lnu-ltc", " dtu-dtn", "atn-ntc"). However, overall statistics like the MAP may hide performance irregularities among queries, and in this regard Tomlinson [9] presented examples demonstrating that, while a given search strategy may improve retrieval performance for some queries, it may lead to decreases for others.

Moreover, the data in Table 1 shows that when the number of search terms increases (from T, TD to TDN), retrieval effectiveness usually increases also. The average improvement is of about 33.4% result when comparing title-only (or T) with TDN queries for the Portuguese collection, 31.3% when comparing the French corpus, and 6.4% for the Bulgarian collection.

Table 1. MAP of single searching strategies

Query Model	French T 50 queries	French TD 50 queries	French TDN 50 queries	Portug. T 50 queries	Portug. TD 50 queries	Portug. TDN 50 queries
	Mean average precision					
Prosit	0.2895	0.3696	**0.3961**	0.2755	0.3438	0.3697
Okapi	**0.3029**	**0.3754**	0.3948	**0.2873**	**0.3477**	**0.3719**
Lnu-ltc	0.2821	0.3437	0.3703	0.2611	0.3338	0.3517
dtu-dtn	0.2726	0.3365	0.3633	0.2571	0.3221	0.3338
atn-ntc	0.2809	0.3328	0.3507	0.2458	0.3076	0.3433
ltn-ntc	0.2588	0.3066	0.3232	0.2149	0.2535	0.2740
ntc-ntc	0.1862	0.2175	0.2335	0.1553	0.1868	0.2221

Query Model	Bulgarian T 49 queries	Bulgarian TD 49 queries	Bulgarian TDN 49 queries	Hungarian TD 50 queries	Hungarian TD-decomp 50 queries	Hungarian TD-light 50 queries
Prosit	**0.2662**	**0.3030**	**0.3132**	0.3420	0.3390	0.3359
Okapi	0.2350	0.2760	0.2819	**0.3501**	**0.3391**	**0.3410**
Lnu-ltc	0.2268	0.2737	0.2800	0.3301	0.3273	0.3249
dtu-dtn	0.2288	0.2575	0.2522	0.3401	0.3341	0.3280
atn-ntc	0.2340	0.2618	0.2578	0.3215	0.3179	0.3199
ltn-ntc	0.1679	0.2031	0.2076	0.2853	0.2820	0.2856
ntc-ntc	0.1781	0.1967	0.2074	0.2208	0.2099	0.2245

With the Hungarian collection, we automatically decompounded long words (composed by more than 8 characters) using our own algorithm [3]. In this experiment, both the compound words and their components were left in both documents and queries (under the label "TD-decomp" in the bottom part of Table 1). Using the TD queries and the Okapi model, we obtained a MAP of 0.3391, revealing a decrease of 3.1% when compared to an indexing approach that did not use decompounding (0.3501). Based on the five best retrieval schemes, the average performance decrease was around 1.6%. Using a lighter stemmer (fewer rules) for the Hungarian language (retrieval performance listed under the label "TD-light" in Table 1), the average difference in MAP over the five best retrieval schemes was around 2%, and in favor of the original stemming approach. Tordai & de Rijke [10] also evaluated various stemming algorithms for the Hungarian languages, finding that a light stemming approach might prove effective for a morphologically rich language such as Hungarian.

It has been observed that pseudo-relevance feedback (PRF or blind-query expansion) seemed to be a useful technique for enhancing retrieval effectiveness. In this study, we adopted Rocchio's approach [4] with α = 0.75, β = 0.75, whereby the system was allowed to add m terms extracted from the k best ranked documents from the original query. To evaluate this proposition, we used the Okapi and the Prosit probabilistic models and enlarged the query by the 10 to 20 terms retrieved from the 3 to 10 best-ranked articles.

Table 2 depicted the best results obtained with the PRF technique for the Okapi model. This demonstrates that the optimal parameter setting seemed to be collection-dependant. Moreover, performance improvement also seemed to be collection-dependant, with the French corpus showing an increase of 9.2% (from a mean average precision of 0.3754 to 0.4099), 5.2% for the Portuguese collection (from 0.3477 to 0.3668), 1.3% for the Hungarian collection (from 0.3501 to 0.3545), and 0.8% for the Bulgarian corpus (from 0.2704 to 0.2726). In Table 2, the baseline used for our statistical testing was the MAP calculated before the query was automatically expanded. In this case, it is interesting to note that our statistical testing does always detect any significant difference.

Table 2. MAP using blind-query expansion (Okapi model)

	Mean average precision			
Query TD Model	French 50 queries	Portuguese 50 queries	Bulgarian 49 queries	Hungarian 50 queries
Okapi	0.3754	0.3477	0.2760	0.3501
k docs/ m terms	3/10 0.3967	3/15 0.3656	3/15 0.2500	3/10 **0.3545**
	5/15 0.4034	5/15 **0.3668**	5/15 0.2553	5/10 0.3513
	10/15 **0.4099**	10/15 0.3626	10/15 **0.2778**	5/15 0.3490
	10/20 0.4075	10/20 0.3601	10/20 0.2718	10/15 0.3492

4 Data Fusion and Official Results

It is assumed that combining different search models should improve retrieval effectiveness, due to the fact that different document representations might retrieve different pertinent items and thus increase the overall recall [11]. On the other hand, when combining different search schemes, we might suppose that these various IR strategies are more likely to rank the same relevant items higher on the list than they would non-relevant documents (viewed as outliers). In this current study we combined the two probabilistic models Okapi and Prosit using the data fusion operators defined in [2].

Table 3 shows the exact specifications of our best-performing official monolingual runs. In these experiments, we combined the Okapi and the Prosit probabilistic models using the Z-Score (see [2]) data fusion operator for the French and Portuguese corpora. For the Hungarian and Bulgarian collection, our best results were achieved using the Prosit model (see Table 3).

Table 3. Description and MAP of our best official monolingual runs

Run name	Lan.	Query	Model	Query exp.	Combined	MAP
UniNEfr1	French	TD	Okapi	3 docs/10 terms		
		TD	Prosit	5 docs/50 terms	Z-scoreW	**0.4207**
UniNEpt2	Portug.	TD	Okapi	3 docs/15 terms		
		TD	Prosit	5 docs/60 terms	Z-scoreW	**0.3875**
UniNEbg3	Bulgarian	TD	Prosit	5 docs/30 terms	n/a	**0.2839**
UniNEhu3	Hungarian	TD	Prosit	5 docs/40 terms	n/a	**0.3889**

5 Bilingual Information Retrieval

For the bilingual track, we chose English as the language to be used for submitting queries for automatic translation into the four different languages. We used seven different machine translation (MT) systems and three bilingual dictionaries ("Babylon," "Ectaco," and "Medios"). The freely available translation tools used in our experiments are listed below:

1.	Systran	www.systranlinks.com
2.	Google	www.google.com/language_tools
3.	FreeTranslation	www.freetranslation.com
4.	InterTran	www.tranexp.com/
5.	WorldLingo	www.worldlingo.com/
6.	BabelFish	babelfish.altavista.com/
7.	Promt	webtranslation.paralink.com/
8.	Babylon	www.babylon.com
8.	Ectaco	www.ectaco.co.uk/free-online-dictionaries
10.	Medios	consulting.medios.fi/dictionary.

When using the different bilingual dictionaries to translate an English request word-by-word, more than one translation was usually provided, in an unspecified order. We thus decided to pick either the first translation available (labeled "Babylon 1" or "Ectaco 1") or the first two terms available (labeled "Babylon 2").

Our experiments show that Google provided the best translation for the French collection and Promt for the Portuguese corpus. The FreeTranslation and Promt MT systems usually obtain satisfactory retrieval performances for both these languages. For French, the BabelFish and Systran translation systems worked well. For Bulgarian and Hungarian, we found only a few translation tools, and unfortunately their overall performance levels were not very good.

Table 4 shows the retrieval effectiveness for various query translation combinations when using the Okapi probabilistic model. The top part of the table indicates the exact query translation combination used while the bottom part shows the MAP obtained with our combined query translation approach. In order to select which query translations would be combined, we made use of our prior findings [2] as well as our own intuition before selecting best translation tools. As can be seen in Table 4, the resulting retrieval performances depicted are sometimes better than the best single translation scheme, as shown in the row labeled "Best single" (e.g., the "Comb 1" strategy for French, or the "Comb 3" or "Comb 5" strategies for Portuguese, "Comb 2" for Bulgarian, and "Comb 5" for Hungarian). From a statistical perspective however these combined query translation approaches did not perform better than the best single translation tool (except "Comb 3" for the Portuguese corpus).

Finally, Table 5 lists the parameter settings used for our best performing official runs in the bilingual task. For each experiment, queries were written in English in order to retrieve documents in the other target languages. Before

Table 4. MAP of various combined translation devices (Okapi model)

	Mean average precision			
TD queries Model	French 50 queries	Portuguese 50 queries	Bulgarian 49 queries	Hungarian 50 queries
Comb 1	Systran+Promt	Promt+Bab 1	Inter+all 2	Inter+Ecta 1
Comb 2	Lingo+Bab 1	Promt+Inter	Ecta 1+Bab 2	Inter+Bab 1
Comb 3	Free+Promt +Babylon 1	Prompt+Free +Babylon 1		Bab 1+Med 2 +Ectaco 1
Comb 4	Lingo+Promt +Babylon 1	Prompt+Inter +Babylon 1	Inter+Ecta 1 +Babylon 2	Inter+Bab 1 +Ectaco 1
Comb 5		Prompt+Free +Inter+Bab 1		Inter+Bab 1+ Med 2+Ecta 1
Best single	0.3259	0.2673	0.0800	0.1822
Comb 1	**0.3274**	0.2849	0.0831	0.1845
Comb 2	0.3089	0.2749	**0.0962**	0.1876
Comb 3	0.3246	0.2977		0.1966
Comb 4	0.3228	0.2955	0.0908	0.2005
Comb 5		**0.2978**		**0.2183**

combining the result lists we automatically expanded the translated queries using a pseudo-relevance feedback method (Rocchio's approach in this case).

6 Monolingual Domain-Specific Retrieval: GIRT

In the domain-specific retrieval task (called GIRT), the three available corpora are composed of bibliographic records extracted from various sources in the social sciences domain. Theses collections contain a total of 397,218 documents or about 590 MB, written for the most part in German. A typical record in this collection contains a title, an abstract, a set of manually assigned keyword, and some additional information of less importance from an IR perspective (e.g., authors' name, publication date, etc.). The GIRT corpus thus allowed us to evaluate the impact of manually assigned descriptors and compare them to an indexing scheme, based only on the information contained in the corresponding article's title and abstract sections. To tackle this we evaluated all of the GIRT

Table 5. Description and MAP of our best official bilingual runs

From EN to ...	French 50 queries	Portuguese 50 queries	Bulgarian 49 queries	Hungarian 50 queries
IR 1 (k d./m t.)	Okapi (10/10)	Okapi (10/30)	Prosit (3/50)	Prosit (3/50)
IR 2 (k d./m t.)		Prosit (10/20)		
Data fusion		Z-scoreW		
Translation tools	Comb3	Comb4	Comb3	Comb5
MAP	**0.3467**	**0.3404**	**0.1399**	**0.2882**
Run name	UniNEbifr2	UniNEbipt1	UniNEbibg3	UniNEbihu3

collection (denoted "all" in Table 6) or only the titles and abstracts taken from the bibliographic records (under the label "TI & AB"). In our experiments, the decrease in mean average precision was around 14.4% for the German corpus and 36.5% for the English GIRT collection.

Table 6. MAP of various single searching strategies (GIRT corpus)

	Mean average precision				
Language	German	German	English	English	Russian
Query TD	all	TI & AB	all	TI & AB	all
Model	25 queries	25 queries	25 queries	25 queries	25 queries
Prosit	0.4249	**0.3659**	**0.4645**	**0.2948**	0.2270
Okapi	**0.4353**	0.3645	0.4604	0.2854	0.2742
Lnu-ltc	0.3977	0.3307	0.4234	0.2712	0.2577
dtu-dtn	0.3789	0.3236	0.3936	0.2738	**0.3003**
atn-ntc	0.3914	0.3458	0.4102	0.2681	0.2695
ltn-ntc	0.3724	0.3146	0.3448	0.2158	0.2636
ntc-ntc	0.2765	0.2452	0.2859	0.2023	0.1393

Our best performing official runs in the monolingual GIRT task are listed in Table 7. For each language, we submitted the first run using a data fusion operator ("Z-ScoreW" in this case). For all runs, we automatically expanded the queries using a blind relevance feedback method (Rocchio's in our experiments), hopping to improve retrieval effectiveness.

Table 7. Description and MAP of our best official GIRT runs

Run name	Lan.	Query	Model	Query exp.	Combined	MAP
UniNEgde1	GE	TD	Okapi	5 d. / 10 t.		
		TD	Prosit	10 d. / 125 t.	Z-scoreW	**0.4921**
UniNEgen1	EN	TD	Okapi	5 d. / 10 t.		
		TD	Prosit	10 d. / 50 t.	Z-scoreW	**0.5065**
UniNEgru2	RU	TD	Okapi	5 d. / 20 t.	n/a	**0.2774**

7 Conclusion

In this sixth CLEF evaluation campaign, we proposed a general stopword list and a light stemming procedure (removing only inflections attached to nouns and adjectives) for the Bulgarian and Hungarian languages. Based on two different probabilistic IR models and five vector-processing schemes (see Table 1), we found that the Okapi or the Prosit models provide the best retrieval performances for all the different languages. Compared to the classical $tf \cdot idf$ model, this approach results in mean average precision improvements of 72% for the French corpus (TD queries, Okapi), 86% for the Portuguese (TD queries, Okapi), 58% for the Hungarian (TD queries, Okapi), and 54% for the Bulgarian (TD queries,

Prosit). When query size is increased from title-only (T) to the longest request formulation (TDN), retrieval performance is also increased (33% for Portuguese, 31% for French, 21% for Hungarian).

As in previous evaluation campaigns we were able to confirm that pseudo-relevance feedback based on Rocchio's model would usually improve mean average precision for the French and Portuguese language, even though this improvement is not always statistically significant (see Table 2). For the other languages (Bulgarian and Hungarian), this blind query expansion did not improve mean average precision from a statistical point of view. In an effort to hopefully enhance retrieval performance, we could use a data fusion approach to combine two or more IR models. The use of this search strategy did however require building two inverted files, thus doubling the search time needed.

The automatic decompounding of Hungarian words and its impact in IR remains an open question and our preliminary experiments provide no clear and precise answers (our decompounding scheme did however decrease retrieval performance slightly, as shown in bottom part of Table 1).

In the bilingual task, the freely available translation tools perform reasonably well for both the French and Portuguese languages (based on the three best translation tools, the MAP compared to the monolingual search is around 85% for the French language and 72.6% for the Portuguese). For the less frequently used languages Bulgarian and Hungarian, the freely available translation tools (either the bilingual dictionary or the MT system) do not perform well. Their MAP is around 50% for Hungarian, and 30% for Bulgarian compared to the retrieval performance of a monolingual search.

In the GIRT task (Table 6), the probabilistic models (either Okapi or Prosit) usually results in better retrieval performances. Moreover, when taking manually assigned descriptors into account, mean average precision improves by around 36.5% for the English corpus and 14.4% for the German collection.

Acknowledgments. The authors would like to also thank the CLEF-2005 task organizers for their efforts in developing various European language test-collections, and C. Buckley from SabIR for giving us the opportunity to use the SMART system. This research was supported in part by the Swiss National Science Foundation under Grant #21-66 742.01.

References

1. Savoy, J.: Combining Multiple Strategies for Effective Monolingual and Cross-Lingual Retrieval. IR Journal, **7** (2004) 121–148
2. Savoy, J.: Data Fusion for Effective European Monolingual Information Retrieval. In: Peters, C., Clough, P.D., Jones, G.J.F., Gonzalo, J., Kluck, M., Magnini, B.(Eds.): Multilingual Information Access for Text, Speech and Images. Lecture Notes in Computer Science: Vol. 3491. Springer, Heidelberg (2005), 233–244
3. Savoy, J.: Report on CLEF-2003 Monolingual Tracks: Fusion of Probabilistic Models for Effective Monolingual Retrieval. In: Peters, C., Braschler, M., Gonzalo, J., Kluck, M. (Eds.): Advances in Cross-Language Information Retrieval. Lecture Notes in Computer Science: Vol. 3237. Springer, Heidelberg (2004), 322–336

4. Buckley, C., Singhal, A., Mitra, M., Salton, G.: New Retrieval Approaches Using SMART. In Proceedings TREC-4. NIST Publication #500-236, Gaithersburg (1996) 25–48
5. Singhal, A., Choi, J., Hindle, D., Lewis, D.D., Pereira, F.: AT&T at TREC-7. In Proceedings TREC-7. NIST, Publication #500-242, Gaithersburg (1999) 239–251
6. Robertson, S.E., Walker, S., Beaulieu, M.: Experimentation as a Way of Life: Okapi at TREC. Information Processing & Management, **36** (2000) 95–108
7. Amati, G., van Rijsbergen, C.J.: Probabilistic Models of Information Retrieval Based on Measuring the Divergence from Randomness. ACM Transactions on Information Systems, **20** (2002) 357–389
8. Savoy, J.: Statistical Inference in Retrieval Effectiveness Evaluation. Information Processing & Management, **33** (1997) 495–512
9. Tomlinson, S.: European Ad Hoc Retrieval Experiments with Hummingbird SearchServer™ at CLEF 2005. In *this volume*
10. Tordai, A., de Rijke, M.: Hungarian Monolingual Retrieval at CLEF 2005. In *this volume*
11. Vogt, C.C., Cottrell, G.W.: Fusion via a Linear Combination of Scores. IR Journal, **1** (1999) 151–173

Socio-Political Thesaurus in Concept-Based Information Retrieval

Mikhail Ageev[1,2], Boris Dobrov[1,2], and Natalia Loukachevitch[1,2]

[1] Research Computing Center of Moscow State University (MSU NIVC), Leninskie Gory, Moscow 119992, Russia
{ageev, dobroff, louk}@mail.cir.ru
[2] NCO Center for Information Research

Abstract. In CLEF 2005 experiments we used a bilingual Russian-English Socio-Political Thesaurus that we developed over more than 10 years as a tool for automatic text processing in information retrieval tasks. The same resource and the same algorithms were used for the ad-hoc and domain–specific task.

1 Introduction

Our group participated in two tasks: Ad-Hoc and Domain Specific Task. In both tasks we used the same resource (our bilingual Russian-English Socio-Political Thesaurus) and the same algorithms.

We developed the Socio-Political Thesaurus since 1994. Its domain is very broad covering the domain of contemporary social relations (the socio-political domain). Therefore the thesaurus includes a lot of terminology of sub-domains of the social sphere such as politics, economy, law, defense, industry, scientific policy, education, sport, arts and others, and also thematic words and expressions of general language.

The Socio-Political Thesaurus includes more than 32 thousand concepts, 78 thousand Russian terms and 85 thousand English terms.

In construction of the thesaurus we combined three different methodologies:

– the methods of construction of **information retrieval thesauri** (information retrieval context, analysis of terminology, terminology-based concepts, a small set of relation types),
– the development of **wordnets** for various languages (word-based concepts, detailed sets of synonyms, description of ambiguous text expressions),
– ontology and **formal ontology** research (strictness of relations description, necessity of many-step inference).

2 Socio-Political Domain

There are several genres of documents of considerable social significance because they concern not only specific professionals, but also life of various social groups of the population. These genres of documents are: legal and normative documents, international treaties, newspaper articles, and news reports.

C. Peters et al. (Eds.): CLEF 2005, LNCS 4022, pp. 141 – 150, 2006.

These different types of documents have very important similarity in their deep content. They describe (discuss, regulate) public and social relations existing in the contemporary society. The conceptual similarity leads to considerable intersection of the vocabulary and of the terminology used in these genres of texts.

The reason of this phenomenon is that all these texts can be considered as documents of the same "poly-thematic" domain – a domain describing life of the contemporary society. We call this domain the "socio-political" domain [11]. The socio-political domain largely comprises terminologies of many specific domains as state policy, economy, law, finance, social sphere and many others (see Fig. 1).

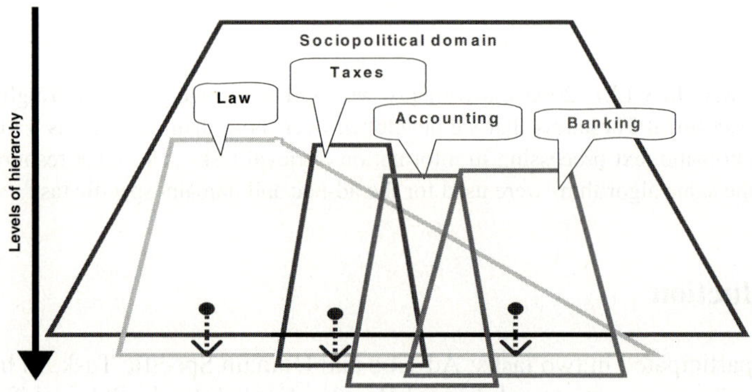

Fig. 1. Interrelations of specific domains within socio-political domain

On the other hand a lot of documents of this domain containing technical terms are understandable by non-professionals. In our opinion, it means that there exists an intermediate area where the general conceptual system and the upper levels of conceptual systems of specific domains intersect, and the socio-political domain is this intermediate area.

Development of linguistic resources or ontologies for the socio-political domain is very productive:

- they can be used for automatic text processing of important types of documents,
- they can serve as a rich source for development of resources and ontologies in specific domains.

Since 1994 we develop a concept-based resource for automatic text processing called Socio-Political Thesaurus.

3 Thesaurus

3.1 Structure of the Thesaurus

The Socio-Political Thesaurus is a hierarchical net of concepts. We consider it as a kind of a linguistic ontology. The concepts of the Thesaurus originate from senses of language expressions, that is single words or multiword expressions.

The main unit of the Socio-Political Thesaurus is a concept. When a new concept is introduced into the Thesaurus, it is necessary to assign its name. The name of a concept has to be clear and unambiguous for native speakers. In the Russian-English thesaurus a concept has to have a name in Russian and a name in English. These names are used in different representations of text processing results.

A concept has a set of linguistic expressions that can be used for reference to the concept in texts. A set of linguistic expressions of a concept is called 'text entries of a concept' and can be considered as a synonymic row. In the Russian-English thesaurus a concept has a set of Russian text entries and set of English text entries. These text entries are used to recognize a concept in texts.

Concepts often have more than 10 text entries including single nouns, verbs, adjectives and noun or verb groups. For example, a set of English text entries of the concept *JUDICIAL COURT* looks as follows: *court, court authorities, court instance, court of judiciary, court of jurisdiction, court of justice, court of law, judicature, judicial bodies, judicial court, judicial organ, judicial tribunal, law court, tribunal*. The concept *COURT SENTENCE* has 19 text entries including such as *sentence by the court, sentence of conviction, judgement of conviction* and others.

A concept within the Thesaurus has relations with other concepts. The main types of relations are taxonomic relations and a specific set of conceptual relations based on ontological dependence relations [3]. This set of relations was experimentally confirmed to be effective in information retrieval applications [8, 9].

The main principle of the description of relations in a thesaurus intended for automatic text processing is that the described relations have not to depend on the textual context [9], for example, any birch is a tree (the taxonomic relation), and any forest consists of trees (the relation of ontological dependence: forests can not exist without trees).

Contemporary thesaurus standards and manuals also stress that the relations in information retrieval thesauri have not to depend on the textual context [4, 16]. In comparison to other thesauri in our thesaurus we apply relations of ontological dependence as such context-free relations.

So the types of conceptual relations in the Thesaurus are:

- taxonomic relations,
- generalized part-whole relations describing internal characteristics of entities (physical parts, properties, participants for situations). In establishing of part-whole relations we use an important rule: concept-parts have to be ontologically dependent from concept-wholes. Therefore in the Thesaurus a tree is not a part of a forest (in fact, only the concept *FOREST TREE* can be described as a part of the concept *FOREST*). This rule provides transitivity of part-whole relations of the Thesaurus,
- external relations of ontological dependence. So in the Thesaurus the concept FOREST is described as a dependent concept from the concept TREE, because forests can not exist without trees, but trees can grow in many others places, not only in forests,
- related term (RT) relation is used for description of relations between very similar concepts not merged to the same concept.

Taxonomic relations and part-whole relations (with the above mentioned restrictions) are considered as transitive. Taxonomic relations, part-whole relations and external relations are hierarchical relations. Therefore a concept of the Thesaurus can have a set of hierarchically lower concepts – a tree of the concept. These trees can be used for query expansion.

3.2 Development of Thesaurus

In 1994 we started the development of the Socio-Political Thesaurus using semi-automatic methods to find multiword terms in text collections of official documents and newspaper articles. Our procedure of term acquisition consisted of two stages. At the first stage term-like expressions were automatically identified in the texts of the corpus. Rules defining term-like expressions included syntactical and lexical conditions. At the second stage our specialists had to look through the revealed expressions, choose terms from them and add new terms to the Thesaurus. This procedure was used during four years: we processed more than 200 Mb of texts and collected more than 200 thousand term-like expressions. It was stopped because it became difficult to find new useful terms, and the terminology coverage became very high.

Now the Thesaurus continues to grow (approximately 2000 concepts each year). This growth is due to several factors:

- the use of the Thesaurus in applications reveals additional useful concepts,
- analysis of new but already frequent words and expressions in text collections of the socio-political domain (normative documents, newspapers),
- adding more specific issues (usually discussed only in professional documents) of such domains as banking, taxes, customs duties, accounting and others. "Professional" concepts are usually located in the lower levels of the hierarchy of the Thesaurus.

The Thesaurus was translated into English (in fact, most concepts received sets of English text entries) and now contains more than 85 thousand English text entries [10]. Several applications of the Thesaurus as a bilingual resource concern processing of documents in English, for example, documents of European Court for Human Rights.

3.3 Comparison to Other Resources

The Socio-Political Thesaurus differs from conventional information retrieval thesauri and from such linguistic resources as WordNet [12] and EuroWordNet [2].

In developing a conventional information retrieval thesaurus the goal is to describe terms necessary for the representation of the main topics of each documents [6]. More specific terms are not included. Ambiguous terms are provided with scope notes and comments convenient for human subjects. In fact a conventional information retrieval thesaurus describes an artificial language based on the real language of a certain domain. To index documents human subjects have to use their domain, common sense, and grammatical knowledge not described in a thesaurus. Therefore conventional information retrieval thesauri created for manual indexing are hard to be utilized in an automatic indexing environment [13, 14, 15]. To be effective in automatic text processing a thesaurus needs to include a lot of information that is usually missed in thesauri for manual indexing such as considerably more concepts and terms, ambiguous text expressions, many levels of hierarchy as we did in the Socio-Political Thesaurus.

The Socio-Political Thesaurus is based on senses of linguistic expressions (words and multiword expressions), has means for description of lexical ambiguity similar to such linguistic resources as WordNet and EuroWordNet. At the same time there are important distinctions:

- concepts in the Thesaurus are the same for all parts of speech;
- inclusion of multiword expressions to the Thesaurus's net is regulated with strict but more liberal rules [1]. It is possible to add a new multiword expression that looks as a syntactically compositional phrase if it brings new information to the thesaurus knowledge. Our policy is to find as many such useful multiword expressions as possible,
- descriptions of concepts include much thematic information: possible situations, participants, properties and so on,
- onceptual relations in the Socio-Political Thesaurus are designed for and tested in information retrieval tasks.

Comparing the Socio-Political Thesaurus to existing ontologies we would like to stress that it is the largest linguistic ontology in the very important and broad domain of contemporary public and social relations. The specially narrowed system of relations allows us to develop resources working in real information retrieval applications.

4 Thesaurus-Based Text Processing

The processing of all received texts in Russian and English includes several stages:

- extraction of formal parameters of documents (source, date, authors and so on),
- morphological analysis,
- terminological analysis – matching with Thesaurus terms including lexical disambiguation procedures. After this stage the conceptual index for a document can be built. This index does not depend on the initial language of a document,
- thematic analysis – construction of thematic representation of texts based on conceptual relations described in the Thesaurus. The thematic representation simulates the topical structure of a text dividing all terms of the text to thematic nodes of sense-related terms [7]. The technique is based on such properties of texts as local cohesion [5] and global coherence. During this stage weights of concepts in the conceptual index are determined. The concepts weights in a text depend not only on frequencies of concepts but of presence of semantically related concepts in the same text.

After processing the documents and all types of extracted information (formal parameters, word and conceptual indexes) are loaded to a version of University information system RUSSIA (www.cir.ru) (see Fig. 2).

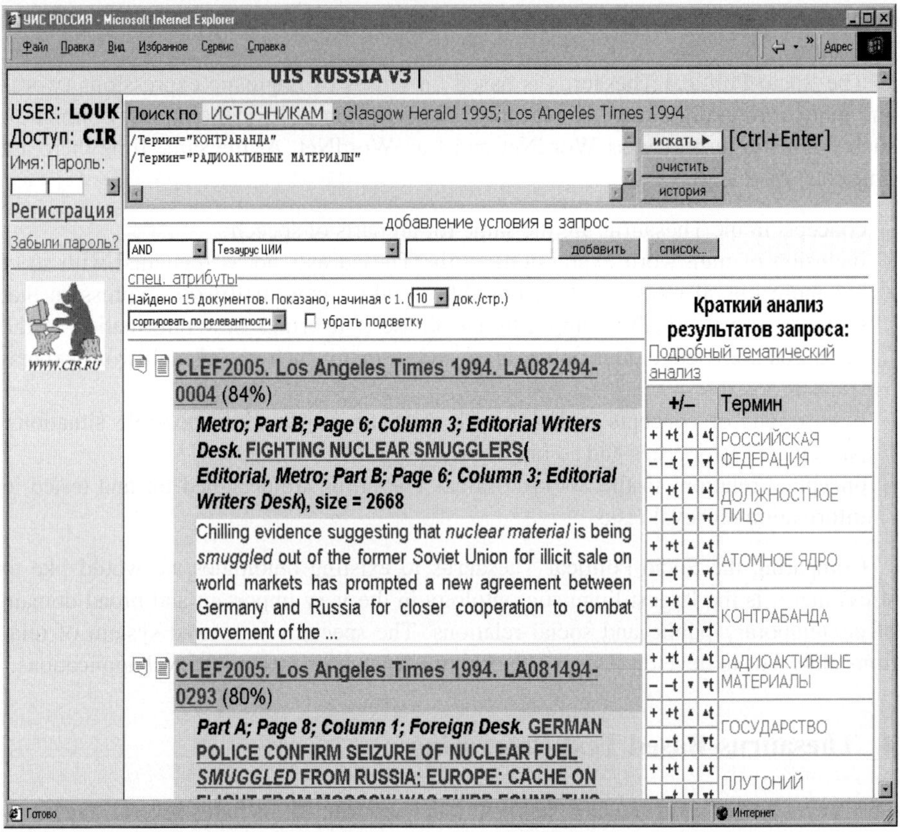

Fig. 2. Cross-lingual conceptual information retrieval in University information system RUSSIA (www.cir.ru)

The thesaurus-based retrieval in our system is independent of a language used in a query and in a text, and a retrieval set can contain texts in both languages.

The right column of the screen shows concepts specific for the retrieval set. Top-rank terms are computed using a technique similar to blind relevance feedback.

A user can modify the query, add or delete the concepts of the right column from the query using only one mouse click. Names of these concepts can be also formulated in both languages. Therefore a user can refine a query using his/her native language, and only after this refinement stage a user has to begin reading or translation of texts in another language.

5 Processing of CLEF Topics and Results of Experiments

The main idea of thesaurus-based processing of CLEF topics was as follows.

We supposed that matching of topics with Thesaurus concepts has to highlight important entities and miss abstract words that can be easily substituted by other words in documents of the collection. The ambiguity of terms in the Thesaurus is much lower than for the general vocabulary [11]. So we decided to construct Boolean queries only from Thesaurus concepts found in a topic.

All parts of topics were compared to the Thesaurus concepts. Figure 3 shows Topic C264 and the Thesaurus concepts found in its zones. In parentheses text entries of a concept, different from concept names, are indicated.

Query:	*Concepts:*
<Ru-title> **Контрабанда радиоактивных материалов** *</Ru-title>* *<EN-title>* **Smuggling** of **Radioactive Materials** *</EN-title>*	• ***КОНТРАБАНДА / CONTRABAND*** *(smuggling)* • ***РАДИОАКТИВНЫЕ МАТЕРИАЛЫ / RADIOACTIVE MATERIALS***
<Ru-desc> Найти документы по **незаконной торговле** между **странами радиоактивными материалами** *</Ru-desc>*| <EN-desc> Find documents on **illicit trafficking** between **countries** of **radioactive substances and nuclear materials**. </EN-desc>	• ***НЕЗАКОННАЯ ТОРГОВЛЯ / ILLICIT TRADE*** *(illicit trafficking)* • ***ГОСУДАРСТВО / STATE*** *(country)* • ***РАДИОАКТИВНЫЕ МАТЕРИАЛЫ / RADIOACTIVE MATERIALS*** *(radioactive substances, nuclear materials)*
<Ru-narr> Релевантными являются документы, содержащие сообщения о **незаконной торговле** или **контрабанде радиоактивных материалов** или **ядерных отходов** как гражданского, так и **военного** происхождения. *</Ru-narr>* *<EN-narr>* Any document reporting cases of **criminal trafficking** or **smuggling** of both civilian and military **nuclear material** or **radioactive waste** over **national borders** is relevant *</EN-narr>*	• ***НЕЗАКОННАЯ ТОРГОВЛЯ / ILLICIT TRADE*** *(criminal trafficking)* • ***КОНТРАБАНДА / CONTRABAND*** *(smuggling)* • ***РАДИОАКТИВНЫЕ МАТЕРИАЛЫ / RADIOACTIVE MATERIALS*** *(nuclear material)* • ***РАДИОАКТИВНЫЕ ОТХОДЫ*** *(ядерные отходы)* ***/ NUCLEAR WASTE*** • ***ОБОРОНА*** *(военный)* ***/NATIONAL DEFENSE****(military)* • ***ГОСУДАРСТВЕННАЯ ГРАНИЦА / NATIONAL BORDER*** *- is absent in the Russian version of the topic.*

Fig. 3. Topic C264 and thesaurus concepts found in its zones

Let us denote concepts found in the title of a topic as $C_{t1} \ldots C_{tn}$, concepts found in the description of a topic - $C_{d1} \ldots C_{dm}$, concepts found in the narrative of a topic – concepts $C_{n1} \ldots C_{nk}$.

The search of documents included several steps. New documents received at every next step are added to the end of the document list received from previous steps.

Step 1. In the first step we suppose that main entities of a topic are named in the title. Concepts found in the description and the narrative give information about additional properties of concepts from the title.

Then the main type of topic representation was as follows:

$$(C_{t1} \text{ and } \ldots \text{ and } C_{tn}) \text{ and } (C_{d1} \text{ or } \ldots \text{ or } C_{dm} \text{ or } C_{n1} \text{ or } \ldots \text{ or } C_{nk})$$

Fig.2 shows results of retrieval of the query for topic 264

$$(C_{t1} \text{ and} \ldots \text{and } C_{tn}) = \textit{CONTRABAND} \text{ and } \textit{RADIOACTIVE MATERIALS}.$$

Step 2. We try to expand a query using Thesaurus concepts subordinate to the concepts of a query. But it is well-known that the context of a concept in a query can restrict expansion of this concept. Therefore in this stage for expansion we try to justify expansion with a technique similar to blind relevance feedback. For expansion we use only that subordinate concepts of the query concepts that are top-ranked 20 concepts from the top-ranked 100 documents. The list of such top-ranked concepts is shown in the right column of the screen.

Sub-ordinate concepts are added using OR to their super-ordinate concepts, forming disjunction. For example at this stage for query 264 “Smuggling of Radioactive Materials” the concepts *URAN* and *PLUTONIUM* are added to concept *RADIOACTIVE MATERIALS*. So we receive the disjunction

(*RADIOACTIVE MATERIALS* or *URAN* or *PLUTONIUM*)

We fulfil expanded queries and add subordinate concepts while new such concepts appear.

Step 3. At this stage we continue to expand the initial query. Now we use full trees of lower concepts for title concepts (C_{t1} and ..and C_{tn}). So at this stage we work with the following query

$$(C_{t1+tree} \text{ and ..and } C_{tn+tree}) \text{ and } (C_{d1} \text{ or ..or } C_{dm} \text{ or } C_{n1} \text{ or .. or } C_{nk})$$

Step 4. At this step we reduce initial query to concepts only from the title, so we have the query

$$(C_{t1} \text{ and } \ldots \text{ and } C_{tn}).$$

Step 5. Concepts from the title are expanded with lower concepts

$$(C_{t1+tree} \text{ and } \ldots \text{ and } C_{tn+tree})$$

Step 6. At this stage we change AND of title concepts to OR and return concepts from the description and narrative to the query Step

$$(C_{t1+tree} \text{ or } \ldots \text{ or } C_{tn+tree}) \text{ and } (C_{d1} \text{ or } \ldots \text{ or } C_{dm} \text{ or } C_{n1} \text{ or } \ldots \text{ or } C_{nk})$$

Step 7. At last all concepts of a topic are used in OR-query

$$(C_{t1+tree} \text{ or } \ldots \text{ or } C_{tn+tree}) \text{ or } (C_{d1} \text{ or } \ldots \text{ or } C_{dm} \text{ or } C_{n1} \text{ or } \ldots \text{ or } C_{nk})$$

Results of our runs in the ad-hoc and domain-specific tasks are shown in figure 4.

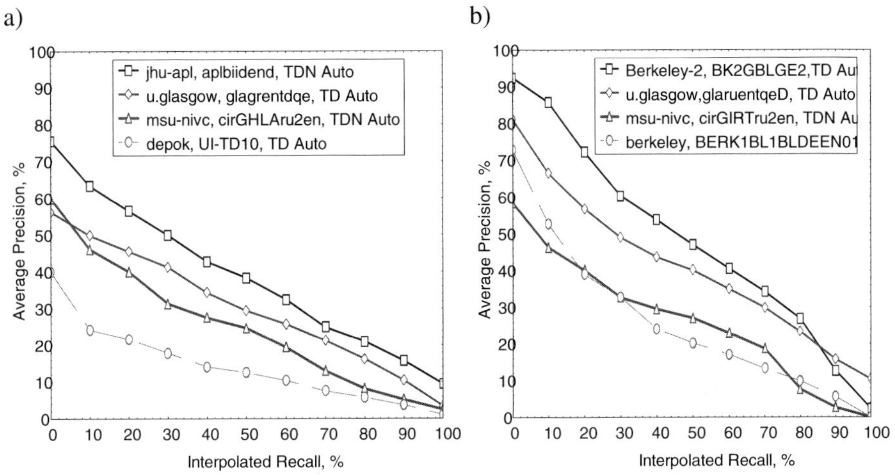

Fig. 4. CLEF2005 -Top 4 participants of a) Ad-Hoc Bilingual X2EN, b) Domain Specific Bilingual X2EN

6 Conclusion

During more than 10 years we developed the bilingual Russian-English Socio-Political Thesaurus as a resource for automatic text processing in a broad domain of social relations of the contemporary society.

We considered the Thesaurus as a resource useful for application in two tasks of CLEF: in the ad-hoc task based on newspapers and the domain-specific task based on social sciences documents. For automatic processing of documents and queries we used only the Socio-Political Thesaurus and therefore we can state that the concepts of the Thesaurus indeed provide broad coverage of newspaper texts, scientific abstracts and corresponding CLEF queries.

In current experiments we did not apply such methods as vector models or pseudo-relevance feedback. Our next goal is to find the better combination of the thesaurus-based techniques and the best-known information retrieval techniques.

Acknowledgments

Partial support for this research is provided by the Russian Foundation for Basic Research through grant # 03-01-00472.

References

1. Bentivogli, L., Pianta, E.: Extending WordNet with Syntagmatic Information. In: International Wordnet Conference (GWC – 2004) (2004) 47-53
2. Climent, S., Rodriguez, H., Gonzalo J.: Definitions of the links and subsets for nouns of the EuroWordNet project. - Deliverable D005, WP3.1, EuroWordNet, LE2-4003. (1996)
3. Guarino, N.: Some Ontological Principles for Designing Upper Level Lexical Resources. In: Proceedings of First International Conference on Language Resources and Evaluation (2000)
4. Guidelines for the Construction, Format and Management of Monolingual Thesauri (Z39.19). – NISO (1993)
5. Hirst, G., St-Onge, D.: Lexical Chains as representation of context for the detection and correction malapropisms, In: Fellbaum, C. (ed.): WordNet: An electronic lexical database and some of its applications, Cambridge, MA: The MIT Press (1997)
6. LIV (Legislative Indexing Vocabulary): Congressional Research Service. The Library of Congress. Twenty-first Edition (1994)
7. Loukachevitch, N., Dobrov, B.: Thesaurus-Based Structural Thematic Summary in Multilin-gual Information Systems. Machine Translation Review, 11 (2000) 10-20
8. Loukachevitch, N., Dobrov, B.: Evaluation of Thesaurus on Sociopolitical Life as Informa-tion Retrieval Tool. In: Gonzalez Rodriguez, M., Paz Suarez Araujo, C. (eds.): Proceedings of Third International Conference on Language Resources and Evaluation (LREC2002), Vol.1 Gran Canaria, Spain (2002) 115-121
9. Loukachevitch, N., Dobrov, B.:. Development of Ontologies with Minimal Set of Conceptual Relations. In: Proceedings of Fourth International Conference on Language Resources and Evaluation (LREC2004), Vol.6 (2004) 1885-1889
10. Loukachevitch, N., Dobrov, B.: Development of Bilingual Domain-Specific Ontology for Automatic Conceptual Indexing. In: Proceedings of Fourth International Conference on Language Resources and Evaluation (LREC2004), – Vol.6 (2004) 1993—1996
11. Loukachevitch, N., Dobrov, B.: Sociopolitical Domain as a Bridge from General Words to Terms of Specific Domains. In: Proceedings of Second International WordNet Conference GWC 2004. (2004) 163-168
12. Miller, G., Beckwith, R., Fellbaum, C., Gross, D., Miller, K.,: Five papers on WordNet, CSL Report, 43, Cognitive Science Laboratory, Princeton University (1990)
13. Salton, G.: Automatic Text Processing - The Analysis, Transformation and Retrieval of Information by Computer. Addison-Wesley, Reading, MA (1989)
14. Soergel, D., Lauser, B., Liang, A., Fisseha, F., Keizer, J., Katz, S.: Reengineering Thesauri for New Applications: the AGROVOC Example. – Journal of Digital Information. Volume 4, Issue 4. - Article No. 257 (2004) 03-17
15. Tudhope, D., Alani, H., Jones, Cr.: Augmenting Thesaurus Relationships: Possibilities for Retrieval. Journal of Digital Libraries. Volume 1, Issue 8 (2001)
16. Will, L.: Thesaurus consultancy. In Roe, Sandra K., Thomas, Alan R. (eds.): The thesaurus: review, renaissance and revision. New York London: Haworth (2004)

The Performance of a Machine Translation-Based English-Indonesian CLIR System

Mirna Adriani and Ihsan Wahyu

Faculty of Computer Science
University of Indonesia
Depok 16424, Indonesia
mirna@cs.ui.ac.id, ihsanw101@mhs.cs.ui.ac.id

Abstract. We describe our participation in the Indonesian-English bilingual task of the 2005 Cross-Language Evaluation Forum (CLEF). We translated an Indonesian query set into English using a commercial machine translation tool called *Transtool* and attempted to improve retrieval effectiveness using a query expansion technique. However, since our initial retrieval effectiveness was low, the query expansion technique had a negative impact on performance.

1 Introduction

This year the University of Indonesia IR-Group participated in the bilingual task of the Cross Language Evaluation Forum (CLEF) i.e., testing English-Indonesian CLIR. We used a commercial machine translation software called *Transtool*[1] to translate an Indonesian query set into English. Indonesian (it is also known as Bahasa Indonesia; Bahasa means language) is the national language of Indonesia which is spoken by more than 200 million people. Indonesian texts use the alphabetical characters so there is no special treatment required in handling them. We learned from our previous work [1, 2] that freely available dictionaries on the Internet could not correctly translate many Indonesian terms, as their vocabulary was very limited. We thus hoped that using machine translation we could improve our result this time.

2 The Query Translation Process

As a first step, we manually translated the original CLEF query set from English into Indonesian. We then translated the resulting Indonesian queries back into English using *Transtool.*

2.1 Query Expansion Technique

Adding translated queries with relevant terms (query expansion) has been shown to improve CLIR effectiveness [1, 3]. A well-known query expansion technique is *pseudo relevance feedback* [4, 5]. This technique is based on the assumption that the

[1] See http://www.geocities.com/cdpenerjemah/.

C. Peters et al. (Eds.): CLEF 2005, LNCS 4022, pp. 151 – 154, 2006.

top few documents initially retrieved are indeed relevant to the query, and should contain other terms that are also relevant to the query. These terms are added to the original query. We applied this technique in this work. To choose the relevant terms from the top ranked documents, we used the *tf*idf* term weighting formula [4]. We added a certain number of noun terms that have the highest weight scores.

3 Experiment

We participated in the bilingual task, querying English documents with Indonesian topics. The English document collection contains 190,604 documents from two English newspapers, the *Glasgow Herald* and the *Los Angeles Times*. We opted to use the topic title and description fields to formulate our queries. The query translation process was performed fully automatically using *Transtool*. Using the topic titles, the average length of the Indonesian queries derived was 3.1 words, while the average length of the original English titles was 2.6 words; and the average length of the English queries translated automatically from Indonesian using *Transtool* was 2.7 words. Using the topic descriptions, the average length of the Indonesian description queries derived was 12.1 words; the average length of the original English topic descriptions was 9.5 words; and the average length of the translated English description queries was 11.3 words. The number of Indonesian words that cannot be translated into English was 10 for the topic titles and 26 for the topic descriptions.

We then applied a pseudo relevance-feedback query-expansion technique to the queries that had been translated using the machine translation tool. We used the top 20 documents from the collection to extract the expansion terms. Only noun terms were used to expand the query. We used the Monty Tagger[2] to identify noun terms in the top 20 documents.

In these experiments, we used Lucene[3] information retrieval system which is based on the *vector space model* [4] to index and retrieve the documents.

4 Results

Our work focused on the bilingual task using Indonesian queries to retrieve documents in the English collections. Table 1 shows the result of our experiments.

The retrieval performance of the title-based queries dropped 43.70% below that of the equivalent monolingual retrieval. The retrieval performance of the description-based queries dropped 26.77% below that of the equivalent monolingual queries.

The retrieval performance using a combination of title and description queries dropped 47.83% below that of the equivalent monolingual queries.

The title-based queries were then expanded using noun terms from the top 20 documents using the pseudo relevance feedback technique [4]. Adding 10 noun terms reduced the retrieval performance by 28.25%, however, adding 20 noun terms reduced the retrieval performance slightly less, i.e., by 21.11% (see Table 2).

---

[2] See http://web.media.mit.edu/~hugo/montytagger/.

[3] See http://lucene.apache.org/.

Table 1. Average retrieval precision of the monolingual runs of the title, description and combination of title and description topics and their translation queries using the machine translation

Task	Monolingual	CLIR (translation)	% Change
Title	0.2810	0.1582	- 43.70%
Description	0.2364	0.1731	- 26.77%
Title + Description	0.3508	0.1830	- 47.83%

Table 2. Average retrieval precision of the title-based queries using the query expansion technique with top-20 document method

Query translation using MT (title)	10 terms added	20 terms added
0.1582 (0%)	0.1135 (-28.25%)	0.1248 (-21.11%)

Table 3. Average retrieval precision of the description-based queries using the query expansion technique with top-20 document method

Query translation using MT (description)	10 terms added	20 terms added
0.1731 (0%)	0.0936 (-45.92%)	0.0907 (-47.60%)

Next, the description-based queries were expanded using noun terms from the top 20 documents using the pseudo relevance feedback technique. Adding 10 noun terms reduced the retrieval performance by 45.92% and adding 20 noun terms reduced the retrieval performance further by 47.60% (see Table 3).

Table 4. Average retrieval precision of the title and the description-based queries using the query expansion technique with top-20 document method

Query translation using MT (description + title)	10 terms added	20 terms added
0.1830 (0%)	0.1285 (-29.78%)	0.1190 (-34.97%)

Finally, the title and description based queries were expanded using noun terms from the top 20 documents using the pseudo relevance feedback technique. Adding 10 noun terms reduced the retrieval performance by 29.78% and adding 20 noun terms reduced the retrieval performance further by 34.97% (see Table 4).

5 Summary

Our results demonstrate that the retrieval performance of queries that were translated using machine translation for Bahasa Indonesia was about 53%-74% of that of the equivalent monolingual queries. The pseudo relevance feedback technique that is commonly used to improve retrieval performance did not improve performance in this case. In fact, the longer the query, the worse the effect of using the query expansion technique. In our experiments, adding noun terms to the translated queries lowered retrieval performance to 37%-41% of that of the equivalent monolingual queries. With such a short time available, we were not able to try different approaches to this task. We hope that we will obtain better results in our next participation in CLEF.

References

1. Adriani, M., van Rijsbergen, C. J.: Term Similarity Based Query Expansion for Cross Language Information Retrieval. In: Abiteboul, Serge; Vercouste, Anne-Marie (eds.): Research and Advanced Technology for Digital Libraries, Third European Conference (ECDL'99). Lecture Notes in Computer Science, Vol. 1696. Springer-Verlag, Berlin (1999) 311-322
2. Adriani, M.: Ambiguity Problem in Multilingual Information Retrieval. In: Peters, Carol (ed.): Cross-Language Evaluation Forum 2000. Lecture Notes in Computer Science, Vol. 2069. Springer-Verlag, Berlin (2001)
3. Ballesteros, L. and Croft, Bruce W.: Resolving Ambiguity for Cross-language Retrieval. In Proceedings of the 21st International SIGIR Conference on Research and Development in Information Retrieval. ACM (1998) 64-71
4. Salton, G., McGill, M. J: Introduction to Modern Information Retrieval. McGraw-Hill, New York (1983)
5. Attar, R. and Fraenkel, A. S.: Local Feedback in Full-Text Retrieval Systems. Journal of the Association for Computing Machinery 24 (1977) 397-417

Exploring New Languages with HAIRCUT at CLEF 2005

Paul McNamee

The Johns Hopkins University Applied Physics Laboratory
11100 Johns Hopkins Road
Laurel, MD 20723-6099 USA
paul.mcnamee@jhuapl.edu

Abstract. JHU/APL has long espoused the use of language-neutral methods for cross-language information retrieval. This year we participated in the ad hoc cross-language track and submitted both monolingual and bilingual runs. We undertook our first investigations in the Bulgarian and Hungarian languages. In our bilingual experiments we used several non-traditional CLEF query languages such as Greek, Hungarian, and Indonesian, in addition to several western European languages. We found that character n-grams remain an attractive option for representing documents and queries in these new languages. In our monolingual tests n-grams were more effective than unnormalized words for retrieval in Bulgarian (+30%) and Hungarian (+63%). Our bilingual runs made use of *subword translation*, statistical translation of character n-grams using aligned corpora, when parallel data were available, and web-based machine translation, when no suitable data could be found.

1 Introduction

HAIRCUT[1] is a Java-based information retrieval system that has been developed at the Johns Hopkins University Applied Physics Laboratory. An early version of HAIRCUT was created for use in the TREC-6 evaluation. One of the original issues that we wanted to investigate with the HAIRCUT system was whether character n-gram tokenization was an effective technique for ad hoc text retrieval. Earlier work using n-grams had been viewed with skepticism [3] and it was our intent to compare n-grams and words in an identical framework (*i.e.,* keeping the retrieval system constant). Our early results were promising and we found that the use of n-grams conveys substantial advantages when non-English collections were used [7].

JHU/APL was a participant in the first CLEF evaluation, and since then, we have been able to apply our techniques in the ten languages explored in the ad hoc tasks, as well as in Chinese, Japanese, Korean (at NTCIR), and Arabic (at TREC). We have found n-gram tokenization to be surprisingly effective across these diverse languages. We believe n-grams are effective, in part, because they account for morphological variation and provide robustness in the face of slight orthographic mismatching. N-grams also eliminate the need to perform decompounding (*e.g.,* in German) or word segmentation (*e.g.,* in Chinese).

---

[1] HAIRCUT stands for the Hopkins Automated Information Retriever for Combing Unstructured Text.

C. Peters et al. (Eds.): CLEF 2005, LNCS 4022, pp. 155 – 164, 2006.

In addition to the use of character n-gram tokenization we make use of a statistical language model of retrieval and combination of evidence from multiple retrievals. For bilingual retrieval we include pre-translation query expansion using comparable collections, statistical translation from aligned parallel collections, and when translation resources are scarce, reliance on language similarity alone. This year we continue experimenting with a technique we first applied at the CLEF 2003 evaluation: *subword translation*, translation of the constituent n-grams in queries rather than words [9]. For translation we used aligned parallel corpora instead of bilingual wordlists, when possible, and other resources (*e.g.*, Web-based MT) when not. Subword translation attempts to overcome obstacles in dictionary-based translation, such as word lemmatization, matching of multiword expressions, and inability to handle out-of-vocabulary words such as common surnames [13].

We submitted official runs for the monolingual and bilingual tracks. For all of our runs we used the HAIRCUT system and a statistical language model similarity calculation. Some of our official runs were based solely on n-gram processing; however, we thought that by using a combination of n-grams and words or stemmed words better performance could be obtained.

2 Methods

HAIRCUT supports several ways of representing documents using an order independent, bag-of-terms model. Note we are frequently using character n-grams, not words as indexing terms. Our general approach is to process the text of each document, reducing all terms to lower-case. Words were deemed to be white-space delimited tokens in the text; however, we preserve only the first 4 digits of a number and we truncate any particularly long tokens (those greater than 35 characters in length). We make no attempt at compound splitting. Once words are identified we optionally perform transformations on the words to create indexing terms (*e.g.*, stemming using the Snowball stemmer). Starting in 2003 we began removing diacritical marks, believing that they are of little importance. So-called stopwords are retained in our index and the dictionary is created from all words present in the corpus. At query time we ignore high frequency terms for reasons of efficiency, and because such terms typically add little to query performance. (By default, query terms occurring in greater than 20% of documents are ignored.)

We continue to use a statistical language model for retrieval akin to those presented by Ponte and Croft [14] and Hiemstra [4] with Jelinek-Mercer smoothing [5] (*i.e.*, linear interpolation). In this model, the probability of relevance is given as:

$$P(D \mid Q) - \prod_{q \in Q} [\alpha P(q \mid D) + (1 - \alpha) P(q \mid C)],$$

where Q is a query, D is a document, C is the collection as a whole, and α is a smoothing parameter. The probabilities on the right side of the equation are replaced by their maximum likelihood estimates when scoring a document. The language model has the advantage that term weights are mediated by the corpus. It has been our experience that this type of probabilistic model outperforms a vector-based cosine model or a binary independence model with Okapi BM25 weighting.

Character n-grams, sequences of n consecutive characters, have been used for a number of tasks in human language technology (*e.g.*, spelling correction [15], diacritics restoration [12], and language identification [1]). Their use for IR dates to the mid-1970s where they were used primarily as a technique to decrease dictionary size. At that time $n=2$ or $n=3$ were typical lengths, and for a fixed alphabet size a substantial reduction in memory requirements could be realized. Over time as physical memory costs fell significantly, research in the mid-1990s led to n-grams being considered as an alternative indexing representation to words or stemmed words (see [3]). There are several variations on n-gram indexing; here we concentrate on overlapping character n-grams of a fixed length (typically $n=4$ or $n=5$). For the text 'prime_minister' and $n=7$ the resulting n-grams are: '_prime_', 'prime_m', 'rime_mi', 'ime_min', 'me_mini', 'e_minis', 'minist', 'ministe', 'inister', and 'nister_'. The single n-gram 'ime_min' that occurs at the word boundary is fairly distinct indicator of the query phrase 'prime minister' and it would not be generated from a sentence like 'the finance minister ordered prime rib for lunch' which might cause a false match using words alone as indexing terms.

3 Monolingual Task

3.1 Official Submissions

For our monolingual work we created indexes for each language using the permissible document fields appropriate to each collection. Our four basic methods for tokenization were unnormalized words, stemmed words obtained through the use of the Snowball stemmer (when available), 4-grams, and 5-grams. Information about each index is shown in Table 1 (below).

Selection of 4-grams and 5-grams as indexing terms was based on a comprehensive study across the CLEF languages that investigated n-gram length [10] and established that 4-grams and 5-grams seem to work equally well for monolingual retrieval. Our language model requires a single smoothing constant; we used $\alpha=0.3$ with both words and stems, and $\alpha=0.5$ with 4-grams and 5-grams. Each of our base runs used blind relevance feedback (queries expanded to 60 terms; terms selected and weighted using 20 top-ranked and 75 low-ranked documents from the top 1000). Figure 1 charts performance using our four different term indexing strategies, in isolation. In the Bulgarian and Hungarian languages, substantial benefits were seen when n-grams were used – 30% and 63% relative improvements, respectively. In the other

Table 1. Summary information about the test collection and index data structures

language	#docs	#rel	index size (MB) / unique terms (1000s)			
			words	stems	4-grams	5-grams
BG	67341	778	57 / 67	---	154 / 193	251 / 769
EN	166754	2063	143 / 302	123 / 236	504 / 166	827 / 916
FR	177450	2537	129 / 328	107 / 226	393 / 159	628 / 838
HU	49530	939	59 / 549	---	121 / 150	200 / 741
PT	210734	2904	178 / 418	140 / 254	529 / 174	868 / 907

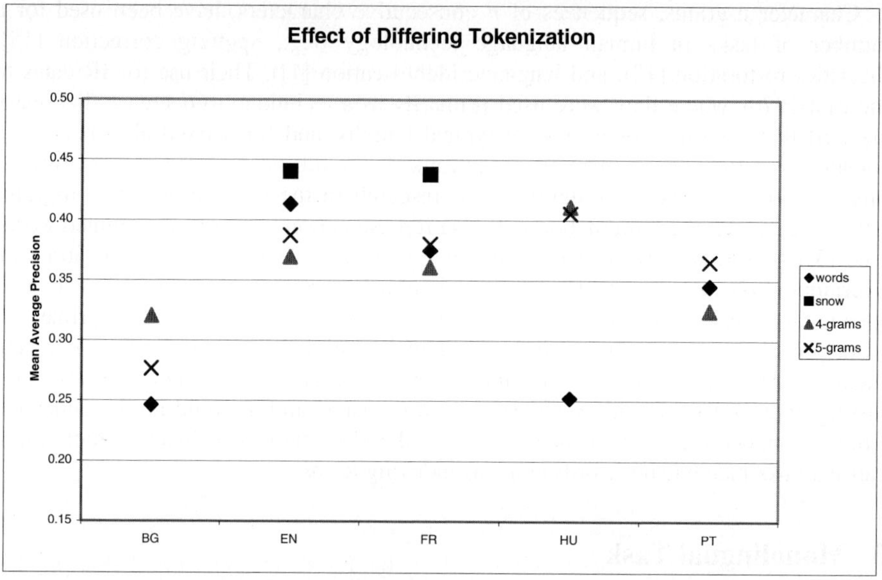

Fig. 1. Relative effectiveness of tokenization methods on the CLEF 2005 test sets

Table 2. Official results for monolingual task

run id	Fields	Terms	MAP	Rel. Found	Relevant
aplmobgc	TD	4+5	0.3058	706	778
aplmobgd	**TD**	**4**	**0.3203**	**678**	**778**
aplmobge	TD	5	0.2768	699	778
aplmoena	**TD**	**5+snow**	**0.4346**	**1930**	**2063**
aplmoenb	TD	4+snow	0.4222	1900	2063
aplmoenc	TD	4+5	0.3898	1877	2063
aplmoend	TD	4	0.3692	1808	2063
aplmoene	TD	5	0.3873	1889	2063
aplmofra	TD	5+snow	0.4114	2422	2537
aplmofrb	**TD**	**4+snow**	**0.4122**	**2427**	**2537**
aplmofrc	TD	4+5	0.3765	2283	2537
aplmofrd	TD	4	0.3608	2109	2537
aplmofre	TD	5	0.3801	2274	2537
aplmohuc	TD	4+5	0.4063	893	939
aplmohud	**TD**	**4**	**0.4112**	**893**	**939**
aplmohue	TD	5	0.4056	891	939
aplmoptc	TD	4+5	0.3610	2446	2904
aplmoptd	TD	4	0.3246	2343	2904
aplmopte	**TD**	**5**	**0.3654**	**2450**	**2904**

languages, n-grams performed similarly to words and somewhat worse than the use of stemmed words (*e.g.,* in English and French). Our previous experience has shown that n-grams produce larger benefits in languages with greater morphological complexity.

Our submitted runs were based on a combination of several base runs using various options for tokenization. Our method for combination is to normalize scores by probability mass and to then merge documents by score. All of our submitted runs were automatic runs and used only the title and description topic fields. We produced three to five runs in each language that were created from combinations of the base runs. Runs were labeled *aplmoxx[a-e]*, where *xx* indicates the language of interest. Runs whose names end with a terminal 'a' were produced by combining a 5-gram base run with a stemmed word base run; a terminal 'b' indicates fusion of a 4-grams and stemmed words; terminal 'c' is used for runs that used both 4-grams and 5-grams; the suffix 'd' indicates solitary use of 4-grams; and, a terminal 'e' indicates the use of 5-grams alone. Monolingual performance based on mean average precision is reported in Table 2.

3.2 Post-hoc Experiments Using N-Gram Stemming

The use of character n-gram indexing benefits retrieval accuracy in Bulgarian and Hungarian (see Figure 1). This improvement comes at a several fold increase in disk space usage and query execution times compared to the use of ordinary words. This is because each word produces multiple n-grams. To address this issue we used a technique where a single n-gram is selected as a representation for each word. This results in an inverted index that is no larger than a word or stemmed word index, but one which hopefully results in performance close to that obtained when all n-grams, including word spanning n-grams, are retained. In these experiments the least frequently occurring n-gram is retained for each word in a document (as in [8]). For example, using 4-grams in English, the words juggle, juggles, juggler, juggled, and juggling are all represented by 'jugg'. This works better than the Porter stemmer,

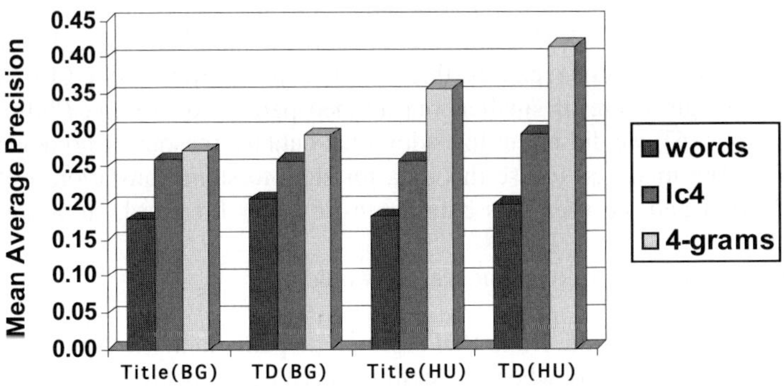

Fig. 2. Effectiveness of least-common n-gram stemming in Bulgarian and Hungarian

which fails to produce the same stem for these five words; however, n-gram stemming, like any stemmer, makes mistakes.

In Figure 2 (below) the use of least-common 4-gram stemming is compared to the use of plain words and the full set of character 4-grams. The least-common n-grams perform on par with n-grams and substantially better (*i.e.,* 25-50% relative improvement) over plain words in both Bulgarian and Hungarian.

4 Bilingual Task

Our preferred approach to bilingual retrieval is based on the following procedure: (1) apply pre-translation query expansion using the source language CLEF corpus; (2) translate terms statistically using aligned parallel corpora, where terms can be words, stems, or n-grams; and, (3) perform retrieval using the query terms that were projected into the target language, possibly with additional relevance feedback. We have had good success using aligned parallel corpora to extract statistical translations. Others have also relied on corpus-based translation; however, we recently demonstrated significant improvements in bilingual performance by translating character n-grams directly. We call this '*subword translation.*' Additionally we also translate stemmed words and words. This year we were only able to use this technique for the English, French, and Portuguese target collections as we lacked parallel resources in Bulgarian and Hungarian.

For the 2002 and 2003 campaigns we relied on a single source for parallel texts, the Official Journal of the E.U. [16], which is published in the official languages (20 languages as of May 2004). The Journal is available in each of the E.U. languages and consists mainly of governmental topics, for example, trade and foreign relations. For the CLEF 2003 evaluation we had obtained 33 GB of PDF files that we distilled into approximately 300 MB of alignable text, per language. In December 2003 we began the process of mining archival issues of the Journal, beginning with 1998. This process took nearly five months. We obtained data from January 1998 through April 2004 – over six years of data. This is nearly 80 GB of PDF files, or roughly 750 MB of plain text per language. We extracted text using the *pdftotext* program; however this software cannot extract the Greek data set; we were left with data in ten languages, from which 45 possible alignments are possible. Though focused on European topics, the time span is three to ten years after the CLEF document collection. Though aware of smaller, but aligned parallel data (*e.g.,* Philip Koehn's Europarl corpus [6]) we did not utilize additional data for reasons of homogeneity and convenience. We managed to use this data for stem-to-stem translation in the CLEF 2004 evaluation and we used this data again this year for word, stem, and n-gram translation.

To align data between two languages, we would:

- convert the data from PDF format to plain text (this introduced some errors, especially when processing diacritical marks in the earlier years);
- apply rules for splitting the text into sections (the data was page-aligned, we desired paragraph-sized chunks); and,
- align files using Church's *char_align* [2].

To induce a translation for a given source language term, we proceed by:

- identifying documents (i.e., approximately paragraphs) containing the source language term;
- examining the set of corresponding documents from the target language portion of the aligned collection;
- producing a score for each term that occurs in at least one of the target language paragraphs (more on this below); and,
- finally, selecting the single term with the largest translation score for the source language term.

Our method for scoring candidate translations does not require translation model software such as GIZA++. Rather, we rely on information theoretic scores (*e.g.,* symmetric conditional probability or mutual information) to rank terms. We adopt the same technique we rely on for pseudo relevance feedback – a method we have developed called *affinity sets*. Terms are weighted based on their inverse document frequency (IDF) and the difference between their relative frequency in the set of documents under consideration and the global set of documents. This measure is related to mutual information; however, we believe our technique is more general as it permits the set of documents to be identified through any means, including potentially, query-specific attempts at retrieval and translation.

We performed pairwise alignments between languages pairs, for example, between English and Portuguese. Once aligned, we indexed each pairwise-aligned collection using the technique described earlier on the CLEF-2005 document collections. That is, we created four indexes per sub-collection, per language – one each of words, stems, 4-grams and 5-grams. This year, rather than create a translation dictionary for every term in a source language index, we translated terms on demand using the algorithm presented above. So far we have been using 1-best translation, but we can generate multiple weighted translations for each term. We have not found this necessary as techniques such as pre-translation query expansion are capable of generating many terms related to a query; thus the harm introduced by a dubious translation is lessened. Our experience on the CLEF 2003 and 2004 bilingual test sets led us to believe that direct translation of 5-grams would likely be the most effective single technique, but that combination using runs generated by translating multiple term types might yield an improvement [11].

Unfortunately, our data from the Official Journal of the EU did not cover two of the target language collections (*i.e.,* Bulgarian and Hungarian). To support translation to or from these languages we relied on query translation using web-based machine translation. We also used MT to use the Greek and Indonesia query sets against English documents. The online services we used are located at:

- http://babelfish.altavista.com (GR to EN)
- http://www.toggletext.com/kataku_trial.php (IN to EN)
- http://www.bultra.com/test_e.htm (BG to/from EN)
- http://www.tranexp.com/ (HU to/from EN)

As can be seen in Table 3 (below), our results using corpus-based subword translation achieved bilingual performance between 78% and 87% of our best monolingual runs for the given target language. Table 4 details our results using available machine translation software. The resultant bilingual performance depends heavily on the individual translation engine used (from 26% to 85% of our best monolingual baselines). In some cases the result of fusing multiple runs using different target-side tokenization of the machine translation output resulted in an improvement, for example, run *aplbiidend* had a 4% absolute improvement in mean average precision of *aplbiidena*, which used 5-grams alone. In a couple of cases we directly compared the use of 4-grams and 5-grams on the MT output and found the results to be very similar (*e.g.*, compare *aplbienbg[a/e]* and *aplbienhu[a/e]*).

Table 3. JHU/APL's official results for bilingual task using corpus-based translation

Run id	Source	Target	Fields	Terms	MAP	% Mono	Rel. Found	Relevant
aplbienfrc	EN	FR	TD	5-grams	0.3442	78.62%	2108	2537
aplbienptb	EN	PT	TD	5-grams	0.3130	85.39%	2053	2904
aplbiesptb	ES	PT	TD	5-grams	0.3185	87.16%	2268	2904

Table 4. JHU/APL's official results for bilingual task using machine translation

Run id	Source	Target	Fields	Terms	MAP	% Mono	Rel. Found	Relevant
aplbigrena	GR	EN	TD	5-grams	0.2418	54.94%	1388	2063
aplbihuena	HU	EN	TD	5-grams	0.1944	44.17%	1363	2063
aplbiidena	ID	EN	TD	5-grams	0.3313	75.28%	1698	2063
aplbiidend	ID	EN	TD	w/s/4/5	0.3728	84.71%	1796	2063
aplbienbga	EN	BG	TD	5-grams	0.0833	26.01%	438	778
aplbienbge	EN	BG	TD	4-grams	0.0959	29.94%	423	778
aplbienhua	EN	HU	TD	5-grams	0.2235	54.35%	718	939
aplbienhue	EN	HU	TD	4-grams	0.2458	59.78%	729	939

In Bulgarian and Hungarian it seems that 4-grams may have a slight advantage over 5-grams, though additional testing should be performed to verify that the differences are statistically significant. However, the use of n-grams over raw words seems clearly indicated.

5 Conclusions

JHU/APL participated in the ad hoc tasks in the CLEF 2005 evaluation, using our language-neutral approach that prominently features character n-gram tokenization and statistical translation using aligned parallel corpora. This year we had to rely on web-based machine translation for mappings between several language pairs, for which we had been unable to obtain suitable parallel data. We compared words, a popular suffix stemmer, and n-grams of lengths four and five on the monolingual collections, all using the same retrieval engine and language model similarity metric. We found that n-grams continued to work well for monolingual retrieval, though their superiority was only apparent in Bulgarian and Hungarian. We also demonstrated that an efficient approximation to n-gram indexing that retrains only a single candidate n-gram for each word is a quite effective surrogate form of stemming.

We continued to combine runs produced through disparate retrievals, which, in the past, we have seen a modest (*e.g.,* 10% relative) improvement. This year, however, we noted that our single-best tokenization method outperformed merging of disparate runs (compare Figure 1 and the results in Table 2).

For bilingual retrieval we employed subword translation in several official runs with good effect. However we still lack parallel corpora for Bulgarian and Hungarian. We would like to expand on these experiments if we can locate appropriate data. Our results from this year agree with previous findings that character n-grams remain effective and an attractive alternative, especially in languages with complex morphology or ones in which resources (*e.g.,* morphological analyzers or stemmers) are difficult to obtain or use. Our recipe for bilingual retrieval appears effective, but is best accomplished when parallel data are available.

References

1. W. B. Cavnar and J. M. Trenkle, ‘N-Gram Based Text Categorization.’ In: *Proceedings of the Third Symposium on Document Analysis and Information Retrieval*, pp. 161-169, 1994.
2. K.W. Church, ‘Char_align: A program for aligning parallel texts at the character level.’ *Proceedings of the 31st Annual Meeting of the Association for Computational Linguistics*, pp. 1-8, 1993.
3. M. Damashek, ‘Gauging Similarity with n-grams: Language-Independent Categorization of Text.’ *Science*, 267:843-848, 1995.
4. D. Hiemstra, *Using Language Models for Information Retrieval.* Ph. D. Thesis, Center for Telematics and Information Technology, The Netherlands, 2000.
5. F. Jelinek and R. Mercer, ‘Interpolated Estimation of Markov Source Parameters from Sparse Data’. In Gelsema ES and Kanal LN eds., *Pattern Recognition in Practice*, North Holland, pp. 381-402, 1980.
6. P. Koehn, ‘Europarl: A multilingual corpus for evaluation of machine translation.’ Unpublished, http://www.isi.edu/ koehn/ publications/europarl/.
7. J. Mayfield, P. McNamee and C. Piatko, "The JHU/APL HAIRCUT System at TREC-8". In E. Voorhees and D. Harman (eds.), *Proceedings of the Eighth Text REtrieval Conference (TREC-8)*, NIST Special Publication 500-246, Gaithersburg, Maryland, 2000.
8. J. Mayfield and P. McNamee, ‘Single N-gram Stemming.’ *Proceedings of the 26th Annual International Conference on Research and Development in Information Retrieval (SIGIR-2003)*, Toronto, Ontario, pp. 415-416, July 2003.
9. P. McNamee and J. Mayfield, ‘JHU/APL Experiments in Tokenization and Non-Word Translation.’ *Working Notes of the CLEF 2003 Workshop*, pp. 19-28, 2003.
10. P. McNamee and J. Mayfield, ‘Character N-gram Tokenization for European Language Text Retrieval’. In *Information Retrieval*, 7(1-2):73-97, 2004.
11. P. McNamee and J. Mayfield, ‘Translating Pieces of Words.’ *Proceedings of the 28th Annual International Conference on Research and Development in Information Retrieval (SIGIR-2005)*, Salvador, Brazil, pp. 643-644, August 2005.

12. R. Mihalcea and V. Nastase, 'Letter Level Learning for Language Independent Diacritics Restoration.' In: *Proceedings of the 6th Conference on Natural Language Learning (CoNLL-2002)*, pp. 105-111, 2002.
13. A. Pirkola, T. Hedlund, H. Keskusalo, and K. Järvelin, 'Dictionary-Based Cross-Language Information Retrieval: Problems, Methods, and Research Findings', *Information Retrieval*, 4:209-230, 2001.
14. J. M. Ponte and W. B. Croft, 'A Language Modeling Approach to Information Retrieval.' In: *Proceedings of the 21st Annual International ACM SIGIR Conference on Research and Development in Information Retrieval*, Melbourne, Australia, pp. 275-281, 1998.
15. E. M. Zamora, J. J. Pollock, and A. Zamora, 'The Use of Trigram Analysis for Spelling Error Detection.' *Information Processing and Management 17:305-316, 1981.*
16. http://europa.eu.int/

Dublin City University at CLEF 2005: Multi-8 Two-Years-On Merging Experiments

Adenike M. Lam-Adesina and Gareth J.F. Jones

School of Computing, Dublin City University, Dublin 9, Ireland
{adenike, gjones}@computing.dcu.ie

Abstract. This year Dublin City University participated in the CLEF 2005 Mulit-8 Two-Years-On multilingual merging task. The objective of our experiments was to test a range of standard techniques for merging ranked lists of retrieved documents to see if consistent trends emerge for lists generated using different information retrieval systems. Our results show that the success of merging techniques can be dependent on the retrieval system used, and in consequence the best merging techniques to adopt cannot be recommended independent of knowing the retrieval system to be used.

1 Introduction

Multilingual information retrieval (MIR) refers to the process of retrieving relevant documents from collections in different languages in response to a user request in a single language. Standard approaches to MIR involve either translating the search topics into the document languages, performing cross-language information retrieval (CLIR), and then merging the ranked document sets produced for each language to form a single multilingual retrieved list, or translating the document collections into the expected topic language merging the translated collections, and then effectively performing monolingual information retrieval in the topic language. In CLEF 2003 we showed that translating the document collections into the topic language using a standard machine translation system and then merging them to form a single collection for retrieval, can result in better retrieval performance than translating the topics and then merging after CLIR retrieval [1]. However, document translation is not always practical, particularly if the collection is very large or the translation resources are limited. For MIR using topic translation and merging retrieved lists of potentially relevant documents, the different statistics of the individual collections and the varied topic translations mean that the scores of documents in the separate lists will generally be incompatible, and thus that merging is a non-trivial process.

The CLEF 2005 Multilingual merging task aims to encourage researchers to focus directly on the merging problem. Retrieval results for merged collections of noisy document translations illustrate the level of retrieval effectiveness that is possible for MIR tasks. Many CLIR experiments using topic translation have demonstrated high levels of effectiveness relative to monolingual information retrieval for individual languages. The challenge for merging is to reliably achieve similar or better MIR by combining CLIR results, than using a single combined collection of translated documents.

C. Peters et al. (Eds.): CLEF 2005, LNCS 4022, pp. 165 – 169, 2006.

Merging strategies explored previously for multilingual retrieval tasks at CLEF and elsewhere have generally produced disappointing results. Previously standardised evaluation tasks incorporating multilingual merging have been combined with the document retrieval stage. It has thus not been possible to distinguish quality of retrieval from the effectiveness of merging, or any dependency between the retrieval methods adopted and the most effective merging algorithm. The idea of the CLEF 2005 merging task is to explore the merging of provided precomputed ranked lists to enable direct comparison of the behaviour of merging strategies between different retrieval systems.

Many different techniques for merging separate result lists to form a single list have been proffered and tested in recent years. All of the techniques suggest that making an assumption that the distribution of relevant documents in the results sets of retrieval from individual collections is similar is not true [2]. Hence, straight merging of relevant documents from the sources will result in poor combination. However, none of the proposed more complex merging techniques have really been demonstrated to be consistently effective.

For our participation in the merging track at CLEF 2005 we applied a range of standard merging strategies to the two provided sets of ranked lists. Our aim was to compare the behaviour of these methods for the two sets of ranked documents in order to learn something about concepts that might be consistently useful or poor when merging ranked lists.

This paper is organized as follows: Section 2 overviews the merging techniques explored in this paper, Section 3 gives our experimental results, and Section 4 draws conclusions and considers strategies for further experimentation.

2 Merging Strategies

The aim of a merging strategy for MIR is to include as many relevant documents at the highest ranks in the merged list as possible. This section overviews the merging strategies used in our experiments. The basic idea is to modify the scored weight of each retrieved document to take account of the characteristics of the retrieval methods used to generate it, or the collection from which it has been retrieved to improve the compatibility of scores before combining the lists.

This score adjustment may take account of factors such as maximum and/or minimum matching scores in each list, or the distribution of matching scores in each list. Another factor available is to select documents for inclusion in the combined list in proportion to the relative size of the collections from which they are drawn. This works on the assumption that similar relative number of relevant documents will be found in each collection. While the process for search topic generation for the multilingual CLEF tasks mean that this will often be a reasonable assumption for these tasks, it will more however often not be the case for many topics in working systems. We include exploration of all these factors to explore their effectiveness for multilingual merging in CLEF tasks.

The schemes used in our experiments were as follows:

$$p = doc\_wgt$$

$$t = doc\_wgt * rank$$

$$d = \frac{doc\_wgt - \min\_wt}{\max\_wt - \min\_wt}$$

$$r = (\frac{doc\_wgt - \min\_wt}{\max\_wt - \min\_wt}) * rank$$

$$q = (\frac{doc\_wgt - g\min\_wt}{g\max\_wt - g\min\_wt}) * rank$$

$$b = \frac{doc\_wgt - \min\_wt}{\max\_wt - \min\_wt * rank}$$

$$m1 = (\frac{doc\_wgt - gmean\_wt}{gstd\_wt}) + (\frac{gmean\_wt - g\min\_wgt}{gstd\_wt})$$

$$m2 = (m1) * rank$$

doc_wgt = the initial document weight
gmax_wt = the global maximum weight, i.e. the highest document weight from all collections for a given query
gmin_wt = the global minimum weight, i.e. the lowest document weight from all collections for a given query
gmean_wt = the global median weight, i.e. the mean document weight from all collections for a given query,

$$gmean\_wt = \frac{\sum_{i=0}^{n} doc\_wgt_i}{totdocs}$$

totdocs = total number of retrieved documents per query across all retrieval methods
max_wt = the individual collection maximum weight for a given query
min_wt = the individual collection minimum weight for a given query
gstd_wt = the standard deviation weight calculated as,

$$\sqrt{\frac{1}{n-1}\sum_{i=1}^{n}(doc\_wgt_i - gmean\_wt)^2}$$

rank = a parameter to control the effect of size of collection - a collection with more documents gets a higher rank (value ranges between 1 and 1.5).

where *p, t, d, r, q, b, m1 and m2* are the new document weight for all documents in all collections, and the results are labelled with the appropriate letter for the new document weight used.

Method *p* is used as a baseline using the raw document scores from the retrieved lists without modification. A useful merging scheme should be expected to improve on the performance of the *p* scheme. The *rank* factor was adjusted empirically using the 20 training topics provided for the merging task.

3 Experimental Results

Results for our experiments using these merging schemes are shown in Tables 1 and 2. Our official submissions to CLEF 2005 are marked *.

Tables 1 and 2 show merging results using CLIR runs provided by Hummingbird and the University of Neuchâtel respectively. Results are shown for precision at cutoff of

Table 1. Merging results using the provided Hummingbird ranked lists

Run-id	P10	% chg.	P30	% chg.	MAP	% chg.	Rel. Ret.	chg.
dcu.hump*	0.518	-	0.396	-	0.2086	-	2982	-
dcu.humd	0.373	-28.0	0.347	-12.4	0.1775	-14.9	2965	-17
dcu.humr	0.455	-12.1	0.364	-8.0	0.1932	-7.4	2964	-18
dcu.humq	0.4576	-11.6	0.363	-8.2	0.2005	-3.9	2752	-230
dcu.humb	0.320	-32.2	0.293	-26.1	0.1596	-23.5	2950	-32
dcu.humt*	0.408	-21.3	0.328	-17.3	0.1734	-16.9	2442	-540
dcu.humm1*	0.480	-7.2	0.382	-3.6	0.1988	-4.7	2873	-109
dcu.humm2*	0.465	-10.1	0.363	-8.4	0.1846	-11.5	2846	-136

Table 2. Merging results using the provided Prosit ranked lists from the University of Neuchâtel

Run-id	P10	% chg.	P30	% chg.	MAP	% chg.	Rel. Ret.	chg.
dcu.Prositqgp*	0.450	-	0.446	-	0.3103	-	4404	-
dcu.Prositqgd	0.485	+7.7	0.444	-0.4	0.2931	-5.5	4552	+148
dcu.Prositqgr	0.495	+10.0	0.446	0.0	0.3011	-3.0	4544	+140
dcu.Prositqgq	0.465	+3.3	0.446	+0.1	0.3192	+2.9	4469	+65
dcu.Prositqgb	0.472	+5.0	0.441	-1.1	0.2834	-8.7	4538	+134
dcu.Prositqgt*	0.460	+2.2	0.446	0.0	0.3201	+3.2	4477	+73
dcu.Prositqgm1*	0.475	+5.6	0.459	+3.0	0.3241	+4.5	4486	+82
dcu.Prositqgm2*	0.470	+4.4	0.461	+3.4	0.3286	+5.9	4512	+108

10 and 30 documents, Mean Average Precision (MAP) and the total number of relevant documents retrieved. The raw score merging scheme *p* is taken as a baseline and changes for each scheme are shown for each data set with respect to the reported metrics.

The most obvious results are that the more complex merging schemes are shown in Table 2 to generally improve performance by a small amount for the Prosit data, but in Table 1 in all cases reduce performance for the Hummingbird data with respect to both the precision measures and the number of relevant retrieved. This appears to offer an answer to one of the questions associated with the CLEF merging task, namely whether the same merging techniques will always be found to be effective for different sets of ranked lists for a common merging task generated using alternative information retrieval systems. The reasons for this difference in behaviour need to be investigated. This analysis will hopefully provide insights into the selection of appropriate merging strategies or the development of merging strategies which will operate more consistently when merging different sets of ranked lists. There are some other observations of consistent behaviour which can be made be. It can be seen that there is no consistent relationship between the variation in precision measures and the number of relevant documents retrieved for the different merging schemes. Schemes with better precision can be accompanied by lower relevant retrieved and vice versa. This is most notable for the *b* results where good relevant retrieved (in relative terms) is accompanied by a large reduction in MAP for both data sets.

4 Conclusions

Results of our merging experiments for CLEF 2005 indicate that the behaviour of merging schemes varies for different sets of ranked lists. The reasons for this behaviour are not obvious, and further analysis is planned to attempt to better understand this behaviour as a basis for the extension of these techniques for merging or the proposal of new ones.

References

1. Di Nunzio, G.M., Ferro, N, and Jones, G.J.F.: CLEF 2005: Multilingual Track Overview, Proceedings of the CLEF 2005: Workshop on Cross-Language Information Retrieval and Evaluation, Vienna, Austria, 2005.
2. Lam-Adesina, A.M. and Jones, G.J.F.: Exeter at CLEF 2003: Experiments with Machine Translation for Monolingual, Bilingual and Multilingual Retrieval, Proceedings of the CLEF 2003 Workshop on Cross-Language Information Retrieval and Evaluation, Trondheim, Norway, pages 271-285, 2003.
3. Savoy, J.: Report on CLEF-2003 Multilingual Tracks, Proceedings of the CLEF 2003 Workshop on Cross-Language Information Retrieval and Evaluation, Trondheim, Norway, pages 64-73, 2003.

Applying Light Natural Language Processing to Ad-Hoc Cross Language Information Retrieval

Christina Lioma, Craig Macdonald, Ben He,
Vassilis Plachouras, and Iadh Ounis

University of Glasgow, G12 8QQ, UK
{xristina, craigm, ben, vassilis, ounis}@dcs.gla.ac.uk

Abstract. In the CLEF 2005 Ad-Hoc Track we addressed the problem of retrieving information in morphologically rich languages, by experimenting with language-specific morphosyntactic processing and light Natural Language Processing (NLP). The diversity of the languages processed, namely Bulgarian, French, Italian, English, and Greek, allowed us to measure the effect of system-specific features upon the retrieval of these languages, and to juxtapose that effect to the role of language resources in Cross Language Information Retrieval (CLIR) in general.

1 Introduction

The driving force behind our participation in CLEF 2005 has been to explore the effect of morphologically rich languages across a set Information Retrieval (IR) platform, in terms of system-specific features and language resources. From the outset it was anticipated that this effect would be considerable, not only from a computational perspective, i.e. technical implementation issues involving character encodings, but most importantly with reference to the availability and quality of language resources provided for the said languages, such as stemmers and lexica.

This year's language selection formed a representative sample of some of the major branches of the IndoEuropean family of languages, spanning from the Slavonic branch, to the Latin, the Germanic, and even the Hellenic branch. We used the same retrieval platform as reported in CLEF 2004 [6], on top of which we added selective language-specific Natural Language Processing (NLP).

This paper is organised as follows. Section 2 presents an overview of the linguistic foundations of this work, with special note being made to the language processing approaches adopted. Section 3 presents and discusses our monolingual and bilingual runs. Section 4 concludes with a summary of the approaches tested and the extent of their success.

2 Linguistic Background

Natural Language Processing is considered essential to the retrieval of highly inflectional languages, of rich morphology and syntax. The validity of this statement has been tested for Greek-English IR. Moreover, noun phrase extraction,

C. Peters et al. (Eds.): CLEF 2005, LNCS 4022, pp. 170–178, 2006.

a popular NLP application that purports to capture constituent structure, and thus add an extra dimension to the conceptual content of a given text as rendered by single words, has been put to the test for monolingual French and bilingual Italian-French retrieval. Noun phrase identification and extraction has been realised using our in-house Noun Phrase (NP) extractor, which identifies noun phrases on the basis of their syntactic features alone, and independently of corpus statistics. The said NP extractor, which can currently process English, French, Italian, and German, is designed to target both nested and discontinuous noun phrases, with an adjustable maximum thershold of terms allowed between members of a broken noun phrase, and no limitations with regards to the length of a given noun phrase.

Additional NLP applications utilised in the context of this work include light syntactic analysis, achieved by a probabilistic part-of-speech (POS) tagger, lemmatisation, and morphological analysis [10,14]. Unfortunately, the unavailability of such technology for Bulgarian meant that only French, Italian, English, and Greek were subjected to this type of examination. The part-of-speech tagsets used for the aforementioned languages adhere to the Penn TreeBank Tagset conventions [7], with a few exceptions. These exceptions stem from the fact that languages are not always syntactically isomorphic. The collective part-of-speech tags used are presented in Table 1. The initials in square brackets relate to the specific language to which the said tags are exclusive. DE, EN, FR, GR and IT stand for German, English, French, Greek and Italian respectively. The class distinction refers to the linguistic distinction between function words and content words [4]. Tags falling under the closed class are assigned to words bearing very little to nil content. Such words are peripheral to the semantic load of their environment, and exist mainly to modify and/or regulate a given sentence. These are the types of words usually representing noise in the context of IR, and normally excluded from the index via stopword lists. Open class tags, on the other hand, are, by and large, associated to the main content carriers, which are the most likely to satisfy the information need. These types of words are often morphologically productive, through inflection, conjugation, and so on, creating thus an extra hurdle to the retrieval of information. This type of problem is commonly addressed by stemming.

3 Monolingual and Bilingual Runs

The main motivation behind our participation in CLEF 2005 was to examine the performance of a set IR platform across an interesting span of lexically and morphosyntactically dissimilar languages, by revealing the extent to which retrieval models and system tuning issues are accountable for the performance of IR on a per language basis, and subsequently pay due heed to the role of language resources in the retrieval of the said languages.

We used our existing retrieval platform, which accommodates a range of matching models and a strong query expansion baseline [6]. Specifically, for the matching process, we selected the models BM25 [9], TF-IDF, as well as the

Table 1. Part-of-Speech Tagset and Class Classification

POS	Tag	Class	POS	Tag	Class
Abbreviation	ABR	Open	Ordinal Number	ORD	Closed
Adjective	JJ	Open	Possessive Ending [EN]	POS	Closed
Adverb	RB	Open	Possessive Wh-Pronoun	WP$	Closed
Auxiliary Verb	MD	Closed	Postposition [DE, GR]	POSTP	Closed
Cardinal Number	CD	Closed	Predeterminer	PDT	Closed
Conjunction	CC	Closed	Preposition	IN	Closed
Determiner	DT	Closed	Preposition with Article [FR, GR, IT]	ORD	Closed
Digit	DIG	Closed	Proclitic Noun Modifier [GR, IT]	PRN	Closed
Existentialist "there" [EN]	EX	Closed	Pronoun	PP	Closed
Foreign Word	FW	Open	Proper Noun	NP	Open
Future Tense Particle [GR]	FUT	Closed	Quantifier [GR, IT]	QUANT	Closed
Interjection	UH	Closed	Special Preposition "to"	TO	Closed
List Item Marker	LS	Closed	Subjunctive Particle [GR]	SUBJ	Closed
Main Verb	VV	Open	Symbol	SYM	Closed
Modal Verb	MD	Closed	Truncated Word	TR	Open
Negation Particle [FR, GR]	NEG	Closed	Wh-Adverb [EN]	WRB	Closed
Noun	NN	Open	Wh-Determiner [EN]	WDT	Closed

following Divergence from Randomness (DFR) models [1]: InexpB2, InexpC2, PL2, and DLH. For query expansion, we opted for Bo1 and Bo2 [1,8]. With the exception of the non-parametric weighting model DLH, the parameter setting of our models was realised on an empirical basis. Specifically, the matching model parameters, namely c for the DFR models, and b for BM25, were set as follows. For Bulgarian and English-Bulgarian, $c = 1.5$ and $b = 1$; for English and Greek-English, $c = 1.15$ and $b = 1$; for French and Italian-French, $c = 1$ and $b = 1$. Similarly, the query expansion *terms*/*documents*(t/d) ratio was set as follows. For Bulgarian, $t/d = 25/5$; for English-Bulgarian, $t/d = 30/5$; for English and Greek-English, $t/d = 20/5$; for French, $t/d = 20/5$; for Italian-French, $t/d = 30/5$. This manifold of matching and expansion models was implemented in our Terrier retrieval platform [8].

We received our baptism of fire with Bulgarian and Greek, both of which share enough morphosyntactic and lexical complexity between them to render the need for language processing resources absolutely imperative.

Bulgarian is a Slavonic language, marked by its rich morphology and syntax, as well as by the strong lexical influence of Old Slavonic [2]. The lack of language processing resources meant that the collection was simply stemmed and indexed, without any supplementary morphosyntactic analysis. This is highly unfortunate, as even the simplest syntactic analysis could have provided the most interesting insights into the content distribution for Bulgarian. The lack of a working Bulgarian stemmer meant that stemming was realised using the Russian version of the freely available Snowball stemmer [12]. For the English - Bulgarian retrieval, the freely available Skycode machine translation system was used to translate text between the two languages [11]. The performance of the above Bulgarian and English - Bulgarian runs is summarised in Table 2. The top row relates to the topic fields used in each run, while the first column informs as

Table 2. Bulgarian and English-Bulgarian Mean Average Precision (MAP)

		Title+Description			Title+Description+Narrative		
	Model	BG	EN-BG	% mono	BG	EN-BG	% mono
Query Expansion False	BM25	0.2360	**0.1337**	56.65%	0.2174	0.1392	64.03%
	DLH	0.2211	*0.1290*	58.34%	0.2036	0.1316	64.64%
	InexpB2	0.2410	0.1266	52.53%	0.2202	0.1392	63.21%
	InexpC2	**0.2436**	0.1305	53.57%	**0.2268**	**0.1455**	64.15%
	PL2	0.2363	0.1294	54.76%	0.2203	*0.1344*	61.01%
	TF-IDF	0.2338	0.1326	56.71%	0.2173	0.1385	63.74%
Query Expansion True	BM25	**0.2662**	0.1718	64.54%	**0.2576**	**0.1864**	72.36%
	DLH	0.2409	0.1534	63.68%	0.2277	*0.1668*	73.25%
	InexpB2	0.2461	0.1538	62.49%	0.2419	0.1731	71.56%
	InexpC2	0.2618	0.1640	62.64%	0.2457	0.1846	75.13%
	PL2	*0.2514*	0.1685	67.02%	*0.2412*	*0.1799*	74.58%
	TF-IDF	0.2658	**0.1732**	65.16%	0.2574	0.1860	72.26%

to whether query expansion was used or not. BG indicates monolingual Bulgarian runs, and $EN-BG$ indicates bilingual English-Bulgarian runs. The column headed $\%mono$ relates to the difference between the monolingual and bilingual performance of corresponding runs. Submitted runs are printed in italics, and optimal runs appear in boldface.

The figures displayed in Table 2 reveal the powerful modifying influence of translation on retrieval performance, which appears to be even stronger for shorter and unexpanded topics. The overall performance of the collective matching models remains coherent throughout, as confirmed by the absence of any sharp score fluctuations. This relative stability and uniformity delineates the need for additional language processing resources for Bulgarian, the evidence of which would weigh more heavily on retrieval performance than that of simple stemming.

The second newcomer in our selection of languages was Greek, a highly inflectional Hellenic language [5]. The complexity of addressing a language as morphologically rich as Greek was accentuated by the stark lack of stemming resources. This problem received a clean treatment with the employment of a rigorous part-of-speech tagger and morphological analyser for Greek, developed by Xerox [14]. For each term in the topics, the corresponding part-of-speech and lemma was produced. When faced with two alternatives, both were selected. Closed class terms (Table 1) were rejected to reduce noise, while lemmas were automatically translated into English using Babelfish machine translation technology [3]. The performance of these runs, contrasted to their equivalent English monolingual equivalents, is presented in Table 3, in a layout similar to the one described for Table 2.

The scores presented in Table 3 are analogous to the scores relating to Bulgarian retrieval in Table 2, confirming the considerable effect of translation on the performance of the bilingual runs. Even so, the overall retrieval scores for Greek-English retrieval are significantly closer to their monolingual equivalent

Table 3. English and Greek-English Mean Average Precision (MAP)

		Title+Description			Title+Description+Narrative		
	Model	EN	GR-EN	% mono	EN	GR-EN	% mono
Query Expansion False	BM25	**0.4255**	**0.2930**	68.86%	0.4255	0.2240	52.64%
	DLH	0.4089	0.2802	68.52%	0.4089	0.2149	52.55%
	InexpB2	0.4115	0.2724	66.20%	**0.4303**	*0.2295*	53.55%
	InexpC2	0.3851	0.2758	71.62%	0.4268	**0.2386**	55.90%
	PL2	0.3634	0.2574	70.83%	0.4042	0.2126	52.60%
	TF-IDF	0.4240	0.2888	68.11%	0.4240	0.2229	52.57%
Query Expansion True	BM25	0.4556	0.3151	69.16%	0.4556	0.3151	69.16%
	DLH	0.4561	0.3128	68.58%	0.4561	0.3128	68.58%
	InexpB2	0.4307	*0.2935*	68.14%	0.4433	0.3117	70.31%
	InexpC2	0.3923	0.2678	68.49%	0.4301	0.3088	71.80%
	PL2	0.3961	0.2488	62.81%	0.4347	0.2838	65.29%
	TF-IDF	**0.4671**	**0.3168**	67.82%	**0.4671**	**0.3168**	67.82%

runs, than the overall English - Bulgarian scores are to the monolingual Bulgarian scores. This comparison underlines the auxiliary service rendered to the Greek topics by the employment of morphological analysis and lemmatisation. The performance of the bilingual Greek-English runs is in complete agreement with our primary tenet that the automatic processing of more or less recondite languages, such as Greek, cannot be entirely successful without being "aided and abetted" by some sort of morphosyntactic analysis. Stemming has been widely used in retrieval to account for this need, but it should be considered neither complete nor unique as an answer. Light syntactic analysis and lemmatisation have been shown to assist retrieval with success. Nevertheless, in order to have a measure of the relation between stemming and lemmatisation, further experimentation is needed, which would juxtapose the effect of the said methods on Greek-English retrieval.

The method used for French retrieval consisted of a variation to the monolingual French strategy tested in CLEF 2004 [6]. We opted for a less aggressive stemming approach, which targets mainly inflectional variants. Additionally, a probabilistic part-of-speech tagger [10] provided a pellucid syntactic analysis of the topics. Closed class tokens (Table 1) were removed to reduce noise. Noun phrases were extracted using the NP extractor described in the preceding section. In the case of Italian - French retrieval, Italian noun phrases were extracted and translated separately into French, using the freely available Worldlingo machine translation system [13]. The performance of the French monolingual and bilingual runs, both with the above mentioned language processing (POS - NP true) and without (POS - NP false), is presented in Table 4. Submitted runs are printed in italics, and optimal runs appear in boldface.

Table 4 reveals that the combination of part-of-speech analysis and noun phrase extraction (POS NP) is associated with better retrieval performance at all times. A point of interest is that this combination appears to benefit monolingual retrieval more than it assists bilingual retrieval. This can be deduced by the fact

Table 4. French and Italian-French Mean Average Precision (MAP)

			Title+Description			Title+Description+Narrative		
		Model	FR	IT-FR	% mono	FR	IT-FR	% mono
POS NP True	Query Expansion False	BM25	0.3199	0.2068	64.58%	0.3316	**0.2334**	70.39%
		DLH	**0.3228**	*0.2066*	64.00%	**0.3371**	0.2305	68.38%
		InexpB2	0.3171	0.2011	63.42%	0.3274	0.2245	68.57%
		InexpC2	0.3098	0.1984	64.04%	0.3198	0.2212	69.17%
		PL2	0.3092	0.2070	66.95%	*0.3206*	*0.2291*	71.46%
		TF-IDF	0.3195	**0.2073**	64.88%	0.3300	0.2328	70.54%
	Query Expansion True	BM25	0.3702	0.2763	74.63%	0.3761	0.2941	78.20%
		DLH	***0.4017***	0.2731	67.99%	**0.4198**	0.3029	72.15%
		InexpB2	0.3569	0.2444	68.48%	0.3596	0.2734	76.03%
		InexpC2	0.3480	0.2435	69.97%	0.3527	0.2676	75.87%
		PL2	*0.3765*	0.2626	69.75%	0.3809	*0.2883*	75.69%
		TF-IDF	0.3718	**0.2769**	74.47%	0.3778	**0.3045**	80.60%
POS NP False	Query Expansion False	BM25	0.3013	0.2025	67.21%	0.3083	0.2246	72.85%
		DLH	0.3007	0.1978	65.78%	0.3042	0.2184	71.79%
		InexpB2	**0.3027**	0.1976	65.28%	**0.3144**	0.2209	70.26%
		InexpC2	0.2961	0.1954	65.99%	0.3072	0.2179	70.93%
		PL2	0.2921	**0.2028**	69.43%	0.2976	0.2218	74.53%
		TF-IDF	0.3024	0.2023	66.90%	0.3087	**0.2255**	73.05%
	Query Expansion True	BM25	0.3575	0.2722	76.14%	0.3592	0.2876	80.07%
		DLH	0.3530	0.2584	73.20%	**0.3823**	**0.3015**	78.86%
		InexpB2	0.3576	0.2486	69.52%	0.3557	0.2928	82.32%
		InexpC2	0.3421	0.2425	70.88%	0.3432	0.2781	81.03%
		PL2	0.3469	0.2566	73.97%	0.3606	0.2843	78.84%
		TF-IDF	**0.3578**	**0.2748**	76.80%	0.3661	0.2989	81.64%

that the difference between the monolingual and bilingual runs is higher when POS NP is used (29.58% on average), than when it is not (26.78% on average), at all times. This observation is indicative of the fact that even though light NLP can be of significant assistance to IR, it cannot counter the shortcomings of insufficient translation resources.

The NP extractor presented above was evaluated as follows. Noun phrases were identified manually. For each noun phrase that was identified correctly by the NP extractor, a single point was added to the evaluation score. For each noun phrase that was not identified by the NP extractor, or for each non-noun phrase that was wrongly identified as a noun phrase by the NP extractor, a point was deducted. The final score of the NP extractor was compared to the manual score. Overall, the NP extractor was shown to be 88.4% accurate at identifying and extracting noun phrases for the French CLEF 2005 topic set, and 88.8% for the English. More importantly, the relation between the identification and extraction of noun phrases and the overall retrieval precision was found to be statistically significant, as per the Wilcoxon Matched-Pairs Signed-Rank Test ($p\text{-}value = 7.821e^{-10}$). Figure 1 illustrates this conclusion.

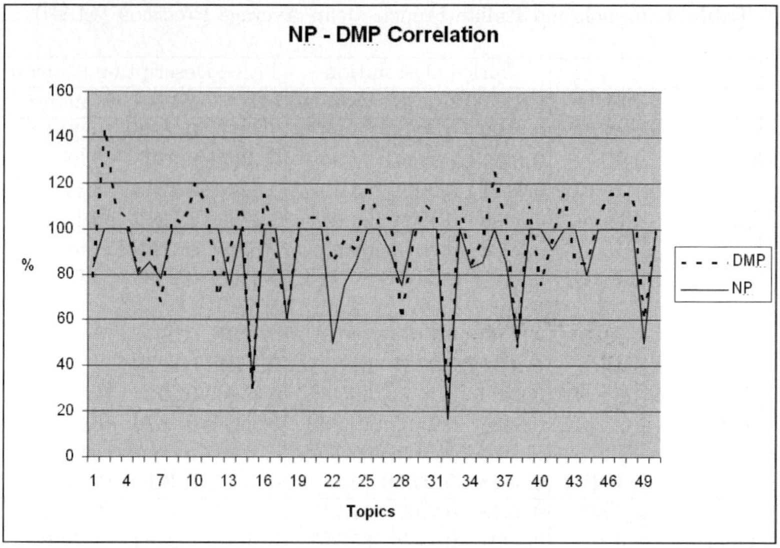

Fig. 1. Noun Phrase (NP) Extraction vs Difference from Median Precision (DMP) for French Monolingual IR

Figure 1 graphically displays the performance of the NP extractor and the difference from the median precision for our best-scoring French monolingual run as follows. The x-axis relates to the individual topics, while the y-axis relates to the percentage of the difference of firstly, the NP Extractor score from the manual score, for the NP Extractor, and secondly, the difference between the precision our best-scoring French run and the Median Precision score of all corresponding submitted runs. The said comparison throws light to the direct and strong link between the extraction of noun phrases and the overall retrieval precision, especially with respect to the median precision. Noun phrase extraction is an acknowledged procedure, and applying it to IR seems an obvious extension, without however making it the supreme arbiter. Further investigation would be required to ascertain the causal nexus between noun phrase extraction and retrieval precision.

As a conclusion, a note should be made with regards to the general performance of our retrieval platform for Bulgarian, Greek, English, French, and Italian. Figure 2 graphically plots the Mean Average Precision score (y-axis) achieved by each matching model employed for each language, or language combination, described in this paper. From the data exhibited in Figure 2, it becomes evident that runs, as clustered by language, tend to favour and disfavour specific models. Hence, DLH provides satisfying results for monolingual French retrieval. BM25, TF-IDF, and PL2 remain consistent throughout. Very frequently, the performance of all six matching models overlaps, and especially so in the case of bilingual runs. System stability aside, this trend emphasises the stultifying effect of translation on retrieval performance, as, in all cases, the overlap consists of

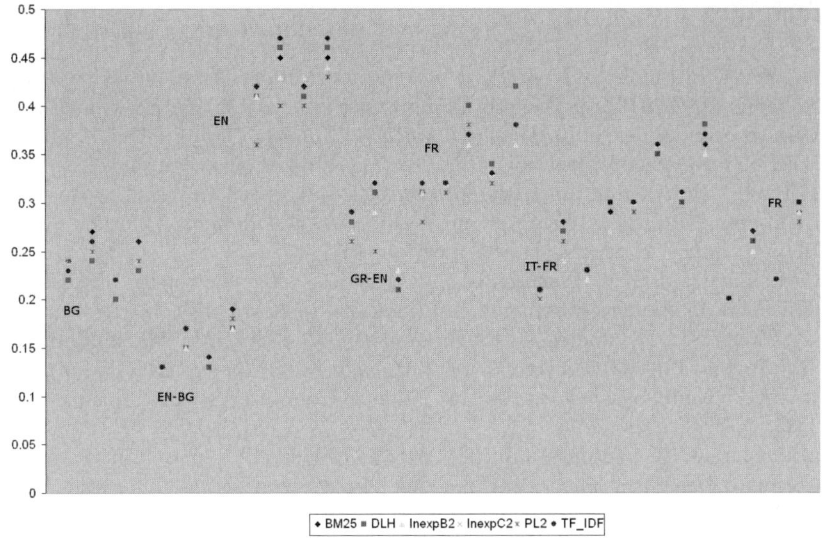

Fig. 2. Comparison of Matching Models per Language

a drop, rather than an increase of score. These results confirm the suitability of our retrieval platform for the retrieval of the aforementioned languages. In addition, they support our research scope that the poor quality and/or lack of suitable language resources for morphologically rich languages has formed an exigent set of circumstances, which cannot be addressed solely by conventional system-specific issues, such as model tuning, query expansion, and so on.

4 Conclusion

Our participation in the CLEF 2005 Ad-Hoc track for Bulgarian, English-Bulgarian, French, Italian-French, and Greek-English retrieval was shown to be successful, with a difference from the Median Precision of the collective submitted runs ranging between +1.135 (for Bulgarian) and +7.830 (for English - Greek), thus scoring second place in the English-Bulgarian and Greek-English retrieval, and third place in the monolingual French retrieval. On a collective basis, poor or no language resources were at all times associated with consistently low retrieval performance. On an individual basis, lemmatisation was shown to be a satisfactory replacement of stemming for Greek, while noun phrase extraction was shown to benefit retrieval directly and consistently for French and Italian-French. We have shown that light morphosyntactic processing can assist the retrieval of information for highly inflectional languages, and by doing so, we have carried our initial contention *a posse ad esse* successfully.

References

1. G. Amati. *Probabilistic Models for Information Retrieval based on Divergence from Randomness.* PhD thesis, Dept of Computing Science, University of Glasgow, 2003.
2. H.I. Aronson. *Bulgarian Inflectional Morphophonology.* Mouton, The Hague, 1968.
3. Babelfish Machine Translation. URL: http://babelfish.altavista.com/.
4. L. Bauer. *Introducing Linguistic Morphology.* Edinburgh University Press, 1988.
5. B. Joseph, I. Philippaki-Warburton. *Modern Greek: A Linguist's Grammar.* Croom Helm (Lingua Descriptive Series), London, 1987.
6. C. Lioma, B. He, V. Plachouras and I. Ounis. The University of Glasgow at CLEF 2004: French Monolingual Information Retrieval with Terrier. In Peters, C., Clough, P. D., Jones, G. F. J., Gonzalo, J., Kluck, M., Magnini, B. (eds.): *Multilingual Information Access for Text, Speech and Images: Results of the Fifth CLEF Evaluation Campaign.* Lecture Notes in Computer Science, Springer-Verlag, 2005.
7. M.P. Marcus, B. Santorini and M.A. Marcinkiewicz. Building a Large Annotated Corpus for English: The Penn Treebank. In *Computational Linguistics*, Volume 19, Number 2, pp. 313–330, 1993.
8. I. Ounis, G. Amati, V. Plachouras, B. He, C. Macdonald, and D. Johnson. Terrier Information Retrieval Platform. In *Proceedings of ECIR 2005*, LNCS vol. 3408, pp. 517–519, 2005. URL: http://ir.dcs.gla.ac.uk/terrier/.
9. S.E. Robertson. Okapi at TREC-3. In Harman, D. K. (eds.): *Overview of the Third Text Retrieval Conference (TREC-3)*, NIST, 2005.
10. H. Schmidt. Probabilistic Part-of-Speech Tagging Using Decision Trees. In Jones, D., Somers, H. (eds.): *New Methods in Language Processing Studies.* Computational Linguistics, UCL Press, 1997.
11. Skycode Machine Translation. URL: http://webtrance.skycode.com/online.asp/
12. Snowball stemmers. URL: http://snowball.tartarus.org/.
13. Worldlingo Machine Translation. URL: http://www.worldlingo.com/.
14. Xerox Greek Language Analysis. URL: http://www/xrce.xerox.com/competencies/content-analysis/demos/greek/

Four Stemmers and a Funeral: Stemming in Hungarian at CLEF 2005

Anna Tordai[1] and Maarten de Rijke[2]

[1] Informatics Institute, University of Amsterdam
Kruislaan 403, 1098 SJ Amsterdam
atordai
[2] mdr@science.uva.nl

Abstract. We developed algorithmic stemmers for Hungarian and used them for the ad-hoc monolingual task for CLEF 2005. Our goal was to determine what degree of stemming is the most effective. Although on average the stemmers did not perform as well as the the best n-gram, we found that stemming over a broad range of suffixes especially on nouns is highly useful.

1 Introduction

In our participation in the CLEF ad-hoc task this year, we focused exclusively on monolingual retrieval for Hungarian. This is the first year Hungarian is part of CLEF, and it is an ideal opportunity to test our work on the effects of stemming in Hungarian. Previous work on languages that are morphologically richer than English, such as Finnish, indicate that there should be benefits from morphological analysis such as stemming, lemmatization, and compound analysis [4, 5, 6]. We have developed a number of suffix-stripping algorithms of varying impact, all focusing on inflectional suffixes. Our goal is to determine the degree of stemming that would prove beneficial for retrieval effectiveness in terms of both precision and recall. We expect to see improvements in recall for all stemmers, but in addition, we hope that our "light" stemmers keep precision at an acceptable level. The "heavy" stemmer we developed is also expected to improve recall, but hurt precision.

The paper is organized as follows. Section 2 describes the traits of the Hungarian language that are important from an information retrieval point of view. Section 3 contains a description of the algorithmic stemmers along with an evaluation. Section 4 describes the retrieval system we used. Section 5 concerns the experiments we performed, finally followed by a conclusion in Section 6.

2 Hungarian Morphology

Hungarian is an agglutinative language remotely related to Finnish and Estonian, and a member of the Ob-Ugric languages [8]. The Hungarian language is highly inflectional, rich in compound words, and has an extensive inflectional

C. Peters et al. (Eds.): CLEF 2005, LNCS 4022, pp. 179–186, 2006.

and derivational morphology. To illustrate this, nouns have 16 to 24 cases depending on the classification system. By adding person, number and possession, a single noun may have as many as 1400 forms [3]. Adjectives similarly may have around 2700 different forms. Verbs have fewer forms, with person, number, tense and transitivity adding up to 59. These numbers merely illustrate the inflectional variety of the language. Additionally, there is an extensive system of derivational suffixes, many of them changing the part of speech of a word.

Compound words are frequent in Hungarian, presenting an additional challenge for retrieval. Compound nouns can be formed by two nouns or a participle and a noun. Adjectives can also be formed by the combination of a noun and adjective. Compounding was not addressed at this time.

3 Algorithmic Stemmers

In this section we describe and evaluate the stemmers used in our retrieval experiments.

3.1 Description of the Stemmers

The stemmers were built in the Snowball language [11] and are rule-based stemmers focusing on inflectional suffixes in Hungarian. Using the Szeged Corpus [1], which is a collection of annotated texts ranging from novels, children's essays, legal texts, newspaper articles to computer books, we created a list of the most frequent types of morphosyntactic tags. This helped to determine which suffixes appear most often in the text and guided the construction of the stemmers.

We developed four types of stemmers:

- *Light1* – handling frequent noun cases, plural and frequent owners.
- *Light2* – handling all noun cases, plural and frequent owners.
- *Medium* – handling frequent noun cases, plural, frequent owners and frequent verb tenses.
- *Heavy* – handling most inflectional suffixes.

The lightest stemmer, *Light1*, only handles 14 frequent noun cases, plural and the most frequent possessive cases. It is the least invasive stemmer but we think it will still have a significant impact. Of all the nouns in the Szeged corpus 26% were in uninflected form. The most frequent types of suffixes cover 36% of the nouns. These were the ones targeted by *Light1* with the exception of the single letter suffix 'k' indicating plurality. Even without it, at least half of all nouns should be indexed in their stem form. Since adjectives have the same case, number and possession suffixes as nouns, they also become stemmed along with numerals which also share a number of cases with nouns.

The second stemmer, *Light2*, is similar to *Light1* except it handles 21 noun cases instead of just 14. Also removing single letter suffixes such as the accusative 't' and superessive 'n'. The *Light1* and *Light2* stemmers both take word length into account, making sure the remainder is at least a valid vowel-consonant combination.

The third stemmer, *Medium*, removes 12 frequent noun cases, plural, possession and combinations of ownership and plurality. It also handles frequent verb tense-person-number combinations as well as the degree of adjectives. Suffixes forming ordinals and fractions out of numerals were removed.

The last stemmer, *Heavy*, is the most aggressive, removing 21 noun cases, handling plurality and possession. For verbs it handles infinitive, indicative, conditional and subjunctive moods.

3.2 Evaluating the Stemming Algorithms

The stemmers were evaluated both intrinsically and extrinsically. For the intrinsic evaluation, we used Paice's method based on error counting [9]. According to this method, two values determine the quality of a stemmer: *understemming* and *overstemming*. In order to determine these values, a list of words is separated into conceptual groups formed by semantically and morphologically related words. This is the target, and an ideal stemmer should conflate words to these conceptual groups.

The stemmers were used to stem the word list, and following the Paice method their correspondence to the conceptual groups was measured. This resulted in an understemming (UI) and overstemming measure (OI). To determine the general relative accuracy of the stemmers, we use a measure, called *error rate relative to truncation*, or ERRT. It is useful for deciding on the best overall stemmer in cases where one stemmer is better in terms of understemming but worse in terms of overstemming. To calculate the ERRT we created a baseline using length truncation by reducing the words in the world list to their n first letters where n was 9, 10, 11 and 12. The overstemming and understemming measure of these truncated lists defines the truncation line. The values of any reasonable stemmers are found between this line and the origin. Figure 1 shows the UI and OI values for each stemmer with the truncation line. Generally, the further the stemmer is from this line, the better it performs on the word lists. By drawing a line that passes through the origin, the datapoint identified by the pair (UI,OI) consisting of the stemmer's understemming and overstemming index, respectively, and that intersects the truncation line, we obtain the distances necessary to calculate the ERRT value of each stemmer. These are the distance from the origin to the stemmer's (UI,OI) divided by the distance from the origin to the intersection with the truncation line. Low overstemming and understemming indexes are the desired feature in a stemmer. Stemmers that are closer to the origin have lower UI and OI values which means the distance is also shorter. The 'best' stemmer would also have the lowest ERRT value compared to the rest.

Table 1 contains the UI, OI and ERRT values for each of the four stemmers used. As expected, *Light1*, being the lightest stemmer, has the highest understemming index, while *Heavy* has the lowest value. The high value for understemming for *Light1* indicates that it leaves many words unstemmed or just understemmed. The reverse is true for the overstemming index. The *Medium*

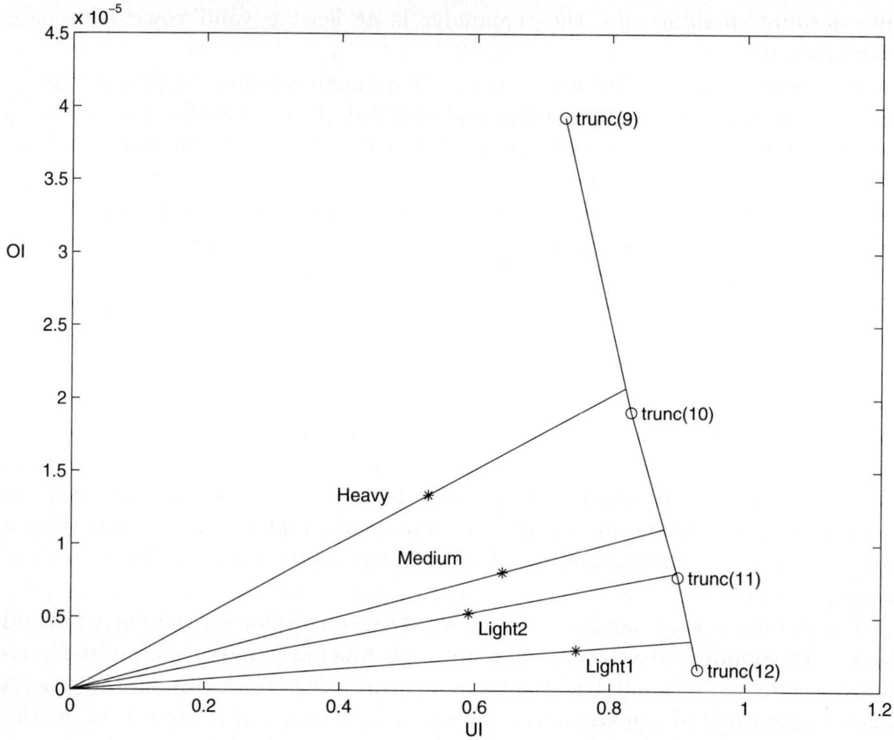

Fig. 1. *UI* × *OI* plot with the *ERRT* distances

stemmer has a lower understemming and higher overstemming index than *Light2* which, at first sight, seems surprising. However, 54% of the words in the list are nouns, and since *Light2* removes all noun cases, just like *Heavy* but unlike *Light1* and *Medium*, these scores make sense. The *Medium* stemmer focuses on some frequent noun cases and verbs. Verbs form only 23% of the word list so the reason for the somewhat unexpected values is simply due to the fact that the *Medium* stemmer stems fewer words than *Light2*. Overall, when it comes to stemming a word list, a stemmer handling all noun cases yields better results than one restricted to the most frequent noun cases and verb tenses. We suspect that this will apply to a lesser extent for retrieval, as words are unique in the word list unlike in a normal corpus.

An examination of the errors in the word list showed that there are difficulties for the stemmers such as overstemming and homonymy. The overstemming of terms such as *nemzet* (nation) to the invalid *nemz* could be alleviated by an exceptions list containing frequent words. Homonymy, for instance with the term *nevet* meaning either 'to laugh' or the accusative form of 'name', can only be solved by looking at the context of the word.

The high ERRT value of *Light1* indicates that although it has very low overstemming it leaves too many words understemmed making it too light. The same

Table 1. Performance of the stemmers on the word-groups

	UI	OI	ERRT
Light1	0.75	0.0000028	0.81
Light2	0.59	0.0000053	0.66
Medium	0.64	0.0000081	0.73
Heavy	0.53	0.0000134	0.65

is true for the *Medium* stemmer, because it focuses on verbs even though there are fewer verbs than nouns in the word list. In this sense, *Light2* and *Heavy* come out as winners having the lowest ERRT values. What would this mean when used in an information retrieval setting? An analysis of English topics used in CLEF 2004 showed that after stopping, over 65% of the words were nouns, only 10% verbs and 12% adjectives. A post submission analysis confirmed these findings for the 2005 Hungarian topics, with 60% of nouns, 23% adjectives and 17% verbs after stopping. Thus, even if a stemmer only concentrates on stemming nouns it should still have an impact on either recall or precision or both. Based on the ERRT values we expect the runs with *Light2* and *Heavy* stemmers to yield a better recall than the other two stemmers and the baseline (no stemming at all). At the same time, precision will probably be negatively affected by the *Heavy* stemmer. These results suggest that the run with *Light2* should have the highest recall and precision values since it has a low understemming ratio and should still stem a large percentage of words.

4 Retrieval Setup

Now that we have described the stemmers, we turn to our retrieval experiments. We used Lucene (off-the-shelf) for indexing and retrieval with a standard vector space model [7]. In addition, we used a stopword list which was created using the Szeged Corpus [1]. We created a list from the 300 most frequent words in the corpus. Numbers and homonyms were removed from the list and it was expanded with pronouns. The result was a list of 188 words.[1] Both the index and queries were stopped. Diacritics were left untouched.

For more information on the ad-hoc track and the collection see [2, 10]. The document collection was encoded in UTF-8. As the Snowball stemmers were created for ISO Latin encoding, the entire collection was converted into ISO Latin 1 encoding without any loss of textual data.

5 The Experimental Results

5.1 Runs

The results of the official CLEF 2005 experiments have been discussed in our Working Notes [12]. We ran the same experiments with some small alterations

[1] The stopword list is available at `http://ilps.science.uva.nl/Resources/`.

such as changes in the stopword list and the separation of hyphenated words. We also performed some new experiments with 4- and 5-grams.

We extended the stopword list with extra terms that appear in practically every query and do not aid retrieval such as *keressünk* (let us search) and *cikk* (article) and their variations. This small change boosted the Mean Average Precision (MAP) and R-precision scores by an average of 0.5.

Additionally we ran experiments with n-grams, this time testing 4-grams and 5-grams. The *4-gram* run returned the highest MAP and R-precision of all the runs.

Analysis of the official runs [12] showed that some relevant documents weren't retrieved because the hyphenated terms in the query and documents were not separated. To this end we performed a new experiment with the best stemmer, Heavy, where we separated hyphenated words in both document collection and queries. The MAP scores and precision scores improved somewhat as a result.

Table 2. Overview of *MAP* scores and *R-precision* scores for the runs. Best scores are in bold face

	MAP	R-prec	% Relevant Docs Retrieved
Light1	0.2245	0.2477	74.7
Light2	0.2911	0.3017	79.1
Medium	0.2417	0.2591	77.2
Heavy	0.2935	0.2921	79.8
Heavy minus hyphen	0.3099	0.3048	83.1
Base	0.1831	0.2096	62.9
4-Gram	**0.3303**	**0.338**	**83.6**
5-Gram	0.3002	0.3057	82.4

Table 2 shows that the *4-gram* has the best performance with respect to MAP, R-precision and number of relevant documents retrieved. Amongst the algorithmic stemmers the *Heavy* stemmer has the highest MAP and R-precision score closely followed by *Light2*. *Medium* scored lower and *Light1* has the worst scores. Overall, when comparing the stemmer scores with the score of the base run, any kind of stemming is better than no stemming at all.

Although the results are to some extent what we had expected, we need to perform a statistical test to determine if there is any significant difference between the methods and stemmers.

We wanted to know if the results of the four different stemming algorithms was significantly different and whether the *4-gram* performed significantly better than the *Heavy* stemmer. A repeated measures ANOVA was performed and showed significant effects for the factor 'stemmer' for both MAP ($F = 12.52$, $df = 5$, $p < 0.01$) and R-precision ($F = 6.99$, $df = 5$, $p < 0.05$); there is a significant difference in the results of the four different stemmers. The results of the *4-gram* however did not differ significantly from the *Heavy* stemmer in both MAP and R-precision.

We examined four queries more closely to find out what the difference is between the performance of the *4-gram* and the *Heavy* stemmer. For the queries

C285 and C298 the *4-gram* outperformed the *Heavy* stemmer. In both cases the queries contained compound words such as *abortuszellenes* (anti-abortion) and *atomerőmű* (nuclear power station). The *4-gram* found the relevant documents containing terms like *abortusz* (abortion) and erőmű (power station) while the *Heavy* run did not.

For the queries C272 and C273 the *Heavy* run outperformed the *4-gram* run. In these cases the queries contained compound words like *kelet-európai* (Eastern European) and *előélete* ('previous life') as well as other frequent words that resulted in the low ranking of the relevant documents by the *4-gram* run.

6 Conclusion

We compared the performance of four different algorithmic stemmers using two forms of evaluation. In Section 3 we found that the *Light2* and *Heavy* stemmers worked best. This has been confirmed by the findings in Section 5 where we also determined that the *Light2* and *Heavy* stemmers worked significantly better for retrieval than *Medium* and *Light1*. This effectively means that stemming nouns and with them adjectives (the two are linked because of similar morphology) is important and makes a difference for retrieval. The stemming of verbs does not seem to have a significant impact.

The *4-gram* had the highest average scores of all the runs, but for this data, it was not significantly higher than the scores of the best stemmer. The *4-gram* has an advantage over our algorithmic stemmers. It is a stemmer and compound splitter all in one. However, as there is no control over what is being 'split' or 'stemmed' this may lead to negative effects on the ranking of the documents when compared to the stemmer.

The next step would be the development of a compound splitter to use in combination with the stemmers. There is also room for improvement on the stemmers themselves, allowing them to handle more irregular forms and increase the number of correct stems.

Acknowledgements

Maarten de Rijke was supported by the Netherlands Organization for Scientific Research (NWO) under project numbers 017.001.190, 220-80-001, 264-70-050, 354-20-005, 612-13-001, 612.000.106, 612.000.207, 612.066.302, 612.069.006.

Bibliography

[1] Szeged Corpus. A morpho-syntactically annotated and POS tagged Hungarian corpus, 2005.

[2] G. M. Di Nunzio, N. Ferro, G. J. F. Jones, and C. Peters. Clef 2005: Ad hoc track overview. URL: `http://www.clef-campaign.org/2005/working_notes/workingnotes2005/dinunzio05.pdf`.

[3] T. Erjavec and M. Monachini. Specifications and notation for lexicon encoding. Technical report, COP Project 106 MULTEXT - East, December 17, 1997.

[4] S. Fissaha Adafre, W.R. van Hage, J. Kamps, G.L. de Melo, and M. de Rijke. The University of Amsterdam at CLEF 2004, 2004.

[5] V. Hollink, J. Kamps, C. Monz, and M. de Rijke. Monolingual document retrieval for European languages, *Information Retrival*, 7:33-52 2004.

[6] T. Korenius, J. Laurikkala, K. Jarvelin, and M. Juhola. Stemming and lemmatization in the clustering of finnish text documents. In *Proceedings of the Thirteenth ACM conference on Information and knowledge management*, 2005, pages 625–633.

[7] Lucene. The Lucene search engine. URL: http://jakarta.apache.org/lucene/.

[8] B. Megyesi. The Hungarian language. URL: http://www.speech.kth.se/~bea/hungarian.pdf.

[9] C.D. Paice. Method for evaluation of stemming algorithms based on error counting. *Journal of The American Society for Information Science*, 47(8):632–649, 1996.

[10] C. Peters. What happened in clef 2005. URL: http://www.clef-campaign.org/2005/working_notes/workingnotes2005/peters05.pdf.

[11] Snowball. The Snowball string processing language. URL: http://snowball.tartarus.org/, 2005.

[12] A. Tordai and M. de Rijke. Hungarian monolingual retrieval at clef 2005. 2005. URL: http://www.clef-campaign.org/2005/working_notes/workingnotes2005/tordai05.pdf.

ENSM-SE at CLEF 2005: Using a Fuzzy Proximity Matching Function

Annabelle Mercier, Amélie Imafouo, and Michel Beigbeder

École Nationale Supérieure des Mines de Saint-Étienne,
158 cours Fauriel, 42023 Saint-Etienne Cedex 2, France
{annabelle.mercier, imafouo, mbeig}@emse.fr

Abstract. Starting from the idea that the closer the query terms in a document are to each other the more relevant the document, we propose an information retrieval method that uses the degree of fuzzy proximity of key terms in a document to compute the relevance of the document to the query. Our model handles Boolean queries but, contrary to the traditional extensions of the basic Boolean information retrieval model, does not use a proximity operator explicitly. A single parameter makes it possible to control the proximity degree required. We explain how we construct the queries and report the results of our experiments in the ad-hoc monolingual French task of the CLEF 2005 evaluation campaign.

1 Introduction

In the information retrieval domain, systems are based on three basic models: the Boolean model, the vector model and the probabilistic model. These models have many variations (extended Boolean models, models based on fuzzy sets theory, generalized vector space model,...) [1]. However, they are all based on weak representations of documents: either sets of terms or bags of terms. In the first case, what the information retrieval system knows about a document is whether it contains a given term or not. In the second case, the system knows the number of occurrences – the *term frequency*, *tf* – of a given term in each document. So whatever the order of the terms in the documents, they share the same index representation if they use the same terms. Noteworthy exceptions to this rule are most of the Boolean model implementations which propose a NEAR operator [2]. This operator is a kind of AND but with the constraint that the different terms are within a window of size n, where n is an integral value. The set of retrieved documents can be restricted with this operator. For instance, it is possible to discriminate between documents about "data structures" and those about "data about concrete structures". Using this operator results in an increase in precision of the system [3]. But the Boolean systems that implement a NEAR operator share the same limitation as any basic Boolean system: these systems are not able to rank the retrieved documents because with this model a document *is* or *is not* relevant to a query. Different extensions have been proposed to the basic Boolean systems to circumvent this limitation. These extensions represent the documents with some kind of term weights. Most of the time these weights are

C. Peters et al. (Eds.): CLEF 2005, LNCS 4022, pp. 187–193, 2006.

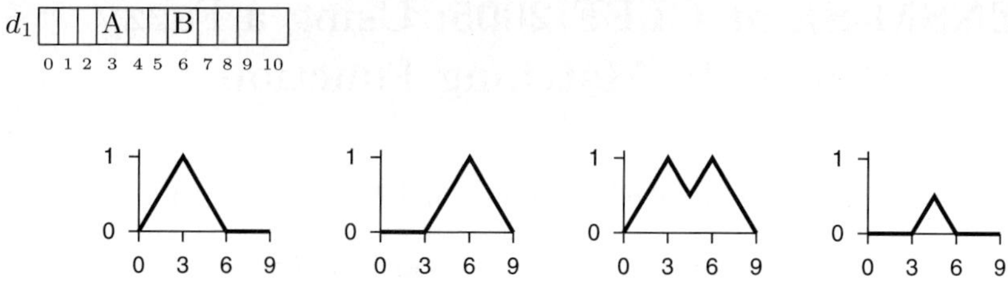

Fig. 1. Document 1 – In order, w_A^{d1}, w_B^{d1}, $w_{A\,\mathrm{OR}\,B}^{d1}$ and $w_{A\,\mathrm{AND}\,B}^{d1}$ are displayed

computed on a *tf* basis. Some combining formulas are then applied to compute the document score given the term weights and the query tree. But these extensions are not compatible with the NEAR operator. Some researchers have thus proposed models that attempt to directly score the documents by taking into account the proximity of the query terms within them.

2 Uses of Proximity

Three methods have been proposed to score documents taking into account different sets of intervals containing the query terms. These methods differ in the set of intervals that are selected in a first step, and then in the formulas used to compute the score for a given interval. The method of Clarke et al. [4] selects the shortest intervals that contain all the query terms (this constraint is relaxed if there are not enough retrieved documents), so the intervals cannot be nested. In the method of Hawking et al. [5], for each query term occurrence, the shortest interval containing all the query terms is selected, thus the selected intervals can nest. Rasolofo et al. [6] chose to select intervals only containing *two* terms of the query, but with the additional constraint that the interval is shorter than five words.

Moreover, passage retrieval methods indirectly use the notion of proximity. In fact, in several methods, documents are ranked by selecting documents which have passages with a high density of query terms, that is to say documents where the query terms are near to each other [7,8,9]. The next section presents our method which scores documents on the basis of term proximity.

3 Fuzzy Proximity Matching

To address the problem of scoring the documents taking into account the relative order of the words in the document, we have defined a new method based on a *fuzzy proximity* between each position in the document text and a query. This fuzzy proximity function is summed up over $\mathbb{Z}$ to score the document.

We model the fuzzy proximity to an occurrence of a term with an influence function f that reaches its maximum (value 1) at the value 0 and decreases on each side down to 0. Different types of functions (Hamming, rectangular,

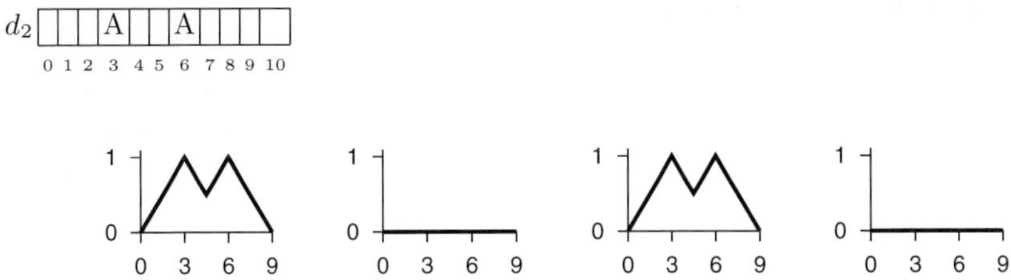

Fig. 2. Document 2 – In order, w_A^{d2}, w_B^{d2}, $w_{A\,\mathrm{OR}\,B}^{d2}$ and $w_{A\,\mathrm{AND}\,B}^{d2}$ are displayed

gaussian, etc.) can be used. In the following, the examples and the experiments will be based on a triangular function $x \mapsto \max(\frac{k-|x|}{k}, 0)$. The constant k controls the support of the function and this support represents the extent of influence of each term occurrence. A similar parameter can be found for other shapes.

So, for a query term t, the fuzzy proximity function to the occurrence at position i of the term t is $x \mapsto f(x-i)$. Now, we define the term proximity function w_t^d which models the fuzzy proximity at the position x in the text to the term t by combining the fuzzy proximity functions of the different occurrences of the term t:

$$x \mapsto w_t^d(x) = \max_{i \in Occ(t,d)} f(x-i)$$

where $Occ(t,d)$ is the set of the positions of the term t in the document d and f is the influence function.

Figures 1 and 2 show the fuzzy proximity functions $w_A^{d_1}$, $w_B^{d_1}$, $w_A^{d_2}$, and $w_B^{d_2}$ to the terms A and B in the documents d_1 and d_2.

The query model is the classical Boolean model: A tree with terms on the leaves and OR or AND operators on the internal nodes. At an internal node, the proximity functions of the sons of this node are combined in the query tree with the usual fuzzy set theory formulas. So the fuzzy proximity is computed by

$$w_{q\,\mathrm{OR}\,q'}^d = \max(w_q^d, w_{q'}^d)$$

for a disjunctive node and by

$$w_{q\,\mathrm{AND}\,q'}^d = \min(w_q^d, w_{q'}^d)$$

for a conjunctive node. With a post-order tree traversal a fuzzy proximity function to the query can be computed at the root of the query tree as the fuzzy proximity functions are defined on the leaves.

So we obtain a function w_q^d from $\mathbb{Z}$ to the interval $[0,1]$. The result of the summation of this function is used as the score of the document:

$$s(q,d) = \sum_{x=-\infty}^{+\infty} w_q^d(x) \ .$$

Thus, the computed score $s(q,d)$ depends on the fuzzy proximity functions and enables document ranking according to the query term proximity in the documents.

4 Experiments and Evaluation

We carried out experiments within the context of the CLEF 2005 evaluation campaign in the ad-hoc monolingual French task[1]. We used the retrieval search engine LUCY[2] which is based on the Okapi information retrieval model [10] to index this collection. It was easy to adapt this tool to our method because it keeps the positions of the terms occurring in the documents in the index. Thus, we extended this tool to compute the relevance score values for our fuzzy proximity matching function.

Documents in the CLEF 2005 test collection are newspapers articles in XML format from *SDA* and *Le Monde* of the years 1994 and 1995. For each document (tag `<DOC>`), we keep the fields `<DOCNO>` with the tag and the document number, the textual contents of the tags `<TX>`, `<LD>`, `<TI>`, `<ST>` for *SDA French* and `<TEXT>`, `<LEAD1>`, `<TITLE>` for *Le Monde* 1995. We used the topics and the relevance judgements to evaluate the different methods by the `trec_eval` program.

4.1 Building the Queries

Each topic is composed of three tags: `<FR-title>`, `<FR-desc>`, `<FR-narr>`. Two sets of queries were built for our experiments.

Automatically built queries. For this set, a query is built with the terms from the title field where the stop words[3] are removed. Here is an example with the topic #278. The original topic is expressed by:

```
<top>
<num> 278 </num>
<FR-title> Les moyens de transport pour handicapés</FR-title>
<FR-desc> A quels problèmes doivent faire face les personnes
handicapées physiques lorsquelles empruntent les transports
publics et quelles solutions sont proposées ou adoptées?
</FR-desc>
<FR-narr> Les documents pertinents devront décrire les
difficultés auxquelles doivent faire face les personnes
diminuées physiquement lorsquelles utilisent les transports
publics et/ou traiter des progrès accomplis pour résoudre ces
problèmes.
</FR-narr>
</top>
```

First, the topic number and the title field are extracted and concatenated:

```
278 moyens transport handicapés
```

---

[1] http://clef.isti.cnr.it/

[2] http://www.seg.rmit.edu.au/lucy/

[3] Removed stop words: à, aux, au, chez, et, dans, des, de, du, en, la, les, le, par, sur, uns, unes, une, un, d', l'.

From this form, the queries are automatically built by simple derivations:

Lucy: `278 moyens transport handicapés`
conjunctive fuzzy proximity: `278 moyens & transport & handicapés`
disjunctive fuzzy proximity: `278 moyens | transport | handicapés`

Manually built queries. They are built with all the terms from the title field and some terms from the description field. The general idea was to build conjunctions (which are the basis of our method) of disjunctions. The disjunctions are composed of the plural form of the terms and some derivations to compensate the lack of a stemming tool in LUCY. Sometimes some terms from the same semantic field were grouped together in the disjunctions.

Queries for the method implemented in the LUCY tool are flat queries composed of different inflectional and/or derivational forms of the terms. Here is an example for topic #278:

fuzzy proximity: 278 `(moyen | moyens) & (transport | transports) & (handicap | handicapé | handicapés)`
Lucy: 278 `moyen moyens transport transports handicap handicapé handicapés`

4.2 Building the Result Lists

The Okapi model and our fuzzy method with different values of k were compared. It is known that the Okapi method gives one of the best performances. However, a previous study showed that proximity based methods improve retrieval [11]. If one of our experiments with our proximity based method does not retrieve enough documents (one thousand for the CLEF experiments), then its results list is supplemented by documents from the Okapi result list that have not yet been retrieved by the proximity based method.

4.3 Differents Runs

In the official runs, the queries used with our method were:

1. the conjunction of the terms automatically extracted from the title field with $k = 20$ (run `RIMfuzzET020`) and with $k = 50$ (run `RIMfuzzET050`);
2. manually built queries with terms from the three fields with $k = 50$ (run `RIMfuzzLemme050`) and with $k = 80$ (run `RIMfuzzLemme080`).

For the runs `RIMLucyET` and `RIMLucyLemme` where the Okapi method was used, the queries are flat (bag of terms). These runs were produced by using the native LUCY search engine and they provide the baselines for the comparison with our method. The recall precision results are provided in Table 4.3.

With the values chosen for the parameter k in the official runs, the Lucy method performs better than the fuzzy proximity ones with automatic queries.

Table 1. Official runs with automatically and manually built queries. The columns display the precision for the runs `RIMLucyET`, `RIMfuzzET050`, `RIMfuzzET020`, `RIMLucyLemme`, `RIMfuzzLemme080`, et `RIMfuzzLemme050`. In boldface, the best result in a row, and in italics the second one.

	Automatic queries			Manual queries (lemmatisation)		
Recall	Lucy	Prox. AND k=50	Prox. AND k=20	Lucy	Prox. k=80	Prox. k=50
0	**62**	*59*	57	68	**70**	*68*
10	**45**	*44*	44	**49**	*49*	48
20	**33**	32	*33*	39	**41**	*41*
30	**26**	25	*25*	31	*33*	**33**
40	21	*21*	**21**	25	*28*	**28**
50	19	*19*	**19**	21	**22**	*21*
60	**14**	14	*14*	17	**18**	*18*
70	*11*	11	**11**	13	**14**	*14*
80	7	**8**	*8*	8	**10**	*10*
90	4	4	4	5	**6**	*6*
100	1	1	1	1	*1*	**1**

Table 2. Unofficial runs with automatically and manually built queries. In boldface, the best result in a row, and in italics the second one.

	Automatic queries			Manual queries (lemmatisation)		
Recall	Lucy	Prox. AND k=100	Prox. AND k=200	Lucy	Prox. k=100	Prox. k=200
0	**62**	60	*61*	68	**72**	*71*
10	**45**	*44*	43	49	*50*	**51**
20	**33**	33	*33*	39	*40*	**41**
30	**26**	*26*	26	31	*33*	**34**
40	21	*21*	**21**	25	*28*	**28**
50	**19**	*19*	19	21	**22**	*22*
60	**15**	*14*	14	17	*18*	**18**
70	**11**	*11*	11	13	**14**	*14*
80	7	**8**	*8*	8	*10*	**10**
90	**4**	*4*	4	5	**6**	*6*
100	*1*	**1**	1	1	**1**	*1*

But when manual queries are used the results of our method are better or equal than the Lucy ones.

In some unofficial runs, other values of k were used to enlarge the area of influence of the terms occurrences. In Table 2 we notice that the larger the area the better the results. Our fuzzy proximity method performs better with manual queries because more documents are retrieved with our method because of the disjunctions of the differents forms of a term and of some quite synonymous terms. So the proximity between query terms is the main factor to select and rank documents.

5 Conclusion

We have presented our information retrieval model which takes into account the position of the query terms in the documents to compute the relevance scores. We experimented this method on the CLEF 2005 Ad-Hoc French test collection.

We note that the higher the area of influence of a term the better the results are. In further experiments, we will use a more flexible influence function which will make it possible to dynamically adapt the value of the k constant to the desired number of retrieved documents. We think also that the results could be improved by using an automatic stemming procedure and eventually a thesaurus in order to retrieve more documents with our method.

References

1. Baeza-Yates, R., Ribeiro-Neto, B.: Modern Information Retrieval. ACM Press / Addison-Wesley (1999)
2. Salton, G., McGill, M.J.: Introduction to Modern Information Retrieval. McGraw-Hill Book Company (1983)
3. Keen, E.M.: Some aspects of proximity searching in text retrieval systems. Journal of Information Science **18** (1992) 89–98
4. Clarke, C.L.A., Cormack, G.V., Tudhope, E.A.: Relevance ranking for one to three term queries. Information Processing and Management **36**(2) (2000) 291–311
5. Hawking, D., Thistlewaite, P.: Proximity operators - so near and yet so far. In Harman, D.K., ed.: The Fourth Text REtrieval Conference (TREC-4), Department of Commerce, National Institute of Standards and Technology (1995) 131–143
6. Rasolofo, Y., Savoy, J.: Term proximity scoring for keyword-based retrieval systems. In: 25th European Conference on Information Retrieval Research. Number 2633 in LNCS, Springer (2003) 207–218
7. Wilkinson, R.: Effective retrieval of structured documents. In: SIGIR '94, Proceedings of the 17th annual international ACM SIGIR conference on Research and development in information retrieval, Springer-Verlag New York (1994) 311–317
8. de Kretser, O., Moffat, A.: Effective document presentation with a locality-based similarity heuristic. In: SIGIR '99: Proceedings of the 22nd ACM SIGIR Annual International Conference on Research and Development in Information Retrieval, ACM (1999) 113–120
9. Kise, K., Junker, M., Dengel, A., Matsumoto, K.: Passage retrieval based on density distributions of terms and its applications to document retrieval and question answering. In Dengel, A., Junker, M., Weisbecker, A., eds.: Reading and Learning: Adaptive Content Recognition. Volume 2956 of Lecture Notes in Computer Science., Springer (2004) 306–327
10. Robertson, S.E., Walker, S., Jones, S., Hancock-Beaulieu, M.M., Gatford, M.: Okapi at trec-3. In Harman, D.K., ed.: Overview of the Third Text REtrieval Conference (TREC-3), Department of Commerce, National Institute of Standards and Technology (1994) 109–126
11. Mercier, A.: Étude comparative de trois approches utilisant la proximité entre les termes de la requête pour le calcul des scores des documents. In: INFORSID 2004. (2004) 95–106

Bulgarian and Hungarian Experiments with Hummingbird SearchServer^{TM} at CLEF 2005

Stephen Tomlinson

Hummingbird, Ottawa, Canada
stephen.tomlinson@hummingbird.com
http://www.hummingbird.com/

Abstract. Hummingbird participated in the Bulgarian and Hungarian monolingual information retrieval tasks of the Ad-Hoc Track of the Cross-Language Evaluation Forum (CLEF) 2005. In the ad hoc retrieval tasks, the system was given 50 natural language queries, and the goal was to find all of the relevant documents (with high precision) in a particular document set. We conducted diagnostic experiments with different techniques for matching word variations and handling stopwords. We found that the experimental stemmers significantly increased mean average precision for both languages. Analysis of individual topics found that the algorithmic Bulgarian and Hungarian stemmers encountered some unanticipated stopword collisions. A comparison to an experimental 4-gram technique suggested that Hungarian stemming would further benefit from decompounding.

1 Introduction

Hummingbird SearchServer[1] is a toolkit for developing enterprise search and retrieval applications. The SearchServer kernel is also embedded in other Hummingbird products for the enterprise.

SearchServer works in Unicode internally [3] and supports most of the world's major character sets and languages. The major conferences in text retrieval experimentation (CLEF [2], NTCIR [6] and TREC [9]) have provided judged test collections for objective experimentation with SearchServer in more than a dozen languages.

This paper describes experimental work with SearchServer for the task of finding relevant documents for natural language queries in Bulgarian and Hungarian using the CLEF 2005 Ad-Hoc Track test collections.

2 Methodology

2.1 Indexing

Our indexing approach was mostly the same as last year [10]. Accents were not indexed except for the combining breve in Bulgarian. The apostrophe was

[1] SearchServer^{TM}, SearchSQL^{TM}and Intuitive Searching^{TM} are trademarks of Hummingbird Ltd. All other copyrights, trademarks and tradenames are the property of their respective owners.

C. Peters et al. (Eds.): CLEF 2005, LNCS 4022, pp. 194–203, 2006.

treated as a word separator for the investigated languages. The custom text reader, cTREC, was updated to maintain support for the CLEF guidelines of only indexing specifically tagged fields.

Some stop words were excluded from indexing (e.g. "the", "by" and "of" in English). For these experiments, the stop word lists for Bulgarian and Hungarian were based on Savoy's lists (of May 2005) [8].

By default, the SearchServer index supports both exact matching (after some Unicode-based normalizations, such as decompositions and conversion to upper-case) and morphological matching (e.g. inflections, derivations and compounds, depending on the linguistic component used).

2.2 Searching

We experimented with the SearchServer CONTAINS predicate. Our test application specified SearchSQL to perform a boolean-OR of the query words. For example, for Bulgarian topic 279 whose Title was "Референдуми в Швейцария" (Swiss referendums), a corresponding SearchSQL query would be:

```
SELECT RELEVANCE('2:3') AS REL, DOCNO
FROM CLEF05BG
WHERE FT_TEXT CONTAINS 'Референдуми'|'в'|'Швейцария'
ORDER BY REL DESC;
```

(Note that "в" is a stopword for Bulgarian so its inclusion in the query wouldn't actually add any matches.)

Most aspects of the SearchServer relevance value calculation are the same as described last year [10]. Briefly, SearchServer dampens the term frequency and adjusts for document length in a manner similar to Okapi [7] and dampens the inverse document frequency using an approximation of the logarithm. These calculations are based on the stems of the terms (roughly speaking) when doing morphological searching (i.e. when SET TERM_GENERATOR 'word!ftelp/inflect' was previously specified). The SearchServer RELEVANCE_METHOD setting was set to '2:3' and RELEVANCE_DLEN_IMP was set to 750 for all experiments in this paper.

2.3 Diagnostic Runs

For the diagnostic runs listed in Table 1, the run names consist of a language code ("BG" for Bulgarian and "HU" for Hungarian) followed by one of the following labels:

- "neu": The run found word variations based on the experimental Neuchatel stemmer for the language [8]. These stemmers were algorithmic (i.e. they were not based on a lexicon for the language). The /inflect option (SET TERM_GENERATOR 'word!ftelp/inflect') was specified.
- "neunos": Same as "neu" except that /nostop was additionally specified which prevents query terms from being discarded if all of their stems are stopwords

Table 1. Mean Scores of Diagnostic Title-only runs

Run	FRS	Success@1	Success@5	Success@10	MRR	MAP
BG-neuall	0.782	15/49 (31%)	38/49 (78%)	41/49 (84%)	0.500	0.255
BG-neunos	0.781	16/49 (33%)	38/49 (78%)	41/49 (84%)	0.507	0.263
BG-4gram	0.758	20/49 (41%)	32/49 (65%)	40/49 (82%)	0.525	0.264
BG-neu	0.749	15/49 (31%)	35/49 (71%)	39/49 (80%)	0.476	0.259
BG-none	0.685	14/49 (29%)	30/49 (61%)	35/49 (71%)	0.440	0.195
HU-4gram	0.834	24/50 (48%)	39/50 (78%)	45/50 (90%)	0.619	0.341
HU-neunos	0.789	26/50 (52%)	36/50 (72%)	42/50 (84%)	0.625	0.287
HU-neuall	0.788	25/50 (50%)	37/50 (74%)	41/50 (82%)	0.614	0.280
HU-neu	0.788	25/50 (50%)	37/50 (74%)	42/50 (84%)	0.613	0.274
HU-neuposs	0.769	24/50 (48%)	36/50 (72%)	41/50 (82%)	0.588	0.271
HU-none	0.671	17/50 (34%)	30/50 (60%)	37/50 (74%)	0.464	0.184

(note that stopwords themselves were still not found because they were not indexed).

- "neuall": Same as "neu" except that a separate index was used which did not stop any words from being indexed (specifying /nostop would make no difference with this index).
- "neuposs" (HU only): Same as "neu" except that the remove_possessive function of the stemmer was not called.
- "4gram": Same as "neuall" except that the run used a different index which primarily consisted of the 4-grams of terms, e.g. the word 'search' would produce index terms of 'sear', 'earc' and 'arch'. No stemming was done; searching used the IS_ABOUT predicate (instead of the CONTAINS predicate) with morphological options disabled to search for the 4-grams of the query terms.
- "none": The run disabled morphological searching. (The run used the same index as "neu" but SET TERM_GENERATOR '' was specified so that variations from stemming were not matched.)

The diagnostic runs just used the Title field of the topic.

2.4 Retrieval Measures

Traditionally in ad hoc retrieval experiments, the primary evaluation measure is "average precision". For a topic, it is the average of the precision after each relevant document is retrieved (using zero as the precision for relevant documents which are not retrieved). By convention, it is based on the first 1000 retrieved documents for the topic. "Mean Average Precision" (MAP) is the mean of the average precision scores over all of the topics (i.e. all topics are weighted equally).

If one wishes to focus on just the first relevant document, the traditional measure is "Reciprocal Rank" (RR). For a topic, it is $\frac{1}{r}$ where r is the rank of the first row for which a desired page is found, or zero if a desired page was not found. "Mean Reciprocal Rank" (MRR) is the mean of the reciprocal ranks over all the topics.

An experimental measure we have created is "First Relevant Score" (denoted "FRS"). Like reciprocal rank, it is based on just the rank of the first relevant retrieved for a topic. FRS is 1.08^{1-r} where r is the rank of the first row for which a desired page is found, or zero if a desired page was not found.

"Success@n" is the percentage of topics for which at least one relevant document was returned in the first n rows.

2.5 Statistical Significance Tables

For tables comparing 2 diagnostic runs (such as Table 2), the columns are as follows:

- "Expt" specifies the experiment. The language code is given, followed by the labels of the 2 runs being compared. The difference is the first run minus the second run. For example, "BG neu-none" specifies the difference of subtracting the scores of the Bulgarian 'none' run from the Bulgarian 'neu' run (of Table 1).
- "ΔMAP" is the difference of the mean average precision scores of the two runs being compared (and "ΔFRS" is the difference of the (mean) FRS scores).
- "95% Conf" is an approximate 95% confidence interval for the difference (calculated from plus/minus twice the standard error of the mean difference). If zero is not in the interval, the result is "statistically significant" (at the 5% level), i.e. the feature is unlikely to be of neutral impact (on average), though if the average difference is small (e.g. <0.020) it may still be too minor to be considered "significant" in the magnitude sense.
- "vs." is the number of topics on which the first run scored higher, lower and tied (respectively) compared to the second run. These numbers should always add to the number of topics (49 for Bulgarian, 50 for Hungarian).
- "3 Extreme Diffs (Topic)" lists 3 of the individual topic differences, each followed by the topic number in brackets (the topic numbers range from 251 to 300). The first difference is the largest one of any topic (based on the absolute value). The third difference is the largest difference in the other direction (so the first and third differences give the range of differences observed in this experiment). The middle difference is the largest of the remaining differences (based on the absolute value).

3 Results of Morphological Experiments

In the per-topic analysis, the official topic translations were used as much as possible. Online translation services were consulted at times ([5] was sometimes helpful for Hungarian, and we found the Russian-to-English translations at [1] often worked for Bulgarian). Prof. Savoy also assisted with some Bulgarian words.

3.1 Impact of Stemming

Table 2 isolates the impact of stemming on the average precision measure (e.g. "BG neu-none" is the difference of the "BG-neu" and "BG-none" runs of Table 1). For both languages, the increase in mean average precision was statistically significant (i.e. zero was not in the approximate 95% confidence interval). In FRS, there was higher variance, and only the increase for Hungarian was statistically significant. Note that for some queries, it was still better to only match the original query form (not variations from stemming); SearchServer allows this option to be controlled for each query term at search-time.

Table 2 shows that topic 279 (Swiss referendums) was substantially affected by stemming for both languages, so we examine it for each language:

- HU-279 (Svájci népszavazások): Without Hungarian stemming, no document contained both of the query terms. No relevant document contained the query word 'népszavazások'. Only some of the relevant documents even contained 'Svájci' (and lots of non-relevants also did). With stemming, average precision was 87 points higher from extra matches such as 'népszavazáson', 'népszavazás', 'népszavazást', 'népszavazással', 'svájciak', 'Svájc', 'Svájcban', 'Svájcot' and 'Svájcról'.
- BG-279 (Референдуми в Швейцария): With Bulgarian stemming, average precision was 58 points higher from extra matches for 'referendums' such as референдум and референдума.

Table 2. Impact of Stemming on Average Precision and First Relevant Score

Expt	ΔMAP	95% Conf	vs.	3 Extreme Diffs (Topic)
HU neu-none	0.090	(0.038, 0.143)	32-11-7	0.87 (279), 0.77 (294), −0.12 (265)
BG neu-none	0.064	(0.005, 0.123)	29-15-5	0.90 (271), 0.58 (279), −0.50 (258)
	ΔFRS			
HU neu-none	0.117	(0.024, 0.209)	19-10-21	1.00 (271), 0.98 (294), −0.83 (262)
BG neu-none	0.064	(−0.042, 0.170)	16-17-16	0.96 (294), 0.86 (269), −0.87 (273)

3.2 Impact of Experimental /nostop Option

Table 3 isolates the impact of using the SearchServer /nostop option. The option affected only a few of the Bulgarian and Hungarian topics. The /nostop option prevents query terms from being discarded if all of their stems are stopwords (note that stopwords themselves are still not found because they are not indexed). The default is to not use /nostop because past experiments otherwise found a lot of spurious matches in some languages (such as Finnish and Korean). We investigate some of the topics flagged in Table 3:

- HU-265 (A Deutsche Bank szerzeményei (Deutsche Bank Takeovers)): The query word 'Bank' stemmed to 'ban' (in) which was a stopword, so by default, the word 'Bank' was not matched in the documents. With the /nostop

Table 3. Impact of /nostop Option on Average Precision and First Relevant Score

Expt	ΔMAP	95% Conf	vs.	3 Extreme Diffs (Topic)
HU nos-neu	0.013	(−0.005, 0.031)	3-1-46	0.40 (292), 0.13 (265), −0.03 (282)
BG nos-neu	0.005	(−0.003, 0.012)	2-2-45	0.17 (273), 0.06 (267), −0.01 (257)
	ΔFRS			
BG nos-neu	0.031	(−0.010, 0.072)	3-1-45	0.80 (273), 0.57 (267), −0.05 (257)
HU nos-neu	0.001	(−0.014, 0.015)	1-1-48	0.26 (292), 0.00 (253), −0.23 (282)

option, 'Bank' was matched and average precision was 13 points higher. (Incidentally, this issue is presumably why Table 2 shows that stemming scored 12 points lower on HU-265; without stemming, 'Bank' was found in the documents.) Perhaps this issue would not have arisen with a lexical stemmer which would preserve the meaning more closely.

- HU-292 (Német városok újjáépítése (Rebuilding German Cities)): The query word 'Német' (German) stemmed to 'nem' (not) which was a stopword and so this useful word was dropped from the query by default. With the /nostop option, average precision was 40 points higher.
- HU-282 (Elítéltekkel szembeni durva bánásmód (Prison Abuse)): In this topic, the default scored higher. Using /nostop changed the rank of the first relevant from 3 to 7. The stopword list contained 'szemben' (in front of), and the query word 'szembeni' presumably is a related noise word, and discarding it was useful. The /nostop option kept 'szembeni', which only occurred in 319 documents, so it had a high enough weighting from inverse document frequency to hurt precision.
- BG-273 (Разширяването на НАТО (NATO Expansion)): НАТО (NATO) stemmed to НА (on) which was a stopword, so the default behaviour removed a key word from the query. With /nostop, the first relevant score was 80 points higher.
- BG-267 (Най-добрите чуждоезикови филми (∼ Foreign Language Films)): The query word филми (films) stemmed to филм (film) which surprisingly was a stopword, so the default behaviour discarded a key query term. Our supplier [8] has confirmed that this was an error in the May 2005 version of the Bulgarian stopword list.
- BG-257 (Етническото прочистване на Балканите (Ethnic Cleansing in the Balkans)): The query word Балканите (Balkans) stemmed to балкан (Balkan mountain) which surprisingly was a stopword. Even though it turned out that precision was a little higher without the Balkans term in this case, in general this appears to be another error in the May 2005 stopword list.

In the topics we examined, in 3 cases the default behaviour of dropping useful terms may have been from the stemmers for Bulgarian and Hungarian being algorithmic instead of lexical (a lexical stemmer typically does not change the meaning of a word, except when words are ambiguous). It appears for algorithmic stemmers it may be better to use the /nostop option by default.

In another 2 cases, it appears the stoplist was in error, which illustrates the usefulness of the CLEF judged test collections: they enable an analyst who does not understand a language to find issues in a resource for the language and make inferences about its quality.

3.3 Impact of Indexing All Words

Table 4 isolates the impact of indexing all words (i.e. of not using a stopword list). None of the mean differences were statistically significant, but there were some large per-topic differences in average precision which we investigate:

Table 4. Impact of Indexing All Words on Average Precision and First Relevant Score

Expt	ΔMAP	95% Conf	vs.	3 Extreme Diffs (Topic)
HU all-nos	−0.006	(−0.021, 0.008)	7-7-36	−0.33 (292), −0.05 (265), 0.05 (274)
BG all-nos	−0.008	(−0.034, 0.018)	16-17-16	−0.55 (271), −0.14 (268), 0.20 (295)
	ΔFRS			
BG all-nos	0.001	(−0.008, 0.010)	3-4-42	0.13 (263), −0.07 (268), −0.07 (271)
HU all-nos	−0.000	(−0.010, 0.009)	1-3-46	0.16 (282), −0.04 (299), −0.14 (292)

- HU-292 (Német városok újjáépítése (Rebuilding German Cities)): We saw earlier that this topic benefitted from the /nostop option (average precision up 40 points), but when indexing all words, average precision fell back (33 points). The reason was that the common word 'nem' (not) was now indexed, so 'Német' (German), which stems to 'nem' with the algorithmic stemmer, had a much lower inverse document frequency than before, and this useful word received less weight. (Even if it had received more weight, there would have been potential confusion with all the indexed occurrences of 'nem'.)
- BG-271 (Бракове между хомосексуални (Gay Marriages)): The stopword между (between) was not in the 2 relevant documents. When it was indexed, its inclusion caused some non-relevants to be preferred, and average precision dropped 55 points.
- BG-295 (Пране на пари (Money Laundering)): This topic scored higher when indexing all words. Surprisingly, the word пари (money) was a stopword, another error in the May 2005 stoplist. It was fine that на (on) was a stopword.

In practice, indexing all words may not be so troublesome because it is typically easy for users to omit noise words from the query, and stemming issues can be worked around by disabling the finding of word variants (SearchServer makes it optional at search-time).

3.4 Comparison to 4-Grams

Compound words appear to be fairly common in Hungarian, but the algorithmic stemmer did not perform decompounding, a technique we have found to be useful for languages such as Finnish [10]. However, [4] has found that using 4-grams as index terms works well in ad hoc ranking experiments for many European languages, including compound-word languages. Table 5 compares our 4-gram runs to the stemming runs which indexed all words (because we did not use stopwords with our 4-gram index). As anticipated, there was a statistically significant increase in mean average precision for Hungarian. We look at the largest per-topic differences for Hungarian:

Table 5. 4-grams vs. Stems in Average Precision and First Relevant Score

Expt	ΔMAP	95% Conf	vs.	3 Extreme Diffs (Topic)
HU 4gr-all	0.060	(0.018, 0.103)	32-17-1	0.46 (255), 0.33 (292), −0.30 (283)
BG 4gr-all	0.009	(−0.028, 0.046)	25-24-0	0.50 (258), 0.25 (254), −0.33 (285)
	ΔFRS			
HU 4gr-all	0.046	(−0.036, 0.128)	15-15-20	1.00 (286), 0.93 (261), −0.81 (251)
BG 4gr-all	−0.024	(−0.093, 0.045)	17-14-18	−0.82 (274), 0.56 (270), 0.59 (288)

- HU-255 (Internetfüggők (Internet Junkies)): Average precision was 46 points higher with 4-grams for this topic (a compound word). The stemmer found the 3 relevant documents which contained 'internetfüggő' or the original query word 'internetfüggők'. 4-grams found all 6 relevant documents by matching other variants such as 'Internetfüggőség' (Internet dependence), 'internetfüggőséggel' and 'internetfüggőségben'. 4-grams also matched other potentially helpful words such as 'internet', 'internetezők', 'internetezés', 'komputerfüggőséget' and 'függővé'. But 4-grams also produced unwanted matches, such as 'intervallum' (interval) and 'Szinte' (as good as); these both came from the 4-gram 'inte'. If the stemmer had just additionally matched 'Internetfüggőség', all 6 relevants would have been found.
- HU-292 (Német városok újjáépítése (Rebuilding German Cities)): On this topic, 4-grams still just found 1 of the 2 relevant documents, but it moved it from rank 3 to 1 (compared to the stemming run). While 4-grams additionally matched 'újjáépítik', the bigger advantage was probably that the 4-gram method did not match 'nem' which we know from earlier was a troublesome match for the stemming run.
- HU-283 (James Bond-filmek (James Bond Films)): On this topic, the 4-gram run scored 30 points lower in average precision than the stemming run. The 4-gram run favored documents with the 'filmek' pattern (which corresponded to three 4-grams ('film', 'ilme' and 'lmek') and so it received roughly 3 times the weight compared to the stemming run). However, the relevant documents tended not to use 'filmek'; instead they tended to use other variants matched by the stemmer such as 'film', 'filmet', 'filmnél', 'filmben' and 'filmhez'.

– HU-286 (Futballsérülések (Football Injuries)): This topic had no matches in the stemming run, but a relevant document was ranked first in the 4-gram run. 4-gram matches in the relevant documents included 'futballista', 'futballkapus' (goalkeeper), 'futballválogatott', 'vállsérülést', 'vállsérüléssel', 'vállsérülés', 'sérülés' (injury), 'sérült' and 'sérültet'. This might be a case for which decompounding would be helpful.
– HU-261 (Jövendőmondás (Fortune-telling)): The run which used stemming only matched the one document that contained 'jövendőmondást' and (the original form) 'jövendőmondás' and it was judged non-relevant, so it scored 0 on this topic. The 4-gram run returned 1 of the 3 relevant documents at rank 2 (the others weren't ranked in the top 100). Matches in the relevant document included 'jövendölők' and 'jövendőmondók'. The latter of these perhaps could have been matched with additional stemming rules, but the former would require a stemmer to do decompounding (or, if the user had decompounded the query, the latter would require index-time decompounding to match).

N-gram approaches typically produce larger indexes and its queries can be slower for common word-searching cases. SearchServer can find character sequences inside European words without n-gramming if the user specifies wildcards (though an n-gram index may help performance for wildcard queries). We're not aware of them being used in practice for European language retrieval, except perhaps by web search engines for url indexing.

4 Submitted Runs

Table 6 lists the mean scores of the runs submitted for assessment in May 2005. In the identifiers (e.g. "humBG05tde"), 't' and 'd' indicate that the Title and Description field of the topic were used (respectively), and 'e' indicates that query expansion from blind feedback on the first 2 rows was used (see last year's paper [10] for more details). From the Description fields for Bulgarian, instruction words such as "find", "relevant" and "document" were automatically removed (based on looking at some older topic lists, not this year's topics; this step was skipped for Hungarian because we lacked an older topic list).

Table 6. Mean Scores of Submitted Runs

Run	FRS	Success@1	Success@5	Success@10	MRR	MAP
humBG05t	0.749	15/49 (31%)	35/49 (71%)	39/49 (80%)	0.476	0.259
humBG05td	0.815	18/49 (37%)	39/49 (80%)	42/49 (86%)	0.537	0.275
humBG05tde	0.752	21/49 (43%)	35/49 (71%)	38/49 (78%)	0.549	0.298
humHU05t	0.788	25/50 (50%)	37/50 (74%)	42/50 (84%)	0.613	0.274
humHU05td	0.838	23/50 (46%)	41/50 (82%)	43/50 (86%)	0.614	0.306
humHU05tde	0.835	22/50 (44%)	38/50 (76%)	45/50 (90%)	0.602	0.331

The submitted Bulgarian and Hungarian Title-only runs (i.e. "humBG05t" and "humHU05t" of Table 6) correspond to the "neu" diagnostic runs (i.e. "BG-neu" and "HU-neu" of Table 1).

References

1. AltaVista's Babel Fish Translation Service. http://babelfish.altavista.com/tr
2. Cross-Language Evaluation Forum web site. http://www.clef-campaign.org/
3. Andrew Hodgson. Converting the Fulcrum Search Engine to Unicode. *Sixteenth International Unicode Conference*, 2000.
4. Paul McNamee and James Mayfield. JHU/APL Experiments in Tokenization and Non-Word Translation. *Proceedings of CLEF 2003.*
5. MTA SZTAKI: English-Hungarian, Hungarian-English Online Dictionary. http://dict.sztaki.hu/english-hungarian
6. NTCIR (NII-NACSIS Test Collection for IR Systems) Home Page. http://research.nii.ac.jp/~ntcadm/index-en.html
7. S. E. Robertson, S. Walker, S. Jones, M. M. Hancock-Beaulieu and M. Gatford. Okapi at TREC-3. *Proceedings of TREC-3*, 1995.
8. Jacques Savoy. CLEF and Multilingual information retrieval resource page. http://www.unine.ch/info/clef/ (visited May 2005)
9. Text REtrieval Conference (TREC) Home Page. http://trec.nist.gov/
10. Stephen Tomlinson. Finnish, Portuguese and Russian Retrieval with Hummingbird SearchServer™ at CLEF 2004. *Proceedings of CLEF 2004.*

Combining Passages in the Monolingual Task with the IR-n System

Fernando Llopis and Elisa Noguera

Grupo de investigación en Procesamiento del Lenguaje Natural y Sistemas de Información
Departamento de Lenguajes y Sistemas Informáticos
University of Alicante, Spain
{llopis, elisa}@dlsi.ua.es

Abstract. The paper describes our participation in the monolingual tasks at CLEF 2005. We submitted results for the following languages: French, Portuguese, Bulgarian and Hungarian, using a passage retrieval system. We focused on a version of this system that combines passages of different size to improve retrieval performance. After an analysis of our experiments and of the official results at CLEF, we find that our passage retrieval combination model achieves considerably improved scores.

1 Introduction

Information Retrieval systems based on passages (PR) [2] determine the relevance of a document with respect to a query on the basis of the similarity of different fragments of the document to the query. The PR model not only makes it possible to better locate relevant documents, but also allows us to find the most relevant part of the document accurately. For this reason, we think that PR systems could be used profitably in other tasks, such as Question Answering (QA).

2 IR-n System

The IR-n system [3] is a PR system which uses passages with a fixed number of sentences. This provides the passages with some syntactical content.

In this section the main characteristics of the IR-n system are presented and details are given on the combined passages version of the system used in CLEF 2005.

Similarity measures. The IR-n system uses several similarity measures: cosine [4], pivoted cosine [6] and okapi [5]. The values of parameters (k1,b,avg) can be easily updated in order to improve results. On the whole, our experiments show that we obtain the best results using Okapi measures. We have also evaluated the results obtained with normalization.

C. Peters et al. (Eds.): CLEF 2005, LNCS 4022, pp. 204–207, 2006.

Query expansion. Most IR systems use query expansion techniques [1] based on adding the most frequent terms contained in the most relevant documents to the original query. The IR-n architecture allows us to use query expansion based on either the most relevant passages or the most relevant documents. In CLEF 2004, we obtained better results using the most relevant passages.

Combined passages. For this year's experiments, we have developed a technique called 'combined passages'. The technique consists of applying strategies, which are similar to those used to merge lists of relevant document in the multilingual task, to lists of relevant passages of different sizes. The lists which are obtained have been combined using four methods. Table 1 shows different methods used to obtain the ranking of scores. Method 1 merges the lists and if a document is in several lists it will have the highest score. Method 2 computes the average of the scores. Methods 3 and 4 are the same as Methods 1 and 2, respectively, but apply normalization. This normalization is carried out subtracting the score of each document RSV_k from the minimum score of the list and dividing by $max(RSV_K) - min(RSV_k)$.

Table 1. Data fusion methods

Number	Method	Formula
1	MAX	$max(RSV_k)$
2	SUM	$sum(RSV_k)$
3	MAX RSVnorm	$max((RSV_k - min(RSV_k))/(max(RSV_k) - min(RSV_k))$
4	SUM RSVnorm	$sum((RSV_k - min(RSV_k))/(max(RSV_k) - min(RSV_k))$

3 Training

We trained the 'combined passage' system on the following languages: English, French and Portuguese using the CLEF 2003 (English and French) and CLEF 2004 (Portuguese) collections. Query expansion techniques were also tested for all languages.

Fixed size passages. Several experiments were performed to determine the size of the passages and the values of the parameters in the Okapi system in order to obtain the best results. The passage size is the same for all languages (8 sentences), with the exception of French where it was 9 sentences.

Fixed size passages with query expansion. Our experiments with query expansion tried to fix the number of terms to be added to the original query and the number of documents (passages) to be taken into account. We also tested the use of passages of different sizes. We obtained the best results with 10 terms in every test, and the 5 or 10 most relevant passages were used, depending on the specific language.

Query expansion using fixed-size passages allows us to improve system performance by between 3.6% and 7.2%, depending on the language.

Table 2. CLEF 2005 official results. Monolingual tasks

Language	Run	AvgP	Dif
French	CLEF Average	35.30	
	IRn-fr-vexp	35.90	+1.7%
	IRn-fr-fexp	34.85	
	IRn-fr-vnexp	30.70	
Portuguese	CLEF Average	33.29	
	IRn-pt-vexp	36.03	+8.2%
	IRn-pt-fexp	34.46	
	IRn-pt-vnexp	33.15	
Hungarian	CLEF Average	29.00	
	IRn-hu-vexp	31.74	+9.4%
	IRn-hu-fexp	30.55	
	IRn-hu-vnexp	30.36	
Bulgarian	CLEF Average	22.00	
	IRn-bu-vexp	17.46	
	IRn-bu-fexp	17.58	
	IRn-bu-vnexp	17.87	-18.0%

Combined passages. The combined passages method consists in using the similarity values provided by passages of different sizes from the same document in order to calculate the document similarity. Three passage sizes have been defined: small, medium and big. Experiments were carried out using one passage of each type. First the similarity of each passage with respect to the query is obtained. Document similarity is then calculated using one of the four methods described previously. The combined method that gives the best results is Method 2 (SUM without normalization). Our experiments showed that the results improved for all languages, except French, using this method compared with those for the fixed passage system.

Combined passages with query expansion. We carried out the same tests with query expansion and the results improved for all languages, although the increase was not significant for Portuguese. The best combined method for English and Portuguese was again Method 2 (SUM), but for French it was Method 1 (MAX). The combined passage system shows an improvement in performance of between 3.1% and 7.7% depending on the language.

4 Results at CLEF 2005

We submitted three runs[1] for each language in our participation in CLEF 2005. The best parameters, i.e. those that gave the best results in system training, were used in all cases.

[1] 'fexp' fixed method with query expansion, 'vexp' combined method with query expansion and 'vnexp' combined method without query expansion.

The official results for each run are shown in Table 2. The version IRn-xx-vnexp is taken as reference. Like other systems which use query expansion techniques, this version improves performance with respect to the base system. Our results are appreciably above average in all languages, except for Bulgarian where they are below average.

5 Conclusions and Future Work

We have described a passage retrieval system which combines the similarity values of three different sized passages from a document in order to obtain a similarity value for the document with respect to the query. This technique has given us an improvement in system performance of approximately 4% with respect to the version which only uses a fixed size passage. The architecture of the IR-n system allows us to use this combined model without any significant increase in system response times. In the future, we intend not only to improve this system, but also to apply it to the Question Answering task.

Acknowledgements

This research has been partially funded by the Spanish Government under project CICyT number TIC2003-07158-C04-01 and by the Valencian Government under project numbers GV04B-276 and GV04B-268.

References

1. Aitao Chen and Fredric C. Gey. Combining query translation and document translation in cross-language retrieval. In *CLEF 2003*, LNCS, pages 108–121, Trondheim, Norway, 2003. Springer-Verlag.
2. M. Kaskziel and J. Zobel. Passage retrieval revisited. In *Proceedings of the 20th annual International ACM Philadelphia SIGIR*, pages 178–185, 1997.
3. F. Llopis. *IR-n: Un Sistema de Recuperación de Información Basado en Pasajes.* PhD thesis, University of Alicante, 2003.
4. G. Salton. Automatic text processing: The transformation, analysis, and retrieval of information by computer. 1989.
5. Savoy J. Fusion of probabilistic models for effective monolingual retrieval. In *CLEF 2003*, LNCS, Trondheim, Norway, 2003. Springer-Verlag.
6. A. Singhal, C. Buckley, and M. Mitra. Pivoted document length normalization. In *Proceedings of the 19th Annual International ACM SIGIR*, pages 21–29, 1996.

Weighting Query Terms Based on Distributional Statistics

Jussi Karlgren, Magnus Sahlgren, and Rickard Cöster

Swedish Institute of Computer Science, Box 1263 SE-164 29 KISTA, Sweden
{jussi, mange, rick}@sics.se
http://www.sics.se

Abstract. This year, the SICS team has concentrated on query processing and on the internal topical structure of the query, specifically compound translation. Compound translation is non-trivial due to dependencies between compound elements. This year, we have investigated topical dependencies between query terms: if a query term happens to be non-topical or noise, it should be discarded or given a low weight when ranking retrieved documents; if a query term shows high topicality its weight should be boosted. The two experiments described here are based on the analysis of the distributional character of query terms: one using similarity of occurrence context between query terms globally across the entire collection; the other using the likelihood of individual terms to appear topically in individual texts. Both – complementary – boosting schemes tested delivered improved results.

1 Query Terms and Their Internal Relations

This year, the SICS team decided to concentrate on query processing and on the internal topical structure of the query: we have identified this as one of the major bottlenecks for cross-lingual access systems. Previous years, the SICS team has investigated, among other issues, how to translate compounds [1]. Compound translation is non-trivial due to dependencies between compound elements and has been treated in various ways in the treatment of compounding languages such as Swedish [2,3,4,5, e.g.] as well as other languages [6, e.g.]. We decided this year to investigate the topical dependencies between query terms, under the hypothesis that the complexity of translating compounds is a special case of the more general case of understanding the respective topicality of query terms.

The question under investigation is how much each query term contributes in terms of topicality in the documents of the collection under consideration. If a query term happens to be non-topical or noise, it should be discarded or given a low weight when ranking retrieved documents; if a query term shows high topicality its weight should be boosted. Our base system is used with two different enhancements to test the hypothesis that boosting topically active terms is beneficial for retreival results.

C. Peters et al. (Eds.): CLEF 2005, LNCS 4022, pp. 208–211, 2006.

2 Baseline Retrieval System

The French target collection and the French topics were lemmatized and normalized using the commercially available FDG tools from Connexor Oy, described in several publications [7, e.g.].[1] The text retrieval engine used for our experiments is based on a standard retrieval system being developed at SICS. A more detailed description of the system is provided in the CLEF paper from 2002 [8].

In retrieval, query terms are weighted by a combination of standard tf-idf metrics with pivoted document length normalization [9] and a boosting procedure where documents containing several of the query terms are boosted higher than documents with the equivalent number of occurrences. In effect, the more query terms that are matched in a document, the higher the boosting weight, but the final weight for that document is not necessarily higher than for a document that has fewer matching terms.

The French target collection was indexed by the system and the translated French queries were used to retrieve texts from the French collection without manual intervention.

3 Term Selection Using Distributional Statistics

In this experiment, we use distributional information to weight words selected from the query description field. The idea is to select words with similar distributional properties, since they can be assumed to indicate similar topics. As an example, consider query number 251, where supposedly the term *"médecine"* is a good descriptor. We would then want to boost the weight of query words that are topically similar to *"médecine"* but that occur in other documents (it would be no point in selecting words that occur in *exactly* the same documents, since we retrieve those documents anyway by using the term *"médecine"*). Considering the example query, we would supposedly like to include words such as *"homéopathie", "chiropractie", "acupuncture", and "thérapie"*. Our hypothesis is that we can use second-order co-occurrence information to find such query words.

The difference between first-order and second-order co-occurrences is that words with a first-order co-occurrence relation are words that co-occur, while words with a second-order co-occurrence relation are words that typically *do not* co-occur, but occur in similar contexts. An example of the former type of relation is associative relations, such as "doctor" – "cure", and an example of the latter type is synonyms, such as "doctor" – "physician". We use *second-order* co-occurrences, since we want to find words with similar distributional statistics that *do not* occur in the same documents, but that occur in the same *type of contexts.* Using first order co-ocurrences would merely find words that occur in similar documents, which is not beneficial for the adhoc Information Retrieval task, since those documents are found by the system by default.

[1] Thanks to Timo Järvinen and Connexor Oy for performing the morphological analysis of the data.

Table 1. Summary of results

	Average precision	Precision at 20	Above median	At median	Below median
V	0.3135	0.420	14	9	27
B	0.3174	0.421	15	11	24
K	0.3271	0.427	21	1	27

Our approach is based on Random Indexing[10,11], a technique for the efficient and tractable analysis of co-occurrence statistics. Random Indexing incrementally collects distributional data for terms in the text collection under consideration and can be used to build a vector space based on those data. In this experiment we use Random Indexing[2] to collect second-order co-occurrences to accumulate a word space in which words with similar distributional properties are located close to each other. We compute distributional similarity between words using the cosine of the angles between "context vectors" that represent their distributional profiles. The cosine values are then used to weight the words in the query description field.

4 Probabilistic Models: Katz' γ

Using an analysis of query term distribution in the target collection, Katz' γ is calculated for each term in the query. This can be understood as the estimated probability for the term to appear at least twice in any given text and is calculated by as the relative frequency of texts with at least two occurrences of the term under consideration to texts with only one occurrence of it. The intuition underlying Katz' γ is that singleton occurrences may be happenstance noise whereas repeated occurrences of a term are likely to be topical [12]; the intuition behind our use of the measure is that terms that often are likely to be topical are likely to be of more interest as regards query relevance than terms that often occur non-topically.

5 Three Submissions and Their Results

A summary of results is shown in table 1. The first submission (V) used the baseline system without modification. The second submission (B) boosted query terms according to their location in the vector space as provided by random key indexing by multiplying the standard tf.idf score with the cosine between it and the closest neighbor of the other query terms. The third submission (K) boosted terms that are likely to be topical by multiplying the standard tf.idf score with its γ. The results were reasonably good with half of the fifty queries on or above median. The two boosting schemes proved to deliver improved results.

[2] Parameters settings for the Random Indexing process: 1000-dimensional vectors; 1% non-zero elements in the index vectors; 2+2-sized distance weighted context window.

6 Conclusions

The results of the boosting schemes delivered uncontroversially improved results. One scheme examined the individual character of the terms; the other the relation between query terms. These are two different avenues of analysis and will most likely provide different (and even better) results if pursued further. These results will also provide impetus for the further study of translation of complex terms — the question which first prompted this set of experiments in the first place.

References

1. Cöster, R., Sahlgren, M., Karlgren, J.: Selective compound splitting of swedish queries for boolean combinations of truncated terms. In Peters, C., Braschler, M., Gonzalo, J., Kluck, M., eds.: 4th Workshop of the Cross–Language Evaluation Forum (CLEF 2003), Lecture Notes in Computer Science (LNCS), Springer, Heidelberg (2004)
2. Ahlgren, P.: The Effects of Indexing Strategy-Query Term Combination on Retrieval Effectiveness in a Swedish Full Text Database. PhD thesis, Department of Library and Information Science, University College of Borås, Borås, Sweden (2004)
3. Dalianis, H.: Improving search engine retrieval using a compound splitter for swedish. In: Proceedings of the 15th Nordic Conference of Computational Linguistics, Joensuu, Finland, University of Joensuu (2005)
4. Hedlund, T.: Dictionary-Based Cross-Language Information Retrieval: Principles, System Design and Evaluation. PhD thesis, Department of Information Science, University of Tampere, Tampere, Finland (2003)
5. Karlgren, J.: Compound terms and their constituent elements in information retrieval. In: Proceedings of the 15th Nordic Conference of Computational Linguistics, Joensuu, Finland, University of Joensuu (2005)
6. Braschler, M., Ripplinger, B.: How effective is stemming and decompounding for german text retrieval? Information Retrieval **7** (2004) 291–306
7. Tapanainen, P., Järvinen, T.: A non-projective dependency parser. In: Proceedings of the 5th Conference on Applied Natural Language Processing, Association for Computational Linguistics (1997) 64–71
8. Sahlgren, M., Karlgren, J., Cöster, R., Järvinen, T.: SICS at CLEF 2002: Automatic query expansion using random indexing. In: The CLEF 2002 Workshop. (2002)
9. Singhal, A., Buckley, C., Mitra, M.: Pivoted document length normalization. In: Proceedings of the 19th International Conference on Research and Development in Information Retrieval, Zürich, Switzerland, ACM SIGIR (1996) 21–29
10. Kanerva, P., Kristofersson, J., Holst, A.: Random indexing of text samples for latent semantic analysis. In: Proceedings of the 22nd Annual Conference of the Cognitive Science Society, Erlbaum (2000) 1036
11. Karlgren, J., Sahlgren, M.: From words to understanding. In Uesaka, Y., Kanerva, P., Asoh, H., eds.: Foundations of Real-World Intelligence. CSLI Publications (2001)
12. Katz, S.: Distribution of content words and phrases in text and language modelling. Natural Language Engineering **2** (1996) 15–60

Domain-Specific Track CLEF 2005: Overview of Results and Approaches, Remarks on the Assessment Analysis

Michael Kluck[1] and Maximilian Stempfhuber[2]

[1] Stiftung Wissenschaft und Politik (SWP), German Institute for International and Security Affairs, Ludwigkirchplatz 3-4, 10719 Berlin, Germany
michael.kluck@swp-berlin.org

[2] Informationszentrum Sozialwissenschaften (IZ), Lennéstrasse 30, 53113 Bonn, Germany
stempfhuber@iz-soz.de

Abstract. The challenge of the CLEF domain-specific track is to map user queries in one language to documents in different languages adapting the systems used to the vocabulary and wording of the social science domain. In addition to a general overview of this track and its tasks, some details on the approaches of the participating groups and their results are reported. One of the outcomes is the considerable improvement in results if the retrieval systems make use of the thesauri provided or the intellectually assigned descriptors. Other findings for IR in a domain-specific context are also given. Finally, considerations on the topic creation and assessment processes are made on the basis of empirical data mainly from the GIRT corpus.

1 The Domain-Specific Track with GIRT and RSSC in the CLEF 2005 Campaign

The domain-specific track aims at mono- and cross-language information retrieval on structured scientific data. The challenge of the CLEF domain-specific track is to map user queries in one language to documents in different languages, adapting the retrieval systems and translation components to the domain-specific vocabulary and wording, and to merge the results in one result list. This track studies retrieval in a domain-specific context using two social science databases:

- the German Indexing and Retrieval Test database (GIRT) (fourth version GIRT-4: German/English pseudo-parallel corpus with identical documents in the GIRT4-DE and the GIRT4-EN part) with 302,638 documents in total (see [1], [2], [3]),
- the new Russian Social Science Corpus (RSSC) with 94,581 documents, which contains mainly short references on social science literature with a bias towards economy (see http://www.socionet.ru and http://socionet.org/bd-en.htm).

The task of mapping user queries (which are called topics in the CLEF context) was split into different sub-tasks for the 2005 campaign:

C. Peters et al. (Eds.): CLEF 2005, LNCS 4022, pp. 212 – 221, 2006.

1. Monolingual task:
    a. German topics against German data GIRT4-DE,
    b. English topics against English data GIRT4-EN,
    c. Russian topics against Russian data RSSC;
2. Bilingual task:
    a. German topics against English data GIRT4-EN,
    b. German topics against Russian data RSSC,
    c. English topics against German data GIRT4-DE,
    d. English topics against Russian data RSSC,
    e. Russian topics against German data GIRT4-DE,
    f. Russian topics against English data GIRT4-EN;
3. Multilingual task:
    a. German topics against all data GIRT4-DE, GIRT4-EN, RSSC,
    b. English topics against all data GIRT4-DE, GIRT4-EN, RSSC,
    c. Russian topics against all data GIRT4-DE, GIRT4-EN, RSSC.

In the context of these sub-tasks the participating groups carried out their retrieval experiments and delivered the top-ranked 1,000 documents for each topic (a 'run') they worked on. The runs of all groups were then merged per topic (pooled) and the top-ranked 60 documents of each pool were assessed for relevance.

The domain-specific task attracted 8 participating groups (two of them from UC Berkeley), and produced a total of 76 runs: 40 monolingual runs, 33 bilingual runs and 3 multilingual runs. For 27 runs the topic language was German, for 33 runs English, and for 16 runs Russian (see Table 1).

Table 1. Sub-tasks by topic languages

Sub-task	Participants	Runs	Topic Language		
			DE	***EN***	***RU***
Multilingual	1	3	1	1	1
Bilingual X to DE	5	15		14	1
Bilingual X to EN	4	13	7		6
Bilingual X to RU	3	5	2	3	
Monolingual DE	6	17	17		
Monolingual EN	6	15		15	
Monolingual RU	5	8			8
Sum	8	76	27	33	16

In Table 2 the number of judged runs is compared to the figures for 2003 and 2004. The distribution of data sources and topic languages are also indicated, and grouped to the sub-tasks. Unlike the previous years, all possible variations of the sub-tasks have been tried at least once. In particular, the Russian topic language was used frequently, not only for the newly added RSSC corpus.

The following groups participated in the domain-specific track: IRIT, Toulouse, France (see [4]), Moscow State University, Russia (see [5]), University California, Berkeley, United States (2 groups, one paper: see [6]), University Glasgow, UK (no

Table 2. Data sources, topic languages and runs 2003 - 2005

Data source	***Topic language***	***Judged runs***					
		2005	*2004*	*2003*	***2005***	*2004*	*2003*
GIRT4-DE	DE	**17**	8	13	*Monolingual*		
GIRT4-EN	EN	**15**	7	4	***40***	15	17
RSSC	RU	**8**	-	-			
RSSC	DE	**2**	-	-	*Bilingual*		
RSSC	EN	**3**	-	-	***33***	*16*	*5*
GIRT4-DE	EN	**14**	6	1			
GIRT4-DE	RU	**1**	0	2			
GIRT4-EN	DE	**7**	10	1			
GIRT4-EN	RU	**6**	0	1			
GIRT4-DE, GIRT4- EN, RSSC	DE or EN or RU				*Multilingual*		
		3	-	-	***3***	-	-
All runs		***76***	***31***	***22***			

paper available), University Hagen, Germany (see [7]), University Hildesheim, Germany (see [8]), University Neuchâtel, Switzerland (see [9]).

2 Main Approaches and Results

The approaches and results of the eight groups participating in the domain-specific track are reported in detail in this volume; the relevant papers are divided between this section and the ad-hoc section. Here, we provide an overview.

The information retrieval systems explicitly mentioned by the participants are based on logistic regression, on vector models or on probabilistic models such as OKAPI or Prosit.

The majority of groups made use of query expansion, and most of them used the thesauri provided with the corpora for this purpose (German-English Thesaurus for the Social Sciences with an additional German-Russian wordlist provided for GIRT, and a Russian-English Socio-Political Thesaurus for the RSSC), while IRIT made use of WordNet. When comparing the results of the groups with the query processing used, we found that whenever the thesauri were used for query expansion or translation, the results significantly improved. The same improvement was found if the descriptor field of the documents (with intellectually assigned keywords from the thesaurus) was included in the processing of the documents; for example the University of Neuchâtel reported an improvement of 14% to 37% in this case [9]. On the other hand Berkley-2 had success with using the thesaurus terms for query enhancement: based on title/description words of the topic, thesaurus term that are highly associated with them were suggested using different weighting strategies.[6]

Other interesting details in the approaches tried were:

- For the translation of topics (title or title and description) several machine translation systems were used, compared, and/or combined: L+H Power-translator, Systran/Babelfish, Promt, WorldLingo, IMTranslator, Free-Translation, Eurodictautom.
- Some groups concentrated on data fusion aspects.
- Besides linguistic treatment in the form of stemmers, POS, and de-compounding the extraction of semantically related concepts or WordNet concepts was also applied.

Some groups experimented with blind or pseudo-relevance feedback which seems to improve results in many, but not all cases.

With respect to the results, some groups emphasized the importance of robustness of the methodology they used and of high-quality results on a per topic basis rather than high average precision over all queries.

The following figures show some comparative statistics of the bilingual runs of any topic language used against the German GIRT4 corpus (fig. 1), and of monolingual runs with Russian as topic language against the Russian RSSC corpus (fig. 2). All results and comparisons are available at http://clef.isti.cnr.it/2005/working_notes/workingnotes2005/appendix_a.pdf .

3 Topic Creation and Relevance Assessment

The topic creation and the relevance assessment are directly related processes with high influence on evaluation results. Both are therefore analyzed periodically. This

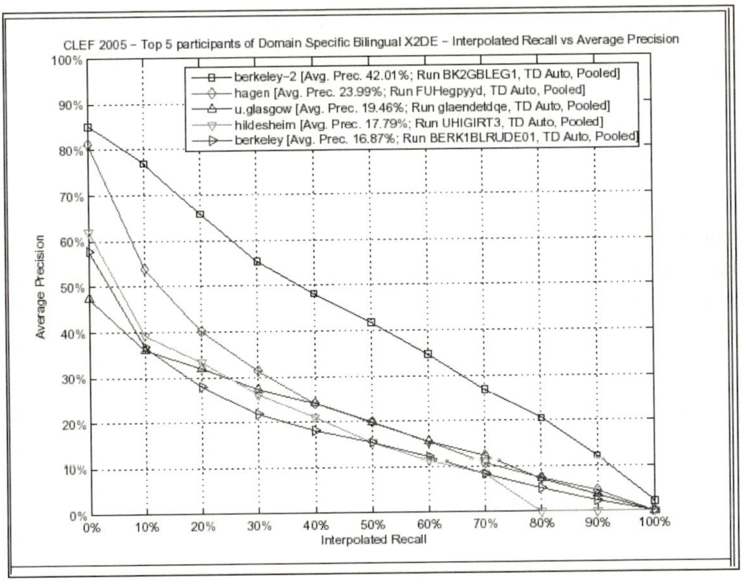

Fig. 1. Top 5 Participants for Bilingual X to German

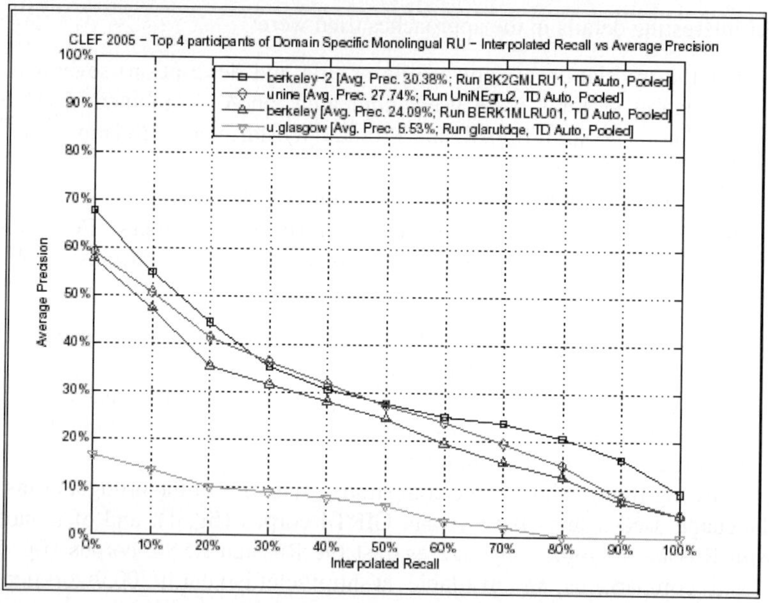

Fig. 2. Top 4 Participants for Monolingual Russian

year we give some insight into the topic creation process for social science queries and into the process of relevance assessment and re-assessment of the results.

3.1 Topic Creation for the Domain-Specific Task

A topic – a fictive information need of a user – contains a headline (title), a one sentence-query (description), and a detailed abstract of the intention of the query (narrative). The narrative also comprises the conditions for the relevance judgment of any single document including negations or exclusion criteria. These three topic elements or any combination of them may be used for processing the query by the retrieval systems, whereas a run with the title and the description elements is mandatory. For further details on the topic creation rules for the ad-hoc track, which also apply for the domain-specific track, see [10].

For the 2005 campaign of the CLEF domain-specific track, 25 topics were developed (the usual number for this track), which cover social science queries only. The topics were derived from the content of the documents available in the German GIRT4-corpus, and then translated into English and Russian. They were also spot tested against the Russian RSSC-corpus, to assure at least one hit per topic.

The proposed topics had to fulfill the following criteria:

- Deal with social sciences in a broad sense.
- Be different from the 125 topics of the campaigns 2000 to 2004.
- Can be used as closed and open answer formats, but give clear instructions for the assessors.

- The description element should show the whole intention of the topic in one sentence.
- The narratives should give good advice for the relevance decision of the assessors, especially by giving exclusion criteria and defining interpretation possibilities. The main function was to narrow or enlarge the topic with respect to possible hits in the GIRT or RSSC corpus. If it was known that there were a lot of potentially relevant documents, the narrative contained strong restrictions, in order to cut down the number of possibly relevant documents. If the pre-test showed only a few hits, then the narrative enlarged the scope of relevancy by adding broader conditions.

60 topic proposals were formulated, from which the final 25 topics were taken. These topics found between 5 to 50 relevant documents during the pre-tests. The complex interrelation between topic formulation and relevance assessment is discussed in detail by [11].

3.2 Overview of the Assessments

Out of the RSSC corpus with 94,581 documents, 8,881 documents were pooled and assessed. Of those, 831 documents were judged as relevant, i.e. equal to 9.36 % of the pooled documents. Six of the topics had very few (up to 1 %) or no relevant documents. This low number of relevant documents is – beside others – due to the fact that the topics had to be created before we had good access to the RSSC data (although during the pre-tests all topics were found to have at least one hit), and that the RSSC data contained less text per document than the GIRT4 data. In addition, the topics were directed mainly towards individual and group related social problems whereas the RSSC data was broader in the sense of societal and economic problems. Thus, to some extent there was a mismatch between the topics and the RSSC data which could not be compensated the first time the RSSC data was used in CLEF.

Table 3. Assessment of GIRT4 Results

	all DE docs	*relevant DE docs*	*Non-relevant DE docs*	*proportion of relevant DE docs per topic*	*all EN docs*	*relevant EN docs*	*Non-relevant EN docs*	*proportion of relevant EN docs per topic*	*doc pairs DE-EN*
sum	13,188	2,682	10,506	-	10,060	2.105	7,955	-	3,262
average	527.5	107.3	420.2	20.3%	402.4	84.2	318.2	20.9%	130
min	190	8	38	1.2%	180	6	49	1.0%	67
max	904	318	857	80.0%	611	242	580	75.3%	218
standard deviation	139.9	89.8	163.0	20.0%	111.7	67.7	127.3	18.3%	31.4

For the GIRT4 corpus we assessed many more documents: 23,248. Compared to the CLEF 2004 campaign, there was an increase of assessed documents, but also of the proportion of relevant documents per topic (see Table 3).

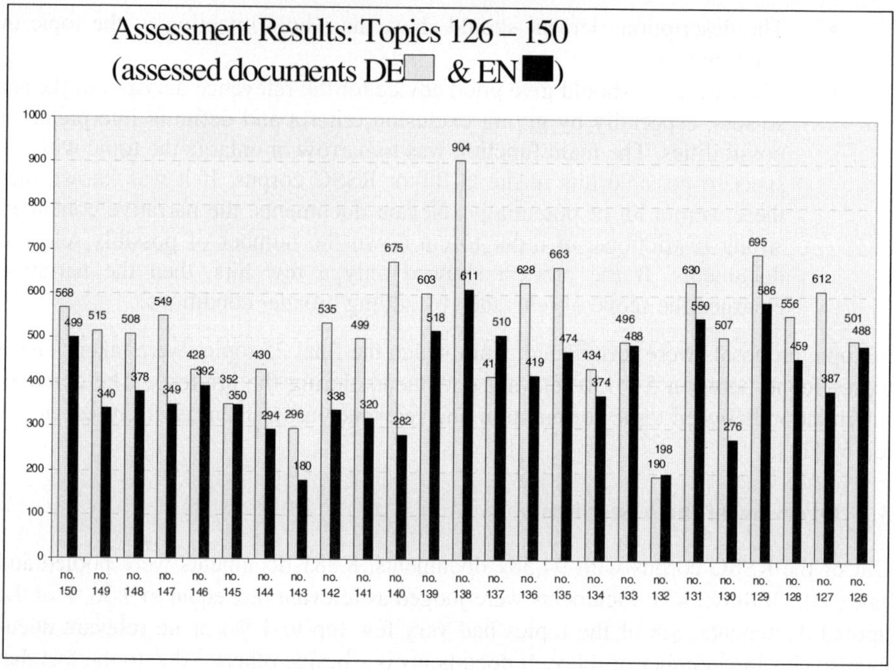

Fig. 3. Number of Assessed Documents per Topic in GIRT4

With respect to the German part of GIRT4, GIRT4-DE, there was a big variation of the number of relevant documents per topic: from 1 % to 80 % with a mean of 20 % (with a standard deviation of 20 %). For GIRT4-EN, the English part of GIRT4, we had 1 % to 75 % relevant documents per topic with a mean of 21 % and a standard deviation of 18 %. A comparison of the number of relevant documents for CLEF 2004 and 2005 is shown in Table 3. There are not only more assessed documents, but also more relevant documents per topic. At the same time the standard deviation of relevant documents per topic has also grown from 56 to 90 for GIRT4-DE and from 45 to 68 for GIRT4-EN.

The systems behaved as expected from theory and from last year's experience: For topics with negative difference of the proportional allotment of relevant documents beyond the standard deviation (i.e. topics with a low number of relevant hits) the retrieval systems were quite effective if a high number of relevant documents was found, but if the proportion of relevant documents was quite low and there were actually few relevant documents, the retrieval systems did not find many of the relevant documents.

For topics with positive difference of proportional allotment of relevant documents beyond the standard deviation (i.e. topics with a high number of relevant hits) the retrieval systems were quite effective, but delivered too many non-relevant documents if the proportional allotment of relevant documents was high. If the number of

Table 4. Comparison GIRT4 Assessment 2004 and 2005

	all DE	relevant DE	proportion relevant DE	all EN	relevant EN	proportion relevant EN
# 2004	9736	1663	17,1%	8556	1235	14,4%
# 2005	13188	2682	20,3%	10060	2105	20,9%
Mean per topic 2004	389,4	66,5		342,2	49,4	
Mean per topic 2005	527,5	107,3		402,4	84,2	

relevant documents found was quite low, the retrieval systems could not process the query effectively as they were not able to distinguish between relevant and non-relevant documents properly.

3.3 Pairs of Relevant Documents in the GIRT Results

As GIRT4 is a parallel corpus of English and German documents, we can see whether a document found in the German part (GIRT4-DE) has a corresponding document found in the English part (GIRT4-EN). These corresponding documents are called pairs. For this reason IZ has created a concordance list of corresponding documents.

Out of the 13,188 German and 10,060 English documents found we could detect 3,262 pairs. This means the assessors made 26,248 judgments, but in 6,524 cases they judged the paired documents as well in German as in English. These judgments were compared and led to conflicting cases in the re-assessment which is described in the next paragraph. For 9,926 German documents, no English equivalent was found by the participants, for 6,789 English documents there were no German equivalents. The document pairs did actually include relevant as well as non-relevant documents. If we restrict the comparison of pairs and non-pairs to relevant documents found by the systems, there were 1,180 German and 708 English documents without their equivalents in the respective language; in total there were 1,332 pairs of relevant documents.

3.4 Re-assessment for the GIRT Corpus

Similarly to last year, two assessors made the judgments – one per language. Both assessors communicated closely when interpreting the relevance of each topic. In some cases (4 topics) the discussion among the assessors led to a new assessment for the whole topic. The assessment work was supported by a newly designed assessment tool, which especially supported the assessment of the parallel corpora. The new assessment tool[1] was build by IZ and is written in Java.

If the assessors judged differently for any document of the pairs, a re-assessment was carried out to make the relevance decisions identical (or keep the different assessments because of the lack of text in one of the corresponding documents). Compared to CLEF 2004, the relative number of changed pairs was nearly the same (about 2 %), although the total number of judged documents has grown. The typology for

[1] See http://www.gesis.org/Forschung/Informationstechnologie/CLEF-DELOS.htm for information on the assessment tool.

changes has been kept the same. Detailed information on this typology and the respective encodings can be obtained in [3]. In 2005 far fewer errors were made by the assessors, but the number of different judgments caused by the lack of text within the respective documents increased significantly.

Table 5. Reasons for Changes of Assessments

Year	2004		2005	
change code / reasons of different judgments	*# docs*	*percent*	*# docs*	*percent*
real mistakes (DE + EN)	120	35,3%	33	6,0%
new interpretation of relevance (DEA + ENA + TE)	201	59,1%	287	51,9%
too short text for equal judgment (TDX + TEX)	19	5,6%	233	42,1%
sum	340	100,0%	553	100,0%

4 Outlook

For the next CLEF campaign we will try to acquire additional Russian social science data, especially documents with longer texts. We are also negotiating with the information provider Cambridge Scientific Abstracts (CSA) about parts of their Sociological Abstracts database which covers the same time period as the GIRT4 corpus, hopefully allowing us to add original English data to the test corpora.

We will smooth the organization of the topic creation and preparation phase to adjust the new topics for all corpora.

Acknowledgements

We greatly acknowledge the partial funding by the European Commission through the DELOS Network of Excellence on Digital Libraries. Again Marco Winter (grad. student of Humboldt-University Berlin) did a huge amount of work in preparing the German assessments and the statistical data. Claudia Henning did the English assessments. Stefan Bärisch developed the greatly improved assessment tool.

References

1. Kluck, M., Gey, F.C.: The Domain-Specific Task of CLEF – Specific Evaluation Strategies in Cross-Language Information Retrieval. In: Carol Peters (ed.): Cross-Language Information Retrieval and Evaluation. Workshop of Cross-Language Evaluation Forum, CLEF 2000, Lisbon, Portugal, September 21-22, 2000, Revised Papers. Berlin: Springer, 48-56, (2001)

2. Kluck, M.: The GIRT Data in the Evaluation of CLIR Systems – from 1997 until 2003. In: Peters, C., Gonzalo, J., Braschler, M., Kluck, M. (eds.): Comparative Evaluation of Multilingual Information Access Systems. 4th Workshop of the Cross-Language Evaluation Forum, CLEF 2003, Trondheim, Norway, August 21-22, 2003, Revised Selected Papers. Lecture Notes in Computer Science, Vol. 3237. Springer-Verlag Berlin Heidelberg New York, 379-393, (2004)
3. Kluck, M.: The Domain-Specific track in CLEF 2004: Overview of the Results and Remarks on the Assessment Process. In: Peters, C., Clough, P., Gonzalo, J., Jones, G.J.F., Kluck, M., Magnini, B. (eds.): Multilingual Information Access for Text, Speech and Images. 5th Workshop of the Cross-Language Evaluation Forum, CLEF 2004, Bath, UK, September 2004, Revised Selected Papers. Lecture Notes in Computer Science, Vol. 3491. Springer-Verlag Berlin Heidelberg New York, 260-270 (2005)
4. Baziz, M., Boughanem, M., Aussenac-Gilles, N.: Evaluating a Conceptual Indexing Method by Utilizing WordNet. (this volume) (2006)
5. Ageev, M., Dobrov, B., Loukachevitch, N.: Socio-Political Thesaurus in Concept-Based Information Retrieval. (this volume) (2006)
6. Petras, V., Gey, F., Larson, R.R.: Domain-Specific CLIR of English, German and Russian Using Fusion and Subject Metadata for Query Expansion. (this volume) (2006)
7. Leveling, J.: A Baseline for NLP in Domain-Specific IR. (this volume) (2006)
8. Hackl, R., Mandl, T.: Domain Specific Mono- and Bilingual English to German Retrieval Experiments with a Social Science Document Corpus. (this volume) (2006)
9. Savoy, J., Berger, P.-Y.: Monolingual, Bilingual, and GIRT Information Retrieval at CLEF-2005. (this volume) (2006)
10. Kluck, M.: Test Collection Report for the CLEF Campaign 2003: Deliverable 3.2.2, Bonn 2003, 10-11, http://www.clef-campaign.org/deliv_avail_to_public/Del322.pdf
11. Kluck, M., Winter, M.: Topic-Entwicklung und Relevanzbewertung bei GIRT: ein Werkstattbericht. In: Mandl, T.; Womser-Hacker, C. (eds.): Effektive Information Retrieval Verfahren in der Praxis. Proceedings Vierter Hildesheimer Evaluierungs- und Retrievalworkshop (HIER 2005), Hildesheim, 20. Juli 2005. Schriften zur Informationswissenschaft, Vol. 45. UVK, Konstanz (2006) to appear

A Baseline for NLP in Domain-Specific IR

Johannes Leveling

Intelligent Information and Communication Systems (IICS)
University of Hagen (FernUniversität in Hagen)
58084 Hagen, Germany
Johannes.Leveling@fernuni-hagen.de

Abstract. The information retrieval (IR) methods employed for the third participation of the University of Hagen in the domain-specific task of the Cross Language Evaluation Campaign (CLEF 2005) provide a baseline for experiments with natural language processing (NLP) methods in domain-specific IR than methods employed in our previous participations. The baseline consists of a combination of state-of-the-art IR methods with NLP methods for document and query processing.

Our monolingual experiments with German documents combine several methods to achieve better performance, including an entry vocabulary module (EVM), query expansion with semantically related concepts, and a blind feedback technique. The monolingual experiments focus on comparing two techniques for constructing database queries: creating a *'bag of words'* and creating a semantic network by means of deep linguistic analysis of the query.

For the bilingual experiments, the English topics are translated into German queries with several machine translation (MT) services publicly available. Each set of translated topics is processed separately with the same techniques as in the monolingual experiments. Evaluation results for official experiments with a staged logistic regression and additional experiments with BM25 are presented.

1 Introduction

This paper presents the results of the third participation of the University of Hagen in the domain-specific GIRT (German Indexing and Retrieval Testdatabase) task in the CLEF campaign. NLP methods as described in the following subsections are part of query processing for the NLI-Z39.50[1] ([1]), a natural language interface for information available on the internet.

For the monolingual experiments in CLEF 2005 two main objectives are pursued: 1) To establish a baseline for comparing the performance between NLP methods in IR, traditional approaches, and their combination. 2) To compare two techniques for creating database queries from the natural language topics: a)

[1] The NLI-Z39.50 was developed as part of the project "Natürlichsprachliches Interface für die internationale Standardschnittstelle Z39.50" and funded by the DFG (Deutsche Forschungsgemeinschaft) within the program "Modernisierung und Rationalisierung in wissenschaftlichen Bibliotheken".

C. Peters et al. (Eds.): CLEF 2005, LNCS 4022, pp. 222–225, 2006.

extracting keywords (*'bag of words'*) and b) applying a deep linguistic analysis by means of a syntactico-semantic parser before creating a database query.

For the bilingual experiments, MT services translate English query topics into German. The resulting translations are processed in separate experiments, employing the query processing techniques for monolingual experiments.

Our experimental setup for domain-specific IR supports a keyword extraction from queries or a deep linguistic analysis of queries (LA=yes/no), i.e. applying NLP methods to produce a semantic network representation (described in [2]); an entry vocabulary module (EVM=yes/no) to map words from an uncontrolled vocabulary to a controlled vocabulary, based on likelihoods of co-occurrence ([3]); blind feedback (BF=yes/no), i.e. extracting terms from top ranked documents for a query reformulation ([4]); and a query expansion with semantically related concepts (QEX=yes/no), including synonyms, hyponyms, and meronyms ([5]).

The document representations result from the morpho-lexical analyses of document titles and abstracts obtained by the WOCADI parser (WOrd ClAss based DIsambiguating parser, [6]). A stemmer and a stopword list consisting of a few hundred entries are applied to the lemmata, because stemming conflates adjectives, adverbs and nouns into a single index term. German noun compounds are analyzed with a lexicon-based decomposition.

Two techniques for query processing are compared. The first technique corresponds to extracting keywords from the topic title and topic description to create a database query as in traditional IR. The topic titles and descriptions are tokenized and word forms are extracted. Some normalization steps such as stopword removal and stemming are employed to produce a database query in the Database Independent Query Representation (DIQR, see [5]). The second query processing technique employs WOCADI to create a semantic network representation of the query according to the MultiNet paradigm ([7]) which is then transformed into a DIQR with a rule-based transformation engine.

For both techniques, the DIQR is mapped to a query in a formal language the database management software supports and submitted to the target database. The document representations were indexed with Cheshire II, which offers staged logistic regression as well as BM25 (OKAPI). The official experiments were based on a staged logistic regression; additional experiments used BM25.

2 Monolingual GIRT Experiments (German – German)

The monolingual GIRT experiments vary in the following parameter settings: using a query expansion with semantically related terms (QEX=yes/no), using an entry vocabulary module (EVM=yes/no), constructing a query from the semantic network obtained by a linguistic analysis of document titles and descriptions with the WOCADI parser or using a traditional keyword extraction (LA=yes/no), and using blind feedback (BF=yes/no). The best official result was obtained using the parameters QEX=yes, EVM=yes, LA=no, and BF=yes (0.3031 MAP in results of official experiments). Processing the queries with a deep linguistic analysis led to a slight decrease in performance (0.3017 MAP).

The best overall result determines the parameters for our new baseline for further experiments with NLP methods in domain-specific IR. It was achieved in the additional experiments with the parameter setting QEX=yes, EVM=yes, LA=yes, and BF=yes (0.3878 MAP) and shows a higher performance when the deep linguistic analysis of queries is used.

A more detailed description of the experimental setup and results are given in [8]. The performance of the best official experiment with respect to mean average precision is better in comparison to our experiments in CLEF 2003 (0.2064 MAP) and CLEF 2004 (0.2482 MAP).

The effect of any single query processing method (corresponding to a single parameter) is still inconclusive, but the combination of all processing methods with a deep linguistic analysis of the query yields the best performance with respect to the number of relevant and retrieved documents and MAP.

3 Bilingual GIRT Experiments (English – German)

Our bilingual GIRT experiments (matching English topics against the German data) are based on various MT services for a translation. For the bilingual retrieval experiments (English – German) with the GIRT document collection, four MT services translate the English topics into German queries: Free translation[2], Systran[3], and WorldLingo[4], and Promt[5].

The best results were achieved by creating a 'bag-of-words query' from the results of the Promt MT (0.2399 MAP in results for official experiments and 0.2807 MAP for the additional experiments). Analyzing query translations with WOCADI often failed, because morpho-syntactical and semantical tests on the translations (such as agreement between subject and verb and selectional restrictions for the complements of an action (verb)) failed for poor translations. Therefore, experiments using the second query processing method to produce a database query showed lower results (0.2111 MAP and 0.2447 MAP, respectively). Thus, potential advantages of a deep linguistic analysis are unavailable and a simple keyword extraction from the morpho-lexical stage in the WOCADI parser performs better.

4 Conclusion

In comparison with the results for the monolingual GIRT task in 2003 and 2004, performance with respect to the MAP for the best official experiment has improved considerably: 0.2064 MAP in 2003, 0.2482 in 2004, and 0.3031 in 2005. Additional experiments employed the ranking scheme BM25, which increased the number of relevant and retrieved documents and the mean average precision

[2] http://www.freetranslation.com/

[3] http://www.systransoft.com/

[4] http://www.worldlingo.com/wl/translate

[5] http://www.e-promt.com/en/

significantly (0.3878 MAP). As indicated by the better performance, the setup for the additional experiments provides a much better baseline for experiments with NLP methods in IR.

The method for constructing a database query using the transformation of the semantic network representation into a database query yields a higher performance than extracting keywords in combination with all other methods applied in these experiments. Results are still inconclusive in which cases NLP methods provide a better performance and even seem to depend on the ranking scheme employed.

The MT services tested did not produce high-quality translations. At the moment, using a keyword extraction yields better performance than a semantic analysis of malformed *translations*.

References

1. Leveling, J., Helbig, H.: A robust natural language interface for access to bibliographic databases. In Callaos, N., Margenstern, M., Sanchez, B., eds.: Proceedings of the 6th World Multiconference on Systemics, Cybernetics and Informatics (SCI 2002). Volume XI., Orlando, Florida, International Institute of Informatics and Systemics (IIIS) (2002) 133–138
2. Leveling, J., Hartrumpf, S.: University of Hagen at CLEF 2004: Indexing and translating concepts for the GIRT task. In Peters, C., Clough, P., Jones, G.J.F., Gonzalo, J., Kluck, M., Magnini, B., eds.: Multilingual Information Access for Text, Speech and Images: 5th Workshop of the Cross-Language Evaluation Forum, CLEF 2004. Volume 3491 of LNCS. Springer, Berlin (2005) 271–282
3. Gey, F.C., Buckland, M., Chen, A., Larson, R.R.: Entry vocabulary – a technology to enhance digital search. In: Proc. of the First International Conference on Human Language Technology, San Diego (2001)
4. Petras, V.: GIRT and the use of subject metadata for retrieval. In Peters, C., Clough, P., Jones, G.J.F., Gonzalo, J., Kluck, M., Magnini, B., eds.: Multilingual Information Access for Text, Speech and Images: 5th Workshop of the Cross-Language Evaluation Forum, CLEF 2004. Volume 3491 of LNCS. Springer, Berlin (2005) 219–225
5. Leveling, J.: University of Hagen at CLEF 2003: Natural language access to the GIRT4 data. In Peters, C., Gonzalo, J., Braschler, M., Kluck, M., eds.: Comparative Evaluation of Multilingual Information Access Systems, 4th Workshop of the Cross-Language Evaluation Forum, CLEF 2003. Volume 3237 of LNCS. Springer, Berlin (2004) 412–424
6. Hartrumpf, S.: Hybrid Disambiguation in Natural Language Analysis. Der Andere Verlag, Osnabrück, Germany (2003)
7. Helbig, H.: Knowledge Representation and the Semantics of Natural Language. Springer, Berlin (2006)
8. Leveling, J.: University of Hagen at CLEF 2005: Towards a better baseline for NLP methods in domain-specific information retrieval. In Peters, C., ed.: Results of the CLEF 2005 Cross-Language System Evaluation Campaign, Working Notes for the CLEF 2005 Workshop. Centromedia, Wien, Österreich (2005)

Domain-Specific CLIR of English, German and Russian Using Fusion and Subject Metadata for Query Expansion

Vivien Petras[1], Fredric Gey[2], and Ray R. Larson[1]

[1] School of Information Management and Systems
University of California, Berkeley, CA 94720 USA
{vivienp, ray}@sims.berkeley.edu
[2] UC Data Archive & Technical Assistance (UC DATA)
University of California, Berkeley, CA 94720 USA
gey@berkeley.edu

Abstract. This paper describes the combined submissions of the Berkeley group for the domain-specific track at CLEF 2005. The data fusion technique being tested is the fusion of multiple probabilistic searches against different XML components using both Logistic Regression (LR) algorithms and a version of the Okapi BM-25 algorithm. We also combine multiple translations of queries in cross-language searching. The second technique analyzed is query enhancement with domain-specific metadata (thesaurus terms). We describe our technique of Entry Vocabulary Modules, which associates query words with thesaurus terms and suggest its use for monolingual as well as bilingual retrieval. Different weighting and merging schemes for adding keywords to queries as well as translation techniques are described.

1 Introduction

For CLEF 2005, the Berkeley group split into two groups (Berkeley 1 and Berkeley 2). Berkeley 1 focused on data fusion techniques whereas Berkeley 2 focused on query expansion techniques using subject metadata. The groups used different probabilistic algorithms and retrieval systems. In this paper, we will report all our results for the domain-specific track but concentrate on describing Berkeley 2's retrieval techniques whereas our paper for the GeoCLEF track will mainly describe Berkeley 1's retrieval techniques (see [9]).

1.1 Fusion

Fusion is a retrieval technique based on the assumption that several different information retrieval systems will retrieve more relevant results than a single retrieval algorithm alone. Lee [10] found that result sets from different retrieval algorithms show similar relevant documents and different non-relevant documents providing criteria for finding relevant documents in a merged set by emphasizing documents found more than once and downweighting documents that are unique to each algorithm.

In [8], the Berkeley 1 group experimented with the fusion of a logistic regression algorithm and the OKAPI BM-25 algorithm. A combination of these two algorithms is also used in the CLEF 2005 experiments.

C. Peters et al. (Eds.): CLEF 2005, LNCS 4022, pp. 226 – 237, 2006.

The search results were combined using the CombMNZ data fusion algorithm developed by Shaw and Fox [16]. The CombMNZ algorithm merges result lists, normalizing the scores in each list and increasing scores for items based on the number of result lists that they appear in, while penalizing items that appear in only a single list.

1.2 Query Expansion Using Subject Metadata

Query expansion has been researched in the information retrieval field for a long time [4]. However, automatic query expansion has been mostly discussed in the context of blind feedback or highly evolved expert systems [e.g. 5]. Thesauri or subject metadata in general are mainly used for manual or interactive query expansion (for an overview, see [17]), but authors report mixed results [6,18] when comparing those techniques to free-text search.

For CLEF 2005, Berkeley's group 2 experimented with Entry Vocabulary Modules (EVMs) to automatically enhance queries with subject metadata terms or to replace query terms with them.

The technique of Entry Vocabulary Modules was designed to serve as an interface between the query vocabulary of the searcher (natural language) and the controlled vocabulary entries of a database. Given any search word or phrase, it will suggest controlled vocabulary terms that represent the concept of the search. A searcher can use these terms to append to his or her query or to substitute his or her own query terms with those controlled vocabulary terms in the hope of achieving a more precise and complete retrieval.

This technique can be used for automatic query expansion if the selection of EVM-suggested thesaurus terms for appending to the query is predetermined (e.g. a number of top-ranked EVM-suggested terms are automatically added to the query).

2 CLEF Domain-Specific Collections

The GIRT collection (German Indexing and Retrieval Test database) consists of 151,319 documents (parallel in English and German) containing titles, abstracts and thesaurus terms in the social science domain. The GIRT thesaurus terms are assigned from the Thesaurus for the Social Sciences [15] and are provided in German, English and Russian. For a detailed description of GIRT and its uses, see [7].

The English GIRT collection contains only 26,058 abstracts (ca. one out of six records) whereas the German collection contains 145,941 - providing an abstract for almost all documents. Consequently, the German collection contains more terms per record to search on. The English corpus has 1,535,445 controlled vocabulary entries (7064 unique phrases) and the German corpus has 1,535,582 controlled vocabulary entries (7154 unique phrases) assigned. On average, 10 controlled vocabulary terms / phrases are appended to each document.

Controlled vocabulary terms are not uniformly distributed. Most thesaurus terms occur less than a 100 times, but 307 occur more than 1,000 times and the most frequent one, "Bundesrepublik Deuschland", occurs 60,955 times.

The Russian Social Science Corpus consists of 94,581 documents containing titles (for all documents) abstracts (for 47,130 documents or 50% of the collection).

Unfortunately for this collection, only 12% of the collection (11,403 documents) have controlled-vocabulary thesaurus terms assigned.

3 Entry Vocabulary Modules

An Entry Vocabulary Module is a dictionary of associations between terms in titles and abstracts in documents and the controlled vocabulary terms associated with the document. If title/abstract words and thesaurus terms co-occur with a higher than random frequency, there exists a likelihood that they are associated. A likelihood ratio statistic is used to measure the association between any natural language term and a controlled vocabulary term. Each pair is assigned an association weight (rank) representing the strength of their association. The higher the rank, the more a thesaurus term represents the concept represented by the document word. The methodology of constructing Entry Vocabulary Modules has been described in detail in [13].

Once an Entry Vocabulary Module is constructed and a table of associations and their weights exist, we can look up a word in the dictionary and find its most highly associated thesaurus term. This is how we find thesaurus terms to associate with the GIRT queries. After experimenting with looking up query title and description words, we found that query title words are sufficient to find relevant thesaurus terms. For all CLEF 2005 experiments, only query title words (after stopword removal) were used for thesaurus term look-up.

If more than one word appears in the query title, we need to merge the results from the thesaurus term look-ups to receive a list of terms for the query as a whole. We experimented with two merging strategies.

For absolute rank merging, an absolute rank for each thesaurus term is calculated by adding the association weights if it is associated with several title words. The five thesaurus terms with the highest rank are then added to the query. The pitfall of this merging strategy is that some associatin pairs have such high weights that other important query word – thesaurus term combinations will be ranked lower no matter what. To avoid this problem, we also tested a round robin merging strategy: for each query word, we looked up the two highest ranked thesaurus terms and added them to the query.

Table 1 shows 2 examples for the different merging strategies and their advantages and disadvantages. For query 138, the first two thesaurus terms in the round robin strategy are highly associated with "insolvent", the second two with "companies". As one can see in the absolute rank strategy, the thesaurus terms for "companies" seem to 'overpower' the ones for "insolvent". Sometimes however, this strategy is prone to errors as topic 143 proves. The words looked up in the EVM are "smoking" and "giving", which is misleading. The absolute rank strategy performs better in this case.

For German with its compounds ("Unternehmensinsolvenzen" instead of "Insolvent Companies" for topic 138), the round robin strategy sometimes only adds two instead of five thesaurus terms to the query, the ranking otherwise being equal to the absolute rank strategy.

For a more in-depth explanation of EVMs and the merging strategies, see our CLEF2005 working paper [12].

Table 1. Comparison of absolute rank and round robin merging for 2 queries

Query 138: Insolvent Companies		Query 143: Giving up Smoking	
Absolute rank merging	*Round robin merging*	*Absolute rank merging*	*Round robin merging*
enterprise	liquidity	smoking	donation
firm	indebtedness	tobacco consumption	social relations
medium-sized firm	enterprise	tobacco	smoking
small-scale business	firm	behavior modification	tobacco consumption
flotation		behavior therapy	

4 Retrieval Techniques

4.1 Berkeley 1 – Fusion

For both the monolingual and bilingual tasks we indexed the documents using the Cheshire II system. The logistic regression algorithm used was the Berkeley TREC-3 algorithm [3], the OKAPI BM-25 algorithm is based on Robertson [14]. The document index entries and queries were stemmed using the Snowball stemmer. Text indexes were created for separate XML elements (such as document titles or dates) as well as for the entire document. The techniques and algorithms used for the domain-specific task were essentially identical to those that we used for the GeoCLEF task and are described in the paper for that track (see [9] for more detail).

4.2 Berkeley 2 – EVM Query Expansion

In all its CLEF submissions, the Berkeley 2 group used a document ranking algorithm based on logistic regression first used in the TREC-2 conference [1]. For all runs, we used stopword lists to remove very common words from collections and queries as well as an implementation of the Muscat stemmer for both English and German and the Snowball stemmer for Russian. For German runs, we used a decompounding procedure developed and described by Aitao Chen [2], which has been shown to improve retrieval results. The decompounding procedure looks up document and query words in a base dictionary and splits compounds when found. As a general procedure, we also use Aitao Chen's blind feedback algorithm [2] in every run. It selects the top 30 ranked terms from the top 20 ranked documents from the initial search to merge with the original query.

Thus, the sequence for processing for retrieval is: query → stopword removal → (decompounding) → stemming → ranking → blind feedback.

5 Retrieval Results – Fusion

The data fusion experiment results did not have a very good performance. Relative to our German and English results, the Russian results look fairly good (we suspect that this may be due to the smaller number of participants). Among the beneficial techniques used in the better-performing Berkeley 2 group runs are 1) query expansion from the thesaurus, 2) automatic decompounding of German words and 3) application of blind relevance feedback. The official submitted runs can be considered preliminary baselines that, we hope, will be improved upon in the future.

The primary approach used by the Berkeley 1 group for query processing is quite similar to that described above, however, no decompounding or blind feedback steps were used, and the ranking algorithms were different, and included multiple ranked sets of results that were then merged using data fusion methods for the final submitted results.

Table 2 shows the average precision for the Berkeley 1 group's submitted runs for the Monolingual tasks. In the monolingual runs, the topic description and title were combined and searched using the TREC3 logistic regression algorithm, and the Okapi BM-25 algorithm. The results of these two searches were then combined using the CombMNZ algorithm. As can be seen by comparison with the results reported by the Berkeley 2 group, the results were not impressive for this task.

Table 2. Average precision scores for Berkeley 1 monolingual title + description runs for German, English and Russian

Run	BERK1MLDE	BERK1MLEN	BERK1MLRU
Avg. precision	0.2314	0.3291	0.2409

Table 3. Average precision scores for Berkeley 1 bilingual title + description runs

run	BERK1 BLDEEN	BERK1 BLDERU	BERK1 BLENDE	BERK1 BLENRU	BERK1 BLRUDE	BERK1 BLRUEN
Languages	German -> English	German-> Russian	English-> German	English-> Russian	Russian-> German->	Russian-> English
Translators	BabelFish L&H	Promt	BabelFish L&H	Promt	Promt	BabelFish Promt
Avg. Precision	0.2398	0.1717	0.1477	0.1364	0.1687	0.2358

Table 3. shows the average precision of the bilingual runs for the Berkeley 1 group. Once again, comparison with Berkeley 2 results for the corresponding tasks shows a significant gap in the performance of the fusion methods when compared to their methods (including decompounding of German Terms, the TREC2 logistic regression algorithm and blind feedback).

Table 4. shows the results for the Berkeley 1 multilingual runs (again using title and description). The results are very low (especially when compared to the Berkeley 2 group Monolingual and Bilingual runs). However these were the top-ranked runs for the DS Multilingual task (of course, they are also, apparently, the *only* submissions for the DS Multilingual task).

It is worth noting that the Berkeley 1 group ran some post-CLEF tests (to verify that the results obtained were not the result of system errors, but instead were the result of the behavior of the fusion operation and the retrieval algorithms used in the

Table 4. Average precision scores for Berkeley 1 multilingual tasks

Run	BERK1MUDEALL	BERK1MUENALL	BERK1MURUALL
Languages	German-> German, English, Russian	English-> German, English, Russian	Russian-> German, English, Russian
Translators	BabelFish L&H Promt	BabelFish L&H Promt	BabelFish Promt
Avg. Precision	0.0294	0.0346	0.0532

CLIR tasks. The tests involved using the TREC2 logistic regression algorithm with blind feedback in place of the TREC3 algorithm while using the same parsing and stemming techniques used the runs reported above, but not using data fusion methods or OKAPI for ranking. The results of these (monolingual only runs) showed considerable improvement for all languages for monolingual retrieval compared to the fusion approach, and were very close to the Berkeley 2 results for title+description English and Russian (0.4472 and 0.2979 Average Precision, respectively). For monolingual German, our post-result was 0.2769 Average Precision. These results highlight the very important effects of using query expansion, and decompounding of German words on performance (as well as choosing the best single algorithm for the task). We believe, however that there may have been some anomalies in the application of the CombMNZ fusion algorithm for some of our tasks, so we intend to do some further investigation of the results in planning for next year's tasks.

6 Retrieval Results – Query Expansion

For more experiments and an in-depth analysis, see our CLEF2005 working paper [16].

6.1 Monolingual Retrieval

For monolingual retrieval, we experimented with three query expansion strategies:

- adding five thesaurus terms retrieved with the EVM absolute rank merging from query title words;
- adding five thesaurus terms from the absolute rank merging strategy (using only query title words) but removing all thesaurus terms from the dictionary that occurred more than a 1,000 times in the document collection, thereby hoping to remove thesaurus terms that would not discriminate effectively;
- adding two thesaurus terms retrieved from the EVM for each query title word using the round robin merging strategy.

For every expansion strategy, we analyze one run where the thesaurus terms are downweighted and one where they are treated as equally important part of the query.

6.1.1 German

As the following table 5 shows, query expansion always improves over the baseline run of title+description if the expanded part is downweighted. If the thesaurus terms are not downweighted, only the round robin strategy improves over the baseline run. However, this case is also the dominating strategy, not only improving the baseline by 13% but also improving on the downweighted strategy and on the other merging strategies.

Table 5. Average precision scores for title + description German Monolingual runs

Run	TD baseline	ABS HW	ABS	ABS -1000 HW	ABS -1000	RR HW	RR
Official run	BK2G MLGG1	BK2G MLGG2		BK2G MLGG3		BK2G MLGG4	
Avg. precision	0.4547	0.4733	0.4369	0.4595	0.3866	0.4936	*0.5144*

ABS	absolute rank strategy
ABS -1000	absolute rank strategy omitting thesaurus terms that occur more than 1000times in the collection
RR	round robin merging
HW	expanded thesaurus terms are downweighted by half in this run

Comparing precision on a query-by-query basis, it becomes clear that downweighting clearly dominates for the absolute rank strategies, whereas not downweighting equally dominates for the round robin strategy although the average precision scores are much closer. In 18 of 25 queries, absolute rank merging with downweighting had a better precision than the not downweighted absolute rank strategy, for the absolute rank –1000 strategy, downweighting achieved a better result in 20 cases. For round robin, not downweighting turned out to be better in 17 of 25 cases compared to downweighting.

6.1.2 English

As table 6 shows, query expansion with EVM suggested thesaurus terms is not as successful for English monolingual retrieval. However, the trend remains the same as in German monolingual retrieval. The round robin strategy without downweighting is still the dominating strategy, improving on the baseline by 6%. For the absolute rank strategies, downweighting works better, although they don't improve on the baseline.

The difference between downweighting or not is more pronounced when looking at the results on a query-by-query basis: in 21 out of 25 cases downweighting is better for the absolute rank strategy and in 20 of 25 cases for the absolute rank –1000 strategy. Not downweighting works better for round robin merging in 14 out of the 25 cases.

Table 6. Average precision scores for title + description English Monolingual runs

Run	TD baseline	ABS HW	ABS	ABS -1000 HW	ABS -1000	RR HW	RR
Official run	BK2G MLEE1	BK2G MLEE2		BK2G MLEE3			
Avg. precision	0.4531	0.4149	0.3462	0.4125	0.3092	0.4697	*0.4818*

In some cases, the absolute strategy seems to make things much worse. This is because it adds thesaurus terms that are too general. But even the round robin strategy doesn't seem to improve precision as much as in German monolingual retrieval. Ironically, it seems that the unique characteristics of the German language (compounds) help in suggesting thesaurus terms that are not only more on the mark but are also compounds themselves retrieving more relevant documents. For example, the thesaurus term *way of life* translates to *Lebensweise* in German. Whereas for English, the retrieval system will look for documents containing "way" and "life" (very general!), the retrieval system will look for "Lebensweise" in German, which is much more precise.

However, it also cannot be overlooked that the English collection contains less text (fewer abstracts) than the German collection to search on. It might be that the added thesaurus terms skew search results in that they take away weight from the free-text search terms ranking documents containing the thesaurus terms higher than ones containing the free-text search terms. This would explain the greater improvement of the downweighting strategies for absolute rank merging as compared to German (precision increases by 20% and 33% for ABS and ABS –1000 in English, whereas only by 8% and 19% in German) and the smaller improvement of not downweighting for round robin (2.5% in English vs. 4% in German).

6.2 Bilingual Retrieval

For bilingual retrieval, we experimented with query expansion and query reformulation using EVMs in addition to query translation. Three translation techniques are compared:

1. Machine translation. We used a combination of the Systran translator (http://babelfish.altavista.com/) and the L & H Power Translator.
2. Thesaurus matching. Words and phrases from the query are looked up in the thesaurus with a fuzzy-matching algorithm and if a matching thesaurus term in the query language is found, the equivalent thesaurus term in the target language is used. See [11] for a more detailed description.
3. EVM. The query title words were submitted to the query language EVM and the round robin merging technique was used to retrieve thesaurus terms. The thesaurus terms in the query language were then replaced by the thesaurus terms in the target language. The query was then reformulated using only thesaurus terms.

We have combined translation techniques by submitting the translated output from the different methods in one and the same run. This increases the number of query words and the danger of introducing more non-discriminating search terms as well as favoring easy to translate terms (they most likely to occur in all methods), but for CLEF, this strategy has worked successfully in previous years. Combining translation methods helps with hard to translate words (higher chance of one method getting it right) and reduces the risk of mis-translation. Table 7 compares combination runs for German-English and English-German retrieval.

For German-English, a combination of all three techniques is clearly the dominating strategy – it seems that adding more words describing the same concept generally improves the precision instead of adding too many non-discriminating terms. It is also worth mentioning that all combination runs perform better than machine translation alone (avg. precision 0.3917), even if one combines thesaurus matching and EVM terms only. In fact, even though lower in precision, this combination performs better in 13 out of 25 cases compared to both the machine translation – thesaurus matching and the machine translation – EVM pairs; a worthy competitor to the commercial translation solutions.

Table 7. Bilingual retrieval combining translation methods

	Machine Translation + Thesaurus Matching	Machine Translation + EVM thesaurus terms	Thesaurus Matching + EVM thesaurus terms	Machine Translation + Thesaurus Matching + EVM thesaurus terms
German-English				
Avg. precision	0.4514	0.4566	0.4346	*0.4803*
English-German				
Avg. precision	0.4201	0.4059	0.4254	*0.4374*

For English-German retrieval, all combination runs seem to perform similarly. However, once again, they clearly outperform machine translation alone (avg. precision 0.3532). Of course, not all combinations work equally well for each query and, sometimes, one translation technique alone works much better.

6.3 Summary

Expanding a query with terms from a thesaurus is like asking an information expert to translate your search strategy into the search language of the database, hopefully providing better search terms than the original search statement. The information expert for this set of experiments is an association dictionary of thesaurus terms and free-text words from titles and abstracts from the collection. Based on title words from the query, thesaurus terms that are highly associated with those words are suggested. Two merging strategies have been tested: absolute rank merging, based on all title words as a set and round robin merging, which suggests two thesaurus terms for each individual query word.

For monolingual retrieval, query expansion with EVM suggested thesaurus terms improves over the baseline of title + description submission by 13% (German) and 6% (English), respectively. Downweighting the added terms performs better for absolute rank but not for the round robin merging. For German, submitting only thesaurus terms (replacing the original query) decreases the average precision over 25 cases, but achieves better precision in 12 individual cases.

For bilingual retrieval, using the thesaurus for translation works surprisingly well. Just using thesaurus terms for the query submission works almost as well as machine translation. Although average precision decreases (9% for English-German and 15% for German-English), EVM suggested thesaurus terms perform better in one third of the queries. A combination of two thesaurus techniques (EVM and thesaurus matching) outperforms machine translation. The combination of machine translation, thesaurus matching and EVM suggested terms outperforms all other strategies.

It has been shown that EVM suggested terms can provide the impact to raise precision for a query – if they are high quality search terms. High quality search terms are those that provide discriminating search power (they occur mostly in relevant documents), describe the information need exactly and, ideally, add new terms to the query. Added terms that are too vague will almost always degrade the performance.

7 Retrieval Results – Russian

The Berkeley 2 group results are summarized by topic in the following table with comparison to overall precision. The highlighted columns are the median performances for monolingual and cross-language IR while the final row is precision averaged over all 25 topics:

Table 8. Berkeley 2 Russian monolingual and bilingual results

Topic	Best Mono	Med Mono	BK2M LRU1	BK2M LRU2	Best CLIR	Med CLIR	BK2B LER1	BK2B LGR1
126	0.5437	0.2004	0.5437	0.2083	0.5182	0.4119	0.421	0.5182
127	0.9036	0.8295	0.9036	0.8789	0.8691	0.6872	0.8691	0.7559
128	0.7085	0.2613	0.2783	0.1973	0.3793	0.2374	0.2594	0.3793
129	0.0596	0.0279	0.0596	0.0095	0.0021	0	0.0021	0.0011
130	0.1227	0.0143	0.0801	0.026	0.0597	0.0061	0.0025	0.0061
131	1	0.0005	1	0.5089	0.5294	0.0976	0.5294	0.2976
132	0.125	0.027	0.125	0.0312	0.304	0.125	0.125	0.1
133	0.1791	0.0606	0.1716	0.1152	0.4643	0.1071	0.3915	0.4643
134	0.3917	0.0992	0.1024	0.0959	0.0913	0.02	0.0913	0.0607
135	0.534	0.1463	0.1419	0.534	0.1876	0.0801	0.1876	0.0257
136	0.6905	0.5087	0.585	0.4324	0.1109	0.022	0.1109	0.1002
137	0.287	0.1797	0.287	0.1855	0.191	0.1114	0.1555	0.191
138	0.5313	0.4702	0.4727	0.3337	0.177	0.0432	0.0432	0.177

Table 8. (*continued*)

139	0.616	0.4282	0.3966	0.4223	0.5145	0.2241	0.2294	0.5145
140	0.0503	0.0368	0.0292	0.0342	0.0358	0.0271	0.0255	0.0271
141	0.2847	0.0454	0.0539	0.2847	0.2086	0.1933	0.1933	0.1344
142	0.7698	0.3085	0.3731	0.2439	0.2886	0.0678	0.0136	0.2886
143	1	0.2667	1	0.45	1	0.7381	0.0094	1
144	0.0402	0.0089	0.0056	0.0091	0.027	0.0137	0.0065	0.0137
145	0.6553	0.5809	0.5335	0.2058	0.6821	0.5949	0.5949	0.6821
146	0.0435	0.0197	0.004	0.0091	0	0	0	0
147	0.125	0	0	0.125	0.0016	0	0.0011	0
148	0.3939	0.2492	0.2405	0.3587	0.1618	0.0639	0.1618	0.0551
149	0.2066	0.0111	0.2066	0.1734	0.088	0.0257	0.088	0.0257
150	0	0	0	0	0.0178	0.0139	0.0139	0.0102
Avg	**0.3887**	**0.1832**	**0.3038**	**0.2349**	**0.2557**	**0.14**	**0.181**	**0.2331**

The first monolingual Russian run (**BK2MLRU1**) and the two bilingual runs (**BK2BLER1, BK2BLER2**) were made using the required Title and Description (TD) fields. The second monolingual run (**BK2MLRU2)** used the Title, Description and Narrative (TDN) fields. The TD run (BK2MLRU1) achieved overall mean average precision of 0.304 with 9 best-of-topic results out of the 25 topics. Interestingly, the TD run performed 30 percent higher than the TDN monolingual run (BK2MLRU2) which had an average precision of only 0.235. We speculate that this is because over half the documents in the collection only have a <TITLE> field and not a <TEXT> field. Topic 150 Поведение во время телепередач (Television Behaviour) retrieved zero relevant documents from all DS monolingual runs, while bilingual runs to the Russian found only two relevant document with best average precision of 0.0178.

The German-Russian bilingual run BK2BLGR1 (MAP of 0.233) performed 29% better than the English-German run BK2BLER1 (MAP of 0.181). Much of this difference can be attributed to topic 143 Отказ от курения (Giving up Smoking) where the German translation seems to have been more accurate than the English one. The German-->Russian precision for topic 143 was 1.0 while the English-->Russian precision was 0.0094.

We believe we achieved our goal of providing a baseline performance for the Russian domain-specific collection of CLEF. We believe our results provide a foundation from which more sophisticated experiments can be developed which leverage the controlled vocabulary indexing of the CLEF DS collections. For the future of CLEF domain-specific Russian to be interesting and successful, substantially more documents will need to have indexing keywords assigned to the documents – 12 % is simply not enough to perform meaningful experiments on the utility of controlled vocabulary.

Acknowledgements

Thanks to Aitao Chen for implementing and permitting the use of the logistic regression formula for probabilistic information retrieval as well as German decompounding and blind feedback in his MULIR retrieval system.

References

1. Chen, A., Cooper, W. and F. Gey (1994). Full text retrieval based on probabilistic equations with coefficients fitted by logistic regression. In: D.K. Harman (Ed.), The Second Text Retrieval Conference (TREC-2): 57-66, March 1994.
2. Chen, A. and F. Gey (2004). "Multilingual Information Retrieval Using Machine Translation, Relevance Feedback and Decompounding." Information Retrieval 7(1-2): 149-182.
3. Cooper, W. S., A. Chen, et al. (1994). Experiments in the probabilistic retrieval of full text documents. Third Text Retrieval Conference (TREC-3), Gaithersburg, MD, National Institute of Standards and Technology Special Publication 500-225
4. Efthimiadis, E. N. (1996). Query Expansion. In Annual Review of Information Systems and Technology (ARIST), edited by M. E. Williams. Medford, NJ: Information Today.
5. Gauch, S. and J. B. Smith (1993). "An expert system for automatic query reformation." Journal of the American Society for Information Science 44(3): 124-36.
6. Jones, S. (1995). "Interactive thesaurus navigation: intelligence rules OK?" Journal of the American Society for Information Science 46(1): 52-9.
7. Kluck, M. (2003). The GIRT Data in the Evaluation of CLIR Systems - from 1997 Until 2003. 4th Workshop of the Cross-Language Evaluation Forum, CLEF 2003. C. A. Peters. Trondheim, Norway, August 21-22, 2003, LNCS 3237, Springer 2004: 376-390.
8. Larson, R. R. (2005). A fusion approach to XML structured document retrieval. Information Retrieval 8: 601-629.
9. Larson, R.R., Gey, F. & Petras, V. (2005). Berkeley at GeoCLEF: Logistic Regression and Fusion for Geographic Information Retrieval. This Volume.
10. Lee, J. H. (1997). Analyses of multiple evidence combination. Proceedings of the 20th Annual International ACM SIGIR Conference on Research and Development in Information Retrieval, July 27-31, 1997, Philadelphia, ACM: 267--276.
11. Petras, V., N. Perelman, et al. (2003). UC Berkeley at CLEF 2003 -- Russian Language Experiments and Domain-Specific Cross-Language Retrieval. 4th Workshop of the Cross-Language Evaluation Forum, CLEF 2003. Trondheim, Norway, August 21-22, 2003, LNCS 3237, Springer 2004: 401-411.
12. Petras, V. (2005). How One Word Can Make all the Difference - Using Subject Metadata for Automatic Query Expansion and Reformulation. Working Notes for the CLEF 2005 Workshop, 21-23 September, Vienna, Austria http://www.clef-campaign.org/2005/working_notes/workingnotes2005/petras05.pdf
13. Plaunt, C., and B. A. Norgard (1998). An Association-Based Method for Automatic Indexing with Controlled Vocabulary. Journal of the American Society for Information Science 49, no. 10 (1998), pp. 888-902.
14. Robertson, S. E. and S. Walker (1997). On relevance weights with little relevance information. Proceedings of the 20th annual international ACM SIGIR conference on Research and development in information retrieval, ACM Press: 16-24.
15. Schott, H. (2000). Thesaurus for the Social Sciences. [Vol. 1:] German-English. [Vol. 2:] English-German. IZ Sozialwissenschaften Bonn, 2000.
16. Shaw, J. A. and E. A. Fox (1994). Combination of multiple searches. Proceedings of the 2nd Text REtrieval Conference (TREC-2), National Institute of Standards and Technology Special Publication 500-215: 243--252.
17. Shiri, A. A., C. Revie, et al. (2002). "Thesaurus-enhanced search interfaces." Journal of Information Science 28(2): 111-22.
18. Sihvonen, A. and P. Vakkari (2004). "Subject knowledge improves interactive query expansion assisted by a thesaurus." Journal of Documentation 60(6): 673-690.

Evaluating a Conceptual Indexing Method by Utilizing WordNet

Mustapha Baziz, Mohand Boughanem, and Nathalie Aussenac-Gilles

IRIT/SIG
Campus Univ. Toulouse III
118 Route de Narbonne
F-31062 Toulouse Cedex 4
{baziz, boughane, aussenac}@irit.fr

Abstract. This paper describes our participation to the English Girt Task of CLEF 2005 Campaign. A method for conceptual indexing based on WordNet is used. Both documents and queries are mapped onto WordNet. Identified concepts belonging to WordNet synsets are extracted from documents and queries and those having a single sense are expanded. All runs are carried out using a conceptual indexing approach. Results prove a primacy of using queries from the title field of the topics and a slight gain of using stemming compared to the non stemming cases.

ACM Categories and Subject Descriptors
H3.3 **[Information Storage And Retrieval]:** Information Search and Retrieval; H.3.1 **[Content Analysis and Indexing]** – *Search process, Retrieval models.*

General Terms: Algorithms, Experimentation.

Keywords: Conceptual Indexing, WordNet, Documents and Query Expansion.

1 Introduction

The objective of our participation to the English GIRT task in 2005, was to evaluate the use of a conceptual indexing method based on the WordNet [3] lexical database. The technique consists in detecting mono and multiword WordNet concepts from both documents and queries and then in using them as a conceptual indexing space. Terms not recognized in WordNet (less than 8%) are also added to complete the representation. Even though they are not useful at the expansion stage, they are used to compare documents and queries at the searching stage.

This paper is organized as follows. In section 2, we describe the synoptic scheme of our system which includes the Mercure search engine . In section 3, the tests required for conceptual indexing are formally described: the concept detection and weighting methods in 3.1, and the disambiguation-expansion method in 3.2. Section 4 reports the official evaluation results compared with the median average obtained by all participating systems. Finally, section 5 gives some conclusions and prospects.

C. Peters et al. (Eds.): CLEF 2005, LNCS 4022, pp. 238 – 246, 2006.

2 Overview of the Approach

In this section, we describe the conceptual indexing method based on WordNet. The principle involves, being given a document (resp. a query), mapping it onto WordNet and then to extract the concepts (mono and multi terms) that belong to WordNet and appear in the text of the document (resp. the query) [1]. The extracted concepts are then weighed and marked using part of speech information (POS) to facilitate their expansion. The *expansion* which we call *Short Expansion* (or SE) amounts to expanding from the document[1] mono sense WordNet terms (having only one sense)

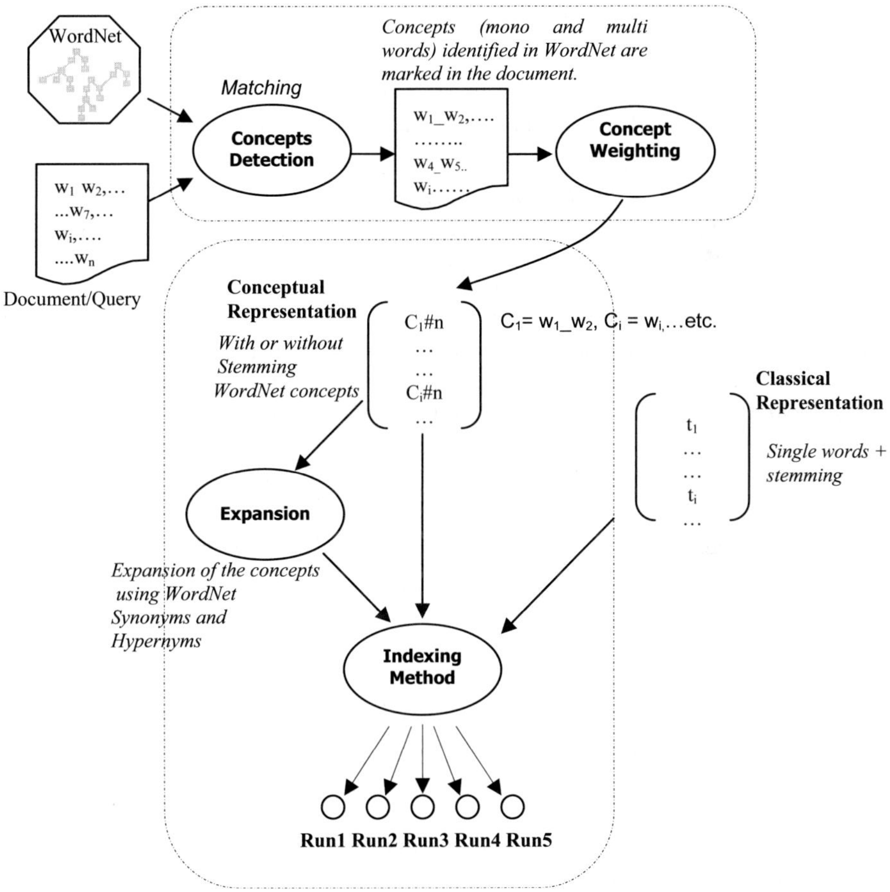

Fig. 1. Description of the indexing method used to generate the different runs

[1] In the following, the word "document" will refer to both queries and documents in the collection.

by using all of their synonyms extracted from the synset[2] they belong to, and only one of their hypernym concepts (belonging to their hypernym synset). The indexing method may or may not use expansion and stemming [5] (according to the run). It includes classical keywords indexing by adding the terms that do not belong to WordNet dictionary.

A total of all, five runs were carried out. They are described in Table2 of section 3.

In the next section we will explain the main steps of our system: the concept detection and weighting methods used to carry out our experiments.

3 Details of Our Approach

3.1 Concepts Detection

Concept detection consists of extracting mono and multiword concepts from documents and queries that correspond to nodes (synsets) in WordNet. Formally, let consider:

$$D= \{w_1, w_2, \ldots, w_n\} \tag{1}$$

the initial document composed of n single words. The result of the concept detection process will be a document D_c. It corresponds to:

$$D_c= \{c_1, c_2, \ldots, c_m, w'_1, w'_{2,\ldots,} w'_{m'}\} \tag{2}$$

where $c_1, c_2, , c_m$ are concepts recognized as WordNet entries. These concepts could be mono or multiword. It may also happen that single words $w'_1, w'_{2,\ldots,} w'_{m'}$ of the initial document (query) do not belong to the WordNet vocabulary. They will not be used for expanding the document (the query). However, they will be added to the final expanded document in order to be used at the search stage.

group_president_and_chief_operating_officer_mike_cramer_called…
group_president_and_chief_operating_officer_mike_cramer_called
group_president_and_chief_operating_officer_mike_cramer
group_president_and_chief_operating_officer_mike
group_president_and_chief_operating_officer
group_president_and_chief_operating
group_president_and_chief
group_president_and
group_president
….
chief_operating_officer_mike_cramer_called
chief_operating_officer_mike_cramer_called
chief_operating_officer_mike_cramer
chief_operating_officer_mike
chief_operating_officer

Concept: **"chief_operating_officer#n"** detected

mike_cramer_called
mike_cramer_called
…

Fig. 2. Concept detection method by combining adjacent words

---

2 WordNet is organised around the notion of Synset (Synonym set). Each Synset contains terms that are synonyms in a given context. Synsets are interrelated by different relations like Hypernymy (Is-a).

To detect concepts in the query, we use an ad hoc technique that relies solely on concatenation of adjacent words to identify compound (multiword) concepts in WordNet. In this technique, two alternative ways may be carried on. The first one would be projecting WordNet on the document : all WordNet multiword concepts are mapped onto the document and those occurring in it. This method has the advantage of creating a reusable resource (a document representation made out of WordNet concepts). Its drawback is the possibility to omit concepts which appear in the document and in WordNet under different forms. For example, if WordNet contains the multiword concept *"solar battery"*, a simple comparison with document would miss the same concept appearing in its plural form *"solar batteries"*. The second way, which we adopt in our experiments, follows an the opposite path, projecting the document onto WordNet: for each multiword candidate concept derived by combining adjacent words in the document, we first question WordNet using these words just as they are, and then we use their base forms if necessary.

Word are combined, as shown in Figure1, according to the longest succession of words for which a concept is detected. In the example of Figure1, the longest concept *"chief_operating_officer#n"* (#n is used for the POS name) is selected although *"chief "* and *"officer"* could also be identified as single word concepts. This concept is defined by WordNet as follow:

> chief executive officer, CEO, chief operating officer -- (the corporate executive responsible for the operations of the firm; reports to a board of directors; may appoint other managers (including a president))

Example of a document after its projection onto WordNet

In Figure 3 below, we can see a document example from the collection (named GIRT-EN19950120120), after its projection onto WordNet conceptual network. For

```
<DOC>
<DOCNO> GIRT-EN19950120120 </DOCNO>
<TITLE-EN>
   establishment#n and development#n of the health_care_delivery#n system#n
   in#n syria#n with regard_to#n morbidity#n especially#r infectious_disease#n
</TITLE-EN>
   ddr
   syria#n
   asia#n
   health_care_delivery#n system#n
   arab#n country#n
   historical#a development#n
   near_east#n
   contagious_disease#n
   developing#n country#n
   epidemiology#n
   morbidity#n
   health#n policy#n
   descriptive#a study#n
   medical#n sociology#n
   health#n policy#n
   sociology#n of developing#n country#n developmental#a sociology#n
</DOC>
```

Fig. 3. An example document from the collection after its projection onto WordNet

example health_care_delivery#n is a concept that belongs to a WordNet synset identified in the document. Words that are not tagged (like "ddr" in this example) do not belong to WordNet terminology.

The notations "#n", "#a", "#v", "#r" are used to indicate the part of speech (POS) of the terms belonging to WordNet. They refer respectively to names, adjectives, verbs and adverbs. For the moment, the POS is not used in the index. We need it only to expand the identified mono-sense WordNet terms.

3.2 WordNet Covering Rate for Documents and Queries

As seen in the previous example, a large majority of the vocabulary used in the collection documents is covered by WordNet. Table1 summarizes the cover rate concerning both queries and documents. More than 92.87% of the vocabulary used in the documents is covered by WordNet and 99.39% (so almost totality!) of the vocabulary used in the queries is covered.

Concerning compound concepts (or multiterms), they represent about 9% for the document and only 7.83% (0.52 compound term in average) for the queries. Multiterms have often only one sense. It is important to use them in our case, as only mono sense terms from the documents and the queries are expanded in our approach.

Table1. Statistics on using WordNet to index the English Girt Collection

Total no of docs: 151319 Total no of queries: 25	Total number of TERMS (CLASSICAL)		WORDNET TERMS ONLY			
			All WN terms		WN compounds terms only	
	Documents	Queries(1)	Documents	Queries(1)	Documents	Queries(1)
Total no of terms	**5 118 187**	**166**	**4 753 566**	**165**	**456 715**	**13**
Average no of terms	**33.82**	**6.64**	**31.41**	**6.6**	**3.01**	**0.52**
% (Wn terms compared to the classical)	-	-	**92.87%**	**99.39%**	**8.92%**	**7.83%**

(1) Only Queries using both Title and Description fields (without expansion) are considered in the table.

3.3 Concepts Weighting

The extracted concepts (single or multiwords) are then weighted as in the classical keywords case according to a kind of TF.IDF which is also a variant of the OKAPI system [1].

Thus, a weight $Weight(t_i, d_j)$ of a term t_i in a document d_j is given by the following formula [2]:

$$Weight(t_i, d_j) = \frac{tf_{ij} * (h_1 + h_2 * \log(\frac{N}{n_i}))}{h3 + h4 * \frac{dl_j}{\Delta d} + h_5 * tf_{ij}} \tag{3}$$

Where:

tf_{ij} : The frequency of the term t_i in the document d_j,

$h_1, h_{2,} h_3, h_4, h_5$: Constants,

n_i : The number of documents containing the term t_i,

N : The total number of documents,

Δ_d : Average document length,

dl_j : Length of document d_j.

The objective of this measure is to attenuate the impact of terms having too much high frequency values.

4 Evaluation

We submitted five official runs to the monolingual English GIRT task ("GIRT_EN"): CWN_T, C_T, CWN_TD, CWNSE_T and CWNSE_TD. The runs are carried out by using title and/or description fields, using or not the term stemming and by performing or not expansion. They are summarized in Table2.

Table 2. Description of the official runs

Run	Description
CWN_T	Title field of the topics is used. No stemming is used for WordNet terms. No expansion is used.
C_T	Title field of the topics is used. Stemming for all terms. No expansion is used.
CWN_TD	Title and Description fields of the topics are used. No stemming is used for WordNet terms. No expansion is used.
CWNSE_T	Short Expansion (SE) is used in Queries. Title field of the topics is used. No stemming is used for WordNet terms.
CWNSE_TD	Short Expansion (SE) is used in Queries. Title and Description fields of the topics are used. No stemming is used for WordNet terms.

The results obtained by the different runs are summarized in Table3. It should be noticed that an error slipped into the program in the name of query 132 (named by error 232). Consequently, the query 132 is not evaluated at all. The first column of Table 3 gives the median average precision (MAP) obtained by our five official runs on all the queries. We give in the second column the same runs when using the query relevance file obtained after submission and with the query 132 corrected.

Concerning the official results, as it can be shown in Figure4, the best results are obtained when using only the title field of the topics and stemming the extracted terms (run C_T). Followed by the run CWN_T where WordNet terms are not stemmed, and then the run CWNSE_T where a short expansion (by synonyms and

Table 3. Official Results obtained for the five submitted runs compared to the median average

	Median Average Precision (MAP)	Non official Results	Increment (%)
CWN_T	0.3411	0.3762	+10,29%
C_T	0.3411	0.3765	+10,38%
CWN_TD	0.3223	0.3574	+10,89%
CWNSE_T	0.3251	0.3579	+10,09%
CWNSE_TD	0.3235	0.3563	+10,14%

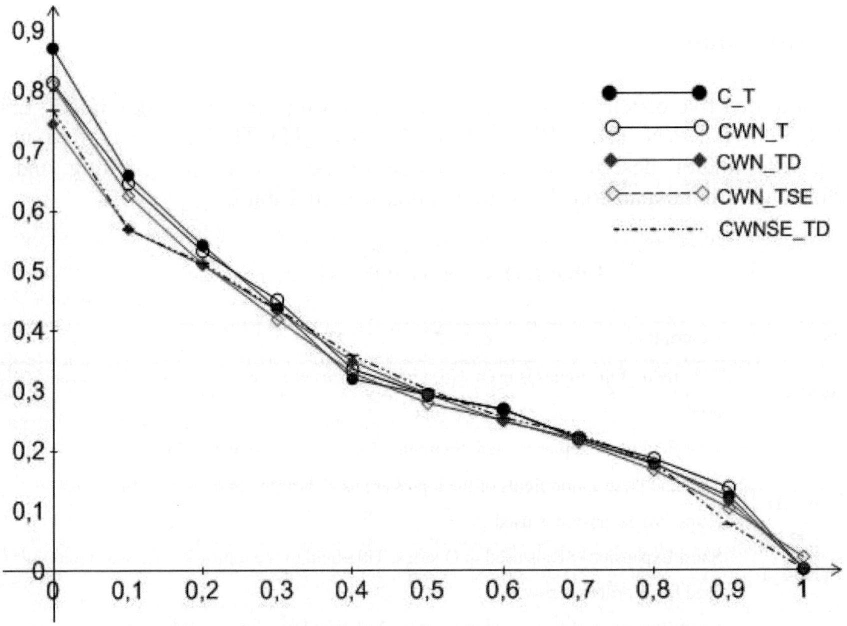

Fig. 4. Recall-Precision curves for the fives submitted runs

one hypernym) is applied to non polysemic terms. The two last runs (CWN_TD and CWNSE_TD) are obtained when both title and description fields are used to build the queries respectively with and without expansion.

Concerning the non official runs, the results follow the same logic while being better than the official ones. The fourth column of Table 3 gives the difference of the global results, for the five runs, between the submitted results and the results obtained after the error has been fixed. Roughly the official results could be enhanced by 10,36% in average for each run by using the query 132 and with changing nothing to the system.

The reason is that the omitted query (132) brings very good results, which also increases the global result. The detailed results of query 132 are given in Table 4 for the five runs.

Table 4. Non official results for the omitted query 132

Run	Num	P5	P10	P15	P20	P30	P100	P1000	MAP
C_T	132	1.0000	1.0000	1.0000	1.0000	1.0000	0.9200	0.1440	0.8854
CWN_T	132	1.0000	1.0000	1.0000	1.0000	1.0000	0.8900	0.1470	0.8791
CWN_TD	132	1.0000	1.0000	1.0000	1.0000	1.0000	0.8900	0.1470	0.8773
CWNSE_T	132	1.0000	1.0000	1.0000	0.9500	0.9000	0.8500	0.1470	0.8196
CWNSE_TD	132	1.0000	0.9000	0.9333	0.9500	0.9333	0.3600	0.0540	0.8192

5 Conclusion

We have evaluated the performances of our conceptual indexing method which consists of matching documents and queries with WordNet. In this method, documents and queries are represented by WordNet nodes. The first remark, when comparing our submitted runs, is that using only title field (runs C_T and CWN_T) from the topics seems to bring the better results than using the title and description fields together. The second remark concerns the use of term stemming. Results showed that stemming indexing terms (run C_T) is slightly better than not stemming them (run CWN_T) when we consider only the first retrieved documents. However, by using a more global judgment (MAP), both cases are close. Another remark concerns the Expansion method used in our experiments. Even though it is made so as to avoid the disambiguation problem (only mono sense terms are expanded), expansion does not seem to bring the best results. The best run is obtained without expansion and by using only the title field of the topics. However, the results obtained by the expansion method, when expanding titles, are better than those obtained when the description fields are used in addition to titles in the queries and without expansion. So we still believe that a more sophisticated expansion method could bring better results [1]. The specificity of the GIRT collection documents could also require some adaptation (to evaluate the usefulness of using hypernymy relation for example).

Another conclusion concerns the suitability of using WordNet for the domain specific collection. It appears that WordNet largely covers the vocabulary of the English GIRT collection (more than 90% for the documents and practically the entire vocabulary of the 25 used queries) and is suitable to be used for this particular collection.

References

1. Baziz M., Boughanem M. and Aussenac-Gilles Nathalie “The Use of Ontology for Semantic Representation of documents”. In Proceeding of Semantic Web and Information Retrieval Workshop (SWIR) held in conjunction with the 27th ACM SIGIR Conference’04, July 25–29, 2004, Sheffield, United Kingdom.
2. Boughanem M., Julien C., Mothe J., Soulé-Dupuy C. "Mercure at TREC-8" Adhoc, Web, CLIR and Filtering tasks. Proceeding of Trec-8, (1999).

3. Miller G., Wordnet: A lexical database. Communication of the ACM, 38(11):39-41, (1995).
4. Okapi at TREC-6, Proceeding of the 6th International Conference on Text Retrieval TREC, Harman D.K. (Ed.), NIST SP 500-236, pages: 125-136, (1997).
5. Porter, M. An algorithm for suffix stripping. Program, 14(3):130-137, July, 1980.

Domain Specific Mono- and Bilingual English to German Retrieval Experiments with a Social Science Document Corpus

René Hackl and Thomas Mandl

University of Hildesheim
Information Science
Marienburger Platz 22, D-31141 Hildesheim, Germany
mandl@uni-hildesheim.de

Abstract. This paper reports experiments in CLEF 2005's domain-specific retrieval track carried out at the University of Hildesheim. The experiments were based on previous experiences with the GIRT document corpus and were run in parallel to the multi-lingual experiments for CLEF 2005. We optimized the parameters of the system with one corpus from 2004 and applied these settings to the domain specific task. In that manner, the robustness of our approach over different document collection was assessed.

1 Introduction

In previous CLEF campaigns, we tested an adaptive fusion system based on the MIMOR model [5] within the domain specific GIRT track [1]. For CLEF 2005, the parameter optimization was based on a French document collection. The parameter settings were applied to the four language document collections of the multilingual task of CLEF 2005 [2]. The basic retrieval engine behind our system is Apache Lucene[1].

In addition, we applied almost the same settings to the domain specific track in order to test the robustness of our system over different collections.

Robustness has become an issue in information retrieval research recently. It has been noted often, that the variance between queries is worse than the variance between systems. There are often very difficult queries which few systems solve well and which lead to very bad results for most systems [3]. Thorough failure analysis can result in substantial improvement. For example, the absence of named entities is a factor which can make queries more difficult overall [6]. As a consequence, a new evaluation track for robust retrieval has been established at the Text Retrieval Conference (TREC). This track does not only measure the average precision over all queries but also emphasizes the performance of the systems for difficult queries. To perform well in this track is more important for the systems to retrieve at least a few

[1] http://lucene.apache.org

C. Peters et al. (Eds.): CLEF 2005, LNCS 4022, pp. 247 – 250, 2006.

documents for difficult queries than to improve the performance on average [8]. In order to allow a system evaluation based on robustness more queries than for a normal ad-hoc track are necessary. The concept of robustness is extended in TREC 2005. Systems need to perform well over different tracks and tasks [8].

For multilingual retrieval, robustness would also be an interesting evaluation concept because the performance between queries differs greatly [6]. Robustness in multilingual retrieval could be interpreted in three ways:

- Stable performance over all topics instead of high average performance (like at TREC)
- Stable performance over different tasks (like at TREC)
- Stable performance over different languages (focus of CLEF)

For the participation in the domain specific track in 2005, we tested the stability of our ad-hoc system for the domain specific track.

2 Domain Specific Retrieval Experiments

Our system was optimized with the French collection of CLEF 2004. The optimization procedure is described in detail elsewhere [2]. The GIRT runs were produced with only slightly different settings.

Previous experiences with the GIRT corpus showed that blind relevance feedback does not lead to good results [4]. Our test runs confirmed that fact and blind relevance feedback was not applied for the submitted runs. Instead, term expansion was based on the thesaurus available for the GIRT data. This thesaurus was developed by the Social Science Information Centre [4]. For the query terms, the fields Broader, Narrower and Related term were extracted from the thesaurus and added to the query for the second run. The topic title weights were set to ten, topic description weights to three and the thesaurus terms were weighted with one. This weighting scheme was adopted from the ad-hoc task.

For the second mono-lingual run UHIGIRT2, we added terms from the multilingual European terminology database Eurodicautom[2] which was also used for the ad-hoc experiments. However, Eurodicautom (EDA) contributed terms for very few queries. Most often, it returned "out of vocabulary". Overall, EDA may not be an appropriate resource for cross language information retrieval within a social science corpus.

As a bilingual GIRT run, one English-to-German experiment was conducted. The query and the thesaurus terms were translated by ImTranslator[3]. In addition, the document field “english-translation” was indexed.

Although, our system has been tested with Russian data at earlier CLEF campaigns and at the ad-hoc task this year, the Russian social science RSSC collection could not be used because it was provided later than the rest of the data.

---

[2] http://europa.eu.int/eurodicautom/Controller

[3] http://freetranslation.paralink.com/

Table 1. Results from the CLEF 2005 Workshop. EDA = Euradicautom

RunID	Languages	Run Type	Fields used	Nr. retrieved rel. docs.	Total rel. docs.	Avg. Prec.
UHIGIRT1	Monolingual German	-	TD	1400	2682	0.220
UHIGIRT2	Monolingual German	IZ thesaurus, EDA	TD	1335	2682	0.193
UHIGIRT3	English-German	IZ thesaurus, EDA ImTranslator	TD	1159	2682	0.178

Concerning robustness, the results are not as good as for systems optimized specifically for the domain specific task. The best system achieves an average precision of 0.42 for the bilingual task. However, the performance of our system is comparable to most other system runs submitted.

3 Outlook

For next year, we intend to implement multi-lingual runs for the domain specific task. The thesaurus use led to a drop in performance. For the future, we intend to develop a more sophisticated strategy to apply thesaurus terms.

For future participations in ad-hoc tasks, we intend to apply the RECOIN (REtrieval COmponent INtegrator)[4] framework [7]. RECOIN is an object oriented JAVA framework for information retrieval experiments. It allows the integration of heterogeneous components into an experimentation system where many experiments may be carried out.

Acknowledgements

We acknowledge the effort of two former graduate students from the University of Hildesheim, Viola Barth and Joachim Pfister who ported the trec_eval tool to Java.

References

1. Hackl, R.; Kölle, R.; Mandl, T.; Womser-Hacker, C.: Domain Specific Retrieval Experiments at the University of Hildesheim with the MIMOR System. In: Advances in Cross-Language Information Retrieval: Third Workshop of the Cross-Language Evaluation Forum, CLEF, Rome, Italy, September 2002. Lecture Notes in Computer Science, Vol. 2785. Springer-Verlag, Berlin Heidelberg New York (2003) 343-348
2. Hackl, R.; Mandl, T.; Womser-Hacker, C.: Ad-hoc Mono- and Multilingual Retrieval Experiments at the University of Hildesheim. In this volume

[4] http://recoin.sourceforge.net

3. Harman, D.; Buckley, C.: The NRRC reliable information access (RIA) workshop. In: Sanderson, M.; Järvelin, K.; Allan, L.; Bruza, P. (eds.): SIGIR 2004: Proceedings of the 27th Annual International ACM SIGIR Conference on Research and Development in Information Retrieval, Sheffield, UK, July 25-29, 2004. ACM, New York (2004) 528-529
4. Kluck, M.: The GIRT Data in the Evaluation of CLIR Systems - from 1997 until 2003. In: Comparative Evaluation of Multilingual Information Access Systems: 4th Workshop of the Cross-Language Evaluation Forum, CLEF, Trondheim, Norway, August 21-22, 2003, Revised Selected Papers. Lecture Notes in Computer Science, Vol. 3237. Springer-Verlag, Berlin Heidelberg New York (2004) 376-390
5. Mandl, T.; Womser-Hacker, C.: A Framework for long-term Learning of Topical User Preferences in Information Retrieval. In: New Library World, 105 (5/6) (2004) 184-195
6. Mandl, T.; Womser-Hacker, C.: The Effect of Named Entities on Effectiveness in Cross-Language Information Retrieval Evaluation. In: Proceedings of the 2005 ACM symposium on Applied computing 2005, Santa Fé, New Mexico March 13 - 17, 2005, Session Information Access and Retrieval (IAR). ACM, New York (2005) 1059-1064
7. Scheufen, J.-H.: RECOIN: Modell offener Schnittstellen für Information Retrieval Systeme und Komponenten. In: Mandl, T.; Womser-Hacker, C. (eds.): Effektive Information Retrieval Verfahren in der Praxis. Proceedings Vierter Hildesheimer Evaluierungs- und Retrievalworkshop (HIER 2005), Hildesheim, 20. Juli 2005. Schriften zur Informationswissenschaft, Vol. 45. UVK, Konstanz (2006) to appear
8. Voorhees, E.: The TREC robust retrieval track. In: SIGIR Forum, 39 (1) (2005) 11-20

Overview of the CLEF 2005 Interactive Track

Julio Gonzalo, Paul Clough, and Alessandro Vallin

Departamento de Lenguajes y Sistemas Informáticos
Escuela Técnica Superior de Ingeniería Informática de la UNED, Madrid
julio@lsi.uned.es
and
Department of Information Studies
Sheffield University, Sheffield
p.d.clough@sheffield.ac.uk
and
ITC-irst
Trento
vallin@itc.it

Abstract. The CLEF Interactive Track (iCLEF) is devoted to the comparative study of user-inclusive cross-language search strategies. In 2005, we have studied two cross-language search tasks: retrieval of answers and retrieval of annotated images. In both tasks, no further translation or post-processing is needed after performing the tasks to fulfill the information need.

In the interactive Question Answering task, users are asked to find the answer to a number of questions in a foreign-language document collection, and write the answers in their own native language. In the interactive image retrieval task, a picture is shown to the user, and then the user is asked to find the picture in the collection.

This paper summarizes the task design, experimental methodology, and the results obtained by the research groups participating in the track.

1 Introduction

In CLEF 2005, user studies have consolidated the two research issues studied in CLEF 2004 as pilot tasks: cross-language question answering and known-item image search.

In the **interactive Question Answering task**, users are asked to find the answer to a number of questions in a foreign-language document collection, and write the answers in their own native language. Subjects must use two interactive search assistants (which are to be compared), pairing questions and systems according to a latin-square design to filter out question and user effects. For this task, we have used a subset of the ad-hoc QA testbed, including questions, collections and evaluation methodology.

In the **interactive image retrieval task**, a picture is shown to the user, and then the user is asked to find the picture in the collection. This was chosen as a realistic task (finding stuff I've seen before) in which visual features could also

C. Peters et al. (Eds.): CLEF 2005, LNCS 4022, pp. 251–262, 2006.

play an important role (users are given a picture instead of a written description of what they have to look for). The target data is the St. Andrews' collection (as used in the ad-hoc image CLEF task), in which images are annotated in English with a number of rich metadata descriptions. Again, each participant group was expected to compare two different search assistants, combining users, queries and systems according to a latin-square desing to filter out query and user effects.

The remainder of this paper describes the experimental design and the results obtained by the research groups for each of these tasks.

2 Image Retrieval Task

The ImageCLEF interactive search task provides user–centered evaluation of cross–language image retrieval systems. In cross–language image search, the object to be retrieved is an image. This is appealing as a CLIR task because often (depending on the user and query) the object to be retrieved (i.e. the image) can be assumed to be language-independent, i.e. there is no need for further translation when presenting results to the user. This makes a good introductory task to CLIR, requiring only query translation to bridge the language gap between the user's query (source) language, and the language used to annotate the images (target language).

Image retrieval can be purely visual in the case of query–by–example (QBE) which is entirely language–independent, but this assumes the user wants to perform a visual search (e.g. find me images which appear visually similar to the one provided). However, users may also want to search for images starting with text-based queries (e.g. Web image search) requiring that texts are associated with the target image collection. For CLIR, the language of the texts used to annotate the images should not affect retrieval, i.e. a user should be able to query the images in their native language making the target language transparent. Effective cross–language image retrieval will involve both text–based and content–based IR (CBIR) methods in conjunction with translation.

The main areas of study for a cross–language image retrieval assistant include:

- How well a system supports user query formulation for images with associated texts (e.g. captions or metadata) written in a language different from the native language of the users. This is also an opportunity to study how the images themselves could also be used as part of the query formulation process.
- How well a system supports query re–formulation, e.g. the support of positive and negative feedback to improve the user's search experience, and how this affects retrieval. This aims to address issues such as how visual and textual features can be combined for query reformulation/expansion.
- How well a system allows users to browse the image collection. This might include support for summarising results (e.g. grouping images by some pre-assigned categorization scheme or by visual feature such as shape, colour or

texture). Browsing becomes particularly important in a CLIR system when query translation fails and returns irrelevant or no results.
- How well a system presents the retrieved results to the user to enable the selection of relevant images. This might include how the system presents the caption to the user (particularly if they are not familiar with the language of the text associated with the images, or some of the specific and colloquial language used in the captions) and investigate the relationship between the image and caption for retrieval purposes.

The interactive image retrieval task in 2004 concentrated on query re–formulation and this has been the focus of experiments in 2005 also, together with the presentation of search results. Groups were not set a specific retrieval goal to enable some degree of flexibility.

2.1 Experimental Procedure

Participants were required to compare two interactive cross–language image retrieval systems (one intended as a baseline) that differ in the facilities provided for interactive retrieval. For example, comparing the use of visual versus textual features in query formulation and refinement. As a cross-language image retrieval task, the initial query was required to be in a language different from the collection (i.e. not English) and translated into English for retrieval. Any text displayed to the user was also required to be translated into the user's source language. This might include captions, summaries, pre-defined image categories etc. ImageCLEF used a within–subject experimental design: users were required to test both interactive systems.

The same search task as 2004 was used: given an image (not including the caption) from the St Andrews collection of historic photographs, the goal for the searcher is to find the same image again using a cross–language image retrieval system. This models the situation in which a user searches with a specific image in mind (perhaps they have seen it before) but without knowing key information thereby requiring them to describe the image instead, e.g. searches for a familiar painting whose title and painter are unknown (i.e. a high precision task or target search [2]).

The interactive ImageCLEF task is run similar to iCLEF 2003 using a similar experimental procedure. However, because of the type of evaluation (i.e. whether known items are found or not), the experimental procedure for iCLEF 2004 (Q&A) is also very relevant and we make use of both iCLEF procedures. The user–centered search task required groups to recruit a minimum of 8 users (native speakers in the source language) to complete 16 search tasks (8 per system). Images which users were required to find are shown in Fig. 1. Users are given a maximum of 5 mins only to find each image. Topics and systems were presented to the user in combinations following a latin–square design to ensure minimisation of user/topic and system/topic interactions.

Participants were encouraged to make use of questionnaires to obtain feedback from the user about their level of satisfaction with the system and how useful

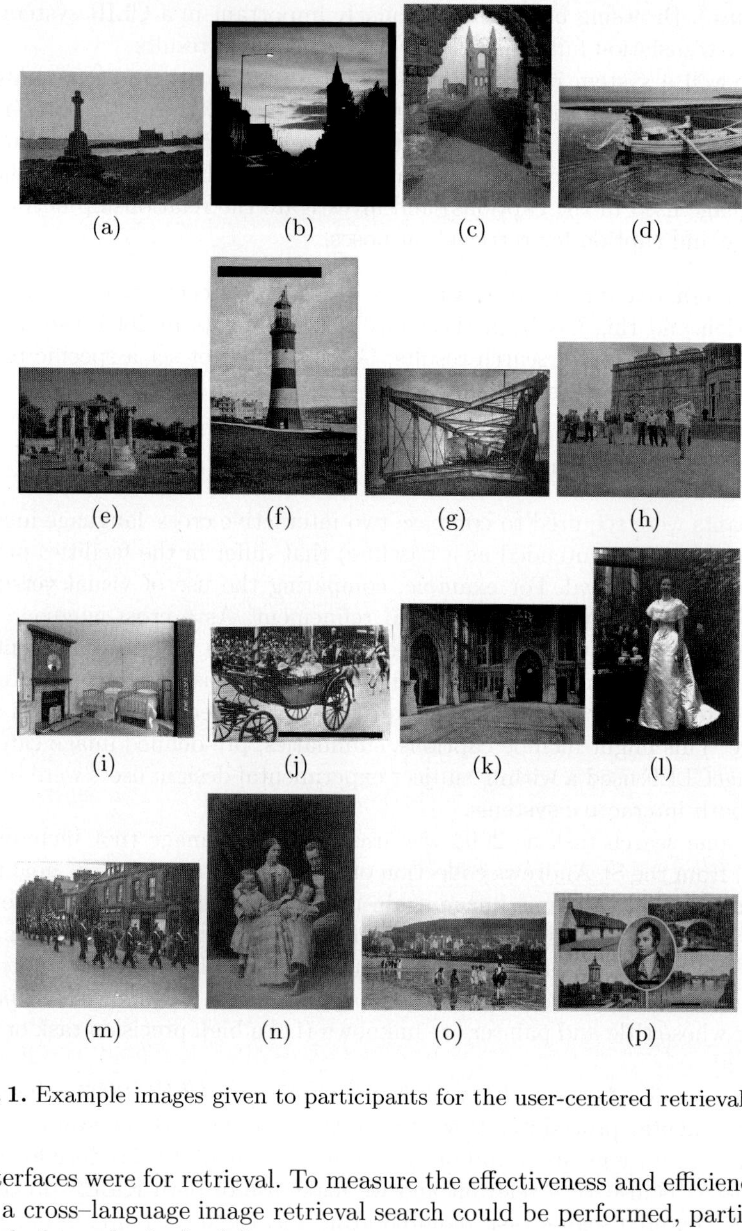

Fig. 1. Example images given to participants for the user-centered retrieval task

the interfaces were for retrieval. To measure the effectiveness and efficiency with which a cross–language image retrieval search could be performed, participants were asked to submit the following information: whether the user could find the intended image or not (mandatory), the time taken to find the image (mandatory), the number of steps/iterations required to reach the solution (e.g. the number of clicks or the number of queries - optional), and the number of images displayed to the user (optional).

2.2 Participating Groups

Although 11 groups signed up for the interactive task, only 2 groups submitted results: Miracle and the University of Sheffield. Miracle compared the same interface but using Spanish (European) versus English versions [8]. The focus of the experiment was whether it is better to use an AND operator to group terms of multi-word queries (in the English system) or combine terms using an OR operator (in the Spanish system). Their aim was to compare whether it is better to use English queries with terms conjuncted (which have to be precise and use the exact vocabulary - maybe difficult for a specialised domain like historical Scottish photographs) or to use the disjunction of terms in Spanish and have the option of relevance feedback (a more "fuzzy" and noisy search but which doesn't require precise vocabulary and exact translations). Their objective was to test the similarity of retrieval performance using both approaches.

Sheffield compared 2 interfaces with the same source language (Italian): one displaying search results as a list, the other organizing retrieved images into a hierarchy of text concepts displayed on the interface as an interactive menu [7]. The aim of the experiment was to determine the usefulness of grouping results using concept hierarchies and investigate translation issues in cross–language image search. Queries were translated using Babelfish and the entire user interface also translated to provide a working system in Italian.

2.3 Results and Discussion

Given only two submissions, conclusions that can be deduced from the interactive task are limited. However, the findings of individual groups were interesting and we summarise their main results to highlight the effectiveness of selected approaches. Miracle found results to be similar for both systems evaluated: English (69% of images found; 102 secs. average search time), Spanish (66% of images found; 113 secs. average search time). Based on investigation of the results and observation of users, a number of interesting points are made: that domain-specific terminology causes problems for cross–language searches (and therefore impacts far greater on queries with a conjunction of terms). In addition, translated Spanish query terms did not match caption terms also causing vocabulary mismatch. From questionnaires, users preferred the English version because the conjunction of terms often gave results users expected (i.e. a set of documents containing all query terms). Miracle also observed users extracting words from captions to further refine their search and user's commented on differences between the expected results of a search for a given keyword and those actually obtained. Users were also allowed to continue searching after the allotted time and in most cases found the relevant image in a short time (less than 1 minute).

The experiments undertaken by Sheffield also highlighted some interesting search strategies by users and problems with the concept hierarchies and interface for cross–language image retrieval. Quantitative results were similar using both a list of images and a menu generated from the concept hierarchies: list (53% of images found; 113 secs. average search time) and menu (47% images found; 139 secs. average search time). Overall users of the Sheffield systems found 82/128 relevant images and users of the Miracle system 86/128 images. The experiments undertaken by Sheffield observed negative effects on search, generation of the concept hierarchy and results display due to translation errors such as mis-translations and un-translated terms. Although based on effectiveness the menu appears to offer no difference compared to presenting results as a list, users preferred the menu (75% vs. 25% for the list) indicating this approach to be an engaging and interesting feature. In particular users liked the compact representation of search results offered by the menu compared to the ranked list.

3 Question Answering Task

3.1 Experiment Design

Participating teams performed an experiment by constructing two conditions (identified as "reference" and "contrastive"), formulating a hypothesis that they wished to test, and using a common evaluation design to test that hypothesis. Human subjects were in groups of eight (i.e., experiments could be run with 8, 16, 24, or 32 subjects). Each subject conducted 16 *search sessions*. A search session is uniquely identified by three parameters: the human subject performing the search, the search condition tested by that subject (reference or contrastive), and the question to be answered. Each team used different subjects, but the questions, the assignment of questions to searcher-condition pairs, and the presentation order were common to all experiments. A latin-square matrix design was adopted to establish a set of presentation orders for each subject that would minimize the effect of user-specific, question-specific and order-related factors on the quantitative task effectiveness measures that were used. The remainder of this section explains the details of this experiment design.

Question set. Questions were selected from the **CLEF 2005 QA question set** in order to facilitate insightful comparisons between automatic and interactive experiments that were evaluated under similar conditions. The criteria to select questions was similar to those used in iCLEF 2004:

- **Answers should not be known in advance** by the human subjects; this restriction resulted in elimination of a large fraction of the initial question set.
- Given that the question set had to be necessarily small, we wanted to **avoid NIL questions** (i.e., questions with no answer. Ideally, it should be possible to find an answer to every question in any collection that a participating team might elect to search.
- We focused on **four question types** to avoid excessive sparseness in the question set: two question types that called for named entities as answers

(PERSON and ORGANIZATION) and two question types that called for temporal or quantitative measures (TIME and MEASURE). The additional restriction of having answers in the largest number of languages forced us to include also some OTHER questions.

The final set of sixteen questions, plus four additional questions for user training, are shown in Table 1.

Table 1. The iCLEF 2005 question set

#	QA#	type	Question
1	0052	MEAS	How old is Jacques Chirac?
2	0105	PERS	Which professor from Bonn received the Nobel Prize for Economics?
3	0131	ORG	Which bank donated the Nobel Prize for Economics?
4	0143	MEAS	How many victims of the massacres in Rwanda were there?
5	0263	ORG	Which institution initiated the European youth campaign against racism?
6	0267	ORG	Which Church ordained female priests in March 1994?
7	0299	OTHER	What was the nationality of most of the victims when the Estonia ferry sank?
8	0362	ORG	Which airline did the plane hijacked by the GIA belong to?
9	0385	OTHER	What disease name does the acronym BSE stand for?
10	0386	ORG	Which country organized "Operation Turquoise"?
11	0397	PERS	Who was the Norwegian Prime Minister when the referendum on Norway's possible accession to the EU was held?
12	0522	TIME	When do we estimate that the Big Bang happened?
13	0535	PERS	Who won the Miss Universe 1994 beauty contest?
14	0573	MEAS	How many countries have ratified the United Nations convention adopted in 1989?
15	0585	MEAS	How many states are members of the Council of Europe?
16	0891	TIME	When did Edward VIII abdicate?
17	0061	ORG	Name a university in Berlin. *(training)*
18	0070	OTHER	Name one of the seven wonders of the world. *(training)*
19	0327	PERS	Which Russian president attended the G7 meeting in Naples? *(training)*
20	0405	OTHER	What minister was Silvio Berlusconi prior to his resignation? *(training)*

Latin-Square Design. One factor that makes reliable evaluation of interactive systems challenging is that once a user has searched for the answer to a question in one condition, the same question cannot be used with the other condition (formally, the learning effect would likely mask the system effect). We adopt a within-subjects study design, in which the condition seen for each user-topic pair is varies systematically in a balanced manner using a latin square, to accommodate this. This same approach has been used in the Text Retrieval Conference (TREC) interactive tracks [3] and in past iCLEF evaluations [6]. Table 2 shows the presentation order used for each experiment.

Evaluation Measures. In order to establish some degree of comparability, we chose to follow the design of the automatic CL-QA task in CLEF-2005 as closely

Table 2. iCLEF 2005 Condition and Topic Presentation Order

user	search order (condition: $A\|B$, question: 1...16)															
1	A1	A4	A3	A2	A9	A12	A11	A10	B13	B16	B15	B14	B5	B8	B7	B6
2	B2	B3	B4	B1	B10	B11	B12	B9	A14	A15	A16	A13	A6	A7	A8	A5
3	B1	B4	B3	B2	B9	B12	B11	B10	A13	A16	A15	A14	A5	A8	A7	A6
4	A2	A3	A4	A1	A10	A11	A12	A9	B14	B15	B16	B13	B6	B7	B8	B5
5	A15	A14	A9	A12	A7	A6	A1	A4	B3	B2	B5	B8	B11	B10	B13	B16
6	B16	B13	B10	B11	B8	B5	B2	B3	A4	A1	A6	A7	A12	A9	A14	A15
7	B15	B14	B9	B12	B7	B6	B1	B4	A3	A2	A5	A8	A11	A10	A13	A16
8	A16	A13	A10	A11	A8	A5	A2	A3	B4	B1	B6	B7	B12	B9	B14	B15

as possible. Thus, we used the same assessment rules, the same assessors and the same evaluation measures as the CLEF QA task:

- Human subjects were asked to designate a supporting document for each answer (we eliminated the exceptions allowed last year, as for instance building an answer from the information in two documents, because in practice no user exploited these alternative possibilities).
- Users were allowed to record their answers in whatever language was appropriate to the study design in which they were participating. For example, users with no knowledge of the document language would generally be expected to record answers in the question language. Participating teams were asked to hand-translate answers into the document language after completion of the experiment in such cases in order to facilitate assessment.
- Answers were assessed by the same assessors that assessed the automatic CL-QA results for CLEF 2005. The same answer categories were used in iCLEF as in the automatic CL-QA track: *correct* (valid, supported answer), *unsupported* (valid but not supported by the designated document(s)), *non-exact* or *incorrect*. The CLEF CL-QA track guidelines at http://clef-qa.itc.it/2005/guidelines.html provide additional details on the definition of these categories.
- We reported the same official effectiveness measures as the CLEF-2005 CL-QA track. Strict accuracy (the fraction of correct answers) and lenient accuracy (the fraction of correct plus unsupported answers) were reported for each condition. Complete results were reported to each participating team by user, question and condition to allow more detailed analyses to be conducted locally.

Suggested User Session. We set a maximum search time of five minutes per question, but allowed our human subjects to move on to the next question after recording an answer and designating supporting document(s) even if the full five minutes had not expired. We established the following typical schedule for each 3-hour session:

Orientation	10 minutes
Initial questionnaire	5 minutes
Training on both systems	30 minutes
Break	10 minutes
Searching in the first condition (8 topics)	40-60 minutes
System questionnaire	5 minutes
Break	10 minutes
Searching in the second condition (8 topics)	40-60 minutes
System questionnaire	5 minutes
Final questionnaire	10 minutes

Half of the users saw condition A (the reference condition) first, the other half saw condition B first. Participating teams were permitted to alter this schedule as appropriate to their goals. For example, teams that chose to run each subject separately to permit close qualitative assessment by a trained observer might choose to substitute a semi-structured exit interview for the final questionnaire. Questionnaire design was not prescribed, but sample questionnaires were made available to participating teams on the iCLEF Web site (http://nlp.uned.es/iCLEF/).

3.2 Experiments

Three groups submitted results:

University of Alicante. This group investigated how much context is needed to recognize answers accurately with a low-medium knowledge of the document language [5]. Their baseline system shows whole passages (maximum context) to users, while the experimental system shows only a clause (minimum context). Both systems highlight query terms, synonyms of query terms and candidate answers to facilitate the task.

University of Salamanca. Their focus has been exploring the use of free online machine translation programs for query formulation and presentation of results [9]. Both systems compared permit entering the query either in the user language or in the target language; in the first case, machine translation is applied to the query before searching the collection. In the reference system, results are displayed without translation; the contrastive system permits translating passages. Users were classified as having "poor" or "good" foreign language skills in four experiments, Spanish to English and Spanish to French.

UNED. This team has compared searching full documents with searching single sentences [4]. Both systems highlight fragments of the appropriate answer type to help locating the answer. In addition, the contrastive system filters out sentences which do not contain expressions of the appropriate answer type.

Table 3 shows the official results for each of the five experiments. Readers are referred to the papers submitted by the participating teams for analyses of results from specific experiments.

Table 3. iCLEF 2005 Q&A results

Group	Users	Docs	Experiment Condition	Accuracy Strict	Accuracy Lenient
Alicante	ES	EN	full passages	.44	.45
Alicante	ES	EN	clauses	.34	.34
Salamanca	ES	EN	good lang. skills / no translation	.50	.53
Salamanca	ES	EN	good lang. skills / translation	.56	.56
Salamanca	ES	EN	poor lang. skills / no translation	.36	.42
Salamanca	ES	EN	poor lang. skills / translation	.39	.45
Salamanca	ES	FR	good lang. skills / no translation	.66	.67
Salamanca	ES	FR	good lang. skills / translation	.69	.73
Salamanca	ES	FR	poor lang. skills / no translation	.63	.70
Salamanca	ES	FR	poor lang. skills / translation	.61	.66
UNED	ES	EN	documents	.53	.53
UNED	ES	EN	sentences with answer type filter	.45	.45

4 Future Work

Although iCLEF experiments continue producing interesting research results, which may have a substantial impact on the way effective cross-language search assistants are built, participation in this track has remain low across the five years of existence of the track. Interactive studies, however, remain as a recognized necessity in most CLEF tracks.

In order to find an explanation for this apparent contradiction, a questionnaire was created to establish reasons for low participation in the interactive ImageCLEF task and sent to all ImageCLEF participants. Seven participants returned their questionnaires and, out of these, 6 stated (the 7th participated in interactive ImageCLEF) their reason for not participating was lack of time, 5 lack of local resources and 4 that interactive experiments involved too much set-up time. Interactive experiments consume resources which many groups do not have.

We can think of a number of measures to solve this problem:

- Lowering the cost of participation. One approach is to provide a common task in which all groups participate, or use a shared multilingual document collection which can be accessed via an API, e.g. Flickr, Yahoo! or Google. This is only a partial solution, because the highest cost comes from recruting, training and monitorizing users for the searching sessions. An alternative is devising an experiment design in which search interfaces are deployed in real working environments, and then study the search logs of real users with

real needs. This is a less controlled environment which could, nevertheless, provide a wealth of information about why and how users search in a cross-language manner.
- Adding value to the experimental setting. For instance, if we could work with online multilingual collections which have large user communities, setting up cross-language search interfaces for them has the additional appeal of being able to provide demonstrations which turn into useful web services for a significant set of web users.

We are currently contemplating the possibility of using a large-scale, web-based image database, such as Flickr (www.flickr.com), for iCLEF experiments. The Flickr database contains over five million images freely accesible via web, daily updated by a large number of users and available for all web users. These images are annotated by the authors with freely chosen keywords in a naturally multilingual manner: most authors use keywords in their native language, some combine more than one language. In addition, photographs have titles, descriptions, colaborative annotations, and comments in many languages. Participating groups would have the opportunity of building search interfaces not only for testing/demo purposes, but also to offer a useful web service with many potential users.

Acknowledgments

We are indebted to Richard Sutcliffe and Christelle Ayache for taking care of the Q&A assessments; Victor Peinado and Fernando López for their assistance with submission processing, Javier Artiles for maintaining the iCLEF web page, and Jianqiang Wang for creating the Systran translations that were made available to the iCLEF teams. Thanks also to Daniela Petrelli for the fruitful discussions about the iCLEF experimental design, and to Carol Peters and Doug Oard for their support. This work has been partially supported by the Spanish Government, project R2D2-Syembra (TIC2003-07158-C04-02).

References

1. P. Clough, H. Müeller, T. Desealers, M. Grubinger, t. Lehmann, J. Jensen and W. Hersh. The CLEF 2005 Cross-Language Image Retrieval Track, in this volume.
2. . J. Cox, M. L. Miller, S. M. Omohundro, and P. N. Yianilos. Pichunter: Bayesian relevance feedback for image retrieval. Proceedings of the 13th International Conference on Pattern Recognition, 3:361–369, 1996.
3. William Hersh and Paul Over. TREC-9 interactive track report. In *The Ninth Text Retrieval Conference (TREC-9)*, November 2000. http://trec.nist.gov.
4. V. Peinado, F. López-Ostenero, J. Gonzalo and F. Verdejo. UNED at iCLEF 2005: automatic highlighting of potential answers In this volume.
5. B. Navarro, L. Moreno-Monteagudo, E. Noguera, S. Vázquez, F. LLopis and A. Montoyo. "How much context do you need?" An experiment about the context size in Interactive Cross-Language Question Answering. In this volume.

6. Douglas W. Oard and Julio Gonzalo. The CLEF 2003 interactive track. In Carol Peters, editor, *Proceedings of the Fourth Cross-Language Evaluation Forum.* 2003.
7. Petrelli, D. and Clough, P.D. Concept Hierarchy across Languages in Text-Based Image Retrieval: A User Evaluation, In this volume.
8. Villena-Román, R., Crespo-García, R.M., and González-Cristóbal, J.C. Boolean Operators in Interactive Search, in this volume.
9. A. Zazo, C. Figuerola, J. Alonso and V. Fernández. iCLEF 2005 at REINA-USAL: Use of Free On-line Machine Translation Programs for Interactive Cross-Language Question Answering. In this volume.

Use of Free On-Line Machine Translation for Interactive Cross-Language Question Answering

Angel Zazo, Carlos G. Figuerola, José Luis A. Berrocal, and Viviana Fernández Marcial

REINA Research Group – Universidad de Salamanca
C/ Francisco de Vitoria 6-16, 37008 Salamanca, Spain
http://reina.usal.es

Abstract. Free on-line machine translation systems are employed more and more by Internet users. In this paper we have explored the use of these systems for Cross-Language Question Answering, in two aspects: in the formulation of queries and in the presentation of information. Two topic-document language pairs were used, Spanish-English and Spanish-French. For each of these, two groups of users were created, depending on the level of reading skills in document language. When machine translation of the queries was used directly in the search, the number of correct answers was quite high. Users only corrected 8% of the translations proposed. As regards the possibility of using machine translation to translate into Spanish the text passages shown to the user, we expected the search of the users with little knowledge of the target language to improve notably, but we found that this possibility was of little help in finding the correct answers for the questions posed in the experiment.

1 Introduction

Question Answering (QA) is one of the most advanced facets in information retrieval. It searches for precise answers to specific questions. The idea is to find a minimum text fragment that will answer the question, using an extensive document collection to do so. When the question and the documents are in different languages, this is called Cross-Language Question Answering (CL-QA). The process becomes complicated if documents are in a language in which the user is rather unskilled.

On-line machine translation systems are free tools becoming more well-known and used by Internet users. For the Cross-Language Evaluation Forum (CLEF) 2005 interactive track (iCLEF), we explored the use of machine translation (MT) for interactive CL-QA. Our intention was to reproduce the normal situation of users with little knowledge of the language of the documents, unable to form the query correctly or to correctly understand a possible answer. In many cases these users resort to on-line MT services to satisfy their information needs. We carried out the experiment with two language pairs: Spanish-English and Spanish-French, in order to see the dependence of the results on the target language. We focused on two aspects:

C. Peters et al. (Eds.): CLEF 2005, LNCS 4022, pp. 263–272, 2006.

1. *The formulation and refinement of the queries.* We wished to analyse the behaviour of users employing an interactive CL-QA system when they can initiate or refine the searches using their own language or the language of the documents.
2. *The possibility of using MT to translate the information shown to the user.* We wished to observe the behaviour of users with little knowledge of the language of the documents when they have the possibility of translating them to their own language and whether this possibility improves the accuracy of the system.

To have a suitable basis for comparison the experiments were carried out with two groups of users for each language pair, each with a different reading level in the language of the documents. This goal was to be able to analyse the behaviour of both types of users.

2 The CLIR System

We actually used as a cross-language information retrieval (CLIR) system a standard document retrieval system that made monolingual searches in the language of the documents. It was based on the vector space model, with different adaptations to translate the questions to the language of the documents and the documents to the language of the user. The system was the same one we used in iCLEF2004 [1], with some modifications.

Text passages were used instead of complete documents, the same as last year, but the possibility of seeing the context of the passage, i.e. the complete document, was excluded, although as we know [1] this reduces the accuracy of the system. This year the passages were made up of at least 50 words (including stop words). If a paragraph had fewer words, it was joined to the following one, and so on as necessary to complete a passage of at least 50 words.

Last year the CLIR system also used an on-line MT system to translate to the target language the questions written in Spanish, but refinement of the searches was only permitted by means of a very limited mechanism of term suggestion (which, by the way, was not greatly appreciated by the users). In this year's experiments the users could refine their searches with greater freedom, both in Spanish and the target language. Interaction with the user was done using standard web forms. The interface permitted the refinement of the searches and the examination of the passages retrieved, with the possibility of translating the latter to the language of the user.

3 The Experiment

We followed the iCLEF guidelines [2] for carrying out the experiment, which indicated what the queries were, how the search should be carried out, which document collections could be used, the questionnaires and the time limit. The

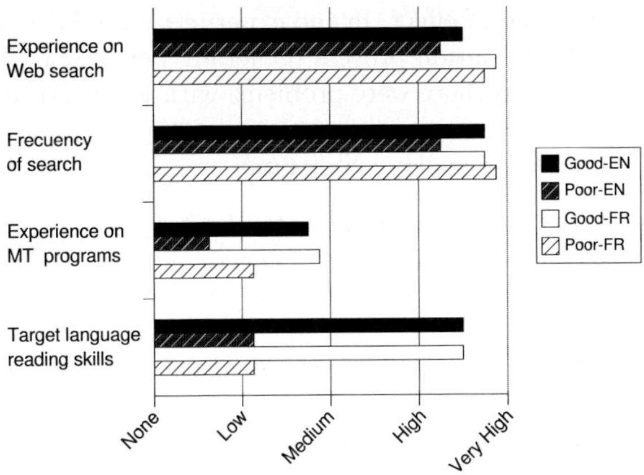

Fig. 1. First questionnaire prior to the experiment

Spanish version of the queries was used in the experiments, and the corresponding document collections in English and French supplied by the CLEF organization.

The experiment was carried out with four groups of users. For each pair of query-document languages, Spanish-English and Spanish-French, two groups of users were created, each with a different reading level in the language of the documents: good and bad (or *poor*). The users were university students whose mother-tongue was Spanish. The groups were named Good-EN, Poor-EN, Good-FR and Poor-FR. The groups with the prefix "Good" were made up of students from the degree course in Translation at the University of Salamanca. These users actually carried out monolingual searches, and their tests served as a referent point for those of the "Poor" group.

Figure 1 shows results of initial questionnaire previously to the searches. For all groups a great deal of experience in Web search was reported. For all users, the frequency of search was close to once or twice a day. Experience of MT programs was small for all groups, but smaller for "Poor" groups. Notice the difference in the knowledge of the target language of both types of groups.

3.1 Machine Translation

On-line machine translation systems are free tools being handled more and more by Internet users. In our experiment we used two of these systems to translate queries or terms from Spanish into the target language and passages from English/French into Spanish:

- Spanish–English: *Google Linguistic Tools* (`http://translate.google.com`)
- Spanish–French: *Systran Online* (`http://w3.systranbox.com`)

Initially we used Google because it did not impose length limit on the input text, but it did not have the Spanish-French translation pair. We thus used Systran for that pair, although sometimes the connection with the Systran server stalled. To avoid this type of effect, in the experiment we did not compute the time employed in the translation process (generally between 1 or 2 seconds for both systems, except when there were problems with the Systran connection).

3.2 Reference and Contrastive Systems

The reference system (*System A*) was a standard document retrieval system based on the vector space model performing monolingual searches in the language of the documents. To formulate the query the users could write the question in Spanish or directly in the target language (Fig. 2). The button labelled "Traducir_y_Buscar" (*Translate and Search*) translated the text entered in the first field into the target language and then immediately made the search. The button labelled "Buscar" (*Search*) carried out the search directly using the terms entered into the second entry field. Before using the system, the users were told how it worked: it was a simple term driven system, and thus the users could use terms instead of questions or sentences. It must be pointed out that, in order to facilitate the typing of the question, in each initial search the field corresponding to Spanish was filled in automatically with the text of the query, and the users were free to use it as such, change it if they wished or enter their own terms in the target language.

Once the search had been carried out, the user was shown an ordered list of retrieved passages (Fig. 3). Within the 5 minutes time limit established for each search, the users could refine the search using the entry fields in the upper part of the interface, both in Spanish and the target language. The lower part of the interface contained fields to fill in the answer and the degree of confidence. The users could abandon the search at any time ('nil' answer), by clicking onto the checkbox button labelled "No encuentro la respuesta" (*I cannot find the answer*). After 5 minutes, a window appeared showing only the lower part of the interface, permitting the user a final chance to write the answer.

The contrastive system (*System B*) was identical to the reference system, except that it allowed for the possibility of translating the passages into Spanish. The button "Traducir este pasaje" (*Translate this passage*) only appeared in this system (see Fig. 3). When clicking this button the original passage and its translation were shown.

4 Results and Discussion

4.1 Difference Between Target Languages

Figure 4 shows the strict accuracy and the average searching time for each group. A priori we did not expect much difference between the groups with a good knowledge of the target language, but it turned out to be large, both in strict accuracy and in average searching time. The users of the Good-FR group needed much less effort to find correct answers to the questions. We believe that the reason for this is the division into passages of text. Considering the set of 16 questions of the experiment, the division in text passages had better results for

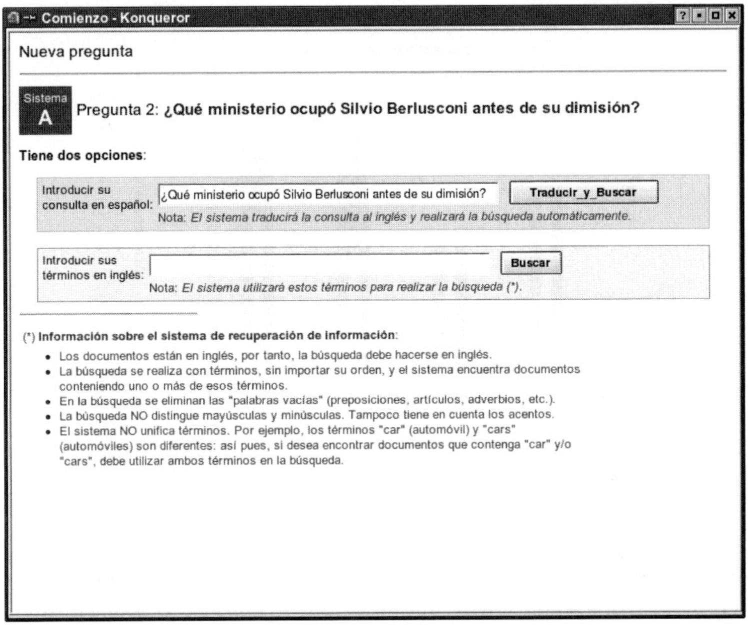

Fig. 2. Initial search of a question

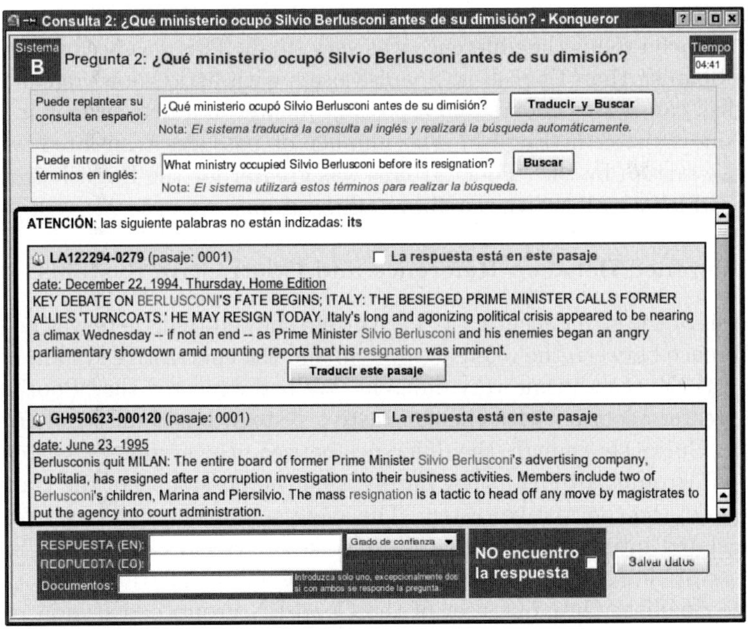

Fig. 3. Ranked list of passages showed to user. Refinement is possible in both reference and contrastive systems.

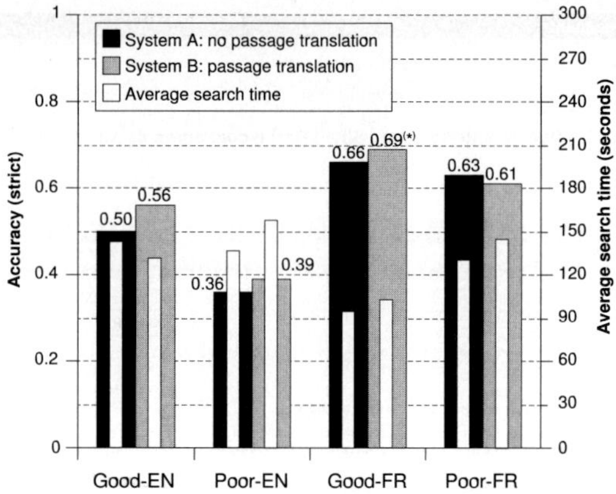

Fig. 4. Strict accuracy and average search time. (*) One 'nil' answer was mistakenly assessed as correct in contrastive system for Good-FR group.

the document collection in French than for the one in English. We should recall that in the experiment the possibility of seeing the context of the passages, i.e. the complete document, was intentionally excluded. If the context of the passages had been available, we believe the difference between the two systems would have been less.

In accordance with what we expected, the groups with a better reading level in the target language obtained greater accuracy than the "Poor" groups, although for both French groups the difference was very small. This was because French is closer to Spanish than English is: Spanish users with little knowledge of French and English can better understand a possible answer in a text written in French than in one written in English. The number of passages translated with the contrastive system by the "Poor" groups was greater for the English group (see Table 1), which corroborates the above affirmation.

4.2 Difference Between Reference and Contrastive Systems

An analysis of the strict accuracy of each group showed that there was no significant difference between the reference system and the contrastive system (Fig. 4). Neither was the search time very different. We had expected the "Poor" groups to have greater accuracy with the contrastive system, but there was hardly any difference. Curiously enough, the difference between the systems was greater for the "Good" groups, although they hardly used the possibility of the translation of passages of the contrastive system. The average number of passages per question translated into Spanish with the contrastive system can be seen in Table 1. No user of the Good-FR group used the possibility of translating the passages into Spanish. Only one user of the Good-EN group had several passages translated from English into Spanish, but said he did it to see the quality of the translation, not because he needed help in the search for answers.

Table 1. Average number of translated passages per topic

Good-EN	Poor-EN	Good-FR	Poor-FR
0.13	3.56	0	1.11

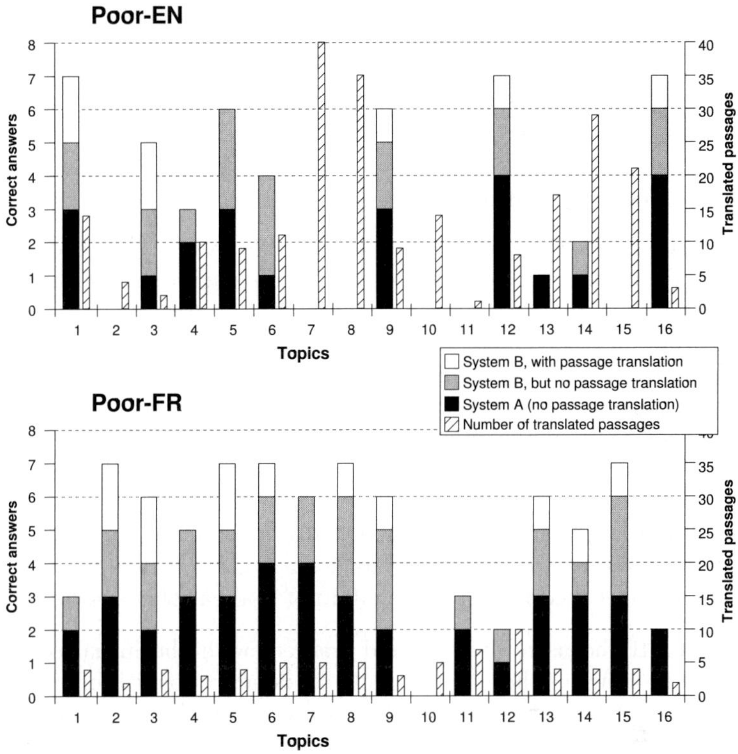

Fig. 5. Correct assessed answers and number of translated passages per topic

For the "Poor" groups, Figure 5 shows the number of correct answers with the reference and contrastive systems for all the questions of the experiment. In the contrastive system the correct answers obtained were differentiated after the user employed the option of translating the passages. Figure 5 also includes the total number of passages translated for each question in the contrastive system. We can see that for both target languages the number of correct answers obtained after having carried out the translation of the passages was low in comparison with the total: 7 out of 48 for English (14.58%) and 12 out of 79 for French (15.19%). It seems that the translation of the passages was of little help to the users in finding correct answers for the particular set of questions in this experiment.

The post-system questionnaires for the reference and contrastive systems were very similar. In general, the contrastive system obtained a better assessment, and the difference was larger in the "Poor" groups. However, these groups did not obtain a significant advantage in accuracy, and the accuracy was less even for the Poor-FR group. According to the results of the final post-search questionnaire, all groups found both systems easy to understand and use. As to which of the systems was considered better in general, the "Good" groups found no differences between them, since, except for one user, they did not make use of the translation possibility of the contrastive system. However, the "Poor" groups indicated that they thought the contrastive system was much better.

All users remarked that the possibility of translating the passages was highly appreciated. Also they noted that it was very useful for locating the possible answer the fact that search terms were displayed in different colour than text.

4.3 Query Formulation and Refinement

Initial Search. Before beginning the search, the users had to choose how to formulate the question: in Spanish or in the language of the documents. As was to be expected, the "Poor" groups began their searches almost exclusively in Spanish. Seventy percent of the users of the Good-EN group and 71% of the Good-FR group also began their searches in Spanish. The percentage is very similar for all the questions. Nevertheless, there were differences among the users: in general, each user employed almost exclusively one of the two methods to begin all their searches. Several of the users who began their searches in Spanish indicated that it was very convenient to use the "Traducir_y_Buscar" button, since the question appeared automatically in the associated field: they let the system make the translation into the target language and then they changed it if they considered it incorrect or if they did not find suitable answers.

Refinement. If the users did not find answers with the initial search, they could refine the search. The refining could be done in Spanish or in the target language. Most of the users refined their searches in the target language. We were able to observe that the way refining is carried out greatly depends on each user. For example, user number 3 in the Poor-EN group carried out most of the refinements in that group. Several users of the Good-EN and Good-FR groups did not refine their searches, although several of their answers were 'nil' answers.

Quality of the Translation. For a term driven document retrieval system, the syntactic or grammatical quality of a translation is of little importance. What is really important is that the translation of the terms be correct in their context. When the search was initiated in Spanish, the number of correct answers without the need to refine the search was high: 71 out of 116 for English (61.21%), and 117 out of 165 for French (70.91%). In the experiment, corrections of the machine translations were made in only a few cases: 21 times in a total of 251 translations (initial search + refinement) from Spanish to English (8.37%) and 21 times in a total of 256 translations from Spanish to French (8.20%). As was to be expected, the groups with a good level in the target language made more corrections than the "Poor" groups. In their comments, several users in the Good-FR group pointed out that they were pleasantly surprised by the quality of the translations of the questions into French.

The errors in translation depended on the language pair in each test. In the use of Google for the translation of Spanish to English, the difficulties were found mainly with three terms: "Economía" (*Economy*), which Google translated as "Economi'a"; the term "Turquesa" (*Turquoise*) which it did not translate because it had a capital letter; and the term "Universo" (*Universe*) which it translated as "Universal". For the Spanish to French translations with Systran, the difficulties were also found with three terms: "Turquesa", which Systran translated as "Turque" (*Turkish*) instead of "Turquoise", and the terms "Noruega" (*Norway*) and "Eduardo", which were not translated because they contained capital letters (the correct translations would have been "Norvège" and "Edouard").

4.4 Failure Analysis

There were fewer answers judged as correct for the tests with English as the target language. We believe this was due to the worse results in the division of passages for the document collection in English and the impossibility of seeing the complete document. If the context of the passages had been available, the accuracy of the systems would have been greater. This justifies in part the high number of unsupported answers in the groups with English as the target language (11%). Other aspects to be taken into account are the incorrect translations, affecting 3 questions, and also imprecise answers for some of the questions. When French was the target languages the errors were due mainly to incorrect translations.

4.5 'Nil' Answers

The mean time for the 'nil' answers was quite uniform for the four groups: about 4 minutes, i.e. the users gave up their searches before the fixed maximum time ran out. This was more pronounced in the second half of each test and denotes tiredness with the experiment. Several users indicated that the test was somewhat tedious: there were many questions, some of them long and complicated.

4.6 Topic 9

The answers to the question "*¿Con el nombre de qu enfermedad se corresponde el acrnimo BSE?*" were judged differently by the English and French assessors. For our tests with the Spanish-English language pair only two answers were affected (one for each group): the accuracy was barely affected by this.

5 Conclusions

The use of free on-line machine translation for interactive CL-QA was explored in two important aspects: in the search process and in the visualization of information. In the first it was found that with direct use the machine translated questions the number of correct answers was high. The fundamental difference was found in language pairs: the results were better for Spanish into French than for Spanish into English. In our case, this differences lies in the fact that French is much closer to Spanish than English is, and the quality of the translation is higher between French and Spanish. The quality of the translation depends on the original and target languages. Other authors have also had this result [3,4].

Regarding visualization, we expected that users with little knowledge of the document language whould to obtain higher accuracy since they could use MT to translate the passages shown to them in another language into Spanish. In fact, all the users manifested in their comments that they valued very positively the possibility of translating into Spanish the passages in the contrastive system. The users in the "Poor" groups thought that the contrastive system was far better. However, for both target languages the number of correct answers obtained after having the passages translated was low in comparison with those obtained without using this option. It seems that the possibility of translating the passages was of little help in finding the correct answers for the questions of the experiment.

Finally, the differences obtained with the languages of the experiments must also be pointed out. The strict accuracy for the Good-EN and the Good-FR groups was quite different. In our view this was due to the importance of the division of the text passages when it is not possible to see the context of the information. If the context of the passages had been available, the accuracy of the systems would have been better in general, and the difference between these groups would have been less.

References

1. Figuerola, C.G., Zazo, A., Alonso Berrocal, J.L., Rodríguez, E.: Interactive and bilingual question answering using term suggestion and passage retrieval. CLEF 2004, Lecture Notes in Computer Science **3491** (2005) 363–370
2. Gonzalo, J., Clough, P., Vallin, A.: Overview of the CLEF 2005 interactive track (In this volume)
3. Jones, G.J., Lam-Adesina, A.M.: Exeter at CLEF 2001: Experiments with machine translation for bilingual retrieval. CLEF 2001, Lecture Notes in Computer Science **2406** (2002) 59–77
4. Kraaij, W.: TNO at CLEF-2001: Comparing translation resources. CLEF 2001, Lecture Notes in Computer Science **2406** (2002) 7893

“How Much Context Do You Need?”: An Experiment About the Context Size in Interactive Cross-Language Question Answering

Borja Navarro, Lorenza Moreno-Monteagudo, Elisa Noguera, Sonia Vázquez, Fernando Llopis, and Andrés Montoyo

NLP Research Group (GPLSI)
Departament of Software and Computing Systems
University of Alicante
Alicante, Spain
{borja, loren, elisa, svazquez, llopis, montoyo}@dlsi.ua.es

Abstract. The main topic of this paper is the context size needed for an efficient Interactive Cross-language Question Answering system. We compare two approaches: the first one (baseline system) shows the user whole passages (maximum context: 10 sentences). The second one (experimental system) shows only a clause (minimum context). As cross-language system, the main problem is that the language of the question (Spanish) and the language of the answer context (English) are different. The results show that large context is better. However, there are specific relations between the context size and the knowledge about the language of the answer: users with poor level of English prefer context with few words.

1 Introduction

In an Interactive Question Answering system, the decision about the correctness of the answer in factotum questions (or usefulness, satisfaction, or helpfulness in analytical questions) depends on the linguistic context in which the possible answer appears [1]. The user decides according to the context. In addition to previous knowledge about the topic and the question itself, the context is the main source of information available for the user in order to decide about the correctness of the answer shown by the system. According to the context, he/she decides if it is necessary a refinement of the question or not.

However, there is a specific problem in Interactive Cross-language Questions Answering: the language in which the answer (and the context of the answer) appears is different from the language of the user and, therefore, the language of the question. The user must deal with a language with null or passive knowledge about it.

The specific question in this experiment is how much context the users need in order to achieve a satisfactory interaction with the system in a language different from the one of the query.

C. Peters et al. (Eds.): CLEF 2005, LNCS 4022, pp. 273–282, 2006.

We have run two systems. The first one (baseline system) is an Information Retrieval System based on passages. This system shows a complete passage of 10 sentences: the maximum context shown to the user.

The interaction with the user based on passages has been improved with two elements:

1. A Name Entities Recognition system. The NE that appears in the passages and in the query, plus the NE of the possible answer, are marked with different colors.
2. Also, the set of synonyms of each (disambiguated) word of the question is shown to the user. If he/she thinks that it is necessary, he/she can re-run the IR system with the synonyms. That is, the user decides if it is better to use an extended query or not.

The second system (experimental system) is a preliminary version of a Question Answering system based on syntactic-semantic patterns. This system calculates the syntactic-semantic similarity between the question and the possible answers. Both are formally represented by means of syntactic-semantic patterns, based on the subcategorization frame of the verb. The system shows the user only the clause in which the possible answer appears. A clause is a linguistic unit smaller than a sentence: it is the minimum context.

In addition to this primary objective about the context size, we have two secondary objectives:

1. As questions are written in a natural language, it is necessary to disambiguate them. We have applied a Word Sense Disambiguation method based on Relevant Domains for the disambiguation of the question.
2. We are developing methods of syntactic-semantic similarity between the question and the possible answer in a bilingual/multilingual framework. As we said before, the experimental system is a QA system based on the syntactic semantic similarity between the verbal subcategorization frame of the question and the verbal subcategorization frame of the possible answers. In this experiment we have obtained preliminary evaluation results.

In the next section, the process of disambiguation, translation and expansion of the question is explained. The baseline system (IR-n system) is explained in Sect. 3 and the QA system based on syntactic-semantic similarity is explained in the Sect. 4. At the end of the paper, the results, conclusions and some problems founded will be shown.

2 Question Translation, Disambiguation and Expansion

The mother tongue of users is Spanish. The questions are written in Spanish and the answers in English. The users have passive knowledge of English: they can understand some words/sentences in English, but they can not formulate a question in English correctly.

The words of the questions were disambiguated with a Word Sense Disambiguation system based on Relevant Domains.

2.1 WordNet Domains and Relevant Domains

WordNet Domains (WND) [2] is an extension of WordNet 1.6 where each synset is annotated with one or more domain labels. These labels are selected from a set of about 250 hundred labels hierarchically organized.

In this work, WND is used to collect examples of domains related to different senses. We use this information to obtain a new resource named Relevant Domains (RD).

In order to obtain RD, we use WND glosses to collect the more relevant and representative domain labels for each word. So the first step to get RD is to use a POS-tagger to obtain all syntactic categories and lemmas of each gloss. For this task we use Tree-tagger [3]. Once the results of the POS-tagger have been obtained, the second step is to create a list of "word-domain" pairs where "word" is each name, verb, adverb or adjective of each gloss and "domain" is the gloss domain label (in WND each gloss has one or more domain labels). We repeat this process with all glosses in WND. Finally we obtain the new resource RD with all this information.

Our purpose is to obtain a resource with all words of WND glosses and their possible domains. Therefore, each word has a list of different domains and these domains will be arranged using two formulas. First of all, we collect the most representative words of a domain with the Mutual Information formula (1) as follows:

$$MI(w, D) = \log_2 \frac{Pr(w|D)}{Pr(w)} \tag{1}$$

w : *word.*
D : *domain.*

Intuitively, a representative word will appear in a domain context more often. But we are interested on the importance of words in a domain, that is, the most representative and common words in a domain. We can appreciate this importance with the Association Ratio (A.R.) formula:

$$AR(w, D) = Pr(w|D) \log_2 \frac{Pr(w|D)}{Pr(w)} \tag{2}$$

This formula A.R. is applied to all words with noun grammatical category obtained from WND glosses. So we arrange pairs of word-domain by A.R. values (bigger to smaller). Next, the same process is applied to verbs, adjectives and adverbs. A proposal in this way has been made in [4], but using Lexicography Codes of WordNet Files.

2.2 WSD Method

Our WSD method is unsupervised and it is based on the hypothesis that words appearing into the same context have quite related senses. In this case, we can take a sentence or a window of words with the ambiguous word as the context.

In order to collect context and the domains of each word by A.R. we need a structure named context vector. Furthermore, each polysemic word in the context has different senses (with their corresponding glosses) and for each sense we need a structure, named sense vector, containing the most representative domains stored by the A.R. formula. In order to obtain the correct word senses in the context, we must measure the proximity between context vector and sense vectors. This proximity is measured by using cosine between both vectors.

2.3 Application to Interactive Task

Part one. First of all we need to disambiguate initial questions. This task needs an automatic translation of questions from Spanish to English.

Step one. Obtaining the Automatic Translation of Questions. In order to obtain the automatic translation of each question we have used three machine translation (MT) systems available on the web: Systran Babelfish.[1], Reverso Soft.[2], and Google.[3] Each one provides its own translation.

Step two. Selecting the Appropriate Translation. We select the most frequent words between all translations. If there isn't any word in common between the three translations we select all words obtained.

Step three. Obtaining the Correct Sense of Words. For this purpose we use our method Relevant Domains [5] to obtain the disambiguation of words selected. This method uses the words of questions as context to construct word sense vectors and select the appropriate sense of each word.

Part two. The next step is using the information provided by our Relevant Domains disambiguation system to expand each question.

Step one. Obtaining Synonym Words. Once we have obtained the correct sense of each word we intend to expand each question with a list of synonyms. That is, we add more information selecting all synonym to each word disambiguated.

This task is possible thanks to the fact that words are disambiguated, so we have only one sense per word. Each sense has associated a synset in WordNet that contains one or more synonyms. With this new information users have the possibility of selecting more words that can appear associated with the answer.

Our method obtains the disambiguation of questions in English, not in Spanish. Although there isn't any problem because we have a direct association of English words and Spanish words with the ILI of EuroWordNet [6]. So for each English word we have a Spanish word with its synonyms. This is the information that users will employ to the iCLEF task.

---

1 http://babelfish.altavista.com/

2 http://www.elmundo.es/traductor/

3 http://www.google.com/language_tools

Step two. Calling the Passages Retrieval System IR-n.
With the words selected by the users we have the information necessary to call the IR-n system for obtaining the possible paragraphs with the correct answer to each question. The expansion of each question with synonyms sets contributes to obtain better results by the IR-n system.

3 Baseline System: Passages Improved with Name Entity Recognition

The baseline system is a Passages Retrieval system. Following with the approach of last years, this model is based on passages with new elements which help the interaction with the user. These new elements are Name Entity Recognition (NER) in the passages and the synonyms of the words.

Our aim is to help the user to find the answer of the query. With this aim the most relevant passages are shown and the words of the query are highlight in the text. Furthermore, the entity type of the answer is detected and the words which are of this type are also highlighted. Finally, the synonyms of the query are shown and they are highlighted in the text.

The passages are extracted by IR-n system. IR-n [7] is a passage retrieval system (RP). RP systems [8] study the appearance of query terms in contiguous fragments of the documents (also called passages). One of the main advantages of these systems is that they allow us to determine not only if a document is relevant or not, but also the detection of the relevant part of the document.

DRAMNERI [9] is a knowledge based Named Entity Recognition system that uses rules and gazetteers in order to identify and classify named entities. This is done sequentially by applying several modules which perform different tasks: tokenization, sentence partition, named entity identification and finally named entity classification.

Firstly, the question in Spanish is presented and following the synonyms of this question which has been obtained by means of the method that is explained in the Sect 2. Next to the synonyms, there is a checkbox which allows the user to carry out the search with query expansion based on synonyms. Moreover, the words and synonyms of the query (only if user has selected the checkbox to carry out query expansion) are highlighted in blue color.

Under the synonyms, this approach lets the user to select the entity type that is expected as an answer. Because of that, a list containing all types of entities that NER detects is shown. The entity which NER has detected as entity type of the answer is selected from the list. Furthermore, the distinct entities detected by NER are shown in the passages. They are highlighted in red color.

When NER is applied to a query, on one hand the entity type of the answer is returned and, on the other hand, all the entities of this type in the text are highlighted. This could be useful for the user because he doesn't need to read all the passage. Firstly he could see if the request is in the marked entities, otherwise the whole passage will be read. Moreover, it has also been included an option that allows to see the whole document. This will be useful if the request is not in the passage but it is in the document.

4 Experimental System: A Question Answering System Based on Syntactic-Semantic Similarity

The experimental system is a Question Answering (QA) system that follows a linguistic oriented approach based on deep linguistic knowledge.

Our objective is to show the user the minimum context necessary to evaluate the correction/utility of the answer. The context is the clause: the set of words related with a verb in a sentence. A clause is formed by one or more nominal or prepositional phrases. Therefore, the system shows the user the possible answer plus the words/phrases that form the clause.

According to their syntactic relations, there are two kinds of clauses: principal clauses (if the verb is the main one of the sentence), and subordinate clauses (if the verb is subordinated).

The intuitive idea behind this approach is that between the question and the answer exists a deep semantic relation: a question is formed by a clause (or more, in complex questions) and the answer appears inside another clause. The objective is to calculate the syntactic-semantic similarity between the question and the clause in which the possible answer appears.

Both, the question and the possible answers, are formally represented as syntactic-semantic patterns. Basically, the syntactic-semantic pattern of a clause is the subcategorization frame of the verb. It is formed by the next components [10] [11]:

1. The verb: each verb forms a syntactic semantic pattern. It is represented by means of its lemma and its sense.
2. The complements of the verb: the set of complements (arguments and adjuncts) that appears with the verb. They are represented by the lemma of the head of the phrase and its sense (or senses, if it is not possible an automatic disambiguation of the ambiguous head nouns). These head nouns are common nouns or proper nouns.

The input of the system is the output of the Passage Retrieval System IR-n. All the passages returned by IR-n system are processed with a PoS_tagger (Treetagger [3]) and a syntactic parser (SUPAR [12]). From this, the system extracts patterns (one for each verb) and stores them in a database of syntactic-semantic patterns. Then all the senses of each head noun and each verb is extracted from EuroWordNet ([6]).

A pattern is extracted from the question too. In this case, the sense of nouns and verbs has been automatically disambiguated.

Once all the patterns are extracted, the system calculates the syntactic-semantic similarity between the question pattern and all the patterns extracted from the passages. This process has two steps:

1. A filter of proper nouns:
   If a proper noun appears in the question, it must appear in the answer. If it does not appear in a pattern, it is not the correct one.[4] At least a proper noun of the question must appear in the answer pattern. If, for example, a question asks about "Thomas Mann", the system accepts all patterns with the proper noun "Thomas", the proper noun "Mann" or both.
2. A syntactic-semantic measure of similarity:
   The system calculates the syntactic-semantic similarity between the question patterns (Pq) and the possible answer pattern (Pa) (the patterns that have been selected in the previous filter), according to the next formula (3):

   $$Sim(Pq, Pa) = \alpha(SimVpq, Vpa) + \beta * NumA_qa + \gamma * NumPN_qa \quad (3)$$

   where
   - $SimVpq - Vpa$ represents the semantic similarity between the verb of the query pattern and the verb of the answer pattern. It is computed by the D. Lin's formula ([13]).[5]
   - $NumA_qa$ represents the number of equal arguments between the query pattern and the answer pattern.
   - $NumPN_qa$ represents the number of equal proper names between the query pattern and the answer pattern.
   - α, β, γ represents the importance of each component.

   The idea behind this formula is that the semantic of the verb establishes the semantic framework of the complete pattern (the subcategorization frame). So both patterns (the question pattern and the answer pattern) must be semantically related mainly by the verb sense. Then, this general semantic relation is specified by the numbers of equal arguments, both commons nouns and proper nouns.

The output of the system is a rank list of patterns, from the most similar with the question pattern up to the less one. For the interactive process, the system shows the user the clause related with each syntactic-semantic pattern. The user must check each clause, until finding the correct answer.

5 Results

In general, the results show that it is better a large context than a small one. That is, the users locate correct answers better with a passage retrieval system (plus name entity recognition) than with a more specific QA system that shows only clauses (Fig. 1).

Three users locate more correct answers with experimental system (small context), and five with baseline system (large context) (Fig. 2).

[4] Or the user will not be able to decide if it is the correct one, because the context doesn't provide enough information in order to decide about the correctness of the clause.

[5] We have used the T. Pedersen's implementation: http://search.cpan.org/t̃pederse/

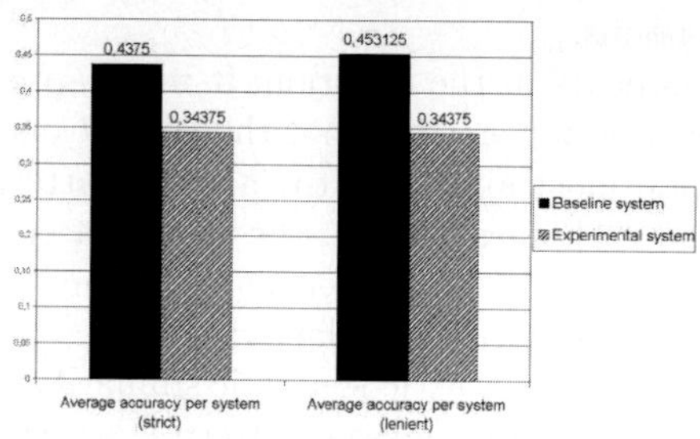

Fig. 1. General results

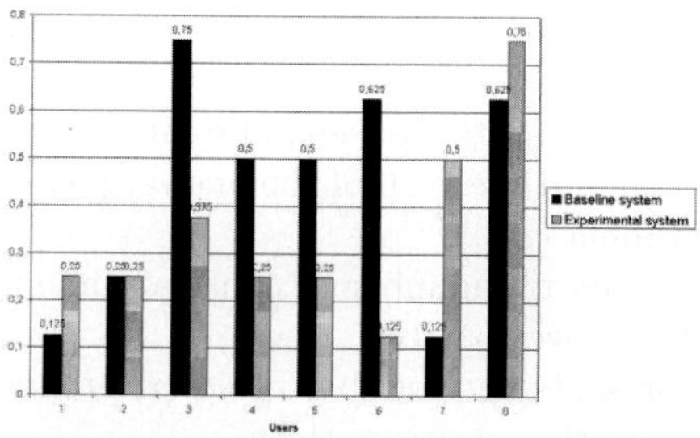

Fig. 2. Results user by user: strict

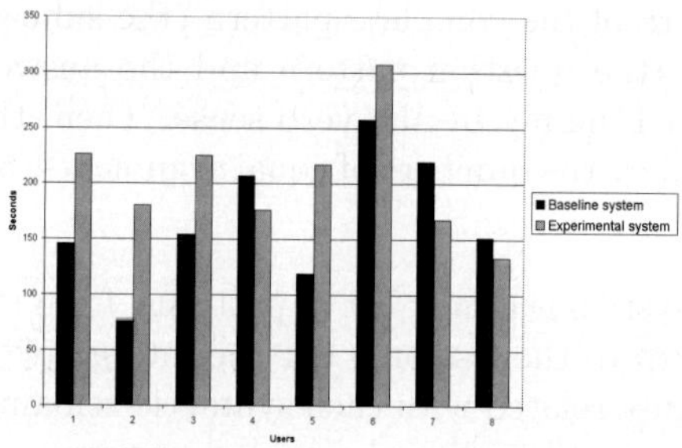

Fig. 3. Time consuming by each user

However, the better results are achieved with both systems: user 3 and user 8. With these results, we think that the improvement of the QA system based on syntactic-semantic patterns will improve the interaction process.

According to the English knowledge of the users, users with low knowledge have reported that they prefer the experimental system, based on clauses. One of them (user 7) has located correct answers with the clauses (0.5 strict accuracy), better than with passages (0.125 strict accuracy).

Comparing the time consumed by each user (Fig. 3), the user that has located correct answers with experimental system (clauses) is the one that has consumed less time (user 8). In general, users have spent much time looking for correct answers, because they tried to find more context in the complete document. In these cases, the context shown by both systems is not sufficient (for example, user 6).

The use of a Name Entity Recognition system has been really useful during the interaction process. All users, except one, report that knowing the name entities of the passage and the possible answer helped them during the localization of the correct answer.

However, users did not use the synonyms and the expansion of the query during the interaction process. Only one user (5) said that the synonyms were really useful to locate the correct answer.

6 Conclusions

It is difficult to establish a fixed context useful for Interactive Question Answering. According to the results of this experiment, for an interactive user interface it is more useful to use passages, in which more context appears, than simple clauses, in which the contexts is formed by few words. Between a large context or a short context, users prefer the large one.

However, for users with poor knowledge of the language of the answer, it is more useful (and fast) to interact with short context. We think that these users have more confident with the systems that the others. This conclusion must be supported by more evidences.

So, for an interactive approach to QA, it is important not only the precision of the system, but also the amount of information that the system shows to the user. This is the information that users need to decide about the correctness or usefulness of the answer.

The use of a name entity recognition system that shows the user the possible answer of a passage is really a useful tool for an optimum interaction. However, the use of synonyms in the interaction process is not useful at all. It is more useful during the automatic expansion of the query.

7 Future Work

This experiment has been a preliminary evaluation of a QA system based on syntactic-semantic patterns. The output of the system is a sentence or clause. It will be improve in order to show only the correct answer.

Acknowledgements

Thank you very much to the users: Pilar, Silvia, Lorena, Sandra, José N., Sergio, Oscar and Mr. Talking Head. This paper has been partially supported by Spanish Government: R2D2 project (TIC 2003-07158-C04-01), CES-ECES project (HUM2004-21127-E) and REXIN project (FIT-340100-2004-14); and Valencian Government: CLASITEX project (GV04B-276) and RECENT project (GV04B-268).

References

1. Maybury, M.T., ed.: New Directions in Question Answering. AAAI Press - MIT Press (2004)
2. Magnini, B., Cavaglia, G.: Integrating Subject Field Codes into WordNet. In Gavrilidou, M., Crayannis, G., Markantonatu, S., Piperidis, S., Stainhaouer, G., eds.: Proceedings of LREC-2000, Second International Conference on Language Resources and Evaluation, Athens, Greece (2000) 1413–1418
3. Schmid, H.: Probabilistic Part-of-Speech Tagging Using Decision Trees. In: Proceedings International Conference on New Methods in Language Processing., Manchester, UK (1994) 44–49
4. Rigau, G., Agirre, E., Atserias, J.: Combining unsupervised lexical knowledge methods for Word Sense Disambiguation. In: Proceedings of joint 35th Annual Meeting of the Association for Computational Linguistics and 8th Conference of the European Chapter of the Association for Computational Linguistics ACL/EACL'97, Madrid, Spain (1997)
5. Vázquez, S., Montoyo, A., Rigau, G.: Using Relevant Domains Resource for Word Sense Disambiguation. IC-AI'04 International Conference **II** (2004)
6. Vossen, P., Bloksma, L., Rodriguez, H., Climent, S., Calzolari, N., Roventini, A., Bertagna, F., Alonge, A., Peters, W.: The EuroWordNet Base Concepts and Top Ontology. Deliverable d017, d034, d036, eurowordnet (le 4003), University of Amsterdam (1997)
7. Llopis, F.: IR-n: Un Sistema de Recuperación de Información Basado en Pasajes. PhD thesis, University of Alicante (2003)
8. Kaskziel, M., Zobel, J.: Passage Retrieval Revisited. In: Proceedings of the 20th annual International ACM Philadelphia SIGIR. (1997) 178–185
9. Toral, A.: DRAMNERI: a free knowledge based tool to Named Entity Recognition. In: Proceedings of the 1st Free Software Technologies Conference. (2005)
10. Navarro, B., Palomar, M., Martínez-Barco, P.: A General Proposal to Multilingual Information Access based on Syntactic Semantic Patterns. In Anje Düsterhöft and Bernhard Thalheim, ed.: Natural Language Processing and Information Systems - NLDB 2003. Lecture Notes in Informatics, GI-Edition, Bonn (2003) 186–199
11. Navarro, B., Palomar, M., Martínez-Barco, P.: Automatic extraction of syntactic semantic patterns for multilingual resources. In: 4th International Conference on Language Resources and Evaluation (LREC), Lisbon (2004)
12. Ferrández, A., Palomar, M., Moreno, L.: An empirical approach to spanish anaphora resolution. Machine Translation. Special Issue on Anaphora Resolution in Machine Translation **14** (1999) 191–216
13. Lin, D.: An information-theoretic definition of similarity. In: Proc. 15th International Conf. on Machine Learning, Morgan Kaufmann, San Francisco, CA (1998) 296–304

UNED at iCLEF 2005: Automatic Highlighting of Potential Answers

Víctor Peinado, Fernando López-Ostenero, Julio Gonzalo, and Felisa Verdejo

NLP Group, ETSI Informática, UNED
c/ Juan del Rosal, 16. E-28040 Madrid. Spain
{victor, flopez, julio, felisa}@lsi.uned.es

Abstract. In this paper, we describe UNED's participation in the iCLEF 2005 track. We have compared two strategies for finding an answer using an interactive question answering system: i) a search system over full documents and ii) a search system over passages (document's paragraphs). We have added an interesting feature to both system in order to facilitate reading: the possibility to enable/disable the highlighting of named entities such as proper nouns, temporal references and numbers likely to contain the right answer.

Our Document Searcher obtained better overall accuracy (0.53 vs. 0.45) but our subjects found browsing passages simpler and faster. However, most of them presented a similar search behavior (regarding time consumption, confidence in their answers and query refinements) using both systems. All our users considered helpful the highlighting of named entities and they all made extensive use of this possibility as a quick way of discriminating between relevant and non relevant documents and finding a valid answer.

1 Introduction

Our participation in iCLEF 2004 [4] focused on comparing two strategies to find an answer using an interactive question answering (QA) system: i) a documents retrieval search engine and; ii) a passages retrieval search engine. We wanted to study what approach was more helpful: browsing documents or passages.

This year we intended to study the impact of automatic highlighting of named entities in both systems. We made use of our simple recognizer, which was able to locate proper nouns, temporal references and numbers, and we added the possibility of enable and disable the emphasis of these named entities. Is it helpful to highlight the named entities in order for the subjects to find a possible answer? How much does the highlighting help the user while browsing documents and while browsing passages?

This paper is divided as follows. In Section 2, we describe the design of the experiments, our testbed and how search sessions are organized. In Section 3, we present our two cross-language search systems. Then, in Section 4, we discuss the official results, analyzing the causes of failure (4.2), the users' and topics' effects

C. Peters et al. (Eds.): CLEF 2005, LNCS 4022, pp. 283–292, 2006.

(4.3 and 4.4) and the cases in which subjects found the answer in the Passages system thanks to the possibility of access the full document (4.5). Lastly, in Section 5, we present some conclusions.

2 Experimental Design

Following the iCLEF 2005 guidelines, [1] we have carried out the comparison of two different cross-language search systems. Eight subjects have searched for the answer of 16 fixed questions in Spanish over a collection of documents written originally in English. The subjects performed eight queries with each system, according to the design of a latin-square proposed by the organization of the task. [3]

The collection of documents consisted of news from 1994 and 1995 taken from *Los Angeles Times* and *Glasgow Herald* newspapers, respectively. In our experiments, we did not use the original documents but a Spanish version translated with *Systran Professional 3.0.* From this translated version of the collection, we made use of the Inquery's API [1] in order to build two different indexes, one for each search system: i) one index whose documents correspond with news articles and; ii) another one in which each document corresponds with a single passage (a paragraph of a news article).

We recruited eight users who were between 19 and 30 years old and had different levels of education, from high school to master degrees. Their mother tongue was Spanish and they all claimed to have between low and medium-high skills in written English comprehension. They were highly familiarized with graphical interfaces and web-based search engines. They also declared to have been using WWW search engines for at least 2-7 years (avg=4.6). On the contrary, none of them had any familiarity using Machine Translation (MT) systems.

We asked the subjects to find a valid answer and select a document supporting it before the time limit. The maximum search time per question was set in five minutes. Once time expired, the system stopped the search and allowed to visualize the subject the set of stored documents, giving her/him a last chance to write an answer. They also had to fill in a pre-search questionnaire about their previous experience with search engines, two post-system questionnaires analyzing their performance and the specific features of each approach, and a final post-search questionnaire about their overall experience.

3 Description of the Reference and Contrastive Systems

3.1 Reference System

Our reference system, henceforth the Documents Searcher, is a simple traditional search engine in which each retrieved document corresponds with a complete news article. Indeed, it has few differences compared to the reference system

[1] For further details, please see `http://nlp.uned.es/iCLEF`.

used last year [4]. We may outline the normal sequence of a subject's actions as follows:

1. The subject types the query terms in Spanish and launches the query.
2. The system makes use of the Inquery's API to retrieve a ranking of relevant documents.
3. The main interface displays only the titles and dates of each document. This interface has additional buttons to discard non-relevant documents, to store a certain document considered interesting, to list already stored documents, and to conclude the search selecting a certain document when an answer has been found.

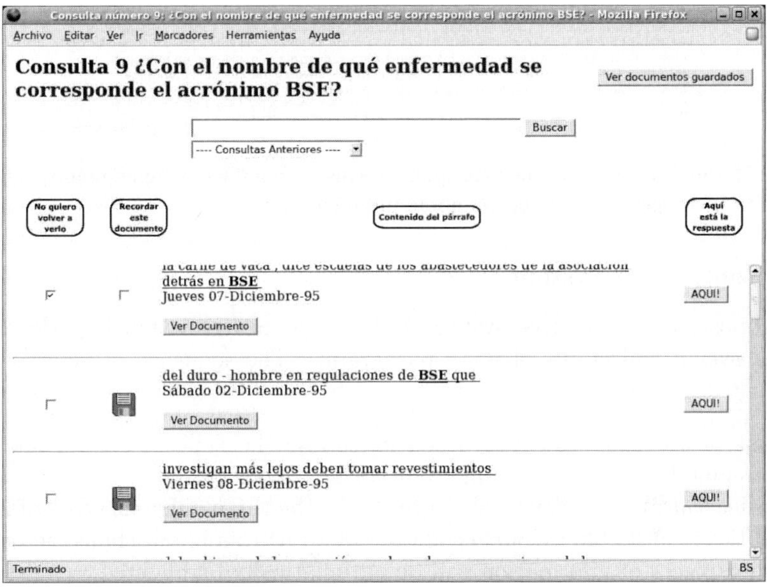

Fig. 1. Documents Searcher's main interface

4. From this main interface, it is possible to visualize the whole document. We have added a feature that did not exist in last year's systems in order to improve the reading: query terms' occurrences appear within the text in boldface. In addition, it is possible to handle some checkboxes in order to enable/disable the highlighting of named entities, such as proper nouns, temporal references, dates and numbers. See Figure 2 for a detailed screenshot showing thc highlighting.
5. Lastly, the subject must type the answer and assign it a confidence value: high or low.

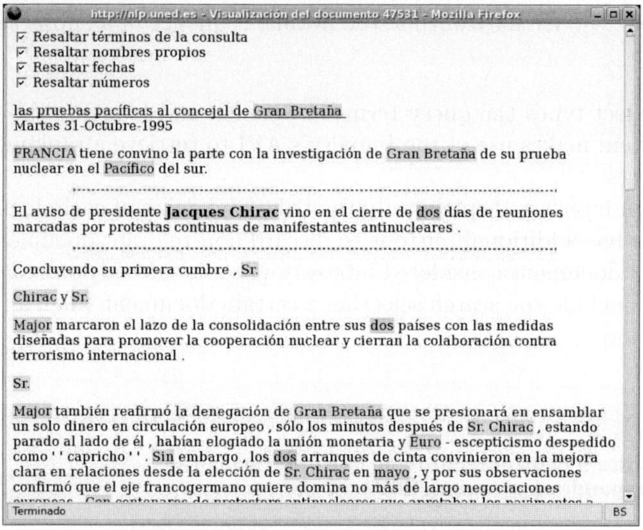

Fig. 2. Highlighted named entities: query terms in boldface, proper nouns in yellow, temporal references in blue and numbers in green

3.2 Contrastive System

We propose, as contrastive system, a Passages Searcher which performs the queries over a collections of news paragraphs. The sequence of actions is the following:

1. First of all, the subject is asked to choose the type of answer she/he is searching for: a proper noun, a date or a number.
   Notice that: i) this distinction agrees with the three different types of named entities identifiable by our recognizer[2] and; ii) this initial choice determines which pieces of information will be automatically highlighted.
   The underlying idea is that, in order to facilitate reading and locating a possible answer, the system will highlight named entities of the same type of the one chosen before submitting the query. For instance, if a subject if looking for a date, it can be useful to automatically emphasize all kind of temporal references.
2. The subject types the query terms in Spanish and launches the query.
3. The system retrieves and shows a ranking of relevant passages. Those passages containing the selected type of answer are promoted by the search engine, and the system automatically highlights query terms and named entities, depending on the initial subject's election.
4. The main interface, as shown in Figure 3, provides also titles and dates of each news article, and has the same buttons that the Documents Searcher to discard and store documents.

[2] We have used a straightforward recognizer which is able to identify proper nouns, temporal references and numbers. See also [5].

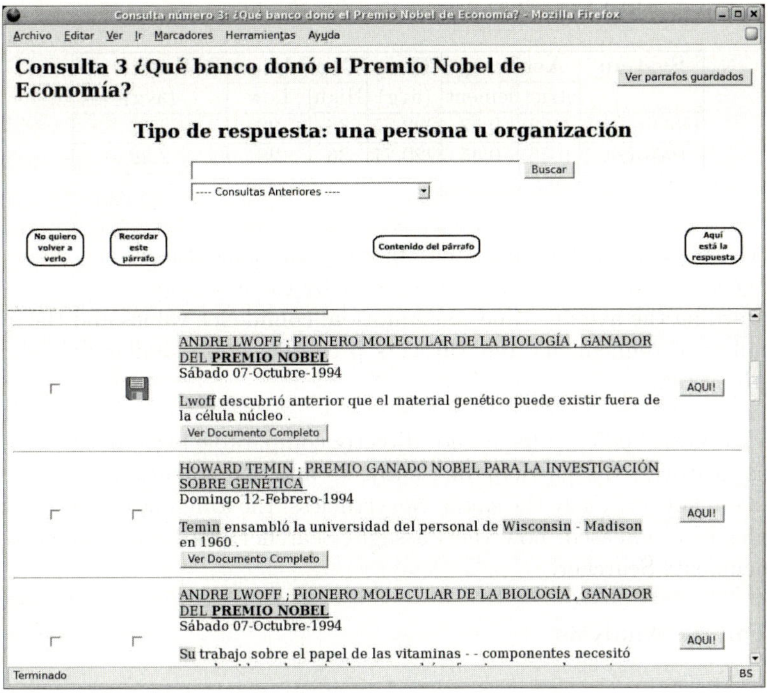

Fig. 3. Passages Searcher's main interface

Unlike last year's experiments, now it is possible to access the complete document the passage makes part of.[3] If this situation takes place, the whole document will clearly show the passage with two dashed lines.

5. When visualizing the full document, it is possible to enable/disable the highlighting of query terms, proper nouns, temporal references and numbers.
6. Lastly, the subject must type the answer and assign it a confidence value: high or low.

4 Results and Discussions

4.1 Comparison Between Systems

From the general results shown in Table 1, we can remark the following:

1. The Documents Searcher obtained better accuracy than the Passages Searcher : 0.53 and 0.45, respectively.

[3] In our participation in iCLEF 2004 [4], we intentionally excluded the possibility of examining the context of a given passage by providing the complete document. All our subjects expressed their complaints because this lack hindered them from understanding the general sense of some short paragraphs. In addition, other works had already analyzed the benefits of allowing the subjects to get the full contents of the documents [2] and we decided to add this feature.

Table 1. Comparison of results for both systems

System	Accuracy		Time	Confidence		Refinements
	strict	lenient	(avg)	High	Low	(avg)
Documents	0.53	0.53	222.25	36	28	2.42
Passages	0.45	0.45	220.77	36	28	2.28

2. Both systems got the same values of strict and lenient accuracy. None of our subject's answers was judged as inexact by the assessors.
3. Regarding the average time consumption, confidence values and the average number of refinements, our subjects present a quite similar behavior with both systems.

The 2004 and 2005 results are not directly comparable because the topics, the systems' features, the participating subjects and the conditions of the experiments were not obviously the same. Nevertheless, the difference between the two strategies has increased: now the Passages Searcher has been 15% worse than the Documents Searcher.

4.2 Failure Analysis

Most of the failure causes was related to mistranslations. As we will discuss below in Section 4.4, sometimes, the MT system did not translated correctly, for instance, translating some terms when it shouldn't and vice versa.

There were also remarkable human errors. Specifically, some users got confused in those topics in which different potential answers (some of them looking contradictory) appeared in the collection (e.g. topics asking for a number of casualties in a incident).

Regarding responsiveness criteria, the results have been strongly language-biased because the same answer was judged in a different way by English and French assessors (see Section 4.4).

4.3 User Effects

The data about accuracy, confidence, number of refinements and time consumption per user are shown in Table 2. Seven out of the eight subjects stated in the questionnaires that they preferred the Passages Searcher. However, six out of eight found more right answers with the Documents Searcher. Some users had some difficulties when using one of the systems. User 7, particularly, obtained poor results with the Passages Searcher, in spite of the fact that she/he spent, on average, 245.38 seconds for each topic. On the contrary, users 2 and 6 performed much worse with the Documents searcher.

Notice that confidence values are generally coherent with the accuracy. Except for users 3 and 6, there are no big differences between the number of answers with a high confidence and the accuracy. For instance, user 6 assigned a high confidence to five of the topics performed with the Documents Searcher

Table 2. Accuracy, confidence, refinements and time (in seconds) per user

User	Accuracy		Confidence				Refinements		Time	
	Docs	Pass	Docs		Pass		Docs	Pass	Docs	Pass
			High	Low	High	Low				
1	.62	.50	4	4	5	3	3.88	2.75	280.36	238.63
2	.25	.50	3	5	5	3	3.5	2.36	275.13	240.75
3	.62	.38	6	2	6	2	1.62	1.36	199.63	197.25
4	.50	.38	4	4	3	5	1.36	1.36	187.88	240.88
5	.75	.62	4	4	5	3	1.75	1.36	251.25	179.75
6	.25	.75	5	3	6	2	1.75	2.25	201.75	179
7	.62	.12	5	3	3	5	2.36	3.38	148.88	245.38
8	.62	.38	5	3	3	5	3.12	3.38	233.13	244.5

but obtained an accuracy of 0.25, representing only two answers assessed as right.

Also, there seems to be a certain correlation between number of query refinements and the experience using our systems, because the three subjects who had already collaborated in 2004 (3, 5, 6) made, on average, fewer refinements than the others.

4.4 Topic Effects

Table 3 shows values about accuracy, confidence, refinements and time consumption per topic. The data clearly pinpoint the difficulties of finding the correct answer for some topics. Those topics in which our subjects obtained poor accuracy, made more refinements and spent longer are:

- 12: *When do we estimate that the Big Bang happened?* In the astronomic domain, the English term "Big Bang" is used as is in Spanish but in our collection it had been translated as *"Gran Estallido"*. This misled most of our subjects and only one of them was able to find a valid answer.
- 13: *Who won the Miss Universe 1994 beauty contest?* As in the previous topic, here there was a translation problem. "Miss Universe" was only partially translated and abbreviated as *"Srta. Universe"* instead of the correct translation that should have been *"Miss Universo"*. Besides, it became complicated even to find a document related to this beauty contest.
- 14: *How many countries have ratified the United Nations convention adopted in 1989?* What made difficult to find a valid answer for this topic was perhaps the huge number of documents related to countries ratifying UN conventions. None of our subjects was able to find a right document with the correct answer.
- 15: *How many states are members of the Council of Europe?* Most of our subject misunderstood the Council of Europe with the European Union.

Topic 9 (*What disease name does the acronym BSE stand for?*) was thought to be an easy topic and its low accuracy deserves a more detailed explanation. While

Table 3. Accuracy, confidence, refinements and time (in seconds) per topic

Topic	Accuracy		Confidence				Refinements		Time	
	Docs	Pass	Docs		Pass		Docs	Pass	Docs	Pass
			High	Low	High	Low				
1	.75	.50	2	2	3	1	3	2.5	270.75	233.75
2	.75	.50	3	1	2	2	2	2	227.25	249.75
3	.25	.50	1	3	3	1	4	2	288	242.5
4	.50	0.00	2	2	1	3	1.5	2.75	203	243.75
5	.25	.50	1	3	2	2	3.75	3	278.25	300
6	.75	.75	3	1	3	1	.75	1.25	268.75	227.5
7	.75	.25	4	0	3	1	.25	1.75	179.75	229.5
8	1.00	1.00	4	0	3	1	1.25	0	126.25	87.25
9	.50	.25	4	0	4	0	.25	.25	73.25	114.25
10	1.00	1.00	3	1	4	0	1.75	1	167	132.25
11	.75	1.00	2	2	4	0	3.25	.25	211.75	160.25
12	.25	0.00	1	3	0	4	4.5	6.5	300	300
13	0.00	0.00	1	3	0	4	5.5	4.5	300	294.75
14	0.00	0.00	0	4	0	4	2.5	3.5	300	300
15	.25	0.00	2	2	0	4	3.5	4	253.25	300
16	.75	1.00	3	1	4	0	1	1.25	108.75	116.75

English assessors considered with good sense that answers different from "Bovine Spongiform Encephalopathy" were wrong, French assessors judged variations of "mad cow disease" as perfectly right and this caused an important language bias. In our case, five of our subjects thought that "mad cow disease" was a valid answer. If we had accepted this answer as right, topic 9 would have obtained a global accuracy of 100%.

On the other hand, topics 8, 10, 11 and 16 turned out to be quite easy. Notice that they got an accuracy of 100% in at least one of the proposed systems and they took our subjects fewer time than other topics.

4.5 From Passages to Documents

We also wanted to analyze the impact of allowing our subject to access the full documents when browsing passages. 29 answers performed with the Passages Searcher was judged as right. In 19 of theses cases, the subject found the answer directly in the passage retrieved by the system, that is, the user wouldn't have needed to visualize the full context. For example, in topic 16 (*When did Edward VIII abdicate?*) the first passage of the ranking contained the answer. In spite of this, most of the subjects used to access the whole document in order to validate the answer and make themselves sure.

On the contrary, when searching topic 8 (*Which airline did the plane hijacked by the GIA belong to?*), the system retrieved passages about GIA's hijackings but it was necessary to check the full context of the paragraph to find out the right answer.

5 Conclusions

In this paper, we have described our participation in the iCLEF 2005 track. We have compared two strategies for finding an answer using an interactive question answering system: i) a search system over full documents and ii) a search system over passages (document's paragraphs). We have added an interesting feature to both system in order to facilitate reading: the possibility to enable/disable the highlighting of named entities such as proper nouns, temporal references and numbers likely to contain the right answer.

The Document Searcher obtained better overall accuracy (0.53 vs. 0.45) but our subjects found browsing passages simpler and faster. However, most of them presented a similar search behavior (regarding time consumption, confidence in their answers and query refinements) using both systems. Besides, we discuss these data focusing on the causes of failure.

All our users considered helpful the highlighting of named entities. They all extensively used the possibility of emphasize proper nouns, dates and numbers, specially while the first reading of a long document. They also appreciated the way the Passages Searcher automatically highlighted named entities, according to their initial choices. This feature helped to quickly discriminate between relevant and non relevant passages.

As shown in other CLEF works, it is necessary to count on a good translation of the documents, using MT systems able to distinguish what should and should not be translated. Therefore, we intend to have a more reliable translation of the collections in the future which will probably improve the overall results of any cross-language information retrieval experiment.

Acknowledgments

The authors would like to thank the participating subjects. We are also grateful to Valentín Sama and Javier Artiles for their collaboration during the recruitment of volunteers and the achievement of the experiments, and to Anselmo Peñas for his valuable remarks about this paper.

This work has been partially supported by the Spanish Government under project R2D2-Syembra (TIC2003-07158-C04-02). Víctor Peinado holds a PhD grant by UNED (*Universidad Nacional de Educación a Distancia*).

References

1. Callan, J. P, Croft, B. W., Harding, S. M.: The Inquery Retrieval System. In: Proceedings of the Third International Conference on Database and Expert Systems Applications. Springer Verlag (1992), 78–83.
2. Figuerola, C.G., Zazo, A. F., Alonso Berrocal, J. L., Rodríguez Vázquez de Aldana, E.: REINA at the iCLEF 2004. In: Results of the CLEF 2004 Evaluation Campaign. Lecture Notes in Computer Science. Springer Verlag (2005), volume 3491.

3. Gonzalo, J., Clough, P., Vallin, A.: Overview of the CLEF 2005 Interactive Track. In: Proceedings of the Cross-Language Evaluation Forum 2005. Lecture Notes of Computer Science (this volume). Springer Verlag (2006).
4. López-Ostenero, F., Gonzalo, J., Peinado, V., Verdejo, F.: Interactive Cross-Language Question Answering: Searching Passages versus Searching Documents. In: Results of the CLEF 2004 Evaluation Campaign. Lecture Notes in Computer Science. Springer Verlag (2005), volume 3491, 323–333.
5. Peinado, V., López-Ostenero, F., Gonzalo, J.: UNED at ImageCLEF 2005: Automatically Structured Queries with Named Entities over Metadata. In: Proceedings of the Cross-Language Evaluation Forum 2005. Lecture Notes of Computer Science (this volume). Springer Verlag (2006).

Effect of Connective Functions in Interactive Image Retrieval

Julio Villena-Román[1,2], Raquel M. Crespo-García[2], and José Carlos González-Cristóbal[1,3]

[1] DAEDALUS – Data, Decisions and Language, S.A.
[2] Universidad Carlos III de Madrid
[3] Universidad Politécnica de Madrid
jvillena@daedalus.es, rcrespo@it.uc3m.es, jgonzalez@daedalus.es

Abstract. This paper presents the participation of the MIRACLE team[1] at the ImageCLEF 2005 interactive search task, in which we compare the efficiency of AND monolingual queries (which have to be precise and use the exact vocabulary, which may be difficult in a specialised search task) versus relevance-guided OR bilingual queries (a fuzzier and noisier search but which doesn't require precise vocabulary and exact translations). User preferences and strategies in the context of cross-lingual interactive image retrieval are also analysed.

1 Introduction

Images are inherently language independent and thus image retrieval can often be seen as a language-independent task. Results (images) can be presented visually, with no text. Even the queries can be done visually, by searching images similar to another one. However, searching images using a text-based query interface, based on image descriptions or metadata is a common scenario. Also, the presentation of the resulting images can be complemented including their corresponding descriptions or using their metadata. Thus, image retrieval integrates with cross-language information retrieval, as users' native language (or even languages) can differ from the language used for labelling the image collection [2].

Queries consisting on several terms can be processed combining their words using either an AND function or an OR function [6]. The AND approach forces the user to use precise vocabulary as query terms must be exactly included in the index for the image to be found. Also, the system responses can be made as precise as wanted, simply by adding more words to the query. However, this is quite difficult to integrate in cross-lingual systems with automatic translation, as many terms may turn out to be ambiguous and accept different translation options. A fuzzier and noisier search results from the OR approach. However, it allows less precise vocabulary and more

[1] This work has been partially supported by the Spanish R+D National Plan, by means of the project RIMMEL (Multilingual and Multimedia Information Retrieval, and its Evaluation), TIN2004-07588-C03-01.

C. Peters et al. (Eds.): CLEF 2005, LNCS 4022, pp. 293 – 296, 2006.

ambiguous translations. In this case, relevance feedback can be used to achieve the search goals instead of image filtering.

According to the user's perspective, the AND approach seems to be more intuitive. Searches can be easily refined by including more search terms if the result set is too large. If too many images have been filtered out from the solution, it can be broadened just by reducing the requirements included in the query. The more specific the query is, the more specific result set is generated. Thus, an immediate sense of control results from this approach, as the solution set reduces its size as the user approaches to the goal.

On the other hand, the OR approach seems to be less effective from the user's point of view. The more terms are included in the query, the more images are probably recovered. Although relevance order is probably more accurate, the user perceives a more generalized, less precise result, as the result set has more images.

In a cross language scenario, the AND approach may be difficult for non-native speakers, particularly in specialised tasks which require domain-specific vocabulary as the one modelled in iCLEF experiment [2]. In such conditions, the OR approach assisted by automatic translation can be a more helpful choice.

This paper analyses the efficiency of AND monolingual queries versus relevance-guided OR bilingual queries. Users' preferences and strategies in the context of interactive image retrieval are also studied. For more information about this experiment, see the detailed description provided in [6].

2 Toolbox

Two systems have been developed to test and compare each search strategy previously described. System A (miraML) implements the AND monolingual approach, whereas System B (miraCL) implements the OR bilingual approach. A similar web-based user interface is used for both of them.

Both systems execute the queries against a common index, built from the collection of images, using Xapian, a publicly available text search engine [8]. Among all the available metadata, only the description of the images is used for generating the index, as it is the field which includes the most useful information for the searches.

Natural language processing techniques are applied before indexing. An ad hoc language-specific parser for English is used to identify different classes of alphanumerical tokens such as dates, proper nouns, acronyms, etc., as well as recognising common compound words. Image descriptions are tokenised, stemmed [5] and stop word filtered to improve searching efficiency.

To evaluate the results, both systems keep a log with the users' queries and the number of results obtained for each one. Searching time is also logged, by means of a timer that is started when the user begins a new topic. The time to execute the queries or to provide the automatic translation is not taken into account for the user time, simply by disabling the timer while performing those operations.

2.1 System A: miraML

miraML is a pure monolingual system. User queries are posed in English, the source language of the image collection. As well as for the image descriptions, a stemming process is applied to all the words included in the query. Query stems are then concatenated with the AND operator before executing the search.

Results are displayed combining visual and textual presentation. The result page shows both the images and their associated textual descriptions. Only the 20 most relevant results are presented to the user, with no pagination.

As a help for the user, a Spanish to English translation textbox is provided, which queries FreeTranslation.com [3], Altavista BabelFish [1], Google Translation [4] and I2E programme (included in Debian Linux distribution). If several options exist for a given term, the user must select the appropriate translation.

2.2 System B: miraCL

miraCL is a cross-lingual (bilingual) Spanish to English image retrieval system. Queries are expressed in the native language of the users, Spanish, and automatically translated into English. A stemming process is applied to the English terms resulting from the translation phase. As the user can include several terms, and each of them can accept different translations, English resulting stems are concatenated with the OR operator and finally executed.

Also, the user may use relevance feedback and ask for similar images to a given list of images. The system builds a new query concatenating the first 25 more relevant keywords of each image in the list.

Just the 20 top results are presented to the user, as in miraML. However, in contrast, the result page only shows the images with their ID and relevance, with no descriptions, because no English text should be shown to the users.

3 Experimental Results

Eight people with similar profiles participated in the experiment (designed according to iCLEF guidelines), all of them Spanish native with a good English skills, five male and three female.

Results show that success rate was similar for both systems (68.75% for system A and 65.63% for B) and also quite independent of searcher, but was somewhat depending on the topic. Some topics (3 and 11) were reported to be more difficult due to specialised vocabulary or lack of expected terms in their descriptions. Differences about systems helpfulness were reported only for a few topics, with very precise or specialised vocabulary. No significant differences between both systems in searching time were found.

Users' subjective impressions were collected by means of personal interviews after the search. Most users preferred System A because they prefer precise queries as they know the target language. But they confessed that, occasionally, the automatic translation provided by the system had helped them to discover the exact search term.

Search strategy differs between users but textual feedback has revealed fundamental. When using System A, searchers usually scrolled the results to add descriptive terms, names and locations appearing in the recovered images to refine the query instead of thinking words on their own.

Most users complained that finding a given image in time often depended on finding the appropriate keyword which not always seemed the most intuitive or representative of the image content.

4 Conclusions and Future Work

Experimental results show no significant difference between the two search strategies evaluated: AND English queries (which have to be precise and use exact vocabulary) versus OR queries in native language, Spanish, sorted by relevance (automatically translated by the system). Search success rate and average searching time are similar for both approaches. However, usability of the systems must be further evaluated, as users seem to be more used to the AND search strategy and because textual feedback (not included in System B) has revealed fundamental.

This promising result may be applied for teaching and/or learning improvement. Spanish students have to read books and references usually written in English, which in many cases is an actual challenge for them and imposes constrains and limitations in their learning rate. According to our experiment, searching in English (System A) or in Spanish (System B) may offer the same searching performance, thus eliminating those constrains and improving the learning process of students.

References

1. BabelFish Altavista. On line http://babelfish.altavista.com [Visited 25/05/2006].
2. Clough, Paul; Müller, Henning; Deselaers, Thomas; Grubinger, Michael; Lehmann, Thomas M.; Jensen, Jeffery; Hersh, William; The CLEF 2005 Cross-Language Image Retrieval Track. This volume.
3. FreeTranslation.com. On line http://www.freetranslation.com [Visited 25/05/2006].
4. Google Translate. On line http://www.google.com/translate_t [Visited 25/05/2006].
5. Porter, M. Snowball. On line http://www.snowball.tartarus.org. [Visited 25/05/2006]
6. Villena-Román, Julio; Crespo-García, Raquel; González-Cristóbal, José Carlos; Boolean operators in Interactive Search. Working Notes of the Cross Language Evaluation Forum 2005, Vienna, 2005.
7. Villena, J.; Martínez, J.L.; Fombella, Jorge; García, A.; Ruiz, A.; Martínez, P.; Goñi, J.M..; and González, J.C. Image Retrieval: The MIRACLE Approach. Comparative Evaluation of Multilingual Information Access Systems (Peters, C; Gonzalo, J.; Brascher, M.; and Kluck, M., Eds.). LNCS, vol. 3237, pp. 621-630. Springer, 2004.
8. Xapian: an Open Source Probabilistic Information Retrieval library. On line http://www.xapian.org. [Visited 25/05/2006]

Using Concept Hierarchies in Text-Based Image Retrieval: A User Evaluation

Daniela Petrelli and Paul Clough

Department of Information Studies, University of Sheffield,
Regent Court, 211 Portobello Street
Sheffield, S1 4DP, UK
{d.petrelli, p.d.clough}@sheffield.ac.uk

Abstract. This paper describes our results from the image retrieval task of iCLEF 2005 based on a comparative user evaluation of two interfaces: one displaying search results as a list; the other organising retrieved images into a hierarchy of concepts displayed on the interface as an interactive menu. Based on a known-item retrieval task, data was analysed with respect to effectiveness, efficiency and user satisfaction. Effectiveness and efficiency were calculated at both the set cut-off time of 5 minutes, and the time after finding the target image (final time). Results showed the list was marginally more effective than the menu at 5 minutes, but the two were equal at final time indicating the menu requires more time to be used effectively. The list was more efficient at both 5 minutes and final time (difference not statistically significant) and users preferred using the menu indicating this could be a potentially interesting and engaging feature for image retrieval.

1 Introduction

Providing an intuitive summary of the search results is considered beneficial for users of IR systems. Different types of summary have been proposed in the past (see, e.g. [1] for a survey) and a variety of clustering techniques have been developed to group documents into topically-coherent sets. This is expected to help users in browsing through search results, obtain an overview of the main topics/themes and help focus their inspection, e.g. by limiting exploration of the results to only those clusters likely to contain relevant documents.

Automatically organising a set of documents based upon concepts derived from the documents themselves is an obviously appealing goal for IR systems: it requires little or no manual intervention and, like unsupervised classification, depends on natural divisions in the data rather than pre-assigned categories (i.e. requires no training data). The generation of concept hierarchies [2] is one such method: it automatically associates terms (or concepts) extracted from a set of documents, and organises them into a hierarchy where each term represents a group of documents related by concept.

This technique has been successfully employed to help users search and browse textual documents [3]. For the iCLEF2005 image retrieval task, we decided to extend this previous work by exploring the use of concept hierarchies for cross-language image retrieval. The language pair used was Italian and English.

C. Peters et al. (Eds.): CLEF 2005, LNCS 4022, pp. 297 – 306, 2006.

2 Experimental Setup

In this task, we evaluated the use of concept hierarchies across language: the retrieved images were organised into a hierarchical menu based on concepts automatically extracted from the image metadata and translated from English into Italian. This interaction mode was compared to a simple list of results (baseline) and in both cases we used a version of the CiQuest system [3]. This was originally developed initially for investigating interactive query expansion with a standard textual document collection (TREC) and modified to satisfy the needs of cross-language users. For query translation, BabelFish[1] was used translate the user's search request (in Italian) into English, the language of the document collection. Use of MT systems for query translation has shown to be a popular approach in recent CLEF campaigns (e.g. [4]). The translated query was then used to search the image collection provided by ImageCLEF: historic photographs from St. Andrews University Library. The standard version of the Okapi search engine was used to perform retrieval: a probabilistic retrieval model based on the BM25 weighting function [5].

In the list interface (the baseline), results were displayed as a ranked list (right-hand side of Figure 1). Images were ranked in descending order of BM25 score, computed between query-caption terms. The entire CiQuest interface (including results) was then translated into Italian using a custom wrapper for the Babelfish online translation service, and finally displayed to the user. Users could view a larger version of the image with caption (translated into Italian) by clicking on the image title.

We are aware of current limitations with the current system, including: (1) users can only view the first 200 images retrieved, and (2) users cannot see the translated query. This latter limitation meant users were not aware of which terms had been translated, or which translation was actually used to search with. This lack of feedback and control contradicts our previous findings [6, 7], however it was considered more important to run the evaluation as we expected this could help us better understand interactive image retrieval and provide useful directions for future research.

Figure 1 shows the menu interface. On the left, a dynamic HTML (DHTML) menu representing the concept hierarchy is displayed. This is dynamically generated from captions of the retrieved set of images. Following Sanderson and Croft [2], words and noun phrases (concepts) are extracted from the captions and organized into a hierarchy of terms. The selection of concepts is based upon term co-occurrence (the same term occurring in multiple captions), term frequency, and statistical relations. The hierarchy is then used to generate the menu whereby each concept is displayed together with an image randomly selected from the set of images associated with that concept. By clicking on the image or concept, the user selects the associated group of images (the size shown in parenthesis). Groups are not mutually exclusive and the same image may appear in more than one group depending on its caption. As the menu is generated by the captions of retrieved images, it is only loosely related to the user's query, i.e. the concepts in the hierarchy may not be those issued by the user. Figure 2 shows how the result of a query is displayed. Here the user has selected the menu item "timpano orientale" (Italian translation for "oriental gable") and the 12 images in the group are displayed in the results list.

---

[1] http://babelfish.altavista.com/ (site accessed: 09/12/2005)

Fig. 1. The system with the cross-language concept hierarchy (menu interface)

3 User Evaluation

Following iCLEF directives [8], a within-subject experimental design was adopted (i.e. each participant tests both interfaces). A Latin-Square was used to fully counter-balance systems and tasks assuring unbiased data are collected. A known-item retrieval task was set for iCLEF 2005: given an image, participants had to find it again from the St. Andrews collection. A total of 16 images were used in the experiment (8 with each interface) and 2 more used for training (one per interface).

An initial briefing explained the experiment to participants and the basic mechanisms of CLIR. Participants then completed an online questionnaire to establish their profiles and attitudes to search before starting a training session with each system prior to completing the actual tasks. Participants were presented with the image to search and required to state their familiarity with it[2]. They were also required to

[2] The goal was to record how confident users felt in retrieving the given image, though it was discovered during the evaluation that the intent was not clear and participants had interpreted the question as if they had previously seen the image.

generate three example queries which could be used to search for the image. The purpose of this was to compare these hypothetical queries with those actually used during the search tasks to see if browsing the hierarchy had an impact on query reformulation.

Participants performed the tasks individually and observed by the authors. They were asked to type queries in Italian to retrieve images with English captions (results were back-translated into Italian before being displayed). Participants' activities were recorded for further behavioural analysis through the logging of system events and recording of activities on video. Participants were given 5 minutes to find the target image, although we did not interrupt searching after the cut-off and encouraged users to complete the task. This was taken into consideration when analysing the data.

Questionnaires to collect participant's opinions were filled in after each session (a variation of those proposed by Chin et al. [9] for testing the usability of systems). They encompassed questions on interface layout and cross-language functionality. Further space was left for personal comments and participants were asked to complete an additional comparison questionnaire at the end of the experiment (stating which system they preferred and what they liked and disliked about each system). Before leaving, participants were invited to express any other opinion or comment on their search experience. The whole evaluation lasted at most 3 hours.

4 Data Analysis

Participants were 8 Italian native speakers (5 male; 3 female), recruited through a Sheffield University mailing list for volunteers. Participants were all students or researchers at the University of Sheffield and each one bilingual (although their level of English language knowledge and UK culture awareness varied[3]). The profile questionnaires showed only 1 participant less than 25 years old (studying for an MSc); the rest between 26 and 44, all with an MSc (working on their PhD) or a PhD (working as research associates).

All participants were computer-literate, and searched the Web daily (50% using a library or commercial search engine rarely; 17% never using commercial search engines). Only 33% had received searching formal training (as part of university courses) but all felt confident in retrieving the information they needed. All participants stated they were aware of machine translation (although no test was performed to verify this) and all stated they had previously performed image search on the Web.

4.1 Quantitative Analysis

As described in section 3, participants were allowed more time to search than the 5 minutes designated by the iCLEF instructions. We therefore analysed performance data at the 5 minute cut-off, as well as at final time.

All the 3 usability measures: effectiveness, efficiency and user satisfaction were used to analyse the results [10, 11]. Effectiveness was measured by the number of

[3] A wider variation was registered with respect to culture awareness depending on the time spent in the UK.

target images retrieved, efficiency through the average time required to find them, and user satisfaction through opinions gathered in the questionnaires.

The global effectiveness was surprisingly identical with 64% of images found with both interfaces. If only those images found in 5 minutes are considered, then the list is more effective (53% versus 47% found). This difference shows that the menu needs more time to be used effectively. The menu success rate also includes cases when the image was found because it was at the top of the list and no interaction with the menu was required to find it (in 53% of the cases the image was found in the results list; in 31% of the cases the image was displayed in the menu and found whilst browsing, and in 16% of the cases it was found via selection - the participant clicked on a sub-menu and the image was found there). By observing interaction we found that participants were particularly pleased when the image was displayed in the menu. This may indicate that the menu has value as a visual summary.

The list interface proved to be the most efficient in both cases. When measured at 5 minutes the list had an average performance of 113s to find the relevant image; the average time of the menu 139s. At final time, list performance was 170s (min 10s; max 643s; median 123s) and menu performance 221s (min 22s; max 617s; median 188s). A Mann-Whitney U Test[4] was conducted to compare performance time and showed no statistically significant difference for both conditions (Z=-1.47, p=0.14 at 5 minutes; Z=-1.75, p=0.08 at final time). Users of the menu seemed to spend time exploring the cluster resulting in fewer queries (256 menu; 282 list). However the difference is not statistically significant (Z=-0.472, p=0.64). The proportion of time spent browsing results impacts on the total interaction time and can only be measured by inspecting the recordings. This is set for future analysis.

Although effectiveness and efficiency of the two conditions were similar, user satisfaction was clearly in favour of the menu: 75% of participants favouring it compared to the list. The menu was also considered easier to use (75% vs. 25%), while the list was stated as easier to learn (75% vs. 25%). The two systems were seen as just slightly different by 87% of participants (13% completely different) but no one rated them as equal showing that the menu is perceived as an important feature. Two participants who favoured the list said: "I found the labels of the images confusing, to the point that I would not know which one to follow" and "sometimes the menu drove me on the wrong path and sidetracked my thought". Among those favouring the menu, the compact format and the (perceived) faster interaction were commented on as important. However, a few participants complained about unclear labels and unrepresentative images for the clusters.

Two questionnaires collected opinions on specific features of each interface. Images were interesting for 86% of participants (14% neutral) while opinions differed with respect to the captions: captions were considered useful by 43%, not useful by 43% and neutral by 14%. The same numbers were obtained for whether users considered the translation quality good enough. In contrast, 72% agreed that viewing captions was useful to verify details in the images (14% disagree, 14% neutral).

The menu was considered easy to learn (87% agree, 13% neutral) and navigate (72% agree, 38% disagree). The majority (62%) considered both text and images

---

4 This test was preferred to the more commonly used t-test because the time distribution was not normal.

useful, while 25% favoured images and 13% text. Images were considered appropriate (87% agree, 13% neutral) and labels were useful to explore the result (75% agree, 25% disagree). Opinions about the organisation of concepts in the hierarchies was less positive with only 37% agreeing concepts were organised in an intuitive progression (38% neutral, 25% disagree), and 37% considering them a manageable number (37% neutral, 26% too many). This could be due to the hierarchy construction method, but also to the poor translation of menu terms (a fact we discovered when inspecting the system behaviour, as discussed below).

Table 1. Summary of ill translations; Golden translation from Garzanti Linguistica

Query	Gold Translation	MT translation
Bianco	white [adjective]	white man
Signora	madam, lady, ms., mrs., woman	mrs.
Vestito	dress, dressed	dressed
reale[famiglia reale]	real, royal [royal family]	real family
Lanterna	lantern	spider
Faro	lighthouse	beacon
Prato	lawn	Prato (an Italian city)
Riva	seaside, (river) bank	river
Sala	hall, sitting room	it knows it
Cappelli	hats	nails head
Coppia	couple	brace
primo piano	foreground	Association of Bologna
bianco e nero	white and black	R-bianco.e.nero
Ingresso	entry, entrance	income
macchine	machines, cars	it blots some

4.2 Qualitative Analysis

Interactions recorded in the log files were analysed for interesting behaviour from input by the user, and translation of queries and menus by Babelfish. Confirming previous studies [7], in 11 queries (2% of the total) participants input English words in an attempt to overcome real (or perceived) limitations of the system. Examples include “bagpipes” and “lighthouse” entered after the system failed to translate the equivalent Italian words. In some cases, participants submitted English terms to search on (e.g. “cottage” and “clubhouse”).

In another 15 cases (3%), queries contained proper names (e.g. “Plymouth”, “Robert Burns”, “Wallace”) or nouns (e.g. “ballgown”, “temple”, “golfers”) picked up from the displayed results. In a further 1% of queries, terms picked up by the user were ill translations (e.g. “randello” shown as the translation of golf club - correct Italian term is “mazza”). Frequently, terms picked up by participants in displayed results and used in follow-up queries failed to be translated correctly. This was always true for ill translations, but also occurred for partially correct English-Italian, e.g. “bridge” translated as “ponticello” (English: “little bridge”), but incorrectly translated into English again when incorporated into the query.

Table 2. Summary of the ill translations by users and tasks (only those terms used by more than one person have been listed)

Term	Ill translation	Correct translation	Users who used it (number of tasks)
macchine	it bolts some	cars	1 (2), 3 (2)
faro	beacon	lighthouse	1 (6), 2 (6), 3 (6), 4 (6), 5 (6), 6 (6), 7 (6), 8 (6)
bianco	white man	white	1 (6, 12), 2 (12), 3 (12, 14), 4 (12), 5 (12), 6 (12), 7 (12), 8 (12)
riva	river	shore/bank	2 (7), 3 (1)
letti	read	beds	3 (9), 4 (9), 8 (9)
reale/reali	real	royal	1 (10), 2 (10), 5 (10), 6 (10), 7 (10), 8 (10)
ingresso	income	entrance (hall)	3 (11), 5 (3), 8 (3, 11)
signora	Mrs.	madam, lady, woman	2 (12), 3 (3)
bianca/bianche	white woman	white	1 (12), 2 (6), 3 (6)
vestito	dressed	dress	5 (12), 6 (12)
coppia	brace	couple	1 (14), 3 (10)

To investigate the success of query translation using MT, translated versions of the queries were compared with the original ones. From a total of 892 valid and unique terms[5], 84% were correctly translated, 11% of terms failed to translate and a further 5% of terms were ill translations. This last kind of translation error includes selecting the wrong sense for terms with multiple senses, or preferring verbs over nouns for the same spelling. In addition, some ill translations were quite inexplicable and bizarre and a summary is given in Table 1. The result was at times unexpected and confusing as, for example, "signora vestito bianco" (English: "lady white dress") retrieved multiple portraits of man as the translated query was "mrs. dressed white man". Participants could not understand why portraits of men were retrieved as the query translation was not displayed.

Some ill translated terms (e.g. faro [lighthouse], bianco [white], reali [real/royals]) or un-translated terms (e.g. carrozza [coach], tempio [temple], ritratto [portrait], cornamuse [bagpipes]) were quite frequent in the corpus and used by all or many users (see Tables 2 and 3). Those terms were observed to frequently correspond to important features of an image (as perceived by the searcher), whereby failing to translate correctly would not only impact retrieval performance, but also force users to generate new terms. In addition, ill translations negatively affected the generation of the menu resulting in erroneous/unclear labels which were then ignored or discarded by participants (even though containing the target image). For example, images of children walking on the seashore were grouped in a set labelled as "remare di bambini" (literally "rowing of children"), while the original text was "children paddling". This results in a conflict between the label and the image as no boat is visible in the image justifying the assigned label "rowing".

[5] This number is the sum of all unique terms used by each participant in each task; stop words and repetitions of the same term by the same user in a task have not been counted.

Table 3. Summary of the non-translated terms by users and tasks (only those terms used by more than one person have been listed)

Term	Translation	Users who used it (topics)
celtica	Celtic	1 (1), 2 (1), 4 (1), 5(1), 7 (1)
citta'	city, town	1 (2, 15), 3 (2)
tempio	temple	1 (5), 2 (5), 3 (5), 4 (5), 5 (5), 6 (5), 7 (5), 8 (5)
vagone/vagoni		1 (7), 2 (7), 3 (7), 4 (7), 5 (7), 6 (7)
carrozza	coach	1 (10), 2 (10), 3 (10), 4 (10), 5 (7, 10), 6 (10), 7 (7, 10), 8 (10)
vetrata/vetrate		1 (11), 2 (12), 6 (11)
lampadario		1 (11), 3 (11), 6 (11), 7 (11), 8 (11)
candelabro		2 (11), 6 (11)
gotico/gotica	Gothic	2 (11), 3 (11), 7 (11)
ritratto	portrait	1 (12, 14, 16), 3 (16), 4 (12, 16), 5 (14), 7 (14), 8 (12, 14)
cornamuse	bagpipes	1 (13), 2 (13), 3 (13), 5 (13), 6(13), 7 (13)
tamburi	drums	1 (13), 2 (13), 3 (13), 4 (13), 6 (13)
lungomare	seashore	4 (15), 5 (15)

Observation of user interaction highlighted another problem: that of asymmetrical translation. Some terms were correctly translated from English to Italian (e.g. "portrait" into "ritratto"), but the translation failed when the Italian term was used in the query (i.e. missing from the Babelfish dictionary). This negatively affected user interaction as often participants picked up specific terms (e.g. "croce Celtica" for "Celtic cross") and used them in follow up queries to focus the search, but instead these failed to improve the results.

Useful comments were collected outside the formal questionnaires. The need to better control the search mechanism by forcing the use of all the terms simultaneously was a shared need. A few participants commented that the menu did not reflect their query and the relation was not straightforward. The two comments must be considered as a pair: forcing an AND retrieval is likely to impact on generation of the hierarchy and consequently on the displayed menu.

Comments on images collected in a set were interesting: participants expected to see visually similar images, but because retrieval and organisation was purely text-based, this was not the case. A further step of visual content clustering would likely satisfy this need, but different interface design could be explored. Indeed a preliminary analysis of interaction behaviour shows two different attitudes in browsing through the menu: some participants used a horizontal approach and looked at all the children before moving to the next one; others proceeded vertically comparing siblings terms, selecting the next one to explore. Both behaviours may result in ignoring part of the menu that might include the wanted image. More effective alternative layouts to represent the result summary many are explored in future research.

5 Discussion

The menu feature did not prove to be more effective or efficient than a simple list display; however it was important for user satisfaction. It seems to engage users more than the list, but requires more interaction time. However, this additional time is not perceived by users as a burden; tediously scrolling the list is. Further work is required to make the generation of concept hierarchies more robust and effective. For example, concepts with translations involving multiple senses should be displayed (or at least highlighted) to avoid the user ignoring good sets because of ill translations.

Users commented positively on the menu as a summary and this feature should be exploited. An improvement would be to dismiss the random selection of the image representing a sub-set in favour of clustering images by visual features inside each group (e.g. by colour or texture). This could generate a range of prototypical images that better represent the contents of each concept. The menu would then summarise the results based on both textual and visual features extracted from the associated metadata (e.g. captions) and low-level content of the images themselves. In addition, different layouts for the summary could be explored (e.g. a table instead of a menu).

As a more general result, the evaluation showed once more that good and consistent (bi-directional) translations are fundamental for CLIR (especially query translation). Furthermore, allowing the user to check (and change) the translated query is important as bilingual users are flexible and able to adapt their search behaviours to overcome limitations of the system.

It also became apparent during the experiment that the hierarchical summary of results is perhaps better suited to exploring a document collection or set of results rather than a high precision task as prescribed by Image CLEF. Further study is planned to determine the effectiveness of image organisation using concept hierarchies for other types of search task.

6 Conclusions and Future Work

The evaluation presented in this paper is the first step in an investigation of the use of concept hierarchies to cluster results in cross-language image retrieval. Results are encouraging, particularly as the users were very positive in their comments about the hierarchical menu.

Further analysis on the collected data is planned. This includes comparing queries across participants for the same query to see how similar/different terms are used, and which were most effective with respect to the image captions. Queries will be also compared to see if list of key terms were used more than fully structured phrases. This is expected to help in identifying which tools could better support searching in the context of images where the text is short and lacks redundancy.

Further work will be carried out to determine the impact of incorrect translation on retrieval performance. The collected corpus of queries will be used in investigating different translation mechanisms (e.g. dictionary-lookup vs. MT) and search algorithms (e.g. Boolean AND vs. BM25). The length and complexity of queries issued by users will also form a part of this investigation. A new interface will be designed to give the user more control over query translation, and provide image clustering based on visual as well as textual features.

Acknowledgements

The authors would like to thank Hideo Joho and Mark Sanderson for their work on concept hierarchies and we are grateful to the 8 participants for assisting us.

References

1. Hearst, M. (1999). "User Interfaces and Visualization". In: Baeza-Yates, R. & Ribeiro-Neto, B. (eds.), *Modern Information Retrieval*, pp. 257-323. New York: ACM Press.
2. Sanderson, M. and Croft, B. (1999) "Deriving concept hierarchies from text" In: *Proceedings of the 22nd ACM Conference of the Special Interest Group in Information Retrieval*, pp. 206-213.
3. Joho, H., Sanderson, M., and Beaulieu, M. (2004) "A Study of User Interaction with a Concept-based Interactive Query Expansion Support Tool". In: McDonald, S. & Tait, J. (eds), *Advances in Information Retrieval, 26th European Conference on Information Retrieval*, pp. 42-56.
4. Savoy, J. and Berger, P. Y. (2005), Selection and Merging Strategies for Multilingual Information Retrieval, In Multilingual Information Access for Text, Speech and Images: Results of the Fifth CLEF Evaluation Campaign, Eds (Peters, C., Clough, P., Gonzalo, J., Jones, G., Kluck, M. and Magnini, B.), Lecture Notes in Computer Science (LNCS), Springer, Heidelberg, Germany, Volume 3491/2005, 597-613.
5. Robertson, S.E., Walker, S., Beaulieu, M.M., Gatford, M. & Payne, A. (1995). "Okapi at TREC-4". In: Harman, D.K. (ed.), *NIST Special Publication 500-236: The Fourth Text REtrieval Conference (TREC-4)*, Gaithersburg, MD. pp. 73-97.
6. Petrelli, D., Beaulieu, M., Sanderson, M, Demetriou, G., Herring, P. (2004) Observing Users Designing Clarity: A Case Study on the User-Centered Design of a Cross-Language Information Retrieval System. JASIST Journal of the American Society for Information Science and Technology, 55 (10): 923-934.
7. Petrelli, D., Levin, S., Beaulieu, M., Sanderson, M. (2005) Which User Interaction for Cross-Language IR? Design Issues and Reflections. JASIST special issue on Multilingual Information Access, 57(5): 709-722.
8. Chin, J. P., Diehl, V. A., Norman, K. L. (1998) Development of an instrument measuring user satisfaction of the human-computer interface. CHI '98. ACM Press, 213-218.
9. Gonzalo, J., Clough, P. and Vallin, A. (2005) Overview of the CLEF 2005 Interactive Track, in this volume.
10. Van Welie, M., van der Veer, G. C., Eliens, A. (1999) Breaking down Usability. Proc. INTERACT99, 613-620.
11. Frokjaer, E., Hertzum, M., Hornbaek, K., Measuring Usability: Are Effectiveness, Efficiency, and User Satisfaction Really Correlated? CHI 2000, 345-352.

Overview of the CLEF 2005 Multilingual Question Answering Track

Alessandro Vallin[1], Bernardo Magnini[2], Danilo Giampiccolo[1], Lili Aunimo[3], Christelle Ayache[4], Petya Osenova[5], Anselmo Peñas[6], Maarten de Rijke[7], Bogdan Sacaleanu[8], Diana Santos[9], and Richard Sutcliffe[10]

[1] CELCT, Italy
{Vallin, Giampiccolo}@celct.it
[2] ITC-Irst, Italy
magnini@itc.it
[3] University of Helsinki, Finnland
aunimo@cs.helsinki.fi
[4] ELDA/ELRA, France
ayache@elda.org
[5] BTB, Bulgaria
petya@bultreebank.org
[6] UNED, Spain
anselmo@lsi.uned.es
[7] University of Amsterdam, The Netherlands
mdr@science.uva.nl
[8] DFKI, Germany, Bogdan
Sacaleanu@dfki.de
[9] Sintef, Norway, Diana
Santos@sintef.no
[10] University of Limerick, Ireland
Richard.Sutcliffe@ul.ie

Abstract. The general aim of the third CLEF Multilingual Question Answering Track was to set up a common and replicable evaluation framework to test both monolingual and cross-language Question Answering (QA) systems that process queries and documents in several European languages. Nine target languages and ten source languages were exploited to enact 8 monolingual and 73 cross-language tasks. Twenty-four groups participated in the exercise. Overall results showed a general increase in performance in comparison to last year. The best performing monolingual system irrespective of target language answered 64.5% of the questions correctly (in the monolingual Portuguese task), while the average of the best performances for each target language was 42.6%. The cross-language step instead entailed a considerable drop in performance. In addition to accuracy, the organisers also measured the relation between the correctness of an answer and a system's stated confidence in it, showing that the best systems did not always provide the most reliable confidence score. We provide an overview of the 2005 QA track, detail the procedure followed to build the test sets and present a general analysis of the results.

C. Peters et al. (Eds.): CLEF 2005, LNCS 4022, pp. 307 – 331, 2006.

1 Introduction

The CLEF QA evaluation campaign conducted in 2005[1] was the result of the experience acquired during the two previous campaigns and of the proposals suggested in last year's workshop in order to make the track more challenging and realistic.

At a first look one realizes that over the years the series of QA evaluation exercises at CLEF has registered a steady increment in the number of participants and languages involved, which is particularly encouraging as multilinguality is one of the main characteristic of these exercises. In fact, in the first campaign, which took place in 2003, eight groups from Europe and North America participated in nine tasks, three monolingual -Dutch, Italian and Spanish- and five bilingual, where questions were formulated in five source languages -Dutch, French, German, Italian- and answer were searched in an English corpus collection. In 2004 eighteen groups took part in the competition, submitting 48 runs. Nine source languages -Bulgarian, Dutch, English, Finnish, French, German, Italian, Portuguese and Spanish- and 7 target languages -all the source languages but Bulgarian and Finnish, which had no corpus available- were considered in the task. In 2005 the number of participants rose to twenty-four, 67 runs were submitted, and 10 source languages -the same as those used in the previous year plus Indonesian- and 9 source languages -the same used as sources, except Indonesian which had no corpus available- were exploit in 8 monolingual and seventy-three cross-language tasks. Moreover, some innovation was introduced concerning the type of questions proposed in the exercise and the metrics used in the evaluation. This edition of QA@CLEF was altogether successful and can be considered a good starting point for next campaigns.

After having described the preparation of test sets, this paper will present the results achieved by the participants, and will briefly sketch some outlines for the future of QA@CLEF.

2 Tasks

The tasks proposed in the 2005 QA campaign were characterized by a basic continuity with what had been done in 2004 [3]. In fact, to the demand for more radical innovation a more conservative approach was preferred, as most organizers opted to further investigate the procedures consolidated in the last two campaigns before moving to the next stage. The task remained basically the same as that proposed in 2005, although some minor changes were actually introduced, i.e. a new type of questions, and two new evaluation measures, namely K1 measure and r value.

Ten source languages -Bulgarian, Dutch, English, Finnish, French, German, Italian, Portuguese, Spanish and, as an experiment, Indonesian- and 9 target languages -all the source languages except Indonesian- were considered at the 2005 CLEF QA track. Eighty-one tasks were setup, 8 monolingual -Bulgarian, Dutch, English, Finnish, French, German, Italian, Portuguese, Spanish- and 73 bilingual. In this way,

[1] For more information about QA@CLEF campaigns visit http://clef-qa.itc.it.

all the possible combinations between source and target languages were exploited, but for two exceptions: Indonesian, being included in a cross-language QA competition, was used only as a source in the Indonesian-English task, meanwhile the monolingual English task was discarded as it has been abundantly tested in past TREC campaigns, according to the decision taken in the previous competition.

As in the previous campaign, for each target language 200 questions were prepared using the topics of the Ad-Hoc track at CLEF, and a gold standard was produced manually searching collections of newspapers and news agencies' articles for answers. The corpora, released by ELRA/ELDA, are large, unstructured, open-domain text collections (see Table 1), whose texts have been SGML tagged. Each document has a unique identifier (docid) that systems had to return together with the answer, in order to support it.

Table 1. Document collections used in CLEF 2005

TARGET LANG..	COLLECTION	PERIOD	SIZE
Bulgarian (BG)	Sega	2002	120 MB (33,356 docs)
	Standart	2002	93 MB (35,839 docs)
Germany (DE)	Frankfurter Rundschau	1994	320 MB (139,715 docs)
	Der Spiegel	1994/1995	63 MB (13,979 docs)
	German SDA	1994	144 MB (71,677 docs)
	German SDA	1995	141 MB (69,438 docs)
English (EN)	Los Angeles Times	1994	425 MB (113,005 docs)
	Glasgow Herald	1995	154 MB (56,472 docs)
Spanish (ES)	EFE	1994	509 MB (215,738 docs)
	EFE	1995	577 MB (238,307 docs)
Finnish	Aamulehti	1994/1995	137 MB (55,344 docs)
French (FR)	Le Monde	1994	157 MB (44,013 docs)
	Le Monde	1995	156 MB (47,646 docs)
	French SDA	1994	86 MB (43,178 docs)
	French SDA	1995	88 MB (42,615 docs)
Italian (IT)	La Stampa	1994	193 MB (58,051 docs)
	Itallian SDA	1994	85 MB (50,527 docs)
	Itallian SDA	1995	85 MB (50,527 docs)
Dutch (NL)	NRC Handelsblad	1994/1995	299 MB (84,121 docs)
	Algemeen Dagblad	1994/1995	241 MB (106,483 docs)
Portuguese (PT)	Público	1994	164 MB (51,751 docs)
	Público	1995	176 MB (55,070 docs)
	Folha	1994	108 MB (51,875 docs)
	Folha	1995	116 MB (52,038 docs)

Although the number of questions was the same as last year, there were changes regarding the type of questions and their distribution. As regards the three major type of questions, namely Factoids (F), Definition (D) and NIL (N), the breakdown, both suggested and real, is shown in Table 2.

Table 2. Test set breakdown according to question type

suggested	F [120]	D [50]	T [30]	NIL [20]
BG	116	50	34	22
DE	135	42	23	20
EN	121	50	29	20
ES	118	50	32	20
FI	111	60	29	20
FR	120	50	30	20
IT	120	50	30	20
NL	114	60	26	20
PT	135	42	23	18

Meanwhile How and Object questions were not included in 2005 task, since they were considered particularly problematic in the evaluation phase, a new subtype of factoid questions was introduced, called *temporally restricted* questions, which is constrained by either an event -e.g. *Who was Uganda's President during Rwanda's war?*-, a date -e.g. *Which Formula 1 team won the Hungarian Grand Prix in 2004?*- or a period of time-e.g. *Who was the President of the European Commission from 1985 to 1995?*. Up to 30 temporally restricted questions could be included in each task.

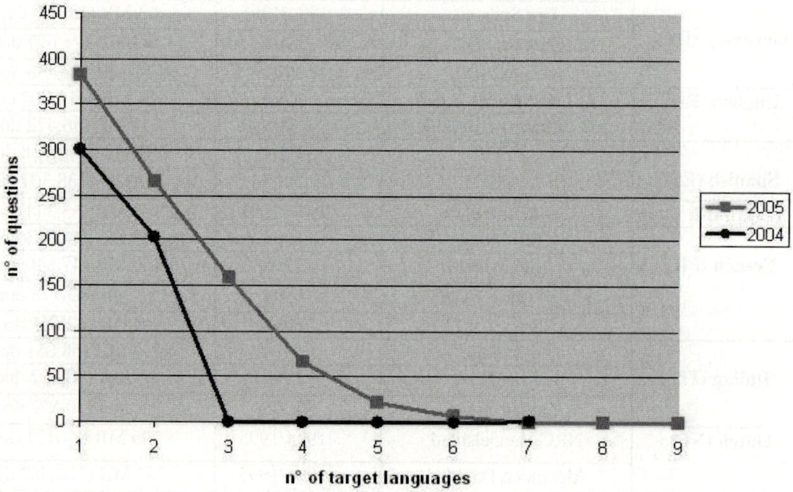

Fig. 1. Question overlapping in 2004 and 2005

As said, in order to increase the overlap between the test sets of different target languages, this year a certain number of topics taken from the Ad-Hoc track at CLEF were assigned to each language and a particular effort was made in order to get general questions, which could easily find an answer also in the other corpora. As a result, no question was actually answered in all 9 languages, but the inter-language partial overlap was increased anyway with respect to the previous edition, as shown in Fig. 1.

The participating systems were asked to retrieve one exact answer for each question –i.e, a snippet of text extracted from the document collections, which provided nothing more or less than the amount of information required. The exact answer had to be also supported by the docid of the text from which it had been taken. Each group was allowed to submit up to two runs per tasks. The results were judged by human assessors as R (ight)/W(rong) –correct or incorrect exact answer; U(nsupported) –if the docid didn't support the answer-; or X (inexact)-if the answer contained more or less information than required. R answers were scored 1, in all other cases the score was 0.

3 Test Set Preparation

The procedure for question generation was the same as that adopted in the previous campaigns. Nine groups were involved in the generation, translation and manual verification of the questions: the Bulgarian Academy of Science, Sofia, Bulgaria (CLPP) was in charge for Bulgarian; the Deutsches Forschungszentrum für Künstliche Intelligenz Saarbrücken, Germany (DFKI) for German; the Evaluations and Language Resources Distribution Agency Paris, France (ELRA/ELDA) for French; the Center for the Evaluation of Language and Communication Technologies Trento, Italy (CELCT) for Italian; Linguateca ICT, Oslo (Norway), for Portuguese; the Universidad Nacional de Educación a Distancia Madrid, Spain (UNED) for Spanish, the University of Amsterdam, The Netherlands for Dutch; the University of Helsinki, Finland for Finnish; the University of Limerick, Ireland for English; and the Department of Computer Science of University of Indonesia joined the activity translating 200 English questions into Indonesian, in order to set up the cross-language Indonesian- English task.

As said, the questions in the test sets addressed large open domain corpora, mostly represented by the same comparable document collections used last year.

According to the consolidate procedure, 100 questions were produced in each target language (except Indonesian), manually searching relevant documents for at least one answer. The questions were then translated into English, so that could be understood and reused by all the other groups. Answers were not translated this year, as it was a time-consuming and basically useless activity [4].

The co-ordinators attempted to balance the difficulty the test sets according to the different answer types of the questions already used in the previous campaigns, i.e. TIME, MEASURE, PERSON, ORGANISATION, LOCATION, and OTHER. HOW and OBJECT questions were not inserted in this exercise because generate ambiguous responses, which are quite difficult to be assessed.

Up to thirty *temporally restricted* questions were allowed, and were themselves classified according to the above mentioned types, i.e., time, measure, etc. Particular care was taken this year in choosing 10% of NIL questions. In fact, some organizers realised that in the previous campaigns NIL questions were quite easily identified by systems, as they were manually generated searching for named entities which were not in the corpora. On the contrary, this time NIL questions were selected randomly from those that seemed to have no answer in the document collections, and were double-checked.

Once the 900 questions were formulated in the original source languages, translated into English and collected in a common XML format, native speakers of each source language, with a good command of English were recruited to translate the English version of all the other questions trying to adhere as much as possible to the original. This process was as challenging as any translation job can be, since many cultural discrepancies and misunderstanding easily creep in. Anyway, as was already pointed out in 2004 ``the fact that manual translation captured some of the cross-cultural as well as cross-language problems is good since QA systems are designed to work in the real world" [3].

Once all the 900 questions were translated into ten source languages -the Indonesian group translated only the final 200 English questions-, 100 additional questions for each target language were selected from the other source languages, so that at the end each language had 200 questions. The added questions were manually verified and searched for answers in the corpus of the respective language. The collection was called *Multi9-05*, and was presented in the same XML format adopted in 2004.

The entire collection is made up of 205 definition questions and 695 factoid, which are quite well balanced according to their types, being divided as follows: 110 MEASURE; 154 PERSON; 136 LOCATION; 103 ORGANISATION, 107 OTHER, 85 TIME. The total number of temporally restricted questions was 149. Although this new kind of questions appeared to be quite interesting, no comprehensive analysis of the results in this group of questions has been made so far, and the experiment requires further investigation.

The *Multi9-05* can now be added to the previous campaigns' collections, which already represent a useful reusable benchmark resource. The proposal to integrate the missing answers with the correct results provided by the systems during the exercise has remained undecided.

4 Participants

The positive trend in terms of participation registered in 2004 was confirmed in the last campaign. From the original 8 groups who participated in 2003 QA task, submitting a total of 19 runs in 9 tasks, the number of competitors went up to twenty-four, which represents an increase of 33% respect to last year, when 18 groups took part in the exercise. The total of submitted runs was sixty-seven.

All the participants in 2005 competition were from Europe, with the exception of group from University of Indonesia which tried the experimental cross-language task Indonesian-English.

Table 3. Number of runs submitted (R) and number of Participants (P)

	BG_t		DE_t		EN_t		ES_t		FI_t		FR_t		IT_t		NL_t		PT_t	
	R	P	R	P	R	P	R	P	R	P	R	P	R	P	R	P	R	P
BG_s	2	2	-	-	1	1	-	-	-	-	-	-	-	-	-	-	-	-
DE_s	-	-	3	2	1	1	-	-	-	-	-	-	-	-	-	-	-	-
EN_s	-	-	3	2			3	2	-	-	1	1	-	-	-	-	1	1
ES_s	-	-	-	-	1	1	13	7	-	-	-	-	-	-	-	-	-	-
FI_s	-	-	-	-	2	1	-	-	2	1	-	-	-	-	-	-	-	-
FR_s	-	-	-	-	4	2	-	-	-	-	10	7	-	-	-	-	-	-
IN_s					1	1												
IT_s	-	-	-	-	2	1	2	1	-	-	1	1	6	3	-	-	-	-
NL_s	-	-	-	-	-	-	-	-	-	-	-	-	-	-	3	2	-	-
PT_s	-	-	-	-	-	-	-	-	-	-	1	1	-	-	-	-	4	3

As shown in table 3, the systems were tested only against 22 of the 81 activated tasks. Monolingual English was discarded this year, as it was in last competition, because the task has been sufficiently investigated in TREC campaigns, and as far as Indonesian is concerned, only the task with English as a target was set up. The non-activated tasks are represented by a blank cell in Table 3.

All nine monolingual tasks (in bold in the table) were tested by at least 1 system, being French (FR) and Spanish (ES) the most chosen languages.

As far as bilingual tasks are concerned, 15 participants altogether chose to test their systems in a cross-language task. English was as usual the most frequent target language, being involved in 8 cross-lingual tasks completed by 9 participants; Spanish was chosen as a target in a cross-language task by three groups, and so was French, meanwhile only one system tried a cross-language task with Portuguese (PT) as a target, i.e. EN-PT. None of the other languages were considered as a target in bilingual tasks.

5 Results

The procedure adopted to assess the systems' outputs was practically the same as the last year. Participants were allowed to submit just one response per question and up to two runs per task, which were judged by human assessors according to correctness and exactness -where correctness expresses whether the answer is clear and pertinent, while exactness evaluates whether the information is either too much or too less. Like in 2004 only exact answers were allowed, and the responses were judged as Right, Wrong, ineXact or Unsupported (when the answer-string contained a correct answer but the returned docid did not support it). As a partial analysis of the inter-tagger agreement has shown, the exactness is still a major problem in evaluation, as most disagreement between judges concerns this parameter.

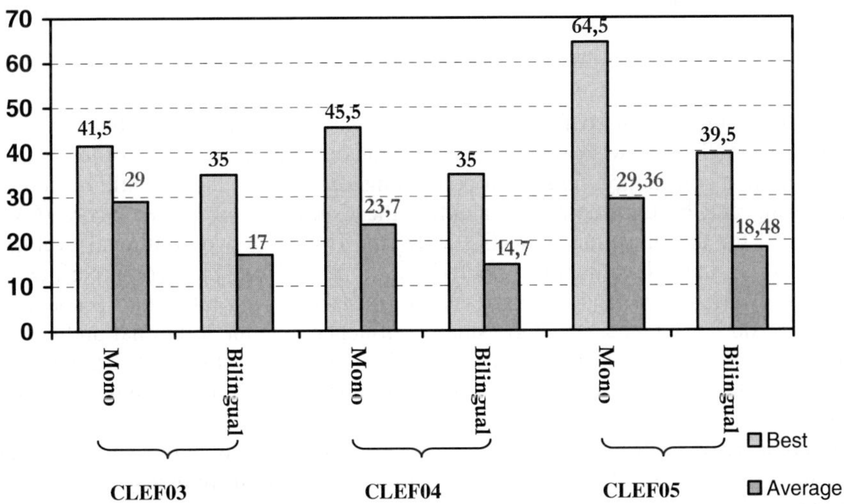

Fig. 2. Best and average results in the QA@CLEF campaigns

Definition questions, which were introduced last year, and were considered particularly difficult also because they could raise problems in assessing their exactness, generally scored quite well, proving that as they are now they are less challenging than one thought. In fact, the answer often consists in the solution of an acronym, when they concern an organisation, or is expressed as an apposition of the proper name, when persons are concerned. As said, the introduction of Temporal Restricted Questions has not been properly analysed yet. It must be said that their number in the test sets was probably too small to provide significant data on their impact on systems' results. Furthermore, some of them were "false temporally restricted" and a system could retrieve an answer without even considering the temporal restriction.

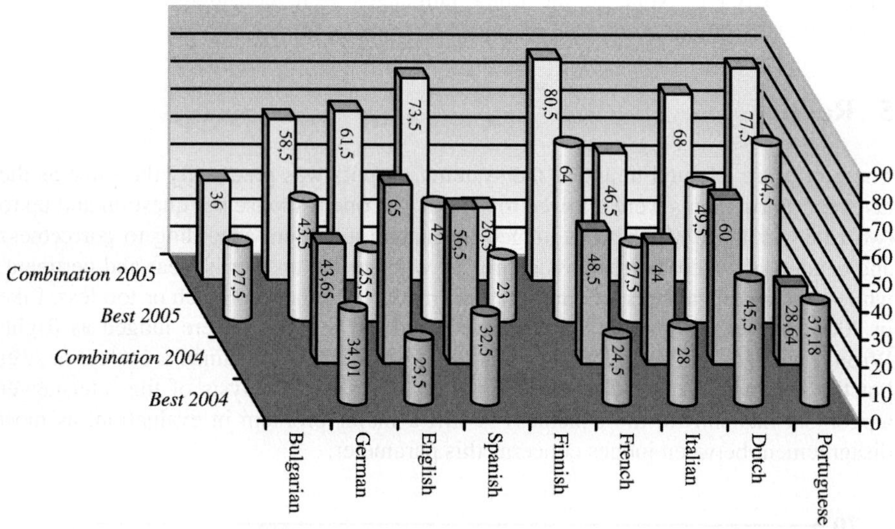

Fig. 3. Best Results and Combinations in QA@CLEF 2004 and 2005

The main measure used for the evaluation was the accuracy, i.e. the fraction of right answers. The answers were returned unranked (i.e. in the same order as in the test set), but a confidence value, that could range between 0 and 1, could be added to each string and be considered to calculate the Confidence-weighted Score (CWS), introduced for the first time in TREC 2002 [6]. This year two additional evaluation measures, i.e. the K1 value and r coefficient, borrowed by [2], were experimentally introduced, in order to find a comprehensive measure which takes into account both accuracy and confidence. Anyway, since confidence was an additional and optional value, only some systems could be assigned the CWS, and consequently the K1 and r coefficient; therefore an analysis based on these measures is not very significant at the moment.

In comparison to last year, the performances of the systems in this campaign show a general improvement, although a significant variation remains among target languages. In fact, in 2004 the best performing monolingual system irrespective of target language (henceforth 'best overall') answered 45.5% of the questions correctly, while the average of the best performances for each target language (henceforth 'average of best') was 32.1%. In 2005 the best overall and average of best figures were 64.5% (in the monolingual Portuguese task)-representing an increase of 19 point- and 42.6% respectively. As far as bilingual tasks are concerned, as usual the cross-lingual step generically entailed a considerable drop in performance. In the following nine sections the results of the runs for each target language are thoroughly discussed. For each target language two kinds of results are given, summarized in two tables. One presents the overall performance, giving the number of right (R), wrong (W), inexact (X), and unsupported (U) answers; the accuracy, in general and on Factoids (F), Definitions (D) and Temporal (T); Precision (P), Recall (R) and F measure for NIL questions; and finally CWS, K1 and r of each run. The second table shows the accuracy of the systems with respect to the answer types, i.e. Definition, sub-classified as Organisation (Or) and Person (Pe), and Factoid and Temporally Restricted, sub-classified as location (Lo), measure (Me), organisation (Or), other (Ot), person (Pe) and time (Ti). Below each answer type, the number of posed questions of that type is shown in square brackets.

The last row of the second table shows a virtual run, called Combination, in which the classification "right answer" is assigned to a question if any of the participating systems found it. The objective of this combination run is to show the potential achievement if one merged all answers and considered the set of answers right, provided that one answer was right.

5.1 Bulgarian as Target

For the first time Bulgarian was addressed as a target language at CLEF 2005. Thus, no comparison can be made with previous results from the same task, but some comments on the present ones are in order.

This year two groups participated in monolingual evaluation tasks with Bulgarian as a target language: IRST, Trento and BTB, LML, IPP, Sofia. Two runs were submitted for Bulgarian-Bulgarian. Both results are below the desired figures (27.50% and 18.50% correct answers), but they outperform their own results from the last year where Bulgarian was used as a source language and English - as a target. Obviously, the Inexact and Unsupported value metrics do not have substantial impact over the final estimations. It seems that as a group the definition questions are the best assessed type (40% and 42%). Then come the factoid ones. The worst performance goes to the temporally restricted questions. Then, NIL questions exhibit better recall than precision. It might be explained by the fact that the systems return NIL when they are not sure in the answer. Only IRST group results provide a confidence weighted score.

It is interesting to discuss the results according to the answer types. Recall that definitions did well as a group. However, when divided further into Organization and Person types, it turns out that the Organization type was better handled by one of the participants, while the Person type was better handled by the other. From non-temporally restricted factoids Organizations and Other have been the most problematic types. From temporally restricted factoids Measure was unrecognized, but the number of these questions was not so high anyway. Person subtype was not detected as well, which is a bit surprising fact.

Table 4. Results in the tasks with Bulgarian as target

run	Right #	Right %	W #	X #	U #	Right % F [116]	Right % D [50]	Right % T [34]	NIL [22] P	NIL [22] R	NIL [22] F	CWS	K1	r
irst051bgbg$_M$	55	27.50	130	13	2	25.00	40.00	17.65	0.15	0.41	0.22	0.144	-0.035	0.160
btb051bgbg$_M$	37	18.50	160	3	-	10.34	42.00	11.76	0.05	0.41	0.10	-	-	-

Most of the problems concerning assessors' agreement were in one `green area': between Wrong and Inexact. Recall that it was also a problem at CLEF 2004. Here we do not have in mind easy cases, such as: What is FARC? The system answered `Columbia' instead of answering `Revolutionary Armed Forces of Colombia' or at least `Revolutionary Armed Forces'. We have in mind subtle cases as follows: (1) too general answers, but still correct (Q: What is ESA? A: `agency' instead of`(European) space agency'), and (2) partial answers, but still correct (Q: Who was proclaimed patron of Europe by the Pope on 31 December 1980? A: `St. Cyril' instead of `St. Cyril and Methodius'). Under the former type we consider answers that are given only some `top ontological' categorization. Under the latter we consider cases, in which part of the answer is presented, but the other part is missing. Very often it concerns questions of measure (Q: How much did Greenpeace earn in 1999? A: '134' instead of '$134 mln.').

Table 5. Results in the tasks with Bulgarian as target (breakdown according to answer type)

run	*Correct Answers*														
	Definition		*Factoid*						*Temporally restricted factoid*					*Total*	
	Or [25]	Pe [25]	Lo [19]	Me [20]	Or [18]	Ot [19]	Pe [20]	Ti [20]	Lo [7]	Me [7]	Or [4]	Ot [4]	Pe [12]	#	%
irst051bgbg$_M$	6	14	6	4	2	3	7	7	-	3	2	-	-	55	27.50
btb051bgbg$_M$	13	8	2	2	1	2	2	3	2	-	2	-	-	37	18.50
combination	16	17	6	4	2	3	7	9	2	3	2	-	1	72	36.00

This year for the first time Bulgarian was tested as a target language at the CLEF track. Two groups made runs on Bulgarian-Bulgarian task. The results are promising in spite of being lower than the half of the correctly recognized answers. So, we consider this a good start. The two extraction systems will be improved on the evaluation feedback. They need to handle better local contexts as well as to try to handle non-local support information.

In the evaluation phase the most problematic still seems to be the definition of the Inexact answer. Inexactness exhibits gradability. In this respect it either should be defined in a more elaborate way (concerning generality and partiality, and per answer type), or there should be introduced a more objective system of final evaluation. Our suggestion is that inexact answers have to contain the head noun of the correct answer. The degree of inexactness depends on the recognized modifiers of the head. If the correct answer is a coordination, then the inexactness is determined also by presence of each coordinates.

5.2 German as Target

There were three research groups that took part in this year's evaluation for the QA-track having German as target language. The number of total system runs submitted by the participants was six, with three runs for every of the two source languages:

German and English. The results of evaluation for every participant group are shown in the tables below.

Table 6. Results in the tasks German as target

run	Right #	Right %	W #	X #	U #	Right % F [135]	Right % D [42]	Right % T [23]	NIL [20] P	NIL [20] R	NIL [20] F	CWS	K1	r
dfki051dede$_M$	87	43.50	100	13	-	35.83	66.00	36.67	0.29	0.65	0.40	0.385	0.095	0.300
fuha051dede$_M$	72	36.00	119	9	-	25.00	70.00	23.33	0.14	1.00	0.25	0.346	0.221	0.665
dfki052dede$_M$	54	27.00	127	19	-	15.00	52.00	33.33	0.28	0.65	0.39	0.227	0.045	0.386
dfki051ende$_C$	46	23.00	141	12	1	16.67	50.00	3.33	0.09	0.10	0.09	0.201	0.060	0.483
dfki052ende$_C$	31	15.50	159	8	2	8.33	42.00	0.00	0.08	0.10	0.09	0.137	0.040	0.564
uhiq051ende$_C$	10	5.00	161	29	-	0.83	18.00	0.00	0.00	0.00	0.00	0.006	-0.310	0.080

For the monolingual German runs the results for definition and temporal questions are better then those for factoid questions. As table 7 shows, within the definition questions, results are better for ORGANIZATION as for PERSON answer types. For factoid questions, best results were attained for TIME, PERSON, LOCATION and ORGANIZATION answer types, in order of their mention, while for temporal questions, results were equally good for PERSON, MEASURE and ORGANIZATION answer types.

Table 7. Results in the tasks with German as target (breakdown according to answer type)

run	*Correct Answers*														
	Definition		*Factoid*						*Temporally restricted factoid*					*Total*	
	Or [29]	Pe [21]	Lo [21]	Me [20]	Or [20]	Ot [19]	Pe [20]	Ti [20]	Lo [4]	Me [13]	Or [3]	Ot [3]	Pe [7]	#	%
dfki051dede$_M$	22	11	7	6	5	3	8	14	2	5	1	-	3	87	43.50
fuha051dede$_M$	20	15	5	2	3	8	5	7	-	4	1	-	2	72	36.00
dfki052dede$_M$	20	6	2	-	3	4	3	6	2	4	1	-	3	54	27.00
combination	**28**	**17**	**10**	**8**	**6**	**10**	**9**	**16**	**2**	**7**	**1**	**-**	**3**	**117**	**58.50**
dfki051ende$_C$	21	4	6	1	-	1	4	8	-	1	-	-	-	46	23.00
dfki052ende$_C$	20	1	2	-	1	1	4	2	-	-	-	-	-	31	15.50
uhiq051ende$_C$	3	6	-	-	-	-	1	-	-	-	-	-	-	10	5.00
combination	**22**	**8**	**7**	**1**	**1**	**2**	**6**	**8**	**-**	**1**	**-**	**-**	**-**	**56**	**28**

For the cross-lingual English-German runs, best results were registered for definition questions, followed by factoid questions, and with poor results by temporal questions. Again, best results for definition questions were for ORGANIZATION answer types and for factoid questions the order of accuracy remains unchanged with respect to the monolingual runs.

Results computed for a "virtual" system, through aggregation of all existing results, show an increase of almost 35% for the monolingual task, and 20% for the cross-lingual task, in accuracy over the best results achieved by participating systems.

5.3 English as Target

Overall, twelve cross-lingual runs with English as a target were submitted. The results are shown in Tables 8 and 9.

The best scoring system overall was DFKI DEEN Run 1 with 25.5%. This score includes all three types of question, i.e. Factoid, Definition and Temporal. For Factoid questions alone, the highest scoring was DLTG FREN Run 1 (20.66%). For Definition questions alone, the highest scoring was DFKI DEEN Run 1 (50%). For Temporal question alone, three systems had an equal top score, DLTG FREN Run 2,

IRST BGEN Run 1 and LIRE FREN Run 2 (all 20.69%). DFKI's main advantage over other systems was their ability to answer definition questions - their score of 50% was well ahead of the next best score of 38% achieved by IRST ITEN Run 1 and IRST ITEN Run 2.

Table 8. Results in the tasks with English as target

run	Right		W	X	U	Right			NIL [20]			CWS	K1	r
	#	%	#	#	#	% F [121]	% D [50]	% T [29]	P	R	F			
dfki051deenC	51	25.50	141	8	-	18.18	50.00	13.79	0.22	0.50	0.31	0.203	0.000	0.322
irst051itenC	47	23.50	145	6	2	19.83	38.00	13.79	0.18	0.35	0.24	0.118	-0.141	0.240
lire052frenC	38	19.00	152	9	1	16.53	24.00	20.69	0.24	0.45	0.31	0.048	-0.201	0.088
irst051bgenC	37	18.50	145	17	1	17.36	20.00	20.69	0.17	0.35	0.23	0.079	-0.270	0.055
dltg051frenC	36	18.00	149	15	-	20.66	12.00	17.24	0.11	0.30	0.16	-	-	-
dltg052frenC	36	18.00	151	13	-	19.83	12.00	20.69	0.10	0.30	0.14	-	-	-
upv051esenC	34	17.00	156	9	1	12.40	28.00	17.24	0.15	0.50	0.23	0.072	-0.105	0.152
lire051frenC	28	14.00	156	14	2	13.22	18.00	10.34	0.21	0.15	0.18	0.043	-0.225	0.237
irst052itenC	26	13.00	168	6	-	5.79	38.00	-	0.22	0.50	0.31	0.114	-0.328	0.414
hels051fienC	25	12.50	164	10	1	12.40	12.00	13.79	0.17	0.55	0.27	0.050	-0.338	0.022
hels052fienC	20	10.00	167	11	2	10.74	8.00	10.34	0.21	0.40	0.27	0.041	-0.332	0.058
uixx051inenC	2	1.00	162	36	-	-	4.00	-	0.40	0.10	0.16	8e-05	-0.770	0.253

Last year, results were only single-judged with all answers to a given question being judged by one assessor using an adapted version of the NIST software. Four assessors each did 50 questions, there being 200 in all. Any issues found by assessors were then discussed and resolved at a series of plenary sessions. This year, all results were double-judged using the same software and with six assessors: Two independently judged questions 1-66, two judged 67-133 and two judged 134-200, there being 200 questions in total once again. The judgements were then automatically compared using the diffutility. A list of variant judgements was then prepared and presented to each pair of assessors for resolution.

The degree of agreement between assessors was found to range between 91.41% and 94.90%, computed as follows: For questions 1-66 there were 66 questions and 12 runs, 792 judgements in all. 68 differences were recorded, so the level of agreement is (792-68)/792, i.e. 91.41%. For questions 67-133, there were 804 judgements with 69 differences recorded, i.e. 91.42% agreement. Finally, for questions 134-200 there were again 804 judgements with 41 differences recorded, i.e. 94.90% agreement.

In almost all cases, points of disagreement could be tracked down to problematic questions which either had no clear answer (but several vague ones) or which had several possible answers depending on the interpretation of the question.

Definition questions were once again included this year but a method of assessing them was not decided upon prior to the competition. In other words, participants did not really know what sort of system to build for definitions and we as assessors were unsure how to go about judging the answers. In consequence we used the same approach as last year: If an answer contained information relevant to the question and also contained no irrelevant information, it was judged R if supported, and U otherwise. If both relevant and irrelevant information was present it was judged X. Finally, if no relevant information was present, the answer was judged W. Two main types of system were used by participants, those which attempted to return an exact factoid-style answer to a question, and those which returned one or more text passages from documents in the collection. Generally, the former type of system is attempting a harder task because it is returning more concise information than is the latter type of system. For this reason, our evaluation method is designed to favour the former type. This was an arbitrary decision, taken in the absence of further guidelines. Our judgements are as accurate as we can make them within our own criteria but we should point out that different criteria could produce different results.

Table 9. Results in the tasks with English as target (breakdown according to answer type)

run	Correct Answers														
	Definition		*Factoid*						*Temporally restricted factoid*					*Total*	
	Or [25]	Pe [25]	Lo [20]	Me [20]	Or [20]	Ot [21]	Pe [20]	Ti [20]	Lo [2]	Me [9]	Or [3]	Ot [5]	Pe [10]	#	%
dfki051deenC	12	13	4	4	5	1	2	6	-	2	-	-	2	51	25.50
irst051itenC	4	15	7	1	3	3	2	8	-	1	-	1	2	47	23.50
lire052frenC	5	7	6	4	4	1	-	5	-	2	1	2	1	38	19.00
irst051bgenC	6	4	7	4	4	1	3	2	-	2	1	-	3	37	18.50
dltg051frenC	2	4	8	4	1	2	2	8	1	2	-	1	1	36	18.00
dltg052frenC	3	3	8	4	1	2	1	8	1	3	-	1	1	36	18.00
upv051esenC	7	7	2	3	3	1	-	6	-	4	-	1	-	34	17.00
lire051frenC	5	4	7	2	1	1	-	5	-	-	2	-	1	28	14.00
irst052itenC	4	15	-	2	2	-	-	3	-	-	-	-	-	26	13.00
hels051fienC	6	-	3	1	2	2	2	5	-	2	-	2	-	25	12.50
hels052fienC	4	-	1	1	2	1	2	6	-	1	-	2	-	20	10.00
uixx051inenC	2	-	-	-	-	-	-	-	-	-	-	-	-	2	1.00
combination	**19**	**23**	**17**	**11**	**10**	**6**	**6**	**13**	**1**	**6**	**2**	**4**	**5**	**123**	**61.50**

Concerning the overall assessment process, we had no procedural difficulties as the format of the data was the same as last year and Michael Mulcahy in particular had already devoted a great deal of time to the adaptation of the software and the development of additional utilities in 2004. Also, most of the assessors were familiar both with the software and with the judgement criteria.

We arrived at two conclusions during the assessment process. Firstly, the main points of difference between assessors in judging answers can be traced back to intrinsic problems associated with certain questions. In other words we need to devote more time to the problem of generating good questions which on the one hand are of the kind which potential users of our systems might pose, and on the other hand have clear answers. We should arrive at objective tests which can be applied to a candidate question and its answers to enable its suitability for use in CLEF to be assessed. Secondly, the situation in respect of definition questions was not ideal for either participants or assessors. This could affect our results for the EN target language as well as their relationship to the results for other target languages.

5.4 Spanish as Target

Seven groups submitted 18 runs having Spanish as target language: 13 of them had also Spanish as source language, 2 had Italian and 3 had English. Notice that is the first time that bilingual runs were submitted.

Table 10 shows the number of correct answers, *CWS*, *K1* and correlation coefficient for all systems. Table 11 shows the number of correct answers for each type of question. Table 12 shows the number of correct answers for each type of temporal restriction.

Table 13 shows the evolution of the most important criteria in the systems performance for the last three years.

The virtual *combination* run was able to answer correctly 73.50% of the questions. The best performing system achieved an overall accuracy of 42% but it only gave a right answer for the 56% of the questions correctly answered by the *combination* run. Thus, we can expect improvements of the systems in a short term.

Table 10. Results in the tasks with Spanish as target

run	Right #	Right %	W #	X #	U #	Right % F [118]	Right % D [50]	Right % T [32]	NIL [20] P	NIL [20] R	NIL [20] F	CWS	K1	r
inao051eses$_M$	84	42.00	110	5	1	28.81	80.00	31.25	0.23	0.80	0.36	-	-	-
tova051eses$_M$	82	41.00	109	7	2	28.81	80.00	25.00	0.24	0.55	0.33	-	-	-
inao052eses$_M$	79	39.50	116	4	1	27.12	80.00	21.88	0.19	0.80	0.31	-	-	-
tova052eses$_M$	77	38.50	113	8	2	23.73	80.00	28.12	0.22	0.55	0.32	-	-	-
upv051eses$_M$	67	33.50	119	13	1	26.27	52.00	31.25	0.19	0.30	0.23	0.218	0.043	0.338
alia051eses$_M$	66	33.00	110	24	-	29.66	40.00	34.38	0.25	0.45	0.32	0.170	-0.273	0.038
aliv051eses$_M$	65	32.50	116	18	1	28.81	46.00	25.00	0.26	0.25	0.26	0.15	-0.224	0.223
alia052eses$_M$	60	30.00	114	26	-	26.27	36.00	34.38	0.24	0.45	0.32	0.153	-0.323	0.038
talp051eses$_M$	58	29.00	122	20	-	27.97	36.00	21.88	0.26	0.70	0.38	0.089	-0.185	-0.011
talp052eses$_M$	54	27.00	133	13	-	25.42	32.00	25.00	0.22	0.65	0.33	0.078	-0.210	-0.043
mira051eses$_M$	51	25.50	138	11	-	26.27	34.00	9.38	0.08	0.10	0.09	0.123	-0.302	0.315
mira052eses$_M$	46	23.00	140	14	-	22.03	34.00	9.38	0.08	0.10	0.09	0.103	-0.343	0.316
upv052eses$_M$	36	18.00	155	9	-	22.88	0.00	28.12	0.10	0.40	0.16	0.128	0.041	0.563
upv051enes$_C$	45	22.50	139	14	2	19.49	34.00	15.62	0.15	0.20	0.17	0.103	-0.033	0.197
mira052enes$_C$	39	19.50	151	8	2	16.95	28.00	15.62	0.17	0.25	0.20	0.088	-0.394	0.227
mira051enes$_C$	39	19.50	153	7	1	16.95	28.00	15.62	0.17	0.25	0.20	0.093	-0.392	0.230
mira051ites$_C$	36	18.00	154	10	-	16.95	26.00	9.38	0.10	0.15	0.12	0.068	-0.437	0.224
mira052ites$_C$	35	17.50	154	11	-	16.95	24.00	9.38	0.10	0.15	0.12	0.071	-0.447	0.219

As shown in Table 11, systems generally behaved better with questions about definitions, locations, persons and organizations. However, when the question type was measure, the accuracy tended to be lower. Indeed, this type of question has turned out to be the most difficult this year. In the factoids without temporal restrictions, the best performing system answered correctly 29.66% of the questions, a very similar accuracy comparing with the results in 2004 (see Table 13).

Concerning questions with temporal restriction, the systems with the best behaviour answered correctly 34.38% of the questions, a similar result comparing with overall accuracy.

Table 11. Results in the tasks with Spanish as target (breakdown according to answer type)

run	*Correct Answers*														
	Definition		*Factoid*						*Temporally restricted factoid*					*Total*	
	Or [25]	Pe [25]	Lo [21]	Me [17]	Or [22]	Ot [19]	Pe [20]	Ti [19]	Lo [6]	Me [7]	Or [6]	Ot [6]	Pe [7]	#	%
inao051eses$_M$	20	20	5	3	4	7	10	5	2	3	2	1	2	84	42.00
tova051eses$_M$	20	20	4	3	8	4	8	7	2	3	1	1	1	82	41.00
inao052eses$_M$	20	20	5	2	5	6	9	5	-	3	2	1	1	79	39.50
tova052eses$_M$	20	20	4	3	8	3	3	7	2	3	1	1	2	77	38.50
upv051eses$_M$	12	14	10	4	5	2	7	3	3	4	-	1	2	67	33.50
alia051eses$_M$	10	10	10	3	7	3	10	2	2	3	2	2	2	66	33.00
aliv051eses$_M$	15	8	8	3	6	2	10	5	4	1	-	-	3	65	32.50
alia052eses$_M$	9	9	9	2	6	4	8	2	2	3	2	2	2	60	30.00
talp051eses$_M$	16	2	11	2	5	4	8	3	1	2	2	1	1	58	29.00
talp052eses$_M$	16	-	12	1	4	3	6	4	2	2	1	1	2	54	27.00
mira051eses$_M$	8	9	7	3	6	4	10	1	-	2	-	-	1	51	25.50
mira052eses$_M$	8	9	6	3	4	2	10	1	-	2	-	-	1	46	23.00
upv052eses$_M$	-	-	10	1	2	2	8	4	3	3	-	-	3	36	18.00
combination	**23**	**24**	**19**	**10**	**16**	**10**	**16**	**10**	**5**	**5**	**3**	**2**	**4**	**147**	**73.50**
upv051enes$_C$	6	11	7	3	3	2	5	3	3	-	-	-	2	45	22.50
mira051enes$_C$	6	8	6	5	2	2	5	-	-	2	1	1	1	39	19.50
mira052enes$_C$	6	8	6	5	2	2	5	-	-	2	1	1	1	39	19.50
mira051ites$_C$	6	7	2	1	4	1	8	4	1	-	-	-	2	36	18.00
mira052ites$_C$	5	7	2	1	4	1	8	4	1	-	-	-	2	35	17.50
combination	**11**	**16**	**10**	**5**	**7**	**5**	**9**	**6**	**3**	**2**	**1**	**1**	**2**	**78**	**39**

As shown in Table 11, when considering the question type, the accuracy scores present small differences. Nevertheless, when the restriction type (date, event and period) is taken into account, the differences are more important (see Table 12).

Table 12. Results of the assessment process for questions with temporal restriction

run	question restriction type		
	date [12]	event [10]	period [10]
alia051eses	3	3	5
alia052eses	3	3	5
aliv051eses	4	3	1
inao051eses	5	2	3
inao052eses	4	1	2
mira051eses	1	2	-
mira052eses	1	2	-
mira051enes	2	2	1
mira052enes	2	2	1
mira051ites	-	3	-
mira052ites	-	3	-
talp051eses	2	3	2
talp052eses	2	4	2
tova051eses	5	-	3
tova052eses	5	1	3
upv051eses	4	3	3
upv052eses	3	3	3
upv051enes	1	3	1
combination	6	8	5

It is worth mentioning that for questions restricted by event, the virtual *combination* run clearly outperforms individual systems separately (low overlapping on correct answers).

In definition questions the best performing system obtained 80% of accuracy. The improvement is remarkable considering that in the 2004 track the best systems answered correctly 70% of the questions.

Regarding NIL questions, the best systems achieved a recall of 0.80. F-measure improvements are also remarkable, with an increase of about 26% with respect to last year (0.30 in 2004 vs. 0.38 in 2005).

Table 13. Evaluation of systems performance with Spanish as target

Year	Best Overall Acc.	Best in Fact	Best in Def	Best NIL (F)	Best r
2003	24.5 %	24.5 %	-	0.25	-
2004	32.5 %	31.11 %	70.00 %	0.30	0.17
2005	42 %	29.66 %	80.00 %	0.38	0.56

Systems have also clearly improved their confidence self-score. While in 2004 the system with higher correlation coefficient (*r*) reached 0.17 [2], in 2005 the highest *r* value was 0.56.

As shown in Table 13, the best performing systems reached and overall accuracy of 24.5%, 32.5% and 42% in 2003, 2004 and 2005, respectively (increasing +71% during the three years).

In order to analyze the *inter-annotator agreement*, we have randomly selected 4 out of 18 runs which have been judged by two assessor with different levels of expertise. Most of the differences among assessors can be found when judging an

Table 14. Results of agreement test of runs with Spanish as target language

run	# Correct (Official)	# Correct (2nd assessor)	# Correct (lenient)	# Correct (strict)	Disagreement #	Kappa	Maximun variation
es1	66	67	71	62	15	0.87	± 2 %
es2	58	63	64	57	11	0.89	± 3 %
en	45	48	51	42	11	0.87	± 4.5 %
it	35	35	39	31	10	0.86	± 2 %

Table 15. Results of agreement test of runs with Spanish as taregt language

run	# Correct (Official)	# Correct (2nd assessor)	# Correct (lenient)	# Correct (strict)	Disagreement #	Kappa	Maximun variation
es1	66	67	71	62	15	0.87	± 2 %
es2	58	63	64	57	11	0.89	± 3 %
en	45	48	51	42	11	0.87	± 4.5 %
it	35	35	39	31	10	0.86	± 2 %

answer as Right or as ineXact. In many cases, an assessor without experience assess as Right an answer that an experienced assessor would judge as ineXact. Table 15 shows the maximum variation of correct answers for these four runs (average = ± 2.9%).

Finally we can conclude that both the improvement in systems' self-evaluation, the scores obtained by the participating systems (73.50% in combination, 42% individually), and the systems' evolution during the last three years, let us expect a significant improvement in Spanish question answering technologies in the near future.

5.5 Finnish as Target

The year 2005 was the first year when Finnish existed as a target language. Only one group submitted runs for this task, and both of the runs were monolingual. The artificial combination run presented in Table 19 shows that the upper bound on the performance of a system that would merge the results of the existing runs and somehow select the right answers from the combined pool of candidate answers is 26.50%. This is by far the lowest monolingual combination run score among the participating languages. The next one is Bulgarian with a combination score of 36.00 % (see Table 5). However, when we calculate the average score for the monolingual runs of each target language, we can see that Finnish is not very far behind, for the average accuracy of the Finnish runs is 21.00%, that of the Bulgarian ones is 23.00%, that of the Italian ones is 24,08%, that of the French ones is 25,20%, and so on. The confidence scores that the systems having Finnish as target assign to the answers only very faintly reflect the assessor's opinion on the correctness of the answer, as can be seen from the correlation coefficient between the system's score and correctness (r) in Table 18.

Table 16. Results in the tasks with Finnish as target

run	Right #	Right %	W #	X #	U #	Right % F [111]	Right % D [60]	Right % T [29]	NIL [20] P	NIL [20] R	NIL [20] F	CWS	K1	r
hels051fifi$_M$	46	23.00	131	23	-	18.92	25	34.98	0.13	0.35	0.19	0.090	-0.202	0.064
hels052fifi$_M$	38	19.00	140	22	-	15.32	23.33	24.14	0.12	0.30	0.17	0.074	-0.230	0.093

The evaluation of the Finnish answers was not straightforward because the evaluation guidelines [1] do not discuss word affixes with regard to the exactness of the answers. Finnish is a highly inflected language where each noun, for example, has 15 different cases. In addition to cases, nouns can also contain possessive suffixes and clitics. Most of the answers to the CLEF questions are noun phrases. The cases, possessive suffixes and clitics typically express meanings that are in the other target languages of the evaluation campaign expressed by separate words such as prepositions, pronouns and adverbs.

Table 17. Results in the tasks with Finnish as target (breakdown according to answer type)

run	*Correct Answers*														
	Definition		*Factoid*						*Temporally restricted factoid*					*Total*	
	Or [27]	Pe [33]	Lo [21]	Me [10]	Or [15]	Ot [20]	Pe [28]	Ti [17]	Lo [4]	Me [5]	Or [5]	Ot [5]	Pe [10]	#	%
hels051fifi$_M$	6	9	4	1	2	1	9	4	1	4	-	1	4	46	23.00
hels052fifi$_M$	8	6	4	1	2	-	7	3	1	3	-	1	2	38	19.00
combination	**8**	**10**	**5**	**1**	**3**	**1**	**11**	**4**	**1**	**4**	**-**	**1**	**4**	**53**	**26.50**

Thus, one single word in Finnish may convey considerably more information than a single word in the other target languages. For example, the word *talossanikin* means *also in my house*. Our understanding of the guidelines was that the answer should be taken from text as such, without any modifications, such as lemmatization. Now, due to the rich affixing, the answer that is not lemmatized may contain additional information that disturbs the evaluator, and he is tempted to judge the answer inexact.

Table 18. Results in the tasks with Finnish as target

run	Right		W	X	U	Right			NIL [20]			CWS	K1	r
	#	%	#	#	#	% F [111]	% D [60]	% T [29]	P	R	F			
hels051fifi$_M$	23	11.50	134	43	-	10.81	6.67	24.14	0.13	0.35	0.19	0.260	-0.316	0.001
hels052fifi$_M$	20	10.00	143	37	-	10.81	5.00	17.24	0.12	0.30	0.17	0.026	-0.331	-0.001

However, judging as inexact all those answers that are not in the form required by the question could not be done, because that is not required according to the guidelines. When deciding how to assess the Finnish answers, we observed how the judgements had been done with regard to cases in the other target languages. For example, in German, the case may cause modifications in the determiner. However, those answers whose head noun is not in the nominative case even though that is the case requested by the question, are marked as correct. For example: Question: *62 D PER Wer ist Goodwill Zwelithini?* Answer: *R 0062 dem König der Zulus*[2]. Thus, we decided to judge as correct in Finnish also those answers that are not in the form required by the question. For example: Question: *65 F PER Kuka on ohjannut elokuvan Hamlet liikemaailmassa?* Answer: *R 0067 Mika Kaurismäen.*[3]. In fact, most of the problematic question forms in the test set for Finnish are of the type where the

---

[2] The question requires the head noun of the answer to be in the nominative case - *der König* - instead of the dative case - *dem König*.

[3] The question requires the answer to be in the nominative case - *Mika Kaurismäki* - instead of the genetive case -*Mika Kaurismäen.*

Table 19. Results in the tasks with Finnish as target (breakdown according to answer type)

run	*Correct Answers*														
	Definition		*Factoid*						*Temporally restricted factoid*					*Total*	
	Or [27]	Pe [33]	Lo [21]	Me [10]	Or [15]	Ot [20]	Pe [28]	Ti [17]	Lo [4]	Me [5]	Or [5]	Ot [5]	Pe [10]	#	%
hels051fifi$_M$	4	-	2	1	2	-	3	4	-	4	-	1	2	23	11.50
hels052fifi$_M$	3	-	1	1	2	-	5	3	-	3	-	1	1	20	10.00
combination	4	-	2	1	3	-	5	4	-	4	-	1	2	26	13.00

answer is given in the genitive case and the case required by the question is the nominative case.

5.6 French as Target

Seven research groups took part in evaluation tasks using French as target language: Synapse Développement (France), CEA-LIST/LIC2M (France), LIMSI-LIR (France), Université de Nantes, LINA (France), Helsinki University (Finland), Universitat Politécnica de Valéncia, UPV (Spain) and TOVA, a joint system between UPV and the Instituto Nacional de Astrofisica Óptica y Electrónica (Mexico). All participating groups took part in the monolingual task: four groups submitted one run and three groups submitted two runs FR-FR. Only Synapse Développement took part in the bilingual tasks. This group submitted three runs, one run per source language: Italian, English and Portuguese. Table 19 shows the results of the assessment of the thirteen submitted runs. This year, many groups participated in the Question Answering tasks with French as a target. It appears that the number of participants for the French task has increased significantly: seven this year as opposed to one last year. The best results were obtained by Synapse Développement for one of the monolingual runs (syna051frfr). This group ranked 2nd and 3rd in the two English-French and Portuguese-French runs which is better than all the other monolingual French runs. The two monolingual runs by the Spanish TOVA group reached the 4th and 5th positions.

Table 20. Results in the tasks with French as target

run	Right #	Right %	W #	X #	U #	Right % F [120]	Right % D [50]	Right % T [30]	NIL [20] P	NIL [20] R	NIL [20] F	CWS	K1	r
syna051frfr$_M$	128	64.00	62	8	2	59.17	86.00	46.67	0.23	0.25	0.24	-	-	-
tova052frfr$_M$	70	35.00	120	10	-	27.50	66.00	13.33	0.14	0.30	0.19	-	-	-
tova051frfr$_M$	69	34.50	121	10	-	26.67	66.00	13.33	0.13	0.25	0.17	-	-	-
upv051frfr$_M$	46	23.00	143	7	4	17.50	46.00	6.67	0.06	0.10	0.07	0.115	-0.048	0.210
hels051frfr$_M$	35	17.50	156	8	1	16.67	22.00	13.33	0.10	0.45	0.17	0.108	-0.196	0.281
upv052frfr$_M$	34	17.00	160	5	1	15.00	20.00	20.00	0.07	0.20	0.10	0.073	-0.057	0.207
lire051frfr$_M$	33	16.50	145	20	2	15.83	14.00	23.33	0.09	-	0.09	0.072	-0.358	0.260
hels052frfr$_M$	33	16.50	157	10	-	15.00	22.00	13.33	0.09	0.40	0.15	0.097	-0.230	0.247
lina051frfr$_M$ *	29	14.50	144	21	3	17.95	6.00	16.67	0.15	0.20	0.17	0.048	-0.470	0.151
lcea051frfr$_M$	28	14.00	165	3	4	18.33	0.00	20.00	0.33	0.05	0.09	-	-	-
syna051enfr$_C$	79	39.50	108	10	3	30.25	72.00	22.58	0.14	0.30	0.19	-	-	-
syna051ptfr$_C$	73	36.50	115	9	3	26.67	68.00	23.33	0.07	0.15	0.10	-	-	-
syna051itfr$_C$	51	25.50	136	11	2	15.00	54.00	20.00	0.13	0.45	0.21	-	-	-

* Results calculated over 197 questions.

The correct answers given for all the runs are presented in table 20, sorted by type of answer (location, measure, organization, etc.). The results show the limits of the system developed by Synapse Développement, which obviously lie in factoid-other (9/20), factoid-measure (10/20) and factoid-time (11/20), whereas results are much better for definition and factoid-person questions. The aim of the virtual run called combination is to provide an upper bound on the possible performance of a system that would merge the existing runs and somehow select the right answers from the combined pool of candidate answers. The best run (syna051frfr) is able to supply 76.19% of the correct answers of combination. This ratio could be enhanced if results for factoid-measure or factoid-time questions were better.

The main problem encountered during the assessment of answers was related to the temporally restricted factoid questions. This year and for the first time in CLEF this kind of questions was included in the test sets. We thought that the generation of this kind of questions would be relatively easy, but did not foresee that the assessment on those questions would be so difficult.

Table 21. Results in the tasks with French as target (breakdown according to answer type)

run	*Correct Answers*														
	Definition		*Factoid*						*Temporally restricted factoid*					*Total*	
	Or [25]	Pe [25]	Lo [20]	Me [20]	Or [20]	Ot [20]	Pe [20]	Ti [20]	Lo [6]	Me [2]	Or [5]	Ot [10]	Pe [7]	#	%
syna051frfr$_M$	21	22	12	10	13	9	16	11	4	1	2	4	3	128	64.00
tova052frfr$_M$	19	14	3	3	7	5	8	7	1	-	1	1	1	70	35.00
tova051frfr$_M$	19	14	3	2	8	5	7	7	1	-	1	1	1	69	34.50
upv051frfr$_M$	9	14	3	5	3	2	4	4	1	-	-	-	1	46	23.00
hels051frfr$_M$	4	7	5	5	3	1	3	3	-	1	1	2	-	35	17.50
upv052frfr$_M$	-	10	3	2	2	1	4	6	3	-	1	1	1	34	17.00
lire051frfr$_M$	3	4	1	4	5	1	2	6	3	1	1	1	1	33	16.50
hels052frfr$_M$	4	7	5	3	2	1	3	4	-	1	1	2	-	33	16.50
lina051frfr$_M$ *	1	2	3	2	2	3	6	5	1	-	1	1	2	29	14.50
lcea051frfr$_M$	-	-	3	4	5	-	6	4	1	-	1	-	4	28	14.00
combination	**23**	**23**	**15**	**16**	**16**	**14**	**18**	**16**	**5**	**2**	**3**	**5**	**5**	**161**	**80.5**
syna051enfr$_C$	21	15	8	6	3	9	6	4	2	-	1	3	1	79	39.50
syna051ptfr$_C$	17	17	6	4	8	7	4	3	4	-	2	1	-	73	36.50
syna051itfr$_C$	15	12	4	6	2	4	1	1	-	1	1	3	1	51	25.50
combination	**21**	**20**	**10**	**10**	**8**	**10**	**8**	**6**	**5**	**1**	**2**	**3**	**2**	**106**	**53**

* Results calculated over 197 questions.

In fact, many temporally restricted factoid questions have not been built properly as there was no logic of restriction at all. The question "In which famous capital was the Eiffel Tower built in 1889?" is a good example. Here, "in 1889" is a redundant information rather than a temporally restriction and will be ignored by the system: the correct answer returned with a document associating the Eiffel Tower to Paris will be a right answer even if it does not specify that the Eiffel Tower was built in 1889.

Therefore, from the beginning of the assessment phase on, many questions arise such as "Should the date be included in the document joined to the answer?", "Should all the items included in the question be found in the document in order to consider the answer as correct?". Now we know how to handle those temporally restricted factoid questions and such problems should not occur next year.

This year, as far as French language is concerned, the best system obtained very good results: 128 correct answers out of 200. In all the QA@CLEF tracks, these are the best results ever obtained for the French used as target language. Moreover, we could see a growing interest in Question Answering from the European research community: the QA@CLEF-2005 attracted more participants in evaluation tasks using French as target language than the previous editions. In addition, the benchmark resources built for these evaluations contributed to the development and the improvement of systems, and could be used again as training resources in the next edition.

5.7 Italian as Target

Three groups participated in the Italian monolingual task, and no one in the other bilingual tasks with Italian as target. A total of six runs were submitted, two each research group: ITC-Irst, the Universidad Politécnica de Valencia (UPV) and a joint experiment by UPV and the Mexican INAOE (Instituto Nacional de Astrofísica, Óptica y Electrónica). As table 21 shows the best system (the one developed by UPV and INAOE) answered correctly to 27.5% of the questions, and the other two systems achieved similar results.

Table 22. Results in the tasks with Italian as target

run	Right		W	X	U	Right			NIL [20]			CWS	K1	r
	#	%	#	#	#	% F [120]	% D [50]	% T [30]	P	R	F			
tova052itit$_M$	55	27.50	135	10	-	23.33	42.00	20.00	0.15	0.55	0.24	-	-	-
tova051itit$_M$	53	26.50	138	9	-	21.67	42.00	20.00	0.16	0.55	0.24	-	-	-
upv_051itit$_M$	51	25.50	142	6	1	20.00	44.00	16.67	0.10	0.15	0.12	0.156	0.012	0.316
upv_052itit$_M$	48	24.00	148	4	-	15.83	50.00	13.33	0.06	0.15	0.09	0.125	-0.200	0.202
irst051itit$_M$	44	22.00	137	17	2	19.17	38.00	6.67	0.17	0.20	0.18	0.129	-0.197	0.267
irst052itit$_M$	38	19.00	145	14	3	14.17	38.00	6.67	0.40	0.10	0.16	0.100	-0.301	0.071

In 2004, two teams had participated in the Italian monolingual task, submitting a total of 3 runs. The best performer had an overall accuracy of 28%, while the average performance was 25.1%. In 2005, the task itself attracted more research groups, and though the best system was approximately as good as the one of last year, the average overall accuracy is slightly worse (i.e. 24%), which probably means that the Italian monolingual test set was more challenging in 2005. As far as the types of questions are concerned, it is interesting to notice that definitional questions proved to be easier than factoids. Between 38 and 50% of definitional questions got a correct answer, while temporally restricted questions were tougher for the three participating systems. Eleven questions (no. 3, 20, 30, 60, 65, 84, 85, 107, 113, 116 and 124) received a correct answer in all the six submitted runs, and five among them are definition questions referred to a person. This suggests that this type of question have often a straightforward answer that appears between brackets or in appositive form within the text. Table 23 shows that the factoids with *location*, *person* and *time* as answer type were the easiest for systems, and if the three systems had worked together, they could have achieved an overall accuracy of 46.5%, which encourages research groups to share tools and resources in the future.

Table 23. Results in the tasks with Italian as target (breakdown according to answer type)

run	*Correct Answers*														
	Definition		*Factoid*						*Temporally restricted factoid*					*Total*	
	Or [25]	Pe [25]	Lo [19]	Me [21]	Or [21]	Ot [19]	Pe [20]	Ti [20]	Lo [4]	Me [4]	Or [3]	Ot [8]	Pe [11]	#	%
tova052itit$_M$	11	10	4	1	7	1	8	7	1	1	-	1	3	55	27.50
tova051itit$_M$	11	10	4	1	7	1	6	7	1	1	-	1	3	53	26.50
upv_051itit$_M$	10	12	6	2	3	2	7	4	1	1	-	-	3	51	25.50
upv_052itit$_M$	11	14	5	-	3	1	6	4	1	1	-	-	2	48	24.00
irst051itit$_M$	5	14	7	-	4	2	5	5	1	-	-	-	1	44	22.00
irst052itit$_M$	5	14	3	-	4	1	3	6	1	-	-	-	1	38	19.00
combination	17	20	9	3	8	4	10	11	3	2	-	1	5	93	46.5

The manual assessment procedure was the same as it was in 2004. Two assessors had a brief training session (based on the 2004 submissions) that aimed at making them familiar with the evaluation tool interface and at solving preliminary doubts.

Both assessors judged all the six runs and then the answers with different judgments were double-checked and received a third, final judgment. Table 24 gives the number of different judgments per run and the inter-assessor kappa coefficient, which is quite high (average value is 0.874).

Table 24. Inter-assessor agreement in the evaluation of the Italian runs

run	*disagreement* different judgments (#)	kappa coefficient
tova052itit	10	0.895
tova051itit	11	0.882
upv_051itit	8	0.909
upv_052itit	9	0.895
irst051itit	17	0.828
irst052itit	15	0.839

A total of 70 disagreement cases were registered, most of them involved the judgment couples R-X (11 cases), R-W (13 cases), U-W (10 cases) and above all X-W (31 cases). Clearly, the evaluation guidelines did not deal extensively with answer exactness, so assessors had some difficulties in deciding which portion of an answer-string was acceptable and which was not. In most of the cases (i.e. 26) where an assessor assigned X and the other W, the third and final judgment was W.

5.8 Dutch as Target

This year two teams that took part in the QA@CLEF track used Dutch as their target language: the University of Amsterdam and the University of Groningen. In total, three runs were submitted, all using Dutch as the source language. All runs were assessed by two assessors, with very high inter-assessor agreement (0.950 for gron051nlnl, and 0.976 for uams051nlnl and uams052nlnl). The results of the evaluation for all runs are provided in Tables 25 and 26.

Table 25. Results in the tasks with Dutch as target

run	Right #	Right %	W #	X #	U #	Right % F [114]	Right % D [60]	Right % T [26]	NIL [20] P	NIL [20] R	NIL [20] F	CWS	K1	r
$gron051nlnl_M$	99	49.50	79	18	4	54.39	50.00	26.92	0.46	0.30	0.36	0.382	0.071	0.302
$uams051nlnl_M$	88	44.00	79	28	5	47.37	45.00	26.92	0.77	0.50	0.61	-	-	-
$uams052nlnl_M$	88	44.00	78	29	5	48.25	43.33	26.92	0.77	0.50	0.61	-	-	-

When scored in terms of the percentage of correct (i.e., correct, exact and supported) answers, the run labelled gron051nlnl (submitted by the University of Groningen) clearly outperforms the two runs submitted by the University of Amsterdam: 49.50% vs. 44% and 44%. When compared to the correct answers in the Groningen run, many of the inexact answers in the Amsterdam runs are caused by incorrect definitions; here is an example:

0094 NLNL What is Eyal?
gron051nlnl: militante joodse groep
uams051nlnl: leider van de extreme-rechtse groep

This observation is confirmed if we take a closer look. In the 200 questions, six initial words occur more than ten times: *Wie* (*Who*), *Wat* (*What*), *Hoe* (*How*), *Welke* (*Which*), *Waar* (*Where*) and *In* (*In*). The performance of the questions with four of the six initial words is similar for the three runs. For *Wat*, Groningen obtains 67% right and Amsterdam 39%. This difference is mainly caused by the problem with the definition answers just mentioned. For *Hoe*, Groningen obtains 63% and Amsterdam 36%. Seven of the eight *Hoe* questions for which only Groningen found the answer, were of the format *Hoe heet DEFINITION?* (*What is the name of DEFINITION?*).

All in all, the Groningen run performs noticeably better than the Amsterdam runs in terms of *precision* --- this is clear from the differences in answers labelled X (inexact): only 18 for Groningen, and as many as 28 and 29 for Amsterdam.

If we drill down a bit further, and consider the detailed results in Table 26, we see that Groningen outperforms Amsterdam on Organisations in the Definitions category, and on Other questions in the Factoid category; Amsterdam is slightly better in Person definitions. On other categories, the differences are very minor or non-existent. There is, however, a noticeable difference in performance on NIL questions, with Amsterdam achieving far higher F-scores than Groningen.

Table 26. Results in the tasks with Dutch as target (breakdown according to answer type)

run	*Correct Answers*														
	Definition		*Factoid*						*Temporally restricted factoid*					*Total*	
	Or [24]	Pe [36]	Lo [30]	Me [9]	Or [11]	Ot [20]	Pe [35]	Ti [9]	Lo [5]	Me [4]	Or [1]	Ot [4]	Pe [12]	#	%
gron051nlnl$_M$	16	14	13	4	3	12	25	5	3	1	-	-	3	99	49.50
uams051nlnl$_M$	9	18	14	2	3	7	23	5	2	-	-	-	5	88	44.00
uams052nlnl$_M$	8	18	14	2	4	7	23	5	2	-	-	-	5	88	44.00
combination	**17**	**24**	**21**	**4**	**6**	**13**	**31**	**7**	**5**	**1**	**-**	**-**	**7**	**136**	**68.00**

To conclude, let's adopt a somewhat alternative perspective. The differences between the Groningen run and the Amsterdam are mainly in the number of inexact answers; in terms of the number of unsupported or wrong answers the differences are negligible. Put differently, in terms of the number of answers that are ``helpful'' [4] i.e., that would help a user meet her information needs, the three runs all perform at the same level: 117 helpful (i.e., correct or inexact) for the Groningen run, and 116 and 117 helpful for the two Amsterdam runs.

5.9 Portuguese as Target

In 2005 there were five runs with Portuguese as target, submitted by three different research teams. In addition to the two participants from last year, SINTEF with the Esfinge system and the University of Évora, we had a newcomer from industry, Priberam, a Portuguese company specialized in NLP products. Although a collection of Brazilian Portuguese news was added to the CLEF collection, no Brazilian participants turned up as yet for CLEF.

Table 27. Results in the tasks with Portuguese as target

run	Right		W	X	U	Right			NIL [18]			CWS	K1	r
	#	%	#	#	#	% F [135]	% D [42]	% T [23]	P	R	F			
prib051ptpt$_M$	129	64.50	55	13	3	67.41	64.29	47.83	0.50	0.11	0.18	-	-	-
ptue051ptpt$_M$	50	25.00	125	22	3	21.48	35.71	26.09	0.10	0.67	0.18	0.250	-0.500	0.000
esfg051ptpt$_M$	46	23.00	139	11	4	23.70	16.67	30.43	0.21	0.78	0.33	-	-	-
esfg052ptpt$_M$	43	21.50	145	10	2	23.70	14.29	21.74	0.22	0.78	0.34	-	-	-
esfg051enpt$_C$	24	12.00	165	9	2	11.11	14.29	13.04	0.12	0.78	0.20	-	-	-

Table 27 presents the five runs. This year there was a first cross-lingual run, from English to Portuguese, by Esfinge, with significantly worse results than the monolingual runs, as might be expected. As to the monolingual results, the Esfinge system showed some improvement as compared to last year, although its best run was still unable to equal PTUE system's score. PTUE's results, however, were slightly worse than last year's. The clear winner in all respects was Priberam's system, which, in fact, was the best participating system in the whole QA@CLEF. Table 28 breaks down the correct answers by kind of entity, as well as provides a combination score: a question is considered answered if any system has been able to provide a right answer (assuming that a user would be able to check easily, in case of multiple answers, the right one). In this, we see that Portuguese language ranks as second, after French.

Table 28. Results in the tasks with Portuguese as target (breakdown according to answer type)

run	*Correct Answers*														
	Definition		*Factoid*						*Temporally restricted factoid*					*Total*	
	Or [15]	Pe [27]	Lo [30]	Me [17]	Or [21]	Ot [15]	Pe [37]	Ti [15]	Lo [5]	Me [1]	Or [2]	Ot [6]	Pe [9]	#	%
prib051ptpt$_M$	12	15	26	11	7	8	25	14	2	-	-	4	5	129	64.50
ptue051ptpt$_M$	5	10	10	1	3	3	10	2	1	-	-	2	3	50	25.00
esfg051ptpt$_M$	1	6	9	4	5	2	9	3	1	-	1	3	2	46	23.00
esfg052ptpt$_M$	-	6	8	3	3	-	13	5	-	-	1	2	2	43	21.50
combination	**12**	**22**	**28**	**13**	**11**	**10**	**27**	**15**	**3**	-	**1**	**6**	**7**	**155**	**77.50**
esfg051enpt$_C$	-	6	3	1	3	1	5	2	-	-	1	2	-	24	12.00
combination	-	**6**	**3**	**1**	**3**	**1**	**5**	**2**	-	-	**1**	**2**	-	**24**	**12.00**

Another relevant remark is that definitions do not seem to be more difficult on average than factoid questions, as was the case last year. We believe, however, that this is due to a considerable simplification of precisely what ``definition questions" are, where they boil down to mainly ask for a person's profession or title. We did some further analysis of the results in order to have other measures of confidence in the systems, which are displayed in table 28. We looked specifically at (i) the cases where no answer was given (*null answer*), which keep the user in a state of ignorance, no matter the system was right in providing the null answer or wrong because it could not find it; (ii) the cases where any user could at once see the answer was rubbish (*rubbish*); and (iii) the cases where the wrong answers could be misleading (*dangerous*). Of course it depends on the ignorance of the questioner, and we were very conservative in imagining total ignorance. Probably most of the ``dangerous" questions would at once be spotted as system's mistakes by an ordinary user -- or at least arise some suspicion.

Table 29. Results in the tasks with Portuguese as target (breakdown of bad answers)

	Incorrect or null answers		
run	null answer	rubbish	dangerous
prib051ptpt	4	13	43
ptue051ptpt	117	3	20
esfg051ptpt	68	41	49
esfg052ptpt	65	34	63
esfg051enpt	121	21	40

The results show that the PTUE system is both the most reliable (less non-NIL wrong answers) and the most conservative system (most empty answers), the more "dangerous" one being Esfinge.

6 Conclusions

This paper presented the Multilingual Question Answering evaluation campaign organized at CLEF 2005. QA@CLEF considerably increased both in number of participants -we are now closer to the Question Answering track at TREC- and also in the number of languages involved. It is also relevant that this year we were able to activate a task with Bulgarian as a target, a language of a new EU member country. A pilot cross-language task with Indonesian as source and English as target has been also activated.

With the organization of the task in its third year, it is now well tested, although involving nine different institutions of as many different countries, and has showed to be able to support the high number of exchanges required by the organization of the task. This is particularly significant considering that all the organizations involved in QA@CLEF guarantee their support on a completely voluntary basis.

The increased number of participants allowed carrying out a number of interesting comparisons among systems participating in the same task (this was one of the drawback of the 2004 campaign). In addition, it is worth mentioning that Question Answering techniques for European languages, being mainly based on NLP tools and resources for the respective languages, demand better tools and resources. In a cross-language perspective the integration of such resources is also crucial.

Finally, having (at least partially) achieved its goal to promote Question Answering for European languages, there is now quite a large scientific community in Europe on Question Answering, and QA@CLEF is now ready to propose its own view on QA, designing a roadmap for next multilingual QA systems.

Acknowledgements. Anselmo Peñas and Valentín Sama Rojo have been partially supported by the Spanish Government under project R2D2-Syembra TIC-2003-07158-C04-02.

Maarten de Rijke was supported by the Netherlands Organization for Scientific Research (NWO) under project numbers 017.001.190, 220-80-001, 264-70-050, 354-20-005, 612-13-001, 612.000.106, 612.000.207, 612.066.302, 612.069.006, and 640.001.501.

Diana Santos and Paulo Rocha were supported by grant POSI/PLP/43931/2001 from the Portuguese Fundação para a Ciência e Tecnologia, co-financed by POSI.

References

1. QA@CLEF 2005 Organizing Committee. Guidelines 2005. http://clefqa.itc.it/2005/guidelines.html
2. Herrera, J., Peñas A., Verdejo, F.: Question answering pilot task at CLEF 2004. In: Peters, C., Clough, P., Gonzalo, J., Jones, Gareth J.F., Kluck, M., Magnini, B. (eds.): Multilingual Information Access for Text, Speech and Images. Lecture Notes in Computer Science, Vol. 3491. Springer-Verlag, Berlin Hidelberg New York (2005) 581–590
3. Magnini, B.,Vallin, A., Ayache, C., Erbach, G., Peñas, A., de Rijke, M., Rocha, P., Simov, K., Sutcliffe, R.: Overview of the CLEF 2004 Multilingual Question Answering Track. In: Peters, C., Clough, P., Gonzalo, J., Jones, Gareth J.F., Kluck, M., Magnini, B. (eds.): Multilingual Information Access for Text, Speech and Images. Lecture Notes in Computer Science, Vol. 3491. Springer-Verlag, Berlin Hidelberg New York (2005) 371-391
4. Santos, D., Rocha, P.: The Key to the First CLEF with Portuguese: Topics, Questions and Answers in CHAVE. In: Peters, C., Clough, P., Gonzalo, J., Jones, Gareth J.F., Kluck, M., Magnini, B. (eds.): Multilingual Information Access for Text, Speech and Images. Lecture Notes in Computer Science, Vol. 3491. Springer-Verlag, Berlin Hidelberg New York (2005) 821-832.
5. Spark Jones, K.: Is question answering a rational task? In: Bernardi, R., Moortgat, M. (eds): Questions and Answers: Theoretical and Applied Perspectives. Second CoLogNETElsNET Symposium. Amsterdam (2003) 24–35
6. Voorhees, E. M.: Overview of the TREC 2002 Question Answering Track. In: Voorhees, E. M. and Buckland, L. P. (eds), Proceedings of the Eleventh Text Retrieval Conference (TREC 2002 NIST Special Publication 500-251, Washington DC (2002) 115 123

A Fast Forward Approach to Cross-Lingual Question Answering for English and German

Robert Strötgen, Thomas Mandl, and René Schneider

University of Hildesheim, Information Science
Marienburger Platz 22, D-31141 Hildesheim, Germany
mandl@uni-hildesheim.de

Abstract. This paper describes the development of a question answering system for mono-lingual and cross-lingual tasks for English and German. We developed the question answering system from a document and retrieval perspective. The system consists of question and answering taxonomies, named entity recognition, term expansion modules, a multi-lingual search engine based on Lucene and a passage extraction and ranking component. The overall architecture and heuristics applied during development are described. We discuss the results at CLEF 2005 and show potential future work.

1 Introduction

The question answering (QA) system developed at the University of Hildesheim for the participation in this years' QA track at CLEF is mainly based on the experience gained from multi-lingual retrieval in previous years. Our system can do mono-lingual QA and cross-lingual retrieval, both for German and English as topic and document language. The architecture of this basic QA system is based on a retrieval engine developed for multi-lingual ad-hoc retrieval [1]. Further components necessary for a QA system [2] and some for system improvement were additionally developed.

As required components we implemented a question and answer taxonomy, a translation utility for automatically translating questions and a passage extraction and ranking passages from the documents. In addition, we integrated a tool for named entity recognition and term expansion. Many of the components were developed by a group of graduate students. All source code was developed using JAVA.

2 Query Processing

The query processing includes the assignment of a question and expected answer type, named entity recognition, translation and stopword removal.

2.1 Question and Answer Taxonomies

A question taxonomy based on the questions of previous QA tracks [4] was developed. It contains eleven question classes and several subclasses for the question types WHO, HOW, WHAT and WHERE and the corresponding answer classes.

C. Peters et al. (Eds.): CLEF 2005, LNCS 4022, pp. 332 – 336, 2006.

An evaluation based on the CLEF QA topics form the years 2003 and 2004 showed that overall, for 73% of the questions, the answer category was assigned correctly. For further 14%, the categorization was partly correct and for another14% of the questions, a wrong category was assigned. The taxonomy was most reliable for the question types WHEN, WITH WHAT and FOR WHAT. Questions starting with WHAT were categorized worst.

2.2 Named Entity Recognition

Previously, we analyzed the impact of named entities on query performance in ad-hoc retrieval and found, that queries are often solved better when named entities are present [6]. As a consequence, we included named entity recognition from the beginning. The goal was, to identify named entities and to create a separate index for them. An analysis of three named entity recognition systems on the CLEF topics showed that the performance was satisfactory and can be improved by training [5].

LingPipe[1] was used as a basic tool. Lingpipe applies a statistical machine learning approach to named entitiy recognition and categorization. For training LingPipe, we used one annotated corpus for each language:

- German: Frankfurter Rundschau with 36 Million word forms (Source: Linguistic Data Consortium, LDC[2])
- English: Reuters News (810.000 news texts)

An evaluation revealed a recognition rate of 60% for correct recognition and 42% for correct categorization into the following four classes: Person (PER), Organization (ORG), Place (LOC) und Miscellaneous (MISC). Named entity recognition was applied to the queries and to the document corpus.

2.3 Query Translation

The key component for cross-lingual QA is a translation utility. As underlying systems, we used Babelfish, FreeTranslation and Linguatec[3]. We tried to avoid the influence of wrongly translated named entities. We replaced all named entities found in the query with a dummy which was not translated by the translation tools. In addition, the named entities were sent to the translation tool without context subsequently. All translated sentences and terms were collected and only stopwords were removed.

2.4 Term Expansion

For retrieving German answers, the translated keywords were expanded using GermaNet[4]. However, to avoid the addition of too many synsets, the expansion was

---

[1] http://www.alias-i.com/lingpipe/
[2] http://www.ldc.upenn.edu/
[3] http://babelfish.altavista.com/, http://www.freetranslation.com/, http://www.linguatec.net/online/ptwebtext/
[4] http://www.sfs.nphil.uni-tuebingen.de/lsd/

only carried out, when GermaNet contained only a single meaning of the word under question. For English, the synonym function of WordNet[5] was used to expand all translated terms. The effect of term expansion has not been evaluated for our system yet.

3 Searching and Passage Retrieval

For stemming, indexing and retrieval we employed Lucene[6] as it has been used in [1]. The system searched with the keywords provided and first returned documents. These were split into passages of size of at least 200 including the remainder until the next punctuation mark.

These passages were again indexed as documents by Lucene and ranked according to a scoring algorithm which rewards the frequency of occurrence of keywords in the passage [3]. The same set of keywords was used for retrieval and ranking. The top ranked passages are returned. A user interface which allows question input and which shows the top three passages has also been developed.

A few heuristics were implemented to improve performance. We focused on named entities especially.

- If named entity is the expected answer type and there are documents in the answer set which contain named entities of the appropriate type, then only these documents are forwarded to the passage extraction.
- If named entity is the expected answer type the most frequent named entities of the expected type within all passages are determined and the first passages containing these named entities are returned.
- If no answer with named entities is found, then the first 90 characters of the most highly ranked passage are returned.
- Trivial answers are not returned. Answers are considered trivial if they contain only one word, if they consist of the name of a known news agency or if the answer string is a subset of the question string.
- When the expected answer type is a named entity, then all the named entities in the first 20 passages are extracted and the most frequent named entity is returned.

The confidence weight returned by the system is the retrieval status value returned by Lucene for the returned passage. NIL is returned when no document is found by Lucene and in this case, a confidence value of 1.0 is assigned.

4 Experiments and Results

The quality of the results was only satisfying for definition questions. For this first participation and considering the focus on named entities, this is acceptable. The results are shown in table 1.

---

[5] http://wordnet.princeton.edu/doc

[6] http://lucene.apache.org/

Table 1. Results for QA system of the University of Hildesheim in 2005

Languages	Question Type	Accuracy
English -> German	Definition	18.00%
English -> German	Factoid	0.83%
English -> German	All	5.00%

The reduced performance is due to several reasons. The time and effort dedicated to evaluation were mainly aimed at system stability and the integration of all tools. Parameter tuning based on previous CLEF experiments were not carried out so far. In addition, this year CLEF required a very short answer. Our system returns passages of at least the length 200 and no further processing is done to extract a short answer. This was probably an advantage for our system for definition questions, where the performance was good.

5 Outlook

The system for QA can be improved by further integrating the question analysis and the search process. So far, the knowledge gained from the question in not fully exploited. Furthermore, the system needs to be evaluated more thoroughly.

Acknowledgements

We would like to acknowledge the work of several students from the University of Hildesheim who implemented the components of the QA system as part of their course work[7]. We also want to thank Maarten de Rijke for his comments on an earlier version of our QA approach.

References

1. Hackl, R.; Mandl, T.; Womser-Hacker, C. (2005): Mono- and Cross-lingual Retrieval Experiments at the University of Hildesheim. In: Peters, C.; Clough, P.; Gonzalo, J.; Kluck, M.; Jones, G.; Magnini, B. (eds): Multilingual Information Access for Text, Speech and Images: Results of the Fifth CLEF Evaluation Campaign. Berlin et al.: Springer [LNCS 3491] pp. 165 – 169
2. Harabagiu, S.; Moldovan, D. (2003): Question Answering. In: *The Oxford Handbook of Computational Linguistics*. Oxford; New York: Oxford University Press, 2003.
3. Light, Marc; Mann, Gideon S.; Riloff, Ellen; Breck, Eric (2001): Analyses for elucidating current question answering technology. In: Journal of Natural Language Engineering, Special Issue on Question Answering Fall-Winter 2001.
4. Magnini, B.; Vallin, A.; Ayache, C.: Erbach, G.; Peñas, A.; de Rijke, M.; Rocha, P.; Simov, K. and Sutcliffe, R. (2005): Multiple Language Question Answering (QA@CLEF). Overview of the CLEF 2004 Multilingual Question Answering Track. In: Working Notes 5th Workshop of the Cross-Language Evaluation Forum, CLEF 2004. Bath, England, http://clef.isti.cnr.it/2004/working_notes/WorkingNotes2004/35.pdf

[7] http://www.uni-hildesheim.de/~rschneid/psws04odqa.html

5. Mandl, T.; Schneider, R.; Schnetzler, P.; Womser-Hacker, C. (2005): Evaluierung von Systemen für die Eigennamenerkennung im cross-lingualen Information Retrieval. In: Gesellschaft für linguistische Datenverarbeitung. Beiträge der GLDV-Frühjahrstagung. Bonn, 30.3. - 01.04. Frankfurt a. M. et al. Peter-Lang.
6. Mandl, T.; Womser-Hacker, C. (2005): The Effect of Named Entities on Effectiveness in Cross-Language Information Retrieval Evaluation. In: Proceedings ACM SAC Symposium on Applied Computing (SAC). Information Access and Retrieval (IAR) Track. Santa Fe, New Mexico, USA. March 13.-17. 2005. S. 1059-1064.

The ŒDipe System at CLEF-QA 2005

Romaric Besançon, Mehdi Embarek, and Olivier Ferret

CEA-LIST
LIC2M (Multilingual Multimedia Knowledge Engineering Laboratory)
B.P.6 - F92265 Fontenay-aux-Roses Cedex, France
{besanconr, embarekm, ferreto}@zoe.cea.fr

Abstract. This article presents Œdipe, the question answering system that was used by the LIC2M for its participation in the CLEF-QA 2005 evaluation. The LIC2M participates more precisely in the monolingual track dedicated to the French language. The main characteristic of Œdipe is its simplicity: it mainly relies on the association of a linguistic pre-processor that normalizes words and recognizes named entities and the principles of the Vector Space model.

1 Introduction

Question Answering is at the edge of Information Retrieval and Information Extraction. This position has led to the development of both simple approaches, mainly based on Information Retrieval tools, and very sophisticated ones, such as [1] or [2] for instance, that heavily rely on Natural Language Processing tools. Previous evaluations in the Question Answering field have clearly shown that high results cannot be obtained with too simple systems. However, it still seems unclear, or at least it is not shared knowledge, what is actually necessary to build a question answering system that is comparable, in terms of results, to the best known systems. This is why we have decided to adopt an incremental method for building Œdipe, the question-answering system of the LIC2M, starting with a simple system that will be progressively enriched. Œdipe was first developed in 2004 for the EQUER evaluation [3] about question answering systems in French. It was designed mainly for finding passage answers and its overall design was not changed for its participation to the French monolingual track of CLEF-QA 2005. The main adaptation we made for CLEF-QA was the addition of a module that extracts short answers in passage answers for definition questions.

2 Overview of the Œdipe System

The architecture of the Œdipe system, as illustrated by Figure 1, is a classical one for a question answering system. Each question is first submitted to a search engine that returns a set of documents. These documents first go through a linguistic pre-processor to normalize their words and identify their named entities.

C. Peters et al. (Eds.): CLEF 2005, LNCS 4022, pp. 337–346, 2006.

The same processing is applied to the question, followed by a specific analysis to determine the type of answer expected for this question. This search is performed through three levels of gisting: first, the passages that are the most strongly related to the content of the question are extracted from the documents returned by the search engine. Then, the sentences of these passages that are likely to contain an answer to the question are selected. These sentences can also be considered as passage answers. Finally, minimal-length answers are extracted from these sentences by locating their phrases that best correspond to the question features.

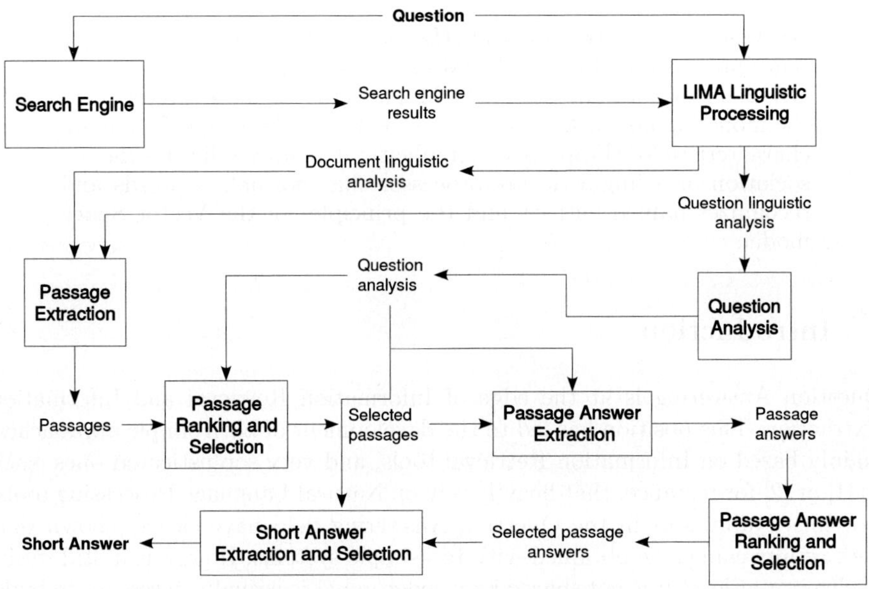

Fig. 1. Architecture of the Œdipe system

3 From Documents to Passages

3.1 LIMA

LIMA [4], which stands for LIc2m Multilingual Analyzer, is a modular linguistic analyzer that performs text processing from tokenization to syntactic analysis for 6 languages[1]. More precisely, for CLEF-QA, the linguistic analysis of both documents and questions relied on the following modules:

– tokenizer
– morphological analysis

[1] These languages are: French, English, Spanish, German, Arabic and Chinese. Full syntactic analysis is only available for French and English but the chunker module exists for the other languages.

- detection of idiomatic expressions
- part-of-speech tagging
- content word identification
- named entity recognition

We did not use LIMA's syntactic analysis for compound extraction. Previous experiments on TREC data showed that for question answering, compounds are useful for selecting documents [5] but are not necessarily interesting for selecting candidate sentences for exact answer extraction. Indeed, there is no reason for an answer to be systematically at a short distance from an occurrence of a compound that is present in the initial question. Compounds were however used for document selection, as they are internally integrated into the search engine we used.

3.2 Search Engine

For the first selection of documents from the collection, we used the LIC2M search engine, that had already participated to the Small Multilingual Track of CLEF in 2003 [6] and 2004 [7]. This search engine is concept-based, which means that it focuses on identifying in a query its most significant concepts, generally represented as multi-terms and named entities, and favors in its results the documents that contain one occurrence of each query concept, or a least the largest number of these concepts, whatever their form[2] and their number of occurrences in documents. The search engine relies on LIMA for the linguistic analysis of both the documents and the queries. The configuration of LIMA was the same as the one described in the previous section, except that the compound extractor was added.

For CLEF-QA, no specific adaptation of the search engine was done. Each question was submitted to the search engine without any pre-processing and the first 50 documents given as result were selected for the next steps.

3.3 Question Analysis

The analysis of questions aims at determining the type of the expected answer. More specifically, it determines if the answer is a named entity or not, and in the first case, the type of the target named entity. We distinguish only 7 types of named entities: person, organization, location, date and time, numerical measure, event and product. Except for the two last ones, they correspond to the types of named entities defined by the MUC evaluations. The analysis of questions is achieved by a set of 248 rules implemented as finite-state automata. These automata are similar to those defined for recognizing named entities and idiomatic expressions in LIMA. Each rule is a kind of lexico-syntactic pattern that can also integrate semantic classes. When it is triggered, it associates the question with one type among the 149 question types we distinguish. As this

[2] The search engine can recognize a concept of the query if it appears in a document as a synonym or a sub-term.

typology heavily relies on the surface form of the questions, a mapping is defined between the question types and the answer types. A question can have several answer types when the rules are not sufficient for choosing among them. This is the case for some ambiguities between persons and organizations.

The rules for question analysis were elaborated following a semi-automatic method, first developed for the EQUER evaluation [8] and that is inspired by Alignment-Based Learning [9]. This method starts from a corpus of questions, made in our case of translated TREC-QA questions[3] and questions from the previous CLEF-QA evaluations. First, the edit distance of Levenshtein is computed for each pair of questions. Then, the Longest Common Substring algorithm is applied for each pair of questions that are close enough in order to extract their common part. The common substrings are sorted to find the question types whereas the distinct parts can be grouped to form classes of entities with similar characteristics:

What is the capital of Yugoslavia?
What is the capital of Madagascar?
question type: what_is_the_capital_of
class of countries: Yugoslavia, Madagascar

This method is implemented by the CoPT tool, developed by Antonio Balvet[4].

3.4 Passage Extraction, Ranking and Selection

After the selection of a restricted set of documents by the search engine, Œdipe delimits the passages of the documents that are likely to contain an answer to the considered question. This delimitation relies on the detection of the areas of documents with the highest density of words of the question. It is done by giving to each position of a document an activation value: when such a position contains a word of the question, a fixed value is added to its activation value and to the activation value of the positions around it (*activSpread* positions on the right and the left sides). Finally, the delimited passages correspond to the contiguous positions of the document for which the activation value is higher than a fixed threshold.

A score is then computed for each extracted passage. This score takes into account three factors:

- the number and the significance of the words of the question that are present in the passage. The significance of a question word is evaluated by its normalized information, computed from 2 years of the *Le Monde* newspaper;
- the presence in the passage of a named entity that corresponds to the expected answer type when the answer type is a named entity;
- the density of the words of the question in the passage.

[3] More precisely, these questions come from the TREC-8, TREC-9 and TREC-10 evaluations and were translated by the RALI laboratory.

[4] Corpus Processing Tools, available at: `http://copt.sourceforge.net`

More precisely, the score of a passage p_i is:

$$score(p_i) = \alpha \cdot wordScore(p_i) + \beta \cdot neScore(p_i) + \gamma \cdot densityScore(p_i) \quad (1)$$

where α,β and γ are modulators[5] and all the scores are between 0.0 and 1.0. The word score is given by:

$$wordScore(p_i) = \frac{\sum_k significance(w_k)}{number\ of\ question\ plain\ words} \quad (2)$$

where w_k is a word of p_i that is a word of the question.

The named entity score is equal to 1.0 if a named entity that corresponds to the expected answer type is present in p_i and to 0.0 otherwise. The density score is defined with respect to a reference size for a passage, given by:

$$reference\ size = 2 * activSpread + number\ of\ question\ words(p_i) \quad (3)$$

If the size of p_i is less than *reference size*, its density score is equal to its maximal value, *i.e.* 1.0. Otherwise, it is attenuated with respect to how much the size of p_i is greater than *reference size*, by being equal to:

$$densityScore(p_i) = \frac{1}{\sqrt{\frac{passage\ size}{reference\ size}}} \quad (4)$$

Once their score is computed, the passages are sorted according to the decreasing order of their score and the first N passages are kept for the further steps[6].

4 From Passages to Answer

Œdipe was first developed as a question answering system dedicated to find passage answers rather than to find short answers. We adapted it for the CLEF-QA evaluation but without changing its overall design. Hence, it first searches for passage answers and then tries to find short answers in them.

[5] For our CLEF-QA run, α and β were equal to 1.0. The value of γ depends on two factors. The first one is the core modulator value set as a parameter (equal to 1.0 in our case). This factor is modulated by :

$$\frac{number\ of\ question\ words(p_i)^4}{(number\ of\ question\ words(p_i) + 1)^4}$$

which makes the density score less important when the number of question words that are present in p_i is high.

[6] N is equal to 20 for this evaluation.

4.1 From Passages to Passage Answers

Œdipe locates a passage answer in each selected passage. This process consists in moving a window over the target passage and to compute a score at each position of the window according to its content. The size of this window is equal to the size of the answer to extract[7]. The extracted answer is the content of the window for its position with the higher score.

The way the window is moved depends on the expected answer type. If the expected answer is not a named entity, the window is moved over each plain word of the passage. Otherwise, it is moved only over the positions where a named entity that corresponds to the expected answer type is present. In both cases, the score computed at each position is the sum of two sub-scores:

- a score evaluating the number and the significance of the question words that are in the window. This score is the same as the word score for passages (see 2);
- a score that is directly equal to the proportion of the named entities of the question that are in the window.

For questions whose expected answer is not a named entity, it is frequent to have several adjacent positions with the same score. When such a case happens with the highest score of the passage, the selected passage answer is taken from the middle of this zone and not from its beginning, as the answer often comes after the words of the question.

Finally, as for passages, all the passage answers are sorted according to the decreasing order of their score. If the score of the highest answer is too low, *i.e.* below a fixed threshold, Œdipe assumes that there is no answer to the considered question.

4.2 From Passage Answers to Short Answers

When the expected answer is a named entity, the extraction of short answers is straightforward: the passage answer with the highest score is selected and the named entity on which the passage answer extraction window was centered is returned as a short answer. In the other case, a search for a short answer based on a small set of heuristics is performed. This search assumes that a short answer is a noun phrase. Hence, Œdipe locates all the noun phrases of the passage answer by applying the following morpho-syntactic pattern:

$$(\mathrm{DET}|\mathrm{NP}|\mathrm{NC})(\mathrm{NC}|\mathrm{NP}|\mathrm{ADJ}|\mathrm{PREP})(\mathrm{ADJ}|\mathrm{NC}|\mathrm{NP})^{8}$$

Then, it computes a score for each of them. This score takes into account both the size of the answer and its context:

[7] The window size was equal to 250 characters for the CLEF-QA evaluation.

[8] DET: article, NP: proper noun, NC: common noun, ADJ: adjective, PREP: preposition.

– its base is proportional to the size of the answer, with a fixed limit;
– it is increased by a fixed value each time a specific element is found in its close context (2 words). This element can be one of the named entities of the question or more generally, an element that is characteristic of the presence of a definition, such as a period, a parenthesis or the verb "to be".

The final score of a short answer is the sum of its passage answer score and of its short answer score. The short answer with the highest score is returned as the answer to the considered question.

5 Evaluation

5.1 Results

We submitted only one run of the Œdipe system for the CLEF-QA 2005 evaluation. For the 200 test questions, Œdipe returned 28 right answers – all of them were answers to factoid questions, with more precisely 6 answers to temporally restricted factoid questions – 3 inexact answers and 4 unsupported answers. Moreover, the detection of a lack of answer by Œdipe was right for only one question among the three it detected whereas 20 questions were actually without any answer. The second column of Table 1 takes up from [10] the best results of the seven participants to the monolingual track for French . As we can see from this table, the results of Œdipe (system 7) are not good but they are not too far from the results of half of the participants.

Table 1. CLEF-QA 2005 results for the French monolingual track

systems	**# right answers**	**score with question difficulty**
1	128	67.5
2	70	30.75
3	46	17.75
4	35	15.25
5	33	17.75
6	29	15
7	**28**	**16.75**

To take into account the fact that all the questions do not have the same level of difficulty, we have computed a specific score (see the last column of Table 1). The difficulty of a question is evaluated by the number of systems that do not return a right answer for it. We computed the mean (denoted M_{diff}) and the standard deviation (denoted SD_{diff}) of the difficulty values for the 200 questions[9] and set the score of a right answer to a question as follows:

[9] These difficulty values were computed from all the runs with French as a target language.

$$\begin{aligned} score &= 0.25 \ \textit{if difficulty} \leq M_{diff} - SD_{diff} \\ score &= 0.5 \ \ \textit{if difficulty} \leq M_{diff} \\ score &= 0.75 \ \textit{if difficulty} \leq M_{diff} + SD_{diff} \\ score &= 1 \ \ \ \ \textit{if difficulty} > M_{diff} + SD_{diff} \end{aligned}$$

This score confirms the fact that the results of Œdipe are not very far from the results of most of the participants and that they could be improved quite quickly as it misses some "easy" questions.

5.2 Discussion

As illustrated by Figure 1, even a simple question answering system such as Œdipe is a complex system and its failures can come from various sources. In this section, we present more detailed results for identifying in which part of Œdipe some answers are "missed". These results were obtained by taking as reference the assessed runs of all the participants to CLEF-QA 2005 with French as target language. This is an incomplete reference as several questions were answered by no participant and there is no guarantee that all the answers to a question were found in the evaluation corpus. But it is a reliable way to compute automatically the minimal score of a question answering system on this corpus.

The first source of missed answers in such system is the retrieval of documents by its search engine. In our case, we have found that the LIC2M search engine returned at least one document with an answer for 132 questions among the 200 test questions, which represents 66% of the questions. Thus, Œdipe found 21.2% of the answers that it could find after the search engine step. More globally, the LIC2M search engine retrieved 262 of the 383 documents with an answer found by all the participants, that is to say 68.4%.

Table 2. Results of the question analysis module

question type	# questions	# correct types	# incorrect types
definition (D)	50	50	0
factoid (F)	120	106	14
temporal factoid (T)	30	23	7

Another important part of a question answering system is the question analysis module because it generally determines what kind of strategy is applied for searching the answer to a question. We have seen in Section 4 that the main distinction in Œdipe from that viewpoint is done between the definition questions and the factoid ones. Table 2 shows the results of the question analysis module of Œdipe on the 200 test questions of CLEF-QA 2005. The first thing to notice is that the classification error rate (10.5%) for these two categories is quite low. Moreover, none definition question is misclassified, which means that the question analysis module is not responsible of the low results of Œdipe for this category of questions.

Table 3. Detailed results of Œdipe for the French monolingual track

# answers/question	exact answer					passage answer				
	MRR[10]	# right answers				MRR	# right answers			
		total	T	D	F		total	T	D	F
1	0.140	28	6	0	22	0.170	34	7	2	25
2	0.147	31	7	0	24	0.182	39	8	2	29
3	0.151	33	7	0	26	0.193	45	8	5	32
4	0.152	34	8	0	26	0.194	46	9	5	32
5	0.152	34	8	0	26	0.197	49	9	7	33
10	0.154	37	8	0	29	0.203	59	9	11	39

The influence of the final modules of Œdipe on its global results is illustrated by Table 3, which gives the number of right exact answers and right passage answers found in the top M answers to the CLEF-QA 2005 questions. More particularly, this table shows that 44.7% of the answers that can be found after the document retrieval step are present in the first 10 passage answers extracted by Œdipe. This percentage is reduced to 37.1% for the first 5 passage answers. For exact answers, it is equal to 28.0% in the first case and to 25.8% in the second one. But the most obvious difference between passage answers and exact answers concerns definition questions: whereas right passage answers are found for some definition questions[11], none right exact answer can be extracted for them. This fact means that our heuristics for extracting exact answers are inefficient, which is actually not a surprise for us as they were developed quickly and not tested on a large scale.

6 Conclusion

We have presented in this article the version of the Œdipe system that participated to the French monolingual track of the CLEF-QA 2005 evaluation. Its results are not very high but they are coherent with the degree of simplicity of the system. The analysis of its results shows that such a simple system can be sufficient to answer around 20% of factoid questions but is totally inefficient for answering to more complex questions such as definition questions. Hence, we will focus our future work on that aspect. Particularly, since the answers to definition questions are often noun phrases, we plan to integrate LIMA's capabilities for syntactic analysis to extract noun phrases instead of using a basic pattern-matching approach. In a more long-term plan, we would like to elaborate an instance-based approach for extracting short answers, which could avoid the building of a set of manual patterns as is often done.

---

10 MRR: Mean Reciprocal Rank, the measure used in the first evaluations of TREC-QA.

11 However, they are proportionally less numerous than for factoid questions.

References

1. Moldovan, D., Harabagiu, S., Girju, R., Moraresc u, P., Novischi, A., Badalescu, A., Bolohan, O.: LCC tools for question answering. In: TREC 2002. (2003)
2. Laurent, D., Séguéla, P.: QRISTAL, système de questions-réponses. In: 12ème Conférence annuelle sur le Traitement Automatique des Langues Naturelles (TALN 2005), Dourdan, France (2005) 53–62
3. Ayache, C.: Campagne EVALDA/EQUER : Evaluation en question-réponse, rapport final de la campagne EVALDA/EQUER. Technical report, ELDA (2005)
4. Besançon, R., Chalendar (de), G.: L'analyseur syntaxique de LIMA dans la campagne d'évaluation EASY. In: 12ème Conférence annuelle sur le Traitement Automatique des Langues Naturelles (TALN 2005), Dourdan, France (2005) 21–24
5. Ferret, O., Grau, B., Hurault-Plantet, M., Illouz, G., Jacquemin, C.: Document selection refinement based on linguistic features for QALC, a question answering system. In: Recent Advances in Natural Language Processing (RANLP 2001). (2001)
6. Besançon, R., Chalendar (de), G., Ferret, O., Fluhr, C., Mesnard, O., Naets, H.: Concept-based Searching and Merging for Multilingual Information Retrieval: First Experiments at CLEF 2003. In: 4th Workshop of the Cross-Language Evaluation Forum, CLEF 2003. (2004) 174–184
7. Besançon, R., Ferret, O., Fluhr, C.: LIC2M experiments at CLEF 2004. In: 5th Workshop of the Cross-Language Evaluation Forum, CLEF 2004. (2005)
8. Balvet, A., Embarek, M., Ferret, O.: Minimalisme et question-réponse : le système Oedipe. In: 12ème Conférence annuelle sur le Traitement Automatique des Langues Naturelles (TALN 2005), Dourdan, France (2005) 77–80
9. van Zaanen, M.: Boostrapping Structure into Language: Alignement-Based Learning. PhD thesis, University of Leeds (2001)
10. Vallin, A., Giampiccolo, D., Aunimo, L., Ayache, C., Osenova, P., Peñas, A., de Rijke, M., Sacaleanu, B., Santos, D., Sutcliffe, R.: Overview of the CLEF 2005 Multilingual Question Answering Track. In: 6th Workshop of the Cross-Language Evaluation Forum, CLEF 2005. (2006)

An XML-Based System for Spanish Question Answering

David Tomás, José L. Vicedo, Maximiliano Saiz, and Rubén Izquierdo

Department of Software and Computing Systems
University of Alicante, Spain
{dtomas, vicedo, max, ruben}@dlsi.ua.es

Abstract. As Question Answering is a major research topic at the University of Alicante, this year two separate groups participated in the QA@CLEF track using different approaches. This paper describes the work of *Alicante 1* group. Thinking of future developments, we have designed a modular framework based on XML that will easily let us integrate, combine and test system components based on different approaches. In this context, several modifications have been introduced, such as a new machine learning based question classification module. We took part in the monolingual Spanish task.

1 Introduction

This year two separate groups participated at the University of Alicante in the QA@CLEF track using different approaches. This paper is focused on the work of *Alicante 1* (run *aliv051eses* in [2]).

Most QA systems are based on pipeline architecture, comprising three main stages: question analysis, document retrieval and answer extraction. These tasks can be isolated in different modules, so that the development of each one could be set apart and afterward integrated as a whole. In order to achieve this goal, we have developed an XML framework that facilitates the communication between the different components of the system, so that we can easily substitute and test new modules into the general framework for further development. Furthermore, the system has suffered several modifications with respect to previous competitions [3] [4] in the different stages of the question answering process.

This paper is organized as follows: in section 2 we describe the system architecture; section 3 outlines the XML framework; section 4 presents and analyses the results obtained at QA@CLEF 2005 Spanish monolingual task; finally, in section 5 we discuss the main challenges for future work.

2 System Description

This approach has evolved from the system developed in our research group [4]. New components and old ones have been fully integrated in a brand new XML framework designed to combine QA processes in a multilingual environment. The system follows the classical three-stages pipeline architecture mentioned above. Next paragraphs describe each module in detail.

C. Peters et al. (Eds.): CLEF 2005, LNCS 4022, pp. 347–350, 2006.

2.1 Question Analysis

This stage carries out two processes: question classification and keyword selection. The first one detects the sort of information claimed by the query, mapping the question into a previously defined taxonomy. Otherwise, keyword selection chooses meaningful terms from the query that help to locate the documents that are likely to contain the answer.

While the keyword extraction module remains the same [4], this year we have replaced the former question classification module, based on hand made lexical patterns, with a new one based on machine learning [1]. After defining the possible answer types (NUMBER, DATE, LOCATION, PERSON, ORGANIZATION, DEFINITION and OTHER), we trained the system with an annotated corpus made up of questions from Question Answering Track in TREC[1] 1999 to 2003 and CLEF 2003 to 2004, to sum up 2793 training questions in Spanish. Thus there is no need to manually tune the module since all the knowledge necessary to classify the questions is automatically acquired.

2.2 Document Retrieval

To accomplish this task we use two different search engines: Xapian[2] and Google[3]. Xapian performs document retrieval over the entire EFE Spanish document collection. The lemmas of the keywords detected in the question analysis stage are used to retrieve the 50 topmost relevant documents from the EFE collection.

In parallel, the same keyword list (not lemmatized this time) is sent to Google search engine through its Web API[4], selecting the 50 top ranked short summaries returned. We store this information for later use as a statistical indicator of answer correctness.

As a novelty, we introduced last year the use of English search to improve the retrieval task [4]. This special search is only performed if the question is mapped to type NUMBER, DATE, PERSON or ORGANIZATION, the classes that are likely to have a language independent answer: numbers, dates, people and company names tend to keep unchanged through languages.

2.3 Answer Extraction

In this stage a single answer is selected from the list of relevant documents retrieved from the EFE Spanish corpus. The set of possible answers is built up extracting all the n-grams (unigrams, bigrams and trigrams in our experiments) from the relevant documents in the EFE collection.

Although the general process is similar to the one we used in previous competitions (explained in detail in [3]), new information has been added to improve the filtering and the final answer selection step.

---

1 Text REtrieval Conference, http://trec.nist.gov

2 http://www.xapian.org

3 http://www.google.com

4 http://www.google.com/api

Filtering is carried out by POS tagging, query class, keywords, definition terms, and stopwords list. Once the filtering process is done, remaining candidate answers are scored taking into account the following information: (1) number of keywords and definition terms that co-occur in the sentence where it appears, (2) the frequency of the answer in the documents and summaries obtained in the retrieval stage, (3) the distance (number of words) between the possible answer and the keywords and definition terms co-occurring in the same sentence, and (4) the size of the answer. All the weights obtained are normalized in order to get a final value between 0 and 1.

3 The XML Framework

Once detailed the different stages of the Question Answering system, we describe the XML framework where all the process takes place. The eXtensible Markup Language (XML) is a general-purpose markup language that has become a standard de facto in inter-system communication, being widely used to facilitate data sharing between applications. We have used it to exchange information between the different modules in our system, building a framework were individual components can be easily interchanged. Thus, new modules can be developed separately and later used in place of old ones in the framework for testing purpose. In order to change a module, we only have to make sure that it fits de XML specification for that process.

We have associated an XML tagset for each stage of the process. Every module adds the XML fragment generated to a common file where the following modules can extract the information required to perform. So, what we finally get is a sort of log file that stores the complete question answering process in XML format. This file can be used to save time testing individual modules, as we have the information needed already stored in the file. For instance, if we just want to test the answer extraction module, we wouldn't need to execute the previous processes as the information might be already stored in the file because of a previous run. Another benefit of this XML framework is that additional tags could be added on demand if extra information storing is required for new modules, having not to change the old modules working as the original structure remains the same.

Although our run was limited to Spanish monolingual task, the framework is prepared to store information in different languages together for multilingual purpose.

4 Results

This year we submitted one run for the Spanish monolingual task. We got an overall result of 32.5%, with 28.81% for factoid questions, 46% por definition and 25% for the temporally restricted, being the seventh best run and achieving the second best performance on factoid questions [2]. These results are very similar to the ones obtained in last year competition [4].

The main goal this year was the design of the XML framework for future developments and the inclusion of a new question classification module based on machine learning. In this sense results are encouraging as there seems to be no lost of performance due to the new module, having the additional benefit of being easily adaptable to new languages for multilingual purpose.

Concerning to the question classification process, almost 77% of the factoid questions were correctly classified (up to 82.5% if we also consider DEFINITION questions), quite promising for a system trained on surface text features.

5 Future Work

In this paper we have described the novelties introduced in our Question Answering system for QA@CLEF 2005 competition. Mainly, a new XML framework has been introduced laying the foundations for future developments. In this framework we can easily introduce new modules and substitute old ones for testing purpose. This year we have introduced a new question classification module that can be trained with different languages, proving to be as competitive as other state-of-the-art systems.

This year's competition reflects the tendency of the systems to use complex linguistic resources and tools, like deep parsing. Our approach deviates from this tendency employing machine learning and statistical information in order to get an easily adaptable system. Therefore, the main goal is to continue the gradual development and integration of new multilingual modules in order to have a system that can deal with many different languages at the same time. To sum up, this can be considered the first step of a full multilingual framework for QA.

Acknowledgements

This work has been developed in the framework of the project CICYT R2D2 (TIC2003-07158-C04) and it has been partially funded by the Spanish Government through the grant BES-2004-3935.

References

1. Tomás, D., Bisbal, E., Vicedo, J.L., Moreno, L. and Suárez, A.: Una aproximación multilingüe a la clasificación de preguntas basada en aprendizaje automático. Procesamiento del Lenguaje Natural, nº 35, pp.391-400, SEPLN, 2005.
2. Vallin, A. et al.: Overview of the CLEF 2005 Multilingual Question Answering Track. In C. Peters (Ed.), Results of the CLEF 2005 Cross-Language System Evaluation Campaign, Vienna, Austria, 2005. Working Notes for the CLEF 2005 Workshop.
3. Vicedo, J.L., Izquierdo, R., Llopis, F. and Muñoz, R.: Question answering in Spanish. In: CLEF, editor, Proceedings CLEF-2003 Lecture Notes in Computer Science, Tronheim, Norwey, August 2003.
4. Vicedo, J.L., Saiz, M. and Izquierdo, R.: Does English help Question Answering in Spanish? In: CLEF, editor, Proceedings CLEF-2004 Lecture Notes in Computer Science, Bath, UK, September 2004.

A Logic Programming Based Approach to QA@CLEF05 Track

Paulo Quaresma and Irene Rodrigues

Departamento de Informática, Universidade de Évora, Portugal
{pq, ipr}@di.uevora.pt

Abstract. In this paper the methodology followed to build a question-answering system for the Portuguese language is described. The system modules are built using computational linguistic tools such as: a Portuguese parser based on constraint grammars for the syntactic analysis of the documents sentences and the user questions; a semantic interpreter that rewrites sentences syntactic analysis into discourse representation structures in order to obtain the corpus documents and user questions semantic representation; and finally, a semantic/pragmatic interpreter in order to obtain a knowledge base with facts extracted from the documents using ontologies (general and domain specific) and logic inference. This article includes the system evaluation under the CLEF'05 question and answering track.

1 Introduction

This paper describes some aspects of a dialogue system that has been developed at the Informatics Department of the University of Évora, Portugal. Namely, the system's ability of answering Portuguese questions supported by the information conveyed by collection of documents.

First, the system processes the documents in order to extract the information conveyed by the documents sentences. This task is done by the *information extraction* module.

Then, using the knowledge base built by the first module, the system is able to answer the user queries. This is done by the *query processing* module.

We use models from the computational linguistic theories for the analysis of the sentences from the document collection and queries. The analysis of the sentence includes the following processes: syntactical analysis uses the Portuguese parser *Palavras* [1] using the constraint grammars framework [2] ; semantical analysis interpreter uses discourse representation theory [3] in order to rewrite sentences parser into a Discourse Representation Structure (DRS); and, finally, semantic/pragmatic interpretation uses ontologies and logical inference in the extraction and retrieval modules.

For the documents collection (Publico and Folha de S. Paulo) used in CLEF05 we obtained over 10 million discourse entities that we had to keep in a Database. In order to integrate the logical inference and the external databases we use ISCO[4,5], a language that extends logic programming.

C. Peters et al. (Eds.): CLEF 2005, LNCS 4022, pp. 351–360, 2006.

The QA system, in order to satisfy CLEF requirements, has to answer queries in Portuguese, supported on information conveyed by a given collection of documents. The answer to a specific question is: a set of words and the identification of the document that contained the answer.

For instance, for the following question: "Who was Emiliano Zapata?"

Our system answers:

"Mexican revolutionary 1877-1919 - document: PUBLICO-19940103-32"

At the moment, the system is able to answer:

— Definition questions

"Quem é Joe Striani? – FSP940126-160 norte-americano guitarrista"

— Temporally restricted factoid questions

"Onde é que caiu um meteorito em 1908 – PUBLICO-19951103-46 sibéria"

— Factoid questions

"Onde é a sede da OMC – PUBLICO-19940506-28 genebra"

This system is an evolution of a previous system evaluated at CLEF 2004 [6]. Some of the existing problems were solved, namely, the need to use a pre-processing information retrieval engine to decrease the complexity of the problem. In this CLEF edition, we were able to solve this major scalability problem via the use of ISCO and its power to connect PROLOG and relational databases.

However, the pre-processing of the collection of documents took more time than we expected and we were not able to answer all the questions to the Folha de S. Paulo newspaper. As we will point out in the evaluation section this was our major problem and it is the reason why our results didn't improve from CLEF04 to CLEF05.

In section 2 the architecture of the system is described. In the following sections 3 and 4 the syntactical analysis and the semantical interpretation modules are detailed. The knowledge representation approach is presented in section 5. Section 6 describes the semantic-pragmatic interpretation of the documents. Section 7 presents the module for query processing and answer generation. In section 8 the evaluation results are presented. Finally, in section 9 some conclusions and future work are discussed.

2 System Architecture

The QA system has two operating modes:

Information extraction: the documents in the collection are processed and as a result a knowledge base is created. The phases of information extraction include (figure 1 present this module processes):

- Syntactical analysis: sentences are processed with the Palavras[1] parser. The result of this process is a new collection of documents with the parsing result of each sentence.
- Semantic analysis: the new collection of sentences is rewritten [3] creating a collection documents with the documents semantic representation, where each document has a DRS (structure for the discourse representation), a list of discourse referents and a set of conditions.

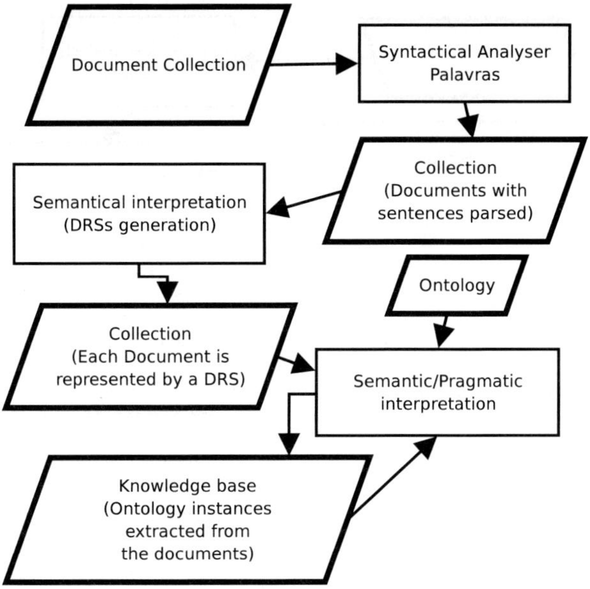

Fig. 1. Document Processing

- Semantic and pragmatic interpretation: the previous collection of documents is processed, using the ontology and, as a result, a knowledge base is built. This knowledge base contains instances of the ontology.

Query processing: this module processes the query and generates the answer, i.e. a set of words and the identification of the document where the answer was found. Figure 2 presents this module diagram. It is composed by the following phases:

- Syntactical analysis: using the parser Palavras[1].
- Semantic analysis: from the parser output, a discourse structure is built, a DRS[3] with the correspondent referents.
- Semantic/Pragmatic interpretation: in this phase some conditions are rewritten taking into account the ontology and generating a new DRS.
- Query Processing: the final query representation is interpreted in the knowledge base through the unification of the discourse entities of the query with documents discourse entities (see section 7).

These processes are described in more detail in the next sections.

3 Syntactical Analysis

Syntactical analysis is done using the PALAVRAS parser from Eckhard Bick[1], This parser gives good morpho-syntactical information and it has a good coverage of the Portuguese language.

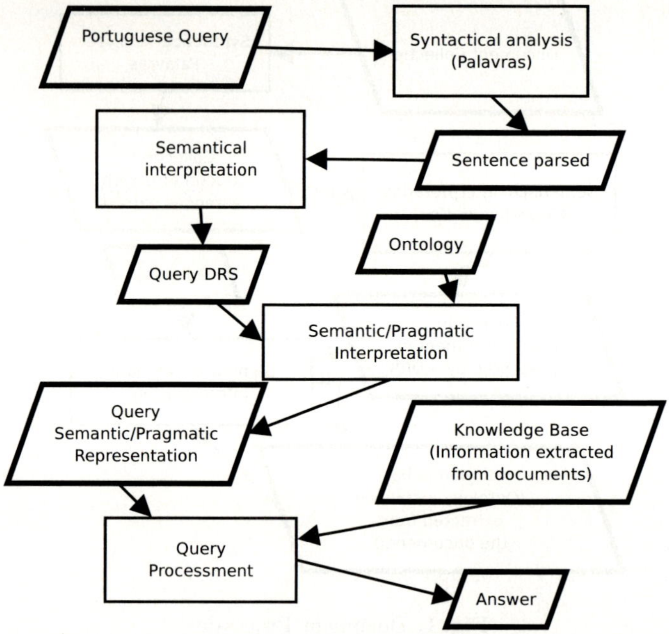

Fig. 2. Query Processing

Below we present an example of the output of Palavras for sentence (3.1):

> Um patologista defendeu que Jimi Hendrix morreu de asfixia após ter ingerido álcool e uma dose excessiva de barbitúricos. (3.1)
> "A pathologist argued that Jimi Hendrix died of asphyxia after drinking alcoholic beverages and an excessive dose of barbiturics".

The syntactical structure of this sentence is the following:

```
sta(fcl, subj(np, n(art('um', 'M', 'S', <arti> ), 'Um'),
          h(n('patologista','M', 'S', <Hprof> ),'patologista')),
      p(v_fin('defender', 'PS', '3S', 'IND'),'defendeu'),
      acc(fcl, sub( conj_s('que'), 'que')),
      subj(prop('Jimi_Hendrix', 'M/F', 'S'), 'Jimi_Hendrix'),
      p(v_fin('morrer', 'PS', '3S', 'IND'), 'morreu'),
      piv(pp, h(prp('dc'),'do'),
          p(np,h(n('asfixia','F','S', <sick> ), 'asfixia'),
            n(pp, h(prp('após'), 'após'),
                    p(icl,p(vp, aux(v_inf('ter'),'ter'),
                          mv(v_pcp('ingerir'), 'ingerido')),
                    acc(n(´álcool','M','S',<cm-liq>), ´álcool'),
                    co(conj_c('e'), 'e'),
                    acc(np, n(art('um', 'F','S',<arti>), 'uma'),
                        h(n('dose','F','S'), 'dose'),
```

```
n(adj('excessivo','F','S'), 'excessiva'),
n(pp, h(prp('de'),'de'),
  p(n('barbitúrico',
      'M','P'),'barbitúricos','.')))))))).
```

This structure is represented in Prolog and is used as the input of the semantic analyzer.

4 Semantic Analysis

The semantic analysis rewrites the syntactical structure in to a discourse representation structure [3], DRS. At present, we only deal with sentences as if they were factual, i.e., sentences with existential quantification over the discourse entities. So, our discourse structures are sets of referents, existentially quantified variables, and sets of conditions, predicates linked by the conjunction *and*.

The semantic interpreter rewrites each syntactic tree into a set of discourse referents and a set of conditions integrated in the document DRS. In order to delay the commitment with an interpretation (the attachment) of prepositional phrases, we use the relation *rel* with 3 arguments, the preposition and two discourse entities, to represent the prepositional phrases.

The semantic/pragmatic interpretation of the predicate *rel* will be responsible to infer the adequate connection between the referents. For instance, the sentence 'A viuva do homem'/ 'The widow of the men', is represented by the following DRS:

```
drs(entities:[A:(def,fem,sing),B:(def,male,sing)],
    conditions:[widow(A), men(B), rel(of,A,B)])
```

As it can be seen in the next section, this representation allows the semantic/pragmatic interpretation to rewrite the DRS, obtaining the following structure:

```
drs(entities:[ A:(def, fem, sing), B:(def, male, sing)],
    conditions:[married(A,B), person(A), person(B), dead(B)])
```

In order to show an example of a syntactical tree transformation into a DRS, we show sentence (3.1) rewritten :

```
drs(entities:[A:(indef,male,sing),B:(def,male/fem,sing),
              C:(def,fem,sing),D:(def,male,sing),
              E:(indef,fem,sing)],
    condições:[pathologist(A),argue(A,B),name(B,'Jimmy Hendrix'),
               died(B),rel(of,B,C),asphyxia(C),rel(after,C,D),
               drinking(D), alcohol(D), dose(D), excessive(D),
               rel(of,D,E), barbiturics(E)])
```

User queries are also interpreted and rewritten into DRS. For instance, the question:

"Como morreu Jimi Hendrix?/How did Jimi Hendrix died?" (4.1)

is transformed into the following discourse structure:

```
drs(entities:[F:(def,male/fem,sing),G:interrog(que),male,sing]
    conditions:[died(F), name(F,'Jimmy Hendrix'), rel(of,F,G)])
```

This representation is obtained because "Como/How" is interpreted as "de que/of what". In the semantic-pragmatic interpretation and in the query processing phase, the structure (4.1) might unify with sentence (3.1) and we may obtain the following answer: "Jimi Hendrix died of asphyxia".

5 Ontology and Knowledge Representation

In order to represent the ontology and the extracted ontology instances (individuals and relations between those individuals), we use an extension to logic programming, ISCO[4,5], which allows Prolog to access databases. This technology is fundamental to our system because we have a very large database of referents: more than 10 millions only for the Público newspaper. Databases are defined in ISCO from ontologies.

The QA system uses two ontologies defined with different purposes:

– an ontology aiming to model common knowledge, such as, geographic information (mainly places), and dates; it defines places (cities, countries, ...) and relations between places.

– an ontology generated automatically from the document collection [7,8]; this ontology, although being very simple, allows the representation of the documents domain knowledge.

The ontology can be defined directly in ISCO or in OWL (Ontology Web Language) and transformed in ISCO [8].

The knowledge extraction process identifies ontology instances, individuals and relations between individuals, and they are inserted as rows in the adequate database table.

Consider sentence (3.1), with semantic representation in page 355, the information extracted from this sentence would generate several tuples in the database. The information extraction process includes a step where first order logical expressions are *skolemized*, i.e., each variable existentially quantified is replaced by a different identifier:

`(123,''Jimmy Hendrix'')` is added to table *name*
`(123)` is added to table *die*
`(124)` is added to table *asphyxia*
`rel(de,123,124)` is added to table *rel*

In the information extraction process, our system uses the first interpretation of each sentence, without taking into account other possible interpretations of the sentence. This is done to prevent the explosion of the number of interpretation to consider for each document sentence. This way we may miss some sentences correct interpretation but the QA system performance does not seem to decrease because the document collection content is redundant (many sentences convey the same meaning).

In order to enable the identification of the document sentence that gives rise to a knowledge base fact, we add information in the database linking referents with the documents and sentences were they appeared. For instance the tuple `(123,'publico/publico95/950605/005',4)` is added to table *referred_in*.

6 Semantic/Pragmatic Interpretation

Semantic/pragmatic interpretation process is guided by the search of the best explanation that supports a sentence logical form in a knowledge base built with the ontology description, in ISCO, and with the ontology instances. This strategy for pragmatic interpretation was initially proposed by [9].

This process uses as input a discourse representation structure, DRS, and it interprets it using rules obtained from the knowledge ontology and the information in the database.

The inference in the knowledge base for the semantic/pragmatic interpretation uses abduction and finite domain constraint solvers.

Consider the following sentence:

"X. é a viuva de Y." ("X. is the widow of Y.".)

which, by the semantic analysis, is transformed into the following structure: one DRS, three discourse referents, and a set of conditions:

```
drs(entities:[A:(def,fem,sing),B:(def,fem,sing),C:(def,male,sing)]
    conditions:[name(A, 'X.'), widow(B), rel(of,B,C), is(A,B)])
```

The semantic/pragmatic interpretation process, using information from the ontology, will rewrite the DRS into the following one:

```
drs(entities:[A:(def,fem,sing), C:(def,male,sing)]
    conditions:[person(A,'X.',alive,widow),
                person(C,'Y.',dead,married),married(A,C)])
```

The semantic/pragmatic interpretation as the rules:

```
widow(A):- abduct( person(A,_,alive,widow)).
rel(of,A,B):- person(A,_,_,widow),
              abduct(married(A,B),person(B,_,dead,married)).
```

The interpretation of *rel(of,A,B)* as

married(A,B),person(B,Name,dead,married) is possible because the ontology has a class *person*, which relates persons with their name, their civil state (single, married, divorced, or widow) and with their alive state (dead or alive).

7 Answer Generation

The generation of the answer is done in two steps:

1. Identification of the database referent that unifies with the referent of the interrogative pronoun in the question.
2. Retrieval of the referent properties and generation of the answer.

As an example, consider the following question:
"Quem é a viuva de X.?" ("Who is the widow of X?")
This question is represent by the following DRS, after syntactical and semantical analysis:

```
drs(entities:[A:(who,male/fem,sing), B:(def,fem,sing),
              C:(def,male,sing)],
    conditions:[is(A,B), widow(B), rel(of,B,C), name(C,'X')])
```

The semantic/pragmatic interpretation of this question is done using the ontology of concepts and it allows to obtain the following DRS:

```
drs(entities:[A:(who,fem,sing), C:(def,male,sing),
    conditions:[person(A,_,alive,widow),
                person(C,'X',dead,married), married(A,C)])
```

The first step of the answer generator is:
To keep the referent variables of the question and to try to prove the conditions of the DRS in the knowledge base. If the conditions can be satisfied in the knowledge base, the discourse referents are unified with the identifiers (skolem constants) of the individuals.
The next step is to retrieve the words that constitute the answer:
In this phase we should retrieve the conditions about the identified referent *A* and choose which ones better characterize the entity. Our first option is to choose a condition with an argument *name* (*name(A,Name)* or as in the example *person(_,Name,_,_)*.
However, it is not always so simple to find the adequate answer to a question. See, for instance, the following questions:
What crimes committed X?
How many habitants has Kalininegrado?
What is the nationality of Miss Universe?
Who is Flavio Briatore?
In order to choose the best answer to a question our systems has an algorithm which takes into account the syntactical category of the words that may appear in the answer and it tries to avoid answers with words that appear in the question. Questions about places or dates have a special treatment involving the access to a database of places or dates.
Note that several answers may exist for a specific question. In CLEF05 we decided to calculate all possible answers and to choose the most frequent one.

8 Evaluation

The evaluation of our system was performed in the context of CLEF – Cross Language Evaluation Forum – 2005. In this forum a set (200) of questions is elaborated by a jury and given to the system. The system's answers are, then, evaluated by the same jury.

Our system had the following results:

25% correct answers (50 answers).

1.5% correct but unsupported answers (3 answers).

11% inexact answers – too many (or too few) words (22 answers).

62.5% wrong answers (125 answers).

The answer-string "NIL" was returned 117 times.

The answer-string "NIL" was correctly returned 12 times.

The answer-strings "NIL" in the reference are 18

The system had 125 wrong answers, but it is important to point out that 105 of these wrong answers were NIL answers, i.e., situations were the system was not able to find any answer to the questions. So, only in 10% of the situations (20 answers) our system gave a really wrong answer.

The major problem with the remaining 105 no-answers is the fact that, due to time constraints we were not able to process the collection of documents from the Folha de S. Paulo newspaper. At present, we do not know how many of these no-answers would be answered by this collection, but we expect our results to improve significantly.

A preliminary analysis of the other incorrect answers showed that the main cause of problems in our system is related with lack of knowledge: wrong syntactical analysis; lack of synonyms; and, mostly, an incomplete ontology. In fact, most problems are related with incorrect pragmatic analysis due to an incomplete ontology.

However, and taking into account that our answers were computed using only one collection of documents (the Público newspaper), and comparing with the CLEF2004 results, we believe our system produced good and promising results. In fact, it showed to have a quite good precision on the non NIL answers: only 10% of these answers were wrong.

9 Conclusions and Future Work

We propose a system for answering questions supported by the knowledge conveyed by a collection of document. The system architecture uses two separate modules: one for knowledge extraction and another one for question answering.

Our system modules uses natural language processing techniques, supported by well known linguistic theories, to analyze the documents and query sentences in every processing phases: syntactic, semantic and pragmatic analysis.

The process of knowledge extraction is defined using logic a programming framework, ISCO, that integrates: representation and inference with ontologies, and the access to external databases to add and retrieve ontology instances. The process of query answering is defined in the same logic programming framework.

The system main source of problems are:

First, poor coverage of the defined ontology: the lack of knowledge in the ontology prevents us of relating query conditions with the document sentences conditions; this explains why system gets 117 NIL answers when it only should get 12.

Next, errors in NLP tools. The PALAVRAS has some troubles in parsing some document and query sentences. The errors in the parsing of a query is more problematic than the problems in the analysis of the document sentences. We hope in the near future to solve the problems in parsing the user queries. The semantic interpretation module, developed by us, also has some problems in rewriting some parser trees. These problems also appear in the processing of the user queries.

As future work, we intend to improve our ontology and our linguistic resources, namely the use of a general domain thesaurus. The improvement of some NLP tools is another area needing much work.

References

1. Bick, E.: The Parsing System "Palavras". Automatic Grammatical Analysis of Portuguese in a Constraint Grammar Framework. Aarhus University Press (2000)
2. Karlsson, F.: Constraint grammar as a framework for parsing running text. In Karlgren, H., ed.: Papers presented to the 13th International Conference on Computational Linguistics. Volume 1753., Helsinki, Finland, Springer-Verlag (1990) 168–173
3. Kamp, H., Reyle, U.: From Discourse to Logic:An Introduction to Modeltheoretic Semantics of Natural Language, Formal Logic and Discourse Representation Theory. Dordrecht: D. Reidel (1993)
4. Abreu, S.: Isco: A practical language for heterogeneous information system construction. In: Proceedings of INAP'01, Tokyo, Japan, INAP (2001)
5. Abreu, S., Quaresma, P., Quintano, L., Rodrigues, I.: A dialogue manager for accessing databases. In: 13th European-Japanese Conference on Information Modelling and Knowledge Bases, Kitakyushu, Japan, Kyushu Institute of Technology (2003) 213–224 To be published by IOS Press.
6. Quaresma, P., Rodrigues, I.: Using dialogues to access semantic knowledge in a web legal IR system. In Moens, M.F., ed.: Procs. of the Workshop on Question Answering for Interrogating Legal Documents of JURIX'03 – The 16th Annual Conference on Legal Knowledge and Information Systems, Utrecht, Netherlands, Utrecht University (2003)
7. Saias, J., Quaresma, P.: Using nlp techniques to create legal ontologies in a logic programming based web information retrieval system. In: Workshop on Legal Ontologies and Web based legal information management of the 9th International Conference on Artificial Intelligence and Law, Edinburgh, Scotland (2003)
8. Saias, J.: Uma metodologia para a construção automática de ontologias e a sua aplicação em sistemas de recuperação de informação – a methodology for the automatic creation of ontologies and its application in information retrieval systems. Master's thesis, University of Évora, Portugal (2003) In Portuguese.
9. Hobbs, J., Stickel, M., Appelt, D., Martin, P.: Interpretation as abduction. Technical Report SRI Technical Note 499, 333 Ravenswood Ave., Menlo Park, CA 94025 (1990)

Extending Knowledge and Deepening Linguistic Processing for the Question Answering System InSicht

Sven Hartrumpf

Intelligent Information and Communication Systems (IICS)
University of Hagen (FernUniversität in Hagen)
58084 Hagen, Germany
Sven.Hartrumpf@fernuni-hagen.de

Abstract. The German question answering (QA) system InSicht participated in QA@CLEF for the second time. It relies on complete sentence parsing, inferences, and semantic representation matching. This year, the system was improved in two main directions. First, the background knowledge was extended by large semantic networks and large rule sets. Second, linguistic processing was deepened by treating a phenomenon that appears prominently on the level of text semantics: coreference resolution. A new source of lexico-semantic relations and equivalence rules has been established based on compound analyses from document parses. These analyses were used in three ways: to project lexico-semantic relations from compound parts to compounds, to establish a subordination hierarchy for compounds, and to derive equivalence rules between nominal compounds and their analytic counterparts. The lack of coreference resolution in InSicht was one major source of missing answers in QA@CLEF 2004. Therefore the coreference resolution module CORUDIS was integrated into the parsing during document processing. The central step in the QA system InSicht, matching semantic networks derived from the question parse (one by one) with document sentence networks, was generalized. Now, a question network can be split at certain semantic relations (e.g. relations for local or temporal specifications). To evaluate the different extensions, the QA system was run on all 400 German questions from QA@CLEF 2004 and 2005 with varying setups. Some extensions showed positive effects, but currently they are minor and not statistically significant. The paper ends with a discussion why improvements are not larger, yet.

1 Introduction

The German question answering (QA) system InSicht participated in QA@CLEF for the second time. This year, the system was improved in two main directions. First, the background knowledge was extended by large semantic networks and rule sets. InSicht's query expansion step produces more alternative representations using these resources; this is expected to increase recall. A second direction

C. Peters et al. (Eds.): CLEF 2005, LNCS 4022, pp. 361–369, 2006.

for improvement was to deepen linguistic processing by treating a phenomenon that appears prominently on the level of text semantics: coreference resolution.

The paper starts with a summary of the basic InSicht system (Sect. 2). Then, the most important improvements since QA@CLEF 2004 are described (Sect. 3). The resulting system is evaluated on the 400 German questions from QA@CLEF 2004 and 2005 (Sect. 4). The contribution of different modifications is investigated by running the system with different setups. Some conclusions appear in the final Sect. 5.

2 Overview of InSicht

The semantic QA system InSicht ([1]) relies on complete sentence parsing, inferences, and semantic representation matching. It comprises six main steps.

In the *document processing* step, all documents from a given collection are preprocessed by transforming them into a standard XML format (CES, corpus encoding standard, http://www.cs.vassar.edu/CES/) with word, sentence, and paragraph borders marked up by XML elements. Then, all preprocessed documents are parsed by the WOCADI parser ([2]), yielding a syntactic dependency structure and a semantic network representation of the MultiNet formalism ([3]) for each sentence.

In the second step (*query processing*), WOCADI parses the user's question. Determining the sentence type (here, often a subtype of *question*) is especially important because it controls some parts of two later steps: query expansion and answer generation. The system does not deal with (expected) answer types or similar concepts; every semantic network for a document sentence that matches a semantic network for the question and can be reformulated by InSicht as a natural language expression leads to a candidate answer.

Next comes *query expansion*: Equivalent and similar semantic networks are derived by means of lexico-semantic relations from a computer lexicon (HaGenLex, see [4]) and a lexical database (GermaNet), equivalence rules, and inference rules like entailments for situations (applied in backward chaining). The result is a set of disjunctively connected semantic networks that try to cover many different sentence representations that (explicitly or implicitly) contain an answer to the user's question.

In the fourth step (*semantic network matching*), all document sentences matching a semantic network from query expansion are collected. A two-level approach is chosen for efficiency reasons. First, an index of concepts (disambiguated words with IDs from HaGenLex) is consulted with the relevant concepts from the query networks. Second, the retrieved documents are compared sentence network by sentence network to find a match with a query network.

Answer generation is next: natural language generation rules are applied to matching semantic networks and try to generate a natural language answer from the deep semantic representations. The sentence type and the semantic network control the selection of answer rules. The rules also act as a filter for uninformative or bad answers. The results are tuples of generated answer string, answer score, supporting document ID, and supporting sentence ID.

To deal with typically many candidate answers resulting from answer generation, an *answer selection* step is required at the end. It implements a strategy that combines a preference for more frequent answers and a preference for more elaborate answers. The best answers (by default only the best answer) and the supporting sentences (and/or the IDs of supporting sentences or documents) are presented to the questioner.

3 Improvements over the System for QA@CLEF 2004

InSicht has been improved in several areas since QA@CLEF 2004. The most notable changes affect document processing, query expansion, coreferences, and semantic network matching.

3.1 Document Processing

The coverage of the WOCADI parser has been increased so that for 51.4% of all QA corpus sentences a full semantic network is produced (compared with 48.7% for QA@CLEF 2004, see [1]). This was achieved by extending the lexicon HaGenLex and by refining the parser. The concept index (a mapping from concept IDs to document IDs), which is used by the matcher for reducing run time, provides more efficient creation and lookup operations than last year because the external binary tree was replaced by the freely available system *qdbm* (Quick Database Manager, http://qdbm.sourceforge.net/).

3.2 More Query Expansions

A new source of lexico-semantic relations and equivalence rules has been established: compound analyses. WOCADI's compound analysis module determines structure and semantics of compounds when parsing a text corpus. The 470,000 compound analyses from parsing the German QA@CLEF corpus and the GIRT corpus were collected. Only determinative compounds (where the right compound part (base noun) is a hypernym of the compound) were considered.

In the first use of compound analyses, lexico-semantic relations are projected from compound parts to compounds. Given a compound, synonyms and hyponyms[1] of each compound part are collected by following corresponding relations in the lexicon. Then, each element from the Cartesian product of these alternatives is looked up in the compound analyses mentioned above. If it exists with a given minimal frequency (currently: 1), a relation is inferred based upon the relations between corresponding parts. In case of a contradiction (e.g. the first parts are in a hyponymy relation while the second parts are in a hypernymy relation), no relation is inferred. This algorithm delivered 16,526 relations: 5,688

[1] Hypernyms can be ignored because hypernymy is the inverse relation of hyponymy and all inferable relations will also be produced when treating the compound analyses containing the corresponding hypernym.

(sub "riesenpython.1.1" "riesenschlange.1.1")
  'giant python' 'giant snake'
(sub "rollhockeynationalmannschaft.1.1" "hockeymannschaft.1.1")
  'roller hockey national team' 'hockey team'
(subs "weizenexport.1.1" "getreideexport.1.1")
  'wheat export' 'crop export'
(syno "metrosuizid.1.1" "u-bahnselbstmord.1.1")
  'metro suicide' 'underground train self-murder'
(syno "rehabilitationskrankenhaus.1.1" "rehaklinik .1.1")
  'rehabilitation hospital' 'rehab hospital (clinic)'
(syno "wirtschaftmodell.1.3" "ökonomiemodell.1.3")
  '(economy) model' 'economy model'

Fig. 1. Examples of inferred lexico-semantic relations for compounds

subordination edges[2] and 10,838 synonymy edges. All of them are lexico-semantic relations between compounds. Some examples are shown in Fig. 1.

A more direct use of compound analyses is the extraction of subordination edges representing a hyponymy relation between a compound and its base noun (or adjective). This process led to 387,326 new edges.

A third use of automatic compound analyses is the production of equivalence rules for complement-filling compounds. One can generate for such compounds an equivalence to an analytic form, e.g. between *Reisimport* ('*rice import*') and *Import von Reis* ('*import of rice*').[3] Currently, only compounds where the base noun has exactly one complement in the lexicon that can (semantically) be realized by the determining noun are treated in this way, so that for 360,000 analyzed nominal compounds in the QA corpus around 13,000 rules were generated. Three simplified MultiNet rules are shown in Fig. 2. Variables are preceded by a question mark. The attribute *pre* contains preconditions for variables occurring on both sides of an equivalence rule. The MultiNet relation PREDS corresponds to SUBS and instantiates (or subordinates) not just a single concept but a set of concepts. The relations AFF (affected object) and RSLT (result of a situation) stem from the HaGenLex characterization of the direct object of the base nouns *Konsum* ('*consumption*'), *Sanierung* ('*sanitation*'), and *Erzeugung* ('*production*'). Such an equivalence rule fired only for question qa05_023 (*Welcher frühere Fußballspieler wurde wegen Drogenkonsum verurteilt?*, '*Which former soccer player was convicted of taking drugs?*') because most questions from QA@CLEF 2004 and 2005 are not related to such compounds.

Another set of rules available to this year's InSicht stems from parsing verb glosses from GermaNet (a German WordNet variant) and further automatic formalization (see [5] for details). Each rule relates one verb reading with one or

[2] MultiNet uses a SUB, SUBR, or SUBS edge for a nominal compound depending upon the noun's ontological sort.

[3] By way of a lexical change relation, the representations of both formulations are linked to the representation of a formulation with a verb: *Reis importieren* ('*to import rice*').

```
((pre ((member ?r1 (preds subs))))
  (rule ((?r1 ?n1 "drogenkonsum.1.1") ; 'drug consumption'
    ↔
    (?r1 ?n1 "konsum.1.1")
    (aff ?n1 ?n2)
    (sub ?n2 "droge.1.1")))
  (name "compound_analysis.sg.drogenkonsum.1.1"))
((pre ((member ?r1 (preds subs))))
  (rule ((?r1 ?n1 "gebäudesanierung.1.1") ; 'building sanitation'
    ↔
    (?r1 ?n1 "sanierung.1.1")
    (aff ?n1 ?n2)
    (sub ?n2 "gebäude.1.1")))
  (name "compound_analysis.sg.gebäudesanierung.1.1"))
((pre ((member ?r1 (preds subs))))
  (rule ((?r1 ?n1 "holzerzeugung.1.1") ; 'wood production'
    ↔
    (?r1 ?n1 "erzeugung.1.1")
    (rslt ?n1 ?n2)
    (sub ?n2 "holz.1.1")))
  (name "compound_analysis.sg.holzerzeugung.1.1"))
```

Fig. 2. Three automatically generated rules for compounds involving a complement of the base noun

more other verb readings. None of these rules fired during query expansion of QA@CLEF questions. This was not too much of a surprise because the rule set is quite small (around 200 rules). Nevertheless, this path seems promising as soon as more German glosses become available (e.g. from GermaNet or Wikipedia).

If the parser delivers several alternative results for a question, all alternatives are used in the query expansion step. For example, question qa04_018 (*Nenne eine französische Zeitung.*, '*Name a French newspaper.*') contains the ambiguous noun *Zeitung* which has two readings: an institutional reading (*The newspaper hired new reporters.*) and an information container reading (*I put the newspaper on the table.*). Due to the limited context of the question, both readings lead to semantic networks with equal scores. Both alternatives are passed to the remaining steps of InSicht, so that both readings can be matched in documents. It would be detrimental to restrict query parsing to one reading if the documents contained only answers with the other reading. The inclusion of query parse alternatives led to some additional answers.

3.3 Coreference Resolution for Documents

Looking at last year's questions that turned out to be hard to answer for most systems (see [1] for error classes and frequencies) and looking at some other test questions, the lack of coreference resolution was identified as one major source of errors. (This lack caused 6% of InSicht's wrong empty answers for questions from QA@CLEF 2004.) Therefore the coreference resolution module CORUDIS

(COreference RUles with DIsambiguation Statistics, [2,6]) was integrated into the parsing during document processing. If a coreference partition of mentions (or markables) from a document is found the simplified and normalized document networks are extended by networks where mentions are replaced by mentions from the corresponding coreference chain in that partition. For example, if document network d contains mention m_i and m_i is in a nontrivial (i.e. $n > 1$) coreference chain $\langle m_1, \ldots, m_i, \ldots, m_n \rangle$ the following networks are added to the document representation:

$$d_{m_i|m_1}, \ldots, d_{m_i|m_{i-1}}, d_{m_i|m_{i+1}}, \ldots, d_{m_i|m_n}$$

The notation $d_{m_1|m_2}$ denotes the semantic network d with the semantics of mention m_1 substituted by the semantics of mention m_2. Some mention substitutions are avoided if no performance improvement is possible or likely (e.g. if the semantic representations of m_1 and m_2 are identical), but there is still room for beneficial refinements.

The usefulness of coreference resolution for QA is exemplified by question qa05_098 (*Welcher Vertrag läuft von 1995 bis 2004?*, '*Which treaty runs from 1995 till 2004?*'). InSicht can answer it only with coreference resolution. Document FR940703-000358 contains the answer distributed over two neighboring sentences, as shown in example (1):

(1) *Bundesbauministerin Irmgard Schwaetzer (FDP) und der*
Federal building minister Irmgard Schwaetzer (FDP) and the
Regierende Bürgermeister Eberhard Diepgen (CDU) haben am
governing mayor Eberhard Diepgen (CDU) have on-the
Donnerstag [einen weiteren Vertrag über den Ausbau Berlins zum
Thursday a further treaty about the extension Berlin's to-the
Regierungssitz]$_i$ unterzeichnet. [Der von 1995 bis 2004 laufende
government-seat signed. The from 1995 till 2004 running
Vertrag]$_i$ hat ein Volumen von 1,3 Milliarden Mark.
treaty has a volume of 1.3 billions mark.
'*Federal building minister Irmgard Schwaetzer (FDP) and the governing mayor Eberhard Diepgen (CDU) signed [another treaty about Berlin's extension to the seat of government]$_i$ on Thursday. [The treaty, which runs from 1995 till 2004,]$_i$ has a volume of 1.3 billion marks.*'

Only if the coreference between the coindexed constituents is established, the answer can be exactly found by a deep approach to QA.

The CORUDIS module is not yet efficient enough (which is not surprising because finding the best coreference partition of mentions is NP-hard) so that the search had to be limited by parameter settings in order to reduce run time. On the down side, this caused that only for 40% of all texts a partition of mentions was found. Therefore the improvements achievable by coreference resolution can be increased by making CORUDIS more robust.

Coreference resolution has been rarely described for natural language processing (NLP) applications. For example, [7] presented and extrinsically evaluated several coreference resolution modules but the application restricts coreferences to mentions that could be relevant for the given information extraction task. In contrast, WOCADI's coreference resolution module treats all mentions that meet the MUC definition of a markable ([8]).

3.4 More Flexible Matching by Splitting Question Networks

Last year's InSicht matched semantic networks derived from a question parse with document sentence networks one by one. A more flexible approach turned out to be beneficial for IR and geographic IR (see [9]); so it was tested in InSicht's QA mode, too. The flexibility comes from the fact that a question network is split if certain graph topologies exist: a network is split in two networks at CIRC, CTXT (nonrestrictive and restrictive context, respectively), LOC (location of objects or situations), and TEMP (temporal specification) edges. The resulting parts are conjunctively connected. For example, no single document sentence contains an answer to question qa05_168: *Was ist Belgiens zweitgrößte Stadt?* ('*What is Belgium's second largest city?*'), but a sentence of document FR941016-000033 talks about *der zweitgrößten Stadt Antwerpen* ('*the second largest city Antwerp*') and the cotext provides the local comparison frame *Belgien* ('*Belgium*'). Splitting question networks can lead to wrong non-NIL answers, but for the questions from QA@CLEF 2004 and 2005 it resulted only in more right answers.

4 Evaluation

The current InSicht QA system has been evaluated on the QA@CLEF questions from the monolingual German task of the years 2004 and 2005. To investigate the impact of different improvements described in Sect. 3 the setup was varied in different ways, as can be seen in the second and third column of Table 1. The evaluation metrics reported are the number of right, inexact, and wrong non-NIL answers and the K1-measure (see [10] for a definition).

For better comparison, the results for InSicht's official run at QA@CLEF 2004 are shown, too. The K1-measure was much lower than this year because the confidence score of last year's system was tuned for confidence-weighted score (CWS). Now, InSicht tries to optimize the K1-measure because the K1-measure seems to be a more adequate metric for evaluating QA systems ([10]). This optimization was successful: InSicht achieved the highest K1-measure and the highest correlation coefficient r (of all systems that deliver confidence scores) although some systems returned more right answers than InSicht.

To experiment with cross-language QA, a machine translation of questions was employed. After the machine translation system Systran (as provided on the web) had translated the 200 English questions (from QA@CLEF 2005) into German, they were passed to the standard InSicht system. The number of right answers dropped by around 50%, which was mainly due to incorrect or ungrammatical translations. Some translation problems seemed to be systematic, so that a simple postprocessing component could correct some wrong translations, e.g. the temporal interrogative adverb *when* was translated as *als* instead of *wann*.

Table 1. Results for the German question sets from QA@CLEF 2004 and 2005. *lexsem* stands for lexico-semantics relations projected to compounds and *hypo* for hyponymy relations for compounds (Sect. 3.2). S is the set of relations where query networks can be split (Sect. 3.4). W_{nn} is the number of wrong non-NIL answers; R (X) is the number of right (inexact) answers. All other answers were wrong NIL answers. The number of unsupported answers was always zero.

Question Set	Setup		Results			
	Query Expansion	Matching	R	X	W_{nn}	K1
2004	*the official run for*	*QA@CLEF 2004*	67	7	0	–03271.000.
2004	lexsem	no coreference, $S = \{\text{LOC}\}$	83	6	0	0285.000.
2004	lexsem	coreference, $S = \{\text{LOC}\}$	83	6	0	0285.000.
2005	*the official run for*	*QA@CLEF 2005*	72	9	1	021.000.
2005	lexsem	no coreference, $S = \{\}$	80	7	1	026.000.
2005	lexsem	no coreference, $S = \{\text{LOC}\}$	84	7	1	028.000.
2005	lexsem	coreference, $S = \{\text{LOC}\}$	84	8	0	028.000.
2005	lexsem, hypo	coreference, $S = \{\text{LOC}\}$	86	8	0	029.000.

5 Conclusion

The QA system InSicht was extended by large semantic networks and numerous equivalence rules derived from automatic compound analyses. The linguistic processing was deepened by integrating the coreference resolution module CORUDIS into document processing.

When evaluated on all 400 German questions from QA@CLEF 2004 and 2005, some of these extensions showed positive effects. But the effects are minor and not yet statistically significant. The reasons need further investigation but here are three observations.

First, the differences in the semantic representation of the test set questions and the semantic representation of document sentences are often small and do not require the kind of knowledge that was generated. For more diverse test sets, positive effects may become more obvious.

On the other extreme, there are some questions that need more inference steps than currently produced by query expansion. The matching approach is quite strict (precision-oriented, while for example the QA system described by [11] is recall-oriented) and can require long inference chains in order to find answers. The main hindrance to building such chains are missing pieces of formalized inferential knowledge, like axioms for MultiNet relations and meaning postulates for lexical concepts. Some parts of this knowledge can be automatically generated, see for example Sect. 3.2.

A third explanation regards the quality of some NLP modules. The still limited recall values of the parser (see Sect. 3.1), the coreference resolution module (see Sect. 3.3), and other modules can cause that an inferential link (e.g. a coreference between two nominal phrases) is missing so that a question remains unanswered and a wrong empty answer is produced. Such negative effects are typical for applications building on deep syntactico-semantic NLP. Therefore the robustness of some modules will be increased in order to answer more questions.

References

1. Hartrumpf, S.: Question answering using sentence parsing and semantic network matching. In [12] 512–521
2. Hartrumpf, S.: Hybrid Disambiguation in Natural Language Analysis. Der Andere Verlag, Osnabrück, Germany (2003)
3. Helbig, H.: Knowledge Representation and the Semantics of Natural Language. Springer, Berlin (2006)
4. Hartrumpf, S., Helbig, H., Osswald, R.: The semantically based computer lexicon HaGenLex – Structure and technological environment. Traitement automatique des langues **44**(2) (2003) 81–105
5. Glöckner, I., Hartrumpf, S., Osswald, R.: From GermaNet glosses to formal meaning postulates. In Fisseni, B., Schmitz, H.C., Schröder, B., Wagner, P., eds.: Sprachtechnologie, mobile Kommunikation und linguistische Ressourcen – Beiträge zur GLDV-Tagung 2005 in Bonn. Peter Lang, Frankfurt am Main (2005) 394–407
6. Hartrumpf, S.: Coreference resolution with syntactico-semantic rules and corpus statistics. In: Proceedings of the Fifth Computational Natural Language Learning Workshop (CoNLL-2001), Toulouse, France (2001) 137–144
7. Zelenko, D., Aone, C., Tibbetts, J.: Coreference resolution for information extraction. In Harabagiu, S., Farwell, D., eds.: ACL-2004: Workshop on Reference Resolution and its Applications, Barcelona, Spain, Association for Computational Linguistics (2004) 24–31
8. Hirschman, L., Chinchor, N.: MUC-7 coreference task definition (version 3.0). In: Proceedings of the 7th Message Understanding Conference (MUC-7). (1997)
9. Leveling, J., Hartrumpf, S., Veiel, D.: Using semantic networks for geographic information retrieval. This volume
10. Herrera, J., Peñas, A., Verdejo, F.: Question answering pilot task at CLEF 2004. In [12] 581–590
11. Ahn, D., Jijkoun, V., Müller, K., de Rijke, M., Schlobach, S., Mishne, G.: Making stone soup: Evaluating a recall-oriented multi-stream question answering system for Dutch. In [12] 423–434
12. Peters, C., Clough, P., Gonzalo, J., Jones, G.J.F., Kluck, M., Magnini, B., eds.: Multilingual Information Access for Text, Speech and Images: 5th Workshop of the Cross-Language Evaluation Forum, CLEF 2004. Volume 3491 of LNCS. Springer, Berlin (2005)

Question Answering for Dutch Using Dependency Relations*

Gosse Bouma, Jori Mur, Gertjan van Noord,
Lonneke van der Plas, and Jörg Tiedemann

Rijksuniversiteit Groningen, Information Science, PO Box 716 9700 AS Groningen
The Netherlands
{g.bouma, j.mur, g.j.m.van.noord, m.l.e.van.der.plas, j.tiedemann}@rug.nl

Abstract. Joost is a question answering system for Dutch which makes extensive use of dependency relations. It answers questions either by table look-up, or by searching for answers in paragraphs returned by IR. Syntactic similarity is used to identify and rank potential answers. Tables were constructed by mining the CLEF corpus, which has been syntactically analyzed in full.

1 Introduction

Joost is a monolingual QA system for Dutch which makes heavy use of syntactic information. Most questions are answered by retrieving relevant paragraphs from the document collection, using keywords from the question. Next, potential answers are identified and ranked using a number of clues. Apart from obvious clues, we also use syntactic structure to identify and rank answer strings. A second strategy is based upon the observation that certain question types can be anticipated, and the corpus can be searched off-line for answers to such questions. Whereas previous approaches have used regular expressions to extract the relevant relations, we use patterns of dependency relations. To this end, the whole corpus has been analyzed syntactically.

In the next section, we describe the building blocks of our QA system. In section 3, we describe Joost. In section 4, we discuss the results of Joost on the CLEF 2005 QA task.

2 Preliminaries

Syntactic Preprocessing. The Alpino-system is a linguistically motivated, wide-coverage, grammar and parser for Dutch in the tradition of HPSG. It consists of over 500 grammar rules and a large lexicon of over 100.000 lexemes. Heuristics have been implemented to deal with unknown words and ungrammatical or out-of-coverage sentences (which may nevertheless contain fragments

* This research was carried out as part of the research program for *Interactive Multimedia Information Extraction*, IMIX, financed by NWO, the Dutch Organisation for Scientific Research.

C. Peters et al. (Eds.): CLEF 2005, LNCS 4022, pp. 370–379, 2006.

that are analyzable). The grammar provides a 'deep' level of syntactic analysis. The output of the system is a dependency graph. [1] shows that the accuracy of the system, when evaluated on a test-set of 500 newspaper sentences, is over 88%, which is in line with state-of-the-art systems for English.

Alpino includes heuristics for *recognizing* proper names. For the QA task, named entity *classification* was added. To this end, we collected lists of personal names (120K), geographical names (12K), organization names (26k), and miscalleneous items (2K). The data was primarily extracted from the Twente News Corpus, a collection of over 300 million words of newspaper text, which comes with relevant annotation. For unknown names, a maximum entropy classifier was trained, using the Dutch part of the shared task for CONLL 2003.[1] The accuracy on unseen CONLL data of the resulting classifier (which combines dictionary look-up and a maximum entropy classifier) is 88.2%.

The Dutch text collection for CLEF was tokenized and segmented into (4.1 million) sentences, and parsed in full. We used a Beowulf Linux cluster of 128 Pentium 4 processors[2] to complete the process in about three weeks. The dependency trees are stored as XML.

Reasoning over Dependency Relations. Several researchers have attempted to use syntactic information, and especially dependency relations, in QA [2,3,4,5]. We have implemented a system in which dependency patterns derived from the question must be matched by equivalent dependency relations in a potential answer. The dependency analysis of a sentence gives rise to a set of dependency relations of the form ⟨`Head/HIx, Rel, Dep/DIx`⟩, where `Head` is the root form of the head of the relation, and `Dep` is the head of the dependent. `Hix` and `DIx` are string indices, and `Rel` the dependency relation. For instance, the dependency analysis of sentence (1-a) is (1-b).

(1) a. Mengistu kreeg asiel in Zimbabwe (*Mengistu was given asylum in Zimbabwe*)

b. { ⟨`krijg/2, su, mengistu/1`⟩, ⟨`krijg/2, obj1, asiel/3`⟩, ⟨`krijg/2, mod, in/4`⟩, ⟨`in/4, obj1, zimbabwe/5`⟩ }

A dependency pattern is a set of (partially underspecified) dependency relations:

(2) { ⟨`krijg/K, obj1, asiel/A`⟩, ⟨`krijg/K, su, Su/S`⟩ }

A pattern may contain variables, represented here by (words starting with) a capital. A pattern P matches a set of dependency relations R if $P \subset R$, under some substitution of variables.

Equivalences can be defined to account for syntactic variation. For instance, the subject of an active sentence may be expressed as a PP-modifier headed by *door* (*by*) in the passive:

---

1 `http://cnts.uia.ac.be/conll2003/ner/`

2 which is part of the High-Performance Computing centre of the University of Groningen

(3) Aan Mengistu werd asiel verleend door Zimbabwe (*Mengistu was given asylum by Zimbabwe*)

The following equivalence accounts for this:

$\{\langle$`V/I,su,S/J`$\rangle\} \Leftrightarrow \{\langle$`word/W,vc,V/I`$\rangle, \langle$`V/I,mod,door/D`$\rangle, \langle$`door/D,obj1,S/J`$\rangle\}$

Here, the verb *word* is (the root form of) the passive auxiliary, which takes a verbal complement headed by the verb `V`.

Given an equivalence $Lhs \Leftrightarrow Rhs$, substitution of Lhs in a pattern P by Rhs gives rise to an equivalent pattern P'. A pattern P now also matches with a set of relations R if there is some equivalent pattern P', and $P' \subset R$, under some substitution of variables.

We have implemented 13 additional equivalence rules, to account for, among others, word order variation within appostions, the equivalence of genitives and *van*-PPs, equivalence between appositions and simple predicative sentence, coordination, and relative clauses. In [6], we show that the inclusion of equivalence rules has a positive effect on various components of our QA system.

Off-line Retrieval. Off-line methods have proven to be very effective in QA [7]. Before actual questions are known, a corpus is exhaustively searched for potential answers to specific question types (`capital, abbreviation, year of birth, ...`). The answers are extracted from the corpus off-line and stored in a structured table for quick and easy access.

[8] show that extraction patterns defined in terms of dependency relations are more effective than regular expression patterns over surface strings. Following this observation, we used the module for dependency pattern matching to exhaustively search the parsed corpus for potential answers to frequently occurring question types. For instance, the pattern in (4) extracts information about organizations and their founders.

(4) $\{\langle$`richt_op/R, su, Founder/S`$\rangle, \langle$`richt_op/R, obj1, Founded/O`$\rangle\}$

The verb *oprichten* (*to found*) can take on a wide variety of forms (active, with the particle *op* split from the root, participle, and infinitival, either the founder or the organization can be the first constituent in the sentence, *etc.* In all cases, modifiers may intervene between the relevant constituents:

(5) a. **Minderop** richtte **de Tros** op toen .... (*M. founded the Tros when...*)
b **Kasparov** heeft **een nieuwe Russische Schaakbond** opgericht en... (*Kasparov has founded a new Russian Chess Union and...*)

The pattern in (4) suffices to extract this relation from both of the examples above. Equivalence rules can be used to deal with other forms of syntactic variation. For instance, once we define a pattern to extract the country and its capital from (6-a), equivalence rules ensure that the alternative formulations in (6-b)-(6-c) match as well. Table 1 lists all the relations we extracted.

Table 1. Size of extracted relation tables. Each second and third column list the overall number of extracted tuples and extracted unique tuples (types) respectively.

Relation	tuples	uniq	Relation	tuples	uniq	Relation	tuples	uniq
Abbreviation	21.497	8.543	Currency	6.619	222	Function	77.028	46.589
Age	22.143	18520	Died Age	1.127	834	Inhabitants	708	633
Born Date	2356	1.990	Died Date	583	544	Nobel Prize	169	141
Born Loc	937	879	Died Loc	664	583			
Capital	2.146	515	Founded	1.021	953			

(6) a. de hoofdstad van Afghanistan, Kabul (*the capital of Af'stan, Kabul*)
b. Kabul, de hoofdstad van Afghanistan (*Kabul, the capital of Af'stan*)
c. Afghanistans hoofdstad, Kabul (*Af'stan's capital, Kabul*)

Extracting ISA relations. Fine-grained named entity classification based on labels obtained from appositions (i.e. *president Jeltsin, the island Awaji*), is useful for answering WH-questions and definition questions [9,10]. From the fully parsed Dutch CLEF text collection, we extracted 602K unique apposition tuples, consisting of a noun (used as class label) and a named entity. The resulting table contains, for instance, 112 names of *ferry boats* (*Estonia, Anna Maria Lauro, Sally Star* etc.) and no less than 2951 national team coaches (*Bobby Robson, Jack Charlton, Menotti, Berti Vogts* etc.). By focussing on the most frequent label for a named entity, most of the noise can be discarded. For instance, *Guus Hiddink* occurs 17 times in the extracted apposition tuples, 5 times as *bondscoach* (*national team chef*), and once with various other labels (*boss, colleague, guest, newcomer, ...*). In [11], we show that automatically acquired class labels for named entities improve the performance of our QA system on *which* questions and definition questions.

3 Joost

In this section, we describe the components of our QA system, Joost. Depending on the question class, questions are answered either by table look-up, or by a combination of IR and linguistic techniques. Potential answers are ranked on the basis of a score which combines, among others, IR-score, frequency of the answer, and the amount of overlap in dependency relations between question and the sentence from which the answer was extracted.

Question Analysis. Each incoming question is parsed by Alpino. To improve parsing accuracy on this specific task, the disambiguation model was retrained on a corpus which contained annotated and manually corrected dependency trees for 650 quiz questions.[3] For CLEF 2005, we used a model which was trained on data which also included (manually corrected dependency trees of) the CLEF 2003 and 2004 questions. It achieved an accuracy of 97.6 on CLEF 2005 questions.

[3] From the *Winkler Prins spel*, a quiz game made available to us by *Het Spectrum, bv.*

On the basis of the dependency relations returned by the parser the question class is determined. Joost distinguishes between 29 different question classes. 18 question classes are related to the relation tuples that were extracted off-line. Note that a single relation can often be questioned in different ways. For instance, whereas a frequent question type asks for the meaning of an acronym (*What does the abbreviation RSI stand for?*), a less frequent type asks for the abbreviation of a given term (*What is the abbreviation of Mad Cow Disease?*). The other 11 question classes identify questions asking for an amount, the date or location of an event, the (first) name of a person, the name of an organization, *how*-questions, WH-questions, and definition questions.

For each question class, one or more syntactic patterns are defined. For instance, the following pattern accounts for questions asking for the capital of a country:

$$(7)\quad \left\{ \begin{array}{ll} \langle \texttt{wat/W, wh, is/I} \rangle, & \langle \texttt{is/I, su, hoofdstad/H} \rangle \\ \langle \texttt{hoofdstad/H, mod, van/V} \rangle, & \langle \texttt{van/V, obj1, Country/C} \rangle \end{array} \right\}$$

Depending on the question class, it is useful to identify one or two additional arguments . For instance, the dependency relations assigned to the question *Wat is de hoofdstad van Togo?* (*What is the capital of Togo?*) match with the pattern in (7), and instantiate `Country` as *Togo*. Therefore, the question class `capital` is assigned, with `Togo` as additional argument. Similarly, *Who is the king of Norway?* is classified as `function(king,Norway)`, and *In which year did the Islamic revolution in Iran start?* is classified as `date(revolution)`.

Some question classes require access to lexical semantic knowledge. For instance, to determine that *In which American state is Iron Mountain?* asks for a location, the systeem needs to know that *state* refers to a location, and to determine that *Who is the advisor of Yasser Arafat?* should be classifed as `function(advisor,Yasser Arafat)`, it needs to know that *advisor* is a function. We obtained such knowledge mainly from Dutch EuroWordNet [12]. The list of function words (indicating function roles such as *president, queen, captain, secretary-general, etc.*) was expanded semi-automatically with words from the corpus that were distributionally similar to those extracted from EWN (see [11] for details).

Question classification was very accurate for the CLEF 2005 questions. There were a few cases where the additional arguments selected by the system did not seem the most optimal choice. Two clear mistakes were found (e.g. *What is the currency of Peru?* was classified as `currency(of)` and not as `currency(Peru)`).

Information Retrieval. For questions which cannot be answered by the relation tables, traditional keyword-based information retrieval (IR) is used to narrow down the search space for the linguistically informed part of the QA system which identifies answers. On the basis of keywords from the question, the IR system retrieves relevant passages from the corpus.

Keywords are derived from the question using its content words. Function words and other irrelevant words are removed using a static stop word list. We implemented an interface to seven publicly available IR engines. We selected

Zettair [13] as the underlying system in our experiments because of speed and recall performance. The entire CLEF QA corpus (in its tokenized plain text version) has been indexed using the IR engine with its standard setup.

Earlier experiments have shown that a segmentation into paragraphs leads to good IR performance for QA. We used the existing markup in the corpus to determine the paragraph boundaries. This resulted in about 1.1 million paragraphs (including headers that have been marked as paragraphs). We did experiments with additional pre-processing, e.g., including proper lemmatization (using Alpino root forms) but we could not improve the IR performance compared to the baseline using standard settings. However, we did include labels of named entities found by Alpino in each paragraph as additional tokens. This makes it possible to search for paragraphs including certain types of named entities (e.g. location names and organizations) and special units (e.g. measure names and temporal expressions).

For the QA@CLEF 2005 data, we used Zettair to return the 40 most relevant paragraphs for a query. This gives an answer recall (for questions which have an answer in the text collection) of 91%. On average, 4.74 paragraphs are required to find an answer, and half of the answers are found in the top 2 paragraphs.

Answer Identification and Ranking. For questions that are answered by means of table look-up, the relation table provides an exact answer string. For other questions, it is necessary to extract answer strings from the set of paragraphs returned by IR. Given a set of paragraph id's, we retrieve from the parsed corpus the dependency relations for the sentences occurring in these paragraphs.

Various syntactic patterns are defined for (exact) answer identification. For questions asking for the name of a person, organization, or location, or for an amount or date, a constituent headed by a word with the appropriate named entity class has to be found. As all of these occur frequently in the corpus, usually many potential answers will be identified. An important task is therefore to rank potential answers.

The following features are used to determine the score of a short answer A extracted from sentence S:

- **Syntactic Similarity** The proportion of dependency relations from the question which match with dependency relations in S.
- **Answer Context** A score for the syntactic context of A.
- **Names** The proportion of proper names, nouns, and adjectives from the query which can be found in S and the sentence preceding S.
- **Frequency** The frequency of A in all paragraphs returned by IR.
- **IR** The score assigned to the paragraph from which A was extracted.

The score for syntactic similarity implements a preference for answers from sentences with a syntactic structure that overlaps with that of the question. Answer context implements a preference for answers that occur in the context of certain terms from the question. Given a question classified as `date(Event)`, for instance, date expressions which occur as a modifier of `Event` are preferred over date expressions occurring as sisters of `Event`, which in turn are preferred over dates which have no syntactic relation to `Event`.

The overall score for an answer is the weighted sum of these features. Weights were determined manually using previous CLEF data for tuning. The highest weights are used for Syntactic Similarity and Answer Context. The highest scoring answer is returned as the answer.

Ranking of answers on the basis of various features was initially developed for IR-based QA only. Answers found by table look-up were ranked only by frequency. Recently, we have started to use the scoring mechanism described above also for answers stemming from table look-up. As the tables contain pointers to the sentence from which a tuple was extracted, we can easily go back to the source sentence, and apply the scoring mechanisms described above.[4] Using more features to rank an answer provides a way to give the correct answer to questions like *Who is the German minister of Economy?*. The function table contains several names for German ministers, but does not distinguish between different departments. The most frequent candidate is *Klaus Kinkel* (54 entries), who is minister of foreign affairs. The correct name, *Günter Rexrodt*, occurs only 11 times. Using Syntactic Similarity and Names as an additional features, Joost manages to give the correct answer.

Special Cases. We did not implement techniques which deal specifically with temporally restricted questions (i.e. *Which volcano erupted in June 1991?*). The mechanism for scoring potential answers takes into account the syntactic similarity and the overlap in names (including date expressions) between question and answer sentence, and this implements a preference for answers which are extracted from contexts referring to the correct date. Note that, as the same scoring technique is used for answers found by table look-up, this strategy should also be able to find the correct answer for questions such as *Who was the mayor of Moscow in 1994?*, for which the function table might contain more than one answer.

General WH-questions, such as (8), are relatively difficult to answer. Whereas for most question types, the type of the answer is relatively clear (i.e. it should be the name of a person or organization, or a date, etc.), this is not the case for WH-questions.

(8) a. Which fruit contains vitamin C?
  b. Which ferry sank southeast of the island Utö?

To improve the performance of our system on such questions, we made use of two additional knowledge sources. From EuroWordNet, we imported all hypernym relations between nouns. Question (8-a) is assigned the question class `which(fruit)`. We use the hypernym relations to assign a higher score to answers which are hypernyms of `fruit`.[5] As EuroWordNet does hardly include

[4] As no IR is involved in this case, the IR score is set to 1 for all answers.

[5] Unfortunately, EuroWordNet only contains two hypernyms for the synset *fruit*, none of which could be used to identify an answer to (8-a).

proper names, we also used the ISA-relations extracted from appositions containing a named entity, as described in section 2. Question (8-b) is assigned the question class `which(ferry)`. Candidate answers that are selected by Joost are: *Tallinn, Estonia, Raimo Tiilikainen* etc. Since, according to our apposition database, *Estonia* is the only potential answer which ISA ferry, this answer is selected.

CLEF 2005 contained no less than 60 definition questions (i.e. *What is Sabena?, Who is Antonio Matarese?*). We used the ISA-relations extracted from appositions to answer such questions. More in particular, our strategy for answering definition questions consisted of two phases:

- Phase 1: The most frequent class found for a named entity is selected.
- Phase 2: The sentences which mention the named entity and the class are retrieved and searched for additional information which might be relevant. Snippets of information that are in a adjectival relation or which are a prepositional complement to the class label are selected.

A disadvantage of focussing on class labels is that the label itself is not always sufficient for an adequate definition. Therefore, in phase 2 we expand the class labels with modifiers which typically need to be included in a definition. For the question *What is Sabena?*, our system produces *Belgian airline company* as answer.

4 Evaluation

As shown in table 2, our QA performs well on factoid questions and definitions. It is unclear to us at the moment what the explanation is for the fact that the system performed less well on temporally restricted questions.

Table 2. Results of the CLEF evaluation

Question Type	# questions	correct answers	
		#	%
Factoid	114	62	54.39
Temporally Restricted Factoid	26	7	26.92
Definition	60	30	50
Overall	200	99	49.5

Of the 140 factoid questions, 46 questions were assigned a type corresponding to a relation table. For 35 of these questions, an answer was actually found in one of the tables. The other 11 questions were answered by using the IR-based strategy as fall-back. 52 of the 60 definition questions were answered by the strategy described in section 3. For the other definition questions, the general IR-based strategy was used as fall-back. Three definition questions received NIL as an answer.

Parsing errors are the cause of some wrong or incomplete answers. The question *Who is Javier Solana?*, for instance, is answered with *Foreign Affairs*, which is extracted from a sentence containing the phrase *Oud-minister van buitenlandse zaken Javier Solana* (*Ex-minister of foreign affairs, Javier Solana*). Here, *Javier Solana* was erroneously analyzed as an apposition of *affairs*. Similarly, the wrong answer *United Nations* for the question *What is UNEP?*, which was extracted from a sentence containing *the environment programme of the United Nations (UNEP)*, which contained the same attachment mistake.

A frequent cause of errors were answers that were echoing (part of) the question. Currently, the system only filters answers which are a literal substring of the question. This strategy fails in cases like *Q: Where is Bonn located? A:* `in Bonn`. and *Q: In which city does one find the famous Piazza dei Miracoli? A:* `at the Piazza dei Miracoli`. It seems these cases could be easily filtered as well, although in some cases substantial overlap between question and answer does lead to a valid answer (e.g Q: *What is the name of the rocket used to launch the satellite Clementine?* A: `Titan rocket`).

Our strategy for answering definition questions seemed to work reasonably well, although it did produce a relatively large number of inexact answers (of the 18 answers that were judged inexact, 13 were answers to definition questions). This is a consequence of the fact that we select the most frequent class label for a named entity, and only expand this label with adjectival and PP modifiers that are adjacent to the class label (a noun) in the corresponding sentence. Given the constituent *the museum Hermitage in St Petersburg*, this strategy fails to include *in St Petersburg*, for instance. We did not include relative clause modifiers, as these tend to contain information which is not appropriate for a definition. However, for the question, *Who is Iqbal Masih*, this leads the system to answer *twelve year old boy*, extracted from the constituent *twelve year old boy, who fought against child labour and was shot sunday in his home town Muritke.* Here, at least a part of the relative clause (i.e. *who fought against child labour*) should have been included in the answer.

5 Conclusion

We have shown that dependency parsing of both questions and the full document collection is useful for developing an adequate QA system. Dependency patterns can be used to search the corpus exhaustively for answers to frequent question types and for class labels for named entities, which are used to improve the performance of the system on *which*-questions and definition questions. Selection of the most likely answer to a question uses a syntactic similarity metric based on dependency relations.

We have used a limited number of equivalences over dependency relations. An obvious next step is to expand this set with equivalences derived automatically from the parsed corpus (i.e. as in [14]). The syntactic techniques we employ operate exclusively on individual sentences. In the future, we hope to extend this to techniques which operate on the paragraph level by integrating, among others, a component for coreference resolution. In the near future, we also hope to be able to use dependency relations to boost the performance of IR [15].

References

1. Malouf, R., van Noord, G.: Wide coverage parsing with stochastic attribute value grammars. In: IJCNLP-04 Workshop Beyond Shallow Analyses - Formalisms and statistical modeling for deep analyses, Hainan (2004)
2. Katz, B., Lin, J.: Selectively using relations to improve precision in question answering. In: Proceedings of the workshop on Natural Language Processing for Question Answering (EACL 2003), Budapest, EACL (2003) 43–50
3. Litkowski, K.C.: Use of metadata for question answering and novelty tasks. In Voorhees, E.M., Buckland, L.P., eds.: Proceedings of the eleventh Text Retrieval Conference (TREC 2003), Gaithersburg, MD (2004) 161–170
4. Mollá, D., Gardiner, M.: Answerfinder - question answering by combining lexical, syntactic and semantic information. In: Australasian Language Technology Workshop (ALTW) 2004, Sydney (2005)
5. Punyakanok, V., Roth, D., Yih, W.: Mapping dependency trees: An application to question answering. In: The 8th International Symposium on Artificial Intelligence and Mathematics (AI&Math 04), Fort Lauderdale, FL (2004)
6. Bouma, G., Mur, J., van Noord, G.: Reasoning over dependency relations for QA. In: Proceedings of the IJCAI workshop on Knowledge and Reasoning for Answering Questions (KRAQ), Edinburgh (2005) 15–21
7. Fleischman, M., Hovy, E., Echihabi, A.: Offline strategies for online question answering: Answering questions before they are asked. In: Proc. 41st Annual Meeting of the Association for Computational Linguistics, Sapporo, Japan (2003) 1–7
8. Jijkoun, V., Mur, J., de Rijke, M.: Information extraction for question answering: Improving recall through syntactic patterns. In: Coling 2004, Geneva (2004) 1284–1290
9. Pasca, M.: Acquisition of categorized named entities for web search. In: Proceedings of the Thirteenth ACM conference on Information and knowledge management. (2004) 137 – 145
10. Pantel, P., Ravichandran, D.: Automatically labeling semantic classes. In Susan Dumais, D.M., Roukos, S., eds.: HLT-NAACL 2004: Main Proceedings, Boston, Massachusetts, USA, Association for Computational Linguistics (2004) 321–328
11. van der Plas, L., Bouma, G.: Automatic acquisition of lexico-semantic knowledge for question answering. In: Proceedings of Ontolex 2005 – Ontologies and Lexical Resources, Jeju Island, South Korea (2005)
12. Vossen, P.: Eurowordnet a multilingual database with lexical semantic networks (1998)
13. Zobel, J., Williams, H., Scholer, F., Yiannis, J., Hein, S.: The Zettair Search Engine. Search Engine Group, RMIT University, Melbourne, Australia. (2004)
14. Lin, D., Pantel, P.: Discovery of inference rules for question answering. Natural Language Engineering **7** (2001) 343–360
15. Tiedemann, J.: Integrating linguistic knowledge in passage retrieval for question answering. In: Proceedings of EMNLP 2005, Vancouver (2005) 939–946

Term Translation Validation by Retrieving Bi-terms

Brigitte Grau, Anne-Laure Ligozat, Isabelle Robba, and Anne Vilnat

LIR group, LIMSI-CNRS, BP 133 91403 Orsay Cedex, France
firstName.lastName@limsi.fr

Abstract. For our second participation to the Question Answering task of CLEF, we kept last year's system named MUSCLEF, which uses two different translation strategies implemented in two modules. The multilingual module MUSQAT analyzes the French questions, translates "interesting parts", and then uses these translated terms to search the reference collection. The second strategy consists in translating the question into English and applying QALC our existing English module. Our purpose in this paper is to analyze term translations and propose a mechanism for selecting correct ones. The manual evaluation of bi-terms translations leads us to the conclusion that the bi-term translations found in the corpus can confirm the mono-term translations.

1 Introduction

This paper presents our second participation to the Question Answering task of the CLEF evaluation campaign. This year we have participated in two tasks: a monolingual task (in French) for which we submitted one run, and a bilingual task (questions in French, answers in English) for which we submitted two runs. Concerning the bilingual task, we used the same two strategies as last year:

- translation of selected terms issued of the question analysis module, then search in the collection; this first system is called MUSQAT
- question translation thanks to a machine translation system, then application of QALC our monolingual English system

Most systems make use of only one of these strategies [6], but our system, MUSCLEF[1], follows both approaches, by combining MUSQAT and QALC. In this article, we focus on the evaluation of the different translation techniques used in MUSCLEF. This study leads us to propose a mechanism for selecting correct term translations.

We will first present an overview of our system (section 2), then we will focus on our recognition of terms in documents, realized by Fastr (3), and their translation (4). We will then present an evaluation of these translations (5) followed by results concerning term validation (6) and our global results at the QA task (7).

C. Peters et al. (Eds.): CLEF 2005, LNCS 4022, pp. 380–389, 2006.

2 Overview of MUSCLEF

MUSCLEF architecture is illustrated in Figure 1. First, its question analysis module aims at deducing characteristics, which may help to find answers in selected passages. These characteristics are: the expected answer type, the question focus, the main verb, and some syntactic characteristics. They are deduced from the morpho-syntactic tagging and syntactic analysis of the question. For this campaign, we developed a grammar of question and used the Cass robust parser[1] to analyze the English questions that were translated using Reverso[2].

We conducted a quick evaluation of our French question analysis, which revealed that 77% of the French questions were attributed the correct expected answer types. We corrected some of the errors, and a more up-to-date question anlysis reached 97% of correct type attribution. Though these results are quite satisfactory, the question analysis is much deteriorated on the translated questions, and this problem will have to be taken into account for next year's evaluation.

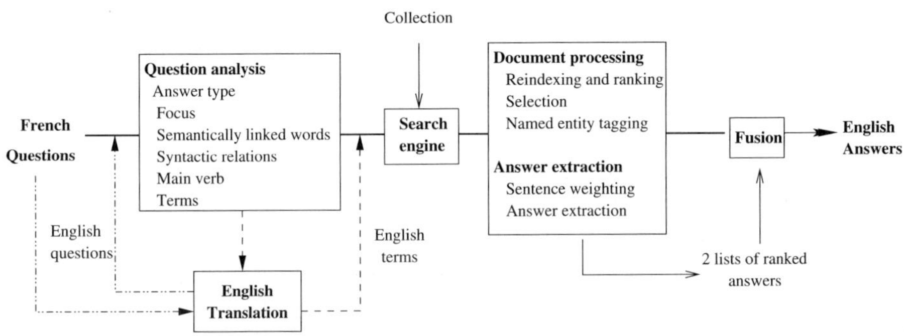

Fig. 1. MUSCLEF architecture

A new type of questions, temporally restricted questions, was introduced in this year's campaign. We have adjusted the question analysis to the category of the question. When a temporal restriction was to be found, we tried to detect it, and to classify it according to the three following types: date, period, and event. The answering strategy was then adapted to the type of temporal constraint.

On the 29 temporally restricted French questions, 18 of them contained dates or periods, and 12 contained event-related restrictions (one question contained both). Our system was able to detect and classify the dates and periods for all 18 questions, the classification consisting in separating dates and periods, and for the periods, in detecting if the period concerned days, months or years.

For querying the CLEF collection and retrieving passages we used MG[3]. Retrieved documents are then processed: they are re-indexed by the question terms

[1] http://www.vinartus.net/spa/
[2] http://www.reverso.net
[3] MG for Managing Gigabytes http://www.cs.mu.oz.au/mg/

and their linguistic variants, reordered according to the number and the kind of terms found in them, so as to select a subset of them.

Named entity recognition processes are then applied. The answer extraction process relies on a weighting scheme of the sentences, followed by the answer extraction itself. We apply different processes according to the kind of expected answer, each of them leading to propose weighted answers.

The first run we submitted corresponds to the strategy implemented in MUSQAT: translation of selected terms. For the second run, we added a final step consisting in comparing the results issued from both strategies: the translated questions and the translated terms. This module named fusion, computes a final score for each potential answer. Its principle is to boost an answer if both chains ranked it in the top 5 propositions, even with relatively low scores.

3 Searching Terms and Variants

Term recognition in retrieved documents is performed by FASTR, a transformational shallow parser for the recognition of term occurrences and variants ([3]). Terms are transformed into grammar rules and the single words building these terms are extracted and linked to their morphological and semantic families.

The morphological family of a single word w is the set $M(w)$ of terms in the CELEX database ([2]) which have the same root morpheme as w. For instance, the morphological family of the noun *maker* is made of the nouns *maker*, *make* and *remake*, and the verbs *to make* and *to remake*. The semantic family of a single word w is the union $S(w)$ of the synsets of WordNet1.6 ([4]) to which w belongs. A synset is a set of words that are synonymous for at least one of their meanings. Thus, the semantic family of a word w is the set of the words w' such that w' is considered as a synonym of one of the meanings of w. The semantic family of *maker*, obtained from WordNet1.6, is composed of three nouns: *maker, manufacturer, shaper* and the semantic family of *car* is *car, auto, automobile, machine, motorcar.* Variant patterns that rely on morphological and semantic families are generated through metarules. They are used to extract terms and variants from the document sentences in the selected documents.

For instance, the following pattern, named $NtoSemArg$, extracts the occurrence *making many automobiles* as a variant of the term *car maker*:

$$NN(car)NN(maker)->$$
$$VM('maker')RP?PREP?ART?(JJ|NN|NP|VBD|VBG)0-3NS('car')$$

In this pattern, NN are nouns and NP proper nouns, RP are particles, $PREP$ prepositions, ART articles, and VBD, VBG verbs. $VM('maker')$ is any verb in the morphological family of the noun *maker* and $NS('car')$ is any noun in the semantic family of *car*.

Relying on the above morphological and semantic families, *auto maker, auto parts maker, car manufacturer, make autos,* and *making many automobiles* are extracted as correct variants of the original term *car maker* through the set of metarules used for the QA-track experiment. Unfortunately, some incorrect variants are extracted as well, such as *make those cuts in auto* produced by the preceding metarule.

4 Term Translation in MUSQAT

In order to achieve term translation we considered the easiest method, which consists in using a bilingual dictionary to translate the terms from the source language to the target language. Last year, we chose Magic-dic[4], a GPL dictionary, because of its increasing capacity: terms can be added by any user, but they are verified before being integrated, and to prevent its incompleteness, we used this year another dictionary FreeDict[5] and merged their translations. FreeDict had added 424 different translations of the 690 words. However, these new translations are mainly other synonyms rather than new translations of unknown words. For example the query for the French word *mener* to Magic-Dic gives the following results: *conduct, lead, guide*; while *accord* is only translated by *agreement*. FreeDict added five translations for *accord*: accord, accordance, concurrence, chord, concord, and gave translations for *frontière* that was unknown by MagicDic. However, *occidental* (western) remained not translated.

We illustrate the strategy defined in our multilingual module MUSQAT on the following example: *"Quel est le nom de la principale compagnie aérienne allemande?"*, which is translated in English *"What is the name of the main German airline company?"*.

The first step is the parsing of the French question that provides a list of the mono-terms and all the bi-terms (such as *adjective/common noun*) which are in the question, and eliminates the stop words. The bi-terms are useful, because they allow a disambiguation by giving a (small) context to a word. In our example, the bi-terms (in their lemmatized form) are: *principal compagnie, compagnie aérien, aérien allemand*; and the mono-terms: *nom, principal, compagnie, aérien, allemand.*

With the help of the dictionaries, MUSQAT attempts to translate the bi-terms (when they exist), and the mono-terms. All the proposed translations are taken into account. All the terms are grammatically tagged. If a bi-term cannot be directly translated, it is recomposed from the mono-terms, following the English syntax. For our example, we obtained for the bi-terms: *principal company/main company, air company, air german*; and for the mono-terms: *name/appellation, principal/main, company, german.*

When a word does not exist in the dictionaries, we keep it as it is without any diacritic, which is often relevant for proper nouns. Then, all the words are weighted relatively to their existence in a lexicon that contains the vocabulary found in the Latimes of the Trec collection, so that each word is weighted according to its specificity within this corpus. If a word is not found in this lexicon, we search with MG if documents contain it (or rather its root because MG indexing was made using stemming). If it is not the case, MUSQAT eliminates it from

[4] http://magic-dic.homeunix.net/

[5] http://www.freedict.de/

the list of translated terms. In this way, MUSQAT discarded 72 non-translated words (out of 439 non-translated mono-terms, the remaining ones often being proper nouns). As we form boolean requests, it was important not to keep non existing words.

English terms plus their categories (given by the Tree Tagger) were then given as input to the other modules of the system, instead of the original words. The translation module did not try to solve the ambiguity between the different translations. We account on the document retrieval module to discard irrelevant translations. This module has been improved this year: it always selects passages (the collection was preliminary split), but in a very smaller number. It first generates boolean requests, based on proper nouns, numbers and specificity of the words. It aims at retrieving 200 passages maximum, and makes the smaller request with the more specific terms so as to obtain a minimum number of passages, set to 50. Each term of the request is made of the disjunction of the different translations. If the boolean query retrieves too few or too much documents, passage retrieval is made thanks to a ranked research with a query that hold all the terms. If there are synonyms for certain terms, relevant documents are then retrieved with these synonyms. If a word is incoherent within the context, we suppose its influence is not sufficient to generate noise. This hypothesis can only be verified if the question is made of several words.

5 Magic-Dic Term Evaluation

We manually evaluated the bi-term translations for the 200 questions of CLEF04 given by this module. Table 1 presents the results of this evaluation.

The system found 375 bi-terms. Among them, 135 are correct translated bi-terms (OK) such as *CERN member*. 24 are bi-terms contextually false i.e. for which one word is not a good translation in the context of this bi-term, such as *accretion hormone* instead of *growth hormone* to translate *hormone de croissance*. 74 bi-terms are due to an erroneous bi-term constitution (False Bi-Terms), such as *able animal* in question asking to *Give an animal able to...*. Finally, 142 bi-terms (a) are completely erroneous translations (False Translation), such as *overground escort* instead of *main company* (110) or (b) have a translation which was absent from the dictionary (Absent Translations), such as *olympique*, where the French word has been kept instead of the English term*olympic* (32).

It is obvious on this table that a lot of terms are wrong for different reasons. We decided to confirm those that must be kept by considering their presence or absence in the selected documents. To do so, we used FASTR results to evaluate the bi-terms or their variants which are retrieved in the documents. Table 2 shows the results of this evaluation. The second column gives the results obtained by FASTR without considering the semantic variations. The third column includes these semantic variations. The last column indicates the percentage of bi-terms FASTR confirms, taking into account the semantic variations.

The correct bi-terms are mostly confirmed by FASTR. The contextually false bi-terms obtain a rather high percentage of confirmation due to the semantic

Table 1. MagicDic terms evaluation

Bi-Terms	#	%
OK	135	36
Contextually False	24	6.4
False	74	19.7
False Transl	110	29.3
Absent Transl	32	8.5
Total False	240	64
Total	375	

Table 2. MagicDic terms validated by Fastr

Bi-terms	#	#retrieved without sem.var.	#retrieved including sem.var.	%
OK	135	61	83	61.5
Context. False	24	4	7	29.2
False	74	11	15	20.3
False Transl	110	7	19	17.3
Absent Transl	32	0	0	0
Total	375	82	120	32

variations which lead to recognize correct synonyms of non accurate translated terms. The false bi-terms can be considered as co-occurrences rather than bi-terms. As co-occurrences, they are retrieved by FASTR in the documents and just a few false translations are retrieved.

6 Evaluation of Terms Extracted from Question Translations

We also proceeded to a similar evaluation of the terms extracted from the questions translated last year by Systran.

As a first step we proceeded to an evaluation of the question translations themselves. We evaluated the syntactic quality of the translations, and classified them in correct, false, or quite correct. Table 3 recapitulates these results.

Table 3. Questions translations evaluation

Questions	Correct	Quite Correct	False	Total
#	73	12	115	200
%	36.5	6.0	57.5	100

Table 4. Evaluation of terms from translated questions

Bi-Terms	#	%
OK	126	75.4
Contextually False	0	0
False	41	24.6
False Transl	0	0
Absent Transl	0	0
Total False	41	24.6
Total	167	

We also evaluated the terms extracted from these translated questions by our monolingual system QALC. We use the same notations as in table 1. Results are given in Table 4.

These results are quite interesting: despite the moderate quality of the translations, QALC is able to identify good terms from these questions. We can also notice that we obtain a smaller number of terms following this procedure because there is only one translation by word.

7 Results

Table 5 gives the results that our system obtained at the CLEF04 and CLEF05 campaigns, with the different strategies: (a) with the translation of the terms (MUSQAT), (b) with QALC applied on the translated questions and searching the collection. The evaluation was made by an automatic process that looks for the answer patterns in the system answers, applying regular expressions. These results were computed with 178 answer patterns that we built for the 200 questions of CLEF04 and 188 for the CLEF05 questions.

The first line indicates the number of correct answers found in the 5 first sentences given by MUSQAT (using term translation) and QALC. The second line, "NE answers", gives the number of correct answers on questions the system categorized as waiting for a Named Entity (the total is 107 in CLEF04 for MUSQAT and 97 for QALC and 91 in CLEF05 for MUSQAT and 66 for QALC). Our total number of questions for this category is far beyond the real number in CLEF05. The third line, "non NE answers", concerns the other questions (the complement to 178 in CLEF04 and to 188 in CLEF05).

Results are presented when the system just gives one answer and when it gives 5 answers. The last line indicates the best official result of our system on the 200 questions. The official score of MUSQAT was 22 (11%) in CLEF04 and 28 (14%) in CLEF05, thus we can observe that merging answers obtained by different strategies enabled a significant gain. We also can notice that if our CLEF05 system better selects sentences, it is less efficient on extracting the named entity answers.

According to the manual evaluation results of bi-terms translations, we have tested an automatic process for filtering Magic-dic translations on CLEF04

Table 5. Results at CLEF04 and CLEF05

		MUSQAT04	QALC04	MUSQAT05	QALC05
Sentences	5 first ranks	56 (31 %)	65 (37 %)	78 (41 %)	87(46 %)
NE answers	Rank 1	17	26	16	9
	5 first ranks	32	37	24	11
Non NE answers	Rank 1	7	3	16	16
	5 first ranks	12	8	22	24
Total	Rank 1	24	29	32	25
	%	12%	14.5%	17%	13%
	5 first ranks	44	45	46	35
Fusion (official results)		38 (19 %)		38 (19 %)	

questions. So, if a bi-term or a variant form was found in the selected documents, we kept it as a valid translation and we kept its lemmas as valid mono-term translations. When a validated translation existed for a term, the non-validated translations were taken out. When no translation of a bi-term was found in corpus, we assumed that mono-term translations were wrong and we kept Systran translations. In order to improve the coverage of our translation, we added Systran translation for terms absent from the dictionary.

In this way, we selected 253 bi-terms in 112 questions, and added 37 translations, with 12 bi-terms, which concerns 35 questions. The last improvement consisted in adding Systran translations that were different from Magic-dic translations (138 terms in 96 questions) to the filtered terms. This last set of terms was composed of 1311 translations for 836 terms in 200 questions (522 terms with 1 translation, 199 with 2 translations, 81 with 3 translations, 25 with 4 translations, 6 with 5 translations and 3 with 6 translations).

We tested MUSQAT with this new selection. Results are shown Table 6. We see that MUSQAT finds relevant documents for 7 additional questions (increase of 4%).

Table 6. MUSQAT new results

		MUSQAT
Sentences	5 first ranks	67
NE answers	Rank 1	25
	5 first ranks	41
Non NE answers	Rank 1	4
	5 first ranks	10
Total	Rank 1	29 (14,5%)
	5 first ranks	51

MUSQAT extracts 7 additional correct answers in the top 5 short answers, with 29 answers in rank 1. MUSQAT obtains here slightly better results than QALC with Systran translations, both for short and long answers. We also measured the number of questions for which the selection process based on

FASTR indexing provides documents containing the answer pattern. In the original MUSQUAT, it was possible to find the answer for 80% of questions. Term selection allows to improve this value to 85%.

These improvements are not significant enough so we had not incorporated them in this year's version, even if we think that this kind of translation validation is worth being tried. So we plan to realize bi-term validation on a larger corpus. Concerning the absence of translations, we began to increase manually our dictionary from lexicons and gazetteers we use for named entities recognition, specially for acronyms and location names, and we plan to use a bilingual aligned corpus.

8 Conclusion

In [7], we can find the results of all participants to CLEF 2005, in all question-answering tasks. For the monolingual task the average of best scores is 42.6%, while for the cross-language task it is 24.5%. The best score for monolingual task is obtained in Portuguese task with 64.5% of right answers, and the best score for cross-language task is obtained in an English-French run with 39.5% of right answers. The best score for task with English language as a target is 25.5% (with German as source language). As always, cross-language task results are far lower than monolingual task results.

Our system MUSCLEF was ranked third among the 12 systems participating to the task with English as target language. Thanks to the use of a second dictionary, we improved MUSQAT results. Moreover, both systems MUSQAT and QALC got better results concerning sentence selection (+10%), because we modified the elaboration of the query sent to the search engine, allowing us to retrieve more relevant documents.

But in spite of these enhancements, our final results remained exactly the same as last year's: 19%. This can be explained by two reasons: firstly, due to a technical problem, we could not use this year the web resource; secondly the question analysis module was much deteriorated on the translated questions.

Nevertheless, this second participation to CLEF evaluation was encouraging, and we plan to continue to improve our system; doing for example a better selection of good translations thanks to the multi-terms, as explained in this paper and also in [5].

References

1. G. Bourdil, F. Elkateb-Gara, O. Ferret, B. Grau, G. Illouz, B. Mathieu, L. Monceaux, I. Robba and A. Vilnat. 2005. Answering French questions in English by exploiting results from several sources of information. *LNCS, Vol 3491, Revised selected papers from Workshop CLEF 2004*, p.470-481.
2. CELEX. 1998. http://www.ldc.upenn.edu/readme_files/celex.readme.html, UPenns, Eds., *Proceedings of Consortium for Lexical Resources.*
3. C. Jacquemin. 1999. Syntacti and paradigmatic representations of term variation. *Proceedings of ACL 1999*, p.341-348.

4. C. Fellbaum. 1998. WordNet: An Electronic Lexical Database. Cambridge, MA: MIT Press.
5. M. Negri, H. Tanev and B. Magnini. 2003. Bridging languages for question-answering: Diogene at CLEF 2003. *Working Notes of CLEF 2003 workshop, 21-22 August, Trondheim, Norway.*
6. C. Peters, M. Braschler, G. Di Nunzio and N. Ferro, CLEF 2004: Ad Hoc Track Overview and Results Analysis, *Fifth Workshop of the Cross–Language Evaluation Forum (CLEF 2004), Lecture Notes in Computer Science (LNCS), Springer, Heidelberg, Germany.*
7. A. Vallin, D. Giampiccolo, L. Aunimo, C. Ayache, P. Osenova, A. Peas, M. de Rijke, B. Sacaleanu, D. Santos, R. Sutcliffe. 2005 Overview of the CLEF 2005 Multilingual Question Answering Track. *Working Notes of CLEF 2005 workshop, 21-23 September, Vienna, Austria.*

Exploiting Linguistic Indices and Syntactic Structures for Multilingual Question Answering: ITC-irst at CLEF 2005

Hristo Tanev[1], Milen Kouylekov[1], Bernardo Magnini[1], Matteo Negri[1], and Kiril Simov[2]

[1] Centro per la Ricerca Scientifica e Technologica ITC-irst
{tanev, kouylekov, magnini, negri}@itc.it
[2] Bulgarian Academy of Sciences
kivs@bultreebank.org

Abstract. We participated at four Question Answering tasks at CLEF 2005: the Italian monolingual (**I**), Italian-English (**I/E**), Bulgarian monolingual (**B**), and Bulgarian-English (**B/E**) bilingual task. While we did not change the approach in the Italian task (**I**), we experimented with several new approaches based on linguistic structures and statistics in the **B**, **I/E**, and **B/E** tasks.

1 Introduction

We participated in four QA tasks at CLEF 2005: the Italian monolingual (**I**), Italian-English (**I/E**), Bulgarian monolingual (**B**), and Bulgarian-English (**B/E**) bilingual task.

Regarding the Italian monolingual task (**I**), our system was the same as the one used at CLEF 2003 and CLEF 2004 (see [8] for detailed description).

We participated for the first time in task **B** and therefore we had to build a new QA system for Bulgarian using some tools and resources from the on-line QA system "Socrates" [10].

We experimented in the cross-language tasks with two novel approaches: a tree edit distance algorithm for answer extraction and syntactic based Information Retrieval (IR). Although these syntactic based approaches did not have a significant impact on the overall performance, we regard them as a step towards introducing more sophisticated methods in Cross-language QA. Moreover, we tested a new model for indexing and retrieving of syntactic structures, which improved the document retrieval and allowed for efficient exploitation of a syntactically pre-parsed corpus.

The rest of the paper is structured as follows: Section 2 provides a brief overview of the QA approaches based on syntactic structures, Section 3 describes the syntactic tree edit distance algorithm which we used for answer extraction, Section 4 introduces our syntactic indexing and Information Retrieval (IR) model, Section 5 describes our new system for QA in Bulgarian "Socrates 2", Section 6 provides an overview of our CLEF results, and Section 7 outlines our directions for research in the future.

C. Peters et al. (Eds.): CLEF 2005, LNCS 4022, pp. 390–399, 2006.

2 Using Syntactic Information for Question Answering

Our multilingual QA system DIOGENE participated at CLEF 2003 and 2004 relying mainly on a multilingual statistical module which mines the Web to validate the candidate answers (see [6] for details). However, this approach depends on the coverage, speed, and accessibility of public domain search engines such as Google or Yahoo.

In this clue, we carried out two experiments for exploitation of syntactic information. Our experiments were inspired by the fact that many QA systems consider syntactic information. For example, the top performing system in the recent years in the TREC QA track - the LCC System [7] uses deep syntactic parsing and representation in logical form. Deep syntactic analysis is used also by the *Shapaqa* system [1].

One of the best performing system in the TREC 2004 track was created in the QA group from the university of Singapore [2] whose approach uses pre-extracted syntactic patterns and approximate dependency relation matching.

In [9] the authors built a QA system based on a mapping algorithm that is a modification of the *edit distance* algorithm presented in [13] for syntactic trees.

3 Answer Extraction Using Tree-Edit Distance

We carried out tree-edit distance answer extraction in the Italian-English cross-language task. Our approach performs three basic steps for each question:

1. We translate the question from Italian to English using the AltaVista translation engine and a list of pre-processing and post-processing translation rules.
2. We retrieve pre-parsed sentences from our syntactic index SyntNet (see Sect.4.1).
3. We extract the candidate answers and rank them considering the tree edit distance between the affirmative form of the question and the retrieved sentences.

3.1 Edit Distance on Dependency Trees

After we extract candidate sentences which are likely to contain the answer, we used a modification of the *tree edit distance* algorithm presented in [9] and [13], in order to identify the sentence closest to the question in terms of edit distance and to extract the answer from it. We adapted our algorithm to use dependency syntactic trees from a parsed corpus (we used MiniPar [4] to obtain the parse trees).

Since the [13] algorithm does not consider labels on edges, while dependency trees provide them, each dependency relation R from a node A to a node B has been re-written as a complex label B-R concatenating the name of the destination node and the name of the relation. All nodes except the root of the tree are relabelled in such way. The algorithm is directional: we aim to find the best (i.e. less costly) sequence of edit operations that transform the dependency tree of the candidate answer sentence into the dependency tree of the question affirmative form. According to the constraints described above, the following transformations are allowed:

- **Insertion**: insert a node from the dependency tree of question affimative form into the dependency tree of the candidate answer sentence.
- **Deletion**: delete a node N from the dependency tree of the answer sentence. When N is deleted all its children are attached to the parent of N. It is not required to explicitly delete the children of N as they are going to be either deleted or substituted on a following step.
- **Substitution**: change the label of a node $N1$ in the answer sentence tree into a label of a node $N2$ of the question tree. Substitution is allowed only if the two nodes share the same part-of-speech. In case of substitution the relation attached to the substituted node is updated with the relation of the new node.

To adapt the algorithm we addressed the following problems:

1. Transform the dependency tree of the question into the dependency tree corresponding to it's affirmative form.
2. Reorder the tree nodes to create an order of the children.
3. Estimate the costs of the delete, insert and replace operations.

The dependency tree of the question is transformed into affirmative form using a set of hand written rules which are activated according to the question and answer types. For some answer types a simple hand-crafted pattern that represents the most frequent syntactic relations between the question focus and the answer of the question was used. Questions with such answer types are questions that have a measure as an answer (height, length, etc.)

The edit distance algorithm presented in [9] and [13] requires an ordering on the children of the syntactic tree. We imposed an order on the children of a node in the tree based on the lexicographic order of the words and the syntactic relation.

In [9] the authors use add-hoc costs of the basic edit operations. In our approach we decided to define more precisely these costs using statistical infomation. To do this, we define a weight of each single word representing its relevance through the inverse document frequency (IDF), a measure commonly used in Information Retrieval. If N is the number of documents in a text collection and N_w is the number of documents of the collection that contain word w, then the IDF of this word is given by the formula:

$$idf(w) = \log \frac{N}{N_w} \quad (1)$$

The weight of the *insertion* operation is the IDF of the inserted word. The most frequent words (e.g. stop words) have a zero cost of insertion. In the current version of the system we are still not able to implement a good model that estimates the cost of the deletion operation. In current experiments we set the cost of deletion to 0. To determine the cost of substitution we used a distributional similarity based thesaurus available at *http://www.cs.ualberta.ca/~lindek/downloads.htm*. For each word, the thesaurus lists up to 200 most similar words and their similarities. The cost of a *substitution* is calculated by the following formula:

$$subs(w_1, w_2) = ins(w_2) * (1 - sim(w_1, w_2)) \tag{2}$$

where w_1 is the word from the candidate answer sentence that is being replaced by the word w_2 from the question and $sim(w_1, w_2)$ is the similarity between w_1 and w_2 in the thesaurus multiplied by the similarity between the syntactic relations which dominate w_1 and w_2. The similarity between relations is learned from a parsed local corpus. The similarities have values from 1 (very similar) to 0 (not similar). If there is no similarity, the cost of substitution is equal to the cost of inserting the word *w2*.

3.2 Answer Extraction

All the sentences retrieved by the IR module of the system are sorted based on the edit distance between their syntactic trees and the affirmative form of the question. As candidate answers we extracted noun phrases part of the syntactic tree of the sentences with the lowest edit distance score.

4 Syntactic Based Information Retrieval

4.1 Syntactic Network

The *Syntactic Network (SyntNet)* is a formalism for representation of a set of dependency syntactic graphs (input graph set) produced from a dependency parser. Equal sub-structures from the input graph set are merged in one structure in SyntNet. This property facilitates identification of repeated sub-structures, allows for efficient calculation of their frequency, and makes possible efficient mining of structures which span over certain words. This last property was extensively used in our syntactic based IR experiment.

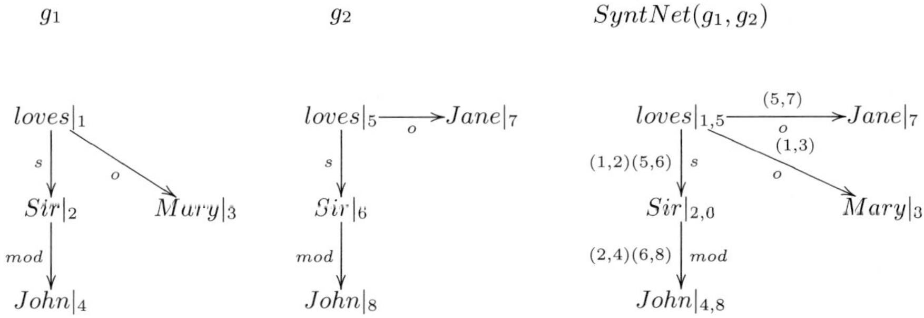

Fig. 1. Two parse trees and their Syntactic Network

SyntNet models an input graph set in which each of the graphs represents the syntax of a sentence from a text corpus. In a dependency syntactic graph the vertices are labelled with words or word lemmas and part of speech. In the dependency graphs each two words w and w' are connected with a directed edge if and only if w governs w' . Edges in the dependency graph are labelled with syntactic relations (see Fig.1).

When the SyntNet is built from the input graph set, all vertices labelled with the same word and part of speech are merged in one vertex. Moreover, all equally labelled dependency edges which connect equally labelled vertices in the same direction are merged in one edge. Therefore, in SyntNet each vertex and edge usually represents more than one vertex and edge from the input graph set. In Fig.1 two dependency graphs g_1 and g_2, representing the sentences "Sir John loves Mary" and "Sir John loves Jane", are merged in one SyntNet - $SyntNet(g_1, g_2)$. Each vertex in g_1 and g_2 is labelled with an unique number (e.g. $John_{|4}$, $John_{|8}$). Edges may be represented via number pairs - the number of the vertex from which the edge begins and the number of the vertex in which the edge enters (e.g. the edge $loves_{|1} \rightarrow Sir_{|2}$ in g_1 is represented with the pair (1,2)). When equally labelled vertices from the input graph set (e.g. g_1 and g_2) are merged into one vertex in the Syntactic Network (e.g. $SyntNet(g_1, g_2)$ on Fig.1), their numerical labels are put together in a numerical set which labels the aggregate vertex (e.g. $John_{|4,8}$). When several edges are merged into one edge in the Syntactic Network, their numerical representations form a set of numerical pairs which label the aggregate edge in SyntNet. For example, the aggregate edge (*loves*, *Sir*) in $SyntNet(g_1, g_2)$ is labelled with the pairs (1,2) and (5,6) which refer to two equally labelled edges (*loves*, *Sir*) from g_1 and g_2. These numerical labels in the SyntNet allow for tracing repeating structures and calculating their frequency. For example, in $SyntNet(g_1, g_2)$ on Fig.1 we may trace the numerical labels in the sub-structure $John \leftarrow Sir \leftarrow loves$ and we can see that two possible paths exist following the numerical labels on the edges of the Syntactic Network : $(4 \leftarrow 2 \leftarrow 1)$ and $(8 \leftarrow 6 \leftarrow 5)$. Each of these paths corresponds to one occurrence of the sub-structure in the input graph sequence, therefore the above mentioned sub-construction appears two times.

4.2 Syntactic-Based Sentence Retrieval

Indexing the English CLEF Collection. We parsed the English CLEF collection of texts with MiniPar [4] and built a SyntNet representation from the parsed sentences. With respect to the original MinPar output, we make a small change: We put the prepositions as edge labels and delete them as vertices. The SyntNet model was implemented as a relational database under the MySQL platform.

Our syntactic-based Information Retrieval algorithm exploits the syntactic structure of the sentences in the text collection in order to compute how syntactically close the question keywords are. The main difference between the syntactic IR and the tree edit distance algorithm, described in the previous section, is that the syntactic IR ignores completely the syntactic structure of the question and processes it as a set of keywords. In cross-language settings this allows for word by word question translation making use of a multilingual approach described earlier in [8]. The advantage of ignoring the question structure in cross-language mode is that the QA process becomes less sensible to incorrect question translations as far as the keywords are translated correctly.

We experimented with syntactic IR in the cross-language Bulgarian-English and Italian-English tasks. We used the SyntNet both for tracing of syntactic constructions in the manner described in Sect.4.1, as well as the calculation of IDF for the words.

We apply the following algorithm:

1. The retrieving process begins with identification of the *keyword vertices* - the vertices in SyntNet which represent the question keywords. As an example let's consider the question "What is the relation between John and Mary?" and the SyntNet on Fig.1. Keyword vertices in SyntNet are $John$ and $Mary$. Each keyword vertex has a weight assigned - derived from its IDF.
2. We use the numerical indices to trace paths in the SyntNet up from each keyword vertex. In this way we find all the vertices that stay above the question keywords in some of the sentences in the corpus. For example, from "John" we can trace in upward direction the two paths $(4 \leftarrow 2 \leftarrow 1)$ and $(8 \leftarrow 6 \leftarrow 5)$. Both numerical paths represent the construction "Sir John loves" in sentences g_1 and g_2. When tracing up from a keyword vertex kv (e.g. "John"), we record for each vertex v (e.g. "loves"), we encounter on our way, what is the distance between v and kv. This distance is calculated from the sum of the IDF of the vertices which stay between kv and v. We will call these vertices *intermediate vertices*. For example, an intermediate vertex between "John" and "loves" is "Sir".

   Keyword vertices which appear as intermediate vertices contribute 0 to the distance. Moreover, if there is some distributional similarity between an intermediate vertex and any of the key vertices, this intermediate vertex contributes to the distance only a part of its IDF. (We measure distributional similarity between words using a syntactic distributional approach similar to [5])

   We will denote thus calculated distance by $|kv\ v|$. It models the quantity of information in the path between kv and v which is not shared with the question.

   For example, the distance between "John" and "loves" will be equal to:

$$|John\ loves| = IDF(Sir).(1 - similarity(Sir, John)) \qquad (3)$$

3. In step 2 we have found all the vertices which stay above the keyword vertices in different sentences. If one and the same vertex stays above several keywords in a sentence, it is a root of a tree whose leaves are these keyword vertices. For each such vertex v which is a root of a tree spanning over keywords $kwQv_1, kwQv_2, ..., kwQv_n$, we define:

$$syntscore(v) = \frac{\sum_{kwQv_i} IDF(kwQv_i)}{I(Q) + \sum_{kwQv_i} |kwQv_i\ v| + IDF(v)} \qquad (4)$$

where I(Q) is the sum of the IDF of all the question keywords. If v is a keyword vertex, $IDF(v)$ in the above formula is considered to be 0. This score we call *syntactic context score.* It shows how similar the keyword spanning tree is to the question in terms of lexical content.

4. Finally, the score of a sentence S is calculated as:

$$score(s) = \max_{v \in S} syntscore(v).\frac{I(Q \cap S)}{I(Q)} \tag{5}$$

In this formula $I(Q \cap S)$ is the sum of the IDF of the question keywords which appear in the sentence. This formula combines the highest syntactic context score in the sentence and the relative quantity of the information that the question shares with that sentence.

For the processing steps which follow the sentence retrieval, only the top ranked sentences are considered. As a last stage DIOGENE system performs answer extraction and Web based answer validation to choose the best answer [6] from the retrieved sentences.

5 A QA System for Bulgarian – "Socrates 2"

In order to participate in the monolingual Bulgarian task, we decided to build a QA system for Bulgarian which uses certain templates from the "Socrates" on-line QA system [10], but also incorporates answer extraction techniques for questions for which no patterns exist. We call this system "Socrates 2". Moreover, we decided to build a linguistic index of the Bulgarian CLEF collection in which each word is represented with its lemma and part of speech. In this index the separate sentences were represented rather than whole documents.

5.1 Question Processing

"Socrates 2" performs question classification on the basis of simple superficial templates. It classifies the question into one of the following categories: definition questions and questions which require person, location, organization, year, date, manner, reason, or generic name as an answer.

5.2 Building the Linguistic Index

Instead of relying on standard search engines, we developed our own sentence retrieval engine and linguistic index for the Bulgarian CLEF collection. The text collection was split into sentences and automatically annotated with part-of-speech tags and word lemmas using the LINGUA system [11]. This linguistic annotation and the IDF of each word were encoded in the linguistic index which backs up our sentence retrieval module.

5.3 Sentence Retrieval

All the sentences which contain at least one of the question keywords are taken into consideration. Sentences are ranked using the following formula: $score(S) = \frac{I(Q \cap S)}{I(Q)}$. Information content of the question $I(Q)$ is measured as a sum of the IDF of its keywords. The quantity of the shared information content $I(Q \cap S)$ is the sum of the IDF of the question keywords which appear in the sentence.

5.4 Answer Extraction

For definition questions we adapted and used templates and rules already implemented in the "Socrates" on-line demo. Since these templates were already tested and tuned using real on-line users questions submitted to the Socrates Web site (http://tanev.dir.bg/Socrat.htm), we did not make any significant improvements in the system of rules.

We did not develop any specific strategy for the temporal questions, rather they were treated as factoid ones. For identification of factoid answers we created rules for extraction of generic names (without specifying if the name designates location, person, organization, or other entity), dates, and numbers. All other answer candidates like noun phrases which are not names or verb phrases were ignored.

When extracting candidate answers for factoid and temporal questions, our system considers the top 200 ranked sentences whose score is greater than 0.5. Moreover, only the sentences which have score greater than 0.1 of the score of the top ranked sentence are taken into consideration. In this way, we avoid to extract answers from sentences which does not contain enough question keywords.

Name Identification. In the general case, our name identification system considers a candidate for a name each sequence of words which begin with capital letters. However, a capitalized word in the beginning of the sentence is considered a part of a name, only if it is found in the dictionary of proper names integrated in the LINGUA morphological processor [3] or it is an unknown word. Usually, this strategy recognizes properly the names, however we noticed that often two names appear next to each other, which causes errors in the name recognition. In such cases we apply a name splitting algorithm which splits a sequence of capitalized words $N_1 N_2 N_3 ... N_n$ after the first one, if $P(N_1|N_2 N_3) < limit$.

Answer scoring and ranking. The score of a candidate answer A in a sentence S is calculated taking into account the IDF and the distance in tokens to each of the question keywords (kw_i) in the sentence: $score(A, S) = \sum_{kw_i \in Q \cap S} \frac{IDF(kw_i)}{1+\sqrt{|A\ kw_i|}}$. This formula gives higher score to the candidate answers which appear close to the most important question keywords (having high IDF). When two candidate answers have equal score, the system prefers the one which appears more often in the top ranked sentences.

6 Evaluation

We submitted one run at the monolingual Bulgarian task using our new system "Socrates 2". We produced two runs in the Italian monolingual task (in the second run keyword density was considered together with the Web validation score). Regarding the Italian-English task, we run the two experiments described in the previous sections. In the first run we used syntactic IR for factoid and temporal questions and in the second run we used tree edit distance algorithm for factoids. We used syntactic based IR also in the Bulgarian-English cross-language task. In all the tasks we used the multilingual template-based approach for answering definition questions [12]. The results of all the tasks are shown on Table 1.

Table 1. QA Performance at CLEF 2005

Task	*Overall*	*Def. (%)*	*Factoid (%)*	*Temp. (%)*
Italian (Web)	22.0	38.0	19.2	6.7
Italian (Web+kw.density)	19.0	38.0	14.2	6.7
Bulgarian	27.5	40.0	25.0	17.7
Italian/English (SyntNet)	23.5	38.0	19.8	13.8
Italian/English (edit distance)	13.0	38.0	5.8	0
Bulgarian/English (SyntNet)	18.5	20.0	17.4	20.7

The Impact of the Syntactic IR. We compared our syntactic based IR descibed in Sec.4.2 with another approach which ranks the sentences according to the sum of the IDF of the question keywords present in the sentence. Evaluation was carried out on 90 randomly selected factoid and temporal questions from the **I/E** task. For each question we took the top ranked sentence from both approaches and tested it for the correct answer. The syntactic IR returned a correct answer in the first sentence for 37.8% of the questions, while the bag-of-words approach for 33.3%.

Although the 4.5% improvement in accuracy may not seem significant, it is enough to demonstrate how the syntactic information can contribute to the performance of the IR module.

7 Conclusions and Future Directions

At CLEF 2005 we experimented with linguistic indices for Bulgarian and English. The Bulgarian QA system based on the linguistic index achieved promising results considering the simplicity of the QA approach. We tested two novel approaches based on syntax: one for IR and the other for answer extraction. An evaluation of the questions from the **I/E** task showed that syntactic based IR outperforms the bag-of-words IR by 4.5%.

In our future work we intend to examine the potential of the tree edit distance algorithms and the SyntNet model for linguistically motivated information search and QA.

References

1. Buchholz, S.: Using Grammatical Relations, Answer Frequencies and the World Wide Web for TREC Question Answering. In Proceeding of the Tenth Text Retrieval Conference (2001), 496–503.
2. Cui, H., Li, K., Sun, R., Chua, T., Kan, M: University of Singapore at the TREC-13 Question Answering Main Task. In Proceedings of the Thirteenth Text Retrieval Conference (2005)
3. Krushkov, H.: Modelling and Building of Machine Dictionaries and Morphological processors. Ph.D. Thesis, University of Plovdiv (1997) (in Bulgarian)
4. Lin, D.: Dependency-based evaluation of MINIPAR. In Proceedings of the Workshop on Evaluation of Parsing Systems at LREC (1998) Granada, Spain.
5. Lin, D.: Automatic Retrieval and Clustering of Similar Words. In Proceedings of COLING-ACL (1998)
6. Magnini, B., Negri, M., Prevete, R., Tanev, H.: Is it the Right Answer? Exploiting Web Redundancy for Answer Validation. Association for Computational Linguistics 40th Anniversary Meeting (ACL-02) (2002) Pennsylvania, Philadelphia.
7. Moldovan, D., Harabagiu, S., Girju, R., Morarescu, P., Lacatsu, F., Novischi, A.: LCC Tools for Question Answering. In Proceedings of The Eleventh Text Retrieval Conference (2003)
8. Negri, M., Tanev, H., Magnini, B. Bridging Languages for Question Answering: DIOGENE at CLEF 2003. CLEF 2003 Working Notes (2003). Trondheim, Norway
9. Punyakanok., V.,Roth, D. and Yih, W.: Mapping Dependencies Trees: An Application to Question Answering In Proceedings of AI & Math (2004)
10. Tanev, H.: Socrates: A Question Answering Prototype for Bulgarian Recent Advances in Natural Language Processing III, Selected Papers from RANLP 2003. John Benjamins (2004) Amsterdam/Philadelphia
11. Tanev, H. an Mikov, R.: Shallow Language Processing Architecture for Bulgarian. In Proceedings of COLING 2002 Taipei, Taiwan
12. Tanev, H., Kouylekov, M., Negri, M., Coppola, B., Magnini, B.: Multilingual Pattern Libraries for Question Answering : a Case Study for Definition Questions. In Proceedings of LREC 2004. Lisbon, Portugal
13. Zhang, K., Shasha, D.: Fast algorithm for the unit cost editing distance between trees. Journal of algorithms, vol. 11, December (1990) , 1245–1262

The TALP-QA System for Spanish at CLEF 2005

Daniel Ferrés, Samir Kanaan, Alicia Ageno, Edgar González, Horacio Rodríguez, and Jordi Turmo

TALP Research Center, Universitat Politècnica de Catalunya
Jordi Girona 1-3, 08043 Barcelona, Spain
{dferres, skanaan, ageno, egonzalez, horacio, turmo}@lsi.upc.edu

Abstract. This paper describes the TALP-QA system in the context of the CLEF 2005 Spanish Monolingual Question Answering (QA) evaluation task. TALP-QA is a multilingual open-domain QA system that processes both factoid (normal and temporally restricted) and definition questions. The approach to factoid questions is based on in-depth NLP tools and resources to create semantic information representation. Answers to definition questions are selected from the phrases that match a pattern from a manually constructed set of definitional patterns.

1 Introduction

This paper describes TALP-QA, a multilingual open-domain Question Answering (QA) system under development at UPC for the past 3 years. A first version of TALP-QA for Spanish was used to participate in the CLEF 2004 Spanish QA track (see [5]). From this version, a new version for English was built and was used in TREC 2004 [6], an improvement of this version is what is presented here. The main changes of the system architecture with respect to the prototype used in the CLEF 2004 evaluation are: i) factoid and definition questions are treated using different architectures, ii) new modules have been designed to deal with temporally restricted questions, iii) Named Entity Recognition and Classification (NERC) and Question Classification modules have been improved.

In this paper the overall architecture of TALP-QA and its main components are briefly sketched, the reader can consult [5] and [6] for more in depth description of this architecture. Most of the paper describes with some details the improvements over the previous system that have been included for this evaluation. We also present an evaluation of the system used in the CLEF 2005 Spanish QA task for factoid, temporally restricted factoid, and definition questions.

2 Factoid QA System

The system architecture for factoid questions has three subsystems that are executed sequentially without feedback: Question Processing (QP), Passage Retrieval (PR) and Answer Extraction (AE). This section describes the three main subsystems and a Collection Pre-processing process.

C. Peters et al. (Eds.): CLEF 2005, LNCS 4022, pp. 400–409, 2006.

2.1 Collection Pre-processing

We pre-processed the document collection (EFE 1994 and EFE 1995) with linguistic tools (described in [5]) to mark the part-of-speech (POS) tags, lemmas, Named Entities (NE), and syntactic chunks. Then, we indexed the collection and we computed the *idf* weight at document level for the whole collection. We used the *Lucene*[1] Information Retrieval (IR) engine to create an index with two fields per document: i) the lemmatized text with NERC and syntactic information, ii) the original text (forms) with NER (not classified) and syntactic information.

2.2 Question Processing

A key point in QP is the Question Classification (QC) subtask. The results from QC in our previous attempt (in CLEF 2004) were low (58.33% accuracy). As was explained in [5] the low accuracy obtained is basically due to two facts: i) the dependence on errors of previous tasks [5], ii) the question classifier was trained with the manual translation of questions from TREC 8 and TREC 9 (about 900 questions). The classifier performs better in English (74% (171/230)) than in Spanish (58.33% (105/180)), probably due to the artificial origin of the training material.

We decided to build a new QP module with two objectives: i) improving the accuracy of our QC component and ii) providing better material for allowing a more accurate semantic pre-processing of the question. The QP module is split into five components, we will next describe these components focusing on those that have been changed from our previous system (see [5] for details):

- **Question Pre-processing.** This subsystem is basically the same component of our previous system with some improvements. For CLEF 2005 (for Spanish) we used a set of general purpose tools produced by the UPC NLP group: *Freeling* [2], *ABIONET* [3], *Tacat* [1], *EuroWordNet* (EWN), and *Gazetteers* [5]. These tools are used for the linguistic processing of both questions and passages. The main improvements on these tools refer to:
  - **Geographical gazetteers.** Due to the limited amount of context in questions, the accuracy of our NER and NEC components suffers a severe fall, specially serious when dealing with locatives (a 46% of NEC errors in the CLEF 2004 questions analysis were related with locatives). For this reason, we used geographical gazetteers to improve the accuracy of the NEC task. The gazetteers used were: a subset of 126,941 non-ambiguous places from the GEOnet Names Server (GNS)[2], the *GeoWorldMap*[3] gazetteer with approximately 40,594 entries (countries, regions and important cities), and *Albayzin Gazetteer* (a gazetteer of 758 place names of Spain existing in the speech corpus Albayzin [4]).

[1] http://jakarta.apache.org/lucene
[2] GNS. http://earth-info.nga.mil/gns/html
[3] Geobytes Inc.: http://www.geobytes.com/

- **FreeLing Measure Recognizer and Classifier.** A module for a fine-grained classification of measures and units has been created. This module was added to *Freeling* and it recognises the following measure classes: *acceleration*, *density*, *digital*, *dimension*, *energy*, *extent*, *flow*, *frequency*, *power*, *pressure*, *size*, *speed*, *temperature*, *time*, and *weight*.
- **Temporal expressions grammar.** This process recognises complex temporal expressions both in the questions and in the passages. It is a recogniser based on a grammar of temporal expressions (composed by 73 rules) which detects four types of such expressions:
  * *Date*: a specific day (e.g. "July 4th 2000"), a day of the week (e.g. "Monday"), months, and years.
  * *Date_range*: a period of time, spanning between two specific dates or expressions such as "in 1910" (which would be equivalent to the period between January 1st 1910 and December 31st 1910), but also the seasons or other well-known periods of the year.
  * *Date_previous*: the period previous to a date (e.g. "before 1998").
  * *Date_after*: the period subsequent to a date (e.g. "after March 1998").

  Moreover, in all the four types, not only absolute dates or periods are detected, but also dates relative to the current date, in expressions such as "el próximo viernes" (next Friday),"ayer" (yesterday), or "a partir de mañana" (from tomorrow on). These relative dates are converted into absolute according to the date of the document in which they are found.

The application of the language dependent linguistic resources and tools to the text of the question results in two structures:

- **Sent**, which provides lexical information for each word: form, lemma, POS tag (Eagles tagset), semantic class of NE, list of EWN synsets and, finally, whenever possible the verbs associated with the actor and the relations between some locations (specially countries) and their gentiles (e.g. nationality).
- **Sint**, composed of two lists, one recording the syntactic constituent structure of the question (basically nominal, prepositional and verbal phrases) and the other collecting the information of dependencies and other relations between these components.

– **Question Refinement.** This module contains two components: a tokenizer and a parser (processing the lexical structure of Question Pre-processing step). The tokenizer refines and sometimes modifies the sent structure. Basically the changes can affect the NEs occurring in the question and their local context (both the segmentation and the classification can be affected). Taking evidences from the local context a NE can be refined (e.g. its label can change from location to city), reclassified (e.g. passing from location to organization), merged with another NE, etc. Most of the work of the tokenizer relies on a set of trigger words associated to NE types, especially locations. We have collected this set from the Albayzin corpus (a corpus of about 6,887 question patterns in Spanish on Spain's geography domain, [4]). The parser uses a DCG grammar learned from the Albayzin corpus and tuned with the

CLEF 2004 questions. In addition of triggers, the grammar uses a set of introducers, patterns of lemmas as "dónde" (where), "qué ciudad" (which city), etc. also collected from Albayzin corpus.

- **Environment Building.** The semantic process starts with the extraction of the semantic relations that hold between the different components identified in the question text. These relations are organized into an ontology of about 100 semantic classes and 25 relations (mostly binary) between them. Both classes and relations are related by taxonomic links. The ontology tries to reflect what is needed for an appropriate representation of the semantic environment of the question (and the expected answer). The environment of the question is obtained from *Sint* and *Sent*. A set of about 150 rules was assembled to perform this task. Only minor changes have been performed in this module, so refer to [5] for details.
- **Question Classification.** This component uses 72 hand made rules to extract the Question Type (QT). These rules use a set of introducers (e.g. 'where'), and the predicates extracted from the environment (e.g. location, state, action,...) to detect the QT (currently, 25 types). The QT is needed by the system when searching the answer. The QT focuses the type of expected answer and provides additional constraints.
- **Semantic Constraints Extraction.** Depending on the QT, a subset of useful items of the environment has to be selected in order to extract the answer. Sometimes additional relations, not present in the environment, are used and sometimes the relations extracted from the environment are extended, refined or modified. We define in this way the set of relations (the semantic constraints) that are supposed to be found in the answer. These relations are classified as mandatory, (MC), (i.e. they have to be satisfied in the passage) or optional, (OC), (if satisfied the score of the answer is higher). In order to build the semantic constraints for each question a set of rules (typically 1 or 2 for each type of question) has been manually built. Although the structure of this module has not changed from our CLEF 2004 system, some of the rules have been modified and additional rules have been included for taking profit of the richer information available for producing more accurate Semantic Constraints (a set of 88 rules is used).

2.3 Passage Retrieval

The Passage Retrieval subsystem is structured using the *Lucene* Information Retrieval system. The PR algorithm uses a data-driven query relaxation technique: if too few passages are retrieved, the query is relaxed first by increasing the accepted keyword proximity and then by discarding the keywords with the lowest priority. The reverse happens when too many passages are extracted. Each keyword is assigned a priority using a series of heuristics fairly similar to [9]. The Passage Retrieval subsystem has been improved with the following components:

- **Temporal Constraints Keywords Search.** When a keyword is a temporal expression, the PR system returns passages that have a temporal expression that satisfies the constraint detected by our temporal grammar.

– **Coreference resolution.** We apply a coreference resolution algorithm to the retrieved passages. This algorithm is applied to enhance the recall in the Answer Extraction modules. We use an adaptation of the limited-knowledge algorithm proposed in [10]. We start by clustering the Named Entities in every passage according to the similarity of their forms (trying to capture phenomena as acronyms). For Named Entities classified as Person we use a first name gazetteer[4] to classify them as masculine or feminine. By the clustering procedure we get the gender information for the occurrences of the name where the first name does not appear. After that, we detect the omitted pronouns and the clause boundaries using the method explained in [7], and then apply the criteria of [10] to find the antecedent of reflexive, demostrative, personal and omitted pronouns among the noun phrases in the 4 previous clauses.

2.4 Factoid Answer Extraction

After PR, for factoid AE, two tasks are performed in sequence: Candidate Extraction (CE) and Answer Selection (AS). In the first component, all the candidate answers are extracted from the highest scoring sentences of the selected passages. In the second component the best answer is chosen.

– **Candidate Extraction.** The answer extraction process is carried out on the set of passages obtained from the previous subsystem. These passages are segmented into sentences and each sentence is scored according to its semantic content (see [8]). The linguistic process of extraction is similar to the process carried out on questions and leads to the construction of the environment of each candidate sentence. The rest is a mapping between the semantic relations contained in this environment and the semantic constraints extracted from the question. The mandatory restrictions must be satisfied for the sentence to be taken into consideration; satisfying the optional constraints simply increases the score of the candidate. The final extraction process is carried out on the sentences satisfying this filter.

  The knowledge source used for this process is a set of extraction rules with a credibility score. Each QT has its own subset of extraction rules that leads to the selection of the answer. The application of the rules follows an iterative approach. In the first iteration all the semantic constraints must be satisfied by at least one of the candidate sentences. If no sentence has satisfied the constraints, the set of semantic constraints is relaxed by means of structural or semantic relaxation rules, using the semantic ontology. Two kinds of relaxation are considered: i) moving some constraint from MC to OC and ii) relaxing some constraint in MC substituting it for another more general in the taxonomy. If no candidate sentence occurs when all possible relaxations have been performed the question is assumed to have no answer.

[4] By Mark Kantrowitz, `http://www-2.cs.cmu.edu/afs/cs/project/ai-repository/ai/areas/nlp /corpora/names`

– **Answer selection.** In order to select the answer from the set of candidates, the following scores are computed for each candidate sentence: i) the rule score (which uses factors such as the confidence of the rule used, the relevance of the OC satisfied in the matching, and the similarity between NEs occurring in the candidate sentence and the question), ii) the passage score, iii) the semantic score (defined previously) , iv) the relaxation score (which takes into account the level of rule relaxation in which the candidate has been extracted). For each candidate the values of these scores are normalized and accumulated in a global score. The answer to the question is the candidate with the best global score.

3 Definitional QA System

The Definitional QA System has three phases: Passage Retrieval, Sentence Extraction, and Sentence Selection. In the first phase, an index of documents has been created using Lucene. The search index has two fields: one with the lemmas of all non-stop words in the documents, and another with the lemmas of all the words of the documents that begin with a capital letter. The target to define is lemmatized, stopwords are removed and the remaining lemmas are used to search into the index of documents. Moreover, the words of the target that begin with a capital letter are lemmatized; the final query sent to Lucene is a complex one, composed of one sub-query using document lemmas and another query containing only the lemmas of the words that begin with a capital letter. This second query is intended to search correctly the targets that, although being proper names, are composed or contain common words. For example, if the target is "Sendero Luminoso", documents containing the words "sendero" or "luminoso" as common names are not of interest; the occurrence of these words is only of interest if they are proper names, and as a simplification this is substituted by the case the words begin with a capital letter. The score of a document is the score given by Lucene. Once selected a number of documents (50 in the current configuration), the passages (blocks of 200 words) that refer to the target are selected for the next phase.

The objective of the second phase is to obtain a set of candidate sentences that might contain the definition of the target. As definitions usually have certain structure, as appositions or copulative sentences, a set of patterns has been manually developed in order to detect these and other expressions usually associated with definitions (for example, <phrase> , <target>, or <phrase> "ser" <target>). The sentences that match any of these patterns are extracted.

In the last step, one of the sentences previously obtained has to be given as the answer. In order to select the most likely sentence, an assumption has been made, in the sense that the words most frequently co-occurring with the target will belong to its definition. Thus, the frequency of the words (strictly, their lemmas) in the set of candidate sentences is computed and the sentence given as answer is the one whose words sum up a higher value of relative frequency.

4 Results

This section evaluates the behaviour of our system in CLEF 2005. We evaluated the three main components of our factoid QA system and the global results:

- **Question Processing.** This subsystem has been manually evaluated for factoid questions (see Table 1) in the following components: POS-tagging, NER and NE Classification (NEC) and QC. These results are accumulatives.

Table 1. Results of Question Processing evaluation

Question Type	Subsystem	Total units	Correct	Incorrect	Accuracy	Error
FACTOID	POS-tagging	1122	1118	4	99.64%	0.36%
	NE Recognition	132	129	3	97.73%	2.27%
	NE Classification	132	87	45	65.91%	34.09%
	Q. Classification	118	78	40	66.10%	33.89%
TEMPORAL	POS-tagging	403	402	1	99.75%	0.25%
	NE Recognition	64	56	8	87.50%	12.50%
	NE Classification	64	53	11	82.81%	17.19%
	Q. Classification	32	27	5	84.37%	15.62%

- **Passage Retrieval.** This subsystem was evaluated using the set of correct answers given by the CLEF organization (see Table 2). We computed two measures: the first one (called *answer*) is the accuracy taking into account the questions that have a correct answer in its set of passages. The second one (called *answer+docID*) is the accuracy taking into account the questions that have a minimum of one passage with a correct answer and a correct document identifier in its set of passages. For factoid questions the two runs submitted differ in the parameters of the passage retrieval module: i) the maximum number of documents retrieved was 1200 (run1) and 1000 (run2), ii) the windows proximity was: (run1: 60 to 240 lemmas; run2: 80 to 220 lemmas), iii) the threshold for minimum passages: 4 (run1) and 1 (run2), iv) the maximum number of passages retrieved: 300 (run1) and 50 (run2).

Table 2. Passage Retrieval results (accuracy)

Question type	Measure	run1	run2
FACTOID	Acc. (*answer*)	78.09% (82/105)	76.19% (80/105)
	Acc. (*answer+docID*)	64.76% (68/105)	59.05% (62/105)
TEMPORAL	Acc. (*answer*)	50.00% (13/26)	46.15% (12/26)
	Acc. (*answer+docID*)	34.61% (9/26)	30.77% (8/26)

- **Answer Extraction.** The evaluation of this subsystem (see Table 3) uses the *answer+docID* and *answer* accuracies described previously.

Table 3. Factoid Answer Extraction results (accuracy)

Question Type	Accuracy Type	run1	run2
FACTOID	Acc. (*answer*)	29.27% (24/82)	26.25% (21/80)
	Acc. (*answer+docID*)	35.29% (24/68)	33.87% (21/62)
TEMPORAL	Acc. (*answer*)	15.38% (2/13)	33.33% (4/12)
	Acc. (*answer+docID*)	22.22% (2/9)	50.00% (4/8)

– **Global Results.** The overall results of our participation in CLEF 2005 Spanish monolingual QA task are listed in Table 4.

Table 4. Results of TALP-QA system at CLEF 2005 Spanish monolingual QA task

Measure	run1	run2
Total Num. Answers	200	200
Right	58	54
Wrong	122	133
IneXact	20	13
Unsupported	0	0
Overall accuracy	29.00% (58/200)	27.00% (54/200)
Accuracy over Factoid	27.97% (33/118)	25.42% (30/118)
Accuracy over Definition	36.00% (18/50)	32.00% (16/50)
Accuracy over Temporal Factoid	21.88% (7/32)	25.00% (8/32)
Answer-string "NIL" returned correctly	25.92% (14/54)	22.41% (13/58)
Confidence-weighted Score	0.08935 (17.869/200)	0.07889 (15.777/200)

5 Evaluation and Conclusions

This paper summarizes our participation in the CLEF 2005 Spanish monolingual QA evaluation task. Out of 200 questions, our system provided the correct answer to 58 questions in run1 and 54 in run2. Hence, the global accuracy of our system was 29% and 27% for run1 and run2 respectively. In comparison with the results of the last evaluation (CLEF 2004), our system has reached a small improvement (24% and 26% of accuracy). Otherwise, we had 20 answers considered as inexact. We think that with a more accurate extraction phase we could extract correctly more questions and reach easily an accuracy of 39% . We conclude with a summary of the system behaviour for the three question classes:

– **Factoid questions**. The accuracy over factoid questions is 27.97% (run1) and 25.42% (run2). Although no direct comparison can be done using another test collection, we think that we have improved slightly our factoid QA system with respect to the results of the CLEF 2004 QA evaluation (18.89% and 21.11%) in Spanish. In comparison with the other participants of the CLEF 2005 Spanish QA track, our system has obtained good results in the following type of questions: location and time. On the other hand, our system has obtained a poor performance in the classes: measure and other.

  - **Question Processing.** In this subsystem the Question Classification component has an accuracy of 66.10%. This result means that there is no great improvement with respect to the classifier used in CLEF 2004 (it reached a 58% of accuracy). These values are influenced by the previous errors in the POS, NER and NEC subsystems. On the other hand, NEC errors have increased substantially with respect to the previous evaluation. NEC component achieved an error rate of 34.09%. This is the most serious drawback of the QP phase and needs an in depth analysis for the next evaluation.
  - **Passage Retrieval.** We evaluated that 78.09% (run1) and 76.19% (run2) of questions have a correct answer in their passages. Taking into account the document identifiers the evaluation shows that 64.76% (run1) and 59.05% (run2) of the questions are really supported. This subsystem has improved substantially its results in comparison with the CLEF 2004 evaluation (48.12% and 43.12% of *answer+docID* accuracy).
  - **Answer Extraction.** The accuracy of the AE module for factoid questions for which the answer and document identifier occurred in our selected passages was of 35.29% (run1) and 33.87% (run2). This means that we have improved our AE module, since the results for this part in CLEF 2004 were 23.32% (run1) and 28.42% (run2), evaluated only with answer accuracy. This is the subsystem that performs worst and needs a substantial improvement and tuning.
- **Definition questions.** This subsystem has reached a performance of 36% (run1) and 32% (run2) of right answers. The difference between the two runs lies in the different priority values assigned to each definitional pattern. The system has failed mainly in giving exact answers. The main cause of error has been the failure to correctly extract the exact sentence defining the target, as in 15 questions there were more words than just the definition, and thus the answer was marked as inexact. Otherwise, 33 questions would have had a right answer, and thus a 66% performance would have been achieved.
- **Temporal Factoid Questions.** The accuracy over temporal factoid questions is 21.88% (run1) and 25.00% (run2). We detected poor results in the PR subsystem: the accuracy of PR with answer and document identifiers is 34.61% (run1) and 30.77% (run2). These results are due to the fact that some questions are temporally restricted by events. These questions need a special treatment, different from the one for factoid questions.

Acknowledgements

This work has been partially supported by the European Commission (CHIL, IST-2004-506909), the Spanish Research Department (ALIADO, TIC2002-04447-C02), the Ministry of Universities, Research and Information Society (DURSI) of the Catalan Government, and the European Social Fund. Daniel Ferrés is supported by a UPC-Recerca grant from Universitat Politècnica de Catalunya (UPC). TALP Research Center, is recognized as a Quality Research Group (2001

SGR 00254) by DURSI. The authors would like to express their gratitude in particular to Lluís Padró.

References

1. J. Atserias, J. Carmona, I. Castellón, S. Cervell, M. Civit, L. Márquez, M.A. Martí, L. Padró, R. Placer, H. Rodríguez, M. Taulé, and J. Turmo. Morphosyntactic Analisys and Parsing of Unrestricted Spanish Text. In *Proceedings of the 1st International Conference on Language Resources and Evaluation, LREC*, pages 603–610, Granada, Spain, May 1998.
2. Xavier Carreras, Isaac Chao, Lluís Padró, and Muntsa Padró. FreeLing: An Open-Source Suite of Language Analyzers. In *Proceedings of the 4th International Conference on Language Resources and Evaluation, LREC*, Lisbon, Portugal, 2004.
3. Xavier Carreras, Lluís Màrquez, and Lluís Padró. Named Entity Extraction using AdaBoost. In *Proceedings of CoNLL-2002*, pages 167–170. Taipei, Taiwan, 2002.
4. J. Diaz, A. Rubio, A. Peinado, E. Segarra, N. Prieto, and F. Casacuberta. Development of Task-Oriented Spanish Speech Corpora. In *Procceedings of the First International Conference on Language Resources and Evaluation*, pages 497–501, Granada, Spain, May 1998. ELDA.
5. Daniel Ferrés, Samir Kanaan, Alicia Ageno, Edgar González, Horacio Rodríguez, Mihai Surdeanu, and Jordi Turmo. The TALP-QA System for Spanish at CLEF 2004: Structural and Hierarchical Relaxing of Semantic Constraints. In Carol Peters, Paul Clough, Julio Gonzalo, Gareth J. F. Jones, Michael Kluck, and Bernardo Magnini, editors, *CLEF*, volume 3491 of *Lecture Notes in Computer Science*, pages 557–568. Springer, 2004.
6. Daniel Ferrés, Samir Kanaan, Edgar González, Alicia Ageno, Horacio Rodríguez, Mihai Surdeanu, and Jordi Turmo. TALP-QA System at TREC 2004: Structural and Hierarchical Relaxation Over Semantic Constraints. In *Proceedings of the Text Retrieval Conference (TREC-2004)*, 2005.
7. A. Ferrández and J. Peral. A computational approach to zero-pronouns in Spanish. In *Proceedings of the 38th Annual Meeting of the Association for Computational Linguistics, (ACL'2000)*, 2000.
8. Marc Massot, Horacio Rodríguez, and Daniel Ferrés. QA UdG-UPC System at TREC-12. In *Proceedings of the Text Retrieval Conference (TREC-2003)*, pages 762–771, 2003.
9. D. Moldovan, S. Harabagiu, M. Pasca, R. Mihalcea, R. Goodrum, R. Gîrju, and V. Rus. LASSO: A tool for surfing the answer net. In *Proceedings of the Eighth Text Retrieval Conference (TREC-8)*, 1999.
10. M. Saiz-Noeda. *Influencia y aplicación de papeles sintácticos e información semántica en la resolución de la anáfora pronominal en español.* PhD thesis, Universidad de Alicante, 2002.

Priberam's Question Answering System for Portuguese

Carlos Amaral, Helena Figueira, André Martins, Afonso Mendes, Pedro Mendes, and Cláudia Pinto

Priberam Informática
Av. Defensores de Chaves, 32 - 3° Esq.
1000-119 Lisboa, Portugal
{cma, hgf, atm, amm, prm, cp}@priberam.pt

Abstract. This paper describes the work done by Priberam in the development of a question answering (QA) system for Portuguese. The system was built using the company's natural language processing (NLP) workbench and information retrieval technology. Special focus is given to question analysis, document and sentence retrieval, as well as answer extraction stages. The paper discusses the system's performance in the context of the QA@CLEF 2005 evaluation.

1 Introduction

Portuguese was introduced as one of the working languages in the 2004 CLEF campaign, allowing pioneering work in QA for this language [1,2,3]. Priberam's approach to this year's QA@CLEF relies on previous work done for the Portuguese module of TRUST[1] (Text Retrieval Using Semantic Technologies), a project whose aim was the development of a multilingual semantic search engine capable of processing and answering NL questions in English, French, Italian, Polish and Portuguese [4,5]. In TRUST, the system searches a set of plain text documents (either in a local hard disk or in the Web) and returns a ranked list of sentences containing the answer. The goal of QA@CLEF is similar, except that it must extract a unique exact answer.

The architecture of this QA system is built upon a standard approach. After the question is submitted, it is categorized according to a question typology and, through an internal query, a set of potentially relevant documents is retrieved. Each document contains a list of sentences which were assigned the same category as the question. Sentences are weighted according to their semantic relevance and similarity with the question. Next, these sentences are reexamined and the parts containing possible answers are extracted and weighted. Finally, a single answer is chosen among all candidates.

The next section addresses the tools and resources developed or used in the system's underlying NLP. Section 3 provides an overview of the engine architecture. Section 4 discusses the experimental results in QA@CLEF. Section 5 presents conclusions and guidelines for future work.

[1] See `http://www.trustsemantics.com`.

C. Peters et al. (Eds.): CLEF 2005, LNCS 4022, pp. 410–419, 2006.

2 A Workbench for NLP

Previous work on the development of linguistic technology for FLiP, Priberam's proofing tools package for Portuguese[2], as well as on the construction of the Portuguese module of TRUST, required building a workbench for NLP [6]. It includes lexical resources, software tools, statistical information extracted from corpora, and other tools and resources adapted to the task of QA.

2.1 Lexical Resources

The lexical resources comprise several lexical databases, such as a wide coverage lexicon, a thesaurus and a multilingual ontology.

The lexicon contains, for each lexical unit, information about POS, sense definitions, semantic features, subcategorization and selection restrictions, ontological and terminological domains, English and French equivalents and semantic relations. For the QA@CLEF monolingual task, the English and French equivalents are not used, since their purpose is mainly performing cross-language tasks.

The thesaurus provides a set of synonyms for each lexical unit, allowing, by means of query expansion, to retrieve documents and sentences that contain synonyms of the question's keywords, improving the information retrieval stage.

A major lexical component of the workbench is the multilingual ontology [4]. Initially designed by Synapse Développement, the French partner of TRUST, it was translated into all the languages of the consortium[3]. The combination of the ontology information of all TRUST languages provides a bidirectional translation mechanism, having English language as an intermediate. This enables operating in a cross-language environment, for instance, to obtain answers in French for questions in Portuguese. Synapse carried out such an experiment and submitted a Portuguese-French run to this year's bilingual task of QA@CLEF [7].

Lexical resources also include question identifiers, i.e., semantically labelled words related with typical question domains. For instance, the <DIMENSION> label includes measuring units (and their abbreviations), nouns, adjectives and verbs related with dimension, distance and measurement.

2.2 Software Tools

The lexical resources are the basis of software tools like *SintaGest*. Priberam's SintaGest is an interactive tool that allows building and testing a grammar for any language[4]. It provides a practical way to code contextual rules (for morphological disambiguation and NE recognition) and production rules to build a context-free grammar (CFG). The NE recognizer groups sequences of proper

[2] FLiP includes a grammar checker, a spell checker, a thesaurus, a hyphenator for both European and Brazilian Portuguese, bilingual dictionaries and a verb conjugator. An online version is available at `http://www.flip.pt`.

[3] The ontology is designed to incorporate additional languages in future projects.

[4] Besides the European and Brazilian Portuguese grammars, SintaGest is currently being tested with Polish.

nouns into a single token and classifies it semantically according to the context. For instance, the sequence *rio de São Domingos* [São Domingos river] is classified as a toponym. SintaGest also allows to perform tasks related with QA, such as writing patterns to categorize questions and extract answers. The rules can be tested on corpora and compiled to generate optimized low-level information. For more details on SintaGest, see [6].

Together with SintaGest, several modules have been developed to perform more specific tasks, like morphological disambiguation. This is done in two stages: first, the contextual rules defined in SintaGest are applied; then, remaining ambiguities are suppressed with a statistical POS tagger based on a second-order hidden Markov model (HMM), using the Viterbi algorithm [8,9]. The priors were estimated by processing partially tagged corpora, among them the *CETEMPúblico* collection from the Portuguese newspaper *Público*[5]. For more details, see [4].

2.3 Question Categorization

Classifying questions is a key task during question analysis, since it allows filtering out unrelated documents and applying better tuned answer extraction rules. We use a (flat) set of 86 categories, defined for TRUST by Synapse. Table 1 illustrates some of these categories.

Table 1. Examples of categories of question

Category	Example
<DENOMINATION>	"Nomeie um cetáceo." [Name a cetacean.]
<DATE OF EVENT>	"Em que dia foi inaugurada a Torre Eiffel?" [On what day was the Eiffel Tower inaugurated?]
<TOWN NAME>	"Em que cidade fica o campo de concentração de Auschwitz?" [In what city is the Auschwitz concentration camp located?]
<FUNCTION>	"Quem é Jorge Sampaio?" [Who is Jorge Sampaio?]

Common approaches for categorization use simple patterns, for instance regular expressions. However, these have the disadvantage of being too focused on string patterns, discarding other useful features. Our approach overcomes these limitations by using more powerful patterns. SintaGest provides the interface for writing, testing and compiling such patterns. They were validated with the *CLEF Multieight-04*[6] corpus [10].

Each pattern is a sequence of *terms* with the possible types: `Word` (a literal word or expression), `Root` (a lemma), `Cat` (a POS tag with optional lexical-semantic features), `Ont` (an ontology entry), `QuestIdent` (a question identifier),

[5] Available at `http://acdc.linguateca.pt/cetempublico`.

[6] Available at `http://clef-qa.itc.it/2005`.

or `Const` (a previously defined constant making use of the other identifiers). Prefix `Any` is used to build disjunctive terms, like `AnyWord`. Constants are often used to make patterns simple and generic. An example of a constant definition is `Const Ergonym = Cat(N(,,,,,ERG))`, stating that an ergonym[7] is any noun with the semantic feature `ERG`. Terms may be conjugated (e.g. `Word(casa) & Cat(N)` means the common noun *casa* [house], and not a form of the verb *casar* [to marry]). A term may also be optional (e.g. in `Word(casa)?` the `?` denotes optionality), and distances may be defined (e.g. `Word(quem) Distance(1,3) Word(presidente)` means that between *quem* [who] and *presidente* [president] there can be a minimum of 1 and a maximum of 3 words).

Table 2. Examples of patterns for category <FUNCTION>

```
// Example of a question answer block encoding QPs and QAPs:
Question (FUNCTION)
    : Word(quem) Distance(0,3) Root(ser) AnyCat(Nprop, ENT) = 15
     // e.g. ''Quem é Jorge Sampaio?''
    : Word(que) QuestIdent(FUNCTION_N) Distance(0,3) QuestIdent(FUNCTION_V) = 15
     // e.g. ''Que cargo desempenha Jorge Sampaio?''
Answer
    : Pivot & AnyCat (Nprop, ENT) Root(ser) {Definition With Ergonym?} = 20
     // e.g. ''Jorge Sampaio é o {Presidente da República}...''
    : {NounPhrase With Ergonym?} AnyCat (Trav, Vg) Pivot & AnyCat (Nprop, ENT) = 15
     // e.g. ''O {presidente da República}, Jorge Sampaio...''
    ;
```

```
// Example of an answer block encoding APs:
Answer (FUNCTION)
    : QuestIdent(FUNCTION_N) = 10
    : Ergonym = 10
    ;
```

These patterns are used not only to categorize questions, but also general sentences, and even to extract answers. There are actually 3 kinds of patterns:

1. *Question patterns* (QPs), to assign categories to questions. More than one category per question is allowed, to avoid difficult decisions at early stages.
2. *Answer patterns* (APs), to assign categories to a sentence during indexation, meaning that it may contain answers for questions with those categories.
3. *Question answering patterns* (QAPs), to extract a possible answer.

When a question matches a QP, a category is assigned to the question and a set of QAPs is activated. Then, documents containing sentences with categories common to the question (previously determined during indexation via the APs) are analysed. The active QAPs are then applied to each sentence in order to extract the possible answers.

Table 2 shows examples of QPs, APs and QAPs. Each pattern includes a heuristic score following the = sign to establish a priority. The `With` command

[7] The word *ergonym* (from Greek *ergon* 'work' and *onoma* 'name') designates here a person's profession, job, function, post, etc.

between terms means that the second term must be verified somewhere inside the first term. QAPs include an extra term, named `Pivot`, to signal keywords that are present both in the question and in the matched sentence (see Sect. 3.2), as well as a sequence of terms delimited by curly brackets, to signal the words that are to be extracted as a possible answer.

3 System Description

The architecture of Priberam's QA system is fairly standard. It involves five major tasks: (*i*) the indexing process, (*ii*) the question analysis, (*iii*) the document retrieval, (*iv*) the sentence retrieval, and (*v*) the answer extraction.

3.1 Indexing Process

Indexation is an off-line procedure during which a set of documents is processed to collect information in index files. Previous work on this subject has been done during the development of LegiX, Priberam's juridical information system[8].

The Portuguese target collection of QA@CLEF 2005 had 210734 documents. For each, the system collects its most relevant ontological and terminological domains and, for each sentence, their question categories, determined through the APs referred in Sect. 2.3. After morphological disambiguation and exclusion of stop-words, it collects as key elements for indexation the lemmas and heads of derivation. Special words as numbers, dates, NEs and proper nouns are flagged. Multiple word expressions are indexed as well as each word that composes them.

For performance reasons, each word in the index is stored with a reference not only to the target documents, but also to the sentences' indices inside each document. This accelerates the document retrieval stage, as described in Sect. 3.3.

3.2 Question Analysis

The question analyser is the first on-line module of the system. It receives a NL question q, that is first lemmatized and morphologically disambiguated (see Sect. 2.2). It then proceeds to categorization.

As described in Sect. 2.3, we use 86 categories in a flat structure and build QPs to categorize the questions. When this stage ends, the following information has been gathered: (*i*) one or more question categories, $\{c^1, c^2, \ldots, c^m\}$, (*ii*) a list of active QAPs to be later applied during answer extraction (see Sect. 3.5), and (*iii*) a score σ^{QP} for each question pattern that matched the question.

The next step is the extraction of pivots. Pivots are the key elements of the question, and they can be words, expressions, NEs, phrases, numbers, dates, abbreviations, etc. For each pivot, we collect its lemma w_L, its head of derivation w_H, its POS, its synonyms $w_S^1, \ldots, w_S^n$ provided by the thesaurus (Sect. 2.1), and flags to indicate if it is a special word. Together with the above mentioned question categories, the relevant ontological and terminological domains in the question, $\{o^1, o^2, \ldots, o^p\}$, are also collected.

[8] For more information about LegiX, see `http://www.legix.pt`.

3.3 Document Retrieval

After analysing the question, a query is submitted to the index using as search keys the pivot lemmas, their heads of derivation, their synonyms, the ontological domains and the question categories.

Let w_L^i, w_H^i and $w_S^{i,j}$ denote resp. the i-th pivot lemma, its head of derivation, and its j-th synonym. Each of these synonyms has a weight $\rho(w_S^{i,j}, w_L^i)$ to reflect its semantic proximity with the original pivot lemma w_L^i. Denote by c^i and o^i resp. the i-th possible category for the question and the j-th relevant ontological or terminological domain. For each word, calculate a weight $\alpha(w)$:

$$\alpha(w) = \alpha_{POS}(w) + K_{ilf} ilf(w) + K_{idf} idf(w) \tag{1}$$

In (1), α_{POS} reflects the influence of the POS on the pivot's relevance. We consider NEs more important than common nouns, and these more important than adjectives or verbs, so $\alpha_{POS}(NE) \geq \alpha_{POS}(N) \geq \alpha_{POS}(ADJ) \geq \alpha_{POS}(V)$. Yet in (1), K_{ilf} and K_{idf} are fixed parameters for interpolation, while ilf and idf denote resp. the *inverse lexical frequency* (the logarithm of the inverted relative frequency of the word in corpora) and the commonly used inverse document frequency [11]. We opted not to include a tf term for the word frequency in the document, because of the relatively small size of each document.

Let d be a particular document in the collection, and define $\delta_L(d, w_L) = 1$ if d contains the lemma w_L and 0 otherwise. Define $\delta_H(d, w_H)$ in the same way for the head of derivation w_H, and $\delta_C(d, c)$ and $\delta_O(d, o)$ analogously for the question category c and the ontological domain o. The document score σ^d becomes:

$$\begin{aligned}\sigma^d = \sum_i \max \Big\{ & K_L \delta_L(d, w_L^i)\alpha(w_L^i), K_H \delta_H(d, w_H^i)\alpha(w_H^i), \\ & \max_j K_S \delta_L(d, w_S^{i,j})\alpha(w_S^{i,j})\rho(w_S^{i,j}, w_L^i) \Big\} + \\ + K_C \max_i \delta_C(d, c^i) &+ K_O \max_i \delta_O(d, o^i),\end{aligned} \tag{2}$$

where K_L, K_H, K_S, K_C and K_O are constants with $K_L > K_H > K_S$ to reward matches of lemmas, stronger than those of heads of derivation and synonyms.

The score in (2) is fine-tuned to take into account the pivot proximity in the documents. In the end, the top 30 documents are retrieved to be analysed at sentence level. To avoid the need of analysing the whole text, each document contains a list of indices of sentences where the pivot matches occur.

3.4 Sentence Retrieval

This module takes as input a set of documents, where sentences that match the pivots are marked. The engine can also analyse the k sentences before and after, where k is configurable. However, this could make processing at this stage to cost too high. Besides, to take full profit of this, additional techniques would be required to find connections among close sentences, for instance through anaphora resolution. Hence, for now we set $k = 0$.

Let s be a particular sentence. After parsing s, a score σ^s is calculated taking into account: (*i*) the number of pivots matching s, (*ii*) the number of pivots having in common the lemma or the head of derivation with some token in s, (*iii*) the number of pivot synonyms matching s, (*iv*) the order and proximity of the pivots in s, (*v*) the existence of common question categories between q and s, (*vi*) the number of ontological and terminological domains characterizing q also present in s, and (*vii*) the score σ^d of the document d that contains s.

Partial matches are also considered: if only one word of a given NE is found in a sentence (e.g. *Fidel* of the anthroponym *Fidel Castro*), it contributes with a lower weight than if it is a complete match. To save efforts in the subsequent answer extraction module, sentences below a threshold are discarded.

3.5 Answer Extraction

The input of the answer extractor is a set $\{s, \sigma^s\}$ of scored sentences potentially containing answers. Each sentence is tested against the QAPs that were activated during the question analysis (see Sect. 3.2). Notice that these QAPs are directly linked with the QP that matched the question (see Table 2). As said in Sect. 2.3, each QAP specifies what part of the sentence is to be extracted as a possible answer; it also includes a score to reflect the pertinence of the foreseen answer.

Suppose that s matches a specific QAP. The curly bracketed terms in the QAP extract one or more candidate answers (note that a single pattern can match s in several ways). Answers that are substrings of others are discarded, unless their score is higher. Those containing question pivots are not allowed, unless they are part of NEs (e.g. *Deng Nan* is allowed as an answer to "Quem é a filha de Deng Xiao Ping?" [Who is Deng Xiao Ping's daughter?]).

Let σ^{QAP} and σ^{QP} be resp. the scores of the QAP and of the QP it is linked to, and a a candidate answer extracted from s. We calculate the score σ^a as:

$$\sigma^a = K_s\sigma^s + K_{QP}\sigma^{QP} + K_{QAP}\sigma^{QAP} + \sum \sigma^{rew} - \sum \sigma^{pen}, \tag{3}$$

where K_s, K_{QP} and K_{QAP} are interpolating constants, and $\sum \sigma^{rew} - \sum \sigma^{pen}$ is the total amount of rewards minus the total amount of penalties applied when processing the QAP. These rewards and penalties are small quantities, the first due to optional terms in the QAP that are verified, and the second due to variable distances, which penalize (linearly) the final score (see Sect. 2.3).

The answer scores $\{\sigma^a\}$ are adjusted with additional rewards that reflect the repeatability of each answer in the collection. To overcome repeated erroneous answers, only sentences above a threshold contribute to those rewards.

Finally, the system outputs the answer with the highest score, $\hat{a} = \arg\max_a \sigma^a$, or "NIL" if none is available. Currently, no confidence score is measured to check if $\hat{a}$ really answers q. This is something to be done in the future.

4 Results

The details of the CLEF experiment are described in [12]. Table 3 displays the final results for Priberam's QA system.

Table 3. Results by type of question

Question ↓ Answer →	R	W	X	U	Total	Acc. (%)
Factoid (F)	91	38	5	1	135	67.4
Definition (D)	27	7	8	0	42	64.2
Temporally restricted factoid (T)	11	10	0	2	23	47.8
Total	129	55	13	3	200	**64.5**

The F-questions and D-questions statistics add to a satisfactory accuracy of the system, whose performance is comparable to that of the best scored systems in recent evaluation campaigns [13]. Several reasons contribute to the lower accuracy of T-questions. Firstly, we do not index dates differently from other keywords. For instance, *25 de Abril de 1974* and *25/4/1974* are indexed as different terms. Hence, we do not force the date to be in the sentence that answers a T-question, leading sometimes to inexact answers. In the future, we intend to index dates in a numeric format, taking into account the documents' dates, and converting relative temporal references (e.g. *ontem* [yesterday]) to absolute ones.

The system's major flaw (responsible for about 16.5% of failures) is related with the candidate answers' extraction: when it fails, the extraction patterns are either too lenient, causing overextraction, or too strict, causing underextraction. Anaphora resolution and setting the value of k to a nonzero value (see Sect. 3.4) to check the answer in close sentences, could improve the system's performance.

The second major flaw (8.0% of failures) is the handling of NIL questions. NIL recall is quite low (11%) because no confidence score is computed. Often, the answer sentence matches only one pivot of a question, which sometimes is too weak a match. Besides, we do not require exclusivity for some question categories. For example, questions like "Qual é o comprimento de..." [What is the length of...] should not have another category besides <DIMENSION>, which demands a numeric answer with an appropriate measure unit.

The third flaw (6.5% of failures) has to do with the choice of the final answer (see Sect. 3.5). Occasionally, the correct answer is ranked in the second position right after the wrong answer that was chosen. Not very frequently, the system had to choose between answers equally scored.

The last flaw (4.5% of failures) reveals that the system sometimes misses the document containing the answer, during the document retrieval stage. One instance occurred with question 30 "Que percentagem de crianças não tem comida suficiente no Iraque?" [What percentage of children does not have enough food in Irak?]. The system did not retrieve the sentence containing the answer: "[...] entre 22 e 30 por cento das crianças iraquianas estão gravemente mal nutridas". In this case, the query expansion related *iraquianas* [Iraqis] to *Iraque* [Iraq], but was not able to establish a synonymic relation between *não tem comida suficiente* [does not have enough food] and *mal nutridas* [badly nourished]. One way to obviate this is to increase the factor K_O in (2), when comparing the ontology domains of the question with those of the documents. In this particular case, the words *comida* (question) and *nutridas* (answer) are grouped under the same domain: metabolism/nutrition.

The CLEF evaluation showed that Brazilian Portuguese was not a relevant problem for a system that only used a European Portuguese lexicon. There were not many questions with exclusive Brazilian spelling or Brazilian terms, and the system was able to retrieve correct answers from Brazilian target documents.

5 Conclusions and Future Work

This paper described Priberam's QA system and its evaluation in QA@CLEF 2005. The system is based on the NLP technology developed for TRUST, and the results suggest that the choices are in the right track.

The architecture of the system is similar to many others, yet it distinguishes itself by the indexation of morphologically disambiguated words at sentence level and by the query expansion using heads of derivation and synonyms. The use of the workbench described in Sect. 2 allows an easy coding and maintenance of several NLP features, making the system scalable.

Despite the encouraging results, the system has a long way to go before it can be efficient in a generic environment. Some improvements to be implemented in a near future concern the question/answer matching, the syntactic treatment of questions and answers, anaphora resolution, and semantic disambiguation. We intend to further exploit the ontology's potential, since it can be a very useful resource during the stages of document and sentence retrieval by introducing semantic knowledge. This implies performing document clustering based on the ontology domains, and inferring from question analysis those that should be predominant in the target documents. Future work will also address list and how- questions, and the refinement of the QA system for Web searching.

This NLP technology is being currently used in M-CAST (Multilingual Content Aggregation System based on TRUST Search Engine), an European eContent project whose aim is the development of a multilingual platform to search large text collections, such as Internet libraries, press agencies, scientific databases, etc. This participation will lead to greater enhancements, especially on the extraction of answers from books, which may prove to be quite different from extracting from newspaper articles.

Acknowledgements

Priberam Informática would like to thank the partners of the NLUC[9] consortium, namely Synapse Développement, for sharing its experience and knowledge. Priberam would also like to express its thanks to the CLEF organization and to Linguateca for preparing and supervising the Portuguese evaluation. Finally, we would like to acknowledge the support of the European Commission in TRUST (IST-1999-56416) and M-CAST (EDC 22249 M-CAST) projects.

[9] Natural Language Understanding Consortium (http://www.nluc.com).

References

1. Santos, D., Rocha, P.: CHAVE: Topics and questions on the Portuguese participation in CLEF. In: Working Notes for the CLEF 2004 Workshop, Bath, UK, 15-17 Sep. (2004)
2. Quaresma, P., Quintano, L., Rodrigues, I., Saias, J., Salgueiro, P.: The University of Évora approach to QA@CLEF-2004. In: Working Notes for the CLEF 2004 Workshop, Bath, UK, 15-17 Sep. (2004)
3. Costa, L.: First evaluation of Esfinge – a question-answering system for Portuguese. In: Working Notes for the CLEF 2004 Workshop, Bath, UK, 15-17 Sep. (2004)
4. Amaral, C., Laurent, D., Martins, A., Mendes, A., Pinto, C.: Design and Implementation of a Semantic Search Engine for Portuguese. In: Proc. of 4th Int. Conf. on Language Resources and Evaluation (LREC 2004), Lisbon, Portugal, 26-28 May. (2004) Also available at `http://www.priberam.pt/docs/LREC2004.pdf`.
5. Laurent, D., Varone, M., Amaral, C., Fuglewicz, P.: Multilingual Semantic and Cognitive Search Engine for Text Retrieval Using Semantic Technologies. In: Pre-proc. of the 1st Workshop on International Proofing Tools and Language Technologies, Patras, Greece, 1-2 July. (2004)
6. Amaral, C., Figueira, H., Mendes, A., Mendes, P., Pinto, C.: A Workbench for Developing Natural Language Processing Tools. In: Pre-proc. of the 1st Workshop on International Proofing Tools and Language Technologies, Patras, Greece, 1-2 July. (2004) Also available at `http://www.priberam.pt/docs/WorkbenchNLP.pdf`.
7. Laurent, D., Séguéla, P., Nègre, S.: Cross Lingual Question Answering using QRISTAL for CLEF 2005. In: Working Notes for the CLEF 2005 Workshop, Vienna, Austria, 21-23 Sep. (2005)
8. Thede, S., Harper, M.: A second-order hidden Markov model for part-of-speech tagging. In: Proc. of the 37th Annual Meeting of the ACL, Maryland. (1999)
9. Manning, C.D., Schütze, H.: Foundations of Statistical Natural Language Processing (2nd printing). The MIT Press, Cambridge, Massachusetts (2000)
10. Magnini, B., Vallin, A., Ayache, C., Erbach, G., Peñas, A., de Rijke, M., Rocha, P., Simov, K., Sutcliffe, R.: Overview of the CLEF 2004 multilingual QA track. In: Working Notes for the CLEF 2004 Workshop, Bath, UK, 15-17 Sep. (2004)
11. B.-Yates, R., R.-Neto, B.: Modern Information Retrieval. ACM Press (1999)
12. Vallin, A., Giampiccolo, D., Aunimo, L., Ayache, C., Osenova, P., Peñas, A., de Rijke, M., Sacaleanu, B., Santos, D., Sutcliffe, R.: Overview of the CLEF 2005 multilingual question answering track. In: Working Notes for the CLEF 2005 Workshop, Vienna, Austria, 21-23 Sep. (2005)
13. Voorhees, E.: Overview of the TREC 2004 QA Track. In: Proc. of the 13th Text Retrieval Conf. (TREC 2004), Gaithersburg, Maryland, 16-19 Nov. (2005)

A Full Data-Driven System for Multiple Language Question Answering*

Manuel Montes-y-Gómez[1], Luis Villaseñor-Pineda[1], Manuel Pérez-Coutiño[1]
José Manuel Gómez-Soriano[2], Emilio Sanchís-Arnal[2], and Paolo Rosso[2]

[1] Instituto Nacional de Astrofísica, Óptica y Electrónica (INAOE), Mexico
{mmontesg, villasen, mapco}@inaoep.mx
[2] Universidad Politécnica de Valencia (UPV), Spain
{jogomez, esanchis, prosso}@dsic.upv.es

Abstract. This paper describes a full data-driven system for question answer ing. The system uses pattern matching and statistical techniques to identify the relevant passages as well as the candidate answers for factoid and definition questions. Since it does not consider any sophisticated linguistic analysis of questions and answers, it can be applied to different languages without requiring major adaptation changes. Experimental results on Spanish, Italian and French demonstrate that the proposed approach can be a convenient strategy for monolingual and multilingual question answering.

1 Introduction

The amount of documents available online is increasing every day. As a consequence, better information retrieval methods are required to achieve the needed information. Question Answering (QA) systems are information retrieval applications whose aim is to provide inexperienced users with a flexible access to the information. These systems allow users to write a query in natural language and to obtain not a set of documents which contain the answer, but the concise answer itself [9]. That is, given a question like: "Where is the Popocatepetl located?", a QA system must respond "Mexico", instead of just returning a list of documents related to the volcano.

Recent developments in QA use a variety of linguistic resources to help in understanding the questions and the documents. The most common linguistic resources include: part-of-speech taggers, parsers, named entity extractors, dictionaries, and WordNet [1,5,6]. Despite promising results, these approaches have two main inconveniences: (i) the construction of such linguistic resources is very complex; and (ii) these resources are highly binding to a specific language.

In this paper we present a QA system that allows answering factoid and definition questions. This system is based on a full *data-driven approach* [2], which requires minimum knowledge about the lexicon and the syntax of the specified language. Mainly, it is supported by the idea that the questions and their answers are commonly

* This work is a revised version of the paper "INAOE-UPV Joint Participation at CLEF 2005: Experiments in Monolingual Question Answering", previously published in the CLEF 2005 working notes (www.clef-campaign.org/2005/working_notes/).

C. Peters et al. (Eds.): CLEF 2005, LNCS 4022, pp. 420–428, 2006.

expressed using the same set of words, and therefore, it simply uses a lexical pattern matching method to identify relevant document passages and to extract the candidate answers.

The proposed approach has the advantage of being adaptable to several different languages, in particular to moderately inflected languages such as Spanish, English, Italian and French. Unfortunately, this flexibility has its price. To obtain a good performance, the approach requires the use of a redundant target collection, that is, a collection in which the answers to questions occur more than once. On one hand, this redundancy increases the probability of finding a passage containing a simple lexical matching between the question and the answers. On the other hand, it enhances the answer extraction, since correct answers tend to be more frequent than incorrect responses.

The proposed system also uses a set of heuristics that attempt to capture some regularities of language and some stylistic conventions of newsletters. For instance, it considers that most named entities are written with an initial uppercase letter, and that most concept definitions are usually expressed using a very small number of fixed arrangements of noun phrases. This kind of heuristics guides the extraction of the candidate answers from the relevant passages.

2 System Overview

Figure 1 shows the general architecture of our system, which is divided into two main modules. One focuses on answering factoid questions. It considers the tasks of: (i) *passage indexing*, where documents are preprocessed, and a structured representation of the collection is built; (ii) *passage retrieval*, where the passages with the greatest probability to contain the answer are recovered from the index; and (iii) *answer extraction*; where candidate answers are ranked and the final answer recommendation of the system is produced.

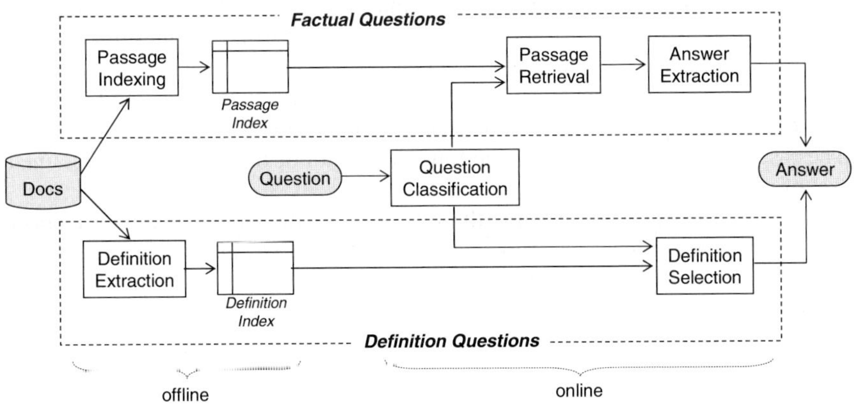

Fig. 1. Block diagram of the system

The other module concentrates on answering definition questions. It includes the tasks of: (i) *definition extraction*; where all possible pairs of acronym-meaning and person-position[1] are located and indexed; and (ii) *definition selection*, where the relevant data pairs are identified and the final answer of the system is generated.

The following sections describe in detail these modules.

3 Answering Factoid Questions

3.1 Passage Retrieval

The Passage Retrieval (PR) method is specially suited for the QA task [4]. It allows retrieving the passages with the highest probability to contain the answer, instead of simply recovering the passages sharing a subset of words with the question.

Given a user question, the PR method finds the passages with the relevant terms (non-stopwords) using a classical information retrieval technique based on the vector space model. Then, it measures the similarity between the *n*-gram sets of the passages and the user question in order to obtain the new weights for the passages. The weight of a passage is related to the largest *n*-gram structure of the question that can be found in the passage itself. The larger the *n*-gram structure, the greater the weight of the passage. Finally, it returns to the user the passages with the new weights.

3.1.1 Similarity Measure

The similarity between a passage *d* and a question *q* is defined by (1).

$$sim(d,q)=\frac{\sum_{j=1}^{n}\sum_{\forall x\in Q_j} h(x(j),D_j)}{\sum_{j=1}^{n}\sum_{\forall x\in Q_j} h(x(j),Q_j)} \qquad (1)$$

Where $sim(d, q)$ is a function which measures the similarity of the set of *n*-grams of the passage *d* with the set of *n*-grams of the question *q*. D_j is the set of *j*-grams of the passage *d* and Q_j is the set of *j*-grams that are generated from the question *q*. That is, D_1 will contain the passage unigrams whereas Q_1 will contain the question unigrams, D_2 and Q_2 will contain the passage and question bigrams respectively, and so on until D_n and Q_n. In both cases, *n* is the number of question terms.

The result of (1) is equal to 1 if the longest *n*-gram of the question is contained in the set of passage *n*-grams.

The function $h(x(j), D_j)$ measures the relevance of the *j*-gram $x(j)$ with respect to the set of passage *j*-grams, whereas the function $h(x(j), Q_j)$ is a factor of normalization[2]. The function *h* assigns a weight to every question *n*-gram as defined in (2).

$$h(x(j),D_j)=\begin{cases}\sum_{k=1}^{j} w_{\hat{x}_k(1)} & \text{if } x(j)\in D_j\\ 0 & \text{otherwise}\end{cases} \qquad (2)$$

[1] In general, we consider the extraction of person-description pairs.

[2] We introduce the notation $x(n)$ for the sake of simplicity. In this case $x(n)$ indicates the *n*-gram *x* of size *n*.

Where the notation $\hat{x}_k(1)$ indicates the *k*-th unigram included in the *j*-gram *x*, and $w_{\hat{x}_k(1)}$ specifies the associated weight to this unigram. This weight gives an incentive to the terms –unigrams– that appear rarely in the document collection. Moreover, this weight should also discriminate the relevant terms against those (e.g. stopwords) which occur often in the document collection.

The weight of a unigram is calculated by (3):

$$w_{\hat{x}_k(1)} = 1 - \frac{\log\left(n_{\hat{x}_k(1)}\right)}{1+\log(N)} \tag{3}$$

Where $n_{\hat{x}_k(1)}$ is the number of passages in which appears the unigram $\hat{x}_k(1)$, and *N* is the total number of passages in the collection. We assume that the stopwords occur in every passage (i.e., *n* takes the value of *N*). For instance, if the term appears once in the passage collection, its weight will be equal to 1 (the maximum weight), whereas if the term is a stopword, then its weight will be the lowest.

3.2 Answer Extraction

This component aims to establish the best answer for a given question. In order to do that, it first determines a small set of candidate answers, and then, it selects the final unique answer taking into consideration the position of the candidate answers inside the retrieved passages.

The algorithm applied to extract the most probable answer from the given set of relevant passages is described below[3]:

1. Extract all the unigrams that satisfy some given typographic criteria. These criteria depend on the type of expected answer. For instance, if the expected answer is a named entity, then select the unigrams starting with an uppercase letter, but if the expected answer is a quantity, then select the unigrams expressing numbers.
2. Determine all the *n*-grams assembled from the selected unigrams. These *n*-grams can only contain the selected unigrams and some stopwords.
3. Rank the *n*-grams based on their compensated frequency. The compensated frequency of the *n*-gram *x*(*n*) is computed as follows:

$$F_{x(n)} = \frac{1}{n}\sum_{i=1}^{n}\sum_{j=1}^{n-i+1}\frac{f_{\hat{x}_j(i)}}{\sum_{\forall y \in G_i} f_{y(i)}} \tag{4}$$

   where G_i indicates the set of *i*-grams, *y*(*i*) represents the *i*-gram *y*, $\hat{x}_j(i)$ is the *j*-th *i*-gram included in *x*(*n*), $f_{y(i)}$ specifies the frequency of occurrence of the *i*-gram *y*, and $f_{x(n)}$ indicates the compensated frequency of *x*(*n*).
4. Select the top five *n*-grams as candidate answers.
5. Compute a ranking score for each candidate answer. This score is defined as the weight of the first retrieved passage (refer to formula 1) that contains the candidate answer.

[3] For more details please refer to (Del-Castillo et al., 2004).

6. Select as the final response the candidate answer with the greatest ranking score. If two or more of the candidate answers have the same ranking score, then select the one with the greatest compensated frequency.

4 Answering Definition Questions

Our system uses an alternative method to answer definition questions. This method makes use of some regularities of language and some stylistic conventions of news letters to capture the possible answer for a given definition question. A similar approach was presented in [7,8].

The process of answering a definition question considers two main tasks. First, the *definition extraction*, which detects text segments containing a description of a term (in particular we consider descriptions related to person's positions and organization's acronyms). Then, the *definition selection*, where the most relevant description for a given question term is identified and the final answer of the system is generated.

4.1 Definition Extraction

The regularities of language and the stylistic conventions of news letters are captured by two basic lexical patterns. These patterns allow the construction of two different definition catalogs. The first one includes a list of pairs of acronym-meaning. The other one consists of a list of person-position couples.

In order to extract the acronym-meaning pairs we use an extraction pattern based on the use of parentheses:

$$w_1 \textit{<meaning>} \; (\textit{<acronym>}) \tag{5}$$

In this pattern, w_1 is a lowercase non stopword, *<meaning>* is a sequence of words starting with an uppercase letter (that may also include some stopwords), and *<acronym>* indicates an uppercase single word.

By means of this pattern we could identify pairs like [*AAPNP – la Asociación de Armadores de Pesca del Norte Portugués*]. In particular, this pair was extracted from the following paragraph:

> *"El pasado 3 de enero la Asociación de Armadores de Pesca del Norte Portugués (AAPNP) acusó al ministro de Asuntos Marítimos, Eduardo Azevedo Soares, de favorecer a los pesqueros españoles."*

In contrast, the extraction of person-position pairs is guided by the occurrence of a special kind of appositive phrase. This information is encapsulated in the following extraction pattern.

$$w_1 \; w_2 \textit{<description>} \; , \textit{<referent>} \; [,|.] \tag{6}$$

Where w_1 represents any word, except for the prepositions "of" and "in", w_2 is an article, *<description>* is a free sequence of words, and *<referent>* indicates a sequence of words starting with an uppercase letter.

Applying this extraction pattern over the below paragraph we caught the pair [*Manuel Concha Ruiz – jefe de la Unidad de Trasplantes del hospital cordobés*].

> "*... no llegó a Córdoba hasta las 19:30 horas, se llevó a cabo con un corazón procedente Madrid y fue dirigida por el jefe de la Unidad de Trasplantes del hospital cordobés, Manuel Concha Ruiz.*"

4.2 Definition Selection

The main quality of the above extraction patterns is their generality: they can be applied to different languages without requiring major adaptation changes. However, this generality causes the patterns to often extract non-relevant information, i.e., information that does not indicate an acronym-meaning or person-position relation. For instance, when applying the pattern (6) to the next text segment we identified the incorrect pair [*Manuel H. M. – otros dos pasajeros de este vehículo*].

> *"También el conductor del Opel Corsa, Antonio D.V., de 24 años, y los ocupantes Andrés L.H., de 24, y Francisco F.L, de 21, resultaron con heridas graves, mientras que los otros dos pasajeros de este vehículo, Manuel H.M., de 29, y Miguel J.M., de 25, resultaron con heridas leves".*

Since the catalogs contain a mixture of correct and incorrect definition pairs, it is necessary to do an additional process in order to select the most probable answer for a given definition question. This process is supported on the idea that the correct information is more redundant than the incorrect one. It considers the following two criteria:

1. The most frequent definition in the catalog has the highest probability to be the correct answer.
2. The larger and, therefore, more specific definitions tend to be the more pertinent answers.

In order to increase the opportunity of selecting the correct answers, the definition catalogs must be cleaned before the execution of this process. We consider two main actions: (i) the removal of stopwords at the beginning of descriptions –acronym meanings and person positions; and (ii) the elimination of the acronym meanings having fewer words than letters in the acronym.

The following example illustrates the selection process. Assume that the user question is "*who is Manuel Conde?*", and that the definition catalog contains the records shown below. Then, the method selects the description "*presidente de la Comisión de Paz del Parlamento Centroamericano (PARLACEN)*" as the most probable answer.

> *Manuel Conde: gobierno de Serrano*
> *Manuel Conde: gobierno de Jorge Serrano (1991-1993)*
> *Manuel Conde: gobierno de Jorge Serrano*
> *Manuel Conde: ex presidente de la COPAZ que participó en la primera etapa*
> *Manuel Conde: presidente de la Comisión de Paz del Parlamento Centroamericano (PARLACEN)*
> *Manuel Conde: presidente de la Comisión de Paz del Parlamento Centroamericano (PARLACEN)*

5 Evaluation Results

This section presents the evaluation results of our system at the QA@CLEF2005 monolingual tracks for Spanish, Italian and French. In the three languages, the evaluation exercise consisted of answering 200 questions of three basic types: factoid, definition and temporal restricted. In all cases, the target corpora were collections of news articles. Table 1 shows some general numbers on the evaluation data set.

Table 1. The evaluation data set

	Target corpora	Question set		
	# sentences	Factoid	Definition	Temporal
Spanish	5,636,945	118	50	32
Italian	2,282,904	120	50	30
French	2,069,012	120	50	30

Figure 2 shows our global results on the three languages[4]. The Spanish results were better than those for Italian and French. However, we obtained the best evaluation result in Italian. In this case the average precision was of 24.1%. In the monolingual Spanish and French tasks we achieved the second best results. In Spanish, the best result was of 42% and the average precision of 31.7%. In French, the best precision was of 64%, and the average of 34%.

Figure 3 detail our results by question types. It can be noticed that we are significantly better in answering definition questions. However, the numbers indicate that

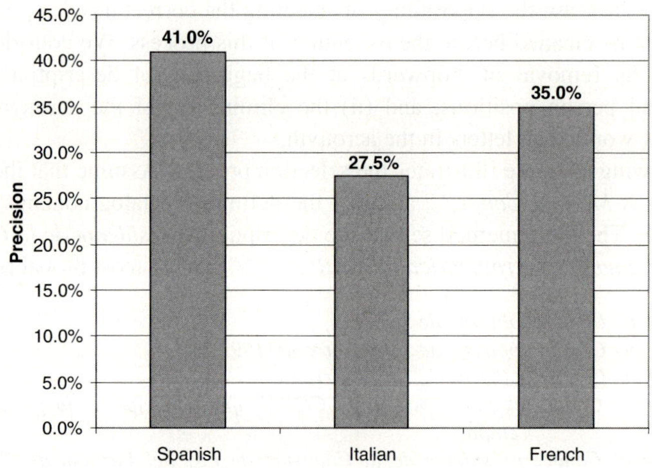

Fig. 2. Overall accuracy results

[4] Since our system only distinguishes between factoid and definition questions, we treated the temporal-restricted questions as simple factoid.

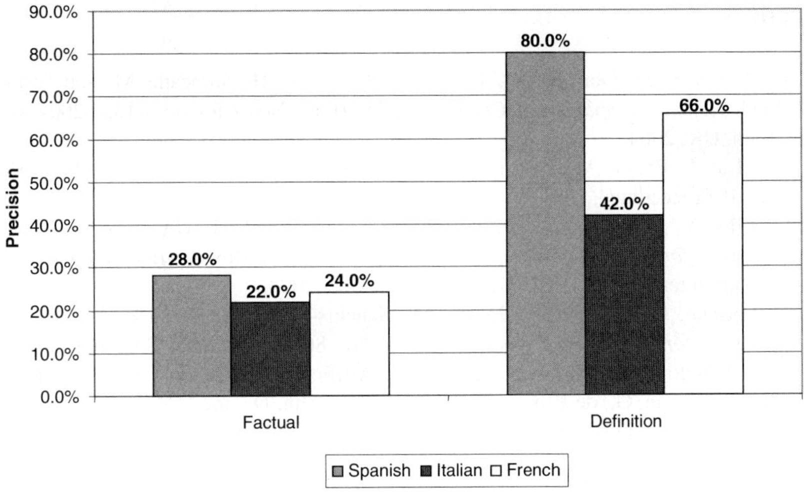

Fig. 3. Accuracy on factoid and definition questions

the method for answering factoid questions is language independent, while the approach for answering definition questions tends to be more language dependent.

6 Conclusions

This paper presented a question-answering system based on a full *data-driven approach*. The system is supported by the idea that the questions and their answers are commonly expressed using the same words, and therefore, it simply uses pattern matching and statistical techniques to identify the relevant passages as well as the candidate answers for factoid and definition questions.

The experiments on Spanish, Italian and French showed the potential and portability of our approach. They also indicated that our method for answering factoid question, which is based on the matching and counting of *n*-grams, is *language-independent*. However, it greatly depends on the redundancy of the answers in the target collection. On the contrary, the method for answering definition questions is very precise. Nevertheless, we cannot conclude anything about its language independence.

Futere work includes improving the ranking score for factoid questions, in order to reduce the dependence on the data redundancy. We also plan to design a technique to discover extraction patterns on the Web. This will help in decreasing the language dependence of our method for answering definition questions.

Acknowledgements. This work was done under partial support of CONACYT (Project Grant 43990), R2D2 (CICYTTIC2003-07158-C04-03), and ICT EU-India (ALA/95/23/2003/077-054). We would also like to thank the CLEF organization committee.

References

1. Ageno, A., Ferrés, D., González, E., Kanaan, S., Rodríguez H., Surdeanu, M., and Turmo, J. *TALP-QA System for Spanish at CLEF-2004*. Working Notes for the CLEF 2004 Workshop, Bath, UK, 2004.
2. Brill, E., Lin, J., Banko, M., Dumais, S., and Ng, A. *Data-intensive Question Answering*. TREC 2001 Proceedings, 2001.
3. Del-Castillo, A., Montes-y-Gómez, M., and Villaseñor-Pineda, L. *QA on the web: A preliminary study for Spanish language*. Proceedings of the 5th Mexican International Conference on Computer Science (ENC04), Colima, Mexico, 2004.
4. Gómez-Soriano, J.M., Montes-y-Gómez, M., Sanchis-Arnal, E., Rosso P. *A Passage Retrieval System for Multilingual Question Answering*. 8th International Conference on Text, Speech and Dialog, TSD 2005. Lecture Notes in Artificial Intelligence, vol. 3658, 2005.
5. Jijkoun, V., Mishne, G., de Rijke, M., Schlobach, S., Ahn, D., and Müller, K.. *The University of Amsterdam at QA@CLEF 2004*. Working Notes for the CLEF 2004 Workshop, Bath, UK, 2004.
6. Pérez-Coutiño, M., Solorio, T., Montes-y-Gómez, M., López-López, A., and Villaseñor-Pineda, L. *The Use of Lexical Context in Question Answering for Spanish*. Working Notes for the CLEF 2004 Workshop, Bath, UK, 2004.
7. Ravichandran D. and Hovy E. *Learning Surface Text Patterns for a Question Answering System*. In ACL Conference, 2002.
8. Saggion, H. *Identifying Definitions in Text Collections for Question Answering*. LREC 2004.
9. Vicedo, J.L., Rodríguez, H., Peñas, A. and Massot, M. *Los sistemas de Búsqueda de Respuestas desde una perspectiva actual*. Revista de la Sociedad Española para el Procesamiento del Lenguaje Natural, n.31, 2003.

Experiments on Cross–Linguality and Question–Type Driven Strategy Selection for Open–Domain QA*

Günter Neumann and Bogdan Sacaleanu

LT–Lab, DFKI, Saarbrücken, Germany
neumann@dfki.de, bogdan@dfki.de

Abstract. We describe the extensions made to our 2004 QA@CLEF German/English QA-system, toward a fully German-English/English-German cross-language system with answer validation through web usage. Details concerning the processing of factoid, definition and temporal questions are given and the results obtained in the monolingual German, bilingual English-German and German-English tasks are briefly presented and discussed.

1 Introduction

The basic functionality of a cross–lingual open–domain question answering (abbreviated as ODQA) system is simple: given a Natural Language query in one language (for example German) find answers for that query in textual documents written in another language (for example English). In contrast to a standard cross-language IR system, the natural language questions are usually well-formed NL–query clauses (instead of a set of keywords), and the identified answers should be *exact* answer strings (instead of complete documents containing the answers).

Since 2003, cross-lingual systems are evaluated as part of a special track at Clef. This year, the task was to process 200 questions of type `factoid`, `temporally restricted`, and `definition`, and to return for each question one exact answer (together with the identifier of the document source from which the answer was extracted) or NIL, if no answer could be found. Last year only factoid and definition questions were tackled.

Starting from our 2004–system (cf. [1]), the major efforts we spend for the QA track at Clef 2005 were focused on:

- improving cross–lingual methods
- development of a component–oriented ODQA-core architecture

* The work presented in this paper has been funded by the BMBF project Quetal, FKZ 01 IW C02. Many thanks to Rob Basten for his support in the development of the component for handling temporally restricted questions, Yuan Ye for his support in data collection and annotation for the definition handlers, and Aljeandro Figuero for his support in the implementation of the web validation strategy.

C. Peters et al. (Eds.): CLEF 2005, LNCS 4022, pp. 429–438, 2006.

- processing definition and temporally restricted questions
- exploration of web-based answer validation

Beside that we also decided to take part in three different tasks:

1. monolingual German ODQA: here we we improved our result from last year from 23.5% to 43.5% this year
2. German-English ODQA: here we achieved with 25.5% accuracy a minor improvement compared with our 2004–result (23.5%)
3. English-German ODQA: this was our first participation in this task and we achieved a result of 23% accuracy

In all three tasks, we obtained the best results. We will now describe some interesting technical aspects of our 2005–system – named QUANTICO – before presenting and discussing the results in more detail.

2 System Overview

Based on a number of experiments we made during the development of our ODQA–technology, we developed the hypothesis that a structural analysis of un-structured documents towards the information needs of questions, will support the retrieval of relevant small textual information units through *informative* IR-queries. However, since we cannot foresee all the different users interests or questions especially in the *open–domain context*, a challenging research question is: How detailed can the structural analysis be made without putting over a "straitjacket" of a particular interpretation on the un-structured source? Thus, there is a trade–off between off-line and on-line document annotation. Questions and answers are somewhat related in that questions influence the information geometry and hence, the information view and access, cf. [2].

Based on this insights, we developed the ODQA–architecture as depicted in figure 1. The idea behind the specific design is the assumption that an off-line annotation of the data collection supports an answer type oriented indexing and answer extraction process through the selection of query–type specific strategies (cf. sec. 3 for more details; a similar approach is also used by [3]). Furthermore, a sentence–oriented preprocessing determining only sentence boundary, named entities (NE) and their co-reference, as well as NE–anchored tuples (see sec. 6) turned out to be a useful level of off–line annotation, at least for the Clef-type of questions.

In order to achieve a high degree of flexibility of the ODQA–core components in future applications, an important design decision was to a use a central QA-Controller: based on the result of the NL—question analysis component, the QAController decides which of the following strategies will be followed:

- Definition Question
- Temporal Question
- Factoid Question

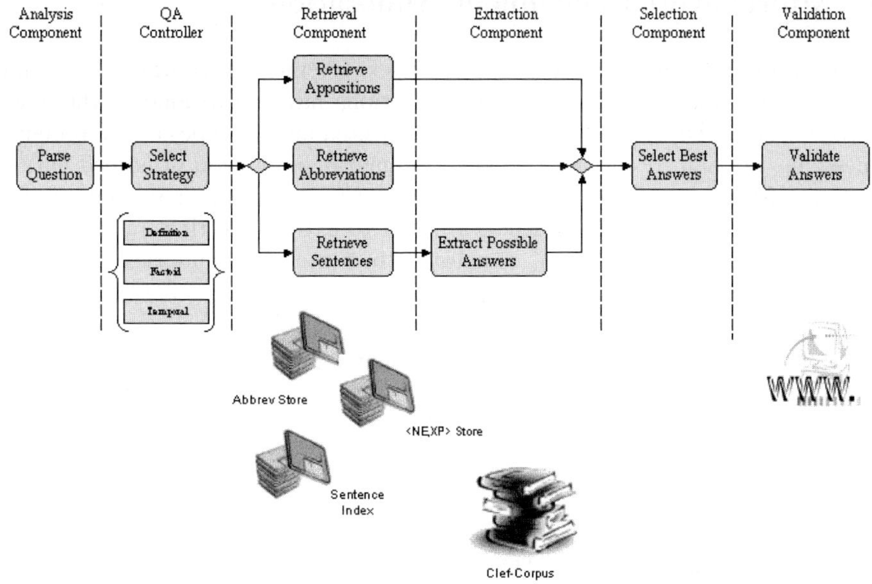

Fig. 1. The architecture of QUANTICO

For each of the above-mentioned tasks, a strategy corresponds to different settings of the components. For the Factoid Question strategy, for example, the Retrieval Component considers sentences as information units (see sec. 4 and 5 for more details); the Answer Extraction Component defines classes of instances for one of the entity types PERSON, ORGANIZATION, LOCATION, DATE and NUMBER; the Answer Selection Component considers relevant information as being the one more closed (distance metric) to the question keywords and with the most coherent context.

3 Question Analysis

The main purpose of the NL question analysis in the context of a open–domain QA-system is to determine the question–type, the expected answer type, the set of relevant keywords, and the set of recognized NE–instances in order to guide information search and answer processing. In our system, the question–type is used to select different answer strategies. For example, for a question of type *abbreviation*, possible answers are looked–up in special data bases (automatically filled with data from the Clef corpus), where for questions of type *completion* the full–text search is activated. In a similar way, specific strategies for the treatment of definition and temporally restricted questions are handled (cf. 6). For more information on the syntactic and semantic aspects of our robust NL question analysis component, see [1].

4 Multi–layered Document Annotation

Beside word indexing and retrieval of raw text documents as information units relevant to a question, pre-emptive annotations have been done to the whole data collection. Driven by the controlled expected answer types of the potential questions, i.e. named entities types, a systematic annotation of named entities and co-reference resolution of both named entities and personal pronouns has been undertaken to the documents, in order to extend the IR-component with entity-based indices. Moreover, annotation of sentence boundaries, allowed us an accurate evaluation of IR-results along the information unit size. Based on

Table 1. Precision of retrieval for different unit types and top N units retrieved. We have alternatively considered the following retrieval units: documents, passages, sentences – and their NE-annotated correspondents (marked by *).

Unit–Type/#N	1	5	10	20	30	40	50	100
Sentences*	37.9	58.2	65.8	69.6	70	72.1	74	75.9
Sentence	28.4	53.1	60.1	67	70	72.7	72.7	74.6
Paragraph*	39.8	63.2	68.3	73.4	74	75.3	76.5	77.8
Paragraph	31.6	60.7	67.7	71.5	74	77.2	77.2	80.3
Document*	47.4	69.6	76.5	80.3	81	82.9	82.9	83.5
Document	46.2	68.3	77.8	82.2	82	83.5	84.1	85.4

experiments with the question set of previous CLEF competitions on the information retrieval unit and the indexation unit (see table 4), we have confined the first to the sentence level and added named entities and abbreviations, along words, as basic indexing units. By doing this, we could query the IR component not only by keywords extracted from the questions, but also by NE types corresponding to their expected answer types. This will not only narrow the amount of data being analyzed for answer extraction, but will also guarantee the existence of an answer candidate.

Even though we registered a decrease in precision of almost 10% with annotated sentences over raw documents as information units, we reduced the amount of "to be processed" data by a range of 30 and dispensed with the use of a passage retrieval component.

5 Treatment of Factoid Questions

Factoid questions require a single fact as answer, which has been restricted to a limited class of named entities (PERSON, ORGANIZATION, etc.) for the CLEF competition. Based on our named entities extended indices, a fixed number of sentences containing at least an instance of the expected answer type are being processed for answer extraction. Extracting the answers consists in gathering all those named entities corresponding to the expected answer type as possible answers to the question, whereby information from the retrieval component (i.e., score, frequency of answer) is taken into account. Selection of best answers is based on a distance measure, which takes into consideration the number of overlapping words between the question words and the answers' context, the overlap cohesion (as distance between the question words) and the candidate cohesion (the distance between the answer and its most closed question words). The number of cross-document occurrences of the possible answers adds lastly to the weight to be computed for the best answer candidate.

6 Treatment of Definition and Temporally Restricted Questions

Definition Questions. Definition questions, asking about instances of PERSON and ORGANIZATION entity types, have been approached by making use of structural linguistic patterns known to be used with explanatory and descriptive goals. Both appositions:

> "Silvio Berlusconi, the Italian prime-minister, visited Germany."

and abbreviation-extension structural patterns:

> "In January 1994, Canada, the United States and Mexico launched the North American Free Trade Agreement (NAFTA) and formed the world's largest free trade area."

were used for this purpose.

Based on a corpus of almost 500 Mbytes textual data from the Clef corpus for every language taken into consideration (German and English), two indices were created corresponding to pairs of phrases of the form (see also fig. 1 where the (NE,XP) and abbreviation store memorize these indices).

> (Silvio Berlusconi, the Italian prime-minister)

and

> (NAFTA, North American Free Trade Agreement)

The Retrieval Component for the Definition Question strategy uses these indices and considers the phrases on the right hand as the information units containing the possible answer, if the corresponding matching left elements of such tuples have also been identified during the Query Analysis Component.

Temporally Restricted Questions. In order to fulfill the requirements of the 2005 qa@clef task description, we developed specific methods for the treatment of temporally restricted questions, e.g., questions like "Who was the German Chancellor in the year 1980?", "Who was the German Chancellor between 1970 and 1990?", or "Who was the German Chancellor when the Berlin Wall was opened?". It was our goal, to process questions of this kind on basis of our existing technology following a *divide-and-conquer* approach, i.e., by question decomposition and answer fusion. The highly flexible design of QUANTICO actually supported us in achieving this goal. Two methods were implemented:

1. The existing methods for handling factoid questions were used without change to get initial answer candidates. In a follow–up step, the temporal restriction from the question was used to check the answer's temporal consistency.
2. A temporally restricted question Q is decomposed into two sub–questions, one referring to the "timeless" proposition of Q, and the other to the temporally restricting part. For example, the question "Who was the German Chancellor when the Berlin Wall was opened?" is decomposed into the two sub–questions "Who was the German Chancellor'" and "When was the Berlin Wall opened?". The answers for both are searched for independently, but checked for consistency in a follow–up answer fusion step. In this step, the identified explicit temporal restriction is used to instantiate the implicit time restriction.

The decomposition of such questions into sub–questions is helpful in cases, where the temporal restriction is only specified implicitly, and hence can only be deduced through application of specific inference rules. Note that the decomposition operation is mainly *syntax driven*, in that it takes into account the grammatical relationship of the sub– and main clauses identified and analysed by QUANTICO' parser SMES, cf. [4].

Through evaluation of a number of experiments, it turned out that processing of question with method 1.) leads to higher precision, and processing of questions using method 2.) leads to increased recall (see also [5]). An initial evaluation of our Clef–results also suggest, that the methods are critically dependant on the Named Entity recognizer's capability to properly recognize time and date expressions (see section 9).

7 Cross-Lingual Methods

Two strategies were used for answering questions asked in a language different from that used for documents containing the answer. Both strategies employ online translation services (Altavista, FreeTranslation, etc.) to solve the language barrier, but with different processing steps: before and after the Analysis Component (see also figure 2).

The **before–method** translated the question string in an earlier step, resulting in several automatic translated strings, of which the best one was then passed on to the Retrieval Component after having been analyzed by the Query Analysis Component. This was the strategy we used in the English–German task. To be more precise: the English source question was translated into several alternative German questions using online MT services. Each German question was then parsed with SMES, QUANTICO's German parser. The resulting query object was then weighted according to its linguistic well–formedness and its completeness wrt. query information (question type, question focus, answer–type). The assumption behind this weighting scheme is that "a translated string s_1 is of greater utility for subsequent processes than another translated string s_2, if the linguistic analysis of s_1 is more complete than the linguistic analysis of s_2."

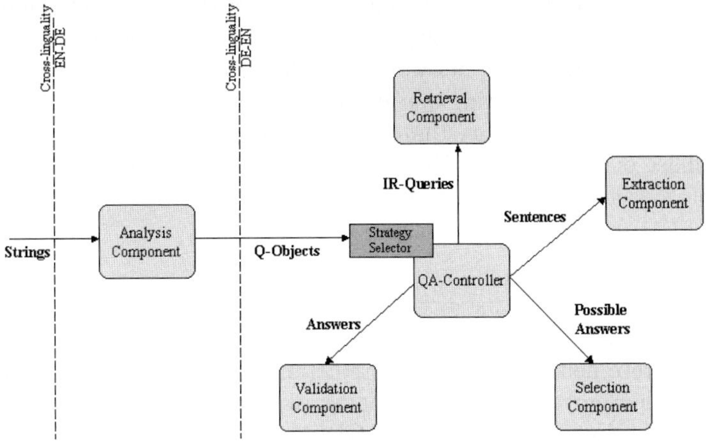

Fig. 2. The architecture of QUANTICO: cross–lingual perspective

The **after–method** translated the formalized result of the Query Analysis Component by using the question translations, a language modeling and a word alignment tool for creating a mapping of the formal information need from the source language into the target language. We used this strategy in the German–English task along two lines (using the following German query as example: *In welchem Jahrzehnt investierten japanische Autohersteller sehr stark?*):

1. translations as returned by the on-line MT systems are being ranked according to a language model

   In which decade did Japanese automakers invest very strongly? (0.7)
   In which decade did Japanese car manufacturers invest very strongly? (0.8)
2. translations with a satisfactory degree of resemblance to a natural language utterance (i.e. linguistically well-formedness), given by a threshold on the language model ranking, are aligned according to several filters: dictionary filter - based on MRD (machine readable dictionaries), PoS filter - based on statistical part-of-speech taggers, and cognates filter - based on string similarity measures (dice coefficient and LCSR (lowest common substring ratio)).
   In: [in:1] true 1.0
   welchem: [which:0.5] true 0.5
   Jahrzehnt: [decade:1] true 1.0
   investierten: [invest:1] true 1.0
   japanische: [japanese:0.5] true 0.5
   Autohersteller: [car manufacturers:0.8, automakers:0.1] true 0.8
   sehr: [very:1] true 1.0
   stark: [strongly:0.5] true 0.5

The CLEF evaluation gives evidence that both strategies are comparable in results, whereby the last one is slightly better, due to the fact of not being forced to choose a best translation, but working with and combining all the translations available. That is, considering and combining several, possible different, translations of the same question, the chance of catching a translation error in an earlier phase of the work–flow becomes higher and propagating errors through the whole system becomes less certain.

8 Web Validation

Our previous Clef–systems where "autistic" in the sense that we did not make use of the Web, neither for answer prediction nor for answer validation. Since we will fuse our current ODQA–technology with the Web in the near future, we started the development of web–based ODQA–strategies. Using the 2004 qa@clef as a testbed, we implemented an initial prototype of a web–validator realizing the following approach: Starting point are the M–best answer candidates found by QUANTICO using the Clef corpus only. Then, for each answer candidate a Google query is constructed from the answer and the the internal representation of the NL–query. The question–answer pair is sent to Google and the resulting total frequency count (TFC) is used to sort the set of answer candidates according to the individual values of TFC. The answer with the highest TFC is then selected as the best answer. The underlying assumption here is, that an IR–query consisting of the NL query terms and the correct answer term will have a higher redundancy on the Web, than one using a false answer candidate. Of course, applying such a method successfully presupposes a *semantic independency* between answer candidates. For this kind of answers, our method seemed to work quite well. However, for answer candidates, which stand in a certain "hidden" relationship (e.g., because a ISA–relation exists between the two candidates), the current method is not sufficient. This is also true for those answer candidates which refer to a different timeline or context than that, preferred by the Web search engine.

9 Results and Discussion

This year, we took part in three tasks: 1.) monolingual German (DE2DE), 2.) cross–lingual English/German (EN2DE), and 3.) cross–lingual German/English (DE2EN). at this point, we would like to stress, that in all different tasks, the *same* ODQA–core machinery was used, extended only for handling the cross–lingual aspects.

The results can be found in tables 2 (DE2DE), 3 (EN2DE), and 4 (DE2EN), respectively. For the tasks DE2DE and EN2DE we submitted two runs: one without web validation (the runs dfki051dede and dfki051ende) and one with web–validation (the runs dfki052dede and dfki052ende). For the task DE2EN, we only submitted one run without web validation. The system performance for the three tasks was as follows: for the task DE2DE, QUANTICO needs approx. 3

sec. for one question–answering cycle (about 10 minutes for all 200 questions); for the task EN2DE, QUANTICO needs approx. 5 sec. (about 17 minutes for all 200 questions), basically due to the extra time, the online machine translation needs. The task DE2EN needs the most computation resources due to online translation, alignment, language model use, etc. (actually approx. 50 minutes are used for all 200 questions).

Table 2. Results in the task German–German

	R		W	X	U	F	D	T
dfki051dede	87	43.50	100	13	-	35.83	66.00	36.67
dfki052dede	54	27.00	127	19	-	15.00	52.00	33.33

Table 3. Results in the task English–German

	R		W	X	U	F	D	T
dfki051ende	46	23.00	141	12	1	16.67	50.00	3.33
dfki052ende	31	15.50	159	8	2	8.33	42.00	0.00

Table 4. Results in the task German–English

	R		W	X	U	F	D	T
dfki051deen	51	25.50	141	8	-	18.18	50.00	13.79

As can be seen from the tables 2 and 3, applying the web validation component (for the best 3 answers determined by QUANTICO) does lead to a system performance loss. At the time of writing this report, we have not yet performed a detailed analysis, but it seems that the lack of contextual information causes the major problems, when computing the Google IR–query. Additional problems could be:

– the number of German web documents might be still too low, for taking into account redundancy effectively
– the correct answer extracted from the Clef–corpus does not exist on the web but a "alternative" answer candidate; in that case, the alternative answer candidate would get a higher rank
– the Clef corpus consists of newspaper articles from 1994 and 1995; thus, the Clef corpus might actually be too old for being validated by the Web, especially if questions referring not to historical events, but to daily news
– in case of EN2DE, web validation is performed with the German query terms, which resulted from automatic machine translation; errors through the translation of complex and long questions had a negative effect on the recall of the web search

However, a first comparison of the assessed results obtained for the task DE2DE, showed that the web validation is useful. Comparing the two runs dfki051dede and dfki052dede (cf. table 2), a total of 51 different assignments were observed (e.g., an answer correct in run dfki051dede, was wrong in run dfki052dede). Actually, 13 questions (of which 8 are definition questions), which where answered incorrectly in dfki051dede, were now answered correctly in run dfki052dede. 28 questions, which were answered correctly in dfki051dede, were answered wrongly in dfki052dede. However, a closer look showed that about half of this errors, are due to the fact, that we actually performed web validation without taking into account the correct timeline. We assume that enhancing the Google IR–query with respect to Clef–corpus consistent timeline (1994/95) will improve the performance of our web validation strategy.

References

1. Neumann, G., Sacaleanu, S.: Experiments on robust nl question interpretation and multi-layered document annotation for a cross-language question/answering system. In: Clef 2004. Volume 3491., Springer-Verlag LNCS (2005) 411–422
2. Rijsbergen, C.V.: The Geometry of Information Retrieval. Cambridge University Pres (2004)
3. Moldovan, D., Harabagui, S., Clark, C., Bowden, M., Lehmann, J., Williams, J.: Experiments and analysis of lcc's two qa systems over trec 2004. In: Proceedings of The Thirteenth Text Retrieval Conference (TREC 2004), Gaithersburg, USA (2004)
4. Neumann, G., Piskorski, J.: A shallow text processing core engine. Computational Intelligence **18**(3) (2002) 451–476
5. Basten, R.: Answering open-domain temporally restricted questions in a multilingual context. Master's thesis, University of Twente and LT-lab DFKI (2005)

QUASAR: The Question Answering System of the Universidad Politécnica de Valencia

José Manuel Gómez-Soriano, Davide Buscaldi, Empar Bisbal Asensi, Paolo Rosso, and Emilio Sanchis Arnal

Dpto. de Sistemas Informáticos y Computación (DSIC),
Universidad Politécnica de Valencia, Spain
{jogomez, dbuscaldi, ebisbal, prosso, esanchis}@dsic.upv.es

Abstract. This paper describes the QUASAR Question Answering Information System developed by the RFIA group at the Departamento de Sistemas Informáticos y Computación of the Universidad Politécnica of Valencia for the 2005 edition of the CLEF Question Answering exercise. We participated in three monolingual tasks: Spanish, Italian and French, and in two cross-language tasks: Spanish to English and English to Spanish. Since this was our first participation, we focused our work on the passage-based search engine while using simple pattern matching rules for the Answer Extraction phase. As regards the cross-language tasks, we had to resort to the most common web translation tools.

1 Introduction

The task of Question Answering (QA) systems is, basically, to retrieve the answer of an user-given question expressed in natural language from an unstructured document collection. In the case of the cross-language QA the collection is constituted by documents written in a language different from the one used in the query, which increases the task difficulty.

A QA system can be divided, usually, into three main modules: Question Analysis, document or Passage Retrieval (PR) and Answer Extraction (AE). The principal aim of the first module is to recognize the type or category of the expected answer (e.g. if it is a Person, Quantity, Date, etc.) from the user question, even if in many systems it also performs the extraction of additional information from the query [1,2]. The second module obtains the passages (or pieces of text) which contain the terms of the question. Finally, the answer extraction module uses the information collected by the previous modules in order to extract the correct answer.

QUASAR (*QUestion AnSwering And information Retrieval*) is a QA system based on the JIRS[1] Passage Retrieval engine, which has been fine-tuned for the QA task, whereas most QA systems use classical PR methods [3,4,5,2]. One of the most valuable characteristics of JIRS is that it is language independent, because during the question and passage processing phases the lexicon and any knowledge

[1] http://leto.dsic.upv.es:8080/jirs

C. Peters et al. (Eds.): CLEF 2005, LNCS 4022, pp. 439–448, 2006.

of the syntax of the corresponding language are not used. The Question Analysis module uses a SVM approach combined with pattern rules. Due to the fact that this was our first participation in the CLEF QA task, the AE module was developed using simple pattern-matching rules, and therefore the results were somewhat coarse, due both to the small number of question categories and to the lack of time to define all the needed patterns.

2 Description of QA System

The architecture of our QA system is shown in Fig.1.

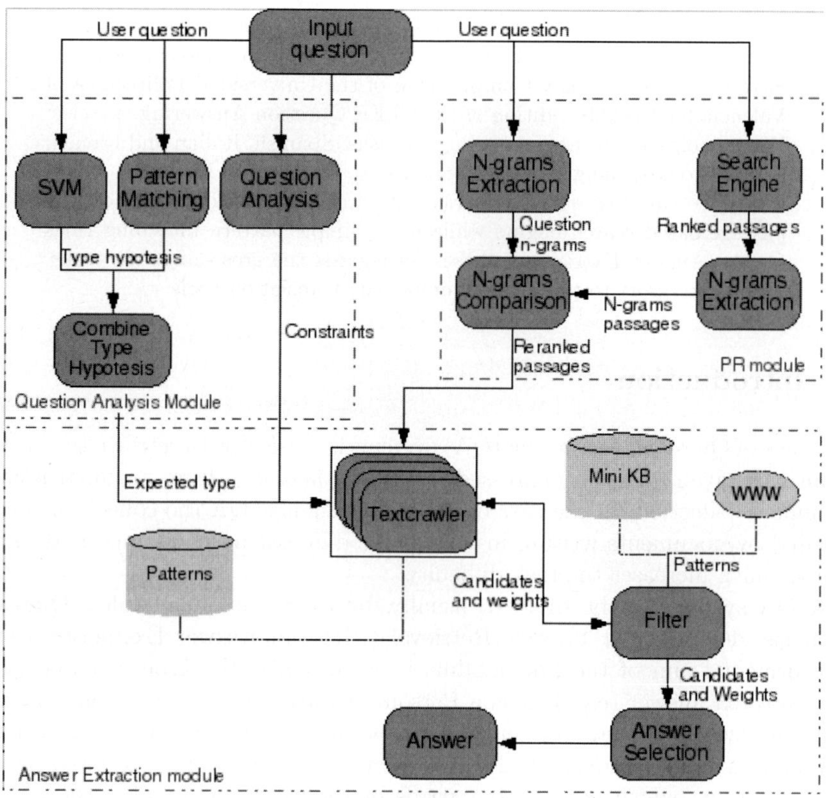

Fig. 1. Main diagram of the QA system

A user provides a question and this is handed over to the *Question Analysis* and *Passage Retrieval* modules. Next, the *Answer Extraction* obtains the answer from the expected type, constraints and passages returned by *Question Analysis* and *Passage Retrieval* modules.

2.1 Question Analysis

The main objective of this module is to derive the expected answer type from the question text. This is a crucial step of the processing since the Answer Extraction module uses a different strategy depending on the expected answer type. Errors in this phase account for the 36.4% of the total number of errors in Question Answering, as reported by Moldovan et al. [6]. The different answer types that can be treated by our system are shown in Table 1.

Table 1. QC pattern classification categories

L0	L1	L2
NAME	ACRONYM	
	PERSON	
	TITLE	
	LOCATION	COUNTRY
		CITY
		GEOGRAPHICAL
DEFINITION		
DATE	DAY	
	MONTH	
	YEAR	
	WEEKDAY	
QUANTITY	MONEY	
	DIMENSION	
	AGE	

A SVM classifier trained over a corpus of 1,393 questions in English and Spanish from the past TREC[2] QA test sets has been coupled with a simple pattern-based classifier. The answers of both classifiers are evaluated by a sub-module that selects the most specific category between the ones returned by the classifiers. For instance, the answer extraction module applies a specialized strategy if the expected type of the answer is "COUNTRY", that is a sub-category of "LOCATION". The patterns are organized in a 3-level hierarchy, where each category is defined by one or more patterns written as regular expressions. For instance, the Italian patterns for the category "city" are: `.*(che|quale) .*citt\'a .+` and `(qual|quale) .*la capitale .+` . Questions that do not match any defined pattern are labeled with *OTHER*. In the case of Italian and French questions, only the pattern-based system was used, because of the unavailability of corpora for these languages.

Another operation performed by this module is to analyze the query with the purpose of identifying the constraints to be used in the AE phase. These constraints are made by sequences of words extracted from the POS-tagged query by means of POS patterns and rules. For instance, any sequence of nouns (such as "ozone hole") is considered as a relevant pattern. The POS-taggers used

[2] http://trec.nist.gov

were the SVMtool[3] for English and Spanish, and the TreeTagger[4] for Italian and French.

We distinguish two classes of constraints: *target* constraints, which can be considered the object of the question, and *contextual* constraints, which keep the information that has to be included in the retrieved passage in order to have a chance of success in extracting the correct answer. There is always one target constraint and zero or more contextual constraints in each question. For example, in the following question: "*How many inhabitants were there in Sweden in 1989?*" *inhabitants* is the target constraint, while *Sweden* and *1989* are the contextual constraints. Usually questions without contextual constraints are *definition* questions. For instance, in "*Who is Jorge Amado?*" the target constraint is *Jorge Amado* and there are no contextual constraints.

In the case of the Cross-language task, the module needs to work with an *optimal* translation of the input query. In order to obtain it, first the question is translated using the following web tools: *Google*, *Systran*, *Babelfish* and *Freetrans*[5]. Afterwards, optimal translation is obtained comparing the web occurrences of their *trigram chains.* A *trigram chain* is obtained as follows: let $w = (w_1, ..., w_n)$ be the sequence of the words in the translation, then a trigram chain is a set of trigrams $T = \{(w_1, w_2, w_3), (w_2, w_3, w_4), \ldots, (w_{n-2}, w_{n-1}, w_n)\}$. Then each of the trigrams $t \in T$ is submitted to a web search engine (we opted for MSN Search[6]) as a string: "$w_i w_{i+1} w_{i+2}$", obtaining the web count $c(t)$ of that trigram. The weight of each trigram chain (and therefore of the corresponding translation) is obtained by means of Formula 1.

$$W(T) = \prod_{t \in T} \hat{c}(t) \quad \text{where} \quad \hat{c}(t) = \begin{cases} \log c(t) & c(t) > 1 \\ 0.1 & c(t) \leq 1 \end{cases} \tag{1}$$

The optimal translation is the one with the highest trigram chain weight. It is important to observe that this translation is not passed to the JIRS module, that works with all the translations (passages retrieved by means of the good translations will achieve a better weight), but only to the Answer Extraction module.

2.2 Passage Retrieval

The user question is handed over also to the JIRS Passage Retrieval system, more specifically to its *Search Engine* and *N-grams Extraction* components. Passages with the relevant terms (i.e., without stopwords) are found by the *Search Engine* using the classical IR system. Sets of 1-grams, 2-grams, ..., n-grams are extracted from the extended passages and from the user question. In both cases, n will be the number of question terms.

---

[3] http://www.lsi.upc.edu/ nlp/SVMTool/

[4] http://www.ims.uni-stuttgart.de/projekte/corplex/TreeTagger/

[5] http://translate.google.com, http://www.systranbox.com, http://babelfish.altavista.com, http://ets.freetranslation.com

[6] http://search.msn.com

A comparison between the n-gram sets from the passages and the user question is done in order to obtain the weight of each passage. The weight of a passage will be heavier if the passage contains greater n-gram structures of the question.

For instance, suppose the question is "*Who is the President of Mexico?*" and the system retrieve two passages: one with the expression "*...**Vicente Fox** is the President of Mexico...*", and the other one with the expression "*...**Carlo Azeglio Ciampi** is the President of Italy...*". Of course, the first passage must have more importance because it contains the 5-gram "*is the President of Mexico*", whereas the second passage only contains the 4-gram "*is the President of* ". In order to calculate the weight of n-grams of every passage, first the most relevant (i.e., the largest) n-gram in the passage is identified and assigned a weight equal to the sum of all term weights. After this, other less relevant n-grams are searched. The weight of the n-grams included in the largest n-gram is computed as the sum of all their weight terms divided by two, in order to avoid their weight being the same of the complete n-gram. The weight of every term is computed by (2):

$$w_k = 1 - \frac{\log(n_k)}{1 + \log(N)} \quad . \tag{2}$$

Where n_k is the number of passages in which the associated term to the weight w_k appears and N is the number of system passages. We made the assumption that stopwords occur in every passage (i.e., n_k takes the value of N). For instance, if the term appears once in the passage collection, its weight will be equal to 1 (the greatest weight). Whereas if it is a stopword its weight will be the lowest.

Due to the question writing style, sometimes a term unrelated to the question can obtain a greater weight than those assigned to the Name Entities (NEs) [7]. Therefore, the (2) is changed to give more weight to the NEs than to other question terms, forcing their presence in the top-ranked passages. NEs are identified only by means of typographical patterns (such as words starting with uppercase letters or numbers). Once the terms are weighted, these are normalized in order that the sum of all terms is 1.

2.3 Answer Extraction

The input of this module is constituted by the n passages returned by the PR module and the constraints (including the expected type of the answer) obtained through the *Question Analysis* module. A *TextCrawler* is instantiated for each of the n passages with a set of patterns for the expected type of the answer and a pre-processed version of the passage text. Some patterns can be used for all languages; for instance, when looking for proper names, the pattern is the same for all languages. The pre-processing of passage text consists in separating all the punctuation characters from the words and in stripping off the annotations

[7] NEs are names of persons, organizations, places, dates, etc. NEs are the most important terms of the question and it does not make sense return passages which do not contain these words.

of the passage. It is important to keep the punctuation symbols because we observed that they usually offer important clues for the individuation of the answer: for instance, it is more frequent to observe a passage containing "*The president of Italy, Carlo Azeglio Ciampi*" than one containing "*The president of Italy **is** Carlo Azeglio Ciampi*" ; moreover, movie and book titles are often put between quotes.

The positions of the passages in which occur the constraints are marked before passing them to the TextCrawlers. Some spell-checking function has been added in this phase by using Levenshtein distance to compare strings. The TextCrawler begins its work by searching all the passage's substrings matching the expected answer pattern. Then a weight is assigned to each found substring s, depending on the positions of the constraints, if s does not include any of the constraint words. Let us define $w_t(s)$ and $w_c(s)$ as the weights assigned to a substring s as a function, respectively, of its distance from the target constraints (3) and the context constraints (4) in the passage.

$$w_t(s) = \max_{0<k\leq|p(t)|} close(s, p_k(t)) \tag{3}$$

$$w_c(s) = \frac{1}{|c|}\sum_{i=0}^{|c|} \max_{0<j\leq|p(c_i)|} near(s, p_j(c_i)) \tag{4}$$

Where c is the vector of contextual constraints, $p(c_i)$ is the vector of positions of the constraint c_i in the passage, t is the target constraint and $p(t)$ is the vector of positions of the target constraint t in the passage. *Close* and *near* are two proximity function defined as:

$$close(s, p) = \exp\left(-\left(\frac{d(s,p)-1}{5}\right)^2\right) \tag{5}$$

$$near(s, p) = \exp\left(-\left(\frac{d(s,p)-1}{2}\right)^2\right) \tag{6}$$

Where p is a position in the passage and $d(s,p)$ is computed as:

$$d(s,p) = \min_{i\in\{0,|s|-1\}} \sqrt{(s_i - p)^2} \tag{7}$$

Where s_i indicates the position of the i-th word of the substring s. The proximity functions can roughly be seen as fuzzy membership functions, where $close(s,p)$ means that the substring s is adjacent to the word at the position p, and $near(s,p)$ means that the substring s is not far from the word at position p. The 2 and 5 values roughly indicate the range within the position p where the words are considered really "close" and "near", and have been selected after some experiments with the CLEF2003 QA Spanish test set. Finally, the weight is assigned to the substring s in the following way:

$$w(s) = \begin{cases} w_t(s) \cdot w_c(s) & \text{if } |p(t)| > 0 \wedge |c| > 0 \\ w_c(s) & \text{if } |p(t)| = 0 \wedge |c| > 0 \\ w_t(s) & \text{if } |p(t)| > 0 \wedge |c| = 0 \\ 0 & \textit{elsewhere.} \end{cases} \quad (8)$$

This means that if in the passage have been found both the target constraint and the contextual constraints, the product of the weights obtained for every constraint will be used; otherwise, only the weight obtained for the constraints found in the passage will be used.

Usually, the type of expected answer directly affects the weighting formula. For instance, the "DEFINITION" questions (such as "Who is Jorge Amado?") usually contain only the target constraint, while "QUANTITY" questions (such as "How many inhabitants are there in Sweden?") contain both target and contextual constraints. For the other question types the target constraint is rarely found in the passage, and weight computation relies only on the contextual constraints (e.g. "From what port did the ferry Estonia leave for its last trip?", port is the target constraint but it is not mandatory in order to found the answer, since it is most common to say "The Estonia left from Tallinn", from which the reader can deduce that Tallinn is -or at least has- a port, than "Estonia left from the port of Tallinn").

The filter module takes advantage of some knowledge resources, such as a mini knowledge base or the web, in order to discard the candidate answers which do not match with an allowed pattern or that do match with a forbidden pattern. For instance, a list of country names in the four languages has been included in the knowledge base in order to filter country names when looking for countries. When the filter rejects a candidate, the TextCrawler provide it with the next best-weighted candidate, if there is one.

Finally, when all TextCrawlers end their analysis of the text, the *Answer Selection* module selects the answer to be returned by the system. The following strategies have been developed:

- Simple voting (SV): The returned answer corresponds to the candidate that occurs most frequently as passage candidate.
- Weighted voting (WV): Each vote is multiplied for the weight assigned to the candidate by the TextCrawler and for the passage weight as returned by the PR module.
- Maximum weight (MW): The candidate with the highest weight and occurring in the best ranked passage is returned.
- Double voting (DV): As simple voting, but taking into account the second best candidates of each passage.
- Top (TOP): The candidate elected by the best weighted passage is returned.

SV is used for every "NAME" type question, while WV is used for all other types. For "NAME" questions, when two candidates obtain the same number of votes, the Answer Selection module looks at the DV answer. If there is still an ambiguity, then the WV strategy is used. For other types of question, the module use directly the MW. TOP is used only to assign the confidence score to the answer, obtained by dividing the number of strategies giving the same answer by the total number of strategies (5), multiplied for other measures depending on the number of passages returned (n_p/N, where N is the maximum number of passages that can be returned by the PR module and n_p is the number of passages actually returned) and the averaged passage weight. The weighting of NIL answers is slightly different, because it is computed as $1 - n_p/N$ if $n_p > 0$, 0 elsewhere.

In our system, candidates are compared by means of a partial string match, therefore *Boris Eltsin* and *Eltsin* are considered as two votes for the same candidate. Later, the Answer Selection module returns the answer in the form occuring most frequently.

For this participation we developed an additional web-corrected weighting strategy, based on web counts of the question constraints. With this strategy, the MSN Search engine is initially queried with the target and contextual constraints, returning p_c, the number of pages containing them. Then, for each of the candidate answers, another search is done by putting the candidate answer itself together with the constraints, obtaining p_a pages. Therefore, the final weight assigned to the candidate answer is multiplied by p_a/p_c. This could be considered a sort of web-based answer validation [7], even if in this case the web weight may not be decisive for answer selection.

3 Experiments and Results

We submitted two runs for each of the following monolingual tasks: Spanish, Italian and French, whereas only one run was submitted for the Spanish-English and English-Spanish cross-language tasks. The second runs (labelled *upv_052*) of the monolingual tasks use the web-corrected weighting strategy, whereas the first runs use the clean system, without recourse to the web. In Table 2 we show the overall accuracy obtained in all the runs.

It can be observed that the web weighting produced worse results, even if the 0.00% obtained for the *upv_052eses* run for definition questions could be due to an undetected problem (network failure). Definition questions obtained better results than other kinds of questions, and we suppose this is due to the ease in identifying the target constraint in these cases. Moreover, the results for the Spanish monolingual tasks are better than the other ones, and we believe this is due mostly to the fact that the question classification was performed combining the results of the SVM and pattern classifiers, whereas for French and Italian the expected type of the answer was obtained only via the pattern-based classifier. Another reason could be that the majority of the preliminary experiments were done over the CLEF2003 Spanish corpus, therefore resulting in the definition of more accurate patterns for the Spanish Answer Extractor.

The average precision obtained by our best run in monolingual Spanish for the questions having "OTHER" type was 4.8%, well below the average precision over questions of types for which a strategy has been implemented (26.9%),

Table 2. Accuracy results for the submitted runs. Overall: overall accuracy, factoid: accuracy over factoid questions; definition: accuracy over definition questions; tr: accuracy over temporally restricted questions; nil: precision over nil questions; conf: confidence-weighted score.

task	run	overall	factoid	definition	tr	nil	conf
es-es	upv_051	33.50%	26.27%	52.00%	31.25%	0.19	0.21
	upv_052	18.00%	22.88%	0.00%	28.12%	0.10	0.12
it-it	upv_051	25.50%	20.00%	44.00%	16.67%	0.10	0.15
	upv_052	24.00%	15.83%	50.00%	13.33%	0.06	0.12
fr-fr	upv_051	23.00%	17.50%	46.00%	6.67%	0.06	0.11
	upv_052	17.00%	15.00%	20.00%	20.00%	0.07	0.07
en-es	upv_051	22.50%	19.49%	34.00%	15.62%	0.15	0.10
es-en	upv_051	17.00%	12.40%	28.00%	17.24%	0.15	0.07

as expected. The best results were obtained for the "LOCATION.COUNTRY" category ($\sim$ 92%), thanks to the use of the nation lists as knowledge source.

Taking into account that this was our first participation to the CLEF, we considered satisfied with the results obtained by our system. QUASAR classified in the top positions (considering participants and not runs) in all the monolingual tasks we participated in, and classified first in the English-Spanish cross-language task. Results obtained in Italian were very close to those achieved by the best system, particularly thanks to the good performance in "DEFINITION" questions. On the other hand, results in French were particularly disappointing in spite of the ranking, since in this case the system obtained the worst results both in factoid and temporally restricted questions.

The most remarkable result achieved by QUASAR at CLEF QA 2005 was that it resulted the system returning the highest Confidence Weight Scores (CWS) among all the participants.

4 Conclusions and Further Work

The obtained results show that QUASAR is a promising system for Question Answering for Spanish, Italian and French languages, even if much work is still needed in order to obtain the results of the best systems. The main drawback of the system is constituted by the cost of defining patterns for the Answer Extraction module: many experiments are needed in order to obtain a satisfactory pattern, and this has to be done for each expected answer type in each category. Moreover, apart from some well-defined categories for which a pattern can be defined, in other cases is almost impossible to identify a pattern that can match with all the answers of such questions. Therefore, we plan to use in the future both machine learning approaches in order to master this problem, together with more knowledge bases, since the small country database allowed the attainment of good results for the COUNTRY questions. In the cross-language task, the Passage Retrieval module worked well despite the generally acknowledged low quality of web translations, allowing to obtain results slightly worse than those obtained in the monolingual task.

Acknowledgments

We would like to thank R2D2 CICYT (TIC2003-07158-C04-03) and ICT EU-India (ALA/95/23/2003/077-054) research projects for partially funding this work. A special acknowledgement to Manuel Montes y Gómez for support during his stay at the Universidad Politécnica de Valencia.

Finally, we would like to thank also the CLEF 2005 organization committee (this work is a revised version of the paper "Monolingual and Cross-language QA using a QA-oriented Passage Retrieval System").

References

1. Harabagiu, S., Moldovan, D., Pasca, M., Mihalcea, R., Surdeanu, M., Bunescu, R., Girju, R., Rus, V., Moraraescu, P.: Falcon: Boosting knowledge for answer engines. In: Proceedings of Text REtrieval Conference (TREC-9). (2000)
2. Neumann, G., Sacaleanu, B.: Experiments on robust nl question interpretation and multi-layered document annotation for a cross-language question/answering system. In: Workshop of the Cross-Lingual Evaluation Forum (CLEF 2004), Bath, UK (2004)
3. Magnini, B., Negri, M., Prevete, R., Tanev, H.: Multilingual question/answering: the DIOGENE system. In: The 10th Text REtrieval Conference. (2001)
4. Aunimo, L., Kuuskoski, R., Makkonen, J.: Cross-language question answering at the university of helsinki. In: Workshop of the Cross-Lingual Evaluation Forum (CLEF 2004), Bath, UK (2004)
5. Vicedo, J.L., Izquierdo, R., Llopis, F., Muoz, R.: Question answering in spanish. In: Workshop of the Cross-Lingual Evaluation Forum (CLEF 2003), Trondheim, Norway (2003)
6. Moldovan, D., Pasca, M., Harabagiu, S., Surdeanu, M.: Performance issues and error analysis in an open-domain question answering system. In: Proceedings of the 40th Annual Meeting of the Association for Computational Linguistics, New York, USA (2003)
7. Magnini, B., Negri, M., Tanev, H.: Is it the right answer? exploiting web redundancy for answer validation. In: Proceedings of the 40th Annual Meeting of the Association for Computational Linguistics. (2002)

Towards an Offline XML-Based Strategy for Answering Questions

David Ahn, Valentin Jijkoun, Karin Müller,
Maarten de Rijke, and Erik Tjong Kim Sang

ISLA, University of Amsterdam, Kruislaan 403
1098 SJ Amsterdam, The Netherlands
{ahn, jijkoun, kmueller, mdr, erikt}@science.uva.nl

Abstract. The University of Amsterdam participated in the Question Answering (QA) Track of CLEF 2005 with two runs. In comparison with previous years, our focus this year was adding to our multi-stream architecture a new stream that uses offline XML annotation of the corpus. We describe the new work on our QA system, present the results of our official runs, and note areas for improvement based on an error analysis.

1 Introduction

For our participation in question answering (QA) tracks at past editions of both CLEF and TREC, we have developed a *multi-stream* QA architecture which incorporates several different approaches to identifying candidate answers, complemented with filtering and ranking mechanisms to choose the best answer [1, 2, 4, 5]. For the 2005 edition of the QA@CLEF track, we devoted some effort to improving this architecture, in particular the table stream (see §2.2). Also, to accommodate the new temporally restricted questions, a dedicated module was developed (§2.3). Most of our efforts, however, were aimed at implementing XQuesta, a pure QA-as-XML-retrieval stream, in which the target collection is automatically annotated with linguistic information at indexing time, incoming questions are converted to semistructured queries, and evaluation of these queries yields a ranked list of candidate answers.

While our system provides *wrong* answers for less than 40% of the test questions, we identified obvious areas for improvement. First, we should work on definition extraction so that both questions asking for definitions and questions requiring resolving definitions can be better answered. Second, we should examine inheritance of document links in the answer tiling process to help the associated module avoid unsupported answers. Most importantly, we should improve our answer filtering module to ensure that the semantic class of the generated answer corresponds with the class required by the question.

The paper is organized as follows. In §2, we describe the architecture of our QA system, including improvements and additions for QA@CLEF 2005. In §3, we describe the new XQuesta stream. In §4, we detail our official runs. In §4, we discuss the results we obtained and give a preliminary analysis of the performance of different components of the system. We conclude in §5.

C. Peters et al. (Eds.): CLEF 2005, LNCS 4022, pp. 449–456, 2006.

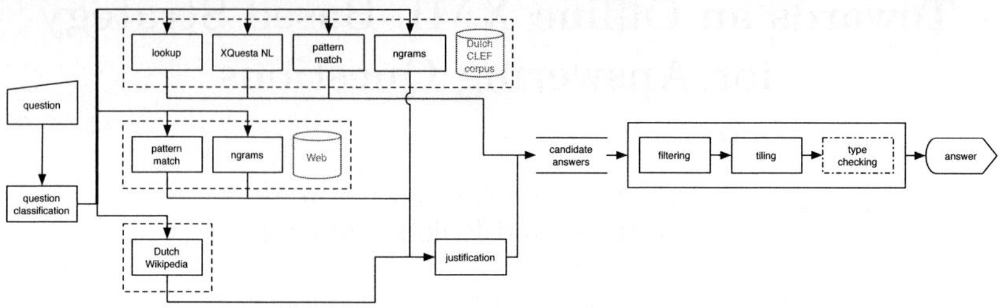

Fig. 1. Quartz-2005: the University of Amsterdam's Dutch Question Answering System

2 System Overview

Essentially, our system architecture implements multiple copies of a standard QA architecture. Each copy (or *stream*) is a complete standalone QA system that produces ranked answers, though not necessarily for all types of questions. The overall system's answer is then selected from the combined pool of candidates through a combination of merging and filtering techniques. For a reasonably detailed discussion of our QA system architecture we refer to [2]. A diagram of the system architecture is given in Figure 2.

The first stage of processing, *question processing*, is common to all the streams. Each of the 200 questions is tagged, parsed, and assigned a question class based on our question classification module. Finally, the expected answer type is determined. See §3.2 for more details about question processing for the XQuesta stream, in particular.

There are seven streams in our system this year, four of which use the CLEF corpus to answer questions and three of which use external sources of information. Four streams are unchanged from our system for last year's evaluation [2]: the *Pattern Match* and *Ngrams* streams for each of the CLEF corpus and the web. The focus of our efforts this year resulted in our XQuesta stream, which is described in §3. We also added a stream that consults Wikipedia (§2.1) and expanded the table stream (§2.2).

The methods we employ to merge, filter, and choose among the answer candidates generated by the seven streams, as well as to *justify* answers (i.e., find supporting documents in the Dutch CLEF corpus for answers obtained outside the corpus), also remain unchanged from our system for last year's evaluation, except for the temporally restricted questions new to this year's evaluation. For these questions, we re-rank candidate answers using temporal information; see §2.3 for more details.

2.1 Wikipedia Stream

Like our streams that consult the web rather than the Dutch CLEF corpus, this stream also uses an external corpus—the Dutch Wikipedia (`http://nl.wikipedia.org`), an open-content encyclopedia in Dutch. However, since this corpus is much cleaner than newspaper text, the stream operates in a different manner. First, the *focus* of the question—usually the main named entity—is identified. Then, this entity's encyclopedia entry is looked up; since Wikipedia is standardized to a large extent, this information has a template-like nature. Finally, using knowledge about the templates used in Wikipedia, information such as DATE-OF-DEATH and FIRST-NAME can easily be extracted.

2.2 Improvements to the Table Stream

To the tables used in 2004, we have added a table which contains definitions extracted offline with two rules: one extracts definitions from appositions, and the other creates definitions by combining proper nouns with preceding common nouns. This table is used in parallel with the existing roles table, which contains definitions only for people. The new table contains more than three times as many entries (611,077) as the existing one.

Unlike earlier versions of the table module, all tables are now stored in SQL format and made available in a MySQL database. The type of an incoming question is converted to sets of tuples containing three elements: table, source field, and target field. The table code searches in the source field of the specified table for a pattern and, when a match is found, keeps the contents of the corresponding target field as a candidate answer. Ideally, the search pattern would be computed by the question analysis module but currently we use separate code for this task. The table code also uses backoff strategies (case insensitive vs. case sensitive, exact vs. inexact match) in case a search returns no matches.

The table fields only contain noun phrases that are present in the text. This means that they can be used for answering questions such as *Who is the President of Serbia?* because phrases such as *President of Serbia* can usually be found in the text. However, in general, this stream cannot be used for answering questions such as *Who was the President of Serbia in 1999?* because the modifier *in 1999* often does not follow the profession.

2.3 Temporal Restrictions

Twenty-six questions in this year's QA track are tagged as *temporally restricted.* Such questions ask for information relevant to a particular time; the time in question may be given explicitly by a temporal expression (or *timex*), as in:

(1) *Q0094: Welke voetballer ontving "De Gouden Bal" in 1995?*
Which footballer won the European Footballer of the Year award in 1995?

or it may be given implicitly, with respect to another event, as in:

(2) *Q0008: Wie speelde de rol van Superman voordat hij verlamd werd?*
Who played the role of Superman before he was paralyzed?

Our system takes advantage of these temporal restrictions to re-rank candidate answers for these questions. Because there is already a module to annotate timexes (see §3.1), we limit ourselves to temporal restrictions signalled by timexes. Handling event-based restrictions would require identifying (and possibly temporally locating) events, which is a much more difficult problem.

For each temporally restricted question, the temporal re-ranker tries to identify an explicit temporal restriction by looking for temporal prepositions (e.g., *in*, *op*, *tijdens*, *voor*, *na*) and timexes in the question. If it succeeds, it proceeds with re-ranking the candidate answers.

For each candidate answer, timexes occurring in sentences containing the answer and question focus (if there is one) are extracted from the justification document, along with the document timestamp. The re-ranker checks whether these timexes are compatible with the restriction. For each compatible timex, the score for the candidate answer is boosted; for each incompatible timex, the score is lowered. The logic involved in checking compatibility of a timex with a temporal restriction is relatively straightforward; the only complications come in handling times of differing granularities.

3 XQuesta

The XQuesta stream implements a QA-as-XML-retrieval approach [6, 7]. The target collection is automatically annotated with linguistic information offline. Then, incoming questions are converted to semistructured queries, and evaluation of these queries yields a ranked list of candidate answers. We describe the three stages in detail.

3.1 Offline Annotation

We automatically processed the Dutch QA collection, identifying sentences and annotating them syntactically and semantically. We used the TnT tagger [3] to tag the collection for parts of speech and syntactic chunks, with the CGN corpus [8] as training data. The same tagger, trained on CoNLL-2002 data [9] was used to identify named entities, and a hand-coded rule-based system, to identify temporal expressions.

In total, we use four annotation layers. The first layer provides information about part-of-speech tags:

(3) `<LID>`*de*`</LID>` `<ADJ>`*machtige*`</ADJ>` `<N>`*burgemeester*`</N>` `<VZ>`*van*`</VZ>`
the powerful mayor of ...

Example (4) shows the second annotation layer: non-recursive syntactic chunks—noun phrases (NP), verb phrases (VP) and prepositional phrases (PP).

(4) `<NP>`*de machtige burgemeester*`</NP>` `<PP>`*van*`</PP>` `<NP>`*Moskou*`</NP>` ,
`<NP>`*Joeri Loezjkov*`</NP>` , `<VP>`*veroordeelt*`</VP>` `<NP>`*dat*`</NP>`

Example (5) shows the third annotation layer: named entities—persons (PER), organizations (ORG), locations (LOC), and miscellaneous entities (MISC).

(5) *de machtige burgemeester van* `<NE type="LOC">`*Moskou*`</NE>` ,
`<NE type="PER">`*Joeri Loezjkov*`</NE>` , *veroordeelt dat*

The next two examples show annotation of temporal expressions, normalized to ISO 8601 format.

(6) *Luc Jouret werd in* `<TIMEX val="1947">`*1947*`</TIMEX>` *geboren.*
Luc Jouret was born in 1947.
(7) *Ekeus verliet Irak* `<TIMEX val="1994-10-06">`*donderdagmorgen*`</TIMEX>`
Ekeus left Iraq Thursday morning

Normalization is more complicated in Example (7); in order to determine that *donderdagmorgen* refers to 1994-10-06, the system uses the document timestamp (in this case, 1994-10-08) and some simple heuristics to compute the reference.

The four annotation layers of the collection are stored in separate XML files to simplify maintenance. Whenever the XQuesta stream requests a document from the collection, all annotations are automatically merged into a single XML document providing full simultaneous access to all annotated information.

3.2 Question Analysis

The current question analysis module consists of two parts. The first part determines possible question classes, such as DATE_BIRTH for the question shown in Example (8).

(8) *Q0014: Wanneer is Luc Jouret geboren?*
When was Luc Jouret born?

We use 31 different question types, some of which belong to a more general class: for example, DATE_BIRTH and DATE_DEATH are subtypes of the class DATE. The assignment of the classes is based on manually compiled patterns.

The second part of our question analysis module is new. Depending on the predicted question class, an expected answer type is assigned. The latter describes syntactic, lexical or surface requirements to be met by the possible answers. The restrictions are formulated as XPath queries, which are used to extract specific information from our preprocessed documents. E.g., the XPath queries corresponding to question types PERSON and DATE are `NE[@type="PER"]` and `TIMEX[@val=~/^\d/]`, respectively. Table 1 displays the manually developed rules for mapping the question classes to the expected answer types.

3.3 Extracting and Ranking Answers

As described in §3.2, incoming questions are mapped to retrieval queries (the question text) and XPath queries corresponding to types of expected answers.

Retrieval queries are used to locate relevant passages in the collection. For retrieval, we use nonoverlapping passages of at least 400 characters starting and ending at paragraph boundaries. Then, the question's XPath queries are evaluated on the top 20 retrieved passages, giving lists of XML elements corresponding to candidate answers. For example, for the question in Example (8) above, with the generated XPath query "`TIMEX[@val=~/^\d/]`", the value "*1947*" is extracted from the annotated text in Example (6).

The score of each candidate is calculated as the sum of retrieval scores of all passages containing the candidate. Furthermore, the scores are normalized using web hit counts, producing the final ranked list of XQuesta's answer candidates.

Table 1. Overview of the mapping rules from question classes to answer types

Question class	Restrictions on the type of answer
ABBREVIATION	word in capital letters
AGE	numeric value, possible word: jarige
CAUSE_REASON	sentence
CITY_CAPITAL	LOC
COLOR	adjective
DATE_DEATH, DATE_BIRTH, DATE	TIMEX, digital number
DEFINITION_PERSON	sentence
DEFINITION	noun phrase or sentence
DISTANCE	numeric value
DISTINCTION	noun phrase or a sentence
EXPANSION	MISC or ORG, noun phrase
HEIGHT	numeric value
LANGUAGE	MISC
LENGTH	numeric value
LOCATION	LOC
MANNER	sentence
MONETARY_UNIT	MISC
NAME	named entity
NUMBER_PEOPLE	numeric value, noun phrase
NUMBER	numeric value
ORGANIZATION	ORG
PERSON	PER
SCORE, SIZE, SPEED, SUM_OF_MONEY	numeric value
SYNONYM_NAME	PER
TEMPERATURE, TIME_PERIOD	numeric value

4 Results and Analysis

We submitted two Dutch monolingual runs. The run uams051nlnl used the full system with all streams described above and final answer selection, while uams052nlnl, on top of this, used an additional stream: the XQuesta stream with paraphrased questions. We generated paraphrases simply, by double-translating questions (from Dutch to English and then back to Dutch) using Systran, an automatic MT system. Question paraphrases were only used for query formulation at the retrieval step; question analysis (identification of question types, expected answer types and corresponding XPath queries) was performed on the original questions. Our idea was to see whether paraphrasing retrieval queries would help to find different relevant passages and lead to more correctly answered questions.

The two runs proved to be quite similar. Different answers were only generated for 13 of the 200 questions. The results of the assessment were even more similar. Both runs had 88 correct answers and 5 unsupported answers. Run uams051nlnl had one less inexact answer than uams052nlnl (28 vs. 29) and one more wrong answer (79 vs. 78). We were surprised about the large number of inexact answers. When we examined the inexact answers of the first run, we found that a disproportional number of these were generated for definition questions: 85% (only 30% of the questions ask for definitions). Almost half of the errors (13 out of 28) were caused by the same problem: determining where a noun phrase starts, for example, *leader of the extreme right group* as an answer to *What is Eyal?* where *extreme right group* would have been correct. This extraction problem also affected the answers for questions that provided a definition and asked for a name. We expect that this problem can be solved by a check of the semantic class of the question focus word and head noun of the answer, both in the answer extraction process and in answer postprocessing. Such a check would also have prevented seven of the 15 other incorrect answers of this group.

When we examined the assessments of the answers to the three different question types, we noticed that the proportion of correct answers was the same for definition questions (45%) and factoid questions (47%) but that temporally restricted questions seemed to cause problems (27% correct). Of the 18 incorrect answers in the latter group, four involved an answer which would have been correct in another time period (questions Q0078, Q0084, Q0092 and Q0195). If these questions had been answered correctly, the score for this category would have an acceptable 46% (including the incorrectly assessed answer for Q0149).

The temporal re-ranking module described in §2 did make a small positive contribution. For two temporally restricted questions, the highest ranking candidate answer before the temporal re-ranking module was applied was incorrect, but the application of the temporal re-ranking module boosted the correct answer to the top position. Additionally, the temporal re-ranking module never demoted a correct answer from the top position.

The answers to the temporally restricted questions are indicative of the overall problems of the system. Of the other 14 incorrect answers, only five were of the expected answer category while nine were of a different category. In the 62 answers to factoid and definition questions that were judged to be wrong, the majority (58%) had an incorrect answer class. An extra answer postprocessing filter that compares the semantic category of the answer and the one expected by the question would prevent such mismatches.

Our system produced five answers which were judged to be unsupported. One of these was wrong, one was right, and a third was probably combined from different answers, with a link to a document containing only a part of the answer being kept. The remaining two errors were probably also caused by a document link which should not have been kept but the reason for this is unknown.

This error analysis suggests three possible improvements. First, we should work on definition extraction so that questions asking for definitions and questions requiring the resolution of definitions can be better answered. Second, we should examine inheritance of document links in the answer tiling process to make sure that the associated module avoids unsupported answers. Most importantly, we should improve answer filtering to make sure that the semantic class of the generated answer corresponds with the class required by the question.

5 Conclusion

Most of our efforts for the 2005 edition of the QA@CLEF track were aimed at implementing XQuesta, a "pure" QA-as-XML-retrieval stream, as part of our multi-stream question answering architecture. For XQuesta, the target collection is automatically annotated with linguistic information at indexing time, incoming questions are converted to semistructured queries, and evaluation of these queries gives a ranked list of candidate answers. The overall system provides *wrong* answers for less than 40% of the questions. Our ongoing work is aimed at addressing the main sources of error: definition extraction, inheritance of document links in answer tiling, and semantically informed answer filtering.

Acknowledgments

This research was supported by various grants from the Netherlands Organization for Scientific Research (NWO). Valentin Jijkoun, Karin Müller, and Maarten de Rijke were supported under project number 220-80-001. Erik Tjong Kim Sang and Maarten de Rijke were supported under project number 264-70-050. David Ahn and Maarten de Rijke were supported under project number 612.066.302. In addition, Maarten de Rijke was also supported by grants from NWO, under project numbers 017.001.190, 365-20-005, 612-13-001, 612.000.106, 612.000.207, 612.069.006, and 640.001.501.

References

[1] D. Ahn, V. Jijkoun, G. Mishne, K. Müller, M. de Rijke, and S. Schlobach. Using Wikipedia at the TREC QA track. In E. Voorhees and L. Buckland, editors, *The Thirteenth Text Retrieval Conference (TREC 2004)*, Gaithersburg, Maryland, 2005.

[2] D. Ahn, V. Jijkoun, K. Müller, M. de Rijke, S. Schlobach, and G. Mishne. Making stone soup: Evaluating a recall-oriented multi-stream question answering stream for Dutch. In e. a. C. Peters, editor, *Multilingual Information Access for Text, Speech and Images: Results of the Fifth CLEF Evaluation Campaign.* Springer Verlag, 2005.

[3] T. Brants. *TnT – A Statistical Part-Of-Speech tagger.* Saarland University, 2000.

[4] V. Jijkoun, G. Mishne, and M. de Rijke. How frogs built the Berlin Wall. In *Proceedings CLEF 2003*, LNCS. Springer, 2004.

[5] V. Jijkoun, G. Mishne, C. Monz, M. de Rijke, S. Schlobach, and O. Tsur. The University of Amsterdam at the TREC 2003 Question Answering Track. In *Proceedings TREC 2003*, pages 586–593, 2004.

[6] K. Litkowksi. Use of metadata for question answering and novelty tasks. In *Proceedings of the Twelfth Text REtrieval Conference (TREC 2003)*, 2004.

[7] P. Ogilvie. Retrieval using structure for question answering. In e. a. V. Mihajlovic, editor, *Proceedings of the First Twente Data Management Workshop*, 2004.

[8] I. Schuurman, M. Schouppe, H. Hoekstra, and T. van der Wouden. CGN, an Annotated Corpus of Spoken Dutch. In *Proceedings of the 4th International Workshop on Linguistically Interpreted Corpora (LINC-03).* Budapest, Hungary, 2003.

[9] E. Tjong Kim Sang. Introduction to the CoNLL-2002 Shared Task: Language-Independent Named Entity Recognition. In *Proceedings of CoNLL-2002*, pages 155–158. Taipei, Taiwan, 2002.

AliQAn, Spanish QA System at CLEF-2005*

S. Roger[1,2], S. Ferrández[1], A. Ferrández[1], J. Peral[1], F. Llopis[1], A. Aguilar[1], and D. Tomás[1]

[1] Natural Language Processing and Information Systems Group
Department of Software and Computing Systems
University of Alicante, Spain
[2] Natural Language Processing Group
Department of Computing Sciences
University of Comahue, Argentina
{sroger, sferrandez, antonio, jperal, llopis, dtomas}@dlsi.ua.es, antonia_agl@yahoo.es

Abstract. Question Answering is a major research topic at the University of Alicante. For this reason, this year two groups participated in the QA@CLEF track using different approaches. In this paper we describe the work of *Alicante 2* group. This paper describes AliQAn, a monolingual open-domain Question Answering (QA) System developed in the Department of Language Processing and Information Systems at the University of Alicante for CLEF-2005 Spanish monolingual QA evaluation task. Our approach is based fundamentally on the use of syntactic pattern recognition in order to identify possible answers. Besides this, Word Sense Disambiguation (WSD) is applied to improve the system. The results achieved (overall accuracy of 33%) are shown and discussed in the paper.

1 Introduction

This year two groups have taken part in the QA@CLEF track using different approaches. In this paper we describe the work of *Alicante 2* (run *alia51eses* and *alia52eses* in [9]) .

Question Answering (QA) is not a simple task of Information Retrieval (IR). A QA system must provide concise answers to questions stated by the user in natural language.

The research in open domain QA has mainly focused around English due to the advances in IR and Natural Language Processing (NLP). However, the Cross-Language Evaluation Forum Campaigns (CLEF) provide a multilingual forum for evaluation of QA systems in languages other than English. Multilingual open domain QA systems have been recognized as an important issue for the future of information search.

* This research has been partially funded by the Spanish Government under project CICyT number TIC2003-07158-C04-01 and by the Valencia Government under project numbers GV04B-276 and GV04B-268.

C. Peters et al. (Eds.): CLEF 2005, LNCS 4022, pp. 457–466, 2006.

Nowadays, there are several types of implementations of Spanish QA systems. Generally, most of the systems are based on NLP tools [2,5,7,8], such as Part of Speech (PoS) taggers, syntactic parsers, etc. On the other hand, some other approaches use machine learning and statistical models [3] like Hidden Markov Models in order to find the answer. Also, there are systems that combine NLP tools with statistical data redundancy techniques [10,11].

The systems based on NLP tools are complex because of the number of different NLP tools that they use. Moreover, a good integration between them is needed. Our system has been developed during the last two years in the Departament of Language Processing and Information Systems at the University of Alicante. It is based on complex pattern matching using NLP tools. Furthermore, Word Sense Disambiguation (WSD) is applied to improve the system.

As usual, in our approach, three tasks have been defined: question analysis, selection of relevant passages and extraction of the answer.

The rest of this paper is organized as follows: section two describes the structure and functionality of the system. Afterwards, the achieved results are shown and discussed in section three and finally, section four details our conclusions and future work.

2 System Description

2.1 Overview

In this section, the structure and functionality of our approach to open domain Spanish QA system are detailed. The next paragraph presents the phases of the QA process.

Our approach is based fundamentally on syntactic analysis of the questions and the Spanish documents (the EFE collection in this case), where the system tries to localize the answer. In order to make the syntactic analysis, SUPAR [4] system is used, which works in the output of a PoS tagger [1]. SUPAR performs partial syntactic analysis that lets us identify the different grammatical structures of the sentence. Syntactic blocks (SB) are extracted, and they are our basic syntactic unit to define patterns.

Using the output of SUPAR we are going to identify three types of SB: verb phrase (VP), simple nominal phrase (NP) and simple prepositional phrase (PP). For example in the sentence: *Hillary Clinton was in Jerusalem*, the obtained list of SB is: [NP, hillary*clinton] [VP, to be] [PP, in: jerusalem].

The overall architecture of our system (Figure 1) is divided in two main phases: Indexation phase and Search phase.

- **Indexation phase.** Indexation phase consists of arranging the data where the system tries to find the answer of the questions. This process is a main step to accelerate the process. Two different indexation are carried out: IR-n and QA indexation. The first one is carried out by IR-n system and it is independent from the second one, in which more syntactic and semantic information is stored. For example, the QA indexation stores the NP, VP

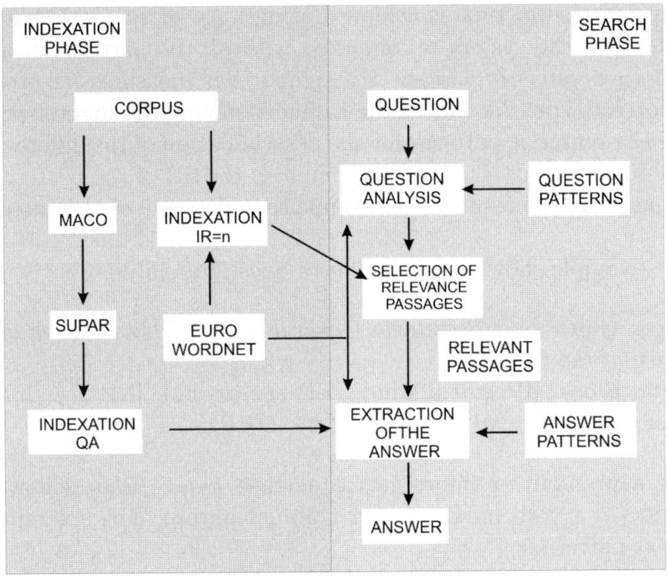

Fig. 1. System architecture

and PP obtained from the parsing, and it also stores the results of the WSD process.
- **Search phase**. This phase follows the most commonly used scheme. The three main modules of our approach are: Question Analysis, Selection of Relevant Passages and Extraction of the Answer.

These modules are described below. Previously, the used annotation is commented. The symbols "[ ]" delimit a SB (NP, VP and PP), *"sp"* is a preposition of a PP, the term *"ap"* indicates that PP is an apposition of the previous nominal head, *SOL* is the place where the answer can be found and the symbols *"[...]"* indicate some irrelevant SB for the search.

2.2 Question Analysis

In this step the system carries out two tasks: 1) To detect the type of information that the answer has to satisfy to be a candidate of answer. 2) To select the question terms (keywords) that make possible to locate those documents that can contain the answer.

We have based on WordNet Based-Types and EuroWordNet Top-Concepts in order to develop our taxonomy that consists of the next categories: person, group, object, place, place city, place capital, place country, abbreviation, event, numerical quantity, numerical economic, numerical age, numerical measure, numerical period, numerical percentage, temporary year, temporary month, temporary date and definition.

The expected answer type is achieved using a set of syntactic patterns. The question posed to the system is compared with all the patterns of all the categories. For each category a score is assigned that measures its probability of being the correct type. We choose the category having the highest probability.

We have 173 syntactic patterns for the determination of the different semantic category of our ontology. The system compares the SB of the patterns with the SB of the question, the result of the comparison determines the category of the question.

The next example shows the behavior of question analysis:

- Question: *Quién es el Secretario General de la ONU? (Who is the General Secretary of the ONU?)*
- Syntactic Block: [IP *quién*](who), [VP *ser*](to be), [NP *secretario_general* [PP, *de: onu*]] *(General Secretary of the ONU)*

We have a pronoun or interrogative particle *quién (who)* followed by two syntactic blocks: a verb phrase and a nominal phrase. This example matches with the next pattern:

[IP, *quién* | *quiénes*] *(who)* [VP, *ser*] *(to be)* [NP, *hipónimo persona*] *(hyponim person)*

therefore, the category of the question is *person*.

For each SB of the pattern, we keep a flag in order to determine whether the SB of the question is considered for the next stage of the QA process or not.

2.3 Selection of Relevant Passages

This second module of the QA process creates and retrieves passages using IR-n system [6]. The goal of IR-n system is to extract a set of passages, where at least one passage contains the answer for the input question.

The inputs of IR-n are the detected keywords in question analysis, IR-n returns a list of passages where we apply the extraction of the answer process. Furthermore, the objective of this task is reducing complexity of the process of searching the solution by means of reducing the amount of text in which the system searches for the answer.

2.4 Extraction of the Answer

The final step of QA is the extraction of the answer. In this module, the system takes the set of retrieved passages by IR-n and tries to extract a concise answer to the question.

Moreover, the type of question, SB of the question and a set of syntactic patterns with lexical, syntactic and semantic information are used in order to find a possible answer.

As shown in the next list, the system use the following NLP techniques.

- *Lexical level.* Grammatical category of answer must be checked according to the type of the question. For example, if we are searching for a *person*, the proposed SB as possible answer has to contain at least a noun.
- *Syntactic level.* Syntactic patterns have been defined. Those let us look for the answer inside the recovered passages.
- *Semantic level.* Semantic restrictions must be checked. For example, if the type of the question is *city* the possible answer must contain a hyponym of *city* in EuroWordNet. Semantic restrictions are applied according to the type of the questions. Some types are not associated with semantic restrictions, such as *quantity.*

In order to design and group the patterns in several sets, the cases of the question are used. The patterns are classified in the following three cases:

- ***Case 1.*** In the question, one SB of type NP or PP is only detected. For example:
  - Question: *Who is the president of Yugoslavia?*
    We only have a SB, the verb *to be* that is not used to find the answer because it is a copulative verb.
  - SB: *[NP, president [PP, of: Yugoslavia]]*
- ***Case 2.*** A VP is detected in the question. This verb expresses an action that must be used in order to search the answer. For example:
  - Question: *Who did write Star Trek?*
  - SB: *[VP, to write] [NP, star∗trek]*
- ***Case 3.*** VP is preceded by a NP or PP. In this case we used three sections to find out the possible answer.
  - Question: *Which team did win the NBA tournament?*
  - SB: *[NP, team] [VP, to win] [NP, NBA∗tournament]*

When the system tries to find a possible answer in a sentence, first, the SB of the question are localized in the text, secondly the system attempts to match the pattern in the sentence. If this has been possible, then a possible answer has been found that must be appraised using lexical and semantic restrictions according to the type of the question. The Spanish QA system has about 60 patterns, the number of patterns that is processed in each sentence depends on the type of the question. Therefore, a question of case 1 and type "*person*" processes different patterns than a question of case 1 and type "*place_city*".

The next example shows the used pattern and the behavior the extraction of the answer: `[SOL[PP, sp: NP1]]` [...] `[VP]`[...] `[NP2]`

First, NP2 (or PP2) and VP are searched by the system, afterward the NP1 with the answer must be found. Next example shows the process:

- **Question:** Qué presidente de Corea del Norte murió a los 80 años de edad? (Which North Korea's president died at the age of 80?)
- **Type:** person

- **Case:** 3
- **List of SB:** [NP, north∗korea∗president] [VP, to death] [PP, at: age [PP, of: 80]
- **Text:** [...] Kim Il Sung, presidente de Corea del Norte, murió ayer a los 82 años [...] ([...] Kim Il Sung, president of North Korea, died yesterday at the age of 80 [...])
- **List of SB of sentence:** [...] [NP, kim∗il∗ sung [PP, apposition: president [PP, of: north∗korea]]] [VP, to death] [PP, at: age [PP, of: 80] [...]
- **Answer:** Kim Il Sung

Value of the Solution. In order to select the answer from a set of candidates, each possible answer is scored. The calculation of the value of the solution on each pattern is described in this subsection of the paper.

The score of a candidate is structured in three phases: comparison of the terms inside a nominal head of a SB with the terms of the nominal head of another SB, comparison of a SB of the question with a SB of the text and weighting of a pattern according to the different SB.

Comparison of the Terms of a Nominal Head. When the system is comparing two terms, the system does not only contemplate the literal value of terms, also checks the relations between these terms in EuroWordNet. So, weighting of terms is calculated using the equation 1, where N is the number of terms inside nominal head and pt_i is the value of the terms that is calculated using EuroWordNet (*1 same lemma, 0.8 synonym and 0.6 hyponim*).

$$Pt = \frac{\sum_{i=1}^{N} pt_i}{N} \tag{1}$$

The equation 2 shows the process of comparison between the terms *"old Bosnian leader"* and *"senior Bosnian sailor"* obtaining the following results:

$$Pt = \frac{0.8 + 1 + 0}{3} = 0.6 \tag{2}$$

where *old* and *senior* have a synonym relation and both SB contain the lemma Bosnian. If the number of terms is different, the system divides using the greater number.

Comparison of the SB. In our approach, the comparison of the SB occurs in two kinds of circumstances. When the SB of the question is localized in the text in order to apply a pattern and when the system is analizing a SB to find the answer.

The first type of comparison is called "*value of terms*", this measure can be affected by fixed circumstances, such as: *Depth of appearance*: the terms of the SB of the question may not appear as nominal heads in a SB of the text. *Excess or missing of modifiers*: if the nominal head of the question has more or less modifiers its value is penalized. *Appearance of terms, but some complements are missing*: when the system detects only the term of the question in the text, then it continues the searching until it is able to find the complements.

The second type of comparison of SB is the calculation of the *value of solution*, this value is calculated when it is searching for a possible answer. It takes into account a set of evaluation rules according to the type of the question, such as: *Lexical restrictions*: grammatical category of the answer depends on the type of the question. For example, a question of type "persona (person)" the answer must have at least a proper noun or common noun. *Semantic restrictions*: the system obtains the answer according to semantic relations such as hyponimy. For example, a question of type "ciudad (city)" the answer must be a hyponym of "ciudad (city)" in EuroWordNet. *Ad-hoc restrictions*: an example of this kind of restriction is founded in the questions of type "fecha (date)", when the system penalizes the value of solution if the answer does not contain day, month and year.

Comparison of the Patterns. When the system is evaluating a pattern in the text, a set of circumstances are considerated in order to provide the value of solution. The total value of an answer is defined by the equation 3, where N is the number of retrieved SB of the question, vt_i is the value of terms of each SB, d is the distance between the localized SB in the text and vs is the value of solution. As shown in the equation 3, vs is 30% of total and the remaining ones is the 70%.

$$Vr = (\frac{\sum_{i=1}^{N} vt_i}{N} - d * 0.1) * 0.7 + vs * 0.3 \tag{3}$$

Final Evaluation of Patterns. The system generates a list of candidate solutions, where each solution has been obtained in a passage. If two solutions have the same value for a question, the system chooses one considering the proposed order by IR-n.

Spanish QA system must determine when a question has an answer or not. In order to do that we suggest an threshold that indicates if an answer is a solution or not. A question has an answer if its Vr is higher than 0.5.

Next, an example (question 114, *In Workshop of Cross-Language Evaluation Forum (CLEF 2003)*) of resolution of one question, where system chooses the correct solution since the Vr is higher than 0.5.

- **Question:** A qué primer ministro abrió la Fiscalía de Milán un sumario por corrupción? (Of which prime minister the Office of the public prosecutor of Milan opened a summary for corruption?)
- **Type:** person
- **Case:** 3
- **List of BS:**
  - **NP1:** ([NP, primer*ministro])
  - **VP:** ([VP, abrir])
  - **NP2:**([NP, fiscalia [PP, de: milan]])([NP, sumario [PP, por: corrupcion]])

- **Text where is a correct solution:** "[...] la **Fiscalía de Milán abrió**, hoy martes, un **sumario** al **primer ministro**, *Silvio Berslusconi*, por un supuesto delito de **corrupción** [...]"
- **Value of the solution:** 0.93
- **Text where is an incorrect solution:** "[...] **primer ministro** y líder socialista, *Bettino Craxi*, al que el pasado 21 de septiembre Paraggio **abrió** un **sumario** relacionado con el proyecto Limen por supuestos delitos de **corrupción** [...]"
- **Value of the solution:** 0.52
- **Answer:** Silvio Berlusconi

As the previous example shows, the system chooses the correct answer among several possible solutions. The correct answer has been chosen due to the *value of terms.*

In the sentence, with the right answer, the value of terms is higher than in other sentences. Although, the VP and NP1 are in both sentences, the NP2 is just completely in the first sentence.

Table 1. General results obtained for each runs

Run	alia051eses-assessed	alia052eses-assessed
Right	66	60
Inexact	24	26
Unsupported	0	0
Wrong	110	114
Presicion(NIL)	0.25	0.24
Recall(NIL)	0.45	0.45
Accuracy over:		
overall questions	33.00%	30.00%
Factoid questions	29.66%	26.27%
Definition questions	40.00%	36.00%
Temporal Restricted Factoid questions	34.38%	34.38%

Table 2. Accuracy over questions

Type	Right	Inexact	Number Questions
Factoid	35	10	118
Definition	20	13	50
Temporal	11	1	32
Total	66	24	200

3 Results

This section describes some tables related with the results and the evaluation of our system in CLEF-2005. The proposed system was applied to the set of 200 questions, all of them was supported by our system.

For the development of our system we used as training set the questions developed for CLEF-2003 and CLEF-2004 questions.

During this test process many faults were detected in the tools used in the lexical and morphological phases. The analysis of question 145 of CLEF-2003 shows one of these errors:

- *Quién es el ministro de economía alemán? (Who's the German Minister of Finance?)*

The term *Alemán* is not in the prepositional phrase where the term *economía* is, because of *economía* is tagged as feminine and *alemán* is tagged as masculine. So, when searching for SB in the corpus to find an answer for the questions, it gives wrong answers.

We submitted two runs. The first run was obtained applying the system after repairing the lexical and morphological errors that we have detected (alia051eses) while the second run (alia52eses) performed QA process without repairing theses faults. Table 1 shows the results for each run and how these errors lowered our system performance giving wrong answers.

Inexact answers also lowers the system performance and in our system, these are due to errors in parsing process. An answer was judged inexact when the answer string contained more or less than just the correct answer, ie. the system finds this answer in the text but it does not extract the part of the information needed to return it as an answer. Our system returned 24 inexact answers (see Table 1). We may obtain a higher level of performance (45%) if we take into account that these inexact answers include the expected answer.

Table 2 shows that the accuracy over temporal questions was 34.38%, ie. we have obtained 11 right answers over 32. This is considered a good score because no special mechanism was developed.

Questions are split into three categories: factoid, definition and temporal. According to table 9 of [9], our proposal scored in first position in the factoid and temporal questions, but we were able to answer correctly only 40% of the definition questions. Thus, we expect to improve the precision of the temporal questions in a short period of time.

4 Conclusion and Future Work

For our first participation in the QA@CLEF track, we proposed a QA system designed to search Spanish documents in response to Spanish queries. To do so we used a Spanish syntactic analyzer in order to assist in identifying the expected answers and the solution of the question.

All track questions have been processed by our systema. The results showed overall accuracy levels of 33%.

As previously mentioned, the accuracy of our system is affected by the precision of the tools we employ in its development (alia52eses). These are encouraging results that show the potential of the proposed approach, taking into account that the use of patterns is a less expensive recourse compared with other proposals.

Ongoing work on the system is focused on multilingual task, temporal question treatment and the incorporation of knowledge to those phases that can be useful to increase the our system performance.

References

1. S. Acebo, A. Ageno, S. Climent, J. Farreres, L. Padró, R. Placer, H. Rodriguez, M. Taulé, and J. Turno. MACO: Morphological Analyzer Corpus-Oriented. *ESPRIT BRA-7315 Aquilex II, Working Paper 31*, 1994.
2. A. Ageno, D. Ferrés, E. González, S. Kanaan, H. Rodríguez, M. Surdeanu, and J. Turmo. TALP-QA System for Spanish at CLEF-2004. *In Workshop of Cross-Language Evaluation Forum (CLEF)*, pages 425 – 434, 2004.
3. C. de Pablo, J.L. Martínez-Fernández, P. Martínez, J. Villena, A.M. García-Serrano, J.M. Goñi, and J.C. González. miraQA: Initial experiments in Question Answering. *In Workshop of Cross-Language Evaluation Forum (CLEF)*, pages 371 – 376, 2004.
4. A. Ferrández, M. Palomar, and L. Moreno. An Empirical Approach to Spanish Anaphora Resolution. *Machine Translation. Special Issue on Anaphora Resolution In Machine Translation*, 14(3/4):191–216, December 1999.
5. J. Herrera, A. Peñas, and F. Verdejo. Question Answering Pilot Task at CLEF 2004. *In Workshop of Cross-Language Evaluation Forum (CLEF)*, pages 445 – 452, 2004.
6. F. Llopis and J.L. Vicedo. Ir-n, a passage retrieval system. *In Workshop of Cross-Language Evaluation Forum (CLEF)*, 2001.
7. E. Méndez-Díaz, J. Vilares-Ferro, and D. Cabrero-Souto. COLE at CLEF 2004: Rapid prototyping of a QA system for Spanish. *In Workshop of Cross-Language Evaluation Forum (CLEF)*, pages 413 – 418, 2004.
8. M. Pérez-Coutiño, T. Solorio, M. Montes y Gómez, A. López-López, and L. Villaseñor-Pineda. The Use of Lexical Context in Question Answering for Spanish. *In Workshop of Cross-Language Evaluation Forum (CLEF)*, pages 377 – 384, 2004.
9. A. Vallin, B. Magnini, D. Giampiccolo, L. Aunimo, C. Ayache, P. Osenova, A. Peña, M. de Rijke, B. Sacaleanu, D. Santos, and R. Sutcliffe. Overview of the CLEF 2005 Multilingual Question Anwering Track. *In Workshop of Cross-Language Evaluation Forum (CLEF)*, 2005.
10. J.L. Vicedo, R. Izquierdo, F. Llopis, and R. Muñoz. Question Answering in Spanish. *Comparative Evaluation of Multilingual Information Access Systems: 4th Workshop of the Cross-Language Evaluation Forum, CLEF, Trondheim, Norway, August 21-22, 2003, Revised Selected Papers.Lecture Notes in Computer Science*, 3237/2004:541, 2003.
11. J.L. Vicedo, M. Saiz, and R. Izquierdo. Does English helps Question Answering in Spanish? *In Workshop of Cross-Language Evaluation Forum (CLEF)*, pages 419 – 424, 2004.

20th Century Esfinge (Sphinx) Solving the Riddles at CLEF 2005

Luís Costa

Linguateca at SINTEF ICT
Pb 124 Blindern, 0314 Oslo, Norway
luis.costa@sintef.no

Abstract. Esfinge is a general domain Portuguese question answering system. It tries to take advantage of the steadily growing and constantly updated information freely available in the World Wide Web in its question answering tasks. The system participated last year for the first time in the monolingual QA track. However, the results were compromised by several basic errors, which were corrected shortly after. This year, Esfinge participation was expected to yield better results and allow experimentation with a Named Entity Recognition System, as well as try a multilingual QA track for the first time. This paper describes how the system works, presents the results obtained by the official runs in considerable detail, as well as results of experiments measuring the import of different parts of the system, by reporting the decrease in performance when the system is executed without some of its components/features.

1 Esfinge Overview

The sphinx in the Egyptian/Greek mythology was a demon of destruction that sat outside Thebes and asked riddles to all passers-by. She strangled all the people unable to answer [1], but times have changed and now Esfinge has to answer questions herself. Fortunately, CLEF organization is much more benevolent when analysing the results of the QA task.

Esfinge (http://www.linguateca.pt/Esfinge/) is a question answering system developed for Portuguese which is based on the architecture proposed in Eric Brill [2]. Brill suggests that it is possible to get interesting results, applying simple techniques to large quantities of data.

Esfinge starts by converting a question into patterns of plausible answers. These patterns are queried in several collections (the CLEF text collections and the Web) to obtain snippets of text where the answers are likely to be found.

Then, the system harvests these snippets for word n-grams. The n-grams will be later ranked according to their frequency, length and the patterns used to recover the snippets where the n-grams were found (these patterns are scored a priori). Several simple techniques are used to discard or enhance the score of each of the n-grams. The answer will be the top ranked n-gram or NIL if none of the n-grams passes all the filters.

C. Peters et al. (Eds.): CLEF 2005, LNCS 4022, pp. 467 – 476, 2006.

2 Strategies for CLEF 2005

In CLEF 2004, several problems compromised Esfinge's results. The main objectives for CLEF 2005 were to correct these problems, and to participate in the multilingual tasks.

This year, in addition to the European Portuguese text collection (Público), the organization also provided a Brazilian Portuguese collection (Folha de São Paulo). This new collection improved the performance of Esfinge, since one of the problems encountered last year was precisely that the document collection only had texts written in European Portuguese, but some of the answers discovered by the system were written in the Brazilian variety and were therefore difficult to support in a European Portuguese collection [3].

IMS Corpus Workbench [4] was used to encode the document collections. Each document was divided in sets of three sentences. Last year other text unit sizes were tried (namely 50 contiguous words and one sentence), but the results using three sentence sets were slightly better. The sentence segmentation and tokenization was done using the Perl Module Lingua::PT::PLNbase developed by Linguateca and freely available at CPAN.

Two different strategies were tested for the PT-PT monolingual task. In the first one, the system searched for the answers in the Web and used the CLEF document collection to confirm these answers (Run 1). This experiment used the strategy described in another paper by Brill [5]. In the second experiment, Esfinge searched for the answers in the CLEF document collection only (Run 2). The other only difference between the two runs was that since the answers in Run 2 were only searched for in CLEF document collection, it was not necessary to check whether there was a document in the collection supporting them.

For each question in the QA track, Esfinge performed the following tasks:

Question Reformulation. The question is submitted to the question reformulation module. This module uses a pattern file that associates patterns of questions with patterns of plausible answers. The result is a set of pairs (answer pattern, score). Some patterns were added this year to the patterns file, based on last year questions. The following pattern is one of the patterns included in that file:

Onde ([^\s?]) ([^?]*)\??/"$2 $1"/20*

It means that for a question including the word *Onde* (Where*)*, followed by some words, a possible pattern for an answer will be the words following the one immediately after *Onde*, followed by the word after *Onde* in a phrase pattern.

As an example, take the question *Onde fica Lillehammer?* (Where is Lillehammer located?). This generates the pattern *"Lillehamer fica"* with a score of 20, which can be used to search for documents containing an answer to the question.

Passage Extraction. The patterns obtained in the previous module are submitted to Google (or searched in the document collection, in Run2). Then, the system extracts the document snippets {S1, S2 … Sn} from Google results pages (or sets of three sentences, in Run2).

It was detected in the experiments made with the system that certain types of sites may compromise the quality of the returned answers. To overcome this problem a list of address patterns which are not to be considered (the system does not consider documents stored in addresses that match these patterns) was created. This list includes patterns such as *blog*, *humor*, *piadas* (jokes). These patterns were created manually, but in the future it may be rewarding to use more complex techniques to classify web pages [6].

Another improvement over last year experiments was that when no documents are recovered from the Web, the system tries to recover them from the CLEF document collection. When searching in the document collection, the stop-words without context are discarded. For example in the query *"o" "ditador" "cubano" "antes" "da" "revolução"* (the Cuban dictator before the revolution), the words *o* and *da* are discarded whereas in the query *"o ditador cubano antes da revolução"* (phrase pattern) they are not discarded. Last year the 22 most frequent words in the CETEMPúblico corpus [7] were discarded. This year in addition to those, some other words were discarded. The choice of these words was the result of the tests performed with the system. Some examples are *chama* (is called), *fica* (is located), *país* (country) and *se situa* (is). One may find these words in questions, but using them in the search pattern increases the difficulty to find documents containing its answers. An example is the question *Com que país faz fronteira a Coreia do Norte?* (What country does North Korea border on?). It is more likely to find sentences like *A Coreia do Norte faz fronteira com a China* (North Korea borders with China) than sentences including the word *país*.

When the system is not able to recover documents from the Web, nor from the CLEF document collection, one last attempt is made by stemming some words in the search patterns. First, the system uses the *jspell* morphological analyser [8] to check the PoS of the various words in each query. Then, the words classified as common nouns, adjectives, verbs and numbers are stemmed using the module Lingua::PT::Stemmer freely available at CPAN, implementing a Portuguese stemming algorithm proposed by Moreira & Huyck [9]. This provides the system with more general search patterns that are used to search documents in the document collection.

If documents are retrieved using any of the previous techniques, at the end of this stage the system has a set of document passages {P1, P2 … Pn} hopefully containing answers to the question. If no documents are retrieved, the system stops here and returns the answer NIL (no answer found).

N-gram Harvesting. The first task in this module consists in computing the distribution of word n-grams (from length 1 to length 3) of the first 100 document passages retrieved in the previous module. The system uses the Ngram Statistic Package (NSP) [10] for that purpose.

Then, the word n-grams are ordered using the following formula:

N-gram score = $\sum (F * S * L)$, through the first 100 document passages retrieved in the previous module where:

F = N-gram frequency
S = Score of the search pattern that recovered the document
L = N-gram length

At the end of this stage, the system has an ordered set of possible answers {A1 … An}.

Named Entity Recognition/Classification in the N-grams. This module was included in this year's participation, hoping that the use of a named entity recognition (NER) system could improve the results (at least for some types of questions).

An extra motivation for using a NER system was the HAREM (Evaluation Contest of Named Entity Recognition Systems for Portuguese) [11], which boosted the development or improvement of already existent NER systems for Portuguese. One of the participants was SIEMES [12] which was developed by the Linguateca team in Porto, and obtained the second best F-measure.

SIEMES detects and classifies named entities in a wide range of categories. Esfinge used a sub-set of these categories: Human, Country, Settlement (includes cities, villages, etc), Geographical Locations (locations with no political entailment, like for example Africa), Date and Quantity.

Esfinge uses a pattern file that associates patterns of questions with the type of expected result. The following pattern is included in that file:

Quant(o|a)s./VALOR TIPO="QUANTIDADE*

This pattern means that a question starting with *Quantos* (how many – masculine form) or *Quantas* (how many – feminine form) probably has a QUANTIDADE (quantity) type answer.

What the system does in this module is to check whether the question matches with any of the patterns in the "question pattern"/"answer type" file. If it does, the 200 best scored word n-grams are submitted to SIEMES. Then the results returned by SIEMES are analyzed to check whether the NER system recognizes named entities classified as one of the desired types. If such named entities are recognized, they are pushed to the top in the ranking of possible answers.

The NER system is used in the "Who" questions in a slightly different way. First, it checks whether a person is mentioned in the question. If that happens, the NER system is not invoked on the candidate answers (example: *Who is Fidel Ramos?*). However there are some exceptions to this rule and some special patterns to deal with them too (example: *Who is John Lennon's widow?*). When no person is mentioned in the question, the NER system is invoked to find instances of persons for "Who" questions.

N-gram Filtering. In this module the list of possible answers (by ranking order) is submitted to a set of filters, namely:

- A filter that discards words contained in the questions. Ex: the answer *Satriani* is not desired for the question *Quem é Joe Satriani?* (Who is Joe Satriani?) and should be discarded.
- A filter that discards answers contained in a list of 'undesired answers'. This list was built with the help of Esfinge log file. The frequency list of all the solutions provided by Esfinge to the 2004 CLEF QA track questions was computed (not only the best answer, but all the answers that managed to go through all the system filters). The list of 'undesired answers' was built with this frequency list and some common sense. The words in the fore mentioned list are frequent words that do not really answer questions alone (like *pessoas*/persons, *nova*/new, *lugar*/place, *grandes*/big, *exemplo*/example). Later some other answers were added to this list, as a result of tests performed with the system. The list includes now 92 entries.

- A filter that uses the morphological analyser *jspell* [8] to check the PoS of the various tokens in each answer. This filter is only used when the system can not predict the type of answer for the question (using the "question pattern"/"answer type" file) or when SIEMES is not able to find any answer of the desired type. Jspell returns a set of possible PoS tags for each token. Esfinge considers some PoS as "interesting": adjectives, common nouns, numbers and proper nouns. All answers whose first and final token are not classified as one of these "interesting" PoS are discarded.

Find Document Supporting an Answer. This module checks whether the system finds a document supporting an answer in the collection. It is only used when the system retrieved documents from the Web. When the system cannot retrieve documents from the Web, it tries to retrieve them from the CLEF document collection, and since the n-grams are extracted from these documents there is no need for this module. It searches the document collection for documents containing both the candidate answer and a pattern obtained from the question reformulation module.

Search for Longer Answers. The motivation to use this very simple module arose from the analysis of last year's results and some additional tests. Sometimes the answers returned by the system were fragments of the right answers. To minimize this problem, a very simple algorithm was implemented this year. When an answer passes all the filters in the previous module, the system does not return that answer immediately and stops, as last year. Instead, it checks whether there are more candidate answers containing the answer which was found. Each of these candidate answers is submitted to the filters described previously and, if one of them succeeds in passing all the filters, this candidate answer becomes the new answer to be returned as result.

Final Answer. The final answer is the candidate answer with the highest score in the set of candidate answers which are not discarded by any of the filters described above. If all the answers are discarded by the filters, then the final answer is NIL (meaning that the system is not able to find an answer in the document collection).

EN-PT Multilingual Task. A run for the EN-PT multilingual task was also submitted. In this experiment the questions were translated using the module Lingua::PT::Translate freely available at CPAN. This module provides an easy interface to the Altavista Babelfish translating tool.

After the translation this experiment followed the algorithm described for the PT-PT monolingual task in Run 1 (the run using the Web, which seemed to have the best results).

3 Overview of the Results

This section presents and discusses Esfinge's official results at CLEF 2005. To create the tables, the question set was divided in categories that intend to check how well the various strategies used by Esfinge perform. Some categories are related to types of entities which the NER system can identify, like "People", "Places", "Quantities" and "Dates". Some other categories are more pattern-oriented like the categories "Which X" and "What is X".

Table 1. Results by type of question

Type of question	No. of Q. in 2005	No. (%) of exact answers			No. of Q. in 2004	No. (%) of exact answers Esfinge 2004
		Run 1 PT-PT	Run 2 PT-PT	Run EN-PT		
People	47	11 (23%)	15 (32%)	5 (11%)	43	8 (19%)
(Que|Qual) X[1]	36	9 (25%)	5 (14%)	6 (17%)	42	7 (17%)
Place	33	9 (27%)	7 (21%)	2 (6%)	41	7 (17%)
Quem é <HUM>[2]	27	6 (22%)	6 (22%)	6 (22%)	17	2 (12%)
Quantity	18	4 (22%)	3 (17%)	1 (6%)	23	4 (17%)
Date	15	3 (20%)	5 (33%)	2 (13%)	15	0 (0%)
Que é X[3]	15	2 (13%)	0 (0%)	0 (0%)	15	1 (7%)
Como se chama X[4]	5	4 (80%)	2 (40%)	2 (40%)	0	0 (0%)
Nomeie X[5]	4	0 (0%)	0 (0%)	0 (0%)	3	1 (33%)
Total	200	48 (24%)[6]	43 (22%)	24 (12%)	199	30 (15%)

[1)] Which X, [2)] Who is <HUM>, [3)] What is X, [4)] What is X called, [5)] Name X, [6)] The official result has 46 right answers, but during the evaluation of the results I found two more right answers.

From table 1 we see that there is no significant difference between the two runs submitted for the Portuguese source/Portuguese target (PT-PT). The run that used the Web (Run 1) got slightly better results, as last year. One can also see that the results of Run 1 are more homogenous than the ones in the second run. Some results are consistently bad, like definitions not involving people (What is X) and naming (Name X). This suggests that the techniques used in Esfinge are not suitable to answer these types of questions and therefore new features need to be implemented to deal with them. The results of the second run for the questions of type "People" and "Date" are better both comparing to the other types of questions and to the same type of questions in the first run. Comparing this year's results with the results of Esfinge's best run last year, one can see that the system improved consistently in almost all types of questions.

Regarding the English source/Portuguese target task (EN-PT), the success rate was significantly lower for the answers of type "People" and "Place", which contributed in a large degree to the weak results in this first participation. On the other hand, in the questions of type "Who is <HUM>" the results were similar to the monolingual runs because these questions are easier to translate than the aforementioned ones.

4 Error Analysis

Esfinge keeps a log file, where it registers all analysed word n-grams for each of the questions, as well as the reason why they were rejected when that was the case. Table 2 provides the results of the detailed error analysis performed for each of the runs. During this error analysis, each of the wrongly answered questions was studied in order to find the first reason for failure.

Table 2. Causes for wrong answers

Problem	No. of wrong answers		
	Run 1 PT-PT	Run 2 PT-PT	Run EN-PT
Translation	-	-	96
No documents retrieved in the document collection	52	51	18
No documents retrieved containing the answer	22	4	12
Tokenization	16	1	2
Answer length >3	10	9	8
Answer scoring algorithm	26	58	25
Missing patterns in "question pattern"/"answer type" file	6	6	1
Named Entity Recognition	7	20	4
Filter "answer contained in question"	1	1	1
Filter interesting PoS	0	1	0
Filter "documents supporting answer"	10	4	9
Search for more complete answers algorithm	2	2	0
Total	152	157	176

Not surprisingly, the most frequent types of errors are tightly connected to the techniques used in each run. For example in the first run there are more problems related to the documents recovered not containing the answer and to the filter "documents supporting answer" due to the greater difficulty in having a precise document retrieval in the Web compared with retrieval in the CLEF document collection.

The second run, on the other hand, had more precise document retrieval, but more problems in the following steps like the answer scoring algorithm and the use of the NER system.

As expected, the main difficulty in the EN-PT run relies in the translation: more than half of the errors are caused by inexact translations. The machine translation (MT) system usually does not translate acronyms, names of places and nationalities (some examples in the question set were *CFSP*, *WMO*, *Cuban* and *Portuguese*). On the other hand, sometimes it translates titles of books or films literally (like *The Life of Galileo* or *Kieslowski on Kieslowski*) when the name for which this works are known in Portuguese is not a direct translation. It would be advisable to use a multilingual ontology prior to invoking the MT system in order to avoid some of these errors.

5 Some Considerations About the Questions

The error analysis is not only useful to find the reasons behind system errors. Here and there one is confronted with some interesting cases. I will describe two of them.

The question *Who is Josef Paul Kleihues?* does not have an answer in the document collection according to the organization, but is this really true? There is a document with the following text (freely translated from the Portuguese original):

People from Galicia like good architecture. In Santiago de Compostela, besides the "Centro Galego de Arte Contemporânea" designed by Siza Vieira, a gym was built in the historical center designed by the German Josef Paul Kleihues.

One of Esfinge's runs returned the answer *Arquitectura* (architecture) giving as support the text from where the previous passage was extracted. One may question which answer would be more useful for a hypothetical user: NIL or the answer provided by Esfinge? It would be even more useful if the system was able to return the whole passage.

Another curious example is the question *Which was the largest Italian party?*. On one of the runs, Esfinge returned the answer *Força Itália* supporting it with a document stating that *Força Itália is* the largest Italian party (it was true at the time the document was written). The committee of judges considered this answer wrong, but in my opinion the answer provided by the system was acceptable, because the question is ambiguous regarding the temporal context [13]. There is no clear definition of when is the present time neither in the question itself nor in CLEF guidelines.

I think that this kind of question is confusing and polemic even for humans, therefore not particularly useful to evaluate QA systems.

6 Additional Experiments

The error analysis (condensed on table 2) provided an insight on the problems affecting system performance.

Some effort was invested in the problems that seemed easier to solve. Namely on the "Error in tokenization", "Problems with the NER system" and "Missing patterns in the file question pattern/answer type". The results of the system after this improvement using the same strategy as in Run 1 are presented in table 3 (Run 3). The table also gives an insight on how each part of the system helps global performance: the results

Table 3. Results in the PT-PT task after improvements in the system using the first run strategy

Type of question	No. of questions	No. (%) of exact answers		
		Run 3	No NER	No PoS Filtering
People	47	14 (30%)	9 (19%)	13 (28%)
(Que|Qual) X	36	11 (31%)	--	7 (19%)
Place	33	10 (30%)	9 (27%)	12 (36%)
Quem é <HUM>	27	7 (26%)	--	3 (11%)
Quantity	18	3 (17%)	1 (6%)	3 (17%)
Date	15	8 (53%)	3 (20%)	6 (40%)
Que é X	15	4 (27%)	--	2 (13%)
Como se chama X	5	3 (60%)	--	2 (40%)
Nomeie X	4	1 (25%)	--	0 (0%)
Total	200	61 (31%)	48 (24%)	48 (24%)

obtained either without using the NER system or without using the morphological analyser are presented ("No NER" and "No PoS filtering" respectively). One can see that (in different types of questions) both these components are helping the system.

The cause for the better results this year could be the possibility that this year questions were easier than last year, but an experiment where the system was applied to the 2004 questions after the improvements and using the same strategy as in Run 1 had better results with last year questions as well. The experiment got 28% exact answers whereas Esfinge's best run last year achieved only 15% exact answers.

7 Concluding Remarks

Esfinge improved comparing to last year: the results are better both with this year and last year questions. Another conclusion is that the two tested strategies perform better with different types of questions, which suggests that both are still worthwhile to experiment, study further and possibly combine.

The experiments performed to check how each part of the system helps global performance demonstrated that (in different types of questions) both the NER system and the morphological analyser improve the system performance.

The detailed error analysis presented in this paper allows the creation of groups of questions with similar challenges for the system which can be used for its further testing and improvement.

Acknowledgements

I thank Diana Santos for reviewing previous versions of this paper, Alberto Simões for the hints on using the Perl Modules "jspell", "Lingua::PT::PLNbase" and Lingua::PT::Translate, Luís Sarmento, Luís Cabral and Ana Sofia Pinto for supporting the use of the NER system SIEMES and Paul Rayson for supporting the use of CLAWS Web Tagger [14] (unfortunately the PT-EN multilingual task run was not finished in time). This work is financed by the Portuguese Fundação para a Ciência e Tecnologia through grant POSI/PLP/43931/2001, co-financed by POSI.

References

1. Wikipedia: http://en.wikipedia.org/wiki/Sphinx/
2. Brill, E.: Processing Natural Language without Natural Language Processing. In: Gelbukh, A. (ed.): *CICLing 2003*. LNCS 2588. Springer-Verlag Berlin Heidelberg (2003) pp. 360-9
3. Costa, L.: First Evaluation of Esfinge - a Question Answering System for Portuguese. In Peters C., Clough P., Gonzalo J., Jones G., Kluck M. & Magnini B. (eds.), *Advances in Cross-Language Information Retrieval: Fifth Workshop of the Cross-Language Evaluation Forum (CLEF 2004)* (Bath, UK, 15-17 September 2004), Heidelberg, Germany: Springer. Lecture Notes in Computer Science, pp. 522-533
4. Christ, O., Schulze, B.M., Hofmann, A. & Koenig, E.: The IMS Corpus Workbench: Corpus Query Processor (CQP): User's Manual. University of Stuttgart, March 8, 1999 (CQP V2.2)

5. Brill, E., Lin, J., Banko, M., Dumais, S. & Ng, A.: Data-Intensive Question Answering. In: Voorhees, E.M. & Harman, D.K. (eds.): *Information Technology: The Tenth Text Retrieval Conference, TREC 2001*. NIST Special Publication 500-250. pp. 393-400
6. Aires, R., Aluísio, S. & Santos, D.: User-aware page classification in a search engine. In *Proceedings of Stylistic Analysis of Text for Information Access, SIGIR 2005* Workshop (Salvador, Bahia, Brasil, 19 August 2005)
7. Santos, D. & Rocha, P.: Evaluating CETEMPúblico, a free resource for Portuguese. In: *Proceedings of the 39th Annual Meeting of the Association for Computational Linguistics* (Toulouse, 9-11 July 2001) pp. 442-449
8. Simões, A. M. & Almeida, J.J.: Jspell.pm - um módulo de análise morfológica para uso em Processamento de Linguagem Natural. In: Gonçalves, A. & Correia, C.N. (eds.): *Actas do XVII Encontro da Associação Portuguesa de Linguística (APL 2001)* (Lisboa, 2-4 October 2001). APL Lisboa (2002) pp. 485-495
9. Orengo, V. M. & Huyck, C.: A Stemming algorithm for the Portuguese Language. In *8th International Symposium on String Processing and Information Retrieval (SPIRE'2001)* (Laguna de San Rafael, Chile, 13-15 November 2001), IEEE Computer Society Publications, pp. 183-193
10. Banerjee, S. & Pedersen, T.: The Design, Implementation, and Use of the Ngram Statistic Package. In: *Proceedings of the Fourth International Conference on Intelligent Text Processing and Computational Linguistics* (Mexico City, February 2003) pp. 370-381
11. Santos D., Seco N., Cardoso N. & Vilela R.: HAREM: An Advanced NER Evaluation Context for Portuguese. In *Proceedings of the 5th International Conference on Language Resources and Evaluation (LREC'2006)* (Genoa, Italia, 22-28 May 2006)
12. Sarmento, L.: SIEMÊS - a named entity recognizer for Portuguese relying on similarity rules. In *VII Encontro para o processamento computacional da língua portuguesa escrita e falada (PROPOR'2006)* (Itatiaia, RJ, Brasil, 13-17 May 2006)
13. Santos, D., Cardoso, N.: Portuguese at CLEF 2005: Reflections and Challenges (this volume)
14. Rayson, P. & Garside, R.: The CLAWS Web Tagger. ICAME Journal, no. 22. The HIT-centre - Norwegian Computing Centre for the Humanities, Bergen (1998), pp. 121-123

Question Answering Experiments for Finnish and French

Lili Aunimo and Reeta Kuuskoski

Department of Computer Science
University of Helsinki, P.O. Box 68
FIN-00014 UNIVERSITY OF HELSINKI, Finland
{aunimo, rkuuskos}@cs.helsinki.fi

Abstract. This paper presents a question answering (QA) system called *Tikka*. *Tikka's* approach to QA is based on question classification, semantic annotation and answer extraction pattern matching. *Tikka's* performance is evaluated by conducting experiments in the following tasks: monolingual Finnish and French and bilingual Finnish-English QA. *Tikka* is the first system ever reported to perform monolingual textual QA in the Finnish language. This is also the task in which its performance is best: 23 % of all questions are answered correctly. *Tikka's* performance in the monolingual French task is a little inferior to its performance in the monolingual Finnish task, and when compared to the other systems evaluated with the same data in the same task, its performance is near the average. In the bilingual Finnish-English task, *Tikka* was the only participating system, and - as is expected - its performance was inferior to those attained in the monolingual tasks.

1 Introduction

A question answering (QA) system is a system that receives as input the information need of a user expressed as a natural language question or statement and that produces as output the answer to that information need. The answer can be a snippet of natural language text, a picture, an expression in a formal language, etc., depending on the question. QA has been studied since the late 1950's, see e.g. [1]. Current research on QA is focused around open-domain factual text-based (or textual) QA, where the database from which answers are sought consists of unstructured text documents [2]. The QA system that is presented in this paper, *Tikka*, is a multilingual open-domain factual text-based QA system. The experimental results are based on evaluation data provided by the CLEF 2005 Multilingual Question Answering Track [3]. For a detailed description of the data and the task, see the QA track overview paper [3].

Figure 1 shows the system architecture of *Tikka*. The input to the system is a question in Finnish or French. The *question analysis* component forms the query terms for document retrieval, determines the class of the question and its topic and target words, and passes these on to the *answer extraction* component. The *answer extraction* component performs document retrieval using the given

C. Peters et al. (Eds.): CLEF 2005, LNCS 4022, pp. 477–487, 2006.

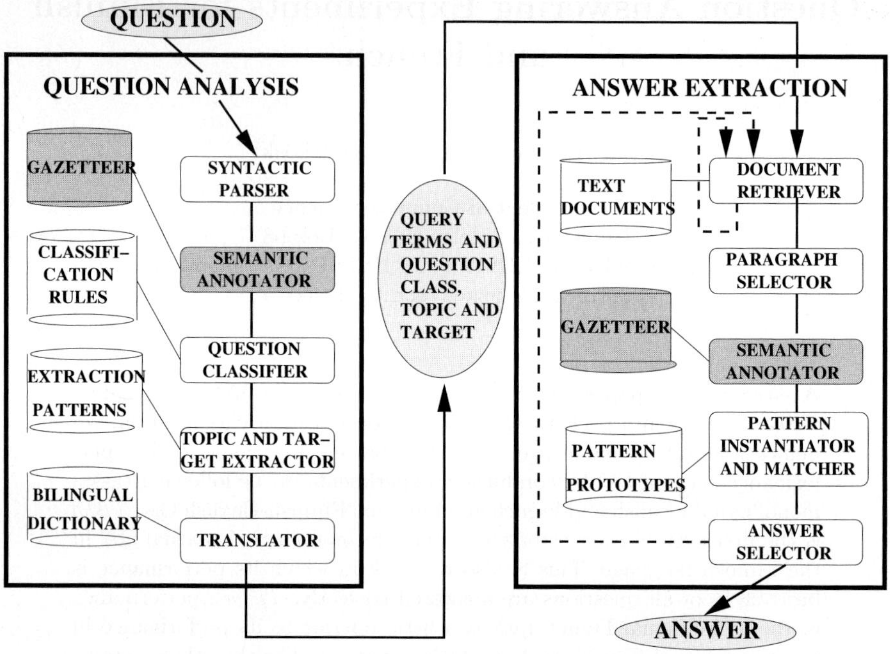

Fig. 1. The system architecture of *Tikka*. *Tikka* has two main components: question analysis and answer extraction. Both components use the same semantic annotator, which is illustrated by gray in the figure. The left hand side of each component lists the databases used by it. The rectangles on the right hand side illustrate the software modules.

query terms, annotates the retrieved text paragraphs semantically, instantiates the class specific answer extraction patterns with potential topic and target words, uses the patterns to extract answers from text, scores them and selects the one to be returned as output. The answer can be in English, Finnish or French. If the question and answer are not expressed in the same language, translation of relevant words is performed in the *question analysis* component.

The rest of this paper is organized as follows: Sections 2, 3 and 4 describe the architecture of *Tikka* in detail and the methods used, starting with the question analysis and answer extraction components and finishing with the semantic annotator. Section 5 presents an analysis of the experimental results. The results themselves are given in the QA track overview paper [3]. Finally, Section 6 concludes and discusses some future work.

2 Question Analysis

The question analysis component of the QA system consists of five software modules: 1) the syntactic parser for Finnish, 2) the semantic annotator, which is detailed in Section 4, 3) the question classifier, 4) the topic and target extractor

Table 1. The availability and output of the five modules of question analysis illustrated with the same example sentence for the target languages English, Finnish and French. Answer extraction with these same questions is illustrated in Table 2.

Module	**Example**		
	English	**Finnish**	**French**
	D FI EN Mikä on WWF ?	D FI FI Mikä on WWF?	D FR FR Qu'est-ce que la WWF?
(1) Parser	1 Mikä mikä subj:>2 &NH PRON SG NOM 2 on olla main:>0 &+MV V ACT IND PRES SG3 3 WWF wwf &NH N		N/A
(2) Semantic Annotator	N/A		Qu'est-ce que <organization> la WWF</organization>?
(3) Classifier	Organization		
(4) T & T Extractor	Topic: WWF Target: N/A		
(5) FI → EN	WWF	N/A	

and 5) the translator, which is described in the system description of the previous version of *Tikka*, that participated in QA@CLEF 2004 [4]. All these modules, along with the databases they use, are illustrated in Figure 1.

Table 1 shows through an example how question analysis is performed. First, a natural language question is given as input to the system, for example: *D FI EN Mikä on WWF?* [1]. Next, the Finnish question is parsed syntactically and the French question is annotated semantically. Then both questions are classified according to the expected answer type, and the topic and target words are extracted from them. The expected answer types are determined by the Multinine Corpus [3], and they are: *LOCATION, MEASURE, ORGANIZATION, OTHER, PERSON* and *TIME*. The target words are extracted or inferred from the question and they further restrict the answer type, e.g. age, kilometers and capital city[5]. The topic words are words extracted from the question that - in a sentence containing the answer to the question - carry old information. For example, in the question *What is WWF?*, *WWF* is the topic because in the answer sentence *WWF is the World Wide Fund for Nature.*, *WWF* is the old information and *the World Wide Fund for Nature* is the new information. The old and new information of a sentence are contextually established [6]. In our case, the question is the context. In *Tikka*, topic words are useful query terms along with the target words, and they are also used to fill slots in the answer pattern prototypes.

3 Answer Extraction

The answer extraction component consists of five software modules: 1) the document retriever, 2) the paragraph selector, 3) the semantic annotator, 4) the

[1] D stands for a definition question and FI EN means that the source language is Finnish and the target language is English. In English, the question means *What is WWF?*

pattern instantiator and matcher and 5) the answer selector. All these modules, along with the databases that they use, are illustrated in Figure 1. The dotted arrows that go from the document retriever back to itself as well as from the answer selector back to the document retriever illustrate that if no documents or answers are found, answer extraction starts all over.

3.1 An Example

Table 2 shows through an example how answer extraction is performed. First, the question analysis passes as input to the component the query terms, the topic and target of the question and the classification of the question. Next, document retrieval is performed using the query terms. If the document retrieval succeeds, the paragraphs containing at least one query word are filtered out for further processing and they are annotated semantically. class-specific set of pattern prototypes is instantiated with the topic word and with a possibly existing target word. Each pattern prototype has a score, which reflects its accuracy. The score ranges between 1 and 9. Instantiated patterns are then matched against semantically annotated paragraphs, and answer candidates are extracted. For

Table 2. The output of the five different modules of answer extraction illustrated with examples. The examples are the same as in Table 1, and the processing in this table is a continuation of the question analysis illustrated in that table.

Module	**Example**		
	English	**Finnish**	**French**
	Query terms: WWF, Topic: WWF, Target: N/A, Classification: organization		
(1) Document retriever	22 docs retrieved 22 docs inspected	76 docs retrieved, 30 docs inspected	313 docs retrieved, 10 docs inspected
(2) Paragraph selector	70 paragraphs selected	99 paragraphs selected	39 paragraphs selected
(3) Semantic Annotator	See Table 5		
(4) Pattern I & M	12 instantiated patterns match 1 unique answer	12 instantiated patterns match 11 unique answers	18 instantiated patterns match 4 unique answers
(5) Answer selector	only one answer	chooses the answer with the highest score, 18	chooses the answer with the highest score, 8
	1 GH951213-000131 World Wide Fund for Nature	0.25 AAMU19950818-000016 Maailman Luonnon Säätiö	0.75 ATS.940527.0086 le Fonds mondial pour la nature

the example illustrated in Table 2, the pattern prototype and the corresponding instantiated pattern that matches the Finnish answer are:

```
Prototype:  ((<[a-z]+>[^<>]+<\/[a-z]+> )+)\( (<[a-z]+>)?TOPIC(<\/[a-z]+>)? \)Score:9
Pattern:    ((<[a-z]+>[^<>]+<\/[a-z]+> )+)\( (<[a-z]+>)?Wwf(<\/[a-z]+>)? \)Score:9
```

The text snippet that matched the above pattern is in Table 5. (The patterns are case insensitive.) Only at least partly semantically annotated candidates can be extracted. The score of a unique answer candidate is the sum of the scores of the patterns that extracted the similar answer instances, or more formally:

$$score(answer) = \sum_{i \ in \ A} patternScore(i), \tag{1}$$

where A is the set of similar answers and $patternScore(i)$ is the score of the pattern that has matched i in text. The confidence value of a non-NIL answer candidate is determined by the candidate's score and by the total number of candidates. This is illustrated in Figure 2. For example, if the total number of candidates is between 1 and 5, and the score of the candidate is 17 or greater, confidence is 1, but if the score of the candidate is between 1 and 16, confidence is 0.75. If the confidence score 1 is reached, the answer is selected and no further answers are searched. Otherwise, all paragraphs are searched for answers, and the one with the highest score is selected.

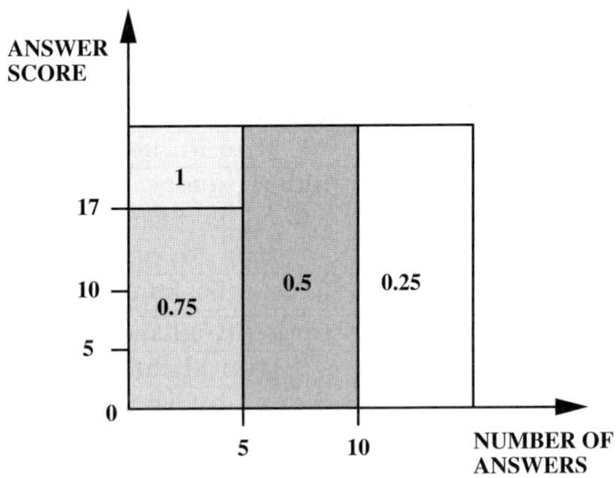

Fig. 2. The confidence value of a non-NIL answer is a function of the answer's score and the number of unique answer candidates.

If document retrieval does not return any documents, or no answer is extracted from the paragraphs, *Tikka* has several alternative ways in which to proceed, depending on which task it is performing and how many times document retrieval has been tried. This is illustrated in Table 3. As can be seen from the table, if no documents are retrieved in the first iteration, the parameter settings of the retrieval engine are altered and document retrieval is performed again in the monolingual Finnish and bilingual Finnish-English tasks. However, in the monolingual French task the system halts and returns NIL with a confidence of 1 as an answer. In the monolingual Finnish task, the system halts after the second try, but in the bilingual English-Finnish task, document retrieval is performed for a third time if either no documents are retrieved or no answer is found. Alternatively, in the monolingual Finnish task and the bilingual task, if documents are retrieved, but no answers are found after the first try, document retrieval is tried once more. In all tasks, the system returns a confidence value of 1 for the NIL answer if no documents are found and a confidence value of 0 for the NIL answer if documents are found but no answer can be extracted.

Table 3. The parameters for document retrieval used in different runs and in different iterations of the same run. *MinS* stands for the minimum similarity value between query and document and *MaxD* stands for the maximum number of documents to be retrieved. The maximum number of iterations is in monolingual Finnish runs 2, in monolingual French runs 1, and in Bilingual English runs 3.

<table>
<tr><th colspan="5">Monolingual Finnish</th></tr>
<tr><th>Iterations</th><th colspan="4">Run id: hels051fifi</th></tr>
<tr><th></th><th>index</th><th>query</th><th>minS</th><th>maxD</th></tr>
<tr><td>(1) →</td><td>filemma</td><td>boolean</td><td>0,65</td><td>30</td></tr>
<tr><td>(2) if no documents →</td><td>fistem</td><td>ranked</td><td>0,65</td><td>20</td></tr>
<tr><td>(2) else if no answers →</td><td>fistem</td><td>ranked</td><td>0,3</td><td>20</td></tr>
<tr><th>Iterations</th><th colspan="4">Run id: hels052fifi</th></tr>
<tr><td>(1) →</td><td>fistem</td><td>boolean</td><td>0,65</td><td>30</td></tr>
<tr><td>(2) if no documents →</td><td>filemma</td><td>ranked</td><td>0,65</td><td>20</td></tr>
<tr><td>(2) else if no answers →</td><td>filemma</td><td>ranked</td><td>0,3</td><td>10</td></tr>
<tr><th colspan="5">Monolingual French</th></tr>
<tr><th>Iterations</th><th colspan="4">Run id: hels051frfr</th></tr>
<tr><th></th><th>index</th><th>query</th><th>minS</th><th>maxD</th></tr>
<tr><td>(1) →</td><td>frstem</td><td>boolean</td><td>0,65</td><td>NONE</td></tr>
<tr><th>Iterations</th><th colspan="4">Run id: hels052frfr</th></tr>
<tr><td>(1) →</td><td>frbase</td><td>boolean</td><td>0,26</td><td>10</td></tr>
<tr><th colspan="5">Bilingual Finnish-English</th></tr>
<tr><th>Iterations</th><th colspan="4">Run id: hels051fien</th></tr>
<tr><th></th><th>index</th><th>query</th><th>minS</th><th>maxD</th></tr>
<tr><td>(1) →</td><td>enstem</td><td>boolean</td><td>0,65</td><td>100</td></tr>
<tr><td>(2) if no documents →</td><td>enstem</td><td>ranked</td><td>0,5</td><td>20</td></tr>
<tr><td>(3) if no answers →</td><td>enstem</td><td>ranked</td><td>0,3</td><td>20</td></tr>
<tr><th>Iterations</th><th colspan="4">Run id: hels052fien</th></tr>
<tr><td>(1) →</td><td>enstem</td><td>boolean</td><td>0,55</td><td>100</td></tr>
<tr><td>(2) if no documents →</td><td>enstem</td><td>ranked</td><td>0,5</td><td>20</td></tr>
<tr><td>(3) if no answers →</td><td>enstem</td><td>ranked</td><td>0,2</td><td>20</td></tr>
</table>

3.2 Document Retrieval

The document retrieval module of *Tikka* consists of the vector space model [7] based search engine Lucene [2] and of the document indices for English, Finnish and French newspaper text built using it. *Tikka* has one index for the English document collection, two indices for the Finnish document collection and two for the French document collection. In each of the indices, one newspaper article forms one document. The English index (enstem) is a stemmed one. It is stemmed using the implementation of Porter's stemming algorithm [8] included in Lucene. One index (filemma) to the Finnish collection is created using the lemmatized word forms as index terms. A syntactic parser is used for the lemmatization. The other Finnish index (fistem) consists of stemmed word forms. The stemming is

[2] http://lucene.apache.org/java/docs/index.html

done by Snowball [9] project's [3] stemming algorithm for Finnish. A Snowball stemmer is also used to create one of the indices for French (frstem). The other French index (frbase) is built using the words of the documents as such. All indices are case-insensitive.

In the document retrieval phase, Lucene determines the similarity between the query (q) and the document (d) in the following way [10]:

$$similarity(q,d) = \sum_{t \; in \; q} tf \; (t \; in \; d) \cdot idf(t) \cdot boost(t.field \; in \; d) \cdot lengthNorm(t.field \; in \; d), \tag{2}$$

where tf is the term frequency factor for the term t in the document d, and $idf(t)$ is the inverse document frequency of the term. The factor *boost* adds more weight to the terms appearing in a given field, and it can be set at indexing time. The last factor is a coefficient that normalizes the score according to the length of the field. After all the scores regarding a single query have been calculated, they are normalized from the highest score if that score is greater than 1. Since we do not use the field specific term weighting, the two last terms of the formula can be discarded, and the formula is equal to calculating the dot product between a query with binary term weights and a document with $tfidf$ [11] term weights.

Lucene does not use the pure boolean information retrieval (IR) model, but we simulate the conjunctive boolean query by requiring all of the query terms to appear in each of the documents in the result set. This differs from the pure boolean IR model in that the relevance score for each document is calculated using Equation 2, and the documents are ordered according to it. This is what the term *boolean* means in Table 3. In the same table, the term *ranked* means a normal Lucene query where all of the query words are not required to appear in the retrieved documents.

4 Semantic Annotation

Semantic annotation is in many ways a similar task to named entity recognition (NER). NER is commonly done based on preset lists of names and patterns [12] or using machine learning techniques [13]. The main difference between NER and semantic annotation is that the first one aims at recognizing proper names whereas the second aims at recognizing both proper names and common nouns.

In *Tikka*, French questions and selected paragraphs from the search results are annotated semantically. We have 14 semantic classes that are presented in Table 4. The lists of names consist mainly of proper nouns, but some common nouns are added for the analysis of the questions. For instance, in the lists for the class *organization*, there are proper names denoting companies and other organizations (*IBM, Toyota, British Museum*), but also some common nouns referring to organizations in each language (*school, union*). As can be seen from Table 4, the *organization* list in English is significantly shorter than those in

[3] http://snowball.tartarus.org/

Table 4. The semantic classes and the number of items in the corresponding list of names for each language

Class	English	French	Finnish	Class	English	French	Finnish
person	3704	3704	3704	unit	31	35	44
country	265	215	252	measure	51	50	34
language	109	79	637	award	15	15	7
nationality	57	177	85	color	22	20	29
capital	277	211	277	profession	95	246	127
location	5339	5440	5314	time	56	38	38
organization	37	968	212	event	29	21	15

other two languages. This is due to the commercial NER that is used in addition to our own semantic annotator.

The semantic annotator uses a window of two words for identifying the items to be annotated. In that way we can only find the entities consisting of one or two words. The external NER that is used in the English annotation is able to identify person names, organizations and locations. Hence, there are no limitations on the length of entities on these three classes in English. For Finnish, we exploit a syntactic parser for part of speech recognition to eliminate the words that are not nouns, adjectives or numerals. For French, the semantic annotator builds solely on the text as it is without any linguistic analysis.

Table 5. Examples of semantically annotated text snippets in English, Finnish and French, retrieved from newspaper text and answering the question *What is WWF?*. It is question number 136 and 278 in the multinine corpus [3] and it is used as an example in the Tables 1 and 2.

Lang.	Example
English	The <organization>World Wide Fund for Nature</organization> (<organization>WWF</organization>) reported that only <measure>35,000</measure> to <measure>50,000</measure> of the species remained in mainly isolated pockets .
Finnish	<organization>Maailman Luonnon Säätiö</organization> (<ne>WWF</ne>) vetoaa kaikkiin <country>Suomen</country> metsästäjiin , ettei <person>Toivoa</person> ja sen perhettä ammuttaisi niiden <unit>matkalla</unit> toistaiseksi tuntemattomille talvehtimisalueille .
French	<ne>La</ne> décision de <organization>la Commission</organization> baleinière internationale (<ne>CBI</ne>) de créer un sanctuaire pour les cétacés est "une victoire historique" , a commenté <time>vendredi</time> <ne>le Fonds</ne> mondial pour la nature (<organization>WWF</organization>)

In the text to be annotated, persons are identified based on a list of first names and the subsequent capital word. The subsequent capital words are added to the list of known names in the document. In this way the family names appearing alone later in the document can also be identified to be names of a person. The *location* gazetteer consists of names of large cities that are not capitals and of the names of states and other larger geographical items. To the class *measure* belong numerals and numeric expressions, for instance *dozen*. *Unit* consists of terms such as *percent, kilometer*. The *event* class is quite heterogeneous, since to it belong terms like *Olympics, Christmas, war* and *hurricane*. The items in the *time* list are names of the months, days of the week etc. Example annotations for each of the languages can be seen in Table 5.

5 Analysis of Results

Tikka was evaluated by participating in the monolingual Finnish and French tasks and in the bilingual Finnish-English task. The evaluation results are described in detail in Section 4 (Results) of the QA track overview paper [3], where the runs produced by *Tikka* are marked with the prefix *hels*. In each of the tasks, two different parameter settings (run 1 and run 2) for the document retrieval component were tested. These settings are listed in Table 3. The results of the runs are shown in Figure 3. We can observe that the difference between runs is not very big for the French monolingual run. The accuracy of the artificial combination run [4] (C) is not much higher than that of the the French monolingual run 1, which means that almost all answers given by the runs are equal. On the contrary, there is a difference of 4 points between the accuracies of the two monolingual Finnish runs, and in addition, as the difference between run 1 and the combination run for Finnish is 3.5 points, we can conclude that some of the correct answers returned by run 2 are not included in the set of correct answers given by run 1. This means that the different parameter settings of the

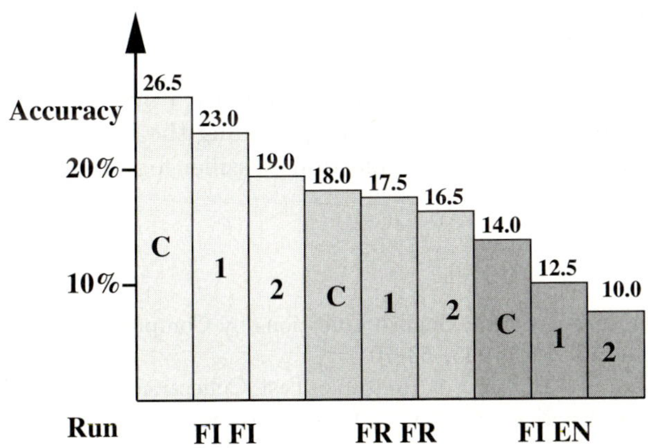

Fig. 3. A histogram showing the percentage of correct answers (i.e. the accuracy) in *Tikka's* submitted test runs and in the artificial combination run. The very light gray represents the monolingual runs for Finnish, the darker gray represents the monolingual French runs and the darkest gray represents the bilingual Finnish-English runs.

[4] In this case, the artificial combination run represents a run where the system is somehow able to choose for each question the better answer from the two answers provided by the runs 1 and 2. For more information on the combination runs, see the track overview paper [3].

runs produced an effect on *Tikka's* overall performance. Between the runs, both the parameters for type of index and the maximum number of documents were altered. In the bilingual Finnish-English task, some difference between the runs can be observed, but the difference is not as big as in he monolingual Finnish task.

6 Conclusions and Future Work

Tikka is a QA system that uses pattern based techniques to extract answers from text. In the experiments presented in this paper, its performance is evaluated in the following tasks: monolingual Finnish and French and bilingual Finnish-English QA. Its performance in the monolingual French task is near the average. In the monolingual Finnish task, *Tikka* is the only existing system, and it performed better than in the monolingual French task. In the bilingual Finnish-English task, *Tikka* was the only participating system, as well, and its performance was inferior to those attained in the monolingual tasks.

In the future, as the document database is not very big (about 1.6 GB), the documents could be annotated semantically before indexing. This would speed up the interactive processing time and the semantic classes could be used as fields in index creation. In addition, indexing based on paragraph level instead of document level might raise the ranking of the essential results and it would speed up the processing time of the interactive phase.

Acknowledgments

The authors thank Connexor Ltd [5] for providing the Finnish and English parsers and NE recognizers, Kielikone Ltd [6] for providing the bilingual dictionary and Juha Makkonen for providing the question classifier for Finnish.

References

1. Simmons, R.F.: Answering English Questions by Computer: A Survey. Communications of the ACM **8** (1965) 53–70
2. Lin, J., Katz, B.: Building a Reusable Test Collection for Question Answering. Journal of the American Society for Information Science and Technology (2005) In Press.
3. Magnini, B., Vallin, A., , Aunimo, L., C.Ayache, Erbach, G., Penas, A., de Rijke, M., Rocha, P., Simov, K., Sutcliffe, R.: Overview of the CLEF 2005 Multilingual Question Answering Track. In Peters, C., Borri, F., eds.: Proceedings of the CLEF 2005 Workshop, Vienna, Austria (2005) To appear.

---

[5] http://www.connexor.com

[6] http://www.kielikone.fi/en

4. Aunimo, L., Kuuskoski, R., Makkonen, J.: Finnish as Source Language in Bilingual Question Answering. In Peters, C., Clough, P.D., Jones, G.J.F., Gonzalo, J., Kluck, M., Magnini, B., eds.: Multilingual Information Access for Text, Speech and Images: 5th Workshop of the Cross-Language Evaluation Forum, CLEF 2004, Bath, UK, September 15-17, 2004, Revised Selected Papers. Volume 3491 of Lecture Notes in Computer Science., Springer Verlag (2005)
5. Aunimo, L., Makkonen, J., Kuuskoski, R.: Cross-language Question Answering for Finnish. In Hyvönen, E., Kauppinen, T., Salminen, M., Viljanen, K., Ala-Siuru, P., eds.: Proceedings of the 11th Finnish Artificial Intelligence Conference STeP 2004, September 1-3, Vantaa, Finland. Volume 2 of Conference Series – No 20., Finnish Artificial Intelligence Society (2004) 35–49
6. Quirk, R., Greenbaum, S., Leech, G., Svartvik, J.: A Comprehensive Grammar of the English Language. Longman (1985)
7. Salton, G.: The SMART Retrieval System: Experiments in Automatic Document Processing. Prentice Hall (1971)
8. Porter, M.F.: An Algorithm for Suffix Stripping. Program **14** (1980) 130–137
9. Porter, M.: Snowball: A Language for Stemming Algorithms (2001) Available at http://snowball.tartarus.org/texts/introduction.html[22.8.2005].
10. Hatcher, E., Gospodnetić, O.: Lucene in Action. Manning Publications Co. (2004)
11. Jones, K.S.: A Statistical Interpretation of Term Specificity and its Application in Retrieval. Journal of Documentation **28** (1972) 11–21
12. Volk, M., Clematide, S.: Learn - Filter - Apply - Forget. Mixed Approaches to Named Entity Recognition. In: Proceedings of the 6th International Workshop of Natural Language for Information Systems, Madrid, Spain (2001)
13. Bikel, D.M., Schwartz, R., Weischedel, R.M.: An Algorithm that Learns What's in a Name. Machine Learning **34** (1999) 211 – 231

MIRACLE's Cross-Lingual Question Answering Experiments with Spanish as a Target Language*

César de Pablo-Sánchez[1], Ana González-Ledesma[2], José Luis Martínez-Fernández[1,4], José María Guirao[3], Paloma Martínez[1], and Antonio Moreno[2]

[1] Universidad Carlos III de Madrid
{cesar.pablo, paloma.martinez}@inf.uc3m.es
[2] Universidad Autónoma de Madrid
{ana, sandoval}@maria.lllf.uam.es
[3] Universidad de Granada
jmguirao@ugr.es
[4] DAEDALUS S.A. - Data, Decisions and Language, S.A.
jmartinez@daedalus.es

Abstract. Our second participation in CLEF-QA consited in six runs with Spanish as a target language. The source languages were Spanish, English an Italian. miraQA uses a simple representation of the question that is enriched with semantic information like typed Named Entities. Runs used different strategies for answer extraction and selection, achieving at best a 25'5% accuracy. The analysis of the errors suggests that improvements in answer selection are the most critical.

1 Introduction

This paper presents and analyzes the results of our second participation in the CLEF-QA task. At this moment, miraQA, is based on a standard pipeline architecture and uses only shallow linguistic analysis. In contrast, we have added semantic resources for NE recognition. The approach and tools differ from our last year participation[2] but we aim to combine both of them in a near future.

In Section 2 we present the system and the tools that have been used. Results are outlined in Section 3 with a detailed analysis of the errors and the modules that originate them. Section 4 presents some conclusions and future improvements.

2 System Description

MIRACLE's contribution to CLEF QA 2005 is an almost new development based on the experience acquired after last year. Our aim was to achieve an architecture

* This work has been partially supported by the Spanish R+D National Plan, by means of the project RIMMEL Multilingual and Multimedia Information Retrieval, and its Evaluation), TIN2004-07588-C03-01.

C. Peters et al. (Eds.): CLEF 2005, LNCS 4022, pp. 488–491, 2006.

where we could do further experiments and perform semi-automatic evaluation with the resources generated at previous CLEF editions like MultiEight[3]. The system is composed of Question Analysis, Sentence Retrieval and Answer Selection modules.

2.1 Resources and Tools

The system integrates individual resources from MIRACLE's group toolbox, open source components and web resources such as:

1. STYLUS[1] (DAEDALUS linguistic processor). This tool was initially developed for spell and grammar checking. It produces all possible POS tags, lemmas and analysis for a word using a large dictionary of Spanish. The tool contains resources for recognition of collocations and other complex tokens. It has been extended with semantic information that it is used to recognize Named Entities.
2. Xapian[2], an open source probabilistic information retrieval engine that uses Okapi BM25 model.
3. Systran[3], was used to translate questions from English and Italian to Spanish.

2.2 Question Analysis

Question classification is achieved using linguistic rules produced after the study and generalization of CLEF 2004 Spanish data. Definitional questions are classified into definitions about organizations and persons. For factual and temporal questions a hierarchical taxonomy based on Sekine's NE hierarchy [4] is used, albeit simplified. Some new types are added also as abbreviations or properties, short descriptions or titles for a person or an organization. The taxonomy for factual and temporal questions is composed of 22 different concepts. The classification proceeds in three steps:

1. question is analyzed using STYLUS
2. features for classification are extracted based on some simple heuristics. Features include question stem, question focus, NE types and verb lemmas as the more salient.
3. classification performed with a manually coded decision tree and compiled word lists of question focus.

After question classification the question is represented as a list of relevant terms. Some terms are believed to harm retrieval effectivenes so they are filtered and are not used to query the collection, although they are used in answer selection.

[1] http://www.daedalus.es [Visited 18/11/2005]
[2] http://www.xapian.org. [Visited 13/07/2005]
[3] http://www.systransoft.com. [Visited 13/07/2005]
[4] http://nlp.cs.nyu.edu/ene/ . [Visited 18/08/2005]

Table 1. Error analysis for mira052eses

Module	*Error*(%)
Question analysis	25.98
Document retrieval recall	20.81
Answer extraction recall	11.83
Answer selection	40.84

2.3 Document and Sentence Retrieval

Documents are indexed off-line using Xapian and Snowball stemmers[5]. At retrieval time, the first N results returned by the engine are analyzed using STYLUS tools. Sentences are scored and filtered according to the number of content terms that they have in common with the query.

2.4 Answer Selection

Rules for extraction are dependent of the expected answer type. They are expressed as a FSA that evaluates boolean predicates over annotated tokens. Predicates check for orthographic, morphological, syntactic and semantic features. Our general strategy is to favor high recall.

After extraction, similar candidate answers are conflated and the one with the highest score is used as the representative of the group. Final scores are assigned in two steps. Runs 051 score answers according to the inverse frequency of relevants terms in the sentence. Runs 052 used a weighted combination of tf*issf (inverted selected sentence frequency) terms and median distance from keywords to answers. In a second step, redundancy is considered by computing the linear combination of the score and the ratio of documents that supports the same answer.

3 Results

We have submitted for evaluation six runs for three different language pairs [4]. Different run series used different ranking function and different strategy for OTHER and MANNER questions. The best results were achieved in mira051eses run but the difference is not significant. As expected, accuracy is lower for cross-lingual runs with a loss between 6% and 7.5%.

The system processes temporal questions in a similar way to factual questions and the accuracy obtained for the former ones is much lower than for the latter ones. The system performs better for definition questions than for the rest of types in absolute numbers. In contrast, compared to other systems with Spanish as a target language, miraQA is answering better factual questions, in particular questions of the PERSON class.

[5] http://www.snowball.tartarus.org. [Visited 13/07/2005]

3.1 Error Analysis

We have performed a detailed analysis of the errors produced by our system. We have try to point a single source of errors although this is complicated in a pipelined QA system, as the interplays and design decisions in any of the modules affects the subsequent ones.

3.2 Cross-Lingual Runs

Questions in cross-lingual runs are translated using Systran and redirected to the spanish QA pipeline. While the classification accuracy for the Spanish questions is 80,5%, for English decreases to 77% and for Italian down to 63,5%. This is due to grammatical errors and the incorrect translations of some question stems. Besides, retrieval performance decreases because of lexical choice up to 13,04%. Despite these problems, answer accuracy only decreases between 6% (English) and 7,5% (Italian). A detailed analysis of the results shows that new correct answers are found in cross-lingual runs that compensate for some other errors. Synonyms that are used in translation allow to retrieve different sentences as well as imposed different weights in the ranking functions.

4 Conclusions and Future Work

Results from the previous sections suggest that performance could be easily improved by means of using better answer selection techniques. Answers are correctly extracted at least for 55% of the questions if all the documents are considered . We believe that better ranking functions and candidate answer filters in the style of our CLEF 2004 system would help us to improve the system. We also plan to explore the use of effective lexical information as the analysis of cross-lingual runs suggests.

References

1. Abney S., Collins M., and Singhal. A., Answer extraction. In Procceeding of Advances in Natural Language Processing 2000, (2000).
2. De Pablo-Sánchez C., Martínez-Fernández J.L., Martínez P., and Villena, J., miraQA: Experiments with Learning Answer Context Patterns from the Web. (2005) in C. Peters et al (Editors), LNCS, Vol. 3491, Springer Verlag (2005).
3. Magnini, B., Vallin, A., Ayache, C., Erbach, G., Peñas, A., de Rijke, M., Rocha, P., Simov, K. and Sutcliffe, R., Overview of the CLEF 2004 Multilingual Question Answering Track, in C. Peters et al (Editors), LNCS, Vol. 3491, Springer Verlag (2005).
4. Vallin A., Giampiccolo D., Aunimo L., Ayache C., Osenova P.,Peñas A., de Rijke M., Sacaleanu B., Santos D., Sutcliffe R., Overview of the CLEF 2005 Multilingual Question Answering Track. (In this volume). (2006)

The Role of Lexical Features in Question Answering for Spanish

Manuel Pérez-Coutiño, Manuel Montes-y-Gómez,
Aurelio López-López, and Luis Villaseñor-Pineda

Instituto Nacional de Astrofísica, Óptica y Electrónica (INAOE)
Luis Enrique Erro No. 1, CP 72840, Sta. Ma. Tonantzintla, Pue., México
{mapco, mmontesg, allopez, villasen}@inaoep.mx

Abstract. This paper describes the prototype developed in the Language Technologies Laboratory at INAOE for the Spanish monolingual QA evaluation task at CLEF 2005. The proposed approach copes with the QA task according to the type of question to solve (factoid or definition). In order to identify possible answers to factoid questions, the system applies a methodology centered in the use of lexical features. On the other hand, the system is supported by a pattern recognition method in order to identify answers to definition questions. The paper shows the methods applied at different stages of the system, with special emphasis on those used for answering factoid questions. Then the results achieved with this approach are discussed.

1 Introduction

Current information requirements call for efficient mechanisms capable of interaction with users in a natural way. Question Answering (QA) systems have been proposed as a feasible option for the creation of such mechanisms. Moreover, the research in this field shows a constant growth both in interest as well as in complexity [3]. This paper presents the prototype developed in the Language Technologies Laboratory at INAOE[1] for the Spanish monolingual QA evaluation task at CLEF 2005. The experiments performed this year by our group are a progression of our efforts reported last year [5] in the following aspects; a) the approach for answering factoid questions is centered in the analysis of the near context related to each named entity selected as candidate answer; b) the context used to discriminate candidate and final answers relies on the lexical information gathered by a shallow language processing (POS and named entities tagging) and statistical parameters. On the other hand, there are some important changes in the prototype architecture that allowed the system to have an improvement in performance (recall) at the initial stages of the QA task. At the same time, there have been some simplifications in the general architecture, which have allowed to get more control and flexibility in order to evaluate multiple system configurations and reduce error propagation from initial stages. For instance, we have applied a shallow question classification process instead of a fine grain question

[1] http://ccc.inaoep.mx/labtl/

C. Peters et al. (Eds.): CLEF 2005, LNCS 4022, pp. 492 – 501, 2006.

classification; and the answer discrimination process relies only on the information located in the target documents, discarding internet searching and extraction modules of our previous prototype.

This paper is focused on the discussion of the proposed methodology for factoid question answering. Nevertheless, a section is presented with a brief description of the methods used for answering definition questions. The rest of this paper is organized as follows; section two describes the architecture of the prototype; from section three to section six the internal processes of the system are discussed; section seven discusses the results achieved by the system; and finally section eight contains our conclusions and discusses further work.

2 Prototype Architecture

As stated before, the system is based on the methodology proposed in the previous year [5] but with some significant modifications in the prototype. Figure 1 shows the main blocks of the system. Here the treatment of factoid and definition questions occurs separately.

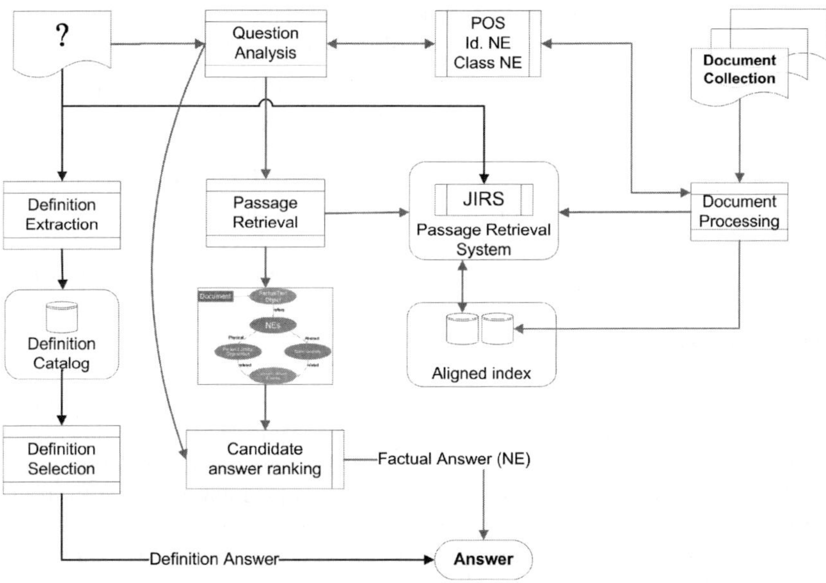

Fig. 1. Block diagram of the system. Factoid and definition questions are treated separately. Factoid questions require the following stages: question processing, document processing, searching, and answer selection. Definition questions use a pattern approach for definition extraction and selection processes.

Factoid questions resolution relies on a hybrid system involving the following stages: *question processing*, which includes the extraction of named entities and lexical context from the question, as well as question classification to define the semantic class of the answer expected to respond to a given question; *document processing*, where the preprocessing of the supporting document collection is done in parallel by a *passage retrieval system (PRS)* and a shallow NLP (similar to that performed in question processing); *searching*, where a set of candidate answers is gathered from a representation of the passages retrieved by the PRS; and finally *answer extraction*, where candidate answers are analyzed, weighted and ranked in order to produce the final answer recommendation of the system.

On the other hand, definition questions are treated directly with a method supported by a couple of lexical patterns that allow finding and selecting the set of possible answers. The following sections describe each of these stages.

3 Question Processing

QA systems traditionally perform a question processing stage in order to know in advance the semantic class of the answer expected for a given question and thus, reduce the searching space to only those information fragments related to instances of the semantic class previously determined. Our prototype implements this stage following a straightforward approach involving these steps:

1. Question is parsed with a set of heuristic rules in order to get its semantic class.
2. Question is tagged with the MACO POS tagger [1]
3. Named entities of the question are identified and classified using MACO.

The first step is responsible of identifying the semantic class of the expected answer. In the experiments performed with the training data set, we observed that when the number of classes was minimal (just 3 classes: date, quantity and proper noun) it was possible to achieve similar results in precision to those achieved when we used a finer classification, for instance person, organization, location, quantity, date and other. Steps 2 and 3 produce information used later on, during searching to match questions and candidate answer context, contributing to the weighting scheme.

4 Document Processing

The prototype implements a hybrid approach for document processing that has allowed simplifying and increasing performance in this stage. The processing of target documents consists of two parts, first the whole document collection is tagged with MACO[1], gathering the POS tags as well as named entities identification and classification for each document in the collection. The second part of this stage is performed by the JIRS [2] passage retrieval system (PRS), that creates the index for the searching process. The index built by JIRS and the tagged collection are aligned phrase by phrase for each document in the collection. In this way, the system can retrieve later the relevant passages for a given question with JIRS, and then use their tagged form for the answer extraction process.

5 Searching

The searching stage is also performed in two steps. As we mentioned, the first step is to retrieve the relevant passages for the given question. This step is performed by JIRS, taking as input the question without any previous processing.

JIRS is a PSR specially suited for question answering. JIRS ranks the retrieved passages based on the computation of a weight for each passage. The weight of a passage is related to the size of the n-gram structure of the question that can be found in the passage. The larger the n-gram structure, the greater the weight assigned to the passage. The following example illustrates this concept.

Given the question "*Who is the president of Mexico?*", suppose that two passages returned the following text segments: "*Vicente Fox is the president of Mexico...*" (p_1) and "*The president of Spain visited Mexico in last February...*" (p_2).

The original question is divided into five sets of *n*-grams (5 is the number of question terms after removing the question word *Who*), these sets are the following:

5-gram: {"is the President of Mexico"}
4-gram: {"is the President of", "the President of Mexico"}
3-gram: {"is the President", "the President of", "President of Mexico"}
2-gram: {"is the", "the President", "President of", "of Mexico"}
1-gram: {"is", "the", "President", "of", "Mexico"}

Then, the five sets of *n*-grams from the two passages are gathered. The passage p_1 contains all the *n*-grams of the question (the 5-gram, the two 4-grams, the three 3-grams, the four 2-grams and the five 1-grams of the question). Therefore the similarity of the question with this passage is 1.

The sets of *n*-grams of the passage p_2 contain only the "*the President of*" 3-gram, the "*the President*" and "*President of*" 2-grams and the following 1-grams: "*the*", "*President*", "*of*" and "*Mexico*". The similarity for this passage is lower than that for p_1 because the second passage is quite different with respect to the original question, although it contains all the relevant terms of the question.

A previous evaluation of JIRS [2] shows that the possible answer to a given question is found among the first 20 passages retrieved for over 60% of the training set.

Once the relevant passages are selected, the second step requires the POS tagged form of each passage in order to gather the representation used to extract the answer. Due to some technical constraints we were unable to finish the implementation for the alignment of the tagged collection and the JIRS index before test set release. Therefore the tagging of relevant passages was performed online with the annoyance of a couple extra hours for such processing.

Tagged passages are represented in the same way as proposed in [4] where each retrieved passage is modeled by the system as a factual text object whose content refers to several named entities[2] even when it could be focused on a central topic. The model assumes that the named entities are strongly related to their lexical context, especially to nouns (subjects) and verbs (actions). Thus, a passage can be seen as a set of entities and their lexical context. Such representation is used later in order to match the question representation against the set of best candidates gathered from passages.

---

[2] The semantic classes used rely on the capability of the named entity classifier, and could be one of these: persons, organizations, locations, dates, quantities, and miscellaneous.

6 Answer Extraction

6.1 Answering Factoid Questions

The system does not differentiate between simple and temporally restricted factoid questions in order to extract their possible answer. Given the set of retrieved passages and their representations (named entities and their contexts) the system computes a weight for each candidate answer (named entity) based on two main factors: a) the activation and deactivation of some features at different steps of the system, and b) the assigned weight computed with the formula 1.

The features listed in table 1 allow us to configure the system in order to change its behavior. For instance, deactivate the question classification step by allowing the final answer selection to rely only on statistical computations. The opposite case could be, deactivate frequency features and let the final answer selection to rely on the matching between question and candidate answers context.

$$\omega_A = \frac{t_q}{n} * \left(\frac{NE_q \cap NE_A}{|NE_q|} + \frac{C_q \cap C_A}{|C_q|} + \frac{F_A(P_i)}{F_A(P)} + \left(1 - \frac{P_i}{k-1}\right) \right) \quad (1)$$

i=1..k; k=number of passages retrieved by JIRS

Where t_q is 1 if the semantic class of the candidate answer is the same as that of the question and 0 in other case; n is a normalization factor based on the number of activated features, NE is the set of named entities in the question (q) or in the candidate answer (A); C is the context either for question (q) or candidate answer (A); $F_A(P_i)$ is the frequency of occurrence of the candidate answer in the passage i; $F_A(P)$ is the total frequency of occurrence of the candidate answer in the passages retrieved; and $1-(P_i/k-1)$ is an inverse relation for the passage ranking returned by JIRS.

Table 1. Features list used in factoid question answering

Features	Function
1. Question classification	Activate question classification step
2. No. Classes	Defines the number of classes to use in question and named entity classification.
3. Context elements	Define the elements included as part of a name entity context. They could be: named entities, common names, verbs, adjectives, adverbs, etc.
4. Context length	Number of elements at left and right of a named entity to include in the context.
5. Question Named Entities	Defines whether passages not containing named entities of the question are allowed.
6. Context match	Intersection
7. Frequency of occurrence	Number of times that a named entity appears as candidate answer in the same passage.
8. JIRS ranking	Position of passage as retuned by JIRS.
9. Passage length	Number of phrases in the passage retrieved.

Once the system computes the weight for all candidate answers, these are ranked by decreasing order, taking as answer that with the greatest weight.

6.2 Answering Definitions

The method for answering definition questions exploits some regularities of language and some stylistic conventions of news notes to capture the possible answer for a given definition question. A similar approach was presented in [6,7].

The process of answering a definition question considers two main tasks. First, the definition extraction, which detects the text segments that contains the description or meaning of a term (in particular those related with the name of a person or an organization). Then, the definition selection, where the most relevant description of a given question term is identified and the final answer of the system is generated.

6.2.1 Definition Extraction

The language regularities and the stylistic conventions of news notes are captured by two basic lexical patterns. These patterns allow constructing two different definition catalogs. The first one includes a list of pairs of acronym-meaning. The second consists of a list of referent-description pairs.

In order to extract the acronym-meaning pairs we use an extraction pattern based on the use of parentheses.

$$w_1 \textit{<meaning>} \; (\textit{<acronym>}) \qquad \text{(i)}$$

In this pattern, w_1 is a lowercase non-stop word, *<meaning>* is a sequence of words starting with an uppercase letter (that can also include some stop words), and *<acronym>* indicates a single word also starting with an uppercase letter.

By means of this pattern we could identify pairs like [*PARM – Partido Auténtico de la Revolución Mexicana*].

In contrast, the extraction of referent-description pairs is guided by the occurrence of a special kind of appositive phrases. This information was encapsulated in the following extraction pattern.

$$w_1 \; w_2 \textit{<description>} \; , \textit{<referent>} \; , \qquad \text{(ii)}$$

Where w_1 may represent any word, except a preposition, w_2 is a determiner, *<description>* is a free sequence of words, and *<referent>* indicates a sequence of words starting with an uppercase letter or appearing in the stop words list.

Applying this extraction pattern we could find pairs like [*Alain Lombard - El director de la Orquesta Nacional de Burdeos*].

6.2.2 Definition Selection

The main advantage of the extraction patterns is their generality. However, this generality causes the patterns to often extract non relevant information, i.e., information that does not indicate a relation acronym-meaning or concept-description.

Given that the catalogs contains a mixture of correct and incorrect relation pairs, it is necessary to do an additional process in order to select the most likely answer for a given definition question. The proposed approach is supported by the idea that, on one hand, the correct information is more abundant than the incorrect, and on the other, that the correct information is redundant.

Thus, the process of definition selection considers the following two criteria:

1. The more frequent definition in the catalog has the highest probability to be the correct answer.
2. The largest and therefore more specific definitions tend to be the more pertinent answers.

The following example illustrates the process. Assuming that the user question is "*who is Félix Ormazabal?*", and that the definition catalog contains the records showed below. Then, the method selects the description "*diputado general de Alava*" as the most likely answer.

Félix Ormazabal: Joseba Egibar:
Félix Ormazabal: candidato alavés:
Félix Ormazabal: diputación de este territorio:
Félix Ormazabal: presidente del PNV de Alava y candidato a diputado general:
Félix Ormazabal: nuevo diputado general
Félix Ormazabal: diputado Foral de Alava
Félix Ormazabal: través de su presidente en Alava
Félix Ormazaba : diputado general de Alava
Félix Ormazabal: diputado general de Alava
Félix Ormazabal: diputado general de Alava

7 Experiments and Results

This section discusses some training experiments and the decision criteria used to select the configuration of the experiments evaluated at QA@CLEF2005 monolingual track for Spanish. Given that we have used the same modules for answering definition questions in all our runs for monolingual QA, including those described in "A Full Data-Driven System for Multiple Language Question Answering" (also in this volume), the discussion on these results and some samples have been documented in that paper. The rest of this document is intended to discuss the results on factoid question answering.

7.1 Training Experiments

As we mentioned earlier, the approach used in our system is similar to that used in [5], an analysis of such system showed that it was necessary to experiment with different values for the parameters involved in the answer extraction stage (see table 1). For instance, in [5] the system relied on a document model considering only nouns or verbs at left and right of named entities, within a lexical context of four elements. In order to improve our approach we performed several experiments using context lengths from four elements to the whole passage retrieved. We also tested different elements for the lexical context: i.e. nouns, proper nouns, verbs, adjectives and adverbs. Table 2 shows some configurations tested with the training set. Then, figure 2 shows the results achieved with the training set applying the configurations showed in table 2. Notice that these results correspond to the factoid question answering.

Table 2. Configurations of some experiments performed with the training set. First column refers to the features listed in table 1.

	Exp. 1	Exp. 2	Exp. 3	Exp. 4	Exp. 5	Exp. 6	Exp. 7	Exp. 8	Exp. 9
1	No	Yes	Yes	No	Yes	No	Yes	No	Yes
2	0	D,Q,NP	D,Q,P,O,G	0	D,Q,NP	0	D,Q,NP	0	D,Q,NP
3	V,NC,NE	V,NC,NE	V,NC,NE	V,NC,NE	V,NC,NE	V,NC,NE,QA	V,NC,NE,QA	V,NC,NE,QA	V,NC,NE,QA
4	4	4	4	4	4	8	8	Passage	Passage
5	1	1	1	1	1	1	1	1	1
6	Yes	Yes	Yes	Yes	Yes	Yes	Yes	Yes	Yes
7	Yes	Yes	Yes	Yes	Yes	Yes	Yes	Yes	Yes
8	Yes	Yes	Yes	Yes	Yes	Yes	Yes	Yes	Yes
9	3	3	3	1	1	1	1	1	1

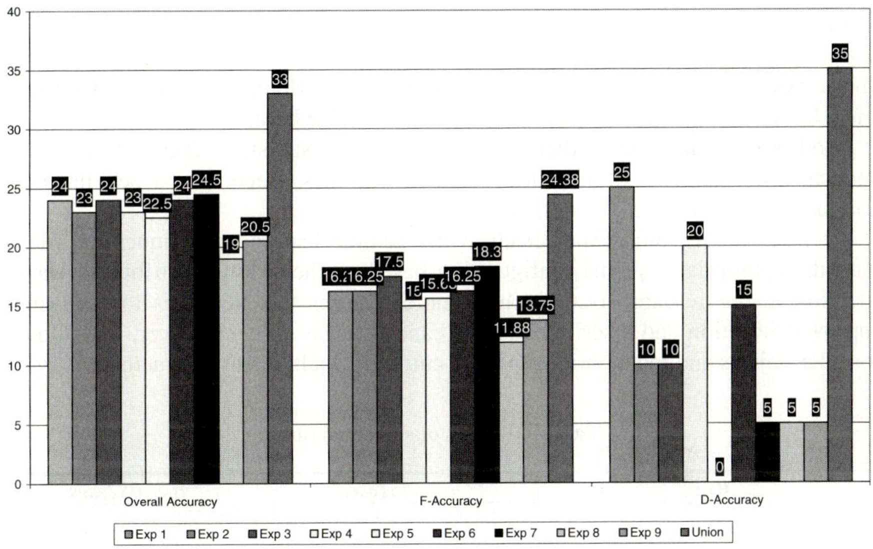

Fig. 2. Results achieved with training set, applying the configurations showed in table 2

Figure 2 shows that the best performance was achieved with the "Exp. 7" which combines the following feature values, first the system classifies the question as one of the following classes: Date, Question, Proper Noun (which includes person, organizations and locations); next the system retrieves the relevant passages with length = 1 phrase, and builds the proper representation for each named entity found in it. At this stage, the context is formed by 8 elements at the left and right of the named entity and considers verbs, common names, named entities and adjectives. The extraction stage filters those candidate answers whose context does not contain any of the question named entity, and finally computes the weight for each candidates according to formula 1 (see table 2 for exp. 7 configuration).

Another interesting experiment was the analysis of the questions answered by this method. We estimate that the "union" of the results gathered with the configurations showed in table 2 could reach over 24% if the best configuration was selected online, i.e., for each question select the best configuration of the system which could return an accurate answer.

7.2 Evaluation

We participated in the evaluation with two runs, both were executed using the same configuration of experiment 7 (see table 2). The first one (inao051eses) analyzes the first 800 passages retrieved by JIRS, while our second run (inao052eses) analyzes only the first 100 passages retrieved by JIRS. Table 3 shows the results of the evaluation.

Despite the fact that our results (for factoid questions) were over 10% better than last year and one of the best for temporally restricted factoid questions, we believe that the approach described is close to its accuracy limit. The methodology is best suited for questions whose answer is commonly found in the near context of some reformulation of the question into the passages, while for other, more elaborated factoid questions, it is unable to identify the right answer. That is the case of questions whose expected answer is an object or some entity which can not be identified *a priori* by the shallow NLP used or without a knowledge base.

Another point to note is that in some cases, the statistical factor given by the frequency of occurrence of a candidate answer becomes a secondary aspect that could lead to a wrong selection of an answer.

We have begun some experiments with machine learning techniques in order to learn the appropriate system configuration based on the question attributes. Another direction in our research is to include more features that allow us to perform an improved selection and discrimination of candidate answers, moreover, that allow to consider objects and more entities that are currently excluded by the methodology.

Table 3. Results of submitted runs

Run	*inao051eses*	*inao052eses*
Right	84 (34F + 40D + 10 TRF)	79 (32F + 40D + 7 TRF)
Wrong	110	116
ineXact	5	4
Unsupported	1	1
Overall Accuracy	42.00%	39.50%
Factoid Questions	28.81%	27.12%
Definition Questions	80.00%	80.00%
Temporally Restricted Factoid Questions	31.25%	21.88%
Answer string "NIL"	Precision= 0.23 Recall=0.80 F-score=0.36	Precision= 0.19 Recall=0.80 F-score=0.31

8 Conclusions

This paper has presented an approach for QA in Spanish centered on the use of lexical features for factoid question resolution that is complemented with a pattern matching approach for definition question resolution. The results achieved in the monolingual track for Spanish have improved compared to our previous year performance by over 10% on factoid questions and over 30% on definition questions. It is important to note that the approach was able to answer over 30% of temporally restricted factoid questions without additions or modifications to the proposed approach.

We have begun to work in two directions: first the inclusion of additional features that allow us to respond questions whose answer is not necessarily expressed as a reformulation of the question into the target documents. Currently our work in this direction is based on the syntactic analysis of the retrieved passages, and in the inclusion of external knowledge. The second direction of research is the automatic selection of features *online* in order to get the best performance of the system for a given question.

Acknowledgements. This work was done under partial support of CONACYT (Project Grants U39957-Y and 43990), SNI-Mexico, and the Human Language Technologies Laboratory at INAOE. We also want to thank the CLEF as well as EFE agency for the resources provided.

References

1. Carreras, X. and Padró, L. *A Flexible Distributed Architecture for Natural Language Analyzers.* In Proceedings of the LREC'02, Las Palmas de Gran Canaria, Spain, 2002.
2. Gómez-Soriano, J.M., Montes-y-Gómez, M., Sanchis-Arnal, E., Rosso P. *A Passage Retrieval System for Multilingual Question Answering.* 8th International Conference on Text, Speech and Dialog, TSD 2005. Lecture Notes in Artificial Intelligence, vol. 3658, 2005.
3. Magnini B., Vallin A., Ayache C., Erbach G., Peñas A., Rijke M., Rocha P., Simov K., Sutcliffe R., *Overview of the CLEF 2004 Multilingual Question Answering Track.* In Working Notes for the Cross Language Evaluation Forum Workshop, (CLEF-2004), Carol Peters and Francesca Borri (Eds.), September 2004, Bath, England, ISTI-CNR, Italy 2004.
4. Pérez-Coutiño M., Solorio T., Montes-y-Gómez M., López-López A. and Villaseñor-Pineda L., *Toward a Document Model for Question Answering Systems.* In Advances in Web Intelligence. Lecture Notes in Artificial Intelligence, vol. 3034, Springer-Verlag 2004.
5. Pérez-Coutiño M., Solorio T., Montes-y-Gómez M., López-López M. and Villaseñor-Pineda L., *Question Answering for Spanish Supported by Lexical Context Annotation*, In Multilingual Information Access for Text, Speech and Images, Proceedings of the 5th Workshop of the Cross-Language Evaluation Forum (CLEF 2004), Peters C, et al. (Eds.), Lecture Notes in Computer Science, vol. 3491, Springer 2005.
6. Ravichandran D. and Hovy E. *Learning Surface Text Patterns for a Question Answering System.* In ACL Conference, 2002.
7. Saggion, H. *Identifying Definitions in Text Collections for Question Answering.* LREC 2004.

Cross-Language French-English Question Answering Using the DLT System at CLEF 2005

Richard F.E. Sutcliffe, Michael Mulcahy, Igal Gabbay, Aoife O'Gorman, and Darina Slattery

Documents and Linguistic Technology Group, Department of Computer Science and Information Systems, University of Limerick, Limerick, Ireland
{Richard.Sutcliffe, Michael.Mulcahy, Igal.Gabbay, Aoife.OGorman, Darina.Slattery}@ul.ie

Abstract. This paper describes the main components of the system built by the DLT Group at Limerick for participation in the QA Task at CLEF. The document indexing we used was again sentence-by-sentence but this year the Lucene Engine was adopted. We also experimented with retrieval query expansion using Local Context Analysis. Results were broadly similar to last year.

1 Introduction

This article outlines the participation of the Documents and Linguistic Technology (DLT) Group in the Cross Language French-English Question Answering Task of the Cross Language Evaluation Forum (CLEF).

2 Architecture of the CLEF 2005 DLT System

2.1 Outline

The basic architecture of our factoid system is standard in nature and comprises query type identification, query analysis and translation, retrieval query formulation, document retrieval, text file parsing, named entity recognition and answer entity selection.

2.2 Query Type Identification

As last year, simple keyword combinations and patterns are used to classify the query into a fixed number of types. Currently there are 69 categories plus the default 'unknown'. Sample types with queries from this year can be seen in Table 1.

2.3 Query Analysis and Translation

This stage is almost identical to last year. We start off by tagging the Query for part-of-speech using XeLDA [7]. We then carry out shallow parsing looking for

C. Peters et al. (Eds.): CLEF 2005, LNCS 4022, pp. 502 – 509, 2006.

Table 1. Some of the Question Types used in the DLT system. The second column shows a sample question from this year for each type. Translations are listed in the third column.

Question Type	Example Question	Google Translation
who	0018 'Qui est le principal organisateur du concours international "Reine du futur" ?'	Who is the main organizer of the international contest "Queen of the Future"?
when	0190 'En quelle année le président de Chypres, Makarios III est-il décédé ?'	What year did the president of Cyprus, Makarios III, die?
how_many3	0043 'Combien de communautés Di Mambro a-t-il crée ?'	How many communities did Di Mambro found?
what_country	0102 'Dans quel pays l'euthanasie est-elle autorisée si le patient le souhaite et qu'il souffre de douleurs physiques et mentales insupportables ?'	In which country is euthanasia permitted if requested by a patient suffering intolerable physical or mental pain?
how_much_rate	0016 'Quel pourcentage de personnes touchées par le virus HIV vit en Afrique ?'	What percentage of people infected by HIV lives in Africa?
unknown	0048 'Quel contrat a cours de 1995 à 2004 ?'	Which contract runs from 1995 to 2004?

various types of phrase. Each phrase is then translated using three different methods. Two translation engines and one dictionary are used. The engines are Reverso [4] and WorldLingo [6] which were chosen because we had found them to give the best overall performance in various experiments.

The dictionary used was the Grand Dictionnaire Terminologique [2] which is a very comprehensive terminological database for Canadian French with detailed data for a large number of different domains. The three candidate translations are then combined – if a GDT translation is found then the Reverso and WorldLingo translations are ignored. The reason for this is that if a phrase is in GDT, the translation for it is nearly always correct. In the case where words or phrases are not in GDT, then the Reverso and WorldLingo translations are simply combined.

The types of phrase recognised were determined after a study of the constructions used in French queries together with their English counterparts. The aim was to group words together into sufficiently large sequences to be independently meaningful but to avoid the problems of structural translation, split particles etc which tend to occur in the syntax of a question, and which the engines tend to analyse incorrectly.

The structures used were number, quote, cap_nou_prep_det_seq, all_cap_wd, cap_adj_cap_nou, cap_adj_low_nou, cap_nou_cap_adj, cap_nou_low_adj, low_nou_low_adj, low_nou_prep_low_nou, low_adj_low_nou, nou_seq and wd. These were based on our observations that (1) Proper names usually only start with a capital letter with subsequent words uncapitalised, unlike English; (2) Adjective-Noun combinations either capitalised or not can have the status of compounds in French and hence need special treatment; (3) Certain noun-preposition-noun phrases are also of significance.

As part of the translation and analysis process, weights are assigned to each phrase in an attempt to establish which parts are more important in the event of query simplification being necessary.

2.4 Retrieval Query Formulation

The starting point for this stage is a set of possible translations for each of the phrases recognised above. For each phrase, a boolean query is created comprising the various alternatives as disjunctions. In addition, alternation is added at this stage to take account of morphological inflections (e.g 'go'<->'went', 'company'<->'companies' etc) and European English vs. American English spelling ('neighbour'<->'neighbor', 'labelled'<->'labeled' etc). The list of the above components is then ordered by the weight assigned during the previous stage and the ordered components are then connected with AND operators to make the complete boolean query. This year we added a component which takes as input the query terms, performs Local Context Analysis (LCA) using the indexed document collection and returns a set of expansion terms. LCA can find terms which are related to a topic by association. For example if the input is 'Kurt Cobain' one output term could be 'Nirvana'. These terms are added to the search expresson in such a way that they boost the relevance of documents which contain them without their being required.

2.5 Document Retrieval

A major change this year was the adoption of the Lucene search engine [3] instead of DTSearch [1]. Lucene was used to index the LA Times and Glasgow Herald collections, with each sentence in the collection being considered as a separate document for indexing purposes. This followed our observation that in most cases the search keywords and the correct answer appear in the same sentence. We use the standard query language.

In the event that no documents are found, the conjunction in the query (corresponding to one phrase recognised in the query) with the lowest weight is eliminated and the search is repeated.

2.6 Text File Parsing

This stage is straightforward and simply involves retrieving the matching 'documents' (i.e. sentences) from the corpus and extracting the text from the markup.

2.7 Named Entity Recognition

Named Entity (NE) recognition is carried out in the standard way using a mixture of grammars and lists. The number of NE types was increased to 75 by studying previous CLEF and TREC question sets.

2.8 Answer Entity Selection

Answer selection was updated this year so that the weight of a candidate answer is the sum of the weights of all search terms co-occurring with it. Because our system works by sentence, search terms must appear in the same sentence as the candidate answer. The contribution of a term reduces with the inverse of its distance from the candidate.

Table 2. Results by Query Type for 2005 Cross-Language French-English Task. The columns C and NC show the numbers of queries of a particular type which were classified correctly and not correctly. Those classified correctly are then broken down into Right, ineXact, Unsupported and Wrong for each of the two runs Run 1 and Run 2.

Query Type	**Classif.**		**Correct Classification**							
			Run 1				**Run 2**			
	C	**NC**	**R**	**X**	**U**	**W**	**R**	**X**	**U**	**W**
abbrev_expand	0	0	0	0	0	0	0	0	0	0
award	1	0	0	0	0	1	0	0	0	1
company	3	0	0	0	0	3	0	0	0	3
distance	2	0	0	0	0	2	0	0	0	2
film	0	0	0	0	0	0	0	0	0	0
how_many3	10	3	3	0	0	7	4	0	0	6
how_much_money	3	0	1	1	0	1	1	1	0	1
how_much_rate	4	0	0	0	0	4	0	0	0	4
how_old	1	0	0	0	0	1	0	0	0	1
pol_party	3	0	0	0	0	3	0	0	0	3
population	1	0	1	0	0	0	1	0	0	0
profession	1	0	0	0	0	1	0	1	0	0
title	1	0	0	0	0	1	0	0	0	1
tv_network	0	0	0	0	0	0	0	0	0	0
what_capital	1	0	1	0	0	0	1	0	0	0
what_city	4	0	2	0	0	2	2	0	0	2
what_country	5	0	1	0	0	4	1	0	0	4
when	11	0	4	0	0	7	4	0	0	7
when_date	1	0	0	0	0	1	0	0	0	1
when_month	1	0	1	0	0	0	1	0	0	0
when_year	4	0	3	0	0	1	3	0	0	1
where	3	0	2	0	0	1	2	0	0	1
who	30	0	2	0	0	28	1	0	0	29
unknown	33	24	5	1	0	27	5	1	0	27
Subtotals	**123**	**27**	**26**	**2**	**0**	**95**	**26**	**3**	**0**	**94**
def_org	20	0	2	2	0	16	2	1	0	17
def_person	25	0	4	9	0	12	3	8	0	14
def_unknown	0	5	0	0	0	0	0	0	0	0
Subtotals	**45**	**5**	**6**	**11**	**0**	**28**	**5**	**9**	**0**	**31**
Totals	**168**	**32**	**32**	**13**	**0**	**123**	**31**	**12**	**0**	**125**

2.9 Temporally Restricted Questions

This year an additional question type was introduced, temporally restricted factoids. We did not have time to make a study of this interesting idea so instead we simply processed them as normal factoids. Effectively this means that any temporal restrictions are analysed as normal syntactic phrases within the query, are translated and hence become weighted query terms. As with all phases, therefore, the weight assigned depends on the syntactic form of the restriction and not on any estimate of its temporal restricting significance. This approach was in fact quite successful (see results table and discussion).

Table 3. Results by query type for incorrectly classified questions. Once again, results are broken down into Right, ineXact, Unsupported and Wrong for each of the two runs Run 1 and Run 2.

Query Type	Incorrect Classification							
	Run 1				Run 2			
	R	X	U	W	R	X	U	W
abbrev_expand	0	0	0	0	0	0	0	0
award	0	0	0	0	0	0	0	0
company	0	0	0	0	0	0	0	0
distance	0	0	0	0	0	0	0	0
film	0	0	0	0	0	0	0	0
how_many3	1	0	0	2	1	0	0	2
how_much_money	0	0	0	0	0	0	0	0
how_much_rate	0	0	0	0	0	0	0	0
how_old	0	0	0	0	0	0	0	0
pol_party	0	0	0	0	0	0	0	0
population	0	0	0	0	0	0	0	0
profession	0	0	0	0	0	0	0	0
title	0	0	0	0	0	0	0	0
tv_network	0	0	0	0	0	0	0	0
what_capital	0	0	0	0	0	0	0	0
what_city	0	0	0	0	0	0	0	0
what_country	0	0	0	0	0	0	0	0
when	0	0	0	0	0	0	0	0
when_date	0	0	0	0	0	0	0	0
when_month	0	0	0	0	0	0	0	0
when_year	0	0	0	0	0	0	0	0
where	0	0	0	0	0	0	0	0
who	0	0	0	0	0	0	0	0
unknown	3	0	0	21	3	0	0	21
Subtotals	**4**	**0**	**0**	**23**	**4**	**0**	**0**	**23**
def_org	0	0	0	0	0	0	0	0
def_person	0	0	0	0	0	0	0	0
def_unknown	0	2	0	3	1	1	0	3
Subtotals	**0**	**2**	**0**	**3**	**1**	**1**	**0**	**3**
Totals	**4**	**2**	**0**	**26**	**5**	**1**	**0**	**26**

2.10 Definition Questions

50 definition questions were also included in the set of 200 queries for this year, with the remaining 150 being factoid (some temporally restricted, some not). At no stage have we made any study of these questions. For TREC we developed a very primitive

component and so this was simply incorporated into the present system. Queries are first classified as def_organisation, def_person or def_unknown. The target is identified in the query (usually the name of an organisation or person). For an organisation query, a standard list of phrases is then added to the search expression, each suggesting that something of note is being said about the organisation. Example phrases are 'was founded' and 'manufacturer of'. All sentences including the target term plus at least one significant phrase are returned. These are concatenated to yield the answer to the question. This approach does work on occasion but the result is rarely concise. For def_person queries the method is the same, but using a different set of phrases such as 'brought up', 'founded' etc. If the categoriser is unable to decide between def_organisation and def_person, it assigns def_unknown which results in both sets of patterns being used.

3 Runs and Results

3.1 Two Experiments

We submitted two runs which differed only in their use of LCA. Run 1 used it while Run 2 did not.

3.2 Results

Results are summarised by query type in Tables 2 and 3. Concerning query classification it shows for each query type the number of queries assigned to that type which were correctly categorised along with the number incorrectly categorised. The overall rate of success was 84% which compares closely with the 85% achieved in the same task last year. This figure includes 33 queries which were 'correctly' classified as unknown. If these are not included then the figure becomes 67.5%. Effectively, answering these 33 queries (16.5% of the entire collection) lies outside the envisaged scope of the system.

The performance in Run 1 can be summarised as follows. Taking all queries together (i.e. definitions and both types of factoid), 32 of the 168 queries classified properly were correctly answered. Of the 32 queries not classified properly, 4 were still answered correctly. Overall performance was thus 36 / 200, i.e. 18%. For Run 2, 31 of the 168 classified properly were answered correctly with an additional 5 of the 32 not classified properly still being right. This also gives a figure of 36 / 200, i.e. 18%. Our best figure for last year was in Run 1 where 19% was achieved. However, there were no definition questions in 2004 and this year we were able to devote little or no time to developing a component for these. If we consider just the factoid figures, performance in both runs is 26+4 / 150 i.e. 20%.

In terms of our overall position in the French-English task (see Table 6 in the QA summary paper) we are only in positions 5 and 6 out of 12 with the best performance being DFKI German-English at 25.50%. However, it turns out that the main difference between ourselves and high scoring competitors is in the definition questions where they score well and we do poorly. If we consider the performance in factoid questions, broken down into two types, non-temporally restricted and temporally restricted, our performance in the former is 20.66% in Run 1 and 19.83% in Run 2 while in the latter it is 17.24% in Run 1 and 20.69% in Run 2. This makes Run 1 the best system in the group for non-temporally restricted questions alone, and Run 2 the best equal system with LIRE French-English Run 2 for temporally restricted questions alone.

As mentioned above, we devoted very little time to definitions and hence our very poor result of 6 / 50 correct i.e. 12%. The judgement of definitions was quite strict (we were responsible for it) with any response containing both relevant and non-relevant information being judged as ineXact not Right. This probably explains why the scores assigned to systems in the English target task were lower than in some other tasks.

3.3 Platform

We used a Dell PC running Windows NT and having 256 Mb RAM. The majority of the system is written in SICStus Prolog 3.11.1 [5] with Part-of-Speech tagging, Web translation and Local Context Analysis components being written in Java.

4 Conclusions

The overall performance was 18% which compares with 19% last year and 11.5% the year before. We were able to do very little work on the system this year and in addition there were 50 definition questions for which we only had a very primitive module inherited from our TREC system. If we exclude definitions, our performance compares more favourably with the other systems with Run 1 being the best system overall for normal factoids and Run 2 being equal best with LIRE for temporally restricted factoids.

Run 1 was our first experiment with Local Context Analysis for term expansion at the document retrieval stage. Informal observations have shown that this method provides very good expansion terms which are semantically related by topic and context. However, these experiments did not show any significant advantage for LCA compared to Run 2 which did not use it. Overall performance of the two runs was identical. Performance on non-temporal factoids was marginally better with the LCA (20.66% vs. 19.83%) but it was worse on temporal factoids (17.24% vs. 20.69%). Further analysis is necessariy to see why this was the case.

Definitions are an interesting category of question and we intend to devote much more time to them next year. We are hoping that the specification of a definition and the precise means by which it can be evaluated will be worked out in the mean time. A major defect of our approach is that it is imprecise. Under our strict scoring, accuracy was only 12%. However, we could easily have considered our inexact answers as correct. This would increase our score from 6 / 50 to 17 / 50, i.e. an improvement from 12% to 34%. To put this another way, if we were to select from the answer sentences more carefully, we could improve our algorithm considerably.

In CLEF generally, performance in the cross-lingual tasks is much lower than in the monolingual ones. One interesting experiment would be to eliminate the translation component from our system, thus making it monolingual, and then to try it on the English version of the same test collection. The level of performance would of course be higher and by measuring the difference we would be able to estimate how much information we are at present losing in the translation stage.

References

1. DTSearch: www.dtsearch.com
2. GDT: http://w3.granddictionnaire.com/btml/fra/r_motclef/index1024_1.asp
3. Lucene: http://jakarta.apache.org/lucene
4. Reverso: http://grammaire.reverso.net/textonly/default.asp
5. SICStus: http://www.sics.se/isl/sicstuswww/site/index.html
6. WorldLingo: http://www.worldlingo.com/products_services/worldlingo_translator.html
7. XeLDA: http://www.temis-group.com/temis/XeLDA.htm

Finding Answers to Indonesian Questions from English Documents

Mirna Adriani and Rinawati

Faculty of Computer Science
University of Indonesia
Depok 16424, Indonesia
mirna@cs.ui.ac.id, rinaw101@mhs.cs.ui.ac.id

Abstract. We present a report on our participation in the Indonesian-English question-answering task of the 2005 Cross-Language Evaluation Forum (CLEF). In this work we translated an Indonesian query set into English using a commercial machine translation tool called *Transtool.* We used linguistic tools to find the answer to a question. The answer is extracted from a relevant passage and is identified as having the relevant tagging as the query.

1 Introduction

Finding the correct answer to a question in documents is a challenging task, and this is the main research topic in CLEF Question Answering task. The question and the documents must be analyzed in order to find the correct answer to the question. There are several techniques that have been used to handle the QA task, such as parsing and tagging [6] the sentence in the question, in documents [4], in paragraph [8], and in passages [2,3].

The University of Indonesia IR-Group participated in the bilingual Question-Answering (QA) task at the Cross Language Evaluation Forum (CLEF) 2005: the Indonesian-English QA. We opted to do the Indonesian-English QA because we were interested in studying the effectiveness of linguistic tools, including machine translation, in translating queries and finding good answers to the queries in documents.

In this work we use entity tagger and part of speech tagger to tag the question and find the correct answer by analyzing the passage in documents that has the highest score based on their tags and the similarity between words in the passage and in the question.

2 The Question Answering Process

A number of steps were performed on the queries that we received from CLEF. The original English queries were translated into Indonesian manually. Our approach is similar to the work that has been done by Li and Croft [6].

C. Peters et al. (Eds.): CLEF 2005, LNCS 4022, pp. 510 – 516, 2006.

The query-answering process proceeds in the following stages:

1. Question categorization
2. Passage identification/building
3. Passage tagging
4. Passage scoring
5. Answer identification.

First, we classified the Indonesian question (query) according to the type of the question. We identified the question type based on the question word found in the query.

The Indonesian question was then translated into English using a machine translation tool. We used a commercial machine translation software called *Transtool*[1] to translate an Indonesian query set into English. We learned from our previous work [1] that freely available dictionaries on the Internet did not provide sufficiently good translation terms, as their vocabulary was very limited. We hoped that we could achieve better results using a machine translation approach.

The resulting English query was then used to retrieve the relevant documents from the collection through an information retrieval system. The contents of a number of documents at the top of the list were then split into passages.

The passages were then tagged using linguistic tagging (annotation) tools to identify the type of words in the passages.

The passages were then scored using an algorithm, and the answer to the question is extracted from the passage with the highest score.

2.1 Categorizing the Questions

Each question category, which is identified by the question word in the question, points to the type of answer that is looked for in the documents. The Indonesian question-words used in the categorization are:

dimana, dimanakah, manakah (where)	points to <location>
apakah nama (what),	points to <location>
siapa, siapakah (who)	points to <person>
berapa (how many)	points to <measure>
kapan (when)	points to <date>
organisasi apakah (what organization)	points to <organization>
apakah nama (which)	points to <location>
sebutkan (name)	points to < other>

By identifying the question type, we can predict the kind of answer that we need to look for in the document. The Indonesian question was tagged using a question tagger that we developed according to the question word that appears in the question. This approach is similar to those used by Clark et al. [2] and Hull [4]. However, we ignored the tagging on the question when we ran the query through the IR system to retrieve the documents.

---

[1] See http://www.geocities.com/cdpenerjemah.

2.2 Building Passages

Next, the Indonesian question was translated into English using machine translation. The resulting English query was then run through an information retrieval system as a query to retrieve a list of relevant documents. We used *Lemur*[2] information retrieval system to index and retrieve the documents. The contents of the top 50 relevant documents were split into passages. Each passage contains two sentences where the second sentence is repeated in the next passage as the first sentence. The sentence in the documents was identified using a sentence parser to identify the beginning and the end of a sentence.

2.3 Tagging the Passage

The passages were then run through an entity tagger to get the entity annotation tags. The entity annotation tagger identifies words of known entity types, and tags them with the entity type tags, such as person, location, and organization. For example, *<organization> UN*, the word *UN* is identified as an organization so it gets the organization tag. In this work, we compared two linguistic tagger tools, *Lingpipe*[3] and *Monty Tagger*[4].

Lingpipe analyzes English words and annotates them with tags to indicate location, organization, and person, where applicable. The annotation tags are used to find the candidate answer based on the type of the question, for example, a word with location tag is a good candidate answer to a *where* question, and a word with a person tag is a good candidate answer to a *who* question. Since *Lingpipe* can only identify person, location, and organization, we have developed our own tagger to identify date and measurement.

The *Monty* tagger analyzes English words and adds tags to indicate parts of speech such as NN, NNP for nouns, and CD for numbers, etc. We established a rule set specifying that terms with NN tags are the answers to location type questions, and terms with CD tags are the answers to date-type questions, and so forth.

2.4 Scoring the Passages

Passages were scored based on their probability of answering the question. We employed a similar scoring technique as the one used by Li and Croft [4]. The scoring rules are as follows:

1. Give 0 to a passage if its tag is not the same as the query tag.
2. Give 0 to a passage if the number of words in the query is smaller than some specified threshold, otherwise give the passage a score equal to the number of matching words in the passage (*count_m*).
3. The threshold is defined as follows:
    a. Threshold = $count\_q$ if $count\_q < 4$
    b. Threshold = $count\_q/2.0 + 1.0$ if $4 \le count\_q \le 8$

[2] See http://www.lemurproject.org/.
[3] See http://www.alias-i.com/lingpipe.
[4] See http://web.media.mit.edu/~hugo/montytagger.

c. Threshold = count_q/3.0 + 2.0 if *count_q* > 8
Where *count_q* is the number of the words in the English query.

4. Add 0.5 if all words in the English query are found in the passage.
5. Add 0.5 if the order of words in the passage is the same as the query.
6. Calculate the final score of the passage:
   Score = score + *count_m* / *passage_size*

where:
count_m = the number of matching words in the passage.
passage_size = the number of the words in the passage.

Once the passages obtained their scores, the top 20 scoring with the appropriate tags – e.g., if the question type is person (the question word "*who*") then the passages must contain the person tag – were then taken to the next stage.

2.5 Finding the Answer

The top 20 passages were analyzed to find the best answer. The probability of a word being the answer to the question is inversely proportional to the number of words in the passage that separate the candidate word and the word in the query. For each word that has the appropriate tag, its distance from a query word found in the passage is computed. The candidate word that has the smallest distance is the final answer to the question.

For example:

- Question: What is the **capital** of <*LOCATION*> Somalia?
- Passage:
  – Here there is no coordination. <*PERSON*> Steffan de Mistura – UNICEF representative in the Somali **capital**, <*LOCATION*> **Mogadishu**, and head of the anti-cholera team – said far more refugees are crowded together here without proper housing or sanitarian than during the <*LOCATION*> **Somalia** crisis. And many are already sick and exhausted by the long trek from <*LOCATION*> **Rwanda**.

The distance between the question word *capital* and *Mogadishu* is 1, between the question word *capital* and *Rwanda* is 38. So, *Mogadishu* becomes the final answer since its distance to the question word *capital* is the smallest one (closest).

3 Experiment

In this work, we used the collection from CLEF that contains English documents from the *Glasgow Herald* and the *Los Angeles Times*. There are 200 questions (queries) in this year's QA task.

Our work focused on the bilingual task using Indonesian questions to find answers in English documents. The Indonesian questions were obtained by manually translating the English questions. The average number of words in the original English questions is 8.50 words and in the Indonesian questions is 7.89 words. The

Indonesian questions were then translated back into English using *Transtool* to retrieve relevant English documents from the collection. The average number of words in the translated English queries is 8.94 words.

3.1 Results

Using the Monty tagger to tag words in the passages, only two correct answers were found (Table 1). There were 36 inexact (ambiguous) answers and 162 wrong answers. One of the reasons why the result was so poor was because our tagger did not provide specific enough tagging to the passages. As a result, the tagging in most passages was too general. For example NN tags could be the answer to questions about location or about organization.

Table 1. Evaluation of the QA result using the Monty tagger

Task : Bilingual QA	Evaluation
W (wrong)	162
U (unsupported)	0
X (inexact)	36
R (right)	2

Among answers that were evaluated as inexact, 9 answers contain the correct words from the correct source documents, but the answers also contain irrelevant words, and 27 answers contain the correct words but from irrelevant source documents (Table 2).

Table 2. Evaluation of the inexact answers, obtained using the Monty tagger

Inexact Answer	Evaluation
Relevant document + correct answer	9
Unrelevant document + correct answer	27

Using the *Lingpipe* tagger to tag words in the passages, only 2 correct answers were found (Table 3). There were 28 inexact (ambiguous) answers and 170 wrong answers.

Table 3. Evaluation of the QA result using the *Lingpipe* tagger

Task : Bilingual QA	Evaluation
W (wrong)	170
U (unsupported)	0
X (inexact)	28
R (right)	2

Among the answers evaluated as inexact there are 9 answers that contain the correct words from the correct relevant documents, but also irrelevant words, 19 answers contain the correct words but from irrelevant source documents (Table 4).

Table 4. Evaluation of the inexact answers, obtained using the *Lingpipe* tagger

Inexact Answer	Evaluati on
Relevant document + correct answer	9
Unrelevant document + correct answer	19

3.2 Analysis

There was no difference between using the *Monty* tagger and the *Lingpipe* tagger, as far as the number of correct answers is concerned. However, in terms of the number of wrong answers, the result of using the *Monty* tagger is better than that using the *Lingpipe* tagger. One of the main reasons was because the *Lingpipe* tagger did not recognize or misidentified words in the passages. Moreover we did not define syntactic rules that recognize sequences of part of speech tags to be the answer to certain types of question as in the work of Pasca [8] and Moldovan [7].

The poor results in translating the Indonesian queries into English using the machine translation software also reduced the performance of the queries. There were 8 Indonesian words that could not be translated into English. Also, there were 13 queries that contain English words that have different meanings than their counterparts in the original English queries. For example, the Indonesian word *markas*, it was translated into *station* whose meaning is not the same as the word *based* in the original English query. This problem needs to be sorted out first before considering the next steps. Perhaps combining the machine translation and dictionary approaches can reduce the number of Indonesian words that cannot be translated into English.

Another problem is that there were a number of correct answers that were judged as not correct because they were not come from the same documents as in the relevant judgment file. This had severely reduced the number of correct answers that our group produced. After evaluating the documents in the relevant judgment file from CLEF, we found out that there are several documents that are not in the top 50 documents that contain the correct answers which our algorithm managed to identify.

4 Summary

Our first experience in doing the QA task has provided us with valuable lessons and ideas for improving our result in the future, such as using better machine translation, applying query expansion to the translated queries, and better scoring system for the passages.

The result of using the algorithm that we developed in this work was relatively poor. Our plan for the future is to use better linguistic tools and improve the scoring algorithm to produce more accurate answers.

References

1. Adriani, M. and van Rijsbergen, C. J. Term Similarity Based Query Expansion for Cross Language Information Retrieval. In Proceedings of Research and Advanced Technology for Digital Libraries (ECDL'99). Springer Verlag, Paris (1999) 311-322
2. Clarke, C. L. A., Cormack, G.G., Kisman, D. I. E. and Lynam, K. Question Answering by Passage Selection. In NIST Special Publication: The 9th Text retrieval Conference (2000)
3. Clarke, Charles L.A., Cormack, Gordon V. and Lynam, Thomas R. Exploiting Redundancy in Question Answering. In Proceeding of ACM SIGIR. New Orleans (2001)
4. Hull, David. Xerox TREC-8 Question Answering Track Report. In NIST Special Publication: The 8th Text Retrieval Conference (1999)
5. Li, Xiaoyan dan Croft, Bruce. Evaluating Question-Answering Techniques in Chinese. In NIST Special Publication: The 10th Text Retrieval Conference (2001)
6. Manning, C.D. and Schutze, H. Foundations of Statistical Natural Language Processing. The MIT Press, Boston (1999)
7. Moldovan, D. et.al. Lasso: A Tool for Surfing the Answer Net. In NIST Special Publication: The 8th Text Retrieval Conference (1999)
8. Pasca, Marius and Harabagiu, Sanda. High Performance Question Anwering. In Proceeding of ACM SIGIR. New Orleans (2001)

BulQA: Bulgarian–Bulgarian Question Answering at CLEF 2005

Kiril Simov and Petya Osenova

Linguistic Modelling Laboratory,
Bulgarian Academy of Sciences, Bulgaria
{petya, kivs}@bultreebank.org

Abstract. This paper describes the architecture of a Bulgarian–Bulgarian question answering system — **BulQA**. The system relies on a partially parsed corpus for answer extraction. The questions are also analyzed partially. Then on the basis of the analysis some queries to the corpus are created. After the retrieval of the documents that potentially contain the answer, each of them is further processed with one of several additional grammars. The grammar depends on the question analysis and the type of the question. At present these grammars can be viewed as patterns for the type of questions, but our goal is to develop them further into a deeper parsing system for Bulgarian.

1 Introduction

This paper describes the architecture and the linguistic processing of a question answering system for Bulgarian — **BulQA**. The system has three main modules: *Question analysis module*, *Interface module*, *Answer extraction module*. The *Question analysis module* deals with the syntactic and semantic interpretation of the question. The result of this module is independent from task and domain representation of the syntactic and semantic information in the question. The *Interface module* bridges the interpretation received from the first module to the input necessary for the third module. The *Answer extraction module* is responsible for the actual detection of the answer in the corresponding corpus. This architecture has the advantage that it allows the poly-usage of the same modules in different tasks, such as Bulgarian as source language in a multilingual question answering, or Bulgarian as a target language. In fact, only *the Interface module* has to be re-implemented in order to tune the connection between Bulgarian modules and the modules for the other languages.

In CLEF 2005 we have used the *Question analysis module* for two tasks: Bulgarian-English QA and Bulgarian-Bulgarian QA. The former is very similar to our participation at the CLEF 2004 ([5]) and for that reason is remains out of this paper's scope.

However, being participants in both tasks, we had to implement two versions of the *Interface module*. For the Bulgarian-English QA task the *Answer searching module* is based on the Diogene system ([4]) implemented at the ITC-Irst, Trento, Italy. For the Bulgarian-Bulgarian task we had implemented our own *Answer*

C. Peters et al. (Eds.): CLEF 2005, LNCS 4022, pp. 517–526, 2006.

searching module. This paper describes it in more detail. Also the paper discusses the necessary resources and processing for answer support in different contexts. In this way we delimit the future developments of the system.

The structure of the paper is as follows: in section 2 we discuss language technology adaptation for the analysis of Bulgarian questions; section 3 describes the interface module; in section 4 we present the answer extraction approach on the basis of additional grammars. Section 5 comments on the necessary language resources and processing for more complicated answer supporting; the last section reports on the results of the question answering track and concludes the paper.

2 Linguistic Processing of the Corpus and the Questions

2.1 Processing the Corpus

The processing of the corpus is done in two steps: off-line and runtime. The goal is as much as possible processing to be done prior to the actual usage in the answer searching. The off-line processing tools are as follows: tokenization, named-entity recognition, morphological analyzer, neural-network based morphosyntactic disambiguation, chunking. These are the very basic tools which were widely used in our previous systems. We consider the results of these tools as reliable. For an overview of the available language resources and tools of Bulgarian and how they were used for Bulgarian-English task at CLEF 2004 see [5]. The result of this preprocessing of the corpus is stored as a set of XML documents with some indexing for searching with XPath language, which is implemented in the CLaRK system — [6]. Although the results of the preprocessing are still not very deep, they allow us to save time during the answer searching. In future we intend to extend the processing with additional information.

The runtime processing of the corpus is based on additional partial parsing modules that are tuned to the type of the questions, the type of the answer and to the type of the content of the questions. Thus we constructed new modules, such as specific partial analyses (we developed new partial grammars for more complex NPs with a semantic categorization, such as time, location and others). The reason these new processing modules have not been included in the off-line processing is that they depend too much on the information from the questions. Thus, they are likely to produce a wrong analysis if there is no appropriate information. The runtime processing is done only for a few documents that are retrieved from the corpus on the basis of the keywords derived from the questions.

2.2 Processing the Questions

The processing of questions is similar to the off-line processing of the corpus. In fact, we have enhanced the processing from the last year. The processing is mainly connected to the use of more elaborate semantic lexicon and module for processing of time expressions (i.e. dates, periods and event marking adverbials) in order to manage questions with temporal restrictions.

Here is an example of the analysis of the question "Koj kosmicheski aparat trygva za Lunata na 25 yanuari 1994 g.?" (in English: *Which space probe started for the Moon on 25 January 1994?*):

```
<analysis group="BTB">
   <NPA>
     <Pron><w ana="Pie-os-m" bf="koj">Koj</w></Pron>
     <A><w ana="Amsi" bf="kosmicheski">kosmicheski</w></A>
     <N><w ana="Ncmsi" bf="aparat">aparat</w></N>
   </NPA>
   <V><w ana="Vpiif-o3s" bf="trygvam">trygva</w></V>
   <PP>
     <Prep><w ana="R" bf="za">za</w></Prep>
     <N><name ana="Ncfsd" sort="LocNE" bf="Luna">Lunata</name></N>
   </PP>
   <PP sort="On_Date">
     <Prep><w ana="R" bf="na">na</w></Prep>
     <NPA sort="Date">
        <M><w ana="Mc--i" bf="25">25</w></M>
        <N><w ana="Ncmsi" bf="yanuari">yanuari</w></N>
        <M><w ana="Mc--i" bf="1994">1994</w></M>
        <N><abbr ana="Ncfsi" cat="lex" sort="Time"
            type="contr" exp="godina" bf="godina">g.</abbr></N>
     </NPA>
   </PP>
   <pt>?</pt>
</analysis>
```

Here each common word is annotated within the following XML element ⟨*w ana="MSD" bf="LemmaList"*⟩*wordform*⟨*/w*⟩, where the value of attribute *ana* is the correct morpho-syntactic tag for the wordform in the given context. The value of the attribute *bf* is a list of the lemmas assigned to the wordform. Names are annotated within the following XML element ⟨*name ana="MSD" sort="Sort"*⟩*Name*⟨*/name*⟩, where the value of the attribute *ana* is the same as above. The value of the attribute *sort* determines whether this is a name of a person, a location, an organization or some other entity. The abbreviations are annotated in a similar way, and additionally they have *type* and *exp* attributes which encode the type of the abbreviation and its extension.

The next level of analysis is the result of the chunk grammars. In the example there are two *NPA* elements (NPA stands for a noun phrase of head-adjunct type), a lexical *V* element (lexical verb) and two *PP* elements. Also, one of the noun phrases is annotated as a date expression with a sort attribute with value: *Date*. This information is percolated to the preposition phrase which is annotated with the relation label *On_Date*. This is a result of the combination of the preposition meaning and the category of the noun phrase. The noun in the other prepositional phrase is annotated as a LOCATION name. The result of this analysis had to be translated into the format which the answer extraction module uses as an input.

3 Interface Module

Here we describe the implemented interface module which translates the result of the question analysis module into the template necessary for the system, which extracts the answers of the questions. This module is an extension of the module we have implemented for the Bulgarian-English task. The main difference is that we do not transfer the question analyses into DIOGENE's type of template with English translations of the keywords, but instead we define a set of processing steps for the Answer searching module. The processing steps are of two kinds: corpus processing and document processing. The first processing step retrieves documents from the corpus that potentially contain the relevant answers. The second one analyzes additionally the retrieved documents in order to extract the answer(s). The process includes the following steps:

- Determining the head of the question.
  The determination of the question head was performed by searching for the chunk which contains the interrogative pronoun. There were cases in which the question was expressed with the help of imperative forms of verbs: *nazovete* (name-plural!), *kazhete* (point out-plural!; say-plural!). After the chunk selection we classify the interrogative pronoun within a hierarchy of question's heads. In this hierarchy some other elements of the chunks — mainly prepositions — play an important role as well.
- Determining the head word of the question and its semantic type.
  The chunk determined in the previous step also is used for determining the head word of the question. There are five cases. First, the chunk is an NP chunk in which the interrogative pronoun is a modifier. In this case the head noun is the head word of the question. For example, in the question: **What nation** *is the main weapons supplier to Third World countries?* the noun 'nation' is the head word of the question. In the second case the chunk is a PP chunk in which there is an NP chunk similar to the NP chunk from the previous case. Thus, again the head noun is a head word for the question. For example, in the question: **In what music genre** *does Michael Jackson excel?* the noun 'genre' is the head word of the question. Third, the interrogative pronoun is a complement of a copula verb and there is a subject NP. In this case the head word of the question is the head noun of the subject NP chunk of the copula. For example, in the question: **What** *is a basic ingredient of Japanese cuisine?* 'ingredient' is the head of the question. The fourth case covers the questions with imperative verbs. Then again the head of the question is the head noun of the complement NP chunk. For example, in the question: *Give a symptom of the Ebola virus.* the noun 'symptom' is the head of the question. The last case covers all the remaining questions. Then the head word of the question is the interrogative phrase (or word) itself. For example, in the question: **When** *was the Convention on*

the Rights of the Child adopted? the head of the question is the interrogative word 'when'. The semantic type of the head word is determined by the annotation of the words with semantic classes from the semantic dictionary. When there are more than one semantic classes we add all of them. The type of the interrogative pronoun is used later for disambiguation. If no semantic class is available in the dictionary, then the class 'other' is assigned.

– Determining the type of the question.
  The type of the question is determined straightforwardly by the semantic type of the head word. For the recognition of the questions with temporal restriction we count on the preprocessing of the questions and the assigned temporal relations. As temporal restriction we consider such expressions that are not part of the head of the question.
– Determining the keywords of the question and their part of speech.
  The keywords are determined by the non-functional words in the question. Sometimes it is possible to construct multi-token keywords, such as names (Michael Jackson), terms or collocations. For the Bulgarian-Bulgarian task this is important when there are special rules for query generation for document retrieval (see next section). We also used gazetteers of abbreviated forms of the most frequent organizations in English. This was very helpful in finding the correct answers to the Definition Organization questions because in many cases these abbreviations lack Cyrillic counterparts, and thus the search is very direct even in the Bulgarian corpus. Only the extensions seem to have systematically Cyrillic counterparts, and therefore they need more complex processing sometimes.

4 Answer Extraction and Validation

The answer extraction is a two-step process: first, the documents possibly containing the answer are retrieved from the corpus; then the retrieved documents are additionally processed with special partial grammars which depend on the type of answer, the type of the question and the found keywords in the document. We can view these grammars as patterns for the different types of questions.

As it was mentioned above, for document retrieval we are using CLaRK system. The corpus is presented as a set of XML documents. The search is done via XPath language enhanced with index mechanism over the (selected) content of each document. The initial step of the answer extraction is done via translating of the keywords from the analysis of the question into an XPath expression. This expression selects the appropriate documents from the corpus. The expression itself is a disjunctive where each disjunct describes some combinations of keywords and their variants. The variants are necessary because the keywords in the question bear different degree of informativeness with respect to the answer (see the discussion below on the answer support). For example, for named entities we constructed different (potential) representations: *Michael Jackson* can be *M. Jackson* or only *Jackson*. Where possible, we convert the corresponding keyword to a canonical form (for example, dates) and we simply match the canonical forms from the corpus and the question.

Definition questions provide one key word or expression. Thus, they are easily trackable at this stage. For example ('Who is Nelson Mandela?' has a key expression 'Nelson Mandela'). However, the factoid questions are more difficult to process even at that general stage. Obviously, the reason is that the question key words are not always the best answer-pointers. This is the reason we to develop our own search engine instead of a standard one. This envisages future developments when we will maximally use the implicit lexical information and incorporate more reasoning along the lines of contemporary investigations of paraphrases, entailment and different degrees of synonymy.

When the documents are retrieved, they are additionally processed in the following way: first, the keywords (the ones from the question and its variants or synonymical expressions) are selected. Then special partial grammars (implemented as cascaded regular grammars in the CLaRK System) are run within the contexts of the keywords. These grammars use the information about the type of the answer and how it is connected to the keywords. The context of a single keyword (or phrase) can be explored by several different grammars and (potentially) several possible answers. If we found more than one answer we apply some additional constraints to select one of them as result. In case no answer was found, the NIL value is returned.

The implementation of this architecture is done in the CLaRK system. The pattern grammars are still not enough with respect to the different kinds of questions. Thus, for other types of questions the resources that we have for Bulgarian are not suffice for real question answering, and only some opportunistic patterns can be implemented. As we would like to develop the system along the lines of knowledge rich question answering systems we did not try to implement many such opportunistic patterns, but more effort was invested in classification of the contexts that support the answers. Next section is an attempt to characterize the processing that we would like to incorporate in the future developments.

5 Discourse Requirements for Answer Support

As stated in CLEF 2005 guidelines, each type of question has an abstract corresponding answer type, but when the answer is in a real context, there exists a scale with respect to the answer acceptability. And the concrete answer must be mapped against this scale. The change of the context can change the answer grade in the scale. In this section we will try to give some examples of answers supported by different contexts.

We consider the text as consisting of two types of information: (1) ontological classes and relations, and (2) world facts. The ontological part determines generally the topic and the domain of the text. We call the corresponding "minimal" part of ontology implied by the text *ontology of the text*. The world facts represent an instantiation of the ontology in the text. Both types of information are called uniformly 'semantic content of the text'. Both components of the semantic content are connected to the syntactic structure of the text. Any (partial) explication of the semantic content of a text will be called *semantic annotation of the text*[1]. The semantic content of a question includes some required, but underspecified element(s) which has(have) to be specialized by the answer in such a way that the specialization of the semantic content of the question has to be true with respect to the actual world.

We consider a textual element a to be an supported answer of a given question q in the text t if and only if the semantic content of the question with the addition of the semantic annotation of the textual element a is true in the world[2].

Although the above definition is quite vague it gives some ideas about the support that an answer receives from the text in which it is found. The semantic annotation of the answer comprises all the concepts applicable for the textual element of the answer and also all relations in which the element participated as an argument[3]. Of course, if we had the complete semantic annotation of the corpus and the question, it would be relatively easy to find a correct answer of the question into the corpus, if such exists. Unfortunately, such an explication of the semantic annotation of the text is not feasible with the current NLP technology. Thus we are forced to search for an answer using partial semantic annotations. In order to give an idea of the complexity necessary in some cases we would like to mention that the context which has to be explored can vary from a phrase (one NP), to a clause, a sentence, a paragraph, the whole article or even the whole issues. The required knowledge can be linguistic relations, discourse relations, world knowledge, inferences above the semantic annotation.

Here are some examples of dependencies with different contexts and a description of the properties necessary to interpret the relations:

Relations within NP. Bulgarian nominal phrase is very rich in its structure. We will consider the following models:

NP :- NP NP

This model is important for two kinds of questions: definition questions for people and questions for measurement. The first type of question is represented by the abstract question "Koj e Ime-na-chovek?" (Who is Name-of-a-Person?): Koj e Nikolaj Hajtov? (Who is Nikolaj Hajtov?). As it was discussed in [7] some of the possible patterns that can help us to find the answer to the question are: "NP Name", "Name is NP" where the Name is the name from the question and NP constitutes the answer. The first pattern is from the type we consider here. The other one and some more patterns are presented below. Although it is a very simple pattern the quality of the answer extraction depends on the quality of the grammar for nominal phrase. The first NP can be quite complicated and recursive. Here are some examples:

[NP klasikyt] [NP Nikolaj Hajtov]
(the classic Nikolaj Hajtov)
[NP golemiya bylgarski pisatel] [NP Nikolaj Hajtov]

---

1 Defined in this way the semantic annotation could contain also some pragmatic information and actual world knowledge.

2 World such as it is described by the corpus.

3 We consider the case when the answer denotes a relation to be a concept.

(the big Bulgarian writer Nikolaj Hajtov)
[NP zhiviyat klasik na bylgarskata literatura] [NP Nikolaj Hajtov]
(the alive classic of the Bulgarian literature Nikolaj Hajtov)
[CoordNP predsedatel na syyuza na pisatelite i zhiv
klasik na bylgarskata literatura] [NP Nikolaj Hajtov]
(chair of the committee of the union of the writers and alive
classic of the Bulgarian literature Nikolaj Hajtov)

As it can be seen from the examples, the first NP can comprise a head noun and modifiers of different kinds: adjectives, prepositional phrases. It also can exemplify coordination. Thus, in order to process such answers, the system needs to recognize correctly the first NP. This step is hard for a base NP chunker (being nonrecursive), but when it is combined with semantic information and a named-entity module, then the task is solvable. A characteristic for the first NP is that the head noun denotes a human. If such nouns are mapped to ontological characteristics, the work of the tool is facilitated.

Another usage of this NP recursive model concerns measurement questions, such as: "Kolko e prihodyt na "Grijnpijs" za 1999 g.?" (How much is the income of Greenpeace for 1999?). The answers to such questions have the following format: "number", "noun for number", "noun for measurement". For example, "[NP 300 miliona] [NP dolara]" (300 million dollars). The NPs are relatively easy to recognize, but their composition remains unrecognized in many cases and the systems return partial answers like '300 million' or only '300'. However, without the complete measurement information such an answer is not quite correct and is discarded.

Problems arise when there are longer names of organizations with embedded PPs or with contacting PPs which are not part of them. The systems often return some NP, but the thing is that they suggest either the dependant NP as an answer instead of the head one, or an NP, which is a part of a PP not modifying the head NP. An example for the first case is the answer to the question: What is FARC? The system answered 'Columbia' instead of answering 'Revolutionary Armed Forces of Colombia' or at least 'Revolutionary Armed Forces'. An example for the second case is the answer to the question: What is CFOR?. It was 'Bosnia' instead of 'command forces' (in Bosnija).

Another interesting case is when the first NP has the form AP NP where AP is a relational adjective connecting the noun with another noun like: italianski (Italian)− >Italy, ruski (Russian)− >Russia, etc. In this case the answer of questions like "Ot koya strana e FIAT?"(Where does FIAT come from?) or "Na koya strana e prezident Boris Yelcin?" (Of which country Boris Yelcin is the president?) is encoded within the adjective. This means that we should have lexicons, which are interrelated in order to derive the necessary information even when it is indirectly present in the text. Note that this does not hold only within NPs. For example, the answer of the question 'Who was Michael Jackson married to?' could be 'Michael Jackson's ex-wife Debby'. Of course, here the relation is more complex, because there is a relation not only between 'marry' and 'wife', but also temporal mapping between 'was married' and 'ex-wife'.

NP :- (Parenthetical NP) | (NP Parenthetical)
Such NP patterns are relevant for definition questions about the extensions of acronyms: Kakvo e BMW? (What is BMW?). Very often the answers are presented in the form of an NP, which is the full name of the organization and the corresponding acronym is given as a parenthetical expression in brackets, or the opposite. In this case two gazetteers: of acronyms and the corresponding organization names would be of help. Additionally, we have to rely on opportunistic methods as well, because it is not possible to have all the new occurrences in pre-compiled repositories. Then, the case with the extension as parenthesis is easier to handle than the opposite case. Recall the problems with defining the boundaries of a complex name.

NP :- NP RelClauss
Here the main relations are expressed via the following relative pronoun. It is a kind of local coreference. Let us consider the example: 'Mr Murdoch, who is the owner of several newspapers'. We can trace who is Murdoch through the relative clause. However, sometimes it might be tricky, because in complex NPs we do not know whether the relative clause modifies the head NP or the dependant one. For example, in the phrase: 'the refugee camp in the city, which is the biggest in the country', we cannot know whether the camp or the city is the biggest in the country.

Relations within a clause (sentence). In order to derive the relevant information, very often we need the availability of relations among paraphrases of the same event. This idea was discussed in [1], [2] and [3] among others. For that task, however, the corpus should be annotated with verb frames and the grammatical roles of their arguments. Additionally, lists of possible adjuncts are also needed, because they are mapped as answer types to questions for time, measure, location, manner. Thus we have to go beyond the argument structure annotation. The ideal lexical repository should include relations between semantic units, such as if something is a location, you can measure distance to it; if something is an artefact, you can measure its cost etc. Also, the classical example with the entailment like: if you write something, then you are its author, can be derived from a rich explanatory dictionary, which is properly parsed.

Discourse relations. They are necessary, when the required information cannot be assessed locally. When some popular politician is discussed in the newspaper, it might be the case that he is addressed only by his name, not the title: 'Yaser Arafat' instead of 'the Palestinian leader Yaser Arafat'. In such cases we need to navigate through wider context and then the marked coreferential relations become a must: Yaser Arafat is mentioned in the sentence, then in the next one he is referred to as 'the Palestinian leader' and finally, as 'he'. Here we could rely on anaphora resolution tools and on some gathered encyclopedic knowledge.

World knowledge. We usually rely on our world knowledge when there is more specific information in the questions and more general in the candidate answers. For example, to the question 'Who is Diego Armando Maradona?' we found answers only about 'Diego Maradona' or 'Maradona'. For this case we could be sure that all these names belong to the same person. However, there could be trickier cases like both Bush - father and son. If the marker 'junior' or 'senior' is not there, then we have to rely on other supportive markers like temporal information or some events that are connected with the one or the other.

6 Results and Outlook

The result from our Bulgarian-Bulgarian QA track can be viewed as a preliminary test of our QA system. We got the following statistics: 37 out of the 200 extracted answers were correct, 160 were wrong and 3 inexact. The distribution of the correct answers among the question categories is as follows: 21 definition questions: 13 for organizations and 8 for persons; 16 factoid questions: 2 for locations, 2 for measure, 1 for organizations, 2 for other categories, 2 for persons, and 3 for time. For the temporal restricted questions: 2 for locations and 2 for organizations.

Our plans for future work are to build on our experience from CLEF 2005 participation. We plan to implement more pattern grammars and to enrich the resources for Bulgarian in two aspects: (1) qualitative – better integration of the available resources and tools, and (2) quantitative – creation of more support grammars for the off-line procedure.

References

1. Ido Dagan and Oren Glickman. Probabilistic Textual Entailment: Generic Applied Modeling of Language Variability. Learning Methods for Text Understanding and Mining Workshop. (2004)
2. Milen Kouylekov and Bernardo Magnini. Recognizing Textual Entailment with Tree Edit Distance Algorithms. PASCAL Challenges Workshop. (2005)
3. Dekang Lin and Patrick Pantel. Discovery of Inference Rules for Question Answering. In: Natural Language Engineering 7(4). (2001) 343–360
4. Matteo Negri, Hristo Tanev and Bernardo Magnini. Bridging Languages for Question Answering: DIOGENE at CLEF-2003. Proceedings of CLEF-2003, Norway. (2003) 321–330
5. Petya Osenova, Alexander Simov, Kiril Simov, Hristo Tanev, and Milen Kouylekov. Bulgarian-English Question Answering: Adaptation of Language Resources. In: (Peters, Clough, Gonzalo, Jones, Kluck, and Magnini eds.) Fifth Workshop of the Cross–Language Evaluation Forum (CLEF 2004), Lecture Notes in Computer Science (LNCS), Springer, Heidelberg, Germany. (2005)
6. Kiril Simov, Zdravko Peev, Milen Kouylekov, Alexander Simov, Marin Dimitrov and Atanas Kiryakov. CLaRK — an XML-based System for Corpora Development. Proceedings of the Corpus Linguistics 2001 Conference. (2001) 558–560.
7. Hristo Tanev. Socrates: A Question Answering Prototype for Bulgarian. In: Proceedings of RANLP 2003, Bulgaria. (2003) 460–466

The Query Answering System PRODICOS

Laura Monceaux, Christine Jacquin, and Emmanuel Desmontils

Université de Nantes, Laboratoire LINA,
2 rue de la Houssinière, BP92208,
44322 Nantes cedex 03,
France
{christine.jacquin, laura.monceaux, emmanuel.desmontils}@univ-nantes.fr

Abstract. In this paper, we present the PRODICOS query answering system which was developed by the TALN team from the LINA institute. We present the various modules constituting our system and for each of them the evaluation is shown. Afterwards, for each of them, the evaluation is put forward to justify the results obtained. Then, we present the main improvement based on the use of semantic data.

1 Introduction

In this paper, we present the PRODICOS query answering system which was developed by the TALN team from the LINA institute. It was our first participation to the CLEF evaluation campaign. We had decided to participate to the monolingual evaluation task dedicated to the French language. This campaign enables us to analyse the performances of our system. Firstly, we present the various modules constituting our system and for all of them, the evaluation is shown. Afterwards, for each of them, the evaluation is put forward to justify the results obtained. Secondly, we present the expected improvement based on used of semantic data: the EuroWordnet thesaurus [1] and topic signatures [2].

2 Overview of the System Architecture

The PRODICOS query answering system is divided into three parts (figure 1):

- question analysis module;
- sentence extraction module (extracts sentences which might contain the answer);
- answer extraction module (extracts the answer according to the results provided by the previous module).

The modules of the PRODICOS system are based on the use of linguistic knowledge, in particular lexical knowledge coming from the EuroWordnet thesaurus [1] and syntactic knowledge coming from a syntactic chunker which has been developed by our team (by the use of the TreeTagger tool [3]).

C. Peters et al. (Eds.): CLEF 2005, LNCS 4022, pp. 527–534, 2006.

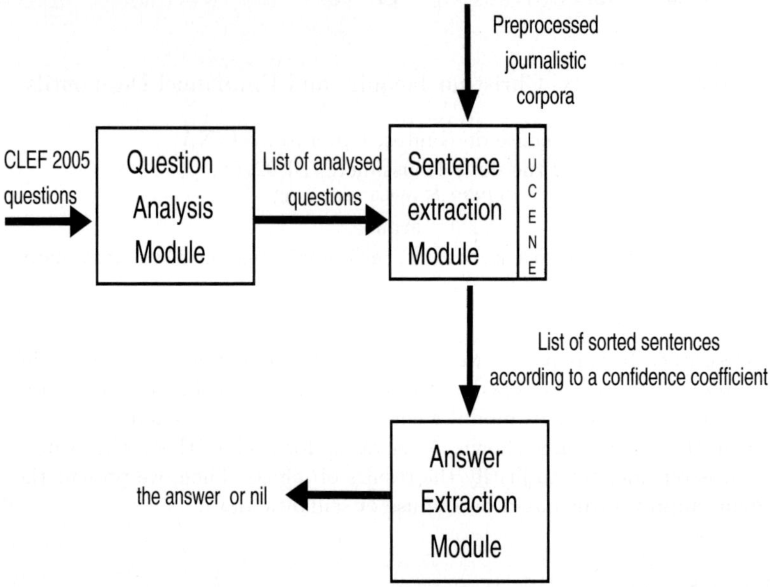

Fig. 1. The PRODICOS System

The system has participated to the CLEF 2005 evaluation campaign for the monolingual query answering task dedicated to the french language. This campaign enables us to make a first evaluation of the system. It allows us to compute the performances of the various modules of the system in order to analyse their weaknesses and the possible need of semantic knowledge. We present, in the next sections, in greater detail, the various modules which belong to the PRODICOS system and the linguistic tools used to implement them. In parallel, we analyse in detail the results for each system module.

3 Question Analysis Module

The question analysis module aims to extract relevant features from questions that will make it possible to guide the answer search. The strategy for performing an answer search depends on the question type. Indeed, searching the right answer to a definition question like "*Qu'est ce que les FARC ?*" will be completely different as performing the same search on a factual question like "*Qui a tué Lee Harvey Oswald ?*". The first and main feature which comes from the question analysis is then the question type. It will not only help to determine the strategy to perform an answer search but also it will make it possible to select rules to extract other important features from questions (answer type, question focus). We defined twenty question types which correspond to a simplified syntactic form of the question[1] (for example the type `QuiVerbeGN`). The question type makes also it possible to verify the answer type that will be retrieved. The answer type may be a named entity (Person, Location-State, Location-City, Organization...), or a numerical entity (Date, Length, Weight, Financial-Amount...). The question focus corresponds to a word or a word group involved in the question. Its main particularity is that, generally around it, the answer is present within the passages which may contain the answer.

In order to construct these rules, some other rules were written based on syntactic and semantic knowledge. Indeed, by using TreeTagger tool, we built rules making it possible to extract the questions chunk (noun phrase,adjective phrase, adverb phrase, prepositional phrase, verb phrase). According to the obtained syntactic chunks, we have written rules which make it possible to extract, from the questions, information like question focus, principal verb,... [5]. Concerning semantics, with the help of EuroWordnet Thesaurus, we built lists of words which are hyponyms of some predefined words which are considered as categories. For example, president, singer, director... are hyponyms of person. These lists enable us to identify for certain question type the answer type. For example, for the question "*Quel est le premier ministre de la France ?*" (answer type: `QuelEtreGN`), the word "*ministre*" (head of the noun phrase: "*premier ministre*") makes it possible to determine that the answer type must be a person.

For example, if the question is "*Qui a construit le Reichstag à Berlin ?*", the analysis of this question is:

1. Question type: `QUI`
2. Answer type: `PERSON`, `ORGANIZATION`
3. Focus: *Reichstag*
4. Chunks segmentation: `<GN>` *Qui* `<GN>` `<NV>` *a construit* `</NV>` `</GN>` *le Reichstag* `</GN>` `<GP>` *à Berlin* `</GP>` ?
   (GN: nominal group, NV: verbal group, GP: prepositional group)
5. Verb: *construire*
6. Proper nouns: *Berlin, Reichstag*

We evaluated the question analysis by calculating, for each extracted information, the percentage of correct features (table 1).

For each information type, the rate of correct information is satisfactory (higher than 74%). Mistakes encountered in the question focus determination were generated by the chunking process. Most of the time, they come from an incomplete recognition of word groups but rarely from a bad tagging of a word group. Mistakes concerning answer type come from a lack of semantic information or the use of some incorrect rules.

4 Sentence Extraction Module

The goal of this module is to extract from the journalistic corpora the most relevant sentences which seem to answer to the question (ie, the sentences which

[1] excepted for definitional questions [5].

Table 1. Evaluation of the question analysis module

Information	Percentage
Question type	99.0
Answer type	74.0
Verb	83.5
Question focus	74.5

might contain the answer). Firstly, the corpora are processed and marked with XML annotation in order to locate the beginning and the end of the article and of the sentences. The corpora are then annotated with part-of-speech and lemma by using the TreeTagger tool.

Then, the corpora are indexed by the Lucene search engine [11]. The indexing unit used is the sentence. For each question, we then build a Lucene request according to the data generated by the question analysis step. The request is built according to a combination of some elements linked with the "or" boolean operator. The elements are: question focus, named entities, principal verbs, common nouns, adjectives, numerical entities.

For a particular request, the sentence extraction module provides a sorted sentence list which answers to the request. The sort criterion is a confidence coefficient associated with each sentence in the list. It is determined according to the number and the category of the question elements which are found in sentences. For example, if the question focus belongs to a sentence, the confidence coefficient of this sentence is high, because the question focus is very important for the answer extraction step. Experimentally, we have defined the weight of each category, they are given in table 2. The confidence coefficient is computed by summing all the weights linked to the elements found in a selected sentence. It is then normalized. The confidence coefficient belongs to the value interval $[0, 1]$. When the sentence extraction module stops, only the 70 sentences with the highest confidence coefficient are kept.

After the CLEF 2005 evaluation campaign, we have studied the position of the first sentences, belonging to the list of returned sentences, which contain the right answer (we except the queries whose answer was NIL) (table 3).

As conclusion, we argue that (for queries whose answers are not NIL) more than 63% of them are available in the 5 first ones of the result set. This seems

Table 2. Weight associated with question elements

Element category	Weight
question focus	40
named entities	40
principal verb	15
common noun	10
cardinal number	10
adjective	10

Table 3. Sentence extraction process evaluation

Sentence position	Percentage of present answer
first sentence	40.9
2-5 sentences	22.7
6-10 sentences	9.4
+10 sentences	9.4
no sentences	17.6

to be a satisfactory result. But, have we obtained so good results because of the strategy used to build the CLEF 2005 queries? Indeed, answers are often situated in sentences which contain the same words as those used for the queries.

Before this evaluation campaign, we planned to use semantic information in order to improve the sentence extraction process. But after these satisfactory obtained results, we doubt of the systematical use of semantics for improving this process. Indeed, the systematical use of semantics leads possibly to have more noise in the results. We are now working in this direction in order to determine, in which cases the use of semantics brings noise in the result and in which cases semantics helps to determine sentences which contain the right answer. In this aim, we are studying the contribution of topic signature techniques (we present this technique at the end of this article).

For the next campaign, we plan to study more in detail, the elements which would constitute the Lucene requests. The results would also be improved if we take into account the noun phrases in the requests (for example "*tour eiffel*" or "*Michel Bon*"). For this evaluation, in the case of the second noun phrase, the process provides the sentence: "*Les ingrats en seront pour leurs frais : Michel Huet va ici jusqu'à décerner, preuves à l'appui la présence de plusieurs espéces de lichens sur les pierres de Notre-Dame, un brevet de bonne conduite à l'atmosphére parisienne !*". However, the process retrieves separately the named entity "*Michel*" and the adjective "*Bon*". This sentence is not an answer to the request, but this error occurs because the noun phrase is not used as a request element.

Finally, the results would also be improved, if this module did not only provide sentences as results but also passages (ie a set of sentence). For some questions, we could then use a reference tool in order to find the answer to the question.

5 Answer Extraction Module

We have developped two strategies to extract the answer to questions:

- when the answer type was been determined by the question analysis step, the process extracts, from the list of sentences provided by the previous step, the named entities or the numerical entities closest to the question focus (if this last is detected). Indeed, the answer is often situated close to the question focus. For locating named entities, NEMESIS tool [6] is used. It was developed by our research team. Nemesis is a french proper name recognizer for large-scale information extraction, whose specifications have been elaborated through corpus investigation both in terms of referential categories and graphical structures. The graphical criteria are used to identify proper names and the referential classification to categorize them. The system is a classical one: it is rule-based and uses specialized lexicons without any linguistic preprocessing. Its originality consists on a modular architecture which includes a learning process.

- when the answer type is not available, the process uses syntactical patterns in order to extract answers. Indeed, according to the question type, certain syntactical patterns can be employed. These patterns were built by taking into account the presence of the question focus and its place compared to the answer. For example, for the question "*Qu'est ce que les FARC ?*" whose category is definitional, the system uses the following pattern: `GNRep ( GNFocus )`. We give here an example of sentence where the system applies the previous pattern in order to find an answer: "*Les deux groupes de guérilla toujours actifs,* `<GNRep>` *les Forces armées révolutionnaires de Colombie* `</GNRep>` (`<GNFocus>` *FARC* `</GNFocus>`) *et , dans une moindre mesure , l'Armée de libération nationale (ELN, castriste) exécutent des paysans accusés d'être des informateurs ou des guérilleros ayant déposé les armes.*". According to the pattern, the system extracts the answer ("*Les Forces armées révolutionnaires de Colombie*").

Following our system evaluation for the french monolingual task, we have obtained the following results:

Table 4. Evaluation of the question answering system

Answer type	Number of right answer
Numerical entity	7
Named entity	14
NIL	3
Definition	3
Other queries	2

The results are not satisfactory, because we only recover 29 correct answers. After analysing the results, we observed that the majority of correct answers correspond to queries whose answers were a named entity or a numerical entity. Moreover, as seen in paragraph 3, for the question analysis step, 26% of the answer types for definitional questions were incorrect. We can then easily improve the process for these question types. On the other hand, the use of syntactic patterns is not satisfactory for the system for several reasons:

- the chunk analyser is not complete;
- the syntactic patterns were built according to learning techniques. The process has been trained on a restricted set of questions(100) coming from an

old evaluation campaign. Then, some question types were not linked to their own answer extraction patterns;
– we do not use semantic patterns in order to extract answers.

6 Conclusion and Prospects

The system has not obtained a high number of correct answers, but it was its first evaluation campaign. The interest for this participation is to highlight changes which can easily improve the system results. Twenty-five questions among the proposed questions were particular definitional questions. For these questions, the answer was the meaning of an abbreviation. If we used an abbreviation recognizer, we would be able to answer to 19 of these question types (the 6 others are abbreviations coming from a foreign language and whose meaning is given in french in the retrieved sentences). The syntactic patterns, used in the answer extraction module, do not cover the totality of the question types set. Indeed, the learning process was performed on a small sample of questions (100) coming from old evaluation campaigns. Several types of question were not present in this sample. The major improvement was to perform the learning process on an other more complete sample and also to add new syntactic patterns manually.

Prospectively, we will be studying the use of semantics in order to improve the query answering system by the use of semantics based techniques.

The Wordnet thesaurus is often used for semantic processing of textual data. One of the principal difficulties is to determine "the right sense" for polysemous terms. In spite of a weak rate of polysemia in Wordnet (approximately 18%), in practice, the need to disambiguate terms is frequent (78% of the terms are polysemous in a corpus like SemCor) [7]. Methods to disambiguate a term are numerous [9]. These methods, although powerful, appear limited when the context is small or the structure is weak. A method seems interesting in these situations: the use of the topic signatures [8].

This method, like others [10], uses the Web as a corpus. The first step to disambiguate a term is to build a corpora of HTML documents associated with each sense of this polysemous term. From these corpora, sets of terms are associated with all the different senses of the polysemous term. Then, either by using the X2 function [8] or by using the tf.idf measure [2], the sets are reduced according to the terms which make it possible to discriminate the senses of the polysemous term: the topic signatures.

From these topic signatures, it is then possible to determine the sense of a term according to its context. Regarding QA systems, we think that topic signatures make it possible to improve the process at various levels. Firstly, during the analysis of the question, it makes it possible to improve the disambiguation of the terms. Indeed, the very poor context of the question does not always make it possible to decide which is the correct sense. Secondly, the set of terms associated with a given sense makes it possible to improve the request provided to the search engine and also to optimize the identification of the passages where the answer might be found.

References

1. Vossen P. : "EuroWordNet: A Multilingual Database with Lexical Semantic", editor Networks Piek Vossen, university of Amsterdam, 1998.
2. Agirre E., Lopez de Lacalle O. : "topic signature for all WordNet nominal senses", Publicly available, LREC 2004.
3. Schmid H. "Improvements in Part-of-Speech Tagging with an Application To German". In Armstrong, S., Chuch, K. W., Isabelle P., Tzoukermann, E. & Yarowski, D. (Eds.), NaturalLanguage Processing Using Very Large Corpora, Dordrecht: Kluwer Academic Publisher.1999
4. Fellbaum, C. (1998). WordNet: An Electronic Lexical Database. Cambridge, MA: MIT Press.
5. Monceaux L. : "Adaptation du niveau d'analyse des interventions dans un dialogue - application à un système de question - réponse", These en informatique, Paris Sud, ORSAY, LIMSI (2003)
6. Fourour, N. : "Identification et catégorisation automatiques des entités nommées dans les textes franais", These en informatique, Nantes, LINA(2004)
7. De Loupy C. : "Evaluation des taux de synonymie et de polysḿie dans un texte", TALN2002, Nancy, pp.225-234
8. Agirre E., Ansa 0., Hovy E., Martinez D. : "Enriching very large ontologies using WWW.", Proceeding of the Ontology Learning Workshop ECAI 2000
9. Ide N., Véronis J.: Word Sense Disambiguation: The State of the Art. Computational Linguistics, 1998, 24(1)
10. Mihalcea R., Moldovan D.I. : "An Automatic Method for Generating Sense Tagged Corpora.", Proceeding of AAAI'99, 1999, pp. 461-466
11. Lucene search engine: http://lucene.apache.org/java/docs/

The CLEF 2005 Cross–Language Image Retrieval Track

Paul Clough[1], Henning Müller[2], Thomas Deselaers[3], Michael Grubinger[4], Thomas M. Lehmann[5], Jeffery Jensen[6], and William Hersh[6]

[1] Department of Information Studies, Sheffield University, Sheffield, UK
p.d.clough@sheffield.ac.uk
[2] Medical Informatics Service, Geneva University and Hospitals, Geneva Switzerland
henning.mueller@sim.hcuge.ch
[3] Lehrstuhl für Informatik VI, RWTH Aachen, Germany
deselaers@cs.rwth-aachen.de
[4] School of Computer Science and Mathematics, Victoria University, Australia
michael.grubinger@research.vu.edu.au
[5] Department of Medical Informatics, Medical Faculty, RWTH Aachen, Germany
lehmann@computer.org
[6] Biomedical Informatics, Oregon Health and Science University, Portland, OR, USA
hersh@ohsu.edu, jensejef@ohsu.edu

Abstract. This paper outlines efforts from the 2005 CLEF cross–language image retrieval campaign (ImageCLEF). Aim of the CLEF track is to explore the use of both text and content–based retrieval methods for cross–language image retrieval. Four tasks were offered in ImageCLEF: ad–hoc retrieval from an historic photographic collection, ad–hoc retrieval from a medical collection, an automatic image annotation task, and a user–centered (interactive) evaluation task. 24 research groups from a variety of backgrounds and nationalities (14 countries) participated in ImageCLEF. This paper presents the ImageCLEF tasks, submissions from participating groups and a summary of the main findings.

1 Introduction

ImageCLEF[1] conducts evaluation of cross–language image retrieval and is run as part of the Cross Language Evaluation Forum (CLEF) campaign. The ImageCLEF retrieval benchmark was previously run in 2003 [1] and 2004 [2] with the aim of evaluating image retrieval from multilingual document collections. Images by their very nature are language independent, but often they are accompanied by texts semantically related to the image (e.g. textual captions or metadata). Images can then be retrieved using primitive features based on pixels which form the contents of an image (e.g. using a visual exemplar), abstracted features expressed through text, or a combination of both. The language used to express the associated texts or textual queries should not affect retrieval, i.e.

[1] See http://ir.shef.ac.uk/imageclef/

C. Peters et al. (Eds.): CLEF 2005, LNCS 4022, pp. 535–557, 2006.

an image with a caption written in English should be searchable in languages other than English.

ImageCLEF 2005 provided tasks for system–centered evaluation of retrieval systems in two domains: historic photographs and medical images. These domains offer realistic (and different) scenarios in which to test the performance of image retrieval systems and offer different challenges and problems to participants. A user–centered search task was also run using the same historic photographs, and is further described in the interactive CLEF (iCLEF) overview [3]. A major goal of ImageCLEF is to investigate the effectiveness of combining text and image for retrieval and promote the exchange of ideas which may help improve the performance of future image retrieval systems.

ImageCLEF has already seen participation from both academic and commercial research groups worldwide from communities including: Cross–Language Information Retrieval (CLIR), Content–Based Image Retrieval (CBIR), medical information retrieval and user interaction. We provide participants with the following: image collections, representative search requests (expressed by both image and text) and relevance judgements indicating which images are relevant to each search request. Campaigns such as CLEF and TREC have proven invaluable in providing standardised resources for comparative evaluation for a range of retrieval tasks and ImageCLEF aims to provide the research community with similar resources for image retrieval. In the following sections of this paper we describe separately each search task: Section 2 describes ad–hoc retrieval from historic photographs, Section 3 ad–hoc retrieval from medical images, and Section 4 the automatic annotation of medical images. For each we briefly describe the test collections, the search tasks, participating research groups, results and a summary of the main findings.

2 Ad–Hoc Retrieval from Historic Photographs

Similar to previous years (see, e.g. [2]), the goal of this task is: given multilingual text queries, retrieve as many relevant images as possible from the provided image collection (the St. Andrews collection of historic photographs[2]). Queries for images based on abstract concepts rather than visual features are predominant in this task, thereby limiting the success of using visual retrieval methods alone. Either these concepts cannot be extracted using visual features and require extra external semantic knowledge (e.g. the name of the photographer), or images with different visual properties may be relevant to a search request (e.g. different views of a city). However based on feedback from participants in 2004, search tasks for 2005 were chosen to reflect more visually–based queries.

2.1 Data and Search Tasks

The St. Andrews collection consists of 28,133 images, all of which have associated structured captions written in British English (the target language). The captions consist of 8 fields (shown in Figure 1), and further examples can be found

[2] `http://specialcollections.st-and.ac.uk/photcol.htm`

Short title: Rev William Swan.
Long title: Rev William Swan.
Location: Fife, Scotland
Description: Seated, 3/ 4 face studio portrait of a man.
Date: ca.1850
Photographer: Thomas Rodger
Categories: [ministers][identified male][dress - clerical]
Notes: ALB6-85-2 jf/ pcBIOG: Rev William Swan ( ) ADD: Former owners of album: A Govan then J J? Lowson. Individuals and other subjects indicative of St Andrews provenance. By T. R. as identi ed by Karen A. Johnstone " Thomas Rodger 1832-1883. A biography and catalogue of selected works".

Fig. 1. An example image and caption from the St. Andrews collection

in [4] and the St. Andrews University Library[3]. Participants were given 28 topics, the main themes based on the analysis of log files from a web server at St. Andrews university, knowledge of the collection and discussions with maintainers of the image collection. After identifying main themes, queries were modified to test various aspects of cross-language and visual search. A custom–built IR system was used to identify suitable topics (in particular those topics with an estimated 20 and above relevant images). A complexity score was developed by the authors to categorise topics with respect to linguistic complexity [5].

Each topic consisted a title (a short sentence or phrase describing the search request in a few words), and a narrative (a description of what constitutes a relevant or non–relevant image for that search request). Two example images per topic were also provided, the envisaged uses being to test relevance feedback (both manual and automatic) and query–by–example searches[4]. Both topic title and narratives were translated into the following languages: German, French, Italian, Spanish (European), Spanish (Latin American), Chinese (Simplified), Chinese (Traditional) and Japanese. Translations of title only were also generated for 25 languages including: Russian, Croatian, Bulgarian, Hebrew and Norwegian. All translations were provided by native speakers and verified by at least one other native speaker.

2.2 Relevance Assessments

Relevance assessments were performed by staff at the University of Sheffield in a manner similar to previous years (see [1,2]). The top 50 results from all submitted runs were used to create image pools giving an average of 1,376 (max: 2,193 and min: 760) images to judge per topic. The authors judged all topics to create a "gold standard" and at least two further assessments were obtained for each topic. Assessors used a custom–built tool to make judgements accessible on–line enabling them to log in when and where convenient. Assessors were asked to judge every image in the topic pool, but also to use interactive search and judge: searching the collection using their own queries to supplement the image pools with further relevant images.

[3] `http://www-library.st-andrews.ac.uk/`

[4] See `http://ir.shef.ac.uk/imageclef2005/adhoc.htm` for an example.

Assessments were based on a ternary classification scheme: (1) relevant, (2) partially relevant and (3) not relevant. Based on these judgements, various combinations were used to create the set of relevant images (qrels). As in previous years we used the `pisec-total` set: those images judged as relevant or partially–relevant by the topic creator and at least one other assessor.

2.3 Participating Groups

In total, 19 groups registered for this task and 11 submitted results (including 5 new groups compared to last year) giving a total of 349 runs (all of which were evaluated). Participants were given queries and relevance judgements from 2004 as training data and access to a CBIR system (GIFT/Viper). Descriptions of individual techniques used can be found in descriptions by the participants:

- CEA from France [6]
- National Institute of Informatics (NII) from Japan [7]
- University of Alicante (Computer Science) from Spain [8]
- Chinese University of Hong Kong (CUHK) [9]
- Dublin City University (DCU - Computer Science) from Ireland [10]
- University Hospitals Geneva from Switzerland [11]
- University of Indonesia (Computer Science) [12]
- Daedalus and Madrid University from Spain (Miracle) [13]
- National Taiwan University (NTU) from Taiwan [14]
- University of Jaén (Intelligent Systems) from Spain [15]
- UNED from Spain [16]

In summary, five groups experimented with combining both text and visual runs [6,9,10,12,14]. Groups experimented with merging visual and textual runs [10,12,14], and using visual runs to reorder the text runs [6,9]. Purely visual runs were submitted by University Hospitals Geneva [11] and NTU [14] and provide a visual baseline against which to compare mixed approaches.

Most groups made use of relevance feedback (in the form of pseudo relevance feedback) to perform query expansion and improve subsequent runs. Of particular interest are: NII who used a learned word association model to improve a language model [7], Alicante who used an ontology created automatically created from the St. Andrews collection to relate a query with several image categories [8] and UNED who experimented with creating structured queries based on identifying named entities in the caption fields [16].

Some groups focused on dealing with specific languages (e.g. Chinese [14], Japanese [7], Spanish [16] and Indonesian [12]); others used generic tools (e.g. freely available MT systems) to tackle larger numbers of languages [8,13]. A voting-based strategy was developed joining three different systems of participating universities: University of Alicante, University of Jaén and UNED [8].

Participants were asked to categorise their submissions by the following dimensions: query language, type (automatic or manual), use of feedback (typically relevance feedback is used for automatic query expansion), modality (text only, image only or combined) and the initial query (visual only, title only, narrative

Table 1. Ad–hoc experiments listed by query language

Query Language	#Runs	#Participants
English	69	9
Spanish (Latinamerican)	36	4
German	29	5
Spanish (European)	28	6
Chinese (simplified)	21	4
Italian	19	4
French	17	5
Japanese	16	4
Dutch	15	4
Russian	15	4
Portuguese	12	3
Greek	9	3
Indonesian	9	1
Chinese (traditional)	8	2
Swedish	7	2
Filipino	5	1
Norwegian	5	1
Polish	5	1
Romanian	5	1
Turkish	5	1
Visual	4	2
Bulgarian	2	1
Croatian	2	1
Czech	2	1
Finnish	2	1
Hungarian	2	1

only or a combination). A summary of submissions by these dimensions is shown in Table 3. No manual runs were submitted, and a large proportion of text runs used only information from the titles. Table 1 provides a summary of submissions by query language. At least one group submitted for each language [13], the most popular (non-English)being French, German and Spanish (European).

2.4 Results

Results for submitted runs were computed using the latest version of trec_eval[5] from NIST (v7.3). Submissions were evaluated using uninterpolated Mean Average Precision (MAP), Precision at rank 10 (P10), and the number of relevant images retrieved (RelRetr) from which we compute recall (the proportion of relevant retrieved). Table 2 summarises the top performing systems in the ad–hoc task by language based on MAP. The highest English (monolingual) retrieval score is 0.4135, with a P10 of 0.5500 and recall of 0.8434. The relatively high recall score, but low MAP and P10 scores indicate that relevant images are being retrieved at lower rank positions. The highest monolingual score is obtained using combined visual and text retrieval and relevance feedback (see [9]).

The highest cross–language MAP is Chinese (traditional) for the NTU submission which is 97% of highest monolingual score. Retrieval performance is variable across language with some performing poorly, e.g. Romanian, Bulgarian, Czech, Croatian, Finnish and Hungarian. Although these languages did not

[5] http://trec.nist.gov/trec_eval/trec_eval.7.3.tar.gz

Table 2. Systems with highest MAP for each language in the ad–hoc retrieval task

Language	MAP	Recall	Group	Run ID	Init. Query	Feedback	Modality
English	0.4135	0.5500	CUHK	CUHK-ad-eng-tv-kl-jm2	title+img	with	text+img
Chinese (Trad)	0.3993	0.7526	NTU	NTU-CE-TN-WEprf-Ponly	title+narr	with	text+img
Spanish (Lat)	0.3447	0.7891	Alicante, Jaen	R2D2vot2SpL	title	with	text
Dutch	0.3435	0.4821	Alicante, Jaen	R2D2vot2Du	title	with	text
German	0.3375	0.4929	Alicante, Jaen	R2D2vot2Ge	title	with	text
Spanish (Euro)	0.3175	0.8048	UNED	unedESENent	title	with	text
Portuguese	0.3073	0.7542	Miracle	imirt0attrpt	title	without	text
Greek	0.3024	0.6383	DCU	DCUFbTGR	title	with	text
French	0.2864	0.7322	Jaen	SinaiFrTitleNarrFBSystran	title+narr	with	text
Japanese	0.2811	0.7333	Alicante	AlCimg05Exp3Jp	title	with	text
Russian	0.2798	0.6879	DCU	DCUFbTRU	title	with	text
Italian	0.2468	0.6227	Miracle	imirt0attrit	title	without	text
Chinese (Sim)	0.2305	0.6153	Alicante	AlCimg05Exp3ChS	title	with	text
Indonesian	0.2290	0.6566	Indonesia	UI-T-IMG	title	without	text+img
Turkish	0.2225	0.6320	Miracle	imirt0allftk	title	without	text
Swedish	0.2074	0.5647	Jaen	SinaiSweTitleNarrFBWordlingo	title	without	text
Norwegian	0.1610	0.4530	Miracle	imirt0attrno	title	without	text
Filipino	0.1486	0.3695	Miracle	imirt0allffl	title	without	text
Polish	0.1558	0.5073	Miracle	imirt0attrpo	title	without	text
Romanian	0.1429	0.3747	Miracle	imirt0attrro	title	without	text
Bulgarian	0.1293	0.5694	Miracle	imirt0allfbu	title	without	text
Czech	0.1219	0.5310	Miracle	imirt0allfcz	title	without	text
Croatian	0.1187	0.4362	Miracle	imirt0attrcr	title	without	text
Finnish	0.1114	0.3257	Miracle	imirt0attrfi	title	without	text
Hungarian	0.0968	0.3789	Miracle	imirt0allfhu	title	without	text
Visual	0.0829	0.2834	Geneva	GE_A_88	visual	without	img

have translated narratives available for retrieval, it is more likely low performance results from limited availability of translation and language processing resources and difficult language structure (e.g. results from CLEF 2004 showed Finnish to be a very challenging language due to its complex morphology). Hungarian performs the worst at 23% of monolingual, however it is encouraging to see participation in CLEF for these languages. On average, MAP for English is 0.2840 (P10=0.3933 and Recall=0.6454) and across all languages MAP is 0.2027 (P10=0.2985 and Recall=0.5737) – see Table 3. Using the Mann-Whitney U test for two-independent samples, this difference is significant (at $p < 0.05$).

Table 3 shows the average MAP score averaged across all submissions by query dimension. We also include standard deviation (SD), median and highest MAP scores because the arithmetic mean is distorted by outliers in the data distribution. There is also a wide variation in counts for each dimension, therefore results are only an indication of effects on performance for each dimension.

From Table 3, it would appear that runs using some kind of feedback (e.g. query expansion) perform approximately 14.8% better than those without. From Figure 3 this appears true for individual topics also and mean differences are significant at $p < 0.05$. Also from Table 3 it appears that combined text and visual runs perform on average 31.5% better than text runs alone (based on average MAP). However, low retrieval scores due to translation draw the text–only results down. If we compare text–only scores for the 5 groups who submitted text and visual runs, the MAP score is 0.2723, approximately 12.1% lower than the combined runs. This difference is significant at $p < 0.05$ using the Mann-Whitney U test. As expected, visual–only runs perform poorly for this task.

2.5 Discussion

The variety of submissions in the ad–hoc task this year has been pleasing with six groups experimenting with both visual and text-based retrieval methods and five

Table 3. MAP results for each query dimension

Dimension	type	#Runs	#Groups	Mean Average Precision (MAP) Mean (SD)	Median	Highest
Language	English	69	9	0.2840 (0.1441)	0.3574	0.4135
	non-English	277	10	0.2027 (0.0784)	0.2143	0.3993
Feedback	yes	142	9	0.2399 (0.1119)	0.2482	0.4135
	no	207	10	0.2043 (0.0887)	0.2069	0.4030
Modality	image	3	2	0.0749 (0.0130)	0.0819	0.0829
	text	318	11	0.2121 (0.0976)	0.2170	0.4115
	text+image	28	5	0.3098 (0.0782)	0.3023	0.4135
Initial Query	image only	4	3	0.1418 (0.1342)	0.0824	0.3425
	title only	274	11	0.2140 (0.0975)	0.2246	0.4115
	narr only	6	2	0.1313 (0.0555)	0.1298	0.1981
	title+narr	57	6	0.2314 (0.0929)	0.2024	0.4083
	title+image	4	1	0.4016 (0.0126)	0.4024	0.4135
	title+narr+image	4	1	0.3953 (0.0153)	0.3953	0.4118

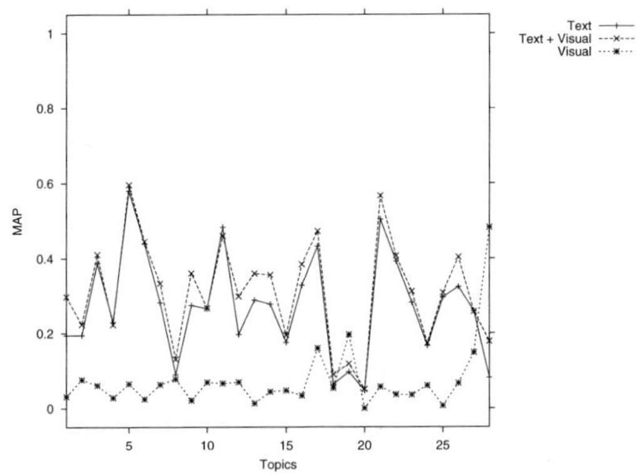

Fig. 2. Comparison between average MAP for visual and text runs from 5 groups using text and visual methods

groups combining the two (although the number of runs submitted as combined is lower than 2004). As in 2004, a combination of text and visual approaches appears to give highest retrieval effectiveness (based on MAP) indicating this is still an area for research.

Considering individual topics, Figure 2 shows improvements for 19 topics based on comparing text–only and text+visual results for the 5 groups who submitted combined runs. In particular we observe clear improvements for topics such as "aircraft on the ground" and "portrait views of mixed sex groups" where a combination of using visual features and semantic knowledge gained from the associated text caption improves over using a single approach. In addition, certain topics do seem better suited to a visual–only approach including topics 28 ("colour pictures of woodland scenes around St. Andrews") and 19 ("composite postcards of Northern Ireland") which obtain the highest MAP results. This begins to indicate the kinds of topics that are likely to perform well and for which visual cues are likely effective for retrieval (i.e. the set of relevant images are themselves visually similar).

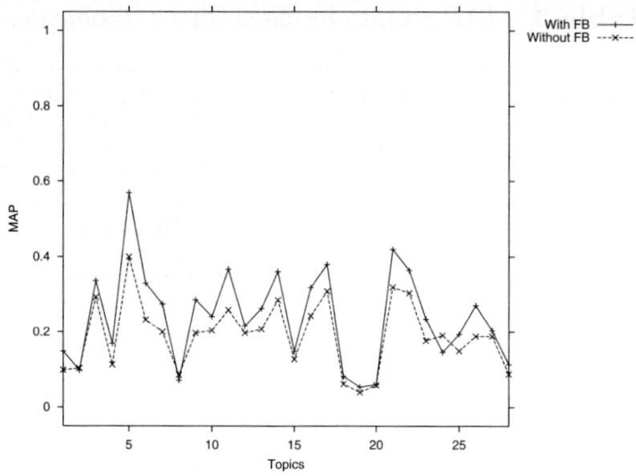

Fig. 3. Comparison between average MAP for runs with/without feedback (FB)

Figure 2 also show that results vary widely across topic, and as expected some are much "harder" than others. For example, topics 8 ("building covered in snow"), 18 ("woman in white dress") and 20 ("royal visits to Scotland (not Fife)") are consistently the lowest scoring topics (based on average and highest MAP scores). The "easiest" topics appear to be topics 5 ("animal statue") and 21 ("monument to poet Robert Burns"). This requires further investigation and we have started analysis based on a measure of topic difficulty [5].

We wanted to offer a wider range of languages in 2005, of which 13 of these obtained runs from at least two groups (compared to 10 in 2004). It would seem that the focus for many groups in 2005 has been translation (and query expansion) with more use made of both title and narrative than 2004. However, it is interesting to see languages such as Chinese (traditional) and Spanish (Latin American) perform above European languages such as French, German and Spanish (European) which performed best in 2004.

Although topics were designed to be more suited to visual retrieval methods (based on comments from participants in 2004), the topics are still dominated by semantics and background knowledge; pure visual similarity still plays a less significant role. The current ad-hoc task is not well-suited to purely visual retrieval because colour information, which typically plays an important role in CBIR, is ineffective due to the nature of the St. Andrews collection (historic photographs). Also unlike typical CBIR benchmarks, the images in the St. Andrews collection are very complex containing both objects in the foreground and background which prove indistinguishable to CBIR methods. Finally, the relevant image set is visually different for some queries (e.g. different views of a city) making visual retrieval methods ineffective. This highlights the importance of using either text-based IR methods on associated metadata alone, or combined with visual features. Relevance feedback (in the form of automatic query expansion) still plays an important role in retrieval as also demonstrated by submissions in 2004: a 17% increase in 2005 and 48% in 2004 (see Figure 3).

We are aware that research in the ad-hoc task using the St. Andrews collection has probably reached a plateau. There are obvious limitations with the existing collection: mainly black and white images, domain-specific vocabulary used in associated captions, restricted retrieval scenario (i.e. searches for historic photographs) and experiments with limited target language (English) are only possible (i.e. cannot test further bilingual pairs). To address these and widen the image collections available to ImageCLEF participants, we have been provided with access to a new collection of images from a personal photographic collection with associated textual descriptions in German and Spanish (as well as English). This is planned for use in the ImageCLEF 2006 ad-hoc task.

3 Ad–Hoc Retrieval from Medical Image Collections

Domain–specific information retrieval is increasingly important, and this holds especially true for the medical field, where patients, clinicians, and researchers have their particular information needs [17]. Whereas information needs and retrieval methods for textual documents have been well researched, there has been little investigation of information needs and search system use for images and other multimedia data [18], even less so in the medical domain. ImageCLEFmed is creating resources to evaluate information retrieval tasks on medical image collections. This process includes the creation of image collections, query tasks, and the definition of correct retrieval results for these tasks for system evaluation. Some of the tasks have been based on surveys of medical professionals and how they use images [19].

Much of the basic structure is similar to the non–medical ad–hoc task, such as the general outline, the evaluation procedure and the relevance assessment tool used. These similarities will not be described in detail in this section.

3.1 Data Sets Used and Query Topics

In 2004, only the Casimage[6] dataset was made available to participants [20], containing almost 9.000 images of 2.000 cases, 26 query topics, and relevance judgements by three medical experts [21]. Casimage is also part of the 2005 collection. Images present in Casimage include mostly radiology modalities, but also photographs, Powerpoint slides and illustrations. Cases are mainly in French, with around 20% being in English and 5% without annotation. For 2005, we were also given permission to use the PEIR[7] (Pathology Education Instructional Resource) database using annotation based on the HEAL[8] project (Health Education Assets Library, mainly Pathology images [22]). This dataset contains over 33.000 images with English annotations, with the annotation being on a per image and not a per case basis as in Casimage. The nuclear medicine database of MIR, the Mallinkrodt Institute of Radiology[9] [23], was also made available to us for ImageCLEFmed. This dataset contains over 2.000 images mainly from

[6] http://www.casimage.com/

[7] http://peir.path.uab.edu/

[8] http://www.healcentral.com/

[9] http://gamma.wustl.edu/home.html

nuclear medicine with annotations provided per case and in English. Finally, the PathoPic[10] collection (Pathology images [24]) was included into our dataset. It contains 9.000 images with extensive annotation on a per image basis in German. Part of the German annotation is translated into English. As such, we were able to use a total of more than 50.000 images, with annotations in three different languages. Through an agreement with the copyright holders, we were able to distribute these images to the participating research groups.

The image topics were based on a small survey administered to clinicians, researchers, educators, students, and librarians at Oregon Health & Science University (OHSU)[19]. Based on this survey, topics for ImageCLEFmed were developed along the following axes:

- Anatomic region shown in the image;
- Image modality (x–ray, CT, MRI, gross pathology, ...);
- Pathology or disease shown in the image;
- abnormal visual observation (eg. enlarged heart).

As the goal was to accommodate both visual and textual research groups, we developed a set of 25 topics containing three different groups of topics: those expected to work most effectively with a visual retrieval system (topics 1–12), those where both text and visual features were expected to perform well (topics 13–23), and semantic topics, where visual features were not expected to improve results (topics 24–25). All query topics were of a higher semantic level than the 2004 ImageCLEF medical topics because the 2005 automatic annotation task provided a testbed for purely visual retrieval/classification. All 25 topics contained one to three images, with one having an image as negative feedback. The topic text was provided with the images in the three languages present in the collections: English, German, and French. An example for a visual query of the first category can be seen in Figure 4.

A query topic requiring more than purely visual features is shown in Figure 5.

3.2 Relevance Judgements

The relevance assessments were performed by graduate students who were also physicians in the OHSU biomedical informatics program. A simple interface was used from previous ImageCLEF relevance assessments. Nine judges, all medical doctors except for one image processing specialist with medical knowledge, performed the relevance judgements. Half of the images for most of topics were judged in duplicate.

To create the pools for the judgements, the first 40 images of each submitted run were used to create pools with an average size of 892 images. The largest pool size was 1.167 and the smallest one 470. It took the judges an average of about three hours to judge the images for a single topic. Compared to the purely visual topics from 2004 (around one hour of judgement per topic containing an average of 950 images), the judgement process took much longer per

[10] http://alf3.urz.unibas.ch/pathopic/intro.htm

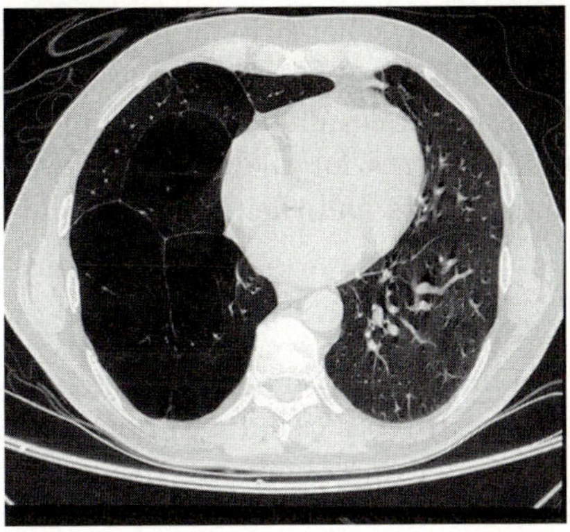

Show me chest CT images with emphysema.
Zeige mir Lungen CTs mit einem Emphysem.
Montre–moi des CTs pulmonaires avec un emphysème.

Fig. 4. An example of a query that is at least partly solvable visually, using the image and the text as query. Still, use of annotation can augment retrieval quality. The query text is presented in three languages.

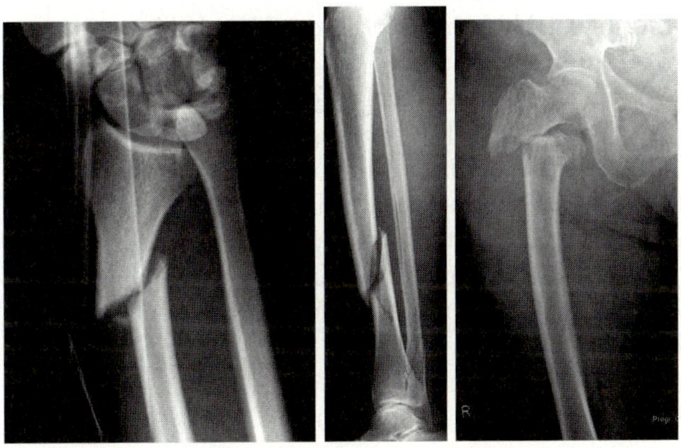

Show me all x–ray images showing fractures.
Zeige mir Röntgenbilder mit Brüchen.
Montres–moi des radiographies avec des fractures.

Fig. 5. A query requiring more than visual retrieval but visual features can deliver hints to good results

image. This was most likely due to the semantic topics requiring the judges to verify the text and/or an enlarged version of the images. The longer time might also be due to the fact that in 2004, all images were pre–marked as irrelevant, and only relevant images required a change, whereas this year we did not have anything pre–marked. Still, this process was generally faster than most text research judgements, and a large number of irrelevant images could be sorted out quickly.

We use a ternary judgement scheme including relevant, partially–relevant, and non–relevant. For the official qrels, we only used images judged as relevant (and not those judged partially relevant). For the topics judged by two persons, we only used the first judgements for the official relevance. (Later we plan to analyse the duplicate judgements and their effect on the results of runs.)

3.3 Participants

The medical retrieval task had 12 participants in 2004 when it was purely visual task and 13 in 2005 as a mixture of visual and non-visual retrieval. Only 13 of the 28 registered groups ended up submitting results, which was likely due to the short time span between delivery of the images and the deadline for results submission. Another reason was that several groups registered very late, as they did not have information about ImageCLEF beforehand, but were still interested in the datasets also for future participations. As the registration to the task was free, they could simply register to get this access.

The following groups registered but were finally not able to submit results for a variety of reasons:

- University of Alicante, Spain
- National Library of Medicine, Bethesda, MD, USA
- University of Montreal, Canada
- University of Science and Medical Informatics, Innsbruck, Austria
- University of Amsterdam, Informatics department, The Netherlands
- UNED, LSI, Valencia, Spain
- Central University, Caracas, Venezuela
- Temple University, Computer science, USA
- Imperial College, Computing lab, UK
- Dublin City University, Computer science, Ireland
- CLIPS Grenoble, France
- University of Sheffield, UK
- Chinese University of Hong Kong, China

In the end, 13 groups (two from the same laboratory but different groups in Singapore) submitted results for the medical retrieval task, including a total of 134 runs. Only 6 manual runs were submitted. Here is a list of their participation including a description of submitted runs:

National Chiao Tung University, Taiwan: submitted 16 runs in total, all automatic. 6 runs were visual only and 10 mixed runs. They use simple visual features (color histogram, coherence matrix, layout features) as well as text retrieval using a vector–space model with word expansion using Wordnet.

State University of New York (SUNY), Buffalo, USA: submitted a total of 6 runs, one visual and five mixed runs. GIFT was used as visual retrieval system and SMART as textual retrieval system, while mapping the text to UMLS.

University and Hospitals of Geneva, Switzerland: submitted a total of 19 runs, all automatic runs. This includes two textual and two visual runs plus 15 mixed runs. The retrieval relied mainly on the GIFT and easyIR retrieval systems.

RWTH Aachen, Computer science, Germany: submitted 10 runs, two being manual mixed retrieval, two automatic textual retrieval, three automatic visual retrieval and three automatic mixed retrieval. Fire was used with varied visual features and a text search engine using English and mixed–language retrieval.

Daedalus and Madrid University, Spain: submitted 14 runs, all automatic. 4 runs were visual only and 10 were mixed runs; They mainly used semantic word expansions with EuroWordNet.

Oregon Health and Science University (OHSU), Portland, OR, USA: submitted three runs in total, two of which were manual. One of the manual runs combined the output from a visual run using the GIFT engine. For text retrieval, the Lucene system was used.

University of Jaen, Spain: had a total of 42 runs, all automatic. 6 runs were textual, only, and 36 were mixed. GIFT is used as a visual query system and the LEMUR system is used for text in a variety of configurations to achieve multilingual retrieval.

Institute for Infocomm research, Singapore: submitted 7 runs, all of them automatic visual runs; For their runs they first manually selected visually similar images to train the features. These runs should probably have been classified as a manual runs. Then, they use a two–step approach for visual retrieval.

Institute for Infocomm research – second group , Singapore: submitted a total of 3 runs, all visual with one being automatic and two manual runs The main technique applied is the connection of medical terms and concepts to visual appearances.

RWTH Aachen – medical informatics, Germany: submitted two visual only runs with several visual features and classification methods of the IRMA project.

CEA, France: submitted five runs, all automatic with two being visual, only and three mixed runs. The techniques used include the PIRIA visual retrieval system and a simple frequency–based text retrieval system.

IPAL CNRS/ I2R, France/Singapore: submitted a total of 6 runs, all automatic with two being text only and the other a combination of textual and visual features. For textual retrieval they map the text onto single axes of the MeSH ontology. They also use negative weight query expansion and mix visual and textual results for optimal results.

University of Concordia, Canada: submitted one visual run containing a query only for the first image of every topic using only visual features. The technique applied is an association model between low–level visual features and high–level concepts mainly relying on texture, edge and shape features.

In Table 4 an overview of the submitted runs can be seen with the query dimensions.

Table 4. Query dimensions of the submissions for the medical retrieval task

Dimension	type	#Runs (%)
Run type	Automatic	128 (95.52%)
Modality	image	28 (20.90%)
	text	14 (10.45%)
	text+image	86 (64.18%)
Run type	Manual	6 (4.48%)
Modality	image	3 (2.24%)
	text	1 (0.75%)
	text+image	2 (1.5%)

3.4 Results

This section gives an overview of the best results of the various categories and performs some more analyses. Table 5 shows all the manual runs that were submitted with a classification of the techniquae used for retrieval.

Table 5. Overview of the best manual retrieval results

Run identifier	visual	textual	MAP	P10
OHSUmanual.txt		x	0.2116	0.4560
OHSUmanvis.txt	x		0.1601	0.5000
i2r-vk-avg.txt	x		0.0921	0.2760
i2r-vk-sem.txt	x		0.06	0.2320
i6-vistex-rfb1.clef	x	x	0.0855	0.3320
i6-vistex-rfb2.clef	x	x	0.077	0.2680

Table 6 gives the best 5 results for textual retrieval only and the best ten results for visual and for mixed retrieval. The results for individual topics varied widely, and further analysis will attempt to explore why this was so. If we calculate the average over the best system for each query we would be much closer to 0.5 than to what the best system actually achieved, 0.2821. So far, non of the systems optimised the feature selection based on the query input.

3.5 Discussion

The results show a few clear trends. Very few groups performed manual submissions using relevance feedback, which was most likely due to the need for more resources for such evaluations. Still, relevance feedback has shown to be extremely useful in many retrieval tasks and the evaluation of it seems extremely necessary, as well. Surprisingly, in the submitted results, relevance feedback did not seem to give a much superior performance compared to the automatic runs. In the 2004 tasks, the relevance feedback runs were often significantly better than without feedback.

We also found that the topics developed were much more geared towards textual retrieval than visual retrieval. The best results for textual retrieval were much higher than for visual retrieval only, and a few of the poorly performing textual runs appeared to have indexing problems. When analysing the topics in

Table 6. Overview of the best automatic retrieval results

Run identifier	visual	textual	MAP	P10
IPALI2R_Tn		x	0.2084	0.4480
IPALI2R_T		x	0.2075	0.4480
i6-En.clef		x	0.2065	0.4000
UBimed_en-fr.T.BI2		x	0.1746	0.3640
SinaiEn_okapi_nofb		x	0.091	0.2920
I2Rfus.txt	x		0.1455	0.3600
I2RcPBcf.txt	x		0.1188	0.2640
I2RcPBnf.txt	x		0.1114	0.2480
I2RbPBcf.txt	x		0.1068	0.3560
I2RbPBnf.txt	x		0.1067	0.3560
mirabase.qtop(GIFT)	x		0.0942	0.3040
mirarf5.1.qtop	x		0.0942	0.2880
GE_M_4g.txt	x		0.0941	0.3040
mirarf5.qtop	x		0.0941	0.2960
mirarf5.2.qtop	x		0.0934	0.2880
IPALI2R_TIan	x	x	0.2821	0.6160
IPALI2R_TIa	x	x	0.2819	0.6200
nctu_visual+text_auto_4	x	x	0.2389	0.5280
UBimed_en-fr.TI.1	x	x	0.2358	0.5520
IPALI2R_TImn	x	x	0.2325	0.5000
nctu_visual+text_auto_8	x	x	0.2324	0.5000
nctu_visual+text_auto_6	x	x	0.2318	0.4960
IPALI2R_TIm	x	x	0.2312	0.5000
nctu_visual+text_auto_3	x	x	0.2286	0.5320
nctu_visual+text_auto_1	x	x	0.2276	0.5400

more detail, a clear division becomes evident between the developed visual and textual topics. However, some of the topics marked as visual actually had better results using a textual system. Some systems performed extremely well on a few topics but then extremely poorly on other topics. No system was the best system for more than two of the topics.

The best results were clearly obtained when combining textual and visual features most likely due to the fact that there were queries for which only a combination of the feature sets works well.

4 Automatic Annotation Task

4.1 Introduction, Idea, and Objectives

Automatic image annotation is a classification task, where an image is assigned to its correspondent class from a given set of pre–defined classes. As such, it is an important step for content–based image retrieval (CBIR) and data mining [25]. The aim of the *Automatic Annotation Task* in ImageCLEFmed 2005 was to compare state–of–the–art approaches to automatic image annotation and to quantify their improvements for image retrieval. In particular, the task aims at finding out how well current techniques for image content analysis can identify the medical image modality, body orientation, body region, and biological system examined. Such an automatic classification can be used for multilingual image annotations as well as for annotation verification, e.g., to detect false information held in the header streams according to Digital Imaging and Communications in Medicine (DICOM) standard [26].

4.2 Database

The database consisted of 9.000 fully classified radiographs taken randomly from medical routine at the Aachen University Hospital. 1.000 additional radiographs

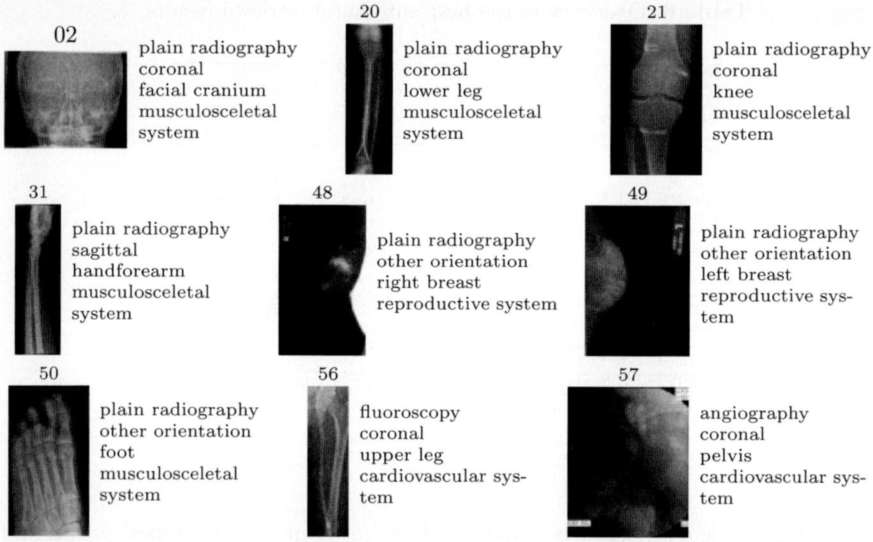

Fig. 6. Example images of the IRMA 10.000 database together with their class and annotation

for which classification labels were unavailable to the participants had to be classified into one of the 57 classes, from which the 9.000 database images come from. Although only 57 simple class numbers were provided for ImageCLEFmed 2005. The images are annotated with the complete IRMA code, a multi–axial code for image annotation [27]. The code is currently available in English and German. It is planned to use the results of such automatic image annotation tasks for further textual image retrieval tasks in the future.

Some example images together with their class number and their complete English annotation are given in Figure 6.

4.3 Participating Groups

In total 26 groups registered for participation in the automatic annotation task. All groups have downloaded the data but only 12 groups submitted runs. Each group had at least two different submissions. The maximum number of submissions per group was 7. In total, 41 runs were submitted which are briefly described in the following.

CEA: CEA from France, submitted three runs. In each run different feature vectors were used and classified using a k–Nearest Neighbour classifier (k was either 3 or 9). In the run labelled `cea/pj-3.txt` the images were projected along horizontal and vertical axes to obtain a feature histogram. For `cea/tlep-9.txt` histograms of local edge pattern features and colour features were created, and for `cea/cime-9.txt` quantified colours were used.

CINDI: The CINDI group from Concordia University in Montreal, Canada used multi–class SVMs (one–vs–one) and a 170 dimensional feature vector consisting of colour moments, colour histograms, cooccurence texture features, shape moment, and edge histograms.

Geneva: The medGIFT group from Geneva, Switzerland used various different settings for gray levels, and Gabor filters in their medGIFT retrieval system.

Infocomm: The group from Infocomm Institute, Singapore used three kinds of 16x16 low–resolution–map–features: initial gray values, anisotropy and contrast. To avoid overfitting, for each of 57 classes, a separate training set was selected and about 6.800 training images were chosen out of the provided 9.000 images. Support Vector Machines with RBF (radial basis functions) kernels were applied to train the classifiers which were then employed to classify the test images.

Miracle: The Miracle Group from UPM Madrid, Spain used GIFT and a decision table majority classifier to calculate the relevance of each individual result in `miracle/mira20relp57.txt`. In `mira20relp58IB8.txt` additionally a k–nearest neighbour classifier with $k = 8$ and attribute normalisation is used.

Montreal: The group from University of Montreal, Canada submitted 7 runs, which differ in the features used. They estimated, which classes are best represented by which features and combined appropriate features.

mtholyoke: For the submission from Mount Holyoke College, MA, USA, Gabor energy features were extracted from the images and two different cross–media relevance models were used to classify the data.

nctu–dblab: The NCTU–DBLAB group from National Chiao Tung University, Taiwan used a support vector machine (SVM) to learn image feature characteristics. Based on the SVM model, several image features were used to predict the class of the test images.

ntu: The group from National Taiwan University used mean gray values of blocks as features and different classifiers for their submissions.

rwth–i6: The Human Language Technology and Pattern Recognition group from RWTH Aachen, Germany had two submissions. One used a simple zero–order image distortion model taking into account local context. The other submission used a maximum entropy classifier and histograms of patches as features.

rwth–mi: The IRMA group from Aachen, Germany used features proposed by Tamura et al to capture global texture properties and two distance measures for downscaled representations, which preserve spatial information and are robust w.r.t. global transformations like translation, intensity variations, and local deformations. The weighting parameters for combining the single classifiers were guessed for the first submission and trained on a random 8.000 to 1.000 partitioning of the training set for the second submission.

ulg: The ulg (University of Liége) method is based on random sub–windows and decision trees. During the training phase, a large number of multi–size subwindows are randomly extracted from training images. Then, a decision tree model is automatically built (using Extra Trees and/or Tree Boosting), based on normalised versions of the subwindows, and operating directly on pixel values. Classification of a new image similarly entails the random extraction of subwindows, the application of the model to these, and the aggregation of subwindows predictions.

4.4 Results

The error rates range between 12.6 % and 73.3 % (Table 7). Based on the training data, a system guessing the most frequent group for all 1.000 test images would result with 70.3 % error rate, since 297 radiographs of the test set were from class 12. A more realistic baseline of 36.8 % error rate is computed from an 1–nearest–neighbour classifier comparing downscaled 32×32 versions of the images using the Euclidean distance.

Interestingly, the classes are very different in difficulty. The average classification accuracy ranges from 6.3 % to 90.7 %, and there is a tendency that classes with less training images are more difficult. For example, images from class 2 were extremely often classified to be from class 44: on average 46% of the images from class 2 were classified to be from class 44. This is probably partly due to a much higher a–priori probability for class 44, which has 193 images in the training set while class 2 only has 32 training images. Classes 7 and 8 are often classified to be from class 6, where once again class 6 is much better represented in the training data. Furthermore, quite a few classes (6,13,14,27,28,34,44,51,57) are often misclassified to be from class 12, which is by far the largest class in the training data. This strongly coincides with the fact that class 12 is the class with the highest classification accuracy: 90.7% of the test images from class 12 were classified correctly. The three classes with the lowest classification accuracies, that is those three classes were on the average most of the images were misclassified, together have less then 1% of the training data.

4.5 Discussion

Similar experiments have been described in the literature. However, previous experiments have been restricted to a small number of categories. For instance, several algorithms have been proposed for orientation detection of chest radiographs, where lateral and frontal orientation are distinguished by means of image content analysis [28,29]. In a recent investigation, Pinhas and Greenspan report error rates below 1 % for automatic categorisation of 851 medical images into 8 classes [30]. In previous investigations, error rates between 5.3% and 15% were reported for experiments with 1617 of 6 [31] and 6,231 of 81 classes, respectively. Hence, error rates of 12 % for 10.000 of 57 classes are plausible.

As mentioned before, classes 6, 7, and 8 were frequently confused. All show parts of the arms and thus look extremely similar (Fig. 6). However, a reason for

Table 7. Resulting error rates for the submitted runs

submission	error rate [%]
rwth-i6/IDMSUBMISSION	12.6
rwth_mi-ccf_idm.03.tamura.06.confidence	13.3
rwth-i6/MESUBMISSION	13.9
ulg/maree-random-subwindows-tree-boosting.res	14.1
rwth-mi/rwth_mi1.confidence	14.6
ulg/maree-random-subwindows-extra-trees.res	14.7
geneva-gift/GIFT5NN_8g.txt	20.6
infocomm/Annotation_result4_I2R_sg.dat	20.6
geneva-gift/GIFT5NN_16g.txt	20.9
infocomm/Annotation_result1_I2R_sg.dat	20.9
infocomm/Annotation_result2_I2R_sg.dat	21.0
geneva-gift/GIFT1NN_8g.txt	21.2
geneva-gift/GIFT10NN_16g.txt	21.3
miracle/mira20relp57.txt	21.4
geneva-gift/GIFT1NN_16g.txt	21.7
infocomm/Annotation_result3_I2R_sg.dat	21.7
ntu/NTU-annotate05-1NN.result	21.7
ntu/NTU-annotate05-Top2.result	21.7
geneva-gift/GIFT1NN.txt	21.8
geneva-gift/GIFT5NN.txt	22.1
miracle/mira20relp58IB8.txt	22.3
ntu/NTU-annotate05-SC.result	22.5
nctu-dblab/nctu_mc_result_1.txt	24.7
nctu-dblab/nctu_mc_result_2.txt	24.9
nctu-dblab/nctu_mc_result_4.txt	28.5
nctu-dblab/nctu_mc_result_3.txt	31.8
nctu-dblab/nctu_mc_result_5.txt	33.8
cea/pj-3.txt	36.9
mtholyoke/MHC_CQL.RESULTS	37.8
mtholyoke/MHC_CBDM.RESULTS	40.3
cea/tlep-9.txt	42.5
cindi/Result-IRMA-format.txt	43.3
cea/cime-9.txt	46.0
montreal/UMontreal_combination.txt	55.7
montreal/UMontreal_texture_coarsness_dir.txt	60.3
nctu-dblab/nctu_mc_result_gp2.txt	61.5
montreal/UMontreal_contours.txt	66.6
montreal/UMontreal_shape.txt	67.0
montreal/UMontreal_contours_centred.txt	67.3
montreal/UMontreal_shape_fourier.txt	67.4
montreal/UMontreal_texture_directionality.txt	73.3
Euclidean Distance, 32x32 images, 1-Nearest-Neighbor	36.8

the common misclassification in favour of class 6 might be that there are by a factor of 5 more training images from class 6 than from classes 7 and 8 together.

Given the confidence files from all runs, classifier combination was tested using the sum and the product rule in such a manner that first the two best confidence files were combined, then the three best confidence files, and so forth. Unfortunately, the best result was 12.9%. Thus, no improvement over the current best submission was possible using simple classifier combination techniques.

Having results close to 10% error rate, classification and annotation of images might open interesting vistas for CBIR systems. Although the task considered here is more restricted than the *Medical Retrieval Task* and can thus be considered easier, techniques applied will probably be apt to be used in future CBIR applications. Therefore, it is planned to use the results of such automatic image annotation tasks for further, textual image retrieval tasks.

5 Conclusions

ImageCLEF has continued to attract researchers from a variety of global communities interested in image retrieval using both low–level image features and associated texts. This year we have improved the ad–hoc medical retrieval by enlarging the image collection and creating more semantic queries based on realistic information needs of medical professionals. The ad–hoc task has continued to attract interest and this year has seen an increase in the number of translated topics and those with translated narratives. The addition of the IRMA annotation task has provided a further challenge to the medical side of ImageCLEF and proven a popular task for participants, covering mainly the visual retrieval community. The user–centered retrieval task, however, remains with low participation, mainly due to the high level of resources required to run an interactive task. We will continue to improve tasks for ImageCLEF 2006 mainly based on feedback from participants.

A large number of participants only registered but finally did not submit results. This means that the resources are very valuable and already access to the resources is a reason to register. Still, only if we have participants submitting results with different techniques, is there really the possibility to compare retrieval systems and developed better retrieval for the future. So for 2006 we hope to receive much feedback for tasks and many people who register, submit results and participate in the CLEF workshop to discuss the presented techniques. Further information can be found in [32,33].

Acknowledgements

This work has been funded by the EU Sixth Framework Programme within the Bricks project (IST contract number 507457) and the SemanticMining project (IST NoE 507505). The establishment of the IRMA database was funded by the German Research Community DFG under grant Le 1108/4. We also acknowledge the support of National Science Foundation (NSF) grant ITR–0325160.

References

1. Clough, P., Sanderson, M.: The CLEF 2003 cross language image retrieval track. In Peters, C., Gonzalo, J., Braschler, M., Kluck, M., eds.: Comparative Evaluation of Multilingual Information Access Systems: Results of the Fourth CLEF Evaluation Campaign, Lecture Notes in Computer Science (LNCS), Springer, Volume 3237 (2004) 581–593
2. Clough, P., Müller, H., Sanderson, M.: The CLEF 2004 cross language image retrieval track. In Peters, C., Clough, P., Gonzalo, J., Jones, G., Kluck, M., Magnini, B., eds.: Multilingual Information Access for Text, Speech and Images: Results of the Fifth CLEF Evaluation Campaign, Lecture Notes in Computer Science (LNCS), Springer, Volume 3491 (2005) 597–613
3. Gonzalo, J., Paul, C., Vallin, A.: Overview of the CLEF 2005 interactive track. In: Proceedings of Cross Language Evaluation Forum (CLEF) 2005 Workshop, Vienna, Austria. (2005)
4. Clough, P., Sanderson, M., Müller, H.: A proposal for the CLEF cross language image retrieval track (ImageCLEF) 2004. In: The Challenge of Image and Video Retrieval (CIVR 2004), Dublin, Ireland, Springer LNCS 3115 (2004)
5. Grubinger, M., Leung, C., Clough, P.: Towards a topic complexity measure for cross–language image retrieval. In: Proceedings of Cross Language Evaluation Forum (CLEF) 2005 Workshop, Vienna, Austria. (2005)
6. Besançon, R., Millet, C.: Data fusion of retrieval results from different media: Experiments at ImageCLEF 2005. In: Proceedings of Cross–Language Evaluation Forum (CLEF) 2005 Workshop, Vienna, Austria. (2005)
7. Inoue, M.: Easing erroneous translations in cross–language image retrieval using word associations. In: Proceedings of Cross Language Evaluation Forum (CLEF) 2005 Workshop, Vienna, Austria. (2005)
8. Izquierdo-Beviá, R., Tomás, D., Saiz-Noeda, M., Vicedo, J.L.: University of Alicante in ImageCLEF2005. In: Proceedings of Cross Language Evaluation Forum (CLEF) 2005 Workshop, Vienna, Austria. (2005)
9. Hoi, S.C.H., Zhu, J., Lyu, M.R.: CUHK at ImageCLEF 2005: Cross–language and cross–media image retrieval. In: Proceedings of Cross Language Evaluation Forum (CLEF) 2005 Workshop, Vienna, Austria. (2005)
10. Jones, G.J., McDonald, K.: Dublin city university at CLEF 2005: Experiments with the ImageCLEF St. Andrews collection. In: Proceedings of Cross Language Evaluation Forum (CLEF) 2005 Workshop, Vienna, Austria. (2005)
11. Müller, H., Geissbühler, A., Marty, J., Lovis, C., Ruch, P.: The use of MedGIFT and EasyIR for imageCLEF 2005. In: Proceedings of Cross Language Evaluation Forum (CLEF) 2005 Workshop, Vienna, Austria. (2005)
12. Adriani, M., Arnely, F.: Retrieving images using cross–lingual text and image features. In: Proceedings of Cross Language Evaluation Forum (CLEF) 2005 Workshop, Vienna, Austria. (2005)
13. Martínez-Fernández, J., Villena Román, J., García-Serrano, A.M., González-Cristóbal, J.C.: Combining textual and visual features for image retrieval. In: Proceedings of Cross Language Evaluation Forum (CLEF) 2005 Workshop, Vienna, Austria. (2005)
14. Chang, Y.C., Lin, W.C., Chen, H.H.: A corpus–based relevance feedback approach to cross–language image retrieval. In: Proceedings of Cross Language Evaluation Forum (CLEF) 2005 Workshop, Vienna, Austria. (2005)

15. Martín-Valdivia, M., Garcí-Cumbreras, M., Dí-Galiano, M., Ureña López, L., Montejo-Raez, A.: The university of jaén at ImageCLEF 2005: Adhoc and medical taskseasing erroneous translations in cross–language image retrieval using word associations. In: Proceedings of Cross Language Evaluation Forum (CLEF) 2005 Workshop, Vienna, Austria. (2005)
16. Peinado, V., López-Ostenero, F., Gonzalo, J., Verdejo, F.: UNED at ImageCLEF 2005: Automatically structured queries with named entities over metadata. In: Proceedings of Cross Language Evaluation Forum (CLEF) 2005 Workshop, Vienna, Austria. (2005)
17. Hersh, W.R., Hickam, D.H.: How well do physicians use electronic information retrieval systems? Journal of the American Medical Association **280** (1998) 1347–1352
18. Markkula, M., Sormunen, E.: Searching for photos – journalists' practices in pictorial IR. In Eakins, J.P., Harper, D.J., Jose, J., eds.: The Challenge of Image Retrieval, A Workshop and Symposium on Image Retrieval. Electronic Workshops in Computing, Newcastle upon Tyne, The British Computer Society (1998)
19. Hersh, W., Müller, H., Gorman, P., Jensen, J.: Task analysis for evaluating image retrieval systems in the ImageCLEF biomedical image retrieval task. In: Slice of Life conference on Multimedia in Medical Education (SOL 2005), Portland, OR, USA (2005)
20. Müller, H., Rosset, A., Vallée, J.P., Terrier, F., Geissbuhler, A.: A reference data set for the evaluation of medical image retrieval systems. Computerized Medical Imaging and Graphics **28** (2004) 295–305
21. Rosset, A., Müller, H., Martins, M., Dfouni, N., Vallée, J.P., Ratib, O.: Casimage project – a digital teaching files authoring environment. Journal of Thoracic Imaging **19** (2004) 1–6
22. Candler, C.S., Uijtdehaage, S.H., Dennis, S.E.: Introducing HEAL: The health education assets library. Academic Medicine **78** (2003) 249–253
23. Wallis, J.W., Miller, M.M., Miller, T.R., Vreeland, T.H.: An internet–based nuclear medicine teaching file. Journal of Nuclear Medicine **36** (1995) 1520–1527
24. Glatz-Krieger, K., Glatz, D., Gysel, M., Dittler, M., Mihatsch, M.J.: Webbasierte Lernwerkzeuge für die Pathologie – web–based learning tools for pathology. Pathologe **24** (2003) 394–399
25. Lehmann, T.M., Güld, M.O., Deselaers, T., Schubert, H., Spitzer, K., Ney, H., Wein, B.B.: Automatic categorization of medical images for content–based retrieval and data mining. Computerized Medical Imaging and Graphics **29** (2005) 143–155
26. Güld, M., Kohnen, M., Keysers, D., Schubert, H., Wein, B., Bredno, J., Lehmann, T.: Quality of DICOM header information for image categorization. In: Proceedings of the SPIE conference Photonics West, Electronic Imaging, special session on benchmarking image retrieval systems. (2002) 280–287
27. Lehmann, T.M., Schubert, H., Keysers, D., Kohnen, M., Wein, B.B.: The IRMA code for unique classification of medical images. In: Medical Imaging. Volume 5033 of SPIE Proceedings., San Diego, California, USA (2003)
28. Pietka, E., Huang, H.: Orientation correction for chest images. Journal of Digital Imaging **5** (1992) 185–189
29. Boone, J.M., Seshagiri, S., Steiner, R.: Recognition of chest radiograph orientation for picture archiving and communications systems display using neural networks. Journal of Digital Imaging **5(3)** (1992) 190–193
30. Güld, M.O., Keysers, D., Deselaers, T., Leisten, M., Schubert, H., Ney, H., Lehmann, T.M.: Comparison of global features for categorization of medical images. In: Medical Imaging 2004. Volume 5371 of SPIE Proceedings. (2004)

31. Keysers, D., Gollan, C., Ney, H.: Classification of medical images using non–linear distortion models. In: Proceedings Bildverarbeitung für die Medizin, Berlin, Germany (2004) 366–370
32. Müller, H., Clough, P., Hersh, W., Deselaers, T., Lehmann, T.M., Geissbuhler, A.: Using heterogeneous annotation and visual information for the benchmarking of image retrieval systems. In: Proceedings of the SPIE conference Photonics West, Electronic Imaging, special session on benchmarking image retrieval systems, San Diego, USA (2006)
33. Müller, H., Clough, P., Hersh, W., Deselaers, T., Lehmann, T., Geissbuhler, A.: Axes for the evaluation of medical image retrieval systems - the ImageCLEF experience. In: Proceedings of the of ACM Multimedia 2005 (Brave New Topics track), 6–12 November, Singapore (2005) 1014–1022

Linguistic Estimation of Topic Difficulty in Cross-Language Image Retrieval

Michael Grubinger[1], Clement Leung[1], and Paul Clough[2]

[1] School of Computer Science and Mathematics, Victoria University, Melbourne, Australia
michael.grubinger@research.vu.edu.au, clement@matilda.vu.edu.au
[2] Department of Information Studies, Sheffield University, Sheffield, UK
p.d.clough@sheffield.ac.uk

Abstract. Selecting suitable topics in order to assess system effectiveness is a crucial part of any benchmark, particularly those for retrieval systems. This includes establishing a range of example search requests (or topics) in order to test various aspects of the retrieval systems under evaluation. In order to assist with selecting topics, we present a measure of topic difficulty for cross-language image retrieval. This measure has enabled us to ground the topic generation process within a methodical and reliable framework for ImageCLEF 2005. This document describes such a measure for topic difficulty, providing concrete examples for every aspect of topic complexity and an analysis of topics used in the ImageCLEF 2003, 2004 and 2005 ad-hoc task.

1 Introduction

Benchmarks for image retrieval consist of four main elements: a collection of still natural images like [1] or [2]; a representative set of search requests (called queries or topics); a recommended set of performance measures carried out on ground truths associated with topics [3, 4]; and benchmarking events like [5] and [6] that attract participants to make use of the benchmark.

The topic selection process is a very important part of any benchmarking event. In order to produce realistic results, the topics should not only be representative of the (image) collection, but also reflect realistic user interests/needs [7]. This is achieved by generating the topics against certain dimensions, including the estimated number of relevant images for each topic, the variation of task parameters to test different translation problems, its scope (e.g. broad or narrow, general or specific), and the difficulty of the topic.

Hence, as the types of search request issued by users of visual information systems will vary in difficulty, a dimension of complexity with respect to linguistic complexity for translation would help to set the context. Thus, there is a need for a measure of topic difficulty that expresses the level of difficulty for retrieval systems to return relevant images in order to ground the topic generation process within a methodical and reliable framework.

As image retrieval algorithms improve, it is necessary to increase the average difficulty level of topics each year in order to maintain the challenge for returning

C. Peters et al. (Eds.): CLEF 2005, LNCS 4022, pp. 558 – 566, 2006.

participants. However, if topics are too difficult for current techniques, the results are not particularly meaningful. Furthermore, it may prove difficult for new participants to obtain good results and prevent them from presenting results and taking part in comparative evaluations (like ImageCLEF). Providing a good variation in topic difficulty is therefore very important as it allows both the organizers (and participants) to observe retrieval effectiveness with respect to topic difficulty levels.

Quantification of task difficulty is not a new concept; on the contrary, it has been applied to many areas including information retrieval [8], machine learning [9], parsing and grammatical formalisms [10], and language learning in general [11]. Other papers include the discussion of syntactic complexity in multimedia information retrieval [12] and a measure of semantic complexity for natural language systems [13].

Recent work has shown the introduction of a clarity score [14] as an attempt to quantify query difficulty. This clarity score measures the difference between the query language model and the corresponding document language model and shows a positive correlation with the query's average precision. The Divergence From Randomness (DFR) scoring model [15] also showed positive correlation to query precision. Another very promising approach [16] estimates query difficulty based on the agreement between the top results of the full query and the top results of its sub-queries.

This work, however, presents an alternative linguistic approach for a measure of topic difficulty for cross-language image retrieval, based on the analysis of the grammatical sentence elements of the topics. Section 2 presents the definition of the proposed measure fore topic difficulty. Section 3 classifies and analyses the topics used at the ImageCLEF ad-hoc tasks from 2003 to 2005. Section 4 finally outlines further improvement of the proposed measure and other future work.

2 A Measure for Cross-Language Topic Difficulty

The linguistic approach for a measure of topic difficulty in cross-language image retrieval tasks that is described hereinafter is based on the hypothesis that more linguistically complex topics result in lower MAP scores due to the requirement of more complex retrieval and translation approaches. The proposed scale for topic difficulty starts at 0 and is unlimited as far as the level of difficulty is concerned. Expressed as a positive integer, the higher the value d, the higher the topic difficulty (Equation 1):

$$0 \leq d_k < \infty \tag{1}$$

The cross-language topic difficulty d for topic k is calculated by summing up the individual topic elements $E_k(i)$ of the topic sentence plus the valency factor V_k,

$$d_k = \sum_{i=1}^{N} E_k(i) + V_k \tag{2}$$

where N is the total number of topic elements and $E_k(i)$ the ith *element* of the topic k, with $E_k(i)$ defined as:

$$E_k(i) = \begin{cases} 1, & \text{if topic element } i \text{ has to be translated and is not meta-data.} \\ 0, & \text{else.} \end{cases} \quad (3)$$

and V_k the valency factor for topic k:

$$V_k = \begin{cases} 1, & \text{if valency } v_k > 2. \\ 0, & \text{else.} \end{cases} \quad (4)$$

The topic elements $E_k(i)$ include nouns (used as subject, direct object, indirect object or in other cases), qualifying attributes of nouns (adjectives) and their cardinality (numerals); verbs and qualifying attributes of verbs (adverbs); time, place, manner and reason adjuncts; and the logic expressions AND and NOT. In cross-language retrieval, a topic element just contributes to topic difficulty if the element has to be translated and queries for image content directly and not for meta-data like the photographer or the date of the image (see Equation 3).

Each of the elements can occur more than once in a topic sentence (e.g. a topic can have two adjectives, like "*traditional Scottish* dancers"). However, logical OR constructs do not increase the difficulty level if they can be expressed differently (for example: *boys or girls* is the same as *children*).

The *Valency* v_k of a topic sentence k is the number of arguments that a verb takes in that sentence. For topics with verbs having a valency higher than two (v_k>2), the difficulty level is incremented by one (see Equation 4) due to the additional challenge of actually having to detect the grammatical relationships between subject (nominative case), direct object (accusative case) and indirect object (dative case).

In general, d_k=0 implies that no translation is necessary and a simple keyword search would suffice for effective retrieval. An example for such a topic would be a German query *David Beckham* on an English document collection, as *David Beckham* requires no translation from German to English. If the same query is formulated in a language that does require a translation, like the Latvian equivalent *Daivide Bekhema*, the topic difficulty would produce a different score (in this case d_k=1). Hence, the same topics can produce different topic difficulty scores in different languages.

3 Evaluation of Query Difficulty at ImageCLEF

The ImageCLEF retrieval benchmark was established in 2003 with the aim of evaluating image retrieval from multilingual document collections [5, 6]. This section presents the results of the new measure for cross-language topic difficulty applied to the 2003, 2004 and 2005 ad-hoc tasks using the St. Andrews historic photographic collection [1]. A strong negative correlation of the topic difficulty measure with the average Mean Average Precisions (MAP) of the participants in 103 topics and up to eight languages demonstrates the robustness of the proposed measure.

3.1 ImageCLEF 2005

In the ImageCLEF 2005 ad-hoc task [17], participants were provided with 28 topics translated into 33 different languages. Table 1 shows an analysis of topic difficulty for each of the topic titles in English.

Table 1. Topic difficulty analysis for English topic titles

k	Topic Title	Topic Analysis	d_k
1	aircraft on the ground	subject, place adjunct	2
2	people gathered at bandstand	subject, verb, place adjunct	3
3	dog (in) sitting (position)	subject, verb	2
4	steam ship docked	subject, verb	2
5	animal statue	subject	1
6	small sailing boat	adjective, subject	2
7	fishermen in boat	subject, place adjunct	2
8	building covered in snow	subject, verb, manner adjunct	3
9	horse pulling cart or carriage	subject, verb, direct object (or direct object)	3
10	sun pictures, Scotland	subject, place adjunct	2
11	Swiss mountain (scenery)	adjective, subject	2
12	postcard from Iona, Scotland	subject, place adjunct	2
13	stone viaduct with several arches	subject, manner adjunct	2
14	people at the marketplace	subject, place adjunct	2
15	golfer putting on green	subject, verb, place adjunct	3
16	waves (breaking) on beach	subject, place adjunct	2
17	man or woman reading	subject (or subject), verb	2
18	woman in white dress	subject, adjective, manner adjunct	3
19	composite postcards of Northern Ireland	adjective, subject, place adjunct, adjective	4
20	royal visit to Scotland (not Fife)	adjective, subject, place adjunct, exclusion	4
21	monument to Robert Burns	subject	1
22	building with waving flag	subject, manner adjunct, adjective	3
23	tomb inside church or cathedral	subject, place adjunct (or place adjunct)	2
24	close-up pictures of bird	subject, genitive noun	2
25	arched gateway	adjective, subject	2
26	portrait pictures of mixed-sex groups	subject, adjective, genitive noun	3
27	woman or girl carrying basket	subject (or subject), verb, direct object	3
28	colour pictures of woodland scenes around St. Andrews	adjective, subject, genitive noun, place adjunct	4

Topic 5 *animal statue* presents an example of a fairly easy topic containing just one topic element (subject) and thus having a topic difficulty of d_5=1. This is also the query with the highest MAP across all participants and languages (see Table 2).

In contrast, topic 20 *royal visits to Scotland (not Fife)* is an example of a rather difficult topic. It comprises four topic elements, the adjective *royal*, the noun *visit* used as a subject, the place adjunct *to Scotland*, and the logical expression *not Fife*, adding up to a topic difficulty of d_{20}=4. Unsurprisingly, this topic produced a very low MAP across all participants and languages (see Table 2).

Like in Table 1, the difficulty levels have been calculated for all alphabetical languages (Romanic alphabet) with more than 10 submitted runs: German (GER), Latin-American Spanish (SPA-L), European Spanish (SPA-E), Italian (ITA), French (FRA), Portuguese (POR), and Dutch (NED).

A total of 11 research groups submitted 349 runs and produced the following Mean Average Precision scores for each topic (Table 2).

Table 2. Average MAP (Mean Average Precision) values for alphabetical languages with more than 10 submitted runs (with their topic difficulty in parenthesis)

k	ENG	GER	SPA – L	SPA - E	ITA	FRA	POR	NED	ALL
1	0.26 (2)	0.00 (2)	0.04 (2)	0.11 (2)	0.12 (2)	0.28 (2)	0.00 (2)	0.20 (2)	0.13 (2.00)
2	0.46 (3)	0.03 (3)	0.00 (3)	0.02 (3)	0.00 (3)	0.07 (4)	0.24 (3)	0.00 (2)	0.12 (3.00)
3	0.43 (2)	0.39 (3)	0.26(2)	0.26 (2)	0.26 (2)	0.43 (2)	0.29 (2)	0.44 (2)	0.35 (2.13)
4	0.28 (2)	0.20 (2)	0.18 (3)	0.16 (3)	0.04 (3)	0.11 (3)	0.03 (3)	0.10 (2)	0.15 (2.63)
5	0.70 (1)	0.71 (1)	0.68 (2)	0.70 (2)	0.65 (2)	0.36 (2)	0.77 (2)	0.61 (2)	0.58 (1.75)
6	0.50 (2)	0.49 (2)	0.38 (2)	0.10 (2)	0.36 (2)	0.15 (2)	0.45 (2)	0.48 (2)	0.31 (2.00)
7	0.35 (2)	0.06 (2)	0.31 (2)	0.25 (2)	0.39 (2)	0.31 (2)	0.27 (2)	0.33 (2)	0.26 (2.00)
8	0.08 (3)	0.05 (2)	0.06 (3)	0.06 (3)	0.07 (3)	0.20 (3)	0.07 (3)	0.05 (3)	0.09 (2.88)
9	0.32 (3)	0.23 (3)	0.34 (3)	0.34 (3)	0.17 (3)	0.14 (2)	0.25 (3)	0.45 (3)	0.27 (2.88)
10	0.32 (2)	0.22 (2)	0.26 (3)	0.24 (3)	0.24 (3)	0.28 (3)	0.28 (3)	0.29 (2)	0.24 (2.63)
11	0.50 (2)	0.14 (2)	0.66 (2)	0.20 (2)	0.09 (2)	0.15 (2)	0.10 (2)	0.06 (2)	0.34 (2.00)
12	0.29 (2)	0.30 (2)	0.26 (3)	0.28 (3)	0.32 (3)	0.32 (3)	0.24 (3)	0.31 (2)	0.23 (2.50)
13	0.37 (2)	0.26 (2)	0.27 (3)	0.31 (3)	0.07 (3)	0.27 (3)	0.26 (3)	0.22 (2)	0.26 (2.50)
14	0.13 (2)	0.42 (2)	0.44 (2)	0.45 (2)	0.15 (2)	0.40 (2)	0.74 (2)	0.49 (2)	0.36 (2.00)
15	0.35 (3)	0.15 (3)	0.19 (3)	0.08 (3)	0.13 (3)	0.06 (3)	0.14 (3)	0.16 (3)	0.15 (3.13)
16	0.41 (3)	0.40 (3)	0.33 (3)	0.42 (3)	0.33 (3)	0.43 (3)	0.39 (3)	0.04 (2)	0.30 (2.75)
17	0.47 (2)	0.46 (2)	0.36 (2)	0.07 (2)	0.33 (2)	0.47 (2)	0.55 (2)	0.46 (2)	0.37 (2.00)
18	0.08 (3)	0.08 (3)	0.08 (3)	0.08 (3)	0.04 (3)	0.09 (3)	0.04 (2)	0.11 (3)	0.08 (2.88)
19	0.22 (4)	0.00 (4)	0.00 (4)	0.00 (4)	0.00 (4)	0.00 (4)	0.00 (4)	0.03 (4)	0.05 (4.00)
20	0.06 (4)	0.03 (4)	0.03 (4)	0.03 (4)	0.04 (4)	0.07 (4)	0.05 (4)	0.08 (4)	0.07 (4.00)
21	0.48 (1)	0.44 (1)	0.46 (1)	0.48 (1)	0.46 (1)	0.55 (1)	0.37 (1)	0.43 (1)	0.39 (1.00)
22	0.32 (3)	0.43 (3)	0.39 (3)	0.39 (3)	0.34 (3)	0.29 (3)	0.21 (3)	0.43 (3)	0.36 (3.00)
23	0.48 (2)	0.34 (2)	0.33 (2)	0.06 (2)	0.02 (2)	0.08 (2)	0.26 (2)	0.54 (2)	0.22 (2.00)
24	0.22 (2)	0.25 (2)	0.15 (2)	0.12 (2)	0.16 (2)	0.17 (2)	0.23 (2)	0.26 (2)	0.19 (2.00)
25	0.45 (2)	0.13 (2)	0.07 (2)	0.11 (2)	0.03 (2)	0.38 (2)	0.22 (2)	0.06 (2)	0.19 (2.00)
26	0.53 (3)	0.36 (3)	0.22 (3)	0.15 (3)	0.08 (3)	0.29 (2)	0.10 (3)	0.37 (3)	0.25 (2.88)
27	0.35 (3)	0.28 (3)	0.14 (3)	0.15 (3)	0.21 (3)	0.29 (3)	0.08 (3)	0.33 (3)	0.22 (3.00)
28	0.13 (4)	0.13 (3)	0.12 (4)	0.10 (4)	0.10 (3)	0.12 (4)	0.09 (4)	0.15 (3)	0.11 (3.63)

In order to establish the existence of a relation between the level of difficulty and results obtained from ImageCLEF submissions, the correlation coefficient ρ_{dy} is calculated for each of the languages, using Pearson's formula:

$$\rho_{dy} = \frac{Cov(D,Y)}{\sigma_d \sigma_y} \quad (5)$$

where

$$-1 \leq \rho_{dy} \leq 1 \quad (6)$$

and

$$Cov(D,Y) = \frac{1}{N} \sum_{k=1}^{N} (d_k - \mu_d)(y_k - \mu_y) \quad (7)$$

where D corresponds to the array of difficulty levels d_k and Y to their respective MAP results. N is the number of topics, μ the mean and σ the standard deviation.

Figure 1 shows that a strong negative correlation exists between the level of topic difficulty and the average MAP of submitted ImageCLEF results (the higher the topic difficulty score, the lower the MAP score).

The correlations of ENG, SPA-L, ITA, FRA, POR and ALL are significant at the 0.01 level, SPA-E and GER at the 0.05 level. Dutch, showing the weakest correlation of just -0.329, did not pass the significance test. This is due to inaccurate translation of topic numbers 2, 16 and 25. If these three topics are omitted, Dutch shows a negative correlation of -0.482 that is significant at the 0.05 level (0.015).

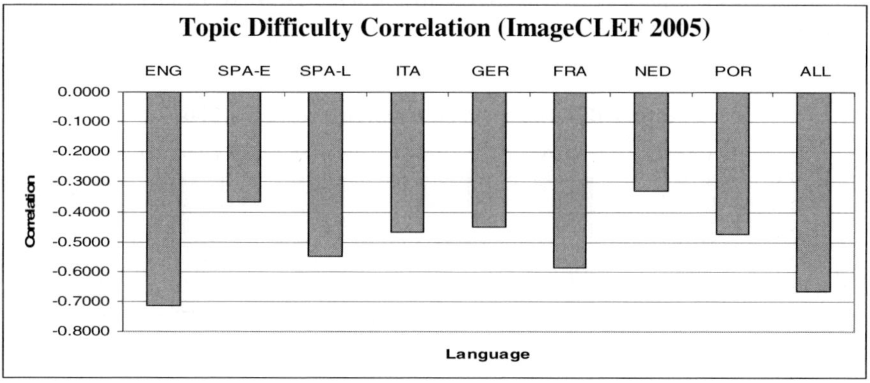

Fig. 1. Correlation between topic difficulty score and MAP for ImageCLEF 2005 submissions

3.2 ImageCLEF 2004

In ImageCLEF 2004 [6], twelve participating groups submitted 190 runs to the ad-hoc task. Similar to results in section 3.1, the levels of topic difficulty were calculated for all 25 topics and compared with the average MAP results for languages with more than 10 submissions.

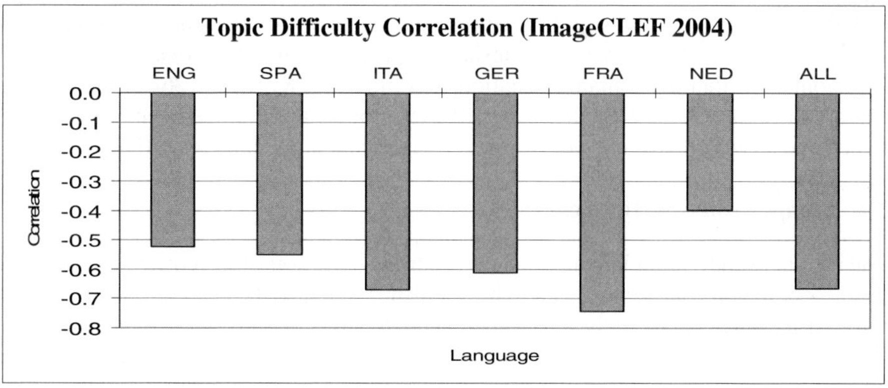

Fig. 2. Topic difficulty correlation for ImageCLEF 2004

Figure 2 shows, again, a strong negative correlation. The correlation factor $\rho_{x,y}$ is always stronger than -0.4, reaches more than -0.6 for Italian and German and even more than -0.7 for French. All correlation are significant at the 0.01 level except for Dutch (NED) which is significant at the 0.05 level.

3.3 ImageCLEF 2003

In ImageCLEF 2003 [5], four participating groups submitted 45 runs to the ad-hoc task. Similar to results in sections 3.1 and 3.2, the levels of topic difficulty were calculated for all 50 topics and compared with the average MAP results for languages with more than 5 submissions.

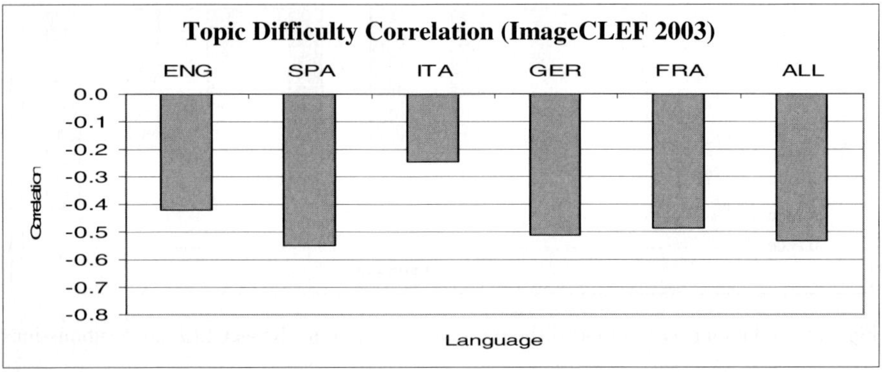

Fig. 3. Topic difficulty correlation for ImageCLEF 2003

The results shown in Figure 3 demonstrate a very strong negative correlation again. Like in 2004 and 2005, the correlation factor $\rho_{x,y}$ is always stronger than -0.4 (except for Italian which is due to a couple of inaccurate translations that produced surprising results). The correlations are significant at the 0.01 level for all the languages except for English which is significant at the 0.05 level.

Italian did not pass the significance test, again due to the inaccurate translation of several topics. An assessment of translation quality of the 2003 ImageCLEF topics [18] points out that the Italian translation of topics 2, 5, 8, 16, 19, 26, 29, 40, 43, 46, and 47 shows a very low quality score. If these topics are omitted in the calculation, Italian shows a correlation of -0.378 that is significant at the 0.05 level (0.019).

3.4 Comparison over the Years

The results of individual languages show a certain variation of the correlation over the years. While some languages (French, Spanish, German) show a consistent correlations in all three years, others (English, Dutch) considerably vary over the years. However, it is felt that this inconsistency is not so much due to the fact that the topic difficulty estimation works better for some languages than for others than due to the following reasons:

Firstly, a varying number of research groups participated in different years using several different techniques, e.g. with and without query expansion, with and without the additional use of a content-based retrieval system, topic titles only or topic titles and narrative descriptions, etc. Further, different translation sources and different translation qualities also lead to varying results over the years.

The nature of queries too changed over the years in response to participants' comments and feedback. While 2004, for example, saw more specific topics including meta-data, the topics in 2005 were of a more general and visual nature.

Moreover, the level of difficulty was increased over the years too, as mentioned in Section 1. While in 2003 and 2004 the average topic difficulty level was nearly the same (1.86 and 1.90 respectively), it was increased to 2.47 in 2005 to keep up the challenge for returning participants. And indeed, the average MAP across all submitted runs dropped to 0.23 in 2005 (compared to 0.32 in 2003 and 0.30 in 2004), which is an indicator that the topics were a little bit too difficult in 2005.

Finally, the number of participants and especially the number of submitted runs has increased each year. Hence, the results and correlations are more and more meaningful each year as they do not depend so much on the performance of just a few participants (389 submitted runs in 2005 compared to 45 runs in 2003).

4 Conclusion and Future Work

In this paper, we present a measure for the degree of topic difficulty for search requests of cross-language image retrieval. Establishing such a measure is beneficial when creating benchmarks such as ImageCLEF in that it is possible to categorise results according to a level of complexity for individual topics. This can help explain results obtained when using the benchmark and provide some kind of control and reasoning over topic generation.

Examples illustrating various aspects of the linguistic structure of the difficulty measure and motivating its creation have been presented. Comparing the level of difficulty for topics created in ImageCLEF 2003 to 2005 for the ad-hoc task with MAP scores from submitted runs by participating groups have shown a strong negative correlation indicating that more linguistically complex topics result in much lower MAP scores due to the requirement of more complex translation approaches.

Future work will involve the improvement and refinement of the proposed measure and further verification by analysing results from the 2006 ImageCLEF ad-hoc task. Further investigation could include the correlation of the topic difficulty measure with translation quality measures [18] and the comparison with alternative approaches [14,16].

References

1. Clough, P., Sanderson, M., Reid, N.: The Eurovision St Andrews Photographic Collection (ESTA), Image CLEF Report, University of Sheffield, UK (February 2003).
2. Grubinger, M., Leung, C.: A Benchmark for Performance Calibration in Visual Information Search, In Proceedings of 2003 Conference of Visual Information Systems, Miami, Florida, USA (September 24-26, 2003) 414 – 419.
3. Leung, C., Ip, H.: Benchmarking for Content Based Visual Information Search. In Laurini ed. Fourth International Conference on Visual Information Systems (VISUAL'2000), Lecture Notes in Computer Science, Springer Verlag, Lyon, France (November 2000), 442 – 456.

4. Müller, H., Müller, W., Squire, D., Marchand-Millet, S., Pun, T.: Performance Evaluation in Content Based Image Retrieval: Overview and Proposals. Pattern Recognition Letters, 22 (5), (April 2001), 563 – 601.
5. Clough, P., Sanderson, M.: The CLEF 2003 cross language image retrieval task. In Proceedings of the Cross Language Evaluation Forum (CLEF) 2003, Trondheim, Norway, Springer Verlag, (2004).
6. Clough, P., Müller, H., Sanderson, M.: Overview of the CLEF cross-language image retrieval track (ImageCLEF) 2004. In C. Peters, P.D. Clough, G. J. F. Jones, J. Gonzalo, M. Kluck, and B. Magnini, editors, Multilingual Information Access for Text, Speech and Images: Result of the fifth CLEF evaluation campaign, Lecture Notes in Computer Science, Springer Verlag, Bath, England (2005).
7. Armitage, L., Enser, P.: Analysis of User Need in Image Archives. Journal of Information Science, 23 (4), (1997), 287 – 299.
8. Bagga, A., Biermann, A.: Analysing the complexity of a domain with respect to an information extraction task. In Proceedings of the tenth International Conference on Research on Computational Linguistics (ROCLING X), (August 1997), 175 – 194.
9. Niyogi, P.: The Informational Complexity of Learning from Examples. PhD Thesis, MIT. (1996).
10. Barton, E., Berwick, R., Ristad, E.: Computational Complexity and Natural Language. The MIT Press, Cambridge, Massachusetts (1987).
11. Ristad, E.: The Language Complexity Games. MIT Press, Cambridge, MA, (1993).
12. Flank, S.: Sentences vs. Phrases: Syntactic Complexity in Multimedia Information Retrieval. NAACL-ANLP 2000 Workshop: Syntactic and Semantic Complexity in Natural Language Processing Systems (2000).
13. Pollard, S., Biermann, A.: A Measure of Semantic Complexity for Natural Language Systems. NAACL-ANLP 2000 Workshop: Syntactic and Semantic Complexity in Natural Language Processing Systems (2000).
14. Cronen-Townsend, S., Zhou, Y., Croft, W.B.: Predicting Query Performance, In Proceedings of the 25th Annual International ACM SIGIR Conference on Research and Development in Information Retrieval 2002, ACM Press (2002), 299 – 306.
15. Amati, G., Carpineto, C., Romano, G.: Query Difficulty, Robustness and Selective Application of Query Expansion. In Proceedings of the 25th European Conference on Information Retrieval (ECIR 2004), Sunderland, Great Britain (2004), 127 – 137.
16. Yom-Tov, E., Fine, S., Carmel, D., Darlow, A.: Learning to Estimate Query Difficulty. In Proceedings of the 28th Annual International ACM SIGIR Conference on Research and Development in Information Retrieval 2005, ACM Press (2005).
17. Clough, P., Müller, H., Deselaers, T., Grubinger, M., Lehmann, T., Jensen, J., Hersh, W.: The CLEF 2005 Cross-Language Image Retrieval Track, Proceedings of the Cross Language Evaluation Forum 2005, Springer Lecture Notes in Computer science, (2006) - to appear.
18. Clough, P.D., Sanderson, M.: Assessing Translation Quality for Cross-Language Image Retrieval, In Proceedings of Cross Language Evaluation Forum (CLEF) 2003, Trondheim, Norway, Springer Verlag (2004).

Dublin City University at CLEF 2005: Experiments with the ImageCLEF St Andrew's Collection

Gareth J.F. Jones and Kieran McDonald

Centre for Digital Video Processing & School of Computing
Dublin City University, Dublin 9, Ireland
{gjones, kmcdon}@computing.dcu.ie

Abstract. The aim of the Dublin City University's participation in the CLEF 2005 ImageCLEF St Andrew's Collection task was to explore an alternative approach to exploiting text annotation and content-based retrieval in a novel combined way for pseudo relevance feedback (PRF). This method combines evidence from retrieved lists generated using text-based and content-based retrieval to determine which documents will be assumed relevant for the PRF process. Unfortunately the experimental results show that while standard text-based PRF improves upon a no feedback text-only baseline, at present our new approach to combining evidence from text-based and content-based retrieval does not give further improvement.

1 Introduction

Dublin City University's participation in the CLEF 2005 ImageCLEF St Andrew's collection task [1] explored a novel approach to pseudo relevance feedback (PRF) combining evidence from separate text-based and content-based retrieval runs. The underlying text retrieval system is based on a standard Okapi model for document ranking and PRF [2]. Three sets of experiments are reported for the following topic languages: Chinese (simplified), Dutch, French, German, Greek, Italian, Japanese, Portuguese, Russian and Spanish (european), along with corresponding monolingual English results as a baseline for comparison. Topics were translated into English using the online Babelfish machine translation engine. The first set of experiments establish baseline retrieval performance without PRF, the second set of experiments incorporate a standard PRF stage, and finally the third set investigates our new combined method for PRF.

This paper is organised as follows: Section 2 briefly outlines the details of our standard retrieval system and describes our novel PRF method, Section 3 gives results for our experiments, and finally Section 4 concludes the paper.

2 Retrieval System

2.1 Standard Retrieval Approach

Our basic experimental retrieval system is a local implementation of the standard Okapi retrieval model [2]. Documents and search topics are processed to remove

C. Peters et al. (Eds.): CLEF 2005, LNCS 4022, pp. 567–573, 2006.

stopwords from the standard SMART list, and suffix stripped using the Snowball implementation of Porter stemming [3] [4]. The resulting terms are weighted using the standard BM25 weighting scheme with parameters ($k1$ and b) selected using the CLEF 2004 ImageCLEF test collection data as a training set.

Standard PRF was carried out using query expansion. The top ranked documents from a baseline retrieval run were assumed relevant. Terms from these documents were ranked using the Robertson selection value (RSV) [2], and the top ranked terms added to the original topic statement. The parameters of the PRF stage were again selected using the CLEF 2004 ImageCLEF test set.

2.2 Combining Text and Content-Based Retrieval for PRF

The preceding text-based retrieval methods have been shown to work reasonably effectively for the St Andrew's ImageCLEF task in earlier workshops [5]. However, this approach makes no use of the document or topic images. In our participation in the CLEF 2004 ImageCLEF task we attempted to improve text-only based retrieval by performing a standard data fusion summation combination of retrieved ranked lists from text-only retrieval and the provided context-based retrieval lists generated using the GIFT/Viper system. The results of these combined lists showed little difference from the text-only runs [5].

Analysis of the GIFT/Viper only runs for the CLEF 2004 task showed them to have very poor recall, but reasonable precision at high cutoff levels. However, further investigation of this showed that this good high cutoff precision is largely attributable to a good match on the topic image which is part of the document collection. This topic image is relevant for the topic and typically found at rank position one. Our analysis suggests that there is little to be gained from data fusion in this way, certainly when content-based retrieval is based on low-level features. Indeed it is perhaps surprising that this method does not degrade performance relative to the text-only retrieval runs.

Nevertheless, we were interested to see if the evidence from content-based retrieval runs might be usefully combined with the text-only retrieval runs in a different way. For our CLEF 2005 experiments we hypothesized that documents retrieved by both the text-based and content-based methods are more likely to be relevant than documents retrieved by only one system. We adapted the standard PRF method to incorporate this hypothesis as follows. Starting from the top of lists retrieved independently using text-based retrieval with the standard PRF method and content-based retrieval, we look for documents retrieved by both systems. Documents retrieved by both systems are assumed to be relevant and are used to augment the assumed relevant document set for a further run of the text-only based retrieval system with the standard query expansion PRF method.

For this investigation content-based retrieval used our own image retrieval system based on standard low-level colour, edge and texture features. The colour comparison was based on 5×5 regional colour with HSV histogram dimensions $16 \times 4 \times 4$. Edge comparison used Canny edge with 5×5 regions quantized into 8 directions. Texture matching was based on the first 5 DCT co-efficients, each

Table 1. Text-only baseline retrieval runs using Babelfish topic translation

		English	Chinese (s)	Dutch	French	German	Greek
Prec.	5 docs	0.557	0.264	0.471	0.393	0.486	0.379
	10 docs	0.500	0.254	0.436	0.375	0.418	0.404
	15 docs	0.460	0.250	0.402	0.355	0.374	0.386
	20 docs	0.427	0.230	0.377	0.323	0.343	0.370
Av Precision		0.355	0.189	0.283	0.244	0.284	0.249
% chg.		—	-46.8%	-20.3%	-31.3%	-20.0%	-29.9%
Rel. Ret.		1550	1168	1213	1405	1337	1107
chg. Rel. Ret.		—	-382	-337	-145	-213	-443

		English	Italian	Japanese	Portuguese	Russian	Spanish (e)
Prec.	5 docs	0.557	0.300	0.393	0.407	0.379	0.336
	10 docs	0.500	0.296	0.368	0.368	0.354	0.325
	15 docs	0.460	0.269	0.336	0.343	0.329	0.307
	20 docs	0.427	0.266	0.311	0.323	0.314	0.280
Av Precision		0.355	0.216	0.259	0.243	0.247	0.207
% chg.		—	-39.2%	-27.0%	-31.5%	-30.4%	-41.7%
Rel. Ret.		1550	1181	1304	1263	1184	1227
chg. Rel. Ret.		—	-369	-246	-287	-366	-323

quantized into 3 values for 3×3 regions. The scores of the three components were then combined in a weighted sum and the overall summed scores used to rank the content-based retrieved list.

3 Experimental Results

The settings for the Okapi model were optimized using the CLEF 2004 ImageCLEF English language topics as follows: $k1 = 1.0$ and $b = 0.5$. These parameters were used for all test runs reported in this paper.

3.1 Baseline Retrieval

Table 1 shows baseline retrieval results for the Okapi model without application of feedback. Monolingual results for English topics are shown in the left side column for each row. Results for each translated topic language relative to English are then shown in the other columns. From these results we can see that cross-language performance is degraded relative to monolingual by between around 20% and 45% for the different topic languages with respect to MAP, and by between 150 and 450 for the total number of relevant documents retrieved. These results are in line with those that would be expected for short documents with cross-language topics translated using a standard commercial machine translation system.

Table 2. Text-only PRF retrieval runs using Babelfish topic translation

		English	Chinese (s)	Dutch	French	German	Greek
Prec.	5 docs	0.529	0.257	0.450	0.407	0.443	0.439
	10 docs	0.500	0.275	0.425	0.407	0.407	0.432
	15 docs	0.467	0.274	0.407	0.393	0.393	0.410
	20 docs	0.432	0.261	0.382	0.373	0.375	0.396
Av Precision		0.364	0.213	0.308	0.283	0.308	0.302
% chg.		—	-41.5%	-15.4%	-22.3%	-15.4%	-17.0%
Rel. Ret.		1648	1320	1405	1580	1427	1219
chg. Rel. Ret.		—	-328	-243	-68	-221	-429

		English	Italian	Japanese	Portuguese	Russian	Spanish (e)
Prec.	5 docs	0.529	0.264	0.350	0.379	0.371	0.336
	10 docs	0.500	0.279	0.346	0.346	0.357	0.321
	15 docs	0.467	0.255	0.326	0.324	0.350	0.295
	20 docs	0.432	0.245	0.329	0.316	0.338	0.286
Av Precision		0.354	0.215	0.268	0.247	0.280	0.224
% chg.		—	-40.9%	-26.4%	-32.1%	-23.1%	-38.5%
Rel. Ret.		1648	1223	1331	1364	1335	1360
chg. Rel. Ret.		—	-425	-317	-284	-313	-288

3.2 Standard Pseudo Relevance Feedback

Results using the CLEF 2004 ImageCLEF data with the English language topics were shown to be optimized on average by assuming the top 15 documents retrieved to be relevant and by adding the resulting top 10 ranked terms to the original topic, with the original terms upweighted by a factor of 3.5 relative to the expansion terms.

Table 2 shows results for applying PRF with these settings. The form of the results table is the same as that in Table 1. From this table we can see that PRF is effective for this task for all topic languages. Further the reduction relative to monolingual retrieval in each case is also generally reduced. Again this trend is commonly observed for cross-language information retrieval tasks.

Performance for individual topic languages can be improved by selecting the parameters separately, but we believed that optimizing for individual topic languages would lead to overfitting to the training topic set. To explore this issue, we performed an extensive set of post evaluation experiments varying $k1$ and b using the CLEF 2005 test collection. Results of these experiments showed that in all cases average precision and the total number of relevant documents retrieval can be improved slightly. In a few cases relatively large improvements were observed (for example, for PRF with Japanese topics average precision improved from 0.268 to 0.303, and with Italian topics from 0.215 to 0.266). There was a very wide variation in the optimal $k1$ and b for the various topic languages, and often between baseline and PRF runs for the same language. For further comparison we ran a similar set of experiments to optimize $k1$ and b for the

Table 3. PRF retrieval runs incorporating text and image retrieval evidence using Babelfish topic translation

		English	Chinese (s)	Dutch	French	German	Greek
Prec.	5 docs	0.529	0.264	0.443	0.407	0.443	0.414
	10 docs	0.504	0.268	0.432	0.411	0.414	0.429
	15 docs	0.460	0.271	0.402	0.393	0.391	0.405
	20 docs	0.432	0.259	0.375	0.373	0.371	0.393
Av Precision		0.365	0.210	0.306	0.282	0.308	0.298
% chg.		—	-42.7%	-16.2%	-22.7%	-15.6%	-18.4%
Rel. Ret.		1652	1318	1405	1578	1428	1218
chg. Rel. Ret.		—	-334	-247	-74	-224	-434

		English	Italian	Japanese	Portuguese	Russian	Spanish (e)
Prec.	5 docs	0.529	0.264	0.343	0.371	0.371	0.343
	10 docs	0.504	0.279	0.350	0.350	0.354	0.318
	15 docs	0.460	0.248	0.321	0.319	0.350	0.291
	20 docs	0.432	0.241	0.325	0.309	0.339	0.284
Av Precision		0.365	0.215	0.268	0.247	0.279	0.224
% chg.		—	-41.1%	-26.6%	-32.3%	-23.6%	-38.6%
Rel. Ret.		1652	1227	1336	1366	1331	1361
chg. Rel. Ret.		—	-425	-316	-286	-321	-291

CLEF 2004 ImageCLEF collection. We observed similar variations in optimal values between the topic languages, baseline and PRF runs, and also generally between the 2004 and 2005 topic sets for the same language and run condition. This variation between topic sets would appear to justify our original decision to adopt the same $k1$ and b values for all our submitted test runs.

3.3 Text and Image Combined Pseudo Relevance Feedback

The combination of features for content-based image retrieval was also optimized using the CLEF 2004 ImageCLEF task using only the topic and document images. Based on this optimization the matching scores of the features were combined as follows: $0.5 \times colour + 0.3 \times edge + 0.2 \times texture$.

The selection depth of documents in the ranked retrieved text-based and image-based lists from which the additional assumed relevant set could be selected was also determined using the CLEF 2004 ImageCLEF data. We carried out extensive investigation of the optimal search depth for a range of topic languages. There was no apparent reliable trend across the language pairs, and we could not be confident that values chosen for a particular pair on the training data would be suitable for a new topic set. Based on analysis of overall trends across the set of language pairs, we decided to set the search to a depth of 180 retrieved documents for the text-only list and for the image-only list to a rank of 20 documents. Documents occurring in both lists down to these rank positions were assumed to be relevant and added to the text-only run top 15 documents assumed to be relevant for term selection in text-only PRF.

Results from these experiments are shown in Table 3. Comparing these results to those using the standard PRF method in Table 2 we observe very little change in the results. In general the results for our new method are marginally reduced in comparison to the standard method. Examination of the outputs from the component systems revealed that the main reason for the similarity between results in Tables 2 and 3 is that very few additional assumed relevant documents are found in the comparison of the text-only and image-only retrieval lists. This arises largely due to the failure of the image-only retrieval system to retrieve relevant documents within the upper ranks[1] of the retrieved lists. Thus when comparing the text-only and image-only retrieved lists very few matches were found. The poor performance of the image-only retrieval system is to be expected since we are using standard low-level image matching techniques on the St Andrew's collection which is very heterogeneous, but we had hoped that combining with the text-only evidence would prove useful.

Similar to the text-only runs, it is likely that these results could be improved marginally by adjusting the search depth of the lists for the PRF stage. However post fitting to the test data does not represent a realistic search scenario, is unlikely to give any clear increase in results, and, as shown in the previous section, will generally not be reliable for different topic sets and languages.

4 Conclusions and Further Work

Results from our experiments for the CLEF 2005 St Andrew's ImageCLEF task show expected performance trends for our baseline system and a PRF augmented text-based retrieval system each using the standard Okapi model. Our proposed new PRF approach combining retrieval lists from text-based and image-based retrieval for this task failed to improve on results obtained using a standard PRF method. A clear reason for the failure of this technique is the absence of relevant documents in the ranked lists retrieved by the image-only retrieval system. Despite the current results, it would be interesting to explore this technique further in a task where the image collection is more homogeneous and image-based retrieval is more effective.

References

[1] Clough, P., Müeller, H., Deselaers, T., Grubinger, M., Lehmann, T., Jensen, J., and Hersh, W.: The CLEF 2005 Cross-Language Image Retrieval Task, Proceedings of the CLEF 2005: Workshop on Cross-Language Information Retrieval and Evaluation, Vienna, Austria, 2005.

[2] Robertson, S. E., Walker, S., Jones, S., Hancock-Beaulieu, M. M., and Gatford, M.,: Okapi at TREC-3. In D.K. Harman, editor, Proceedings of the Third Text REtrieval Conference (TREC-3), pages 109-126. NIST, 1995.

[1] In determining the system parameters we explored searching the image retrieval lists to a depth of 200 documents for our new combination method.

[3] *Snowball* toolkit `http://snowball.tartarus.org/`
[4] Porter, M. F.: An algorithm for suffix stripping. *Program* 14:10-137, 1980.
[5] Jones, G. J. F., Groves, D., Khasin, A., Lam-Adesina, A. M., Mellebeek, B., and Way, A.: Dublin City University at CLEF 2004: Experiments with the ImageCLEF St Andrew's Collection, Proceedings of the CLEF 2004: Workshop on Cross-Language Information Retrieval and Evaluation, Bath, U.K., pp653-663, 2004.

A Probabilistic, Text and Knowledge-Based Image Retrieval System

Rubén Izquierdo-Beviá, David Tomás, Maximiliano Saiz-Noeda, and José Luis Vicedo

Departamento de Lenguajes y Sistemas Informáticos.
Universidad de Alicante. Spain
{ruben, dtomas, max, vicedo}@dlsi.ua.es

Abstract. This paper describes the development of an image retrieval system that combines probabilistic and ontological information[1]. The process is divided in two different stages: indexing and retrieval. Three information flows have been created with different kind of information each one: word forms, stems and stemmed bigrams. The final result combines the results obtained in the three streams. Knowledge is added to the system by means of an ontology created automatically from the St. Andrews Corpus. The system has been evaluated at CLEF05 image retrieval task.

1 Introduction

An image retriever is an IR system that discovers relevant images. Mainly, there are two approaches to Image Retrieval [1]. On the one hand we have Content-Based Image Retrieval (CBIR). This approach deals with primitive features of the image using computer vision techniques. On the other hand there are techniques based on the text that describes the image. Moreover, there are hybrid ones that combine both approaches.

Our system combines probabilistic and automatic extracted knowledge from the text that describes the image. We have initially used a probabilistic information retrieval system: Xapian[2]. The knowledge is incorporated using an ontology created automatically from the St. Andrews Corpus.

2 The System

Our system relies on Xapian, a probabilistic and boolean information retrieval system. The process is divided in two stages: indexing and retrieval.

2.1 Indexing

In this stage, we process the text of the image and create three indexes using words, stems and stemmed bigrams. The text is analyzed by means of a set of

[1] This work has been partially supported by the Spanish Government (CICYT) with grant TIC2003-07158-c04-01.

[2] The Xapian Project, http://www.xapian.org

C. Peters et al. (Eds.): CLEF 2005, LNCS 4022, pp. 574–577, 2006.

patterns and several fields are extracted from it. We assign a weight to each field, depending on the relevance of the information contained on it. The fields extracted and the weights selected are shown in table 1.

Table 1. Weights assigned to each field in the image file

FIELD	Headline	Short title	Description	Data	Photographer	Location	Notes
WEIGHT	5	4	1	3	3	0	8

For each image we create a document to be indexed. This document consists of weighted tokens extracted from the text that describes the image. Tokens can be words, stems and stemmed bigrams. In this way we create three indexes using different tokens. The weight assigned to each token is:

$$W_{token} = \begin{cases} 100 * field\_weight \text{ if 1st letter is uppercase} \\ 50 * field\_weight \text{ if 1st letter is lowercase} \end{cases} \quad (1)$$

2.2 Retrieval

In the retrieval stage, for each query topic we make three retrievals (one for each index) and combine the results to get a single list of ranked documents.

The first step prepares the query to be processed by the retrieval system. Stop words are removed and words are processed to obtain stems and stemmed bigrams. The retrieval process can be summarized in these steps:

1. Retrieval in the corresponding index
2. Apply relevance feedback to expand the query[3]
3. Retrieve with the expanded query
4. Enrich the results with the ontology information

As a result we obtain three document lists, one for each index. The next step is to combine them to get the final result: a single list of weighted documents. Each information stream provides a different kind of information, and thus, each stream must have a different weight. We analyzed the system's performance to obtain the best weight tuning considering the contribution of each information flow. The weights assigned to stem, word and bigram flows are: 0.5, 0.1 and 0.3, respectively. When combining, each document is scored by the sum of its flow

[3] Xapian allows us to apply relevance feedback by selecting a number of documents considered relevant. We have selected the first twenty three documents due to some experiments over the ImageCLEF 2004 query set reveal that this is the number of documents suitable to get the best results.

scores multiplied by their corresponding weight ($0.5 * W_{Flow} + 0.1 * W_{Word} + 0.3 * W_{Bigram}$).

3 Multilingual View

We have used an automatic online translator to deal with multilingual features. The process consists on translating the query topics into English and then use the monolingual system described in the previous section. We compared several translators in order to select the best performing one. This analysis was carried out using the ImageCLEF2004 query set and the St. Andrews Corpus. The translators reviewed were Babel[4], Reverso[5], WordLingo[6], Epals[7] and Prompt[8]. The best performance was achieved by WordLingo.

4 Ontology

The ontology has been created automatically from the St. Andrews Corpus. Each image in this corpus has a field called <CATEGORIES>. We can extract the words contained in the rest of the fields and match them with these categories. In this way, we created an ontology, where each category is related to the images belonging to it through the words that describe these images (category descriptor vector).

The ontology is used as follows: the system computes the similarity between the query and the categories using the category descriptor vectors, and the weight obtained boosts document similarity in the relevant document lists previously obtained in the retrieval stage. This way, the relevance of documents having any category in common with relevant categories is increased according to the relevance of the category obtained.

5 Experiments and Results

Four experiments have been carried out combining different features and techniques. The features merged in the different experiments are: the kind of tokens used (stem, words, bigrams), the fields selected and their weights, the weights for flow combination, the use of ontology and the use of automatic feedback.

With these features we developed over 100 experiments. The characteristics and results of the best ones are shown in table 2.

As shown, *Experiment3* provides the best performance. It uses stems, words and bigrams implementing feedback and category knowledge. Stream combination and ontology information improve the overall performance.

[4] http://world.altavista.com/

[5] http://www.reverso.net/

[6] http://www.worldlingo.com/en/products_services/worldlingo_translator.html

[7] http://www.epals.com/translation/translation.e

[8] http://translation2.paralink.com/

Table 2. Feature selection for each retrieval experiment

	STEM	WORD	BIGRAM	CATS.	FEEDBACK	MAP
Baseline	X					0.3944
Experiment1	X	X	X			0.3942
Experiment2	X	X	X		X	0.3909
Experiment3	X	X	X	X	X	0.3966

6 Conclusions and Future Work

In this paper we have presented an image retrieval method based on probabilistic and knowledge information. The system implements a text-based multimedia retrieval system. We have used Xapian, a probabilistic and boolean information retrieval system, and an ontology created automatically from the St. Andrews Corpus.

We can conclude that our system has reached a high performance with a simple idea: the combination of different information streams and the use of knowledge.

Having in mind CLEF05 competition [2] and comparing our results with other participant systems, our system performs better than CBIR (visual retrieval) approaches and our results are also above the average MAP for different features combination in text-based systems. Our best result (*Experiment3*) reached 0.3966 for English, taking into account that the average MAP for English runs is 0.2084. *Experiment3* implements feedback, while the average MAP for runs using feedback is 0.2399. Finally, we used only title as query, with the average MAP for runs using title being 0.2140.

The system can be improved in different ways. First consider the use of NLP to improve the information retrieval [3]. Another task to be developed is the creation and management of the ontology, that is, the use of knowledge in the retrieval process [4].

References

1. Paul Clough and Mark Sanderson and Henning Muller: The CLEF Cross Language Image Retrieval Track (imageCLEF) 2004. In: Working Notes for the CLEF 2004 WorkShop, Bath, United Kingdom (2004)
2. Paul Clough, Henning Muller, Thomas Deselaers, Michael Grubinger, Thomas M. Lehmann, Jeery Jensen, William Hersh: The CLEF 2005 Cross-Language Image Retrieval Track. In: Proceedings of the Cross Language Evaluation Forum 2005, Springer Lecture Notes in Computer science, Viena, Austria (2006 (to appear))
3. Lewis, D.D., Jones, K.S.: Natural language processing for information retrieval. Communications of the ACM 39(1) (1996) 92101
4. Kashyap, V.: Design and creation of ontologies for environmental information retrieval, proceedings of the 12th workshop on knowledge acquisition, modeling and management (kaw'99), ban, canada, october 1999. In: KAW'99 Conference. (1999)

UNED at ImageCLEF 2005: Automatically Structured Queries with Named Entities over Metadata

Víctor Peinado, Fernando López-Ostenero, Julio Gonzalo, and Felisa Verdejo

NLP Group, ETSI Informática, UNED
c/ Juan del Rosal, 16. E-28040 Madrid. Spain
{victor, flopez, julio, felisa}@lsi.uned.es

Abstract. In this paper, we present our participation in the ImageCLEF 2005 ad-hoc task. After a pool of preliminary tests in which we evaluated the impact of different-size dictionaries using three distinct approaches, we proved that the biggest differences were obtained by recognizing named entities and launching structured queries over the metadata. Thus, we decided to refine our named entities recognizer and repeat the three approaches with the 2005 topics, achieving the best result among all cross-language European Spanish to English runs.

1 Introduction

In this paper, we describe the experiments submitted by UNED to the ImageCLEF 2005 ad-hoc task [1]. First, we try a first pool of preliminary experiments using the ImageCLEF 2004 testbed and the Spanish official topics, performed in order to study the impact of different-size dictionaries in the final results. Then, we describe UNED's participation in the ImageCLEF 2005 track. Given the benefits of recognizing named entities in the topics in order to structure the queries, we decided to improve our recognition process. We performed three approaches over the 2005 testbed obtaining the first and third best cross-lingual runs in European Spanish.

2 Previous Experiments

After our official participation in ImageCLEF 2004 [2], we applied the following three approaches with six different bilingual dictionaries to the query translation [3]: i) a naive baseline using a word by word translation of the topic titles; ii) a strong baseline based on Pirkola's work [4]; and iii) a structured query using the named entities with field search operators and Pirkola's approach.

The differences among dictionaries were not statistically relevant in most cases. However, the fact of identifying named entities in the topics and launching structured queries over the metadata turned out to be the key of the overall improvements. Since we were able to outperform our official results, we decided to improve our resources and try the same approaches with the new topics.

C. Peters et al. (Eds.): CLEF 2005, LNCS 4022, pp. 578–581, 2006.

3 Experimental Settings

The testbed provided to ImageCLEF 2005 ad-hoc task participants was the St Andrews image collection. The participants were given 28 topics, each containing a title and a narrative fragment with verbose details about an information need. Unlike last year's edition, in 2005 two distinct set of Spanish topics, which tried to show the local variants of the language, were provided: one European Spanish translation and another Latin-American version. Even though the topics had wholly been compiled into Spanish, we only took the short titles in our experiments.

We also had our bilingual dictionary complied from different lexicographic sources such as Vox, EuroWordNet and FreeDict. Lastly, our search engine was developed using the Inquery's API.

4 Proper Nouns, Temporal References and Numbers Found

Some improvements have been done in our named entities recognition process with respect to our last year's edition. Now, we can locate more complex multiword proper nouns and temporal references by attaching several simple entities of the same type usually connected by articles, prepositions and conjunctions. And so, our recognizer is able to locate some Spanish named entities such as the ones shown in Table 1.

Table 1. Examples of Spanish named entities: proper nouns and organizations, temporal references and cardinal numbers located in the EFE news agency corpus

organizations
Alta Comisaría de las Naciones Unidas para los Refugiados
Orquesta Sinfónica de la Radio Bávara
Comisión Nacional del Mercado de Valores
temporal references and dates
ocho de la tarde de ayer 31 de diciembre
domingo 2 de enero de 1994
16,30 de ayer viernes
cardinal numbers
20.000 millones
treinta y cuatro
ochocientos sesenta millones

In Table 2, we show the named entities located in the ImageCLEF 2005 European Spanish topics. It is worth mentioning that the topics proposed this year contained fewer expressions likely to be named entities than last year. Indeed, no temporal reference or number was located and we could only take advantage of the improvements of the recognizer in 6 out of 28 topics. Regarding the precision

Table 2. Named entities identified in the 2005 topics

topic #	Entities identified
10	imágenes del [$_{PN}$ Sol], [$_{PN}$ Escocia]
12	postales de [$_{PN}$ Iona], [$_{PN}$ Escocia]
19	postales compuestas con imágenes de [$_{PN}$ Irlanda del Norte]
20	visita real a [$_{PN}$ Escocia] (excepto a [$_{PN}$ Fife])
21	monumento al poeta [$_{PN}$ Robert Burns]
28	fotografías a color de bosques alrededor de [$_{PN}$ St. Andrews]

of this recognizer, notice that the entities located in this year's topics are the same as the ones that a user would have manually selected.

5 Submitted Runs

We submitted five different runs, based on the same experiments we had already tested in Section 2. First, one monolingual run in order to establish the maximum precision that we could achieve using our resources. Then, a naive run building the queries with a simple word by word translation.

We also submitted two runs based on the strong baseline with the synonymy's operators which allowed us to enrich and expand the translations while minimizing the noise. Lastly, we repeated the run adding field search operators.

6 Results and Discussion

The official results obtained by our five runs are shown in Table 3. First of all, it is worth mentioning that our cross-lingual run enriched with named entities `unedESENEnt` obtained the best MAP score among all official cross-lingual runs having European Spanish as the topic language. Its counterparts without using the named entities `unedESEN` and `unedESAmerEN` got comparable results: 0.28 (3rd position in European Spanish) and 0.26, respectively. On the other hand, our simpler cross-lingual run achieved 0.19.

In spite of the apparently poor result obtained by our monolingual run, the small difference regarding our best cross-lingual run, whose MAP score represents 94% of `unedmono`'s one, is remarkable. This leads `unedESENEnt` even closer than our last year's best strategy.

Table 3. Results of our official runs

run	MAP	variation
unedmono	.34	–
unedESENEnt	.32	94%
unedESEN	.28	82%
unedESAmerEN	.26	76%
unedESENnaive	.19	56%

7 Conclusions

In this paper, we have presented our participation in the ImageCLEF 2005 ad-hoc task. After a pool of preliminary experiments using the ImageCLEF 2004 testbed, which allowed us to outperform our official participation, we decided to refine our named entities recognizer and repeat the same approach with the 2005 topics, achieving the best result among all cross-language European Spanish to English runs.

Automatic query structuring seems an effective strategy to improve cross-language retrieval on semi-structured texts. Remarkably, no sophisticated named entity recognition machinery is required to benefit from query structuring. Of course, it remains to be checked whether this result holds on collections with different metadata fields and different textual properties.

Acknowledgments

This work has been partially supported by the Spanish Government under the project R2D2-Syembra (TIC2003-07158-C04-02). Víctor Peinado holds a PhD grant by UNED (*Universidad Nacional de Educación a Distancia*).

References

1. Clough, P., Müller, H., Deselears, T., Grubinger, M., Lehmann, T. M., Jensen, J., Hersh, W.: The CLEF 2005 Cross-Language Image Retrieval Track. In: Proceedings of the Cross-Language Evaluation Forum 2005. Springer Lecture Notes of Computer Science (to appear).
2. Peinado, V., Artiles, J., López-Ostenero, F., Gonzalo, J., Verdejo, F.: UNED at Image CLEF 2004: Detecting Named Entities and Noun Phrases for Automatic Query Expansion and Structuring. In: Cross Language Evaluation Forum, Working Notes for the CLEF 2004 Workshop. Springer Lecture Notes of Computer Science (2005), 3491:643–652.
3. Peinado, V., López-Ostenero, F., Gonzalo, J., Verdejo, F.: Searching Cross-Language Metadata with Automatically Stuctured Queries. In: European Conference on Research and Advanced Technology for Digital Libraries (ECDL 2005). Springer Lecture Notes of Computer Science (2005), 3652:529-530.
4. Pirkola, A.: The Effects of Query Structure and Dictionary Setups in Dictionary-Based Cross-Language Information Retrieval. In: Proceedings of SIGIR'98, 21st ACM International Conference on Research and Development in Information Retrieval (1998) 55–63.

Easing Erroneous Translations in Cross-Language Image Retrieval Using Word Associations

Masashi Inoue

National Institute of Informatics, Tokyo, Japan
m-inoue@nii.ac.jp

Abstract. When short queries and short image annotations are used in text-based cross-language image retrieval, small changes in word usage due to translation errors may decrease the retrieval performance because of an increase in lexical mismatches. In the ImageCLEF2005 ad-hoc task, we investigated the use of learned word association models that represent how pairs of words are related to absorb such mismatches. We compared a precision-oriented simple word-matching retrieval model and a recall-oriented word association retrieval model. We also investigated combinations of these by introducing a new ranking function that generated comparable output values from both models. Experimental results on English and German topics were discouraging, as the use of word association models degraded the performance. On the other hand, word association models helped retrieval for Japanese topics whose translation quality was low.

1 Introduction

One of the goals of research on information retrieval (IR) systems is to overcome a shortage of meaningfully retrieved documents. In text-based ad-hoc image retrieval, when annotations are used as the target of query matching, an insufficient retrieval is often the result of term-mismatch. The words in a query do not appear in most annotations, because often there are few words in image annotations.

When a query and image annotations are described in different languages, and there needs to be translation process that brings diversity in the lexical expressions of a concept, a term-mismatch problem becomes more severe. As a result, the IR performance often degrades. In ImageCLEF2005, we studied the effect of word association models on mitigating such phenomena. We employed a probabilistic word-by-word query translation model structure [1], although in our models, the actual translation took place by an MT system outside of the retrieval model and the translation in the model was, in effect, a monolingual word expansion [2]. We tested our approach in the setting where both queries and annotations were short. Monolingual English-to-English, cross-lingual German-to-English, and cross-lingual Japanese-to-English image retrievals were compared.

C. Peters et al. (Eds.): CLEF 2005, LNCS 4022, pp. 582–591, 2006.

One finding from our experiments was that when a simple word-matching strategy failed to retrieve a relevant image because of an erroneous translation, the use of a word association model could improve the word-matching. In our runs, a recovery effect was observed only in Japanese-to-English translations, being an example of translation between disparate languages.

In the following text, we first describe the experimental conditions, and then introduce the retrieval models and ranking functions. Next, we discuss the experimental results, and finally, we conclude the paper.

2 Data Preparation

2.1 Test Collection

The test collection used was the ImageCLEF2005 St Andrews Library photographic collection that was prepared for ad-hoc retrieval tasks [3]. This consisted of 28, 133 images and their captions in English, with 28 topics in a variety of languages. Each caption had nine fields assigned by experts. Among these, we used only short title fields that were considered to be the simplest form of annotation. The mean length of the short titles was 3.43 words.

The retrieval topics was described using two fields: short description (title) and long description (narrative). They were the translations of original English topics. In our experiments, we used only the titles, which can be regarded as the approximation of users' queries. We examined English, German, and Japanese topics. The mean length of the queries was 4.18 words for English, 4.39 words for German, and 5.96 words for Japanese. We considered English topics as the baseline, German topics as the relatively easy task, and Japanese topics as the relatively hard task. Here, by 'easy' we mean that the current state-of-the art accuracy of machine translation (MT) for that language is high, and retrieval can be conducted in nearly the same fashion as the original (English) language. Similarly, by 'hard', we mean that queries differ substantially from the source language after undergoing the machine translation process. According to the results of ImageCLEF2004 that consisted of the same image dataset as ImageCLEF2005 but with different topics, German topics yielded the highest average mean average precision (MAP) score after English, and Japanese topics yielded the lowest average MAP scores for the top five systems [4].

The size of the vocabulary was 9, 945 for both image annotations and queries. Although we were also interested in the use of visual information, we did not use it either for queries or for annotations. Therefore, the retrieval was purely textual. Details of data pre-processings are explained in [5].

2.2 Query Translation

Our approach to cross-language retrieval was to use query translation. According to previous experiments on ImageCLEF ad-hoc data, query translation generally outperforms document translation [6]. Although a combination of query translation and document translation may be promising, we only considered query translation for now. German and Japanese topics were translated into English, the document language, using the Babelfish web-based MT system[1], and the complete list of translation results can be found in the Appendix of [5].

By analysing the translation results, we confirmed that German topics were 'easy' and Japanese topics were 'hard', in terms of the number of translation errors. In this paper, we define an error in machine translation as being the generation of words that invokes a mismatch between the queries and the annotations. For example, if a word is translated into 'photographs' when it should be translated to 'pictures', for a human observer, this difference has little effect in understanding sentences that contain the word 'photographs'. However, for image retrieval in particular, where only short text descriptions are available, such a difference may change the results of retrieval dramatically. For example, when all the relevant images are annotated as 'pictures', the system cannot retrieve anything, and therefore, this translation is considered an error. These errors can be observed only indirectly by comparing IR performances on the original topics and the translated topics. Therefore, in the following qualitative analysis, we only describe the errors that can be analysed qualitatively.

First, we examined the overall quality of German–English translations. Some notable errors were found in the translation of prepositions. For example, 'on' was translated as 'at', and 'from' was translated as 'of'. Other typical errors were the inappropriate assignment of imprecise synonyms. For example, 'ground' was replaced by 'soil'. (Details of the errors are given in [5].) Despite these errors, in most translations of German topics, the basic meanings were similar to the original English. Among 28 topics (titles), four topics were translated exactly as in the original English. This result confirms the relatively high accuracy of German–English MT.

For Japanese-to-English translations, however, the quality of translation was worse. As in the German-to-English translations, the Japanese-to-English translations contained errors in prepositions. Errors that were peculiar to the Japanese-to-English translations were the excessive use of definite articles and relative pronouns. More seriously, some of the Japanese words could not be translated at all. Untranslated words were 'aiona (Iona)', 'nabiku (waving)', and 'sentoandoryusu (St Andrews)'. The problem was that the untranslated words were often proper nouns, which can be useful for distinguishing relevant documents from irrelevant documents. Although this out-of-vocabulary problem occurred in German-to-English translations too, the effect of missing proper nouns was less severe, because the spellings were the same for both English and German, and for the indexing purposes, they did not need to be translated.

3 Retrieval Process After Translation

3.1 Retrieval Models

We introduce retrieval models based on the unigram language models and word association models. The baseline model was a simple unigram keyword-matching

[1] http://babelfish.altavista.com

document model denoted by `diag`. For the query of the length K, $\mathbf{q}=\{q_1, ..., q_K\}$, the likelihood of $\mathbf{q}$ being generated from $\mathbf{d}_n$, the nth document or image, is $\prod_{k=1}^{K} P(q_k|\mathbf{d}_n)$. Here, we assume independence between query words, $P(\mathbf{q}) = \prod_{k=1}^{K} P(q_k)$, although this is not always true for the ImageCLEF2005 topics, where titles are sometimes sentential and word orders have meaning. For the word association model, we estimated the following transitive probabilities from the jth word to the ith word in the vocabulary, $P(w_i|w_j)$. When the above two models are combined, the following represents the process of query generation:

$$\prod_{k=1}^{K} \sum_{i=1}^{V} P(q_k|w_i)P(w_i|\mathbf{d}_n). \tag{1}$$

The word association models can be estimated in various heuristic ways. We tried two methods, and in both methods, we regarded the frequency of the co-occurrence of two words as being the measure of word association. If two words co-occurred, then they were assumed to be related. The first method counted self-co-occurrences, where a word is regarded as co-occurring with itself as well as other co-occurrences. Values for each term pair were estimated as follows

$$P(w_i|w_j) = \frac{\#(w_i, w_j)}{\sum_{i=1}^{V} \#(w_i, w_j) + \#(w_i)} \quad \text{where } i \neq j, \tag{2}$$

$$P(w_i|w_j) = \frac{\#(w_i, w_j) + \#(w_i)}{\sum_{i=1}^{V} \#(w_i, w_j) + \#(w_i)} \quad \text{where } i = j. \tag{3}$$

Here, $\#(w_i, w_j)$ represents the frequency of co-occurrence of w_i and w_j (i.e., the appearance of the two words in the same image annotation), and $\#(w_i)$ represents the frequency of occurrence of w_i. This procedure strengthens self-similarities in the model and is termed `cooc`. The second method counted purely co-occurring pairs, and was named `coocp`. Values for each term pair were estimated as follows

$$P(w_i|w_j) = \frac{\#(w_i, w_j)}{\#(w_j)} \quad \text{where } \#(w_j) > 0. \tag{4}$$

When we consider the matrix representations of above association probabilities, the baseline model that did not use a word association model can be interpreted as using an identity matrix and we denoted this as `diag`. Note that these models were estimated before the arrival of any queries and the computation at the time of query focused on score calculation.

3.2 Ranking Functions

Our runs were divided into two groups according to the ranking function employed. In the first group, documents were ranked according to the query–log likelihood of the document models. The ranking function can be written as

$$\log L = \sum_{k=1}^{K} \log \sum_{i=1}^{V} P(q_k|w_i)P(w_i|\mathbf{d}_n). \tag{5}$$

Runs based on these functions are marked with `log_lik` in Table 1.

In general, when an expansion method is involved, the number of terms matched between queries and documents increases. Consequently, the scores of documents given by the first scoring measure `log_lik` are larger in models with an expansion method than in those without an expansion method. Thus, the first scoring measure was not suitable for a comparison of the output scores between different models. The output combination method that will be introduced in Sect. 3.3 requires comparable scores from different models. Therefore, we heuristically derived the second measure. In the second group of runs, documents were ranked according to the accumulated information for all the matched words. First, we transformed the variables for the probability of a query word, q_k, $P(q)$, to $F_q = e^{(\log P(q))^{-1}}$ where $P(q)$ was either $P(q|\mathbf{d}_n)$ or $\sum_{i=1}^{V} P(q|w_i)P(w_i|\mathbf{d}_n)$, and was considered only when $P(q) \neq 0$. Then, the new ranking function can be defined as

$$\log L' = \sum_{k=1}^{K} \log \frac{1}{F_{q_k}}. \tag{6}$$

We regarded $\log \frac{1}{F_{q_k}}$ as the information on query word, q. A document with a higher score was assumed to have more information on the query than one with a lower score. Runs based on this measure are marked with `vt_info` in Table 1.

3.3 Model Output Combination

When the `vt_info` measure is used, the combination of different models at the output level can be performed because their scores are directly comparable. First, two sets of document scores and corresponding document indices from two models were merged. Then they were sorted in descending order of scores. For each document, the higher score was retained. This process assumed that lower scores usually corresponded to a lack of knowledge about the documents, and thus were less reliable. From the merged rank, the top M documents were extracted as the final result. This can be considered as an example of the raw score method [7]. Here, the scores are calculated by taking only matched terms into account. Strictly, this is not a single association model, however, for simplicity of notation, we denote it as `dc` association model to represent the combination of `diag` and `cooc`.

4 Experimental Results

The MAP scores in Table 1 are based on runs we conducted considering the 1,000 top scores for each of the 28 topics. On comparing our runs to those of other participants, the overall performance was found to be deficient. This is due

Table 1. Summary of the mean average precision scores (Figures in bold face represent the best performances for each language)

Ranking Function	log-lik			vt-info			
Association Model	diag	cooc	coocp	diag	cooc	coocp	dc
English	**0.0301**	0.0195	0.0065	0.0144	0.0110	0.0018	0.0149
German	**0.0215**	0.0077	0.0022	0.0110	0.0059	0.0064	0.0114
Japanese	0.0109	0.0120	0.0087	0.0118	0.0116	0.0078	**0.0121**

to the restricted textual information we used and the oversimplification of our retrieval models and pre-processings. Because we were interested in a comparison between query languages and the use of word association models, we will not discuss further the overall performance here.

First, we considered the difference between the models. In both English and German, our best run was achieved using the `diag` model, which we had considered as the simplest baseline. All models employing word association underperformed for these two languages. There are two possible explanations for this result. The first reason may be that there was no need to relax the limitation of exact term matching. Some relevant documents could be retrieved by word-by-word correspondence and other relevant documents could not be reached by word-level expansion. For example, the relevant images for topic 28 should be colour images. However, the textual description itself does not inform if an image is in colour or is monochrome. When such visual information is the dominant factor in determining relevance, changes in word-matching do not influence the retrieval results. The second reason may be that the word association models were not learned adequately, so they could not help with connecting query words and document words. Separation of the two types of influences in the final rankings is open to question.

For the model output combination method (`dc`), Figure 1 shows whether the `dc` or `diag` model performed better in monolingual English-English retrieval when the `vt_info` measure was used. The bars for each topic represent the difference between the average precision scores of two models on the top 1,000 ranks. In Topics 11 and 25, the `dc` method worked better than the `diag` method did by taking advantages of the `cooc` method. Interestingly, Topics 11 and 25 that gave average precision gains in the `dc` model were not the most successful topics in `cooc`. For example, when the `cooc` model was used, Topic 2 benefited more. These results means that the gain achieved by the output combination was not simply derived by the quality of association model, but was provided by the merging process. Let us now look at the final ranking in detail. Figure 2 shows which of the two methods, `diag` or `cooc`, determined the position of the images in the merged ranking for monolingual (English-to-English) retrieval. The diamond symbols represent documents whose ranks were given by the precision-oriented `diag` models, and the square symbols represent documents whose ranks were given by the recall-oriented `cooc` models. Note that these figures do not

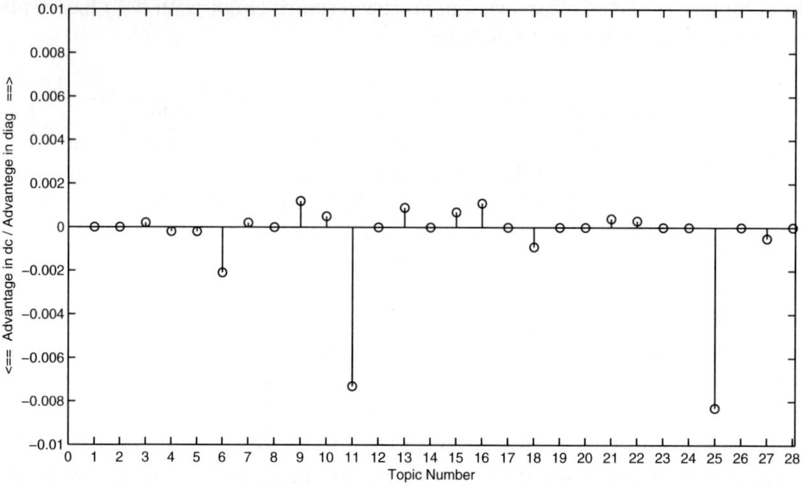

Fig. 1. Superiority of the two models in terms of resulting average precision for each topic (English-English retrieval evaluated on the top 1,000 ranks) when the `vt-info` measure was used

hold information on the relevance of the documents, and the rank interlacing may have degraded the quality of the ranking.

As can be seen in Figure 2, the `diag` model dominated the top scores. We had expected this tendency, because an exact-matching scheme should have higher confidence in its outputs when queries can find their counterparts. What was unexpected was that in most of the topics, the dominance of the `diag` model often ranged from the top rank to about the 1,000th rank, and the scores given by `cooc` models appeared only in the lower ranks. Because we had considered only the top 1,000 ranks, the resulting MAP scores were determined almost solely by the `diag` model. Top-ranked documents are usually more important to a user, and with this in mind, we must consider a better way of rank merging so as not to miss any opportunity to swap top-ranked documents.

Next, we examined the effects of translations by comparing the three topic languages in baseline models. Basically, as we expected, monolingual topics performed best, German topics were in second place, and the performances of the Japanese topics were the worst. This order can be understood by the influence of translation errors, as discussed in Sect. 2.2. Particularly, the most serious problem in translation errors was the generation of out-of-vocabulary words. Most of the English topics after removal of any out-of-vocabulary words still made sense, whereas translated German and Japanese topics suffered from word scarcity. The table in Appendix A is the translation results of Japanese topics. It also shows which words were not contained in the target dataset or the short titles of images in our case. Note that, here by 'out-of-vocabulary', we mean unknown words for the IR models and not for the MT systems, as discussed in Sect. 2.2. The problem of these out-of-vocabulary words may be mitigated by

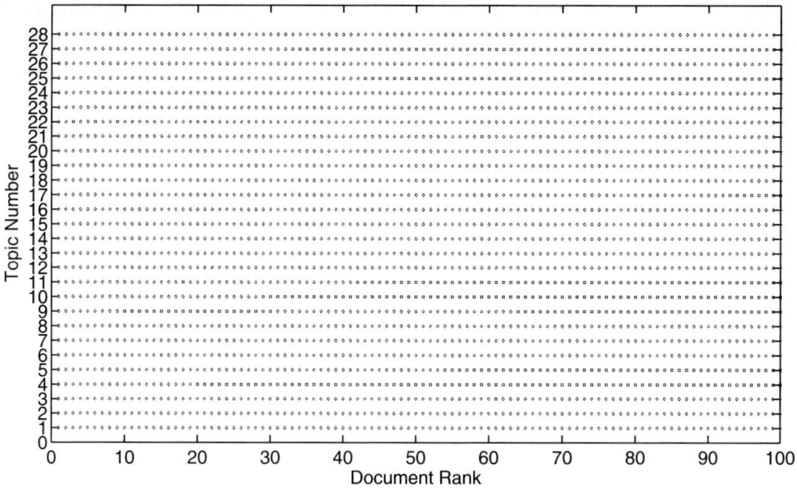

Fig. 2. Model dominance for the `dc` method in the top 100 scale (The diamond symbols represent documents whose ranks were given by the `diag` models, and the square symbols represent documents whose ranks were given by the `cooc` models)

using stemming, pseudo-relevance feedback, and use of external knowledge on the word associations. Investigation of their effect on the IR performance is a topic for future work.

Concerning the relationships between the topic languages and the association models, as we can see in Table 1, for the `log_lik` ranking function, direct word-matching models performed better than word association models in English and German topics. In contrast, in Japanese topics, the use of word association models (`cooc`) improved the performance. When English and Japanese topics were compared, because the only difference between languages was the presence or absence of translations, the positive effect of word association in Japanese topics may be attributed to the poor quality of translations. Therefore, word association models may be seen as the restoration of translation errors that caused mismatches in the retrieval process. When we also consider German topics, the relationship becomes more complex. Even though German topics contained some translation errors, the degradation of performance using `cooc` was more severe in German than in English. This result may be better understood by considering additional languages with various translation difficulties.

5 Discussion

In our experiments, we observed that the use of word association models may help recover query translation errors that arise in MT systems. However, the performances of our models were inadequate as standard systems. For simplicity, we did not incorporate the following established techniques: 1) inverse document frequency (idf) factor, 2) stop words elimination, and 3) document length normalization. These may be integrated into the IR process to demonstrate the general applicability of our method.

There are other ways of utilizing word associations which may be of considerable benefit. We fixed the association models before the querying time. However, together with relevance feedback or pseudo-relevance feedback, association models can be estimated (e.g., [8]). Although the practicality of the construction of word association models from scratch is debatable, because the users' load may be too high, modification of already estimated associations at querying time using feedbacks will be an interesting extension of our approach. Another situation may arise when words are expanded more than once. In our runs, we used an MT system with a single output. If we had used an MT system that outputs multiple candidates with their confidence scores, then the MT system would have performed the soft expansion by itself. The combined effect of the expansion by the MT system and that by the IR system is an interesting future topic.

6 Conclusions

Text-based cross-language image retrieval that relies on short descriptions is considered to be less robust with respect to translation errors. In our experiments using the ImageCLEF2005 ad-hoc test collection, estimated word association models helped with the retrieval of Japanese topics when machine translation into English performed poorly. This recovery effect produced by word expansion may become clearer by comparing various languages with different degrees of translation difficulty.

References

1. Kraaij, W., de Jong, F.: Transitive CLIR Models. In: RIAO, Vaucluse, France (2004) 69–81
2. Inoue, M., Ueda, N.: Retrieving Lightly Annotated Images Using Image Similarities. In: SAC '05: Proceedings of the 2005 ACM symposium on Applied computing, NY, USA (2005) 1031–1037
3. Clough, P., Müller, H., Deselaers, T., Grubinger, M., Lehmann, T.M., Jensen, J., Hersh, W.: The CLEF 2005 Cross-language Image Retrieval Track. In: Proceedings of the Cross Language Evaluation Forum 2005. Springer Lecture Notes in Computer science (to appear)
4. Clough, P., Müller, H., Sanderson, M.: The CLEF Cross Language Image Retrieval Track (ImageCLEF) 2004. In: ImageCLEF2004 Working Note. (2004)
5. Inoue, M.: Recovering Translation Errors in Cross Language Image Retrieval by Word Association Models. In: ImageCLEF2005 Working Note. (2005)
6. Clough, P.: Caption vs. Query Translation for Cross-language Image Retrieval. In: ImageCLEF2004 Working Note. (2004)
7. Hiemstra, D., Kraaij, W., Pohlmann, R., Westerveld, T.: Translation Resources, Merging Strategies, and Relevance Feedback for Cross-language Information Retrieval. In: Lecture Notes in Computer Science. Volume 2069. (2001) 102–115
8. Xiang Sean Zhou, T.S.H.: Unifying Keywords and Visual Contents in Image Retrieval. IEEE Multimedia **9** (2002) 23–33

A Out-of-Vocabulary Words in Queries

This appendix contains the table of out-of-vocabulary and in-vocabulary words in the translated Japanese queries. Due to the limitation of space, we omit the tables for English and translated German queries. In the table below, the words in italic did not appear in the image annotations (out-of-vocabulary). Thus, only the words in bold face were effectively used. Note that our experimental procedure did not involve a stemming process and the presence of out-of-vocabulary words may be exaggerated.

Table 2. Translated Japanese queries

Topic No.	Translated Titles
1	*terrestrial airplane*
2	**the people** *who* **meet in the field music hall**
3	**the dog** *which sits* **down**
4	**the steam ship** *which* **is** *docked* **to the pier**
5	*image* **of** *animal*
6	*smallsized* **sailing ship**
7	**fishermen on boat**
8	**the building** *which* **the snow** *accumulated*
9	**the horse** *which* **pulls the load carriage and the carriage**
10	**photograph of sun Scotland**
11	**the Swiss mountain scenery**
12	**the** *illustrated postcards* **of Scotland and island**
13	**the** *elevated* **bridge of the** *stonework which* **is** *plural* **arch**
14	**people of market**
15	**the golfer** *who does* **the** *pad* **with the green**
16	**the** *wave which washes* **in the beach**
17	**the man or the woman** *who reads*
18	**woman of white dress**
19	*illustrated postcards* **of the** *synthesis* **of** *province*
20	**the Scottish visit of king family other** *than* **fife**
21	**poet Robert Burns' monument**
22	**flag building**
23	**grave inside church and large** *saintly* **hall**
24	*closeup* **photograph of bird**
25	**gate of arch** *type*
26	**portrait photograph of man and woman** *mixed* **group**
27	**the woman or the girl** *who has* **the** *basket*
28	*colour* **picture of forest scenery of every place**

A Corpus-Based Relevance Feedback Approach to Cross-Language Image Retrieval

Yih-Chen Chang[1], Wen-Cheng Lin[2], and Hsin-Hsi Chen[1]

[1] Department of Computer Science and Information Engineering
National Taiwan University
Taipei, Taiwan
ycchang@nlg.csie.ntu.edu.tw, hhchen@csie.ntu.edu.tw
[2] Department of Medical Informatics
Tzu Chi University
Hualien, Taiwan
denislin@mail.tcu.edu.tw

Abstract. This paper regards images with captions as a cross-media parallel corpus, and presents a corpus-based relevance feedback approach to combine the results of visual and textual runs. Experimental results show that this approach performs well. Comparing with the mean average precision (MAP) of the initial visual retrieval, the MAP is increased from 8.29% to 34.25% after relevance feedback from cross-media parallel corpus. The MAP of cross-lingual image retrieval is increased from 23.99% to 39.77% if combining the results of textual run and visual run with relevance feedback. Besides, the monolingual experiments also show the consistent effects of this approach. The MAP of monolingual retrieval is improved from 39.52% to 50.53% when merging the results of the text and image queries.

1 Introduction

In cross-language image retrieval, users employ textual queries in one language and example images to access image database with text descriptions in another language. It becomes practical because many images associating text like captions, metadata, Web page links, and so on, are available nowadays. Besides, the neutrality of images to different language users resolves the arguments that users not familiar with the target language still cannot afford to understand the retrieved documents in cross-language information retrieval.

Two types of approaches, i.e., content-based and text-based approaches, are usually adopted in image retrieval [1]. Content-based image retrieval (CBIR) uses low-level visual features to retrieve images. In such a way, it is unnecessary to annotate images and translate users' queries. However, due to the semantic gap between image visual features and high-level concepts [2], it is still challenging to use a CBIR system to retrieve images with correct semantic meaning. Integrating textual information may help a CBIR system to cross the semantic gap and improve retrieval performance.

Recently, many approaches have tried to combine text- and content-based methods for image retrieval. A simple approach is conducting text- and content-based retrieval

C. Peters et al. (Eds.): CLEF 2005, LNCS 4022, pp. 592 – 601, 2006.

separately and merging the retrieval results of the two runs [3, 4]. In contrast to the parallel approach, a pipeline approach uses textual or visual information to perform initial retrieval, and then uses the other feature to filter out irrelevant images [5]. In these two approaches, textual and visual queries are formulated by users and do not directly influence each other. Another approach, i.e., transformation-based approach [12], mines the relations between images and text, and uses the mined relations to transform textual information into visual one, and vice versa.

To formulate the cross-media translation between visual and textual representations, several correlation-based approaches have been proposed. Mori, Takahashi and Oka [6] divided images into grids, and then the grids of all images were clustered. Co-occurrence information was used to estimate the probability of each word for each cluster. Duygulu, *et al.* [7] used blobs to represent images. First, images are segmented into regions using a segmentation algorithm like Normalized Cuts [8]. All regions are clustered and each cluster is assigned a unique label (blob token). The Expectation-Maximization (EM) algorithm [9] is used to construct a probability table that links blob tokens with word tokens. Jeon, Lavrenko, and Manmatha [10] proposed a cross-media relevance model (CMRM) to learn the joint distribution of blobs and words. They further proposed continuous-space relevance model (CRM) that learned the joint probability of words and regions, rather than blobs [11]. Lin, Chang and Chen [12] transformed a textual query into visual one using a transmedia dictionary.

The above approaches use the relation between text and visual representation as a bridge to translate image to text. However, it is hard to learn all relations between all visual and textual features. Besides, the degree of ambiguity of the relations is usually high. For example, visual feature "red circle" may have many meanings such as sun set, red flower, red ball, *etc.* Similarly, the word "flower" may have different looks of images, e.g., different color and shape. In contrast to the transmedia dictionary approach [12], this paper regards images with captions as a cross-media parallel corpus to transform visual features to textual ones. The text descriptions of the top-*n* retrieved images of the initial image retrieval are used for feedback to conduct a second retrieval. The new textual information can help us determine the semantic meaning of a visual query, and thus improve retrieval performance.

The rest of the paper is organized as follows. Section 2 presents the proposed approach and Section 3 shows the experimental results in bilingual ad hoc retrieval task at ImageCLEF2005. Section 4 provides some discussion and Section 5 ends the paper with concluding remarks.

2 A Corpus-Based Relevance Feedback Approach

In this paper, we translate visual and textual features without learning correlations. We treat the images along with their text descriptions as an aligned cross-media parallel corpus, and a corpus-based method transforms a visual query to a textual one. Figure 1 shows the concept of this approach.

In cross-language image retrieval, given a set of images $I=\{i_1, i_2, \ldots, i_m\}$ with text descriptions $T_{I,L1}=\{t_1, t_2, \ldots, t_m\}$ in language $L1$, users issue a textual query Q_{L2} in

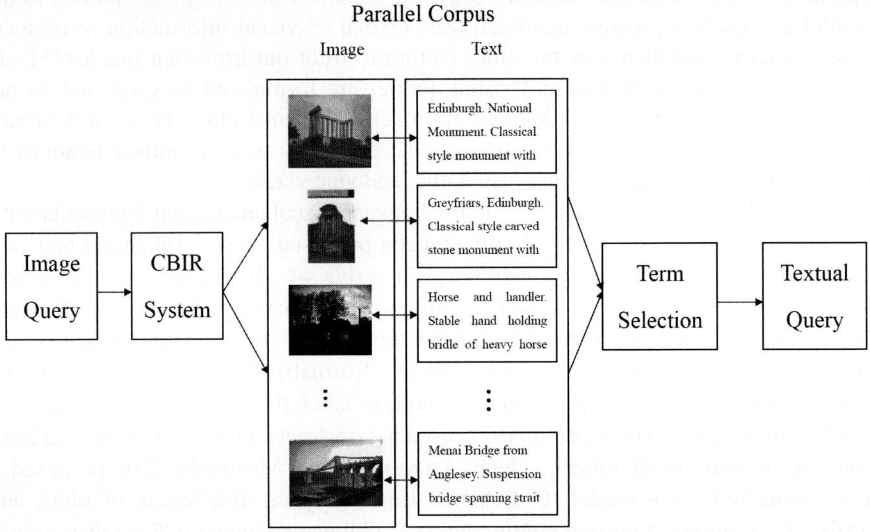

Fig. 1. Key concept of a corpus-based approach

language $L2$ ($L2 \neq L1$) and example images $E=\{e_1, e_2, \ldots, e_p\}$ to retrieve relevant images from I. At first, we submit example images E as initial query to a CBIR system, e.g., VIPER [13], to retrieve images from I. The retrieved images are $R=\{r_{i1}, r_{i2}, \ldots, r_{in}\}$ and their text descriptions are $T_{R,L1}=\{t_{ri1}, t_{ri2}, \ldots, t_{rin}\}$ in language $L1$. Then, we select terms from the text descriptions of the top k retrieved images to construct a new textual query. The new textual query can be seen as a translation of initial visual query by using a corpus-based approach. We submit the new textual query to a text-based retrieval system, e.g., Okapi [14], to retrieve images from I. That is latter called a *feedback run*.

Figure 2 shows how to integrate the feedback process into a cross-language image retrieval system. In addition to the visual feedback run, we also conduct a text-based run using the textual query in the test set. We use the method proposed in ImageCLEF 2004 [15] to translate textual query Q_{L2} into query Q_{L1} in language $L1$, and submit the translated query Q_{L1} to the Okapi system to retrieve images. The results of textual run and visual feedback run can be combined. The similarity scores of images in the two runs are normalized and linearly combined using equal weight.

3 Experimental Results

In the experiments, we used historic photographs from the St. Andrews University Library[1] [16]. There are 28,133 photographs, which are accompanied by a textual description written in British English. The ImageCLEF test collection contains 28

[1] http://www-library.st-andrews.ac.uk/

topics, and each topic has text description in different languages and two example images. In our experiments, queries are in traditional Chinese. Figure 3 shows an image and its description. Figure 4 illustrates a topic in English and in Chinese.

The text-based retrieval system is Okapi IR system, and the content-based retrieval system is VIPER system. The <HEADLINE> and <CATEGORIES> sections, and the record body of English captions are used for indexing. The weighting function is BM25. Chinese queries and example images are used as the source queries.

In the formal runs, we submitted four Chinese-English cross-lingual runs, two English monolingual runs and one visual run in CLEF 2005 image track. In English monolingual runs, using narrative or not using narrative will be compared. In the four cross-lingual runs, combining with visual run or not combining with visual run, and using narrative or not using narrative will be compared. The details of the cross-lingual runs and visual run are described as follows.

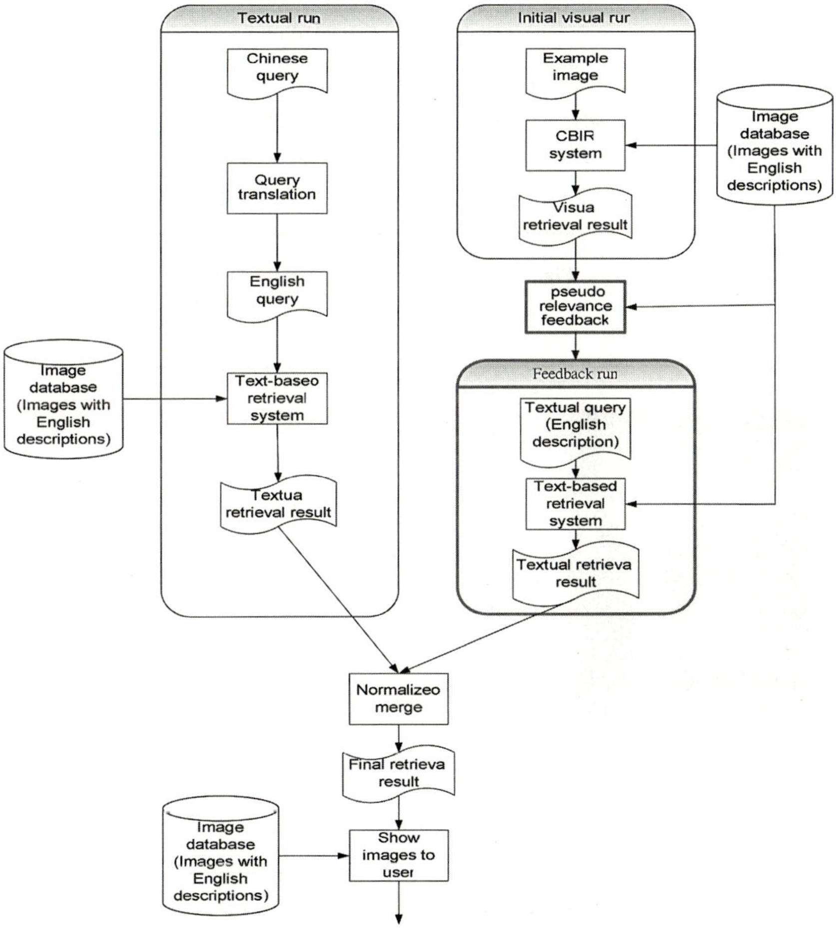

Fig. 2. A cross-language image retrieval system

<DOC>
<DOCNO> stand03_1041/stand03_9914.txt </DOCNO>
<HEADLINE> Azay le Rideau. Bridge. </HEADLINE>
<TEXT>
<RECORD_ID> JEAS-.000032.-.000045 </RECORD_ID>
Azay le Rideau.
Round tower with conical roof attached to large three-storey building; low bridge spanning still water to right.
1907
John Edward Aloysius Steggall
Indre et Loire, France
JEAS-32-45 pc/jf
<CATEGORIES>
[towers - round], [towers - conical roofed], [France urban views], [France all views]
</CATEGORIES>
<SMALL_IMG>
stand03_1041/stand03_9914.jpg
</SMALL_IMG>
<LARGE_IMG>
stand03_1041/stand03_9914_big.jpg
</LARGE_IMG>
</TEXT>
</DOC>

Fig. 3. An image and its description

<top>
<num> Number: 17 </num>
<title> man or woman reading </title>
<narr>
Relevant images will show men or women reading books or a paper. People performing any other activity are not relevant.
</narr>
</top>

<top>
<num> Number: 17 </num>
<title>
正在閱讀的男人或女人
</title>
</top>

Fig. 4. A Topic in English and in Chinese

(1) NTU-adhoc05-CE-T-W
This run employs textual queries (title field only) to retrieve images. We use the query translation method as proposed for CLEF 2004 [15] to translate Chinese queries into English ones, and the Okapi IR system retrieves images based on a textual index.
(2) NTU-adhoc05-CE-TN-W-Ponly
This run uses textual queries (title plus narrative fields). Only the positive information in narrative field is considered. The sentences that contain phrase "are not relevant" are removed to avoid noise [17].
(3) NTU-adhoc05-EX-prf
It is a visual run with pseudo relevance feedback. VIPER system provided by ImageCLEF retrieves the initial results, and the text descriptions of the top 2 images are used to construct a textual query. The textual query is submitted to Okapi IR system to retrieve images.
(4) NTU-adhoc05-CE-T-WEprf
This run merges the results of NTU-adhoc05-CE-T-W and NTU-adhoc05-EX-prf. The similarity scores of images in the two runs are normalized and linearly combined with equal weight 0.5.
(5) NTU-adhoc05-CE-TN-WEprf-Ponly
This run merges the results of NTU-adhoc05-CE-TN-W-Ponly and NTU-adhoc05-EX-prf.
(6) NTU-adhoc05-EE-T-W
This run is a monolingual run by using title field only.
(7) NTU-adhoc05-EE-TN-W-Ponly
This run is a monolingual run by using title and narrative fields.

Two unofficial runs shown as follows are also conducted for comparison.

(8) NTU-adhoc05-EE-T-WEprf
This run merges the results of NTU-adhoc05-EE-T-W and NTU-adhoc05-EX-prf.
(9) VIPER
This run is the initial visual run.

Tables 1 and 2 show the experimental results of official runs and unofficial runs, respectively. The Mean Average Precision (MAP) of the textual query using title and narrative is better than that of the textual query using title only, but the difference is not significant. That is,

NTU-adhoc05-CE-TN-W-Ponly > NTU-adhoc05-CE-T-W,
NTU-adhoc05-CE-TN-WEprf-Ponly > NTU-adhoc05-CE-T-WEprf, and
NTU-adhoc05-EE-TN-W-Ponly > NTU-adhoc05-EE-T-W.

Besides, the MAP of integrating textual and visual queries by using corpus-based relevance feedback approach is much better than that of textual query only. That is,

NTU-adhoc05-CE-T-WEprf > NTU-adhoc05-CE-T-W,
NTU-adhoc05-CE-TN-WEprf-Ponly > NTU-adhoc05-CE-TN-W-Ponly, and
NTU-adhoc05-EE-T-WEprf > NTU-adhoc05-EE-T-W.

Although the MAP of initial visual run is only 8.29%, the effects from relevance feedback improve the performance significantly. Figure 5 illustrates the average precision of each query using NTU-adhoc05-EE-T-WEprf (EE+EX), NTU-adhoc 05-CE-T-WEprf (CE+EX), NTU-adhoc05-EE-T-W (EE), NTU-adhoc05-EX-prf

Table 1. Results of official runs

Run	Features in Query		MAP
	Text	Visual	
NTU-adhoc05-CE-T-W	Chinese (Title)	None	0.2399
NTU-adhoc05-CE-TN-W-Ponly	Chinese (Title+ Positive Narrative)	None	0.2453
NTU-adhoc05-CE-T-WEprf	Chinese (Title)	Example image	0.3977
NTU-adhoc05-CE-TN-WEprf-Ponly	Chinese (Title+ Positive Narrative)	Example image	0.3993
NTU-adhoc05-EX-prf	English (feedback query)	Example image (initial query)	0.3425
NTU-adhoc05-EE-T-W	English	None	0.3952
NTU-adhoc05-EE-TN-W-Ponly	English (Title+ Positive Narrative)	None	0.4039

Table 2. Performances of unofficial runs

Run	Features in Query		MAP
	Text	Visual	
NTU-adhoc05-EE-T-WEprf	English (Title)	Example image	0.5053
Initial Visual Run (VIPER)	None	Example image	0.0829

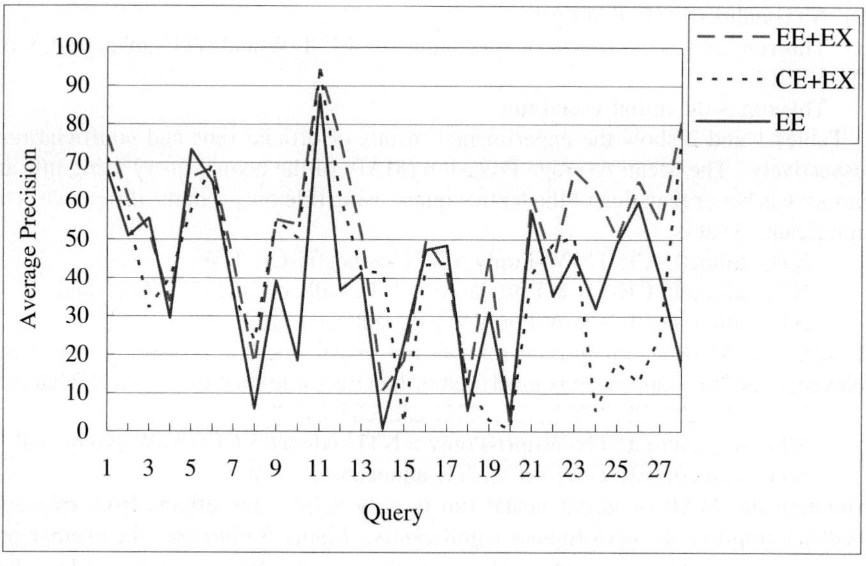

Fig. 5. Average precision of each query

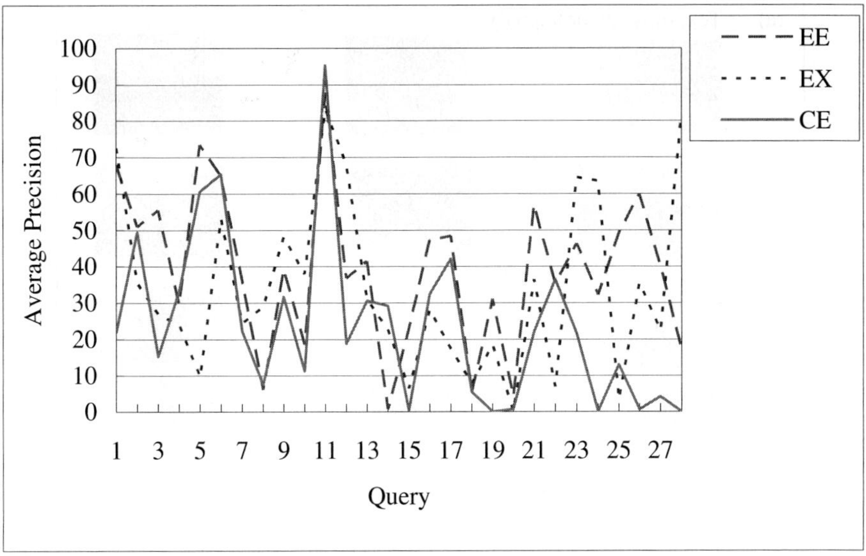

Fig. 5. Average precision of each query (*Continued*)

(EX), and NTU-adhoc05-CE-T-W (CE). In summary, EE +EX > CE+EX ≅ EE > EX > CE > visual run.

4 Discussion

The MAP of monolingual retrieval using the title field only is 39.52%. Comparing with our performance at ImageCLEF 2004 [15], i.e., 63.04%, topics of this year is more general and more visual than those of last year, e.g., waves breaking on beach, dog in sitting position, *etc*. The MAP of Chinese-English cross-lingual run (23.99%) is 60.70% of that of English monolingual run (39.52%). It shows that there are still many errors in language translation.

The MAP of initial visual run, i.e., VIPER, is not good enough. Text-based runs, even cross-lingual runs, perform much better than initial visual run. It shows that semantic information is very important for the queries of this year. After relevance feedback, the performance is increased dramatically from 8.29% to 34.25%. The result shows that the feedback method transforms visual information into textual one. Combining textual and visual feedback runs further improves retrieval performance.

Figure 6 shows the first three returned images of query "aircraft on the ground". For monolingual case, the images containing aircrafts not on the ground are reported wrongly. For cross-lingual case, "地面上的飛機" is translated to "aircraft above the floor", which captures wrong images. For visual case, the feedback query "aircraft in military air base" captures more relevant images. This is because aircrafts in military air base are very likely to be parked and thus are on the ground.

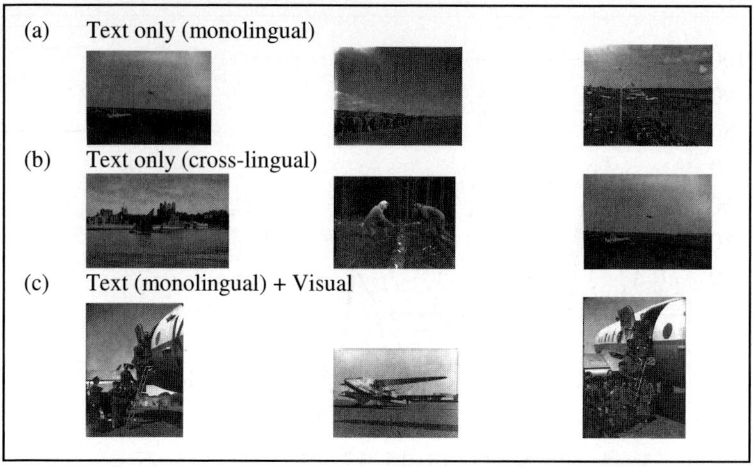

Fig. 6. Retrieval results of query "Aircraft on the Ground"

5 Conclusion

An approach of combining textual and image features is proposed for Chinese-English image retrieval. A corpus-based feedback cycle is performed after CBIR. Comparing with the MAP of monolingual IR (i.e., 39.52%), integrating visual and textual queries achieves better MAP in cross-language image retrieval (39.77%). It indicates part of translation errors is resolved. The integration of visual and textual queries also improves the MAP of the monolingual IR from 39.52% to 50.53%. It reveals the integration provides more information. The MAP of Chinese-English image retrieval is 78.2% of the best monolingual text retrieval in ImageCLEF 2005. The improvement is the best among all the groups.

Acknowledgements

Research of this paper was partially supported by National Science Council, Taiwan, under the contracts NSC 94-2752-E-001-001-PAE and NSC 94-2213-E-002-076.

References

1. Goodrum, A.A.: Image Information Retrieval: An Overview of Current Research. Information Science, 3(2). (2000) 63-66.
2. Eidenberger, H. and Breiteneder, C.: Semantic Feature Layers in Content-based Image Retrieval: Implementation of Human World Features. In: Proceedings of International Conference on Control, Automation, Robotic and Vision. (2002).
3. Besançon, R., Hède, P., Moellic, P.A., and Fluhr, C.: Cross-Media Feedback Strategies: Merging Text and Image Information to Improve Image Retrieval. In: 5th Workshop of the Cross-Language Evaluation Forum, LNCS 3491. (2005) 709-717.

4. Jones, G.J.F., Groves, D., Khasin, A., Lam-Adesina, A., Mellebeek, B., and Way, A.: Dublin City University at CLEF 2004: Experiments with the ImageCLEF St. Andrew's Collection. In: 5th Workshop of the Cross-Language Evaluation Forum, LNCS 3491. (2005) 653-663.
5. Baan, J., van Ballegooij, A., Geusenbroek, J.M., den Hartog, J., Hiemstra, D., List, J., Patras, I., Raaijmakers, S., Snoek, C., Todoran, L., Vendrig, J., de Vries, A., Westerveld, T., and Worring, M.: Lazy Users and Automatic Video Retrieval Tools in the Lowlands. In: Proceedings of the Tenth Text REtrieval Conference. National Institute of Standards and Technology (2002) 159-168.
6. Mori, Y., Takahashi, H. and Oka, R.: Image-to-Word Transformation Based on Dividing and Vector Quantizing Images with Words. In: Proceedings of the First International Workshop on Multimedia Intelligent Storage and Retrieval Management. (1999).
7. Duygulu, P., Barnard, K., Freitas, N. and Forsyth, D.: Object Recognition as Machine Translation: Learning a Lexicon for a Fixed Image Vocabulary. In: Proceedings of Seventh European Conference on Computer Vision, Vol. 4. (2002) 97-112.
8. Shi, J. and Malik, J.: Normalized Cuts and Image Segmentation. IEEE Transactions on Pattern Analysis and Machine Intelligence, 22(8). (2000) 888-905.
9. Dempster, A.P., Laird, N.M., and Rubin, D.B.: Maximum Likelihood from Incomplete Data via the EM Algorithm. Journal of the Royal Statistical Society, Series B, 39(1). (1977) 1-38.
10. Jeon, J., Lavrenko, V. and Manmatha, R.: Automatic Image Annotation and Retrieval using Cross-Media Relevance Models. In: Proceedings of the 26th Annual International ACM SIGIR Conference on Research and Development in Information Retrieval. (2003) 119-126.
11. Lavrenko, V., Manmatha, R. and Jeon, J.: A Model for Learning the Semantics of Pictures. In: Proceedings of the Seventeenth Annual Conference on Neural Information Processing Systems. (2003).
12. Lin, W.C., Chang, Y.C. and Chen, H.H.: Integrating Textual and Visual Information for Cross-Language Image Retrieval. In: Proceedings of the Second Asia Information Retrieval Symposium, LNCS 3689. (2005) 454-466.
13. Squire, D.M., Müller, W., Müller, H., and Raki, J.: Content-Based Query of Image Databases, Inspirations from Text Retrieval: Inverted Files, Frequency-Based Weights and Relevance Feedback. In: Scandinavian Conference on Image Analysis. (1999) 143-149.
14. Robertson, S.E., Walker, S. and Beaulieu, M.: Okapi at TREC-7: Automatic Ad Hoc, Filtering, VLC and Interactive. In: Proceedings of the Seventh Text REtrieval Conference. National Institute of Standards and Technology (1998) 253-264.
15. Lin, W.C., Chang, Y.C. and Chen, H.H.: From Text to Image: Generating Visual Query for Image Retrieval. In: 5th Workshop of the Cross-Language Evaluation Forum, LNCS 3491. (2005) 664-675.
16. Clough, P., Müller, H., Deselaers, T., Grubinger, M., Lehmann, T.M., Jensen, J., and Hersh, W.: The CLEF 2005 Cross-Language Image Retrieval Track, Proceedings of the Cross Language Evaluation Forum 2005, Springer Lecture Notes in Computer science, 2006 - to appear.
17. Feng, K.M. and Chen, H.H.: Effects of Positive and Negative Information Needs on Information Retrieval. Bulletin of the College of Engineering, National Taiwan University, 90. (2004) 35-42.

CUHK at ImageCLEF 2005: Cross-Language and Cross-Media Image Retrieval

Steven C.H. Hoi, Jianke Zhu, and Michael R. Lyu

Department of Computer Science and Engineering
The Chinese University of Hong Kong
Shatin, N.T., Hong Kong
{chhoi, jkzhu, lyu}@cse.cuhk.edu.hk

Abstract. In this paper, we describe our studies of cross-language and cross-media image retrieval at the ImageCLEF 2005. This is the first participation of our CUHK (The Chinese University of Hong Kong) group at ImageCLEF. The task in which we participated is the "bilingual ad hoc retrieval" task. There are three major focuses and contributions in our participation. The first is the empirical evaluation of language models and smoothing strategies for cross-language image retrieval. The second is the evaluation of cross-media image retrieval, i.e., combining text and visual contents for image retrieval. The last is the evaluation of bilingual image retrieval between English and Chinese. We provide an empirical analysis of our experimental results, in which our approach achieves the best mean average precision result in the monolingual query task in the campaign. Finally we summarize our empirical experience and address the future improvement of our work.

1 Introduction

Although content-based image retrieval (CBIR) has received considerable attention in the community [1], there are so far only a few benchmark image datasets available. The CLEF (Cross Language Evaluation Forum) organization began the ImageCLEF campaign from 2003 for benchmark evaluation of cross-language image retrieval [2]. ImageCLEF 2005 offers four different tasks: bilingual ad hoc retrieval, interactive search, medical image retrieval and an automatic image annotation task [2]. This is the first participation of our CUHK (The Chinese University of Hong Kong) group at ImageCLEF. The task in which we participated this year is the "bilingual ad hoc retrieval".

In the past decade, traditional information retrieval has mainly focused on document retrieval problems [3]. Along with the growth of multimedia information retrieval, which has received ever-increasing attention in recent years, cross-language and cross-media retrieval have been put forward as an important research topic in the community [2]. The cross-language image retrieval problem is to tackle the multimodal information retrieval task by unifying the techniques from traditional information retrieval, natural language processing (NLP), and traditional CBIR solutions.

C. Peters et al. (Eds.): CLEF 2005, LNCS 4022, pp. 602–611, 2006.

In this participation, we offer our main contributions in three aspects. The first is an empirical evaluation of language models and smoothing strategies for cross-language image retrieval. The second is an evaluation of cross-media image retrieval, i.e., combining text and visual contents for image retrieval. The last is the design and empirical evaluation of a methodology for bilingual image retrieval spanning English and Chinese sources.

The rest of this paper is organized as follows. Section 2 introduces the TF-IDF retrieval model and the language model based retrieval methods. Section 3 describes the details of our implementation for this participation, and outlines our empirical study on the cross-language and cross-media image retrieval. Finally, Section 4 concludes our work.

2 Language Models for Text Based Image Retrieval

In this participation, we have conducted extensive experiments to evaluate the performance of Language Models and the influences of different smoothing strategies. More specifically, two kinds of retrieval models are studied in our experiments: (1) The TF-IDF retrieval model, and (2) The KL-divergence language model based methods. The smoothing strategies for Language Models evaluated in our experiments [4] are: (1) the Jelinek-Mercer (JM) method, (2) Bayesian smoothing with Dirichlet priors (DIR), and (3) Absolute discounting (ABS).

2.1 TF-IDF Similarity Measure for Information Retrieval

We incorporate the TF-IDF similarity measure method into the Language Models (LM) [3]. TF-IDF is widely used in information retrieval, which is a way of weighting the relevance of a query to a document. The main idea of TF-IDF is to represent each document by a vector in the size of the overall vocabulary. Each document D_i is then represented as a vector $(w_{i1}, w_{i2}, \cdots, w_{in})$ if n is the size of the vocabulary. The entry $w_{i,j}$ is calculated as: $w_{ij} = TF_{ij} \times \log(IDF_j)$, where TF_{ij} is the term frequency of the j-th word in the vocabulary in the document D_i, i.e. the total number of occurrences. IDF_j is the inverse document frequency of the j-th term, which is defined as the number of documents over the number of documents that contain the j-th term. The similarity between two documents is then defined as the cosine of the angle between the two vectors.

2.2 Language Modeling for Information Retrieval

Language model, or the statistical language model, employs a probabilistic mechanism to generate text. The earliest serious approach for a statistical language model may be tracked to Claude Shannon [5]. To apply his newly founded information theory to human language applications, Shannon evaluated how well simple n-gram models did at predicting or compressing natural text. In the past, there has been considerable attention paid to using the language modeling techniques for text document retrieval and natural language processing tasks [6].

The KL-Divergence Measure. Given two probability mass functions $p(x)$ and $q(x)$, $D(p||q)$, the Kullback-Leibler (KL) divergence (or relative entropy) between p and q is defined as

$$D(p||q) = \sum_x p(x) log \frac{p(x)}{q(x)} \tag{1}$$

One can show that $D(p||q)$ is always non-negative and is zero if and only if $p = q$. Even though it is not a true distance between distributions (because it is not symmetric and does not satisfy the triangle inequality), it is often still useful to think of the KL-divergence as a "distance" between distributions [7].

The KL-Divergence Based Retrieval Model. In the language modeling approach, we assume a query q is generated by a generative model $p(q|\theta_Q)$, where θ_Q denotes the parameters of the query unigram language model. Similarly, we assume a document d is generated by a generative model $p(q|\theta_D)$, where θ_Q denotes the parameters of the document unigram language model. Let $\hat{\theta}_Q$ and $\hat{\theta}_D$ be the estimated query and document models, respectively. The relevance of d with respect to q can be measured by the negative KL-divergence function [6]:

$$-D(\hat{\theta}_Q||\hat{\theta}_D) = \sum_w p(w|\hat{\theta}_Q) logp(w|\hat{\theta}_D) + (-\sum_w p(w|\hat{\theta}_Q) logp(w|\hat{\theta}_Q)) \tag{2}$$

In the above formula, the second term on the right-hand side of the formula is a query-dependent constant, i.e., the entropy of the query model $\hat{\theta}_Q$. It can be ignored for the ranking purpose. In general, we consider the smoothing scheme for the estimated document model as follows:

$$p(w|\hat{\theta}_D) = \begin{cases} p_s(w|d) & \text{if word } w \text{ is present} \\ \alpha_d p(w|\mathcal{C}) & \text{otherwise} \end{cases} \tag{3}$$

where $p_s(w|d)$ is the smoothed probability of a word present in the document, $p(w|\mathcal{C})$ is the collection language model, and α_d is a coefficient controlling the probability mass assigned to unseen words, so that all probabilities sum to one [6]. We discuss several smoothing techniques in detail below.

2.3 Several Smoothing Techniques

In the context of language modeling study, the term "smoothing" can be defined as the adjustment of the maximum likelihood estimator of a language model so that it will be more accurate [4]. As we know that a language modeling approach usually estimates $p(w|d)$, a unigram language model based on a given document d, one of the simplest methods for smoothing is based on the maximum likelihood estimate as follows:

$$p_{ml}(w|d) = \frac{c(w;d)}{\sum_w c(w;d)} \tag{4}$$

Unfortunately, the maximum likelihood estimator will often underestimate the probabilities of unseen words in the given document. Hence, it is important to employ smoothing methods that usually discount the probabilities of the words seen in the text and assign the extra probability mass to the unseen words according to some model [4].

Some comprehensive evaluation of smoothing techniques for traditional text retrieval can be found in literature [8,4]. They have been an important tool to improve the performance of language models in traditional text retrieval. To achieve efficient implementations for large-scale tasks, three representative methods are selected in our scheme, which are popular and relatively efficient. They are discussed in turn below.

The Jelinek-Mercer (JM) Method. This method simply employs a linear interpolation of the maximum likelihood model with the collection model, using a coefficient λ to control the influence:

$$p_\lambda(\omega|d) = (1-\lambda)p_{ml}(\omega|d) + \lambda p(\omega|\mathcal{C}) \tag{5}$$

It is a simple mixture model. A more general Jelinek-Mercer method can be found in [9].

Bayesian Smoothing with Dirichlet Priors (DIR). In general, a language model can be considered as a multinomial distribution, in which the conjugate prior for Bayesian analysis is the Dirichlet distribution with parameters [4] $(\mu p(\omega_1|\mathcal{C}), \mu p(\omega_2|\mathcal{C}), \ldots, \mu p(\omega_n|\mathcal{C}))$. Thus, the smoothing model can be given as:

$$p_\mu(\omega|d) = \frac{c(\omega;d) + \mu p(\omega|\mathcal{C})}{\sum_\omega c(\omega;d) + \mu} \tag{6}$$

Note that μ in the above formula is a DIR parameter that is usually estimated empirically from training sets.

Absolute Discounting Smoothing (ABS). The absolute discounting method subtracts a constant from the counts of seen words for reducing the probabilities of the seen words, meanwhile it increases the probabilities of unseen words by including the collection language model. More specifically, the model can be represented as follows:

$$p_\delta(\omega|d) = \frac{\max(c(\omega;d) - \delta, 0)}{\sum_\omega c(\omega;d)} + \sigma p(\omega|\mathcal{C}) \tag{7}$$

where $\delta \in [0,1]$ is a discount constant and $\sigma = \delta|d|_\mu/|d|$, so that all probabilities sum to one. Here $|d|_\mu$ is the number of unique terms in document d, and $|d|$ is the total count of words in the document, i.e., $|d| = \sum_\omega c(\omega;d)$.

Table 1 summarizes the three methods in terms of $p_s(\omega|d)$ and α_d in the general form. In the table, for all three cases, a larger parameter value of λ, μ or δ means it involves more smoothing in the language model. Typically, these parameters can be estimated empirically by training sets. Once the smoothing parameters are given in advance, retrieval tasks using of the three methods above can be deployed very efficiently.

Table 1. Summary of three smoothing methods evaluated in our submission

Method	$p_s(\omega\|d)$	α_d	parameter
JM	$(1-\lambda)p_{ml}(\omega\|d)+\lambda p(\omega\|\mathcal{C})$	λ	λ
DIR	$\frac{c(\omega;d)+\mu p(\omega\|\mathcal{C})}{\sum_\omega c(\omega;d)+\mu}$	$\frac{\mu}{\sum_\omega c(\omega;d)+\mu}$	μ
ABS	$p_\delta(\omega\|d)=\frac{\max(c(\omega;d)-\delta,0)}{\sum_\omega c(\omega;d)}+\frac{\delta\|d\|_\mu\delta}{\|d\|}p(\omega\|\mathcal{C})$	$\frac{\delta\|d\|_\mu}{\|d\|}$	δ

3 Cross-Language and Cross-Media Image Retrieval

In this section, we describe our experimental setup and development at the ImageCLEF 2005, in which we have participated in the bilingual ad hoc image retrieval task. In addition, we empirically analyze the results of our submission.

3.1 Experimental Setup and Development

The goal of the bilingual ad hoc retrieval task is to find as many relevant images as possible for each given topic. The St. Andrew collection is used as the benchmark dataset for the ad hoc retrieval task. There are 28 queries in total for each language. More details about the task can be found in [2].

For the bilingual ad hoc retrieval task, we have studied the query tasks in English and Chinese (simplified). Both text and visual information are used in our experiments. To evaluate the language models correctly, we employ the *Lemur* toolkit[1]. A list of standard stopwords is used in the parsing step.

To evaluate the influence on the performance of using the different schemes, we produce the results using a variety of configurations. Tables 2 shows the configurations and the experimental results in detail. In total, 36 runs with different configurations are provided in our submission.

3.2 Empirical Analysis on the Experimental Results

In this subsection, we empirically analyze the experimental results of our submission. The goal of our evaluation is to check how well the language model performs for cross-language image retrieval and what kinds of smoothing achieve better performance. Moreover, we are interested in comparing performance between the bilingual retrieval with Chinese queries and the monolingual retrieval with the normal English queries.

Empirical Analysis of Language Models. Figure 1 and Figure 2 plot the curves of *Precision* vs. *Recall* and the curves of *Precision* vs. *Number of Returned Documents*, respectively. From the experimental results shown in Figure 1 and Figure 2 as well as in Table 2, we can observe that the KL-divergence

[1] http://www.lemurproject.org/.

Table 2. The configurations and official testing results of our submission

Run ID	Language	QE	Modality	Method	MAP
CUHK-ad-eng-t-kl-ab1	english	without	text	KL-LM-ABS	0.3887
CUHK-ad-eng-t-kl-ab2	english	with	text	KL-LM-ABS	0.4055
CUHK-ad-eng-t-kl-ab3	english	with	text	KL-LM-ABS	0.4082
CUHK-ad-eng-t-kl-jm1	english	without	text	KL-LM-JM	0.3844
CUHK-ad-eng-t-kl-jm2	english	with	text	KL-LM-JM	0.4115
CUHK-ad-eng-t-kl-di1	english	without	text	KL-LM-DIR	0.3820
CUHK-ad-eng-t-kl-di2	english	with	text	KL-LM-DIR	0.3999
CUHK-ad-eng-t-tf-idf1	english	without	text	TF-IDF	0.3510
CUHK-ad-eng-t-tf-idf2	english	with	text	TF-IDF	0.3574
CUHK-ad-eng-tn-kl-ab1	english	without	text	KL-LM-ABS	0.3877
CUHK-ad-eng-tn-kl-ab2	english	with	text	KL-LM-ABS	0.3838
CUHK-ad-eng-tn-kl-ab3	english	with	text	KL-LM-ABS	0.4083
CUHK-ad-eng-tn-kl-jm1	english	without	text	KL-LM-JM	0.3762
CUHK-ad-eng-tn-kl-jm2	english	with	text	KL-LM-JM	0.4018
CUHK-ad-eng-tn-kl-di1	english	without	text	KL-LM-DIR	0.3921
CUHK-ad-eng-tn-kl-di2	english	with	text	KL-LM-DIR	0.3990
CUHK-ad-eng-tn-tf-idf1	english	without	text	TF-IDF	0.3475
CUHK-ad-eng-tn-tf-idf2	english	with	text	TF-IDF	0.3660
CUHK-ad-eng-v	english	without	vis	Moment-DCT	0.0599
CUHK-ad-eng-tv-kl-ab1	english	without	text+vis	KL-LM-ABS	0.3941
CUHK-ad-eng-tv-kl-ab3	english	with	text+vis	KL-LM-ABS	0.4108
CUHK-ad-eng-tv-kl-jm1	english	without	text+vis	KL-LM-JM	0.3878
CUHK-ad-eng-tv-kl-jm2	english	with	text+vis	KL-LM-JM	0.4135
CUHK-ad-eng-tnv-kl-ab2	english	with	text+vis	KL-LM-ABS	0.3864
CUHK-ad-eng-tnv-kl-ab3	english	with	text+vis	KL-LM-ABS	0.4118
CUHK-ad-eng-tnv-kl-jm1	english	without	text+vis	KL-LM-JM	0.3787
CUHK-ad-eng-tnv-kl-jm2	english	with	text+vis	KL-LM-JM	0.4041
CUHK-ad-chn-t-kl-ab1	chinese	without	text	KL-LM-ABS	0.1815
CUHK-ad-chn-t-kl-ab2	chinese	with	text	KL-LM-ABS	0.1842
CUHK-ad-chn-t-kl-jm1	chinese	without	text	KL-LM-JM	0.1821
CUHK-ad-chn-t-kl-jm2	chinese	with	text	KL-LM-JM	0.2027
CUHK-ad-chn-tn-kl-ab1	chinese	without	text	KL-LM-ABS	0.1758
CUHK-ad-chn-tn-kl-ab2	chinese	with	text	KL-LM-ABS	0.1527
CUHK-ad-chn-tn-kl-ab3	chinese	with	text	KL-LM-ABS	0.1834
CUHK-ad-chn-tn-kl-jm1	chinese	without	text	KL-LM-JM	0.1843
CUHK-ad-chn-tn-kl-jm2	chinese	with	text	KL-LM-JM	0.2024

LM denotes Language Model, KL denotes Kullback-Leibler divergence based, DIR denotes the smoothing using the Dirichlet priors, ABS denotes the smoothing using Absolute discounting, and JM denotes the Jelinek-Mercer smoothing.

language model outperforms the simple TF-IDF retrieval model significantly (around 5%). In the evaluation of the smoothing techniques, we observe that the Jelinek-Mercer smoothing and the Absolute discounting smoothing yield better results than the Bayesian smoothing with the Dirichlet priors (DIR).

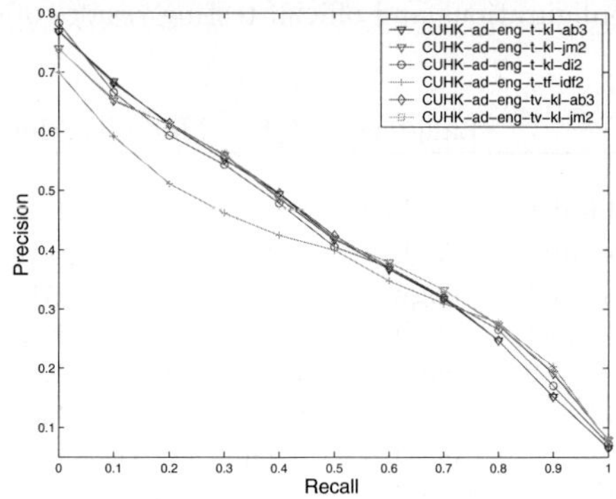

Fig. 1. Experimental Result of Precision vs. Recall with Selected Configuration

More specifically, from Figure 2(b), we see that the Jelinek-Mercer smoothing achieves the best result when the number of returned documents is less than or equal to 13, while the Absolute discounting smoothing method achieves the best when the number of returned documents is greater than 13. Finally, from the official testing results [2], our approach achieves the best MAP (Mean Average Precision) result among all submissions on the monolingual query. This shows that the language model method is the state-of-the-art approach for text based image retrieval.

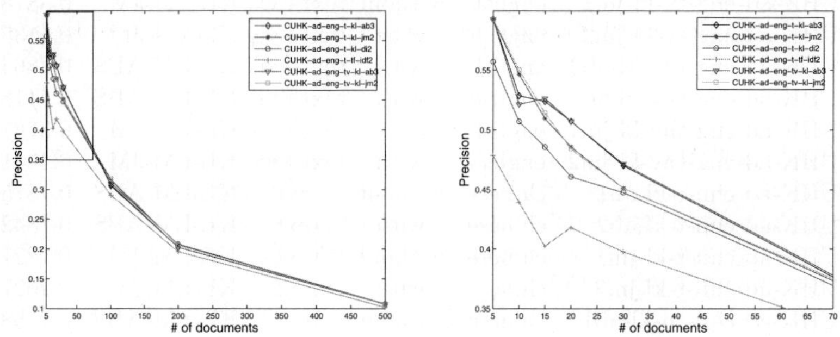

(a) (b)

Fig. 2. Experimental Result of Precision vs. Number of Returned Documents with Selected Configuration. (a) shows the original comparison on 500 returned documents; (b) shows the detailed comparison on 70 returned documents.

Cross-Language Retrieval: Chinese-To-English Query Translation. To deal with the Chinese queries for retrieving English documents, we first adopt a Chinese segmentation tool from the Linguistic Data Consortium (LDC) [10], i.e., the "LDC Chinese segmenter" [2], to extract the Chinese words from the

[2] http://www.ldc.upenn.edu/Projects/Chinese/seg.zip.

given query sentences. The segmentation step is an important step toward effective query translation. Figure 3 shows the Chinese segmentation results of part queries. We can see that the results can still be improved.

For the bilingual query translation, the second step is to translate the extracted Chinese words into English words using a Chinese-English dictionary. In our experiment, we employ the LDC Chinese-to-English Wordlist [10]. The final translated queries are obtained by combining the translation results.

From the experimental results shown in Table 2, we can observe that the mean average precision of Chinese-to-English queries is about half of the monolingual queries. There are many ways that we could improve this performance. One is to improve the Chinese segmentation algorithm. Some post-processing techniques may be effective for improving the performance. Also, the translation results can be further refined. Finally, one can better tune the results by adopting various Natural Language Processing techniques [11].

Cross-Media Retrieval: Re-Ranking Scheme with Text and Visual Content. In this task we study the combination of text and visual contents for cross-media image retrieval. We suggest the re-ranking scheme to combine text and visual contents. For a given query, we first rank the images using the language modeling techniques. We then re-rank the top ranked images by measuring the similarity of visual content to the query images.

In our experiment, two kinds of visual features are used: texture and color features. For texture, the discrete cosine transform (DCT) is engaged to calculate coefficients that multiply the basis functions of the DCT. Applying the DCT to

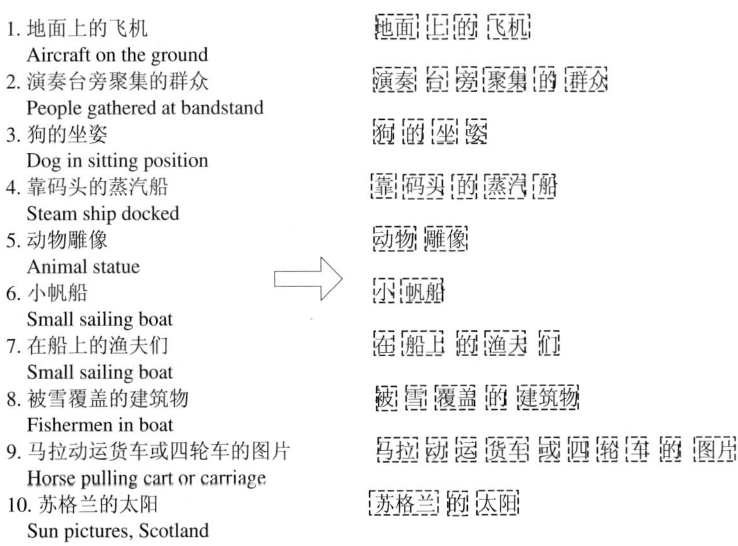

Fig. 3. Chinese segmentation results of part Chinese (Simplified) queries. Each dashed box represents a segmented Chinese word from the given English query.

an image yields a set of coefficients to represent the texture of the image. In our implementation, a block-DCT (block size 8x8) is applied on a normalized input image, which generates 256 DCT features. For color, color moment is employed to represent the images. For each image, 9 color moment features are extracted. Thus, in total, each image is represented by a 265-dimensional feature vector.

As shown in Table 2, the MAP performance of the retrieval results using only visual information is only about 6%; this is much lower than the approaches using text information, which yielded over 40%. From the experimental results, we observe that the re-ranking scheme produces only a marginal improvement compared with the text-only approaches. However, there are some reasons that explain the results. One is that the engaged visual features may not be able to discriminate between the images effectively. Another is that relevant images of the same queries in the ground truth may vary significantly in visual content, which makes it difficult for low-level features to discriminate between relevant and irrelevant images. In the future, two important research directions that could improve the performance are studying more effective techniques of low-level features, and finding more elegant methods of combining text and visual contents. Moreover, if users' logs of relevance feedback are available, that may also help the retrieval task.

Query Expansion for Information Retrieval. In general, Query Expansion (QE) refers to adding further terms to a text query (e.g. through pseudo-relevance feedback or a thesaurus) or adding further image samples to a visual query. From the experimental results in Table 2, we observe that most of the queries are greatly enhanced by adopting query expansion. The average improvement for all the queries is around 1.71%, which accounts for 4.14% of the maximum MAP of 41.35%. It is interesting to find that QE especially benefits considerably from the Jelinek-Mercer smoothing method; in this case, the mean gain with QE is about 2.49%, which accounts for 6.02% of the maximum MAP of 41.35%. Note that the number of feedback documents or samples usually strongly influences the improvement achieved with QE schemes. In our experiments, this number is estimated empirically from the official training set.

4 Conclusions

In this paper, we report our empirical studies of cross-language and cross-media image retrieval in the ImaegCLEF 2005 campaign. We address three major focuses and contributions. The first is the evaluation of Language Models and the smoothing strategies for cross-language image retrieval. We empirically show that the Language modeling approach is the state-of-the-art approach for text-based cross-language image retrieval. Among the smoothing techniques, the Jelinek- Mercer smoothing and the Absolute discounting smoothing perform better than the Bayesian smoothing with the Dirichlet priors. The second is the evaluation of cross-media image retrieval. We observe that the combination of text and visual contents gives only a marginal improvement. We can study more effective low-level features to improve this performance. The last is the evaluation of the bilingual image retrieval between English and Chinese. In our experiments, the mean average precision of Chinese-to-English Queries is about half of the monolingual queries. In future work, we can study more effective natural language processing techniques to improve this performance.

Acknowledgements

The work described in this paper was fully supported by Innovation and Technology Fund (Project No. ITS/105/03), and the Shun Hing Institute of Advanced Engineering (SHIAE) at CUHK.

References

1. A. W. M. Smeulders, M. Worring, S. Santini, A. Gupta, and R. Jain, "Content-based image retrieval at the end of the early years," *IEEE Transactions on Pattern Analysis and Machine Intelligence*, vol. 22, no. 12, pp. 1349–1380, 2000.
2. P. Clough, H. Müeller, T. Deselaers, M. Grubinger, T. Lehmann, J. Jensen, and W. Hersh, "The CLEF 2005 cross language image retrieval track," in *Proceedings of the Cross Language Evaluation Forum 2005.* Springer Lecture Notes in Computer science, 2005.
3. R. Baeza-Yates and B. Ribeiro-Neto, *Modern Information Retrieval.* Addison Wesley, 1999.
4. C. Zhai and J. Lafferty, "A study of smoothing methods for language models applied to ad hoc information retrieval," in *ACM International SIGIR Conference (SIGIR'01)*, 2001, pp. 334–342.
5. C. E. Shannon, "Prediction and entropy of printed English," *Bell Sys. Tech. Jour.*, vol. 30, pp. 51–64, 1951.
6. C. Zhai and J. Lafferty, "Model-based feedback in the kl-divergence retrieval model," in *Proc. Tenth International Conference on Information and Knowledge Management (CIKM2001)*, 2001, pp. 403–410.
7. T. M. Cover and J. A. Thomas, *Elements of Information Theory.* Wiley, 1991.
8. D. Hiemstra, "Term-specific smoothing for the language modeling approach to information retrieval: the importance of a query term," in *Proceedings 25th ACM SIGIR conference*, 2002, pp. 35–41.
9. F. Jelinek and R. Mercer, "Interpolated estimation of markov sourceparameters from sparse data," *Pattern Recognition in Practice*, pp. 381–402, 1980.
10. "http://www.ldc.upenn.edu/projects/chinese/."
11. C. Manning and H. Schütze, *Foundations of Statistical Natural Language Processing.* The MIT Press, 1999.

The University of Jaén at ImageCLEF 2005: Adhoc and Medical Tasks

M.T. Martín-Valdivia[1], M.A. García-Cumbreras[1], M.C. Díaz-Galiano[1], L.A. Ureña-López[1], and A. Montejo-Raez[1]

University of Jaén. Departamento de Informática
Grupo Sistemas Inteligentes de Acceso a la Información
Campus Las Lagunillas, Ed. A3, e-23071, Jaén, Spain
{maite, magc, mcdiaz, laurena, amontejo}@ujaen.es

Abstract. In this paper, we describe our first participation in the ImageCLEF campaign. The SINAI research group participated in both the ad hoc task and the medical task. For the first task, we have used several translation schemes as well as experiments with and without Pseudo Relevance Feedback (PRF). A voting-based system has been developed, for the ad hoc task, joining three different systems of participant Universities. For the medical task, we have also submitted runs with and without PRF, and experiments using only textual query and using textual mixing with visual query.

1 Introduction

This is the first participation for the SINAI research group at the ImageCLEF competition. We have accomplished the ad hoc task and the medical task [1].

As a cross language retrieval task, a multilingual image retrieval based on query translation can achieve high performance, more than a monolingual retrieval. The ad hoc task involves to retrieve relevant images using the text associated with each image query.

The goal of the medical task is to retrieve relevant images based on an image query. This year, a short text is associated with each image query. We first compare the results obtained using only textual query versus results obtained combining textual and visual information. We have accomplished several runs with and without Pseudo Relevance Feedback (PRF). Finally, we have used different methods to merge visual and text results.

The next section describes the ad hoc experiments. In Section 3, we explain the experiments for the medical task. Finally, conclusions and proposals for work are presented in Section 4.

2 The Ad Hoc Task

The goal of the ad hoc task is, given a multilingual query, to find as many relevant images as possible from an image collection.

C. Peters et al. (Eds.): CLEF 2005, LNCS 4022, pp. 612–621, 2006.

The proposal of the ad hoc task is to compare results with and without PRF, with or without query expansion, using different methods of query translation or using different retrieval models and weighting functions.

2.1 Experiment Description

In our experiments we have used nine languages: English, Dutch, Italian, Spanish, French, German, Danish, Swedish, and Russian. The dataset is the same used in 2004: St Andrews. The St Andrews dataset consists of 28,133 photographs from the St Andrews University Library photographic collection which holds one of the largest and most important collections of historic photography in Scotland. The collection numbers in excess of 300,000 images, 10% of which have been digitized and used for the ImageCLEF ad hoc retrieval task. All images have an accompanying textual description consisting of 8 distinct fields. These fields can be used individually or collectively to facilitate image retrieval. The collections have been preprocessed, using stopwords and the Porters stemmer.

The collection has been indexed using LEMUR IR system[1], it is a toolkit that supports indexing of large-scale text databases, the construction of simple language models for documents, queries, or subcollections, and the implementation of retrieval systems based on language models as well as a variety of other retrieval models.

We have used online Machine Translator for each language pair, using English as pivot language. One parameter for each experiment is the weighting function, such as Okapi or TFIDF. Another is the use or not of PRF.

2.2 Results and Discussion

Tables 1, 2, 3, 4, 5, 6, 7, 8, and 9 show a summary of experiments submitted and results obtained for the seven languages used.

The results obtained show that in general the application of query expansion improves the results. Only one Italian experiment without query expansion gets a better result. In the case of the use of only title or title + narrative, the results are not conclusive, but the use of only title seems to produce better results.

Table 1. Summary of results for the ad hoc task (Dutch)

Experiment	Initial Query	Expansion	MAP	%MONO	Rank
SinaiDuTitleFBSystran	title	with	0.3397	66.5%	2/15
SinaiDuTitleNoFBSystran	title	without	0.2727	53.4%	9/15

2.3 Joint Participation

For the ad hoc task we have also made a joint participation within the R2D2 project framework. We have integrated our system and the ones belonging to the UNED group from Madrid and the system from the University of Alicante (UA).

[1] `http://www.lemurproject.org/`

Table 2. Summary of results for the ad hoc task (English)

Experiment	Initial Query	Expansion	MAP	%MONO	Rank
SinaiEnTitleNarrFB	title + narr	with	0.3727	n/a	31/70
SinaiEnTitleNoFB	title	without	0.3207	n/a	44/70
SinaiEnTitleFB	title	with	0.3168	n/a	45/70
SinaiEnTitleNarrNoFB	title + narr	without	0.3135	n/a	46/70

Table 3. Summary of results for the ad hoc task (French)

Experiment	Initial Query	Expansion	MAP	%MONO	Rank
SinaiFrTitleNarrFBSystran	title + narr	with	0.2864	56.1%	1/17
SinaiFrTitleNarrNoFBSystran	title + narr	without	0.2227	43.6%	12/17
SinaiFrTitleFBSystran	title	with	0.2163	42.3%	13/17
SinaiFrTitleNoFBSystran	title	without	0.2158	42.2%	14/17

Table 4. Summary of results for the ad hoc task (German)

Experiment	Initial Query	Expansion	MAP	%MONO	Rank
SinaiGerTitleFBSystran	title	with	0.3004	58.8%	4/29
SinaiGerTitleFBPrompt	title	with	0.2931	57.4%	5/29
SinaiGerTitleNoFBPrompt	title	without	0.2917	57.1%	6/29
SinaiGerTitleNarrFBSystran	title + narr	with	0.2847	55.7%	7/29
SinaiGerTitleNarrFBPrompt	title + narr	with	0.2747	53.8%	10/29
SinaiGerTitleNoFBSystran	title	without	0.2720	53.2%	13/29
SinaiGerTitleFBWordlingo	title	with	0.2491	48.8%	16/29
SinaiGerTitleNarrNoFBSystran	title + narr	without	0.2418	47.3%	17/29
SinaiGerTitleNarrNoFBPrompt	title + narr	without	0.2399	47.0%	18/29
SinaiGerTitleNoFBWordlingo	title	without	0.2217	43.4%	19/29
SinaiGerTitleNarrFBWordlingo	title + narr	with	0.1908	37.4%	21/29
SinaiGerTitleNarrNoFBSWordlingo	title + narr	without	0.1860	36.4%	22/29

Table 5. Summary of results for the ad hoc task (Italian)

Experiment	Initial Query	Expansion	MAP	%MONO	Rank
SinaiItTitleNoFBSystran	title	without	0.1805	35.3%	12/19
SinaiItTitleFBSystran	title	with	0.1672	32.7%	13/19
SinaiItTitleNarrNoFBSystran	title + narr	without	0.1585	31.0%	14/19
SinaiItTitleNoFBWordlingo	title	without	0.1511	29.6%	15/19
SinaiItTitleNarrFBSystran	title + narr	with	0.1397	27.3%	16/19
SinaiItTitleFBWordlingo	title	with	0.1386	27.1%	18/19

Table 6. Summary of results for the ad hoc task (Russian)

Experiment	Initial Query	Expansion	MAP	%MONO	Rank
SinaiRuTitleFBSystran	title	with	0.2229	43.6%	11/15
SinaiRuTitleNoFBSystran	title	without	0.2096	41.0%	12/15

Table 7. Summary of results for the ad hoc task (Spanish European)

Experiment	Initial Query	Expansion	MAP	%MONO	Rank
SinaiSpEurTitleFBPrompt	title	with	0.2416	47.3%	5/33
SinaiSpEurTitleFBEpals	title	with	0.2292	44.9%	7/33
SinaiSpEurTitleNoFBPrompt	title	without	0.2260	44.2%	8/33
SinaiSpEurTitleNarrFBEpals	title + narr	with	0.2135	41.8%	11/33
SinaiSpEurTitleNoFBEpals	title	without	0.2074	40.6%	16/33
SinaiSpEurTitleNarrFBSystran	title + narr	with	0.2052	40.2%	20/33
SinaiSpEurTitleNoFBSystran	title	without	0.1998	39.1%	21/33
SinaiSpEurTitleNoFBWordlingo	title	without	0.1998	39.1%	22/33
SinaiSpEurTitleFBSystran	title	with	0.1965	38.5%	23/33
SinaiSpEurTitleFBWordlingo	title	with	0.1965	38.5%	24/33
SinaiSpEurTitleNarrNoFBEpals	title + narr	without	0.1903	37.3%	25/33
SinaiSpEurTitleNarrNoFBPrompt	title + narr	without	0.1865	36.5%	27/33
SinaiSpEurTitleNarrNoFBSystran	title + narr	without	0.1712	33.5%	28/33
SinaiSpEurTitleNarrFBSystran	title + narr	with	0.1605	31.4%	29/33
SinaiSpEurTitleNarrNoFBSWordlingo	title + narr	without	0.1343	26.3%	31/33
SinaiSpEurTitleNarrFBWordlingo	title + narr	with	0.1182	23.1%	32/33

Table 8. Summary of results for the ad hoc task (Spanish Latinamerican)

Experiment	Initial Query	Expansion	MAP	%MONO	Rank
SinaiSpLatTitleFBPrompt	title	with	0.2967	58.1%	8/31
SinaiSpLatTitleNoFBPrompt	title	without	0.2963	58.0%	9/31
SinaiSpLatTitleNoFBEpals	title	without	0.2842	55.6%	11/31
SinaiSpLatTitleNoFBSystran	title	without	0.2834	55.5%	12/31
SinaiSpLatTitleNoFBWordlingo	title	without	0.2834	55.5%	13/31
SinaiSpLatTitleFBSystran	title	with	0.2792	54.7%	14/31
SinaiSpLatTitleFBWordlingo	title	with	0.2792	54.7%	15/31
SinaiSpLatTitleFBEpals	title	with	0.2606	51.0%	16/31
SinaiSpLatTitleNarrNoFBSystran	title + narr	without	0.2316	45.3%	19/31
SinaiSpLatTitleNarrFBPrompt	title + narr	with	0.2259	44.2%	20/31
SinaiSpLatTitleNarrFBSystran	title + narr	with	0.2026	39.7%	21/31
SinaiSpLatTitleNarrFBEpals	title + narr	with	0.2001	39.2%	22/31
SinaiSpLatTitleNarrNoFBPrompt	title + narr	without	0.1992	39.0%	23/31
SinaiSpLatTitleNarrNoFBEpals	title + narr	without	0.1900	37.2%	24/31
SinaiSpLatTitleNarrNoFBSWordlingo	title + narr	without	0.1769	34.6%	25/31
SinaiSpLatTitleNarrFBWordlingo	title + narr	with	0.1459	28.6%	27/31

Table 9. Summary of results for the ad hoc task (Swedish)

Experiment	Initial Query	Expansion	MAP	%MONO	Rank
SinaiSweTitleNoFBSystran	title	without	0.2074	40.6%	2/7
SinaiSweTitleFBSystran	title	with	0.2012	39.4%	3/7

We have developed a voting system among them. For English, Dutch, French, German, Italian, Russian and Spanish we have done a combination between UA and SINAI. UA, UNED and SINAI systems have been only combined for Spanish. The parameters selected are the use of feedback and the use of query titles and automatic translation. The voting was developed using the weights of each document in each retrieved list.

The results are shown in the Table 10. The ranks are shown in brackets.

Table 10. Summary of results for the voting-based collaborative system

Language	SINAI	UA	UNED	SINAI-UA	SINAI-UA-UNED
Dutch	0.3397(2/15)	0.2765(8/15)	-	0.3435(1/15)	-
English	0.3727(30/70)	0.3966(14/70)	-	0.4080(7/70)	-
French	0.2864(1/17)	0.2621(6/17)	-	0.2630(5/17)	-
German	0.3004(4/29)	0.2854(7/29)	-	0.3375(1/29)	-
Italian	0.1805(11/19)	0.2230(4/19)	-	0.2289(2/19)	-
Russian	0.2229(11/15)	0.2683(3/15)	-	0.2665(5/15)	-
Spanish (eur)	0.2416(5/33)	0.2105(12/33)	0.3175(1/33)	0.2668(4/33)	0.3020(2/33)
Spanish (lat)	0.2967(8/31)	0.3179(2/31)	0.2585(17/31)	0.3447(1/31)	0.3054(4/31)

As we can see the voting system improves the results for the Dutch, English, German, Italian and Spanish-latinoamerican languages.

3 The Medical Task

The main goal of medical task is to improve the retrieval of medical images from heterogeneous and multilingual document collections containing images as well as text. This year, queries have been formulated with example images and a short textual description explaining the research goal. For the medical task, we have used the list of retrieved images by GIFT[2] [2] which was supplied by the organizers of this track. Also, we used the text of topics for each query. For this reason, our efforts concentrated on manipulating the text descriptions associated with these images and in mixing the partial results lists. Thus, our experiments only use the list provided by the GIFT system in order to expand textual queries. Textual descriptions of the medical cases have been used to try to improve retrieval results.

3.1 Textual Retrieval System

In order to generate the textual collection we have used the images and their annotations.

The entire collection consists of 4 datasets (CASImage, Pathopic, Peir and MIR) containing about 50,000 images. Each subcollection is organized into cases that represent a group of related images and annotations. Each case consists in

[2] http://www.gnu.org/software/gift/

a group of images and an optional annotation. The collection annotations are in XML format. The majority of the annotations are in English but a significant number is also in French (CASImage) and German (Pathopic), with a few cases that do not contain any annotation at all. The quality of the texts is variable between collections and even within the same collection.

We generated a textual document per image, where the identifier number of document is the name of the image and the text of document is the XML annotation associated with this image. The XML tags and unnecessary fields such as *LANGUAGE* were removed. If there were several images of the same case, the text was copied several times.

We have used English language for the document collection as well for the queries. Thus, French annotations in CASImage collection were translated to English and then were incorporated with the collection. Pathopic collection has annotation in both English and German language. We only used English annotations in order to generate the Pathopic documents and German annotations were discarded.

Finally, we have added the text associated with each query topic as documents. In this case, if a query topic includes several images, the text was also copied several times.

Once the document collection was generated, experiments were conducted with the LEMUR retrieval information system. We have used the 3 different weighting schemes available: TFIDF, Okapi and Kl-divergence.

3.2 Experiment Description

Our main goal is to investigate the effectiveness of combining text and image for retrieval. For this, we compare the obtained results when we only use the text associated with the query topic and the results when we merge visual and textual information.

We have accomplished a first experiment that we have used as baseline case. This experiment simply consists of taking the text associated with each query as a new textual query. Then, each textual query is submitted to the LEMUR system. The resulting list is directly the baseline run. This result list from LEMUR system contains the most similar cases with respect to the text and a weighting (the relevance). The weighting was normalized based on the highest weighting in the list to get values between 0 and 1.

The remaining experiments start from the ranked lists provided by the GIFT. The organization provides a GIFT list of relevant images for each query. For each list/query we have used an automatic textual query expansion of the first five images from the GIFT lists. We have taken the text associated with each image in order to generate a new textual query. Then, each textual query is submitted to the LEMUR system and we obtain five new ranked lists. Again, the resulting lists were normalized to 1. Thus, for each original query we have six partial lists. The last step consists of merging these partial result lists using some strategy in order to obtain one final list with relevant images ranking by relevance. Figure 1 describes the process.

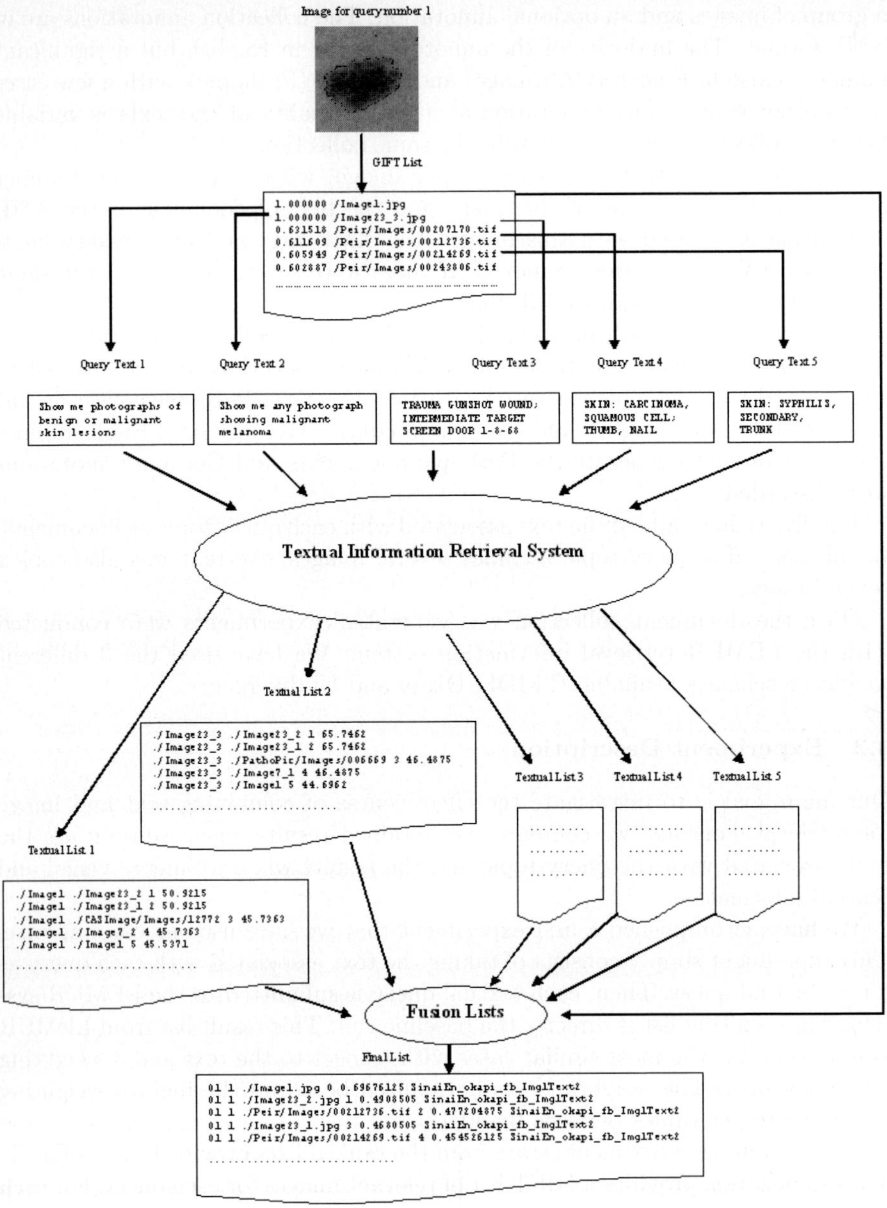

Fig. 1. The merging process of result lists

The merging of the visual and textual results was done in various ways:

1. **ImgText4:** The final list includes the images present in at least 4 partial lists independently of these lists are visual or textual. In order to calculate the final image relevance simply we sum the partial relevance and divide by the maximum number of lists where the images are present.
2. **ImgText3:** This experiment is the same as ImgText4 but the image must be in at least 3 lists.
3. **ImgText2:** This experiment is the same as ImgText4 but the image must be in at least 2 lists.
4. **Img1Tex4:** The final list includes the images present in at least 4 partial lists, but the image is necessary to be in the GIFT list (i.e., the image must be in the GIFT list and in at least other 3 textual lists). In order to calculate the final image relevance we simply sum the partial relevance and divide by the maximum number of lists where the images are present.
5. **Img1Text3:** This experiment is the same as Img1Text4, but the image must be in at least 3 lists (the GIFT list and at least 2 textual lists).
6. **Img1Text2:** This experiment is the same as Img1Text4, but the image must be in at least 2 lists (the GIFT list and at least 1 textual list).

These 6 experiments and the baseline experiment (that only uses textual information of the query) have been accomplished with and without PRF for each weighting schemes (TFIDF, Okapi and Kl-divergence). In summary, we have submitted 42 runs: 7 (different experiments)*2 (PRF and no PRF) * 3 (weighting schemes).

3.3 Results and Discussion

Tables 11 and 12 show the official results for medical task (text only and mixed retrieval). The total runs submitted for text were only 14 and for mixed retrieval 86. Best results were obtained when using Okapi without PRF for *text only* runs (experiment SinaiEn_okapi_nofb_Topics.imageclef2005) and using Kl-divergence with PRF and ImgText2 experiment for *mixed retrieval* runs (experiment SinaiEn_kl_fb_ImgText2.imageclef2005).

Table 11. Performance of official runs in Medical Image Retrieval (text only)

Experiment	Precision	Rank
IPALI2R_TIan (best result)	0.2084	1
SinaiEn_okapi_nofb_Topics.imageclef2005	0.091	5
SinaiEn_okapi_fb_Topics.imageclef2005	0.0862	6
SinaiEn_kl_fb_Topics.imageclef2005	0.079	7
SinaiEn_kl_nofb_Topics.imageclef2005	0.0719	8
SinaiEn_tfidf_fb_Topics.imageclef2005	0.0405	10
SinaiEn_tfidf_nofb_Topics.imageclef2005	0.0394	12

Table 12. Performance of official runs in Medical Image Retrieval (mixed text+visual)

Experiment	Precision	Rank
IPALI2R_Tn (best result)	0.2084	1
SinaiEn_kl_fb_ImgText2.imageclef2005	0.1033	24
SinaiEn_kl_fb_Img1Text2.imageclef2005	0.1002	28
SinaiEn_okapi_fb_Img1Text2.imageclef2005	0.0992	31
SinaiEn_okapi_nofb_Img1Text2.imageclef2005	0.0955	33
SinaiEn_kl_nofb_ImgText2.imageclef2005	0.0947	34
SinaiEn_okapi_nofb_ImgText2.imageclef2005	0.0931	36
SinaiEn_okapi_fb_ImgText2.imageclef2005	0.0905	39
SinaiEn_kl_fb_ImgText3.imageclef2005	0.0891	41
SinaiEn_kl_nofb_Img1Text2.imageclef2005	0.0884	42
SinaiEn_okapi_nofb_ImgText3.imageclef2005	0.0867	43
SinaiEn_kl_fb_Img1Text3.imageclef2005	0.0845	44
SinaiEn_okapi_fb_ImgText3.imageclef2005	0.0803	47
SinaiEn_kl_nofb_ImgText3.imageclef2005	0.0781	48
SinaiEn_okapi_nofb_Img1Text3.imageclef2005	0.0779	49
SinaiEn_okapi_fb_Img1Text3.imageclef2005	0.0761	50
SinaiEn_kl_nofb_Img1Text3.imageclef2005	0.0726	52
SinaiEn_okapi_nofb_ImgText4.imageclef2005	0.0685	53
SinaiEn_tfidf_fb_Img1Text2.imageclef2005	0.0678	54
SinaiEn_kl_nofb_ImgText4.imageclef2005	0.0653	57
SinaiEn_kl_nofb_Img1Text4.imageclef2005	0.0629	59
SinaiEn_kl_fb_ImgText4.imageclef2005	0.062	60
SinaiEn_kl_fb_Img1Text4.imageclef2005	0.0602	61
SinaiEn_okapi_nofb_Img1Text4.imageclef2005	0.0596	62
SinaiEn_tfidf_nofb_Img1Text2.imageclef2005	0.0582	63
SinaiEn_okapi_fb_Img1Text4.imageclef2005	0.055	64
SinaiEn_okapi_fb_ImgText4.imageclef2005	0.0547	65
SinaiEn_tfidf_fb_ImgText2.imageclef2005	0.0481	69
SinaiEn_tfidf_fb_Img1Text3.imageclef2005	0.0474	70
SinaiEn_tfidf_fb_ImgText3.imageclef2005	0.0713	76
SinaiEn_tfidf_nofb_Img1Text3.imageclef2005	0.0412	77
SinaiEn_tfidf_nofb_ImgText2.imageclef2005	0.0395	79
SinaiEn_tfidf_fb_ImgText4.imageclef2005	0.0386	80
SinaiEn_tfidf_fb_Img1Text4.imageclef2005	0.0372	82
SinaiEn_tfidf_nofb_ImgText3.imageclef2005	0.0362	83
SinaiEn_tfidf_nofb_Img1Text4.imageclef2005	0.0339	84
SinaiEn_tfidf_nofb_ImgText4.imageclef2005	0.0336	85

There are no significant differences between results obtained with Okapi and Kl-divergence schemes. However, the worst results were obtained with the TFIDF scheme.

On the other hand, the use of only two lists is better than mixing three or four lists of partial results. A substantial difference in the inclusion or not of the images in the GIFT list (Img1Text$X$ experiments) is not appraised, either.

4 Conclusion and Further Works

In this paper, we have presented the experiment carried out in our first participation in the ImageCLEF campaign. We have only tried to verify if the use of textual information increases the effectiveness of the systems. Evaluation results show that the use of textual information significantly improves the retrieval.

The incorporation of some natural language processing techniques such as word sense disambiguation (WSD) or named entity recognition (NER) will focus our future work. We also plan to use some machine learning algorithms in order to improve the lists merging process. Thus, we should do a comparative study for different fusion methods using basic algorithms (such as Round-Robin or Raw Scoring) and machine learning algorithms (such as logistic regression, neural networks and support vector machines).

Acknowledgements

This work has been partially supported by a grant from the Spanish Government, project R2D2 (TIC2003-07158-C04-04).

References

1. Clough P., Henning Mller, Thomas Deselaers, Michael Grubinger, Thomas M. Lehmann, Jeffery Jensen, William Hersh, The CLEF 2005 Cross-Language Image Retrieval Track, Proceedings of the Cross Language Evaluation Forum 2005, Springer Lecture Notes in Computer science, 2006 - to appear.
2. Müller, H., Geissbhler, A., Ruch., P.: Report on the CLEF experiment: Combining image and multi-lingual search medical image retrieval. In Proceedings of the Cross Language Evaluation Forum (CLEF 2004), 2004

Data Fusion of Retrieval Results from Different Media: Experiments at ImageCLEF 2005

Romaric Besançon and Christophe Millet

CEA-LIST/LIC2M, BP 6 92265 Fontenay-aux-Roses CEDEX - France
{besanconr, milletc}@zoe.cea.fr

Abstract. The CEA-LIST/LIC2M develops both multilingual text retrieval systems and content-based image indexing and retrieval systems. These systems are developed independently. The merging of the results of the two systems is one of the important research interests in our lab. We tested several simple merging techniques in the ImageCLEF 2005 campaign. The analysis of our results show that improved performance can be obtained by appropriately merging the two media. However, an a-priori tuning of the merging parameters is difficult because the performance of each system highly depends on the corpus and queries.

1 Introduction

The ImageCLEF campaign aims at studying cross-language image retrieval, that potentially uses text and image matching techniques. The CEA-LIST/LIC2M participated in ImageCLEF 2005 to perform experiments on merging strategies to integrate the results obtained from the cross-language text retrieval system and the content-based image retrieval (CBIR) system that are developed in our lab.

We participated in the three tasks of the ImageCLEF 2005 campaign: ad hoc, medical and annotation tasks. More information on each task can be found in the overview paper of the ImageCLEF track [1]. For both retrieval tasks (ad hoc and medical), text and visual information were provided for the queries. We applied the same strategy for the two retrieval tasks, using our retrieval systems independently on text and visual queries and applying *a posteriori* merging strategies on the results. The annotation task is an image classification task that rely only on the image indexing techniques. Our participation in this task was useful to determine the relevance of the image indexing techniques used in our CBIR system for the medical images used in this task and develop adapted classifiers.

We present in section 2 the retrieval systems for text and image and the merging strategies used. We then present the results obtained for the ad hoc task and the medical task in sections 3 and 4 respectively. The strategy and results for the annotation task are presented in section 5.

C. Peters et al. (Eds.): CLEF 2005, LNCS 4022, pp. 622–631, 2006.

2 Retrieval Systems

2.1 Multilingual Text Retrieval System

The multilingual text retrieval system used for these experiments is a general-domain system which has not been specially adapted to work on the ImageCLEF collections. In particular, no special treatment has been performed to take into account the specific structure of the documents (such as photographer's name, location, date for the captions and description, diagnosis, clinical presentation in the medical annotations) or to take into account the specificities of medical texts (specialized vocabulary). Notice that this system is not only cross-lingual but multilingual, because it integrates a concept-based merging technique to merge results found in each target language. Its basic principle is briefly described here.

Document and query processing. The documents and queries are processed using a linguistic analyzer that performs in particular part-of-speech tagging, lemmatization, compound and named entities extraction. The elements extracted from the documents are indexed into inverted files. The elements extracted from the queries are used as query "*concepts*". Each concept is reformulated into a set of *search terms* for each target language, either using a monolingual expansion dictionary (that introduces synonyms and related words), or using a bilingual dictionary.

Document Retrieval. Each search term is searched in the index, and documents containing the term are retrieved. All retrieved documents are then associated with a *concept profile*, indicating the presence of query concepts in the document. This concept profile depends on the query concepts, and is language-independent (which allow merging results from different languages). Documents sharing the same concept profile are clustered together, and a weight is associated with each cluster according to its concept profile and to the weight of the concepts (the weight of a concept depends on the weight of each of its reformulated term in the retrieved documents). The clusters are sorted according to their weights and the first 1000 documents in this sorted list are retrieved.

2.2 Content-Based Image Retrieval System

The CBIR system used for these experiments is the system PIRIA (Program for the Indexing and Research of Images by Affinity)[2], developed in our lab. For each query image, the system returns a ranked list of similar images. The similarity is obtained by a metric distance on image signatures, that rely on several indexers: principally *Color*, *Texture* and *Shape* if the segmentation of the images is relevant. The system takes into account geometric transformations and variations like rotation, symmetry, mirroring, etc. PIRIA is a global one-pass system, feedback or "relevant/non relevant" learning methods are not used.

Color Indexing. This indexer first quantifies the image, and then, for each quantified color, it computes how much this color is connex. It can also be described as a border/interior pixel classification [3]. The distance used for the color indexing is a classical L2 norm.

Texture Indexing. A global texture histogram is used for the texture analysis. The histogram is computed from the Local Edge Pattern descriptors [4]. These descriptors describe the local structure according to the edge image computed with a Sobel filtering. We obtain a 512-bins texture histogram, which is associated with a 64 bins color histogram where each plane of the RGB color space is quantized into 4 colors. Distances are computed with a L1 norm.

Shape Indexing. The shape indexer used consists of a projection of the edge image along its horizontal and vertical axes. The image is first resized in 100x100. Then, the Sobel edge image is computed and divided into four equal sized squares (up left, up right, bottom left and bottom right). Then, each 50x50 part is projected along its vertical and horizontal axes, thus giving a 400-bins histogram. The L2 distance is used to compare two histograms.

2.3 Search and Merging Strategy

For both ad hoc and medical task, the queries contain textual and visual information. Textual information is used to search relevant text documents with the text retrieval system. For ad hoc task, each text document corresponds to a single image: the images corresponding to the relevant texts are then given as results. For the medical task, a text document may be associated with several images. In that case, the score obtained by the text documents is given to each image it is associated with, and the first 1000 images in this image list are kept.

Independently, visual information was used by the CBIR system to retrieve similar images. Queries contain several images: a first merging has been performed internally in the PIRIA system to obtain a single image list from the results of each query image: the score associated with result images is set to the max of the scores obtained for each query image.

The results obtained by each system are merged using a merging strategy that consist in assigning to each document a score equal to a weighted sum of the scores obtained by each system. This merging is parameterized by a coefficient α: for a query q and an image document d retrieved for this query, the merging score is

$$s(d) = \alpha \times s'_T(d) + (1-\alpha) \times s'_I(d) \qquad (1)$$

where $s'_T(d)$ is a normalized score of the text retrieval system and $s'_I(d)$ a normalized score of the image retrieval system.

We tested several normalization schemes for the individual scores, that have been used for multilingual information retrieval data fusion (for instance in [5]). These different normalization schemes are presented in Table 1. The *normMax* scheme normalizes the score by the maximal score s_{max} obtained for this query. The *normRSV* normalizes the score taking into account the range of the scores of the documents retrieved for the query. The *Z-score* normalizes the score taking into account the mean s_{mean} and the standard deviation s_σ of the scores the documents retrieved for the query.

We also tested a *conservative* merging strategy that gave good performance in the ImageCLEF 2004 campaign [6]. By *conservative*, we mean that we use

Table 1. Normalization schemes for the scores in the merging strategy

normMax	$s'_X(d) = \frac{s_X(d)}{s_{max}}$
normRSV	$s'_X(d) = \frac{s_X(d) - s_{min}}{s_{max} - s_{min}}$
Z-score	$s'_X(d) = \frac{s_X(d) - s_{mean}}{s_\sigma} + \delta$ with $\delta = \frac{s_{mean} - s_{min}}{s_\sigma}$

the results obtained by one system only to reorder the results obtained by the other (results can be added at end of list if the number of documents retrieved by main system is less than 1000). The score of a document retrieved by the first system is modified using equation 1. Documents retrieved only by the second system are ignored.

3 Results for the Ad Hoc Task

We present in Table 2 the results obtained for the ad hoc task by each retrieval system independently: text retrieval has been performed on English, French and Spanish queries, using either the title only (T) or the title and the narrative (T+N); CBIR has been performed using texture and color indexers.

Text results show that average precision is better when using the title only, but the number of relevant documents is generally better when using also the narrative part (except for French, for which it is a bit worse): the narrative introduces more words that allow to increase the total number of documents retrieved, but also introduces more noise, which makes the precision decrease.

CBIR results for the StAndrews collection are quite poor, which confirms that this collection, composed of old, often monochrome, photographs, is not well adapted to the kind of image indexers we use, that rely mostly on color for segmentation, and that the queries rely mostly on the text descriptions of the images, as we already noticed in our previous experiments in ImageCLEF [6].

Table 2. Ad hoc task: results of single text and CBIR systems: mean average precision (*map*), number of relevant documents (*relret*) and recall at 1000 documents (*r1000*)

	text retrieval						CBIR	
	eng		fre		spa		texture	color
	T	T+N	T	T+N	T	T+N		
map	**0.246**	0.224	**0.186**	0.146	**0.191**	0.151	**0.0677**	0.0657
relret	1246	**1401**	**1237**	1184	1085	**1153**	**367**	330
r1000	65%	**73.1%**	**64.6%**	61.8%	56.6%	**60.2%**	**19.2%**	17.2%

We present in Table 3 the results obtained with the merging of the two systems, using the texture indexer for the CBIR system, and the title only for the

Table 3. Ad hoc task: comparative results for the merging strategies

eng				fre				spa			
α	NMax	NRSV	NZ	α	NMax	NRSV	NZ	α	NMax	NRSV	NZ
1	0.246	0.246	0.246	1	0.186	0.186	0.186	1	0.191	0.191	0.191
0.9	0.274	0.259	0.262	0.9	0.214	**0.211**	0.208	0.9	0.208	0.207	0.207
0.8	**0.281**	**0.265**	0.268	0.8	**0.221**	0.21	0.211	0.8	0.212	0.209	0.209
0.7	0.275	0.258	**0.271**	0.7	0.204	0.188	0.217	0.7	**0.222**	0.213	0.213
0.6	0.26	0.244	0.27	0.6	0.176	0.164	**0.22**	0.6	0.219	0.214	0.214
0.5	0.236	0.227	0.244	0.5	0.162	0.163	0.205	0.5	0.217	**0.215**	**0.215**

text retrieval system. The results are presented for the different merging scores and for different values of the merging coefficient α ($\alpha = 1$ corresponds to the text-only search)[1].

These results show that the merging of text and image results can increase the mean average precision by a gain from 14% up to 18%, depending on the query language. A signed-ranks Wilcoxon test show that this improvement is significant. The best value for α depends on the language and the normalization scheme, but a value of 0.7 seems to give good performances (differences with surrounding values are not significant). All normalization schemes seems to give similar results.

Similar results are presented in Table 4 using the conservative merging strategy, for α between 0.5 and 0.7. Since the CBIR results are worse that the text retrieval results, we chose the text retrieval as base for conservative merging. The difference between best scores using conservative merging and best scores using a simple merging is between +1.5% and +5%, but is not significant, according to the Wilcoxon test. However, best results for the conservative merging strategy are obtained for smaller values of α (since no new documents are added, conservative strategy allow to use more information from the second results for reordering of the main results).

Table 4. Ad hoc task: comparative results for the conservative merging strategies

eng				fre				spa			
α	NMax	NRSV	NZ	α	NMax	NRSV	NZ	α	NMax	NRSV	NZ
0.7	0.28	0.28	0.282	0.7	**0.22**	0.22	0.217	0.7	0.223	0.218	0.225
0.6	**0.281**	**0.281**	**0.287**	0.6	0.217	0.218	0.222	0.6	0.225	0.223	0.23
0.5	0.276	0.278	0.283	0.5	0.212	**0.223**	**0.224**	0.5	**0.227**	**0.228**	**0.233**

As a complementary information, we computed the overlap and inclusion ratios on relevant and non-relevant documents. These measures are defined by:

$$R_{overlap} = \frac{2 \times |R_1 \cap R_2|}{|R_1| + |R_2|} \qquad NR_{overlap} = \frac{2 \times |NR_1 \cap NR_2|}{|NR_1| + |NR_2|}$$
$$R_{inclusion}(i) = \frac{|R_1 \cap R_2|}{|R_i|} \qquad NR_{inclusion}(i) = \frac{|R_1 \cap R_2|}{|NR_i|} \tag{2}$$

[1] Values of α below 0.5 are not presented but do not give better results.

where R_i (resp. NR_i) is the set of relevant (resp. non-relevant) documents retrieved by the system i.

The overlap and inclusion ratios for the results on the ad hoc task are presented in Table 5 (these values are average values on all text/image result combination, for the different query languages and the different image indexers). These

Table 5. Ad hoc task: average overlap and inclusion ratios

text/image	R	NR
overlap	23.2%	4.15%
inclusion(text)	17.3%	4.42%
inclusion(image)	69.05%	4.03%

ratios show that the overlap on relevant documents is much higher than on the non-relevant ones, which is a good indicator that the merging of the results can improve the performance of the system [7,8]. On the other hand, the inclusion ratios show that almost 70% of the relevant documents found by the CBIR system where also found by the text retrieval system. This figure reinforces the idea that a conservative merging should be a good strategy, even though the experimental results are comparable to simple merging.

4 Results for the Medical Task

We present in Table 6 the results obtained in the medical task by each retrieval system independently: the text retrieval results are given for English and French queries, the CBIR results are given for the texture and color indexers. The text retrieval results are lower than for the ad hoc task, which can be explained by the lack of specialized linguistic resources adapted to medical data (for the analysis and the translation of the queries). Average precision of the CBIR results is also surprisingly low: results obtained on medical images in previous experiments were reasonably high [6]. However, the medical image collection of ImageCLEF 2005 is much larger and varied than previous collections, which could explain these results.

We present in Table 6 the results obtained using the different merging strategies, using the results of the texture indexer for the CBIR system, with different

Table 6. Medical task: results of single text and CBIR systems: mean average precision (*map*), number of relevant documents (*relret*) and recall at 1000 documents (*r1000*)

	text retrieval		CBIR	
	eng	fre	texture	color
map	0.0843	0.0899	**0.0465**	0.0307
relret	999	1059	**822**	643
r1000	32.8%	34.8%	**27%**	21.1%

Table 7. Medical task: comparative results for the merging strategies

eng				fre			
α	NMax	NRSV	NZ	α	NMax	NRSV	NZ
1	0.084	0.084	0.084	1	0.09	0.09	0.09
0.8	0.11	**0.11**	0.106	0.8	**0.129**	**0.127**	**0.127**
0.7	0.114	0.105	**0.107**	0.7	**0.129**	0.126	**0.127**
0.6	**0.118**	0.108	0.106	0.6	0.127	0.124	0.12

values of the merging coefficient α. A significant improvement is noticed with the merging of the results, that is higher that for the ad hoc task (around 40%). The results of the tests performed to evaluate the conservative merging are not presented here but lead to conclusions similar to the ones derived from the ad hoc task results: best results are obtained for smaller values of α (around 0.5), but are not significantly better than the best results obtained with simple merging. The average values of overlap and inclusion ratios on the results of the medical task are presented in Table 8, for all queries and for each type of queries separately (this values are averaged on English and drench queries only). As for the

Table 8. Medical task: average overlap and inclusion measures

	all		visual		mixed		semantic	
text/image	R	NR	R	NR	R	NR	R	NR
overlap	21.4%	3.24%	27.2%	3.0%	15.0%	3.3%	36.6%	3.9%
inclusion(text)	20.4%	3.25%	23.5%	3.2%	16.5%	3.3%	26.4%	4.0%
inclusion(image)	34.4%	3.23%	41.2%	2.9%	20.1%	3.2%	95.5%	3.8%

ad hoc task, the overlap on relevant document is much higher than the overlap on non-relevant documents, which confirms that a merging strategy will improve the results. But the overall inclusion ratios also show that the relevant images retrieved by the text and image retrieval systems are different: 2/3 of the relevant images found by the image retrieval were not found by the text retrieval. Hence the two systems are really complementary, which explains the important improvement of the results when using the merging strategy. As far as query types are concerned, the intuition is verified for the semantic queries, for which more than 95% of the relevant documents found by the CBIR system were found by the text retrieval system.

5 Annotation Task

Table 9 present the results obtained for the annotation task. We tested several image indexers, several classifiers and possible merges of results obtained independently from different classifiers.

We first tested simple k-Nearest Neighbor classifiers using the three indexers described in section 2 (Color, Texture and Shape). For these classifiers, the strategy is the following: for each candidate image, the CBIR system returns an ranked list of the most similar images, associated with their distance to the candidate image. The k nearest images are selected in the list. A confidence score is then associated with each class, defined by the sum of the inverse distance of each image among the first k that belongs to the class. Each confidence score is then scaled linearly so that the sum of all scores for all classes is equal to 1.

Different values of k have been tested for each indexer (from 1 to 13, except 2-NN which is equivalent to 1-NN here), and evaluated with the leave-one-out method. Best values k were 3 for the shape indexer, 6 for the texture indexer and 9 for the color indexer.

As we could expect, the shape indexer performs better than the others, since all the images in the database are in grey levels, which is the kind of images the shape indexer is designed for, whereas the color and texture indexers are not well adapted to this kind of images (remember that the texture indexer includes a 64-bins color histogram).

Table 9. Results for the automatic annotation task

single classifier	error rate
9-NN Color	46.0%
6-NN Texture	42.5%
3-NN Shape	36.9%
4-NN Texture-Grey	35.1%
SVM Shape	**30.7%**

merged classifiers	error rate
6-NN Texture/3-NN Shape	33.6%
6-NN Texture-Grey/3-NN Shape	30.3%
6-NN Texture-Grey/SVM Shape	**25.5%**

In order to improve the results, we merged the confidence scores of the two best classifiers (6-NN Texture and 3-NN Shape), using a weighted sum parameterized by a coefficient α (as in equation 1). This merging can improve the error rate from 36.9% to 33.6% (for $\alpha = 0.6$).

Further improvement can be obtained by adapting the texture indexer to grey level images, replacing the 64-bins color histogram of the Texture indexer by a 64-bins grey level histogram: this new indexer is called *Texture-Grey*. With this indexer, an error rate of 35.1% is obtained with a 4-Nearest Neighbor, which is the best result obtained for a single indexer. Merging the 4-NN Texture-Grey and 3-NN Shape can further decrease the error rate to 30.3% (with α around 0.5).

Another source of improvement is the classifier model. We are currently replacing the K-Nearest Neighbor classifier with Support Vector Machine (SVM) classifiers: for each class, we can build a binary SVM classifier where the images in the class to learn are considered as positive examples, and images from the other classes are considered as negative examples. This results in 57 classifiers. So far, we have learned and tested these SVMs using the Shape indexer as features (this classifier is called Shape-SVM). Preliminary results are very promising: we obtain an error rate of 30.7% without any tuning of the SVM parameters. This classifier can also be merged with the k-NN classifiers described above. We obtain an error rate of 25.5% when merging it with the 4-NN Texture-Grey.

A more detailed analysis of the results show that the algorithm proposed here does not deal well with unbalanced data: in the training data, the class 12 is the largest class with 2567 images, which represents more than 1/4 of the training set (9000 images), and is much larger than the second class: class 34 with 883 training images. In the test set, we noticed that among a total of 297 images belonging to class 12, only 3 (1%) were misclassified, whereas among the 255 misclassified images, 54 were classified in class 12 (21%). A solution to this problem could be to weight the examples for the learning phase of the SVMs, giving smaller weights to the examples of larger classes.

In any case, merging different classifiers allow to decrease the error rate by at least 5%, when the classifiers are significantly different (for instance, the shape and the texture indexers). On the other hand, merging similar indexers (for instance, Shape-SVM and 3-NN Shape indexers) only allow to decrease the error rate by less than 1% in the best case.

6 Conclusion

We experimented on the ImageCLEF 2005 campaign collections several data fusion strategies to merge the results obtained independently by retrieval systems that work on different media: text and image. The results obtained show that this merging can increase the overall performance of the search system: a well-tuned *a posteriori* merging of the results obtained by two general purpose systems can improve the mean average precision by at least 15% and up to 40%.

The difficulty relies on the tuning of the merging strategy. We used a simple weighted sum of the scores given by each system but the importance given to each system should rely on the performance of the system on a particular corpus, that is not easily predicted (for instance, the best strategy for the ImageCLEF 2004 medical task appears to be opposite to the best strategy for ImageCLEF 2005 medical task, that has a more varied corpus and more difficult visual queries).

Further experiments will be undertaken to try to make the systems give a confidence score associated with its results and adapt the merging strategy according to this confidence. Other more sophisticated merging strategies (such as using logistic regression) will also be considered.

References

1. Clough, P., Müller, H., Deselaers, T., Grubinger, M., Lehmann, T.M., Jensen, J., Hersh, W.: The clef 2005 cross-language image retrieval track. In: Proceedings of the Cross Language Evaluation Forum 2005. Springer Lecture Notes in Computer science (2006)
2. Joint, M., Moëllic, P.A., Hède, P., Adam, P.: PIRIA : A general tool for indexing, search and retrieval of multimedia content. In: SPIE Electroning Imaging 2004, San Jose, California USA (2004)
3. Stehling, R.O., Nascimento, M.A., Falco., A.X.: A compact and efficient image retrieval approach based on border/interior pixel classification. In: CIKM '02: Proceedings of the eleventh international conference on Information and knowledge management, McLean, Virginia, USA (2002)

4. Cheng, Y.C., Chen, S.Y.: Image classification using color, texture and regions. Image and Vision Computing **21** (2003)
5. Savoy, J., Berger, P.Y.: Report on clef-2005 evaluation campaign: Monolingual, bilingual, and girt information retrieval. In: Working Notes of the Cross Language Evaluation Forum 2005. (2005)
6. Besançon, R., Hède, P., Moëllic, P.A., Fluhr, C.: Cross-media feedback strategies: Merging text and image information to improve image retrieval. In Peters, C., Clough, P., Gonzalo, J., Jones, G., Kluck, M., Magnini, B., eds.: Multilingual Information Access for Text, Speech and Images, Springer (2005)
7. Lee, J.H.: Analyses of multiple evidence combination. In: Proceedings of the 20th Annual International ACM SIGIR conference on Research and Development in Information Retrieval, Philadelphia (1997) 267–276
8. McCabe, M.C., Chowdhury, A., Grossman, D.A., Frieder, O.: A unified environment for fusion of information retrieval approaches. In: CIKM. (1999) 330–334

Combining Visual Features for Medical Image Retrieval and Annotation

Wei Xiong[1], Bo Qiu[1], Qi Tian[1], Changsheng Xu[1],
S.H. Ong[2], and Kelvin Foong[3]

[1] Institute for Infocomm Research, 21 Heng Mui Keng Terrace, Singapore 119613,
{wxiong, visqiu, tian, xucs}@i2r.a-star.edu.sg
[2] Department of Electrical and Computer Engineering,
National University of Singapore, Singapore 117576
eleongsh@nus.edu.sg
[3] Department of Preventive Dentistry,
National University of Singapore,Singapore 119074
pndfwc@nus.edu.sg

Abstract. In this paper we report our work using visual feature fusion for the tasks of medical image retrieval and annotation in the benchmark of ImageCLEF 2005. In the retrieval task, we use visual features without text information, having no relevance feedback. Both local and global features in terms of both structural and statistical nature are captured. We first identify visually similar images manually and form templates for each query topic. A pre-filtering process is utilized for a coarse retrieval. In the fine retrieval, two similarity measuring channels with different visual features are used in parallel and then combined in the decision level to produce a final score for image ranking. Our approach is evaluated over all 25 query topics with each containing example image(s) and topic textual statements. Over 50,000 images we achieved a mean average precision of 14.6%, as one of the best performed runs. In the annotation task, visual features are fused in an early stage by concatenation with normalization. We use support vector machines (SVM) with RBF kernels for the classification. Our approach is trained over a 9,000 image training set and tested over the given test set with 1000 images and on 57 classes with a correct classification rate of about 80%.

1 Introduction

ImageCLEF is an international campaign in Cross Language Evaluation Forum (CLEF)for image retrieval. ImageCLEFmed is a component task relating to medical image collections and it contains two sub tasks in 2005: retrieval and annotation. Using results from ImageCLEFmed 2004 (8725 radiology pathology images over 26 query topics) [1], this year's retrieval task retrieves images from more than five thousand images and some associated text descriptions, evaluated over 25 challenging query topics. Given 9000 training images, the annotation task is to classify 1000 test images into 57 classes in terms of their anatomic regions, imaging modalities, etc., based on visual features only. This annotation task is

C. Peters et al. (Eds.): CLEF 2005, LNCS 4022, pp. 632–641, 2006.

also rather challenging as the collections contain more than 57 classes and are rather imbalanced. For more information, readers may refer to related documents in this volume [2]. Below we will report our work in two parts: retrieval and annotation.

In the retrieval task, each of the 25 query topics contains topic statements in English, French and German, and a collection of images for each topic. Normally one or two example images for the desired result for the topic are supplied. One query also contains a negative example as a test. These queries are divided into visually possible queries (topics 1–11), mixed visual/semantic queries (topics 12-22) and semantic (rather textual) queries (topics 23-25). Since we will use visual features alone, it would be very challenging for us to handle topics 12-25. This has been proven by the submitted results of this forum: the best run of the mixtures of textual and visual retrievals is almost twice good as that of runs using visual-only retrievals. These retrieval tasks are very challenging because visual variations within each query topic are large whereas differences among different query topics are small.

Medical image annotation can be regarded as an interpretation of medical images. In the annotation task of ImageCLEFmed 2005, the annotation is to label an image to one of 57 given classes. They were labelled with IRMA codes [3] according to multi-axial medical information but not released publically for the test data.

In addition to the large variance within a class and similarity between classes, one particular difficulty is the severe population imbalance among the 57 classes. In the training data, for example, one class has around 1000 images, another class has more than 2500 samples, while most of the classes have far fewer images. Nearly 80% of images belong to 20 of the 57 classes in the training sets. It is still a challenging research topic to classify multi-class imbalance data. Our strategy is to choose suitable features and classifiers and their parameters based on simulation experiments by separating a small portion of the training data for testing and the rest for training. Our final submitted results are produced with optimal classifiers and parameters resulting from the simulations.

2 Multiple Feature Descriptions

In this section, we describe the visual features used in our work. A survey of visual features useful for general CBIR can be found in [4]. We have employed color, shape, and texture characteristics at the pixel level, the region level and the entire image level.

Global Color and Layout Property. Color images use three color channels. Most gray images use one channel only. However there are some that still employ three channels. This channel information can be used directly to classify images. Besides, the image layouts differ consistently, e.g., the ultrasound images are almost triangles. They form features set $\mathbf{F}_1$.

Low Resolution Pixel Map at Pixel Levels. Images in the database, even in the same class, vary in size and may have translations. Resizing them into a thumbnail [5,6] of a fixed size, through introducing distortions, may overcome the above difficulties in representing the same class of images in the database. It is a reduced and low-resolution version from the original image in the database ignoring its original size. A 16-by-16 image pixel map, called an "icon", is used. Examples are shown in Figure 1. They look more similar visually than their original versions. These so-called "icons" are extensively used in face recognition and have proven to be effective [5]. We have also applied them to medical image retrieval [7]. They are feature set $\mathbf{F}_2$. Texture features (contrast, anisotropy and polarity) are also computed. An example of these features is shown in the lower row of Figure 1. For ease of comparison, they are then resized to 16-by-16 maps, called LRPMs. Our experiments find that the three kinds of LRPMs (of the initial images, of contrast and anisotropy) are best for annotation tasks. We call them feature set $\mathbf{F}_4$.

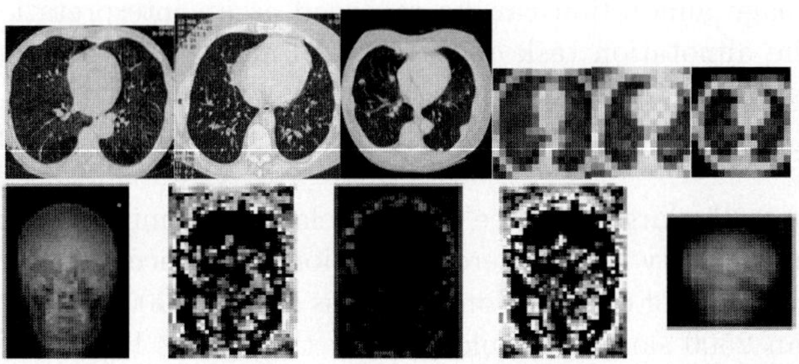

Fig. 1. Examples of original images and their respective low-resolution maps. Upper row: the left three images are original ones in the same class and the right three images are their respective reduced versions. Lower row: An original image (left most) and its texture features (contrast, anisotropy, polarity, from left to right), as well as its "icon".

Blob Feature at Object/Image Level. We consider both regional and image-wide color, texture and shape features. Local regions are segmented using GMM and EM in a joint color-texture-spatial feature vector space. The largest 10 regions are identified and represented by the elliptical harmonics. First 20 coefficients are used for each region. We have also included the global color histogram and texture histogram over the whole image. The above regional features and the global features form feature set $\mathbf{F}_3$, referred to as "blob" in this paper [8]. The feature vector is 352-dimensional. For a more detailed description of the specific usage, see our previous work [7,9].

3 Retrieval Methodology

This section presents the retrieval methodology used in this work. The basic processing flow of our approach is illustrated in Figure 3. Above the dashed

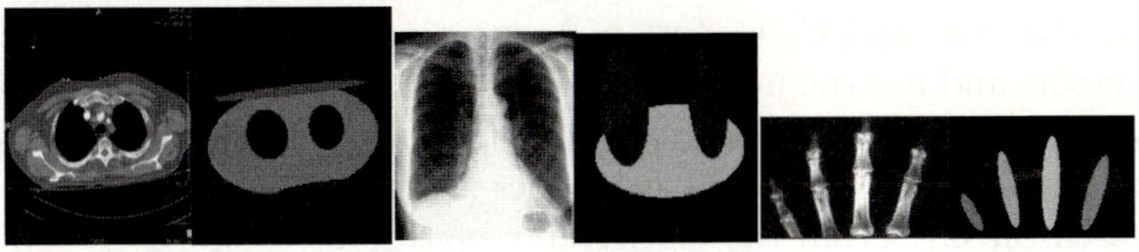

Fig. 2. Examples of original images and their respective blob representations. Three pairs of examples are shown here: the left one is the original image and the right one is its blob representation.

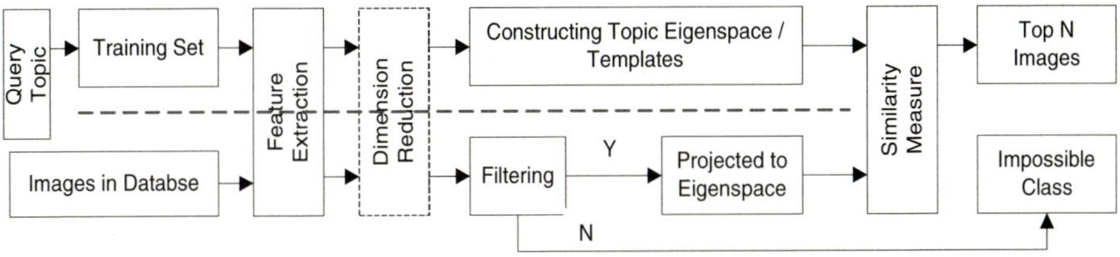

Fig. 3. A diagram of the processing flow

horizontal line are processing procedures for any given query and below the line are procedures for the images in the test databases.

Before retrieval, we browse the four databases provided, especially the CASImage database used for training. For the j-th query topic, j=*1,...,25*, some more semantically similar images (which may be visually different) are chosen to form a set $Q^j_{n_j}$ of n_j training images. For each image, some raw features, such as color, geometrical and texture properties, are extracted to form a $p \times 1$ feature vector $\mathbf{x_i} = (x_{i1}, x_{i2}, \cdots, x_{ip})$ for image i.

Principal components are analyzed upon a set of such features. (We will provide more details later.) An eigenspace E_j is set up for each query topic j, $j = 1, \ldots, 25$. Feature dimension may also be reduced, which is illustrated as a dashed box. The feature vector of a test image $\mathbf{x_i} = (x_{i1}, x_{i2}, \ldots, x_{ip})$ is then projected to E_j. The similarity is measured in E_j.

This procedure is repeated for all test images to generate a similarity ranked list for them. For the test image, pre-filtering is introduced using $\mathbf{F}_1$. Those images that are impossible to be similar are excluded earlier (denoted by "N"). Only those which pass (indicated by "Y") will go to the final comparison stage. In this final stage, two parallel engines are introduced for similarity measures. They use independent sets of features "icon" and "blob", representing local and global characteristics, respectively.

More specifically, we analysis principal components and utilize them in two ways. The first is for feature dimension reduction. The second is used to design similarity measuring functions [7,10]. Given a training dataset $Q^j_{n_j}$ with n_j images: $\mathbf{X} = (\mathbf{x}_1, \mathbf{x}_2, \cdots, \mathbf{x}_{n_j})^T$, the generating matrix can be constructed as in [7,10]

$$\mathbf{C}_1 = \mathbf{X}\mathbf{X}^{\mathrm{T}}, \quad \text{or}, \quad \mathbf{C}_2 = \mathbf{X}^{\mathrm{T}}\mathbf{X}. \tag{1}$$

Here $\mathbf{C}_1$ is of $n_j \times n_j$ and $\mathbf{C}_2$ is of $p \times p$. As mentioned before, n_j is the number of images/vectors and p is the number of features. $\mathbf{C}_1$ is used to generate templates of this dataset and $\mathbf{C}_2$ is used to reduce the dimension of the feature space when necessary. Supposing m out of n eigenvalues (λ_i) and their eigenvectors ($\mathbf{u}_i$) are chosen based on $\mathbf{C}_1$. From the eigenvector matrix $\mathbf{U} = (\mathbf{u}_1, \mathbf{u}_2, \cdots, \mathbf{u}_m)^T$, the template vectors $\mathbf{V} = (\mathbf{v}_1, \mathbf{v}_2, \cdots, \mathbf{v}_m)^T$ are given by using

$$\mathbf{v}_i = \frac{1}{\sqrt{\lambda_i}} \mathbf{X}^T \mathbf{u}_i, \;\; i = 1, ..., m. \tag{2}$$

Given a test image set, its feature matrix $\mathbf{Y}$ is reconstructed by

$$\mathbf{Y}' = \mathbf{V}\mathbf{V}^T\mathbf{Y}, \tag{3}$$

with a least square error

$$s = \|\mathbf{Y} - \mathbf{Y}'\| . \tag{4}$$

The similarity-measuring functions η_2 and η_3 have the same form of this error but with different feature sets as parameters.

The weighted summation rule [11,12] is used to fuse them as

$$d = w_1 s_1 + w_2 s_2, \tag{5}$$

where s_1 and s_2 are the similarities computed above using different feature sets $\mathbf{F}_1$ and $\mathbf{F}_2$ and where w_1 and w_2 are weighted coefficients subject to $0 \leq w_1, w_2 \leq 1$, $w_1 + w_2 = 1$. The resulting distance d serves as the final score for ranking: the larger the score is, the less similar the query and the test image are.

4 Annotation Methodology

We use support vector machines as the classifiers in this annotation task. Primarily SVM tackles the binary classification problem. The objective is to find an optimal separating hyper-plane (OSH) that correctly classifies feature data points as accurately as possible as well as separating the points of two classes to the greatest extent possible. The approach is to map the training data into a higher dimensional (possibly infinite) space and formulate a constrained quadratic programming problem for the optimization.

SVM for multiple-classes classification is still under development. Generally there are two types of approaches. One type has been to incorporate multiple class labels directly into the quadratic solving algorithm. Another more popular type is to combine several binary classifiers. The one we utilize here, SVM^{Torch}, which is free software, belongs to the latter. We choose radial basis functions (RBF) shown in Equation (6) as the nonlinear mapping kernels:

$$K(\mathbf{x}, \mathbf{y}) = e^{-\|\mathbf{x}-\mathbf{y}\|^2/2\sigma^2} . \tag{6}$$

For the RBF case, the number of centers, the centers themselves, the weights, and the threshold are all produced automatically by the SVM training. The standard variance σ and the parameter C, controlling the tradeoff between training error and the margin, are experimentally determined. Equation (4) is derived from principle component analysis (PCA) and tested in our experiments as comparison. However, the results are not as good as the SVM.

5 Experiments

5.1 Retrieval Experiments

In this campaign, we use visual features alone for all topic retrieval tasks including those that require text information. Experiments start with the selection of training data. For each topic, we manually choose a number of images in the test database to represent the visual varieties of the query topic. Three undergraduate engineering students without medical background selected these images. The only criterium is the visual appearance of the images. Consequently, there are doubtless many incorrectly chosen images and the numbers of images are larger. The more correct the visual varieties of the query topic we can collect into the training set, the better the representation is semantically. This is done offline before retrieval.

We have also referred to the results from the baseline work from medGIFT [13]. Table 2 lists the number of images, n_j, collected for each query topic. Here "q", "a", and "b" refer to the query topic and the number of images for two sets of training data, respectively. The total number of images in the training set "a" is 4789 with a mean 191.56 for each topic. In other words, 9.573% of the 50026 test images are used for training, which is a small portion. For training set "b", there are 3874 images in total (i.e., 7.744% of the 50026 test images) with a mean 154.96 for each topic.

Next, we compute all three feature sets $\mathbf{F}_1$, $\mathbf{F}_2$ ("icon") and $\mathbf{F}_3$ ("blob") for all images including those for training and testing. The similarity measuring function η_1 is a unit function for binary classification in terms of $\mathbf{F}_1$. Design η_2 and η_3 according to Equations (1) to (4) using $\mathbf{F}_2$ and $\mathbf{F}_3$ respectively. We combine their results according to Equation (5) with the same coefficients ($w_1 = w_2 = 0.5$).

Table 1. Number of images in the training set for each of 25 query topics

q	1	2	3	4	5	6	7	8	9	10	11	12	13
a	460	161	79	142	146	194	19	9	107	257	33	418	382
b	457	161	79	117	96	24	19	9	107	257	39	360	371

q	14	15	16	17	18	19	20	21	22	23	24	25
a	420	105	40	316	161	181	190	149	44	23	571	179
b	140	167	26	286	141	176	150	56	44	10	468	117

Table 2. MAPs of seven runs submitted to ImageCLEFmed 2005

Group	Run	MAP	Group	Run	MAP
1 (set "a")	I2RbPBnf	0.1067	2 (set "a")	I2Rfus	0.1455
1 (set "a")	I2RcPBnf	0.1114	3 (set "b")	I2RbP1nf	0.0928
1 (set "a")	I2RbPBcf	0.1068	3 (set "b")	I2RcP1nf	0.0934
1 (set "a")	I2RcPBcf	0.1188			

We submitted seven retrieval runs. Table 2 lists their labels and their performance in terms of mean average precision (MAP). They are divided into 3 groups as shown in Table 2. Only Group 3 "I2Rfus" utilizes all techniques mentioned above. Other runs in Groups 1 and 2 use parts of the techniques for comparison. In Group 1, two subgroups are further divided in terms of the feature sets used. Subgroup 1 uses "blob" and Subgroup 2 uses "icon". In each subgroup, we have two members, some using prefiltering ("I2RbPBcf" and "I2RcPBcf") while others ("I2RbPBnf" and "I2RcPBnf") do not.

We observe that use of the "icon" feature set normally yields slightly higher MAP than using the "blob" feature set. This is clear by comparing respectively "I2RbPBnf" (0.1067) against "I2RcPBnf" (0.1068), and "I2RbPBcf" (0.1114) against "I2RcPBcf" (0.1188). The binary classifier in Stage 1 improves the entire system performance. To see this effect, we can compare "I2RbPBnf" (0.1067) against "I2RbPBcf" (0.1114) and "I2RcPBnf" (0.1068) against "I2RcPBcf" (0.1188), respectively. The improvement is more significant when using the "icon" feature set (11.24%) than using the "blob" set (with 4.4%). Group 2 is the fusion of "I2RcPBnf" and "I2RcPBcf" where the weights are equal. It achieves the best results (MAP=14.55%).

It is important to select more examples to form a training set for each query topic before retrieval. In order to have a comparison, some of images (the underlined numbers in Table 1) are removed from the representation sets of some topics. We repeat experiments "I2RbPBnf" (0.1067) against "I2RcPBnf" (0.1068) but using these new training sets (Set "b"). This results in "I2RbP1nf" (using "blob" with MAP=0.0928) and "I2RcP1nf" (using "icon" with MAP=0.0934) in Group 3. Again, "icon" features have slightly better precision performance. Comparing experiments vertically using the two training sets, one finds that performance of Group 3 drops down using either feature set. This shows that the representation of the query topic using the training set is indeed important.

5.2 Annotation Experiments

In the following experiments, for each set of runs, the average accuracy (AA) is used as the annotation performance index. AA is defined as the percentage of the total number of test images correctly classified for the 57 classes. If not indicated otherwise, the 9000 training images are partitioned into 9 equal parts for each class, 8 of them as training data, the remaining part as test data.

Simulation experiments with PCA. According to our past work [10], the PCA method using blob features achieves good results in image retrieval. Here the average accuracy is 0.5026. However, here using texture features, we got 0.6977. Using either feature set, almost all the images are trapped into a few 'attractive' classes. Many other classes are assigned no images. This is due to the severly imbalanced data distribution. Thus PCA is not good for this annotation task.

Simulation experiment with SVM. We utilize SVM^{Torch} using the RBF kernel with the standard variance σ and the margin control parameter C. We change these parameters and evaluate the classifiers on many features and their fused features. The best results using these features are 0.6311 for "blob" alone, 0.7725 for LRPM features alone, 0.8318 for texture alone, while the fusion of all("blob+LRPM+texture") gives 0.889.

Influence of training dataset size. Generally speaking, the larger the training set, the better the classification result will be. However, in this work, a larger training set may produce worse results. For example, only change the number of training images of class 12, out of 2563 samples, while keeping others unchanged, we got AA=0.8890 for 600 training samples, AA=0.8727 for 1000 training samples and AA=0.8413 for 1500 training samples.

Experiments on the real test data. With the conclusions from the above simulation experiments, the 'SVM+Blob+LRPM +texture' fused feature is chosen. Unfortunately, in our submission result to ImageCLEFmed 2005, Blob was not included, resulting in AA=0.7940. Our latest result is 0.8070, both results with C=20, σ = 0.809. AAs of 11 classes are higher than 0.9, containing 505 correctly classified images in all 515 images; AAs of 23 classes are from 0.5 to 0.9, containing 270 correctly classified images in all 356 images; in the last 23 classes with the AAs below 0.5, there are 129 images in total, and only 32 images are correctly classified. This shows that, with the features above, SVM is not good at classifying small classes with few samples.

As seen there is a severe population imbalance among the training dataset. The largest class contains 2563 samples (class 12), while the smallest class has only 9 samples (class 51, 52). In many cases, too many training samples will cause the over-fitting problem. One of the solutions is to define a threshold to limit the numbers of training samples. For example, the threshold is set to 300. Then each of 57 training datasets is to be capped to 300 training samples for each class. Using soft margin SVM, when the threshold increases from 500, it will have little influence to AA. If using PCA, the threshold will do influence AA greatly. This is another reason we choose SVM rather than PCA. The parameter AA is more sensitive to SVM parameter std (i.e. σ), but less to C, as shown in the left two sub-figures of Figure 4.

Finally, we calculate the precision and the recall of each class and plot them in a two-dimensional graph in the right sub-figure in Figure 4. There is only one point for each class on the graph. G is the best region because the points in this region have high recall and precision; B is the worst region because its points have low recall and precision. For a multi-class problem, a convincing results would have most of its classes in region G.

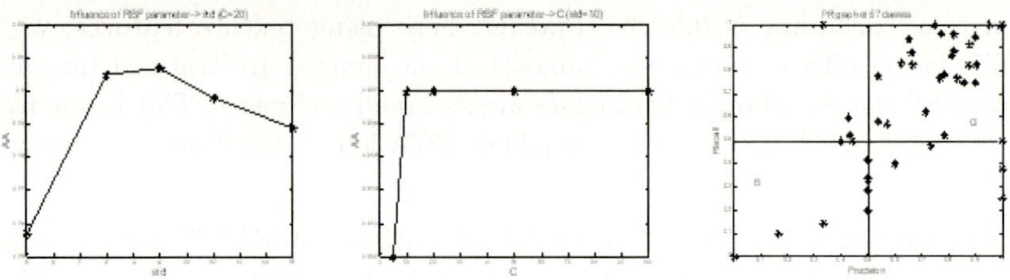

Fig. 4. Experiments for the annotation task using all fused features. Left and middle: influence of SVM parameters to average precision. Right: Precision and recall graph showing the performance of 57 classes.

6 Discussion and Conclusion

We have reported our efforts to the medical image retrieval task and annotation task in the ImageCLEFmed 2005. In the retrieval work, we manually select some training images for each topic before retrieval. These images span an eigen-space for each topic and similarity metrics are defined based on it. A pre-filtering process is used to act as a coarse topic image filter before the two similarity measures for fine topic retrieval. To achieve higher performance, two similarity measuring channels are used. They use different sets of features and operate in parallel. Their results are then combined to form a final score for similarity ranking. We have not used relevance feedback during the retrieval. In our experiments, only visual features are applied to not only the 11 visual-retrieval-possible topics, but also those 13 topics needing textual information. We have submitted seven runs in this track. Our best approach utilizes multiple sets of features with pre-filtering and fusing strategies, which enables us to achieve very good performance in the visual-only group.

In our annotation work, an SVM classifier using fusion of some texture features and blob features provides our best result (AA= 80.7%). We have achieved this by tuning the parameters based on simulations over training data. A precision-recall graph is helpful to give an overview of performance over each class.

References

1. Clough, P., Sanderson, M., Müller, H.: The CLEF 2004 cross language image retrieval track. In Peters, C., P. Clough, J.G., Jones, G., Kluck, M., Magnini, B., eds.: Lecture Notes in Computer Science (LNCS). Multilingual Information Access for Text, Speech and Images: Results of the Fifth CLEF Evaluation Campaign, Heidelberg, Germany, Springer (2005) in print.
2. Clough, P., Müller, H., Deselaers, T., Grubinger, M., Lehmann, T.M., Jensen, J., Hersh, W.: The CLEF 2005 cross language image retrieval track. In: Proceedings of the Cross Language Evaluation Forum 2005, Lecture Notes in Computer Science, Springer (2006) to appear.

3. Lehmann, T., Wein, B., Keysers, D., Bredno, J., Gld, M., Thies, C., Schubert, H., Kohnen, M.: Image retrieval in medical applications: The IRMA approach. In: VISIM Workshop: Information Retrieval and Exploration in Large Medical Image Collections, Fourth International Conference on Medical Image Computing and Computer-Assisted Intervention, Utrecht, Netherland (2001)
4. Yang, Z., Kuo, C.C.J.: Survey on image content analysis, indexing, and retrieval techniques and status report of MEPG-7. Tamkang Journal of Science and Engineering **2** (1999) 101–118
5. Belhumeur, P.N., Hespanha, J.P., Kriegman, D.J.: Eigenfaces vs. fisherfaces: Recognition using class specific linear projection. IEEE Transactions on pattern analysis and machine intelligence **19** (1997) 711–720
6. Howarth, P., Yavlinsky, A., Heesch, D., Rüger, S.: Visual features for content-based medical image retrieval. In: Proceedings of Cross Language Evaluation Forum (CLEF) Workshop 2004, Bath, UK (2004)
7. Xiong, W., Qiu, B., Tian, Q., Xu, C., Ong, S.H., Foong, K., Chevallet, J.P.: Multipre : A novel framework with multiple parallel retrieval engines for content-based image retrieval. In: ACM Multimedia 2005, Hilton, Singapore (2005) 1023–1032
8. Carson, C., Belongie, S., Greenspan, H., Malik, J.: Recognition of images in large databases using color and texture. IEEE Transactions on pattern analysis and machine intelligence **24** (2002) 1026–1038
9. Xiong, W., Qiu, B., Tian, Q., Müller, H., Xu, C.: A novel content-based medical image retrieval method based on query topic dependent image features (QTDIF). Proceedings of SPIE **5748** (2005) 123–133
10. Xiong, W., Qiu, B., Tian, Q., , Xu, C., Ong, S.H., Foong, K.: Content-based medical image retrieval using dynamically optimized regional features. In: The IEEE International Conference on Image Processing 2005. Volume 3., Genoa, Italy (2005) 1232–1235
11. Alkoot, F., Kittler, J.: Experimental evaluation of expert fusion strategies. Pattern Recognition Letters **20** (1999) 1361–1369
12. Kuncheva, L.I.: A theoretical study on six classifier fusion strategies. IEEE Transactions on pattern analysis and machine intelligence **24** (2002) 281–286
13. Müller, H., GeissbMühler, A., Ruch, P.: Report on the CLEF experiments: Combining image and multi-lingual search for medical image retrieval. In Peters, C., P. Clough, J.G., Jones, G., Kluck, M., Magnini, B., eds.: Lecture Notes in Computer Science (LNCS). Multilingual Information Access for Text, Speech and Images: Results of the Fifth CLEF Evaluation Campaign, Heidelberg, Germany, Springer (2005) in print.

A Structured Visual Learning Approach Mixed with Ontology Dimensions for Medical Queries

Jean-Pierre Chevallet[1,4], Joo-Hwee Lim[2], and Saïd Radhouani[3,4]

[1] IPAL-CNRS, Institute for Infocomm Research
viscjp@i2r.a-star.edu.sg
[2] Institute for Infocomm Research
21 Heng Mui Keng Terrace, Singapore 119613
joohwee@i2r.a-star.edu.sg
[3] Centre universitaire d'informatique
24, rue Général-Dufour, CH-1211 Genève 4, Switzerland
Said.Radhouani@cui.unige.ch
[4] Université Joseph Fourier, CLIPS-IMAG France

Abstract. Precise image and text indexing requires domain knowledge and a learning process. In this paper, we present the use of an ontology to filter medical documents and of visual concepts to describe and index associated images. These visual concepts are meaningful medical terms with associated visual appearance from image samples that are manually designed and learned from examples. Text and image indexing processes are performed in parallel and merged to answer mixed-mode queries. We show that fusion of these two methods are of a great benefit and that external knowledge stored in an ontology is mandatory to solve precise queries and provide the overall best results.

1 Introduction

The medical domain requires indexing of images and text with precise meaning. Content Based Information Retrieval (CBIR) in the medical domain requires the use of *external explicit knowledge* both for image and textual data. For images, this knowledge is in semantic local features that can be learned from examples (rather than handcrafted with a lot of expert input) and do not rely on robust region segmentation. For text, this requires use of an ontology to force the presence of key terms and to discard inconsistent terms.

In order to manage large and complex sets of visual entities (i.e., high content diversity) in the medical domain, we developed a structured learning framework to facilitate modular design and extract medical visual semantics, *VisMed* terms, that are image regions with semantic meaning to medical practitioners. During image indexing, they are detected in image content, reconciled across multiple resolutions, and aggregated spatially to form local semantic histograms.

The resulting compact and abstract VisMed image indexes can support both similarity-based query and semantic-based query efficiently.

When queries are in the form of example images, both a query image and a database image can be matched based on their distributions of VisMed terms.

C. Peters et al. (Eds.): CLEF 2005, LNCS 4022, pp. 642–651, 2006.

In addition, a flexible tiling (FlexiTile) matching scheme has been developed to compare the similarity between two medical images of arbitrary aspect ratios.

When a query is expressed as a text description, it can be translated into a visual query representation that chains the presences of VisMed terms with spatial significance via logical operators (AND, OR, NOT) and spatial quantifiers for automatic query processing based on the VisMed image indexes. Text is filtered via a medical ontology and results are merged with visual querying.

In this paper, we present the VisMed indexing technique (part 2 & 3), the textual indexing process (part 4), and results with fusion of the two (part 5).

2 Learning VisMed Terms for Image Indexing

VisMed terms are typical semantic tokens with visual appearance in medical images (e.g., Xray-bone-fracture, CT-abdomen-liver, MRI-head-brain, photo-skin). They are defined using image region instances cropped from sample images and then modeled and built based on statistical learning. In these experiments, we have adopted color and texture features as well as used support vector machines (SVMs) for VisMed term representation and learning respectively though a framework is not dependent on a particular feature and classifier. This notion of using a visual vocabulary to represent and index image has been applied to consumer images in [1].

Table 1. VisMed terms and numbers of region samples

VisMed Terms	#	VisMed Terms	#
00-angio-aorta-artery	30	01-angio-aorta-kidney	30
02-ct-abdomen-bone	40	03-ct-abdomen-liver	20
04-ct-abdomen-vessel	30	05-ct-chest-bone	30
06-ct-chest-emphysema	30	07-ct-chest-nodule	20
08-path-alzheimer	40	09-path-kidney	50
10-path-leukemia	30	11-photo-face-eye	60
12-photo-face-mouth	30	13-photo-face-nose	30

To compute VisMed terms from training instances, we use SVMs on color and texture features for an image region and denote this feature vector as z. An SVM $\mathcal{S}_k$ is a detector for VisMed term k on z. The classification vector T for region z is computed via the softmax function as:

$$T_k(z) = \frac{\exp^{\mathcal{S}_k(z)}}{\sum_j \exp^{\mathcal{S}_j(z)}}. \tag{1}$$

i.e. $T_k(z)$ corresponds to a VisMed entry in the 39-dimensional vector T adopted in this paper.

A feature vector z has two parts, namely, a color feature vector z^c and a texture feature vector z^t. We compute the mean and standard deviation of each

YIQ color channel and the Gabor coefficients (5 scales, 6 orientations) respectively [1]. Hence the color feature vector z^c has 6 dimensions and the texture feature vector z^t has 60 dimensions. Zero-mean normalization is applied to both the color and texture features. In our evaluation described below, we adopted RBF kernels with modified city-block distance between feature vectors y and z,

$$|y - z| = \frac{1}{2}(\frac{|y^c - z^c|}{N_c} + \frac{|y^t - z^t|}{N_t}) \tag{2}$$

where N_c and N_t are the numbers of dimensions of the color and texture feature vectors respectively. This just-in-time feature fusion within the kernel combines the contribution of color and texture features equally. It is simpler and more effective than other feature fusion methods we have attempted.

After learning, the VisMed terms are detected during image indexing from multi-scale block-based image patches without region segmentation to form semantic local histograms as described in previous work [1,2]. Essentially an image is tessellated into image blocks (e.g. 3×3 grid) and the classification vectors T (Eq. (1)) are summarized within an image block. Suppose a region Z comprises of n small equal regions with feature vectors $z_1, z_2, \cdots, z_n$ respectively. To account for the size of detected VisMed terms in the spatial area Z, the classification vectors are aggregated as

$$T_k(Z) = \frac{1}{n} \sum_i T_k(z_i). \tag{3}$$

To facilitate spatial aggregation and matching of image with different aspect ratios ρ, we design 5 tiling templates for Eq. (3), namely 3×1, 3×2, 3×3, 2×3, and 1×3 grids resulting in 3, 6, 9, 6, and 3 $T_k(Z)$ vectors per image respectively. Since the tiling templates have aspect ratios of 3, 1.5, and 1, the decision thresholds to assign a template for an image are set to their mid-points (2.25 and 1.25) as $\rho > 2.25$, $1.25 < \rho \leq 2.25$, and $\rho \leq 1.25$ respectively based on $\rho = \frac{L}{S}$ where L and S refer to the longer and shorter sides of an image respectively.

3 Medical Image Retrieval Using VisMed Terms

We have applied the VisMed approach on the Medical Image Retrieval task in ImageCLEF 2005. We set out to design VisMed terms that correspond to typical semantic regions in the medical images. We have manually designed 39 VisMed terms relevant to the query topics. Table 1 lists part of VisMed terms and Figure 1 illustrates visual examples.

Based on 0.3% (i.e. 158 images) of the 50,026 images from the 4 collections plus 96 images obtained from the web, we manually cropped 1460 image regions to train and validate 39 VisMed terms using SVMs. As we would like to minimize the number of images selected from the test collection for VisMed term learning, we include relevant images available from the web. For a given VisMed term, the

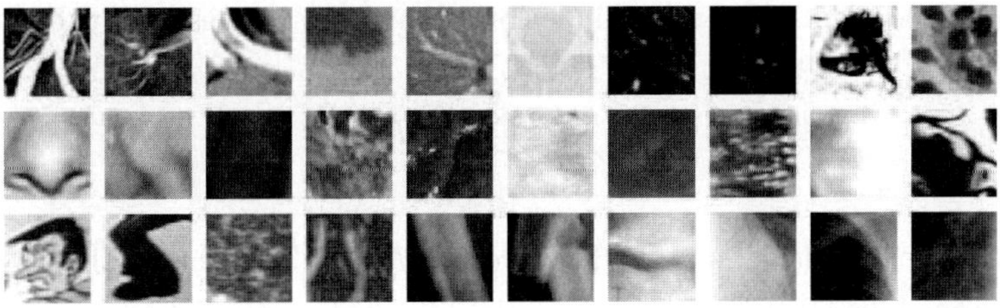

Fig. 1. One visual example each for the VisMed terms

negative samples are the union of the positive samples of all the other 38 VisMed terms. We ensure that they do not contain any of the positive and negative query images given by the 25 query topics.

The odd and even entries of the cropped regions are used as training and validation sets respectively (i.e. 730 each) to optimize the RBF kernel parameter of support vector machines. Both the training and validation sets are then combined to form a larger training set to retrain the 39 VisMed detectors.

3.1 Similarity-Based Retrieval with Visual Query

Given two images represented as different grid patterns, we developed a flexible tiling (FlexiTile) matching scheme to cover all possible matches. For instance, given a query image Q of 3×1 grid and an image Z of 3×3 grid, intuitively Q should be compared to each of the 3 columns in Z and the highest similarity will be treated as the final matching score. The details of FlexiTile can be found in [2]. In this paper, we denote the similarity between query images $\mathcal{Q}$ and database image Z as $\lambda(\mathcal{Q}, Z)$.

3.2 Semantics-Based Retrieval with Text Query

A new visual query language, Query by Spatial Icons (QBSI), has been developed to combine pattern matching and logical inference [1]. A QBSI query is composed as a spatial arrangement of visual semantics. A Visual Query Term (VQT) P specifies a region R where a VisMed i should appear and a query formulus chains these terms up via logical operators. The truth value $\mu(P, Z)$ of a VQT P for any image Z is simply defined as

$$\mu(P, Z) = T_i(R) \tag{4}$$

where $T_i(R)$ is defined in Equation (3).

As described above, the medical images are indexed as 3×1, 3×2, 3×3, 2×3, and 1×3 grids, depending on their aspect ratios. When a query involves the presence of a VisMed term in a region larger than a single block in a grid and its semantics prefers a larger area of presence of the VisMed term to have a good match (e.g. entire kidney, skin lesion, chest x-ray images with tuberculosis), Equation (4) will become

$$\mu(P, Z) = \frac{\sum_{Z_j \in R} T_i(Z_j)}{|R|} \tag{5}$$

where Z_j are the blocks in a grid that cover R and $|R|$ denotes the number of such blocks. This corresponds to a spatial universal quantifier ($\forall$).

On the other hand, if a query only requires the presence of a VisMed term within a region regardless of the area of the presence (e.g. presence of a bone fracture, presence of micro nodules), then the semantics is equivalent to the spatial existential quantifier ($\exists$) and Equation (4) will be computed as

$$\mu(P, Z) = \max_{Z_j \in R} T_i(Z_j) \tag{6}$$

A QBSI query $\mathcal{P}$ can be specified as a disjunctive normal form of VQT (with or without negation),

$$\mathcal{P} = (P_{11} \wedge P_{12} \wedge \cdots) \vee \cdots \vee (P_{c1} \wedge P_{c2} \wedge \cdots) \tag{7}$$

Then the query processing of query $\mathcal{P}$ for any image Z is to compute the truth value $\mu(\mathcal{P}, Z)$ using appropriate logical operators using min/max fuzzy operations. For the query processing in ImageCLEF 2005, a query text description is manually translated into a QBSI query with the help of a visual query interface [1] that outputs an XML format to state the VisMed terms, the spatial regions, the Boolean operators, and the spatial quantifiers. As an illustration, query 02 "Show me x-ray images with fractures of the femur" is translated as "$\forall$ xray-bone $\in$ whole $\wedge$ $\forall$ xray-pelvis $\in$ upper $\wedge$ $\exists$ xray-bone-fracture $\in$ whole" where "whole" and "upper" refer to the whole image and upper part of an image respectively.

3.3 Combining Similarity- and Semantics-Based Retrieval

If a query topic is represented with both query images and text description, we can combine the similarities resulting from query processing using the FlexiTile matching scheme [2] and the fuzzy matching scheme. A simple scheme would be a linear combination of $\lambda(\mathcal{Q}, Z)$ and $\mu(\mathcal{P}, Z)$ with $\omega \in [0, 1]$

$$\rho(\mathcal{Q}, \mathcal{P}, Z) = \omega \cdot \lambda(\mathcal{Q}, Z) + (1 - \omega) \cdot \mu(\mathcal{P}, Z) \tag{8}$$

where ρ is the overall similarity and the optimal ω can be determined empirically using even sampling at 0.1 intervals. In the following, we present the process of text only for separated indexing.

4 Using Ontology Dimensions for Text

We have noticed that textual queries refer to particular notions we call "dimensions" like anatomy, pathology and modality. These dimensions are relative to an ontology: dimensions are sub tree of a medical ontology. Hence we have made the obvious assumption that relevant document to a query with dimensions are the one that fulfils correctly to these dimensions. For the CLEF medical queries, we have only used three dimensions of the MESH ontology: `Anatomy [A]`, `Diseases [C]` and `Analytical, Diagnostic and Therapeutic Techniques and Equipment [E]`. The question we faced for this experiment was how to take into account these dimensions into an Information Retrieval System. We developed two solutions: a query filtering Boolean method based on ontology dimensions and a negative weight term vector expansion based also on ontology dimensions.

When we want to take into account the notion of dimension relative to an ontology, it means that the query usually focuses on one instance or possible value in one dimension and excludes all others. For example, if we are searching for images about one special body region of the dimension Anatomy from the ontology, the choice of a body region explicitly *excludes* other body regions. If the query is about "Abdomen" then all documents that are about an other body region are irrelevant. It is then clear that the use of dimension of an ontology leads to express the notion of term exclusion at the query level. Unfortunately, there is no way for the Vector Space Model to express such term exclusions. For this reason, we developed a negative query expansion.

4.1 Negative Query Expansion Using Ontology

We make the hypothesis that *a document containing many different terms from the same ontology dimension is less relevant than a document containing terms from different ontology dimensions.* Negative query expansion tests this hypothesis. For a given query term t belonging to the medical ontology, negative query expansion changes the query weight $Q(t_i)$ for all terms t_i belonging to the same dimension of t but not on the same sub tree. The new query vector Q' is computed from the original query vector Q by a negative uniform spreading of the term t weight $Q(t)$.

$$Q'(t_i) = \begin{cases} Q(t_i) - Q(t)/|T_{neg}(t)| & \text{if } t_i \in T_{neg}(t) \\ Q(t_i) & \text{else} \end{cases} \tag{9}$$

The function $T_{neg}(t)$ returns the set of terms in the same dimension as t but that belong to other sub trees that t belongs to (see formula (10)). For a given ontology, if function $T_{dim}(t)$ returns all terms belonging to the same dimension than t, $T_{sub}(t)$ returns all sub terms of t and $T_{up}(t)$ returns all upper terms of t in the tree structure of the ontology, then we define:

$$T_{neg}(t) = T_{dim}(t) - T_{sub}(t) - T_{up}(t) - \{t\} \tag{10}$$

Following example shows an extended query where some null terms weight of the `Anatomy` dimension of `head` term are added with negative value:

```
<vector id="11" size="5">
<c id="head" w="0.4149327576"/>
<c id="mri" w="0.3636860549"/>
<c id="sagittal" w="0.6271265149"/>
<c id="chest" w="-0.0345777298"/>
<c id="liver" w="-0.0345777298"/>
<c id="skin" w="-0.0345777298"/>
<c id="abdomen" w="-0.0345777298"/>
<c id="kidney" w="-0.0345777298"/>
...
```

This extension changes the usual way vector space model is defined, as only positive weight are used for defining both document and query vectors.

4.2 Filtering by Ontology Dimensions

The second use of the ontology is a query dimension selection. The basic idea is to split the initial query Q into several sub queries, each addressing one ontology dimension. Our goal is to give some terms priority depending on the ontology dimension they belong to. For that purpose, we use Boolean expressions on the sub query. It is a Boolean pre-filtering technique on top of the Vector Space Model system.

At first, we split terms of the query Q into sub queries Q_i according to their dimension i. Then, we query the whole document collection using Q_i and select document in which at least one term of Q_i appears and obtains a sub set $\mathcal{D}_i$ of the collection. These sets of document are precise because they contain explicitly dimensions terms that are in the query.

In order to solve the original multidimensional query, we finally combine these dimensions using a Boolean expression. A conjunction forces dimensions to be present together. We can reduce this constraint using a disjunction. We compute this Boolean dimension constraint formula using all sub sets $\mathcal{D}_i$. We obtain a final sub set of document $\mathcal{D}_f$ that has been filtered by the ontology in two ways: first having at least one term from the query from a given dimension, and second by selecting some dimension to appears together in the selected document. For example, for an initial query Q containing three dimensions, sub query Q_1, Q_2 and Q_3 are build, and $\mathcal{D}_1$, $\mathcal{D}_2$, $\mathcal{D}_3$ document sets are obtained. If we decide that a relevant document must include dimension 1 and dimension 2 or only dimension 3, we compute the filtered sub document set by the boolean formula $\mathcal{D}_f = (\mathcal{D}_1 \cap \mathcal{D}_2) \cup \mathcal{D}_3$.

After this filtering, the next step is to query this sub set $\mathcal{D}_f$ using the full original query Q using the classical Vector Space Model, that gives us the final document ranking. A similar approach based on term pre-filtering before Vector Space Model querying has been apply in multilingual CLEF [3]. We can combine this filtering techniques with negative expansion when applying query in input of the VSM.

4.3 Indexing Process

The first treatment applied to the collection is some XML correction and some re-tagging actions. The XML correction is just the transformation of some characters like '<'), that should not appear in XML documents. For the MIR collection, we have noticed a strong regularity in the document framework, and we have decided to reconstruct a documents framework by replacing some regular texts like "Brief history" into XML tags. Before the tagging we selected the fields we believed were worth value to be indexed. This step is important because putting all the document fields into the index could result in noise, and avoiding some could lead to silence. We also decided to index all texts after computing the part of speech (POS) of all documents in the collection. The simple treeTager [4] was used for this task. For the indexing part, we used the XIOTA experimental system [5].

Starting from the part of speech tagging, all documents from the same language were processed following a parallel path. The resulted in three sets of indexing for each of the three languages: French, English and German. We used filtering on POS tags instead of the classical stopwords method, keeping only nouns, adjectives and abbreviations[1]. This resulted in a term vector for each document in a given language. Documents in a given language from all collection were merged in the same indexing matrix. We used the classical `ltc` indexing scheme of the vector space model for both query and document vectors. Each query language was used to query the corresponding index matrix. We finally fused all three language results by selecting only the best matching value when same document was retrieved from several languages at the same time. Taking the maximum value between languages emphasized the language where matching was more efficient.

5 Results

5.1 Results on Text Only

For CLEF 2005, we limited ourselves to only two actual dimensions, anatomy and modality, for all three languages. We also used a reduced term set for query negative expansion. Boolean pre-filtering[2] was used to force at least one ontology dimension to be present into the relevant document. Using this filter we obtained a MAP of 0.2075 (run `IPALI2R_T`), which was the second best value of all text-only runs.

To use negative query expansion, we reduced the size of the ontology to reduce computation. With the combination of the two methods, we obtained the best overall text-only CLEF results with a MAP of 0.2084 (run run `IPALI2R_Tn`).

[1] In the TreeTager notation is it the list NOM,ADJ,ABR,JJ,NN,NNS,NP,ADJD, ADJA,NE.

[2] In fact, we have technically a post-filtering which is equivalent to pre-filtering. Post-filtering is here possible due to the relative small number of documents in this test collection.

Table 2. Combination of filtering and expansion

Dimension filtering	no expansion	negative expansion
None	17.25%	17.32%
At least one dimension	20.75%	20.84%
Anatomy and Pathology	-	21.39%

We explain this results by the fact document that are focus more clearly on one concept in one dimension are more precise and tend to be rank in better position than document that mixes different concept into the same ontology dimension.

Table 2 shows a summary of results combining negative expansion and ontology filtering. Using the Vector Space Model on documents tagged with the POS analyzer, without taking into account the query dimensions, we obtain a MAP of 0.1725. Negative query expansion resulted in a small improvement to 0.1732. We obtained a larger improvement when forcing the document to answer to at least one dimension. In that case, we also maintained the small benefit of the negative expansion. Finally, the best results for this collection were obtained by forcing only two dimensions: anatomy and pathology. This result is query dependent and is probably due to the fact that modality is not always explicit in documents.

5.2 Mixing Textual and Visual

Merging text and visual results produced enhancement of our results. To compute the new raking list from images and text, we had the hypothesis that absolute relevance status value should be comparable. We then only had to rescale the RSV of the two lists using a linear transformation so that the RSV of the top document was always equal to 1. We then tested two simple merging techniques: for each document in both ranked list, either we kept the best (max) ranking value or computed an average value. Keeping the best value follows the hypothesis that either one media (text or image) is better, as computing the average supposes that both are always equally participating to the ranking.

Our results (see table 3) showed that both visual and textual participated in the ranking. This combination outperformed both text only and image only by a large amount (e.g., an increase 35% in MAP over only text). This combination outperformed all other methods used in 2005.

Table 3. Textual and visual mixed results

Run	Fusion Method	negative query exp.	results MAP
IPALI2R_TIan	Average	YES	28.21%
IPALI2R_TIa	Average	NO	28.19%
IPALI2R_TImn	Max	YES	23.25%
IPALI2R_TIm	Max	NO	23.12%

6 Conclusion

For this collection, the quality of text indexing seems to have a greater influence than expected, probably because queries are related to a focused domain, where a term is not really ambiguous and is related to a strong and precise meaning. The results we have obtained for this participation shows the value of the use of *explicit knowledge* when solving precise queries. Benefits of mixing text and image are also very clear. The use of an ontology seems useful both as a final filtering and as a negative query expansion.

This work has been done under the IPAL I2R laboratory, a joint lab founded by CNRS and Université Joseph Fourier from the French side and A-STAR from the Singaporean side. This work has also been done in relation with the Centre Universitaire d'Informatique of Switzerland. Finally this work is part of the ISERE project founded by the French Ministry of Foreign Affairs.

References

1. Lim, J., Jin, J.: A structured learning framework for content-based image indexing and visual query. Multimedia Systems Journal **10** (2005) 317–331
2. Lim, J., Chevallet, J.P.: Vismed: a visual vocabulary approach for medical image indexing and retrieval. In: Proc. of AIRS 2005. (2005) 84–96
3. Guyot, J., Radhouani, S., Falquet, G.: Ontology-based multilingual information retrieval. In: CLEF Workhop, Working Notes Multilingual Track, Vienna, Austria. (2005)
4. Schmid, H.: Probabilistic part-of-speech tagging using decision trees. In: Proceedings of International Conference on New Methods in Language Processing. (1994)
5. Chevallet, J.P.: X-iota: An open xml framework for ir experimentation application on multiple weighting scheme tests in a bilingual corpus. Lecture Notes in Computer Science (LNCS), AIRS'04 Conference Beijing **3211** (2004) 263–280

FIRE in ImageCLEF 2005: Combining Content-Based Image Retrieval with Textual Information Retrieval

Thomas Deselaers, Tobias Weyand, Daniel Keysers,
Wolfgang Macherey, and Hermann Ney

Lehrstuhl für Informatik VI, RWTH Aachen University, Aachen, Germany
surname@informatik.rwth-aachen.de

Abstract. In this paper the methods we used in the 2005 ImageCLEF content-based image retrieval evaluation are described. For the medical retrieval task, we combined several low-level image features with textual information retrieval. Combining these two information sources, clear improvements over the use of one of these sources alone are possible.

Additionally we participated in the automatic annotation task, where our content-based image retrieval system, FIRE, was used as well as a second subimage based method for object classification. The results we achieved are very convincing. Our submissions ranked first and the third in the automatic annotation task out of a total of 44 submissions from 12 groups.

1 Introduction

It is known that in content-based image retrieval (CBIR) benchmarking of systems is a major problem. ImageCLEF, as part of the Cross Language Evaluation Forum, is a major step towards creating standard benchmarking tasks and setting up competitions to compare content-based image retrieval systems. One of the main conclusions that can be drawn from the 2004 and 2005 ImageCLEF image retrieval evaluations is that textual information and user feedback, if available, can greatly improve the results. This is especially true if the queries are of semantic nature, as it is intrinsically difficult to solve them using visual information alone.

Particularly in real life applications, for example, in medicine, where textual information is available and pictures alone are not sufficient to describe a medical case, any available information should be used. If, for example, the query image is a microscopy of a bacteria culture, a standard image retrieval system will easily find other pictures of bacteria cultures, but it will hardly be able to distinguish between different kinds of bacteria. With additional textual query information like "Coli bacteria", the query, and thus the result is more precise.

Since we obtained the best score in the category "visual information only, no user interaction" in the 2004 ImageCLEF evaluation, it was an interesting challenge to extend our FIRE system[1] towards the use of textual information.

[1] http://www-i6.informatik.rwth-aachen.de/~deselaers/fire.html

C. Peters et al. (Eds.): CLEF 2005, LNCS 4022, pp. 652–661, 2006.

Other groups had already proposed approaches combining textual information retrieval and content-based image retrieval, e.g. [1, 2, 3].

In this paper, we describe the techniques we used for the 2005 ImageCLEF evaluation. In particular, we describe how textual information retrieval and content-based image retrieval were combined.

The 2005 ImageCLEF involved four tasks: automatic annotation, medical image retrieval, bilingual information retrieval, and interactive retrieval. We participated in the automatic annotation task and the medical image retrieval task. Our approach to the medical retrieval task is described in Section 2, the two approaches to the automatic annotation task are described in Section 3.

2 Medical Retrieval Task

For the medical retrieval task in the 2005 ImageCLEF Image Retrieval Evaluation, 25 queries were given. Each query was defined by a short textual query description and one to three example images. One query contained a negative example image, all other example images were positive. A more detailed description of the task and an overview of the results can be found in [4]. In the following we describe the setup of the FIRE-system, for the medical retrieval task.

2.1 Decision Rule

Given a set of positive example images Q^+ and a (possibly empty) set of negative example images Q^- a score $S(Q^+, Q^-, X)$ is calculated for each image X from the database:

$$S(Q^+, Q^-, X) = \sum_{q \in Q^+} S(q, X) - \sum_{q \in Q^-} S(q, X). \tag{1}$$

where $S(q, X) = e^{-D(q,X)}$ is the score of database image X with respect to query q. $D(q, X)$ is a weighted sum of distances calculated according to

$$D(q, X) := \sum_{m=1}^{M} w_m \cdot d_m(q_m, X_m). \tag{2}$$

Here, q_m and X_m are the mth feature of the query image q and the database image X, respectively. d_m is the corresponding distance measure, and w_m is a weighting coefficient. For each d_m, $\sum_{X \in \mathcal{B}} d_m(Q_m, X_m) = 1$ is enforced by re-normalization. Given a query (Q^+, Q^-), the images are ranked according to descending score and the K images X with the highest scores $S(Q^+, Q^-, X)$ are returned by the retriever.

Due to the lack of suitable training data, the weightings w_m were chosen heuristically based on experiences from earlier experiments with other data.

2.2 Textual Information Retrieval

To incorporate textual information in FIRE, we decided to use an existing textual information retrieval engine [5]. The text retrieval engine implements a variant of the Smart-2 retrieval metric, which is based on the well-known *term frequency inverse document frequency* (tf-idf) metric. The textual information is preprocessed by removing function words that are considered to be of no importance to the actual retrieval process (so called *stopping*). The stop word list used comprises 319 of the most frequently occurring function words in the English language. After all texts are stopped, the remaining words are reduced to their stems using Porter's stemming algorithm [6]. The stemmed words form the index terms that are used to index the text documents provided in addition to the image data. In our implementation of the Smart-2 retrieval metric we use the following definition of the inverse document frequency:

$$\mathrm{idf}(t) := \log \left\lfloor \frac{K}{n(t)} \right\rfloor \tag{3}$$

Here, t denotes an index term, and K is the number of text documents. Due to the floor operation in Eq. (3) a term weighting will be zero if it occurs in more than half of the documents. According to [7], each index term t in a document $\mathbf{d}$ is associated with a weighting $g(t, \mathbf{d})$ which depends on the ratio of the logarithm of the term frequency $n(t, \mathbf{d})$ to the logarithm of the average term frequency $\overline{n}(\mathbf{d})$

$$g(t, \mathbf{d}) := \begin{cases} \left[1 + \log n(t, \mathbf{d})\right] / \left[1 + \log \overline{n}(\mathbf{d})\right] & \text{if } t \in \mathbf{d} \\ 0 & \text{if } t \notin \mathbf{d} \end{cases} \tag{4}$$

with $\log 0 := 0$ and

$$\overline{n}(\mathbf{d}) = \frac{\sum_{t \in \mathcal{T}} n(t, \mathbf{d})}{\sum_{t \in \mathcal{T}: n(t, \mathbf{d}) > 0} 1} \tag{5}$$

The logarithms in Eq. (4) prevent documents with high term frequencies from dominating those with low term frequencies. In order to obtain the final term weightings, $g(t, \mathbf{d})$ is divided by a linear combination of a pivot element c and the number of singletons $n_1(\mathbf{d})$ in document $\mathbf{d}$:

$$\omega(t, \mathbf{d}) := \frac{g(t, \mathbf{d})}{(1 - \lambda) \cdot c + \lambda \cdot n_1(\mathbf{d})} \tag{6}$$

with $\lambda = 0.2$ and

$$c = \frac{1}{K} \sum_{k=1}^{K} n_1(\mathbf{d}_k) \quad \text{and} \quad n_1(\mathbf{d}) := \sum_{t \in \mathcal{T}: n(t, \mathbf{d}) = 1} 1 \tag{7}$$

Unlike tf-idf, only query terms are weighted with the inverse document frequency $\mathrm{idf}(t)$:

$$\omega(t, \mathbf{q}) = \left[1 + \log n(t, \mathbf{q})\right] \cdot \mathrm{idf}(t) \tag{8}$$

The SMART-2 retrieval function is then defined as the product over the document and query specific index term weightings:

$$f(\mathbf{q}, \mathbf{d}) = \sum_{t \in T} \omega(t, \mathbf{q}) \cdot \omega(t, \mathbf{d}) \tag{9}$$

To use the textual information for image retrieval, each image has to be attached to at least one (possibly empty) text document. These text documents are used in the image retrieval process described above. To determine the distance $d_{\text{text}}(q_m, X_m)$ between a query image q with query text q_m and a database image X with attached text X_m, first the textual information retriever is queried using the query text. Then, the textual information retriever returns the list of all documents from the database that it considers relevant. These documents are ranked by the retrieval status value (RSV) R which is high for documents similar to the query and low for dissimilar documents. The distance $d(q_m, X_m)$ is then calculated as

$$d_{\text{text}}(q_m, X_m) = \begin{cases} R_{\text{max}} - R_X & \text{if } X \in \text{list of relevant documents} \\ \rho & \text{otherwise} \end{cases} \tag{10}$$

where R_{max} is the maximum of all returned RSVs, R_X is the RSV for image X, q_m and X_m are the query text and the text attached to image X, respectively, and ρ is a sufficiently large constant, chosen so as to make sure that images whose texts do not appear in the list of relevant objects have high distances. Note that the case where $\rho = R_{\text{max}}$ corresponds to assigning an RSV of 0 to all non-relevant texts. The resulting distances $d_{\text{text}}(q_m, X_m)$ are used in the retrieval process described in the previous section.

2.3 Image Features

In the following we describe the visual features we used in the evaluation. These features are extracted offline from all database images.

Appearance-based Image Features. The most straightforward approach is to directly use the pixel values of the images as features. For example, the images might be scaled to a common size and compared using the Euclidean distance. In optical character recognition and for medical data, improved methods based on image features usually obtain excellent results [8, 9, 10].

In this work, we have used 32×32 versions of the images. These have been compared using Euclidean distance. It has been observed that for classification and retrieval of medical radiographs, this method serves as a reasonable baseline.

Color Histograms. Color histograms are widely used in image retrieval [11, 12, 13], and constitute one of the most basic approaches. To demonstrate performance improvements, image retrieval systems are often compared to a system using only color histograms. The color space is partitioned and for each partition the pixels with a color within its range are counted, resulting in a representation of the relative frequencies of the occurring colors. In accordance with [12], we use the Jeffrey divergence to compare histograms.

Tamura Features. Tamura et al. propose six texture features corresponding to human visual perception: *coarseness*, *contrast*, *directionality*, *line-likeness*, *regularity*, and *roughness* [14]. From experiments testing the significance of these features with respect to human perception, it has been concluded that the first three features are the most important. Thus in our experiments we use coarseness, contrast, and directionality to create a histogram describing the texture [11] and compare these histograms using the Jeffrey divergence [12].

Global Texture Descriptor. In [11] a texture feature consisting of several parts is described: *Fractal dimension* measures the roughness or the crinkliness of a surface [15]. *Coarseness* characterizes the grain size of an image. *Entropy* is used as a measure of disorderedness or information content in an image. The *Spatial gray-level difference statistics* (SGLD) describes the brightness relationship of pixels within neighborhoods. It is also known as co-occurrence matrix analysis [16]. The *Circular Moran autocorrelation function* measures the roughness of the texture. For the calculation a set of autocorrelation functions is used [17].

Invariant Feature Histograms. A feature is called invariant with respect to certain transformations if it does not change when these transformations are applied to the image. The transformations considered here are translation, rotation, and scaling. In this work, invariant feature histograms as presented in [18] are used. These features are based on the idea of constructing features invariant with respect to certain transformations by integration over all considered transformations. The resulting histograms are compared using the Jeffrey divergence [12]. Previous experiments have shown that the characteristics of invariant feature histograms and color histograms are very similar and that invariant feature histograms often outperform color histograms [19].

3 Automatic Annotation Task

In the automatic annotation task, the objective was to classify 1,000 images into one of 57 classes using 9,000 training images. We participated in the automatic annotation task using two different methods. Method A is identical to the approach we have chosen for the medical retrieval task, except that here no textual information was available, and that we used appearance-based image features and Tamura Texture Features only, as we know from earlier experiments that these features perform well on medical radiographs [20].

Method B is a general object recognition method using histograms of image patches and discriminative training of log-linear models [21, 22].

The parameters of method A were optimized using 1,000 images from the 9,000 training images as a development set and the remaining 8,000 images for training. The parameters of method B were chosen as they work best on the Caltech database [23, 24, 22].

A more detailed description of the task and a detailed analysis of the results can be found in [4].

Table 1. Error rates [%] using different features on the IRMA 10,000 validation data

feature	distance	dev corpus	test corpus
32×32 thumbnails	Euclidean	25.3	36.8
X×32 thumbnails	IDM	13.0	12.6
Tamura texture histogram	JSD	33.1	46.0

3.1 Method A: Image Distortion Model

Method A uses our CBIR system FIRE and a subset of the above described features consisting of thumbnails of the images of the sizes 32×32 and $X \times 32$ and Tamura texture histograms. Error rates using these features alone are given in Table 1.

Some experiments with different weightings of Tamura features and thumbnails on our development corpus have shown that using the image distortion model alone outperforms the combinations. In particular, the combination of image distortion model (weighted 5) and Tamura texture features (weighted 2) is interesting, as this performed best in previous experiments on smaller versions of the IRMA database [20]. In our experiments, this combination yielded an error rate of 13.5% on the development corpus. Using the image distortion model alone yielded an error rate of 13.0% for the development data. Thus, we decided to use the image distortion model for our submission.

3.2 Method B: Object Recognition with Subimages and Discriminative Training

For method B an object recognition and classification approach using histograms of image patches and maximum entropy training to classify the 1,000 test images was used [21, 22].

To reduce the time and memory requirements for the clustering process, we used only 4,000 images for estimating the Gaussian mixture model. Nonetheless, we created the histograms for all training images and we used all histograms for the discriminative training of the log-linear model.

The model submitted used multi-scale features where the first PCA component was discarded to account for brightness changes and 4096-dimensional histograms. This combination was reported to work best on the Caltech database [23] and in the PASCAL Visual Object Classes Challenge [25]. The model achieved an error rate of 13.9% and thus is slightly better than the model by Raphaël Marée who follows a similar approach [26].

4 Experiments and Results

In the following the exact setups of the submitted runs for the automatic annotation task and the medical retrieval task are described and the results are discussed. Furthermore, we discuss our methods, point to errors we made, and present results of experiments that were conducted after the evaluation taking into account the lessons learned.

4.1 Automatic Annotation Task

Our submission using model A ranked first in the automatic annotation task. The submission following the object recognition approach ranked third. In total, 44 runs were submitted by 12 groups. The second rank was obtained by the IRMA group[2] using an approach similar to our model A and the fourth rank was obtained by the University of Liège, Belgium using an approach with image patches and boosted decision trees. A clear improvement over the baseline result of 36.8% error rate can be observed. This baseline result is obtained by a nearest neighbor classifier using 32x32 thumbnails of the images and Euclidean distance.

4.2 Medical Retrieval Task

For the medical retrieval task, we used the features described in Section 2.3 with different weightings in combination with text features. In total, we submitted 10 runs which are briefly described here.

Runs using textual information only. We submitted two fully automatic runs, where only textual information was used. These runs were labelled `En` and `EnDeFr`. In `En` only the English texts were used, for `EnDeFr` the English, the German, and the French texts were used and combined with equal weighting.

Runs using visual information only. We submitted three fully automatic runs, where only visual information was used. The runs `5000215`, `0010003`, and `1010111` only differ in the weighting of the image features. The exact weightings can be seen in Table 2. The run labelled `5000215` uses exactly the same setting as our submission to the 2004 ImageCLEF evaluation which had the best score from all 23 submissions in the category "visual features only, no user interaction". From the bad score of 0.06, it can be seen that this year's tasks differ significantly from the task of the previous year.

Runs using visual and textual information. We submitted three fully automatic runs and two runs with relevance feedback where textual and visual information was used. For the run `i6-3010210111`, the features were combined in exactly the way described above. For the runs `i6-3(1010111-min(111))` and `i6-3(3030333)-min(111)` before combining text- and visual features, the minimum distance of all three text distances was first taken for each image. This was done to better account for images that have texts in one language only.

The runs `i6-vistex-rfb1` and `i6-vistex-rfb2` used relevance feedback from the first 20 results of the automatic run `i6-3(1010111-min(111))` and differ only in the user feedback. In both cases the feedback was given by a computer

[2] `http://www.irma-project.org`

Table 2. Overview of the submitted runs for the medical retrieval task and their setup. For each run, the feature weightings and the achieved MAP with badly chosen ρ and with properly chosen ρ is given. (* as feature weight means that for all features marked with * the distance was calculated and the minimum among those was chosen, - means not used, + means that relevance feedback was used).

	textual information only		visual information only			visual and textual information				+relevance feedback	
run	En	EnDeFr-min	1010111	5000215	0010003	3010210111	3(3030333) -min(111)	3(1010111) -min(111)	-	vistex-rfb1	vistex-rfb2
X×32 image features	-	-	1	5	3	3	9	3	1	1	1
32×32 image features	-	-	1	0	0	0	0	3	1	1	1
color histograms	-	-	1	0	1	1	9	3	1	1	1
tamura features	-	-	1	2	0	2	9	3	1	1	1
invariant feat. histo.	-	-	1	1	0	1	9	3	1	1	1
English text	1	*	-	-	-	1	*	*	2	*	*
German text	0	*	-	-	-	1	*	*	0	*	*
French text	0	*	-	-	-	1	*	*	0	*	*
relevance feedback	-	-	-	-	-	-	-	-	-	+	+
score w/ wrong ρ	0.21	0.05	0.07	0.06	0.05	0.07	0.07	0.06	-	0.09	0.08
score w/ properly chosen ρ	0.21	0.15				0.22		0.20	0.25		

scientist familiar with the FIRE system but with little background in medicine. Furthermore, the textual information was not available for the user feedback. Thus, the feedback is based on visual information only.

Table 2 shows an overview of all runs we submitted for the medical retrieval task. Unfortunately, we were unable to test our combination of textual- and visual information retrieval in advance of the competition , which led to a very unlucky choice of ρ in Eq. (10). As a result, any combination with textual information retrieval was adversely affected. The results obtained after the evaluation, where ρ was chosen properly, are significantly improved (Table 2). In particular, using English textual information retrieval only, we could reach a MAP of 0.25 which would have achieved third ranking in the 2005 ImageCLEF evaluation in the category "textual and visual information, no relevance feedback".

5 Conclusion and Outlook

We presented the methods we used in the 2005 ImageCLEF CBIR evaluation. Participating in the automatic annotation task, we obtained the first and third rank. In the medical image retrieval task our results were not satisfying due to improper parameterization. Results with correct settings are presented in this work and results are significantly improved. In particular, the result obtained would have been ranked 3rd in the medical retrieval task in the category “fully automatic runs using textual and visual information”.

References

1. Müller, H., Geissbühler, A.: How to Visually Retrieve Images From the St. Andrews Collection Using GIFT. In: Multilingual Information Access for Text, Speech and Images. Proceedings of the 5th Workshop of the Cross-Language Evaluation Forum. CLEF 2004. Volume 3491 of LNCS., Bath, UK, Springer (2004) 633–642
2. Lin, W.C., Chang, Y.C., Chen, H.H.: From Text to Image: Generating Visual Query for Image Retrieval. In: Multilingual Information Access for Text, Speech and Images. Proceedings of the 5th Workshop of the Cross-Language Evaluation Forum. CLEF 2004. Volume 3491 of LNCS., Bath, UK, Springer (2004) 664–675
3. Alvarez, C., Oumohmed, A.I., Mignotte, M., Nie, J.Y.: Toward Cross-Language and Cross-Media Image Retrieval. In: Multilingual Information Access for Text, Speech and Images. Proceedings of the 5th Workshop of the Cross-Language Evaluation Forum. CLEF 2004. Volume 3491 of LNCS., Bath, UK, Springer (2004) 676–687
4. Clough, P., Mueller, H., Deselaers, T., Grubinger, M., Lehmann, T., Jensen, J., Hersh, W.: The CLEF 2005 Cross-Language Image Retrieval Track. In Proceedings of the Cross Language Evaluation Forum 2005, Springer Lecture Notes in Computer science, 2006 - to appear.
5. Macherey, W., Viechtbauer, H.J., Ney, H.: Probabilistic Aspects in Spoken Document Retrieval. EURASIP Journal on Applied Signal Processing Special Issue on "Unstructured Information Management from Multimedia Data Sources"(2) (2003) 1–12
6. Porter, M.F.: An Algorithm for Suffix Stripping, Morgan Kaufmann, 1980, San Francisco, CA.
7. Choi, J., Hindle, D., Hirschberg, J., Magrin-Changnolleau, I., Nakatani, C., Pereira, F., Singhal, A., Whittaker, S.: An Overview of the At&T Spoken Document Retrieval. In: Proc. 1998 DARPA Broadcast News Transcription and Understanding Workshop, Lansdowne, Va, USA (1998) 182–188
8. Keysers, D., Gollan, C., Ney, H.: Classification of medical images using non-linear distortion models. In: Bildverarbeitung für die Medizin, Berlin, Germany (2004) 366–370
9. Keysers, D., Gollan, C., Ney, H.: Local Context in Non-Linear Deformation Models for Handwritten Character Recognition. In: International Conference on Pattern Recognition. Volume 4., Cambridge, UK (2004) 511–514
10. Keysers, D., Macherey, W., Ney, H., Dahmen, J.: Adaptation in Statistical Pattern Recognition Using Tangent Vectors. IEEE Transactions on Pattern Analysis and Machine Intelligence **26**(2) (2004) 269–274
11. Deselaers, T.: Features for Image Retrieval. Diploma thesis, Lehrstuhl für Informatik VI, RWTH Aachen University, Aachen, Germany (2003)
12. Puzicha, J., Rubner, Y., Tomasi, C., Buhmann, J.: Empirical Evaluation of Dissimilarity Measures for Color and Texture. In: International Conference on Computer Vision. Volume 2., Corfu, Greece (1999) 1165–1173
13. Smeulders, A.W.M., Worring, M., Santini, S., Gupta, A., Jain, R.: Content-Based Image Retrieval: The End of the Early Years. IEEE Transactions on Pattern Analysis and Machine Intelligence **22**(12) (2000) 1349–1380

14. Tamura, H., Mori, S., Yamawaki, T.: Textural Features Corresponding to Visual Perception. IEEE Transaction on Systems, Man, and Cybernetics **8**(6) (1978) 460–472
15. Haberäcker, P.: Praxis der Digitalen Bildverarbeitung und Mustererkennung. Carl Hanser Verlag, München, Wien (1995)
16. Haralick, R.M., Shanmugam, B., Dinstein, I.: Texture Features for Image Classification. IEEE Transactions on Systems, Man, and Cybernetics **3**(6) (1973) 610–621
17. Gu, Z.Q., Duncan, C.N., Renshaw, E., Mugglestone, M.A., Cowan, C.F.N., Grant, P.M.: Comparison of Techniques for Measuring Cloud Texture in Remotely Sensed Satellite Meteorological Image Data. Radar and Signal Processing **136**(5) (1989) 236–248
18. Siggelkow, S.: Feature Histograms for Content-Based Image Retrieval. PhD thesis, University of Freiburg, Institute for Computer Science, Freiburg, Germany (2002)
19. Deselaers, T., Keysers, D., Ney, H.: Features for Image Retrieval – A Quantitative Comparison. In: DAGM 2004, Pattern Recognition, 26th DAGM Symposium. Number 3175 in LNCS, Tübingen, Germany (2004) 228–236
20. Lehmann, T.M., Güld, M.O., Deselaers, T., Keysers, D., Schubert, H., Spitzer, K., Ney, H., Wein, B.: Automatic Categorization of Medical Images for Content-Based Retrieval and Data Mining. Computerized Medical Imaging and Graphics **29** (2005) in press
21. Deselaers, T., Keysers, D., Ney, H.: Discriminative Training for Object Recognition Using Image Patches. In: CVPR 05. Volume 2., San Diego, CA (2005) 157–162
22. Deselaers, T., Keysers, D., Ney, H.: Improving a Discriminative Approach to Object Recognition Using Image Patches. In: DAGM 2005. LNCS, Vienna, Austria (2005) 326–333
23. Fergus, R., Perona, P., Zissermann, A.: Object Class Recognition by Unsupervised Scale-Invariant Learning. In: Conference on Computer Vision and Pattern Recognition, Blacksburg, VG (2003) 264–271
24. Dreuw, P., Keysers, D., Deselaers, T., Ney, H.: Gesture Recognition Using Image Comparison Methods. In: GW 2005, 6th Int. Workshop on Gesture in Human-Computer Interaction and Simulation, Vannes, France (2005)
25. Everingham, M., Gool, L.V., Williams, C., Zisserman, A.: Pascal Visual Object Classes Challenge Results. Technical report, University of Oxford, Oxford, UK (2005)
26. Marée, R., Geurts, P., Piater, J., Wehenkel, L.: Random Subwindows for Robust Image Classification. In Schmid, C., Soatto, S., Tomasi, C., eds.: IEEE Conference on Computer Vision and Pattern Recognition. Volume 1., San Diego, CA, USA, IEEE (2005) 34–40

A Clustered Retrieval Approach for Categorizing and Annotating Images

Lisa Ballesteros and Desislava Petkova

Mount Holyoke College, South Hadley MA 01075, USA
dipetkov|lballest@mtholyoke.edu

Abstract. Images are difficult to classify and annotate but the availability of digital image databases creates a constant demand for tools that automatically analyze image content and describe it with either a category or set of words. We develop two cluster-based cross-media relevance models that effectively categorize and annotate images by adapting a cross-lingual retrieval technique to choose the terms most likely associated with the visual features of an image.

1 Introduction

The exponential growth of multi-media information has created a compelling need for innovative tools for managing, retrieving, presenting, and analyzing image collections. Medical databases, for example, continue to grow as hospitals and research institutes produce thousands of medical images daily. Furthermore, systems that enable search and retrieval of images across languages would facilitate medical diagnoses via the sharing of databases across national boundaries.

Image retrieval techniques can be classified into two types, content based image retrieval (CBIR) and text-based image retrieval (TBIR). CBIR attempts to find images based on visual similarities such as shape or texture. TBIR techniques retrieve images based on semantic relationships rather than visual features and require that descriptive words or annotations have been previously assigned to each image. For collections of realistic size, it is impractical to rely exclusively on manual annotation because the process is both time-consuming and subjective. As a practical alternative, automatic annotation can either supplement or replace manual annotation. The goal is to automatically assign semantically descriptive words to unannotated images.

As with most tasks involving natural language processing, we assume that a training collection of already annotated images is available, from which to learn correlations between words and visual components or *visterms*. We specify the task further by considering annotation to be a cross-lingual retrieval problem: Two languages - textual and visual - are both used to describe images, and we want to infer the textual representation of an image given its visual representation. Therefore, we can think of words being the target language and visterms being the source language. Of course the language of visterms is entirely synthetic, but this CLIR approach does not require language specific knowledge. In fact, it can be used to successfully assign categories or annotations across languages with the visterms serving as an interlingua.

C. Peters et al. (Eds.): CLEF 2005, LNCS 4022, pp. 662–672, 2006.

2 Background

Other researchers have proposed methods for modeling the relationships between words and visual components [11,1,8]. Our approach is a modification of the Cross-media Relevance Model (CMRM) developed by Jeon *et al* [7]. In this case, the visterms of an image to be annotated constitute a query and all candidate words are ranked in terms of their relevance to the visual query. An annotation of any length can be created by selecting the n highest ranked words. More precisely, using a collection T of training images J, the joint probability of observing a word w and the set of visterms derived from an unannotated image $I = \{v_1, ..., v_m\}$ is computed as:

$$P(w, v_1, ..., v_m) = \sum_{J \in T} P(J)P(w|J) \prod_{i=1}^{m} P(v_i|J) \tag{1}$$

where $P(w|J)$ and $P(v|J)$ are maximum-likelihood estimates smoothed with collection frequencies.

$$P(w|J) = (1 - \alpha)\frac{\#(w, J)}{|J|} + \alpha\frac{\#(w, T)}{|T|} \tag{2}$$

$$P(v|J) = (1 - \beta)\frac{\#(v, J)}{|J|} + \beta\frac{\#(v, T)}{|T|} \tag{3}$$

CMRM uses word-visterm co-occurrences across training images to estimate the probability of associating words and visterms together. This method computes the word and visterm distributions $P(\cdot|J)$ of each image separately, so it does not take into account global similarity patterns. We improve CMRM's probability estimates by including information from *clusters* of similar images.

Document clustering within information retrieval is not new [6,12,13,5]. More recently, Liu *et al* [10] investigate clustering in the framework of full text retrieval and show that cluster-based Language Models improve retrieval. They define two models: Cluster Query Likelihood (CQL) and Cluster-based Document Model (CBDM). Both models explore across-document and within-document word co-occurrence patterns to improve the ranking of documents in response to user queries. CQL directly ranks clusters based on $P(Q|C)$, the probability of a cluster C generating the query Q, while CBDM ranks documents similarly, but smooths their language models with the models of their respective clusters. We adapt these techniques to annotate and categorize images by extending the Cross-media Relevance Model to take advantage of cluster statistics in addition to image statistics.

The mathematical definitions for CQL are given by (4),(5),and (6). The formulas for CBDM are similar, with the following differences. First, the clusters, C, of (4) are replaced by individual images, J. Second, the statistics from clusters, C, and the collection, T, in (5) and (6) are replaced by statistics from individual images, J, and from clusters, C, respectively. Note that clusters play different roles in these two models - ranking in CQL and smoothing in CBDM.

$$P(w, v_1, ..., v_m) = \sum_{C \in T} P(C)P(w|C) \prod_{i=1}^{m} P(v_i|C) \quad (4)$$

$$P(w|C) = (1-\gamma)\frac{\#(w,C)}{|C|} + \gamma\frac{\#(w,T)}{|T|} \quad (5)$$

$$P(v|C) = (1-\delta)\frac{\#(v,C)}{|C|} + \delta\frac{\#(v,T)}{|T|} \quad (6)$$

3 Methodology of Categorization and Annotation

Textual representations provided for ImageCLEFmed 2005 are categories rather than annotations. Since we are interested in both categorizing and annotating images, we generate more realistic annotations by breaking up categorical records into sets of individual concepts, yielding a restricted vocabulary of 46 distinct concepts and annotations with a maximum length of six. We define a "concept" to be a comma-separated string. Some of these are literal dictionary words (e.g. "spine"), others are sequences of words (e.g. "radio carpal joint"), and they all identify a single distinctive image property.

We get two kinds of textual representations per image - a category and an annotation. Concepts do not refer directly to objects in the images but describe very high-level, specialized attributes which are not reflected directly by any visual feature. As a result, images that are apparently different can have very similar annotations, i.e. share many concepts. In contrast, all images classified in the same category are visually similar.

We also observe that concepts have an unusual distribution where the six most frequent ones account for more than 75% of the total number of occurrences. In fact, one concept - 'x-ray' - appears in every single image. Both CQL and CBDM would likely be biased in favor of these very frequent concepts, tending to select them rather than rare ones. Since we set the models to generate fixed-length annotations of six concepts (this is the maximum length of training annotations), we would expect the same set of concepts to be assigned over and over.

Recall that both CQL and CBDM compute a set of probabilities $P(w_i|I), i = 1...|V|$, based on the visterms of an image I. These probabilities are used to rank terms w according to their suitability to describe the content of I. The only restriction on the vocabulary V is that it is a finite set of discrete elements. Both categories and individual concepts satisfy this requirement therefore we can use the same implementation to assign either categories or concepts by only changing the input to the system.

We consider each category to be an annotation of length 1. By learning relationships between categories and visterms we can categorize new images directly by assigning the term with the highest probability.

Categories are divided into concepts generating annotations of various lengths. By learning relationships between concepts and visterms we can annotate new images directly by assigning several of the highest probability concepts. Alternatively, we can categorize new images indirectly by representing categories as combinations of concepts:

$$P(\texttt{category}) = P(\texttt{concept}_1, ..., \texttt{concept}_k) = \sum_{i=1}^{k} P(\texttt{concept}_i) \tag{7}$$

Concept distribution across the set of 57 categories varies widely with the most frequent concept appearing in every category. To address this issue we scale frequencies using a TF×IDF weighting scheme. Concept probabilities are computed as

$$P(c_i|J) = \frac{1}{log(\#(c_i, S))} P(c_i|J) \tag{8}$$

where S is the set of categorical definitions. Thus we emphasize concepts that appear in only a few categories and penalize concepts that appear in many categories since they have little discriminatory power. In the rest of the paper, we refer to concepts and categories jointly as terms.

4 Data Processing and Experimental Setup

Preliminary image processing involves extracting visual features to generate an image vocabulary of visterms. Briefly, our representations are generated in the following way. Each image is grid partitioned into regions and the complete set of image regions is partitioned into disjoint groups based on corresponding feature vectors. All regions in a group are given the same unique identifier or *visterm*. Once image processing is complete, our approach relies on a model of the correspondences between terms and visterms, inferred from a set of previously annotated training images.

4.1 Feature Extraction and Visterm Generation

The dataset consists of 9000 training images and 1000 test images. Each image is scaled to 256×256 pixels and divided into a 5×5 square grid. This produces 250,000 regions to be discretized into visterms. Regions are clustered on the basis of visual similarities and each cluster is assigned a unique identifier. Since the ImageCLEFmed collection consists entirely of black-and-white images, we only consider visual features that analyze texture. More specifically, we apply the Gabor Energy and Tamura texture analyses.

The Gabor method [4] measures the similarity between image neighborhoods and specially defined masks to detect spatially local patterns such as oriented lines, edges and blobs. We use a MATLAB implementation courtesy of Shaolei Feng at the Center for Intelligent Information Retrieval, University of Massachusetts at Amherst. This feature computes a 12-bin histogram per image region.

The Tamura features - Coarseness, Directionality and Contrast - are intended to reproduce human visual perception. We use the FIRE Flexible Image Retrieval Engine to extract Tamura features [2]. Given an input image, FIRE creates three output partial images, one for each of the three features. Each 6×6 partial image feature is converted into a 36-dimensional vector.

Visual features describe distinctive image properties. Even if two features both analyze texture, they do so using different calculations and therefore might recognize different characteristics of the texture. On the other hand, we do not want to waste time and resources to extract correlated features, which are equivalent rather than complimentary sources of information. Deselaers *et al* show that Gabor filters and the individual Tamura features are not correlated [3]. Therefore, we investigate two alternatives for combining these features for a more comprehensive texture analysis.

The first combines features at visterm generation. We begin by joining feature vectors produced by each feature into one compound vector, and then cluster to quantize the vectors into visterms. For example, the lengths of Gabor energy and of Coarseness vectors are 12 and 36, respectively. These generate a 250000×48 matrix of feature vectors for the entire collection, which is partitioned into 500 visterms. These theoretically reflect the similarity of regions based both on Gabor energy and Coarseness.

In the second approach (combination at representation), the feature vectors produced by each analysis are clustered separately prior to visterm assignment. Different cluster identifiers are assigned for each feature, e.g. integers from 1 to 500 for Gabor energy and integers from 501 to 1000 for Coarseness, and both types of visterms are assigned to each image. An image has twice as many visterms with approach two, as it does when features are combined at generation (approach one), so their visual representations are longer. Therefore, probability estimates could be closer to the true underlying distribution.

Our experiments show that combining features at generation is not very effective while two features combined at representation work better than either feature alone. Figure 1 graphs the performance of CQL according to error rate, as the number of clusters increases. Figure 2 graphs the same results for CBDM. It is likely that combining features at generation fails because the weaker feature Coarseness is three times as long as the better feature Gabor energy. On the other hand, when combining at representation each feature accounts for 25 out of the 50 visterms per image, so in this respect the features are given equal weight.

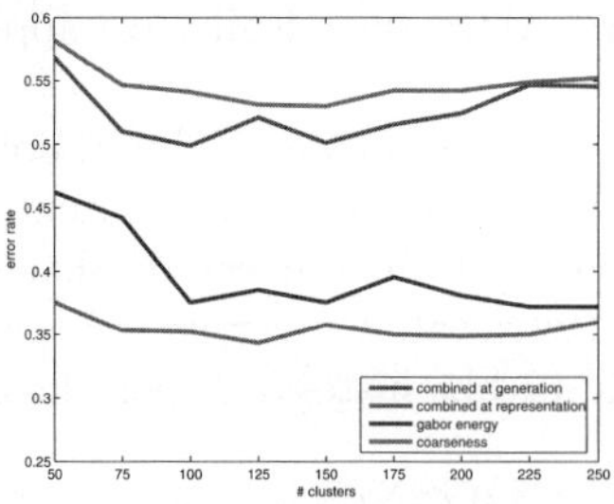

Fig. 1. CQL performance with Gabor energy and Coarseness combined

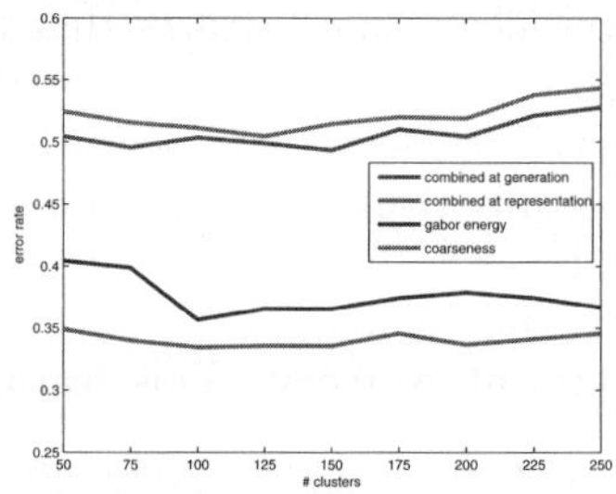

Fig. 2. CBDM performance with Gabor energy and Coarseness combined

4.2 Clustering Techniques

Visterms tend to identify lower-level visual properties, while terms identify higher-level semantic ones. By combining terms and visterms a clustering technique can generate clusters with both visual and semantic coherence. The theoretical framework of cluster-based relevance modeling does not depend on the specific implementation of clustering. We investigate two different clustering techniques, K-means clustering and K-nearest neighbors (KNN) clustering. We compare these to a baseline of clusters based on manually assigned categories.

The K-means algorithm takes the desired number of clusters, K, as input and returns a list of indices indicating to which cluster each point in the partitioned dataset belongs. Initially K elements from the set are selected randomly as cluster centroids. Each remaining element is added to the cluster to which it is most similar, then the centroids are reevaluated. The algorithm refines the partitioning iteratively by repeatedly reevaluating and reassigning until no element changes assignment and the clustering converges.

K-means is a *hard* clustering algorithm which produces mutually exclusive clusters. Performance depends on both the value of K and the initial choice of centroids. The appropriate number of clusters is determined by the dataset configuration which is usually unknown. Even if the value of K is close to the natural number of groupings, given the starting centroid positions, K-means can still get trapped in a local maximum and fail to find a good solution. The method is also sensitive outliers. Because K-means computes centroids as within-cluster averages, an outlier can pull away a centroid away from its true position.

Kurland *et al* propose a clustering method that takes the K-1 nearest neighbors of each training image to form a cluster of size K (KNN) [9]. In contrast to K-means, KNN is a *soft* clustering technique that can assign an element to more than one cluster. KNN generates as many clusters as there are training images, each of size K-1 nearest neighbors.

To find the nearest neighbors of a training image J_k, all images $J_m, m = 1...|T|, m \neq k$, are first ranked according to their similarity to J_k. In our work, language models are generated by smoothing image frequencies with collection frequencies. Then the similarity between J_k and J_m is estimated as $\texttt{sim}(J_k, J_m) = \prod_{i=1}^{|J_k|} P(t_i|J_m)$, where t_i are the terms and visterms of J_k. The ranking process is repeated $|T|$ times - once for each one of the training images in the collection T.

5 Experimental Results

The cluster-based models rely on several smoothing and clustering parameters. These include: α for smoothing terms in image models, β for visterms in image models, γ for terms in cluster models, δ for visterms in cluster models, K for the number of clusters.

We apply 10-fold cross validation to set each parameter, by dividing the 9000 training images into 10 subsets of equal size and optimizing performance by minimizing the error rate. We determine that CQL works best with $\gamma = 0.1$ and

$\delta = 0.2$ while CBDM works best with $\alpha = 0.5, \beta = 0.8, \gamma = 0.5$ and $\delta = 0.3$. We use these values throughout the rest of the experiments.

Cluster quality is closely linked to the choice of visual feature and since the value of K is feature-dependent, we cross-validate it individually for each visual feature. The clustering parameter K is feature-dependent and is selected empirically. For CQL, we use $K = 225$ for Gabor energy, 100 for Coarseness, and 200 for Gabor energy combined with the three Tamura features (Coarseness, Directionality and Contrast). However, in comparison to CQL, CBDM shows a consistent tendency to perform best with fewer but larger clusters, so we set $K=$ 175, 75, and 100, respectively, for Gabor energy, Coarseness, and the combined Tamura features.

5.1 Feature Effectiveness and Evaluation Measures

To get a sense of the relative effectiveness of the extracted features, we compare Coarseness and Gabor energy. The former has highest performance at 100 clusters, the latter at 225, and Gabor energy is the more useful feature (Table 1).

Since images represented with Coarseness visterms are clustered into fewer groups, it is likely that dissimilar images will occasionally be contained in the same cluster. Perhaps Coarseness captures less information about content, yielding poorer discrimination between images. This would be true if the images are naturally structured into more groups, but the clustering algorithm fails to distinguish between some groups based on the Coarseness representations. Although Coarseness appears to extract less useful information than Gabor energy, its

Table 1. Ranking visual features according to their effectiveness as measured by CQL performance on Categorization and Annotation

Categorization Task								
	Ranking via error rate		Ranking via highest precision		Ranking via F-measure		Ranking via mAP	
I.	Gabor + Tamura	.3178	Gabor + Tamura	.6792	Gabor + Tamura	.4125	Gabor	.3800
II.	Gabor	.3722	Gabor	.6527	Gabor	.3724	Gabor + Tamura	.3195
III.	Coarseness	.5078	Coarseness	.5087	Coarseness	.2010	Coarseness	.2412
Annotation Task								
	Ranking via error rate		Ranking via highest precision		Ranking via F-measure		Ranking via mAP	
I.	Gabor energy	.1513	Gabor energy	.8909	Gabor energy	.5560	Gabor energy	.5863
II.	Gabor energy and Tamura	.1516	Gabor energy and Tamura	.8338	Gabor energy and Tamura	.5530	Gabor energy and Tamura	.4137
III.	Coarseness	.2060	Coarseness	.7008	Coarseness	.3546	Coarseness	.3842

texture analysis does not overlap with that of Gabor. Since they identify different image properties, combining the two features proves to be an advantage.

Not all evaluation measures will necessarily suggest the same feature as most effective. Therefore, we compare four measures with respect to categorization and annotation using the CQL model: `error rate`, `precision at 0.0 recall`, `average F-measure`, and `mean average precision`. Smoothing parameters are set as described above. Results are reported in Table 1.

The experiments show that Gabor energy is the best feature for assigning annotations. On the other hand, Gabor energy and Tamura combined is the optimal feature for assigning categories according to all but mean average precision, in which Gabor energy is best. When assigning categories, only the highest ranked category is selected, so we need not be concerned about the tradeoff between recall and precision. On the other hand, when we assign annotations we select several concepts and we are interested in both recall and precision. Based on these distinctions, in the remaining experiments, effectiveness of categorization and annotation are measured via error rate and F-measure, respectively.

5.2 Clustering Effectiveness

Clustering is an important ingredient of our method and the choice of clustering technique can significantly affect performance. We explore two alternatives, K-means and KNN (described in Section 4.2) and compare them with a baseline of manually assigned clusters. Since ImageCLEFmed images are assigned to one particular category, we can assume that categories play the role of cluster labels. It becomes straightforward to partition the collection by putting all images of the same category in a separate cluster. The result is a set of 57 non-overlapping clusters of various lengths, depending on how many training examples from each category are provided. Results are given in Table 2.

Category-clusters give satisfactory performance (Table 2), although are unrealistic for most datasets. K-means gives CQL a statistically significant improvement but slightly hurts CBDM. The results suggest that the medical categories are relatively broad. For example, there might be a category which contains two visually different types of images, and the accuracy of CQL increases as a result of separating them into two different clusters. (We know that K-means breaks

Table 2. Categorization performance of cluster-based CMRM improves with unsupervised clustering (K-means or KNN). 95%-confidence p-values according to the Wilcoxon signed-rank test are reported in parenthesis.

	CQL		CBDM	
	error rate	nonzero categories	error rate	nonzero categories
Categories	.3010	37	.2570	40
K-means	.2650 (.0014)	36	.2630 (.4709)	39
KNN	.2440 (.0166)	40	.2310 (.0006)	46

up some of the category clusters because the value of K is larger than 57. In this way, the system deals with the issue of some clusters not being compact enough. On the other hand cluster compactness has less influence on their usefulness as background models for smoothing; this could explain why the performance of CBDM does not improve. (With CBDM emphasis is on generalization and therefore recall, and with CQL - on correctness and therefore precision.) For collections in which manual categories are narrowly defined, we would expect K-means to generate fewer clusters than the number of categories. This should increase recall, which would have a positive effect both on CQL and CBDM.

CQL and CBDM apply clusters in two conceptually different roles - on one hand, as training examples which are somewhat more general than images, and on the other hand, as background collections which are somewhat more specific than the entire collection. Implicitly, bigger clusters are more useful for generalizing patterns observed in individual images - if the clusters are too small, they would fail to capture some aspects of member images and their content. Therefore, with CBDM we are less concerned about the compactness of the clusters, and can allow some relatively dissimilar elements to join the same cluster.

First, this corroborates our previous conclusion that CQL works well with very compact clusters and CBDM works well with more general clusters. We also observe that categorization performance improves with a statistically significant difference as compared to K-means clustering (Table 2). KNN clusters have more local coherence because they are defined with respect to a particular image. Since by generation a KNN cluster is specific to an image, it is better at describing image context. In addition, the KNN method does not reduce the number of training examples. It generates as many clusters as there are images. On the other hand, K-means creates considerably fewer clusters, which implies that there are fewer observations on which to base the model's probability estimations.

5.3 Cross-Language Annotation and Categorization

All images are annotated with twelve concepts: 6 English concepts and their German translations. The following experiments were designed to test the effectiveness of our clustered relevance models for categorizing and assigning annotations across languages.

As our models are language independent, the accuracy of probability estimates should not be effected by the annotation language. We verify this by partitioning the training set into two groups, one with English annotations and the other with German annotations. Features are extracted from each group of images, then CQL and CBDM models are built for each. We then assign monolingual annotations to each training image, choosing the top 6 English (German) concepts from the models of the training images annotated with English (German). Results showed no significant difference between the accuracy of assigned categories or annotations for either Enlish or German, using either CQL or CBDM.

It is unrealistic to expect manual annotations to be generated and maintained for growing image collections, and is even less likely that multi-lingual annotations will be assigned. We assume that a multi-lingual image collections derived by combining sets of images with monolingual annotations would be easier to generate. Following this assumption, we combine our English and German image subsets to generate a training set of 9000 images, half with English annotations and half with German annotations. Word identifiers are assigned to distinguish English from German words, images are processed for feature extraction, then CQL and CBDM models are generated for the set. We evaluate the models on the 1000 test images, by generating categories and annotations in English and in German.

6 Conclusion

In this work, we analyzed a cluster-based cross-lingual retrieval approach to image annotation and categorization. We described two methods for incorporating cluster statistics into the general framework of cross-media relevance modeling and showed that both build effective probabilistic models of term-visterm relationships. We also discussed how different clustering techniques affect the quality and discriminative power of automatically generated clusters. Finally, we demonstrated an efficient method for combining visterms produced by several visual features.

We regard clustering as a kind of unsupervised classification that offers greater flexibility than manual classification. If the actual categories are too broad, then the system can break them into smaller clusters. If the actual categories are too specific, then it can redefine them by generating bigger clusters. If manually assigned categories are unavailable, the system can create them automatically. The only disadvantage is that automatic clusters do not have explicit textual descriptions, but the word distribution in clusters could be analyzed to build statistical language models.

In the future, we plan to investigate grouping by concept (similar to the method of grouping by category described here but based on annotation words) as an alternative version of soft clustering. We are also interested in analyzing the categorization performance of CQL and CBDM on a collection of true-color images to examine how visual properties influence accuracy.

References

1. Duygulu, P., Barnard, K., de Freitas, N., Forsyth, D.: Object recognition as machine translation: Leaning a lexicon for a fixed image vocabulary. European Conference on Computer Vision (2002)
2. Deselaers, T., Keysers, D., Ney, H.: FIRE - Flexible Image Retrieval Engine. CLEF 2004 Workshop (2004)
3. Deselaers, T., Keysers, D., Ney, H.: Features for image retrieval: A quantitative comparison. DAGM Pattern Recognition Symposium (2004)
4. Fogel, I., Sagi, Dov.: Gabor filters as texture discriminator. Journal of Biological Cybernetics **61** (1989) 102113
5. Hearst, M.A., and Pedersen, J.O.: (1996). Re-examining the cluster hypothesis: Scatter/Gather on retrieval results. ACM SIGIR (1996)

6. Jardine, N. and van Rijsbergen, C.J: The use of hierarchical clustering in information retrieval. Information Storage and Retrieval,**7** (1971) 217–240
7. Jeon, J., Lavrenko, V., Manmatha, R: Automatic image annotation and retrieval using Cross-media relevance models. ACM SIGIR (2003)
8. Jeon, J., Manmatha R.: Using maximum entropy for automatic image annotation. Conference on Image and Video Retrieval (2004)
9. Kurland, O., Lee, L.: Corpus structure, language models, and ad hoc information retrieval. ACM SIGIR (2004)
10. Liu, X., Croft, B.: Cluster-based retrieval using language models. ACM SIGIR (2004)
11. Mori, Y., Takanashi, H., Oka, R.: Image-to-word transformation based on dividing and vector quantizing images with words. MISRM International Workshop (1999)
12. van Rijsbergen, C.J. & Croft, W. B.: Document clustering: An evaluation of some experiments with the Cranfield 1400 collection. Information Processing & Management, **11** (1975) 171–182
13. Voorhees, E.M.: The cluster hypothesis revisited. ACM SIGIR (1985)

Manual Query Modification and Data Fusion for Medical Image Retrieval

Jeffery R. Jensen and William R. Hersh

Department of Medical Informatics & Clinical Epidemiology
Oregon Health & Science University
Portland, Oregon, USA
{jensejef, hersh}@ohsu.edu

Abstract. Image retrieval has great potential for a variety of tasks in medicine but is currently underdeveloped. For the ImageCLEF 2005 medical task, we used a text retrieval system as the foundation of our experiments to assess retrieval of images from the test collection. We conducted experiments using automatic queries, manual queries, and manual queries augmented with results from visual queries. The best performance was obtained from manual modification of queries. The combination of manual and visual retrieval results resulted in lower performance based on mean average precision but higher precision within the top 30 results. Further research is needed not only to sort out the relative benefit of textual and visual methods in image retrieval but also to determine which performance measures are most relevant to the operational setting.

1 Introduction

The goal of the medical image retrieval task of ImageCLEF is to identify and develop methods to enhance the retrieval of images based on real-world topics that a user would bring to such an image retrieval system. A test collection of nearly 50,000 images - annotated in English, French, and/or German - and 25 topics provided the basis for experiments. As described in the track overview paper [1], the test collection was organized from four collections, each of which was organized into cases consisting of one or more images plus annotations at the case or image level (depending on the organization of the original collection).

There are two general approaches to image retrieval, semantic (also called context-based) and visual (also called content-based) [2]. Semantic image retrieval uses textual information to determine an image's subject matter, such as an annotation or more structured metadata. Visual image retrieval, on the other hand, uses features from the image, such as color, texture, shapes, etc., to determine its content. The latter has historically been a difficult task, especially in the medical domain [3]. The most success for visual retrieval has come from "more images like this one" types of queries. There has actually been little research in the types of techniques that would achieve good performance for queries more akin to those a user might enter into a text retrieval system, such as "images showing different types of skin cancers." Some

C. Peters et al. (Eds.): CLEF 2005, LNCS 4022, pp. 673 – 679, 2006.

researchers have begun to investigate hybrid methods that combine both image context and content for indexing and retrieval [3].

Oregon Health & Science University (OHSU) participated in the medical image retrieval task of ImageCLEF 2005. Our experiments were based on a semantic image retrieval system, although we also attempted to improve our performance by fusing our results with output from a content-based search. Data fusion has been used for a variety of tasks in IR, e.g., [4]. Our experimental runs included an automatic query, a manually modified query, and a manual/visual query (the manual query refined with the results of a visual search).

2 System Overview

Our retrieval system was based on the open-source search engine, Lucene. We have used Lucene in other retrieval evaluation forums, such as the Text Retrieval Conference (TREC) Genomics Track [5]. Documents in Lucene are indexed by parsing of individual words and weighting of those words with an algorithm that sums for each query term in each document the product of the term frequency (TF), the inverse document frequency (IDF), the boost factor of the term, the normalization of the document, the fraction of query terms in the document, and the normalization of the weight of the query terms, for each term in the query. The score of document d for query q consisting of terms t is calculated as follows:

$$score(q,d) = \sum_{t \in q} tf(t,d) * idf(t) * boost(t,d) * norm(d,t) * frac(t,d) * norm(q)$$

where: tf(t.d) = term frequency of term t in document d

idf(t) = inverse document frequency of term t
boost(t,d) = boost for term t in document d
norm(t,d) = normalization of d with respect to t
frac(t,d) = fraction of t contained in d
norm(q) = normalization of query q

Lucene is distributed with a variety of analyzers for textual indexing. We chose Lucene's standard analyzer, which supports acronyms, floating point numbers, lowercasing, and stop word removal. The standard analyzer was chosen to bolster precision. Each annotation, within the library, was indexed with three data fields, which consisted of a collection name, a file name, and the contents of the file to be indexed. Although the annotations were structured in XML, we indexed each annotation without the use of an XML parser. Therefore, every XML element was indexed (including its tag) along with its corresponding value.

As noted in the track overview paper, some images were indexed at the case level, i.e., the annotation applied to all images associated with the case. (This applied for the Casimage and MIR collections, but not the PEIR or PathoPIC collections.) When the search engine matched a case annotation, each of the images associated with the case was added to the retrieval output. It was for this reason that we also did a run that filtered the output based on retrieval by a visual retrieval run, in an attempt to focus the output of images by whole cases.

3 Methods

OHSU submitted three official runs for ImageCLEF 2005 medical image retrieval track. These included two that were purely semantic, and one that employed a combination of semantic and visual searching methods.

Our first run (OHSUauto) was purely semantic. This run was a "baseline" run, just using the text in the topics as provided with the unmodified Lucene system. Therefore, we used the French and German translations that were also provided with the topics. For our ranked image output, we used all of the images associated with each retrieved annotation.

For our second run (OHSUman), we carried out manual modification of the query for each topic. For some topics, the keywords were expanded or mapped to more specific terms. This made the search statements for this run more specific. For example, one topic focused on chest x-rays showing an enlarged heart, so we added a term like cardiomegaly. Since the manual modification resulted in no longer having accurate translations, we "expanded" the manual queries with translations that were obtained from Babelfish (http://babelfish.altavista.com). The newly translated terms were added to the query with the text of each language group (English, German, and French) connecting via a union (logical OR). Figure 1 shows a sample query from this run.

In addition to the minimal term mapping and/or expansion, we also increased the significance for a group of relevant terms using Lucene's "term boosting" function. For example, for the topic focusing on chest x-rays showing an enlarged heart; we increased the significance of documents that contained the terms, chest and x-ray and posteroanterior and cardiomegaly, while the default significance was used for documents that contained the terms, chest or x-ray or posteroanterior, or cardiomegaly. This strategy was designed to give a higher rank to the more relevant documents within a given search. Moreover, this approach attempted to improve the precision of the results from our first run. Similar to the OHSUauto run, we returned all images associated with the retrieved annotation.

```
(AP^2 PA^2 anteroposterior^2 posteroanterior^2 thoracic thorax cardiomegaly^3
heart coeur)
```

Fig. 1. Manual query for topic 12

Our third run (OHSUmanviz) used a combination of textual and visual retrieval methods. We took the image output from OHSUman and excluded all documents that were not retrieved by the University of Geneva "baseline" visual run (GE_M_4g.txt). In other words, we performed an intersection (logical AND) between the OHSUman and GE_M_4g.txt runs as a "combined" visual and semantic run.

Consistent with the ImageCLEF medical protocol, we used mean average precision (MAP) as our primary outcome measure. However, we also analyzed other measures output from trec_eval, in particular the precision at N images measures.

4 Results

Our automatic query run (OHSUauto) had the largest number of images returned for each topic. The MAP for this run was extremely low at 0.0403, which fell below the median (0.11) of the 9 submissions in the "text-only automated" category.

The manually modified queries run (OHSUman) for the most part returned large numbers of images. However, there were some topics for which it returned fewer images than the OHSUauto run. Two of these topics were those that focused on Alzheimer's disease and hand-drawn images of a person. This run was in the "text-only manual" category and achieved an MAP of 0.2116. Despite being the only submission in this category, this run scored above any run from the "text-only automatic" category and as such was the best text-only run.

When we incorporated visual retrieval data (OHSUmanviz), our queries returned the smallest number images for each topic. The intent was to improve precision of the results from the previous two techniques. This run was placed in the "text and visual manual" category, and achieved an MAP of 0.1601, which was the highest score in this category. This technique's performance was less than that of our manual query technique. Recall that both our manual and manual/visual techniques used the same textual queries, so the difference in the overall score was a result of the visual refinement.

Figure 2 illustrates the number of images returned by each of the techniques, while Figure 3 shows MAP per topic for each run. Even though the fully automatic query technique consistently returned the largest number of images on a per-query basis, this approach rarely outperformed the others. Whereas the manual query technique did not consistently return large numbers of images for each query, it did return a good proportion of relevant images for each query. The manual/visual query technique found a good proportion of relevant images but clearly eliminated some images that the text-only search found, resulting in decreased performance.

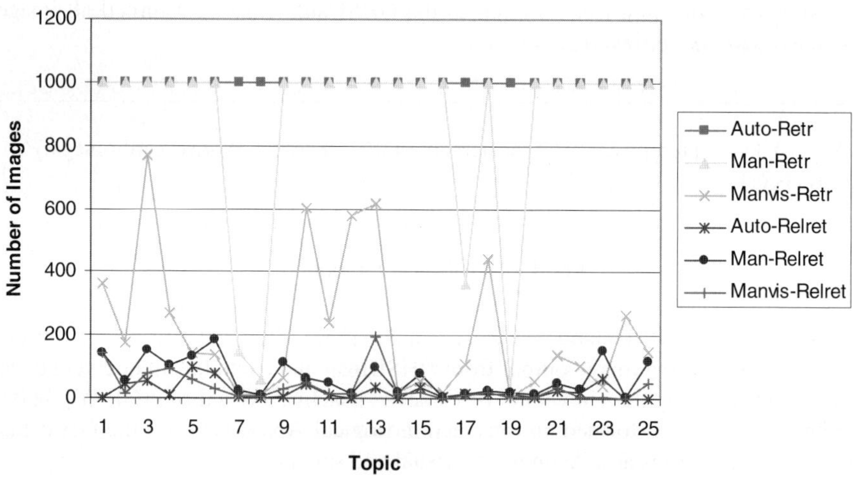

Fig. 2. Number of relevant images and retrieved relevant images for each of the three runs for each topic

Perhaps the most interesting result from all of our runs was comparing the performance based on MAP with precision at top of the output. Despite the overall lower MAP, the OHSUmanvis had better precision starting at five images and continuing to 30 images. The better MAP is explainable by the high precision across the remainder of the output (down to 1,000 images). However, this finding is significant by virtue of the fact that many real-world uses of image retrieval may have users who explore output solely in this range. Figure 4 shows precision at various levels of output, while Figure 5 shows a recall-precision curve comparing the two.

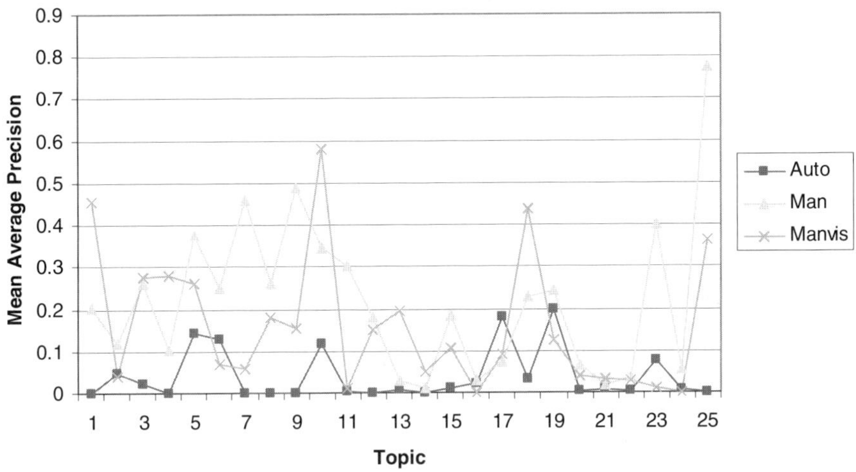

Fig. 3. Mean average precision for each of the three runs for each topic

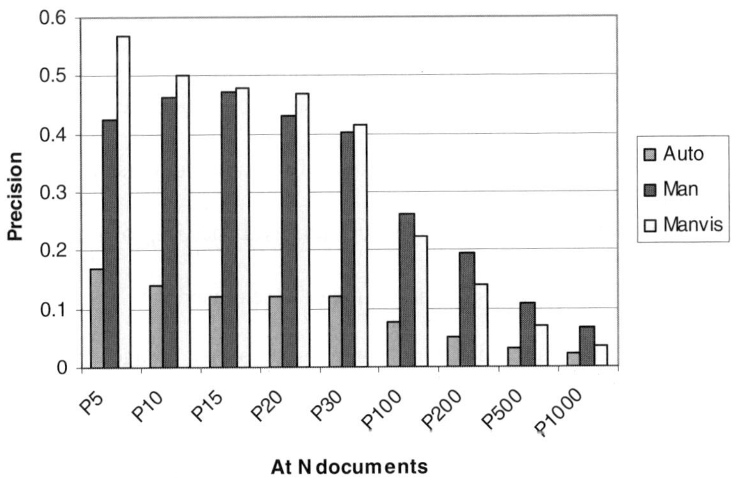

Fig. 4. Average of precision at 5, 10, 15, 20, 30, 100, 200, 500, and 1000 images for each run. The manual plus visual query run has higher precision down to 30 images retrieved, despite its lower mean average precision.

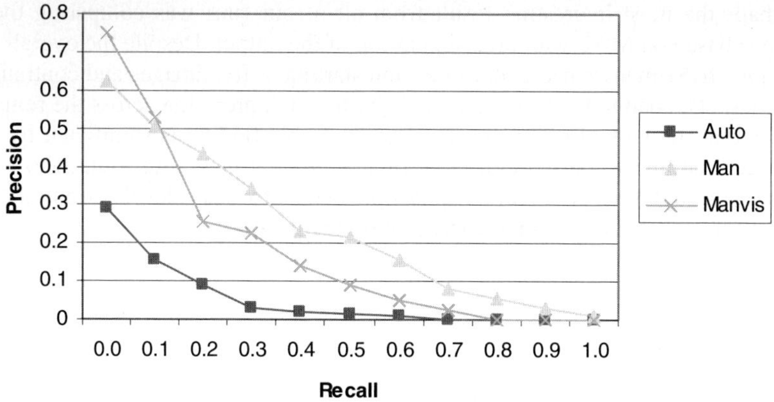

Fig. 5. Recall-precision curves for each run. The manual plus visual query run has a higher precision at low levels of recall (i.e., at the top of image output).

5 Conclusions

Our ImageCLEF medical track experiments showed that manual query modification and use of an automated translation tool provide benefit in retrieving relevant images. Filtering the output with findings from a baseline content-based approach diminished performance overall, but perhaps not in the part of the output most likely to be seen by real users, i.e., the top 30 images.

The experiments of our groups and others raise many questions about image retrieval:

- Which measures coming from automated retrieval evaluation experiments are most important for assessing systems in the hands of real users?
- How would text retrieval methods shown to be more effective in some domains (e.g., Okapi weighting) improve performance?
- How would better approaches to data fusion of semantic and visual queries impact performance?
- Are there methods of semantic and visual retrieval that improve performance in complementary manners?
- How much do these variations in output matter to real users?

Our future work also includes building a more robust image retrieval system proper, which will both simplify further experiments as well as give us the capability to employ real users in them. With such a system, users will be able to manually modify queries and/or provide translation. Additional work we are carrying out includes better elucidating the needs of those who use image retrieval systems based on a pilot study we have performed [6].

References

1. Clough, P., Müller, H., Deselaers, T., Grubinger, M., Lehmann, T., Jensen, J., Hersh W.: The CLEF 2005 cross-language image retrieval track. In: Springer Lecture Notes in Computer Science (LNCS), Vienna, Austria. (2006 - to appear)
2. Müller, H., Michoux, N., Bandon, D., Geissbuhler, A.: A review of content-based image retrieval systems in medical applications-clinical benefits and future directions. International Journal of Medical Informatics, **73** (2004) 1-23
3. Antani, S., Long, L., Thoma, G.R.: A biomedical information system for combined content-based retrieval of spine x-ray images and associated text information. Proceedings of the 3rd Indian Conference on Computer Vision, Graphics and Image Processing (ICVGIP 2002), Ahamdabad, India (2002)
4. Belkin, N., Cool, C., Croft, W.B., Callan, J.P.: Effect of multiple query representations on information retrieval system performance. In: Proceedings of the 16th Annual International ACM SIGIR Conference on Research and Development in Information Retrieval, Pittsburgh, PA. ACM Press (1993) 339-346
5. Cohen, A.M., Bhupatiraju, R.T., Hersh, W.: Feature generation, feature selection, classifiers, and conceptual drift for biomedical document triage, In: The Thirteenth Text Retrieval Conference: TREC 2004 (2004) http://trec.nist.gov/pubs/trec13/papers/ohsu-hersh.geo.pdf
6. Hersh, W., Jensen, J., Müller, H., Gorman, P., Ruch, P.: A qualitative task analysis of biomedical image use and retrieval. MUSCLE/ImageCLEF Workshop on Image and Video Retrieval Evaluation, Vienna, Austria (2005) http://medir.ohsu.edu/~hersh/muscle-05-image.pdf

Combining Textual and Visual Features for Image Retrieval

J.L. Martínez-Fernández[1], Julio Villena Román[1]
Ana M. García-Serrano[2], and José Carlos González-Cristóbal[3]

[1] Universidad Carlos III de Madrid
joseluis.martinez@uc3m.es, jvillena@it.uc3m.es
[2] Facultad de Informática, Universidad Politécnica de Madrid
agarcia@dia.fi.upm.es
[3] DAEDALUS - Data, Decisions and Language, S.A.
jgonzalez@daedalus.es

Abstract. This paper presents the approaches used by the MIRACLE team to image retrieval at ImageCLEF 2005. Text-based and content-based techniques have been tested, along with combination of both types of methods to improve image retrieval. The text-based experiments defined this year try to use semantic information sources, like thesaurus with semantic data or text structure. On the other hand, content-based techniques are not part of the main expertise of the MIRACLE team, but multidisciplinary participation in all aspects of information retrieval has been pursued. We rely on a publicly available image retrieval system (GIFT 4) when needed.

1 Introduction

ImageCLEF is the cross-language image retrieval track which was established in 2003 as part of the Cross Language Evaluation Forum (CLEF), a benchmarking event for multilingual information retrieval held annually since 2000. The scope of ImageCLEF is to collect and provide resources and encourage de exchange of ideas about image retrieval. Images are language independent by nature, but often they are accompanied by texts semantically related to the image (e.g. textual captions or metadata). Images can then be retrieved using primitive features based on their contents (e.g. visual exemplar) or abstract features expressed through text or a combination of both.

Originally, ImageCLEF focused specifically on evaluating the retrieval of images described by text captions using queries written in a different language, therefore having to deal with monolingual and bilingual image retrieval (multilingual retrieval was not possible as the document collection is only in one language) 17. Later, the scope of ImageCLEF widened and goals evolved to investigate the effectiveness of combining text and visual information for retrieval 9.

The MIRACLE team is made up of three university research groups located in Madrid (UPM, UC3M and UAM) along with DAEDALUS, a company founded in 1998 as a spin-off of two of these groups. DAEDALUS is a leading company in linguistic technologies in Spain and is the coordinator of the MIRACLE team. This is the third participation in CLEF 5, 10. As well as bilingual, monolingual and cross

C. Peters et al. (Eds.): CLEF 2005, LNCS 4022, pp. 680 – 691, 2006.

lingual tasks, the team has participated in the adhoc multilingual, Q&A, WebCLEF and GeoCLEF tracks.

This paper describes experiments performed in the bilingual adhoc and medical image retrieval tasks defined in ImageCLEF 2005. For the first task, a semantic driven approach has been tried. Semantic tools used have been: EuroWordnet 2 and structure of the textual image descriptions. A new method for semantic query expansion has been developed, centered on the computation of closeness among the nodes of the EuroWordnet tree, where each node corresponds to a word appearing in the query. An expansion method based on the same idea was previously described in 11. For the second task, different combinations of content-based and text-based subsystems have been tested, trying to improve the results of the content-based system with the addition of text retrieval.

The remainder of the paper is structured as follows: Section 2 describes the techniques and results obtained in the bilingual adhoc task; Section 3 explains the experiments defined for the medical image retrieval task; finally, Section 4 provides some conclusions and future directions to follow in image retrieval.

2 Bilingual Adhoc Task

This year, a special focus on semantics has been made for the bilingual adhoc task. Two main techniques have been developed: the first one, a semantic expansion algorithm, based on EuroWordnet, where the focus is to obtain a common path among the concept tree represented in EuroWordNet. The idea is to make a more fine-grained query expansion than including every synonym for each word in the query. Along with this expansion algorithm morphological information is also used to apply a set of simple rules to identify words introduced by negative particles (such as 'not', 'excluding', etc.) that must not appear in captions of images to be retrieved. The second technique was devoted to the construction of different indexes according to the fields used in image captions. Then several linguistic patterns were automatically built to recognize data included in one of these specialized indexes. These patterns were matched against the queries to focus the search process in some specific indexes. The following subsections describe these techniques.

2.1 Semantic Expansion Using EuroWordnet

EuroWordnet is a lexical database with semantic information in several languages. This resource includes, for a given language, different semantic relations among dictionary entries, also called *concepts*. These relations include: hyperonym, where links with more general concepts are defined, hyponym, where relations with more specific terms are included and synonym, where constructions grouping entries with the same meaning (named *synsets*) are built. All possible meanings for a given concept are part of the EuroWordnet data structure. It is worth mentioning that not all languages are equally covered by EuroWordNet. As can be seen, a tree graph can be built using these semantic relations, and the distance among concepts, i.e., the semantic similarity among concepts, in this tree can be used as a disambiguation method for the terms included in the query 11.

For example, *bank* is defined in EuroWordnet as "*a financial institution that accepts deposits and channels the money into lending activities*" and also as "*sloping land (especially the slope beside a body of water)*" along with eight more different senses. The question arising is: how can be the word *bank* disambiguated when used as part of a query? The answer considered in this work is: by means of the rest of the words appearing with *bank* in the query. That is, some of the synonyms for the words appearing with the word *bank* will overlap with the synonyms of *bank*. If it does not happen hyponyms and hyperonyms of the given words are considered, until some relations among the initial words are found. The senses which are not linked with the senses of other words appearing in the query expression can be discarded. Somehow, the main goal is to find one unique path through the EuroWordnet tree that joins all query words.

By applying this approach, a fewer number of synonyms are included in the expanded query if compared with a rough expansion, where every synonym of a word is included in the expanded query.

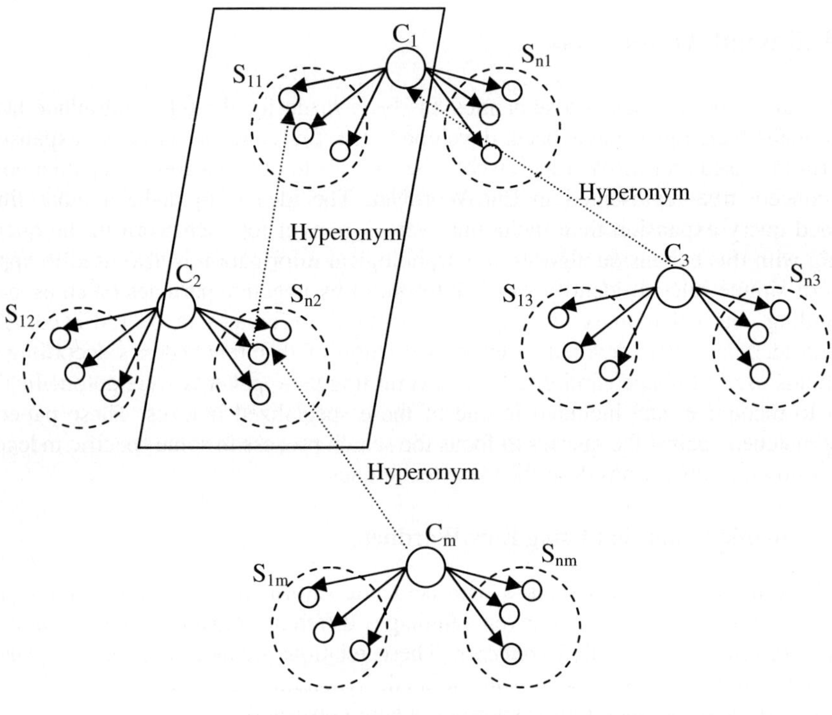

Fig. 1. Hyperonym relations in EuroWordnet

The described situation is depicted in Figure 1. The marked area corresponds to semantically related concepts, where the sense S_{n2} for the concept C_2 (appearing in the query) is related, by a hyperonym relation, with the sense S_{11} for the concept C_1 appearing in the query. In this way, concepts C_1 and C_2 can be expanded including words in S_{11} and S_{n2} sets, discarding the rest of senses, S_{n1} and S_{12}.

The described algorithm has been implemented using Ciao Prolog and an adaptation of the Dijkstra algorithm has been developed to compute the shortest way between two nodes. An efficient implementation of the expansion method has been pursued and, for this reason, not all possible paths among nodes are computed, a maximum of three jumps are allowed to limit execution times to an affordable value.

2.2 Exploiting the Structure of Image Captions

Captions supplied for the St. Andrews image collection are divided in fields, each of them containing specific information such as short title, location, etc. Image textual descriptions are composed of a total of 9 fields. Taking into account this structure, several indexes have been defined, one containing only image descriptions, another one with short title, one more with the photographer, another one with the places shown in the images, one with the dates when the pictures were taken and the last one with the proper nouns that have been identified in the image caption. From data available of previous campaigns, linguistic patterns have been automatically identified which allow the identification of information contained in specific caption fields. These patterns are matched against the query captions trying to determine which of the indexes should be searched or, in other way, which indexes can be discarded during the search process. Some previous work in this line is described in 12, but using named entities to decide which index should be searched. The Xapian[1] search engine has been used to index text representations for the image captions and the ability for this search engine to perform search processes combining independent indexes has been used.

This information distribution allows for the assignment of semantic interpretation for each field and, with a minimum processing for the query, it is possible to search a specific entity over the right index. For example, several queries ask for images taken by a predefined photographer; a simple processing of the query allows for the identification of structures like "... taken by ..." where the name to be searched can be extracted and located over the picture author index. This strategy allows for a fine-grained search process that is supposed to provide better precision figures.

2.3 Evaluation Results

Results produced by the different experiments are grouped according to the languages involved. Table 1 shows the Mean Average Precision (MAP) for the monolingual experiments presented this year by the Miracle group. All the submission IDs shown in the table begin with the prefix 'imir', and the rest of the identifier is built as follows:

- The first two letters denote the field of the topic used in the experiment: 't0', when only the query title is used, 'd0', when only the narrative field is used, and 'dt', when both title and narrative are used to build the query for the search engine.
- The next part of the identifier denotes the linguistic processing applied to the query: 'base', when the processes for the baseline are applied (i.e.: parsing, stopword filtering, special characters substitution and lowercasing and stemming);

[1] Xapian. On line `http://www.xapian.org/`

's', when a morphosyntactical analysis for the query is performed; 'e', when the semantic expansion based on EuroWordnet is applied; 'o', when the operator to combine the expanded words is OR; 'a' when the operator to join expanded query words is a combination of OR operators with AND operators; 'pn', when proper nouns are identified in the text.

- The following part identifies which index (or indexes) is (are) used to retrieve images. Possible values are: 't0', if only the titles of the captions are indexed, 'd0', when only the descriptions for the captions are searched, 'dt', when both titles and descriptions constitute a unique index, 'attr', if indexes for the different caption fields are used (the identified fields are: text, author, date, place), and finally 'allf', when a unique index with the content of all fields is used.
- The next two letters identify the language in which the query is supplied. In monolingual experiments it is English, but for bilingual experiments it can it can identify one from 22 different languages (Bulgarian, Croatian, Czech, Dutch, English, Finnish, Filipino, French, German, Greek, Hungarian, Italian, Japanese, Norwegian, Polish, Portuguese, Romanian, Russian, Spanish - Latin America, Spanish - Spain, Swedish, Turkish and Simplified Chinese.
- Finally, the last two letters identify the language in which the image captions collection is written. At this moment, the target language is always English.

The best result is obtained when the query string, built taken only the topic title, is searched against the combination of attribute indexes (text, place, author, date). As a

Table 1. Mean Average Precision for monolingual runs

Run	MAP
imirt0attren	0.3725
imirt0allfen	0.3506
imirt0based0enen	0.3456
imirt0basedtenen	0.3286
imirt0eod0enen	0.2262
imirt0eotdenen	0.2183
imirtdseod0enen	0.1914
imirtdseotdenen	0.1851
imirt0baset0enen	0.1798
imirt0eot0enen	0.1405
imirtdseot0enen	0.1254
imirtdbased0enen	0.1065
imirtdbasedtenen	0.1039
imird0based0enen	0.1010
imird0basedtenen	0.0972
imirtdbaset0enen	0.0555
imird0baset0enen	0.0545

previous step, the query was processed with a basic procedure (parsing, normalizing words, stopword removal and stemming). This experiment receives the identifier 'imirt0attren'. It should be mentioned that, due to a programming error, duplicate elements were included in the results list, which could blur precision figures. These duplicate entries were deleted (but not substituted), lowering precision figures for the experiments. Besides, there is no a great difference between the MAP of the best experiment, 'imirt0attren', 37%, and the MAP of the next one 'imirt0allfen', 35%, where a unique index is built with the information contained in all the fields included in image captions.

Results for bilingual experiments are also very interesting. In Table 2, the differences among experiments for each language can be noticed. The MAP precision values for the best result for each language are compared. The best bilingual MAP result is 74% of English monolingual, and it is reached for the Portuguese language. Comparing with the best monolingual result, a difference of around 7% in MAP value can be seen.

Table 2. Mean Average Precision for bilingual runs

Run	Query Language	MAP	%
imirt0attren	English	0.3725	100.0%
imirt0attrpt	Portuguese	0.3073	74.3%
imirt0attrdu	Dutch	0.3029	73.3%
imirt0allfsl	Spanish (Latin America)	0.2969	71.8%
imirt0attrfr	French	0.2797	67.6%
imirt0attrja	Japanese	0.2717	65.7%
imirt0attrge	German	0.2559	61.9%
imirt0allfru	Russian	0.2514	60.8%
imirt0attrit	Italian	0.2468	59.7%
imirt0allfgr	Greek	0.2436	58.9%
imirt0attrsp	Spanish (European)	0.2304	55.7%
imirt0allftk	Turkish	0.2225	53.8%
imirt0attrsw	Swedish	0.1965	47.5%
imirt0allfzh	Chinese (simplified)	0.1936	46.8%
imirt0attrno	Norwegian	0.1610	38.9%
imirt0attrpo	Polish	0.1558	37.7%
imirt0allffl	Filipino	0.1486	35.9%
imirt0attrro	Romanian	0.1429	34.6%
imirt0allfbu	Bulgarian	0.1293	31.3%
imirt0allfcz	Czech	0.1219	29.5%
imirt0attrcr	Croatian	0.1187	28.7%
imirt0attrfi	Finnish	0.1114	26.9%
imirt0allfhu	Hungarian	0.0968	23.4%

As already tested in previous campaigns, the translation process between languages introduces a lot of noise, decreasing the precision of the retrieval process. The process followed in the 'imirt0attrpt' experiment is equivalent to the one applied in the best monolingual run, but including a previous translation step using online translators 31415. That is, the topic title is translated from Portuguese into English and then parsed, normalized, stopwords are removed and the rest of words are stemmed. The words forming the query are ORed and searched against the combination of attribute indexes (text, place, author, date). Of course, the previously explained problem with duplicate results in the final list also applies to the bilingual runs submitted.

The MIRACLE team was the only participant for some target languages such as Bulgarian, Croatian, Czech, Filipino, Finnish, Hungarian, Norwegian, Polish, Romanian and Turkish.

3 Medical Image Retrieval Task

In this task (referred as ImageCLEFmed), example images are used to perform a search against a medical image database consisting of images such as scans and x-rays 6 to find similar images. Each medical image or a group of images represents an illness, and case notes in English or French are associated with each illness.

For this purpose, we focused our experiments on fully automatic retrieval, avoiding any manual feedback, and submitted runs both using only visual features for retrieval (content-based retrieval) and also runs using visual features and text (combination of content-based and text-based retrieval).

To isolate from the content-based retrieval part of the process, we relied on GIFT (GNU Image Finding Tool) 4, a publicly available content-based image retrieval system which was developed under the GNU license and allows to perform query by example on images, using an image as the starting point for the search process. GIFT relies entirely on visual information such as colour, shape and texture and thus it doesn't require the collection to be annotated. It also provides a mechanism to improve query results by relevance feedback.

Our approach is based on the multidisciplinary combination of GIFT content-based searches with text-based retrieval techniques. Our system consists of three parts: the content-based retrieval component (mainly GIFT), the text-based search engine and the merging component, which combines the results from the others to provide the final results. We submitted 13 different runs to be evaluated by the task coordinators, which can be divided in two groups:

- *Content-based retrieval*, which includes experiments using GIFT with two different configurations: with and without feedback. When feedback is used, each visual query is introduced into the system to obtain the list of images which are more similar to the visual query. Then the top N results are added to the original visual query to build a new visual query which is again introduced into the system to obtain the final list of results.
- *Content-based and text-based mixed retrieval*, including experiments focused on testing whether the text-based image retrieval could improve the analysis of the content of the image, or vice versa. We were interested in determining how text and image attributes can be combined to enhance image retrieval, in this case, in

the medical domain. As a first step, all the case annotations are indexed using a text-based retrieval engine. Natural language processing techniques are applied before indexing. An adhoc language-specific (for English, German and French) parser 16 is used to identify different classes of alphanumerical tokens such as dates, proper nouns, acronyms, etc., as well as recognising common compound words. Text is tokenized, stemmed 1316 and stop word filtered (for the three languages).

Only one index is created, combining keywords in the three different languages. Two different text-based retrieval engines were used. One was Lucene 8, with the results provided by the task organizers. The other engine was KSite 7, fully developed by DAEDALUS, which offers the possibility to use a probabilistic (BM25) model or a vector space model for the indexing strategy. Only the probabilistic model was used in our experiments. The combination strategy consists on reordering the results from the content-based retrieval using a text-based retrieval. For each ImageCLEFmed query, a multilingual textual query is built with the English, German and French queries. The list of relevant images from the content-based retrieval is reordered, moving to the beginning of the list those images which belong to a case that is in the list of top-1000 cases. The rest of the images remain in the end of the list.

3.1 Evaluation Results

Relevance assessments have been performed by experienced medical students and medical doctors as described in 1. The experiments included in Table 3 have been performed as follows:

- *miraqbase.qtop:* this experiment consists on a content-based-only retrieval using GIFT. Initially the complete image database was indexed in a single collection using GIFT, down-scaling each image to 32x32 pixels. For each ImageCLEFmed query, a visual query is made up of all the images contained in the ImageCLEFmed query. Then, this visual query is introduced into the system to obtain the list of more relevant images (i.e., images which are more similar to those included in the visual query), along with the corresponding relevance values. Although different search algorithms can be integrated as plug-ins in GIFT, finally only the provided separate normalization algorithm has been used in our experiments.
- *mirarf5.qtop:* this run takes the 5 most relevant images for feedback, each one with a value of 1 for its relevance in the visual query. The relevance in the visual query for the original images remains 1.
- *mirarf5.1.qtop:* the same as *mirarf5.qtop* but using a value of 0.5 for the relevance in query of feedback images. The relevance in query for the original images remains 1.
- *mirarf5.2.qtop:* the same as *mirarf5.qtop* but using a value of 0.5 for the relevance in query of the original images.

As shown in Table 3, the best result for the content-based runs was obtained with the base experiment, which means that relevance feedback has failed to improve the

Table 3. Evaluation of content-based runs

Run	MAP	%
mirabase.qtop	0.0942	100.0%
mirarf5.1.qtop	0.0942	100.0%
mirarf5.qtop	0.0941	99.8%
mirarf5.2.qtop	0.0934	99.1%

results (neither to worsen them). This may be due to an incorrect choice of the parameters, but this has to be further studied.

Apart from MIRACLE, other 8 groups participated in this year's evaluation in the content-based-only runs. Only one group is above us in the group ranking, although their average precision is much better than ours. Our pragmatic approach using a "standard" publicly available content-based retrieval engine such as GIFT has proved to be a better approach than other presumably more complex techniques. We still have to test if another selection of indexing parameters (different from image down-scaling to 32x32 pixels and separate normalization algorithm) may provide better results.

For the mixed retrieval experiments, the 10 different runs included in Table 4 were obtained as follows:

- *mirabasefil.qtop, mirarf5fil.qtop, mirarf5.1fil.qtop, mirarf5.2fil.qtop:* these runs consisted on the combination of content-based-only runs with the text-based retrieval obtained with KSite.
- *mirabasefil2.qtop, mirarf5fil2.qtop, mirarf5.1fil2.qtop, mirarf5.2fil2.qtop:* the same experiment, but using Lucene.
- Two other experiments were developed to test if there was any difference in results when using our own content-based GIFT index or using the medGIFT results provided by the task organizers. So, medGIFT was used as the starting point and then the same combination method as described before was applied.
  - *mirabase2fil.qtop*: medGIFT results filtered with text-based KSite results
  - *mirabase2fil2.qtop:* medGIFT results filtered with Lucene results

Results of the content-based and text-based mixed retrieval runs are included in Table 4. The use of relevance feedback provides slightly better precision values. Considering the best runs, the optimum choice seems to be to assume 1.0 for the relevance of the top 5 results and reduce the relevance of the original query images.

Table 4 also shows that the results are better with our own text-based search engine than using Lucene (all runs offer better precision values), at least with the adopted combination strategy. This difference could be attributed to better language dependent pre-processing and removal of stop words.

It is interesting to observe that the worst combination is to take both results provided by the task organizers (content-based medGIFT results and text-based Lucene results), with a performance decrease of 15%.

Table 4. Comparison of mixed retrieval runs

Run	MAP	%	Text Retrieval Engine
mirarf5.2fil.qtop	0.1173	100.0%	KSite
mirarf5fil.qtop	0.1171	99.8%	KSite
mirabasefil.qtop	0.1164	99.2%	KSite
mirabase2fil.qtop	0.1162	99.0%	KSite
mirarf5.1fil.qtop	0.1159	98.8%	KSite
mirarf5fil2.qtop	0.1028	87.6%	Lucene
mirarf5.2fil2.qtop	0.1027	87.6%	Lucene
mirarf5.1fil2.qtop	0.1019	86.9%	Lucene
mirabasefil2.qtop	0.0998	85.1%	Lucene
mirabase2fil2.qtop	0.0998	85.1%	Lucene

Comparing content-based runs with the mixed runs, Table 5 shows[2] that the combination of both types of retrieval offers better performance and even the worst mixed run is better than the best content-based only run. This actually proves that text-based image retrieval can be used to improve the content-based only retrieval, with much superior performance.

Apart from MIRACLE, other 6 groups participated in this year's evaluation in the content-based and text-based runs. In this case, our position in the table shows that the submissions from other groups clearly surpassed our results. Anyway, these results are not bad for us, considering that our main research field is not image analysis.

Table 5. Comparison of content-based and mixed retrieval strategies

Run	MAP	%
mirarf5.2fil.qtop	0.1173	100.0%
mirabase2fil2.qtop	0.0998	85.1%
mirabase.qtop	0.0942	80.0%

It is also interesting to note that most groups managed to improve their results with mixed approaches over the content-based only runs. This is especially visible for the NCTU group, with an improvement from 0.06 to 0.23 (+355%) in MAP.

4 Conclusions

The experiments performed in ImageCLEF 2005 point out some conclusions: regarding to bilingual retrieval, the application of semantic centered techniques must be further tested to assess their usefulness. Obtained results are not conclusive, our best monolingual result is 5% under the best mean average precision obtained by the

[2] The last column in this table shows the difference, in percentage, from the best result.

Chinese University of Hong Kong group, but an interesting research line has been opened. On the other hand, the quality of the translation is decisive for the quality of the retrieval process, as can be seen according to the average precision values for different languages. The degree of development of the translation tools applied 31415 is not the same for all languages and, for those with lower coverage, such as Finnish or Hungarian, MAP figures fall down. Regarding techniques combining text-based with content-based image retrieval, average precision figures can be dramatically improved if textual features are used to support content-based retrieval.

Future works will be focused on improving the semantic expansion algorithm, combined with the use of semantic representations of sentences directed by shallow syntactic information. Regarding content-based retrieval techniques, different indexing features will be tested, along with the application of better quality text-based retrieval techniques.

Acknowledgements

This work has been partially supported by the Spanish R+D National Plan, by means of the project RIMMEL (Multilingual and Multimedia Information Retrieval, and its Evaluation), TIN2004-07588-C03-01. Special mention to our colleagues of the MIRACLE team should be done (in alphabetical order): Francesco Carbone, Michelangelo Castagnone, Juan José Fernández, Ana González-Ledesma, José Mª Guirao-Miras, Sara Lana-Serrano, Paloma Martínez-Fernández, Ángel Martínez-González, Antonio Moreno-Sandoval and César de Pablo-Sánchez.

References

1. Clough, Paul; Müller, Henning; Deselaers, Thomas; Grubinger, Michael; Lehmann, Thomas M.; Jensen, Jeffery; Hersh, William: The CLEF 2005 Cross-Language Image Retrieval Track, Proceedings of the Cross Language Evaluation Forum 2005, Springer Lecture Notes in Computer science, 2006 - to appear
2. "Eurowordnet: Building a Multilingual Database with Wordnets for several European Languages". On line `http://www.let.uva.nl/ewn`. March (1996)
3. FreeTranslation. Free text translator. On line `http://www.freetranslation.com` [Visited 20/07/2005].
4. GIFT: The GNU Image-Finding Tool. On line `http://www.gnu.org/software/gift/` [Visited 15/11/2005]
5. Goñi-Menoyo, José M; González, José C.; Martínez-Fernández, José L.; and Villena, J.: MIRACLE's Hybrid Approach to Bilingual and Monolingual Information Retrieval. CLEF 2004 proceedings (Peters, C. et al., Eds.). Lecture Notes in Computer Science, vol. 3491, pp. 188-199. Springer, 2005
6. Goodrum, A.A.: Image Information Retrieval: An Overview of Current Research. Informing Science, Vol 3 (2) 63-66 (2000)
7. KSite [Agente Corporativo]. On line `http://www.daedalus.es/ProdKSiteAC-E.php` [Visited 15/11/2005]
8. Lucene. On line `http://lucene.apache.org` [Visited 15/11/2005]

9. Martínez-Fernández, José L.; García-Serrano, Ana; Villena, J. and Méndez-Sáez, V.: MIRACLE approach to ImageCLEF 2004: merging textual and content-based Image Retrieval. CLEF 2004 proceedings (Peters, C. et al., Eds.). Lecture Notes in Computer Science, vol. 3491. Springer, 2005
10. Martínez, José L.; Villena, Julio; Fombella, Jorge; G. Serrano, Ana; Martínez, Paloma; Goñi, José M.; and González, José C.: MIRACLE Approaches to Multilingual Information Retrieval: A Baseline for Future Research. Comparative Evaluation of Multilingual Information Access Systems (Peters, C; Gonzalo, J.; Brascher, M.; and Kluck, M., Eds.). Lecture Notes in Computer Science, vol. 3237, pp. 210-219. Springer, 2004
11. Montoyo, A.: Método basado en marcas de especificidad para WSD, In Proceedings of SEPLN, nº 24, September 2000
12. Peinado, V., Artiles, J., López-Ostenero, F., Gonzalo, J., Verdejo, F.: UNED at ImageCLEF 2004: Detecting Named Entities and Noun Phrases for Automatic Query Expansion and Structuring, Lecture Notes in Computer Science, Volume 3491, Aug 2005, Pages 643 - 652
13. Porter, Martin: Snowball stemmers. On line `http:// www.snowball.tartarus.org`. [Visited 15/11/2005]
14. SYSTRAN Software Inc., USA. SYSTRAN 5.0 translation resources. On line `http:// www.systransoft.com` [Visited 13/07/2005].
15. Translation Experts Ltd. InterTrans translation resources. On line `http:// www.tranexp.com` [Visited 28/07/2005]
16. University of Neuchatel. Page of resources for CLEF. On line `http:// www.unine.ch/info/clef/` [Visited 15/11/2005]
17. Villena, Julio; Martínez, José L.; Fombella, Jorge; G. Serrano, Ana; Ruiz, Alberto; Martínez, Paloma; Goñi, José M.; and González, José C.: Image Retrieval: The MIRACLE Approach. Comparative Evaluation of Multilingual Information Access Systems (Peters, C; Gonzalo, J.; Brascher, M.; and Kluck, M., Eds.). Lecture Notes in Computer Science, vol. 3237, pp. 621-630. Springer, 2004

Supervised Machine Learning Based Medical Image Annotation and Retrieval in ImageCLEFmed 2005

Md. Mahmudur Rahman[1], Bipin C. Desai[1], and Prabir Bhattacharya[2]

[1] Dept. of Computer Science, Concordia University, Canada
[2] Institute for Information Systems Engineering, Concordia University, Canada*

Abstract. This paper presents the methods and experimental results for the automatic medical image annotation and retrieval task of ImageCLEFmed 2005. A supervised machine learning approach to associate low-level image features with their high level visual and/or semantic categories is investigated. For automatic image annotation, the input images are presented as a combined feature vector of texture, edge and shape features. A multi-class classifier based on pairwise coupling of several binary support vector machine is trained on these inputs to predict the categories of test images. For visual only retrieval, a combined feature vector of color, texture and edge features is utilized in low dimensional PCA sub-space. Based on the online category prediction of query and database images by the classifier, pre-computed category specific first and second order statistical parameters are utilized in a Bhattacharyya distance measure. Experimental results of both image annotation and retrieval are reported in this paper.

1 Introduction

During the last decade, there have been an overwhelming research interests in medical image classification or annotation and retrieval from different communities [1,2]. Medical images of various modalities (X-ray, CT, MRI, Ultrasound etc.) constitute an important source of anatomical and functional information for the diagnosis of diseases, medical research and education. To search or annotate these large image collections effectively and efficiently poses significant technical challenges, and hence the necessity of constructing intelligent image retrieval and recognition systems. One of the major thrust in this direction is ImageCLEFmed, which is a part of the Cross Language Evaluation Forum (CLEF) [3], a benchmark event for multilingual information retrieval. The main goal of ImageCLEFmed is to create a standard environment for evaluation and improvement medical images retrieval from heterogeneous collections containing images as well as text. The 2005 meeting of ImageCLEFmed focused on two task: image annotation and retrieval. This is the first participation of our research group (CINDI) in ImageCLEF and we have participated in both tasks.

* This work was partially supported by NSERC, IDEAS and Canada Research Chair grants.

C. Peters et al. (Eds.): CLEF 2005, LNCS 4022, pp. 692–701, 2006.

2 Image Annotation Task

In the ImageCLEFmed 2005 automatic image annotation task, the main aim is to determine how well current techniques can identify image modality, body orientation, body region, and biological system examined based on the images in IRMA data set. Here, we investigate a supervised machine learning approach to categorize or annotate images. In supervised classification, we are given a collection of labeled images (training samples), and the problem is to label newly encountered, yet unlabeled images (test samples). Each instance in the training set contains category or class specific labels and several image feature descriptors in the form of a combined feature vector. In this work, effective texture, edge and shape descriptors are used to represent image content at global level and train a multi-class classification system based on several binary support vector machine (SVM) classifiers. The goal of the SVM classification system is to produce a model which will predict target value or category of images with highest probability or confidence in the testing set.

2.1 Feature Representation

The IRMA collection contained mainly monochrome or gray level medical images with specific layout. Hence, we characterize images by texture, edge and shape features, thereby ignoring color information totally. These features are incorporated in a combined feature vector and used as input to the classification system.

Spatially localized texture information are extracted from the gray level co-occurrence matrix (GLCM) [4]. A GLCM is defined as a sample of the joint probability density of the gray levels of two pixels separated by a given displacement d and angle θ. The $G \times G$ gray level co-occurrence matrix p for a displacement vector $d = (dx, dy)$ is defined as [4]:

$$p(i,j) = |((r,s),(t,v)) : (I(r,s) = i, I(t,v) = j)| \tag{1}$$

where $(r,s),(t,v) \in N \times N$, and $(t,v) = (r+dx)(s+dy)$.

Typically, the information stored in a GLCM is sparse and it is often useful to consider a number of GLCM's, one for each relative position of interest. In order to obtain efficient descriptors, the information contained in GLCM is traditionally condensed in a few statistical features. Four GLCM's for four different orientations (horizontal 0°,vertical 90°, and two diagonals 45° and 135°) are obtained and normalized to the entries [0,1] by dividing each entry by total number of pixels. Haralick has proposed a number of useful texture features that can be computed from the GLCM [4]. Higher order features, such as energy, entropy, contrast, homogeneity and maximum probability are measured based on each GLCM to form a five-dimensional feature vector. Finally, a twenty dimensional feature vector is obtained by concatenating the feature vectors of each GLCM for four different orientations.

To represent the edge feature on a global level, a histogram of edge direction is constructed. The edge information contained in the images is processed and generated by using the Canny edge detection algorithm [5] (with $\sigma = 1$, Gaussian masks of size = 9, low threshold = 1, and high threshold = 255). The corresponding edge directions are quantized into 72 bins of 5° each produces a 72 dimensional edge vector. Scale invariance is achieved by normalizing this histograms with respect to the number of edge points in the image.

The global shape of an image is presented in terms of seven invariant moments [6]. These features are invariant under rotation, scale, translation, and reflection of images and have been widely used in a number of applications due to their invariance properties. For a 2-D image, $f(x, y)$, the central moment of order $(p + q)$ is given by

$$\mu_{pq} = \sum_{x} \sum_{y} (x - \overline{x})^p (y - \overline{y})^q f(x, y) \tag{2}$$

Seven moment invariants $(M_1, \cdots, M_7)$ based on the second and third order moments are extracted by utilizing μ_{pq} [6]. $M_1, \cdots, M_6$ are invariant under rotation and reflection, whereas M_7 is invariant only in its absolute magnitude under a reflection.

If f_{t}, f_{e}, and f_{s} are the texture, edge and shape feature vector of an image respectively, then the composite feature vector is formed by simple concatenation of each individual feature vector as $F_{\text{combined}} = (f_{\text{t}} + f_{\text{e}} + f_{\text{s}}) \in \mathbb{R}^d$, where d is the sum of individual feature vector dimension (20 for texture, 72 for edge, 7 for shape, and in total of 99). Thus, the input space for our SVM classifiers is a 99-dimensional space, and each image in the training set corresponds to a point in this space.

2.2 Category Prediction with Multi-class SVM

Support vector machine (SVM) is an emerging machine learning technology which has been used successfully in content-based image retrieval(CBIR) [7]. Given training data $(\boldsymbol{x}_1, \ldots, \boldsymbol{x}_n)$ that are vectors in space $\boldsymbol{x}_i \in \mathbb{R}^d$ and their labels $(y_1, \ldots, y_n)$ where $y_i \in (+1, -1)^n$, the general form of the binary linear classification function is

$$g(x) = \boldsymbol{w} \cdot \boldsymbol{x} + b \tag{3}$$

which corresponds to a separating hyper plane

$$\boldsymbol{w} \cdot \boldsymbol{x} + b = 0 \tag{4}$$

where $\boldsymbol{x}$ is an input vector, $\boldsymbol{w}$ is a weight vector, and b is a bias. The goal of SVM is to find the parameters $\boldsymbol{w}$ and b for the optimal hyper plane to maximize the geometric margin $\frac{2}{||\boldsymbol{w}||}$ between the hyper planes, subject to the solution of the following optimization problem [8]:

$$\min_{\boldsymbol{w}, b, \xi} \quad \frac{1}{2}\boldsymbol{w}^T\boldsymbol{w} + C\sum_{i=1}^{n} \xi_i \tag{5}$$

subject to

$$y_i(\boldsymbol{w}^T\phi(\boldsymbol{x}_i)+b) \geq 1-\xi_i \tag{6}$$

where $\xi_i \geq 0$ and $C > 0$ is the penalty parameter of the error term. Here training vectors $\boldsymbol{x}_i$ are mapped into a high dimensional space by the non linear mapping function $\phi : \mathrm{I\!R}^d \rightarrow \mathrm{I\!R}^f$, where $f > d$ or f could even be infinite. Both the optimization problem and its solution can be represented by the inner product. Hence,

$$\boldsymbol{x}_i \cdot \boldsymbol{x}_j \rightarrow \phi(\boldsymbol{x}_i)^T\phi(\boldsymbol{x}_j) = K(\boldsymbol{x}_i, \boldsymbol{x}_j) \tag{7}$$

where K is a kernel function. The SVM classification function is given by [7]:

$$f(\boldsymbol{x}) = \mathrm{sign}\left(\sum_{i=1}^{n} \alpha_i y_i K(\boldsymbol{x}_i, \boldsymbol{x}) + b\right) \tag{8}$$

A number of methods have been proposed for extension to multi-class problem to separate L mutually exclusive classes essentially by solving many two-class problems and combining their predictions in various ways [7]. One technique, known as pairwise coupling (PWC) or "one-vs-one" is to construct SVMs between all possible pairs of classes. This method uses $L \cdot (L-1)/2$ binary classifiers, each of which provides a partial decision for classifying a data point. PWC then combines the output of all classifiers to form a class prediction. During testing, each of the $L \cdot (L-1)/2$ classifier votes for one class. The winning class is the one with the largest number of accumulated votes. Though the voting procedure requires just pairwise decisions, it only predicts a class label. However, in many scenarios probability estimates are required. In our experiments, the probability estimate approach is used[9]. This produces a ranking of the K classes, with each class assigned a confidence or probability score for each image. This technique is used for the implementation of the multi-class SVM by using the LIBSVM software package [10].

There are 57 categories of images provided in the training set for the image annotation task. So, we define a set of 57 labels where each label characterizes the representative semantics of an image category. Class labels along with feature vectors are generated from all images at the training stage. In testing stage, each un annotated image is classified against the 57 categories using PWC or "one-vs-one" technique. This produces a ranking of the 57 categories, with each category assigned a confidence or probability score to each image. The confidence represents the weight of a label or category in the overall description of an image and the class with the highest confidence is considered to be the class of the image.

3 Image Retrieval Task

In the image retrieval task, we have experimented with a visual only approach; example images are used to perform a search against four different data sets to find similar images based on visual attributes (color, texture, etc.). Currently, most CBIR systems are similarity-based, where similarity between query and target images in a database is measured by some form of distance metrics in feature space [11]. However, retrieval systems generally conduct this similarity matching on a very high-dimensional feature space without any semantic interpretation or paying sufficient attention to the underlying distribution of the feature space. High- dimensional feature vectors not only increase the computational complexity in similarity matching and indexing, but also increase the logical database size. For many frequently used visual features in medical images, their category specific distributions are available. In this case, it is possible to extract a set of low-level features (e.g., color, texture, shape, etc.) to predict semantic categories of each image by identifying its class assignment using a classifier. Thus, an image can be best characterized by exploiting the information of feature distribution from its semantic category.

In the image retrieval task, we have investigated a category based adaptive statistical similarity measure technique on the low-dimensional feature space. For this, we utilized principal component analysis (PCA) for dimension reduction and multi-class SVM for online category prediction of query and database images. Hence, category-specific statistical parameters in low-dimensional feature space can be exploited by the statistical distance measure in real time similarity matching.

3.1 Feature Extraction and Representation in PCA Sub-space

Images in four data sets (CASImage, PathoPic, MIR and Peir) contain both color and gray level images for retrieval evaluation. Hence, color, texture and edge features are extracted for image representation at the global level. As color feature, a 108-dimensional color histogram is created in vector form on hue, saturation, and value (HSV) color space. In HSV, the colors correlates well and can be matched in a way that is consistent with human perception. In this work, HSV is uniformly quantized into twelve bins for hue (each bin consisting of a range of $30°$), three bins for saturation and three bins for value, which results in $12 \cdot 3 \cdot 3 = 108$ bins for color histogram. Many medical images of different categories can be distinguished via their homogeneous texture and global edge characteristics. Hence, global texture and edge features are also extracted as measured for image annotation.

As the dimensions of combined feature vector (108 (color)+ 20 (texture) + 72 (edge) = 200) is large, we need to apply some dimension reduction technique to reduce the computational complexity and logical database size. Moreover, if the training samples used to estimate the statistical parameters are smaller compared to the size of feature dimension, then there could be inaccuracy or singularity for second order (covariance matrix) parameter estimation. The problem of selecting most representative feature attributes is commonly known as dimension reduction. It has been examined by principal component analysis (PCA) [12]. The basic idea of PCA is to find m linearly transformed components so that they explain the maximum amount of variances in the input data. The mathematical steps used to describe the method is as follows:

Given a set of N feature vectors (training samples) $\boldsymbol{x}_i \in \mathbb{R}^d, i = (1, \cdots, N)$, the mean vector μ and covariance matrix C is estimated as

$$\mu = \frac{1}{N}\sum_{i=1}^{N} \boldsymbol{x}_i \quad \text{and} \quad C = \frac{1}{N}\sum_{i=1}^{N}(\boldsymbol{x}_i - \mu)(\boldsymbol{x}_i - \mu)^T \tag{9}$$

Let ν_i and λ_i be the eigenvectors and the eigenvalues of C respectively, then they satisfy the following:

$$\lambda_i = \sum_{i=1}^{N}(\nu_i^T(\boldsymbol{x}_i - \mu))^2 \tag{10}$$

Here, $\sum_{i=1}^{N} \lambda_i$ accounts for the total variance of the original feature vectors set. The PCA method tries to approximate the original feature space using an m-dimensional feature vector, that is using m largest eigenvalues account for a large percentage of variance, where typically $m \ll \min(\mathrm{d}, \mathrm{N})$. These m eigenvectors span a subspace, where $\boldsymbol{V} = [\boldsymbol{v}_1, \boldsymbol{v}_2, \cdots, \boldsymbol{v}_m]$ is the $(d \times m)$-dimensional matrix that contains orthogonal basis vectors of the feature space in its columns. The $m \times d$ transformation $\boldsymbol{V}^T$ transforms the original feature vector from $\mathbb{R}^d \rightarrow \mathbb{R}^m$. That is

$$\boldsymbol{V}^T(\boldsymbol{x}_i - \mu) = \boldsymbol{y}_i \tag{11}$$

where $\boldsymbol{y}_i \in \mathbb{R}^m$ and kth component of the $\boldsymbol{y}_i$ vector is called the kth principal component (PC) of the original feature vector $\boldsymbol{x}_i$. So, the feature vector in the original $\mathbb{R}^d$ space for query and database images can be projected on to the $\mathbb{R}^m$ space via the transformation of $\boldsymbol{V}^T$ [12]. This technique is applied to the composite feature vector, and the feature dimension for subsequent SVM training and similarity matching is reduced.

3.2 Adaptive Statistical Distance Measure

Statistical distance measure, defined as the distances between two probability distributions, finds its uses in many research areas in pattern recognition, information theory and communication. It captures correlations or variations between attributes of the feature vectors and provides bounds for probability of retrieval error of a two way classification problem. Recently, the CBIR community also adopted statistical distance measures for similarity matching [13]. In this scheme, query image q and target image t are assumed to be in different classes and their respective density as $p_{\mathrm{q}}(\boldsymbol{x})$ and $p_{\mathrm{t}}(\boldsymbol{x})$, both defined on $\mathbb{R}^d$. When these densities are multivariate normal, they can be approximated by mean vector μ and covariance matrix C as $p_{\mathrm{q}}(\boldsymbol{x}) = N(\boldsymbol{x}; \mu_{\mathrm{q}}, C_{\mathrm{q}})$ and $p_{\mathrm{t}}(\boldsymbol{x}) = N(\boldsymbol{x}; \mu_{\mathrm{t}}, C_{\mathrm{t}})$, where

$$N(\boldsymbol{x}; \mu, C) = \frac{1}{\sqrt{(2\pi)d|C|}} \exp^{-\frac{1}{2}(\boldsymbol{x}-\mu)^T C^{-1}(\boldsymbol{x}-\mu)} \tag{12}$$

Here, $\mathbf{x} \in \mathbb{R}^m$ and $|\cdot|$ denotes the matrix determinant [14]. A popular measure of similarity between two Gaussian distributions is the Bhattacharyya distance, which is equivalent to an upper bound of the optimal Bayesian classification error probability [14]. Bhattacharyya distance (D_{Bhatt}) between query image q and target image t in the database is given by:

$$D_{\mathrm{Bhatt}}(q,t) = \frac{1}{8}(\mu_{\mathrm{q}} - \mu_{\mathrm{t}})^T \left[\frac{(C_{\mathrm{q}} + C_{\mathrm{t}})}{2}\right]^{-1} (\mu_{\mathrm{q}} - \mu_{\mathrm{t}}) + \frac{1}{2} \ln \frac{\left|\frac{(C_{\mathrm{q}}+C_{\mathrm{t}})}{2}\right|}{\sqrt{|C_{\mathrm{q}}||C_{\mathrm{t}}|}} \qquad (13)$$

where μ_{q} and μ_{t} are the mean vectors, and C_{q} and C_{t} are the covariance matrices of query image q and target image t respectively. Equation (13) is composed of two terms, the first one being the distance between mean vectors of images, while the second term gives the class separability due to the difference between class covariance matrices. In the retrieval experiment, the Bhattacharyya distance measure is used for similarity matching. Here, it is called adaptive due to the nature of online selection of μ and C by the multi-class SVM as discussed in the next section.

3.3 Category Prediction and Parameter Estimation

To utilize category specific distribution information in similarity matching, the multi-class SVM classifier is used as described in Section 2.2 to predict the category of query and database images. Based on the online prediction, the distance measure function is adjusted to accommodate category specific parameters for query and reference images of database. To estimate the parameters of the category specific distributions, feature vectors are extracted and reduced in dimension, as mentioned in Section 3.1; from N selected training image samples. It is assumed that feature of each category will have distinguishable normal distribution. Computing the statistical distance measures between two multivariate normal distributions requires first and second order statistics in the form of μ and C or parameter vector $\theta = (\mu, C)$ as described in previous section. Suppose that there are L different semantic categories in the database, each assumed to have a multivariate normal distribution with μ_i and C_i, for $i \in L$. However, the true values of μ and C of each category usually are not known in advance and must be estimated from a set of training samples N [14]. The μ_i and C_i of each category are estimated as

$$\mu_i = \frac{1}{N_i} \sum_{j=1}^{N_i} \boldsymbol{x}_{i,j} \quad \text{and} \quad C_i = \frac{1}{N_i - 1} \sum_{j=1}^{N_i} (\boldsymbol{x}_{i,j} - \mu_i)(\boldsymbol{x}_{i,j} - \mu_i)^T \qquad (14)$$

where $\boldsymbol{x}_{i,j}$ is sample j from category i, N_i is the number of training samples from category i and $N = (N_1 + N_2 + \ldots + N_{\mathrm{L}})$.

4 Experiments and Results

For the annotation experiment, the following procedure is performed at the training stage:

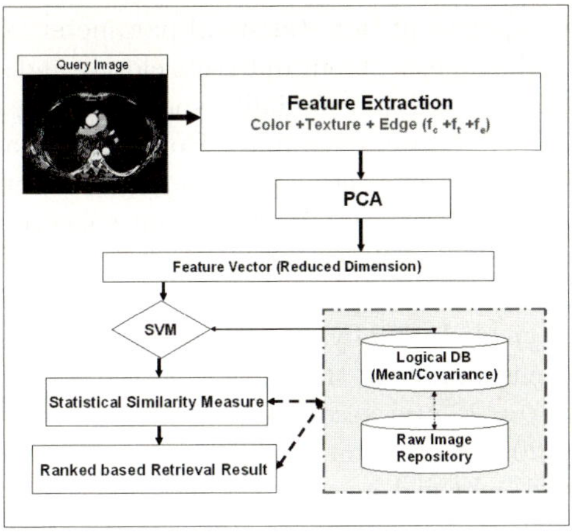

Fig. 1. Block diagram of the retrieval technique

- Consider the radial basis kernel function (RBF) $K(x_i, x_j) = \exp(-\gamma||x_i - x_j||^2), \gamma > 0$
- Use cross-validation (CV) to find the best parameter C and γ
- Use the best parameters C and γ to train the entire training set

There are two tunable parameters while using RBF kernel and soft-margin SVMs in the version space: C and γ. The γ in the RBF kernel controls the shape of the kernel and C controls the trade-offs between margin maximization and error minimization. It is not known beforehand which C and γ are the best for our classification problem. In the training stage, the goal is to identify good values for C and γ, so that the classifier can accurately predict the test data. It may not be useful to achieve high training accuracy (i.e., classifiers accurately predict training data whose class labels are indeed known). Therefore, a 10-fold cross-validation is used with various combinations of γ and C to measure the classification accuracy. In 10-fold cross-validation, the training set is firstly divided into 10 subsets of equal size. Sequentially one subset is tested using the classifier trained on the remaining $9 = 10 - 1$ subsets. Thus, each instance of the entire training set is predicted once and the cross-validation accuracy is the percentage of data, that is correctly classified. A grid-search on C and γ is performed using cross-validation. Pairs of $(C\ ,\ \gamma)$ are tried and the one with the best cross-validation accuracy is picked. We find the best $(C\ ,\ \gamma)$ as (200, 0.01) with the cross-validation rate 54.65%. After the best $(C\ ,\ \gamma)$ is found, the entire training set of 9,000 images is trained again to generate the final classifiers. Finally, the generated classifiers are tested on the 1,000 image testing set of unknown labels to generate the image annotation.

In ImageCLEFmed 2005 automatic image annotation experiment, we have submitted only one run with the above parameters and the classification error rate is 43.3%. Which means, 433 images were misclassified out of 1,000 or accuracy of our system is 56.7% at this moment.

In image retrieval experiment, for statistical parameter estimation and SVM training, we observed the images of four data sets closely and selected 33 different categories based on perceptual and modality specific differences, each with 100 images for generating the training samples. However, for actual evaluation of the similarity measure function, the experiments are conducted on the entire database (around 50,000 images from four different collections).

For SVM training, the reduced feature vector with RBF kernel is used. After 10-fold cross-validation, the best parameters $C = 100$ and $\gamma = 0.03$ with an accuracy of 72.96% is yielded. Finally, the entire training set is trained with these parameters. The dimensionality of the feature vector is reduced to $\mathbb{R}^d \rightarrow \mathbb{R}^m$, where $d = 200$ and $m = 25$ and accounted for 90.0% of the total variances. In the ImageCLEFmed 2005 evaluation, we have submitted only one run with the above parameters and achieved a mean average precision of 0.0072 across all queries, which is very low at this moment compared to other systems. However, the number of features used to represent the images is also low as compared to the superior approaches and images in the training set might not represent the population well.

5 Conclusion and Future Work

This is the first year for the CINDI group takes part in the ImageCLEF campaign and specially in the ImageCLEFmed track. This year, our main goal was to participate and do some initial experiment with the databases provided by the organizer. This paper presents our approaches to automatic image annotation and retrieval based on global image feature contents and multi-class SVM classifier. Despite having 57 categories for annotation, many of them are similar, yet our classification system is still able to provide moderate classification performance. In future, we will investigate region-based local image features and statistical methods that can deal with the challenges of an unbalanced training set, as provided in the current experimental setting. The retrieval performance of our system is inadequate due to the following reasons. First of all, it is very difficult to select a reasonable training set of images with predefined categories from four different data sets with a huge amount of variability in image size, resolution, modality etc. The performance of our system is critical to the appropriate training of multi-class SVM as parameter selection of statistical distance measure is depended on the online category prediction. Secondly, we have only used global image features, which may not be suitable for medical images as large unwanted background dominated in many of these images. In future, we plan to resolve these issues and incorporate text based search approach in addition with the visual based approach.

References

1. Tagare, H. D., Jafe, C., Duncan, J.: Medical image databases: A content-based retrieval approach. Journal of the American Medical Informatics Association. **4 (3)** (1997) 184–198

2. Muller, H., Michoux, N., Bandon, D., Geissbuhler, A.: A review of content-based image retrieval applications -clinical benefits and future directions. International Journal of Medical Informatics. **73:1** (2004) 1–23
3. Clough P., Muller, H., Deselaers, T., Grubinger, M., Lehmann, T. M., Jensen, J., Hersh, W.: The CLEF 2005 Cross-Language Image Retrieval Track. Proceedings of the Cross Language Evaluation Forum 2005. Springer Lecture Notes in Computer science, 2006 - to appear.
4. Haralick, R. M., Shanmugam, Dinstein, I.: Textural features for image classification, IEEE Trans System, Man, Cybernetics. **SMC-3** (1973) 610-621
5. Canny, J.: A computational approach to edge detection. IEEE Trans. Pattern Anal. Machine Intell., **8** (1986) 679–698
6. Hu, M. K.: Visual pattern recognition by moment invariants, IRE Trans. Information Theory. **8** 1962
7. Chapelle, O., Haffner, P., Vapnik, V.: SVMs for histogram-based image classification. IEEE Transaction on Neural Networks. **10(5)** (1999) 1055–1064
8. Burges, C.: A tutorial on support vector machines for pattern recognition. Data Mining and Knowledge Discovery. **2** (1998) 121–167
9. Wu, T. F., Lin, C. J., Weng, R. C.: Probability Estimates for Multi-class Classification by Pairwise Coupling. Journal of Machine Learning Research. **5** (2004) 975–1005
10. Chang, C. C., Lin, C. J.: LIBSVM : a library for support vector machines. (2001) Software available at http://www.csie.ntu.edu.tw/ cjlin/libsvm
11. Smeulder, A., Worring, M., Santini, S., Gupta, A., Jain, R.: Content-Based Image Retrieval at the End of the Early Years. IEEE Trans. on Pattern Anal. and Machine Intell. **22** (2000) 1349–1380
12. Jain, A. K., Bhandrasekaran, B.: Dimensionality and sample size considerations in pattern recognition practice. Handbook of Statistics, **2** (1987) 835–855
13. Aksoy, S., Haralick, R. M.: Probabilistic vs. geometric similarity measures for image retrieval. Proceedings. IEEE Conference on Computer Vision and Pattern Recognition. **2** (2000) 357–362
14. Fukunaga, K.: Introduction to Statistical Pattern Recognition. 2nd edn. Academic Press Professional, Inc. San Diego, CA, USA (1990)

Content-Based Retrieval of Medical Images by Combining Global Features

Mark O Güld, Christian Thies, Benedikt Fischer, and Thomas M. Lehmann

Department of Medical Informatics, RWTH Aachen, Aachen, Germany*
{mgueld, cthies, bfischer}@mi.rwth-aachen.de, lehmann@computer.org

Abstract. A combination of several classifiers using global features for the content description of medical images is proposed. Beside well known texture histogram features, downscaled representations of the original images are used, which preserve spatial information and utilize distance measures which are robust with regard to common variations in radiation dose, translation, and local deformation. These features were evaluated for the annotation task and the retrieval task in ImageCLEF 2005 without using additional textual information or query refinement mechanisms. For the annotation task, a categorization rate of 86.7% was obtained, which ranks second among all submissions. When applied in the retrieval task, the image content descriptors yielded a mean average precision (MAP) of 0.0751, which is rank 14 of 28 submitted runs. As the image deformation model is not fit for interactive retrieval tasks, two mechanisms are evaluated with regard to the trade-off between loss of accuracy and speed increase: hierarchical filtering and prototype selection.

1 Introduction

ImageCLEFmed 2005 [1] consists of several challenges for content-based retrieval [2] on medical images. A newly introduced annotation task poses a classification problem of mapping 1,000 query images with no additional textual information into one of 57 pre-defined categories. The mapping is to be learned based on a ground truth of 9,000 categorized reference images. For the retrieval task, the reference set was expanded to over 50,000 images, compared to 8,725 medical images in 2004. These tasks reflect the real-life constraints of content-based image retrieval in medical applications, as image corpora are large, heterogeneous and additional textual information about an image, especially its content, is not always reliable due to improper configuration of the imaging devices, ambiguous naming schemes, and both inter- and intra-observer variability.

2 The Annotation Task

The annotation task consists of 9,000 images grouped into 57 categories and 1,000 images to be automatically categorized. It should be noted that the category definition is based solely on the aspects of

* This work is part of the IRMA project, which is funded by the German Research Foundation, grant Le 1108/4.

C. Peters et al. (Eds.): CLEF 2005, LNCS 4022, pp. 702–711, 2006.

1. imaging modality, i.e. identification of the imaging device (three different device types)
2. imaging direction, i.e. relative position of the body part towards the imaging device
3. anatomy of the body part examined, and
4. biological system, which encodes certain contrast agents and a coarse description of the diagnostic motivation for the imaging.

Thus, the category definition does not incorporate any diagnosis information, e.g. the detection of pathologies or their quantitative analysis.

2.1 Image Features and Their Comparison

Based on earlier experiments conducted on a similar image set, three types of features and similarity measures were employed [3].

TAMURA et al. proposed a set of texture features to capture global texture properties of an image, namely coarseness, contrast, and directionality [4]. This information is stored in a three-dimensional histogram, which is quantized into $M = 6 \times 8 \times 8 = 384$ bins. To capture this texture information at a comparable scale, the extraction is performed on downscaled images of size 256×256, ignoring their aspect ratio. The query image $q(x, y)$ and the reference image $r(x, y)$ are compared by applying Jensen-Shannon divergence [5] to their histograms $H(q)$ and $H(r)$:

$$d_{\mathrm{JSD}}(q,r) = \frac{1}{2}\sum_{m=1}^{M}\left[H_m(q)\log\frac{2H_m(q)}{H_m(q)+H_m(r)} + H_m(r)\log\frac{2H_m(r)}{H_m(q)+H_m(r)}\right] \tag{1}$$

To retain spatial information about the image content, downscaled representations of the original images are used and the accompanying distance measures work directly on intensity values. It is therefore possible to incorporate a priori knowledge into the distance measure by modelling typical variability in the image data, which does not alter the category that the image belongs to. The cross-correlation function (CCF) from signal processing determines the maximum correlation between two 2D image representations, each one of size $h \times h$:

$$s_{\mathrm{CCF}}(q,r) = \max_{|m|,|n|\le d}\left\{\frac{\sum_{x=1}^{h}\sum_{y=1}^{h}(r(x-m,y-n)-\overline{r})\cdot(q(x,y)-\overline{q})}{\sqrt{\sum_{x=1}^{h}\sum_{y=1}^{h}\left(r(x-m,y-n)-\overline{r}\right)^2}} \cdot \frac{1}{\sqrt{\sum_{x=1}^{h}\sum_{y=1}^{h}\left(q(x,y)-\overline{q}\right)^2}}\right\} \tag{2}$$

Here, $q(x, y)$ and $r(x, y)$ refer to intensity values at a pixel position on the scaled representations of q and r, respectively. Note that s_{CCF} is a similarity measure and the values lie between 0 and 1. CCF includes robustness regarding two very common variabilites among the images: translation, which is explicitly tested within the search window of size $2d+1$, and radiation dose, which is normalized by subtracting the average intensity values $\overline{q}$ and $\overline{r}$. For the experiments, downscaling to 32×32 pixels and a translation window of size $d = 4$ was used, i.e. translation can vary from -4 to $+4$ pixels in both the x- and the y-direction.

While s_{CCF} considers only global displacements, i.e. translations of entire images, and variability in radiation dose, it is suggested to model local deformations of medical images caused by pathologies, implants and normal inter-patient variability. This can be done with an image distortion model (IDM) [6]:

$$d_{\mathrm{IDM}}(q,r) = \sum_{x=1}^{X}\sum_{y=1}^{Y} \min_{|x'|,|y'|\leq W_1} \left\{ \sum_{|x''|,|y''|\leq W_2} || \, r(x+x'+x'', y+y'+y'') - q(x+x'', y+y'')||_2 \right\} \quad (3)$$

Again, $q(x,y)$ and $r(x,y)$ refer to intensity values of the scaled representations. Note that each pixel of q must be mapped on some pixel in r, whereas not all pixels of r need to be the target of a mapping. Two parameters steer d_{IDM}: W_1 defines the size of the neighborhood when searching for a corresponding pixel. To prevent a totally unordered pixel mapping, it is useful to incorporate the local neighborhood as context when evaluating a correspondence hypothesis. The size of the context information is controlled by W_2. For the experiments, $W_1 = 2$, i.e. a 5×5 pixel search window, and $W_2 = 1$, i.e. a 3×3 context patch are used. Also, better results are obtained if the gradient images are used instead of the original images, because the correspondence search will then focus on contrast and be robust to global intensity differences due to radiation dose. It should be noted that this distance measure is computationally expensive as each window size influences the computation time in a quadratic manner. The images were scaled to a fixed height of 32 pixels and the original aspect ratio was preserved.

2.2 Nearest-Neighbor Classifier

To obtain a decision $q \mapsto c \in \{1 \ldots C\}$ for a query image q, a nearest neighbor classifier evaluating k nearest neighbors according to a distance measure is used (k-NN). It simply votes for the category which accumulated the most votes among the k reference images closest to q. This classifier also allows visual feedback in interactive queries.

2.3 Classifier Combination

Prior experiments showed that the performance of the single classifiers can be improved significantly if their single decisions are combined [3]. This is especially true for classifiers which model different aspects of: the image content, such as the global texture properties with no spatial information and the scaled representations, which retain spatial information. The easiest way is a parallel combination scheme, since it can be performed as a post-processing step after the single classifier stage [7]. Also, no assumptions are required for the application, whereas serial or sieve-like combinations require an explicit construction.

For comparability, the distance values (d_{Tamura}, d_{IDM}) are normalized at first over all distances $d(q, r_i), i = 1 \dots N$ between sample q and each reference r_i:

$$d'(q, r_i) = \frac{d(q, r_i)}{\sum_{n=1}^{N} d(q, r_n)} \tag{4}$$

Afterwards, a new distance measure can be obtained by a weighted sum of distance measures d_1, d_2.

$$d_c(q, r) = \lambda \cdot d'_1(q, r) + (1 - \lambda) \cdot d'_2(q, r),\ \lambda \in [0; 1] \tag{5}$$

For a similarity measure s, $d(q, r) := 1 - s(q, r)$ is used and the normalization is performed afterwards. Thus, the parallel combination of the three classifiers results in

$$\begin{aligned} d_{\text{combined}}(q, r) &= \lambda_{\text{Tamura}} \cdot d'_{\text{Tamura}}(q, r) \\ &+ \lambda_{\text{CCF}} \cdot d'_{\text{CCF}}(q, r)) \\ &+ \lambda_{\text{IDM}} \cdot d'_{\text{IDM}}(q, r) \end{aligned} \tag{6}$$

with $\lambda_{\text{Tamura}}, \lambda_{\text{CCF}}, \lambda_{\text{IDM}} \geq 0$ and $\lambda_{\text{Tamura}} + \lambda_{\text{CCF}} + \lambda_{\text{IDM}} = 1$.

2.4 Training and Evaluation on the Reference Set

The combined classification process relies on three parameters: λ_{Tamura}, λ_{CCF} and k for the number of nearest neighbors to be evaluated (λ_{IDM} is linearly dependent). To obtain suitable values for the parameters, the reference set of 9,000 images was split at random into a static training set of 8,000 images and a static test set of 1,000 images. The best parameter values found for this configuration are then applied to the 1,000 query images. For practical reasons, the matrices $D_{\text{Tamura}} = (d_{\text{Tamura}}(q_i, r_j))_{ij}$, $S_{\text{CCF}} = (s_{\text{CCF}}(q_i, r_j))_{ij}$, and $D_{\text{IDM}} = (d_{\text{IDM}}(q_i, r_j))_{ij}$ are computed once. Afterwards, all combination experiments can be performed rather quickly by processing the matrices.

2.5 Use of Class Prototypes

Since the distance computations for the scaled representations are rather expensive, there is – in general – great interest for prototype selection which reduces the required computation time, storage space and might even improve the categorization rate by removing possible outliers in the reference set.

Prototype sets can be obtained in various ways [8]. For simplicity, only random prototype selection and KCentres for K=1 and a simplified variation of it were used. Based on the empirically optimized d_{combined}, a set of category prototypes $R_{\text{prototypes}} \subset R = \bigcup_{c=1 \dots C} R_c$, with R_c being the set of all references belonging to class c, is computed by using KCentres:

$$R_{\text{prototypes}} = \bigcup_{c=1 \dots C} \left\{ \arg \min_{r' \in R_c} \left\{ \sum_{r \in R_c} d_{\text{combined}}(r, r') \right\} \right\} \tag{7}$$

These elements $\{r'_c\}, c = 1..C$ yield the smallest sum of distances to all members of their respective category.

The prototypes are used to obtain a dissimilarity-space representation of the reference images and the unknown images [8]:

$$r \mapsto (d(r, r'_1), \ldots, d(r, r'_C))^{tr} \in I\!R^C \tag{8}$$

$$q \mapsto (d(q, r'_1), \ldots, d(q, r'_C))^{tr} \in I\!R^C \tag{9}$$

For the classification, two representations are compared using Euclidian distance.

3 The Retrieval Task

The retrieval task uses 50,024 images for reference and consists of 25 queries, which are given as a combination of text information and query images, with some queries specifying both positive and negative example images. While the image data for the annotation task only contains grayscale images from mostly x-ray modalities (plain radiography, fluoroscopy, and angiography), the image material in this task is much more heterogeneous: It also contains photographs, ultrasonic imaging and even scans of illustrations used for teaching. Note that the retrieval task demands a higher level of image understanding, since several of the 25 queries directly refer to the diagnosis of medical images, which is often based on local image details, e.g. bone fractures or the detection of emphysema in computed tomography (CT) images of the lungs.

3.1 Image Features and Their Comparison

The content representations described in the previous section only use grayscale information, i.e. color images are converted into grayscale by using color weighting recommended by ITU-R:

$$Y = \frac{6969 \cdot R + 23434 \cdot G + 2365 \cdot B}{32768} \tag{10}$$

In general, however, color is the single most important discriminate feature type on stock-house media and the image corpus used for the retrieval task contains many photographs, color scans of teaching material, and microscopic imaging. Therefore, a basic color feature was employed to compute mean, variance and third order moments for each color channel red R, green G, and blue B. This yields a nine-dimensional feature vector. Euclidean distance with equal weights for each color component is used to compute the distance between two vectors.

3.2 Summation Scheme for Queries Consisting of Multiple Images

Some of the queries do not consist of a single example image, but use several images as a query pool Q: positive and negative examples. For such queries, a simple summation scheme is used to obtain an overall distance:

$$d(Q,r) = \sum_{i=1}^{|Q|} w_i \cdot d'(q_i,r), Q = \bigcup_i \{(q_i,w_i)\}, w_i = \begin{cases} 1: q_i \text{ positive ex.} \\ -1: q_i \text{ negative ex.} \end{cases} \quad (11)$$

4 Results

All results were obtained non-interactively, i.e. without relevance feedback by a human user, and without using textual information for the retrieval task.

4.1 Annotation Task

Table 1 shows the categorization results obtained for the 1,000 unknown images using single classifiers. As IDM is very expensive (see running times below), a serial combination with a faster, but more inaccurate classifier as a filter was also tested. For this, Euclidian distance on 32×32 scaled representations was used and only the 500 closest references were passed to IDM. This cuts computation time down to 1/18, as the costs for the filtering step are negligible.

Table 1. Results for single classifiers

Content representation	Categorization rate in %	
	k=1	k=5
TAMURA texture histogram, Jensen-Shannon divergence	69.3	70.3
32×32, CCF (9×9 translation window)	81.6	82.6
X×32, IDM (gradients, 5×5 window, 3×3 context)	85.0	83.8
X×32, IDM (as above, 32x32 Euclid 500-NN as filter)	84.1	83.5

To obtain the optimal empirical weighting coefficients λ for the parallel combination, an exhaustive search would have been necessary. Instead, a more time-efficient two-step process was employed: First, a combination of the two spatial representations was considered. Afterwards, a combination of the combined spatial representations with the Tamura texture feature was investigated. Both runs tested values for λ increasing at a stepsize of 0.1. The results for these two steps on the *testing set*, i.e. 1,000 images of the 9,000 original reference images, are shown in Tab. 2. The resulting empirical parameter configuration is shown in boldface. When using this parameter set for the classification of the 1,000 images to be categorized, a categorization rate of 86.7% for the 1-NN is obtained.

Using the 57 prototypes obtained via (7) as a representation set, a dissimilarity-space representation for the reference set and the unknown set was computed. The dissimilarity representations were then compared using Euclidian distance. In addition, not only the elements with minimum sum of distances were used, but also the ones with the best $n, n = 2 \ldots 5$ elements per category. This yields 114, 171, 228, and 285 components for the representation vectors. For comparison, experiments were also done for a random pick of $1 \ldots 5$ elements per category,

Table 2. Results on the testing subset, combination of IDM, CCF (left), combination of IDM, CCF, and TAMURA texture (right)

Weights		Categorization rate in %		Weights			Categorization rate in %	
λ_{IDM}	λ_{CCF}	k=1	k=5	λ_{IDM}	λ_{CCF}	λ_{Tamura}	k=1	k=5
0.0	1.0	82.5	80.9	0.00	0.00	1.0	70.8	69.0
0.1	0.9	84.0	82.0	0.07	0.03	0.9	78.1	76.9
0.2	0.8	84.8	83.5	0.14	0.06	0.8	81.4	80.7
0.3	0.7	85.6	84.1	0.21	0.09	0.7	83.5	83.1
0.4	0.6	85.6	84.3	0.28	0.12	0.6	84.6	84.0
0.5	0.5	85.5	84.5	0.35	0.15	0.5	85.5	84.6
0.6	0.4	86.2	84.2	**0.42**	**0.18**	**0.4**	**86.7**	**85.2**
0.7	0.3	**86.6**	**84.5**	0.49	0.21	0.3	86.7	85.1
0.8	0.2	85.9	84.0	0.56	0.24	0.2	86.6	85.1
0.9	0.1	85.5	82.8	0.63	0.27	0.2	86.6	84.9
1.0	0.0	84.7	82.6	0.70	0.30	0.1	86.6	84.5

resulting in representation vectors of the same size. The results are shown in Fig. 1, yielding a best categorization rate of 75.4% when using 2 center prototypes per category from the IDM-based 5-NN as the representation set.

4.2 Retrieval Task

Since no ground truth for the automatic optimization of the parameters is available, only a short visual inspection was done and two runs were submitted. The results are listed in Tab. 3. The result quality is measured by mean average precision (MAP).

Table 3. Results for the retrieval task

λ_{IDM}	λ_{CCF}	λ_{Tamura}	λ_{RGB}	MAP
0.4	0.4	0.2	0.0	0.0659
0.36	0.36	0.18	0.1	0.0751

These results are ranked 19th and 14th among 28 submitted runs in the "visual only, automatic" category of this task, reaching half the MAP of the leading competitor in this category.

4.3 Running Times

Table 4 lists the computation times of the algorithms for the annotation task on a standard Pentium 4 PC running at 2.6 GHz. For the retrieval task, extraction times per image are identical and query time is 5.5 times greater as there are 50,000 references compared to 9,000.

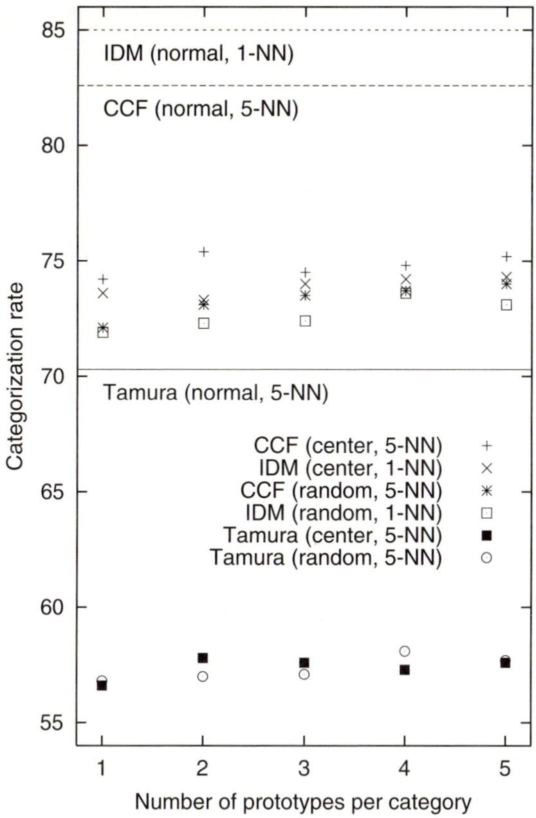

Fig. 1. Results for single classifiers using dissimilarity representation

5 Discussion

The results obtained for the annotation task verify the results obtained on a smaller corpus using leaving-one-out [3]. Note that the rather high weight λ_{Tamura} overemphasizes the role of the texture features in the experiments, as the actual improvement of the categorization rate is statistically insignificant

Table 4. Running times for the annotation task

Content Representation	Extraction [s] (per reference)	Query [s] (per sample)
TAMURA texture histogram, Jensen-Shannon divergence	5	<<1
32×32, CCF (9 × 9 translation window)	3	6
X×32, IDM (gradients, 5 × 5 window, 3 × 3 context)	3	190
X×32, IDM (as above, 32x32 Euclid 500-NN as filter)	6	9

for the 1-NN. It marginally improves the quality of the next nearest neighbors as seen in the results for the 5-NN, which produces slightly better results for interactive queries which list a set of nearest neighbors.

While results for the retrieval task were satisfactory in queries based on grayscale radiographs, other queries, especially from photograpy imaging, had rather poor results, partly due to very basic color feature that was employed. Furthermore, a detailed visual evaluation might have resulted in better tuning of the weighing parameters. This was dropped due to time constraints and it is also unrealistic for real-life applications. Therefore, the results can be considered as a baseline for fully automated retrieval algorithms without feedback mechanisms for parameter tuning. It should also be noted that several queries demand a high level of image content understanding, as they are aimed at diagnosis-related information, which is often derived from local details in the image (Tab. 5).

Table 5. Queries in the retrieval task which directly refer to diagnoses

Query	Semantic constraint
2	fracture of the femur
10	emphysema in lung CT
12	enlarged heart in PA chest radiograph
15	gross pathologies of myocardial infarction
16	osteoarthritis in hand
17	micro nodules in lung CT
18	tuberculosis in chest radiograph
19	Alzheimer's desease in microscopic pathologies
20	chronic myelogenous leukemia in microscopic pathologies
21	bone fracture(s) in radiograph
23	differentiate between malignant and benign melanoma
24	right middle lobe pneumonia

Concerning running times, texture features by TAMURA and CCF are fit for interactive use. By pre-filtering with a computationally inexpensive distance measure, computation time can be severly reduced without sacrificing too much accuracy. In the experiments, pre-filtering clearly outperformed dissimilarity space approaches for both random prototype selection and 1Centres. However, further evaluation of algorithms for prototype selection is necessary. The parallel combination of single classifiers proved very useful, as it improves the categorization results considerably and can also be performed as an easy post-processing step on the distance matrices.

The methods used in this work to describe the image content either preserve no spatial information at all (texture features by TAMURA) or capture it at very large scale, omitting local details important for diagnosis-relevant questions. Using only the image information, such queries cannot be processed with satisfactory quality of the results with a one-level approach. Refering to the concepts described in [9], the methods employed in this paper work on the categorization layer of the content abstraction chain. For a better query completion, subsequent image abstraction steps are required.

References

1. Clough, P., Müller, H., Deselaers, T., Grubinger, M., Lehmann, T.M., Jensen, J., Hersh, W.: The CLEF 2005 Cross-Language Image Retrieval Track. Proceedings of the Cross Language Evaluation Forum 2005, Springer Lecture Notes in Computer Science (to appear).
2. Smeulders, A.W.M., Worring, M., Santini, S., Gupta, A., Jain, R.: Content-based image retrieval at the end of the early years. IEEE Transactions on Pattern Analysis and Machine Intelligence **22**(12) (2000) 1349–1380
3. Güld, M.O., Keysers, D., Deselaers, T., Leisten, M., Schubert, H., Ney, H., Lehmann, T.M.: Comparison of global features for categorization of medical images. Proceedings SPIE **5371** (2004) 211–222
4. Tamura, H., Mori, S., Yamawaki, T.: Textural features corresponding to visual perception. IEEE Transactions on Systems, Man, and Cybernetics **8**(6) (1978) 460–472
5. Puzicha, J., Rubner, Y., Tomasi, C., Buhmann, J.: Empirical evaluation of dissimilarity measures for color and texture. Proceedings International Conference on Computer Vision, 2 (1999) 1165–1173
6. Keysers, D., Gollan, C., Ney, H.: Classification of medical images using non-linear distortion models. Bildverarbeitung für die Medizin 2004, Springer-Verlag, Berlin (2004) 366–370
7. Jain, A.K., Duin, R.P.W., Mao, J.: Statistical pattern recognition: A review. IEEE Transactions on Pattern Analysis and Machine Intelligence **22**(1) (2000) 4–36
8. Pekalska, E., Duin, R.P.W., Paclik, P.: Prototype selection for dissimilarity-based classification. Pattern Recognition (to appear)
9. Lehmann, T.M., Güld, M.O., Thies, C., Fischer, B., Spitzer, K., Keysers, D., Ney, H., Kohnen, M., Schubert, H., Wein, B.B.: Content-based image retrieval in medical applications. Methods of Information in Medicine **43**(4) (2004) 354–361

Combining Textual and Visual Features for Cross-Language Medical Image Retrieval

Pei-Cheng Cheng[1], Been-Chian Chien[2], Hao-Ren Ke[3], and Wei-Pang Yang[1,4]

[1] Department of Computer & Information Science, National Chiao Tung University, 1001 Ta Hsueh Rd., Hsinchu, Taiwan 30050, R.O.C.
{cpc, wpyang}@cis.nctu.edu.tw

[2] Department of Computer Science and Information Engineering, National University of Tainan, 33, Sec. 2, Su Line St., Tainan, Taiwan 70005, R.O.C.
bcchien@mail.nutn.edu.tw

[3] Library and Institute of Information Management, National Chiao Tung University, 1001 Ta Hsueh Rd., Hsinchu, Taiwan 30050, R.O.C.
claven@lib.nctu.edu.tw

[4] Department of Information Management, National Dong Hwa University 1, Sec. 2, Da Hsueh Rd., Shou-Feng, Hualien, Taiwan 97401, R.O.C.
wpyang@mail.ndhu.edu.tw

Abstract. In this paper we describe the technologies and experimental results for the medical retrieval task and automatic annotation task. We combine textual and content-based approaches to retrieve relevant medical images. The content-based approach containing four image features and the text-based approach using word expansion are developed to accomplish these tasks. Experimental results show that combining both the content-based and text-based approaches is better than using only one approach. In the automatic annotation task we use Support Vector Machines (SVM) to learn image feature characteristics for assisting the task of image classification. Based on the SVM model, we analyze which image feature is more promising in medical image retrieval. The results show that the spatial relationship between pixels is an important feature in medical image data because medical image data always has similar anatomic regions. Therefore, image features emphasizing spatial relationship have better results than others.

1 Introduction

In this paper we present the research of the NCTU group at ImageCLEF 2005 [16]. The dataset of medical image retrieval contains about 50,000 images in total from the Casimage, MIR, PEIR, and PathoPIC datasets. Each image of the collection contains annotations in XML format. The majority of the annotations are in English but a significant number are also in French and German. A few cases do not contain any annotation at all. The queries of this task were formulated with example images and a short textual description explaining the research goal.

The participants were asked to accomplish the task with either fully automatic retrieval or retrieval with manual feedback. The query information used can incorporate

C. Peters et al. (Eds.): CLEF 2005, LNCS 4022, pp. 712 – 723, 2006.

the example images or the textual description only, or combine the images and texts together. The main purpose is to evaluate the retrieval of medical images from heterogeneous and multilingual document collections containing images as well as text.

For handling the medical image retrieval task, the NCTU group used two approaches: a content-based approach and text-based approach. The combination of these two approaches using similar weight was also discussed. The content-based approach uses four image features: a Facade scale image feature, Gray Histogram layout, Coherence Moment and Color histogram, extracted from the images directly. The text-based approach processes the annotations based on the vector space model and word expansion using Wordnet [1]. The mixed retrieval of visual and textual data was done by combining the content-based approach and the text-approach with different weights.

In the automatic annotation task, a database of 9,000 fully classified radiographs in 57 classes taken randomly from medical routines is made available and can be used to train a classification system. One thousand radiographs whose classification labels are not available to the participants have to be classified. The aim is to find out how well current techniques can identify image modality, body orientation, body region, and biological system examined based on the images.

In this task we use Support Vector Machines (SVM) to learn image feature characteristics. Based on the SVM model, several image features that consider from the viewpoint of a human observer the invariance in image rotation, shift and illumination are employed in our system. Using these image features, the support vector machines act as classifiers to categorize the 1,000 test images into 57 classes.

In Section 2 of this paper the image features for the content-based approach are described. Section 3 illustrates the text-based approach that processes the multilingual annotations and translation. Section 4 describes the classification method for the automatic annotation task. Section 5 describes our submissions at ImageCLEF 2005 and the ranking results. We provide an explanation and discussion of our experimental results. Finally, Section 6 provides concluding remarks and future direction for medical image retrieval research.

2 Image Features

This section describes the features used for the ImageCLEF 2005 [16] evaluation. In an image retrieval system image features are extracted from pixels of images. To get fast response time the image features should be simple and concise. Further, the image features must include enough meaningful information to represent the image. In this paper we adopt several image features that we have proposed [2], which have good performance in medical image application.

Normalization should be done before quantization to reduce the illuminative influence. In [2], we proposed a relative normalization method concentrating our attention on the contrast of an image. A whole image was separated into four clusters by the K-means method [3]. The four clusters were sorted in ascending order according to their mean values. After clustering, we shifted the mean of the first cluster to a value of 50 and the fourth cluster to 200; then, each pixel in a cluster was multiplied by a relative weight to normalize. Let m_{c1} be the mean value of cluster 1 and m_{c4} be the mean value of cluster 4. The normalization formula of pixel p(x,y) is defined in Eq. (1).

$$p(x,y)_{normal} = (p(x,y) - (m_{c1} - 50)) \times \frac{200}{(m_{c4} - m_{c1})} \quad (1)$$

After normalization, we scaled an image to 128*128 pixels and extracted image features.

2.1 Facade Scale Image Feature

The pixel values of an image are trivial and straight-forward features. For computational efficiency, images are always scaled to a common small size and compared using the Euclidean distance. [4] has shown that optical character recognition and medical image retrieval based on facade image features have obtained excellent results. In this work we scale down an image into 8×8 pixels to form a 64-feature vector as facade scale image feature.

2.2 Gray Histogram Layout

A Color Histogram [5] is a prime image feature for image information retrieval. Histogram methods are invariant in image rotation, and it is easy to implement and have good results in color image indexing. Because numbers of medical images only consist in a gray level, the spatial relationship becomes very important. Medical images always contain particular anatomic regions (lung, liver, head, and so on); therefore, similar images have similar spatial structures. We divide an image into nine sections and calculate their gray level histogram respectively. After normalization, the gray values are quantized into 16 levels for computational efficiency.

In the gray level histogram, the gray value may be quantized into several bins to improve the similarity between adjacent bins. We set an interval range δ to extend the similarity of each gray value. The histogram layout feature estimates the probability of each gray level that appears in a particular area. The probability equation is defined in Eq. (2), where δ is set to 10, p_j is a pixel of the image, and m is the total number of pixels. The gray histogram layout of an image has a total of 144 bins.

$$h_{c_i}(I) = \frac{\sum_{j=1}^{m} \frac{[p_j - \frac{\delta}{2}, p_j + \frac{\delta}{2}] \cap c_i}{\delta}}{m} \quad (2)$$

2.3 Coherence Moment

The semantic gap is a serious problem for designing image representations. State-of-the-art technology still cannot reliably identify objects. The coherence moment feature attempts to describe features from a human observer's viewpoint in order to reduce the semantic gap.

An image is partitioned into four classes by the K-means algorithm. After clustering an image into four classes, we calculate the number of pixels (COH_K), mean gray value (COH_μ) and standard variance of gray value (COH_ρ) in each class. For each class we group connected pixels into eight directions as an object. If an object is bigger than 5% of the whole image, we denote it as a big object; otherwise it is a small object. We count the number of big objects (COH_o) and small objects (COH_v) in each class, and use COH_o and COH_v as parts of image features.

Since we aim to learn how the reciprocal effects pixels, we use the smooth method on the image. If the spatial distribution of pixels in two images is similar, they will also be similar after smoothing. If their spatial distributions are quite different, then they may have a different result after smoothing. After smoothing we cluster an image into four classes and calculate the number of big objects (COH_τ) and small objects (COH_ω). Each pixel will be influenced by its neighboring pixels. Two close objects of the same class may be merged into one object. Then, we can analyze the variation between the two images before and after smoothing. The coherence moment of each class forms a seven-feature vector, (COH_κ, COH_μ, COH_ρ, COH_o, COH_v, COH_τ, COH_ω). The coherence moment of an image is a 56-feature vector that combines the coherence moments of the four classes.

2.4 Color Histogram Features

The color histogram [5] is a basic method and has demonstrated good performance in representing image content. The color histogram method gathers statistics about the proportion of each color as the signature of an image. In this work the colors of an image are represented in the HSV (Hue/Saturation/Value) space, which is closer to human perception than other models, such as RGB (Red/Green/Blue) or CMY (Cyan/Magenta/Yellow). The HSV space is quantized into 18 hues, 2 saturations, and 4 values. Also, we consider an additional 4 levels of gray values and thus have 148 (i.e., 18×2×4+4) bins total. Let C ($|C| = m$) a set of colors (i.e., 148 bins), P_I is represented as Eq. (3), which models the color histogram $H(P_I)$ as a vector in which each bucket h_{c_i} counts the ratio of pixels of P_I in color c_i.

$$H(P_I) = < h_{c_1}(P_I), \ldots, h_{c_m}(P_I) > \tag{3}$$

In many previous studies, each pixel is only assigned to a single color. Consider the following situation: I_1, I_2 are two images and all pixels of I_1 and I_2 fall into c_i and c_{i+1} respectively; I_1 and I_2 are indeed similar to each other, but the similarity computed by the color histogram will regard them as different images. To address this problem we set an interval range δ to extend the color of each pixel and introduce the idea of a partial pixel as shown in Eq.(4),

$$h_{c_i}(P_I) = \frac{\sum_{p \in P_I} \frac{|\alpha_p - \beta_p|}{\delta}}{|P_I|} \tag{4}$$

Let c_{i-1}, c_i, and c_{i+1} stand for a color bin; p is the value of a pixel. $[p - \frac{\delta}{2}, p + \frac{\delta}{2}]$ denotes the interval range δ, $[\alpha_p, \beta_p]$ is the intersection of $[p - \frac{\delta}{2}, p + \frac{\delta}{2}]$ and c_i. The contributions of the pixel to c_i and c_{i-1} are computed as $\frac{|\alpha_p - \beta_p|}{\delta}$ and $\frac{|(p-\delta/2)-\alpha_p|}{\delta}$, respectively. It is clear that a pixel has its contributions not only to c_i but also to its neighboring bins.

Based on the modified color histogram definition, the similarity of two color images q and d is defined in Eq. (5):

$$SIMcolor(H(q),H(d)) = \frac{H(q) \cap H(d)}{|H(q)|} = \frac{\sum_{i=1}^{n} \min(h_i(q), h_i(d))}{\sum_{i=1}^{n} h_i(q)} \tag{5}$$

2.5 Color/Gray Feature

The medical image collection of the ImageCLEF 2005 evaluation contains gray and color images. With color images users are usually attracted by the change of colors more than the positions of objects. Thus, the effective feature in querying a color image is different from querying a gray image. It is obvious that the image is a color or gray value image. When the user queries an image by example, the system first determines whether the example is color or grayscale. If more than 80% of the pixels in an image are in gray values, the image is a gray image; otherwise it is a color image. If the input is a color image, then we set the weight parameter to “C”; if the query image is determined to be a gray valued image, we use the weight parameter of “G,” as shown in Tables 1 and 2.

2.6 Gabor Texture Features

The Gabor image method is adopted to extract texture features from images for image retrieval [13], and has been shown to be very efficient. Gabor filters are a group of wavelets, with each wavelet capturing energy at a specific frequency and a specific direction. Expanding a signal using this basis provides a localized frequency description, therefore capturing local features/energy of the signal. Texture features can then be extracted from this group of energy distributions. The scale (frequency) and orientation tunable properties of the Gabor filter makes it especially useful for texture analysis.

The Gabor wavelet transformation W_{mn} of Image I(x,y) derived from Gabor filters according to [13] is defined in Eq. (6)

$$W_{mn}(x,y) = \int I(x,y) g_{mn}^{*}(x-x_1, y-y_1) dx_1 dy_1 . \tag{6}$$

The mean μ_{mn} and standard deviation σ_{mn} of the magnitude $|W_{mn}|$ are used for the feature vector, as shown in Eq. (7).

$$\mu_{mn}(x, y) = \iint |W_{mn}(x, y)|\, dxdy, \text{ and } \delta_{mn} = \sqrt{\iint (|W_{mn}(x, y)| - u_{mn})^2\, dxdy}. \quad (7)$$

This image feature is constructed by μ_{mn} and σ_{mn} of different scales and orientations. Our experiment uses four (S=4) as the scale and six (K=6) as the orientation to construct a 48-feature vector $\bar{f}$, as shown in Eq. (8).

$$\bar{f} = [u_{00}, \delta_{00}, u_{01}, \delta_{01}, \ldots\ldots, u_{35}, \delta_{35}]. \quad (8)$$

3 Textual Vector Representation

In the ImageCLEFmed collections annotations are in English, French and German. The overall multilingual search process is shown in Fig. 1. Given an initial query Q, the system performs cross-language retrieval and returns a set of relevant documents to the user. We use the representation expressing a query as a vector in the vector space model [6]. The Textual Vector Representation is defined as follows. Let W ($|W| = n$) be the set of significant keywords in the corpus. For a document D, its textual vector representation (i.e., D_T) is defined as Eq. (9),

$$D_T = \langle w_{t_1}(D_T), \ldots, w_{t_n}(D_T) \rangle \quad (9)$$

where the n dimensions indicate the weighting of a keyword t_i in D_T, which is measured by TF-IDF [6], as computed in Eq.(10);

$$w_{t_i}(D_T) = \frac{tf_{t_i, D_T}}{\max tf} \times \log \frac{N}{n_{t_i}} \quad (10)$$

In Eq.(7), $\frac{tf_{t_i, D_T}}{\max tf}$ stands for the normalized frequency of t_i in D_T, max tf is the maximum number of occurrences of any keyword in D_T, N indicates the number of documents in the corpus, and n_{t_i} denotes the number of documents in which a caption t_i appears.

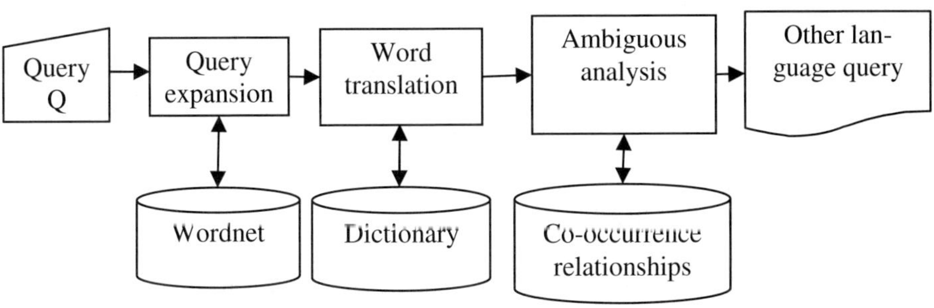

Fig. 1. Text-based multilingual query translation flowchart

Above we introduce the textual vector representation for documents. As for a query Q, one problem is that since Q_T is given in English, it is necessary to translate Q_T into French and German, which are the languages used in the document collection.

A short query usually cannot cover as many useful search terms as possible because of the lack of words. We perform a query expansion process to add new terms to the original query. The additional search terms are taken from a thesaurus – WordNet [1]. Each English term expansion is then translated into one or several corresponding French and German words using a dictionary.[1]

Assuming $AfterExpansion(Q_T) = \{e_1,...,e_h\}$ is the set of all English words obtained after query expansion and query translation, it is obvious that $AfterExpansion(Q_T)$ may contain many words that are incorrect translations or useless search terms. To resolve the translation ambiguity problem, we define *word co-occurrence relationships* to determine final query terms. If the co-occurrence frequency of e_i and e_j in the corpus is greater than a predefined threshold, both e_i and e_j are regarded as useful search terms.

So far, we have a set of search terms, $AfterDisambiguity(Q_T)$, which is presented as Eq.(11),

$$\begin{aligned} AfterDisambiguity(Q_T) = \{e_i, e_j \mid e_i, e_j \in AfterTranslation(Q_T) \\ \& \ e_i, e_j \text{ have a significant co-occurrence}\} \end{aligned} \tag{11}$$

After giving the definition of $AfterDisambiguity(Q_T)$ for a query Q, its textual vector representation (i.e., Q_T) is defined in Eq. (12),

$$Q_T = < w_{t_1}(Q_T),..., w_{t_n}(Q_T) > \tag{12}$$

where $w_{t_i}(Q_T)$ is the weighting of a keyword t_i in Q_T, which is measured as Eq. (10); $w_{c_i}(Q_T)$ indicates whether there exists an $e_j \in AfterDisambiguity(Q_T)$.

In Eq. (13), W is the set of significant keywords as defined before, $\frac{tf_{t_i,Q_T}}{\max tf}$ stands for the normalized frequency of t_i in $AfterDisambiguity(Q_T)$, maxtf is the maximum number of occurrences of any keyword in $AfterDisambiguity(Q_T)$, N indicates the number of images in the corpus, and n_{t_i} denotes the number of images in which a caption t_i appears.

$$w_{t_i}(Q_T) = \left\{ \frac{tf_{t_i,Q_T}}{\max tf} \times \log \frac{N}{n_{t_i}} \right. \tag{13}$$

4 Classification Method

In the automatic annotation task we use Support Vector Machines (SVM) [13] to learn image feature characteristics. SVM is an effective classification method. Its ba-

[1] http://www.freelang.net/

sic idea is to map data into a high-dimensional space and find a separating hyperplane with the maximum margin. Given a training set of instance-label pairs (x_i, y_i), i=1,…,k where $x_i \in R^n$ and $y \in \{1,-1\}^k$, the support vector machines optimizes the solution of the following problem:

$$\underset{w,b,\phi}{Min}(\frac{1}{2}w^T w + C\sum_{i=1}^{k}\phi_i) \text{ and } y_i(w^T\psi(x_i)+b) \geq 1-\phi_i, \phi_i \geq 0 \tag{14}$$

Training vectors x_i are mapped into a higher dimensional space by the function ψ. Then SVM finds a linear separating hyperplane with the maximum margin in this higher dimensional space. $C > 0$ is the penalty parameter of the error term. $K(x_i,x_j) \equiv \psi(x_i)^T \psi(x_j)$ is called the kernel function. In this paper we use LIBSVM [15] to classify the training data with a radial basis function or a polynomial function as the kernel function. The radial basis function (RBF) and the polynomial function used are defined in Eq. (15) and Eq. (16), respectively, whereγ, r, and d are kernel parameters.

$$K(x_i,x_j) = \exp(-\gamma \| x_i - x_j \|^2), \gamma > 0. \tag{15}$$

$$K(x_i,x_j) = (\gamma x_i^T x_j + r)^d, \gamma > 0. \tag{16}$$

5 Experimental Results

In ImageCLEF 2005, the medical image retrieval task contains 25 queries for evaluation. The queries are mixed visual images and semantic textual data. The visual queries use image examples to find similar images; each topic contains at least one image example. The semantic textual queries allow user query by a sentence, from which high-level semantic concepts are directly derived from images with difficulty. The goal is to promote visual and textual retrieval together and find out what works well in which cases.

All submissions of participants in this task were classified into automatic runs and manual runs. With automatic runs the system intervened at the query process without manual assistance. In the automatic category, the methods can be classified into three sub-categories: Text only, Visual only and Mixed retrieval (visual and textual) according to the feature used. The category "Text only" means that systems use textual features only to retrieve relevant images. The "Visual only" category means that systems only use visual image features without combining textual annotation to retrieve similar images. Mixed retrieval means the systems combine visual and textual features to retrieve images.

In this task we have submitted ten runs for the mixed retrieval automatic runs and six runs for the visual only automatic runs. In the content-based approach we combine four proposed image features by weighted adjusting to retrieve related images. We initially set at the system the weight of features without further user intervention. Table 1 lists the query results of visual only runs and the setting weight of four image features. Table 2 lists the results of mixed retrieval runs and the setting weight of image features and textual features. The difference of each run is the weighted setting of features.

The query topics contain color and gray images. We first determine whether the query's image is color or gray by **color/gray feature**. Depending on whether the image is color or grey, we set different weights for the image features. In the Table 1, "C" denotes that the query image is a color image and "G" denotes that the query image is a gray image. We submit six runs for the visual only category. The run "nctu_visual_auto_a8" has the better result in our experiment. The weights of each feature are set equal, which means that four image features have the same importance.

The setting weights of mixed runs and results are listed in table 2. The result of runs 8, 9 and 10 illustrate that combining the visual and textual features will achieve better results than single features. Run 8 assumes that the significant of visual and textual feature are equal. Run 9 emphasizes the weight of visual features and Run 10 emphasizes the weight of textual features. The results show that the text-based approach is better than the content-based approach, but the content-based approach can improve the textual results.

In the ImageCLEF 2005 Automatic Annotation Task we have submitted five SVM-based runs. Table 3 gives an overview of the features and the error rates of the submitted runs. According to the error rate each .1% corresponds to 1 misclassification, because this task has a total of one thousand images to be classified. For the first run a Facade scale feature with 64-feature vectors is used and the radial basis function is chosen as the kernel function of SVM. Both the second run and the third run use all 324 features, but they use different kernel functions for the SVM. The fourth run uses two kinds of features, Facade scale and fuzzy histogram layout, and contains 208 features. The fifth run uses the coherence moment feature only and the radial basis kernel function for SVM.

In the image features used in our experiment the facade scale feature that directly scales down an image contains the most spatial relationships. The fuzzy histogram layout feature divides an image into nine sections, which results in less spatial information than the facade scale feature; however, this feature is more invariant in image shift. The coherence moment factors the image rotation and shift, but cannot carry much spatial information.

In our experiments the first run had the best result, with an error rate of 24.7%. The second run, which had an error rate of 24.9%, used all image features but did not have better results than the first run because the first run contained the most spatial information. Others image features do not improve the description of spatial relationships. The fifth run contained the least spatial information, thus it had the worst results.

In the ImageCLEF 2005 one experiment for a nearest neighbor classifier that scaled down images to 32*32 pixels and used the Euclidean distance for comparison had an error rate of 36.8%, which means that 368 images were misclassified. This experiment used a feature very similar to the facade features; however, the facade image feature scaled down an image to only 8 x 8 pixels. It can be observed that the representation of the facade image feature is more concise and has better results than the 32x32-pixel features. Furthermore, the SVM method has better performance than the Euclidean distance metric.

Table 1. The query results of visual only runs and the weight of visual image features

runs	The weight of Image features								Result	
Image features	Coherence		Gray HIS		Color HIS		Facade		MAP	Rank of runs
detected color or gray	C	G	C	G	C	G	C	G		
visual_auto_a1	0.3	0.2	0.3	0.5	1	0.2	1	1	0.0628	14
visual_auto_a2	0.3	0.2	0.5	0.3	0.3	0.5	1	1	0.0649	10
visual_auto_a3	0.5	1	0.5	1	1	0.5	1	1	0.0661	8
visual_auto_a5	0.1	0.2	0.1	0.5	1	0.5	0.5	1	0.0631	13
visual_auto_a7	0.3	0.2	0.3	0.5	1	0.2	1	0.5	0.0644	11
visual_auto_a8	1	1	1	1	1	1	1	1	0.0672	7

Table 2. The result of mixed retrieval runs and the weight of visual image features and textual features

runs	The weight of Image features													
Image features	Coher-ence		Gray HIS		Color HIS		Facade		visual		textual		MAP	Rank
Color / gray	C	G	C	G	C	G	C	G	C	G	C	G		
visual+Text_1	0.3	0.2	0.3	0.5	1	0.2	1	1	1	1	0.8	0.1	0.227	10
visual+Text_2	0.3	0.2	0.5	0.3	0.3	0.5	1	1	1	1	0.8	0.1	0.212	14
visual+Text_3	0.5	1	0.5	1	1	0.5	1	1	1	1	0.8	0.1	0.228	9
visual+Text_4	0.3	0.2	0.3	0.5	1	0.2	1	1	1	1	1	0.2	0.238	3
visual+Text_5	0.1	0.2	0.1	0.5	1	0.5	0.5	1	1	1	0.8	0.1	0.224	12
visual+Text_6	0.3	0.2	0.3	0.5	1	0.2	1	1	1	1	1	1	0.231	7
visual+Text_7	0.3	0.2	0.3	0.5	1	0.2	1	0.5	1	1	0.8	0.1	0.226	11
visual+Text_8	1	1	1	1	1	1	1	1	1	1	1	1	0.232	6
visual+Text_9	1	1	1	1	1	1	1	1	1	1	0.1	0.1	0.090	22
visual+Text_10	1	1	1	1	1	1	1	1	0.1	0.1	1	1	0.194	15

Table 3. Features for the different submissions and the evaluation results

Submission runs	Image features	SVM kernel function	error rate %
nctu_mc_result_1.txt	Facade scale: 64 vectors	radial basis function	24.7
nctu_mc_result_2.txt	All features: 324 vectors	radial basis function	24.9
nctu_mc_result_3.txt	All features: 324 vectors	polynomial	31.8
nctu_mc_result_4.txt	Facade scale, Histogram layout: 208 vectors	radial basis function	28.5
nctu_mc_result_5.txt	Coherence Moment: 56 vectors	radial basis function	33.8

6 Conclusions

The ImageCLEF 2005 medical image retrieval task offers a good test platform to evaluate the ability of image retrieval technologies. 112 runs were submitted in total for this task. The results of the evaluation show that the method we proposed is excellent. Our best result rank by MAP is 3, so there are is only one system better than ours.

In the experiment results we find that a content-based approach retrieving similar images relies on visual feature, which has less semantic expansion. The text-based approach has better performance than the content-based approach. Combining the textual and visual features will achieve the best results.

The results in the medical retrieval task show that weighted settings between the features is very important. The variation between different settings of weight is extreme. Suitable weight adjusting will improve the results.

In this paper several image features are examined for medical image data. The medical image application is unlike general-purpose images. Medical images have more stable camera settings than general purpose images. Therefore, the spatial information becomes an important factor in medical images, and we must improve the representation regarding spatial relations in these kinds of images.

In the automatic annotation task we use support vector machines as a classifier. This is very efficient but the SVM lacks the ability to select features. The fourth run also contains the Facade scale feature but the results are worse than the first run. In the future we plan to develop feature selection technology for the SVM to improve performance.

References

1. Miller, G: WordNet: A Lexical Database for English, Communications of the ACM (1995) 39-45
2. Cheng, P. C., Chien, B. C., Ke, H. R., and Yang, W. P.:KIDS's evaluation in medical image retrieval task at ImageCLEF 2004, Working Notes for the CLEF 2004 Workshop September, Bath, UK (2004) 585-593
3. Han, J., and Kamber, M.: Data Mining: Concepts and Techniques. Academic Press, San Diego, CA, USA (2001)
4. Keysers, D., Macherey, W., Ney, H., and Dahmen, J.: Adaptation in Statistical Pattern Recognition using Tangent Vectors. IEEE transactions on Pattern Analysis and Machine Intelligence, 26 (2), February (2004) 269-274
5. Swain, M.J. and Ballard, D. H.: Color Indexing, International Journal of Computer Vision, Vol. 7 (1991) 11-32
6. Salton, G. and McGill, M. J.: Introduction to Modern Information Retrieval. New York: McGraw-Hill (1983)
7. Manjunath, B. S., and Ma, W. Y.: Texture features for browsing and retrieval of large image data, IEEE Transactions on Pattern Analysis and Machine Intelligence, Vol. 18 (8), August (1996) 837-842
8. Flickner, M., Sawhney, H., Niblack, W., Ashley, J., Huang, Q., Dom, B., Gorkani, M., Hafner, J., Lee, D., Petkovic, D., Steele, D., Yanker, P.: Query by Image and Video Content: The QBIC system, IEEE Computer 28 (9) (1995) 23-32
9. Carson, C., Thomas, M., Belongie, S., Hellerstein, J. M., Malik, J., Blobworld: A system for region-based image indexing and retrieval, in: D. P. Huijsmans, A. W. M. Smeulders (Eds.), Third International Conference On Visual Information Systems (VISUAL' 99), no. 1614 in Lecture Notes in Computer Science, Springer, Verlag, Amsterdam, The Netherlands (1999) 509-516
10. Belongie, S., Carson, C., Greenspan, H., Malik, J.: Color and texture based image segmentation using EM and its application to content-based image retrieval, in: Proceedings of the International Conference on Computer Vision (ICCV'98), Bombay, India (1998) 675-682

11. Squire, D. M., Muller, W., Muller, H., and Raki, J.: Content-Based Query of Image Databases, Inspirations from Text Retrieval: Inverted Files, Frequency-Based Weights and Relevance Feedback. In Scandinavian Conference on Image Analysis, Kangerlussuaq, Greenland, June (1999)143-149
12. Wang, J. Z., Li, J., and Wiederhold, G.: SIMPLIcity: Semantics-Sensitive Integrated Matching for Picture Libraries. IEEE Transaction on Pattern Analysis and Machine Intelligence, 23 (9), September (2001) 947-963
13. Boser, B., Guyon, I., and Vapnik, V.: A training algorithm for optimal margin classifiers. In Proceedings of the Fifth Annual Workshop on Computational Learning Theory (1992)
14. Manjunath, B. S. and Ma, W. Y.: Texture features for browsing and retrieval of large image data, IEEE Transactions on Pattern Analysis and Machine Intelligence, Vol. (18:8), August (1996) 837-842
15. Chang, C.-C. and C.-J. Lin. LIBSVM: a library for support vector machines. http://www.csie.ntu.edu.tw/~cjlin/libsvm, (2001)
16. Clough, P., Müller, H., Deselaers, T. Grubinger, M., Lehmann, T., Jensen, J., and Hersh, W.: The CLEF 2005 Cross-Language Image Retrieval Track. In: Working Notes of the CLEF 2005 Workshop. (2005)

The Use of MedGIFT and EasyIR for ImageCLEF 2005

Henning Müller, Antoine Geissbühler, Johan Marty,
Christian Lovis, and Patrick Ruch

University and University Hospitals of Geneva, Service of Medical Informatics
24 Rue Micheli-du-Crest, CH-1211 Geneva 14, Switzerland
henning.mueller@sim.hcuge.ch

Abstract. This article describes the use of *medGIFT* and *easyIR* for three of four *ImageCLEF* 2005 tasks. All results rely on two systems: the GNU Image Finding Tool (*GIFT*) for visual retrieval, and *easyIR* for text. For ad–hoc retrieval, two visual runs were submitted. No textual retrieval was attempted, resulting in lower scores than those using text retrieval. For medical retrieval, visual retrieval was performed with several configurations of Gabor filters and grey level/color quantisations as well as combinations of text and visual features. Due to a lack of resources no feedback runs were created, an area where *medGIFT* performed best in 2004. For classification, a retrieval with the target image was performed and the first $N = 1; 5; 10$ results used to calculate scores for classes by simply adding up the scores for each class. No machine learning was performed, so results were surprisingly good and only topped by systems with optimised learning strategies.

1 Introduction

Image retrieval is increasingly important in information retrieval research. Compared to text retrieval little is known about how to search for images, although it has been an extremely active domain in the fields of computer vision and information retrieval [1,2,3,4]. Benchmarks such as ImageCLEF [5,6] allow to evaluate algorithms compared to other systems and deliver insights into the techniques that perform well. Thus, new developments can be directed towards these goals and techniques of well–performing systems can be adapted. More on the tasks can be found in [7].

In 2005, the ad–hoc retrieval task created topics were better adapted for visual systems using the same database as in 2004. The tasks made available contain three images. We submitted two configurations of our system to this task using visual information only.

The medical retrieval task was performed on a much larger database than in 2004 containing a total of more than 50.000 images [8]. The annotation was also more varied, ranging from a few words in a very structured form to completely unstructured paragraphs. This made it hard to preprocess any of the information. Finally, only free–text retrieval was used for our results submission including

C. Peters et al. (Eds.): CLEF 2005, LNCS 4022, pp. 724–732, 2006.

all XML tags. The tasks were much harder and mainly semantic tasks, which made the retrieval by visual means more difficult. Due to a lack of resources we could only submit partial results that did not include any relevance feedback or automatic query expansion.

The automatic annotation task was interesting and challenging at the same time [9]. We did not take into account any of the training data and simply used *GIFT* and a nearest neighbour technique to classify results. Still, the outcome is surprisingly good (6th best submission, 3rd best group) and when taking into account the learning data using an approach as described in [10], these results are expected to get better.

ImageCLEF gave us the opportunity to compare our system with other techniques which are invaluable and will provide us with directions for future research.

2 Basic Technologies Used

For our ImageCLEF participation, we aim at combining content–based retrieval of images with cross–language retrieval applied to textual annotation of the images. Based on the results from last year (2004), we used parameters that were expected to lead to good results.

2.1 Image Retrieval

The technology used for the content–based retrieval of images is mainly taken from the *Viper*[1] project of the University of Geneva. Much information about this system is available [11]. Outcome of the *Viper* project is the GNU Image Finding Tool, *GIFT*[2]. This software tool is open source and can be used by other participants of ImageCLEF. A ranked list of visually similar images for every query topic was made available for participants and will serve as a baseline to measure the quality of submissions. Demonstration versions with a web–accessible interface of *GIFT* were also made available for participants. Not everybody can be expected to install a Linux tool only for such a benchmark. The feature sets that are used by *GIFT* are:

- Local color features at different scales by partitioning the images successively into four equally sized regions (four times) and taking the mode color of each region as a descriptor;
- global color features in the form of a color histogram, compared by a simple histogram intersection;
- local texture features by partitioning the image and applying Gabor filters in various scales and directions, quantised into 10 strengths;
- global texture features represented as a simple histogram of responses of the local Gabor filters in various directions and scales.

[1] `http://viper.unige.ch/`

[2] `http://www.gnu.org/software/gift/`

A particularity of *GIFT* is that it uses many techniques well–known from text retrieval. Visual features are quantised and the feature space is very similar to the distribution of words in texts, corresponding roughly to a Zipf distribution. A simple *tf/idf* weighting is used and the query weights are normalised by the results of the query itself. The histogram features are compared based on a histogram intersection [12].

The medical adaptation of the *GIFT* is called *medGIFT*[3] [13]. It is also accessible as open source and adaptations concern mainly visual features and the user interface that shows the diagnosis on screen and is linked with a radiologic teaching file so the MD can not only browse images but also get the textual data and other images of the same case. Grey levels play a more important role for medical images and their numbers are raised, especially for relevance feedback (RF) queries. The number of the Gabor filter responses also has an impact on the performance and these are changed with respect to directions and scales. We used in total 4, 8 and 16 grey levels and for the Gabor filters we used 4 and 8 directions. Other techniques in *medGIFT* such as a pre–treatment of images [14] were not used for this competition due to a lack of resources.

2.2 Text Search

The basic granularity of the Casimage and MIR collections is the case. A case gathers a textual report, and a set of images. For the PathoPic and PEIR databases annotation exists for every image. The queries contain one to three images and text in three languages. We used all languages as a single query and indexed all documents in one index. Case–based annotation is expanded to all images of the case after retrieval. The final unit of retrieval is the image.

Indexes. Textual experiments were conducted with the easyIR engine[4]. As a single report is able to contain written parts in several languages mixed, it would have been necessary to detect the boundaries of each language segment. Ideally, French, German and English textual segments would be stored in different indexes. Each index could have been translated into the other language using a general translation method, or more appropriately using a domain-adapted method [15]. However, such a complex architecture would require to store different segments of the same document in separate indexes. Considering the lack of data to tune the system, we decided to index all collections using a unique index using an English stemmer, For simplicity reasons, the XML tags were also indexed and not separately treated.

Weighting Schema. We chose a generally good weighting schema of the term frequency - inverse document frequency family. Following weighting convention of the SMART engine, cf. Table 1, we used atc-ltn parameters, with $\alpha = \beta = 0.5$ in the augmented term frequency.

[3] `http://www.sim.hcuge.ch/medgift/`

[4] `http://lithwww.epfl.ch/~ruch/softs/softs.html`

Table 1. Usual *tf-idf* weight; for the cosine normalisation factor, the formula is given for Euclidean space: $w_{i,j}$ is the document term weight, $w_{j,q}$ is the query term weight

Term Frequency	
First Letter	$f(tf)$
n (natural)	tf
l (logarithmic)	$1 + log(tf)$
a (augmented)	$\alpha + \beta \times (\frac{tf}{max(tf)})$, where $\alpha = 1 - \beta$ and $0 < \alpha < 1$
Inverse Document Frequency	
Second Letter	$f(\frac{1}{df})$
n(no)	1
t(full)	$log(\frac{N}{df})$
Normalisation	
Third Letter	$f(length)$
n(no)	1
c(cosine)	$\sqrt{\sum_{i=1}^{t} w_{i,j}^2} \times \sqrt{\sum_{j=1}^{t} w_{j,q}^2}$

2.3 Combining the Two

Combinations of visual and textual features for retrieval are still scarce in the literature [16], so many of the mechanism and fine tuning of the combinations will need more work, especially when the optimisation is based on the actual query. For the visual query we used all images that are present, including one query containing negative feedback. For the text part, the text of all three languages was used as a combined query together with the combined index that includes the documents in all languages. Results lists of the first 1000 documents were taken into account for both the visual and the textual search. Both result lists were normalised to deliver results within the range [0; 1]. The visual result is normalised by the result of the query itself whereas the text was normalised by the document with the highest score. This leads to visual scores that are usually slightly lower than the textual scores in high positions.

To combine the two lists, two different methods were chosen. The first one simply combines the list with different percentages for visual and textual results (textual= 50, 33, 25, 10%). In a second form of combination the list of the first 1000 visual results was taken, and then, all those that were in the first 200 textual documents were multiplied with N–times the value of the textual results.

3 The Ad Hoc Retrieval Task

For the ad–hoc retrieval task we submitted results using fairly similar techniques as those in 2004. The 2005 topics were actually more adapted to the possibilities of visual retrieval systems as more visual attributes were taken into account for the topic creation [7]. Still, textual retrieval is necessary for good results. It is not so much a problem of the queries but rather a problem of the database containing mostly grey or brown scale images of varying quality where automatic treatment such as color indexing is difficult. This should change in 2006 with a new database using mostly consumer pictures of vacation destinations.

We used *GIFT* with two configurations. First, we used the normal *GIFT* engine with 4 grey levels and the full HSV space using the Gabor filter responses in four directions and at three scales. The second configuration took into account 8 grey levels as the 2004 results for 16 grey levels were actually much worse than expected. We also raised the number of directions of the Gabor filters to 8 instead of four. The results of the basic *GIFT* system were made available to all participants and used by several. Surprisingly the results of the basic *GIFT* system remain the best in the test with a MAP of 0.0829, being at the same time the best purely automatic visual system participating. The system with eight grey levels and eight directions for the Gabor filters performed slightly worse and a MAP of 0.0819 was reached. Other visual systems performed slightly lower. The best mono–lingual text systems performed at a MAP of 0.41. Several text retrieval systems performed worse than the visual system for a variety of languages.

4 The Automatic Annotation Task

We were new to automatic annotation as almost everyone and mainly used our system for retrieval, so far. Due to a lack of resources no optimisation using the available training data was performed. Still, the tf/idf weighting is automatically weighting rare features higher which leads to a discriminative analysis.

As techniques we performed a query with each of the 1000 images to classify and took into account the first $N = 1, 5, 10$ retrieval results. For each of these results (i.e. images from the training set) the correct class was determined and this class was augmented with the similarity score of the image. The class with the highest final score became automatically the class selected for the query. For retrieval we used three different settings of the features using 4, 8, and 16 grey levels. The runs with 8 and 16 grey levels also had eight directions of the Gabor filters for indexation. Best results obtained in the competition were from the Aachen groups (best run at 12.6% error rate) that have been working on very similar data for several years, now.

The best results for our system were retrieved when using 5NN and eight grey levels (error rate 20.6%), and the next best results using 5NN and 16 grey levels (20.9). Interestingly, the worst results were obtained with 5NN and 4 grey levels (22.1). Using 10NN led to slightly worse results (21.3) and 1NN was rather in the middle (4 grey levels 21.8; 8 grey levels: 21.1; 16 grey levels 21.7).

In conclusion we can say that all results are extremely close together 20.6-22.1%, so the differences do not seem statistically significant. 5NN seems to be the best but this might also be linked to the fact that some classes have a very small population and 10NN would simply retrieve too many images of other classes to be competitive. 8 levels of grey and 8 directions of the Gabor filters seem to perform best, but the differences are still very small.

In the future, we planned to train the system with the available training data using the algorithm described in [10]. This technique is similar to the market basket analysis [17]. A proper strategy for the training needs to be developed to especially help smaller classes to be well classified. Typically, these classes cause most of the classification problems.

5 The Medical Retrieval Task

Unfortunately, our textual retrieval results contained an indexation error and the results were almost random. The only textual run that we submitted had a MAP of 0.0226. The best textual retrieval systems were at 0.2084 (IPAL/I2R). Due to a limitation of resources, we were not able to submit relevance feedback runs, where *GIFT* usually is strongest. The best feedback system was OHSU with a MAP of 0.2116 for only textual retrieval.

The best visual system is I2R with a MAP of 0.1455. Our *GIFT* retrieval system was made available to participants and was widely used. Again, the basic *GIFT* system obtained the best results among the various combinations in feature space (MAP 0.0941), with only I2R having actually better results but using manual optimisation based on the dataset. The second indexation using 8 grey levels and eight directions of the Gabor filters performs slightly worse at 0.0872.

For mixed textual/visual retrieval, the best results were obtained by IPAL/I2R with MAP 0.2821. Our best result in this category is using 10% textual part and 90% visual part and obtains 0.0981. These results should be much better when using a properly indexed text–based system. The following results were obtained for other combinations: 20% visual: 0.0934, 25%: 0.0929, 33%: 0.0834, 50%: 0.044. When using eight grey levels and 8 Gabor directions: 10% visual: 0.0891, 20%: 0.084, 33%: 0.075, 50%: 0.0407. The results could lead to the assumption that visual retrieval is better than textual retrieval in our case, but this holds only true because of our indexation error.

A second combination technique that we applied used as a basis the results from textual retrieval and then added the visual retrieval results multiplied with a factor $N = 2, 3, 4$ to the first 1000 results of textual retrieval. This strategy proved fruitful in 2004 the other way round by taking first the visual results and then augmenting only the first N=1000 results. The results for the main *GIFT* system were: 3 times visual: 0.0471, 4 times visual 0.0458, 2 times visual 0.0358. For the system with 8 grey levels, the respective results are: 3 times visual 0.0436, 4 times visual 0.0431, 2 times visual 0.0237. A reverse order of taking the visual results first and then augment the textually similar would have led to better results in this case but when having correct results for text as well as for visual retrieval, this needs to be proven.

The MAP scores per topic shown in Figure 1 show that the textual retrieval is extremely low for all but very few queries (GE_M_TXT.txt) compare with the visual results (GE_M_88.TXT and GE_M_4g.txt). For the queries with good text results the mixed retrieval (GE_M_10.txt) is actually much better than

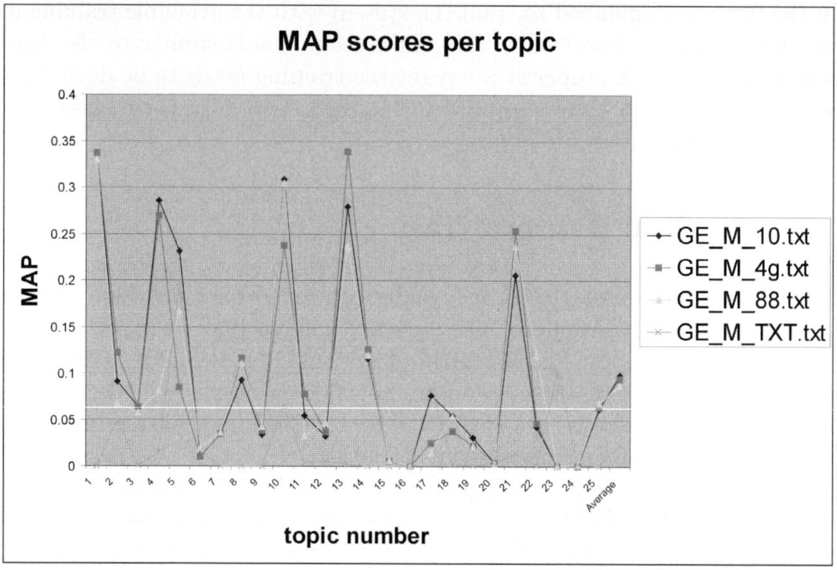

Fig. 1. MAP per topic for four different system configurations

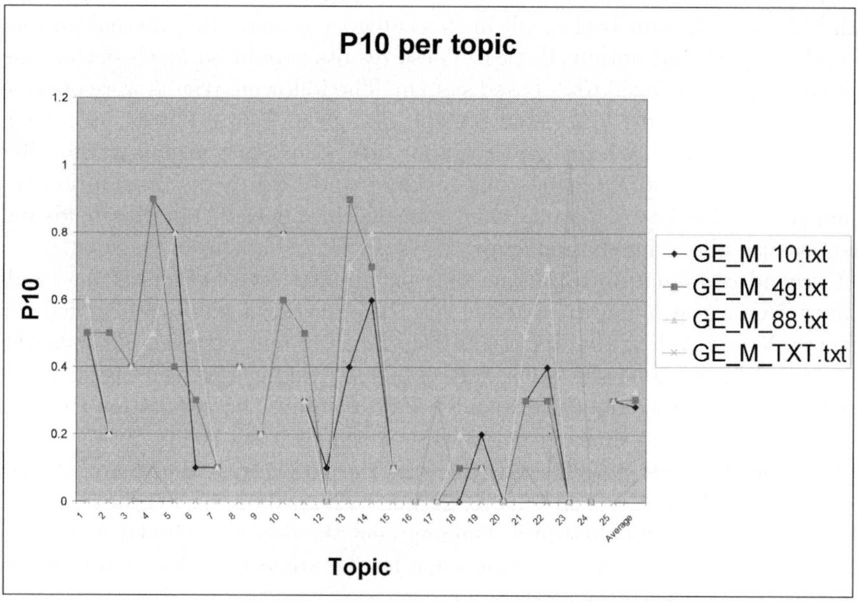

Fig. 2. Precision after ten images retrieved per topic for four different configurations

only textual retrieval. This shows the potential of the mixed runs with correct text retrieval results. Best test retrieval results were 10 times better than ours. The precision after ten retrieval image per topic can be seen in Figure 2. This underlines our previous assumption as most results for the text retrieval receive no relevant images early on, whereas visual retrieval does have very good results. Much more can not be concluded from our submission as several errors prevented better results.

6 Conclusions

Although we did not have any resources for an optimised submission we still learned from the 2005 tasks that the *GIFT* system delivers a good baseline for visual image retrieval and that it is widely usable for a large number of tasks and different images. More detailed results show that the ad–hoc task is hard for visual retrieval even with a more visually–friendly set of queries as the image set does not contain enough color information or clear objects, which is crucial for fully visual information retrieval.

The automatic annotation or classification task proved that our system delivers good results even without learning and shows that information retrieval can also be used well for document classification. When taking into account the available training data these results will surely improve significantly.

From the medical retrieval task not much can be deduced for now as we need to work on our textual indexation and retrieval to find the error responsible for the mediocre results. Still, we can say that *GIFT* is well suited and among the best systems for general visual retrieval. It will need to be analysed which features were used by other systems, especially runs performing better.

For next year we will definitely have to take into account the available training data and we hope as well to use more complex algorithms for example to extract objects form the medical images and limit retrieval to theses objects. Another strong point of *GIFT* is the good relevance feedback and this can surely improve results significantly as well. Already the fact to have a similar databases for two years in a row would help as such large databases need a large time to be indexed and require human resources for optimisation as well.

Acknowledgements

Part of this research was supported by the Swiss National Science Foundation with grants 632-066041 and 205321-109304/1. We also acknowledge the support of the EU FP6 project SemanticMining (IST NoE 507505).

References

1. Smeulders, A.W.M., Worring, M., Santini, S., Gupta, A., Jain, R.: Content–based image retrieval at the end of the early years. IEEE Transactions on Pattern Analysis and Machine Intelligence **22 No 12** (2000) 1349–1380

2. Müller, H., Michoux, N., Bandon, D., Geissbuhler, A.: A review of content–based image retrieval systems in medicine – clinical benefits and future directions. International Journal of Medical Informatics **73** (2004) 1–23
3. Tagare, H.D., Jaffe, C., Duncan, J.: Medical image databases: A content–based retrieval approach. Journal of the American Medical Informatics Association **4** (1997) 184–198
4. Rui, Y., Huang, T.S., Ortega, M., Mehrotra, S.: Relevance feedback: A power tool for interactive content–based image retrieval. IEEE Transactions on Circuits and Systems for Video Technology **8** (1998) 644–655 (Special Issue on Segmentation, Description, and Retrieval of Video Content).
5. Clough, P., Sanderson, M., Müller, H.: A proposal for the CLEF cross language image retrieval track (ImageCLEF) 2004. In: The Challenge of Image and Video Retrieval (CIVR 2004), Dublin, Ireland, Springer LNCS 3115 (2004)
6. Clough, P., Müller, H., Sanderson, M.: Overview of the CLEF cross–language image retrieval track (ImageCLEF) 2004. In Peters, C., Clough, P.D., Jones, G.J.F., Gonzalo, J., Kluck, M., Magnini, B., eds.: Multilingual Information Access for Text, Speech and Images: Result of the fifth CLEF evaluation campaign. Lecture Notes in Computer Science, Bath, England, Springer–Verlag (2005)
7. Clough, P., Müller, H., Deselaers, T., Grubinger, M., Lehmann, T.M., Jensen, J., Hersh, W.: The CLEF 2005 cross–language image retrieval track. In: Springer Lecture Notes in Computer Science (LNCS), Vienna, Austria (2006 – to appear)
8. Hersh, W., Müller, H., Gorman, P., Jensen, J.: Task analysis for evaluating image retrieval systems in the ImageCLEF biomedical image retrieval task. In: Slice of Life conference on Multimedia in Medical Education (SOL 2005), Portland, OR, USA (2005)
9. Lehmann, T.M., Güld, M.O., Deselaers, T., Schubert, H., Spitzer, K., Ney, H., Wein, B.B.: Automatic categorization of medical images for content–based retrieval and data mining. Computerized Medical Imaging and Graphics **29** (2005) 143–155
10. Müller, H., Squire, D.M., Pun, T.: Learning from user behavior in image retrieval: Application of the market basket analysis. International Journal of Computer Vision **56(1–2)** (2004) 65–77 (Special Issue on Content–Based Image Retrieval).
11. Squire, D.M., Müller, W., Müller, H., Pun, T.: Content–based query of image databases: inspirations from text retrieval. Pattern Recognition Letters (Selected Papers from The 11th Scandinavian Conference on Image Analysis SCIA '99) **21** (2000) 1193–1198 B.K. Ersboll, P. Johansen, Eds.
12. Swain, M.J., Ballard, D.H.: Color indexing. International Journal of Computer Vision **7** (1991) 11–32
13. Müller, H., Rosset, A., Vallée, J.P., Geissbuhler, A.: Integrating content–based visual access methods into a medical case database. In: Proceedings of the Medical Informatics Europe Conference (MIE 2003), St. Malo, France (2003)
14. Müller, H., Heuberger, J., Geissbuhler, A.: Logo and text removal for medical image retrieval. In: Springer Informatik aktuell: Proceedings of the Workshop Bildverarbeitung für die Medizin, Heidelberg, Germany (2005)
15. Ruch, P.: Query translation by text categorization. In: Proceedings of the conference on Computational Linguistics (COLING 2004), Geneva, Switzerland (2004)
16. La Cascia, M., Sethi, S., Sclaroff, S.: Combining textual and visual cues for content–based image retrieval on the world wide web. In: IEEE Workshop on Content–based Access of Image and Video Libraries (CBAIVL'98), Santa Barbara, CA, USA (1998)
17. Agrawal, R., Srikant, R.: Fast algorithms for mining association rules. In: Proceedings of the 20th VLDB Conference, Santiago, Chile (1994) 487–499

Retrieving Images Using Cross-Language Text and Image Features

Mirna Adriani and Framadhan Arnely

Faculty of Computer Science
University of Indonesia
Depok 16424, Indonesia
mirna@cs.ui.ac.id, frama101@mhs.cs.ui.ac.id

Abstract. We present a report on our participation in the English-Indonesian image ad-hoc task of the 2005 Cross-Language Evaluation Forum (CLEF). We chose to translate an Indonesian query set into English using a commercial machine translation tool called *Transtool*. We used an approach that combines the retrieval results of the query on text and on image. We used query expansion in our effort to improve the retrieval effectiveness. However, worse retrieval effectiveness was resulted.

1 Introduction

This year we (the IR Group of the University of Indonesia) participated in the bilingual ad-hoc task of the CLEF cross-language image retrieval campaign (ImageCLEF) [5], e.g. Indonesian to English CLIR. We used a commercial machine translation software called *Transtool*[1] to translate an Indonesian query set into English. We learned from our previous work [1, 2] that freely-available dictionaries on the Internet failed to provide correct translations for many query terms, as their vocabulary was very limited. We hoped that we could improve the result using machine translation.

2 The Query Translation Process

As a first step, we translated the original query set from CLEF into Indonesian. Then this Indonesian version of the query set was translated back into English using *Transtool*. After deleting stopwords from the translated English queries, the words were then stemmed using a Porter stemmer. The resulting queries were then used to find relevant documents in the collections.

2.1 Query Expansion Technique

Expanding translation queries by adding relevant terms has been shown to improve CLIR effectiveness. Among the query expansion techniques is the *pseudo relevance*

[1] See http://www.geocities.com/cdpenerjemah/

C. Peters et al. (Eds.): CLEF 2005, LNCS 4022, pp. 733 – 736, 2006.

feedback [3, 5]. This technique is based on an assumption that the top few documents initially retrieved are indeed relevant to the query, and so they must contain other terms that are also relevant to the query. The query expansion technique adds such terms into the translated queries. We applied this technique to this work. To choose the good terms from the top ranked documents, we used the *tf*idf* term weighting formula [3, 5]. We added a certain number of noun terms with the highest weight values.

2.2 Combining the Scores of Text and Image

The short caption that attached to each image in the collections was indexed using *Lucene*[2], an open source indexing and retrieval engine, and the image collection was indexed using GIFT[3]. We combined the scores of text and image retrieval in order to get a better result. The text was given more weight because the image retrieval effectiveness that we obtained from using GIFT was poor. We used the two examples given by CLEF and ran them as query by example through GIFT to search through the collection. We combined the color histogram, texture histogram, the color block, and the texture block in order to get the images that are most similar to the two examples. The text score was given a weight of 0.8 and the image score was given 0.2. These weights were chosen after comparing a number of different weight configurations in our initial experiments.

3 Experiment

The image collection contains 28,133 images from the St. Andrews image collection that have short captions in English. We participated in the bilingual task using Indonesian query topics. We opted to use the query title and the narrative for all of the available 28 topics. The query translation process was performed fully automatic using the *Transtool* machine translation software.

We then applied the pseudo relevance-feedback query-expansion technique to the translated queries. We used the top 20 documents from the *Glasgow Herald* collection to extract the expansion terms.

In these experiments, we used the *Lucene* information retrieval system to index and retrieve image captions (text).

4 Results

Our work was focused on the bilingual task using Indonesian queries to retrieve images from the image collections. The machine translation tool failed to translate three words in the titles and eight words in the narratives. In particular, the machine translation failed to translate Indonesian names of places or locations such as *Skotlandia* (Scotland), *Swis* (Swiss), and *Irlandia* (Ireland) into English. The average number of words in the queries was largely the same as the resulting English version.

---

[2] See http://lucene.apache.org/

[3] See http://savannah.gnu.org/projects/gift/

Table 1 shows the result of our experiments. The retrieval performance of the translation queries obtained using the machine translation-based technique falls below the equivalent monolingual query.

Table 1. Average retrieval precision of the monolingual runs using English queries

Query	Monolingual	Bilingual
Title	0.3538	0.2122 (-40.02%)
Narrative	0.3463	0.1781 (-48.57%)
Title + Narrative	0.3878	0.2082 (-46.31%)

The retrieval precision of the translated title queries was below that of the monolingual retrieval, i.e. by 40.02%. The retrieval effectiveness of translated narrative queries was 48.57% below that of the monolingual retrieval. The retrieval effectiveness of combined translated title and narrative queries was 46.31% below that of the monolingual retrieval.

Table 2. Average retrieval precision of the bilingual runs using Indonesian queries that were translated into English using machine translation

Task : Bilingual	P/R
Title	0.2122
Title + Expansion	0.1485
Title + Image	0.2290
Title + Narrative	0.2082
Title + Narrative + Expansion	0.1931
Title + Narrative + Image	0.2235
Narrative	0.1781
Narrative + Expansion	0.1586
Narrative + Image	0.1981

The retrieval performance of the translated queries using machine translation was best for title only (see Table 2). The effectiveness of narrative-only retrieval was 16.06% worse than that of the title only. By taking the image score into account, in addition to text, the results showed some improvement. For the title-based retrieval, the image score increased the average retrieval precision by 7.91%; for the narrative-based retrieval, the image score increased the average retrieval precision by 11.22%. However, the query expansion technique did not improve the retrieval performance. It decreased the retrieval performance of the title-only retrieval by 30.01% and narrative-only retrieval by 10.94%.

The retrieval effectiveness of combining title and narrative was 1.88% worse than that of the title only retrieval, but was 14.45% better than the narrative only retrieval. The query expansion also decreased the retrieval performance by 7.25% compared to the combined title and narrative queries. Adding the weight of the image to the combined title and narrative scores helped to increase the retrieval performance by 7.34%.

5 Summary

Our results demonstrate that combining the image with the text in the image collections result in better retrieval performance compared to using text only. However, query expansions using general newspaper collections hurt the retrieval performance of the queries. We hope to find a better approach to improve the retrieval effectiveness of combined text and image-based retrieval.

References

1. Adriani, M., van Rijsbergen, C. J.: Term Similarity Based Query Expansion for Cross Language Information Retrieval. In: Abiteboul, Serge; Vercouste, Anne-Marie (eds.): Research and Advanced Technology for Digital Libraries, Third European Conference (ECDL'99). Lecture Notes in Computer Science, Vol. 1696. Springer-Verlag, Berlin (1999) 311-322
2. Adriani, M.: Ambiguity Problem in Multilingual Information Retrieval. In: Peters, Carol (ed.): Cross-Language Evaluation Forum 2000. Lecture Notes in Computer Science, Vol.2069. Springer-Verlag, Berlin (2001)
3. Baeza-Yates, R., Ribeiro-Neto, B.: Modern Information Retrieval. Addison-Wesley, New York (1999)
4. Clough, P., Müller, H., Deselears, T., Grubinger, M., Lehmann, T. M., Jensen, J., Hersh, W.: The CLEF 2005 Cross-Language Image Retrieval Track. In: Proceedings of the Cross-Language Evaluation Forum 2005. Springer Lecture Notes of Computer Science (to appear)
5. Salton, G., McGill, M. J: Introduction to Modern Information Retrieval. McGraw-Hill, New York (1983)

UB at CLEF 2005: Bilingual CLIR and Medical Image Retrieval Tasks

Miguel E. Ruiz and Silvia B. Southwick

State University of New York at Buffalo
School of Informatics,
Dept. of Library and Information Studies
534 Baldy Hall
Buffalo, NY 14260-1020 USA
meruiz@buffalo.edu,
silvias@buffalo.edu
http://www.informatics.buffalo.edu/faculty/ruiz

Abstract. This paper presents the results of the State University of New York at Buffalo in the Cross Language Evaluation Forum 2005 (CLEF 2005). We participated in monolingual Portuguese, bilingual English-Portuguese and in the medical image retrieval tasks. We used the SMART retrieval system for text retrieval in the mono and bilingual retrieval tasks on Portuguese documents. The main goal of this part was to test formally the support for Portuguese that had been added to our system. Our results show an acceptable level of performance in the monolingual task. For the retrieval of medical images with multilingual annotations our main goal was to explore the combination of Content-Based Image Retrieval (CBIR) and text retrieval to retrieve medical images that have clinical annotations in English, French and German. We used a system that combines the content based image retrieval systems GIFT and the well known SMART system for text retrieval. Translation of English topics to French was performed by mapping the English text to UMLS concepts using MetaMap and the UMLS Metathesaurus. Our results on this task confirms that the combination of CBIR and text retrieval improves results significantly with respect to using either image or text retrieval alone.

1 Introduction

This paper presents the results of the State University of New York at Buffalo in CLEF 2005. We participated in three tasks: bilingual English-Portuguese, monolingual Protuguese and medical image retrieval.

Section 2 presents our result for the monolingual Portuguese and bilingual English to Portuguese. Section 3 presents our work for the task of retrieving medical images with multilingual annotations. Section 4 shows our conclusion and future work.

C. Peters et al. (Eds.): CLEF 2005, LNCS 4022, pp. 737–743, 2006.

2 Monolingual and Bilingual Portuguese Tasks

For our monolingual Portuguese and bilingual English-Portuguese tasks we used the SMART information retrieval system [1] modified in house to handle Latin-1 encoding. We also have added several weighting schemes such as pivoted length normalization (Lnu.ltu), and versions of Porter's stemmers for 11 languages. Our main purpose for these tasks was to formaly evaluate the performance of the system using Portuguese documents.

2.1 Document and Query Processing

Documents were preprocessed using a standard Porter stemming algorithm and discarding common Portuguese words using a list of 356 words that was manually constructed. We also added word bigrams that were automatically generated by selecting consecutive words that did not include punctuation or stopwords between them. The word bigrams could include stopwords that are commonly used to form nouns (i.e. "pacto de Varsóvia"). The documents are represented using two ctypes (or index vectors). Queries are pre-processed using the same methods that are used for the documents to generate a representation using two ctypes (stems and bigrams). Similarity between query and document is computed using a generalized vector space model that performs a linear combination of the scores obtained from both ctypes. For the bilingual English to Portuguese retrieval we translate the original English queries using free machine translation services available on the Internet (Systran [1] and Applied Languages [2]). The translated queries are then processed to generate the bigram representation for each query.

Documents were indexed using pivoted length normalization with a pivot equal to the average length of the documents (284.3866) computed over the entire Portuguese collection and a fixed slope value (0.2). We also used pseudo relevance feedback to automatically expand the query assuming that the top n documents are relevant and then select the top m terms ranked according to Rocchio's relevance feedback formula to expand the query [2].

2.2 Results and Analysis

We submitted four runs for the monolingual Portuguese task which cover different strategies for expansion varying the number of documents and terms used for pseudo relevance feedback:

- Aggressive pseudo relevance feedback: expanding queries with 300 terms from the top 10 retrieved documents using Lnu.ltu weights (UBmono-pt-rf1)

[1] Systran translation is available at http://www.google.com/language_tools

[2] Applied Languages offers a free page translation tool available at http://www.appliedlanguage.com/free_translation.shtml

Table 1. Performance of official monolingual Portuguese

	AvgP	number of queries > median
UBmono-pt-rf1	0.3171	17
UBmono-pt-rf2	0.3189	20
UBmono-pt-rf3	0.3162	16
UBmono-pt-comb1	0.3166	20

Table 2. Performance of official bilingual English-Portuguese

	AvgP	% of best Monolingual
UBbi-en-pt-t1	0.1786	56%
UBbi-en-pt-t2	0.1791	56%
UBbi-en-pt-comb1	0.1572	49%
UBbi-en-pt-comb2	0.1787	56%

– Moderate pseudo relevance feedback: expanding queries with the top 30 terms from the top 5 retrieved documents using Lnu.ltu weight (UBmono-pt-rf2)
– Aggressive pseudo relevance feedback with Lnu.ltc weights: expanding the query with 300 terms from the top 10 retrieved documents (UBmono-pt-rf3)
– Combination of all the runs above using a simple addition of normalized scores (UBmono-pt-comb1)

The results for these runs are presented in Table 1. These results show that the current system performs about the same level as the median system in CLEF 2005. Although these results are acceptable there is still room for improvement.

Results for the bilingual English-Portuguese task are presented in Table 2. For this task we submitted four runs that use two different translation systems. For all our runs we used a conservative pseudo relevance feedback expansion that assumes that the top 10 retrieved documents are relevant and then selects the top 30 terms for expanding each query. Our results show that there is a very small difference between the two translations obtained from Systran and Applied Language. It also shows that the combination of both translations does not produce an improvement in retrieval performance. After doing some analysis of the actual translations we found that there are some substantial errors in the queries generated by the machine translation that need to be corrected to achieve a higher performance. In particular there were 14 queries that achieve less than 10% of the monolingual performance and 12 queries that achieve less than 50% of the monolingual performance. We will need to explore other methods to improve performance in these queries.

3 Retrieval of Medical Images with Multilingual Annotations

For our participation in the retrieval of medical images with multilingual annotations this year we used a modified version of the system that we designed for Image-CLEF 2004 [3]. This system combines the GNU Image Finding Tool (GIFT) [4] and the well known SMART information retrieval system [1].

The image retrieval is performed using the ranked list of retrieved images generated by GIFT which was made available to all participants of the image retrieval track [5]. Since this year the queries include a short text description as well as one or more sample images we decided to explore the usage of a tool for maping free text to semantic concepts. For this purpose we used Meta Map [6] which is a tool that maps free text to concepts in the Unified Medical Language System (UMLS)[7]. The UMLS includes the Metathesaurus, the Specialist Lexiocon, and the Semantic Map. The UMLS Metathesaurus combines more that 79 vocabularies. Among these vocabularies, the Medical Subject Headings (MeSH) and several vocabularies include translations of medical English terms to 13 diferent languages.

3.1 Collection Preparation and Indexing

We used the SMART system to create a multilingual database with all the case descriptions of the 4 collections of images (Casimage, MIR, Pathopic, and PIER). The English text associated to each query was processed using Meta Map to obtain a list of UMLS concepts associated to the query [6]. These UMLS concepts are used to locate the corresponding French translations. These translation terms are added to the original English query to generate a bilingual English-French query. Figure 1 shows a schematic representation of the system used for in this task.

The organizers of the conference provided a list of the top 1000 retrieved images returned by GIFT for each of the 25 topics. We used this list as the output of CBIR system. The English version of the queries was processed with Meta Map using a strict model and printing the Concept Unique Identifier (CUI) of the candidate terms. These CUIs were used for retrieving French translations from the UMLS. The resulting French terms were used as the translation of the query. We also use an automatic retrieval feedback with the top 10 retrieved images and case descriptions to generate and expanded query using Rocchio's formula. The images associated to the retrieved textual descriptions were assigned the retrieval score assigned to the retrieved case. The final step combines the results from the CBIR and text retrieval systems using the following formula:

$$W_k = \lambda Iscore_k + \delta Tscore_k \tag{1}$$

where $Iscore_k$ and $Tscore_k$ are the scores assigned to the image k by the image retrieval system and text retrieval system (SMART) respectively , λ and δ are coefficients that weight the contribution of each score. Usually the coefficients are estimated from experimental results.

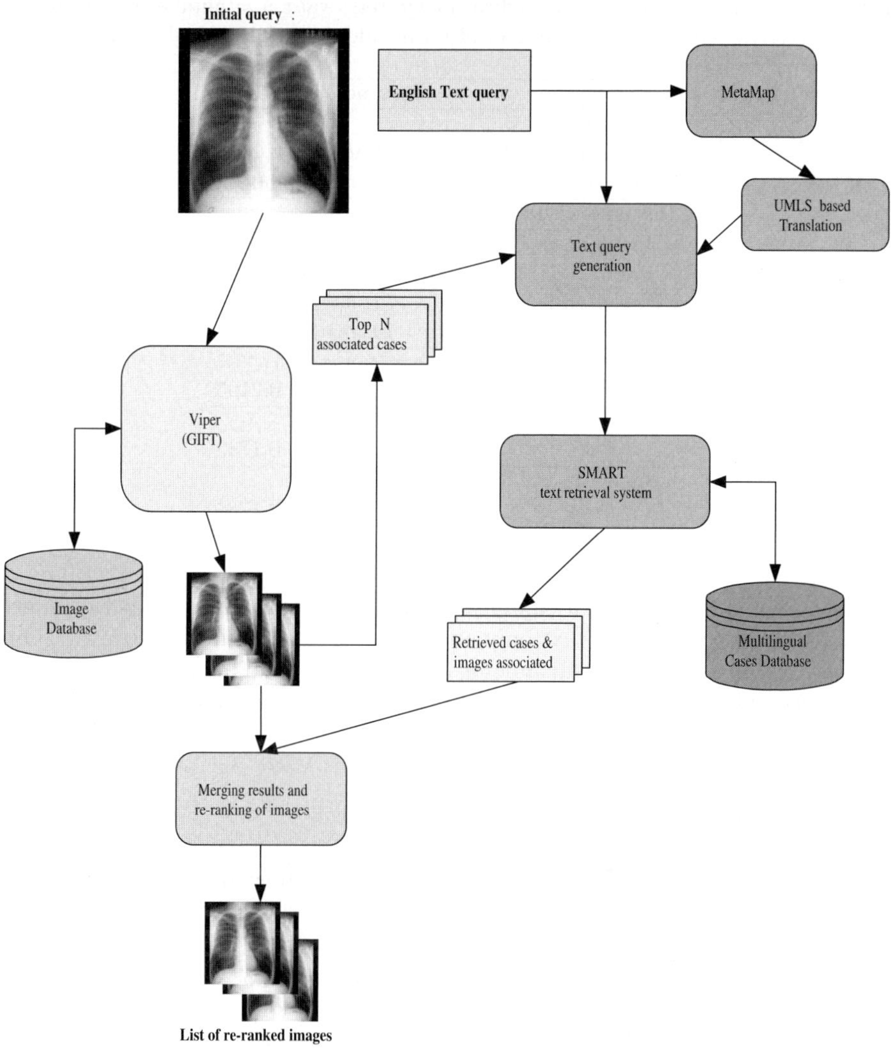

Fig. 1. Diagram of our text and image retrieval system for CLEF 2005

3.2 Results

We submitted five runs that included different weights for the contribution of text and images, and several variations on the number of terms used for expansion (see Table 3). The best combination of our official results were obtained by weighting the text results 3 times higher than the visual results. The parameters for the relevance feedback use the top 10 results (both images and text cases), and expand the queries with the top 50 terms ranked using the Rocchio's formula (with $\alpha = 8$, $\beta = 64$, $\gamma = 16$) [2].

Table 3. Summary of results for medical image retrieval (n = number of documents used for retrival feedback, m = number of terms added to the expanded query)

	Parameters	MAP
Text only		
(UBimed_en-fr.T.Bl)	n=10, m=50	0.1746
Visual only	GIFT results	0.0864
Text and visual		
UBimed_en-fr.TI.1	$\lambda = 1$, $\delta = 3$	
	n= 10, m=50	0.2358
UBimed_en-fr.TI.2	$\lambda = 1$, $\delta = 1$	
	n= 10, m=50	0.1663
UBimed_en-fr.TI.3	$\lambda = 2$, $\delta = 5$	
	n= 10, m=150	0.2195
UBimed_en-fr.TI.4	$\lambda = 2$, $\delta = 5$	
	n= 10, m=50	0.1742
UBimed_en-fr.TI.5	$\lambda = 1$, $\delta = 3$	
	n= 10, m=20	0.1784

This combination shows a significant improvement of retrieval performance (35% with respect to using text only and 173% using only image retrieval). Our runs were fourth over all and among the best 3 systems participating in the conference. The difference between the combined run and both base lines (text only and image only) are statistically significant.

4 Conclusions and Future Work

While our monolingual Portuguese retrieval results show an acceptable level of performace, the bilingual English-Portuguse results show that further research is needed to improve the cross-language retrieval results.

The results obtained in the retrieval of medical images with bilingual annotations show that combining CBIR and text retrieval yields significant improvements in performance. We also confirmed that the translation method based on mapping English concepts to the UMLS Metathesurus to find the appropriate translation to French is an effective alternative to machine translation.

We plan to extend this work to further explore translation issues that affect performance of cross-language retrieval. It seems that using a mapping to a conceptual space before translation could help to improve this process in general.

Acknowledgement

We want to thank the National Library of Medicine for allowing us to use the UMLS and MetaMap programs for this research. Part of this research was conducted at the National Library of Medicine by Miguel E. Ruiz while he was working as a visiting researcher during the summer of 2005.

References

1. Salton, G. (Ed.): The SMART Retrieval System: Experiments in Automatic Document Processing. Englewood Cliff, NJ, Prentice Hall, 1971.
2. Rocchio, J. J.: Relevance feedback in information retrieval. In G. Salton (Ed.) The SMART Retrieval System: Experiments in Automatic Document Processing (pp.313.323). Englewood Cliff, NJ, Prentice Hall, 1971.
3. Ruiz, M. E. and Srikanth, M.: UB at CLEF2004: Cross Language Medical Image Retrieval. In Proceedings of the Cross Language Evaluation Forum 2004, Springer Lecture Notes in Computer science, 2005 - In press.
4. Viper Research Group URL: viper.unige.ch
5. Clough, P and Müller, H and Deselaers, T and Grubinger,M and Lehmann, T M and Jensen, J and Hersh, W : The CLEF 2005 Cross-Language Image Retrieval Track, Proceedings of the Cross Language Evaluation Forum 2005, Springer Lecture Notes in Computer science, 2006 - to appear
6. Aronson, A.: Effective Mapping of Biomedical Text to the UMLS Metathesaurus: The MetaMap Program. Paper presented at the American Medical Informatics Association Conference, 2001.
7. U.S. National Library of Medicine: Unified Medical Language System (UMLS). Bethesda: MD, 2004.

Overview of the CLEF-2005 Cross-Language Speech Retrieval Track

Ryen W. White[1], Douglas W. Oard[1,2], Gareth J.F. Jones[3], Dagobert Soergel[2], and Xiaoli Huang[2]

[1] Institute for Advanced Computer Studies
[2] College of Information Studies
University of Maryland, College Park MD 20742, USA
{ryen, oard, dsoergel, xiaoli}@umd.edu
[3] School of Computing, Dublin City University, Dublin 9, Ireland
Gareth.Jones@computing.dcu.ie

Abstract. The task for the CLEF-2005 cross-language speech retrieval track was to identify topically coherent segments of English interviews in a known-boundary condition. Seven teams participated, performing both monolingual and cross-language searches of ASR transcripts, automatically generated metadata, and manually generated metadata. Results indicate that monolingual search technology is sufficiently accurate to be useful for some purposes (the best mean average precision was 0.13) and cross-language searching yielded results typical of those seen in other applications (with the best systems approximating monolingual mean average precision).

1 Introduction

The 2005 Cross-Language Evaluation Forum (CLEF) Cross-Language Speech Retrieval (CL-SR) track follows two years of experimentation with cross-language retrieval of broadcast news in the CLEF-2003 and CLEF-2004 Spoken Document Retrieval (SDR) tracks [2]. CL-SR is distinguished from CL-SDR by the lack of clear topic boundaries in conversational speech. Moreover, spontaneous speech is considerably more challenging for the Large-Vocabulary Continuous Speech Recognition (referred to here generically as Automatic Speech Recognition, or ASR) techniques on which fully-automatic content-based search systems are based. Recent advances in ASR have made it possible to contemplate the design of systems that would provide a useful degree of support for searching large collections of spontaneous conversational speech, but no representative test collection that could be used to support the development of such systems was widely available for research use. The principal goal of the CLEF-2005 CL-SR track was to create such a test collection. Additional goals included benchmarking the present state of the art for ranked retrieval of spontaneous conversational speech and fostering interaction among a community of researchers with interest in that challenge.

Three factors came together to make the CLEF 2005 CL-SR track possible. First, substantial investments in research on ASR for spontaneous conversational speech have yielded systems that are able to transcribe near-field speech (e.g., telephone

C. Peters et al. (Eds.): CLEF 2005, LNCS 4022, pp. 744 – 759, 2006.

calls) with Word Error Rates (WER) below 20% and far-field speech (e.g., meetings) with WER near 30%. This is roughly the same WER range that was found to adequately support ranked retrieval in the original Text Retrieval Conference (TREC) SDR track evaluations [3]. Second, the Survivors of the Shoah Visual History Foundation (VHF) collected, digitized, and annotated a very large collection (116,000 hours) of interviews with Holocaust survivors, witnesses and rescuers. In particular, one 10,000-hour subset of that collection was extensively annotated in a way that allowed us to affordably decouple relevance judgment from the limitations of current speech technology. Third, a project funded by the U.S. National Science Foundation focused on Multilingual Access to Large Spoken Archives (MALACH) is producing LVSCR systems for this collection to foster research on access to spontaneous conversational speech, and automatic transcriptions from two such systems are now available [1].

Designing a CLEF track requires that we balance the effort required to participate with the potential benefits to the participants. For this first year of the track, we sought to minimize the effort required to participate, and within that constraint to maximize the potential benefit. The principal consequence of that decision was adoption of a known-boundary condition in which systems performed ranked retrieval on topically coherent segments. This yielded a test collection with the same structure that is used for CLEF ad hoc tasks, thus facilitating application of existing ranked retrieval technology to this new task. Participants in new tracks often face a chicken-and-egg dilemma, with good retrieval results needed from all participants before an a test collection can be affordably created using pooled relevance assessment techniques, but the exploration of the design space that is needed to produce good results requires that a test collection already exist. For the CLEF-2005 CL-SR track we were able to address this challenge by distributing training topics with relevance judgments that had been developed using a search-guided relevance assessment process [5]. We leveraged the availability of those training topics by distributing an extensive set of manually and automatically created metadata that participants could use as a basis for constructing contrastive conditions. In order to promote cross-site comparisons, we asked each participating team to submit one "required run" in which the same topic language and topic fields and only automatically generated transcriptions and/or metadata were used.

The remainder of this overview paper is structured as follows. In Section 2 we describe the CL-SR test collection. Section 3 identifies the sites that participated and briefly describes the techniques that they tried. Section 4 looks across the runs that were submitted to identify conclusions that can be drawn from those results. Section 5 concludes the paper with a brief description of future plans for the CLEF CL-SR track.

2 Collection

The CLEF-2005 CL-SR test collection was released in two stages. In Release One (February 15 2005), the "documents," training topics and associated relevance judgments, and scripts were made available to participants to support system development. Release Two (April 15 2005) included the 25 evaluation topics on which sites' runs would be evaluated, one additional script that could be used to perform thesaurus expansion, and some metadata fields that had been absent from Release One. This section describes the genesis of the test collection.

2.1 Documents

The fundamental goal of a ranked retrieval system is to sort a set of "documents" in decreasing order of expected utility. Commonly used evaluation frameworks rely on an implicit assumption that ground-truth document boundaries exist.[1] The nature of oral history interviews challenges this assumption, however. The average VHF interview extends for more than 2 hours, and spoken content that extensive can not presently be easily skimmed. Many users, therefore, will need systems that retrieve passages rather than entire interviews.[2] Remarkably, the VHF collection contains a 10,000 hour subset for which manual segmentation into topically coherent segments was carefully performed by subject matter experts. We therefore chose to use those segments as the "documents" for the CLEF-2005 CL-SR evaluation.

Development of Automatic Speech Recognition (ASR) systems is an iterative process in which evaluation results from initial system designs are used to guide the development of refined systems. In order to limit the computational overhead of this process, we chose to work initially with roughly 10% of the interviews for which manual topic segmentation is available. We chose 403 interviews (totaling roughly 1,000 hours of English speech) for this purpose. Of those 403, portions of 272 interviews had been digitized and processed by two ASR systems at the time that the CLEF-2005 CL-SR test collection was released. A total of 183 of those are complete interviews; for the other 89 interviews ASR results are available for at least one, but not all, of the 30-minute tapes on which the interviews were originally recorded. In some segments, near the end of an interview, physical objects (e.g., photographs) are shown and described. Those segments are not well suited for ASR-based search because few words are typically spoken by the interviewee (usually less then 15) and because we chose not to distribute the visual referent as a part of the test collection. Such segments were unambiguously marked by human indexers, and we automatically removed them from the test collection. The resulting test collection contains 8,104 segments from 272 interviews totaling 589 hours of speech. That works out to an average of about 4 minutes (503 words) of recognized speech per segment. A collection of this size is very small from the perspective of modern IR experiments using written sources (e.g., newswire or Web pages), but it is comparable in size to the 550-hour collection of broadcast news used in the CLEF-2004 SDR evaluation.

As Figure 1 shows, each segment was uniquely identified by a `DOCNO` field in which the `IntCode` uniquely identifies an interview within the collection, `SegId`

---

[1] Note that we do not require that document boundaries be known to the system under test, only that they exist. The TREC HARD track passage retrieval task and the TREC SDR unknown boundaries condition are examples of cases in which the ground truth boundaries are not known to the system under test. Even in those cases ground-truth boundaries must be known to the evaluation software.

[2] Initial studies with 9 teachers and 6 scholars indicated that all teachers and about half the scholars needed segment-based access for the tasks in which they were engaged.

uniquely identifies a segment within the collection, and `SequenceNum` is the sequential order of a segment within an interview. For example, VHF00009-056149.001 is the first segment in interview number 9.

The following fields were created by VHF subject matter experts while viewing the interview. They are included in the test collection to support contrastive studies in which results from manual and automated indexing are compared:

- The `INTERVIEWDATA` field contains all names by which the interviewee was known (e.g., present name, maiden name, and nicknames) and the date of birth of the interviewee. The contents of this field are identical for every segment from the same interview (i.e., for every `DOCNO` that contains the same `IntCode`). This data was obtained from handwritten questionnaires that were completed before the interview (known as the Pre-Interview Questionnaire or PIQ).
- The `NAME` field contains the names of other persons that were mentioned in the segment. The written form of a name was standardized within an interview (a process known as "name authority control"), but not across interviews.
- The `MANUALKEYWORDS` field contains thesaurus descriptors that were manually assigned from a large thesaurus that was constructed by VHF. Two types of keywords are present, but not distinguished: (1) keywords that express a subject or concept; and (2) keywords that express a location, often combined with time in one pre-coordinated keyword. On average about 5 manually thesaurus descriptors were manually assigned to each segment, at least one of which was typically a pre-coordinated location-time pair (usually with one-year granularity)
- The `SUMMARY` field contains a three-sentence summary in which a subject matter expert used free text in a structured style to address the following questions: who? what? when? where?

The following fields were generated fully automatically by systems that did not have access to the manually assigned metadata for any interview in the test collection. These fields could therefore be used to explore the potential of different techniques for automated processing:

- Two ASRTEXT fields contain words produced by an ASR system. The speech was automatically transcribed by ASR systems developed at the IBM T. J. Watson Research Center. The manual segmentation process at VHF was conducted using time-coded videotape without display of the acoustic envelope. The resulting segment boundaries sometimes occur in the middle of a word in the one-best ASR transcript. We therefore automatically adjusted the segment boundaries to the nearest significant silence (a silence with a duration of 2 seconds or longer) if such a silence began within 9 seconds of the assigned boundary time; otherwise we adjusted the segment boundary to the nearest word boundary. The words from the one-best ASR transcript were then used to create an ASR field for the resulting segments. This process was repeated for two ASR systems. The `ASRTEXT2004A` field of the document representation shown in Figure 1 contains an automatically created transcript using the best available ASR system, for which an overall mean WER of 38% and a mean named entity error rate of 32% was computed over portions of 15 held-out interviews. The recognizer vocabulary for this system was primed on an interview-specific basis with person names, locations, organization names and country names mentioned in an extensive pre-interview questionnaire. The `ASRTEXT2003A` field contains an automatically created transcript using an earlier system for which a mean WER of 40% and a mean named entity error rate of 66% was computed using the same held-out data.

- Two AUTOKEYWORD fields contain thesaurus descriptors that were automatically assigned by using text classification techniques. The `AUTOKEYWORD2004A1` field contains a set of thesaurus keywords that were assigned automatically using a k-Nearest Neighbor (kNN) classifier using only words from the `ASRTEXT2004A` field of the segment; the top 20 keywords are included. The classifier was trained using data (manually assigned thesaurus keywords and manually written segment summaries) from segments that are not contained in the CL-SR test collection. The `AUTOKEYWORD2004A2` field contains a set of thesaurus keywords that were assigned in a manner similar to those in the `AUTOKEYWORD2004A1`, but using a different kNN classifier that was trained (fairly) on different data; the top 16 concept keywords and the top 4 location-time pairs (i.e., the place names mentioned and associated dates) were included for each segment.

The three KEYWORD fields in the test collection included only the VHF-assigned "preferred term" for each thesaurus descriptor. A script was provided with the final release of the test collection that could be used to expand the descriptors for each segment using synonymy, part-whole, and is-a thesaurus relationships. That capability could be used with automatically assigned descriptors or (for contrastive runs) with the manually assigned descriptors.

```
<DOC>
<DOCNO>VHF[IntCode]-[SegId].[SequenceNum]</DOCNO>
<INTERVIEWDATA>Interviewee name(s) and birthdate
</INTERVIEWDATA>
<NAME>Full name of every person mentioned</NAME>
<MANUALKEYWORD>Thesaurus keywords assigned to segment
</MANUALKEYWORD>
<SUMMARY>3-sentence segment summary</SUMMARY>
<ASRTEXT2003A>ASR transcript produced in 2003
</ASRTEXT2003A>
<ASRTEXT2004A>ASR transcript produced in 2004
</ASRTEXT2004A>
<AUTOKEYWORD2004A1>Thesaurus keywords from a kNN classifier
</AUTOKEYWORD2004A1>
<AUTOKEYWORD2004A2>Thesaurus keywords from second kNN classifier
</AUTOKEYWORD2004A2>
</DOC>
```

Fig. 1. Document structure in CL-SR test collection

2.2 Topics

The VHF collection has attracted significant interest from scholars, educators, documentary film makers, and others, resulting in 280 topic-oriented written requests for materials from the collection. From that set, we selected 75 requests that we felt were representative of the types of requests and the types of subjects contained in the topic-oriented requests. The requests were typically made in the form of business letters, often accompanied by a filled-in request form describing the requester's project and purpose. Additional materials (e.g., a thesis proposal) were also sometimes available. TREC-style topic descriptions consisting of title, a short description and a narrative were created for the 75 topics, as shown by the example in Figure 2.

```
<top>
<num> 1148
<title> Jewish resistance in Europe
<desc> Provide testimonies or describe actions of Jewish resis-
tance in Europe before and during the war.
<narr> The relevant material should describe actions of only- or
mostly Jewish resistance in Europe. Both individual and group-
based actions are relevant. Type of actions may include survival
(fleeing, hiding, saving children), testifying (alerting the
outside world, writing, hiding testimonies), fighting (parti-
sans, uprising, political security) Information about undiffer-
entiated resistance groups is not relevant.
</top>
```

Fig. 2. Example topic

Only topics for which relevant segments exist can be used as a basis for comparing the effectiveness of ranked retrieval systems, so we sought to ensure the presence of an adequate number of relevant segments for each test topic. For the first 50 topics, we iterated between topic selection and interview selection in order to arrive at a set of topics and interviews for which the number of relevant segments was likely to be sufficient to yield reasonably stable estimates of mean average precision (we chose 30 relevant segments as our target, but allowed considerable variation). At that point we could have selected any 10% of the available fully indexed interviews for the test collection, so the process was more constrained by topic selection than by interview selection. In some cases, this required that we broaden specific requests to reflect our understanding of a more general class of information need for which the request we examined would be a specific case. This process excluded most queries that included personal names or very specific and infrequently used geographical areas. The remaining 25 topics were selected after the interview set was frozen, so in that case topic selection and broadening were the only free variables. All of the training topics are drawn from the first 50; most of the evaluation topics are from the last 25. A total of 12 topics were excluded, 6 because the number of relevant documents turned out to be too small to permit stable estimates of mean average precision (fewer than 5) or so large (over 50% of the total number of judgments) that the exhaustiveness of the search-guided assessment process was open to question. The remaining 6 topics were excluded because relevance judgments were not ready in time for release as training topics and they were not needed to complete the set of 25 evaluation topics. The resulting test collection therefore contains 63 topics, with an additional 6 topics for which embargoed relevance judgments are already available for use in the CLEF-2006 evaluation collection. Participants are asked not to perform any analysis involving topics outside the released set of 63 in order to preserve the integrity of the CLEF-2006 test collection.

All topics were originally authored in English and then re-expressed in Czech, French, German and Spanish by native speakers of those languages to support cross-language retrieval experiments. In each case, the translations were checked by a second native speaker before being released. For the French translations, resource constraints precluded translation of the narrative fields. All three fields are available for the other query languages.

Relevance judgments were made for the full set of 404 interviews, including those segments that were removed from the released collection because they contained only brief descriptions of physical objects. Judging every document for every topic would have required about 750,000 relevance judgments. Even had that been affordable (e.g., by judging each segment for several topics simultaneously), such a process could not be affordably scaled up to larger collections. The usual way this challenge is addressed in CLEF, pooled relevance assessment, involves substantial risk when applied to spoken word collections. With pooled assessment, documents that are not assessed are treated as if they are not relevant when computing effectiveness measures such as mean average precision. When all systems operate on similar feature set (e.g., words), it has been shown that comparable results can be obtained even for systems that did not contribute to the assessment pools. This is enormously consequential, since it allows the cost of creating a test collection to be amortized over anticipated future uses of that collection. Systems based on automatic speech recognition with a relatively high WER violate the condition for reuse, however, since the feature set on which future systems might be based (recognized words) could well be quite different. We therefore chose an alternative technique, search-guided relevance judgment, which has been used to construct reusable test collections for spoken word collections in the Topic Detection and Tracking (TDT) evaluations.

Our implementation of search-guided evaluation differs from that used in TDT in that we search manually assigned metadata rather than ASR transcripts. Relevance assessors are able to search all of the metadata distributed with the test collection, plus notes made by the VHF indexers for their own use, summaries of the full interview prepared by the VHF indexer, and a fuller set of PIQ responses. For interviews that had been digitized by the time assessment was done, relevance assessors could also listen to the audio; in other cases, they could indicate whether they felt that listening to the audio might change their judgment so that re-assessment could be done once the audio became available. The relevance assessment system was based on Lucene, which supports fielded searching using both ranked and Boolean retrieval. The set of thesaurus terms assigned to each segment was expanded by adding broader terms from the thesaurus up to the root of the hierarchy. A threshold was applied to the ranked list, and retrieved segments were then re-arranged by interview and within each interview in decreasing score order. The display order was structured to place interviews with many highly ranked segments ahead of those with fewer. Relevance assessors could easily reach preceding or following segments of the same interview; those segments often provide information needed to assess the relevance of the segment under consideration, and they may also be relevant in their own right.

2.3 Relevance Assessment

Our relevance assessors were 6 graduate students studying history. The assessors were experienced searchers; they made extensive use of complex structured queries and interactive query reformulation. They conducted extensive research on assigned topics using external resources before and during assessment, and kept extensive notes on their interpretation of the topics, topic-specific guidelines for deciding on the level of relevance for each relevance type, and other issues (e.g., rationale for judging specific segments). Relevance assessors did thorough searches to find as many relevant segments as possible and assessed the segments they found for each topic. We employed two processes to minimize the chance of unintentional errors during relevance assessment:

- Dual-assessment: For some training topics, segments were judged independently by two assessors with subsequent adjudication; this process resulted in two sets of independent relevance judgments that can be used to compute inter-annotator agreement plus the one set of adjudicated judgments that were released.
- Review: For the remaining training topics and all evaluation topics, an initial judgment was done by one assessor and then their results were reviewed, and if necessary revised, by a second assessor. This process resulted in one set of adjudicated relevance judgments that were released.

As a result of the above processes, for every topic-segment pair, we have two sets of relevance assessments derived from two assessors, either independent or not. This allowed us to later measure the inter-assessor agreement and thus to gain insight into the reliability of relevance assessments on selected topics.

The search-guided assessments are complemented by pooled assessments using the top 100 segments from 14 runs (i.e., the top two prioritized runs selected from each of the seven participating sites). Participants were requested to prioritize their runs in such a way that selecting the runs assigned the highest priority would result in the most diverse judgment pools. Assessors judged all segments in these pools that had not already been judged as part of the search-guided assessment process. For this process, most topics had just one assessor and no review. A grand total of 58,152 relevance judgments were created for the 403 interviews and 75 topics during the summer months of 2003, 2004, and 2005. These judgments comprised the search-guided assessments from all three summers, plus the pooled assessments from 2005. Of these judgments, 48,881 are specific to the topics and segments in the CLEF-2005 CL-SR test collection. The 9,271 judgments that were not released can be attributed to the 12 topics excluded from the test collection.

Relevance is a multifaceted concept; interview segments may be relevant (in the sense that they help the searcher perform the task from which the query arose) for different reasons. We therefore defined five types of topical relevance, both to guide the thinking of our assessors and to obtain differentiated judgments that could serve as a basis for more detailed analysis than would be possible using binary single-facet judgments. The relevance types that we chose were based on the notion of evidence (rather than, for example, potential emotional impact or appropriateness to an audience). The initial inventory of five relevance types was based on our understanding of historical methods and information seeking processes. The types were then refined during a two-week pilot study through group discussions with our assessors. The resulting types are:

- Provides **direct** evidence
- Provides **indirect**/circumstantial evidence
- Provides **context**
- Useful as a basis for **comparison**
- Provides **pointer** to a source of information

The first two of these match the traditional definition of topical relevance in CLEF; the last three would normally be treated as not relevant in the sense that term is used at CLEF. Each type of relevance was judged on a five-point scale (0=none to 4=high). Assessors were also asked to assess **overall** relevance, defined as the degree to which they felt that a segment would prove to be useful to the search that had originally posed the topic. Assessors were instructed to consider two factors in all assessments: (1) the nature of the information (i.e., level of detail and uniqueness), and (2) the nature of the report (i.e., first-hand vs. second-hand accounts vs. rumor). For example, the definition of direct relevance is: "Directly on topic ... describes the events or circumstances asked for or otherwise speaks directly to what the user is looking for. First-hand accounts are preferred ... second-hand accounts (hearsay) are acceptable." For indirect relevance, the assessors also considered the strength of the inferential connection between the segment and the phenomenon of interest. The average length of a segment is about 4 minutes, so the brevity of a mention is an additional factor that could affect the performance of search systems. We therefore asked assessors to estimate the fraction of the segment that was associated with each of the five categories.[3] Assessors were instructed to treat brevity and degree separately (a very brief mention could be highly relevant). For more detail on the types of relevance see [4].

To create binary relevance judgments, we elected to treat the union of the direct and indirect judgments with scores of 2, 3, or 4 as topically relevant, regardless of the duration of the mention within the segment.[4] A script was provided with the test collection that allowed sites to generate alternative sets of binary relevance scores as an aid to analysis of results (e.g., some systems may do well when scored with direct topical relevance but poorly when scored with indirect topical relevance).

---

[3] Assessments of the fraction of the segments that were judged as relevant are available, but they were not released with the CLEF-2005 CL-SR test collection because the binarization script had not yet been extended to use that information.

[4] We elected not to use the overall relevance judgments in this computation because our definition of overall relevance allowed consideration of context, comparison and pointer evidence in arriving at a judgment of overall relevance.

The resulting test collection contained 63 topics (38 training, 25 evaluation topics), 8,104 segments, and 48,881 6-aspect sets of complex relevance judgments, distributed as shown in Table 1. Although the training and evaluation topic sets were disjoint, the set of segments being searched was the same.

Table 1. Distribution of judgments across training topics and evaluation topics

Topic set	Training	Evaluation
Total number of topics	38	25
Total judgment sets	30,743	18,138
Median judgment sets per topic	787	683
Total segments with binary relevance true	3,105	1,846
Median relevant judgments per topic	51.5	53

Figure 3 shows the distribution of relevant and non-relevant segments for the training and evaluation topics. Topics are arranged in descending order of proportion relevant (i.e., binary relevance true) versus judged for that topic.

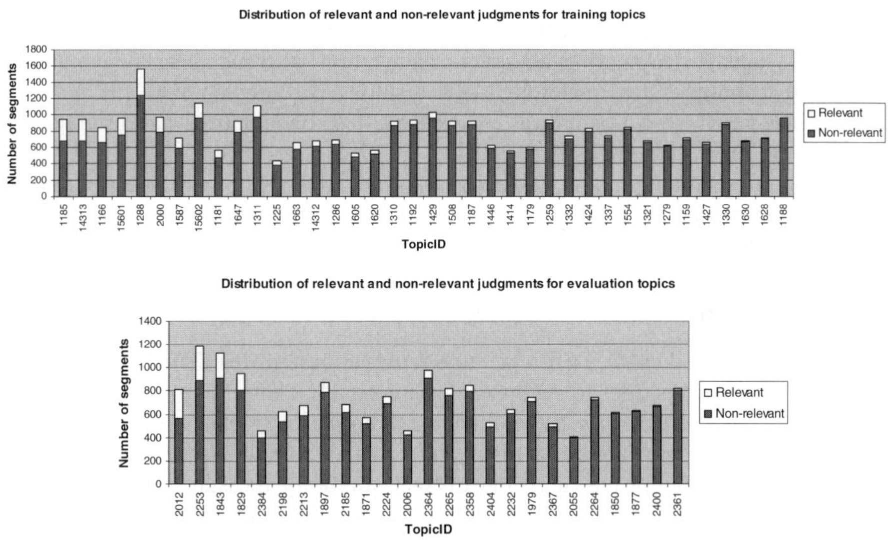

Fig. 3. Distribution of relevant (binary relevance true) and non-relevant segments

To determine the extent of individual differences, we evaluated inter-assessor agreement using two sets of independent judgments for the 28 training topics that were dual assessed. Cohen's Kappa was computed on search-guided binary relevance judgments. The average Kappa score is 0.487, with a standard deviation of 0.188, indicating moderate agreement. The distribution of Kappa scores across different levels of agreement is shown in Table 2.

Table 2. Distribution of agreement over 28 training topics

Kappa range	Slight (0.01 – 0.20)	Fair (0.21 – 0.40)	Moderate (0.41 – 0.60)	Substantial (0.61 – 0.80)	Almost perfect (0.81 – 1.00)
Topics	4	3	12	8	1

3 Experiments

In this section, we describe the run submission procedure and the sites that participated. We accepted a maximum of 5 runs from each site for "official" (i.e., blind) scoring; sites could also score additional runs locally to further explore contrastive conditions. To facilitate comparisons across sites, we asked each site to submit one "required" run using automatically constructed queries from the English title and description fields of the topics (i.e., an automatic monolingual "TD" run) and an index that was constructed without use of human-created metadata (i.e., indexing derived from some combination of `ASRTEXT2003A`, `ASRTEXT2004A`, `AUTOKEYWORD2004A1`, and `AUTOKEYWORD2004A2`, including the optional use of synonyms and/or broader terms for one or both of the `AUTOKEYWORD` fields). The other submitted runs could be created in whatever way best allowed the sites to explore the research questions in which they are interested (e.g., comparing monolingual and cross-language, comparing automatic recognition with metadata, or comparing alternative techniques for exploiting ASR results). In keeping with the goals of CLEF, cross-language searching was encouraged; 40% of submitted runs used queries in a language other than English.

Seven groups submitted runs, and each has provided the following brief description of their experiments; additional details can be found in the working notes paper submitted by each group.

3.1 University of Alicante (ualicante)

The University of Alicante used a passage retrieval system for their experiments in the track this year. Passages in such systems are usually composed of a fixed number of sentences, but the lack of sentence boundaries in the ASR that composed the collection of this track does not allow this feature. To address this issue they used fixed word length overlapping passages and distinct similarity measures (e.g., Okapi) to calculate the weights of the words of the topic according to the document collection. Their experimental system applied heuristics to the representation of the topics in the way of logic forms. The University of Alicante's runs all used English queries and automatic metadata.

3.2 Dublin City University (dcu)

As in Dublin City University's previous participations in CLEF, the basis of their experimental retrieval system was the City University research distribution version of the Okapi probabilistic model. Queries were expanded using pseudo relevance feedback (PRF). Expansion terms were selected from "sentence-based" summaries of the top 5 most assumed relevant documents, where "sentences" in the ASR transcript were derived based on sequential word clusters. All terms within the chosen sentences were then ranked and the top 20 ranking terms selected as expansion terms. Non-English topics were translated to English using SYSTRAN version 3.0. Runs explored various combinations of the ASR transcription, autokeyword and summary fields.

3.3 University of Maryland (umaryland)

The University of Maryland tried automatic retrieval techniques (including blind relevance feedback) with two types of data: manually created metadata and automatically generated data. Three runs used automatic metadata. Submission of the two runs with manual metadata has two main purposes: to set up the best monolingual upper-bound and to compare CLIR with monolingual IR. All runs used the InQuery search engine (version 3.1p1) from the University of Massachusetts.

3.4 Universidad Nacional de Educación a Distancia (uned)

UNED tested different ways to clean documents in the collection. They erased all duplicate words and joined the characters that form spelled words like "l i e b b a c h a r d" into the whole word (i.e., "liebbachard"). Using this cleaned collection they tried a monolingual trigrams approach. They also tried to clean the documents, erasing the less informative words using two different approaches: morphological analysis and part of speech tagging. Their runs were monolingual and cross-lingual.

3.5 University of Pittsburgh (upittsburgh)

The University of Pittsburgh explored two ideas: (1) to study the evidence combination techniques for merging retrieval results based on ASR outputs with human generated metadata at the post-retrieval stage, (2) to explore the usage of Self-Organizing Map (SOM) as a retrieval method by first obtaining the most similar cell on the map to a given search query, then using the cell to generate a ranked list of documents. Their submitted runs used English queries and a mixture of manual and automatically generated document fields.

3.6 University of Ottawa (uottawa)

The University of Ottawa employed an experimental system built using off-the-shelf components. To translate topics from French, Spanish, and German into English, six free online machine translation tools were used. Their output was merged in order to allow for variety in lexical choices. The SMART IR system was tested with many different weighting schemes for indexing the collection and the topics. The University of Ottawa used a variety of query languages and only automatically generated document fields for their submitted runs.

3.7 University of Waterloo (uwaterloo)

The University of Waterloo submitted three English automatic runs, a Czech automatic run and a French automatic run. The basic retrieval method for all runs was

Okapi BM25. All submitted runs used a combination of several query formulation and expansion techniques, including the use of phonetic n-grams and feedback query expansion over a topic-specific external corpus crawled from the Web. The French and Czech runs used translated queries supplied by the University of Ottawa group.

4 Results

Table 3 summarizes the results for all 35 official runs averaged over the 25 evaluation topics, listed in descending order of mean uninterpolated average precision (MAP). Table 3 also reports precision at the rank where the number of retrieved documents equals the number of known relevant documents (Rprec), the fraction of the cases in which judged non-relevant documents are retrieved before judged relevant documents (Bpref) and the precision at 10 documents (P10). Required runs are shown in bold.

Table 3. Official runs

Run name	MAP	Rprec	Bpref	P10	Lang	Query	Document fields	Site
metadata+syn.en.qe	0.313	0.349	0.342	0.480	EN	TD	N,MK,SUM	umaryland
metadata+syn.fr2en.qe	0.248	0.288	0.282	0.368	FR	TD	N,MK,SUM	umaryland
titdes-all	0.188	0.231	0.201	0.364	EN	TD	N,MK,SUM,ASR04,AK1,AK2	upitt
dcusumtit40ffr	0.165	0.218	0.175	0.308	FR	T	ASR04,AK1,AK2,SUM	dcu
dcusumtiteng	0.143	0.199	0.156	0.256	EN	T	ASR04,AK1,AK2,SUM	dcu
titdes-combined	0.142	0.178	0.149	0.360	EN	TD	N,MK,SUM,ASR04,AK1	upitt
uoEnTDN	0.137	0.190	0.163	0.336	EN	TDN	ASR04,AK1,AK2	uottawa
uoEnTD	**0.131**	**0.189**	**0.151**	**0.296**	**EN**	**TD**	**ASR04,AK1,AK2**	**uottawa**
autokey+asr.en.qe	**0.129**	**0.172**	**0.144**	**0.2720**	**EN**	**TD**	**ASR04,AK2**	**umaryland**
Asr.de.en.qe	0.128	0.188	0.146	0.276	EN	TD	ASR04	umaryland
uoFrTD	0.128	0.181	0.155	0.324	FR	TD	ASR04,AK1,AK2	uottawa
uoSpTDN	0.116	0.165	0.142	0.276	SP	TDN	ASR04,AK1,AK2	uottawa
Uw5XETDNfs	0.114	0.191	0.141	0.272	EN	TDN	ASR03,ASR04	uwaterloo
uw5XETDfs	**0.112**	**0.174**	**0.139**	**0.276**	**EN**	**TD**	**ASR03,ASR04**	**uwaterloo**
asr.en.qe	0.110	0.171	0.129	0.280	EN	TD	ASR04	umaryland
dcuala2tit40feng	0.110	0.156	0.131	0.252	EN	T	ASR04,AK1,AK2	dcu
dcuala2tit40ffr	0.106	0.157	0.132	0.260	FR	T	ASR04,AK1,AK2	dcu
uw5XETfs	0.098	0.156	0.127	0.268	EN	T	ASR03,ASR04	uwaterloo
uoGrTDN	0.094	0.138	0.125	0.216	DE	TDN	ASR04,AK1,AK2	uottawa
unedMpos	**0.093**	**0.152**	**0.110**	**0.240**	**EN**	**TD**	**ASR04**	**uned**
unedMmorpho	0.092	0.153	0.110	0.236	EN	TD	ASR04	uned
uw5XFTph	0.085	0.142	0.116	0.256	FR	T	ASR03,ASR04	uwaterloo
UATDASR04AUTOA2	0.077	0.118	0.098	0.224	EN	D	ASR04,AK2	ualicante
UATDASR04LF	**0.077**	**0.123**	**0.095**	**0.192**	**EN**	**TD**	**ASR04**	**ualicante**
titdes-text04a	**0.076**	**0.134**	**0.106**	**0.212**	**EN**	**TD**	**ASR04**	**upitt**
UATDASR04AUTOS	0.074	0.127	0.106	0.240	EN	D	ASR04,AK1,AK2	ualicante
UATDASR04AUTOA1	0.073	0.121	0.102	0.220	EN	D	ASR04,AK1	ualicante
UATDASR04	0.072	0.125	0.090	0.160	EN	D	ASR04	ualicante
uned3gram	0.071	0.112	0.099	0.180	EN	TD	ASR04	uned
dcua2desc40feng	**0.065**	**0.120**	**0.094**	**0.176**	**EN**	**TD**	**ASR04,AK2**	**dcu**
uw5XCTph	0.047	0.075	0.093	0.132	CZ	T	ASR03,ASR04	uwaterloo
unedCLpos	0.037	0.075	0.054	0.120	SP	TD	ASR04	uned
unedCLmorpho	0.037	0.076	0.054	0.120	SP	TD	ASR04	uned
som-allelb	0.012	0.013	0.040	0.012	EN	TDN	N,MK,SUM,ASR04,AK1,AK2	upitt
som-titdes-com	0.004	0.015	0.041	0.012	EN	TD	N,MK,SUM,ASR04,AK1,AK2	upitt

N = Name (Manual), MK = Manual Keywords (Manual), SUM = Summary (Manual).
ASR03 = ASRTEXT2003A (Automatic), ASR04 = ASRTEXT2004A (Automatic).
AK1 = AUTOKEYWORDS2004A1 (Automatic), AK2 = AUTOKEYWORDS2004A2 (Automatic).

Figure 4 compares the required runs across the seven participating sites. The ovals in the figure group runs that are statistically indistinguishable based on a two-tailed Wilcoxon Signed-Rank Test for paired samples at $p<0.05$ across the 25 evaluation topics). The best official run using manual metadata yielded a statistically significant improvement over the strongest results obtained using only automatically generated data.

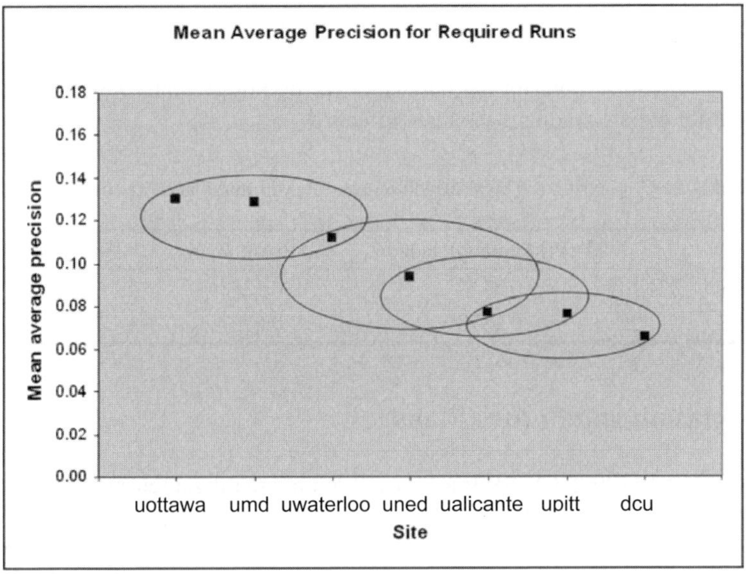

Fig. 4. Plot of mean average precision for required runs

There were 8 cases in which the same site submitted both monolingual and cross-language runs under comparable experimental conditions (i.e., the same query fields and same document fields). Table 4 summarizes those results. Every query language was used. French topics proved to be the most popular for cross-language searching, being used by four of the seven participating teams. Notably, one team achieved cross-language results for French that numerically exceeded their English monolingual mean average precision (although the difference was not statistically significant).

Table 4. Percentage difference in MAP between English and non-English comparable runs

Site (query – document)	En	Cz	De	Fr	Sp
uottawa (TD – ASR04,AK1,AK2)	0.1313	–	–	-3%	–
uottawa (TDN - ASR04,AK1,AK2)	0.1366	–	**–31%**	–	–15%
umaryland (TD – N,K,SUM)	0.3129	–	–	**–21%**	–
uwaterloo (T – ASR03,ASR04)	0.0980	**–52%**	–	–13%	–
uned (TD – ASR04)	0.0934	–	–	–	**–60%**
dcu (T –ASR04,AK1,AK2)	0.1429	–	–	+16%	–

Monolingual baselines constructed in this way are known to be deficient because cross-language retrieval introduces a natural query expansion effect. They are nonetheless useful as a reference condition.

Two sites submitted official runs in which manual metadata and automatic metadata were used under otherwise comparable conditions (i.e., the same query length). As Table 5 shows, the use of manual metadata yielded substantial improvements that were statistically significant. This most likely reflects some combination of indexing by subject matter experts of concepts that were not lexicalized within the segment, ASR deficiencies, and a possible bias in word choices made when writing topic descriptions in favor of more formal language. We do not presently have sufficient evidence to differentiate among these three effects.

Table 5. Comparing retrieval effectiveness for Automatic and Manual metadata

Site	MAP(Manual Metadata)	MAP(Automatic)	Automatic/Manual
umaryland – TD	0.3129	0.1288	41%
upitt – TD	0.1878	0.0757	40%

5 Conclusion and Future Plans

Overall, the CLEF-2005 CL-SR track succeeded in creating a reusable test collection, bringing together a group of researchers with similar interests, and exploring alternative techniques to facilitate access to a large collection of spontaneous conversational speech. We therefore plan to continue the track in 2006. The following options are under consideration: (1) addition of an unknown boundary condition for English using the retrieval effectiveness measures first developed for the TREC SDR evaluation, (2) release of a larger English collection (approximately 900 hours of speech) with an improved word error rate (approximately 25%), and (3) creation of a second test collection containing Czech interviews. We look forward to discussing these and other when we meet in Vienna!

Acknowledgments

The authors would like to thank those who performed the topic translation: Christelle Ayache, Catherine Bosio, Clara Cabezas, Pavel Ircing, Fernando Lopez Ostenero, Pavel Pecina and Victor Peinado. We would also like to thank our relevance assessors: Stefan Papaioannou, Daniel Rubin, Ingo Trauschweizer, Ruth Schachter, Benzion Schwinn and Ariel Segal. Finally we are grateful to Bhuvana Ramabhadran for providing the ASR results, to Martin Franz and J. Scott Olsson for providing the text classification results, and to G. Craig Murray for the thesaurus expansion script. This work has been supported in part by NSF IIS Award 0122466. Any opinions, findings and conclusions or recommendations expressed in this material are those of the authors and do not necessarily reflect the views of the NSF.

References

1. Byrne, W., Doermann, D., Franz, M., Gustman, S., Hajic, J., Oard, D., Picheny, M., Psutka, J., Ramabhadran, B. Soergel, D., Ward, T. and Zhu, W.-J.: Automatic recognition of spontaneous speech for access to multilingual oral history archives. IEEE Transactions on Speech and Audio Processing, Special Issue on Spontaneous Speech Processing. (2004), 12(4): 420-435.
2. Federico, M., Bertoldi, N., Levow, G.-A. and Jones, G. J. F.: CLEF 2004 Cross-Language Spoken Document Retrieval Track. In Proceedings of the CLEF 2004: Workshop on Cross-Language Information Retrieval and Evaluation. (2004).
3. Garafolo, J.S., Auzanne, C.G.P. and Voorhees, E.M.: The TREC Spoken Document Retrieval Track: A Success Story. In Proceedings of the RIAO Conference: Content-Based Multimedia Information Access. (2000), 1-20.
4. Huang, X. and Soergel, D.: Relevance judges' understanding of topical relevance types: An explication of an enriched concept of topical relevance. In Proceedings of the Annual Meeting of the American Society for Information Science and Technology (2004) 156-167.
5. Oard, D., Soergel, D., Doermann, D., Huang, X., Murray, G.C., Wang, J., Ramabhadran, B., Franz, M., Gustman, S., Mayfield, J., Kharevych, L. and Strassel, S.: Building an information retrieval test collection for spontaneous conversational speech. In Proceedings of 27th Annual ACM Conference on Research and Development in Information Retrieval. (2004), 41-48.
6. Soergel, D. and Oard, D.: The MALACH English Speech Retrieval Test Collection. Technical Report, 11 pages, available with the test collection from the Evaluations and Language Resources Distribution Agency (ELDA) (2005).

Using Various Indexing Schemes and Multiple Translations in the CL-SR Task at CLEF 2005

Diana Inkpen, Muath Alzghool, and Aminul Islam

School of Information Technology and Engineering
University of Ottawa
{diana, alzghool, mdislam}@site.uottawa.ca

Abstract. We present the participation of the University of Ottawa in the Cross-Language Spoken Document Retrieval task at CLEF 2005. In order to translate the queries, we combined the results of several online Machine Translation tools. For the Information Retrieval component we used the SMART system [1], with several weighting schemes for indexing the documents and the queries. One scheme in particular led to better results than other combinations. We present the results of the submitted runs and of many un-official runs. We compare the effect of several translations from each language. We present results on phonetic transcripts of the collection and queries and on the combination of text and phonetic transcripts. We also include the results when the manual summaries and keywords are indexed.

1 Introduction

This paper presents the first participation of the University of Ottawa group in CLEF, the Cross-Language Spoken Retrieval (CL-SR) track. We briefly describe the task. Then, we present our system, followed by results for the submitted runs and for many unofficial runs. We experiment with many possible weighting schemes for indexing the documents and the queries. We compare the effect of several translations of the queries and of combining the translations. We look at using phonetic transcriptions of the queries and documents instead of the original ASR-produced text, and at combining the phonetic transcripts with the text. At the end we present the best results when all available information in the collection is used.

The CLEF-2005 CL-SR test collection includes 8104 segments, 75 topics (queries), and 12359 Relevance Judgments. See [3] and [7] for more details. For the documents (segments), we indexed only the ASRTEXT2004A field and the keywords automatically extracted from it. This field contains ASR transcripts of the audio segments, with 38% word error rate. In Section 5.4 we also index the metadata for each segment (manual summaries, thesaurus terms, and person names). The topics provided with the collection were created in English from actual user requests and then translated into Czech, German, French, and Spanish by native speakers.

C. Peters et al. (Eds.): CLEF 2005, LNCS 4022, pp. 760 – 768, 2006.

2 System Overview

The University of Ottawa Cross-Language IR system was built with off-the-shelf components. For translating the queries from French, Spanish, and German into English, several free online machine translation tools were used. Their output was merged in order to allow for variety in lexical choices. All the translations of a title made the title of the translated query; the same was done for the description and narrative fields. For the retrieval part, the SMART IR system [1] was tested with many different weighting schemes for indexing the collection and the queries. The weighting schemes are combinations of term frequency, collection frequency, and length normalization components. For all languages involved in the task, the best results were obtained when all the fields of the queries were used (title, description, and narrative); it still worked well with title plus description, and not as well with title only.

3 Translation

For translating the topics into English we used several online MT tools. The idea behind using multiple translations is that they might provide more variety of words and phrases, therefore improving the retrieval performance. The seven online MT systems that we used for translating from Spanish, French, and German were:

1. http://www.google.com/language_tools?hl=en
2. http://www.babelfish.altavista.com
3. http://freetranslation.com
4. http://www.wordlingo.com/en/products_services/wordlingo_translator.html
5. http://www.systranet.com/systran/net
6. http://www.online-translator.com/srvurl.asp?lang=en
7. http://www.freetranslation.paralink.com

For the Czech language topics we were able to find only one online MT system: http://intertran.tranexp.com/Translate/result.shtml

The Spanish, German, and Czech topics provided by the CLEF organizers contained translations of all the fields (title, description, and narrative). For French the narrative field was not translated by the CLEF organizers, due to lack of time. An example of French query is the following:

<top>
<num>1159
<title>Les enfants survivants en Suède
<desc>Descriptions des mécanismes de survie des enfants nés entre 1930 et 1933 qui ont passé la guerre en camps de concentration ou cachés et qui vivent actuellement en Suède.
</top>

We combined the outputs of the MT systems by simply concatenating all the translations. All seven translations of a title made the title of the translated query; the same was done for the description and narrative fields. An example of combined output, for the above French query, is:

<top>
<num> 1159
<title> surviving children in Sweden
surviving children in Sweden
The children survivors in Sweden
surviving children in Sweden
surviving children in Sweden
The surviving children in Sweden
surviving children in Sweden
<desc> Descriptions of the mechanisms of survival of the children born between 1930 and 1933 who passed the war in concentration camps or hidden and who currently live in Sweden.
Descriptions of the mechanisms of survival of the children born between 1930 and 1933 who passed the war in concentration camps or hidden and who currently live in Sweden.
Descriptions of the survival mechanisms of the born children between 1930 and 1933 that passed the war in concentration camps or hidden and that live currently in Sweden.
Descriptions of the mechanisms of survival of the children born between 1930 and 1933 who passed the war in concentration camps or hidden and who currently live in Sweden.
Descriptions of the mechanisms of survival of the children born between 1930 and 1933 who passed the war in concentration camps or hidden and who currently live in Sweden.
Descriptions of the mechanisms of survival of the children been born between 1930 and 1933 which crossed war in concentration camps or hidden and that live in Sweden nowadays.
Descriptions of the mechanisms of survival of the children born between 1930 and 1933 who passed the war in concentration camps or hidden and who currently live in Sweden.
<narr>
</top>

We used the combined topics for all experiments except those described in section 5.2 which investigate the effectiveness of the individual translations.

4 Retrieval

We used the SMART Information Retrieval (IR) system, originally developed at Cornell University in the 1960s. SMART is based on the vector space model of information retrieval [5]. It generates weighted term vectors for the document collection. SMART preprocesses the documents by tokenizing the text into words, removing common words that appear on its stop-list, and performing stemming on the remaining words to derive a set of terms. When the IR server executes a user query, the query terms are also converted into weighted term vectors. Vector inner-product similarity computation is then used to rank documents in decreasing order of their similarity to the user query.

The newest version of SMART (version 11) offers many state-of-the-art options for weighting the terms in the vectors. Each term-weighting scheme is described as a combination of term frequency, collection frequency, and length normalization components [6]. The description of each component is:

Term Frequency Component

Let *tf* denote the term frequency of a term *t* in the document; then *new_tf* weights the terms according to the following schemes:

none (n) : $new\_tf = tf$

max-norm (m) : $new\_tf = \dfrac{tf}{\max\_tf}$

augmented normalized (a): $new\_tf = 0.5 + 0.5 \cdot \dfrac{tf}{\max\_tf}$

where max_tf is the largest *tf* value in the vector.

log (l): $new\_tf = \ln(tf) + 1.0$

square (s): $new\_tf = tf^2$

Merging of Collection Frequency Component

Let *N* and *df* denote the number of documents in the collection and the number of documents in which term t occurs, respectively; then *new_wt* is defined as follows:

none (n): $new\_wt = new\_tf$

inverse document frequency weight (t): $new\_wt = new\_tf \cdot \log \dfrac{N}{df}$

probabilistic (p): $new\_wt = new\_tf \cdot \log \dfrac{N - df}{df}$

squared (s): $new\_wt = new\_tf \cdot (\log \dfrac{N}{df})^2$

Merging of Vector Normalization

Let *m* denote the number of entries in the vector, then the final weight *norm_wt* is defined as follows:

none (n): $norm\_wt = new\_wt$

sum (s): $norm\_wt = \dfrac{new\_wt}{\sum_m new\_wt}$

cosine (c): $norm\_wt = \dfrac{new\_wt}{\sqrt{\sum_m new\_wt^2}}$

In this paper we employ the notation used in SMART to describe the combined schemes: xxx . xxx. The first three characters refer to the weighting scheme used to index the document collection and the last three characters refer to the weighting scheme used to index the query fields. For example, lpc.atc means that lpc was used for documents and atc for queries. lpc would apply log term frequency weighting (l) and probabilistic collection frequency weighting (p) with cosine normalization to the document collection (c). atc would apply augmented normalized term frequency (a), inverse document frequency weight (t) with cosine normalization (c).

5 Results

Table 1 shows the results of the submitted results on the test data. The evaluation measure we report is standard measures computed with the trec_eval script: MAP (Mean Average Precision). The information about what fields of the topics were indexed in given in the column named Fields: T for title only, TD for title + description, TDN for title + description + narrative. For each run we include an additional description of the experimental settings. For all the required runs we used the indexing scheme lnn.ntn, since it performed best on the training data. This weighting scheme worked better when all fields of the topics are indexed. The results for TDN are slightly better than for TD and better than for T. Table 1 does not present baseline results, but we can say that our submitted results were better than the ones submitted by the other six teams that participated in the task, on the required run.

Table 1. Results of the five submitted runs, for topics in English, French, Spanish, and German. The required run (English, title + description) is in bold.

Language	Run	MAP	Fields	Description
English	uoEnTDN	0.1366	TDN	Weighting scheme: lnn.ntn
English	**uoEnTD**	**0.1313**	**TD**	**Weighting scheme: lnn.ntn**
French	uoFrTD	0.1275	TD	Weighting scheme: lnn.ntn
Spanish	uoSpTDN	0.1156	TDN	Weighting scheme: lnn.ntn
German	uoGrTDN	0.0936	TDN	Weighting scheme: lnn.ntn

5.1 Comparison of Indexing Schemes

Table 2 presents results for various weighting schemes document/topics. There are 3600 possible combinations of weighting schemes: 60 schemes (5 x 4 x 3) for documents and 60 for queries. We tried 240 combinations and we present in the table the results for 15 combinations (the best ones, plus some other ones to show the diversity of the results). lnn.ntn seems to be the best, and there might be a few other weighting schemes that achieve similar performance. Some of the weighting schemes perform best when indexing all the fields of the queries (TDN), some on TD, and some on title only (T). lnn.ntn is best for TDN and TD and lsn.ntn and lsn.atn are best for T. (Note that for mpc.ntn and other schemes that contain the probabilistic term "p", due to a minor bug in Smart, some documents were returned as answer to the same query more than once. In this case, we preprocessed the results to eliminate the duplicates and kept the first 1000 distinct results for each query, to retrieve the same number of documents per query as in the other experiments).

In all the presented experiments we use stemming when indexing the collection and the translated topics (except Section 5.3). We don't present the results here, but when we tried using an English lemmatizer (to produce base forms of inflected words) instead of a stemmer, the results were slightly worse for all settings; when using no-stemming during indexing the performance was much worse. Relevance feedback was not enabled in the SMART system.

5.2 Comparison of Various Translations

Table 3 presents results for each translation produced by the seven online MT tools, from French, Spanish, and German into English. The last column is for the combination of all translations, as explained in Section 3. All the results in the table are for lnn.ntn, TDN (except for French where only TD was available).

The translations from German and the one from Czech had many words that were not translated, they were kept unchanged into the English output of the MT tools. This would explain the lower performance for German and Czech. The MT tool number 6 for French and German seems to obtain better results on the test data than the combination, but this was not the case on the training data. In general, the combination of all translations performs better than the individual translations.

Table 2. Results (MAP scores) of the various weighting schemes, for English topics. In bold are the best scores for TDN, TD, and T.

	Weighting scheme	**TDN**	**TD**	**T**
1	lnn.ntn	**0.1366**	**0.1313**	0.1207
2	lnc.ntn	0.1362	0.1214	0.1094
3	mpc.ntn	0.1283	0.1219	0.1107
4	npc.ntn	0.1283	0.1219	0.1107
5	mpc.mtc	0.1283	0.1219	0.1107
6	mpc.mts	0.1282	0.1218	0.1108
7	mpc.nts	0.1282	0.1218	0.1108
8	npn.ntn	0.1258	0.1247	0.1118
9	lsn.ntn	0.1195	0.1233	**0.1227**
10	lsn.atn	0.0919	0.1115	**0.1227**
11	asn.ntn	0.0912	0.0923	0.1062
12	snn.ntn	0.0693	0.0592	0.0729
13	sps.ntn	0.0349	0.0377	0.0383
14	nps.ntn	0.0517	0.0416	0.0474
15	mtc.atc	0.1138	0.1151	0.1108

Table 3. Results on the output of each Machine Translation system. French, Spanish, German, and Czech (lnn.ntn).

Measure	Translation							
	Fr1	**Fr2**	**Fr3**	**Fr4**	**Fr5**	**Fr6**	**Fr7**	**French**
MAP	0.1209	0.1196	0.1169	0.1200	0.1196	0.1288	0.1196	0.1275
	Sp1	**Sp2**	**Sp3**	**Sp4**	**Sp5**	**Sp6**	**Sp7**	**Spanish**
MAP	0.1130	0.1142	0.1016	0.0991	0.1140	0.1116	0.1142	0.1156
	Gr1	**Gr2**	**Gr3**	**Gr4**	**Gr5**	**Gr6**	**Gr7**	**German**
MAP	0.0908	0.0906	0.0853	0.0900	0.0907	0.0994	0.0906	0.0936
	Czech							
MAP	0.0822							

5.3 Results on Phonetic Transcriptions

In Table 4 we present results for an experiment where the text of the collection and the queries were transcribed into phonetic form and split into n-grams (groups of n sounds, n = 4 in our case) that we used for indexing (without stemming). The phonetic n-grams were produced by the University of Waterloo's group. See [2] for more details.

Table 4. Results on phonetic n-grams, and combination text plus phonetic transcripts for topics in English, and the translations from French, Spanish, German, and Czech. All the runs in this table use lnn.ntn.

Language	MAP	Fields	Description
English	0.0986	T	Phonetic
English	0.1019	TD	Phonetic
English	0.0981	T	Phonetic+Text
English	0.1066	TD	Phonetic+Text
French	0.0931	T	Phonetic
French	0.1052	TD	Phonetic
French	0.0929	T	Phonetic+Text
French	0.1072	TD	Phonetic+Text
Spanish	0.0898	T	Phonetic
Spanish	0.0972	TD	Phonetic
Spanish	0.0948	T	Phonetic+Text
Spanish	0.1009	TD	Phonetic+Text
German	0.0744	T	Phonetic
German	0.0782	TD	Phonetic
German	0.0746	T	Phonetic+Text
German	0.0789	TD	Phonetic+Text
Czech	0.0479	T	Phonetic
Czech	0.0583	TD	Phonetic
Czech	0.0510	T	Phonetic+Text
Czech	0.0614	TD	Phonetic+Text

We wanted to test the hypothesis that the phonetic form might help compensate for the speech recognition errors made when the collection was produced. When the fields TD were indexed, the results are better than when only T is indexed. When combining phonetic and text forms (by simply indexing both phonetic n-grams and text), the result improved compared to using only the phonetic forms. But the MAP scores are lower than the results on the text form of the documents and queries.

5.4 Manual Summaries and Keywords

Table 5 presents the results when all the fields of the document collection were used: the manual keywords and manual summaries in addition to the ASR transcripts and the automatic keywords. The retrieval performance improved a lot, for all the languages. The MAP score jumped from 0.1366 to 0.277 for English, TDN, with the lnn.ntn weighting scheme. The score doubles for English queries, and for the queries translated from the other languages.

Table 5. Results of indexing all the fields of the collections: the manual keywords and summaries, in addition to the ASR transcripts (lnn.ntn)

Language	MAP	Fields	Description
English	0.2771	TDN	Manual fields included
French	0.2473	TD	Manual fields included
Spanish	0.2267	TDN	Manual fields included
German	0.1852	TDN	Manual fields included
Czech	0.1562	TDN	Manual fields included

6 Discussion

We obtained the best retrieval results on the required run among the seven teams that participated in this track. We tried various weighting scheme for indexing the document and query terms. Table 2 shows that performance varies with the weighting scheme; it can be lower for the some of the classic indexing schemes.

In this paper we presented the results on the test queries, but our conclusions also applied on the training queries.

The idea of using multiple translations proves to be good. More variety in the translations would be beneficial. The online MT systems that we used are rule-based systems. Adding translations by statistical MT tools might help, since they produce radically different translations.

On the manual data, the best MAP score we obtained is around 27%, for English topics. On automatic data the best result is around 13% MAP score. This difference shows that the poor quality of the ASR transcripts severely hurts the performance of IR systems on this collection. In future work we plan to investigate methods of removing or correcting some of the speech recognition errors in the ASR transcripts, using semantic coherence measures [4].

References

1. C. Buckley, G. Salton, and J. Allan : Automatic retrieval with locality information using SMART. In Proceedings of the First Text REtrieval Conference (TREC-1), pages 59–72. NIST Special Publication 500-207, March (1993).
2. C. L. A. Clarke : Waterloo Experiments for the CLEF05 SDR Track, in Working Notes for the CLEF 2005 Workshop, September, Vienna, Austria (2005)
3. D. W. Oard, D. Soergel, D. Doermann, X. Huang, G. C. Murray, J. Wang, B. Ramabhadran, M. Franz and S. Gustman : Building an Information Retrieval Test Collection for Spontaneous Conversational Speech, in Proceedings of SIGIR (2004)
4. D. Inkpen and A. Désilets : Semantic Similarity for Detecting Recognition Errors in Automatic Speech Transcripts, in Proceedings of EMNLP 2005, Vancouver, Canada, October (2005)
5. G. Salton : Automatic Text Processing: The Transformation, Analysis, and Retrieval of Information by Computer. Addison-Wesley Publishing Company (1989)
6. G. Salton and C. Buckley : Term-weighting approaches in automatic retrieval. Information Processing and Management, 24(5):513-523 (1988)
7. R. W. White, D. W. Oard, G. J. F. Jones, D. Soergel, X. Huang : Overview of the CLEF-2005 Cross-Language Speech Retrieval Track, in Working Notes for the CLEF 2005 Workshop, September, Vienna, Austria (2005)

The University of Alicante at CL-SR Track

Rafael M. Terol, Manuel Palomar, Patricio Martinez-Barco,
Fernando Llopis, Rafael Muñoz, and Elisa Noguera

Departamento de Lenguajes y Sistemas Informáticos
Universidad de Alicante
Carretera de San Vicente del Raspeig - Alicante - Spain
Tel.: +34965903772; Fax: +34965909326
{rafamt, mpalomar, patricio, llopis, rafael, elisa}@dlsi.ua.es

Abstract. In this paper, the new features that IR-n system applies on the topic processing for CL-SR are described. This set of features are based on applying logic forms to topics with the aim of incrementing the weight of topic terms according to a set of syntactic rules.

1 Introduction

The CL-SR system that is going to be presented in this paper is based on a passage retrieval system called IR-n [1]. This system usually recognizes passages according to a fixed number of sentences. However, the format of spoken documents does not allow this supposition. In this case, the documents are composed by a contiguous set of words with any punctuation mark. Instead of sentences, the CL-SR system recognizes the passages according to a fixed number of words. Moreover, with the aim of incrementing the weights of several words, IR-n system incorporates a new module that applies a set of heuristics to the representation of the topics by way of logic forms.

2 Logic Form Derivation

In order to enhance the performance of our IR-n system, the logic forms of the topics are inferred. Each one of the terms of the topic in the logic form can modify its own weight according to its assert type and the relationships with the rest of the asserts in the logic form. The logic form of a topic (or sentence) is derived through the processing of the dependency tree between the words of the sentence. The MINIPAR [2] toolkit obtains these dependency relationships between the words of the sentence by way of a dependency tree.

2.1 Logic Form Inference

This approach is based on a set of NLP rules that infer several properties from the dependency relationships such as the assert, the assert type, the unique identifier of the assert and the relationships between the different asserts in the logic form. This technique is different from other techniques such as Moldovan's

C. Peters et al. (Eds.): CLEF 2005, LNCS 4022, pp. 769–772, 2006.

[3] that constructs the logic form through the syntactic tree obtained from the output of the syntactic parser. Our logic form, similar to Moldovan's logic form, is based on the format defined by eXtended WordNet [5]. As an example, the logic form "*story:NN(x14) of:IN(x14, x13) varian:NN(x10) NNC(x11, x10, x12) fry:NN(x12) and:CC(x13, x11, x6) emergency:NN(x5) NNC(x6, x5, x7) rescue:NN(x8) NNC(x7, x8, x9) committee:NN(x9) who:NN(x1) save:VB(e1, x1, x2) thousand:NN(x2) in:IN(e1, x3) marseille:NN(x3)*" is derived automatically from the analysis of the dependency relationships between the words of the topic "*The story of Variant Fly and the Emergency Rescue Committee who saved thousands in Marseille*". In this format of logic form each assert has at least one argument. The first argument is usually instantiated with the identifier of the assert and the rest of the arguments are related to the identifiers of other asserts that are related with this assert. For instance, in the assert "*story:NN(x14)*", its type is related to noun *(NN)* and its identifier is instantiated to *x14*; in the assert "*NNC(x11, x10, x12)*", its type is related to composed entity *(NNC)*, its identifier is instantiated to *x11*, and the other two arguments indicate the relationships to other asserts: *x10* and *x12*.

3 Applying Rules to Logic Form to Increment Topic Term Weights

Under several circumstances, some rules are applied to the logic form to increment the weight of the topic terms. This occurs when the assert type corresponds to preposition *(IN)* which second argument instantiates an assert which type matches to noun *(NN)* or derives in a assert which type corresponds to noun, then the term weight associated to this last assert is incremented. This rule generally describes those utterances that have a circumstantial behaviour in the sentence (eg. in Marseille, in concentration camps, in Sweden, of Holocaust experience and so on) and then we consider the nouns (NN assert type) as very relevant words in the topic. This fact means that the term weight of these words (terms) is incremented by 15% of their initial values. Table 1 shows the term weights that the IR-n system associates to the topic "*The story of Variant Fly and the Emergency Rescue Committee who saved thousands in Marseille*". These terms are expressed through their stem form. The logic form inferred for this topic ("*story:NN(x14) of:IN(x14, x13) varian:NN(x10) NNC(x11, x10, x12) fry:NN(x12) and:CC(x13, x11, x6) emergency:NN(x5) NNC(x6, x5, x7) rescue:NN(x8) NNC(x7, x8, x9) committee:NN(x9) who:NN(x1) save:VB(e1, x1, x2) thousand:NN(x2) in:IN(e1, x3) marseille:NN(x3)*") has two asserts whose types are *IN*. The second argument of these asserts are instantiated to *x13* and *x3* respectively. *x13* turns to the asserts *x10*, *x12*, *x5*, *x8* and *x9* which types are *NN*, while the type of *x3* is directly *NN*. Then, according to this rule, these facts mean that the term weights associated with all these asserts have their initial values incremented by 15%.

Table 1. Term weights assigned by IR-n system

Term (stem)	Initial Weight	Final Weight
stori	1.84449	1.84449
fry	6.19484	7.124066
emerg	6.47296	7.443904
rescu	6.19484	7.124066
committe	4.08194	4.694231
save	3.06725	3.06725
thousand	2.33944	2.33944
marseil	5.13363	5.9036745

4 Submitted Runs

The differences among the five submitted runs are basically based on the treatment of the topics and the indexation of a combination of different fields of segments in the document collection. In all the submitted runs we use the indexing and searching processes developed by our IR-n system using English as the query language. we do not use any kind of thesaurus terms as keywords in carrying out the indexing and the searching processes. The following list shows the features of the five submitted runs according to the judgment pool priority order:

- **UATDASR04FL Run.** In this run IR-n system indexed the **AUTOKEYWORD2004A2** field of the segments in the document collection. The English title and description fields of the topics were used in construction of the queries. This was the unique submitted run in which we apply the rules based on the processing of queries in the way of logic forms described in previous section.
- **UATDASR04 Run.** In this run, as in previous submitted run, our IR-n system indexed the **AUTOKEYWORD2004A2** field of the segments in the document collection. As in the following submitted runs, the English description field of the topics was used in the construction of the queries.
- **UATDASR04AUTOA1 Run.** In this run we indexed the **AUTOKEYWORD2004A2** field of the segments in the document collection and a set of thesaurus keywords that were assigned automatically using a k-Nearest Neighbor (kNN) classifier using only words from this transcript.
- **UATDASR04AUTOA2 Run.** In this run IR-n system indexed the **AUTOKEYWORD2004A2** field of the segments in the document collection and a set of thesaurus keywords that were assigned using a different kNN classifier that was trained (fairly) on different data.
- **UATDASR04AUTOS Run.** In this run our IR-n system indexed the **ASRTEXT2004A**, **AUTOKEYWORD2004A1** and **AUTOKEYWORD2004A2** fields of the segments in the document collection.

Table 2. Evaluation Results

run	map	rprec	bpref	rr	p5	p20	p100	p1000
UATDASR04LF	0,0768	0,1230	0,0949	0,4622	0,2160	0,1740	0,1088	0,0324
UATDASR04	0,0724	0,1246	0,0899	0,4377	0,1840	0,1660	0,1036	0,0313
UATDASR04AUTOA1	0,0727	0,1206	0,1018	0,4509	0,2800	0,1740	0,0916	0,0277
UATDASR04AUTOA2	0,0769	0,1181	0,0980	0,4744	0,2640	0,1920	0,0928	0,0290
UATDASR04AUTOS	0,0739	0,1274	0,1056	0,4354	0,2640	0,1880	0,0920	0,0260

5 Results

Table 2 shows the results obtained by our system for each one of the submitted runs. According to the difference between the map scores of the UATDASR04LF (using logic forms) and UATDASR04 (without logic forms) runs, the use of the technique based on logic forms produces an improvement of 6%.

6 Conclusions

In this new release of the CL-SR track at the CLEF 2005 conference we have participated using our CL-SR system based on IR-n system. Our main aim was to evaluate the goodness of the new Logic Form Module of IR-n system. According to our foresight, the obtained scores applying this module (UATDASR04LF) are higher than the ones without it (UATDASR04).

Acknowledgments. This research work has been partially funded by the Spanish Government under project CICyT number TIC2000-0664-C02-02 and PROFIT number FIT-340100- 2004-14 and by the Valencia Government under project numbers GV04B-276 and GV04B-268.

References

1. F. Llopis and E. Noguera. Combining Passages in Monolingual Experiments with IR-n system. In *Workshop of Cross-Language Evaluation Forum (CLEF 2005)*, in this volume, Vienna, Austria, 2005.
2. D. Lin. Dependency-based evaluation of minipar. In *Workshop on the Evaluation of Parsing Systems*, Granada, Spain, 1998.
3. D. Moldovan and V. Rus. Logic Form Transformation of WordNet and its Applicability to Question-Answering. In *Proceedings of 39th Annual Meeting of the Association for Computational Linguistics*, Toulouse, France, 2001.
4. R. M. Terol, P. Martínez-Barco and M. Palomar. Applying Logic Forms to Biomedical Q-A. In *International Symposium on Innovations in Intelligent Systems and Applications (INISTA 2005)*, pages 29–32, Istambul, Turkey, 2004.
5. S. Harabagiu, G. A. Miller, and D. I. Moldovan. WordNet 2 - A Morphologically and Semantically Enhanced Resource. In *Proceedings of ACL-SIGLEX99: Standardizing Lexical Resources*, Maryland, pages 1–8, 1999.

Pitt at CLEF05: Data Fusion for Spoken Document Retrieval

Daqing He and Jae-Wook Ahn

School of Information Sciences
University of Pittsburgh, Pittsburgh, PA 15260 USA
{dah44, jaa38}@pitt.edu

Abstract. This paper describes an investigation of data fusion techniques for spoken document retrieval. The effectiveness of retrievals solely based on the outputs from automatic speech recognition (ASR) is subject to the recognition errors introduced by the ASR process. This is especially true for retrievals on Malach test collection, whose ASR outputs have average word error rate (WER) of 35%. To overcome the problem, in this year CLEF experiments, we explored data fusion techniques for integrating the manually generated metadata information, which is provided for every Malach document, with the ASR outputs. We concentrated our effort on the post-search data fusion techniques, where multiple retrieval results using automatic generated outputs or human metadata were combined. Our initial studies indicated that a simple unweighted combination method (i.e., CombMNZ) that had demonstrated to be useful in written text retrieval environment only generated significant 38% relative decrease in retrieval effectiveness (measured by Mean Average Precision) for our task by comparing to a simple retrieval baseline where all manual metadata and ASR outputs are put together. This motivated us to explore a more elaborated weighted data fusion model, where the weights are associated with each retrieval result, and can be specified by the user in advance. We also explored multiple iterations of data fusion in our weighted fusion model, and obtained further improvement at 2nd iteration. In total, our best run on data fusion obtained 31% significant relative improvement over the simple fusion baseline, and 4% relative improvement over the manual-only baseline, which is a significant difference.

1 Introduction

Spoken documents become more and more popular in people's information seeking activities along with the advance of information technologies, especially the storage and network communication technologies. However, comparing to the studies performed on text base documents, the achievements on retrieving spoken documents are still far less. Recent remarkable advances in the automatic recognition of spontaneous conversational speech makes it even urgent to study effective spoken document retrieval techniques. This is the reason that

C. Peters et al. (Eds.): CLEF 2005, LNCS 4022, pp. 773–782, 2006.

we participated CLEF Spoken Document Retrieval (SDR) track, and our goal is to leverage technologies developed for text retrieval into retrieving spoken documents.

Retrieving spoken documents from Malach test collection, a test collection developed by University of Maryland for retrieving spontaneous conversational speech [6], poses some interesting challenges. Before Malach collection, there have been several spoken document collections, whose documents are mostly news broadcast stories, help desk telephone calls, and political speeches. The documents in the Malach collection, however, are interviews of Holocaust survivors, who talk about their personal stories. Because of the genre, the topics, and the emotion involved, the average Word Error Rate (WER) in machine transcripts of the documents, an indicator of the quality of the ASR output, is around 35%. This imposes a great difficult for searching based on these ASR outputs.

Our major interests for this year's experiments, however, lie on the several forms of human generated metadata associated with the spoken documents. For each document, there are a list of person names mentioned in the documents, the human assigned thesaurus keywords and a brief summary in 2-3 sentences written by the human catalogers during their cataloging process.

We view ASR outputs and human generated metadata as two types of information that are complimentary of each other in retrieval process. On the one hand, ASR outputs provide full and detailed information about the content of the documents, which often could not be totally covered by human generated data. On the other hand, human generated metadata provide focused, human-processed, and high quality information that can be relied on for the accuracy of the retrieval. If we can develop a reliable retrieval method that can combine both information into the retrieval process in such way that their complimentary features can be fully explored, the achieved retrieval effectiveness would be greatly superior than that of any one of them. This is the goal of our studies in this year's CLEF-SDR experiments, and two derived research questions are:

1. how the manual metadata and ASR outputs in Malach collection can be integrated for improving the retrieval effectiveness of the final run?
2. what are the parameters that we can utilize to make the data fusion techniques more effective for our task?

In the rest of this report, we will firstly review some existing data fusion methods in Section 2; discuss in detail the experiment settings in Section 3; then talk about the fusion techniques we developed for the CLEF-SDR experiments in Section 4. Finally we will discuss some further studies in Section 5.

2 Data Fusion

In the literature, the techniques for combining multiple queries, document representations or retrieval results is called "data fusion" [5]. It has been an active topic in text retrieval process, and people have developed many techniques for applying fusion techniques in various retrieval applications. Belkin et al. [1] studied pre-search data-fusion approach by progressively combining Boolean query formulations. Lee [5] provided an analysis of multiple post-search data fusion methods using TREC3 ad hoc retrieval data. Data fusion also has been applied in cross-language information retrieval [3,2], recommendation systems [7], and many other areas.

In post-search data fusion approaches, to properly merge retrieval results that are commonly ranklist of documents, the score associated with each document has to be normalized within that list. A often used normalization scheme (see Equation (1)) utilizes the maximum and minimum scores of a ranklist (i.e., $MaxScore$ and $MinScore$) in the normalization process [5].

$$NormalizedScore = \frac{UnnormalizedScore - MinScore}{MaxScore - MinScore} \tag{1}$$

Fox and Shaw [4] developed several fusion methods for combining multiple evidence, and they named the methods as CombMIN, CombMAX, CombSUM, CombANZ, and CombMNZ (the definitions of them are shown in table 1). Lee [5] studied these methods, and established that CombMNZ is the best among the four in retrieving TREC ad hoc data.

Table 1. Combining functions proposed by Fox and Shaw

CombMIN	minimum of all scores of a document
CombMAX	maximum of all scores of a document
CombSUM	summation of all scores of a document
CombANZ	CombSUM ÷ number of nonzero scores of a document
CombMNZ	CombSUM × number of nonzero scores of a document

3 Experiment Settings

3.1 Malach Test Collection

Malach Test Collection was developed by University of Maryland as part of their effort in Malach project [6]. The collection contains about 7800 segments from 300 interviews of Holocaust survivors. All the segments were constructed manually by catalogers. Each segment contains two automatic speech recognition outputs from the ASR system developed by IBM in 2003 and 2004 respectively. The WER of the two outputs are about 40% and 35% respectively. In addition, there are automatically generated thesaurus terms from a system developed at University of Maryland. Each segment also contains a set of human generated data, including person names mentioned in the segment, average 5 thesaurus labels and 3-sentence summaries.

There are total 63 search topics, 38 of which were available for training, and 25 were held as the testing topics. Each topic is designed in TREC style, which has a title, a description and a narrative (see Figure 1). The topics are available

```
<top> <num> 1148
<title> Jewish resistance in Europe
<desc> Provide testimonies or describe actions of Jewish resistance in
Europe before and during the war.
<narr> The relevant material should describe actions of only- or
mostly Jewish resistance in Europe. Both individual and group-based
actions are relevant. Type of actions may include survival (fleeing,
hiding, saving children), testifying (alerting the outside world,
writing, hiding testimonies), fighting (partisans, uprising, political
security) Information about undifferentiated resistance groups is not
relevant.
</top>
```

Fig. 1. An example of the search topic in Malach Collection

in English, Spanish, Czech, German and French, however, we only used English topics for our studies.

3.2 Indri Search Engine

Our search engine was Indri 1.0, which was a collaboration effort between the University of Massachusetts and Carnegie Mellon University[1]. Its retrieval model is a combination of language model and inference network. We chose it not only because of its state-of-art retrieval effectiveness, but also because it is an open source system, on which we can easily integrated our modifications. Its powerful query syntax is another attraction to us, since we want to specify which index fields should a retrieval be based on for our studies of manual metadata only or automatic data only searches.

3.3 Measures

To study the retrieval results in as wide scenarios as possible, instead of choosing a single measure, we employed a set of evaluation measures, each of which tells us some aspect of the retrieval effectiveness of the search results:

- **mean average precision (MAP)**, the measure aims at giving an emphasis view of precision in a ranklist. Since the ranks of the relevant documents are considered in the measure, this measure gives a reasonable overview of the quality of the ranklist for a given retrieval topic.
- **Precision at 10 (P10)** is a useful measure to examine how many relevant documents there are in the first result screen, which are often the only results viewed by a user.
- **R-Precision (R-PREC)** emphases precision, but avoids the artificial cut-off effect imposed by pre-defined cut-off point, like in P10. The "R" varies according to the number of relevant documents of a given topic.
- **Average Recall at top 1000 returned documents** indicates the quality of the ranklist from the point of recall.

[1] http://newhaven.lti.cs.cmu.edu/indri/.

3.4 Baselines

We established three baselines for evaluating our methods (see Table 2). The first two represent the scenario that no data fusion is performed. We selected a run on ASRTEXT 2004 as the baseline for searching on ASR output, since ASRTEXT 2004 is the better one among the two ASR outputs. This baseline is referred to as *"asr04"*, and is treated as the lower baseline. Ideally, we should use the search on manual transcripts as the upper baseline. Since Malach collection does not provide manual transcripts, we used all manually generated data in the segments as a proximate upper bound baseline (referred as *"manual-only"* baseline). We did not apply blind relevance feedback (BRF) over *"manual-only"* run since BRF over *"manual-only"* baseline using Indri's BRF function generated inferior results. The third baseline is a search on all manual and ASR outputs combined together as if they are different parts of the same document. This represents the simplest data fusion method, and is referred *"simple-fusion"* baseline.

Table 2. Retrieval effectiveness of the three baselines and the CombMNZ run

runs	MAP	R-PREC	P10	Avg-Recall
manual-only	0.2312	0.2836	0.4603	0.5813
asr04	0.0693	0.1139	0.2111	0.3595
simple-fusion	0.1842	0.1985	0.3635	0.5847
autowa1	0.0464	0.0879	0.1683	0.3319
CombMNZ	0.1127	0.1173	0.3079	0.6182

4 Experiments and Results Analysis

4.1 Data Fusion with CombMNZ

The first data fusion method studied in our CLEF-SDR experiments was our implementation of CombMNZ method since Lee demonstrated its superiority over the other three methods [5]. This run merged results from three retrieval runs, the *"manual-only"* baseline, the *"asr04"* baseline, and a retrieval run on the automatic assigned thesaurus keywords called *"AUTOKEYWORD2004A1"* (we call this run *"autokw1"*). Table 2 shows the results of *"CombMNZ"* run and that of the three runs that it was based on. Comparing to the lower *"asr04"* baseline, this combined run has achieved significant improvement by the measures of MAP, P10, and especially Avg-Recall ($P \ll 0.05$ in paired T-tests). However, it shows a significant decrease at MAP, R-PREC, and P10 when compared to the two higher baselines, *"manual-only"* baseline and *"simple-fusion"* baseline ($P \ll 0.05$ in paired T-test). The only improvement it achieved over the two higher baselines is measured by Avg-Recall. This means that *"CombMNZ"* run does return more relevant documents comparing to the two high baselines, but it ranks them badly.

A close examination of the retrieval runs in Table 2 shows that the retrieval effectiveness of the *"manual-only"* run is greatly higher than that of the two automatic runs. For example, the MAP of *"manual-only"* increases about 200%

over *"asr04"*, the better one of the two automatic runs. Therefore, it makes no sense to assume that their contribution to the final fused ranklist is the same, which is the assumption in CombMNZ model. We need a data fusion model that considers the retrieval difference.

4.2 Weighted CombMNZ

The failure of CombMNZ on our data fusion task motivated us to explore a weighted scheme for data fusion based on CombMNZ. A natural place to insert a weight in CombMNZ is to assign a weight of belief for each retrieval run as it is possible to obtain such evidence or belief. In our weighted CombMNZ model (called WCombMNZ model), such belief is used in calculation of the final combined score for a document (see Equation 2).

$$WCombMNZ_i = \sum_{j=1}^{n} (w_j \times NormalizedScore_{i,j}) \times n \tag{2}$$

where w_j is a predefined weight associated with a search result to be combined, n is the number of nonzero scores of document i, and the $NormalizedScore_{i,j}$ is calculated using Equation 1.

Table 3. Retrieval effectiveness of individual runs on the 38 training topics

runs	MAP	R-PREC	P10	Avg-Recall
manual-only	0.1494	0.1823	0.3237	0.4221
asr04	0.0525	0.0754	0.1447	0.2788
autowa1	0.0239	0.0460	0.0816	0.2832

Various methods can be used to obtain the weight w_j for a given ranklist j. In this year's experiment, we firstly used the retrieval effectiveness of those pre-combined runs on the 38 training topics as the weights (the details of the pre-fused runs on the training topics are in Table 3). Therefore, we have four different *"WCombMNZ"* runs (see Table 4), and their retrieval effectiveness evaluated by the four measures are shown in Table 5.

All four WCombMNZ runs are significant higher than the non-weighted *"CombMNZ"* run (paired T-test with $P < 0.05$) when looking at MAP, R-PREC, and P10 as the measures. However, they are still significant lower than the *"manual-only"* run using the same measures.

Since the weights of *"WCombMNZ-1"* generated the best MAP, R-PREC and P10 results, we used those weights to help us explore further the effect of different combinations of the weights. As the difference of the retrieval effectiveness between *"manual-only"* run and the two automatic runs is significantly higher than that between the two automatic runs, we first explored the change of ratio between the weight of *"manual-only"* run and that of the *"asr-04"* and *"autowa1"* runs. The ratios we tested were 2:1 (that is the weight for *"manual-only"* run is 2, and the weights for the two automatic runs were both assigned to be 1

Table 4. Our weighted combination runs

WCombMNZ-1	use the MAP values as the weights
WCombMNZ-2	use the R-PREC values as the weights
WCombMNZ-3	use the P10 values as the weights
WCombMNZ-4	use the Avg-Recall values as the weights

Table 5. Retrieval effectiveness of The first 4 WCmbMNZ runs on total 63 topics

runs	MAP	R-PREC	P10	Avg-Recall
manual-only	0.2312	0.2836	0.4603	0.5813
CombMNZ	0.1127	0.1173	0.3079	0.6182
WCombMNZ-1	0.2137	0.2589	0.4460	0.6008
WCombMNZ-2	0.1987	0.2431	0.4206	0.6254
WCombMNZ-3	0.1967	0.2416	0.4190	0.6253
WCombMNZ-4	0.1783	0.2188	0.3778	0.6215

in WCombMNZ model), 5:1, 10:1, 15:1, and up to 1000:1 (the results are presented in Table 6). We then changed the weight ratio between the *"asr04"* and that of *"autowa1"* to 2:1, which is closer to the weight ratio in *"WCombMNZ-1"*, and varied the weight ratio of the three runs from 4:2:1, 6:2:1, and up to 50:2:1. As shown in Table 6, the ratio between the weight of the *"manual-only"* and that of two automatic runs is the dominate factor in affecting the retrieval performance, and once the ratio between the manual run and the automatic runs is larger than 10, there is not much difference in the retrieval effectiveness evaluated by all measures. However, still none of the fused runs achieves better MAP, R-PREC, and P10 than *"manual-only"*, although they are much closer to the performance of the *"manual-only"* than the two automatic runs, and at the same time, many of them have achieved significant better Avg-Recall than the *"manual-only"* run.

Table 6. Exploring the weight ratios in WCmbMNZ model

runs with ratio	MAP	R-PREC	P10	Avg-Recall	runs with ratio	MAP MAP	R-PREC R-PREC	P10 P10	Avg-Recall
2-1	0.1884	0.2315	0.4032	0.6236	4-2-1	0.1937	0.2354	0.3735	0.6246
5-1	0.2088	0.2590	0.4254	0.6259	6-2-1	0.2047	0.2523	0.4190	0.6253
10-1	0.2133	0.2598	0.4302	0.6240	10-2-1	0.2110	0.2591	0.4238	0.6236
15-1	0.2132	0.2590	0.4381	0.6211	20-2-1	0.2138	0.2599	0.4333	0.6208
20-1	0.2140	0.2581	0.4413	0.6202	30-2-1	0.2144	0.2591	0.4365	0.6207
25-1	0.2131	0.2581	0.4444	0.6129	50-2-1	0.2141	0.2574	0.4444	0.6172
50-1	0.2141	0.2577	0.4429	0.6133	100-2-1	0.2140	0.2575	0.4444	0.6089
100-1	0.2140	0.2583	0.4460	0.6087					
1000-1	0.2132	0.2593	0.4460	0.5995					

4.3 Multiple Iteration of Data Fusion

One exploration within the data fusion framework is "does multiple iterations of data fusion make sense?" To answer this, we conducted several experiments in WCombMNZ model. A total of five retrieval runs were used in the second iteration of data fusion. We kept the *"manual-only"* run since it is the best run so far, and we used the four runs listed in Table 5 *"WCombMNZ-1"* to *"WCombMNZ-4"*. We used a similar scheme to vary the weight ratios among the runs, and we also set all weights to 1 to make WCombMNZ model fall back to CombMNZ so that we can study CombMNZ too. The ratio "2-1" in Table 7 means that the weight for *"manual-only"* is 2, and that for the other four runs is 1.

As shown in Table 7, the *"manual-only"*, in our current retrieval setting, still deserves more weight than the other runs, and the best retrieval results are achieved with the ratio around 10:1. Statistical tests (paired T-test) between the results of the 2nd round fusion runs and that of the *"manual-only"* run demonstrate that 2-iteration fusion data generated significant improvement on average recall, but only the runs with ratio above 10:1 generated significant improvement on P10, and only runs with ratio 10:1 and 15:1 generated significant improvement on MAP. No significant improvement can be achieved on R-PREC.

Table 7. Exploring multiple iterations in data fusion

runs	MAP	R-PREC	P10	Avg-Recall
manual-only	0.2312	0.2836	0.4603	0.5813
2nd-ratio 1-1	0.2119	0.2670	0.4413	**0.6241**
2nd-ratio 2-1	0.2295	0.2720	0.4540	**0.6228**
2nd-ratio 5-1	0.2397	0.2806	0.4778	**0.6200**
2nd-ratio 10-1	**0.2409**	0.2860	**0.4937**	**0.6188**
2nd-ratio 15-1	**0.2400**	0.2853	**0.4968**	**0.6157**
2nd-ratio 20-1	0.2388	0.2856	**0.4810**	**0.6142**
3rd-ratio 1-1	0.2403	0.2876	0.5016	0.6143
3rd-ratio 2-1	0.2393	0.2865	0.4857	0.6142
3rd-ratio 1-2	0.2409	0.2866	0.4984	0.6157
3rd-ratio 1-5	0.2407	0.2867	0.4937	0.6159
3rd-ratio 1-10	0.2408	0.2869	0.4921	0.6168
3rd-ratio 1-15	0.2408	0.2864	0.4921	0.6168
3rd-ratio 1-30	0.2404	0.2869	0.4921	0.6171

We then generated various third round fusion runs using a similar scheme, which include the *"manual-only"* run, and the four second round runs with the ratio 5:1, 10:1, 15:1 and 20:1. The results are shown in Table 7. None of the third round runs could generate statistical significant improvement over the second round runs. It seems that fusions with iteration more than 2 does not justify the extra costs involved compared to the second round fusion runs.

Our multiple iteration experiments tell us that it is usually difficult to obtain a better fusion result over the best pre-fusion run when the retrieval effectiveness of the pre-fusion runs are greatly different to each other. The fusion experiment on *"manual-only"* and the other automatic runs is an example of such fusion. However, significant improvement over the best pre-fusion run could be achieved via multiple iterations of fusion. For example, we achieved significant improvement over the best pre-fusion run in two iterations. Of course, we need further experiments to test the general effectiveness of the multiple iteration fusion.

5 Conclusion

In this paper, we have described an investigation of data fusion techniques for spoken document retrieval. Because of the various characteristics of the documents in the Malach test collection, retrieval based solely on the output from automatic speech recognition (ASR) is well below retrievals on manual generated data. To overcome the problem, we have explored data fusion techniques for integrating the manually generated metadata information with the ASR outputs. We concentrated on the post-search fusion approach, and explored weighted CombMNZ model with different weight ratios and multiple iterations. Our initial results indicate that a simple unweighted combination method, that has been demonstrated to be useful in written retrieval environment [5], only generated significant 38% relative decrease in retrieval effectiveness (Mean Average Precision) for our task by comparing to a simple retrieval baseline where all manual metadata and ASR outputs are put together. Only with the more elaborate weighted combination scheme did we obtain a 31% significant relative improvement over the simple fusion baseline, and 4% relative improvement over the manual-only baseline, which is a significant difference.

Our future work include further experiments on the general effectiveness of the multiple iteration fusion. Other future work will explore the usage of WCombMNZ in other retrieval tasks, where multiple retrieval results can be obtained from one retrieval engine, or even different engines. The third further study we want to work on is to answer the question what is the minimum human generated data to ASR output if the goal is to combine the human generated data with the ASR output to achieve a comparable retrieval effectiveness to a retrieval on manual transcripts.

Acknowledgment

The authors would like to thank Doug Oard, Gareth Jones and Ryen White for their tireless efforts to coordinate CLEF-SDR.

References

1. N.J. Belkin, C. Cool, W.B. Croft, and J.P. Callan. The effect of multiple query representations on information retrieval system performance. In *Proceedings of SIGIR'93*, pages 339–346, 1993.

2. A. Chen. Cross-language retrieval experiments at CLEF 2002. In *Proceedings of CLEF 2002*, pages 28–48, 2002.
3. K. Darwish and D. W. Oard. CLIR Experiments at Maryland for TREC 2002: Evidence Combination for Arabic-English Retrieval. In *Proceedings of TREC 2002*, pages 703–710, 2002.
4. E. A. Fox and J. A. Shaw. Combination of multiple searches. In *Proeedings of the 2nd Text REtrieval Conference (TREC-2)*, pages 243–252, 1994.
5. J. H. Lee. Analyses of multiple evidence combination. In *Proceeding of SIGIR'97*, pages 267–276, 1997.
6. D. W. Oard, D. Soergel, D. Doermann, X. Huang, G. .C Murray, J. Wang, B. Ramabhadran, M. Franz, and S. Gustman. Building an information retrieval test collection for spontaneous conversational speech. In *Proceedings of SIGIR 2004*, page 41–48, 2004.
7. L. M. Rocha. Combination of evidence in recommendation systems characterized by distance functions. In *Proceedings of the 2002 World Congress on Computational Intelligence, FUZZ-IEEE'02*, pages 203–208. IEEE Press, 2002.

UNED@CL-SR CLEF 2005: Mixing Different Strategies to Retrieve Automatic Speech Transcriptions

Fernando López-Ostenero, Víctor Peinado, Valentín Sama, and Felisa Verdejo

NLP Group, ETSI Informática, UNED
c/ Juan del Rosal, 16. E-28040 Madrid. Spain
{flopez, victor, vsama, felisa}@lsi.uned.es

Abstract. In this paper we describe UNED's participation in the CLEF CL-SR 2005 track. First, we explain how we tried several strategies to clean up the automatic transcriptions. Then, we describe how we performed 84 different runs mixing these strategies with named entity recognition and different pseudo-relevance feedback approaches, in order to study the influence of each method in the retrieval process, both in monolingual and cross-lingual environments. We noticed that the influence of named entity recognition was higher in the cross-lingual environment, where MAP scores double when we take advantage of an entity recognizer. The best pseudo-relevance feedback approach was the one using manual keywords. The effects of the different cleaning strategies were very similar, except for character 3-grams, which obtained poor scores compared with other approaches.

1 Introduction

The goal of the CLEF CL-SR 2005 track is to develop and evaluate systems to rank retrieval of spontaneous conversational speech. The corpus used was the MALACH collection, a subset of 8,104 segments of interviews from survivors, liberators, rescuers and witnesses of the Holocaust. Our participation in the track focused on testing and mixing different techniques to improve the retrieval effectiveness: strategies to clean up documents, recognize named entities and refine the queries using different pseudo-relevance feedback approaches.

The effects of the cleaning strategies were very similar for all methods based on full words. The manual keywords turned out to be the best terms to use in a pseudo-relevance feedback approach. When using our entity recognizer, we improved the MAP scores in both monolingual and cross-lingual environments. However, we also noticed that the influence of named entity detection was bigger in the cross-lingual environment, since we had previously used an entity recognizer to detect nouns that should not be translated.

The remaining sections of this paper are divided as follows: in Section 2 we describe our testbed and the design of our submitted runs. In Section 3, we describe the experiments performed after the official evaluation and, in Section 4, we show the results of our 84 runs, analyzing the influence of the named entity

C. Peters et al. (Eds.): CLEF 2005, LNCS 4022, pp. 783–791, 2006.

recognition in monolingual and cross-lingual environments (Section 4.1), cleaning strategies (Section 4.2) and the different pseudo-relevance feedback methods used (Section 4.3). Lastly, in Section 5 we draw some conclusions.

2 Experiment Design

Following the CL-SR CLEF 2005 guidelines [6], we submitted five different runs. After the release of the official evaluation, we performed several other experiments in order to complete our participation.

2.1 Testbed

We used the following data from the collection provided by the track's organizers:

- As transcription, we only took `ASR2004A` since it looked very similar to the alternative transcription called `ASR2003A` and it seemed to contain fewer typos.
- We used the manually written summary of the segment (`SUMMARY`) to check whether the named entity located by our named entity recognizer should be translated or not.
- We also used three different sets of keywords for the pseudo-relevance feedback: one set of manually selected keywords (`MANUALKEYWORD`) and two different automatic sets (`AUTOKEYWORD2004A1` and `AUTOKEYWORD2004A2`).

In order to clean up the automatic transcriptions and remove the typical features of the conversational speech which may be harmful to a retrieval task, we tried the following strategies:

1. When speech recognizers are not able to identify something, they try to spell it out as in *l i e b b a c h a r d*. We decided to join these characters assuming that they formed a unique misrecognized word.

   Besides, in spontaneous speech, it is usual to insert some pet words and repetitions and these were transcribed in the documents. When performing a retrieval process, the results may be affected by these words, so we decided to remove all extra occurrences of the duplicated words. The resulting documents after these first two steps were indexed in a collection that we will refer as CLEAN.
2. In Information Retrieval tasks, the most informative terms are usually nouns, adjectives and verbs[1]. So we used the FreeLing tools[2] in order to generate two new collections of documents with words from these three grammatical categories:

---

[1] See [4] for a successful example of locating and extracting noun phrases in Spanish by using this technique in an IR environment.

[2] For further information, about this toolkit please see `http://www.lsi.upc.es/~nlp/freeling`.

  - First we performed a simple morphological analysis of the CLEAN collection. All words labeled either as a noun, an adjective or a verb were included into what we indexed as the MORPHO collection.
  - Then, we performed a full part of speech tagging, also with the FreeLing tools. This process was a further step and included a POS disambiguation phase in order to select only one of the possible categories for a given word. As in the previous process, only words acting as nouns, adjectives or verbs remained in the resulting index. We will refer this second index as the POS collection.
3. Lastly, we built an additional collection called 3GRAMS by splitting words into 3-grams of characters. We intended to compare the performance of this simple approach with the more complex ones.

We only considered the `TITLE` and `DESCRIPTION` fields of the topics for both English and Spanish, performing the usual word normalization and stop word removal process. For our cross-lingual runs, we used a query translation approach following Pirkola's proposal [5], where alternative translations for a term are taken as synonyms, giving them equal weights.

Concerning the search engine, our system used the Inquery API [2]. In order to build the indexes, all stop words were removed and the remaining terms were stemmed applying the KSTEM algorithm provided by the API.

2.2 Submitted Runs

For our official participation, we submitted five different runs:

- A monolingual run using the 3GRAMS collection and the English topics expressed as 3-grams (`mono-3grams`).
- A monolingual run using the MORPHO collection (`mono-morpho`) and the English topics.
- A cross-lingual run using the MORPHO collection and the Spanish topics translated into English (`trans-morpho`).
- A monolingual run using the POS collection (`mono-pos`).
- A cross-lingual run using the POS collection and the Spanish topics translated into English (`trans-pos`).

Table 1 shows the official results. Our runs were far from the best monolingual and Spanish cross-lingual ones, so there seems to be room for improvement. MAP scores of MORPHO and POS runs were very similar in both monolingual and cross-lingual environments. As expected, POS scored slightly better than MORPHO, but with only two different runs we don't have enough data to conclude whether the POS disambiguation helped in cleaning the documents or not.

Regarding the run based on 3-grams, it reached only 75.6% of our best full word retrieval run `mono-pos`. Again we don't have enough data to conclude if it's more convenient for this task to use full word retrieval or a 3-grams approach.

Just using a bilingual dictionary and Pirkola's approach, our cross-lingual runs reached about 40% of their monolingual counterparts. In some cases (see

Table 1. Results of the submitted runs

Ranking	MAP	Run	Language
1	0.3129	UMD (best English run)	English (monolingual)
5	0.1863	U. Ottawa (best Spanish run)	Spanish (cross-lingual)
20	0.0934	`mono-pos`	English (monolingual)
21	0.0918	`mono-morpho`	English (monolingual)
29	0.0706	`mono-3grams`	English (monolingual)
32	0.0373	`trans-pos`	Spanish (cross-lingual)
33	0.0370	`trans-morpho`	Spanish (cross-lingual)

section 4.1) a bad translation of a named entity might have harmed the cross-lingual search.

With only five different runs it's difficult to draw clear conclusions. According to suggestions of the CL-SR CLEF organizers, we tried additional experiments after the official submission in order to test a more complete approach. These experiments are described in the following section.

3 Additional Experiments

With this second set of experiments, we intended to test the effects of two strategies (named entity identification and pseudo-relevance feedback) and compare all possible combinations in different approaches.

3.1 Named Entity Identification

We used our entity recognizer [3] in order to improve the query structure, identifying possible named entities in the topics. These entities were processed in the following ways in our monolingual and cross-lingual experiments:

- For the monolingual runs, we just identified the named entities appearing in the topics. Then, we structured the query, tagging each of them with Inquery's `#phrase` operator which enabled us to treat the named entity as a single term.
- Our topics were written in Spanish and the collection was written in English thus using the same strategy as above in a cross-lingual environment would not suffice. We needed an effective way to decide if a given named entity should be translated or not. So, we used the recognizer in order to identify named entities in the `SUMMARY` field of the documents. If an entity appeared both in the Spanish topics and the English `SUMMARY`, we assumed this entity should not be translated.

3.2 Pseudo-relevance Feedback

We also decided to test a pseudo-relevance feedback [1] (PRF) approach to check the utility of the keyword fields of the documents. To do that, we built five different indexes:

- A collection called AK1 using the terms in the `AUTOKEYWORD2004A1` field.
- A collection called AK2 using the terms in the `AUTOKEYWORD2004A2` field.
- A collection called AK12 mixing the keywords appearing in both autokeyword fields.
- A collection called MK using the terms in the `MANUALKEYWORD` field.
- A collection called MKAK12 mixing the terms from the three keyword fields.

In order to choose the keyword terms we proceed as follows. First, every automatic keyword was scored according to its order of appearance within a given keyword field, from 20 to 1. If a keyword appeared in more than one field, it was assigned the total sum of the particular scores for each field. We sorted out the terms according to their score and we kept with the top 20. This is the keyword list we used to build the AK12 collection.

Then, to build the MKAK12 collection, we appended the AK12 list to the terms appearing in the `MANUALKEYWORD` field and we selected only the top 20 terms of the resulting list.

And finally, the steps we followed in order to perform the searches with PRF are:

1. Launch a query without keyword expansion and take the 10 most relevant documents retrieved.
2. Take the keywords from these documents and rank them using the same method explained above to combine both automatic keyword fields.
3. Use the top 20 ranked keywords to expand the query.

3.3 Full Set of Runs

Our first intention was to test all possible combinations of each feature: topic language, named entity identification, cleaning method and relevance feedback. We discarded performing the cross-lingual runs using 3-grams since it seemed to us that trying to translate three-character strings was pointless.

Each run was named with the labels of the different features considered. For instance, `mono-noent-morpho-AK2` represents a monolingual run without named entity identification, over the MORPHO collection, performing a pseudo-relevance feedback process using the `AUTOKEYWORD2004A2` field.

$$\underbrace{\begin{pmatrix} \text{mono} \\ \text{trans} \end{pmatrix}}_{\textit{language}} \times \underbrace{\begin{pmatrix} \text{noent} \\ \text{ent} \end{pmatrix}}_{\textit{named entity}} \times \underbrace{\begin{pmatrix} \text{3grams} \\ \text{clean} \\ \text{morpho} \\ \text{pos} \end{pmatrix}}_{\textit{cleaning method}} \times \underbrace{\begin{pmatrix} \text{NO} \\ \text{AK1} \\ \text{AK2} \\ \text{AK12} \\ \text{MK} \\ \text{MKAK12} \end{pmatrix}}_{\textit{relevance feedback}}$$

Fig. 1. Combination of all features

Figure 1 shows all possible values for each feature: 96 different combinations. But, if we exclude the cross-lingual runs with 3-grams equals the 84 runs performed.

4 Results and Discussion

The results of all our runs are shown in Table 2. Our best monolingual run (`mono-ent-morpho-MK`) obtained a MAP improvement of 277.8% with respect to our best submitted monolingual run. In addition, our best cross-lingual run (`trans-ent-pos-MK`) obtained an astonishing improvement of 545.8% with respect to our best submitted cross-lingual run.

The best strategies seem to be pseudo-relevance feedback using the MK or the MKAK12 collections and adding named entity recognition. On the other side the monolingual 3-grams runs scored poorly, reaching only a 30% MAP of our best run.

4.1 Language and Named Entity Effects

In figure 2 we can see the effects of the proper noun detection in both monolingual and cross-lingual runs. The columns represent the different cleaning effects and the relevance-feedback methods. The points in the graphics represent the percentage of MAP increment between a run using named entity detection and the same run not using it. We can infer from these results that structuring monolingual queries by tagging named entities is worthless. But, in cross-lingual runs, identifying words that should remain untranslated seems to be a very effective technique.

For instance, on topic #1113 (*The story of Varian Fry*), the influence of named entity detection is very important, because in Spanish the word "Varian" can be identified as a verbal form of *variar* (to vary, to change) and is wrongly translated as "vary", "deviate" or "fluctuate".

4.2 Cleaning Effects

Regarding the influence of the cleaning method, we can conclude that the best cleaning strategy seems to be MORPHO, but the differences between POS and CLEAN are minimal. Again, character 3-grams are shown to be a bad cleaning strategy when compared with full words approaches.

4.3 Pseudo-relevance Feedback

In figure 3 we compare the differences between the different pseudo-relevance feedback strategies tested. Each point represents the MAP percentage of one PRF method with respect to a corresponding run without using PRF.

It can be noted that:

- The best PRF method is MK (average increment of MAP using the PRF over manual keywords field with respect to no relevance feedback is about

Table 2. Evaluation results (submitted runs in boldface)

MAP	R-Prec	Experiment
0.2595	0.3046	mono-ent-morpho-MK
0.2583	0.3001	mono-ent-pos-MK
0.2557	0.3025	mono-ent-clean-MK
0.2499	0.2879	mono-noent-morpho-MK
0.2498	0.2873	mono-noent-pos-MK
0.2462	0.2860	mono-noent-clean-MK
0.2396	0.2897	mono-ent-pos-MKAK12
0.2353	0.2855	mono-ent-morpho-MKAK12
0.2299	0.2895	mono-ent-clean-MKAK12
0.2284	0.2740	mono-noent-pos-MKAK12
0.2245	0.2711	mono-noent-morpho-MKAK12
0.2224	0.2774	mono-noent-clean-MKAK12
0.2036	0.2444	trans-ent-pos-MK
0.2000	0.2475	trans-ent-clean-MK
0.1982	0.2437	trans-ent-morpho-MK
0.1931	0.2443	trans-ent-pos-MKAK12
0.1880	0.2420	trans-ent-morpho-MKAK12
0.1853	0.2411	trans-ent-clean-MKAK12
0.1025	0.1465	trans-noent-morpho-MK
0.1016	0.1421	trans-noent-pos-MK
0.0994	0.1574	mono-noent-pos-AK12
0.0991	0.1597	mono-ent-pos-AK12
0.0976	0.1378	trans-noent-clean-MK
0.0971	0.1523	mono-noent-morpho-AK12
0.0969	0.1562	mono-ent-morpho-AK12
0.0953	0.1530	mono-noent-clean-AK12
0.0950	0.1582	mono-ent-pos-NO
0.0944	0.1593	mono-ent-clean-NO
0.0937	0.1540	mono-ent-clean-AK12
0.0935	0.1603	mono-ent-morpho-NO
0.0934	**0.1522**	**mono-noent-pos-NO**
0.0927	0.1528	mono-noent-clean-NO
0.0918	**0.1532**	**mono-noent-morpho-NO**
0.0879	0.1254	trans-noent-morpho-MKAK12
0.0874	0.1450	mono-ent-pos-AK2
0.0871	0.1431	mono-noent-pos-AK2
0.0868	0.1431	mono-ent-morpho-AK2
0.0866	0.1522	mono-ent-pos-AK1
0.0865	0.1221	trans-noent-pos-MKAK12
0.0860	0.1500	mono-ent-morpho-AK1
0.0860	0.1473	mono-noent-pos-AK1
0.0857	0.1225	trans-noent-clean-MKAK12
0.0853	0.1372	mono-noent-morpho-AK2
0.0852	0.1468	mono-ent-clean-AK1
0.0846	0.1469	mono-noent-morpho-AK1
0.0841	0.1408	mono-noent-clean-AK1
0.0837	0.1287	trans-ent-pos-AK12
0.0828	0.1382	mono-noent-clean-AK2
0.0827	0.1282	trans-ent-morpho-AK12
0.0826	0.1423	mono-ent-clean-AK2
0.0789	0.1282	trans-ent-clean-AK12
0.0780	0.1134	mono-noent-3grams-MK
0.0769	0.1370	trans-ent-pos-AK1
0.0766	0.1361	trans-ent-morpho-AK1
0.0752	0.1329	trans-ent-clean-AK1
0.0740	0.1127	mono-ent-3grams-MK
0.0735	0.1202	trans-ent-morpho-NO
0.0731	0.1193	trans-ent-pos-NO
0.0731	0.1175	trans-ent-clean-NO
0.0725	0.1198	trans-ent-pos-AK2
0.0717	0.1191	trans-ent-morpho-AK2
0.0715	0.1196	trans-ent-clean-AK2
0.0706	**0.1119**	**mono-noent-3grams-NO**
0.0650	0.1029	mono-ent-3grams-MKAK12
0.0649	0.1125	mono-noent-3grams-MKAK12
0.0601	0.1020	mono-ent-3grams-NO
0.0541	0.0892	mono-ent-3grams-AK12
0.0475	0.0870	mono-ent-3grams-AK1
0.0427	0.0757	mono-ent-3grams-AK2
0.0423	0.0850	mono-noent-3grams-AK12
0.0411	0.0838	mono-noent-3grams-AK1
0.0393	0.0667	mono-noent-3grams-AK2
0.0373	**0.0750**	**trans-noent-pos-NO**
0.0372	0.0746	trans-noent-clean-NO
0.0370	**0.0759**	**trans-noent-morpho-NO**
0.0346	0.0724	trans-noent-pos-AK1
0.0346	0.0687	trans-noent-morpho-AK1
0.0343	0.0713	trans-noent-pos-AK12
0.0342	0.0723	trans-noent-clean-AK1
0.0331	0.0673	trans-noent-morpho-AK12
0.0326	0.0634	trans-noent-clean-AK12
0.0290	0.0664	trans-noent-morpho-AK2
0.0288	0.0663	trans-noent-pos-AK2
0.0282	0.0673	trans-noent-clean-AK2

271.6%), nearly followed by MKAK12 (an average MAP of 90.5% with respect to MK).

- There are no big differences between the use of each automatic keyword field, but PRF using the `AUTOKEYWORD2004A1` field seems to obtain a high MAP score. And, when combining both fields AK12, MAP scores on average 41.51% of MKAK12.

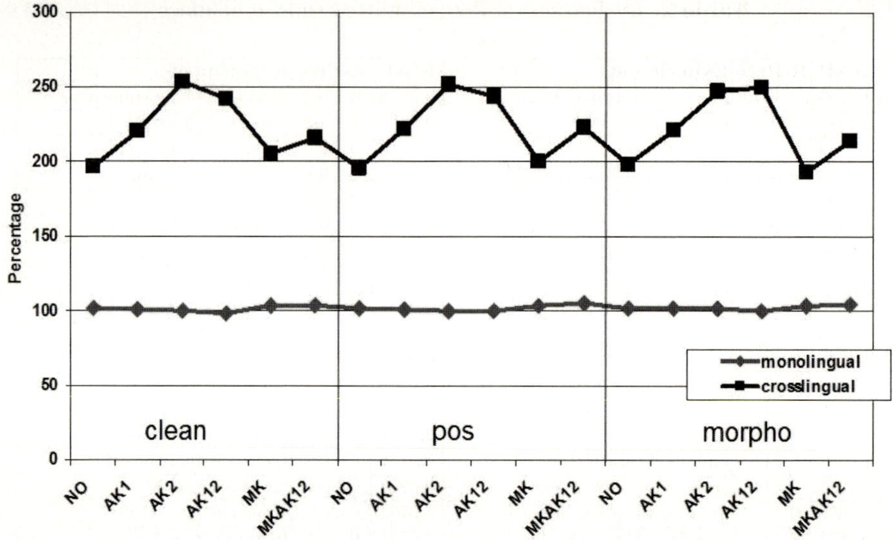

Fig. 2. Influence of named entity detection: monolingual and cross-lingual runs

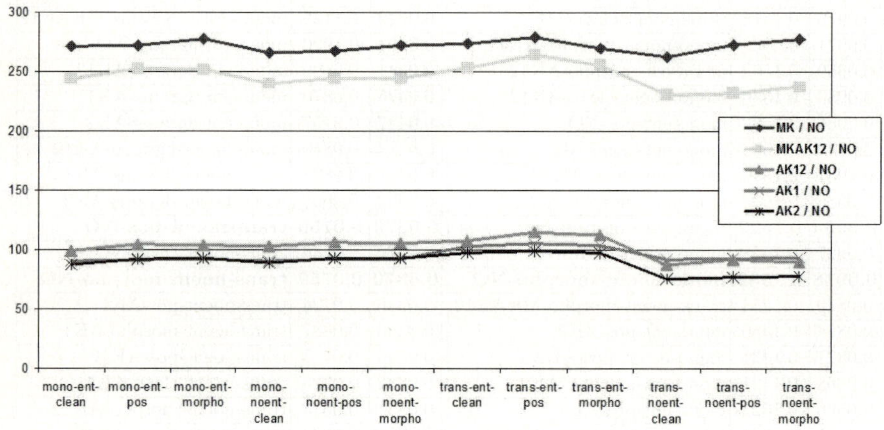

Fig. 3. Influence of pseudo-relevance feedback methods

5 Conclusions and Future Work

In this paper, we have shown different techniques to improve retrieval of automatic speech transcriptions in both monolingual and cross-lingual environments.

- The use of a shallow entity recognizer to identify named entities, seems to be very useful, especially in a cross-lingual environment, where the MAP increases 221.9% on average.

- Cleaning methods based on full words (CLEAN, MORPHO and POS) show no significant differences, but character 3-grams approach can be discarded for this task.
- Pseudo-relevance feedback using manually generated keywords turns out to be the best option to improve retrieval performance, with an average percentage of 271.6% compared to runs without relevance feedback.

As future work we want to try different approaches to identify named entities in automatically generated fields, instead of using the manual summary of the documents. The big improvement in detecting named entities in the cross-lingual environment may be due to the use of the manually generated field, just like the improvement obtained when considering the `MANUALKEYWORDS` field in pseudo-relevance feedback.

Acknowledgments

This work has been partially supported by the Spanish Government under the project R2D2-Syembra (TIC2003-07158-C04-02). Víctor Peinado holds a PhD grant by UNED (*Universidad Nacional de Educación a Distancia*).

References

1. Buckley, C., Salton, G., Allan, J., Singhal, A.: Automatic Query Expansion Using SMART: TREC 3. In: Proceedings of the 3rd Text Retrieval Conference (TREC3), 69–80. National Institute of Standards and Technology (NIST), Gaithesburg, MD, 1995.
2. Callan, J. P., Croft, W. B., Harding, S. M.: The Inquery Retrieval System In: Proceedings of the Third International Conference on Database and Expert Systems Applications. 78–83. Springer-Verlag, 1992.
3. Peinado, V., López-Ostenero, F., Gonzalo, J., Verdejo, F.: UNED at ImageCLEF 2005: Automatically Structured Queries with Named Entities over Metadata. In: Cross Language Evaluation Forum, Working Notes for the CLEF 2005 Workshop, 2005.
4. Peñas, A.: Website Term Browser: Un sistema interactivo y multilingüe de búsqueda textual basado en técnicas lingüísticas. PhD thesis, Departamento de Lenguajes y Sistemas Informáticos, Universidad Nacional de Educación a Distancia, 2002.
5. Pirkola, A.: The Effects of Query Structure and Dictionary Setups in Dictionary-Based Cross-Language Information Retrieval. In: Proceedings of SIGIR'98, 21st ACM International Conference on Research and Development in Information Retrieval, 55–63, 1998.
6. White, R. W., Oard, D. W., Jones, G. J. F., Soergel, D., Huang, X.: Overview of the CLEF-2005 Cross-Language Speech Retrieval Track. In: Cross Language Evaluation Forum, Working Notes for the CLEF 2005 Workshop, 2005.

Dublin City University at CLEF 2005: Cross-Language Speech Retrieval (CL-SR) Experiments

Adenike M. Lam-Adesina and Gareth J.F. Jones

School of Computing, Dublin City University, Dublin 9, Ireland
{adenike, gjones}@computing.dcu.ie

Abstract. The Dublin City University participation in the CLEF 2005 CL-SR task concentrated on exploring the application of our existing information retrieval methods based on the Okapi model to the conversational speech data set. This required an approach to determining approximate sentence boundaries within the free-flowing automatic transcription provided to enable us to use our summary-based pseudo relevance feedback (PRF). We also performed exploratory experiments on the use of the metadata provided with the document transcriptions for indexing and relevance feedback. Topics were translated into English using Systran V3.0 machine translation. In most cases Title field only topic statements performed better than combined Title and Description topics. PRF using our adapted method is shown to be affective, and absolute performance is improved by combining the automatic document transcriptions with additional metadata fields.

1 Introduction

The Dublin City University participation in the CLEF 2005 CL-SR task [1] concentrated on exploring the application of our existing information retrieval methods based on the Okapi model to this data set, and exploratory experiments on the use of the provided document metadata. Our official submissions included both the English monolingual and French bilingual runs. This paper reports additional results for German and Spanish bilingual runs. Topics were translated into English using the Systran V3.0 machine translation system. The resulting English topics were applied to the English document collection.

Our standard Okapi retrieval system incorporates a summary-based pseudo relevance feedback (PRF) stage. This PRF system operates by selecting topic expansion terms from document summaries, full details are described in [2]. However, since the transcriptions of the conversational speech documents generated using automatic speech recognition (ASR) do not contain punctuation, we needed to develop a method of selecting significant document segments to identify documents "summaries". Details of our method for doing this are described in Section 2.1.

The spoken document transcriptions are provided with a rich set of metadata, further details are available in [1]. It is not immediately clear how best to exploit this most effectively in retrieval. This paper reports our initial exploratory experiments in making use of this additional information by merging it with the standard document transcriptions for indexing and relevance feedback.

C. Peters et al. (Eds.): CLEF 2005, LNCS 4022, pp. 792 – 799, 2006.

The remainder of this paper is structured as follows: Section 2 overviews our retrieval system and describes our sentence boundary creation technique, Section 3 presents the results of our experimental investigations, and Section 4 concludes the paper with a discussion of our results.

2 System Setup

The basis of our experimental system is the City University research distribution version of the Okapi system [3]. The documents and search topics are processed to remove stopwords from a standard list of about 260 words, suffix stripped using the Okapi implementation of Porter stemming [4] and terms are indexed using a small standard set of synonyms. None of these procedures were adapted for the CLEF 2005 CL-SR test collection. The documents fields to be indexed for a particular set of experiments were merged into a single document field prior to indexing.

2.1 Term Weighting

Document terms were weighted using the Okapi BM25 weighting scheme developed in [3] calculated as follows,

$$cw(i,j) = \frac{cfw(i) \times tf(i,j) \times (K1+1)}{K1*((1-b)+(b \times ndl(j))) + tf(i,j)}.$$

where *cw(i,j)* represents the weight of term *i* in document *j*, *cfw(i)* is the standard collection frequency weight, *tf(i,j)* is the document term frequency, and *ndl(j)* is the normalized document length. *ndl(j)* is calculated as *ndl(j) = dl(j)/avdl* where *dl(j)* is the length of *j and avdl* is the average document length for all documents. *k1* and *b* are empirically selected tuning constants for a particular collection. *k1* is designed to modify the degree of effect of *tf(i,j)*, while constant *b* modifies the effect of document length. High values of *b* imply that documents are long because they are verbose, while low values imply that they are long because they are multi-topic. The values used for our submitted runs were tuned using the provided training topics.

2.2 Pseudo-relevance Feedback

We apply PRF for query expansion using a variation of the summary-based method described in [2] which has been shown to be effective in our previous submissions to CLEF, including [5] and elsewhere. The main challenge for query expansion is the selection of appropriate terms from the assumed relevant documents. For the CL-SR task our query expansion method operates as follows. A summary is made of the ASR transcription of each of the top ranked documents, which are assumed to be relevant for each PRF. Each document summary is then expanded to include all terms in the metadata fields used in this document index. All non-stopwords in these augmented summaries are ranked using a slightly modified version of the Robertson selection value (rsv) [3] shown in equation (1).

$$rsv(i) = r(i) \times rw(i). \quad (1)$$

where *r(i)* = the total number of relevant documents containing term *i*, and *rw(i)* is the standard Robertson/Sparck Jones relevance weight [3],

$$rw(i) = \log \frac{(r(i)+0.5)(N-n(i)-R+r(i)+0.5)}{(n(i)-r(i)+0.5)(R-r(i)+0.5)}$$

where *r(i)* = is defined as before, *n(i)* = the total number of documents containing term *i*, *R* = the total number of relevant documents for this query, and *N* = the total number of documents

The top ranked terms are then added to the topic. In our modified version of *rsv(i)*, potential expansion terms are selected from the augmented summaries of the top ranked documents, but ranked using statistics from a larger number of assumed relevant ranked documents from the initial run.

2.2.1 Sentence Selection

Our standard process for summary generation is to select representative sentences from the document [6]. Since the transcriptions in the CL-SR document set do not contain punctuation marking, we needed an alternative approach to identifying significant units in the transcription. We approached this using a method derived from Luhn's word cluster hypothesis. Luhn's hypothesis states that significant words separated by not more than 5 non-significant words are likely to be strongly related. Clusters of these strongly related word were identified in the running document transcription by searching for word groups separated by not more than 5 insignificant words, as shown in Figure 1. Note that words appearing between clusters are not included in clusters, but can be ignored for the purposes of query expansion since they are by definition stop words.

… this chapter gives a brief description of the [*data* sets used in *evaluating* the *automatic* relevance *feedback* procedure *investigated* in this *thesis*] and also discusses the extension of …

Fig. 1. Example of Sentence creation

The clusters were then awarded a significance score based on two measures.

Luhn's Keyword Cluster Method. Luhn's method assigns a sentence score for the highest scoring cluster within a sentence. We adapted this method to assign a cluster score as follows:

$$SS1 = \frac{SW^2}{TW}.$$

where *SS1* = the sentence score
SW = the number of bracketed significant words
TW = the total number of bracketed words

For the example in Fig. 1, *SW*=6 and *TW*=14.

Query-Bias Method. This method assigns a score to each sentence based on the number of query terms in the sentence as follows:

$$SS2 = \frac{TQ^2}{NQ}\ .$$

where $SS2$ = the sentence score
TQ = the number of query terms present in the sentence
NQ = the number of terms in a query

The overall score for each sentence (cluster) was then formed by summing these two measures for each sentence.

3 Experimental Investigation

This section describes the establishment of the parameters for our experimental system and then gives results from our investigations.

3.1 Selection of System Parameters

In order to set the appropriate parameters for our feedback runs, we carried out development runs using the CLEF 2005 CL-SR training topics. The Okapi parameters were set as follows $k1$=1.4 b=0.8. For all our PRF runs, 5 documents were assumed relevant for term selection and document summaries comprised the best scoring 4 clusters. The *rsv* values to rank the potential expansion terms were estimated based on the top 20 or 40 ranked assumed relevant documents. The top 20 ranked expansion terms taken from the clusters were added to the original query in each case. Based on results from our previous experiments in CLEF, the original topic terms are up-weighted by a factor of 3.5 relative to terms introduced by PRF. For our submitted runs we used either the Title section (dcu*tit) or the Title and Description (dcu*desc) section of each topic. Our official submitted runs are marked $^+$ the tables of results. Baseline monolingual results using English topics without query expansion are given for comparison for each experimental condition.

For our experiments the document fields were combined as follows:

dcua2 – combination of ASRTEXT2004A and AUTOKEYWORDA1

dcua1a2 – combination of ASRTEXT2004A, AUTOKEYWORDA1 and AUTOKEYWORDA2

dcusum – combination of ASRTEXT2004A, AUTOKEYWORDA1 and AUTOKEYWORDA2 and the SUMMARY

dcuall – combination of ASRTEXT2004A, SUMMARY, NAME and MANUALKEYWORD

3.2 Experimental Results

Tables 1-4 show results of our experiments using these different data combinations for the 25 test topics released for the CLEF 2005 CL-SR task. Results shown are Mean Average Precision (MAP), total relevant documents retrieved (Rr), and precision at cutoffs of 10 and 30 documents. Topic languages used are English, French, German and Spanish. Topics were translated into English using the Systran V3.0 machine translation system. The upper set of results in each table shows

Table 1. Results using a combination of ASRTEXT2004A and AUTOKEYWORDA1, with the Title or Title and Description topic fields. Expansion terms ranked for selection using statistics of 40 top ranked documents.

Run-id	Topic Lang.	MAP	Rr	P10	P30
dcua2desc40f	Baseline	0.050	536	0.148	0.103
	English	0.065[+]	738	0.176	0.140
	French	0.076	744	0.208	0.139
	German	0.041	611	0.116	0.099
	Spanish	0.055	727	0.152	0.109
dcua2tit40f	Baseline	0.070	384	0.228	0.143
	English	0.080	622	0.252	0.151
	French	0.081	708	0.252	0.155
	German	0.056	647	0.184	0.120
	Spanish	0.068	602	0.192	0.129

combined Title and Description topic queries and the lower set Title only topic queries.

Results in Table 1 show results for combination of ASRTEXT2004A with AUTOKEYWORDA1. It can be seen that the PRF method improves results for the English topics in each case. Also that the results using Title only topics are better than those using the combined Title and Description topics with respect to MAP. This result is perhaps a little surprising since the latter are generally found to be perform better and we are investigating the reasons for the results observed here. However, the number of relevant documents retrieved is generally higher when using the combined topics which is to be expected since the topics will contain more terms which can match with potentially relevant documents. Cross-language information retrieval (CLIR) results using French topics are shown to perform better than monolingual

Table 2. Results using a combination of ASRTEXT2004A, AUTOKEYWORDA1 and AUTOKEYWORDA2, with the Title or Title and Description topic fields. Expansion terms ranked for selection using statistics of 40 top ranked documents.

Run-id	Topic Lang.	MAP	Rr	P10	P30
dcuala2desc40f	Baseline	0.046	500	0.188	0.105
	English	0.067	784	0.184	0.148
	French	0.094	773	0.216	0.171
	German	0.046	611	0.096	0.092
	Spanish	0.064	765	0.164	0.128
dcuala2tit40f	Baseline	0.0800	472	0.228	0.160
	English	0.110[+]	727	0.252	0.196
	French	0.106[+]	768	0.260	0.191
	German	0.074	691	0.172	0.149
	Spanish	0.091	679	0.220	0.156

English for both MAP and relevant retrieved. This is again unusual, but not unprecedented in CLIR. Results for translated German and Spanish topics show a reduction compared to the monolingual results.

Table 2 shows results for the same set of experiments as those in Table 1 with the addition of the AUTOKEYWORDA2 metadata to the documents. Results here generally show similar trends to those in Table 1 with small absolute increases in performance in most cases. In this case the performance advantage of French topics over English topics with PRF has largely disappeared for the Title only topics, however, performance for French topics is still much better than for English topics for the combined Title and Description topics.

Table 3. Results using a combination of ASRTEXT2004A, AUTOKEYWORDA1 and AUTOKEYWORDA2 and the SUMMARY section of each document, with the Title or Title and Description topic fields. Expansion terms ranked for selection using statistics of 40 top ranked documents.

Run-id	Topic Lang.	MAP	Rr	P10	P30
dcusumdesc40f	Baseline	0.105	598	0.224	0.171
	English	0.147	889	0.272	0.217
	French	0.154	856	0.260	0.216
	German	0.108	696	0.164	0.137
	Spanish	0.107	860	0.168	0.152
dcusumtit40f	Baseline	0.141	618	0.284	0.216
	English	0.167	770	0.292	0.243
	French	0.165^{+}	837	0.308	0.251
	German	0.110	738	0.220	0.160
	Spanish	0.154	736	0.284	0.130

Table 3 shows results for a further set of experiments with the SUMMARY field added to the document descriptions. All results here show large increases compared to those in Table 2, indicating that the contents of the SUMMARY field are useful descriptions of the documents. The SUMMARY of each document is manually generated and presumably includes important terms which may be good descriptions of the topic of the document and possibly words actually appearing in the document, but incorrectly transcribed by the speech recognition system. The relative performance of monolingual and cross-language topics is the same as that observed in Table 2.

Table 4 shows a final set of experiments combining the ASRTEXT2004A, SUMMARY, NAME and MANUALKEYWORD fields. These results show large improvements over the results shown in previous tables. Performance for Title only and Title and Description combined topics is now similar with neither clearly showing an advantage. Monolingual English performance is now clearly better than results for translated French topics for both topic types, while our PRF method is still shown to be effective. The manually assigned keywords are shown to be particularly useful additional search fields.

Table 4. Results using a combination of ASRTEXT2004A, SUMMARY, NAME and MANUALKEYWORD section of each document, with the Title or Title and Description topic fields. Expansion terms ranked for selection using statistics of 40 top ranked documents.

Run-id	Topic Lang.	MAP	Rr	P10	P30
dcualldesc40f	Baseline	0.221	1031	0.368	0.271
	English	0.283	1257	0.432	0.337
	French	0.257	1122	0.424	0.303
	German	0.229	1001	0.328	0.272
	Spanish	0.247	1160	0.380	0.297
dcualltit40f	Baseline	0.242	736	0.412	0.311
	English	0.307	1009	0.488	0.377
	French	0.276	1136	0.496	0.360
	German	0.205	962	0.360	0.276
	Spanish	0.232	908	0.360	0.268

4 Conclusions and Further Work

Our initial experiments with the CLEF 2005 CL-SR task illustrate that PRF can be successfully applied to this data set, and that the different fields of the document set make varying levels of positive contribution to information retrieval effectiveness. In general in can be seen that manual assigned fields are more useful than the automatically generated ones.

These experiments only represent a small subset of those that are possible with this dataset. In order to better understand the usefulness of document fields and retrieval methods more detailed analysis of these existing results and further experiments are planned. The okapi retrieval model generally produces competitive retrieval results. However, in this case the results achieved are significantly lower than those observed using a parameter setting of the SMART retrieval system [7]. It is important to understand why the standard okapi weighting does not appear to work well with the CLEF 2005 CL-SR test collection, and we will be pursuing this issue as part of our further work.

References

1. White, R. W., Oard, D. W., Jones, G. J. F., Soergel, D., and Huang, X.: Overview of the CLEF-2005 Cross-Language Speech Retrieval Track, Proceedings of the CLEF 2005: Workshop on Cross-Language Information Retrieval and Evaluation,Vienna, Austria, 2005.
2. Lam-Adesina, A. M., and Jones, G. J. F.: Applying Summarization Techniques for Term Selection in Relevance Feedback, Proceedings of the Twenty-Fourth Annual International ACM SIGIR Conference on Research and Development in Information Retrieval, pages 1-9, New Orleans, 2001. ACM.
3. Robertson, S. E., Walker, S., Jones, S., Hancock-Beaulieu, M. M. ,and Gatford, M.: Okapi at TREC-3, Proceedings of the Third Text REtrieval Conference (TREC-3), pages 109-126. NIST, 1995.

4. Porter, M. F.: An Algorithm for Suffix Stripping, Program, 14:10-137, 1980.
5. Luhn. H.P.: The Automatic Creation of Literature Abstracts. IBM Journal of Research and Development, 2(2):159-165, 1958.
6. Jones, G. J. F., Burke, M., Judge, J., Khasin, A., Lam-Adesina, A. M., and Wagner, J.: Dublin City University at CLEF 2004: Experiments in Monolingual, Bilingual and Multilingual Retrieval, Proceedings of the CLEF 2004: Workshop on Cross-Language Information Retrieval and Evaluation, Bath, U.K., pages 207-220, 2004.
7. Tombros, A., and Sanderson, M.: The Advantages of Query-Biased Summaries in Information Retrieval. In proceedings of the Twenty-First Annual International ACM SIGIR Conference Research and Development in Information Retrieval, pages 2-10, Melbourne, 1998. ACM.
8. Inkpen, D., Alzghool, M., and Islam, A. : University of Ottawa's Contribution to CLEF 2005, the CL-SR Track Proceedings of the CLEF 2005: Workshop on Cross-Language Information Retrieval and Evaluation, Vienna, Austria, 2005.

CLEF-2005 CL-SR at Maryland: Document and Query Expansion Using Side Collections and Thesauri

Jianqiang Wang and Douglas W. Oard

College of Information Studies and UMIACS
University of Maryland, College Park, MD 20742, USA
{wangjq, oard}@glue.umd.edu

Abstract. This paper reports results for the University of Maryland's participation in the CLEF-2005 Cross-Language Speech Retrieval track. Techniques that were tried include: (1) document expansion with manually created metadata (thesaurus keywords and segment summaries) from a large side collection, (2) query refinement with pseudo-relevance feedback, (3) keyword expansion with thesaurus synonyms, and (4) cross-language speech retrieval using translation knowledge obtained from the statistics of a large parallel corpus. The results show that document expansion and query expansion using blind relevance feedback were effective, although optimal parameter choices differed somewhat between the training and evaluation sets. Document expansion in which manually assigned keywords were augmented with thesaurus synonyms yielded marginal gains on the training set, but no improvement on the evaluation set. Cross-language retrieval with French queries yielded 79% of monolingual mean average precision when searching manually assigned metadata despite a substantial domain mismatch between the parallel corpus and the retrieval task. Detailed failure analysis indicates that speech recognition errors for named entities were an important factor that substantially degraded retrieval effectiveness.

1 Introduction

Automated techniques for speech retrieval seek to provide users with access to spoken content. The most widely adopted approaches to fully automated content-based speech retrieval rely on the combination of two critical techniques: automatic speech recognition (ASR) and information retrieval (IR). An ASR engine is first used to transcribe digitized audio into text, and text retrieval techniques can then be applied to accomplish the task. However, since ASR is an imperfect process, often there are spoken words that are not recognized correctly. This will lead to word mismatch in the retrieval step. Therefore, improving ASR accuracy (i.e., decreasing the ASR word error rate (WER)) can improve retrieval effectiveness [3]. Early experiments with speech retrieval for broadcast news in the TREC Spoken Document Retrieval (SDR) track showed that modern ranked retrieval techniques are fairly robust in the presence of speech recognition errors. For example, WER as high as 40% were observed to degrade retrieval

C. Peters et al. (Eds.): CLEF 2005, LNCS 4022, pp. 800–809, 2006.

effectiveness by less than 10% [1]. Routinely achieving that level of accuracy for broadcast news is now well within the state of the art.

The challenge of automated access to spoken content is, however, far from completely solved because broadcast news represents only a small portion of the variety of spoken content that information users may be interested in. This year's CLEF Cross-Language Speech Retrieval (CL-SR) track chose oral history interviews. This offers an excellent opportunity to study the application of techniques that have proven to be successful for searching broadcast news to a different domain, while providing opportunities to explore additional issues that are not easily studied in news genre.

In this study, we first wanted to re-examine how speech recognition errors affect IR effectiveness in the domain of oral history. An initial study we conducted in 2004 using a smaller test collection indicated that retrieval effectiveness using ASR results was substantially below what we could obtain when using either manually transcribed text or manually assigned metadata [5]. The improved ASR accuracy and the larger number of topics in the CLEF-2005 CL-SR collection permits a more thorough exploration of the reasons for this effect. Second, query and document expansion using blind relevance feedback are known to improve retrieval effectiveness when applied to broadcast news but we are not aware of similar experiments with any source of spontaneous speech. The availability of a training/evaluation split among the CLEF-2005 CL-SR topics makes it possible to explore this question in a principled manner. Also, the availability of thesaurus keyword synonyms makes it possible to test document expansion in a different way. Finally, the availability of topics in languages other than English facilitates cross-language speech retrieval experiments. We were particularly interested in using translation knowledge learned from parallel texts for query translation in CLIR.

The remainder of this paper is organized as follows. In the next section, we describe the techniques that we applied. Section 3 then presents mean average precision results for our five official submissions and additional experiments that we scored locally using both the training and the evaluation collections. Section 4 augments those results with an initial query-by-query analysis of the effect of ASR errors. The paper then concludes with a few remarks on our future plans.

2 Techniques

In this section we describe the techniques that we used in our experiments.

2.1 Document Expansion Using Blind Relevance Feedback

There are generally two types of errors that an ASR system can produce: (1) failure to recognize some spoken words (2) introduction of spurious words. These problems often occur together: because ASR systems seek to map sounds to words, recognition errors generally lead to mapping the associated sounds to spurious words. Missing words reduce *word-recall* (proportion of spoken words that are recognized) while adding words reduce *word precision* (proportion of recognized words that were spoken). Singhal, et al argue that IR would benefit from high word-recall, and that it would be less influenced by poor word precision [7]. They proposed an approach that they called *document expansion* that enriched each speech document in the collection with additional words selected from a side collection of newswire text in the same subject. The enriched speech documents were then re-indexed so that subsequent searches could match on the words that were added. They found that document expansion yielded substantial improvements in retrieval effectiveness [7,8].

Applying document expansion to the CLEF-2005 CL-SR test collection required that we identify a source of documents that can be used as a basis for expansion. However, it is very difficult to acquire a side collection of documents in the same domain. We instead used 4,377 similar interviews provided by the Survivors the Shoah Visual History Foundation. These interviews were manually segmented and cataloged in the same way as those contained in the test collection. After excluding short segments in which a displayed physical object was the primary referent (this fact is indicated by a manually assigned thesaurus term), We finally formed 168,584 documents, each with an average of 48 words by combining the summary and thesaurus terms of an interview segment. This collection of documents served as the side collection for our document expansion experiment.

The present structure of the test collection imposed some limitations on our document expansion experiments. First, word lattices that encoded alternate hypotheses from the ASR experiments were not available, so it was not possible to limit the expansion words to those that appear somewhere in the word lattice. Singhal, et al had found that such a restriction could be useful [7]. Second, the ASR text for each segment contains an average of 503 words. Query processing time grows roughly linearly with the length of the query, so it would be computationally impractical to use every word produced by ASR as a query, even for this relatively small 8,104-segment test collection. We therefore tried two techniques for ranking terms for query selection: (1) Robertson Sparck Jones offer weights and (2) Okapi BM 25 weights [6]. Experiments with the training set indicated that Okapi weights were the better choice in this case.

Specifically, our implementation of document expansion works as follows. First, we selected top n words for each document based on Okapi BM25 weight to formulate a query for that document. We tried n of 20 and 40 respectively to see how the number of words selected affects document expansion results. Then, we used the formulated query to search the side collection for the most closely related segments based on lexical overlap with the summary and thesaurus term manually created metadata fields. We used InQuery (version 3.1p1) from the University of Massachusetts for this purpose. Next, we selected top m words from top k retrieved segments. Optimal values of m and k depend on the nature of the side collection and the test collection, and in particular on the "closeness" between them. These factors are difficult to characterize without experimentation, so we tried the top 10, 20, 50, and 100 documents, and, for each, the top 10, 20, 30, 40, and 50 words (see Table 2). Terms are ranked by their cumulative

Okapi weight among the top m documents with a restriction that a selected word should appear in at least 3 of the top m documents (this restriction was intended to prevent pathological cases from dominating the results). Finally, the selected words were concatenated with the original ASR text to form a expanded segment that was then available for indexing.

We repeated the entire process for each of the 8,104 segments. With several variants of expanded document collections generated in this way and the original document collection, we were able to use the same set of queries to run a set of directly comparable ranked retrieval experiments. Retrieval results were then compared so that we could compare the relative effectiveness of each parameter setting.

2.2 Document Expansion Using Thesaurus Relationships

Another way to perform document expansion is to add synonyms of each thesaurus term contained in each segment to that segment, now that the thesaurus indicating the synonymy relationship was distributed together with the test collection. In our 2004 experiments, we found that concatenating manually created summaries and manually assigned thesaurus terms yielded better results than indexing either alone. Therefore, we were interested in knowing whether retrieval effectiveness could be further improved by adding synonyms of the thesaurus terms. There are two types of thesaurus terms for each segment in the test collection: manual keywords and automatic keywords. Manual keywords were assigned manually by subject matter experts, while automatic keywords were generated automatically through k-Nearest Neighbors (kNN) classifiers. Consequently, expansion could be applied to either manual keywords, or automatic keywords, or both. However, our initial experiments with the training set showed no gains when synonym expansion was applied to automatic keywords (concatenated with ASR text), so we focused on synonym expansion for manual keywords in our CLEF-2005 experiments. For this synonym expansion experiment, we created the baseline document collection with segments that contain only manual keywords, and the comparative collection with segments that contain both the manual keywords and their synonyms found in the thesaurus. The same set of queries were then used to search relevant segments from the two collections respectively. Finally mean average precisions computed for the two runs were compared.

2.3 Query Expansion Using Blind Relevance Feedback

"Blind relevance feedback" (BRF) is the technique of compensating poorly formulated queries with terms automatically selected from top retrieved documents. It has been shown to work well when the test collection being searched is very large (thus increasing the likelihood that some top-ranked documents will actually be relevant) and when the collection contains text generated through a process with few errors (e.g., professionally edited newswire stories, thus increasing the likelihood that useful expansion terms can be reliably identified).

Unfortunately, the CLEF-2005 CL-SR test collection satisfies neither condition. We nonetheless performed query expansion using the collection to be searched rather than using the available side collection because that provided a cleaner design for exploring the interaction between query and document expansion.

When both expansion techniques were applied, we ran document expansion first, and then used the resulting collection as a basis for query expansion. We tried the top 5, 10, 15, and 20 Okapi words respectively from top 10, 20, or 30 top documents using the training topics and found that top 5 words from top 20 documents gave us the best results. We also tried limiting the our choice of top words to those that appeared in at least 1, 2, or 3 of the top m documents. We found that 2 was the best choice for this parameter on the training topics. Those parameters (top 5 words appearing in at least 2 of the top 20 documents) were therefore used for query expansion in all of our official submissions.

2.4 Cross-Language Retrieval Using Statistical Translation

Cross-language speech retrieval has previously been explored in the context of broadcast news in the Topic Detection and Tracking Evaluations and in the CLEF-2003 and 2004 CL-SDR evaluations. The usual approach has been first transcribing the spoken documents into text with an ASR engine, then translating either the transcribed documents or the query into the other language. Translation can be done using hand-crafted bilingual dictionaries, translation knowledge learned from parallel corpus, or a full-fledged machine translation (MT) systems. Experiments with newswire text have generally indicated that translation statistics learned from parallel texts can be remarkably useful. Corpus-based translation techniques are, however, sensitive to the degree of topical alignment between the corpus from which the translation statistics are learned and the test collection on which the resulting cross-language retrieval system will be evaluated. The CLEF-2005 CL-SR test collection provides an excellent opportunity to begin to characterize this effect because the topical coverage of that collection is quite different from the topical coverage of the large collections of parallel text that have been assembled for use in other tasks.

To produce a statistical translation table from French to English, we ran the freely available Giza++ toolkit[1] with the Europarl parallel corpus [4]. The result is a a three-column table that specifies, for each French-English word pair, the normalized translation probability of the English word given the French word. Unlike dictionary-based techniques, statistical analysis of parallel corpora can yield a potentially infinite set of translation mappings with progressively smaller translation probabilities. Threshold selection to limit the options to the most plausible translations is therefore important. Preliminary experiments on the training set using probabilistic structured queries [2] with multiple translation alternatives did not yield results better than with one-best translation. So, in all the CL-SR experiments reported in this paper, we used one-best translation.

[1] http://www-i6.informatik.rwth-aachen.de/Colleagues/och/software/GIZA++.html

3 Experiment Results

The required run in the CLEF-2005 CL-SR track called for use of the *title* and *description* fields as a basis for formulating queries. We therefore used all words from those fields as the query (a condition we call "TD") for our five official submissions. Stopwords in each query (as well as in each document) were automatically removed by InQuery, which is the retrieval engine that we used for all of our experiments. Stemming of the queries and documents was performed automatically by InQuery using kstem. Statistical significance is reported for $p < 0.05$ by a Wilcoxon signed rank test for paired samples.

3.1 Official Evaluation Results

Table 1 shows the experiment conditions and the Mean Average Precision (MAP) for the five official runs that we submitted. Not surprisingly, the two runs with manual metadata (PIQ person names, manual keywords and their thesaurus synonyms, and segment summary) yielded the best results. Comparing the first two columns reveals that document expansion was indeed helpful (see Section 3.2 for more details on this). Enriching the ASR text with automatically generated keywords (i.e., comparing asr.en.qe with autokey+asr.en.qe) produced a similar beneficial effect.[2] This is consistent with the results we obtained with the training set, in which ASR alone yielded a mean average precision of 0.055, automatic keywords alone produced 0.032, and combining both in a single index yielded 0.066. Comparing the last two columns, CL-SR using one-best translation with synonym-expanded metadata achieved about 79% of monolingual effectiveness under similar conditions.

Table 1. Conditions and results of official runs, TD queries with automatic query expansion. ASR text: ASRTEXT2004A; autokey: AUTOKEYWORD2004A2; metadata: NAME, MANUALKEYWORD, and SUMMARY; synonym: thesaurus synonyms of MANUALKEYWORD.

run name	CL-SR?	doc fields	doc exp?	syn exp?	MAP
asr.en.qe	monolingual	ASR text	×	×	0.1102
asr.de.en.qe	monolingual	ASR text	√	×	0.1275
autokey+asr.en.qe	monolingual	ASR text, autokey	×	×	0.1288
metadata+syn.fr2en.qe	CL-SR	metadata, synonym	×	√	0.2476
metadata+syn.en.qe	monolingual	metadata, synonym	×	√	0.3129

3.2 Document Expansion Results

Table 2 show unofficial results for experiments with document expansion on the evaluation sets respectively. Three parameters were varied: (1) the number of words from each segment used to formulate the expansion query, (2) the

[2] For all the experiments reported in this paper that involve ASR text, we used the ASR text in ASRTEXT2004A.

Table 2. Monolingual retrieval MAP with document expansion. TD queries, 25 test topics. m: the number of top documents used. n: the number of top words selected from top m documents based on Okapi weight.

formulating query with top 40 words					
$m \setminus n$	10	20	30	40	50
10	0.0995	0.0993	0.1004	0.1007	0.1030
20	0.1060	0.1005	0.1055	**0.1072**	0.1063
50	0.1041	0.1048	0.1040	0.1017	0.1048
100	0.1018	0.1010	0.1024	0.1042	0.1029
baseline (without document expansion): 0.0987					

number of top-ranked documents from which expansion words were selected, and (3) the number of expansion words that were selected. All parameter settings produced improvements over the no-expansion condition for both the training and evaluation sets. In our experiment with the training set, 40-word expansion queries and selection of the 20 most selective words from the top 50 documents yielded the best retrieval effectiveness, so that condition was used in our official submission (asr.de.en.qe). This yielded a 6% apparent relative improvement over the unexpanded condition on the evaluation collection that was not statistically significant, far smaller than the 24% statistically significant relative improvement observed on the training collection. Exploration of the parameter space on the evaluation collection indicated that the optimal parameter setting would have yielded less than a 9% relative improvement over the unexpanded condition. This substantial difference between the training and evaluation sets suggests that the utility of document expansion is somewhat variable, and that topic-specific tuning might be productive.

Expanding manually assigned thesaurus terms with synonyms yielded a 4% relative improvement on the training set (0.2848 vs. 0.2748) and a 3% relative reduction on the evaluation set (0.3011 vs. 0.3090), neither of the differences is statistically significant. This somewhat surprising result may reflect a bias in the vocabulary used in the topic descriptions that favors the more "proper" terminology that was designated as the preferred expression for a thesaurus entry.

3.3 Query Expansion Results

Remarkably, query expansion based on blind relevance feedback appeared to be helpful under every condition that we tried (see Table 3), although the observed increases in mean average precision were statistically significant only for two of the five conditions (asr.de.fr2en and autokey+asr). Interestingly, the relative and absolute increases in mean average precision were larger when searching ASR text than when searching metadata. The table shows results on the evaluation topics for the the best parameter settings that were learned using only the training topics, i.e., using top 5 words from top 20 retrieved segments.

Table 3. Query expansion using blind relevance feedback helps speech retrieval, TD queries, 25 test topics, top 5 words from top 20 retrieved documents

	asr.de.en	asr.de.fr2en	autokey+asr	metadata+syn	metadata+syn.fr2en
Unexpanded	0.1048	0.0814	0.1113	0.3011	0.2327
Query Expansion	0.1275	0.1178	0.1288	0.3129	0.2476

4 Failure Analysis

Our best fully automatic official run (autokey+asr.en.qe) yielded just 41% of MAP achieved by our best official run using manual metadata (metadata+syn. en.de). Since the mean across topics masks quite a lot of variation, it is useful to investigate the difference for individual topics. We chose to analyze an unofficial run on 63 title-only queries (by combining the training set and the test set) with ASR text alone (i.e., with no document expansion, no query expansion, and no automatically assigned thesaurus terms). No expansion was applied to the comparative run that used metadata.

Figure 1 shows a query-by-query comparison of average precision between ASR and metadata for the 32 topics for which metadata yielded a mean average precision above 0.2. The light gray bars at the bottom show the average precision achieved for each topic using ASR, while the darker bars above show how much better metadata did. We chose to focus on those 32 topics because the other 31 topics had poor results for both metadata and ASR, hence offered little scope for comparison. After removing stopwords from each of the remaining 32 title queries, we counted the total number of segments that contained a stemmed match for each query word in the ASR text and in the metadata.

We found in every of the six queries (corresponding to Topic 1188, 1630, 2185, 1628, 1187, and 1330) in which at least a query word was completely absent from all 8,104 ASR segments, retrieval effectiveness for the ASR condition was very poor. Interestingly, all of the seven missing words ("volkswagen", "eichmann", "sinti", "roma", "telefunken", "ig", "farben") are proper names that seem to be unique to the domain. A similar pattern is evident to a lesser extent for the other four queries (corresponding to Topic 2400, 1446, 2264, and 1850) that performed similarly poorly with ASR, with "sobibor," "minsk," "wallenberg," and "female," appearing far less in ASR than in metadata. On the other hand, queries contain common proper names (such as "bulgaria," "shanghai," "italy," and "sweden") did not exhibit similar problems. This suggests that domain-tuned techniques for language modeling with the ASR system and/or domain-adapted techniques for accommodating weaknesses in the ASR language model might be a productive line of investigation.

For the rest of 22 queries, query word coverage by both ASR and metadata are quite comparable to each other. Therefore, the relative difference of retrieval effectiveness for those 22 queries between ASR and metadata was not as big as that for the other 10 queries discussed above.

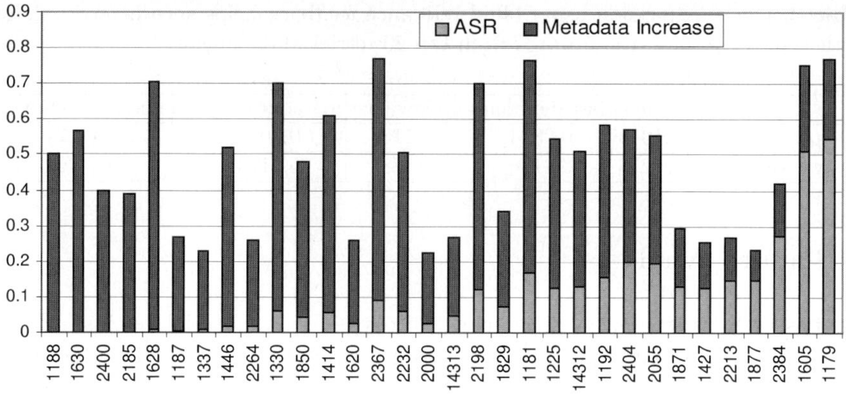

Fig. 1. Query-by-query comparison of average precision between ASR text and metadata, 32 title queries with average precision of metadata equal to or higher than 0.2

5 Conclusion

This year's CLEF CL-SR track has provided an excellent opportunity to study the problem of speech retrieval in a domain other than broadcast news. The availability of a large side collection provided an opportunity to re-examine the potential of document expansion to mitigate the effect of recognition errors. Through a series of experiments with the 38 training topics and the 25 test topics, we were able to show that a combination of document expansion using a side collection and query expansion using the collection being searched could improve speech retrieval effectiveness and that tuning the expansion parameters on a set of 38 training topics yielded near-optimal improvements on the 25 evaluation topics. Despite a domain mismatch between the parallel text and the document collection, cross-language retrieval with French queries yielded 79% of monolingual mean average precision when searching manually assigned metadata. A query-by-query analysis of query term coverage revealed that failure to reliably recognize domain-specific named entities was a possible cause for a substantial number of the cases in which very poor results were observed from ASR-based searches.

Looking at future work, we are interested in at least three ares. First, we plan to develop techniques that can take advantage of word lattices generated by ASR engines instead of one-best ASR Second, we are interested in extending our baseline cross-language speech retrieval results to explore techniques that accommodate both translation and recognition uncertainty. Finally, we hope to explore a broader range of document expansion techniques that include parameter settings that are adapted to observable document characteristics (e.g., length or clarity measures) and sequence-based expansion (e.g., selectively importing location names from earlier segments).

Acknowledgments

The authors would like to thank the MALACH project teams at the University of Maryland, IBM and the Survivors of the Shoah Visual History foundation for creating the test collection. This work has been supported in part by NSF IIS award 0122466 (MALACH). Any opinions, findings, and conclusions or recommendations expressed in this material are those of the authors and do not necessarily reflect the views of the NSF.

References

1. James Allan. Perspectives on information retrieval and speech. In *Information Retrieval Techniques for Speech Applications*, pages 1–10. Springer-Verlag London, UK, 2001.
2. Kareem Darwish and Douglas W. Oard. Probabilistic structured query methods. In *Proceedings of the 21st Annual 26th International ACM SIGIR Conference on Research and Development in Information Retrieval*, pages 338–344. ACM Press, July 2003.
3. John S. Garofolo, Cedric G. P. Auzanne, and Ellen E. Voorhees. The TREC spoken document retrieval track: A successful story. In *Proceedings of the Nineth Text REtrieval Conference (TREC-9)*, 2000. http://trec.nist.dov.
4. Philipp Koehn. Europarl: A multilingual corpus for evaluation of machine translation. unpublished draft. 2002.
5. Douglas W. Oard, Dagobert Soergel, David Doermann, Xiaoli Huang, G. Craig Murray, Jianqiang Wang, Bhuvana Ramabhadran, Martin Franz, Samuel Gustman, James Mayfield, Liliya Kharevych, and Stephanie Strassel. Building an information retrieval test collection for spontaneous conversational speech. In *Proceedings of the 20th International ACM SIGIR Conference on Research and Development in Information Retrieval*, pages 41–38, 2004.
6. S. E. Robertson and Karen Sparck-Jones. Simple proven approaches to text retrieval. Cambridge University Computer Laboratory, 1997.
7. Amit Singhal, John Choi, Donald Hindle, and Fernado Pereira. ATT at TREC-7. In *The Seventh Text REtrieval Conference*, pages 239–252, November 1998. http://trec.nist.gov.
8. Amit Singual and Fernando Pereira. Document expansion for speech retrieval. In *Proceedings of the 22st Annual International ACM SIGIR Conference on Research and Development in Information Retrieval*, pages 34–41. ACM Press, August 1999.

Overview of WebCLEF 2005

Börkur Sigurbjörnsson[1], Jaap Kamps[1,2], and Maarten de Rijke[1]

[1] ISLA, Faculty of Science, University of Amsterdam
[2] Archives and Information Science, Faculty of Humanities, University of Amsterdam
{borkur, kamps, mdr}@science.uva.nl

Abstract. We describe WebCLEF, the multilingual web track, that was introduced at CLEF 2005. We provide details of the tasks, the topics, and the results of WebCLEF participants. The mixed monolingual task proved an interesting addition to the range of tasks in cross-language information retrieval. Although it may be too early to talk about a solved problem, effective web retrieval techniques seem to carry over to the mixed monolingual setting. The multilingual task, in contrast, is still very far from being a solved problem. Remarkably, using non-translated English queries proved more successful than using translations of the English queries.

1 Introduction

The world wide web is a natural setting for cross-lingual information retrieval; web content is essentially multilingual, and web searchers are often polyglots. Even though English has emerged as the lingua franca of the web, planning for a business trip or holiday usually involves digesting pages in a foreign language. The same holds for searching information about European culture, education, sports, economy, or politics. To evaluate systems that address multilingual information needs on the web, a new multilingual web track, called WebCLEF, has been set up as part of CLEF 2005.

Three tasks were organized within this year's WebCLEF track: mixed monolingual, multilingual, and bilingual English to Spanish, with 242 homepage and 305 named page finding queries for the first two tasks, and 67 homepage and 67 named page finding tasks for the third task. All topics, and the accompanying assessments, were created by the participants in the WebCLEF track. In total, 11 teams submitted 61 runs for the three tasks.

The main findings of the WebCLEF track in 2005 are the following. The mixed monolingual task proved an interesting addition to the range of tasks in cross-language information retrieval. Although it may be too early to talk about a solved problem, effective web retrieval techniques seem to carry over to the mixed monolingual setting. The multilingual task, in contrast, is still very far from being a solved problem. Remarkably, using non-translated English queries proved more successful than using translations of the English queries.

The remainder of the paper is organized as follows. In Section 2 we describe the WebCLEF 2005 track in more detail. Section 3 is devoted to a description

C. Peters et al. (Eds.): CLEF 2005, LNCS 4022, pp. 810–824, 2006.

```
<topic>
  <num>WC0005</num>
  <title>Minister van buitenlandse zaken</title>
  <metadata>
    <topicprofile>
      <language language="NL"/>
      <translation language="EN">dutch minister of foreign
        affairs</translation>
    </topicprofile>
    <targetprofile>
      <language language="NL"/>
      <domain domain="nl"/>
    </targetprofile>
    <userprofile>
      <native language="IS"/>
      <active language="EN"/>
      <active language="DA"/>
      <active language="NL"/>
      <passive language="NO"/>
      <passive language="SV"/>
      <passive language="DE"/>
      <passive_other>Faroese</passive_other>
      <countryofbirth country="IS"/>
      <countryofresidence country="NL"/>
    </userprofile>
  </metadata>
</topic>
```

Fig. 1. Example of a WebCLEF 2005 topic

of the runs submitted by the participants, while the results are presented in Section 4. We conclude in Section 5.

2 The Retrieval Tasks

2.1 Collection

For the purposes of the track a new corpus, EuroGOV, was developed [15]. EuroGOV is a crawl of European government-related sites, where collection building is less restricted by intellectual property rights. It is a multilingual web corpus, which contains over 3.5 million pages from 27 primary domains, covering over twenty languages. There is no single language that dominates the corpus, and its linguistic diversity provides a natural setting for multilingual web search.

2.2 Topics

Topic development was in the hands of the participating groups. Each group was expected to create at least 30 monolingual known-item topics, 15 homepages and 15 named page topics. Homepage topics are names of a site that the

Table 1. Summary of participating teams, the number of topics they developed and the number of runs they submitted

Group id	Group name	Subm. topics	Runs Mixed-Mono	Multilingual	BiEnEs
buap	BUAP (C.S. Faculty)	39			5
hummingbird	Hummingbird	30	5		
ilps	U. Amsterdam (ILPS)	162	1	4	
melange	Melange (U. Amsterdam)	30	5	5	
miracle	DAEDALUS S.A.	30	5	5	
ualicante	U. Alicante	30	2		1
uglasgow	U. Glasgow (IR group)	30	5		
uhildesheim	U. Hildesheim	30	3	5	
uindonesia	U. Indonesia	36	3		
uned	NLP Group - UNED	30			2
unimelb	U. Melbourne (NICTA i2d2)	47			
usal	U. Salamanca (REINA)	30	5		
sintef	Linguateca	30			
xldb	U. Lisboa (XLDB Group)	30			
metacarta	MetaCarta Inc	3			
Total		547	34	19	8

user wants to reach, and named page topics concern non-homepages that the user wants to reach. The track organizers assigned languages to groups based on their location and the language expertise available within the group. For each topic, topic creators were instructed to detect identical or similar pages in the collection, both in the language of the target page and in other languages. Many European governmental sites provide translations of (some of) their web pages in a small number of languages, e.g., in additional official languages (if applicable), in languages of some neighboring countries, and/or in English. In addition, participants provided English translations of their topics.

The topic authors were also asked to fill out a form where they provided various types of metadata, including their language knowledge, birth place and residence. This information was used to augment the topics with additional metadata. Figure 1 provides an example of the topic format used at WebCLEF 2005. The track organizers reviewed the topics, suggested improvements, and finally selected the final set of topics.

As few participants had facilities to search the EuroGOV collection during the topic development phase, the organizers provided a Lucene-based search engine for the collection, and the University of Glasgow provided access to the collection through Terrier. Both search engines were at a proof-of-concept level only and were not specially adapted for the task.

Table 1, column 3, shows a summary of the number of topics submitted by each participating team. The WebCLEF 2005 topic set contained 547 topics, 242 homepage topics and 305 named page topics. The target pages were in 11 different languages: Spanish (ES), English (EN), Dutch (NL), Portuguese (PT), German (DE), Hungarian (HU), Danish (DA), Russian (RU), Greek (EL),

Table 2. Number of topics per language for both homepages (HP) and named pages (NP). The languages are sorted by the number of available topics. The bottom part of the table shows how many duplicates/translations were identified. We list both the number of topics having a duplicate/translation and also the total count of duplicates/translations.

	Total	ES	EN	NL	PT	DE	HU	DA	RU	EL	IS	FR
Total	547	134	121	59	59	57	35	30	30	16	5	1
HP	242	67	50	25	29	23	16	11	15	5	1	–
NP	305	67	71	34	30	34	19	19	15	11	4	1
Duplicates (topics)	191	37	47	21	15	38	11	12	8	1	1	–
Duplicates (total)	473	82	109	40	95	90	18	26	11	1	1	–
Translations (topics)	114	25	24	9	4	13	6	15	6	7	5	–
Translations (total)	387	100	47	18	7	39	17	101	11	19	28	–
Readable trans. (topics)	72	17	6	9	2	10	6	9	5	7	1	–
Readable trans. (total)	143	29	8	16	3	26	6	30	6	13	6	–

Table 3. Statistical information on length of queries

	Total	ES	EN	NL	PT	DE	HU	DA	RU	EL	IS	FR
Mean	5.2	6.3	5.7	3.9	5.8	3.3	3.5	3.6	5.8	8.6	3.4	8.0
Median	5	6	5	4	5	3	3	3	6	8.5	4	8
Min	1	2	1	1	2	1	1	1	2	3	2	8
Max	17	13	12	8	17	7	9	7	11	15	4	8
Stdev	2.5	2.3	2.3	1.9	2.6	1.3	1.9	1.7	2.5	3.1	0.9	–

Icelandic (IS), and French (FR). Since topic development depended on language knowledge within participating groups the distribution between languages in the test set varies considerably. Table 2 provides more detailed statistics of the WebCLEF 2005 topic set.

During topic development, topic authors were asked to try to identify duplicates and translations of the target page. Table 2 shows the number of duplicates/translations available. We list both the number of topics having a duplicate/translation and also the total count of duplicates/translations. The category *Readable trans.* refers to the number of translations whose language matches the language knowledge identified by the user. The number of translations naturally varies from one domain to another. As an example, for 78 topics target pages were located in the `eu.int` domain (14% of the topics), and those pages have 232 translations (60% of identified translations). The identification of translations is a difficult and labor intensive process. Due to a lack of resources we have not been able to verify the completeness of duplicate/translation identification. This must be taken into account when interpreting results using the duplicate/translation information.

Tables 3 and 4 show statistics on the length of the original queries and the query translations, respectively. The average number of query terms in the WebCLEF collection is 5.2 terms. This is considerably higher number than is reported

Table 4. Statistical information on the length of the English translations of queries

	Total	ES	EN	NL	PT	DE	HU	DA	RU	EL	IS	FR
Mean	6.2	6.7	5.9	6.1	5.9	5.7	5.6	5.3	7.6	9.9	4.4	7.0
Median	6	6	5	6	6	6	5	5	6	9.5	5	7
Min	1	2	1	2	3	2	1	2	3	3	2	7
Max	15	12	12	12	16	11	12	11	17	19	6	7
Stdev	2.7	2.6	2.3	2.6	2.3	2.0	2.7	2.4	3.4	4.3	1.8	–

Table 5. Statistical information on the language knowledge of the topic creators. Active+ stands for native or active. Passive+ stands for active+ or passive.

	Native	Active	Passive	Active+	Passive+
Mean	1.1	1.8	1.6	2.9	4.4
Median	1	1	2	2	4
Min	1	0	0	1	1
Max	2	10	6	11	17
Stdev	0.26	1.91	1.40	1.99	3.10

in studies of real search engine query logs [7,16], where most queries contain only 1–3 terms, and the average lies around 2.5 terms. We see that the English translations of the queries are even longer than the original queries. This can be explained by the fact that implicit national references had to be made explicit in the English translation, e.g., the Dutch query 'minister van buitenlandse zaken' translates to the query '*Dutch* minister of foreign affairs.'

If we look at the language knowledge of our topic creators, we see that they are truely polyglots. On average, they speak 2.9 different language either at native or active level. Table 5 shows the language knowledge of our users in more detail.

Table 6 shows statistics on the number of topics created by a single autor. For many languages the topics per author ratio seems disproportionally high; we believe that in an IR test collection it is desirable that topics are created by a diverse group of people so as to increase robustness and avoid over-fitting.

2.3 Tasks

Due to limited resources for evaluation all tasks at WebCLEF 2005 were restricted to known-item searches. The following tasks were organized for WebCLEF 2005.

- *Mixed-Monolingual* The mixed-monolingual task is meant to simulate a user searching for a known-item page in an European language. The mixed-monolingual task used the title field of the topics to create a set of monolingual known-item topics.
- *Multilingual* The multilingual task is meant to simulate a user looking for a certain known-item page in a particular European language. The user, however, uses English to formulate her query. The multilingual task used the English translations of the original topic statements.

Table 6. Number of topics per-topic creator. The last line says how many topic creators contributed to each language.

	Total	ES	EN	NL	PT	DE	HU	DA	RU	EL	IS	FR
Mean	19.5	16.8	17.3	8.4	29.5	28.5	17.5	30	30	16	5	1
Median	24	16.5	15	4	29.5	28.5	17.5	30	30	16	5	1
Min	2	2	1	1	29	28	3	30	30	16	5	1
Max	36	29	30	28	30	29	32	30	30	16	5	1
Stdev	11.3	10.4	10.7	9.6	0.7	0.7	20.5	–	–	–	–	–
Count	28	8	7	7	2	2	2	1	1	1	1	1

– *Bilingual English to Spanish* For this task a special topic set was used. It contained a reviewed translation of the Spanish topics. The reviewed and revised translations were provided by the NLP group at UNED.

2.4 Submission

For each of the tasks, teams were allowed to submit up to 5 runs. Each run could contain 50 results for each topic.

2.5 Evaluation

Since each NP and HP topic is developed with a URL in mind, the only judging task is to identify URLs of equivalent (near-duplicate or translated) pages. As described previously, this task was carried out during the topic development phase.

From the assessments obtained during the topic development stage we are able to define a number of qrel sets, including the following.

– *Monolingual* This set of qrels contains for each topic, the target page and all its duplicates.
– *Multilingual* This set of qrels contains for each topic, the target page, its duplicates and all its translations.
– *User readable* This set of qrels contains for each topic, the target, all its duplicates, and all translations which are in a language that the topic author marked as her native/active/passive language.

Each of these qrel sets can be further divided into subsets based on the language of the topic or the domain of the target page. In this report we will only use the language-based subsets.

The main metric used for evaluation was *mean reciprocal rank* (MRR).

3 Submitted Runs

Table 1 shows a summary of the number of runs submitted by each team. The mixed-monolingual task was the most popular task with 34 runs submitted by 9

Table 7. Summary of the runs submitted for the Mixed-Monolingual task. The 'metadata usage' columns indicate usage of topic metadata: topic language (TL), page language (PL), page domain (PD), and user's native or active languages (UN, UA, respectively). For each team, its best scoring non-metadata run is in italics, and its best scoring metadata run is in boldface.

		Metadata usage					
Group id	Run name	TL	PL	PD	UN	UA	MRR
hummingbird	humWC05dp						0.4334
	humWC05dpD	Y	Y	Y			0.4707
	humWC05dplD	Y	Y	Y			**0.4780**
	humWC05p						0.4154
	humWC05rdp						*0.4412*
ilps	*UAmsMMBaseline*						*0.3497*
melange	BaselineMixed						0.0226
	AnchorMixed						*0.0260*
	DomLabelMixed			Y			**0.0366**
	LangCueMixed						0.0226
	LangLabelMixed	Y					0.0275
miracle	*MonoBase*						*0.0472*
	MonoExt			Y			0.1030
	MonoExtAH1PN			Y			0.1420
	MonoExtH1PN			Y			**0.1750**
	MonoExtUrlKy			Y			0.0462
ualicante	**final**	Y					**0.1191**
	final.lang						*0.0000*[1]
uglasgow	*uogSelStem*						*0.4683*
	uogNoStemNLP			Y			**0.5135**
	uogPorStem			Y			0.5107
	uogAllStem	Y		Y			0.4827
	uogAllStemNP	Y		Y			0.4828
uhildesheim	UHi3TiMo						0.0373
	UHiScoMo						0.1301
	UHiSMo						*0.1603*
uindonesia	*UI-001*						*0.2165*
	UI-002			Y			**0.2860**
	UI-003			Y			0.2714
usal	usal0	Y		Y			0.0537
	usal1	Y	Y				0.0685
	usal2	Y		Y			0.0626
	usal3	Y		Y			**0.0787**
	usal4	Y		Y			0.0668

[1] This run had an error in topic-result mapping. Corrected run has MRR of 0.0923.

teams; Table 7 provides details of the runs submitted. The multilingual task was the second most popular task with 19 runs submitted by 4 teams; the details are given in Table 8. For the bilingual English to Spanish task, 8 runs were submitted by 3 teams; consult Table 9 for details.

Table 8. Summary of the runs submitted for the Multilingual task. The 'metadata usage' columns indicate topic metadat usage: topic language (TL), page language (PL), page domain (PD), and the user's native or active languages (UN, UA, respectively). MRR is reported using the monolingual, multilingual, and the user readable assessment sets. For each team, its best scoring non-metadata run is in italics, while its best scoring metadata run is in boldface.

		Metadata usage					MRR		
Group id	Run name	TL	PL	PD	UN	UA	mono	multi	u.r.
ilps	ILPSMuAll						0.0092	0.0097	0.0097
	ILPSMuAllR						0.0157	0.0164	0.0164
	ILPSMuFive						0.0109	0.0117	0.0117
	ILPSMuFiveR						*0.0166*	*0.0175*	*0.0175*
melange	BaselineMulti						0.0082	0.0091	0.0091
	AnchorMulti						0.0074	0.0083	0.0083
	AccLangsMulti				Y	Y	0.0082	0.0092	0.0092
	LangCueMulti						*0.0086*	*0.0092*	*0.0092*
	SuperMulti			Y			**0.0086**	**0.0092**	**0.0092**
miracle	*MultiBase*						*0.0314*	*0.0401*	*0.0387*
	MultiExt			Y			0.0588	0.0684	0.0669
	MultiExtAH1PN			Y			0.0633	0.0736	0.0733
	MultiExtH1PN			Y			**0.0762**	**0.0903**	**0.0902**
	MultiExtUrlKy			Y			0.0338	0.0397	0.0383
uhildesheim	UHi3TiMu						0.0274	0.0282	0.0282
	UHiScoMu						0.1147	0.1235	0.1225
	UHiSMu						*0.1370*	*0.1488*	*0.1479*
	UHi3TiMuBo91						0.0139	0.0160	0.0159
	UHiSMuBo91						0.0815	0.0986	0.0974

Table 9. Summary of the runs submitted for the BiEnEs task. For each team, the score of its best scoring run is in boldface.

Group id	Run name	MRR
buap	BUAP_Full	0.0465
	BUAP_PT10	0.0331
	BUAP_PT40	**0.0844**
	BUAP_PT60	0.0771
	BUAP_PT20	0.0446
ualicante	**BiEn2Es**	**0.0395**
uned	UNED_bilingual_baseline	0.0477
	UNED_bilingual_exp1	**0.0930**

We will now provide an overview of features used by the participating teams. We divide the overview in three parts: *web-specific*, *linguistic*, and *cross-lingual* features.

The teams used a wide variety of web-based features. Many teams indexed titles separately: Hummingbird [17], Miracle [12], U. Alicante [11], U. Glasgow [10],

U. Indonesia [1], and U. Salamanca [5]. A few teams also built special indexes for other HTML tags: Hummingbird, Miracle, and UNED. Several teams used a separate index for anchor text: Melange, U. Glasgow, and U. Salamanca. Miracle also built an index for URL text. Hummingbird, U. Glasgow and U. Salamanca used URL length in their ranking. PageRank was used by Melange and U. Salamanca. Neither U. Amsterdam (ILPS) [9] nor U. Hildesheim [8] used any web-specific features.

The teams also used a wide variety of linguistic features. Language specific stemming was performed by a number of teams: Hummingbird, Melange, U. Alicante, and U. Glasgow. U. Amsterdam (ILPS) limited themselves to a simple accent normalization, but did do a ASCII transliteration for Russian. Miracle extracted proper nouns and keywords and indexed these separately. U. Hildesheim experimented with character tri-grams. U. Indonesia did not use any language specific features. U. Salamanca applied a special stemmer for Spanish.

In the multilingual task, two different techniques were used by participating groups to bridge the gap between query language (English) and target page language. Neither U. Hildesheim nor Miracle used any translation. I.e., both teams simply used the English version of the topics. Both ILPS and Melange used an on-line translator.

In the bilingual English to Spanish task two different approaches were used to translate the English queries to Spanish. UNED used an English to Spanish dictionary, but BUAP [13] and U. Alicante used on-line translators.

4 Results

4.1 Mixed-Monolingual Task

First we look at each team's best scoring baseline run. Figure 2 (left) shows the scores of the 5 best scoring teams. The left-most point shows the MRR over all topics. The successive points show MRR scores for a subset of the topics: one for

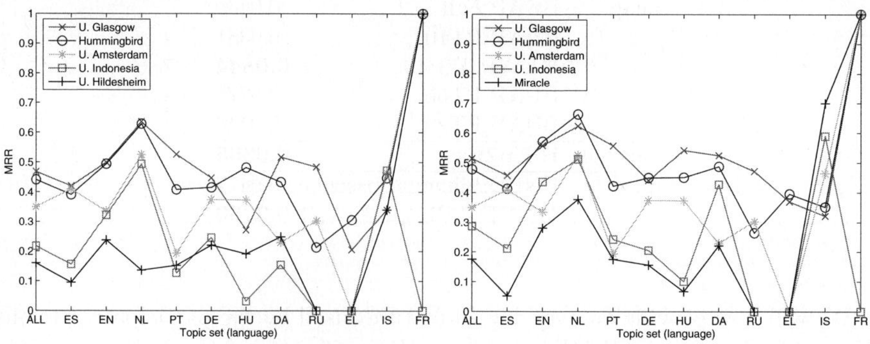

Fig. 2. Scores per-language for the 5 best scoring runs for the Mixed-Monolingual task using MRR. **(Left)**: Best scoring baseline run per team. **(Right)**: Best scoring run per team.

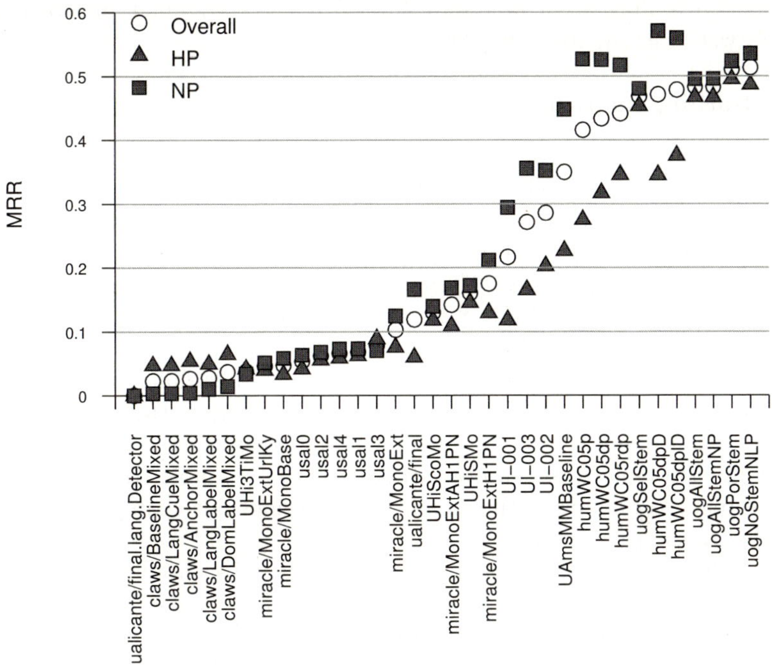

Fig. 3. Homepages vs. named pages

each language. The languages are sorted by the number of topics: from Spanish (ES) with the most topics (134) to French (FR) with only one topic.

Now, let us look at each team's best scoring run, independent of whether it was a baseline run or used some of the topic metadata. Figure 2 (right) shows the scores of the 5 best scoring teams. For the top scoring teams only U. Amsterdam (ILPS) uses no metadata.

Observe that, for each of the top five scoring runs, there is a considerable amount of variation across languages. For some languages the "hardness" seems independent of systems. Most systems score relatively high for Dutch; relatively low for Russian and Greek; but the score for German is close to their average score. The different performance between languages is only partially caused by the "hardness" of the particular language. Since the topics are not the same across languages, the "hardness" of the topics may also play a role.

Let us turn to the use of metadata now. The highest scoring runs are ones that use metadata. No team used user metadata; information about the domain of the target page proved to be the most popular type of metadata, and using it to restrict retrieval systems' outputs seems to be a sensible strategy, as is witnessed by the fact that it's the only type of metadata that each of the 5 top ranking runs uses.

Finally, for many runs, there is a clear gap between scores for NPs and HPs, with the named page queries scoring higher than the home page queries. For the best scoring runs, both types of known-item topics in relative balance. This phenomenon is illustrated in Figure 3, and mirrors a similar phenomenon at TREC's web track in 2003 and 2004 [4].

4.2 Multilingual Task

For the multilingual task we can actually look at 3 tasks. The tasks differ w.r.t. the translations being used in the qrels. Figure 4 (Top row) shows the results if only the target page and its duplicates are considered relevant. The second row shows the results if all translations are added to the relevant set. And the bottom row shows the results if only "user readable" translations are added to the relevant set. From Table 8 we see that the overall MRR increases when translations are added to the relevant set. This effect is, obviously, due to an increase in the amount of relevant pages. There is little difference between the two sets of translations, which may have several causes: the completeness of the translation identification is not known, and there might be a bias toward identifying "readable" translations rather than "un-readable" translations. Note that the relative ranking of the submitted runs does not change if translations are added to the relevant set.

The highest MRR for the multilingual task is substantially lower than the highest MRR for the mixed monolingual task: 0.1370 vs. 0.5135. The top score of the best scoring team on the multilingual task, U. Hildesheim, is over 14% below their top score on the mixed monolingual task. For the teams that score second and third best on the multilingual task, the corresponding differences are even more dramatic (56% for Miracle, and 95% for U. Amsterdam).

The success of the approaches that did not apply translation is interesting and deserves a closer look. Let us look at the 40 topics which received the highest mean MRR over all submitted runs, using the monolingual result set. Thereof, 26 topics are in English. The remaining 14 topics are listed in Table 10. For the high scoring non-English topics we see that proper names are common, such as *Jan-Peter Balkenende*, *Henri Muller*, *Paul Hartling*, *Europol* etc. For these queries a translation is hardly needed.

It is difficult to say whether metadata helped in the multilingual task, since we have very few runs to compare. It is tempting, however, to say that the metadata did indeed help Miracle.

4.3 Bilingual English to Spanish Task

The results for the bilingual English to Spanish task can be seen from Table 9. We refer to the individual participants' papers [11,13,2] for a more detailed analysis of the results.

5 Conclusions

The mixed monolingual task proved an interesting addition to the range of tasks in cross-language information retrieval. A number of participant built effective

Table 10. Non-English queries with the highest mean MRR over all runs submitted to the multilingual track

Topic	Lang.	Original query	English query
WC0528	Dutch	cv balkenende	cv balkenende
WC0185	German	Europa Newsletter	Europa Newsletter
WC0070	French	Le professeur Henri Muller nommé Ambassadeur de l'Hellénisme	Prof. Henri Muller named ambassador for Hellenism
WC0232	Danish	Regeringen Poul Hartling	The cabinet of Poul Hartling
WC0456	Icelandic	upplýsingar um europol	europol factsheet
WC0404	Dutch	CV minister-president Jan-Peter Balkenende	CV of the Dutch prime minister Jan-Peter Balkenende
WC0149	German	Ernst Breit 80. Geburtstag	80th birthday of Ernst Breit
WC0536	German	Interviews mit Staatsminister Rolf Schwanitz	Interviews with Minister of State Rolf Schwanitz
WC0025	Greek	–	Historical sources of the Hellenic parliament
WC0198	Spanish	El Palacio de la Moncloa	Moncloa Palace
WC0327	German	Autobahn Südumfahrung Leipzig	Southern Autobahn Ring Road of Leipzig
WC0202	Danish	Dansk Færøsk kulturfond	danish faroese culture fund
WC0497	Greek	–	Home page of the Hellenic parliament for kids
WC0491	German	Francesca Ferguson Architektur-Biennale 2004	Francesca Ferguson for Germany at achitecture Biennale 2004

systems, that cope well with all eleven languages in the topic set. Specific web-centric techniques or additional knowledge from the metadata fields leads to further improvements. Although it may be too early to talk about a solved problem, effective web retrieval techniques seem to carry over to the mixed monolingual setting. The multilingual task, in contrast, is still very far from being a solved problem. Remarkably, using non-translated English queries proved more successful than using translations of the English queries. A closer look at the best scoring queries revealed that a large portion of them had indeed an English target. As for the best scoring queries which had non-English target, a majority contained a proper name which does not require translation.

WebCLEF 2005 was an important first step toward a cross lingual web retrieval test collection. There are a number of steps that can be taken to further improve the quality of the current test collection. Here we list a few.

– *User data* More user data was collected during topic development phase than was used as topic metadata. This serves as an important resource to better understand the challenges of multilingual web retrieval. The data is available to all groups who participated in the topic development process.
– *Duplicates* It is not clear how complete the duplicate detection is. It remains as future work to investigate this completeness. Furthermore, we need to analyze how incomplete duplicate detection affects system ranking.

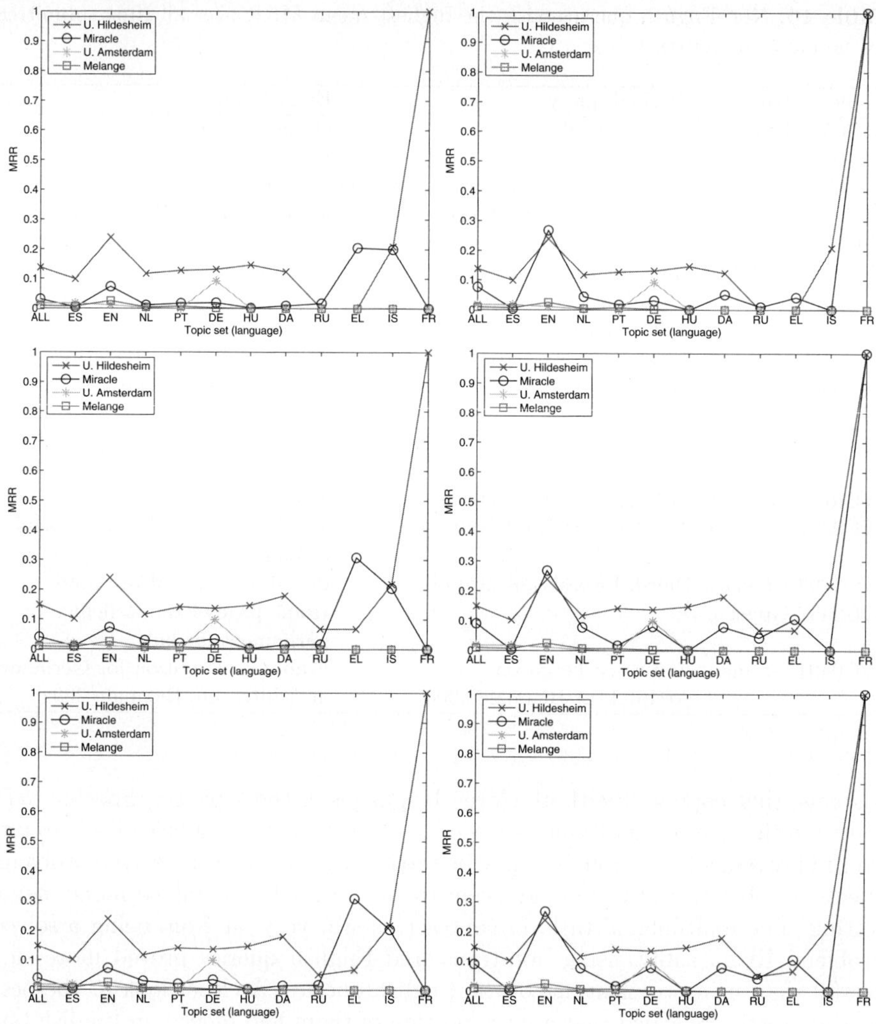

Fig. 4. (Top row): Scores per-language for the best scoring runs for the Multilingual task using MRR and only target pages and duplicates. (Left): Baseline runs. (Right): All runs. **(Second row)**: Scores per-language for the 5 best scoring runs for the Multilingual task using MRR and target pages, duplicates and ALL translations. (Left): Baseline runs. (Right): All runs. **(Bottom row)**: Scores per-language for the best scoring runs for the Multilingual task using MRR and target pages, duplicates and *user readable* translations. (Left): Baseline runs. (Right): All runs.

- *Translations* As with duplicates, the translations are likely to be incomplete. It is rather complicated to achieve complete list of translations. It remains as future work to investigate if the creation of the set of translation can be partly automated.

If we look ahead and speculate about future WebCLEF developments, one important aspect concerns post-submission assessments. This would be important not only to gain some understanding of the issues listed above, but also to drop the limitation to navigational topics and also consider more informational topics [3,14]: understanding these is an important challenge on the multilingual web retrieval agenda [6].

Acknowledgments

We want to thank the participating teams for their valuable input that helped to make this test collection a reality. We are thankful to the University of Glasgow for providing additional search engine access to the collection during the topic development phase. We thank UNED for providing a reviewed set of translations for the bilingual English to Spanish task. We would like to thank Ian Soboroff and TREC for their help with creating the topic development guidelines.

Jaap Kamps was supported by a grant from the Netherlands Organization for Scientific Research (NWO) under project numbers 612.066.302 and 640.001.501. Maarten de Rijke was supported by grants from NWO under project numbers 017.001.190, 220-80-001, 264-70-050, 354-20-005, 612-13-001, 612.000.106, 612.-000.207, 612.066.302, 612.069.006, 640.001.501, and 640.002.501.

References

1. M. Adriana and R. Pandugita. Combining page title and target-domain information for the WebCLEF mixed-monolingual task. In *This Volume*, 2006.
2. J. Artiles, V. Peinado, A. Peñas, J. Gonzales, and F. Verdejo. UNED at WebCLEF 2005. In *This Volume*, 2006.
3. A. Broder. A taxonomy of web search. *SIGIR Forum*, 36(2):3–10, 2002.
4. N. Craswell and D. Hawking. Overview of the TREC-2004 Web Track. In *Proceedings TREC 2004*, 2005.
5. C.G. Figuerola, J.L. Alonzo Berrocal, A.F. Zazo Rodríguez, and E. Rodríguez V. de Aldana. Web page retrieval by combining evidence. In *This Volume*, 2006.
6. F.C. Gey, N. Kando, and C. Peters. Cross-language information retrieval: the way ahead. *Inf. Process. Manage.*, 41(3):415–431, 2005.
7. B.J. Jansen and A. Spink. An analysis of web searching by European AlltheWeb.com users. *Information Processing and Management*, 41(2):361–381, 2005.
8. N. Jensen, R. Hackl, T. Mandl, and R. Strötgen. Web retrieval experiments with the EuroGOV corpus at the University of Hildesheim. In *This Volume*, 2006.
9. J. Kamps, M. de Rijke, and B. Sigurbjörnsson. Combination methods for crosslingual web retrieval. In *This Volume*, 2006.
10. C. Macdonald, V. Plachouras, B. He, C. Lioma, and I. Ounis. University of Glasgow at WebCLEF 2005: Experiments in per-field normalisation and language specific stemming. In *This Volume*, 2006.
11. T. Martínez, E. Noguera, R. Mu noz, and F. Llopis. University of Alicante at the CLEF 2005 WebCLEF Track. In *This Volume*, 2006.

12. Á. Martínez-González, J.L. Martínez-Fernández, C. de Pablo-Sánchez, and J. Villena-Román. MIRACLE at WebCLEF 2005: Combining web specific and linguistic information. In *This Volume*, 2006.
13. D. Pinto, H. Jiménez-Salazar, P. Rosso, and E. Sanchis. BUAP-UPV TPIRS: A system for document indexing reduction at WebCLEF. In *This Volume*, 2006.
14. D.E. Rose and D. Levinson. Understanding user goals in web search. In *Proceedings WWW '04*, pages 13–19, New York, NY, USA, 2004. ACM Press.
15. B. Sigurbjörnsson, J. Kamps, and M. de Rijke. EuroGOV: Engineering a Multilingual Web Corpus. In *This Volume*, 2006.
16. A. Spink, S. Ozmutlu, H. C. Ozmutlu, and B. J. Jansen. U.S. versus European Web searching trends. *SIGIR Forum*, 32(1):30–37, 2002.
17. S. Tomlinson. Danish and Greek Web search experiments with Hummingbird SearchServer™ at CLEF 2005. In *This Volume*, 2006.

EuroGOV: Engineering a Multilingual Web Corpus

Börkur Sigurbjörnsson[1], Jaap Kamps[1,2], and Maarten de Rijke[1]

[1] ISLA, Faculty of Science, University of Amsterdam
[2] Archives and Information Science, Faculty of Humanities, University of Amsterdam
{borkur, kamps, mdr}@science.uva.nl

Abstract. EuroGOV is a multilingual web corpus that was created to serve as the document collection for WebCLEF, the CLEF 2005 web retrieval task. EuroGOV is a collection of web pages crawled from the European Union portal, European Union member state governmental web sites, and Russian governmental web sites. The corpus contains over 3 million documents written in more than 20 different European languages. In this paper we provide a detailed description of the EuroGOV collection.

1 Introduction

The world wide web is a natural setting for cross-lingual information retrieval. This is particularly true in Europe: many European searches are essentially cross-lingual. For instance, when organizing to travel abroad for a business trip or a holiday, planning and booking usually involves digesting pages in foreign languages. Similarly, looking for information about European culture, education, sports, economy, or politics, usually requires making sense of web pages in several languages. A case in point is the current European Union, which has no less than 20 official languages.

The linguistic diversity of European content is "mirrored" by the fact that European searchers tend to be multilingual. Some Europeans are native speakers of multiple languages. Many Europeans have a broad knowledge of several foreign languages, while English functions as the lingua franca of the world wide web. Moreover, many Europeans have a passive understanding of even more languages.

In view of the linguistic diversity of the European web and its searchers, a cross-lingual web retrieval task, called WebCLEF, was launched at CLEF 2005 [3]. Cross-lingual web retrieval requires a new document collection to be constructed, containing web content in many languages. Of course, there are many options for creating such a collection. Multi-lingual documents are abundant on the web. We have chosen to focus on pages of European government-related sites, where collection building is less restricted by intellectual property rights. The resulting collection, which we think of as a European counterpart of the `.GOV` collection [2], is called EuroGOV and has been made available in January 2005 [5]. The crawled pages were cleaned-up and organized in a uniform format, bundled and compressed down to manageable sizes. The collection

C. Peters et al. (Eds.): CLEF 2005, LNCS 4022, pp. 825–836, 2006.

Table 1. List of top-level domains covered in the EuroGOV collection. (Left): Domains which which were considered more important, based on previous/current CLEF interests. (Right): Other domains contained in the collection.

Main domains		Additional domains	
Domain	Country	Domain	Country
`.cz`	Czech Republic	`.at`	Austria
`.de`	Germany	`.be`	Belgium
`.es`	Spain	`.cy`	Cyprus
`.eu.int`	European Union	`.dk`	Denmark
`.fi`	Finland	`.ee`	Estonia
`.fr`	France	`.gr`	Greece
`.hu`	Hungary	`.ie`	Ireland
`.it`	Italy	`.lt`	Lithuania
`.nl`	The Netherlands	`.lu`	Luxemburg
`.pt`	Portugal	`.lv`	Latvia
`.ru`	Russia	`.mt`	Malta
`.se`	Sweden	`.pl`	Poland
`.uk`	United Kingdom	`.si`	Slovenia
		`.sk`	Slovakia

is available under an individual or organizational license restricting its usage to research only; see [5].

In this paper we describe the EuroGOV collection in detail. The paper is organized as follows. We start by describing the crawling process in Section 2. Section 3 then lists various characteristics of the resulting collection, including the domains, the languages, and the link structure. We conclude with some discussion and future outlook in Section 4.

2 Crawling

Our initial plan for building EuroGOV was to obtain a focused crawl from the European Union seed `.eu.int`, and branch into the individual member states' governmental sites. However, restricting a crawler to government-related sites proved highly non-trivial. There is no simple way to tell a European government site apart from any other European site. For some government sites the crawling is smooth and we can easily filter out governmental pages (notable examples include `.gov.uk` and `.regeringen.se`). Most governmental sites, however, have more complex structures, and we could only focus the crawl by providing an explicit list of domains. As an example, we initially crawled 13 different domains to gather pages from the Finnish government. As the following domain list shows, there is no easy way of identifying Finnish governmental domains:

> `defmin.fi`, `formin.finland.fi`, `intermin.fi`, `ktm.fi`, `minedu.fi`, `mmm.fi`, `mintc.fi`, `mol.fi`, `om.fi`, `stm.fi`, `vm.fi`, `vnk.fi`, and `ymparisto.fi`

These differences in domain naming traditions make it difficult to guarantee completeness of the information crawled for some governments. As a result, what we should realistically aim for is that EuroGOV contains the fairly complete content of

- the main government portals, and
- the main ministries

of the countries whose information we want to include in the corpus.

Our crawling process can be divided into three parts. Our initial seed was made by picking 2–3 main governmental sites for each EU member state. The seed contained 40 URLs and was created by referring to a list from the EU portal.[1] After completing several cycles of this crawl we realized that due to the varying structure of governmental sites, the portion of governmental pages covered differed considerably from one country to another. In order to try to get a better harmony in coverage we began a new crawl, now starting with a seed consisting of a list of ministries for a subset of the EU countries. The subset covered 12 countries and was chosen according to CLEF interests. The left column of Table 1 shows the list of main domains. The second seed list consisted of 131 ministries from 9 EU member states (the UK, Sweden, and the EU itself were considered adequately covered in the initial crawl). The seed was created by browsing the main government portals. The third crawl was performed when interest was expressed in including Russian government pages in the crawl. The Russian crawl was created from a single seed: `www.gov.ru`. The final collection was created by combining the three crawls into a single collection of pages.

3 EuroGOV Collection Characteristics

In this section we provide various statistics concerning the collection, including the domains covered, the languages it contains, and its link structure.

3.1 Domains

The EuroGOV collection has pages from the 27 primary domains listed in Table 1. There is a set of 13 main domains, shown on the left-hand side of Table 1, chosen in accordance with current CLEF interests and plans. We have attempted to include a sufficiently large number of pages from these 13 main domain. There are 14 additional domains, shown on the right-hand side of Table 1, from which pages are also included in the collection. The coverage of these additional domains is often less complete than the coverage of the main domains. Note that pages in the languages of the additional domains will 'creep in' anyway. For example, the `eu.int` domain has ample pages in all of the 20 official languages of the European Union.

The EuroGOV collection features more languages and countries than are being used in the WebCLEF 2005 evaluation tasks. We made a deliberate choice to go for this extended list of countries and domains. This will facilitate future task extensions for cross-lingual web retrieval, or re-use of the collection for other

[1] URL: `http://europa.eu.int/abc/governments/index_en.htm`

Table 2. Statistics of the EuroGOV collection over primary domains

Domain	Pages				Size
	Total	Duplicated	Duplicates	Unique	(compressed)
.at	10,065	457	950	9,115	24M
.be	69,011	819	2,066	66,945	115M
.cy	1,972	52	52	1,920	7.9M
.cz	324,496	10,808	25,915	298,581	519M
.de	444,794	1,682	4,658	440,136	1.1G
.dk	2,144	497	519	1,625	5.4M
.ee	16,768	486	3,960	12,808	44M
.es	35,168	3,372	9,297	25,871	298M
.eu.int	374,484	32,838	58,415	316,069	1.9G
.fi	661,559	5,815	85,289	576,270	1.3G
.fr	156,450	11,144	21,894	134,556	545M
.gr	303	10	15	288	416K
.hu	330,822	361	1,082	329,740	1.5G
.ie	12,754	1,431	1,982	10,772	32M
.it	89,836	10,056	17,011	72,825	324M
.lt	10,765	751	1,131	9,634	8.8M
.lu	8,521	52	837	7,684	33M
.lv	317,404	10,357	25,711	291,693	675M
.mt	13,991	1,300	1,372	12,619	57M
.nl	149,949	6,097	18,911	131,038	434M
.pl	66,885	3,746	4,889	61,996	330M
.pt	147,445	2,454	8,744	138,701	753M
.ru	104,659	10,676	20,049	84,610	479M
.se	102,457	2,506	15,068	87,389	155M
.si	12,434	73	224	12,210	27M
.sk	58,020	3,288	3,764	54,256	128M
.uk	66,345	1,688	2,987	63,358	331M
Total	3,589,501	122,816	336,792	3,252,709	11G

purposes. We also feel that this reflects the natural situation when building a 'European' search engine.

The EuroGOV collection contains a total of 3,589,501 pages, and can be compressed in 11 gigabytes of data. Table 2 gives the page counts for each of the primary domains in the collection. The first column lists the primary domains in the collection. The second through fifth columns list the total number of web pages per domain; the number of MD5 checksums (of the page's content) that occur more than once; the number of pages that have a repeated MD5 checksum (and thus the same content as another page); and the number of unique pages. The final, sixth, column lists the total size of the pages when compressed. The five domains with the largest numbers of pages are: Finland (661,599), Germany (444,794), European Union (374,484), Hungary (330,822), Czech Republic (324,496). Although the number of pages per domain varies between 661,559 (Finland) and 303 (Greece), the number of pages is generally sufficient to support the building of a test collection. Specifically, the smallest

Table 3. Breakdown of the EUROGOV collection over document languages

EUROGOV Collection		Domain .eu.int.	
Language	Percentage	Language	Percentage
finnish	20.28%	english	33.26%
german	18.20%	french	18.08%
hungarian	12.58%	german	9.08%
english	10.16%	finnish	6.24%
latvian	8.80%	spanish	5.75%
french	6.98%	dutch	5.29%
swedish	5.32%	danish	5.13%
portuguese	3.93%	portuguese	4.47%
dutch	3.91%	swedish	3.26%
polish	2.14%	greek-iso8859-7	2.92%
italian	1.70%	italian	2.64%
spanish	1.39%	latvian	1.13%
czech-iso8859_2	1.13%	polish	1.05%
slovak-windows1250	0.89%	estonian	0.60%
russian-windows1251	0.60%	lithuanian	0.51%
danish	0.49%	hungarian	0.40%
estonian	0.39%	czech-iso8859_2	0.05%
russian-koi8_r	0.30%	slovak-windows1250	0.04%
slovak-ascii	0.27%	romanian	0.03%
greek-iso8859-7	0.27%	slovak-ascii	0.02%
lithuanian	0.19%	russian-koi8_r	0.02%
irish	0.03%	icelandic	0.01%
welsh	0.01%	russian-windows1251	0.01%

set of pages for one of the main domains is 35,168 (Spain). It is unclear, at this point, to what extent the varying numbers of pages per domain is a result of the available web content, different link structure of different governmental sites, or of our particular choices in crawler software or seed points.

3.2 EuroGOV Language Distributions

What is the distribution of languages in the collection? To answer this question, we applied the TextCat language identification tool [4], which is based on [1], using a restricted set of 30 language models covering the European languages only. Table 3 shows the results for the whole EUROGOV collection, as well as a breakdown for the `.eu.int` domain. Since pages may have little text or mixed language content, language identification may show multiple languages. For over two-thirds of the pages, a single candidate language stands out sufficiently clearly. Below, we analyze the language distribution on these pages.

When looking at the distribution of languages over the whole collection, shown on the left-hand side of Table 3, we see that the most frequent languages are Finnish (20%), German (18%), Hungarian (13%), English (10%), and Latvian (9%). It is a surprizing outcome that languages of the Finno-Ugrian family

Table 4. Breakdown over document languages for selected domains in the EUROGOV collection

Domain `.be.`		Domain `.de.`		Domain `.fi.`		Domain `.fr.`		Domain `.uk.`	
Lang.	Perc.	Lang.	Perc.	Lang.	Perc.	Lang.	Perc.	Lang.	Perc.
french	36.78%	german	97.70%	finnish	81.15%	french	94.25%	english	99.05%
dutch	24.32%	english	1.37%	swedish	11.52%	german	2.49%		
german	21.61%	french	0.74%	english	7.26%	english	2.24%		
english	16.74%					spanish	0.81%		

dominate the collection! The distribution of languages over the collection closely corresponds with the number of pages per domain (in numbers of pages, Finnish ranked first and Hungarian ranked fourth, see Table 2).

A look at the distribution of languages for Germany, France, and the UK, shown in Table 4, confirms this strong correlation between country and official language: In the German domain, 98% of the pages is in German. In the French domain, 94% of the pages are in French, and in the UK domain, 99% of the pages are in English. In countries with more than one official language, such as Finland (with Finnish and Swedish) or Belgium (with Dutch, French, and German), we see more language diversity within the corresponding domains. The language distribution for the Finnish and Belgian domains is also shown in Table 4. Since the languages and domains seem to be closely tied together, the distribution of the mixed language domain of the European Union, shown in Figure 1 and on

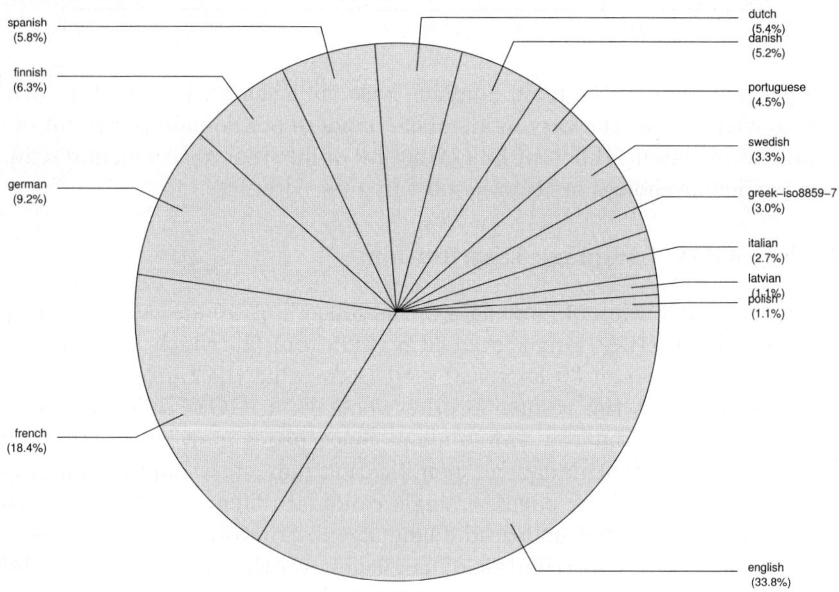

Fig. 1. Language distribution in the `.eu.int` domain

the right-hand side of Table 3, is of great interest. Here, we see that English is the most used language, accounting for 33% of the pages, followed by French (18%) and German (9%). In Appendix A, the language distribution of each of the main top-level domains is given.

3.3 Link Structure

Table 5 lists a number of salient features of the EuroGOV link structure. The second and third columns give the counts of the number of links and the number of realized links (ones whose targets are in EuroGOV; columns 4 and 5 provide the average number of links per page and the average number of realized links per page. The last row but one provides averages over all top level domains, and the last row provides the total number of links in the collection.

The largest numbers of links can be found in the domains with the largest numbers of pages; just under half of the links are realized in the collection. The average number of links per page varies considerably between domains, and the average realized number of links is just over half of the average number of links, although the relative gap between the two numbers varies quite a lot between domains, (e.g., for `it` the average realized fan-out is 84% of all links per page, while it is only 16% for `ru`).

4 Discussion

EuroGOV was thought of as an experimental collection for evaluating cross-lingual web retrieval. As such, the collection serves its purpose well. However, EuroGOV has several limitations which should be taken into account when working with the current collection and planning for possible future extensions of the collection.

- *Completeness*: Quite some effort was put into collecting lists of governmental sites to crawl. This is, however, not a complete list. Especially for the Spanish and Portuguese domains, the collection contains only a very small fraction of the available pages on government-related web sites.
- *Incomplete description of the link structure*: A full link analysis of the EuroGOV collection has not been performed yet. This is not an inherent limitation of the document collection. However, this sort of analysis is important for evaluating whether the collection is a reasonable representative of a realistic web.
- *Empty pages*: The collection contains over 70,000 empty documents. It is not clear why this error ocurred, but it should be avoided in future versions of the collection.
- *Rich document types*: In the EuroGOV collection, document types such as PDF and DOC files appear in the collection in the same format as they were crawled, i.e., their text is not extracted. Furthermore, large documents are truncated to avoid the collection growing too big. A truncated PDF or DOC file does not go down well with several off-the-shelf document parsers.

Table 5. Salient properties of the EuroGOV link structure

Domain	Number of links		Avg # links/page	
	True	Realized	True	Realized
at	438,591	367,590	43.5759	36.5216
be	729,597	340,415	10.5703	4.93191
cy	42,407	33,231	21.5046	16.8514
cz	10,602,034	6,286,711	32.6723	19.3738
de	15,890,499	2,881,943	35.7179	6.47789
dk	33,572	26,158	15.6586	12.2006
ee	291,709	180,085	17.3968	10.7398
es	318,696	218,448	9.0621	6.21156
eu.int	11,754,603	7,402,189	31.3886	19.7663
fi	17,505,000	3,881,257	26.4602	5.86683
fr	6,101,468	5,080,196	38.9990	32.4713
gr	7,973	6,007	26.3135	19.8251
hu	14,412,108	5,345,513	43.5645	16.1583
ie	397,159	279,833	31.1400	21.9408
it	2,435,376	2,048,472	27.1091	22.8024
lt	161,601	87,511	15.0117	8.12922
lu	186,984	146,270	21.9439	17.1658
lv	9,325,789	5,547,302	29.3807	17.4767
mt	273,873	215,417	19.5749	15.3968
nl	7,087,202	3,636,065	47.2635	24.2484
pl	1,632,655	1,187,235	24.4092	17.7499
pt	9,046,688	5,613,440	61.3564	38.0714
ru	4,880,064	783,246	46.6282	7.48379
se	4,766,234	1,280,677	46.5148	12.4984
si	213,239	152,137	17.1497	12.2356
sk	1,167,119	892,326	20.1155	15.3794
uk	1,847,259	1,286,001	27.8407	19.3818
Avg	4,501,833	2,044,655	29.1971	16.9391
Total	121,549,499	55,205,675		

From a web document collection perspective, this is a realistic and interesting scenario. From the perspective of a cross-lingual retrieval collection this scenario might, however, be less desirable since participants might spend too much time on these issues rather than focusing on the multi-lingual aspects of the task.

– *Character Encodings*: Character encoding is very varied in the European Web, especially for non-latin languages and for extended character sets. Added to that, the information about it in the metadata HTTP header is often wrong, because it is automatically produced and people do not know or care to set it right. Again, this adds to the realism of a cross-lingual web document collection, but also requires considerable effort from participants more interested in the multi-lingual aspects of the collection.

Despite its limitations EuroGOV is very suitable for the initial exploration of cross-lingual web search.

The EuroGOV collection is available for WebCLEF participants, but also as a resource for researchers in fields like natural language processing, information retrieval, or document understanding. Details on how to obtain the EuroGOV collection are on the WebCLEF website [5].

Acknowledgments

Thanks to Craig Macdonald for advise at various stages during the creation of EuroGOV, to the Melange group for sharing their normalized links with us, and to Krisztian Balog for help with exploring EuroGOV's link structure.

The building of EuroGOV was supported by the Netherlands Organization for Scientific Research (NWO) under project numbers 017.001.190, 220-80-001, 264-70-050, 354-20-005, 612-13-001, 612.000.106, 612.000.207, 612.066.302, 612.-069.006, 640.001.501, and 640.002.501.

Bibliography

[1] W. B. Cavnar and J. M. Trenkle. N-gram-based text categorization. In *Proceedings of Third Annual Symposium on Document Analysis and Information Retrieval*, pages 161–175, 1994.

[2] .GOV. TREC Web Corpus: .GOV, 2006. URL: `http://es.csiro.au/TRECWeb/govinfo.html`.

[3] B. Sigurbjörnsson, J. Kamps, and M. de Rijke. Overview of WebCLEF 2005. In *This Volume*, 2006.

[4] TextCat. Language identification tool, 2006. URL: `http://odur.let.rug.nl/~vannoord/TextCat/`.

[5] WebCLEF. Cross-lingual web retrieval, 2006. URL: `http://ilps.science.uva.nl/WebCLEF/`.

A Language Distributions in EuroGOV

Czech Republic Top-level domain `.cz`.

Domain .cz.	
Language	Percentage
czech-iso8859_2	71.71%
slovak-ascii	17.03%
english	10.41%

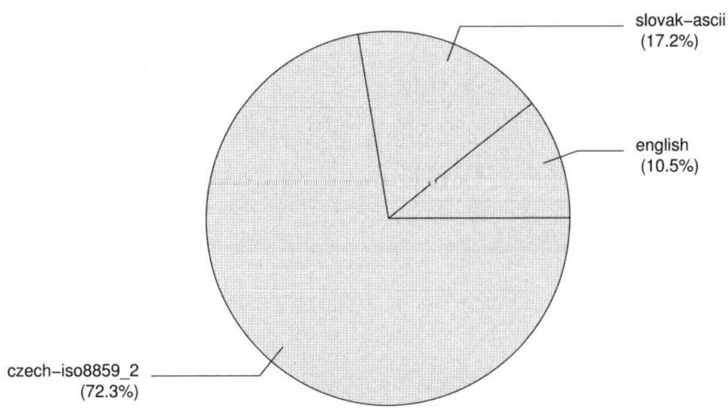

Germany Top-level domain .de.

Domain .de.	
Language	Percentage
german	97.70%
english	1.37%
french	0.74%

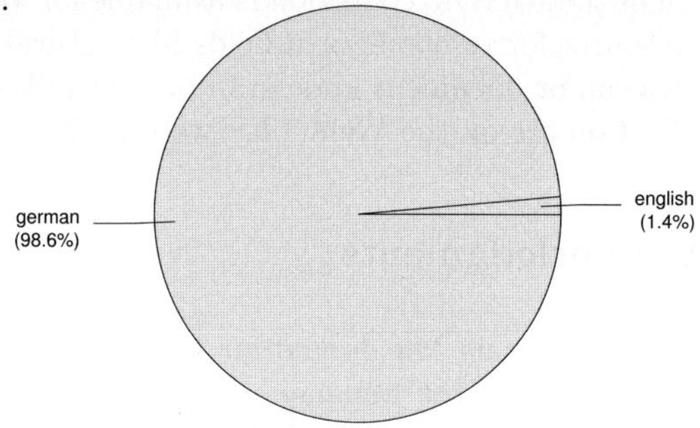

Spain Top-level domain .es.

Domain .es.	
Language	Percentage
spanish	97.20%
english	0.96%
latvian	0.91%
french	0.86%

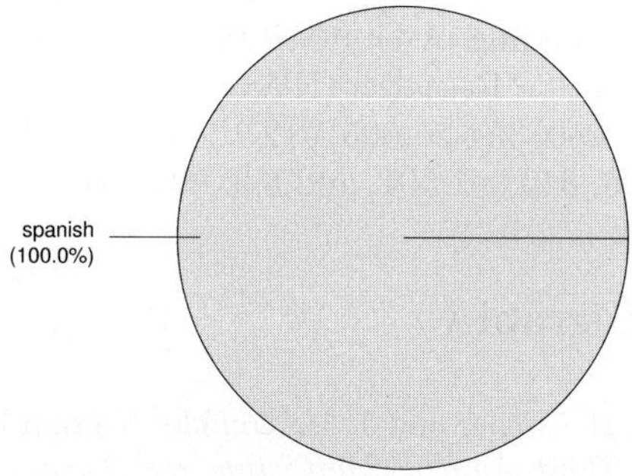

Finland Top-level domain .fi.

Domain .fi.	
Language	Percentage
finnish	81.15%
swedish	11.52%
english	7.26%

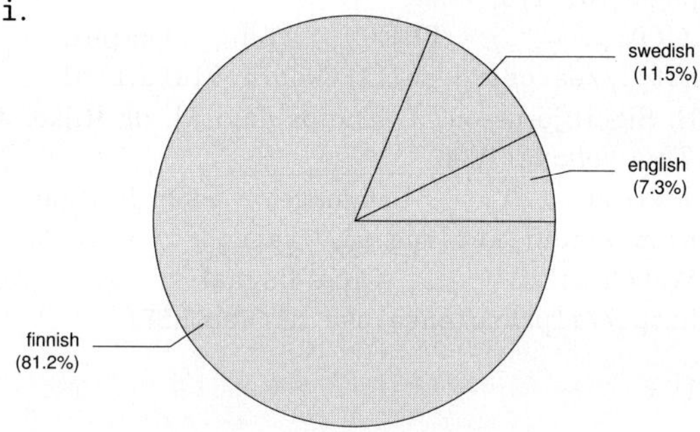

France Top-level domain .fr.

Domain .fr.	
Language	Percentage
french	94.25%
german	2.49%
english	2.24%
spanish	0.81%

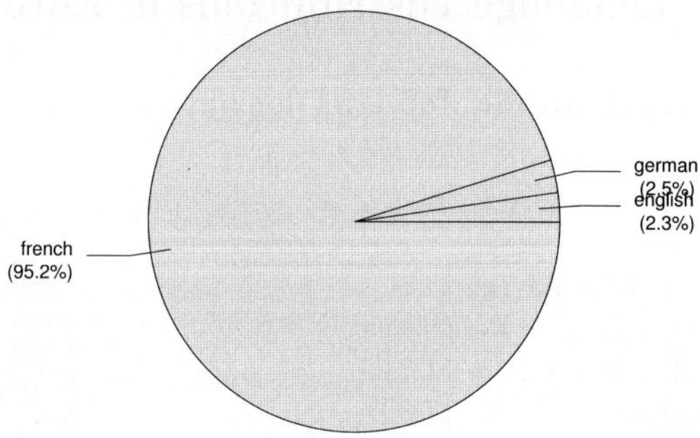

Hungary Top-level domain `.hu`.

Domain `.hu`.	
Language	Percentage
hungarian	99.60%
english	0.31%

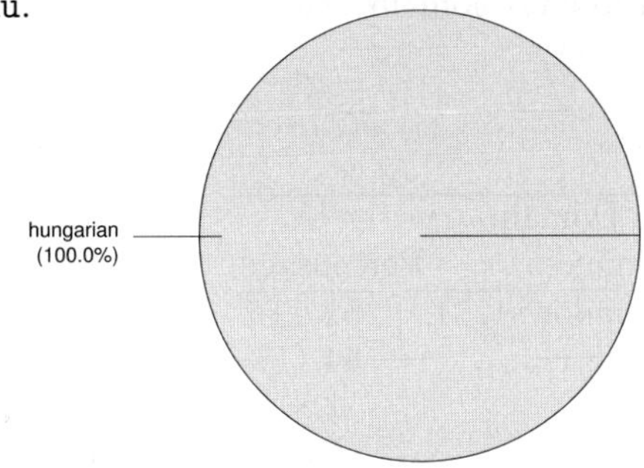

Italy Top-level domain `.it`.

Domain `.it`.	
Language	Percentage
italian	90.15%
english	8.52%
french	0.89%

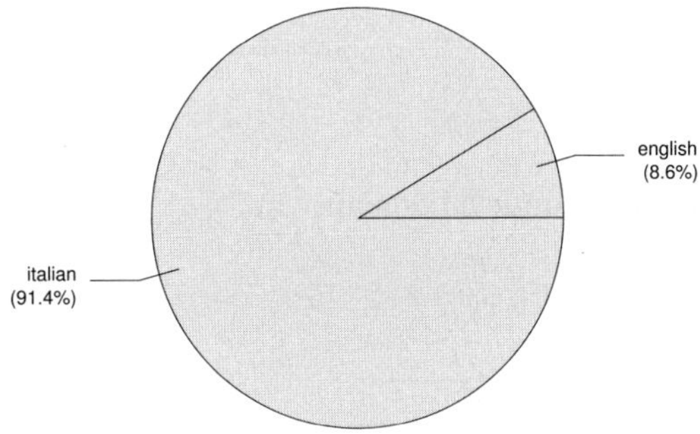

The Netherlands Top-level domain `.nl`.

Domain `.nl`.	
Language	Percentage
dutch	94.39%
english	4.94%

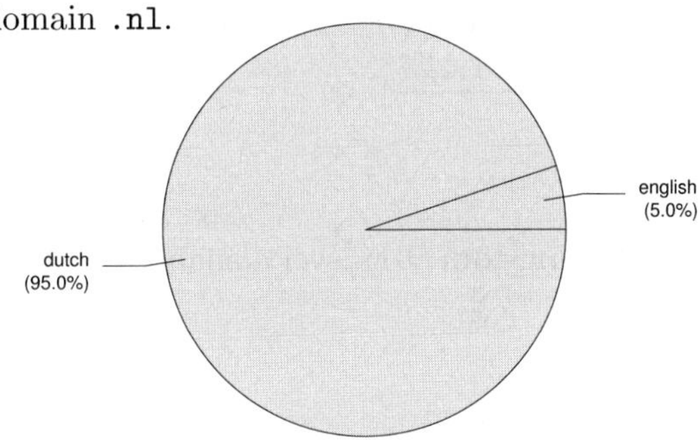

Portugal Top-level domain `.pt`.

Domain `.pt`.	
Language	Percentage
portuguese	98.13%
english	1.72%

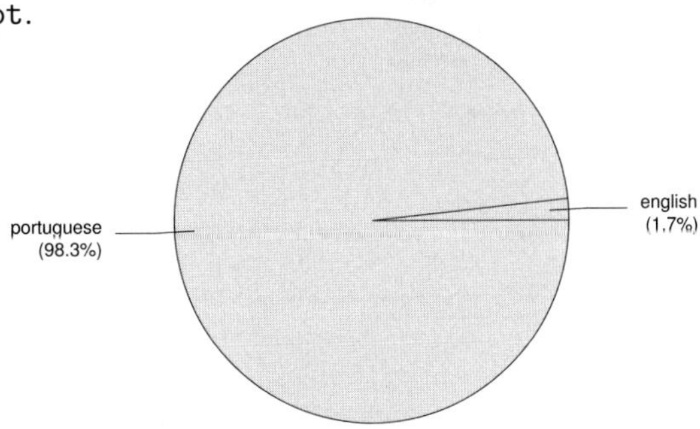

Russia Top-level domain `.ru`.

Domain .ru.	
Language	Percentage
russian-windows1251	52.49%
russian-koi8_r	44.11%
latvian	2.81%
english	0.54%

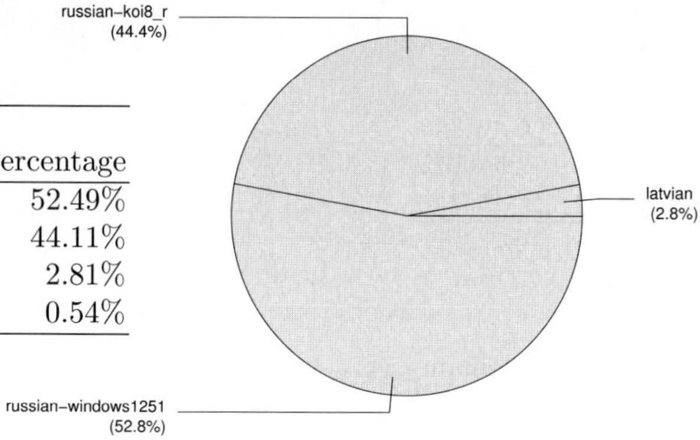

Sweden Top-level domain `.se`.

Domain .se.	
Language	Percentage
swedish	98.45%
english	1.42%

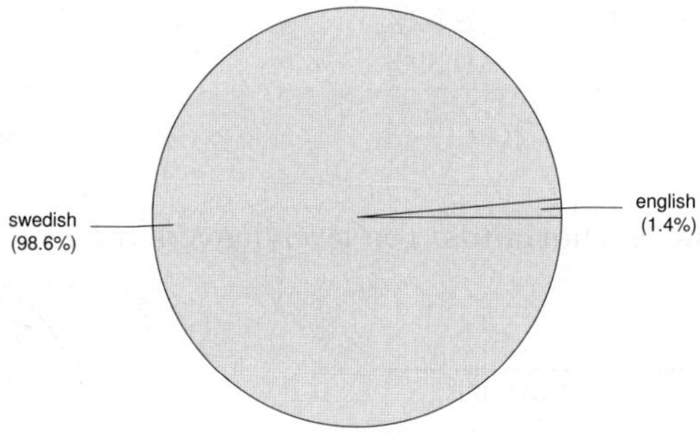

United Kingdom Top-level domain `.uk`.

Domain .uk.	
Language	Percentage
english	99.05%
welsh	0.47%

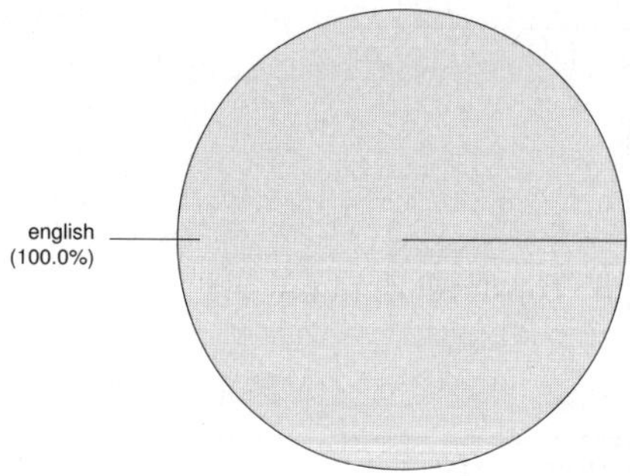

Web Retrieval Experiments with the EuroGOV Corpus at the University of Hildesheim

Niels Jensen, René Hackl, Thomas Mandl, and Robert Strötgen

Universität Hildesheim, Information Science
Marienburger Platz 22, D-31141 Hildesheim, Germany
mandl@uni-hildesheim.de

Abstract. This paper describes web retrieval experiments with the EuroGOV corpus carried out at the University of Hildesheim. For both the multi-lingual and the mixed mono-lingual task, several indexing strategies were tested, all of them based on one mixed language index. After stopword removal, word and n-gram based indexes were developed based on the full document content, part of the content and the document title. Boosting the original topic language with a higher weight in the query and punishing the English translation led to better results for most settings. A title only run gave the best results during post submission runs for the multi-lingual task.

1 Introduction

Web search engines has become a part of every day life for many people. The development of information retrieval systems for the web is faced with many challenges. Systems give different answers to these challenges and it is difficult to judge the effect of decisions during the design of search engine. As a consequence, there is a great need for evaluation in web retrieval. This has led to the development of several evaluation campaigns for web retrieval [9].

Within the Cross Language Evaluation Forum (CLEF), a web track has been created to investigate retrieval methods for multilingual retrieval with web data [14]. For the first time, a large multilingual web corpus has been collected and distributed [13].

In the experiments conducted in this web track, an existing experimental retrieval system was tuned to the challenges of a large web corpus. During these experiments, resources for all languages in the corpus were not available. As a consequence, the experiments were directed toward the goal of implementing a web retrieval system without language specific resources. N-gram indexing [10] and a word index without stemming were implemented. The main engine behind our system is Apache Lucene.

2 Data Pre-processing and Language Identification

A corpus in well formed XML was required to use the system implemented for previous multilingual CLEF experiments [3, 4]. Since the files of the EuroGOV corpus were not released in well formed XML, substantial effort for data

C. Peters et al. (Eds.): CLEF 2005, LNCS 4022, pp. 837 – 845, 2006.

pre-processing was necessary. After preliminary experiments with a Perl-Script, a Java program was developed that transformed the corpus into XML. This allowed a SAX parser to parse the files during indexing. The main issues for transforming the EuroGOV files were pre-declared entities. Ampersand characters and dollar signs needed to be replaced. Remaining unresolved parsing errors probably due to nested CDATA tags left some 20% of all documents only partially indexed. During indexing, the HTML tags were removed from the data. Some HTML tags might improve indexing, however, the focus of the experiments described was the question whether it is possible to implement an efficient solution without language specific resources.

Language identification is an important issue for web retrieval. When the proper language is known, specific resources can be applied. Although many systems are available for language identification and there is a significant amount on research published on the topic [11], it remains a challenge when many languages are involved and for web data. Web data is often multi-lingual, contains different sorts of texts and texts may be short. This difficulty is partially reflected in the language identification list which is part of the web corpus. In this list, the language of 15 % of all documents is unknown and for the others, 2.3 languages are assigned to each document on average.

In order to heuristically assess the quality of the list, we conducted an intellectual analysis of some 700 pages from CZ domain which were not identified as Czech. Some 85% of the language assignments were inaccurate and 4% were wrong [5]. As a consequence, we initiated the development of a new language identification tool with a specific focus on multilingual documents [1]. However, this tool was not ready for the web track experiments and as a consequence, no language specific resources were used.

3 Indexing the EuroGOV Corpus

As mentioned in the introduction, one multilingual index was created. In order to generate a slim index we assembled a multilingual stopword list. The basis for this list were the stopword lists supplied by the Université de Neuchâtel[1] and a list developed specifically for the Czech language [5]. All lists were combined and merged into one file. This multilingual stopword list covers thirteen languages and was used for the indexing process of the corpus. It did not contain stopwords for all eleven topic languages of the web track. The list resulted in the elimination of 52% of all tokens in the corpus. In mono-lingual retrieval, stopword removal should eliminate only some 30% of a corpus [12]. It seems, that tokens which are stopwords in one language also appear in other languages. This is especially true for similar languages and for abbreviations because stopwords are often short and may therefore be used as acronyms in other contexts. This fact might impair performance of an approach without language specific stopword removal. Nevertheless, runs without stopword elimination performed poorly and were disregarded.

[1] Stopword lists: http://www.unine.ch/Info/clef/ verified August 11th 2005.

For our retrieval experiments, we created different multilingual indexes. Two were created with the Lucene StandardAnalyzer[2], which does not implement any linguistic processing apart from word segmentation. That means, no stemming was applied. This does not seem to be a very promising approach considering results of previous CLEF experiments [6]. As a consequence, we considered a language independent approach for indexing. In recent years, character n-gram indexing emerged to be a good choice for information retrieval [10] and we developed tri-, four- and five-gram based indexes for the web track. Most of the basic code for retrieval and n-gram analysis was adopted from previous CLEF ad-hoc experiments [4]. Altogether, four indexing approaches were applied.

Web retrieval has been focusing on exploiting local and global structure in order to improve retrieval. Many systems implement link analysis or anchor text analysis. Also the internal document structure typical for the web has often been analyzed [2]. Their success depends on the nature of the task. For the web track, named page and homepage finding were required, no ad-hoc information needs were included in the topics. For these tasks, link and structure analysis have proven to enhance retrieval quality.

For our system, we applied some robust form of structure analysis focusing on content and title. The first index covered the whole content of the documents whereas the second index cut off after a maximum of 200 characters of content for each individual document. On account of this way of content handling, the sizes of the index dropped from 5 GB to 700 MB. In addition, we indexed only the title for some runs.

Another parameter of our runs was induced by the format of the multi-lingual task. The original version of the topic was given in the language in which the topic was developed. This version needed to be used in the mixed mono-lingual task. In addition, an English version created by human translators was available. The systems could generate further language version by automatic translation. For our multi-lingual experiments, we relied solely on the versions provided. As additional parameter, the weighting between the original version and the English version was modified. We conducted runs with a 10:1, a 1:10 and a 1:1 weighting of the two versions.

All parameters explored in our experiments are displayed in table 1. We did not use any of the metadata that was supplied by the topics due to time and resource constraints. Further details are specified in [7].

Table 1. Parameters for the experiments at the University of Hildesheim

Indexing method	**Document parts indexed**	**Topic field usage and weighting**
word index (no stemming)	full content	original (mixed-mono)
3-gram	content cut-off (first 200 chars.)	original + English (1:1)
4-gram		original + English (10:1)
5-gram	title only	original + English (1:10)

[2] Lucene StandardAnalyzer: http://lucene.apache.org verified on August 11th 2005.

4 Results

Until the deadline of the web track, only six runs could be submitted. Further runs were generated during post experiments. For evaluation of the post runs, a script was provided by the University of Amsterdam. Their results are presented in the following two section, respectively.

All runs were created on an IBM computer with two 64-bit 2.4 GHz processors, 8 GB RAM and 215 GB disc space running Linux 9.3 and Java 1.5. Indexing time varied between 1.5 and 34 hours for a tri-gram title only run and a full content, word based run, respectively. The size of the index for the same runs was 290 MB and 4.9 GB.

4.1 Submitted Experiments

Because of performance and time restrictions, the tri-gram approach was only applied to the title field of the individual documents for the submitted runs. The size of the index dropped to 300 MB for title only which led to a very quick and stable performance at retrieval time. Six different baseline runs were submitted. Results are shown in table 2. For multi-lingual runs, only 1:1 weighting of the two topic fields was applied.

Table 2. Results of submitted WebCLEF 2005 runs

	3-gram, title, mono	3-gram, title, multi	word, cut-off, mono	word, cut-off, multi	word, content, mono	word, content, multi
mean reciprocal rank	0.0373	0.0274	0.1301	0.1147	0.1603	0.137
avg. success at 5	0.0512	0.0402	0.1627	0.1353	0.2011	0.1627
avg. success at 10	0.064	0.0494	0.1883	0.1609	0.2194	0.1927
avg. success at 20	0.075	0.064	0.2322	0.192	0.2523	0.2249

The mono-lingual runs compared poorly to the runs of other participants where language specific methods were applied [14]. Among the multi-lingual runs submitted, the run in the last column in table 2 was the best performing run submitted. It can be seen, that mono-lingual experiments lead to better performance. On average, the monolingual runs differ from the multilingual runs by about 0.0162 MRR points. That might be a hint, that in the setting of the web track at CLEF where homepages and named pages need to be identified, the multi-lingual aspect is especially hard. Furthermore, the inclusion of the English translation actually hurts performance.

Considering the results of the submitted runs it becomes clear that the tri-gram index did not confirm the high expectations. Having those results in mind the method of indexing the corpus with the Lucene StandardAnalyzer turned out to be more effective than the tri-gram strategy.

4.2 Post Submission Experiments

In the post experiments, more parameter combinations could be explored [7]. Many more n-gram runs for the multi-lingual task were generated. Their results are presented in table 3.

Table 3. Results of N-gram Experiments (av Suc = Average Success at X documents)

		title				content cut-off			full content			
		mono ling.	multi 1:1	boost orig. topic	boost transl topic	multi 1:1	boost orig. topic	boost transl topic	mono ling.	multi 1:1	boost orig. topic	boost transl topic
3-gram	MRR	0.037	0.027	0.038	0.014	0.099	0.108	0.099	0.017	0.010	0.017	0.006
	avS 5	0.051	0.040	0.053	0.017	0.106	0.114	0.106	0.024	0.018	0.026	0.007
	avS 10	0.064	0.049	0.062	0.024	0.106	0.114	0.106	0.042	0.024	0.033	0.015
	avS 50	0.064	0.049	0.104	0.051	0.106	0.114	0.106	0.055	0.040	0.053	0.040
4-gram	MRR	0.112	0.084	0.102	0.048	0.050	0.053	0.036	0.025	0.019	0.024	0.011
	avS 5	0.123	0.092	0.112	0.053	0.054	0.055	0.039	0.016	0.012	0.014	0.009
	avS 10	0.123	0.092	0.112	0.053	0.055	0.057	0.041	0.032	0.025	0.032	0.011
	avS 50	0.123	0.092	0.112	0.053	0.055	0.057	0.041	0.045	0.034	0.043	0.018
5-gram	MRR	**0.121**	0.095	0.113	0.057	0.095	0.113	0.057				
	avS 5	0.131	0.103	0.121	0.062	0.103	0.121	0.062				
	avS 10	0.131	0.103	0.121	0.062	0.103	0.121	0.062				
	avS 50	0.131	0.103	0.121	0.062	0.103	0.121	0.062				

Within the post submission experiments, the first n-gram experiments on the full content were conducted. Nevertheless, none of the runs reached the same performance as the best submitted multi-lingual run. That confirmed the results form the submitted runs. Probably, n-gram indexes are sensitive to mixed language indexes and should not be applied in a multi-lingual environment without language identification.

Although n-gram indexing performs poorly, table 3 reveals that for many settings, simply boosting the original topic language 10:1 compared to the English translation version improves performance. That trend was further investigated for the word based indexing method. The ratio for the two query fields were 10 to 1 and vice versa. The results that are shown in table 4 and 5 show that by boosting the title field of the query the results improve by 0.0144 MRR points on average. Applying this procedure, the performance of the multilingual run based on the Lucene StandardAnalyzer Index results in higher MRR values. All of these runs are multi-lingual experiments.

The results confirm that boosting improves the performance. The English translation seems to diminish the quality for most topics. In addition, none of the runs by other participants in the multi-lingual task applying some form of translation of the topic outperformed this run [14]. That hints, that translation does not support named page and homepage finding in a multilingual task.

The best results are achieved with the smallest content type used. These runs are based on the title only. The boosted title only run based on the word index has a mean reciprocal rank (MRR) of 0.212 which is 32% higher than the best submitted run. In addition, a title only runs in the mono-lingual setting also returned the best mono-lingual results of our system (MRR 0.238). The good performance of the title only runs is quite surprising. The titles in the web corpus are often of low quality. They contain very short text and in many cases, the titles are meaningless dummy texts created by content management systems.

Table 4. Translated English Version of Topic Boosted 10 to 1

	3-gram, title	3-gram, content	word, title	word, cut-off	word, content
mean reciprocal rank	0.0139	0.0063	0.123	0.0677	0.0811
avg. success at 5	0.0165	0.0073	0.127	0.0786	0.0987
avg. success at 10	0.0238	0.0146	0.127	0.1079	0.1133
avg. success at 20	0.0293	0.0201	0.127	0.1207	0.1316

Table 5. Original Topic Language Boosted 10 to 1

	3-gram, title	3-gram, content	word, title	word, cut-off	word, content
mean reciprocal rank	0.0379	0.0172	0.212	0.1307	0.1608
avg. success at 5	0.053	0.0256	0.226	0.1609	0.1974
avg. success at 10	0.0622	0.0329	0.226	0.1883	0.2176
avg. success at 20	0.075	0.0439	0.226	0.2285	0.245

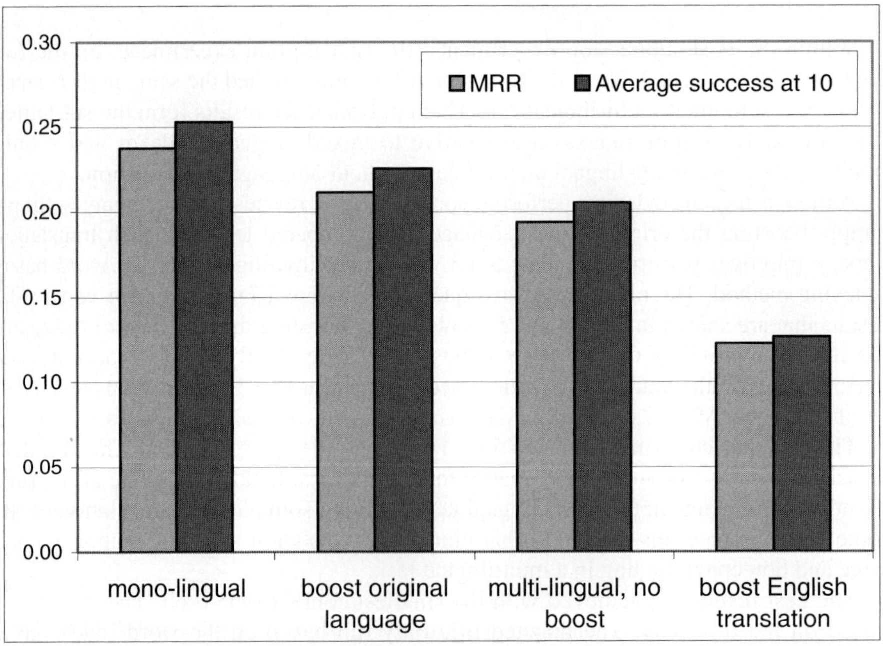

Fig. 1. Comparison of Title Only Runs Based on Words

Looking at all title runs reveals the effect of the original language version of the topic and the English version. As figure 1 shows, the mono-lingual run where only the original version of the topic was used for querying did best. For all other runs, both the original and the English version were used for querying. With increasing weight for the English version, the performance continues to drop. If we consider the first run as a multi-lingual run, it outperforms all other runs including some form of translation.

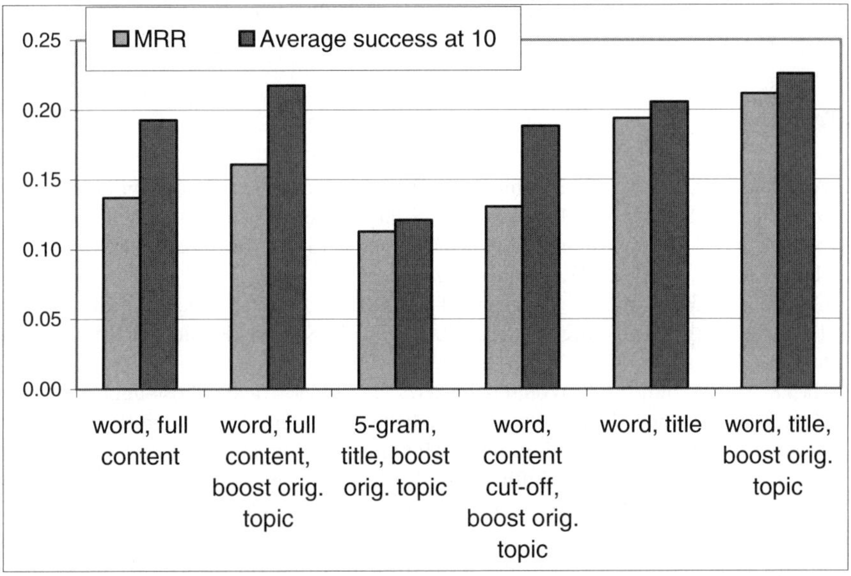

Fig. 2. Comparison of Most Important Multilingual Results

The performance of the most important multilingual runs can be compared in figure 2. It shows the best submitted run on the left which was later improved by boosting (see second run). The third run shown is the best n-gram run which performs worst in this figure. The fourth run is the best run based on the content cut-off at 100 characters and the two most right columns display the best post submission runs based on the title only which was indexed using word segmentation.

5 Conclusion and Outlook

For the first web track at CLEF, we intended to tune our system to be able to cope with a large amount of data. We succeeded in returning valid results for several runs. The experiments reported in this paper show that multilingual web retrieval with a reasonable quality can be implemented in a highly efficient manner by focusing on the title and creating a small and multilingual index. However, there remains ample room for improvement as can be seen from the large gap between multi- and mixed mono-lingual experiments.

For the next CLEF web track, we intend to run the current setup again as a benchmark and to involve the metadata that is being provided by the WebCLEF topics. Furthermore, language dependent resources are planned to be used. However, we need to further investigate the reasons for the good performance of title only and boosted runs. These reasons may foster system improvement in the future.

We also want to include advanced quality measures into consideration. Link based quality measures seem to be integral part of commercial search engines. They have been evaluated at the web track at TREC [2]. Advanced quality measures take more features into account, especially information and design aspects [8].

References

1. Artemenko, O., Mandl, T., Shramko, M., Womser-Hacker, C.: Evaluation of a Language Identification System for Mono- and Multi-lingual Text Documents. In: Proceedings of 2006 ACM SAC Symposium on Applied Computing (SAC). Document Engineering Track (DE). SAC'06, April, 23-27, 2006, Dijon, France.
2. Craswell, N., Hawking, D.: Overview of the TREC-2004 Web Track. In: The Thirteenth Text Retrieval Conference (TREC 2004) NIST Special Publication: SP 500-261. http://trec.nist.gov/pubs/trec13/t13_proceedings.html
3. Hackl, R., Mandl, T.. Womser-Hacker, C.: Mono- and Cross-lingual Retrieval Experiments at the University of Hildesheim. In: Peters, C., Clough, P., Gonzalo, J., Kluck, M., Jones, G., Magnini, B. (eds): Multilingual Information Access for Text, Speech and Images: Results of the Fifth CLEF Evaluation Campaign. Berlin et al.: Springer [Lecture Notes in Computer Science 3491] 2005. pp. 165-169.
4. Hackl, R., Kölle, R., Mandl, T., Ploedt, A., Scheufen, J-H., Womser-Hacker, C.: Multilingual Retrieval Experiments with MIMOR at the University of Hildesheim. In: Peters, C., Braschler, M., Gonzalo, J., Kluck, M. (eds.): Comparative Evaluation of Multilingual Information Access Systems: 4th Workshop of the Cross-Language Evaluation Forum, CLEF 2003, Trondheim, Aug. 21-22, 2003, Revised Selected Papers. Berlin et al.: Springer [LNCS 3237] 2004. pp. 166-173.
5. Hofman Miquel, L: Informations-linguistische Ressourcen für das Information Retrieval in der tschechischen Sprache im Rahmen des Cross Language Evaluation Forums (CLEF). Master Thesis Information Science, University of Hildesheim. 2005. http://web1.bib.uni-hildesheim.de/edocs/2005/504033603/meta/
6. Hollink, V., Kamps, J., Monz, C., de Rijke, M.: Monolingual Document Retrieval for European Languages. In: Information Retrieval 7 (1/2) 2004. pp. 33-52.
7. Jensen, N.: Multilinguales Webretrieval am Beispiel des EuroGOV Korpus. Master Thesis Information Science, University of Hildesheim. 2005. http://web1.bib.uni-hildesheim.de/edocs/2005/503856797/meta/
8. Mandl, T.: The quest for the best pages on the web. In: Information Service & Use. 2005 vol. 25 (2). 2005. pp. 69-76.
9. Mandl, T.: Recent Developments in the Evaluation of Information Retrieval Systems: Moving Toward Diversity and Practical Applications. To appear 2006.
10. McNamee, P., Mayfield, J.: Character N-Gram Tokenization for European Language Text Retrieval. In: Information Retrieval 7 (1/2) 2004. pp. 73-98.
11. McNamee, P.: Language identification: a solved problem suitable for undergraduate instruction. In: Journal of Computing Sciences in Colleges, vol. 20 (3) 2005. pp. 94-101.

12. Savoy, J.: A Stemming Procedure and Stopword List for General French Corpora In: Journal of the American Society for Information Science, vol. 50 (10) 1999. pp. 944–952.
13. Sigurbjörnsson, B., Kamps, J., de Rijke, M.: Blueprint of a Cross-Lingual Web Retrieval Collection. In: Journal of Digital Information Management, vol. 3 (1) 2005. pp. 9-13.
14. Sigurbjörnsson, B., Kamps, J., de Rijke, M.: Overview of the WebCLEF track. In this volume. 2006.

Danish and Greek Web Search Experiments with Hummingbird SearchServer™ at CLEF 2005

Stephen Tomlinson

Hummingbird, Ottawa, Canada
stephen.tomlinson@hummingbird.com
http://www.hummingbird.com/

Abstract. Hummingbird participated in the WebCLEF mixed monolingual retrieval task of the Cross-Language Evaluation Forum (CLEF) 2005. In this task, the system was given 547 known-item queries from 11 languages (134 Spanish, 121 English, 59 Dutch, 59 Portuguese, 57 German, 35 Hungarian, 30 Danish, 30 Russian, 16 Greek, 5 Icelandic and 1 French). The goal was to find the desired page in the 82GB EuroGOV collection (3.4 million pages crawled from government sites of 27 European domains). Our experiments found that stopword processing was more important than anticipated, perhaps because words common in one language may tend to be overweighted by inverse document frequency in a mixed language collection. Extra weight on the document title helped significantly, and extra weight on less deep urls significantly helped home page queries. Stemming was of neutral impact on average, but it made a substantial difference for some individual queries. We analyze several Danish and Greek queries in detail.

1 Introduction

Hummingbird SearchServer[1] is a toolkit for developing enterprise search and retrieval applications. See our ad hoc paper in this volume [10] for more background.

2 Indexing

Our indexing approach was based on the approach we used for TREC Web tasks the previous three years (described in detail in [11]). Briefly, in addition to full-text indexing, the custom text reader cTREC populated particular columns such as TITLE (if any), URL, URL_TYPE and URL_DEPTH. The URL_TYPE was set to ROOT, SUBROOT, PATH or FILE, based on the convention which worked well in TREC 2001 for the Twente/TNO group [13] on the entry page finding task (also known as the home page finding task). The URL_DEPTH

[1] SearchServer™, SearchSQL™and Intuitive Searching™ are trademarks of Hummingbird Ltd. All other copyrights, trademarks and tradenames are the property of their respective owners.

C. Peters et al. (Eds.): CLEF 2005, LNCS 4022, pp. 846–855, 2006.

was set to a term indicating the depth of the page in the site. Examples and the exact rules we used are given in [11].

WebCLEF required a few indexing enhancements compared to TREC. In particular, it wouldn't suffice to assume all the pages were in the ASCII character set. We added a /cs option to our cTREC text reader which used the first recognized 'charset' specification in the page (e.g. from the meta http-equiv tag) to indicate from which character set to convert the page to Unicode (Win_1252 was assumed if no charset was specified).

For the baseline task, in which the system was not to make use of any of the topic metadata such as the specified language of the query, we still indexed with English stopwords (even though the majority of the documents were in other languages). We treated the apostrophe as a term separator (which we normally do for languages other than English, but in this collection, it was also a separator for English). No accents were indexed. English stemming was used on the table, but SearchServer also indexed all the surface forms (after Unicode normalizations such as case normalization), and the baseline runs just searched the surface forms, not the stems.

For 2 of our submitted runs, we labelled the runs as making use of the topic and page language metadata (which were always the same in the mixed monolingual task) along with the page's domain. For these runs, we created a set of language-specific indexes (one for each of the 11 query languages) which used a stemmer and stopfile for that language (for English and Icelandic, we actually used the original baseline index, which had English stems and stopwords). For some of the languages, because we were close to the submission deadline, we also skipped indexing some of the domains to save time (e.g. for Greek, just the 'gr' and 'eu.int' subsets of EuroGOV were included because it was known all the results were in the 'gr' domain) which would have a (probably minor) effect on the inverse document frequencies (minor especially since we always included the 'eu.int' subset in each index). For 9 of the languages (Danish, Dutch, English, French, German, Greek, Portuguese, Russian and Spanish), the lexical stemmer in SearchServer (based on internal stemming component 3.7.0.15) was used. For Hungarian, the Neuchatel stemmer [6] was used (see our companion ad hoc retrieval paper [10] for details). For Icelandic, we used the English index as previously mentioned. For Greek and Russian, we additionally enabled indexing of a few accents because the stemmer was accent-sensitive. When processing queries for these runs, the query was directed to the index for the specified language.

3 Searching

We executed 7 runs in June 2005, though only 5 were allowed to be submitted. All 7 are described here. The first 4 runs were 'baseline' runs which did not use the topic metadata. The other 3 runs made use of the topic metadata (in particular, the domain, and for the last 2 runs, also the language).

humWC05none: This run was a plain content search of the baseline table. No inflections were used. This run was the analog of the "none" runs described in our ad hoc retrieval paper [10]. It used the '2:3' relevance method and document length normalization (SET RELEVANCE_DLEN_IMP 500). The IS_ABOUT predicate was used instead of the CONTAINS predicate (and hence the VECTOR_GENERATOR was set to blank to disable inflections instead of the TERM_GENERATOR), but the relevance calculation was the same. (This run was not submitted.)

humWC05p run: This submitted run was the same as humWC05none except that it put additional weight on matches in the title, url, first heading and some meta tags, including extra weight on matching the query as a phrase in these fields. Below is an example SearchSQL query. The searches on the ALL_PROPS column (which contained a copy of the title, url, etc. as described in [11]) are the difference from the humWC05none run. Note that the FT_TEXT column indexed the content and also all of the non-content fields except for the URL. This run used the same approach as the TREC 2004 humW04pl run [12] except that linguistic inflections were disabled.

```
SELECT RELEVANCE('2:3') AS REL, DOCNO
FROM EGOV
WHERE
 (ALL_PROPS CONTAINS 'Giuseppe Medici' WEIGHT 1) OR
 (ALL_PROPS IS_ABOUT 'Giuseppe Medici' WEIGHT 1) OR
 (FT_TEXT IS_ABOUT 'Giuseppe Medici' WEIGHT 10)
ORDER BY REL DESC;
```

humWC05dp run: This submitted run was the same as humWC05p except that it put additional weight on urls of depth 4 or less. Less deep urls also received higher weight from inverse document frequency because (presumably) they were less common. This run used the same approach as the TREC 2004 humW04dpl run [12] except that linguistic inflections were disabled.

humWC05rdp run: This submitted run was the same as humWC05dp except that it put additional weight on the url type. This run used the same approach as the TREC 2004 humW04rdpl run [12] except that linguistic inflections were disabled.

humWC05dpD0 run: This run was the same as humWC05dp except that the domain information of the topic metadata was used to restrict the search to the specified domain. This run was not submitted.

humWC05dpD run: This submitted run was the same as humWC05dpD0 except that the language information of the topic metadata was used to direct the search to the table for the specified language (i.e. the WHERE clause was the same as for humWC05dpD0, but the FROM clause specified a different table). Inflections were still not used.

humWC05dplD run: This submitted run was the same as humWC05dpD except that the content and title searches included linguistic expansion from language-specific stemming. (Linguistic variations were enabled with SET VECTOR_GENERATOR 'word!ftelp/inflect'; note that the /decompound option (applicable to Dutch and German) was omitted because of an oversight, so for each compound word in a query, all of its stems (from a particular stemming interpretation) needed to be in the same or consecutive words in a document to increase the relevance score.)

4 Results of Web Search Experiments

The 7 runs allow us to isolate 6 'web techniques' which are denoted as follows:

- 'p' (extra weight for phrases in the Title and other properties plus extra weight for vector search on properties): The humWC05p score minus the humWC05none score.
- 'd' (modest extra weight for less deep urls): The humWC05dp score minus the humWC05p score.
- 'r' (extra weight for urls of root, subroot or path types): The humWC05rdp score minus the humWC05dp score.
- 'o' (domain filtering): The humWC05dpD0 score minus the humWC05dp score.
- 's' (stopwords specific to the language and possibly accent-indexing and inverse document frequency changes): The humWC05dpD score minus the humWC05dpD0 score.
- 'l' (linguistic expansion from stemming): The humWC05dplD score minus the humWC05dpD score.

Table 1 lists the mean scores of the 5 submitted runs (and the 2 other diagnostic runs in brackets). It also lists the mean scores over just named page (NP) and home page (HP) queries. Table 2 isolates the differences in 'first relevant score' (FRS) between the runs of Table 1. (To save close to a page, the column headings (and the retrieval measures such as FRS) are just defined in our companion ad hoc paper [10] in this volume.)

Findings from Table 2 include the following:

- The 'p' technique (extra weight for phrases in the Title and other properties plus extra weight for vector search on properties) was of statistically significant benefit for both named pages and home pages, which is consistent with our TREC results [12] except that the benefit was larger at TREC.
- The 'd' technique (modest extra weight for less deep urls) was of statistically significant benefit for home pages and neutral on average for named pages, which is consistent with our TREC results except that the mean benefit for home pages was larger at TREC.
- The 'r' technique (strong extra weight for urls of root, subroot or path types) was less detrimental than we expected for named pages and less helpful than we expected for home pages compared to our TREC results.

Table 1. Mean Scores of Submitted WebCLEF Runs

Run	FRS	Success@1	Success@5	Success@10	MRR
humWC05dplD	0.635	212/547 (39%)	315/547 (58%)	356/547 (65%)	0.478
humWC05dpD	0.627	204/547 (37%)	314/547 (57%)	353/547 (65%)	0.471
(humWC05dpD0)	0.603	197/547 (36%)	303/547 (55%)	343/547 (63%)	0.449
humWC05rdp	0.589	195/547 (36%)	293/547 (54%)	330/547 (60%)	0.441
humWC05dp	0.583	190/547 (35%)	292/547 (53%)	327/547 (60%)	0.433
humWC05p	0.559	182/547 (33%)	276/547 (50%)	318/547 (58%)	0.415
(humWC05none)	0.513	152/547 (28%)	253/547 (46%)	284/547 (52%)	0.365
NP: dplD	0.726	139/305 (46%)	204/305 (67%)	229/305 (75%)	0.560
NP: dpD	0.720	142/305 (47%)	207/305 (68%)	228/305 (75%)	0.571
NP: dpD0	0.698	141/305 (46%)	202/305 (66%)	223/305 (73%)	0.552
NP: rdp	0.662	132/305 (43%)	187/305 (61%)	206/305 (68%)	0.517
NP: dp	0.669	134/305 (44%)	192/305 (63%)	210/305 (69%)	0.526
NP: p	0.669	133/305 (44%)	193/305 (63%)	212/305 (70%)	0.527
NP: none	0.648	119/305 (39%)	187/305 (61%)	203/305 (67%)	0.492
HP: dplD	0.521	73/242 (30%)	111/242 (46%)	127/242 (52%)	0.375
HP: dpD	0.509	62/242 (26%)	107/242 (44%)	125/242 (52%)	0.345
HP: dpD0	0.484	56/242 (23%)	101/242 (42%)	120/242 (50%)	0.319
HP: rdp	0.497	63/242 (26%)	106/242 (44%)	124/242 (51%)	0.345
HP: dp	0.474	56/242 (23%)	100/242 (41%)	117/242 (48%)	0.317
HP: p	0.420	49/242 (20%)	83/242 (34%)	106/242 (44%)	0.275
HP: none	0.343	33/242 (14%)	66/242 (27%)	81/242 (33%)	0.205

Table 2. Impact of Web Techniques on First Relevant Score

Expt	ΔFRS	95% Conf	vs.	3 Extreme Diffs (Topic)
o-NP	0.029	(0.015, 0.042)	44-0-261	1.00 (285), 0.87 (292), 0.00 (289)
s-NP	0.022	(0.007, 0.037)	43-24-238	−0.88 (527), 0.76 (477), 0.87 (116)
p-NP	0.021	(0.007, 0.035)	65-28-212	−0.83 (292), −0.64 (477), 0.59 (415)
l-NP	0.006	(−0.014, 0.025)	47-59-199	1.00 (112), 0.95 (402), −0.78 (157)
d-NP	0.000	(−0.005, 0.005)	24-37-244	0.40 (377), 0.17 (524), −0.14 (423)
r-NP	−0.008	(−0.018, 0.003)	18-49-238	−0.87 (469), −0.46 (528), 0.68 (418)
p-HP	0.077	(0.050, 0.105)	82-19-141	1.00 (101), 0.98 (313), −0.92 (435)
d-HP	0.054	(0.032, 0.075)	64-20-158	1.00 (453), 0.91 (52), −0.40 (290)
s-HP	0.025	(0.005, 0.044)	53-21-168	0.91 (39), −0.76 (346), −0.79 (20)
r-HP	0.023	(−0.009, 0.054)	53-48-141	−1.00 (148), −0.93 (246), 0.92 (32)
l-HP	0.012	(−0.011, 0.036)	41-50-151	0.96 (123), 0.93 (124), −0.68 (324)
o-HP	0.010	(0.003, 0.017)	22-0-220	0.43 (432), 0.40 (507), 0.00 (546)

– The 'o' technique (domain filtering), as expected, never caused the score to go down on any topic (as the 'vs.' column shows) because it just included rows from the known domain. But the benefit was not large on average, so apparently the unfiltered queries usually were not confused much by the extra domains.

- The 's' technique (stopwords specific to the language and possibly accent-indexing and inverse document frequency changes) was a surprise in that it led to a statistically significant benefit for both named pages and home pages. We look at this more below.
- The 'l' technique (linguistic expansion from stemming) was of neutral impact on average, but it could make a substantial difference for individual queries as we will see below.

We focus on Danish and Greek queries below because this is the first time we have had judged test collections for these languages. In particular, we focus on the impact of the 's' and 'l' techniques, i.e. the impacts of stopwords (and accents) and stemming.

4.1 Danish Retrieval

Table 3 lists the mean scores for the 19 Danish named page queries and 11 Danish home page queries, and Table 4 shows the largest per-topic differences in First Relevant Score for each experiment. The following 3 topics particularly illustrate Danish linguistic variations:

Table 3. Mean Scores of WebCLEF Runs on Danish Queries

Run	FRS	Success@1	Success@5	Success@10	MRR
dplD-NP-DA	0.807	12/19 (63%)	14/19 (74%)	15/19 (79%)	0.693
dpD-NP-DA	0.798	11/19 (58%)	15/19 (79%)	16/19 (84%)	0.661
dpD0-NP-DA	0.759	11/19 (58%)	14/19 (74%)	15/19 (79%)	0.632
p-NP-DA	0.758	10/19 (53%)	13/19 (68%)	15/19 (79%)	0.616
dp-NP-DA	0.754	11/19 (58%)	13/19 (68%)	15/19 (79%)	0.629
rdp-NP-DA	0.743	10/19 (53%)	13/19 (68%)	15/19 (79%)	0.593
none-NP-DA	0.704	9/19 (47%)	12/19 (63%)	14/19 (74%)	0.550
rdp-HP-DA	0.336	1/11 (9%)	2/11 (18%)	4/11 (36%)	0.158
dpD-HP-DA	0.320	1/11 (9%)	2/11 (18%)	4/11 (36%)	0.147
dpD0-HP-DA	0.310	0/11 (0%)	2/11 (18%)	3/11 (27%)	0.108
dp-HP-DA	0.310	0/11 (0%)	2/11 (18%)	3/11 (27%)	0.108
dplD-HP-DA	0.301	1/11 (9%)	1/11 (9%)	3/11 (27%)	0.135
p-HP-DA	0.242	0/11 (0%)	1/11 (9%)	2/11 (18%)	0.067
none-HP-DA	0.163	0/11 (0%)	1/11 (9%)	1/11 (9%)	0.052

WC0233: Table 4 shows that the biggest impact of switching to the Danish-specific stopfile was a 71 point increase in FRS on topic 233 (presserum europæiske kantor for bekæmpelse af svig (press room of the european anti fraud office)). Without having 'af' as a stopword, the first relevant rank fell from 2 to 21. This appears to be a similar finding to Greek topic WC0445 (examined below) in that a common word in one language was uncommon enough in the mixed language collection to be assigned a high enough inverse document frequency to cause trouble. (Our Danish stoplist was based on Porter's [4].) With stemming enabled, the rank increased from 2 to 1 for this topic, in part because of an extra 'bekaempelse' match in the meta keywords and also from an extra 'Europaeiske' match in body. The SearchServer stemmer handled the æ vs. ae variation of Danish (the query words used the one-character ligature (æ) while the document words used two letters ('a' and 'e')).

Table 4. Impact of Web Techniques on First Relevant Score, Danish Queries

Expt	ΔFRS	95% Conf	vs.	3 Extreme Diffs (Topic)
p-NP-DA	0.053	(0.003, 0.104)	7-1-11	0.39 (311), 0.25 (329), −0.07 (264)
s-NP-DA	0.040	(−0.037, 0.116)	2-1-16	0.71 (233), 0.12 (329), −0.08 (58)
l-NP-DA	0.008	(−0.050, 0.067)	4-1-14	−0.43 (329), 0.13 (311), 0.25 (219)
o-NP-DA	0.005	(−0.002, 0.013)	2-0-17	0.05 (329), 0.04 (58), 0.00 (481)
d-NP-DA	−0.004	(−0.035, 0.027)	2-4-13	0.14 (454), 0.14 (329), −0.14 (58)
r-NP-DA	−0.011	(−0.027, 0.005)	0-3-16	−0.14 (211), −0.05 (329), 0.00 (232)
p-HP-DA	0.079	(0.013, 0.144)	6-0-5	0.27 (80), 0.23 (48), 0.00 (429)
d-HP-DA	0.068	(−0.076, 0.211)	2-1-8	0.78 (286), 0.02 (392), −0.05 (53)
r-HP-DA	0.027	(−0.013, 0.066)	3-0-8	0.21 (385), 0.07 (286), 0.00 (429)
s-HP-DA	0.011	(−0.034, 0.055)	4-3-4	0.15 (80), 0.07 (286), −0.13 (48)
o-HP-DA	0.000	n/a	0-0-11	0.00 (317), 0.00 (53), 0.00 (429)
l-HP-DA	−0.019	(−0.069, 0.030)	3-2-6	−0.21 (317), −0.13 (48), 0.08 (392)

WC0392: Another interesting Danish stemming case was topic 392 (Rigsombudsmanden i Grønland (the high commissioner of greenland)). With stemming, the rank of the desired page increased from 24 to 19. The extra matches from stemming were 'Rigsombudsmand' and 'Groenland' (the latter occurred in the filenames of img tags, which we indexed). The SearchServer stemmer matched the query form using the Danish o with stroke (ø) with the two-letter variant ('oe').

WC0317: On topic 317 (økologisk landbrug i europa (organic farming in europe)), the rank of the desired page actually fell from 4 to 8 with stemming, even though the additional matches of 'okologisk' (in the meta keywords) and 'landbrugets' look proper. (As an aside, the compound 'landbrugspolitik' was not matched.) The relevance scores of the top documents were close together for this topic, so the fall in rank appears to be a chance result. Note that the cTREC text reader used for these experiments did not normalize the html entity reference 'Ø' to Ø (or most other entity references for that matter, which may have impaired the overall results for some languages). The SearchServer stemmer matched the query form using the Danish o with stroke (ø) with the one-letter variant ('o').

4.2 Greek Retrieval

Table 5 lists the mean scores for the 11 Greek named page queries and 5 Greek home page queries. The top-scoring runs used stemming (run humWC05dplD) or disabled accent-indexing (run humWC05dplD0). The run with accent-indexing and not stemming (humWC05dpD) did not score as highly on average. Table 6 shows that the 'l' technique (stemming, i.e. the dplD score minus the dpD score) was positive on average, while the 's' factor (the dpD score minus the dpD0 score, primarily isolating the impact of stopwords specific to the language, including specifying accent-indexing in the Greek case) was negative, and it lists the topics most affected by each technique in each direction, which we examine below. (In the topic analysis, the translations are based partly on the official topic translations and partly on the online Greek-to-English translation service at [1].)

Table 5. Mean Scores of WebCLEF Runs on Greek Queries

Run	FRS	Success@1	Success@5	Success@10	MRR
dplD-NP-EL	0.536	3/11 (27%)	5/11 (45%)	6/11 (55%)	0.363
dpD0-NP-EL	0.442	3/11 (27%)	5/11 (45%)	5/11 (45%)	0.316
dpD-NP-EL	0.398	1/11 (9%)	4/11 (36%)	5/11 (45%)	0.206
dp-NP-EL	0.306	3/11 (27%)	3/11 (27%)	3/11 (27%)	0.279
rdp-NP-EL	0.297	2/11 (18%)	3/11 (27%)	3/11 (27%)	0.233
p-NP-EL	0.291	3/11 (27%)	3/11 (27%)	3/11 (27%)	0.277
none-NP-EL	0.287	2/11 (18%)	3/11 (27%)	3/11 (27%)	0.232
dpD0-HP-EL	0.657	2/5 (40%)	3/5 (60%)	3/5 (60%)	0.483
dplD-HP-EL	0.571	2/5 (40%)	3/5 (60%)	3/5 (60%)	0.467
rdp-HP-EL	0.571	2/5 (40%)	3/5 (60%)	3/5 (60%)	0.467
dp-HP-EL	0.571	2/5 (40%)	3/5 (60%)	3/5 (60%)	0.467
dpD-HP-EL	0.532	1/5 (20%)	3/5 (60%)	3/5 (60%)	0.340
p-HP-EL	0.480	1/5 (20%)	2/5 (40%)	3/5 (60%)	0.289
none-HP-EL	0.430	1/5 (20%)	2/5 (40%)	2/5 (40%)	0.278

WC0112: Table 6 shows that the biggest impact of Greek stemming was on topic 112 (Πλήρης λίστα των υπουργών και υφυπουργών όλων υπουργείων της Ελληνικής κυβέρνησης (List of ministers and deputy ministers for all the ministries of the Greek government)). The desired page was not retrieved in the top-50 without inflecting because the key query terms were plurals (υπουργών (ministers), υφυπουργών (undersecretaries), υπουργείων (ministries)) while the desired page just contained singular forms (Υπουργός (Minister), Υφυπουργός (Undersecretary), Υπουργείο (Ministry)).

WC0395: Table 6 shows that the next biggest impact of Greek stemming was on topic 395 (Ο ΄Ελληνας πρωθυπουργός και το μήνυμά του (The Greek Prime Minister and his message)). With stemming, the desired page was found at rank

Table 6. Impact of Web Techniques on First Relevant Score, Greek Queries

Expt	ΔFRS	95% Conf	vs.	3 Extreme Diffs (Topic)
l-NP-EL	0.138	(−0.056, 0.333)	5-2-4	1.00 (112), 0.34 (395), −0.15 (403)
o-NP-EL	0.136	(−0.015, 0.288)	3-0-8	0.74 (403), 0.40 (395), 0.00 (266)
d-NP-EL	0.015	(−0.016, 0.046)	1-0-10	0.17 (524), 0.00 (151), 0.00 (266)
p-NP-EL	0.004	(−0.012, 0.020)	1-1-9	0.07 (184), 0.00 (151), −0.03 (524)
r-NP-EL	−0.009	(−0.024, 0.005)	0-2-9	−0.07 (184), −0.03 (524), 0.00 (266)
s-NP-EL	−0.045	(−0.117, 0.028)	1-4-6	−0.34 (395), −0.14 (498), 0.13 (445)
d-HP-EL	0.092	(−0.092, 0.276)	1-0-4	0.46 (366), 0.00 (271), 0.00 (25)
o-HP-EL	0.086	(−0.086, 0.258)	1-0-4	0.43 (432), 0.00 (366), 0.00 (25)
p-HP-EL	0.050	(−0.050, 0.150)	1-0-4	0.25 (366), 0.00 (271), 0.00 (25)
l-HP-EL	0.039	(−0.012, 0.090)	2-0-3	0.12 (366), 0.07 (271), 0.00 (25)
r-HP-EL	0.000	n/a	0-0-5	0.00 (271), 0.00 (366), 0.00 (25)
s-HP-EL	−0.125	(−0.316, 0.066)	1-2-2	−0.43 (432), −0.26 (366), 0.07 (271)

13 instead of 39, a 34 point increase in FRS (in the reciprocal rank measure, this would just be a 5 point increase). Without stemming, the only matching word was του (his) which probably should have been a stopword. With stemming, the query word πρωθυπουργός (Prime Minister) matched the document's variant (Πρωθυπουργού). Because we enabled indexing of Greek accents for our lexical Greek stemmer, the query word μήνυμά (message) did not match the document form Μήνυμα (which did not include an accent on the last character; the first letter is just an lowercase-uppercase difference which all runs handled by normalizing Unicode to uppercase). Note that the humWC05dpD0 run did match Μήνυμα because it did not enable accent-indexing; presumably this is why the s-NP-EL line of Table 6 shows that switching to the Greek-specific stopfile (which enabled accent indexing) decreased FRS 34 points for this topic. For most languages, our lexical stemmers are accent-insensitive; apparently we should investigate doing the same for Greek.

WC0432: Table 6 shows that the biggest impact of switching to the Greek-specific stopfile was a detrimental impact on topic 432 (Είσοδος Ελληνικής ιςτοσελίδας για τη συνέλευση για το μέλλον της Ευρώπης (Greek home page of the convention for the future of Europe)). The desired page was found at rank 12 without accent-indexing but was not retrieved in the top-50 with accent-indexing. The humWC05dpD0 run matched the document title terms which were in uppercase and did not have accents, particularly ΣΥΝΕΛΕΥΣΗ (ASSEMBLY), ΜΕΛΛΟΝ (FUTURE) and ΕΥΡΩΠΗΣ (EUROPE). The corresponding query words had accents: συνέλευση (assembly), μέλλον (future) and Ευρώπης (Europe). This issue would presumably impair the 'p' web technique (extra weight on properties such as the title) because title words are often in uppercase and apparently, in Greek, uppercase words often omit the accents. (Incidentally, the o-HP-EL line of Table 6 shows that domain filtering (restricting to the .gr domain) was useful for this query; without it, even without accent-indexing, the retrieved pages were mostly from the .eu.int domain.)

WC0445: Table 6 shows that the biggest positive impact of switching to the Greek-specific stopfile was on topic 445 (Πληροφορίες επικοινωνίας όλων των υπουργείων της Ελληνικής κυβέρνησης (Contact information of all the ministries of the Greek government)). The reason seems to be that the non-content words in the query (such as των (of) and της (her)) generated spurrious matches in the humWC05dpD0 run (which did not use Greek-specific stopwords), pushing down the desired page from rank 28 to beyond the top-50. Normally, common words have little effect on the ranking because they have a low inverse document frequency (idf), but in this mixed language collection, common words in the Greek documents are still fairly uncommon overall, and hence get relatively more weight. This topic illustrates why stopword processing may be of more importance in mixed language collections than in single language collections.

5 Conclusions

Danish and Greek web search is a microcosm of mixed monolingual web retrieval. Stemming can be quite helpful, accent mismatches are common (especially in the important Title field of web documents), and stopwords common in one language may be over-weighted in a mixed language collection by traditional idf formulations.

References

1. AltaVista's Babel Fish Translation Service. http://babelfish.altavista.com/tr
2. Cross-Language Evaluation Forum web site. http://www.clef-campaign.org/
3. Andrew Hodgson. Converting the Fulcrum Search Engine to Unicode. *Sixteenth International Unicode Conference*, 2000.
4. M. F. Porter. Snowball: A language for stemming algorithms. October 2001. http://snowball.tartarus.org/texts/introduction.html
5. S. E. Robertson, S. Walker, S. Jones, M. M. Hancock-Beaulieu and M. Gatford. Okapi at TREC-3. *Proceedings of TREC-3*, 1995.
6. Jacques Savoy. CLEF and Multilingual information retrieval resource page. http://www.unine.ch/info/clef/
7. Börkur Sigurbjörnsson, Jaap Kamps and Maarten de Rijke. EuroGOV: Engineering a Multilingual Web Corpus. *This volume.*
8. Börkur Sigurbjörnsson, Jaap Kamps and Maarten de Rijke. Overview of WebCLEF 2005. *This volume.*
9. Text REtrieval Conference (TREC) Home Page. http://trec.nist.gov/
10. Stephen Tomlinson. Bulgarian and Hungarian Experiments with Hummingbird SearchServer™ at CLEF 2005. *This volume.*
11. Stephen Tomlinson. Experiments in Named Page Finding and Arabic Retrieval with Hummingbird SearchServer™ at TREC 2002. *Proceedings of TREC 2002.*
12. Stephen Tomlinson. Robust, Web and Terabyte Retrieval with Hummingbird SearchServer™ at TREC 2004. *Proceedings of TREC 2004.*
13. Thijs Westerveld, Wessel Kraaij and Djoerd Hiemstra. Retrieving Web Pages using Content, Links, URLs and Anchors. *Proceedings of TREC 2001.*

Combination Methods for Crosslingual Web Retrieval

Jaap Kamps[1,2], Maarten de Rijke[2], and Börkur Sigurbjörnsson[2]

[1] Archives and Information Science, Faculty of Humanities, University of Amsterdam
[2] ISLA, Faculty of Science, University of Amsterdam
{kamps, mdr, borkur}@science.uva.nl

Abstract. We investigate a range of crosslingual web retrieval tasks using the test suite of the CLEF 2005 WebCLEF track, which features a stream of known-item topics in various languages. Our main findings are: (i) straightforward indexing and retrieval is effective for mixed monolingual web retrieval; (ii) standard machine translation methods are effective for bilingual web retrieval; but (iii) standard combination methods are ineffective for multilingual web retrieval; we analyze the failure and suggest an alternative Z-score normalization that leads to effective multilingual retrieval results.

1 Introduction

The web presents one of the greatest challenges for crosslingual information retrieval. Web data is much noisier than traditional collections of newswire and newspaper data originated from a single source. Also, the linguistic variety in the collection makes it harder to apply language-dependent processing methods such as stemming algorithms. Moreover, the size of the web only allows for methods that scale well, casting doubt on the practicality of language-independent methods such as character n-gramming.

We investigate a range of approaches to crosslingual web retrieval using the test suite of the CLEF 2005 WebCLEF track, featuring a stream of known-item topics in various languages. First, we focus on the *mixed monolingual* task. We aim to evaluate the robustness of modern information retrieval techniques, by applying standard ad hoc retrieval settings for a stream of monolingual topics in various languages. Second, we focus on a range of bilingual retrieval tasks using the English translations of the WebCLEF 2005 topics. Here, our aim is to evaluate the effectiveness of machine translation for known-item search in various languages. Third, we focus on the *multilingual* task, where there is a stream of English topics targeting pages in a range of languages. Here, we investigate whether the effectiveness of straightforward run combinations carries over to crosslingual web retrieval. Such methods have previously been used successfully at earlier CLEF monolingual and multilingual ad hoc retrieval tasks [6, 7].

This paper is structured as follows. In Section 2 we describe our retrieval system as well as the specific approaches to crosslingual web retrieval. Section 3

C. Peters et al. (Eds.): CLEF 2005, LNCS 4022, pp. 856–864, 2006.

describes our mixed monolingual experiments. The next two sections discuss our multilingual experiments, focusing on translations to individual languages in Section 4, and on combinations for all languages in Section 5. Finally, in Section 6, we offer some conclusions regarding our crosslingual web retrieval efforts.

2 System Description

Our retrieval system is based on the Lucene engine with a number of home-grown extensions [3, 9].

For our ranking, we used the default similarity measure in Lucene [9], i.e., for a collection D, document d and query q containing terms t_i:

$$sim(q,d) = \sum_{t \in q} \frac{tf_{t,q} \cdot idf_t}{norm_q} \cdot \frac{tf_{t,d} \cdot idf_t}{norm_d} \cdot coord_{q,d} \cdot weight_t,$$

where

$$\begin{aligned} tf_{t,X} &= \sqrt{\text{freq}(t,X)}, \\ idf_t &= 1 + \log \frac{|D|}{\text{freq}(t,D)}, \\ norm_d &= \sqrt{|d|}, \\ coord_{q,d} &= \frac{|q \cap d|}{|q|}, \text{ and} \\ norm_q &= \sqrt{\sum_{t \in q} tf_{t,q} \cdot {idf_t}^2}. \end{aligned}$$

We indexed the whole collection by simply extracting the full text from the documents. We did not apply any stemming nor did we use a stopword list. We applied case-folding and normalized marked characters to their unmarked counterparts, i.e., mapping ö to o, æ to ae, î to i, etc. The only language specific processing we did was a transformation of the multiple Russian encodings into an ASCII transliteration.

We used the WorldLingo machine translation [12] for translating the English topic statements into eight languages: Dutch, French, German, Greek, Italian, Portuguese, Russian, and Spanish. Combined with the English source topic statements, this gave us short topic statements in nine European languages.

We combine the results for runs with different translations of the topics using both rank-based methods, in particular a straightforward round robin approach, as well as score-based methods, such as the unweighted CombSUM function of Fox and Shaw [2]. The score-based methods were applied after normalizing the similarity scores. First, we use min-max normalization, $s' = \frac{s - min}{max - min}$, with *min* (*max*) the minimal (maximal) score over all topics in the run. The min-max normalization was also used in [8]. Second, we use the Z-score normalization, $s' = \frac{s-\mu_i}{\delta_i}$, with μ_i the mean retrieval status value and δ_i the standard deviation for topic i. A variant of Z-score normalization was used earlier in [11].

3 Mixed Monolingual Experiments

For the mixed monolingual task, we investigate the effectiveness of standard ad hoc retrieval settings for a stream of topics in various languages. We create a single run using the short topic statement in the ⟨title⟩ field of the WebCLEF 2005 topics. Our run uses Lucene's standard ranking formula applied on our full-text index (as discussed in Section 2 above). The resulting run was submitted to the WebCLEF 2005 mixed monolingual task.

Table 1 reports the results of the mixed monolingual run. A number of observations present themselves. First, we see that, on average, the desired page is found in the top three. That is a reassuring result for the mixed monolingual task. Somewhat worrying is the success rate at rank 10, with no relevant page found for over 40% of the topics. Second, when breaking down the score over the two topic types, named page topics score somewhat higher than home page topics, on all measures. This is well-known from other web retrieval tasks [1], which also suggests that the scores for home page finding can be substantially improved using specific web centric techniques such as various document representations and non-content priors [4]. Third, when zooming in on the different topic languages, we see that we score reasonably well over all languages. The exception are the Greek topics; because of a technical problem, the Greek topics were processed as Russian and characters outside the expected character range where treated as noise and removed.

Table 1. Mixed Monolingual Task results by mean reciprocal rank and success at rank 1, 5 and 10

	# Topics	MRR	S@1	S@5	S@10
All topics	547	.3497	.2523	.4589	.5576
Home pages	242	.2263	.1322	.3347	.4380
Named pages	305	.4476	.3475	.5574	.6525
Danish	30	.2288	.1667	.3000	.4333
Dutch	59	.5245	.4068	.6610	.7966
English	121	.3345	.2231	.4628	.5785
French	1	1.000	1.000	1.000	1.000
German	57	.3736	.2456	.5263	.6316
Greek	16	.0000	.0000	.0000	.0000
Hungarian	35	.3731	.2571	.5143	.5714
Icelandic	5	.4654	.4000	.6000	.6000
Portuguese	59	.1934	.1017	.3051	.3898
Russian	30	.3033	.2667	.3333	.4000
Spanish	134	.4091	.3134	.5000	.5970

Table 2. Bilingual results by mean reciprocal rank and success at rank 1, 5 and 10

	Restricted to language					All 547 topics			
	# Topics	MRR	S@1	S@5	S@10	MRR	S@1	S@5	S@10
Dutch	59	.2709	.2203	.3051	.3729	.0540	.0420	.0640	.0823
English	121	.3289	.2149	.4628	.5702	.0882	.0585	.1207	.1499
French	1	1.000	1.000	1.000	1.000	.0303	.0201	.0366	.0494
German	57	.2008	.1754	.1930	.2807	.0447	.0329	.0530	.0695
Greek	16	.0000	.0000	.0000	.0000	.0204	.0146	.0256	.0329
Italian	0	–	–	–	–	.0284	.0201	.0366	.0475
Portuguese	59	.1047	.0508	.1525	.1695	.0412	.0256	.0567	.0713
Russian	30	.0127	.0000	.0333	.0333	.0446	.0293	.0567	.0750
Spanish	134	.2272	.1791	.2687	.3582	.0809	.0603	.0969	.1316

4 Bilingual Experiments

Although there was no separate bilingual task at WebCLEF 2005, the multilingual topics can be used to evaluate the effectiveness of the individual translations, resulting in a whole range of bilingual retrieval experiments. All runs use the English version of the short topic statement in the ⟨translation language="EN"⟩ field of the WebCLEF 2005 topics. We generate the eight translations mentioned in Section 2 above. Note that the nine languages that we cover in total differ somewhat from the languages in the WebCLEF 2005 topic set. The topic set also has topics in Danish, Hungarian, and Icelandic. Furthermore, we have a translation of the English topics into Italian, whereas the topic set contains no topics in Italian.

Table 2 lists the results of the translated queries, both evaluated against the whole topic set, as well as against all topics targeting a page in the language at hand. We see the following. First, when looking at the restricted topic sets, effectiveness varies from total failure (Greek) to perfection (French). The score for the five frequent languages is reasonable compared to those of the mixed monolingual task. Hence, one may conclude that the automatic topic translations are effective. Second, when evaluated over all topics, the scores are generally unimpressive and mirroring the frequency with which a topic of the given language appears in the topic set. This comes as no surprise, given that the topic set covers eleven languages, and each of the topic translations will dominantly target only one of them. Third, the translated topics pick up relevant pages in languages other than the target language. In particular, the Italian topics do pick up a relevant page for 35 of the topics.

5 Multilingual Experiments

We move on to the multilingual task, and investigate the effectiveness of combinations of the individual bilingual runs. We experimented along two dimensions. The first dimension is the number of topic languages:

All translations Assuming that we have no knowledge of the language of the desired pages for each of the topics, it makes sense to use all available translations. That is, we use the topics in all nine languages available.

Five languages Based on knowledge of the languages in the WebCLEF topic set, we restrict the set of languages to those that occur frequently and for which we have reasonable translation methods. That is, we use the topics in the five languages: Dutch, English, German, Portuguese, and Spanish.

Recall that WebCLEF provides a stream of topics, with topics from arbitrary languages. For the multilingual task, we use the English short topic statement. The downside of this is, of course, that finding the targeted page in the source language becomes a formidable problem. The upside is that, at least, the topic language is known, and the same holds for the translations we obtained.

The second dimension we experiment with is trying to exploit this knowledge:

All results Topics in one language may likely retrieve pages in other languages as well. A case in point is WebCLEF topic WC0014, whose English topic statement ("Chancellery at the Spreebogen") could still allow us to retrieve German pages targeted by the German topic statement ("*Bundeskanzleramt am Spreebogen*"). Hence, we may simply use all pages retrieved by a topic of a particular, known language.

Language restricted Since we know the language of the topic in each of the translations, and the intention of the translated topic is to retrieve pages in that language, we may decide to restrict the pages returned by our retrieval system. We do this by restricting retrieved pages to the dominant domains. For example, for a run with the topics translated to Dutch, we restrict pages to come from either the `.nl` or the `.eu.int` domain, and similar for German, we restrict pages to come from either `.de` or `.eu.int`.[1]

Combining the two dimensions naturally suggests four different sets of bilingual runs. These are combined using unweighted CombSUM using the min-max normalization. The resulting four runs were submitted to the WebCLEF 2005 multilingual task.

5.1 CombSUM with Min-Max Normalization

Table 3 reports the result of the multilingual runs. Again, we make a number of observations. First, we see that scores are substantially lower than for the mixed monolingual task. The complexity of the multilingual task can hardly be overestimated: given an English query we have to guess what page in any language has to be returned to the user. Obvious ways of limiting this wealth of options are the use of topic meta-fields, or of sophisticated techniques to extract target language cues. Second, our experiment with the number of translations to use points to the smaller set of five language used frequently in the topic set. It

[1] Note that we mainly aim for precision here, we ignore domains such as `.be` (Belgium) and `.at` (Austria) where Dutch or German pages, respectively, are abundant.

Table 3. Multilingual Task results by mean reciprocal rank and success at rank 1, 5 and 10

Number of	All topics				Home pages				Named pages			
Languages	MRR	S@1	S@5	S@10	MRR	S@1	S@5	S@10	MRR	S@1	S@5	S@10
Nine	.0092	.0055	.0073	.0165	.0072	.0041	.0083	.0124	.0109	.0066	.0066	.0197
Nine, restr.	.0157	.0091	.0201	.0219	.0157	.0124	.0165	.0165	.0158	.0066	.0230	.0262
Five	.0109	.0055	.0091	.0165	.0084	.0041	.0083	.0124	.0129	.0066	.0098	.0197
Five, restr.	.0166	.0091	.0201	.0238	.0163	.0124	.0165	.0207	.0168	.0066	.0230	.0262

is a reassuring fact that the improvement is moderate, and the extended set of translations is far from detrimental to the performance. Note that the extended set includes, for example, Italian, which is not used in any of the topics. Third, our experiment with restricting our intention to pages in the language of the topic translation is successful. Fourth, the single topic language runs in Table 2 are much more effective than the combined multilingual runs, even when evaluated against the total topic set. This is a disappointing result, and clearly indicates that the straightforward run combination is ineffective. On a more positive note, however, the results for the individual translations strongly suggest that more sensible methods are possible.

5.2 Rank-Based Combination: Round Robin

We saw above that the quality of our multilingual run combinations poorly reflects the quality of the individual bilingual runs. If we look, again, at the individual language results in Table 2, we see that already the success rate at rank 1 is higher than the mean reciprocal rank for the combination runs in Table 3. Hence a combination method that preserves the order of the individual runs will be more effective. We apply a straightforward rank-based combination method, round robin, in which the individual bilingual runs are interleaved. Specifically, we only return the same document once per topic, ordering languages alphabetically by their two character iso-codes, resulting in German, Greek, English, Spanish, French, Italian, Dutch, Portuguese, and Russian. Hence, the success rate at rank 1 will be identical to that of the bilingual English to German run evaluated over all topics.

Table 4 shows the results of applying the round-robin combination. Indeed, the rank-based round robin is much more effective than the results for CombSUM

Table 4. Round robin combination results by mean reciprocal rank and success at rank 1, 5 and 10

Number of	All topics				Home pages				Named pages			
Languages	MRR	S@1	S@5	S@10	MRR	S@1	S@5	S@10	MRR	S@1	S@5	S@10
Nine	.0763	.0329	.1335	.1883	.0551	.0248	.0992	.1322	.0930	.0393	.1607	.2328
Nine, restr.	.0535	.0238	.0951	.1298	.0458	.0248	.0785	.0992	.0597	.0230	.1082	.1541
Five	.0944	.0329	.1700	.2194	.0704	.0248	.1198	.1570	.1135	.0393	.2098	.2689
Five, restr.	.0687	.0238	.1243	.1645	.0575	.0248	.0950	.1157	.0776	.0230	.1475	.2033

in Table 3. In fact, the combination of the five frequent languages in the topic set outperforms the best individual language run. The restriction to domains corresponding to the languages of the translations is now detrimental to the performance.

The effectiveness of rank-based round-robin combinations can be attributed to the fact that highly ranked documents in the combination are also highly ranked by some of the bilingual runs. The earlier applied combination method, CombSUM, tends to favor documents receiving scores in several of the bilingual runs. The results show that this is an undesirable behavior for the task at hand. This may be explained by the fact that the task is known-item retrieval, and this single, relevant page is generally retrieved by at most one of the bilingual runs.

5.3 CombSUM with Z-Score Normalization

As we saw in Section 4, each of the bilingual runs is also capable of retrieving relevant documents in another language. That is, we may expect there to be some middle ground in which the combination does largely respect the rankings of pages in the individual bilingual runs, but at the same time does reward pages returned by several runs.

We focus on score normalization. Earlier we used the Min-Max normalization, which results in a simple linear transformation of the original scores into values between 0 and 1. We want to come up with a score normalization that gives a relatively higher weight to top ranking documents. A standard method for score normalization is the Z-score: values are normalized to the number of standard deviations that they are higher (or lower) than the mean score. At first sight, this only makes sense for normally distributed values, for example because documents not retrieved will have the mean score of the retrieved documents. On closer inspection, this will yield exactly the properties we desire. Since the similarity scores will be very skewed, with a long tail approaching zero, the mean and standard deviation will be very small. Hence, the top scoring documents will receive relatively high scores, but the score is steeply declining.

Table 5 shows the results of applying CombSUM combination to relevance scores being normalized with the Z-score value. We see that the Z-score normalization is far more effective than the Min-Max normalization in Table 3. It also improves over the rank-based round robin combination in Table 4.

Table 5. Combination results based on Z-score normalization by mean reciprocal rank and success at rank 1, 5, and 10

Number of	All topics				Home pages				Named pages			
Languages	MRR	S@1	S@5	S@10	MRR	S@1	S@5	S@10	MRR	S@1	S@5	S@10
Nine	.0914	.0494	.1298	.1846	.0659	.0372	.0992	.1364	.1186	.0689	.1705	.2197
Nine, restr.	.0638	.0347	.0859	.1371	.0467	.0289	.0579	.0868	.0674	.0295	.1016	.1705
Five	.1096	.0640	.1609	.2029	.0770	.0413	.1157	.1529	.1352	.0820	.1967	.2590
Five, restr.	.0841	.0475	.1261	.1572	.0649	.0413	.0909	.1074	.0947	.0492	.1475	.2000

Table 6. Combination results based on domain information by mean reciprocal rank and success at rank 1, 5 and 10. Top half: using nine languages. Bottom half: using five languages.

Combination	All topics				Home pages				Named pages			
Method	MRR	S@1	S@5	S@10	MRR	S@1	S@5	S@10	MRR	S@1	S@5	S@10
Min-Max	.0530	.0165	.0731	.1353	.0474	.0165	.0744	.1074	.0574	.0164	.0721	.1574
Round robin	.1382	.0676	.2267	.2834	.1038	.0579	.1612	.2107	.1654	.0754	.2787	.3410
Z-score	.1605	.1042	.2303	.2797	.1104	.0661	.1653	.1983	.2001	.1344	.2820	.3443
Min-Max	.0612	.0219	.0823	.1609	.0523	.0207	.0785	.1281	.0683	.0230	.0852	.1869
Round robin	.1472	.0695	.2358	.2907	.1098	.0620	.1653	.2107	.1769	.0754	.2918	.3541
Z-score	.1676	.1079	.2468	.2852	.1193	.0785	.1777	.2025	.2060	.1311	.3016	.3508

5.4 Exploiting Additional Information: Target Domain

What if our user provides us with further information, such as the language or the domain of the desired page? We investigate this scenario by using some of the additional metadata fields. In particular, we use the additional information about the domain of the target page in the ⟨domain domain="*top-level domain*" /⟩ field. Table 6 shows the results of applying (i) CombSUM combination of the min-max normalization; (ii) round robin; and (iii) CombSUM combination of the Z-score normalization. We see that information about the domain of the desired page can effectively be exploited by all three combination methods. The relative effectiveness of the combination methods mimic the earlier combination scores closely, with the CombSUM method with Z-score normalization the most effective.

6 Conclusions

The EuroGOV collection used at the CLEF 2005 WebCLEF Track is based on a crawl of governmental information from a range of sites. Such a collection of web data is much noisier than traditional collections of newswire and newspaper data originating from a single source. Moreover, the linguistic variety in the collection makes it harder to apply language-specific processing methods such as stemming algorithms. Hence, we simply indexed the collection by extracting the full text from the documents. For our crosslingual web retrieval retrieval experiments we use a stream of known-item topics in various languages. For the *mixed monolingual* task, our main finding is that such a straightforward approach is relatively effective, even without specific web settings. Considering the fact that we are dealing with a stream of topics in eleven languages, and with an even greater number of languages in the collection, this sheds new light on the robustness of modern information retrieval techniques. For bilingual retrieval, we experimented with machine translations of the English queries. The individual query translations are relatively successful in targeting their share of relevant pages. For the *multilingual* task, we experimented with various combination methods. A standard CombSUM combination using Min-Max normalization is ineffective.

This result deviates from earlier experiences with combination methods for corpora in various languages [5], or with known-item retrieval on an English web corpus [10]. We show that rank-based combination methods fare much better, and propose an alternative Z-score normalization method that turns out to be effective for crosslingual web retrieval.

Acknowledgments. We want to thank Valentin Jijkoun for help with the Russian collection. This research was supported by the Netherlands Organization for Scientific Research (NWO) under project numbers 017.001.190, 220-80-001, 264-70-050, 354-20-005, 365-20-005, 612.000.106, 612.000.207, 612.013.001, 612.-066.302, 612.069.006, 640.001.501, and 640.002.501

Bibliography

[1] N. Craswell and D. Hawking. Overview of the TREC-2004 Web Track. In *Proceedings TREC 2004*, 2005.

[2] E. Fox and J. Shaw. Combination of multiple searches. In *The Second Text REtrieval Conference (TREC-2)*, pages 243–252. National Institute for Standards and Technology. NIST Special Publication 500-215, 1994.

[3] ILPS. The ILPS extension of the Lucene search engine, 2005. `http://ilps.science.uva.nl/Resources/`.

[4] J. Kamps. Web-centric language models. In *CIKM'05: Proceedings of the 14th ACM International Conference on Information and Knowledge Management*, pages 307–308, 2005.

[5] J. Kamps and M. de Rijke. The effectiveness of combining information retrieval strategies for European languages. In *Proceedings of the 2004 ACM Symposium on Applied Computing*, pages 1073–1077, 2004.

[6] J. Kamps, C. Monz, M. de Rijke, and B. Sigurbjörnsson. Language-dependent and language-independent approaches to cross-lingual text retrieval. In *Comparative Evaluation of Multilingual Information Access Systems, CLEF 2003*, pages 152–165, 2004.

[7] J. Kamps, S. Fissaha Adafre, and M. de Rijke. Effective translation, tokenization and combination for cross-lingual retrieval. In *Multilingual Information Access for Text, Speech and Images: Results of the Fifth CLEF Evaluation Campaign*, pages 123–134, 2005.

[8] J. Lee. Combining multiple evidence from different properties of weighting schemes. In *Proceedings of the 18th Annual International ACM SIGIR Conference on Research and Development in Information Retrieval*, pages 180–188, 1995.

[9] Lucene. The Lucene search engine, 2005. `http://lucene.apache.org/`.

[10] P. Ogilvie and J. Callan. Combining document representations for known-item search. In *Proceedings of the 26th Annual International ACM SIGIR Conference on Research and Development in Information Retrieval*, pages 143–150, 2003.

[11] J. Savoy. Report on CLEF-2003 multilingual tracks. In *Comparative Evaluation of Multilingual Information Access Systems, CLEF 2003*, pages 64–73, 2004.

[12] Worldlingo. Online translator, 2005. `http://www.worldlingo.com/`.

University of Alicante at the CLEF 2005 WebCLEF Track

Trinitario Martínez, Elisa Noguera, Rafael Muñoz, and Fernando Llopis

Language Processing and Information Systems Research Group
University of Alicante, Spain
{tme, elisa, rafael, llopis}@dlsi.ua.es

Abstract. This paper presents the first experiment done for the CLEF2005 WebCLEF Track. In the present work, we have focused our main efforts in the Spanish part of the Mixed Monolingual task, but we have also participated in several other languages tasks and in the Bilingual English-Spanish task. A passage- based IR system is applied in the retrieval phase. Also a language identifier has been created in order to build a fully automatic system without the need of knowing the topic language.

1 Introduction

Retrieving in a Multi/Crosslingual manner is a natural and common established way for carrying out web searches. The aim of this specific task is to find the correct document according to the description. This paper is structured as follows: the next section describes the collection and topics used, later we explain the corpus processing and retrieving, afterwards we show the results and conclusions, and finally we discuss about future improvements of the system.

2 Processing Phase

2.1 Data Preprocessing

As this is our first participation in this kind of scientific evaluations of IR, we have focused our efforts on Spanish monolingual queries, and have made some other approaches. We have divided the corpus by languages. Once HTML files are extracted:

1.Firstly, *title* and *keywords* fields are collected from the Eurogov corpuss.
2.Secondly, HTML code is replaced by its equivalent in ASCII.
3.Thirdly, regular expressions are used in order to remove special tags.
4.At the end of the process, id, keywords, title and plane text of each document is stored in order to form a plain input for the IR system (TREC format).

2.2 Retrieving Phase: IR-n System

IR-n is a passage retrieval system (RP). RP systems [4] locate in contiguous fragment of text (passages) and improve IR field by proposing a set of solutions to traditional IR systems common problems.

C. Peters et al. (Eds.): CLEF 2005, LNCS 4022, pp. 865 – 868, 2006.

For every language, the resources used were provided by the CLEF organizers (http://www.unine.ch/info/clef). There are stemmers and stopword lists for all languages except for Danish and Dutch. The indexing module has been modified to consider title and keywords tags. Words that are in these labels have more weight than words in the rest of the document in order to increase the value of the documents which have words of the query in the labels over the other ones. Finally, this year for the adhoc task a technique called combined passages has been implemented [5]. It applies fusion methods, which are used in multilingual tasks to combine results with the different size of passages.

3 WebCLEF Tasks

Although we have focused this paper in the Spanish scientific evaluation of IR, other languages have been taken into account. The targeted languages have been:

- Mixed Monolingual: Danish, Spanish, Dutch, German, English and Portuguese.
- Bilingual: English-to-Spanish.

3.1 Mixed Monolingual Task

In the monolingual task, topics have been divided by language so that they can be individually processed by the system.

3.1.1 Language Identification

As a baseline run, we have developed a language detector in order to automatically determine the correct language of the topic. These were the general aproaches:

- Dictionary based (joined dictionaries, specific per-language stopwords)
- Characterised part-of-word terminology (i.e. "ção" in the case of Portuguese)

This technique have been given us a good response in Spanish, English, Portuguese and Danish in other tasks. Also, it was used with Dutch and German. By separating per language the topics and the corpus a faster response of the system is obtained than when the whole corpus is considered.

3.2 BiEnEs Task

Our automatic approach has been performed by a merging of three different on-line translators (Freetranslator[1], BabelFish[2] and InterTran[3]). The main idea is that the words that appear in different translations have more relevancy that those that only appear in one translation.

---

[1] http://www.freetranslation.com/

[2] http://world.altavista.com/

[3] http://www.tranexp.com/win/itserver.htm

4 Results

4.1 Monolingual Task Results

In the process of our first experiment at WebCLEF2005, we focused on the Spanish Topics part of the Mixed Monolingual task. It must be mentioned that Spanish Topics are the greater subset of the topic set, so this is a relatively large subset of the score for WebCLEF2005 topics. We also have been performing experiments with other five languages. In Table 1, average success at ranks 1, 5, 10, 20 and 50 are shown, as well as the MRR. The last column shows the difference between our system and the average results.

Table 1. Mixed Monolingual official results per language

Language	Av. at 1	Av. at 5	Av. at 10	Av. at 20	Av. at 50	MRR	Dif
ES	0.1716	0.3134	0.3433	0 .373	0.4328	0.2377	+4,426
DA	0.0333	0.0667	0.0667	0.0667	0.0667	0.0500	-4,082
DE	0.1579	0.2105	0.2632	0.3158	0.3158	0.1907	-9,424
EN	0.0496	0.0744	0.0826	0.0826	0.0909	0.0614	-15,26
NL	0.1356	0.1525	0.1525	0.1695	0.1695	0.1451	-9,424
PT	0.0508	0.1695	0.1695	0.2034	0.2712	0.0833	-6,200

In Table 2, results for the application of the automatic language identifier in the Mixed Monolingual task are shown. Obviously, these results are equal or lower than the previous ones and they give us an idea about how a mechanized system would response. Identical results means that the language identifier has work perfectly.

Table 2. Mixed Monolingual with automatic language detection results

Language	Av. at 1	Av. At 5	Av. at 10	Av. at 20	Av. at 50	MRR
ES	0.1343	0.2612	0.3134	0.3582	0.4104	0.1995
DA	0.0333	0.0667	0.0667	0.0667	0.0667	0.0500
DE	0.0702	0.1053	0.1579	0.2105	0.2105	0.0942
EN	0.0496	0.0744	0.0826	0.0826	0.0909	0.0614
NL	0.0847	0.1017	0.1017	0.1186	0.1186	0.0943
PT	0.0508	0.0847	0.1017	0.1525	0.2203	0.0656

4.2 Bilingual English-Spanish Results

Clearly, the results obtained in this task are influenced by the results of the Spanish Monolingual task and also by the association of the three mentioned translators.

Table 3. Bilingual English-Spanish task

Av. at 1	Av. at 5	Av. at 10	Av. at 20	Av. at 50	MRR	Dif
0.0299	0.0522	0.0597	0.0746	0.0970	0.0395	-2,5028

5 Conclusions and Future Work

In this paper we have presented the first version of our system in the CLEF 2005 WebCLEF Track. In the Mixed Monolingual Task, in Spanish we are above the average, whilst in other languages the system has a lower performance (we have never worked before with Danish nor Dutch).

In the automatic language detection process, we regret not having a better language identifier. The one used here has been a fast developed attempt, but it is not perfect. In the Bilingual English to Spanish task, the conclusion is clear: general purpose machine translators are not a proper tool, due to the fact that the retrieving collection is focused in a determined scope, such as governmental processes. Our 3-translator association works better than one translator in its own, but this is not the ideal solution yet, and we consider the requirement of a specialized translator a must. Finally, we have found that keyword tags extracted from EuroGOV were adding so much noise to the system, because documents can have several governmental scope keywords. This is why they are not working perfectly and are giving bad results.

Our future work concerns including languages left out in this participation (Hungarian, Polish, French, Greek, Icelandic and Russian); a major challenge here is the need for resources (stemmers, stopwords lists and so on). In addition, we want to experiment with hyperlinks of the HTML documents of the EuroGOV Collection, storing them and establishing some relation between web pages. Also, extraction of the link text string could add more information to retrieve. Further steps include improving the present identifier so it can use n-grams, experimenting without using keyword tags, and extending the system so that the multilingual task can be fully run.

Acknowledgements

This work has been partially supported by the Spanish Government (CiCYT) with grant TIC2003-07158-C04-01 and by the Regional Technology Ministry of Valencia Government by means of the projects with reference GV04B-276 and GV04B-286.

References

[1] Llopis, F., Muñoz, R, Noguera, E., M. Terol, R. IR-n r2: Using normalized passages. CLEF 2004

[2] Callan, J. P.: Passage-Level Evidence in Document Retrieval. In Proceedings of the 17th Annual International Conference on Research and Development in Information Retrieval, London, UK. Springer Verlag (1994) 302-310.

[3] Rafael M. Terol, Patricio Martínez-Barco, Fernando Llopis, Trinitario Martínez: An Application of NLP Rules to Spoken Document Segmentation Task. NLDB 2005: 376-379

[4] M. Kaskziel and J. Zobel. Passage retrieval revisited. In *Proceedings of the 20th annual International ACM Philadelphia SIGIR*, pages 178–185, 1997.

[5] Llopis F., Noguera E. Combining passages in monolingual experiments. In *Workshop of Cross-Language Evaluation Forum (CLEF 2005)*, In this volume, Vienna, Austria, 2005.

MIRACLE at WebCLEF 2005: Combining Web Specific and Linguistic Information

Ángel Martínez-González[1,3], José Luis Martínez-Fernández[2,3], César de Pablo-Sánchez[2], and Julio Villena-Román[2,3]

[1] Universidad Politécnica de Madrid
[2] Universidad Carlos III de Madrid
[3] DAEDALUS - Data, Decisions and Language, S.A.
amartinez@daedalus.es, jmartinez@daedalus.es, cdepablo@inf.uc3m.es, jvillena@daedalus.es

Abstract. This paper describes MIRACLE approach to WebCLEF. A set of independent indexes was constructed for each top level domain of the EuroGOV collection. Each index contains information extracted from the document, like URL, title, keywords, detected named entities or HTML headers. These indexes are queried to obtain partial document rankings, which are combined with various relative weights to test the value of each index. The final aim is to identify which index (or combination of them) is more relevant for a retrieval task, avoiding the construction of a full-text index.

1 Introduction

Linguistic heterogeneity makes the Web a very appropriate setting to evaluate cross-language Information Retrieval systems. Furthermore, web search engines face some challenges not found in other Information Retrieval tasks, such as the huge amount of data to be processed and the different formats. WebCLEF 2005 [3] focuses on known-item search, that is, retrieving a page already known to exist in the collection. This paper describes MIRACLE[1] approach to this task.

Our objectives for this first participation were two-fold: firstly to adapt our existing tools to a web environment and secondly, to evaluate the relative relevance of several of these information sources (such as document URL, title, keywords, detected named entities or HTML headers) in opposition to full-text indexes.

For these purposes, a set of independent indexes was constructed for each top level domain of the collection. Partial searches on each index are performed by applying the BM25 probabilistic ranking model. Finally, these partial lists are combined to get the final result. In different experiments, different weights are given to each set of partial results. The main goal is to evaluate the relative importance of the different information sources that have been indexed for the retrieval process.

The generated indexes were:

[1] This work has been partially supported by the Spanish R+D National Plan, by means of the project RIMMEL (Multilingual and Multimedia Information Retrieval, and its Evaluation), TIN2004-07588-C03-01.

C. Peters et al. (Eds.): CLEF 2005, LNCS 4022, pp. 869 – 872, 2006.

- H1 index, containing document titles and H1 HTML headers [2].
- H2 index, containing headers H2 to H6.
- PN index, containing named entities (proper nouns) found by a detection module.
- Ky index, document keywords given in a META HTML element.
- Url index, containing parsed parts of the document url, removing the query string and taking characters such as '.' ,'/' or '–' as delimiters.

Consequently, the total number of indexes was 85 (5 indexes/domain * 17 domains).

2 Developed Tools

The tools developed by MIRACLE for WebCLEF are explained below:

- *Document extraction and HTML parsing:* based on the El-Kabong HTML processing library. The content or attributes of special tags such as headers, anchors or META tags are extracted. The body is then extracted in plain text format.
- *Named Entities Recognition:* named entities are filtered from plain text using an in-house developed multilingual recognizer. Recognition is based on the evaluation of predicates in a Finite State Automaton. We have explicitly considered Spanish, Portuguese, Italian, French, English, Swedish and Dutch. After WebCLEF we have evaluated the tool with data from the CONLL 2002 shared task and achieved for Spanish 80.49% precision and 88.7% recall rate; the results for Dutch were 66.25% precision and 60% recall rate.
- *Indexing and ranking:* a trie based indexing and retrieval engine developed by MIRACLE has been used for all WebCLEF experiments. This engine supports the use of several variants of probabilistic and vector based ranking formulas with no need of reindexing. For this track only BM25 formula was used.
- *Combination of partial results:* relevance rankings from different indexes are mixed by means of an ad-hoc script that calculates the average relevance allowing to easily assign different weights to different indexes. Techniques described in [1] have been applied.
- *Query language detection:* in the case of the baseline mixed monolingual run, no metadata such as the target language of the query was allowed, so this in-house developed module tried to guess the target language from the words of the query title.

3 Description of the Submitted Runs

The MIRACLE team has taken part in the two main tasks (Mixed Monolingual and Multilingual), submitting five runs for each one of them. A baseline run, using no metadata was mandatory. The other four runs (which will be referred as *extended* in this paper) used supplied metadata (the target domain). In the baseline runs, the language identification tool was employed to guess the target language from the words in the query title. For each query, only the indexes of the top level domain corresponding to the target language and the international INT domain were queried.

In the five Monolingual runs submitted, partial results were combined in the following ways:

- Monobase: this is the baseline run. Relevance of documents is averaged over the five partial results, giving all of them the same weight.
- MonoExt: extended run, combining the results in the same way as in MonoBase.
- MonoExtH1PN: extended run; only H1 and PN considered (with the same weight).
- MonoExtUrlKy: extended run; only Url and Ky considered (with the same weight).
- MonoExtAH1PN: extended run. All indexes are considered, but H1, PN and Ky are considered more relevant, so a weight factor with value 2 is applied.

In the Multilingual runs Multibase, MultiExt, MultiExtH1PN, MultieExtUrlKy and MultiExtAH1PN, partial results were mixed in the same way as in the corresponding monolingual runs.

4 Evaluation

Table 1 contains the MRR scores of all runs submitted by MIRACLE, while Figure 1 shows the average success rate of these runs. The best scoring runs are MonoExtH1PN (0.1750 MRR) for the Mixed Monolingual Task and MuliExtH1PN (0.0762 MRR) for the Multilingual Task.

The expected conclusion is confirmed: titles and named entities are the most valuable sources of information to find known-items. In Multilingual runs results are worse and the effect of different combinations of results is not so significant.

Table 1. MRR scores of all runs submitted by MIRACLE

Mixed Monolingual Task		Multilingual Task	
Run Name	**MRR**	**Run Name**	**MRR**
MonoBase	0.0472	MultiBase	0.0314
MonoExt	0.1030	MultiExt	0.0588
MonoExtH1PN	0.1750	MultiExtH1PN	0.0762
MonoExtUrlKy	0.0462	MultiExtUrlKy	0.0338
MonoExtAH1PN	0.1420	MultiExtAH1PN	0.0633

Our results in the multilingual task are, although worse in absolute terms than the monolingual results, better if considered relative to the other participants, even though our approach was quite simple, with no query or document translation. Elements without translation such as named entities are less noisy and especially valuable for known-item search.

Our results were rather variable with the target language of the topic. The results in languages such as Greek or Russian were much poorer than in other languages, even though the techniques used are language independent (with the partial exception of named entities recognition). This suggests we have had some sort of problem with character sets and encodings, which should be corrected for future participations.

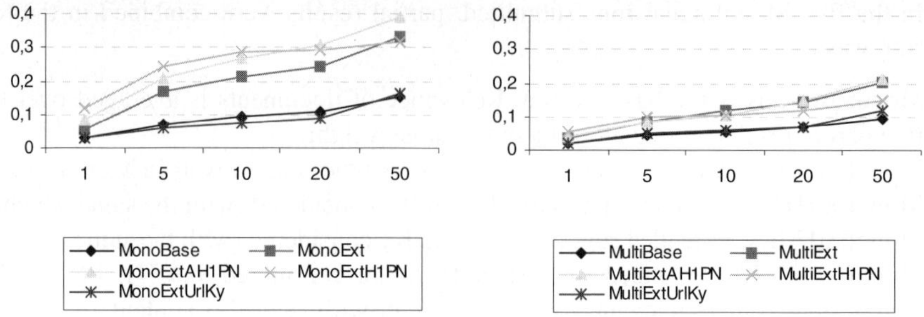

Fig. 1. Average success at n (portion of topics where the known-entity was found at a rank less than or equal to n)

5 Conclusions and Future Work

Obviously, in this first year of WebCLEF track, there were no previous results available and the selection of experiments was somehow based on intuition. Nevertheless, valuable conclusions have been drawn and software tools have been developed. We plan to use and further improve these tools in future participations in order to pursue more ambitious aims.

The low MRR values obtained suggest that the use of a full text index cannot be avoided and this full text index, combined appropriately with the more specific indexes, would probably improve the results. In our next participation, we are also planning to introduce some sort of query translation mechanism. Another improvement would be to consider the hyperlink structure of the collection; a voting algorithm could be used to estimate the relative importance of web pages and this way detect home pages.

References

1. Goñi-Menoyo, J. M., González, J. C., Villena-Román, J.: MIRACLE at Ad-Hoc CLEF 2005: Merging and Combining without Using a Single Approach. Proceedings of the Cross Language Evaluation Forum 2005, Lecture Notes in Computer Science, Springer-Verlag, (2006)
2. Ragget, D., Le Hors, A., Jacobs, I. (Ed.): HTML 4.01 Specification. W3C Recommendation On line http://www.w3.org/TR/html4/, visited 15/07/2005 (1999)
3. Sigurbjörnsson , B., Kamps, J., de Rijke, M. : Overview of WebCLEF 2005. Proceedings of the Cross Language Evaluation Forum 2005, Lecture Notes in Computer Science, Springer-Verlag (2006)

BUAP-UPV TPIRS: A System for Document Indexing Reduction at WebCLEF

David Pinto[1,2], Héctor Jiménez-Salazar[2], Paolo Rosso[1], and Emilio Sanchis[1]

[1] Department of Information Systems and Computation,
UPV, Valencia 46022,
Camino de Vera s/n, Spain
{dpinto, prosso, esanchis}@dsic.upv.es
[2] Faculty of Computer Science, BUAP, Puebla 72570,
Ciudad Universitaria, Mexico
{davideduardopinto, hgimenezs}@gmail.com

Abstract. In this paper we present the results of BUAP/UPV universities in WebCLEF, a particular task of CLEF 2005. Particularly, we evaluate our information retrieval system at the bilingual "English to Spanish" task. Our system uses a term reduction process based on the Transition Point technique. Our results show that it is possible to reduce the number of terms to index, thereby improving the performance of our system. We evaluate different percentages of reduction over a subset of EuroGOV, in order to determine the best one. We observed that after reducing the 82.55% of the corpus, a Mean Reciprocal Rank of 0.0844 was obtained, compared with 0.0465 of such evaluation with full documents.

1 Introduction

High volume of information in Internet led to the development of novel techniques for managing of data, specially when we deal with information in multiple languages. There are sufficient example scenarios in which users may be interested in information which is in a language other than their own native language. A common language scenario is where a user has some comprehension ability for a given language but s/he is not sufficiently proficient to confidently specify a search request in that language. Thus, a search system that can deal with this problem should be of a high benefit. The World Wide Web (WWW) is a natural setting for cross-lingual information retrieval; the European Union is a typical example of a multilingual scenario, where multiple users have to deal with information published in at least 20 languages.

In order to reinforce research in this area, CLEF (Cross-Language Evaluation Forum) has been compiling a set of multi-lingual corpora and promoting the evaluation of multiple multi-lingual information retrieval systems for diverse kinds of data [5]. A particular task for the evaluation of such systems that deal with information on the web has been set up this year as a part of CLEF. This forum was named WebCLEF, and the best description of this particular task

C. Peters et al. (Eds.): CLEF 2005, LNCS 4022, pp. 873–879, 2006.

can be seen in [14]. In WebCLEF, three subtasks were defined within this year: mixed monolingual, multilingual, and bilingual English to Spanish.

This paper reports results on the evaluation of a Cross-Language Information Retrieval System (CLIRS) for the bilingual English to Spanish subtask of WebCLEF 2005. A document indexing reduction is proposed, in order to improve precision of CLIRS and to diminish the storing space on such systems. Our proposal is based on the use of the Transition Point (TP) technique, which is somehow a method that obtains important terms from a document. We evaluate different percentages of TP over a subset of EuroGOV corpus [13], and we observed that it is possible to improve precision results by reducing the number of terms for a given corpus.

The next section describes our information retrieval system in detail. Section 3 briefly introduces the corpus used in our experiments, and the results obtained after evaluation. Finally, a discussion of our experiments is presented.

2 Description of TPIRS

We used a boolean model with Jaccard similarity formula for our CLIRS. Our goal was to determine the behaviour of document indexing reduction in an information retrieval environment. In order to reduce the terms from every document treated, we applied a technique named Transition Point, which is described as follows.

2.1 The Transition Point Technique

The Transition Point (TP) is a frequency value that splits the vocabulary of a document into two sets of terms (low and high frequency). This technique is based on the Zipf Law of Word Ocurrences [18] and also on the refined studies of Booth [2], as well as of Urbizagástegui [17]. These studies are meant to demonstrate that mid-frequency terms are closely related to the conceptual content of a document. Therefore, it is possible to form the hypothesis that terms closer to TP can be used as indexes of a document. A typical formula used to obtain this value is given in equation 1:

$$TP = \frac{\sqrt{8 * I_1 + 1} - 1}{2}, \tag{1}$$

where I_1 represents the number of words with frequency equal to 1 [12] [17].

Alternatively, TP can be localized by identifying the lowest frequency (from the highest frequencies) that it is not repeated in each document; this characteristic comes from the properties of the Booth's law of low frequency words [2]. In our experiments we have used this approach.

Let us consider a frequency-sorted vocabulary of a document; i.e., $V_{TP} = [(t_1, f_1), ..., (t_n, f_n)]$, with $f_i \geq f_{i-1}$, then $TP = f_{i-1}$, iif $f_i = f_{i+1}$. The most important words are those that obtain the closest frequency values to TP, i.e.,

$$TP_{SET} = \{t_i | (t_i, f_i) \in V_{TP}, U_1 \leq f_i \leq U_2\}, \tag{2}$$

where U_1 is a lower threshold obtained by a given neighbourhood percentage of TP (NTP), thus, $U_1 = (1 - NTP) * TP$. U_2 is the upper threshold and it is calculated in a similar way ($U_2 = (1 + NTP) * TP$).

We have used the TP technique in different areas of Natural Language Processing (NLP) like: clustering of short texts [7], categorization of texts [9], keyphrases extraction [10] [16], summarization [3], and weighting models for information retrieval systems [4]. Thus, we believe that there exist enough evidence to use this technique as a terms reduction process.

2.2 Information Retrieval Model

Our information retrieval is based on the Boolean Model, and, in order to rank documents retrieved, we used the Jaccard's similarity function, applied to both, the query and every document of the corpus used. Previously, each document was preprocessed and its index terms were selected (the preprocessing phase is described in section 3.1). For this purpose, several values of a neighbourhood of TP were used as thresholds, as equation 2 indicates.

3 Evaluation

3.1 Corpus

We used a subset of the EuroGOV corpus for our evaluation. This subset was composed by a set of Spanish Internet pages, originally obtained from European government-related sites.

In order to construct this corpus, for every page compiled in the EuroGOV corpus, we determine its language by using TexCat [15], a language identification program widely used. We construct our evaluation corpus with those documents identified as Spanish language.

The preprocessing process consisted of the elimination of punctuation symbols, Spanish stopwords, numbers, html tags, script codes and cascading style sheets codes.

For the evaluation of this corpus, a set of 134 queries was composed and refined, in order to provide gramatically correct "English" queries. Supervised queries (queries and related webpages) were created by the participants in the WebCLEF task, and the particular case of the queries were later reviewed and in some cases corrected in their English translation by the NLP Group at UNED. Queries were distributed in the following way: 67 homepages and 67 named page findings.

We applied a preprocessing phase to this set of queries. First, we used an online translation system [1] in order to translate every query from English to Spanish. After that, an elimination of punctuation symbols, spanish stopwords and numbers was done.

We did not apply a rigorous method of translation, due to the fact that our main goal in our first participation in WebCLEF was to determine the quality of terms reduction in our CLIRS.

[1] http://www.freetranslation.com

3.2 Indexing Reduction

In order to determine the behaviour of document indexing reduction on CLIRS, we submitted to the contest, a set of five runs, which are described as follows.

First Run: → **Full:** This run used "Full documents" as evaluation corpus, and conformed the baseline for our experiments.

Second Run: → **TP10:** This run used an evaluation corpus composed by the reduction of every document, using the TP technique with a neighbourhood of 10% around TP.

Third Run: → **TP20:** This run used an evaluation corpus composed by the reduction of every document, using the TP technique with a neighbourhood of 20% around TP.

Fourth Run: → **TP40:** This run used an evaluation corpus composed by the reduction of every document, using the TP technique with a neighbourhood of 40% around TP.

Fifth Run: → **TP60:** This run used an evaluation corpus composed by the reduction of every document, using the TP technique with a neighbourhood of 60% around TP.

Table 1 shows the size of every evaluation corpus used, as well as the percentage of reduction obtained for each one. As can be seen, the TP technique obtained a big percentage of reduction (between 75 and 89%), which also implies a reduction in time for the indexing process in a CLIRS.

Table 1. Evaluation corpora

Corpus	Size (Kb)	% of Reduction
Full	117,345	0%
TP10	12,616	89.25%
TP20	19,660	83.25%
TP40	20,477	82.55%
TP60	28,903	75.37%

3.3 Results

Table 2 shows the results for every run submitted. The first column indicates the name of each run. The last column shows the Mean Reciprocal Rank (MRR) obtained for each run. Additionally, the average success at different number of documents retrieved is shown; by instance, the second column indicates the average success of the CLIRS at the first answer. The "TP20" approach, obtained fewer than 50 results, and therefore, it average success at 50 was not calculated.

As can be seen, an important improvement was gained by using an evaluation corpus obtained with a neighbourhood of 40% of TP. We were hoping to obtain comparable results with the "Full" run, but as can be seen, the "TP40" run received double the score of the "Full" run when evaluated using MRR.

Table 2. Evaluation results

Corpus	**Average Success at**					**Mean Reciprocal Rank**
	1	**5**	**10**	**20**	**50**	
Full	0.0224	0.0672	0.1119	0.1418	0.1866	0.0465
TP10	0.0224	0.0373	0.0672	0.0821	0.1119	0.0331
TP20	0.0299	0.0448	0.0672	0.1045	–	0.0446
TP40	**0.0597**	0.0970	0.1119	0.1418	**0.2164**	**0.0844**
TP60	0.0522	**0.1045**	**0.1269**	**0.1642**	0.2090	0.0771

Three teams participated at the bilingual "English to Spanish" subtask at WebCLEF. Every team submitted at least one run [1,11,8]. A comparison among the results obtained by each team can be seen in Table 3. Our second place in this contest can be dramatically improved by applying a better translation process and by using a better representation model for our information retrieval system.

Table 3. All teams results

Team Name	**Average Success at**					**Mean Reciprocal Rank over 134 Topics**
	1	**5**	**10**	**20**	**50**	
UNED	**0.0821**	**0.1045**	**0.1194**	0.1343	0.2090	**0.0930**
BUAP/UPV	0.0597	0.0970	0.1119	**0.1418**	**0.2164**	0.0844
ALICANTE	0.0299	0.0522	0.0597	0.0746	0.0970	0.0395

4 Conclusions

We have proposed an index reduction method for a cross-lingual information retrieval system. Our proposal is based on the transition point technique.

After submitting five runs at the bilingual English to Spanish subtask of WebCLEF, we observed that it is possible to reduce terms in the documents that conform the corpus of a CLIRS, not only by reducing the time needed for indexing but also by improving the precision of the results obtained by CLIRS.

Our method is linear in computational time, and therefore it can be used in practical tasks. Until now, results obtained in terms of MRR are very low, but findings show that by applying better techniques of English to Spanish translation of queries, results can be dramatically improved [6].

We were concerned with the impact of indexing reduction on CLIRS, and in the future we hope to improve other components of our CLIRS, for instance, the use of vector space model, in order to improve the MRR.

The TP technique has shown an effective use on diverse areas of NLP, and its best features for NLP, are mainly two: a high content of semantic information and the sparseness that can be obtained on vectors for document representation on models based on the vector space model. On the other hand, its language independence allows to use this technique in CLIRS, that is the matter of WebCLEF.

Acknowledgments

This work was partially supported by BUAP-VIEP 3/G/ING/05, R2D2 (CI-CYTTIC 2003-07158-C04-03), ICT EU-India (ALA/95/23/2003/077-054), and Generalitat Valenciana Grant (CTESIN/2005/12). We would like also thank the CLEF 2005 organising committe (This work is a revised version of the paper "TPIRS: A System for Document Indexing Reduction at WebCLEF").

References

1. J. Artiles, V. Peinado, A. Peñas, F. Verdejo: *UNED at WebCLEF 2005*, Extended abstract in Working notes of CLEF'05, Viena, 2005.
2. A. Booth: *A Law of Ocurrences for Words of Low Frequency*, Information and control, 1967.
3. C. Bueno, D. Pinto, H. Jimenez: *El párrafo virtual en la generación de extractos*, Research on Computing Science Journal, ISSN 1665-9899, 2005.
4. R. Cabrera, D. Pinto, H. Jimenez, D. Vilariño: *Una nueva ponderación para el modelo de espacio vectorial de recuperación de información*, Research on Computing Science Journal, ISSN 1665-9899, 2005.
5. CLEF 2005: *Cross-Language Evaluation Forum*, http://www.clef-campaign.org/, 2005.
6. W. B. Croft: *Language Modeling for Information Retrieval*, The Information Retrieval Series, Vol. 13, Lafferty, John (Eds.), 2003.
7. H. Jimenez, D. Pinto, P. Rosso: *Selección de Términos No Supervisada para Agrupamiento de Resúmenes*, In proceedings of Workshop on Human Language, ENC05, 2005.
8. T. Martínez, E. Noguera, R. Muñoz, F. Llopis: *Web Track for CLEF2005 at ALICANTE UNIVERSTITY*, Extended abstract in Working notes of CLEF'05, Viena, 2005.
9. E. Moyotl, H. Jimenez: *An Analysis on Frequency of Terms for Text Categorization*, Proceedings of XX Conference of Spanish Natural Language Processing Society (SEPLN-04), 2004.
10. D. Pinto, F. Pérez: *Una Técnica para la Identificación de Términos Multipalabra*, In Proceedings of 2nd. National Conference on Computer Science, Mexico, 2004.
11. D. Pinto, H. Jiménez-Salazar, P. Rosso, E. Sanchis: *TPIRS: A System for Document Indexing Reduction on WebCLEF*, Extended abstract in Working notes of CLEF'05, Viena, 2005.
12. B. Reyes-Aguirre, E. Moyotl-Hernández & H. Jiménez-Salazar: *Reducción de Términos Indice Usando el Punto de Transición*, In proceedings of Facultad de Ciencias de Computación XX Anniversary Conferences, BUAP, 2003.
13. B. Sigurbjörnsson, J. Kamps, and M. de Rijke: *EuroGOV: Engineering a Multilingual Web Corpus*, In Proceedings of CLEF 2005, 2005.
14. B. Sigurbjörnsson, J. Kamps, and M. de Rijke: *WebCLEF 2005: Cross-Lingual Web Retrieval*, In Proceedings of CLEF 2005, 2005.
15. TextCat: *Language identification tool*, http://odur.let.rug.nl/ vannord/TextCat/, 2005.

16. M. Tovar, M. Carrillo, D. Pinto, H. Jimenez: *Combining Keyword Identification Techniques*, Research on Computing Science Journal, ISSN 1665-9899, 2005.
17. R. Urbizagástegui: *Las posibilidades de la Ley de Zipf en la indización automática*, Research report of the California Riverside University, 1999.
18. G. K. Zipf: *Human Behavior and the Principle of Least-Effort*, Addison-Wesley, Cambridge MA, 1949.

Web Page Retrieval by Combining Evidence*

Carlos G. Figuerola, José L. Alonso Berrocal,
Angel F. Zazo, and Emilio Rodríguez Vázquez de Aldana

University of Salamanca, REINA Research Group,
reina@usal.es
http://reina.usal.es

Abstract. The participation of the REINA Research Group in WebCLEF 2005 focused in the monolingual mixed task. Queries or topics are of two types: *named* and *home pages*. For both, we first perform a search by thematic contents; for the same query, we do a search in several elements of information from every page (title, some meta tags, anchor text) and then we combine the results. For queries about *home pages*, we try to detect using a method based in some keywords and their patterns of use. After, a re-rank of the results of the thematic contents retrieval is performed, based on Page-Rank and Centrality coeficients.

1 Introduction

Our participation in WebCLEF 2005 focused on the monolingual mixed task in Spanish. The task has a two-fold objective: to find *named web pages* and *home pages*. Each query has a single valid response and both types of queries are mixed and we do not know a priori to which type of query each one pertains.

In principle, the basic approach consists of finding pages whose content is relevant to each query; the valid response is expected to be found among the first pages retrieved and a better or worse positioning depends on the techniques applied in the search.

In cases of queries searching for a *home page* we apply a procedure that reorders the list of documents retrieved, taking into account, besides their similarity to the query, different types of evidence that point to their being *home pages*. A further problem is that we do not know a priori which queries are searching for *home pages* and which are not, so we must include a procedure to analyze the queries and determine which ones are searching for *home pages* and which are not.

The paper is organized as follows: in section 2 we offer a description of the part of the document collection that we worked with; section 3 describes the approach applied; the section following that reports on the experiments carried out and their results and finally, the last section gives our conclusions.

* This research has been partially supported by a grant from the Junta de Castilla y León, project number SA089/04.

C. Peters et al. (Eds.): CLEF 2005, LNCS 4022, pp. 880–887, 2006.

2 The Document Collection

Our participation was limited to the `.es` domain. It has a total of 35,168 documents; not all the pages are `HTML` and it is not always easy to identify the document format; the `Content-type` is empty in many of the documents. For this year, the queries were limited to `HTML` documents and the organizers facilitated a blacklist of 4,365 documents that are not in `HTML`.

Table 1. Blacklist for `.es` domain

Format	Number of docs.
PDF	4040
MS Word	315
empty docs	6

However, there are documents in other formats that are not on the blacklist. Thus, of the 35,168 documents in the `.es` domain, 8642 are not labeled `<HTML>`.

Furthermore, the documents seem to have been truncated to a size of approximately 64K, and in the binary files, such as PDF files, the characters `chr(0)` seem to have been replaced by `chr(32)`.

2.1 Topics

There are 118 topics in Spanish, 59 searching for *home pages* and 59 for *named pages*. The concept of *home page*, however, is fuzzy; the consideration of some of the searched pages as *home* is quite debatable.

In addition, there are some mistakes in the topics set. Thus, some topics are duplicated, or even triplicated. Some of them, with different correct page as answer in the *qrels* file. Some topics are a formulation too wide. By example, topic `WC0098`: *Consejería de Educación y Cultura*; there are, in Spain, 17 Autonomous Communities and every one of them has a Council of Education and Culture. Besides, we have found that many embassies have also a *Consejería de Educación y Cultura*, and there is a lot of embassies. How can a search engine determine which of them is the right answer?

A few topics have as correct answer a page which is not in the `.es` domain. This is, maybe, right; but, since we work only in the .es domain, we cannot find the correct page anyway.

3 Our Approach

As mentioned earlier, the basic idea was to find pages or documents closest to each query, and, in the case of *home page* type queries, prioritize on the list of retrieved documents the pages most likely to be *home pages*. This also obliged us to analyze the queries to determine their type.

The first part of our task, to find the pages most similar to each query, could have been approached using a classic scheme for document retrieval. However, web pages contain informative elements other than the text seen in the windows of navigators. We could thus use these elements to refine the retrieval.

3.1 Combining Evidence

The list of elements that we can take into account in web pages is long, but we focused on the following:

- The body field, which seems to be the most important
- The title field
- The contents of some META tags, as in the case of Description and Keywords
- The anchor text of incoming hyperlinks to a page.

All these elements supply evidence that we can somehow combine to find the pages most similar to each query. There are several ways to make this fusion or combination, and the first choice is whether to do the fusion before making the query or after. We opted to do it afterwards, and therefore the procedure applied was the following:

- build an index with the terms of each of the elements to be taken into account
- execute the query in each of these indexes.
- fuse the results obtained with each of the indexes

For the first step we used our *Karpanta* software [1], based on the well-known vector model, and built indexes of the fields `BODY`, `TITLE`, `META Description`, `META keywords`, and anchor text. The weights of the terms were calculated according to the classical scheme based on $tf \times IDF$ known as `atc`. In all cases the empty words were previously eliminated, applying a list of some 300 words in Spanish; also, an improved s-stemmer [2] was applied.

The sizes of the resulting indexes were uneven, as were the fields or elements on which the indexes were based. Almost all the HTML pages contained a `BODY` field (some only have *java* scripts and the like), but this was not the case for the rest of the indexes. So, 71.5 % of the pages in the `.es` domain contained a `TITLE` field and the mean length of these titles was 40 characters, which means they are very short titles.

The `META Description` tag or field was only present in 16.9 % of the documents, with a mean size of 38.6 characters. Of these documents, in 7.4 % of the cases the `META Description` coincided exactly with that of the `TITLE` field. The keywords (`META Keywords` field) only appeared in 24.7 % of the documents, with a mean of 7.7 words per document. As regards backlinks, 24.7 % of the documents had none (from inside the collection), and those that did receive them did so with a mean of 9 backlinks per document. The text of these backlinks, on the other hand, was very short (18.7 characters), although perhaps very significant. It thus seems clear that, except for the body field, the rest of the elements are limited in importance, since they were not present in large amounts of documents. For the fusion or combination of the resulting lists in each of the retrievals on each index, first the coefficients of similarity were normalized based on the *z-score* [3] and then the normalized lists were fused using the CombMNZ algorithm [4], modified in order to be able to weight differently the results obtained with each index:

$$Score = \sum_{i=1}^{n} score_i \times k_i \times (number\ of\ score\ ! = 0) \qquad (1)$$

There are other fusion procedures that can be applied [4,5,6,7]. Most of them are based on the combination of the coefficients of similarity obtained after executing the query in each index, but it is also possible to work with the positions in the lists of documents retrieved in each index [8]; this algorithm is attractive because of its simplicity, since it is not even necessary to previously normalize the scores or coefficients.

3.2 Finding *home pages*

The first step was to determine which queries are searching for *home pages*. The concept of *home page*, however, is diffuse, and therefore not everyone would consider as *home pages* some of the correct answers to some queries.

In an exploratory phase, different *home pages* of the `.es` domain were examined manually, particularly the `TITLE` field, with the idea that a query that hoped to find that page was probably quite similar to its title. Likewise, the *home page* type queries used in TREC were also consulted manually. They are in English, but once translated can give an idea of the structure and characteristics of this type of query.

During this phase some common elements were found in the structure of the home page queries. This structure has a lot to do with the use of specific terms related to the *home page* being looked for. Thus, pages of this type are those that give entry to the webs of certain institutions: ministries, institutes, schools, etc., and, as a consequence, these words will appear in the query [3].

Furthermore, they appear in certain positions and accompanied, before and after, by certain auxiliary words (articles and other connectors). This allowed us to build a series of patterns of *home page* queries to which a simple heuristic was added: the appearance of expressions such as *home page*, *portal*, etc. Once these supposedly *home page* queries had been identified using this system, the results of a search resolved by means of a combination of evidence such as those seen in the section above were reordered so as to place at the top those pages which, being relevant in the contents, were most likely to be *home pages*.

To determine which of the pages found can be *home pages*, several techniques have been described which are non-exclusive and can be combined with each other. The most well-known techniques use two types of information: the `URL` structure of the page, on the one hand, and links analysis, on the other.

The techniques based on the `URL` structure operate with the depth of that structure. Kraaij, Westerveld and Hiemstra [9] studied the statistical distribution of home pages in the different depth levels of the `URL`, as well as Beitzel and colleagues [3]. Plachouras, Ounis, Rijsbergen and Cacheda [10] also used criteria based on the length of the URL, as did Tomlinson [11].

The techniques based on the analysis of links have also been widely used. Although judged to be of less usefulness in searches by content, they seem to be effective in recognizing *home pages* [12]. Different coefficients have been used, ranging from simple *in* and *out-degrees* [13] to *page-rank* [14] or *HITS* [15]. We tried with *page-rank* [16] and with the *centrality* index [17], both based on backlinks.

4 Experiments Performed

We performed official and unofficial experiments. Our aim was to determine what elements or evidence would be useful in the search for contents and what indexes based on links analysis seemed to be more effective in finding *home pages.*

The official results are shown in Table 2. USAL0 was used as a baseline for comparison and this was carried out with the queries in Spanish on pages in the .es domain. Only the BODY field of the pages was indexed, and all the queries were processed in the same way.

USAL1 combines results from the BODY, META Description fields and the text of the backlinks to each page.

USAL2 adds META Keywords to the fields of USAL1. USAL3 and USAL4 attempt to apply specific methods to locate home pages. From the results of USAL1 an attempt was made to detect *home page* type queries, and the results of these queries were re-ordered with *Page-Rank* in USAL3 and with *Centrality* in USAL4.

4.1 Evaluation

Table 2 shows the results of the official evaluation of the experiments. However, we have seen before some problems about the queries (duplicated ones, right answers in anothers domains). So, we have carried out an unofficial evaluation, removing erroneous topics: duplicated ones (even triplicated), right answers out of the .es domain, badly formulated queries. Classification in *home* and *named pages*, although debatable, we have left it as it was.

Table 2. Results (.es domain only) of the Official Evaluation

	USAL0	USAL1	USAL2	USAL3	USAL4
success at 1	0.1343	0.1642	0.1567	0.1940	0.1567
success at 5	0.3134	0.4254	0.3657	0.4776	0.4179
success at 10	0.3731	0.5000	0.4776	0.5522	0.4925
success at 20	0.3955	0.5970	0.5821	0.6493	0.6269
success at 50	0.6269	0.7463	0.7090	0.7537	0.7313
MRR	0.2193	0.2796	0.2553	0.3214	0.2776

Table 3. Unofficial Evaluation (`.es` domain only)

	USAL0	USAL1	USAL2	USAL3	USAL4
success at 1	0.1622	0.1982	0.1892	0.2162	0.1892
success at 5	0.3694	0.5135	0.4414	0.5586	0.5045
success at 10	0.4324	0.6036	0.5676	0.6486	0.5946
success at 20	0.4595	0.6847	0.6667	0.7207	0.7117
success at 50	0.7117	0.8378	0.7928	0.8468	0.8378
MRR	0.2611	0.3339	0.3045	0.3667	0.3255

Table 4. Most frequent keywords in `.es` domain

Keyword	times
cultura	1864
ministerio	1624
investigacion	1202
spain	1174
administracion	1171
politica	1169
informacion	1169
policy	1168
ministry	1168
research	1168
telecommunications	1168
information	1157
espaa	1157
industria	1126
turismo	1119
comercio	1080
energia	1012
telecomunicaciones	990
industry	962
trade	962
commerce	962
energy	962
tourism	962
parques nacionales	658

4.2 Results

It seems clear that working with more elements than just the `BODY` field improves retrieval; this seems to be true for `TITLE`, `META Description` and anchor text. However, the use of `META Keywords` made the results worse. This may seem surprising (certain simple retrieval systems are based on this field alone), but if we examine the use that the different pages make of it we see that, at the least, it is a strange use. Table 3 shows the keywords expressions (not individual terms) most used in the `.es` part of the collection.

For the most part these are very generic terms, not very useful for searches made in a government collection. Many of them are included in pages also translated into English, and some of them directly in English, without their Spanish counterpart (even though the rest of the page is in Spanish).

A manual examination of some of the pages of the collection showed that there are pages (particularly *home pages* of certain institutions) that have literally hundreds of keywords. In some cases, these long lists of key words are handed down without variation by the rest of the pages in the site. This probably has something to do with certain myths that are circulating on the way in which the search engines find and rank the pages. Some pages repeat the same keyword many times, in the hope that the search engines will place it at the top of the list.

As regards the locating of home pages, it seems that the use of query patterns to distinguish *home page* queries and treat them specifically achieves results, since experiments `USAL3` and `USAL4` showed an improvement over the others. Of these two, *Centrality* provided better results for detecting *home pages. Centrality* is simpler and does not discriminate backlinks, but it seems that the *home pages* are not necessarily the most prestigious.

5 Conclusions

We have described our participation in WebCLEF 2005, based on the retrieval by contents using fusion or a combination of different elements, as well as the use of coefficients from links analysis for locating *home pages.* The use of information elements such as the `TITLE` or anchor text is clearly helpful, despite the fact that the texts of many backlinks are very short. However, the `keywords` entered by the authors of the pages seem to be of little help and do not result in good results. Moreover, the coefficients based on links analysis, such as *Page-Rank* or the simple index of *Centrality*, help to locate *home pages.*

References

1. Figuerola, C.G., Zazo Rodríguez, A., Alonso Berrocal, J.L., Rodríguez, E.: Karpanta: Un motor de búsqueda para la investigación experimental en recuperación de la información. In: IBERSID 2003, Zaragoza, Spain (2003)
2. Figuerola, C.G., Zazo, Á.F., Rodríguez Vázquez de Aldana, E., Alonso Berrocal, J.L.: La recuperación de información en español y la normalización de términos. Revista Iberoamericana de Inteligencia Artificial **8**(22) (2004) 135–145
3. Beitzel, S., Jensen, E., Cathey, R., Ma, L., Grossman, D., Frieder, O., Chowdury, A., Pass, G., Vandermolen, H.: Task classification and document structure for known-item search. In: The Twelfth Text REtrieval Conference (TREC 2003), Gaithersburg, Maryland,2003. NIST Special Publication 500-255 (2003)
4. Fox, E.A., Shaw, J.A.: Combination of multiples searches. In: Overview of the Third Text REtrieval Conference (TREC-3), NIST Special Publication 500-226 (1994) 243–252
5. Lee, J.H.: Combining multiple evidence from different relevance feedback methods. Technical Report, Center for Intelligent Information Retrieval (CIIR), Department of Computer Science, University of Massachusetts (1996)

6. Thompson, P.: A combination of expert opinion approach to probabilistic information retrieval, part 1: The conceptual model. Information Processing and Management **26**(3) (1990) 371–382
7. Basterr, B.T., Cottrell, G.W., Belew, R.K.: Automatic combination of multiple ranked retrieval systems. In: Proceedings of the 17th Annual International ACM-SIGIR Conference on Research and Development in Information Retrieval. Dublin. Ireland, 3–6 July 1994 (Special Issue of the SIGIR Forum), ACM/Springer-Verlag (1994)
8. Lee, J.H.: Analyses of multiple evidence combination. In: SIGIR '97: Proceedings of the 20th Annual International ACM SIGIR Conference on Research and Development in Information Retrieval, New York, NY, USA, ACM Press (1997) 267–276
9. Kraaij, W., Westerveld, T., Hiemstra, D.: The importance of prior probabilities for entry page search. In: 5th Annual International ACM SIGIR Conference, Association for Computing Machinery (2002) 27–34
10. Plachouras, V., Ounis, I., Rijsbergen, C.J.v., Cacheda, F.: University of Glasgow at the Web Track: Dynamic application of hyperlink analysis using the query scope. In: The Twelfth Text REtrieval Conference (TREC 2003), Gaithersburg, Maryland,2003. NIST Special Publication 500-255 (2003)
11. Tomlinson, S.: Robust, Web and Terabyte retrieval with Hummingbird Searchserver at TREC 2004. In: The Thirteen Text REtrieval Conference (TREC 2004), NIST Special Publication 500-261 (2004)
12. Hawking, D., Craswell, N.: Very large scale retrieval and Web search. In Voorhees, E., Harman, D., eds.: TREC: Experiment and Evaluation in Information Retrieval. MIT Press (2005) `http://es.csiro.au/pubs/trecbook_for_website.pdf` (ISBN 0262220733).
13. Yang, K., Albertson, D.: Widit in TREC 2004 genomics, hard, robust and Web tracks. In: The Thirteen Text REtrieval Conference (TREC 2004), NIST Special Publication 500-261 (2004)
14. Zaragoza, H., Craswell, N., Taylor, M., Saria, S., Robertson, S.: Microsoft Cambridge at TREC-13: Web and hard tracks. In: The Thirteen Text REtrieval Conference (TREC 2004), NIST Special Publication 500-261 (2004)
15. Farah, M., Vanderpooten, D.: Novel approaches in text information retrieval. Experiments in the Web track of TREC-2004. In: The Thirteen Text REtrieval Conference (TREC 2004), NIST Special Publication 500-261 (2004)
16. Brin, S., Page, L.: The anatomy of a large-scale hypertextual Web search engine. Computer Networks and ISDN Systems **30**(1–7) (1998) 107–117
17. Kleinberg, J.M., Kumar, R., Raghavan, P., Rajagopalan, S., Tomkins, A.S.: The Web as a graph: measurements, models, and methods. Lecture Notes in Computer Science **1627** (1999)

UNED at WebCLEF 2005

Javier Artiles, Víctor Peinado, Anselmo Peñas,
Julio Gonzalo, and Felisa Verdejo

NLP Group, ETSI Informática, UNED
c/ Juan del Rosal, 16. E-28040 Madrid. Spain
javart@bec.uned.es, {victor, anselmo, julio, felisa}@lsi.uned.es

Abstract. This paper describes the experiments submitted by UNED's NLP Group to the WebCLEF 2005 track in the bilingual English to Spanish task. We present two different runs: i) a simply search over the whole content of the documents; ii) a series of restricted searches over given fields according to their descriptiveness. Our newly developed approach for searching ordered fields performs 80% better than the baseline. We also describe a non-supervised approach to translate out-of-vocabulary words.*

1 Introduction

The basic idea behind the WebCLEF 2005 track was to evaluate cross-language retrieval systems in a web setting. [1]. A huge corpus consisting of a crawl of governmental sites in the European Union was built and 575 known-item topics were developed. The participant systems' goal was to find a particular page for each search topic. The participants were asked to submit a ranked list of results (50 hits maximum) for each known item topic.

For this first participation at the WebCLEF track, we only took part in the bilingual English to Spanish task, that is, using English topics in order to find a web page written in Spanish. For our particular case, the testbed consisted of the 134 English topics for which there were a Spanish target page, and a subset of the corpus made of web pages identified by the track organizers as written either in Spanish or in an unknown language.

This paper is structured as follows: in Section 2 we explain how we processed the collection and built our index. In Section 3, we describe how we dealt with the translation of the English topics into Spanish. Then, in Sections 4 and 5 we comment the submitted runs and the results obtained. Lastly, in Section 6 we draw some conclusions and mention future lines of work.

2 Indexing EuroGOV

The EuroGOV collection contains more than 3.5 million pages from European governmental websites (organized in 27 different national web domains, such as

* This work has been partially supported by the Spanish Government under the project R2D2-Syembra (TIC2003-07158-C04-02). Javier Artiles and Víctor Peinado hold a PhD grant by UNED (*Universidad Nacional de Educación a Distancia*).

C. Peters et al. (Eds.): CLEF 2005, LNCS 4022, pp. 888–891, 2006.

`.uk`, `.de`, `.fr`, `.es`, `.eu`...). In order to work with a smaller dataset, we decided to build a unique index with the Spanish pages, according to the language detection output provided by the track organizers. This subset of the EuroGOV collection was indexed using the Lucene's API.[1]

From the HTML structure of each document, we extracted those fields likely to contain relevant or descriptive information, and we indexed each document by the following fields: title, metadata, headings and body. No further word normalization technique was used except the tokenization provided by Lucene's `StandardAnalyzer` class.

3 Query Translation

The first issue we faced before trying to perform a word by word translation of the topic was to decide which terms we had to translate and which ones we should leave unstranslated. Our hypothesis was that a given word having a higher relative frequency in a collection of documents other than the English one, is not an English word, and hence it must remain untranslated. To do that, for each word in the topic, we simply computed its relative frequency with respect to the number of documents in the corresponding index, as $F(w)_{Lang} = \frac{tf(w)}{N_{Lang}}$.

Given an English word w, if $F(w)_{Spanish} > F(w)_{English}$ we assume that w must remain untranslated. Otherwise, we try to lemmatize and look it up in our dictionary (Vox + EuroWordNet + FreeDict). In spite of the good recall of our dictionary, a few remained without translation. To translate these out-of-vocabulary words, we applied the assumption found in previous works (e.g. [2]) to our particular case: a Spanish document containing the English word w might also contain its translation into Spanish. So, we followed this procedure, as shown in Table 1:

1. We query Google for Spanish pages containing the English word w.
2. We take the 10 most frequent Spanish words (after removing stopwords) from the 40 first snippets retrieved by Google. We call these terms *candidate translations.*
3. We search for English pages containing each candidate and count up every time it co-occurs with w in the 40 first snippets, as a kind of *inverse translation.*
4. Finally, we rank the candidates and choose the most frequent one in steps 2 and 3 as the *ultimate translation.*

4 Submitted Experiments

We decided to use two different approaches to rank the results of our retrieval experiments. And these are the two runs we submitted to the bilingual task:

[1] Official Lucene's website available at `http://lucene.apache.org`.

Table 1. Translating the out-of-vocabulary word *Cantabrian*

Topic: *Strategy for the preservation of the Cantabrian brown bear*
OOV word: Cantabrian
Candidate translations: cantabria (16), spain (14), diccionarios (10), mountains (9), glosarios (6), términos (6), turismo (5), región (5), sea (5)
Ultimate translation: cantabria

baseline. We could launch full boolean queries with the `AND` operator over the whole content of the documents and rank the results according to the search engine output.

ordered field search. We could weight the different fields identified during the indexing (see Section 2) and perform restricted searches over these fields. We establish the following order: title, metadata, headings and body. This ordering, which may seem arbitrary, tries to reflect which fields are likely to contain more descriptive information about the web page itself. In this case, we proceeded as follows:

1. We launch the query over the `title` fields.
2. If we don't get 50 pages, we re-launch the query over the `metadata` fields and append the results, removing any possible duplicate.
3. If we don't have 50 pages yet, we repeat step 2 over the `heading` fields and, if necessary, over the `body` fields and append the results, removing any possible duplicate.

Only if we were not able to reach 50 results, we repeated this process using the `OR` operator.

5 Results and Discussion

Table 2 shows our official results. Our baseline successfully retrieved the target web page in the first position of the ranking only in 2% of the cases, while the proposed system did it in 8% of the cases. Even though we can observe the same behavior when considering positions 5 and 10, the baseline performs clearly better at lower positions. And this may be explained by the fact that, in some cases, we completed the results' ranking re-launching the query with the `OR` operator (see Section4).

Mean Reciprocal Rank (MRR) values are quite low in the baseline (0.05) but improve considerably (+80%) when we perform restricted searches over one field at a time. In spite of the poor results, our ordered field search obtained the best MRR value among all bilingual participants.

Two different factors must be taken into account in order to adequately interpret the results. First, the proposed task is inherently difficult; and then, the selection of a smaller (and more affordable) index, based on the language detection provided by the organization, possibly excluded some relevant web pages.

Table 2. Evaluation results

	baseline	proposal	variation
Avg success at 1	0.02	0.08	+300
Avg success at 5	0.07	0.10	+43
Avg success at 10	0.10	0.12	+20
Avg success at 20	0.17	0.13	-23
Avg success at 50	0.26	0.21	-19
MRR over 134 topics	0.05	0.09	+80

6 Conclusions and Future Work

The tasks proposed is very attractive and we initially signed in for every WebCLEF task. But we soon encountered problems trying to deal with such large amounts of data and we limited our participation to the bilingual English to Spanish task. As final conclusions, we can mention that:

- The partial indexing of EuroGOV seems to be the first shortcoming in the design of our participation. Complete indexing is necessary in order to avoid the loss of relevant pages.
- The strategy of launching restricted searches over the descriptive fields seems to perform reasonably well for known-item tasks. Among the descriptive fields considered, we may also include anchor text.
- The translation method for OOV words seems a very promising tool for cross-language information retrieval tasks but it needs more study and a more careful selection of the candidate translations. However, using external resources such as Google's output are out of our control.

Our future work will be focused on: i) improving the OOV translation method and testing the procedure in different languages for which we have no lexicographic resources; ii) adding anchor texts, which usually containt interesting descriptive information, to our index; and iii) evaluating the system within the Monolingual and Multilingual environments.

References

1. Sigurbjörnsson, B., Kamps, J., de Rijke, M.: Overview of WebCLEF 2005. In: Proceedings of the Cross-Language Evaluation Forum 2005. Springer Lecture Notes of Computer Science (to appear).
2. Vogel, S., Zhang, Y., Huang, F.: Mining Translations of OOV terms from the Web through Cross-Lingual Query Expansion. In: Proceedings of the SIGIR 2005, 2005.

Using the Web Information Structure for Retrieving Web Pages

Mirna Adriani and Rama Pandugita

Faculty of Computer Science
University of Indonesia
Depok 16424, Indonesia
mirna@cs.ui.ac.id, ramap101@mhs.cs.ui.ac.id

Abstract. We present a report on our participation in the mixed monolingual web task of the 2005 Cross-Language Evaluation Forum (CLEF). We compared the result of web page retrieval based on the page content, page title, and a combination of page content and page title. The result shows that using the combination of page title resulted in the best retrieval performance compared to using only page content or page title. Taking into account the number of links referring to a web page and the depth of the directory path in its URL did not result in any significant improvement to the retrieval performance.

1 Introduction

The fast growing amount of information on the web motivated many researchers to come up with a way to deal with such information efficiently. Information retrieval forums such as the Cross Language Evaluation Forum (CLEF) have included research in the web area. In fact, this year CLEF includes web retrieval as one of the topic research tracks. This year we, the University of Indonesia IR-Group, participated in the mixed monolingual WebCLEF - CLEF 2005 task.

The web page contains some characteristics that the newspaper document does not have such as the structure of the web page, anchor text, or URL length. These characteristics have been studied to have positive effects on the retrieval of web pages [2]. This paper reports our attempt to study whether these characteristics can result in better retrieval performance instead of using word frequency alone. We also study if applying a word stemmer to web documents can increase the retrieval performance as with newspaper documents [1].

2 The Retrieval Process

The mixed monolingual task searches for web pages in a number of languages. The queries and the documents were processed using the *Lucene*[1] information retrieval system. Stopword removal was applied only to the English queries and documents.

---

[1] See http://lucene.apache.org.

C. Peters et al. (Eds.): CLEF 2005, LNCS 4022, pp. 892 – 897, 2006.

2.1 Word Stemming

Word stemming has been known to increase the retrieval performance of IR systems with newspaper document collections [1]. In this study, we were interested in knowing if applying the stemmer to the web collection could increase the IR system's performance. We used the Porter stemmer for English [3] and applied word stemming to documents in the collection and the queries for all languages.

2.2 Web Page Scoring Techniques

We employed three different techniques for scoring the relevance of documents in the collection, i.e., based only on the content of the page, based only on the title of the page, and based on the combination of page title and page content.

The first technique takes into account only the content of a web page to find the most relevant web pages to the query. We used the *vector space model* [1, 2] to find the similarity value between the query and the pages. The second technique considers the title of the web page as the only source in finding the relevant pages. The third technique uses the content and the title of the page to find the relevant pages.

2.3 Score Adjustment Based on Web Page Structure

The structure of web page collections is much richer than newspaper document collections commonly used in IR research. We analyzed the structure of web pages in finding the relevant web pages. A web page usually contains many in- (referred by) and out-links (reference to) and has a URL. A portion of URL indicates the directory path where the webpage is kept. This path information can be short or long depending on the directory structure of the web pages. We take into account the number of in-links and the depth of the URL-path in scoring the relevance of a web page.

Web pages that are retrieved using the IR system are then rescored based on the number of in-links (link factor) and the depth the URL path (path factor).

The link factor is based on an assumption that the more referenced a web page is, the more relevant the web page is to the query. We count the number other retrieved web-pages that refer to a web page divided by the maximum of such a number. The path factor of a web page *i*, *Li,* is defined as follows:

- *Li* = (the number other pages referring to page-*i*)/*L-max* if *L-max* $\neq 0$
  where
  - *L-max* is the maximum number of other pages referring to page-*j* for *j*=1 to *M*
  - *M* is the number of web pages retrieved.
- *Li* = 1 if *L-max* = 0.

The path factor is based on an assumption that the lower the directory level depth the more focused the web page on the query topic. We count the depth of the directory level in the path. The path factor of a we page-*i*, *Pi*, is defined as follows:

- *Pi* = *P-min*/(the directory level depth of page-*i*) if *P-min* $\neq 0$
  where
  - P-min is the minimum directory level among all retrieved pages.
- Pi = 1 if *P-min* = 0.

The final score of a retrieved web page-*i* is: $x_1 \times Ii + x_2 \times Li + x_3 \times Pi$ where *Ii* is the original score of the web page based on the vector space ranking algorithm; and x_1, x_2, and x_3 are the weights assigned to *Ii*, *Li*, and *Pi*, respectively.

For example, if the original score of a web page from the IR system is 0.9, the path factor score is 0.33, and the link factor score is 1 and the x_1= 0.6, x_2=0.2, and x_3=0.2, then the page's new score is $(0.6 \times 0.9) + (0.2 \times 0.33) + (0.2 \times 1) = 0.81$.

3 Experiment

The web collection contains over two million documents from the EuroGOV collection. The collection is divided into 27 European language domains. In the mixed monolingual task, the queries are in various languages and are used to find documents in the same language as the queries. There are 547 queries to be used for searching in two categories, namely, the name page search and the homepage search. The average number of words in the queries is 6.29 words.

In these experiments, we used *Lucene* information retrieval system to index and retrieve the documents. *Lucene* is based on the vector space model. *Lucene* is also capable of indexing documents using two separate fields such as the title page and the content, and then searching can be done using either the title page or the content page.

We conducted a number of experiments to see the effects of several aspects of a web page on retrieval. First, we wanted to know if applying a word stemmer to web documents can help improving the retrieval performance. Stemmers have been known to increase the number documents retrieved by decreasing the word variation [1]. We also compared the results of retrieving web documents using the text in the content-only, in the title-only, and in the combination of the title and content of a web page. We then applied techniques that use the path-depth of the URL and the number of links to adjust the ranking score of a web document.

4 Results

Using word stemming in information retrieval systems has been known to increase the retrieval effectiveness, especially with collections containing newspaper articles. In this work, we investigated the effect of using a stemmer for searching a web collection.

Table 1. Mean Reciprocal Mean (MRR) of the stemmed and unstemmed web-pages and queries

Task : Mixed Monolingual	Stemmed	Unstemmed
MRR	0.1722	0.2714
Average success at 1:	0.1133	0.1901
Average success at 5:	0.2285	0.3638
Average success at 10:	0.2815	0.4223
Average success at 20:	0.3327	0.4936
Average success at 50:	0.4241	0.5978

The mean reciprocal rank (MRR) shows that not applying the stemmer to the web pages is more effective than applying the stemmer to the web collection (Table 1). Based on this result, we conducted the following experiments without applying the stemmer to the documents.

The results that we have submitted were produced using the three techniques, namely, based on page content only, based on the title page only, and based on the combination of title page and page content. Table 2 shows the result of our experiments. The mean reciprocal rank (MRR) over 547 queries is 0.2714 for using the page content only, 0.2621 for using the page title only, and 0.2860 for using the combination of page title and page content. The MRR of the title only is 3.42% below that of the page content only. However, the combination of page content and page title performed 5.37% better than the page content only.

Table 2. Mean reciprocal Mean (MRR) of the mixed monolingual queries

Task : Mixed Monolingual	Mean Reciprocal Rank (MRR)
Content	0.2714
Title	0.2621
Content + Title	0.2860

Table 3 shows the average of success of each technique at several ranks. The best result was achieved by using the combination of page content and page title, with average success at 1 = 0.2249, which is consistent with the earlier MRR result. The retrieval performance of the combination of page content and page title is 15.19% better than that of using the page content only, and 6.53% better than that of using page title at rank 1. However, in the top-5 or bigger lists, the page content only technique performed the best.

Table 3. Average of success of the mixed monolingual runs using the content only, the title only, the combination of page content and page title

Task : Mixed Monolingual	Content	Title	Content + title
Average success at 1:	0.1901	0.2102	0.2249
Average success at 5:	0.3638	0.3181	0.3583
Average success at 10:	0.4223	0.3638	0.4186
Average success at 20:	0.4936	0.4132	0.4662
Average success at 50:	0.5978	0.4589	0.5320

We also did some experiments by adjusting the scores of web pages retrieved using the page content technique based on the link and the path depth factors. Table 4 shows that the best result was achieved by considering 60% of the webpage score, 20% of the number of links, and 20% of the URL depth analysis where the retrieval effectiveness increased by 0.67% of the content-only score. Considering 80% of the webpage score, 10% of the number of links, and 10% of the URL depth increased the performance by 0.47% of the content-only score. However, the score decreased by 1.02% when combining 50% of the content, 20% of the number of links, and 20% of the URL depth.

Table 4. Average of success of the mixed monolingual runs using various weight compositions of content only (co), the number of links (ln), and depth of URL path (ur) scores

Task : Mixed Monolingual	Content only	co=0.8, ln=0.1, ur=0.1	co=0.6, ln=0.2, ur=0.2	co=0.5, ln=0.25, ur=0.25
MRR	0.2714	0.2728	0.2781	0.2612
Average success at 1:	0.1901	0.1810	0.1810	0.1664
Average success at 5:	0.3638	0.3693	0.3803	0.3620
Average success at 10:	0.4223	0.4552	0.4589	0.4479
Average success at 20:	0.4936	0.5247	0.5265	0.5247
Average success at 50:	0.5978	0.5960	0.5960	0.5960

Performing similar experiments using the combination of page content and page title technique, we obtained results as shown in Table 5. Table 5 shows that the score adjustment resulted in worse retrieval effectiveness for all weight compositions. The retrieval performance drops were -3.72%, -6.74%, and -8.20% from the original page content and page title technique for the 0.8+0.1+0.1, 0.6+0.2+0.2, and 0.5+0.25+0.25 weight compositions, respectively.

Our result is similar to the work by Westerveld et al. [2] who obtained better results by using other information in addition to the content. The use of links also show that the effect of considering the link in the web pages doesn't have much effect in getting the most relevant web-pages in the highest rank. This result is also similar with the result in the report on TREC [2].

Table 5. Average of success of the mixed monolingual runs using the page content and page title technique (co+ti), the number of links (ln), and depth of the URL path (ur)

Task : Mixed Monolingual	Content + title	co+ti=0.8, ln=0.1, ur=0.1	co+ti=0.6, ln=0.2, ur=0.2	co+ti=0.5, ln=0.2, ur=0.2
MRR	0.2860	0.2488	0.2186	0.2040
Average success at 1:	0.2249	0.1718	0.1426	0.1316
Average success at 5:	0.3583	0.3327	0.2834	0.2724
Average success at 10:	0.4186	0.4004	0.3894	0.3711
Average success at 20:	0.4662	0.4625	0.4589	0.4570
Average success at 50:	0.5320	0.5302	0.5302	0.5302

Applying English Porter stemmer to all documents hurts the retrieval performance compared to non-stemmed documents. The stemmer decreased the MRR for the English and non-English documents in 35% of the web topics.

Since this was our first participation in the WEB task, it took us quite a lot of effort to cope with such large collection. There were several document sets that were damaged, possibly in the process of downloading the files. As a result, we could not index those corrupt files. It is possible that those files were relevant to some of the queries.

The other problem was that we did not prepare *Lucene* to handle non-Latin characters, and so, the retrieval of documents using queries containing such characters was erroneous.

5 Summary

Our results demonstrate that combining the page content and the page title resulted in a better mean reciprocal rank (MRR) compared to searching using the page content only or using the page title only. However the combination of page title and page content achieved the best performance only at rank 1. For higher ranks, using the page-content only technique showed better result compared to using the other two techniques. We hope to improve our results in the future by exploring still other methods. Taking into account the number of links referring to a web page and the depth of the directory path in its URL did not result in any significant improvement of the retrieval performance.

References

1. Baeza-Yates, R., Ribeiro-Neto, B.: Modern Information Retrieval. Addison-Wesley, New York (1999)
2. Craswell, Nick and Hawking, David. Overview of the TREC 2004 Web Track. In NIST Special Publication: The 13th Text Retrieval Conference (2004)
3. Porter, M. F: An algoritm for suffix stripping. Program Vol. 14: 3 (1980) 127-130
4. Salton, Gerard, and McGill, Michael J. Introduction to Modern Information Retrieval. McGraw-Hill, New York (1983)
5. Westerveld, Thijs, Kraaij, Wessel and Hiemstra, Djoerd. Retrieving Web Pages using Content, Links, URLs, and Anchors. In NIST Special Publication: The 10th Text Retrieval Conference (TREC-10) (2001)

University of Glasgow at WebCLEF 2005: Experiments in Per-Field Normalisation and Language Specific Stemming

Craig Macdonald, Vassilis Plachouras, Ben He, Christina Lioma, and Iadh Ounis

University of Glasgow, G12 8QQ, UK
{craigm, vassilis, ben, xristina, ounis}@dcs.gla.ac.uk

Abstract. We participated in the WebCLEF 2005 monolingual task. In this task, a search system aims to retrieve relevant documents from a multilingual corpus of Web documents from Web sites of European governments. Both the documents and the queries are written in a wide range of European languages. A challenge in this setting is to detect the language of documents and topics, and to process them appropriately. We develop a language specific technique for applying the correct stemming approach, as well as for removing the correct stopwords from the queries. We represent documents using three fields, namely content, title, and anchor text of incoming hyperlinks. We use a technique called per-field normalisation, which extends the Divergence From Randomness (DFR) framework, to normalise the term frequencies, and to combine them across the three fields. We also employ the length of the URL path of Web documents. The ranking is based on combinations of both the language specific stemming, if applied, and the per-field normalisation. We use our Terrier platform for all our experiments. The overall performance of our techniques is outstanding, achieving the overall top four performing runs, as well as the top performing run without metadata in the monolingual task. The best run only uses per-field normalisation, without applying stemming.

1 Introduction

One of the main problems when applying language dependent retrieval techniques to multilingual collections is to identify the language in which the documents are written, in order to apply the appropriate linguistic processing techniques, such as stemming, or the removal of the appropriate stopwords. The EuroGOV collection used in WebCLEF 2005 is a crawl of European government Web sites, and includes documents written in a broad range of European languages [13]. Similarly, the used topics in WebCLEF 2005 are provided in any one of 11 different languages, as well as translated in English. We investigate a language specific stemming approach to deal with the multilingual setting. Our approach is based on identifying the language of the documents and the queries, and applying the appropriate stemmer. Our main hypothesis is that applying the

C. Peters et al. (Eds.): CLEF 2005, LNCS 4022, pp. 898–907, 2006.

appropriate stemmer for the language of each document and topic will increase the retrieval effectiveness of the search engine.

The WebCLEF 2005 monolingual task is a typical Web known-item finding search task, consisting of home page and named page finding queries, where there is only one relevant document, and the query corresponds to the name of this document. The evaluation results for similar tasks in the context of the Web track of TREC 2003 [3] and TREC 2004 [4] have shown that the anchor text and title of Web documents are effective sources of evidence for performing retrieval. The URL of Web documents is also very effective for identifying the home pages of Web sites. Therefore, we use the same Web Information Retrieval (IR) techniques in our WebCLEF 2005 participation.

We represent a Web document with three different fields, namely its content, title and the anchor text of its incoming hyperlinks. To apply an appropriate term frequency normalisation, and to combine the information from the different fields, we employ a technique called *per-field normalisation*, which extends *Normalisation 2*, a term frequency normalisation technique from the Divergence From Randomness (DFR) framework [1]. We also use evidence from the length of the document URL path in order to identify relevant home pages.

In all our submitted runs we use per-field normalisation and evidence from the document URL path. Depending on the method used to identify the language of documents and queries, we test various approaches for performing stemming in a robust and appropriate way on the tested multilingual setting. We use our Terrier IR platform [10] to conduct all the experiments.

Our results show that all our submitted runs to WebCLEF 2005 achieved outstanding retrieval performance. In particular, we achieved the overall top four performing runs, as well as the top performing run without the use of metadata in the monolingual task. The results suggest that the per-field normalisation seems to be effective in enhancing the retrieval performance, while there is less benefit from using the URLs of Web documents. In addition, our results suggest that the application of language specific stemming achieves good performance when the language of documents is identified correctly. However, the highest retrieval performance is achieved when no stemming is applied.

The remainder of this paper is organised as follows: Section 2 provides details of our methodology for language specific stemming, per-field normalisation, and evidence from the document URL path. Section 3 describes the experimental setting and our submitted runs to the monolingual task of WebCLEF 2005. We present and discuss the obtained results in Section 4. This paper closes with some concluding remarks in Section 5.

2 Searching a Multilingual Web Test Collection

We describe our proposed techniques for effectively searching a multilingual Web collection for known-item finding queries. As mentioned in the introduction, one major problem with multilingual test collections is how to apply the appropriate linguistic processing techniques, such as stemming, or the removal of the appropriate stopwords. Section 2.1 presents our proposed language specific stemming technique. In addition, Sections 2.2 and 2.3 describe the applied Web IR techniques, namely the per-field normalisation and the evidence from the document URL path, respectively.

2.1 Language Specific Stemming

Stemming has been shown to be effective for ad-hoc retrieval from monolingual collections of documents in European languages [7]. Our main research hypothesis in this work is that applying the correct stemmer to a document and a topic would increase the retrieval effectiveness of the search engine. This would emulate a monolingual IR system, where the correct stemmer for both the language of the documents and topics is always applied.

To test our hypothesis, we use three approaches for processing the text of documents and topics. First, we do not use stemming. Second, we apply Porter's English stemmer to all text, regardless of the language. This approach stems English text, but it does not affect texts written in other languages, with the exception of those terms that contain affixes expected in English terms. Third, we identify the language of each document or topic, and then apply an appropriate stemming approach. The latter technique is called *language specific stemming.*

For identifying the language of documents or topics, we primarily use the TextCat language identification tool [2,15]. However, as the language identification process is not precise – often giving multiple language choices – we choose to supplement document language detection with additional heuristics. For each document, we examine the suggested languages provided by the language identification tool, and look for evidence to support any of these languages in the URL of the document, the metadata of the document, and in a list of "reasonable languages" for each domain. For example, we do not expect Scot Gaelic or Welsh documents in the Web sites of the Hungarian government.

For each of the considered languages, in addition to a stemmer, we assume that there exists an associated stopword list. The language of the queries is identified by either the provided metadata, or the TextCat tool.

2.2 Per-Field Normalisation

The evaluation of Web IR systems with known-item finding queries suggests that using the title of Web documents and, in particular, the anchor text of the incoming hyperlinks results in improved retrieval effectiveness [3,4].

In this work, we take into account the fields of Web documents, that is the terms that appear within particular HTML tags, and introduce one more normalisation method in the Divergence From Randomness (DFR) framework, besides *Normalisation 2* and the normalisation with Dirichlet priors [6]. We call this method *per-field normalisation.* Our introduced method applies term frequency normalisation and weighting for a number of different fields. The per-field normalisation has been similarly applied in [16] using the BM25 formula. In this work, we use a different document length normalisation formula.

Per-field normalisation is useful in a Web context because the content, title, and anchor texts of Web documents often have very different term distributions. For example, a term may occur many times in a document, because of the document's verbosity. On the other hand, a term appearing many times in the anchor text of a document's incoming hyperlinks represents votes for this document [5]. Moreover, the frequencies of terms in the document titles are distributed almost uniformly. Thus, performing normalisation and weighting independently for the various fields allows to take into account the different characteristics of the fields, and to achieve their most effective combination.

The DFR weighting model PL2 is given by the following equation:

$$score(d,Q) = \sum_{t \in Q} \frac{qtfn}{tfn+1} \Big(tfn \cdot \log_2 \frac{tfn}{\lambda} + (\lambda - tfn) \cdot \log_2 e + 0.5 \cdot \log_2 (2\pi \cdot tfn) \Big) \quad (1)$$

where $score(d,Q)$ corresponds to the relevance score of document d for query Q, $\lambda = \frac{F}{N}$ is the mean and variance of a Poisson distribution, F is the total term frequency in the collection, and N is the number of documents in the collection. $qtfn$ is the normalised query term frequency, given by $qtfn = \frac{qtf}{qtf_{max}}$, where qtf is the query term frequency, and qtf_{max} is the maximum query term frequency among the query terms. tfn is given by *Normalisation 2*:

$$tfn = tf \cdot \log_2 (1 + c \cdot \frac{avg\_l}{l}), \quad (c > 0) \quad (2)$$

where tf is the frequency of t in a document d, c is a hyper-parameter, avg_l is the average document length in the collection, and l is the length of d.

Our per-field *Normalisation 2F* extends *Normalisation 2*, so that tfn corresponds to the weighted sum of the normalised term frequencies for each used field f:

$$tfn = \sum_f \Big(w_f \cdot tf_f \cdot \log_2 (1 + c_f \cdot \frac{avg\_l_f}{l_f}) \Big), \quad (c_f > 0) \quad (3)$$

where w_f is the weight of field f, tf_f is the frequency of t in f, avg_l_f is the average length of f in the collection, l_f is the length of f in a particular document, and c_f is a hyper-parameter for each field f. Note that *Normalisation 2* is a special case of *Normalisation 2F*, when the entire document is considered as one field. After defining *Normalisation 2F*, the DFR weighting model PL2 can be extended to PL2F by replacing tfn from Equation (3) in Equation (1).

2.3 Evidence from URL Path Length

In our previous work [11], we found that taking the length of the document URL path component into account is particularly effective in both topic distillation, and home page finding tasks. In particular, the relevance score of the retrieved documents is updated according to the following formula:

$$score(d,Q) := score(d,Q) \cdot \frac{1}{\log_2 (1 + URLPathLen_d)} \quad (4)$$

where $score(d, Q)$ is the relevance score of document d for query Q. The length in characters of the document URL path component is denoted by $URLPathLen_d$. The above formula is applied for a certain number of top ranked documents in order not to introduce noise and not to change the ranking considerably.

In this work, we follow [16] and refine the combination of content analysis and evidence from the document URL path, by adding a score related to the length of the document URL path:

$$score(d, Q) := score(d, Q) + \omega \cdot \frac{\kappa}{\kappa + URLPathLen_d} \quad (5)$$

where ω and κ are free parameters. The parameter κ controls the saturation related to the length of the document URL path. The parameter ω weights the contribution of the document URL path length to the document's relevance score. We apply the above formula to all the retrieved documents.

3 Experimental Setting and Runs

In this section, we present how the above described techniques have been applied for the monolingual task of the WebCLEF 2005. More specifically, we provide details about our experimental setting (Section 3.1) and our submitted runs (Section 3.2).

3.1 Experimental Setting

For all our experiments we used a version of the University of Glasgow's Terrier platform. More details about the platform can be found in [10]. Terrier provides a range of weighting models, from classical models, such as tf-idf and BM25, to models based on the Divergence From Randomness (DFR) framework [1].

To support retrieval from multilingual document collections, such as the EuroGOV [13], it is essential that the IR system accurately and uniquely represents each term in the corpus. To meet this requirement, the correct encoding for each document must be identified prior to indexing. The version of the Terrier platform we used detects the encoding of documents. During the parsing of the collection, we used heuristics, based on the HTTP headers, the META tags, and the TextCat language identifier tool, to determine the correct content encoding for each document. Once the correct encoding is determined, each term is read and converted to UTF-8 encoding. This ensures that we have a correct representation of the documents.

For the language specific stemming technique, we mainly used the Snowball stemmers [14], with the following exceptions: English, where we used Porter's English stemmer; Icelandic, where we used the Danish Snowball stemmer; Hungarian, where we used Hunstem [8]; and Greek, where we did not apply any stemming. The anchor text of the incoming hyperlinks of documents is processed with the stemmer for the language of the source document. For example, when English documents link to a French document, then the anchor text of the French document is stemmed with Porter's English stemmer.

For the per-field normalisation, in all our experiments, we considered three document fields: the content, the title, and the anchor text of its incoming hyperlinks. The values of the hyper-parameters c_f and the weights w_f were automatically set using an extension of our previous work [6], which takes fields into account. The parameters ω and κ employed in the integration of evidence from the document URL path were empirically set using the .GOV TREC Web test collection and the associated known-item finding task from TREC 2003 [3].

3.2 Runs

As described in Section 2.1, we applied several stemming approaches to index the EuroGOV collection. Three indices were built: in the first one, no stemming was applied; in the second one, Porter's English stemmer was applied for all documents; and in the third index, the stemmer deemed appropriate for each document was applied.

We submitted five runs to the monolingual task of WebCLEF 2005, four of which used topic metadata. For all metadata runs, we used the domain topic metadata to limit the URL domain of the returned results. For example, if the topic stated `<domain domain="eu.int"/>`, only results with URLs in the eu.int domain were returned. For two runs, we also used the topic language metadata for detecting the correct stemmer to apply for the query. The official runs we submitted are detailed below:

- `uogSelStem`: This run did not use any metadata. Instead, we used the TextCat language identifier tool [2,15], to identify the language of each topic. The topic was then stemmed using the appropriate stemmer for that language. If TextCat was unable to classify the topic, then the topic was stemmed with the English Porter stemmer. We used the index with language specific stemming. This run tested the accuracy of the language identifier in determining which stemmer to apply to each topic.
- `uogNoStemNLP`: This run used only the domain metadata described above. No stemming was applied neither to the topics, nor to the documents. Additionally, we used a natural language processing technique to deal with acronyms. This run tested the retrieval effectiveness of not applying stemming in this multilingual Web IR setting.
- `uogPorStem`: This run used only the domain metadata described above. Porter's English stemmer was applied to all topics, and the corresponding index was used. This run tested the retrieval effectiveness of applying Porter's English stemmer to all languages in the EuroGOV collection.
- `uogAllStem`: This run used both the domain metadata described above, and the topic language metadata, which allowed the use of the correct stemmer for each topic. We used the index with language specific stemming. This run tested the hypothesis that applying the correct stemmer to both documents and topics would improve results overall.
- `uogAllStemNP`: This run is identical to `uogAllStem`, except that term order in the topics was presumed to be important. We applied a strategy where

the weights of query terms linearly decrease with respect to their position in the query and the query length. The underlying hypothesis is that in Web search, the user will typically enter the most important keywords first, then add more terms to narrow the focus of the search.

The used hyper-parameter and weight values related to the per-field normalisation are shown in Table 1. The used values for the parameters ω and κ are 2.0 and 18.0, respectively, for all the submitted runs.

Table 1. The used values of the hyper-parameters c_c, c_a, c_t, and the weights w_c, w_a and w_t, related to the per-field normalisation of the content, anchor text, and title fields, respectively, for the submitted runs

Run	c_c	c_a	c_t	w_c	w_a	w_t
`uogSelStem`	3.00	100	100	1	40	35
`uogNoStemNLP`	4.10	100	100	1	40	40
`uogPorStem`	3.19	100	100	1	40	40
`uogAllStem`	3.00	100	100	1	40	35
`uogAllStemNP`	3.00	100	100	1	40	35

4 Results and Discussion

Table 2 details the mean reciprocal rank (MRR) achieved by each of our submitted runs in the monolingual task. From initial inspection of the evaluation results, the run `uogNoStemNLP`, which did not apply any stemmers, gives the best MRR, closely followed by the run `uogPorStem`.

Table 2. Mean Reciprocal Rank (MRR) of the submitted runs to the monolingual task. The bold entry indicates the most effective submitted run, and the emphasised entry corresponds to the run without metadata.

Run	Description	MRR
uogSelStem	PL2F, URL, Language Specific Stemming	*0.4683*
`uogNoStemNLP`	PL2F, URL, No Stemming, Metadata, Acronyms	**0.5135**
`uogPorStem`	PL2F, URL, Porter's English Stemmer, Metadata	0.5107
`uogAllStem`	PL2F, URL, Language Specific Stemming, Metadata	0.4827
`uogAllStemNP`	PL2F, URL, Language Specific Stemming, Metadata, Order	0.4828

In Table 3, we have also broken the MRR down into the component languages of the queries, and the home page (HP) and named page (NP) queries. It would appear that Porter's English stemmer is more effective than, either no stemming, or the appropriate Snowball stemmer for Dutch and Russian. English and Portuguese topics give the best performance without any stemming applied. The weighting of the query term ordering showed little retrieval performance

Table 3. Mean Reciprocal Rank (MRR) of the submitted runs to the monolingual task. The bold entries indicate the most effective run for the corresponding set of topics. The numbers in brackets correspond to the number of queries for each language and each type of query. NP and HP stand for the named page and home page finding topics, respectively.

Topic Set		uogSelStem	uogNoStemNLP	uogPorStem	uogAllStem	uogAllStemNP
All	(547)	0.4683	**0.5135**	0.5107	0.4827	0.4828
DA	(30)	0.5168	0.5246	0.5098	**0.5857**	0.5829
DE	(57)	0.4469	0.4414	0.4567	**0.4780**	0.4689
EL	(16)	0.2047	0.3704	0.3659	0.3586	**0.4003**
EN	(121)	0.4988	**0.5578**	0.5240	0.5188	0.5239
ES	(134)	0.4198	0.4571	0.4635	0.4602	**0.4647**
FR	(1)	**1.0000**	**1.0000**	**1.0000**	**1.0000**	**1.0000**
HU	(35)	0.2713	**0.5422**	**0.5422**	0.1142	0.1003
IS	(5)	**0.3400**	0.3222	0.3222	**0.3400**	**0.3400**
NL	(59)	0.6362	0.6226	**0.6551**	0.6444	0.6447
PT	(59)	0.5262	**0.5565**	0.5336	0.5048	0.5028
RU	(30)	0.4838	0.4724	**0.4975**	0.4838	0.4625
NP only	(305)	0.4803	**0.5353**	0.5232	0.4952	0.4956
HP only	(242)	0.4531	0.4862	**0.4949**	0.4669	0.4666
All - HU	(512)	0.4818	**0.5116**	0.5085	0.5078	0.5089

improvement. It was particularly effective for the Greek topics (0.3586 to 0.4003), but showed very little positive or negative change for most languages.

The runs with the correct stemming applied (`uogAllStem` and `uogAllStemNP`) perform very well, with the exception of the Hungarian queries, which are affected considerably. The last row of Table 3 displays the MRR of all runs with all Hungarian topics removed. This shows that stemming makes little difference – the runs `uogAllStem` and `uogAllStemNP` achieve approximately the same MRR as the run `uogPorStem`, and are comparable to the run `uogNoStemNLP`.

The obtained performance when applying the correct stemmer to the Hungarian topics (the runs `uogAllStem` and `uogAllStemNP`) implies that the use of an aggressive stemmer, such as Hunstem [8], which addresses both inflectional and derivational variants, is not appropriate for the tested settings. However, when the language identifier classifies the Hungarian topics (as in `uogSelStem`), performance improves (0.2713 vs. 0.1142).

By comparing the runs `uogAllStem` and `uogSelStem`, we can see that the accuracy of the language classifier has an impact on the retrieval effectiveness (0.4827 vs. 0.4683 from Table 2). However, the effect of the classification accuracy for individual languages varied. For Hungarian topics, when the language identifier did not correctly classify the language of the topics, performance actually improved. The TextCat tool correctly classified 304 out of the 547 topics, while there were only 6 topics for which the identified language was wrong. TextCat did not classify 237 topics, because the input data was not sufficient to make a classification. For these topics, the Porter stemmer was used. Improvement in

MRR is obtained if no stemming is applied to the unclassified topics and the unstemmed index is used (0.4735 vs. 0.4683 from run uogSelStem).

We examined the benefit from using the field-based weighting model PL2F, as well as evidence from the URLs of Web documents (Sections 2.2 and 2.3, respectively). First the documents are represented by the concatenation of the content, title and anchor text fields, and the weighting model PL2 (Equation (1)) is used for retrieval. The hyper-parameter c of the *Normalisation 2* (Equation (3)) is set equal to c_c from run uogNoStemNLP (Table 1). The evaluation shows that this approach seems to be less effective than field-based retrieval with PL2F (0.5018 vs. 0.5135 from the run uogNoStemNLP). If the evidence from the URLs of Web documents is not used for the run uogNoStemNLP, then the obtained MRR is 0.5116, which is slightly lower than 0.5135 obtained from the run uogNoStemNLP. Overall, the field-based weighting model PL2F seems to have a positive impact on the retrieval effectiveness. However, the evidence from the URLs resulted in only a small improvement in retrieval performance.

We also investigated the average topic length, in particular for the German, Spanish, and English topic sets, and found these to be 3.3, 6.3, and 5.7 terms, respectively. In contrast, a recent study by Jansen & Spink [9] found an average length of 1.9, 2.6, and 5.0 terms for German, Spanish, and English queries, respectively. This difference can be due to two reasons. First, the studied queries in [9] are likely to include informational queries [12], which tend to be shorter, thus resulting in a lower average query length. Second, the difference in the average query length could be attributed to the fact that the used topics in WebCLEF 2005 were not representative of real European user search requests on a multilingual collection. Moreover, it's worth noting the distribution of queries in Table 3, where the number of queries by language in fact reflects the participating groups in WebCLEF 2005. Indeed, the creation of the queries and the corresponding relevance assessments was a joint community effort. In the future, it would be interesting to employ topics corresponding to European user search requests from commercial search engine query logs.

Regarding the two types of queries, all our submitted runs performed consistently better on the named page finding queries, than on the home page finding queries. Overall, all our submitted runs to the monolingual task of WebCLEF 2005 were clearly above the median of all the participants' submitted runs. Four of our runs were the best performing runs overall, and our run `uogSelStem` was the best performing run among the compulsory runs without metadata.

5 Conclusions

Our participation in the WebCLEF 2005 has been focused on the correct application of stemmers in a multilingual setting, as well as on the use of different document fields and evidence from the document URL path. We found that applying the correct stemmer for the language of the document and topic was effective in most cases. However, the improvements in retrieval performance from applying the correct stemmer for a language depend on the accuracy of the language identification of topics and documents. Without accurate language identification, retrieval effectiveness is penalised when a different stemmer is applied to a topic and the corresponding target document. The bare-system approach of applying no stemming at all achieved the best performance in the monolingual task.

Regarding the Web IR techniques we used, the per-field normalisation seemed to improve the retrieval performance, while the document URL path length resulted in smaller improvements. In future work, we will be extending per-field normalisation to other common fields of Web documents, such as H1, H2 tags.

References

1. G. Amati. *Probabilistic Models for Information Retrieval based on Divergence from Randomness.* PhD thesis, Dept of Computing Science, University of Glasgow, 2003.
2. W.B. Cavnar and J.M. Trenkle. N-gram-based text categorization. In *Proceedings of SDAIR-94*, pp. 161–175, 1994.
3. N. Craswell, D. Hawking, R. Wilkinson, and M. Wu. Overview of the TREC-2003 Web Track. In *Proceedings of TREC 2003*, 2003.
4. N. Craswell, D. Hawking. Overview of the TREC-2004 Web Track. In *Proceedings of TREC 2004*, 2004.
5. D. Hawking, T. Upstill and N. Craswell. Towards better weighting of anchors. In Proceedings of ACM SIGIR 2004, pp. 512–513, 2004.
6. B. He and I. Ounis. A study of the Dirichlet Priors for term frequency normalisation. In Proceedings of ACM SIGIR 2005, pp. 465–471, 2005.
7. V. Hollink, J. Kamps, C. Monz and M. de Rijke. Monolingual Document Retrieval for European Languages. *Information Retrieval*, 7(1-2):33–52, 2004.
8. Hunspell & Hunstem: Hungarian version of Ispell & Hungarian stemmer. URL: `http://magyarispell.sourceforge.net/`.
9. B.J. Jansen and A. Spink. An analysis of Web searching by European AlltheWeb.com users. *Inf. Process. Manage.*, 41(2):361–381, 2005.
10. I. Ounis, G. Amati, V. Plachouras, B. He, C. Macdonald, and D. Johnson. Terrier Information Retrieval Platform. In *Proceedings of ECIR 2005*, LNCS vol. 3408, pp. 517–519, 2005. URL: `http://ir.dcs.gla.ac.uk/terrier/`.
11. V. Plachouras, B. He, and I. Ounis. University of Glasgow at TREC2004: Experiments in Web, Robust and Terabyte tracks with Terrier. In *Proceedings of TREC 2004*, 2004.
12. D.E. Rose and D. Levinson. Understanding user goals in web search. In Proceedings of the 13th international conference on World Wide Web, pages 13–19, 2004.
13. B. Sigurbjonsson, J. Kamps, and M. de Rijke. EuroGOV: Engineering a Multilingual Web Corpus. In *Proceedings of CLEF 2005 Workshop*, 2005
14. Snowball stemmers. URL: `http://snowball.tartarus.org/`.
15. G. van Noord. TextCat language guesser. URL: http://odur.let.rug.nl/~vannoord/TextCat/.
16. H. Zaragoza, N. Craswell, M. Taylor, S. Saria, and S. Robertson. Microsoft Cambridge at TREC-13: Web and HARD tracks. In *Proceedings of TREC 2004*, 2004.

GeoCLEF: The CLEF 2005 Cross-Language Geographic Information Retrieval Track Overview

Fredric Gey[1], Ray Larson[1], Mark Sanderson[2], Hideo Joho[2], Paul Clough[2], and Vivien Petras[1]

[1] University of California, Berkeley, CA, 94709 USA
gey@berkeley.edu, ray@sims.berkeley.edu, vivienp@sims.berkeley.edu
[2] Department of Information Studies, University of Sheffield, Sheffield, UK
m.sanderson@sheffield.ac.uk, h.joho@sheffield.ac.uk, p.d.clough@sheffield.ac.uk

Abstract. GeoCLEF was a new pilot track in CLEF 2005. GeoCLEF was to test and evaluate cross-language geographic information retrieval (GIR) of text. Geographic information retrieval is retrieval oriented toward the geographic specification in the description of the search topic and returns documents which satisfy this geographic information need. For GeoCLEF 2005, twenty-five search topics were defined for searching against the English and German ad-hoc document collections of CLEF. Topic languages were English, German, Portuguese and Spanish. Eleven groups submitted runs and about 25,000 documents (half English and half German) in the pooled runs were judged by the organizers. The groups used a variety of approaches, including geographic bounding boxes and external knowledge bases (geographic thesauri and ontologies and gazetteers). The results were encouraging but showed that additional work needs to be done to refine the task for GeoCLEF in 2006.

1 Introduction

GeoCLEF is a new track for CLEF 2005. GeoCLEF was run as a pilot track to evaluate retrieval of multilingual documents with an emphasis on geographic search. Existing evaluation campaigns such as TREC and CLEF do not explicitly evaluate geographical relevance. The aim of GeoCLEF is to provide the necessary framework in which to evaluate GIR systems for search tasks involving both spatial and multilingual aspects. Participants were offered a TREC style ad hoc retrieval task based on existing CLEF collections. GeoCLEF was a collaborative effort by research groups at the University of California, Berkeley and the University of Sheffield. Twelve research groups from a variety of backgrounds and nationalities submitted 117 runs to GeoCLEF.

Geographical Information Retrieval (GIR) concerns the retrieval of information involving some kind of spatial awareness. Given that many documents contain some kind of spatial reference, there are examples where geographical references

C. Peters et al. (Eds.): CLEF 2005, LNCS 4022, pp. 908–919, 2006.

(geo-references) may be important for IR. For example, to retrieve, re-rank and visualize search results based on a spatial dimension (e.g. "find me news stories about riots near Dublin City"). In addition to this, many documents contain geo-references expressed in multiple languages which may or may not be the same as the query language. This would require an additional translation step to enable successful retrieval.

For this pilot track 2 languages, German and English, were chosen to be the document languages, while topics were developed in English with topic translations provided for German, Portuguese and Spanish. There were two Geographic Information Retrieval tasks: monolingual (English to English or German to German) and bilingual (language X to English or language X to German, where X was one of English, German, Portuguese or Spanish).

2 Document Collections Used in GeoCLEF

The document collections for this year's GeoCLEF experiments are all newswire stories from the years 1994 and 1995 used in previous CLEF competitions. Both the English and German collections contain stories covering international and national news events, therefore representing a wide variety of geographical regions and places. The English document collection consists of 169,477 documents and was composed of stories from the British newspaper The Glasgow Herald (1995) and the American newspaper The Los Angeles Times (1994). The German document collection consists of 294,809 documents from the German news magazine Der Spiegel (1994/95), the German newspaper Frankfurter Rundschau (1994) and the Swiss news agency SDA (1994/95). Although there are more documents in the German collection, the average document length (in terms of words in the actual text) is much larger for the English collection. In both collections, the documents have a common structure: newspaper-specific information like date, page, issue, special filing numbers and usually one or more titles, a byline and the actual text. The document collections were not geographically tagged or contained any other location-specific information.

3 Generating Search Topics

A total of 25 topics were generated for this year's GeoCLEF. Ten of them were extended from the past CLEF topics and 15 of them were newly created. This section will discuss the processes taken to create the spatially-aware topics for the track.

3.1 Format of Topic Description

We used the format to describe the search topics was designed to highlight the geographic aspect of the topics so that the participants can exploit the information in the retrieval process without extracting the geographic references from the description. A sample topic was shown in Figure 1.

```
<top>
<num> GC001 </num>
<orignum> C084 </orignum>
<EN-title>Shark Attacks off Australia and California</EN-title>
<EN-desc> Documents will report any information relating to shark
attacks on humans. </EN-desc>
<EN-narr> Identify instances where a human was attacked by a
shark, including where the attack took place and the circumstances
surrounding the attack. Only documents concerning specific attacks
are relevant; unconfirmed shark attacks or suspected bites are not
relevant. </EN-narr>
<!-- NOTE: This topic has added tags for GeoCLEF -->
<EN-concept> Shark attacks </EN-concept>
<EN-spatialrelation>near</EN-spatialrelation>
<EN-location> Australia </EN-location>
<EN-location> California </EN-location>
</top>
```

Fig. 1. Topic GC001: Shark Attacks off Australia and California

As can be seen, after the standard data such as the title, description, and narrative, the information about the main concept, locations, and spatial relation which were manually extracted from the title were added to the topics. The above example has the original topic ID of CLEF since it was created based on the past topic. The process of selecting the past CLEF topics for this year's GeoCLEF will be described below.

3.2 Analysis of Past CLEF Topics

Creating a subset of topics from the past CLEF topics had several advantages for us. First of all, it would reduce the amount of effort required to create new topics. Similarly, it would save the resource required to carry out the relevance assessment of the topics. The idea was to revisit the past relevant documents with a greater weight on the geographical aspect. Finally, it was anticipated that the distribution of relevant documents across the collections would be ensured to some extent.

The process of selecting the past CLEF topics for our track was as follows. Firstly, two of the authors went through the topics of the past Ad-Hoc tracks (except Topic 1-40 due to the limited coverage of document collections) and identified those which either contained one or more geographical references in the topic description or asked a geographical question. A total of 72 topics were found from this analysis.

The next stage involved examining the distribution of relevant documents across the collections chosen for this year's track. A cross tabulation was run on the qrel files for the document collections to identify the topics that covered our collections. A total of 10 topics were then chosen based on the above analysis as well as the additional manual examination of the suitability for the track.

One of the characteristics we found from the chosen past CLEF topics was a relatively low granularity of geographical references used in the descriptions. Many referred to countries. This is not surprising given that a requirement of CLEF topics is that they are likely to retrieve relevant documents from as many of the CLEF collections as possible (which are predominately newspaper articles from different countries). Consequently, the geographic references in topics were likely to be to well-known locations, i.e. countries.

However, we felt that the topics with a finer granularity should also be devised to make the track geographically more interesting. Therefore, we decided to create the rest of topics by focusing on each of the chosen collections. 7 topics were created based on the articles of LA Times, and 8 topics were created based on Glasgow Herald. The new topics were then translated into other languages by one of the organisers and the volunteers from the participants.

3.3 Geospatial Processing of Document Collections

Geographical references found in the document collections were automatically tagged. This was done for two reasons: firstly, it was thought that highlighting the geographic references in the documents would facilitate the topic generation process; secondly, it would help assessors identify relevant documents more quickly if such references were highlighted. In the end though only some assessments were conducted using such information.

Tagging was conducted using a geo-parsing system developed in the Spatially-Aware Information Retrieval on the Internet (SPIRIT) project (http://www.geospirit.org/). The implementation of the system was built using the information extraction component from the General Architecture for Text Engineering (GATE) system (see Cunningham et al [4]) with the additional contextual rules especially designed for the geographical entities. The system used several gazetteers such as the SABE (Seamless Administrative Boundaries of Europe) dataset, the Ordnance Survey 1:50,000 Scale Gazetteer for the UK, and the Getty Thesaurus of Geographic Names (TGN). The detail of the geo-parsing system can be found in [2].

4 Participation

4.1 Participants

Twelve groups (including two from Berkeley) signed up to participate in the GeoCLEF task in 2005, the table 1 shows the group names and the sub-tasks in which they submitted runs, of whom eleven completed the task.

4.2 Approaches to Geographic Information Retrieval

The participants used a wide variety of approaches to the GeoCLEF tasks, ranging from basic IR approaches (with no attempts at spatial or geographic reasoning or indexing) to deep NLP processing to extract place and topological clues from the texts and queries. As Table 1 shows, all of the participating groups submitted runs for the Monolingual English task. The bilingual X->EN task actually represents 3 separate tasks, depending on whether the German, Spanish, or Portuguese query sets were used (and likewise for X->DE from English, Spanish or Portuguese). The University of Alicante was the only group to submit runs for all possible combinations of Monolingual and Bilingual tasks including Spanish and Portuguese to both English

Table 1. Participants in GeoCLEF 2005 by task and runs

Group Name	Mono EN	Mono DE	Bilin X→E	Bilin X→DE	Total Runs
California State University, San Marcos	2	0	2	0	4
Grupo XLDB (Universidade de Lisboa)	6	4	4	0	14
Linguateca (Portugal and Norway)†	-	-	-	-	-
Linguit GmbH. (Germany)	16	0	0	0	16
MetaCarta Inc.	2	0	0	0	2
MIRACLE (Universidad Politécnica de Madrid)	5	5	0	0	10
NICTA, University of Melbourne	4	0	0	0	4
TALP (Universitat Politècnica de Catalunya)	4	0	0	0	4
Universidad Politécnica de Valencia	2	0	0	0	2
University of Alicante	5	4	12	13	34
University of California, Berkeley (Berkeley 1)	3	3	2	2	10
University of California, Berkeley (Berkeley 2)	4	4	2	2	12
University of Hagen (FernUniversität in Hagen)	0	5	0	0	5
Total Submitted Runs	53	25	22	17	117
Number of Groups Participating in Task	11	6	5	3	12

(†Note that Linguateca did not submit runs, but worked with the organizers to translate the GeoCLEF queries to Portuguese, which were then used by other groups).

and German. The task with the least participation was for the Bilingual X->DE task. Specific techniques used included:

- Ad-hoc techniques (blind feedback, German word decompounding)
- Question-answering modules
- Gazetteer construction (GNIS, World Gazetteer)
- Geoname Named Entity Extraction
- Term expansion using Wordnet, geographic thesauri
- Toponym resolution
- NLP – Geofiltering predicates
- Latitude-longitude assignment
- Gazetteer-based query expansion

4.2.1 Geofiltering Predicates

One of the most interesting techniques was developed by J Leidner of Linguit GMBH who defined three geofiltering predicates (from most restrictive to least restrictive):

1. ALL-INSIDE which filters out any document which mentions a geographic entity lying outside a query polygon
2. MOST-INSIDE which discards documents that mention more locations outside a query polygon than locations inside
3. ANY-INSIDE which discards only documents which mention no location within the query polygon

5 Relevance Assessment

Assessment was shared by Berkeley and Sheffield Universities. Sheffield was assigned topics 18-25 for the English collections (LA Times, Glasgow Herald);

Berkeley assessed topics 1-17 for English and topics 1-25 for the German collections. Assessment resources were restricted for both groups, which influenced the manner in which assessments were conducted.

Berkeley used the conventional approach of judging documents taken from the pool formed by the top-*n* documents from participants' submissions. In TREC the tradition is to set *n* to 100. However, due to a limited number of assessors, Berkeley set *n* to 60, consistent with the ad-hoc CLEF cutoff. English judgments were conducted by Berkeley authors of this paper, and half of the German judgments were conducted by an external assessor paid €1000 (from CLEF funds). Although restricting the number of documents assessed by so much appears to be a somewhat drastic measure, it was observed at last year's TRECVID that reducing pool depth to as little as 10 had little effect on the relative ordering of runs submitted to that evaluation exercise (see report by Kraaij, Smeaton, Over and Arlandis [5]). More recently Sanderson and Zobel [6] conducted a large study of the levels of error in effectiveness measures based on shallow pools and again showed that error levels were little different from those based on much deeper pools.

Sheffield was able to secure some funding to pay students to conduct relevance assessments, but the money had to be spent before geoCLEF participants were due to submit their results. Assessments had to be conducted before the submission date; therefore, Sheffield used the Interactive Searching and Judging (ISJ) method described by Cormack, Palmer and Clarke [3] and broadly tested by Sanderson and Joho [8]. With this approach to building a set of relevance judgments, assessors for a topic become searchers, who were encouraged to search the topic in as broad and diverse a way as possible, marking any relevant documents found. To this end, an ISJ system was previously built for the SPIRIT project was modified for GeoCLEF.

Sheffield employed 17 searchers (mostly University students), paying each of them (£40) for a half-day session; one searcher worked for three sessions. In each session, two topics were covered. Before starting, searchers were given a short introduction to the system. The authors of the paper also contributed to the assessing process. As so many searchers were found, Sheffield moved beyond the eight topics assigned to it and contributed judgments to the rest of the English topics, overlapping with Berkeley's judgments. For the judgments used in the GeoCLEF exercise, if two documents were found to judged by both Sheffield and Berkeley, Berkeley's judgment was used. The reason for producing such an overlap is the plan to compare judgment quality between the ISJ process and the more conventional pooling approach, which will be forthcoming.

5.1 Relevant Document Overlap

One measure of the completeness of relevant documents found (Recall) is to see what fraction of unique relevant documents were found by the participating groups. Unless there is significant overlap in relevant documents found, we can assume that a substantial number of the total number of relevant documents were not present within the pooled results. For English retrieval, some 41% of relevant document were uniquely found by a participating group.

For German GeoCLEF retrieval, however, fully 54% of relevant documents were found uniquely by the five participating groups, making it almost certain that additional assessment would find additional documents.

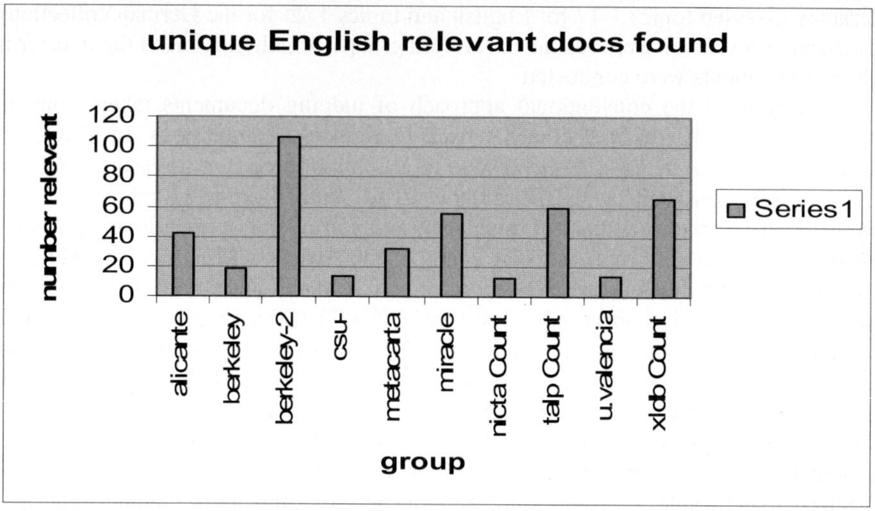

Fig. 2. 418 unique relevant English docs out of 1028 total English relevant (40.7%)

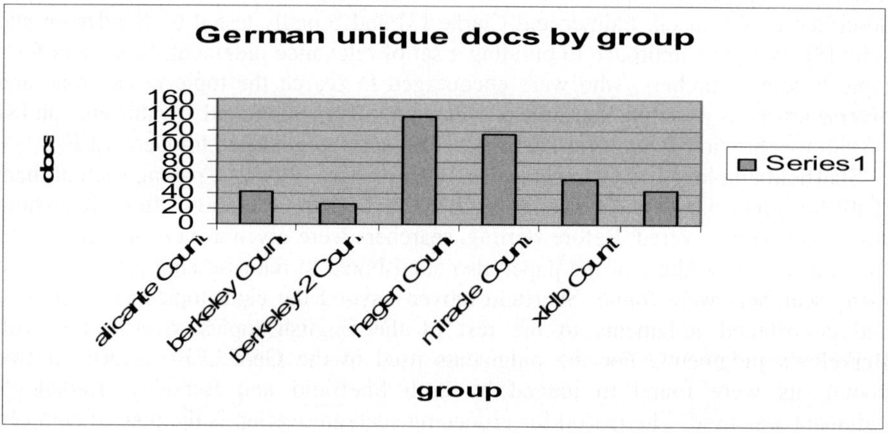

Fig. 3. 427 unique relevant German docs out of 785 total German relevant (54.4%)

This also is an explanation as to why German performance was worse than English performance, as will be described in more detail below.

6 GeoCLEF Performance

6.1 Monolingual Performance

Since the largest number of runs (57) were submitted for monolingual English, it is not surprising that that evaluation is represented by the largest number of groups (11). Monolingual German was carried out by 6 groups submitting 25 runs. The following is a ranked list of performance and results by overall mean average precision using the

TREC_Eval software, displaying best English against best German. We choose only the single best run from each participating group (independent of method used to produce the best run):

Table 2. Best Monolingual Runs by Language

Best monolingual-English-run	MAP	Best monolingual-German-run	MAP
berkeley-2_BKGeoE1	0.3936	berkeley-2_BKGeoD3	0.2042
csu-sanmarcos_csusm1	0.3613	alicante_irua-de-titledescgeotags	0.1227
alicante_irua-en-ner	0.3495	miracle_GCdeNOR	0.1163
berkeley_BERK1MLENLOC03	0.2924	xldb_XLDBDEManTDGKBm3	0.1123
miracle_GCenNOR	0.2653	hagen_FUHo14td	0.1053
nicta_i2d2Run1	0.2514	berkeley_BERK1MLDELOC02	0.0535
linguit_LTITLE	0.2362		
xldb_XLDBENManTDL	0.2253		
talp_geotalpIR4	0.2231		
metacarta_run0	0.1496		
u.valencia_dsic_gc052	0.1464		

One immediately apparent observation is that German performance is substantially below that of English performance. This derives from two sources: Many of the topics were "English" news story-oriented and had few, if any, relevant documents in the German language. Four topics (1, 20, 22, and 25) had no relevant German documents. Topics 18 and 23 had 1 and 2 relevant documents, respectively. By contrast, no English version of the topic had less than 3 relevant documents. The German task seems to have been inherently more difficult, with fewer geographic resources available in the German language to work with.

6.2 Performance Comparison on Mandatory Tasks

A fairer comparison (one usually used in CLEF, TREC and NTCIR) is to compare system performance on identical tasks. The two runs expected from each participating

Table 3. Best Monolingual English Runs for Title-Description Mandatory Task

Recall	CSUSM	Berkeley2	Alicante	Berkeley	NICTA
0.0	0.7634	0.7899	0.7889	0.6976	0.6680
0.1	0.6514	0.6545	0.6341	0.5222	0.5628
0.2	0.5348	0.5185	0.4972	0.4321	0.4209
0.3	0.4883	0.4584	0.4315	0.3884	0.3456
0.4	0.4549	0.3884	0.3776	0.3435	0.2747
0.5	0.3669	0.3562	0.3258	0.2783	0.2217
0.6	0.3039	0.2967	0.2728	0.2221	0.1715
0.7	0.2439	0.2563	0.2072	0.1877	0.1338
0.8	0.1834	0.1963	0.1591	0.1168	0.0908
0.9	0.1040	0.1169	0.0701	0.0525	0.0624
1.0	0.0484	0.0603	0.0314	0.0194	0.0272
MAP	0.3613	0.3528	0.3255*	0.2794*	0.2514*

*CSUSM run is a statistically significant improvement over this run using a paired t-test at 5% probability level.

group were a Title-Description run which used only these fields and a Title-Description-Geotags run which utilized the geographic tag triples (Concept-Location-Operator-Location). The precision scores for best Title-Description runs for monolingual English are as shown in Table 3.

The next mandatory run was to also include (in addition to Title and Description) the contents of the Geographic tags in the topic description. The next table provides performance comparison for the best 5 runs with TD+GeoTags:

Table 4. Best Monolingual Engish Performance for Mandatory Runs Title-Description+GeoTags

Recall	Berkeley2	Alicante	CSUSM	Berkeley	Miracle
0.0	0.8049	0.7856	0.7017	0.6981	0.5792
0.1	0.7144	0.6594	0.5822	0.5627	0.4932
0.2	0.5971	0.5318	0.4612	0.4804	0.4266
0.3	0.5256	0.4675	0.4204	0.4149	0.3516
0.4	0.4534	0.4138	0.3803	0.3460	0.3184
0.5	0.3868	0.3580	0.2937	0.2960	0.2815
0.6	0.3464	0.2924	0.2293	0.2257	0.2231
0.7	0.2913	0.2342	0.1974	0.1869	0.1889
0.8	0.2301	0.1779	0.1451	0.1198	0.1450
0.9	0.1318	0.0823	0.1084	0.0534	0.0928
1.0	0.0647	0.0317	0.0281	0.0243	0.0344
MAP	0.3937	0.3471	0.3032*	0.2924*	0.2653*

*Berkeley2 run is a statistically significant improvement over this run using a paired t-test 1% probability level.

6.3 Bilingual Performance

Fewer groups accepted the challenge of bilingual retrieval. There were a total of 22 bilingual X to English runs submitted by 5 groups and 17 bilingual X to German runs submitted by 3 groups. The table below shows the performance of bilingual best runs by each group for both English and German, independent of method used to produce the run.

Table 5. Best Bilingual Performance

Best bilingual-X→English-run	MAP	Best bilingual-X→German-run	MAP
berkeley-2_BKGeoDE2	0.3715	berkeley-2_BKGeoED2	0.1788
csu-sanmarcos_csusm3	0.3560	alicante_irua-ende-syn	0.1752
alicante_irua-deen-ner	0.3178	berkeley_BERK1BLENDENOL01	0.0777
berkeley_BERK1BLDEENLOC01	0.2753		

Bilingual performance for the mandated retrieval tasks of Title/Description are found in the following figures. The graphs clearly show that bilingual to German was substantially worse than bilingual to English.

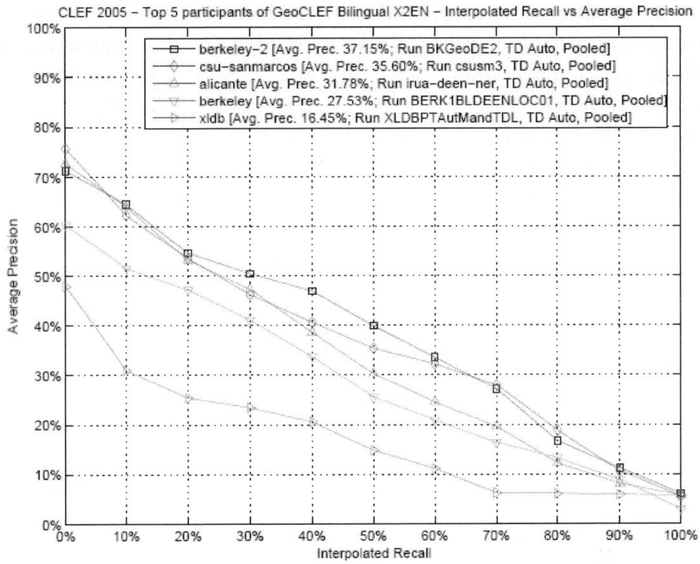

Fig. 4. Best Bilingual X→EN runs for mandatory Title-Description runs

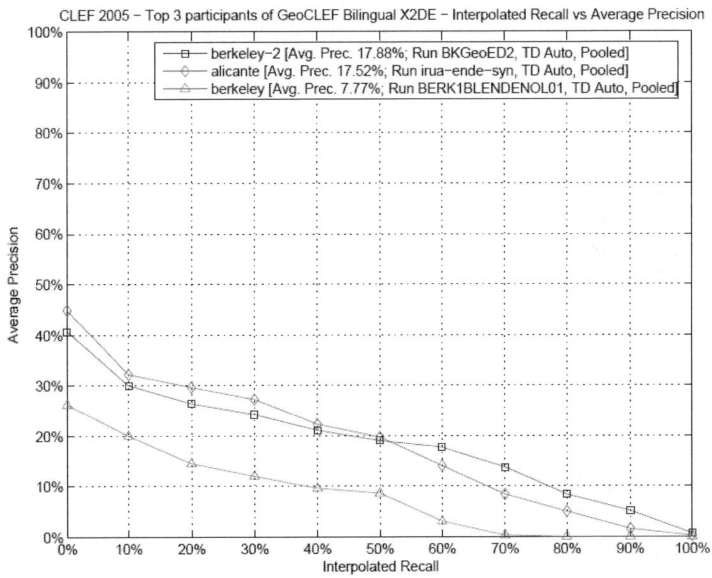

Fig. 5. Best bilingual X→DE runs for mandatory Title-Description runs

7 Conclusions and Future Work

While the results of the GeoCLEF 2005 pilot track were encouraging, both in terms of number of groups/runs participating, but also in terms of interest, there is some question as to whether we have truly identified what constitutes the proper evaluation of geographic information retrieval. One participant has remarked that "The geographic scope of most queries had the granularity of Continents or groups of countries. It should include queries with domain of interest restricted to much smaller areas, at least to the level of cities with 50,000 people."

In addition, the best performance was achieved by groups using standard keyword search techniques. If we believe that *GIR ≠ Keyword Search*, then we must find a path which distinguishes between the two. GeoCLEF will continue in 2006 with additional document languages (Portuguese and Spanish) as well as the scope of the task (i.e. consider more difficult topics such as "find stories about places within 125 kilometers of [Vienna, Viena, Wien]").

Directions which are being taken for GeoCLEF 2006 are:

1. *Additional document Portuguese and Spanish languages.*
2. *Special collections:* Currently the tasks are monolingual and bilingual against the news collections used in the CLEF ad-hoc tasks. For GeoCLEF 2006 a special task of geographic information retrieval topics against an image collection with multilingual text annotations will be done in cooperation with the ImageCLEF organizers.
3. *Task difficulty:* Should we increase the challenge of GeoCLEF 2006? One possible direction to increase task difficulty is to include geospatial distance or locale in the topic, i.e. "find stories about places within 125 kilometers of Vienna" or "Find stories about wine-making along the Mosel River" or "what rivers pass through Koblenz Germany?".Should the task become more of a named entity extraction task (see the next point on evaluation)?
4. *Evaluation:* Do we stick with the relative looseness of ranking documents according to subject and geographic reference? Or should we make the task more of an entity extraction task, like the shared task of the Conference on Computational Natural Language Learning 2002/2003 (CoNLL) found at http://www.cnts.ua.ac.be/conll2003/ner/ . This task had a definite geographic component. In this instance we might have the evaluation be to extract a list of unique geographic names and the recall/precision measures are on the completeness of the list (how many relevant found) and how many are found at rank x (precision) as well as the F measure. Clough and Sanderson have proposed a MUC style evaluation for GIR [1].

Acknowledgments

All effort done by the GeoCLEF organizers both in Sheffield and Berkeley was volunteer labo(u)r. The English assessment was evenly divided with University of California taking half and the Sheffield group taking the other half. Vivien Petras did half the German assessments. At the last minute funding was found part of the German assessment, which might not have been completed otherwise. Similarly groups volunteered the topic translations into Portuguese (thanks to Diana Santos and Paulo Rocha of Linguateca) and Spanish (thanks Andres Montoyo of U. Alicante). In addition a tremendous amount of work was done by the Padua group (thanks Giorgio

Di Nunzio and Nicola Ferro) – we owe them a great debt. Funding to help pay for assessor effort and travel came from the EU projects, SPIRIT and BRICKS. The future direction and scope of GeoCLEF will be heavily influenced by funding and the amount of volunteer effort available.

References

1. Clough, P.D., Sanderson, M. (2004). A Proposal for Comparative Evaluation of Automatic Annotation for Geo-referenced Documents. *In Proceedings of Workshop on Geographic Information Retrieval, SIGIR, 2004.*
2. Clough, P.D. (2005). Extracting Metadata for Spatially-Aware Information Retrieval on the Internet. In *Proceedings of GIR'05 Workshop at CIKM2005*, Nov 4, Bremen, Germany, online.
3. Cormack, G.V., Palmer, C.R. and Clarke, C.L.A. (1998). Efficient Construction of Large Test Collections. In Proceedings of the 21st Annual International ACM SIGIR Conference on Research and Development in Information Retrieval, 282-289.
4. Cunningham, H., Maynard, D., Bontcheva, K., and Tablan, V. (2002). GATE: A Framework and Graphical Development Environment for Robust NLP Tools and Applications. In *Proceedings of ACL'02*. Philadelphia.
5. Kraaij, W., Smeaton, A.F., Over, P., Arlandis, J. (2004). TRECVID 2004 - An Overview. In *TREC Video Retrieval Evaluation Online Proceedings*, http://www-nlpir.nist.gov/projects/tvpubs/tv.pubs.org.html.
6. Sanderson, M. and Joho, H. (2004). Forming Test Collections with No System Pooling. In Järvelin, K., Allan, J., Bruza, P., and Sanderson, M. (eds), *Proceedings of the 27th Annual International ACM SIGIR Conference on Research and Development in Information Retrieval*, 33-40, Sheffield, UK.
7. Sanderson, M and Zobel, J. (2005). Information Retrieval System Evaluation: Effort, Sensitivity, and Reliability. In *Proceedings of the 28th ACM SIGIR conference,* 162-169, Brazil.

MIRACLE at GeoCLEF 2005: First Experiments in Geographical IR

Sara Lana-Serrano[1], José M. Goñi-Menoyo[1], and José C. González-Cristóbal[1,2]

[1] Universidad Politécnica de Madrid
[2] DAEDALUS - Data, Decisions and Language, S.A.
slana@diatel.upm.es, josemiguel.goni@upm.es,
jgonzalez@dit.upm.es

Abstract. This paper presents the 2005 MIRACLE team's approach to Cross-Language Geographical Retrieval (GeoCLEF). The main goal of the GeoCLEF participation of the MIRACLE team was to test the effect that geographical information retrieval techniques have on information retrieval. The baseline approach is based on the development of named entity recognition and geospatial information retrieval tools and on its combination with linguistic techniques to carry out indexing and retrieval tasks.

1 Introduction

The main objective of the MIRACLE[1] team participation in GeoCLEF task [2] has been to make a first contact with Geographical Information Retrieval systems, focusing most of the effort on the resolution of problems related to the geospatial retrieval: creating multilingual gazetteers, geo-entities recognition, processing spatial queries, document tagging, and document and topic expansion. For information retrieval we have used the set of basic components developed for MIRACLE team [3]: stemming, transformation and filtering.

In the development of the Geographical Information Retrieval system we have used different Information Retrieval models: boolean model for geo-entities recognition, probabilistic model for textual information retrieval, and deterministic model for topic expansion.

2 Geo-entity Recognition

The general task of Named Entity Recognition (NER) involves the identification of proper names in the text and their classification as different types of named entities. The lexical resources that are typically included on a NER system are a lexicon and a grammar. The lexicon stores, using one or more lists, a set of well-known names classified according to their type. The grammar is used for disambiguating the entities that match the lexicon entries on more than one list.

---

[1] A description of the MIRACLE team can be found in this volume [2].

C. Peters et al. (Eds.): CLEF 2005, LNCS 4022, pp. 920 – 923, 2006.

The geo-entity recognition process that we have developed involves a lexicon consisting of a gazetteer list of geographical resources and several modules for linguistic processing, carrying tasks such as geo-entity identification and tagging.

For lexicon creation we have coalesced two existing gazetteers: the Geographic Names Information System (GNIS) gazetteer of the U.S. Geographic Survey [4] and the Geonet Names Server (GNS) gazetteer of the National Geospatial Intelligence Agency (NGA) [5]. When used together, they meet the main criteria for gazetteer selection we have taken into account: world-wide scope, free availability, open format, location using longitude and latitude coordinates, and homogeneity and high granularity. However, they have some unsuitable properties for our purposes that we have had to improve:

- They use the geographic area as the only criterion to relate resources. We have provided the gazetteers with a flexible structure that allows us to define other types of relationships between resources; for example based on its language (Latin America, Anglo-Saxon countries) or religion (Catholic, Protestant, Islamic,...).
- The top of the hierarchic relationships between resources is the country. It has been necessary to add new features to all the entries to store information on the continent they belong to.
- The entries are in vernacular language. We have selected the most relevant geographic resources (continents, countries, region, counties/provinces and well-known cities) and translated them into English, Spanish and German.

The gazetteer we have been finally working with has 7,323,408 entries. The Lucene [1] information retrieval engine was used for indexing and searching the gazetteers.

The developed named geo-entity identifier involves several stages: text preprocessing by filtering special symbols and punctuation marks, initial delimitation by selecting tokens with a starting uppercase letter, token expansion by searching possible named entities consisting of more than one word, and filtering tokens that do not match exactly any gazetteer entry.

For the geographical entity tagging we have chosen an annotation scheme that allows us to specify the geographical path to the entity. Each one of the elements of this path provides information of its level in the geographical hierarchy (continent, country, region…) as well as a unique identifier that distinguishes it from the rest of the geographical resources of the gazetteer.

3 Topic Expansion

The topic expansion tool developed consists of three functional blocks:

- *Geo-entity Identifier*: identifies geographic entities using the information stored in the gazetteer.
- *Spatial Relation Identifier*: identifies spatial relationships. It can identify the spatial relations defined in a configuration file. Each entry in this file defines both a spatial relationship and its related regular expressions which define patterns for several languages.

- *Expander*: tags and expands the topic in order to identify the spatial relationships and the geo-entities related to them. This block uses a relational database system to compute the points located in a geographic area whose centroid is known.

4 Description of the Experiments

The baseline approach to processing documents and topic queries is made up of the following sequence of steps:

1. *Extraction*: ad-hoc scripts are run on the files that contain particular documents or topic queries collections, to extract the textual data enclosed in XML marks.
2. *Remove accents*: all document words are normalized by eliminating accents in words. This process is done before the stemming one since the gazetteer consists of normalized entity names.
3. *Geo-entity Recognition* or *Topic Expansion*: All document collections and topics are parsed and tagged using the geo-entity recognition tool and the topic expansion tool introduced in the previous section.
4. *Stopwords filter*: all the words known as stop words are eliminated from the document.
5. *Stemming*: the process known as stemming is applied to each one of the words of the document.
6. *Lowercase words*: all document words and tags are normalized by changing all uppercase letters to lowercase.
7. *Indexing*: once all document collections have been processed, they are indexed. We have used two search engines applying them to different experiments: The indexing and retrieval system based on the *trie* data structure developed by the MIRACLE team [3], and the Apache Jakarta Lucene [1] system.
8. *Retrieval*: once all topic queries have been processed and expanded they are fed to the *trie* or Lucene engine for searching the previously built index. In our experiments we have only used OR combinations on the search terms.

This year, we have submitted only runs for monolingual tracks. In addition to the required experiment (identified with the suffix NOR in the run identifier) we have defined four additional experiments. They are differentiated mainly in the search engine used as well as in the topic processing. The experiments whose run identifier has the prefix GC have used the *trie*-based search engine whereas these ones whose run identifier has the prefix LGC have used Lucene system.

The suffix CS and NCS refer to topic processing. For topics processing we have used topic title, topic description and all the geographical tags provided. In the experiments whose run identifier ends in CS, all the topic text has fed the topic expansion process, whereas for the ones that end in NCS we have only used the text from the geographical tag for topic expansion.

Figure 1 shows the results obtained by the experiments. If we analyze the individual topic results, we can mainly derive the following: the topic expansion process in conjunction with OR based searching transforms documents that do not match the geographical criteria of topics into pertinent documents; the use of high granularity gazetters can convert from topics that are assumed precise to ambiguous topics, making the obtained results considerably worse; and finally, CS experiments provide worse results than NCS experiments since the geo-entity recognition process does not have the capability to distinguish the class of named entities.

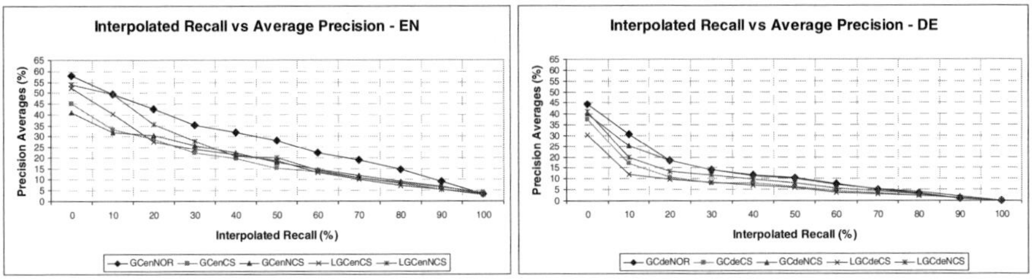

Fig. 1. Results for monolingual English (EN) and German (DE)

5 Conclusions and Future Work

The fundamentals of a geographical information system are the Named Entity Recognition System (NER) in conjunction with the Geographic Information Retrieval (GIR). At this GeoCLEF edition we have tried to attack both aspects of the problem. In order to obtain a solution that approaches better to all the aspects of the problem a great human effort is required.

Future work of the MIRACLE team in this task will be directed to several action lines:

- Improvement of the named entity recognition system adding to it part of speech tagging, classification of the entities and geo-entity disambiguation.
- Incorporation of the improvements obtained by the MIRACLE team, by means of its participation in the ad-hoc track, by using selective or averaging result combination techniques for information retrieval.

References

1. Apache Lucene project. On line http://lucene.apache.org [Visited 2005/10/10].
2. Gey, Frederic; Larson, Ray; Sanderson, Mark; Joho, Hideo; Clough, Paul; and Petras, Vivien. GeoCLEF: The CLEF 2005 Cross-Language Geographical Information Retrieval Track Overview. Proceedings of the Cross Language Evaluation Forum 2005, Springer Lecture Notes in Computer science, 2006 (in this volume).
3. Goñi-Menoyo, José M.; González, José C.; and Villena-Román, J.. MIRACLE at Ad-Hoc CLEF 2005: Merging and Combining without Using a Single Approach. Proceedings of the Cross Language Evaluation Forum 2005, Springer Lecture Notes in Computer science, 2006 (in this volume).
4. U.S. Geological Survey. On line http://www.usgs.gov [Visited 2005/10/10].
5. U.S. National Geospatial Intelligence Agency. On line http://www.nga.mil [Visited 2005/10/10].

University of Alicante at GeoCLEF 2005*

Óscar Ferrández, Zornitsa Kozareva, Antonio Toral, Elisa Noguera, Andrés Montoyo, Rafael Muñoz, and Fernando Llopis

Natural Language Processing and Information Systems Group
Department of Software and Computing Systems
University of Alicante, Spain
{ofe, zkozareva, atoral, elisa, montoyo, rafael, llopis}@dlsi.ua.es

Abstract. For our participation in GeoCLEF 2005 we have developed a system made up of three modules. One of them is an Information Retrieval module and the others are Named Entity Recognition modules based on machine learning and based on knowledge. We have carried out several runs with different combinations of these modules for resolving the proposed tasks. The system scored second position for the tasks against German collections and third position for the tasks against English collections.

1 Introduction

The aim of GeoCLEF 2005 is to retrieve relevant documents by using geographic tags [2]. Nowadays, the fast development of Geographic Information Systems (GIS) involves the need of Geographic Information Retrieval Systems (GIR) that help GIS systems to obtain documents with relevant geographic information.

Our GIR system has been designed to retrieve relevant documents that contain geographic tags. For this reason, our system includes modules for the recognition of geographic entities. We consider that using Information Retrieval (IR) and Named Entity Recognition (NER) is a promising approach to identify relevant documents about specific geographic items.

This paper is organized as follows: next section describes the whole system. Then, we describe the different runs carried out and present the results obtained. Finally, the conclusions about our participation in GeoCLEF 2005 are expounded.

2 System Description

Our system is made up of three modules which explanation follows.

* This research has been partially funded by the Spanish Government under project CICyT number TIC2003-07158-C04-01 and by the Valencia Government under project numbers GV04B-276 and GV04B-268.

C. Peters et al. (Eds.): CLEF 2005, LNCS 4022, pp. 924–927, 2006.

2.1 IR-n: Information Retrieval Module

IR-n is a passage retrieval system. These systems [3] study the appearance of query terms in contiguous fragments of documents. One of the main advantages of these systems is that they allow us to determine not only if a document is relevant or not, but also to detect the relevant parts of this document.

For every language, the resources used were provided by the CLEF organization[1]. These are stemmers and stopword lists (for English and German). Furthermore, we have used a splitter of compound nouns for German.

IR-n system allows using different similarity measures. We have applied IR-n with different measures to the tasks in which we have participated. For every collection the best similarity measure from the ones we have considered has been Okapi [5].

2.2 NERUA: Named Entity Recognition Module Based on Machine Learning

NERUA [1] is a NER system built up of three machine learning techniques: K-nearest neighbours, Maximum Entropy and Hidden Markov Models. The system consists of two phases: entity detection and entity classification. Initially, the system was developed for Spanish using the data sets of CoNLL-2002.

The features behind the method are mainly lexical, contextual, gazetteers, trigger word lists and morphological. However, the high performance of NERUA is due to the weighted voting strategy incorporated during the classification task.

Once developed, NERUA was trained for Portuguese[2] and English. For English we used the CoNLL-2004 corpus provided for semantic role labelling. From this corpus, we considered only the words and the associated Named Entity tags.

2.3 DRAMNERI: Rule-Based Named Entity Recognition Module

DRAMNERI [6] (Dictionary, Rule-based and Multilingual Named Entity Recognition Implementation) is a system that identifies and classifies named entities. It is organized as a sequential set of modules.

The main aim of this system is to be as customizable as possible. Thus, most of the actions it performs and the resources it uses are configurable.

Its modules are entity identification and entity classification. The first is based on regular expression matching; the substrings that match to a regular expression are considered generic entities. The second is applied to the entities detected in the previous step. For classifying these entities we use external evidence (trigger lists) and also internal evidence (gazetteers combined with rules).

3 Results and Discussion

In this section we present and analyse the results of our experimental runs. Our system has participated in all the Monolingual and Bilingual tasks proposed.

1 http://www.unine.ch/info/clef

2 http://poloxldb.linguateca.pt/harem.php

Table 1. GeoClef 2005 officials results for Monolingual tasks

Task	Run	Our AvgP	Position in Ranking	Best AvgP
DE	Mand2	12.27%	2nd	16.08%
EN	IRn+Nerua	34.95%	3rd	39.36%

3.1 Monolingual Tasks

There are two mandatory runs for each task, the first of them uses only the topic title and the topic description (*Mand1*) whereas the other (*Mand2*) uses both the topic title and description plus all the geographic tags. In order to carry out these runs we have applied only IR-n, which obtains the top 1000 ranked documents of the provided collections.

In addition to the mandatory runs we have developed other runs using the NER modules. The first run (*IRn+Nerua*) uses NERUA. This focuses on the recognition of locations. Even though NERUA is built up of three machine learning techniques, because of the large computing time required by these algorithms, we only have used K-nearest neighbours. In a nutshell, this run combines IR-n and NERUA, in such a way that for each passage that IR-n returns, NERUA will consider it relevant depending on the existence of a location entity.

Our second proposed run uses DRAMNERI (*IRn+Dramneri*). We have tailored its configuration to only recognise location entities. Moreover, specific gazetteers of locations, countries and so on have been added. DRAMNERI takes the relevant passages returned from IR-n and analyses them to find specific location entities, if any entity is found then the passage is considered to be relevant.

The last run we have developed (*syn*) consists of an expansion of the topics adding synonyms of the main nouns. This run has only been carried out for English topics. We have used WordNet 1.5 in order to obtain the synonyms.

The best results achieved for each monolingual task are shown in Table 1. Our results are significantly different if the retrieved documents are from the English or German collections. The reason is that the different modules of our system were developed for English and, although we adjusted these modules for German, the resources were not as good as for English.

NERUA improves the result for English, but not for German. This is due to the mentioned reason. DRAMNERI does not obtain the expected results. We consider that more extensive resources like specific gazetteers would be needed.

3.2 Bilingual Tasks

In order to deal with the bilingual task we have followed a similar strategy to the one used in [4]. This strategy consists of merging several translations. For each bilingual task, the same runs developed for monolingual tasks were carried out. Table 2 shows the scores achieved for the bilingual tasks.

The results achieved have been very similar to the results for the monolingual tasks. The problem of lack of resources for German determines this fact again.

Table 2. GeoClef 2005 officials results for Bilingual tasks

Task	Run	Our AvgP	Position in Ranking	Best AvgP
X2DE	syn	17.52%	2nd	17.88%
X2EN	IRn+Nerua	31.78%	3rd	37.15%

The best result against German is achieved by using synonyms. The reason for this is that the performance of our NER systems decreases for German whereas using synonyms in English topics provides valuable information that can be used after the translation into German. Regarding runs against English, no synonym information is available for any source language (Spanish, Portuguese and German). Besides, our NER systems obtain good results for English, and thus, it is expected that the best result is achieved by using them.

4 Conclusion

Our GIR system is made up of an IR module and two NER modules which are used to recognise location entities. Therefore, an appropriate combination of these modules could achieve a good performance for GeoCLEF tasks.

We have carried out several runs for each task by combining our modules. We achieve better results for English tasks. This is because our system was initially designed for English and thus we have better resources for this language.

The main problem we have encountered is the lack of resources. Thus, we propose as future work to look for more adequate resources for languages other than English. Besides, we plan to develop a structured knowledge resource with information about geographic items.

References

1. Ó. Ferrández, Z. Kozareva, A. Montoyo, and R. Muñoz. Nerua: sistema de detección y clasificación de entidades utilizando aprendizaje automático. In *Procesamiento del Lenguaje Natural*, volume 35, pages 37–44, 2005.
2. F. Gey, R. Larson, M. Sanderson, H. Joho, P. Clough, and V. Petras. GeoCLEF: the CLEF 2005 Cross-Language Geographic Information Retrieval Track Overview. In *Proceedings of the Cross Language Evaluation Forum 2005*. Lecture Notes in Computer Science (in this volume), 2006.
3. M. Kaskziel and J. Zobel. Passage retrieval revisited. In *Proceedings of the 20th annual International ACM Philadelphia SIGIR*, pages 178–185, 1997.
4. F. Llopis, R. Muñoz, R. M. Terol, and E. Noguera. IR-n r2 : Using normailized passages. In *Lecture Notes in Computer Science*, volume 3491, 2004.
5. J. Savoy. Fusion of probabilistic models for effective monolingual retrieval. In *4th Workshop of the Cross-Language Evaluation Forum, CLEF 2003*, Lecture notes in Computer Science, Trondheim, Norway, 2003.
6. A. Toral. DRAMNERI: a free knowledge based tool to named entity recognition. In *Proceedings of the 1st Free Software Technologies Conference*, pages 27–31. A Coruña, Spain, July 2005.

Evaluating Geographic Information Retrieval

András Kornai

MetaCarta Inc., 350 Massachusetts Avenue, Cambridge MA 02139, USA
kornai@metacarta.com
http://www.kornai.com

In Memoriam Erik Rauch

Abstract. The processing steps required for geographic information retrieval include many steps that are common to all forms of information retrieval, e.g. stopword filtering, stemming, vocabulary enrichment, understanding Booleans, and fluff removal. Only a few steps, in particular the detection of geographic entities and the assignment of bounding boxes to these, are specific to geographic IR. The paper presents the results of experiments designed to evaluate the geography-specificity of the GeoCLEF 2005 task, and suggests some methods to increase the sensitivity of the evaluation.

1 Introduction

The past 15 years have seen a great deal of controversy about the best way of evaluating Information Retrieval (IR) systems [9]. The *systematic* approach, developed in great depth at TREC [5], is based on fixed collections, repeatable tasks, and uniform figures of merit, carefully keeping human judgment to an absolute minimum. The *user-centric* approach emphasizes the dynamic nature of the collections, the widely divergent paths that knowledge workers may take toward the same IR task, and the inherent difficulties in mapping user satisfaction to standardized figures of merit. This approach advocates detail tracking of individual "use cases" as the main avenue toward agile software development [2]. While the cultural differences between the two groups are as large (and in many ways just as irreconcilable) as those between settled agriculturalists and hunter-gatherers, here we attempt the impossible and chart a middle course for the evaluation of geographic IR. Our starting point will be the MetaCarta user experience, which makes the map interface the focal point of the user's interaction with the data. Faced with a query such as the following:

> *Environmental concerns in and around the Scottish Trossachs.* A relevant document will describe environmental concerns (e.g. pollution, damage to the environment from tourism) in and around the area in Scotland known as the Trossachs. Strictly speaking, the Trossachs is the narrow wooded glen between Loch Katrine and Loch Achray, but the name is now used to describe a much larger area between Argyll and Perthshire, stretching north from the Campsies and west from Callander to the eastern shore of Loch Lomond.

C. Peters et al. (Eds.): CLEF 2005, LNCS 4022, pp. 928–938, 2006.

the user selects a map region containing the Trossachs, and types in a few key phrases such as *pollution* or *environmental damage* or perhaps *tourism damage.* As document icons appear on the map, the user can rapidly scan the excerpts, recognize document stacks that contain documents referring to the exact same location, document clusters that refer to nearby events, and see isolated documents. There is no fixed discovery procedure: once the user gets an overall sense of the spatial density of pollution events in the region, she may decide to zero in on one subregion, perhaps one on the periphery of the original region of interest, perhaps one near the center.

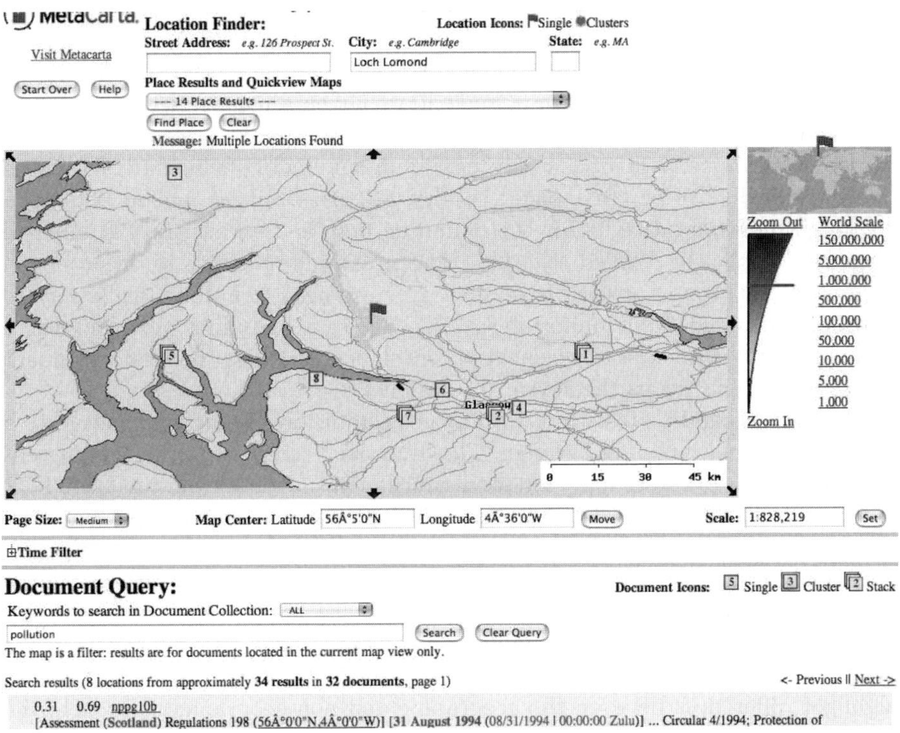

Fig. 1. The MetaCarta interface

On the face of it, there is very little that is repeatable, let alone fully automated, in the discovery process: in particular, it would take very significant natural language parsing capabilities to derive two polygons that capture the "strict" and the "broader" Trossachs as defined above. In Section 2 we describe the processing steps we used, with special emphasis on whether we consider any given step relevant for geographic IR. In Section 3 we describe our experimental results, and consider the larger issue of whether the query texts require true geographical capabilities or are answerable by generic keyword search systems as well. In the concluding Section 4 we offer some suggestions how to make the evaluation task more specific to geographic IR.

2 Systematizing User-Centric Geographic IR

A single iteration of the MetaCarta geographic IR process consists of the user selecting a region (possibly the whole world) and a set of keywords (possibly empty), and viewing the results page. On this page, document icons are returned both on the map and the textual sections, the latter being similar to the results page of most major search engines. How the user proceeds to the next iteration seems very hard to model, especially as different users react to the same display with different strategies. *Geographic query refinement* is a subject of great intrinsic interest, and we will discuss some potential evaluation methods in Section 4, but here we confine ourselves to a single loop. Given a fixed collection of documents, such as the English dataset provided for GeoCLEF, a MetaCarta query has three parameters: `maxdocs` is the maximum number of document IDs we wish to see, typically 10 for "first page" results, `bbleft bbright bbtop bbbottom` are longitudes and latitudes for the bounding box, and an arbitrary number of keywords, implicitly ANDed together. To approximate a single iteration of the geographic IR process at least to some degree, we need to automatically set the `maxdocs` threshold (kept uniformly at 10), derive a bounding box, and select some keywords. Our first experiment was designed to assess the relative impact of the geographic versus the keyword component.

The queries can be submitted, with no geographic processing whatsoever, to a regular (non-geographic) IR system. This was the strategy that the winning entry, the Cheshire II system [8], followed. Since it was evident from the GeoCLEF topic set that the keyword component will have overwhelming impact, we decided that this factor is best controlled by standardizing on a less sophisticated, but widely available (open source) background IR algorithm: we chose Lucene [6]. Further, we decided to standardize to a base level several preprocessing steps known to have significant impact on the outcome of IR evaluations. Since the goal was not to improve performance on the GeoCLEF task but rather to highlight differences between the geographic and non-geographic approach, the sophistication of these preprocessing steps was kept to an absolute minimum.

Defluffing. We manually removed meta-guidance such as *find information about* or *relevant documents will describe* since the relevant documents will not have the words *relevant* or *document* in them. We call this step "defluffing" and perform it using a simple sed script that deletes the words *describing describe Provide provide articles article that discuss particular especially document relevant documents will describe Find Documents stories concerning give_detail statistics about report _any information items relating_to related_to especially _a _ing _s* by global search and replace. Note this step does *not* presume stemming or lowercasing, since we want to defluff irrespective of how we standardize these.

Stopword removal. We defined stopwords as those words that had more than 1% of the frequency of the word *the* in a terabyte corpus we used for frequency analysis. This amounts to filtering out *0 1 A All For In S The This U What a about after all also and any are as at be because between but by can could e first for from has have if in including information is it its more much must name new not now of off on one or order other part people right should such take that the these they this time to two used was were where which will*, a total of 75 words.

Geographic defluffing. We removed geographic metawords in a manner similar to defluffing: when the task description asks for countries involved in the fur trade the word *country* will not be in the docs. These words are *countries country regions region locations location Locations Location cities city*.

Stemming and lowercasing. We performed neither stemming nor lowercasing, because the interaction of these operations with large sets of toponyms leads to many ambiguities not present in the original data. However, the possibility of using a standard (e.g. Porter) stemmer in conjunction with a large list of stemming exceptions (gazetteer entries) is worth keeping in mind. We are less sanguine about lowercasing, since the case distinction is a strong feature on proper names, and entity extraction without case information is noticeably harder.

Query expansion. Vocabulary enrichment, in particular the local techniques pioneered by [1] are now an essential part of IR. The geographic field also offers a particularly attractive way of expanding queries globally, since the hierarchical structure of geography, whereby *Oslo* is subordinated to *Norway* which is subordinated to *Scandinavia* which is subordinated to *Northern Europe* which is subordinated to *Europe*, is fixed once and for all. Here we performed neither local nor global query expansion, but we return to the matter in Section 4.

Query parsing. While our overall strategy was to bring everything down to the lowest common denominator, and we performed no overall query parsing, we made a specific exception for Booleans, since these were often emphasized in the query text. For simplicity, we treated a query such as *Shark Attacks near Australia California* as two queries, *Shark Attacks near Australia* and *Shark Attacks near California* and merged the result sets.

After the steps described above, the topics (only `title` and `desc` fields kept) looks as in Table 1 (autodetected geographic entities are shown in **boldface**).

Note how well the results of stopword removal from the `desc` section approximate the `title` section: aside from the last three topics, (where the `desc` section is really narrative) the two are practically identical. The stopword filtering step was included above very much with this goal in mind – in general, a good IDF weighting scheme will actually obviate the need for stopword filtering, but here we want to make sure that effects are not due to sophisticated integration of the different sections. This is not to say that such integration is worthless: to the contrary, its value is clearly proven by the Cheshire II experiments. However, we wished to take the narrative section out of consideration entirely, because

Table 1. Preprocessed Queries

001 Shark Attacks **Australia California** shark attacks humans
002 Vegetable Exporters **Europe** exporters fresh dried frozen vegetables
003 AI **Latin America** Amnesty International human rights **Latin America**
004 Actions against fur industry **Europe USA** protests violent acts against fur industry
005 Japanese Rice Imports reasons consequences first imported rice **Japan**
006 Oil Accidents Birds **Europe** damage injury birds caused accidental oil spills pollution
007 Trade Unions **Europe** differences role importance trade unions European
008 Milk Consumption **Europe** milk consumption European
009 Child Labor **Asia** child labor **Asia** proposals eliminate improve working conditions children
010 Flooding **Holland Germany** flood disasters **Holland Germany** 1995
011 Roman **UK Germany** Roman **UK Germany**
012 Cathedrals **Europe** particular cathedrals **Europe United Kingdom Russia**
013 Visits American president **Germany** visits President Clinton **Germany**
014 Environmentally hazardous Incidents **North Sea** environmental accidents hazards **North Sea**
015 Consequences genocide **Rwanda** genocide **Rwanda** impacts
016 Oil prospecting ecological problems **Siberia** and **Caspian Sea** Oil petroleum development related ecological problems **Siberia Caspian Sea**
017 American Troops **Sarajevo Bosnia Herzegovina** American troop deployment **Bosnia Herzegovina Sarajevo**
018 Walking holidays **Scotland** walking holidays **Scotland**
019 Golf tournaments **Europe** golf tournaments held European
020 Wind power Scottish Islands electrical power generation using wind power islands **Scotland**
021 Sea rescue **North Sea** rescues **North Sea**
022 Restored buildings Southern **Scotland** restoration historic buildings southern **Scotland**
023 Murders violence South-West **Scotland** violent acts murders South West part **Scotland**
024 Factors influencing tourist industry **Scottish Highlands** tourism industry Highlands **Scotland** factors affecting
025 Environmental concerns around Scottish **Trossachs** environmental issues concerns **Trossachs Scotland**

the user-centric approach rarely, if ever, encounters queries of this sort, and we wished to make the results robust across the choice of `title` and `desc`. After these preprocessing steps, the queries are ready for submission to Lucene. Submission to the MetaCarta engine requires two further steps.

Identifying geographic references. This task is generic to all geographic IR systems, and when we ran the 25 topics through the MetaCarta tagger we found that on the 124 geographic entities we had a precision of 100% (we had no false positives) and a recall of 96.8%: we missed *Scottish Islands* (twice), *Douglas*, and *Campeltown*. This suggests two evaluation paths: on the *discard* path missed entities are treated as plain (nongeographic) text, and on the *pretend* path we pretend the system actually found these. Either way (we found no significant difference between the two), the tagger is close enough to the ideal that the impact of geography is maximized.

Deriving bounding boxes. Construed narrowly, this task may be specific to MetaCarta's query language: we use bounding boxes where others may use polygons, grids, tessellations, or other proximity schemes. Yet we do not wish to construe the task very broadly. In particular, we wish to exclude proximity schemes based on latent semantic indexing, hierarchical position in the gazetteer, or any other method that is entirely free of geographic coordinate information. MetaCarta computes bounding boxes offline (prior to having seen any query). For the experiments (including the submission) the following table was used:

Table 2. Bounding Boxes

```
Asia 25.0 179.9 6.0
Australia 112.9 159.1 -9.1 -54.7
Bosnia Herzegovina 15.7 19.6 45.2 42.5
California -124.4 -114.1 42.0 32.5
Caspian Sea 47.0 54.0 47.0 36.0
Europe -11.0 60.0 72.00 32.00
Germany 5.8 15.0 55.0 47.2
Holland 3.3 7.2 53.5 50.7
Japan 122.9 153.9 45.5 24.0
Latin America -118.0 -35.0 32.0 -55.0
North Sea -4.0 8.0 65.0 51.0
Russia 26.0 60.0 72.0 41.1
Rwanda 28.8 30.8 -1.0 -2.8
Scotland -8.0 0.0 61.0 55.0
Scottish Highlands -8.0 -2.0 59.3 56.0
* Scottish Islands -8.0 0.0 61.0 56.0
Siberia 60.0 179.9  82.0 48.0
* Trossachs -4.5 -4.25 56.5 56.0
United Kingdom -8.6 2.0 60.8 49.0
United States -125.0 -66.0 49.0 26.0
```

Items marked by ∗ did not have a bounding box in the database and reflect manual assignment, a fact that is reflected in our notion of **discard** versus **pretend** evaluation.

3 The Main Experiment

Though the point of the experiment is to compare pure keyword based IR, as exemplified by Lucene, to true geographic IR, as exemplified by MetaCarta, we did not think it appropriate to submit Lucene runs officially, and we submitted only the two pure MetaCarta runs of the five considered here. Needless to say, we used the same `trec_eval` settings to evaluate all five. In the following table, we summarize the `trec_eval` output for the five runs discussed in the text – for the definition of the various figures of merit run `trec_eval -h`.

Table 3. Comparing geographic to keyword search

Run #	**0**	**1**	**2**	**3**	**0+2**
Condition	MC geo	MC keywd	Luc bool	L w/o bool	Cmb MC+L
num_q	22	15	25	25	25
num_ret	1494	1002	820	500	1594
num_rel	895	765	1028	1028	1028
num_rel_ret	289	132	214	144	339
map	0.1700	0.1105	0.1819	0.1653	0.1959
R-prec	0.2155	0.1501	0.2328	0.2040	0.2396
bpref	0.1708	0.1148	0.1796	0.1570	0.1896
recip_rank	0.6748	0.6522	0.5453	0.5970	0.6778
ircl_prn.0.00	0.6837	0.6633	0.6064	0.6344	0.6878
ircl_prn.0.10	0.4178	0.2904	0.5096	0.4757	0.4505
ircl_prn.0.20	0.3443	0.2188	0.3748	0.3338	0.3740
ircl_prn.0.30	0.2977	0.1700	0.1622	0.1765	0.2986
ircl_prn.0.40	0.1928	0.1103	0.1161	0.1453	0.2064
ircl_prn.0.50	0.0971	0.0676	0.0976	0.1301	0.1221
ircl_prn.0.60	0.0435	0.0365	0.0687	0.0680	0.0750
ircl_prn.0.70	0.0261	0.0109	0.0687	0.0430	0.0597
ircl_prn.0.80	0.0130	0.0109	0.0663	0.0410	0.0457
ircl_prn.0.90	0.0000	0.0109	0.0513	0.0063	0.0207
ircl_prn.1.00	0.0000	0.0089	0.0394	0.0063	0.0194
P5	0.4455	0.3467	0.4240	0.4160	0.4640
P10	0.3182	0.2333	0.3680	0.3640	0.3560
P15	0.2667	0.1867	0.3627	0.3227	0.3067
P20	0.2500	0.1867	0.3300	0.2880	0.2820
P30	0.2182	0.1644	0.2360	0.1920	0.2427
P100	0.1141	0.0740	0.0856	0.0576	0.1204
P200	0.0636	0.0410	0.0428	0.0288	0.0660

For *Run 0* we only took the title words, the automatically detected regions, created a query as described above, with `maxdocs` set at 200. Since the system returns results in rank order, to create a first page one can just apply `head` to the result set. When the query implied logical OR rather than AND, we run the queries separately and sorted the results together by relevance. This way, run 0 mimicked a true geographic search where the geographic portion of the query is input through the map interface.

In *Run 1* we used MetaCarta as a pure keyword search engine, where everything, including geographic words, is treated just as a keyword (so the discard and the pretend paths coincide) and the bounding box is set to the whole world. As we expected, this is considerably worse than using geography (MAP 0.11 as opposed to 0.17 in run 0), but leaves some lingering questions.

First, experimenter bias: obviously MetaCarta has a vested interest in proving geographic IR to be better than pure keyword IR – in our eagerness to prove the point, have we perhaps dumbed down our keyword search techniques too much? Second, MetaCarta keyword search, much like Google, is designed to deal with very large document sets and short queries, and is therefore purely conjunctive: if a document does not contain all the keywords it doesn't even surface. To address both these issues, we decided to rerun the test with Lucene, an independent, disjunction-based keyword search engine.

Run 2 uses Lucene with default settings, but the additional benefit of Boolean resolution at query time: just as in Run 0, queries like *Roman cities in the UK and Germany* are broken up in advance as *Roman cities in the UK* and *Roman cities in Germany* and the result sets are merged. *Run 3* is the same, except for the benefit of this manual Boolean resolution: here the entire burden of query parsing is handled by the Lucene disjunction mechanism.

That some mechanism to handle disjunction is needed anyway for the GeoCLEF task, with its relatively small document set and relatively long queries, is evident from the fact that a purely conjunctive system such as MetaCarta did not return any results for a number of topics: obviously no shark attacks took place near both California and Australia, and no Roman city is both in Germany and England.

Run 0+2 is a simple attempt to remedy this defect, using MetaCarta results where available, and reverting to Lucene results for those queries where no MetaCarta results were returned. Remarkably, the use of geography boosts Lucene about as much as manual handling of Booleans did.

4 Conclusions

Overall, the 2005 GeoCLEF task was not one where geographic IR systems could really shine: the best results were obtained by pure keyword systems, and the top two systems, Berkeley [8] and CSU San Marcos [4], both reported neutral and even negative effects from adding geographic information. By our own estimate, in systems tuned to this task, selectively disabling the classic (keyword based) IR strategies as described in Section 1 leads to a factor of four greater loss in performance than selectively disabling the geographic component. Since this was rather predictable from reading through the topics, we felt a need to demonstrate that geography does help after all, and devised our experiment to prove this point, evident though it may be from the user-centric perspective, in the context of a systematic evaluation. From the experiment and the preprocessing leading up to it, several main components of geographic IR emerge that need to be more strongly exercised in future evaluations, we discuss these in turn.

First, the selection of geographic entities was limited, and most of them fit in what MetaCarta calls "Tier 1", a small set (2350 entries) of core place names whose approximate locations are known to everyone with a high school education. With the possible exception of the Scottish Islands (a class better defined by listing than by coherent geography) and the Trossachs (whose boundaries are clearly explained in the narrative task) a system with a small post-hoc gazetteer table could handle most of the questions: the only entries missing from the Tier 1 gazetteer are *Argyll, Ayr, Callander, Loch Achray, Loch Katrine, Loch Lomond, Perthshire, Scottish Islands* and *Trossachs*, and these do not even appear in the non-narrative sections.

Given that the problem of avoiding false positives is increasingly hard as we add more and more entities to the gazetteer, a task that encourages the use of trivial gazetteers will not serve the overall evaluation goals well. As it is, MetaCarta has an F-measure of 98.36%, which would be quite impressive, were it produced on a more realistic test set. Even within this limited set, one has the feeling (perhaps unsubstantiated, the guidelines didn't address the issue) that many of the toponyms are used metonymically. In particular, *Europe* seems to refer to the EU as a political entity rather than to the continent (see in particular topics 4 and 8).

It is not clear that a TREC-style evaluation like CLEF is the ideal forum for evaluating geographic coverage and disambiguation issues: clearly these can be measured more directly as part of a MUC-style named entity recognition task. One possible solution is to standardize on a single entity extraction tool; another is to distribute the extraction results as part of the train and test sets. Either way, it is important to realize that by taking large vocabulary issues off the table we artificially decrease the inherent difficulties of keyword techniques: with the multimillion word vocabularies typical of large gazetteers, the maintenance of good stemmers, obtaining reasonable background frequency estimates, and even correct tokenization are far bigger challenges than experience with small and medium vocabulary keyword-based IR would suggest. With large gazetteers, important multilingual issues such as phonetic spelling and exonyms crop up all the time, and it would fit the CLEF goals well to evaluate systems specifically in this regard.

Second, the issue of geographic proximity needs to be addressed in a more systematic fashion. In real life systems, a question about Hamburg may receive a relevant answer in a document that only discusses Bremen. We do not claim that the bounding box technique used by MetaCarta is ideal, and in fact we would very much like to see a task that would let us explore quantitatively the difference between alternative approaches. But it should be abundantly clear that tacking *in Rwanda* on a query does not make it truly geographic. The easy part of geography, continents and countries, is not any different from any other topic hierarchies. Continents expand to lists of countries rather trivially, but expanding Bordeaux to the list of over five thousand significant chateaux poses formidable knowledge engineering problems (and even if these are somehow surmounted, rare is the IR system that can handle a five thousand term disjunct over millions of documents gracefully).

This is not to say that the only real geographic queries are location questions like *Where was Osama bin Laden last seen?* – to the contrary, we find that even a small geographic hint as in *Bordeaux wine* or *Lexington preschool* is quite sufficient. Since such queries are in fact quite typical, parsing queries into geographic and non-geographic portions is an interesting research, and evaluation, topic. The 2005 descriptive queries offer a fascinating glimpse into problems that are viewed as important research topics such as negation *(Reports regarding canned vegetables, vegetable juices or otherwise processed vegetables are not relevant)*, or high level semantic reasoning (asking e.g. for *consequences, concerns, effects* and other highly abstract concepts generally considered beyond the ken of mainstream IR techniques). We do not deny the importance of these problems, but we question the wisdom of burdening GeoCLEF with these, especially as long as the simpler (but still very hard) query parsing questions remain unaddressed.

Finally, let us return to the question raised at the beginning of this article concerning the nature of the geographic query refinement loop. In the pure keyword search domain, the bulk of the work is spent on finding the right keywords: once these are at hand, at least in a well linked set of documents such as the web, both PageRank [3] and hub/authority counts [7] provide sufficiently good results. In the geographic IR setting, typically there is no link structure (in this respect, the current document collection is very well chosen), and the only queries answered by purely geographic returns are the location questions. But the typical question is not about location, for the user knows it perfectly well at the outset that she is interested in wines from Bordeaux or preschools in Lexington. Rather, the bulk of the work is spent on analyzing the returns with some ordinal criteria (e.g. quality, price, trustworthiness, timeliness) in mind, and a realistic evaluation task would do well to choose a set of documents where some such criteria are easily computed.

Acknowledgements

We thank Doug Cutting for Lucene. Special thanks to Bradley Thompson, Karl Wright, Rachel Dillon, and the whole MetaCarta team, very much including Erik Rauch, whose sudden death fills us all with sorrow.

References

1. Attar, R. and Fraenkel, A.S.: Local Feedback in Full-Text Retrieval Systems. Journal of the ACM vol 24/3 pp 397–417 (1997)
2. Beck, K. et al: Manifesto for Agile Software Development. `http://agilemanifesto.org` (2001)
3. Brin, S. and Page, L.: The Anatomy of a Large-Scale Hypertextual Web Search Engine. WWW7 / Computer Networks 30(1-7): 107-117 (1998)

4. Guillen, R.: CSUSM experiments in GeoCLEF2005. This volume.
5. Harman, D.: Overview of the first Text Retrieval Conference In D. Harman (ed): Proc. 1st TREC, Publ NIST Gaithersburg MD. pp 1-20 (1993)
6. Hatcher, E. and Gospodnetić, O.: Lucene in action. Manning Publications 2004
7. Kleinberg, J.: Authoritative sources in a hyperlinked environment. Journal of the ACM vol 46/5 pp 604–632 (1999)
8. Larson, R.: Chesire II at GeoCLEF. This volume.
9. Sherman, C.: Old Economy Info Retrieval Clashes with New Economy Web Upstarts at the Fifth Annual Search Engine Conference. http://www.infotoday.com/newsbreaks/nb000424-2.htm (2000)

Using the WordNet Ontology in the GeoCLEF Geographical Information Retrieval Task

Davide Buscaldi, Paolo Rosso, and Emilio Sanchis Arnal

Dpto. de Sistemas Informáticos y Computación (DSIC),
Universidad Politécnica de Valencia, Spain
{dbuscaldi, prosso, esanchis}@dsic.upv.es

Abstract. This paper describes how we managed to use the WordNet ontology for the GeoCLEF 2005 English monolingual task. Both a query expansion method, based on the expansion of geographical terms by means of WordNet synonyms and meronyms, and a method based on the expansion of index terms, which exploits WordNet synonyms and holonyms. The obtained results show that the query expansion method was not suitable for the GeoCLEF track, while WordNet could be used in a more effective way during the indexing phase.

1 Introduction

Geographical entities can appear in very different forms in text collections. The problems of using text strings in order to identify a geographical entity are well-known and are related mostly to ambiguity, synonymy and names changing over time. Moreover, since in this case we are not using spatial databases, explicit information of regions including the cited geographical entities is usually missing from texts. Ambiguity and synonymy are well-known problems in the field of Information Retrieval. The use of semantic knowledge may help to solve these problems, even if no strong experimental results are yet available in support of this hypothesis. Some results [1] show improvements by the use of semantic knowledge; others do not [2]. The most common approaches make use of standard keyword-based techniques, improved through the use of additional mechanisms such as document structure analysis and automatic query expansion.

Automatic query expansion is used to add terms to the user's query. In the field of IR, the expansion techniques based on statistically derived associations have proven useful [3], while other methods using thesauri with synonyms obtained less promising results [4]. This is due to the ambiguity of the query terms and its propagation to their synonyms. The resolution of term ambiguity (Word Sense Disambiguation) is still an open problem in Natural Language Processing. Nevertheless, in the case of geographical terms, ambiguity is not as frequent as in the general domain (even if it still represents a major problem: for instance, 16 places named "*Genoa*" can be found in various locations all over the world: one in Italy, another in Australia and the remaining ones in the United States); therefore, better results can be obtained by the use of effective query

C. Peters et al. (Eds.): CLEF 2005, LNCS 4022, pp. 939–946, 2006.

expansion techniques based on ontologies, as demonstrated by the query expansion techniques developed for the SPIRIT project [5].

In our work we used the WordNet ontology only in the geographical domain, by applying a query expansion method, based on the synonymy and meronymy relationships, to geographical terms. The method is based on a similar one we previously developed using queries from the TREC-8[1] adhoc task [6]. It is quite difficult to calculate the number of geographical entities stored in WordNet, due to the lack of an explicit annotation of the synsets, however we retrieved some figures by means the *has_instance* relationship, resulting in 654 cities, 280 towns, 184 capitals and national capitals, 196 rivers, 44 lakes, 68 mountains. As a comparison, a specialized resource like the Getty Thesaurus of Geographic Names (TGN)[2] contains 3094 entities of type "city".

2 Query Reformulation

There can be many different ways to refer to a geographical entity. This may occur particularly for foreign names, where spelling variations are frequent (e.g. *Rome* can be indicated also with its original italian name, *Roma*), acronyms (e.g. *U.K.* or *G.B.* used instead of the extended form *United Kingdom of Great Britain and Northern Ireland*), or even some popular names (for instance, *Paris* is also known as the *ville lumiére*, i.e., the city of light). Each one of these cases can be reduced to the *synonymy* problem. Moreover, sometimes the rhetoric figure of *metonymy* (i.e., the substitution of one word for another with which it is associated) is used to indicate a greater geographical entity (e.g. *Washington* for *U.S.A.*), or the indication of the including entity is omitted because it is supposed to be well-known to the readers (e.g. *Paris* and *France*).

WordNet can help in solving these problems. In fact, WordNet provides synonyms (for instance, {*U.S., U.S.A., United States of America, America, United States, US, USA* } is the synset corresponding to the "*North American republic containing 50 states*"), and meronyms (e.g. *France* has *Paris* among its meronyms), i.e., concepts associated through the "part of" relationship.

Taking into account these observations, we developed a query expansion method in order to take advantage from these relationships. First of all, the query is tagged with POS labels. After this step, the query expansion is done in accordance to the following algorithm:

1. Select from the query the next word (w) tagged as proper noun.
2. Check in WordNet if w has the {*country, state, land*} synset among its hypernyms; if not, return to 1, else add to the query all the synonyms, with the exception of stopwords and the word w, if present; then go to 3.
3. Retrieve the meronyms of w and add to the query all the words in the synset containing the word *capital* in its gloss or synset, except the word *capital* itself. If there are more words in the query, return to 1, else end.

[1] http://trec.nist.gov

[2] http://www.getty.edu/research/conducting_research/vocabularies/tgn/

For example, the query: *Shark Attacks off Australia and California* is POS-tagged as follows: NN/shark, NNS/attacks, PRP/off, NNP/Australia CC/and NNP/California. Since "Shark" and "Attacks" do not have the {*country, state, land*} synset among their hypernyms, therefore Australia is selected as the next w. The corresponding WordNet synset is {*Australia, Commonwealth of Australia*}, with the result of adding "*Commonwealth of Australia*" to the expanded query. Moreover, the following meronym contains the word "capital" in synset or gloss: "*Canberra, Australian capital, capital of Australia - (the capital of Australia; located in southeastern Australia)*", therefore *Canberra* is also included in the expanded query. The next w is *California*. In this case the WordNet synset is {*California, Golden State, CA, Calif.*}, and the words added to the query are "*Golden State*", "*CA*" and "*Calif.*". The following two meronyms contain the word "capital":

- *Los Angeles, City of the Angels - (a city in southern California; motion picture capital of the world; most populous city of California and second largest in the United States)*
- *Sacramento, capital of California - (a city in north central California 75 miles northeast of San Francisco on the Sacramento River; capital of California)*

Moreover, during the POS tagging phase, the system looks for word pairs of the kind "adjective noun" or "noun noun". The aim of this step was to imitate the search strategy that a human would attempt. Stopwords are also removed from the query during this phase. Therefore, the expanded query that is handed over to the search engine is: *"shark attacks" Australia California "Commonwealth of Australia" Canberra "Golden State" CA Calif. "Los Angeles" "City of the Angels" Sacramento.*

For this work we used the Lucene[3] search engine, an open source project freely available from Apache Jakarta. The Porter stemmer [7] was used during the indexing phase, and for this reason the expanded queries are also stemmed by Snowball[4] before being submitted to the search engine itself.

3 Expansion of Index Terms

The expansion of index terms is a method that exploits the WordNet ontology in a somehow opposite way with respect to the query expansion. It is based on *holonyms* instead of meronyms, and uses synonyms too. The indexing process is performed by means of the Lucene search engine, generating two index for each text: a *geo* index, containing all the geographical terms included in the text and also those obtained through WordNet, and a *text* index, containing the stems of text words that are not related to geographical entities. Thanks to the separation of the indices, a document containing "John Houston" will not be retrieved if

[3] http://lucene.jakarta.org

[4] http://snowball.tartarus.org/

the query contains "Houston", the city in Texas. The adopted weighting scheme is the usual *tf-idf*. The geographical terms in the text are identified by means of a Named Entity (NE) recognizer based on maximum entropy[5], and put into the *geo* index, together with all its synonyms and holonyms obtained from WordNet.

For instance, consider the following text:

"`On Sunday mornings, the covered market opposite the station in the leafy suburb of Aulnay-sous-Bois - barely half an hour's drive from central Paris - spills opulently on to the streets and boulevards.`"

The NE recognizer identifies *Paris* as a geographical entity. A search for Paris synonyms in WordNet returns {*Paris, City of Light, French capital, capital of France*}, while its holonyms are:

```
 -> France, French Republic
    -> Europe
       -> Eurasia
          -> northern hemisphere
          -> eastern hemisphere, orient.
```

Therefore, the following index terms are put into the *geo* index: {Paris, City of Light, French capital, capital of France, France, French Republic, Europe, Eurasia, northern hemisphere, eastern hemisphere, orient}. The result of the expansion of index terms is that the above text will be indexed also by words like *France*, *Europe* that were not explicitly mentioned in it.

4 Experimental Results

We submitted only the two mandatory runs, one using the topic title and description fields, and the second including the "concept" and "location" fields. For both runs only the query expansion method was used. For every query the top 1000 ranked documents have been returned by the system. We performed two runs, one with the unexpanded queries, the other one with expansion. For both runs we plotted the precision/recall graph (see Fig. 1) which displays the precision values obtained at each of the 10 standard recall levels.

The obtained results show that our system was the worst among the participants to the exercise [8]. The query expansion technique proved effective only in a few topics (particularly the topic number 16: "Oil prospecting and ecological problems in Siberia and the Caspian Sea"). The worst results were obtained for topic number 5 ("Japanese Rice Imports").

We suppose there are two main explanations for the obtained results: the first is that the keyword grouping heuristic was too simple: for instance, in topic number 5 the words are grouped as: "Japanese Rice" and "Imports", even if the topic description says: "Find documents discussing reasons for and consequences

[5] Freely available from the OpenNLP project: http://opennlp.sourceforge.net

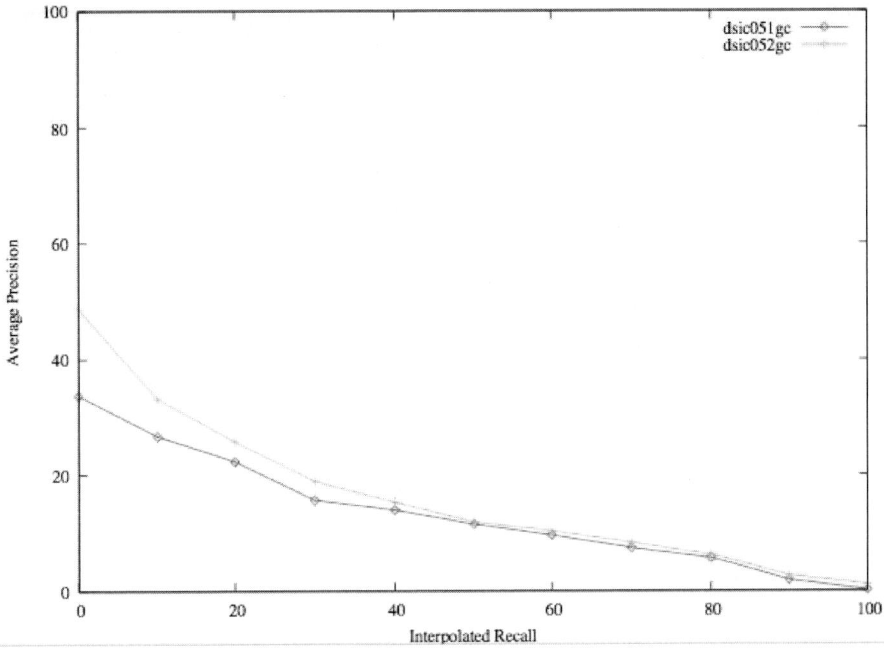

Fig. 1. Interpolated precision/recall graph for the two system runs: *dsic051gc*, using only the topic title and description fields, and *dsic052gc*, using also the "concept" and "location" fields

of the first imported rice in Japan". Therefore, in this case a better grouping should be "Japanese" and "Rice Imports".

Another reason could be that the expansion may introduce unnecessary information. For example, if the user is asking about "shark attacks in California", we have seen that *Sacramento* is added to the query. Therefore, documents containing "shark attacks" and "Sacramento" will obtain an higher rank, with the result that documents that contain "shark attacks" but not "Sacramento" are placed lower in the ranking. Since it is unlikely to observe a shark attack in Sacramento, the result is that the number of documents in the top positions will be reduced with respect to the one obtained with the unexpanded query, with the consequence of achieving a smaller precision.

In order to better understand the obtained results, we compared them with two baselines, the first obtained by submitting to the Lucene search engine the query without the synonyms and meronyms, and the latter by using only the tokenized fields from the topic. For instance, the query *"shark attacks" Australia California "Commonwealth of Australia" Canberra "Golden State" CA Calif. "Los Angeles" "City of the Angels" Sacramento* would be *"shark attacks" Australia California* for the first baseline (without WN) and *shark attacks Australia California* in the second case.

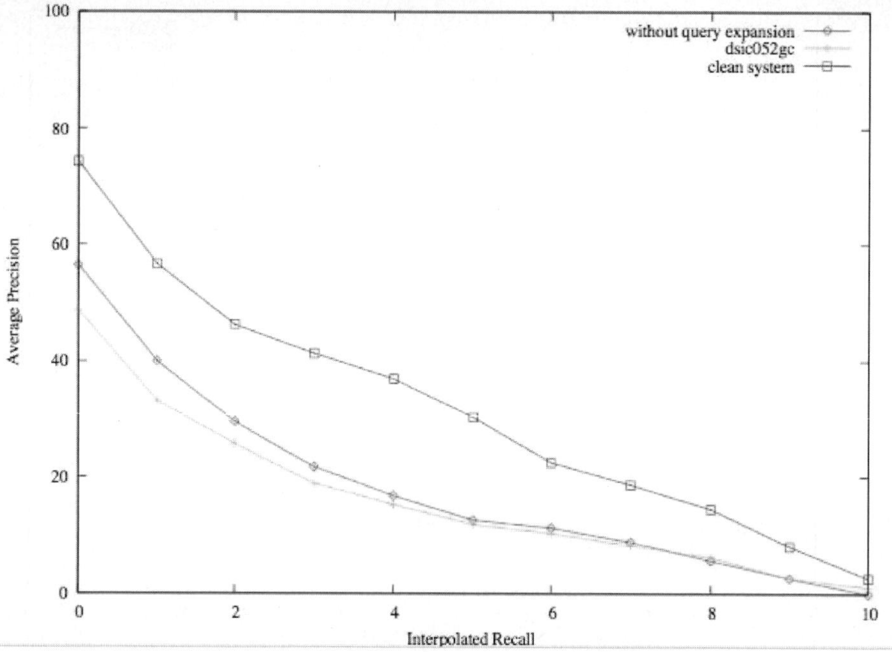

Fig. 2. Comparison of our best run (dsic052gc) with the "without query expansion" baseline and the clean system (neither query expansion nor keyword grouping)

The interpolated precision/recall graph in Fig. 2 demonstrates that both of our explanations for the obtained results are correct: in fact, the system using keyword grouping but not query expansion performs better than the system that uses both; however, this system is still worse than the one that do not use neither the query expansion nor keyword grouping.

The experiments carried out using the expansion of index terms method gave significantly better results than the query expansion, even if, due to the slowness of the indexing process (due principally to the Named Entity recognition), we were not able to send these runs for evaluation to the GeoCLEF; moreover, we were able to complete the indexing of the Glasgow Herald 1995 collection only. The topics (all-fields) were submitted to Lucene as for the simplest search strategy, but using the usual Lucene syntax for multi-field queries (e.g. all the geographical terms were labelled with "geo:"). The obtained results are displayed in Fig. 3.

We compared the results obtained with the standard search (i.e., no term was searched in the geo index). In order to make the difference between the two systems more comprehensible, the following string was submitted to Lucene for topic 1 when using the WordNet-enhanced search based on index term expansion: "text:shark text:attacks geo:california geo:australia", whereas in the case of the standard search method the submitted string was: "text:shark text:attacks text:california text:australia". It can be observed than the results obtained by means of the expansion of index terms method are considerably better than those obtained using query expansion; however, a more detailed study needs to be carried out in order to verify if the results are also better than those obtained with the standard system.

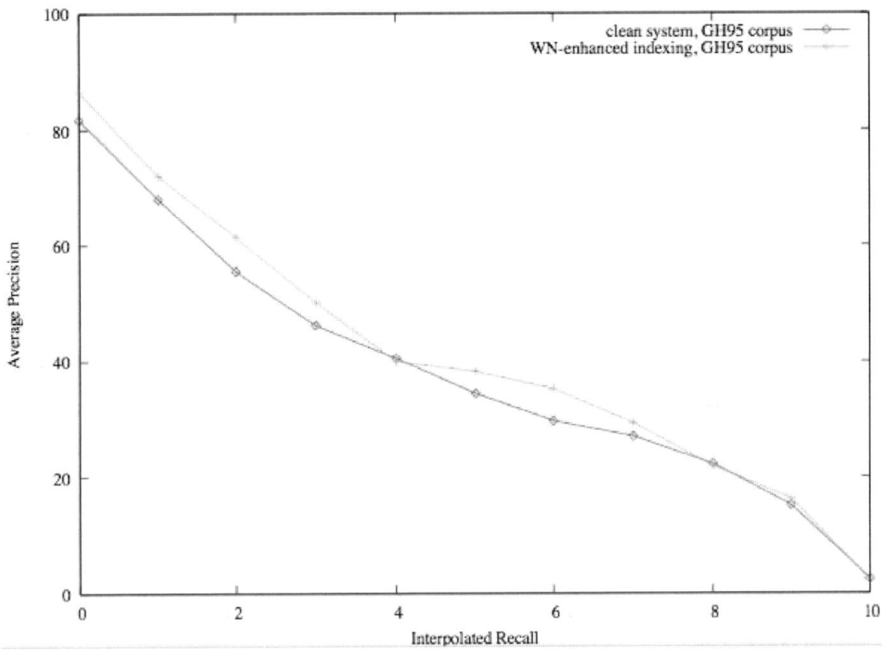

Fig. 3. Results obtained with the expansion of index terms method (*WN-enhanced indexing*), compared with the clean system baseline (indexing restricted to the Glasgow Herald 1995 collection)

5 Conclusions and Further Work

Our query expansion method was tested before only on a set of topics from the TREC-8 collection, demonstrating that a small improvement could be obtained in recall, but with a deterioration of the average precision. However, the results obtained in our participation at the GeoCLEF 2005 did not confirm the previous results. We believe that this was due to the different nature of the searches in the two exercises; more precisely, in theTREC-8 queries the geographical names usually represent political entities: "U.S.A.", "Germany", "Israel", for instance, are used to indicate the American, German or Israeli government (therefore the proposed query expansion method, which added to the query Washington, Berlin or Jerusalem, proved effective), while in GeoCLEF the geographical names just represent a location constraint for the users information needs. In such a context the use of WordNet during the indexing phase proved to be more effective, by adding the synonyms and the holonyms of the encountered geographical entities to each documents index terms. Further work will include experiments over the whole collection with the expansion of index terms method, and a comparison of WordNet with a geographically specialized resource such as the Getty Thesaurus of Geographical Names.

Acknowledgments

We would like to thank R2D2 CICYT (TIC2003-07158-C04-03) and ICT EU-India (ALA/95/23/2003/077-054) research projects for partially supporting this work. We would like to thank also the CLEF 2005 organizing committee (this work is a revised version of the paper "A WordNet-based Query Expansion method for Geographical Information Retrieval").

References

1. Bo-Yeong, K., Hae-Jung, K., Sang-Lo, L.: Performance analysis of semantic indexing in text retrieval. In: CICLing 2004, Lecture Notes in Computer Science, Vol. 2945, Mexico City, Mexico (2004)
2. Rosso, P., Ferretti, E., Jiménez, D., Vidal, V.: Text categorization and information retrieval using wordnet senses. In: CICLing 2004, Lecture Notes in Computer Science, Vol. 2945, Mexico City, Mexico (2004)
3. Xu, J., Croft, W.: Query expansion using local and global document analysis. In: Proceedings of the ACM SIGIR 1996, New York, USA (1996)
4. Voorhees, E.: Query expansion using lexical-semantic relations. In: Proceedings of the ACM SIGIR 1994. (1994)
5. Fu, G., Jones, C., Abdelmoty, A.: Ontology-based spatial query expansion in information retrieval. In: Proceedings of the ODBASE 2005 conference. (2005)
6. Calcagno, L., Buscaldi, D., Rosso, P., Gomez, J., Masulli, F., Rovetta, S.: Comparison of indexing techniques based on stems, synsets, lemmas and term frequency distribution. In: III Jornadas en Tecnología del Habla, Valencia, Spain (2004)
7. Baeza-Yates, R., Ribeiro-Neto, B.: Modern Information Retrieval. Addison-Wesley, Wokingham,UK (1999)
8. Gey, F., Larson, R., Sanderson, M., Joho, H., Clough, P.: Geoclef: the clef 2005 cross-language geographic information retrieval track. In: Working notes for the CLEF 2005 Workshop (C.Peters Ed.), Vienna, Austria (2005)

The GeoTALP-IR System at GeoCLEF 2005: Experiments Using a QA-Based IR System, Linguistic Analysis, and a Geographical Thesaurus

Daniel Ferrés, Alicia Ageno, and Horacio Rodríguez

TALP Research Center, Software Department
Universitat Politècnica de Catalunya
Jordi Girona 1-3, 08043 Barcelona, Spain
{dferres, ageno, horacio}@lsi.upc.edu
http://www.lsi.upc.edu/~nlp

Abstract. This paper describes GeoTALP-IR system, a Geographical Information Retrieval (GIR) system. The system is described and evaluated in the context of our participation in the CLEF 2005 GeoCLEF Monolingual English task.

The GIR system is based on *Lucene* and uses a modified version of the Passage Retrieval module of the TALP Question Answering (QA) system presented at CLEF 2004 and TREC 2004 QA evaluation tasks. We designed a Keyword Selection algorithm based on a Linguistic and Geographical Analysis of the topics. A Geographical Thesaurus (GT) has been built using a set of publicly available Geographical Gazetteers and a Geographical Ontology. Our experiments show that the use of a Geographical Thesaurus for Geographical Indexing and Retrieval has improved the performance of our GIR system.

1 Introduction

This paper describes GeoTALP-IR, a multilingual Geographical Information Retrieval (GIR) system. The paper focuses on our participation in the CLEF 2005 GeoCLEF Monolingual English task [6].

The GIR system is based on *Lucene*, uses a modified version of the Passage Retrieval module of the TALP Question Answering (QA) system presented at CLEF 2004 [4] and TREC 2004 [5]. We designed a Keyword Selection algorithm based on a Linguistic and Geographical Analysis of the topics. A Geographical Thesaurus (GT) has been build using a set of Geographical Gazetteers and a Geographical Ontology.

In this paper we present the overall architecture of GeoTALP-IR and describe briefly its main components. We also present an evaluation of the system used in the GeoCLEF 2005 evaluation.

C. Peters et al. (Eds.): CLEF 2005, LNCS 4022, pp. 947–955, 2006.

1.1 GeoCLEF Task Description

GeoCLEF is a cross-language geographic retrieval task at the CLEF 2005 campaign (consult [6] for more details). The goal of the task is to find as many relevant documents as possible from the document collections, using a topic set. Topics are textual descriptions with the following fields: title, description, narrative, location (e.g. geographical places like continents, regions, countries, cities, etc.) and a geographical operator (e.g. spatial relations like in, near, north of, etc.). See below an example of a topic:

```
<num> GC001 </num>
<orignum> C084 </orignum>
<EN-title> Shark Attacks off Australia and California </EN-title>
<EN-desc> Documents will report any information relating to shark
attacks on humans. </EN-desc>
<EN-narr> Identify instances where a human was attacked by a shark,
including where the attack took place and the circumstances
surrounding the attack. Only documents concerning specific attacks
are relevant; unconfirmed shark attacks or suspected bites are not
relevant. </EN-narr>
<EN-concept> Shark Attacks </EN-concept>
<EN-spatialrelation> near </EN-spatialrelation>
<EN-location> Australia </EN-location>
<EN-location> California </EN-location>
```

2 System Description

2.1 Overview

The system architecture has two phases that are performed sequentially (as shown in Figure 1): Topic Analysis (TA) and Document Retrieval (DR). A collection pre-processing process was carried out in advance.

2.2 Collection Pre-processing

We have used the *Lucene*[1] Information Retrieval (IR) engine to perform the DR task. Before GeoCLEF 2005 we indexed the entire English collections: Glasgow Herald 1995 (GH95) and Los Angeles Times 1994 (LAT94) (i.e. 169,477 documents). We pre-processed the whole collection with linguistic tools (described in the next sub-section) to mark the part-of-speech (POS) tags, lemmas and Named Entities (NE). After this process the collection is analyzed with a Geographical Thesaurus (described in the next sub-section). This information was used to build an index (see an example in Figure 2) that contains the following fields for each document:

– **Form Field:** This field stores the original text (word forms) with the Named Entities recognized.

[1] http://jakarta.apache.org/lucene

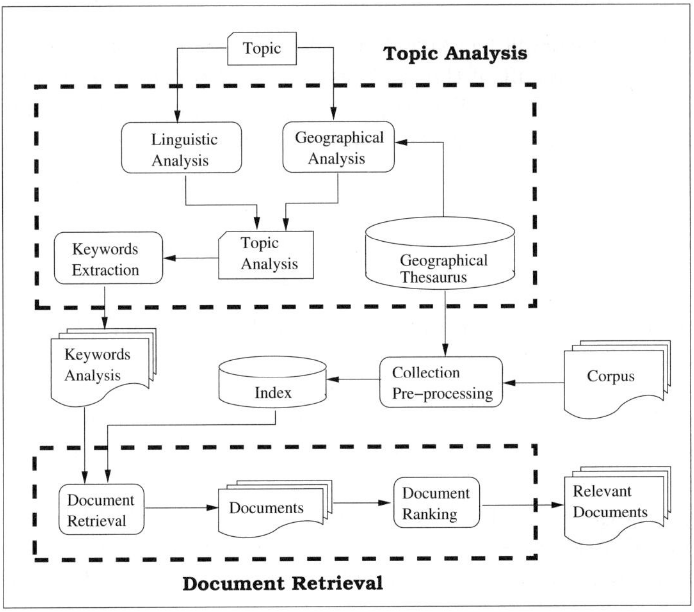

Fig. 1. Architecture of GeoTALP-IR system

Field	Indexed Content
Form	Watson flew off with his wife for a weekend in Barcelona, returned to London on Monday,
Lemma	Watson#NNP#PERSON fly#VBD off#RP with#IN his#PRP$ wife#NN for#IN a#DT weekend#NN in#IN Barcelona#NNP#LOCATION#city ,#, return#VBD to#TO London#NNP#LOCATION#capital on#IN monday#NNP ,#,
Geo	Europe#Europe#Spain#Cataluña#Barcelona#41.383_2.183 Europe#Europe#United_Kingdom#England#London#51.517_-0.105

Fig. 2. Example of an indexed document

- **Lemma Field:** This part is built using the lemmas of the words, the POS tags, and the results of the Named Entity Recognition and Classification (NERC) module and the Geographical Thesaurus.
- **Geo Field:** It contains all NEs classified as *location* or *organization* that appear in the Geographical Thesaurus. This part has the geographical information about these NE: including geographical coordinates and geographical relations with the corresponding places of its path to the top of the geographical ontology (i.e. a city like "Barcelona" contains its state, country, sub-continent and continent). If a NE is an ambiguous location, all the possible ambiguous places are stored in this field.

2.3 Topic Analysis

The goal of this phase is to extract all the relevant keywords from the topics enriching them as a result of the analysis. These keywords are then used by the Document Retrieval phase. The Topic Analysis phase has three main components: a Linguistic Analysis, a Geographical Analysis and a Keyword Selection algorithm.

Linguistic Analysis. This process extracts lexico-semantic and syntactic information using the following set of Natural Language Processing tools:

- **Morphological components**, a statistical POS tagger (*TnT*) [1] and the WordNet 2.0 [3] lemmatizer are used to obtain POS tags and lemmas. We used the *TnT* pre-defined model trained on the Wall Street Journal corpus.
- **A modified version of the Collins parser**, which performs full parsing and robust detection of verbal predicate arguments [2]. See [5] for more details.
- **A Maximum Entropy based NERC**, a Named Entity Recognizer and Classifier that identifies and classifies NEs in basic categories (person, place, organization and other). This NERC has been trained with the CONLL-2003 shared task English data set [9].
- **Gazetteers**, with the following information: location-nationality relations (e.g. Spain-Spanish) and actor-action relations (e.g. write-writer).

Geographical Analysis. The Geographical Analysis is applied to the Named Entities provided by the location tag (<EN-location>), and the Named Entities from the Title and Description tags that have been classified as *location* or *organization* by the NERC module. This analysis has two main components:

- **Geographical Thesaurus:** this component has been built joining three gazetteers that contain entries with places and their geographical class, coordinates, and other information:
  1. *GEOnet Names Server* (GNS)[2]: a gazetteer covering worldwide excluding the United States and Antarctica, with 5.3 million entries. Each gazetteer entry contains a geographical name (toponym) and its geographical coordinates (latitude, longitude), language of the geographical name and other features as country, first administrative division,....
  2. *Geographic Names Information System* (GNIS)[3], it contains information about physical and cultural geographic features in the United States and its territories. This gazetteer has 2.0 million entries, but we used a subset (39,906) of the most important geographical names.
  3. *GeoWorldMap*[4] *World Gazetteer*: a gazetteer with approximately 40,594 entries of the most important countries, regions and cities of the world.

[2] **GNS**. http://gnswww.nima.mil/geonames/GNS/index.jsp

[3] **GNIS**. http://geonames.usgs.gov/geonames/stategaz

[4] Geobytes Inc.: Geoworldmap database containing geographical information and coordinates of cities, regions and countries of the world. http://www.geobytes.com/.

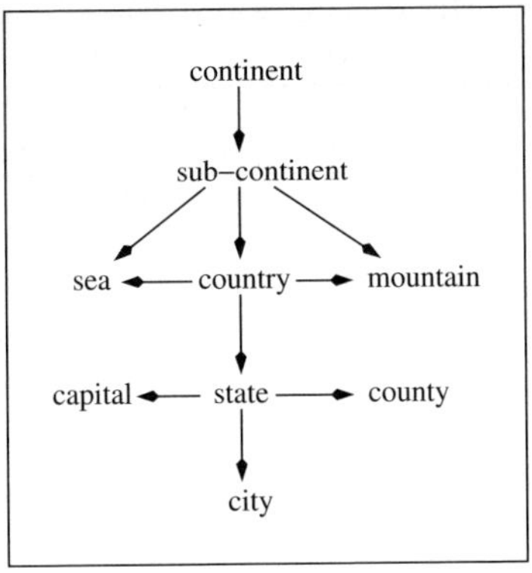

Fig. 3. Geographical ontology

Each one of these gazetteers have a different set of classes. We have mapped this sets to our set of classes (see Figure 3), which includes the most common classes and the most important ones (e.g. country is not common, but is important). The resulting thesaurus contains approximately 3.7 million places with its geographical class. This approach is similar to that used in [7], but they used a limited number of locations (only the 50,000 most important ones).

– **NEC correction filter:** a filter to correct some common errors in the *location-person* and *organization-person* ambiguity classes has been implemented. This filter stores all the NEs classified as *person* in the document; for each one of these NEs it extracts and stores in a hash table all the tokens that compose the NE. Then, for each NE of the document classified as *location* or *organization* it checks whether the NE exists in the document hash. If the NE exists then its class is changed to *person*.

Topic Keywords Selection. We designed an algorithm to extract the most relevant keywords of each topic. These keywords are then passed to the Document Retrieval phase. The algorithm is applied after the Linguistic and Geographical analysis and has the following steps:

1. Initial Filtering. First, all the punctuation symbols and stopwords are removed from the analysis of the title, description and geographical tags.
2. Title Words Extraction. All the words from the title tag are obtained.
3. Description Chunks Filtering. All the Noun Phrase base chunks from the description tag that contain a word with a lemma that appears in one or more words from the title are extracted.
4. Description Words Extraction. The words belonging to the chunks extracted in the previous step and do not have a lemma appearing in the words of the title are extracted.
5. Append Title, Description and Location Words Analysis. The words extracted from the title and description and the geographical tag are appended.

Topic	EN-title	Environmental concerns in and around the Scottish Trossachs
	EN-desc	Find articles about environmental issues and concerns in the Trossachs region of Scotland.
	EN-location	the Scottish Trossachs
Keyword Selection	Title Stopword Filtering	Environmental concerns Scottish Trossachs
	Title Extracted words	Environmental, concerns, Scottish, and Trossachs
	Description Chunks	[environmental issues] [Trossachs region]
	Description Words Extraction	issues and region
	Selected Keywords	Environmental#environmental#JJ concerns#concern#NNS issues#issue#NNS region#region#NN scottish#Scottish#NNP#misc#location("Scotland") Trossachs#trossachs#NNP

Fig. 4. Keyword Selection example

2.4 Document Retrieval

The main function of the Document Retrieval component is to extract relevant documents that are likely to contain the information needed by the user. Document retrieval is performed using the *Lucene* Information Retrieval system. *Lucene* uses the standard tf.idf weighting scheme with the cosine similarity measure, and it allows ranked and boolean queries. The document retrieval algorithm uses a data-driven query relaxation technique: if too few documents are retrieved, the query is relaxed by discarding the keywords with the lowest priority. The reverse happens when too many documents are extracted. Each keyword is assigned a priority using a series of heuristics fairly similar to [8]. For example, a proper noun is assigned a higher priority than a common noun, the adverb is assigned the lowest priority, and stop words are removed.

The main options of the Document Retrieval phase are:

- Query types:
  - Boolean: all the keywords must appear in the documents retrieved. *Lucene* allows boolean queries and returns a score for each retrieved document.
  - Ranked: *Lucene* does ranked queries with tf-idf and cosine similarity.
  - Boolean+Ranked: this mode joins documents retrieved from boolean and ranked queries, giving priority to the documents from the boolean query.
- Geographical Search Mode:
  - Lemma Field: this search mode implies that all the keywords that are Named Entities detected as *location* are searched in the "Lemma" field part of the index.

  - Geo Field: this search means that the NEs tagged as *location* and detected as keywords will be searched at the "Geo" index field.
- Geographical Search Policy:
  - Strict: this search policy can be enabled when the "Geo" Field search is running, and is used to find a *location* with exactly all this ontological path and coordinates for the following classes: country and region. In example, the form used to search "Australia" in the index is:
  Oceania#Oceania#Australia#-25.0_135.0
  - Relaxed: this search policy can also be enabled when the "Geo" field search is running. This mode searches without coordinates. The form used to search "Australia" in the index for this kind of search policy is:
  Oceania#Oceania#Australia
  In this case, the search is flexible and all the cities and regions of Australia will be returned. An example of a location found with the previous query is:
  Oceania#Oceania#Australia#Western_Australia#Perth#-31.966_115.8167

2.5 Document Ranking

This component joins the documents provided by the Document Retrieval phase. If the Query type is *boolean* or *ranked* it returns the first 1000 top documents with their *Lucene* score. In the case of a query mode *boolean+ranked*, it first gives priority to the documents retrieved from the boolean Query and holds their score. The documents provided by the ranked query are added to the list of relevant documents, but their score is then re-scaled using the score of the last boolean document retrieved (the document with lower score of the boolean retrieval). Finally, the first 1000 top documents are selected.

3 Experiments

We designed a set of four experiments that consist in applying different query strategies and tags to an automatic GIR system (see Table 1). Two baseline experiments have been performed: the runs *geotalpIR1* and *geotalpIR2*. These runs differ uniquely in the Query type used: a *boolean+ranked* retrieval in *geotalpIR1* run and only *ranked* retrieval in *geotalpIR2* run. These runs consider the Title and Description tags, and they use the "lemma" index field. The third run (*geotalpIR3*) differs from the previous ones in the use of the Location tag (considering Title, Description and Location) and uses the "Geo" field instead of the "lemma" field. The "Geo" field is used with a Strict Query search policy. This run also performs a *boolean+ranked* retrieval. The fourth run (*geotalpIR4*) is very similar to the third run (*geotalpIR3*), but uses a Relaxed Query search policy.

We can expect a considerable difference between the two first runs and the last ones, because the other ones used an index with geographical knowledge. The fourth run is expected to be better than the third, due to the use of a relaxed search policy, that can increase the recall. On the other hand, we avoided the use

Table 1. Description of the Experiments at GeoCLEF 2005

Run	Run type	Tags	Query Type	Geo. Index	Geo. Search
geotalpIR1	automatic	TD	Boolean+Ranked	Lemma	-
geotalpIR2	automatic	TD	Ranked	Lemma	-
geotalpIR3	automatic	TDL	Boolean+Ranked	Geo	Strict
geotalpIR4	automatic	TDL	Boolean+Ranked	Geo	Relaxed

of the operation tag (e.g. south, in, near,...) because our system is not prepared to deal with this information. Finally, the use of the location tag in the last runs is not so relevant, because our NERC and Geographical Thesaurus are able to detect the place names from the Title and Description tags with high performance.

4 Results

The results of the GeoTalpIR system at the GeoCLEF 2005 Monolingual English task are summarized in Table 2. This table shows the following IR measures for each run: *Average Precision*, *R-Precision*, *Recall*, and the increment over the median of the average precision (0.2063) obtained by all the systems that participated in the GeoCLEF 2005 Monolingual English task.

Table 2. GeoCLEF 2005 results

Run	Tags	AvgP.	R-Prec.	Recall (%)	Recall	Δ AvgP. Diff.(%) over GeoCLEF AvgP.
geotalpIR1	TD	0.1923	0.2249	49.51%	509/1028	-6.78%
geotalpIR2	TD	0.1933	0.2129	49.22%	506/1028	-6.30%
geotalpIR3	TDL	0.2140	0.2377	62.35%	641/1028	+3.73%
geotalpIR4	TDL	**0.2231**	**0.2508**	**66.83%**	**687/1028**	**+8.14%**

The results show a substantial difference between the two first runs and the two last ones, specially in the recall measure: 49.51% and 49.22% respectively in the first and second run (*geotalpIR1* and *geotalpIR2*) and 62.35% and 66.38% respectively in the third and fourth run (*geotalpIR3* and *geotalpIR4*). The recall is also improved by the use of Geographical Knowledge and a relaxed policy over the "Geo" Field as it is seen in run four (*geotalpIR4*). Finally, in the last run (*geotalpIR4*) we obtained results about +8.14% better than the median of the average obtained by all runs (0.2063).

5 Conclusions

This is our first attempt to participate in a IR and GIR task. Our approach is based in a QA-based IR system for Document Retrieval and a Linguistic and

Geographical Analysis of the collections and topics. The use of a Geographical Thesaurus has helped to improve the results of our GIR. As a future work, we propose the following improvements to the system: i) analyzing the topics using WordNet, ii) the use of the spatial operator and narrative tags, iii) improving the boolean IR strategy, and iv) the resolution of geographical ambiguity problems.

Acknowledgements

This work has been partially supported by the European Commission (CHIL, IST-2004-506909) and the Spanish Research Department (ALIADO, TIC2002-04447-C02). Daniel Ferrés is supported by a UPC-Recerca grant from Universitat Politècnica de Catalunya (UPC). TALP Research Center, is recognized as a Quality Research Group (2001 SGR 00254) by DURSI (the Ministry of Universities, Research and Information Society of the Catalan Government). The authors would like to express their gratitude in particular to Mihai Surdeanu.

References

1. T. Brants. TnT – a statistical part-of-speech tagger. In *Proceedings of the 6th Applied NLP Conference, ANLP-2000*, Seattle, WA, United States, 2000.
2. M. Collins. *Head-Driven Statistical Models for Natural Language Parsing.* PhD thesis, University of Pennsylvania, 1999.
3. Christiane Fellbaum, editor. *WordNet: An Electronic Lexical Database.* pub-MIT, 1998.
4. Daniel Ferrés, Samir Kanaan, Alicia Ageno, Edgar González, Horacio Rodríguez, Mihai Surdeanu, and Jordi Turmo. The TALP-QA System for Spanish at CLEF 2004: Structural and Hierarchical Relaxing of Semantic Constraints. In Carol Peters, Paul Clough, Julio Gonzalo, Gareth J. F. Jones, Michael Kluck, and Bernardo Magnini, editors, *CLEF*, volume 3491 of *Lecture Notes in Computer Science*, pages 557–568. Springer, 2004.
5. Daniel Ferrés, Samir Kanaan, Edgar González, Alicia Ageno, Horacio Rodríguez, Mihai Surdeanu, and Jordi Turmo. TALP-QA System at TREC 2004: Structural and Hierarchical Relaxation Over Semantic Constraints. In *Proceedings of the Text Retrieval Conference (TREC-2004)*, 2005.
6. Fredric Gey, Ray Larson, Mark Sanderson, Hideo Joho, Paul Clough, and Vivien Petras. GeoCLEF: the CLEF 2005 Cross-Language Geographic Information Retrieval Track Overview. In *Proceedings of the Cross Language Evaluation Forum 2005*, Lecture Notes in Computer Science. Springer, 2006 (in this volume).
7. Manov, D., Kiryakov, A., Popov, B., Bontcheva, K., Maynard, D., Cunningham, H. Experiments with geographic knowledge for information extraction. In *Proceedings of HLT-NAACL Workshop of Analysis of Geographic References*, 2003.
8. D. Moldovan, S. Harabagiu, M. Pasca, R. Mihalcea, R. Goodrum, R. Gîrju, and V. Rus. LASSO: A tool for surfing the answer net. In *Proceedings of the Eighth Text Retrieval Conference (TREC-8)*, 1999.
9. Erik F. Tjong Kim Sang and Fien De Meulder. Introduction to the CoNLL-2003 Shared Task: Language-Independent Named Entity Recognition. In Walter Daelemans and Miles Osborne, editors, *Proceedings of CoNLL-2003*, pages 142–147. Edmonton, Canada, 2003.

CSUSM Experiments in GeoCLEF2005: Monolingual and Bilingual Tasks

Rocio Guillén

Computer Science Department, California State University San Marcos, USA

Abstract. This paper presents the results of our initial experiments in the monolingual English task and the Bilingual Spanish → English task. We used the Terrier Information Retrieval Platform to run experiments for both tasks using the Inverse Document Frequency model with Laplace after-effect and normalization 2. Additional experiments were run with Indri, a retrieval engine that combines inference networks with language modelling. For the bilingual task we developed a component to first translate the topics from Spanish into English. No spatial analysis was carried out for any of the tasks. One of our goals is to have a baseline to compare further experiments with term translation of georeferences and spatial analysis. Another goal is to use ontologies for Integrated Geographic Information Systems adapted to the IR task. Our initial results show that the geographic information as provided does not improve significantly retrieval performance. We included the geographical terms appearing in all the fields. Duplication of terms might have decreased gain of information and affected the ranking.

1 Introduction

Geographic Information Retrieval (GIR) is aimed at the retrieval of geographic data based not only on conceptual keywords, but also on spatial information. Building GIR systems with such capabilities requires research on diverse areas such as information extraction of geographic terms from structured and unstructured data; word sense disambiguation, which is geographically relevant; ontology creation; combination of geographical and contextual relevance; and geographic term translation, among others.

Research efforts on GIR are addressing issues such as access to multilingual documents, techniques for information mining (i.e., extraction, exploration and visualization of geo-referenced information), investigation of spatial representations and ranking methods for different representations, application of machine learning techniques for place name recognition, development of datasets containing annotated geographic entities, among others. [4]. Other researchers are exploring the usage of the World Wide Web as the largest collection of geospatial data.

The purpose of GeoCLEF 2005 is to experiment with and evaluate the performance of GIR systems when geographic operators and geographic locations are added. Four tasks were considered, two monolingual and two bilingual. We

C. Peters et al. (Eds.): CLEF 2005, LNCS 4022, pp. 956–962, 2006.

participated in two tasks, one monolingual and one bilingual. For the monolingual task we worked with both topics and collection in English, for the bilingual task we worked with topics in Spanish and documents in English.

In this paper we describe our initial experiments in the English monolingual task and the bilingual task with topics in Spanish and documents in English. We used the Terrier Information Retrieval (IR) platform to run our initial experiments, and built an independent module for the translation of the topics from Spanish into English. We used Terrier because it has performed successfully in monolingual information retrieval tasks (CLEF2004 and TREC2004). Our goal is to have a baseline for further experiments with our component for translating georeferences from Spanish into English, and addition of spatial analysis. Another goal is to use ontologies for integrated geographic information systems and adapt/create ontologies for GIR systems. Further experiments were run after we submitted our results. We used Indri, which is a new language modeling retrieval engine.

The paper is organized as follows. In Section 2 we present our work in the English monolingual task including an overview of Terrier. Additionally we describe further work with Indri. Section 3 describes our setting and experiments in the bilingual task. Experimental results are discussed in Section 4, and we present our conclusions and future work in Section 5.

2 Monolingual Task

In this section we first give an overview of the IR platform used in the initial experiments. Next we present an overview of Indri used in later experiments after the official runs were submitted. The purpose was to compare results to verify our conclusion that the geographic information as used does not improve the effectiveness of the retrieval, but it decreased.

Terrier is a platform for the rapid development of large-scale Information Retrieval (IR) systems. It offers a variety of IR models based on the Divergence from Randomness (DFR) framework ([3],[9]). The framework includes more than 50 DFR models for term weighting. These models are derived by measuring the divergence of the actual term distribution from that obtained under a random process ([2]).

Both indexing and querying of the documents were done with Terrier. The document collections to be indexed were the LA Times (American) 1994 and the Glasgow Herald (British) 1995. There were 25 topics. Documents and topics were processed using the English stopword list (571 words) built by Salton and Buckley for the experimental SMART IR system [1], and the Porter stemmer. We worked with the InL2 term weighting model, which is the Inverse Document Frequency model with Laplace after-effect and normalization 2. Our interpretation of GeoCLEF's tasks was that they were not exactly classic ad-hoc tasks, hence we decided to use a model for early precision. Our goal was to experminet with other models, but we ran out of time.

The risk of accepting a term is inversely related to its term frequency in the document with respect to the elite set, a set in which the term occurs to a relatively greater extent than in the rest of the documents. The more the term occurs in the elite set, the less the term frequency is due to randomness. Hence the probability of the risk of a term not being informative is smaller. The Laplace model is utilized to compute the information gain with a term within a document. Term frequencies are calculated with respect to the standard document length using a formula referred to as normalization 2 shown below.

$$tfn = tf.log(1 + c\frac{sl}{dl})$$

tf is the term frequency, *sl* is the standard document length, and *dl* is the document length, c is a parameter. We used $c = 1.0$ for short queries, which is the default value, and $c = 7.0$ for long queries. Short queries in our context are those which use only the topic title and topic description; long queries are those which use the topic title, topic description, topic concept, topic spatial-relation and topic location. We used these values based on the results generated by the experiments on tuning for BM25 and DFR models done by He and Ounis [8]. They carried out experiments for TREC (Text REtrieval Conference) with three types of queries depending on the different fields included in the topics given. Queries were defined as follows: 1) short queries are those where only the title field is used, normal; 2) normal queries are those where only the description field is used; and 3) long queries are those where title, description and narrative are used.

Indri is a new language modeling retrieval engine developed at UMass [6] derived from the Lemur project. It was written to handle question answering and web retrieval tasks using large corpora. Indri can be used to build an index/repository with the application *buildindex* and run queries using the index built with the application *runquery*. Buildindex can build repositories from formatted documents, HTML documents, text documents and PDF files. It also handles HTML/XML documents. Runquery evaluates queries using one or more indexes or repositories generating the results as a ranked list of documents. We only created indexes and ran queries.

The indexing process in Indri creates the following data structures for the collection of documents (corpus).

- A compressed inverted file for the collection including term position information.
- Compressed inverted extent lists for each field indexed in the collectionn.
- A vector for each document, which includes term position information and field position information.
- A random-access compressed version of the corpus text.

The document vectors are compressed arrays of numbers, where each number corresponds to some term in the collection.

The Indri query language is based on the Inquery system [7]. It can handle simple queries as well as complex queries. It allows phrase matching, synonyms, weighted expressions, Boolean filtering, numeric fields, proximity operators. To run queries we first translated the topics into Indri query language. This process was not necessary in Terrier. An example of a query using title and description is shown in Figure 1.

```
<query>#combine(Shark Attacks off Australia and California
 Documents will report any information relating to shark
attacks on humans)</query>
```

Fig. 1. Sample query in Indri

Query extension was done in Terrier using the default mechanism, which extracts the informative terms from the top-returned documents. In Indri we used pseudorelevance feedback with the first 20 documents and 20 terms.

3 Bilingual Task

For the bilingual task we worked with Spanish topics and English documents. We built a component, independent of Terrier and Indri, to translate the topics from Spanish into English. All the information within the tags was translated except for the narrative, because we did not consider the narrative for any of the two runs that we submitted. Topics in Spanish were preprocessed by removing diacritic marks and stopwords using a list of 351 Spanish words from SMART. Diacritic marks were also removed from the stopwords list and duplicates were eliminated. Plural stemming was then applied. The last step was to perform word-by-word translation without considering word ordering and syntactic differences between Spanish and English. For instance, Topic 8 *Consumo de leche en Europa* was mapped into "consumption milk europe". However, we took into account abbreviations and different spellings. For instance, in Topic 3 the title *AI en Latinoamerica* was mapped to "amnesty international latinamerica latin-america latin america". The new set of topics thus created was then used to run two monolingual tasks in English (see section above).

4 Experimental Results

Four runs were submitted as official runs, two for the GeoCLEF2005 monolingual task, and two for the GeoCLEF2005 bilingual task. In Table 1 we report the results for the English monolingual task.

Table 1. English Monolingual Retrieval Performance

Run Id	Topic Fields	Avg Prec.	Recall Prec.
csusm1	title, description	36.13	37.61
csusm2	title, description, geographic tags	30.32	33.66

Our retrieval results for the first official run performed well above average for most of the topics, except for Topics 7 and 8. The performance of the run adding geographic tags did not improve as it was originally expected. It decreased in general. The average precision of topics 5, 6, 7, 9 and 20 was below the MAP. We have run experiments with different values for the c parameter, however the results did not vary signigicantly. Official results show that our best run MAP was 0.3613, second to the best MAP that was 0.3936. The precision score for our best Title-Description run was 0.3613, which evaluators considered a statistically significant improvement over other runs using a paired t-test at 5% probability level. The precision score for our best Title-Description-Geographic-tags run was 0.3032. For a detailed description of the task and results see [5].

Evaluation of experimental results using Indri are shown in Table 2.

Table 2. English Monolingual Retrieval Performance with Indri

Run Id	Topic Fields	Avg Prec.	Recall Prec.
indri1	title, description	26.94	28.01
indri1	title, description, geographic tags	13.62	14.37

Indri did not perform as well as Terrier. However results show that adding geographic tags did not improve performance in both systems, but decreased performance in approximately 19% for Terrier and over 50% for Indri.

4.1 Bilingual Task

The results for the two official runs submitted for the bilingual task are shown in Table 3. Our results performed well above average for 13 out of the 25 topics, and below average for 7 of the topics with only the title and the description. For the run using additional geographic tags the results performed above the median precision average for 15 topics acoording to the evaluation sent by the organizers of GeoCLEF2005.

Word-by-word translation did not perform as well in general. One of the factors may be word ordering. Another factor could be the addition of abbreviations and full names. The latter occurred because the information gain starts decreasing at some point. Further experiments and study of the search algorithm will provide us with more accurate data. One of our goals in the future is to extend the translation component to do more than word-to-word translation.

Table 3. Bilingual (Spanish → English) Retrieval Performance

Run Id	Topic Fields	Avg Prec.	Recall Prec.
csusm3	title, description	35.60	37.17
csusm4	title, description, geographic tags	31.23	33.50

We are not reporting further results because we did not run experiments with Indri for this task.

Comparison of retrieval performance between the monolingual task and the bilingual task, which was run as a monolingual task shows that the average precision using the title and description performed better in the former task. The average precision using the title, description and geographic tags was better in the bilingual task than in the monolingual task.

Performance comparison with the other participating groups provided by the evaluators [5] show that our best monolingual-English run (without Geographic tags) was the second best over all runs. For the first mandatory run (Title and Description) our results were the best with respect to recall. For the second mandatory run (Title, Description and Geographic tags) our results came third with respect to recall.

Performance comparison with the other participating groups show that our best bilingual-X-English run (without Geographic tags) was second to the overal best.

5 Conclusions and Future Work

In this paper we presented work on monolingual and bilingual geographical information retrieval. We used Terrier to run our experiments, and an independent translation component built to map Spanish topics into English topics. The results were evaluated in the GeoCLEF2005 track of CLEF2005. Later we ran experiments using Indri for the monolingual task only.

Experimental results show the following. The use of geographical information did not improve retrieval performance significantly in our work. Repetition of geographical terms seems to have affected gain of information negatively. In our very first experiments we used additional geographical information to the one provided, which resulted in very poor results. Translated geographic information performed better than using the original English tags. Further experimentation using Indri, another IR system, confirmed our conclusion that geographical information did not improve performance. We are starting to investigate the translation of spatial relations and contextual relevance to GIR and the use of ontologies.

References

1. http://ftp.cs.cornell.edu/pub/smart/.
2. Lioma, C., He, B., Plachouras, V., Ounis, I.: The University of Glasgow at CLEF2004; French monolingual information retrieval with Terrier. In Working notes of the CLEF 2004 Workshop, Bath, UK, 2004.
3. Ounis, I., Amati, G., Plachouras, V., He, B., Macdonald, C., Johnson, D.: Terrier information retrieval platform. In Proceedings of the 27th European Conference on Information Retrieval (ECIR 05), 2005. http://ir.dcs.ga.ac.uk/terrier/
4. Purves, R., Jones, C. editors : SIGIR2004: Workshop on Geographic Information Retrieval, Sheffield, UK, 2004.

5. Gey, F., Larson, R., Sanderson, M., Joho, H., Clough, P., Petras, V.: GeoCLEF: the CLEF2005 Cross-Language Geographic Information Retrieval Track Overview Proceedings of the Cross Language Evaluation Forum 2005, Springer Lecture Notes in Computer Science, 2006 (in this volume).
6. Allan, J., Callan, J., Collins-Thompson, K., Croft, B., Feng, F., Fosher, D., Lafferty, L., Larkey, L., Metzler, D., Truong, T.N., Ogilvie, P., Si, L., Strohman, T., Turtle, H., Yau, L., Zhai, C. : The Lemur toolkit for language modeling and information retrieval, 2005. http://www.cs.cmu.edu/~lemur/
7. Callan, J., Croft, B., Harding, S. : The INQUERY retrieval system. In *DEXA-92*, pp. 78-83.
8. He, B., Ounis, I. : A study of parameter tuning for the frequency normalization. Proceedings of the twelfth international conference on Information and knowledge management, New Orleans, LA, USA, 2003.
9. Amati, G., van Rijsbergen, C.J. : Probabilistic Models of Information Retrieval Based on Measuring the Divergence from Randomness. *ACM Transactions on Information Systems.* Vol. 20(4), pp:357-389.

Berkeley at GeoCLEF: Logistic Regression and Fusion for Geographic Information Retrieval

Ray R. Larson[1], Fredric C. Gey[2], and Vivien Petras[1]

[1] School of Information Management and Systems
{ray, vivienp}@sims.berkeley.edu
[2] UC Data Archive and Technical Assistance
gey@berkeley.edu
University of California, Berkeley, CA, USA

Abstract. In this paper we will describe the Berkeley (groups 1 and 2 combined) submissions and approaches to the GeoCLEF task for CLEF 2005. The two Berkeley groups used different systems and approaches for GeoCLEF with some common themes. For Berkeley group 1 (Larson) the main technique used was fusion of multiple probabilistic searches against different XML components using both Logistic Regression (LR) algorithms and a version of the Okapi BM-25 algorithm. The Berkeley group 2 (Gey and Petras) employed tested CLIR methods from previous CLEF evaluations using Logistic Regression with Blind Feedback. Both groups used multiple translations of queries in for cross-language searching, and the primary geographically-based approaches taken by both involved query expansion with additional place names. The Berkeley1 group used GIR indexing techniques to georeference proper nouns in the text using a gazetteer derived from the World Gazetteer (with both English and German names for each place), and automatically expanded place names in topics for regions or countries in the queries by the names of the countries or cities in those regions or countries. The Berkeley2 group used manual expansion of queries, adding additional place names.

1 Introduction

For GeoCLEF 2005 the Berkeley IR research group split into two groups (Berkeley1 and Berkeley2). Berkeley2 used the same techniques as used in previous CLEF evaluations with some new query expansion experiments for GeoCLEF, while Berkeley1 tried some alternative algorithms and fusion methods for both the GeoCLEF and Domain Specific tasks. This paper will describe the results of both on the techniques used by the Berkeley1 group for GeoCLEF and the results of our official submissions, as well as some additional tests using versions of the algorithms employed by the Berkeley2 group. The main technique being tested is the fusion of multiple probabilistic searches against different XML components using both Logistic Regression (LR) algorithms and a version of the Okapi BM-25 algorithm. We also combine multiple translations of queries in

C. Peters et al. (Eds.): CLEF 2005, LNCS 4022, pp. 963–976, 2006.

cross-language searching. Since this is the first time that the Cheshire II system has been used for CLEF, this approach can at best be considered a very preliminary base testing of some retrieval algorithms and approaches. This paper is organized as follows: In the next section we discuss the retrieval algorithms and fusion methods used by the Berkeley1 group for the submitted runs. We then discuss the Berkeley2 group algorithms. We will then discuss the specific approaches taken for indexing and retrieval in GeoCLEF and the results of the submitted runs for each group. We also compare our official submitted results to some additional runs with alternate approaches conducted later. Finally we present conclusions and discussion of lessons learned in GeoCLEF 2005.

2 Berkeley1 Retrieval Algorithms and Fusion Operators

The algorithms and fusion combination methods used by the Berkeley1 group are implemented as part of the Cheshire II XML/SGML search engine, as described in [7] and in the CLEF notebook paper[6]. The system also supports a number of other algorithms for distributed search and operators for merging result lists from ranked or Boolean sub-queries.

2.1 Logistic Regression Algorithm

The basic form and variables of the *TREC3 Logistic Regression* (LR) algorithm used by Berkeley1 was originally developed by Cooper, et al.[3]. It provided good full-text retrieval performance in the TREC3 ad hoc task and in TREC interactive tasks [4] and for distributed IR [5]. As originally formulated, the LR model of probabilistic IR attempts to estimate the probability of relevance for each document based on a set of statistics about a document collection and a set of queries in combination with a set of weighting coefficients for those statistics. The statistics to be used and the values of the coefficients are obtained from regression analysis of a sample of a collection (or similar test collection) for some set of queries where relevance and non-relevance has been determined.

Much of our recent focus for the Cheshire II system has been on exploiting the structure of XML documents (including the GeoCLEF documents) as a tree of XML elements. We define a "document component" as an XML subtree that may include zero or more subordinate XML elements or subtrees with text as the leaf nodes of the tree. Naturally, a full XML document may also be considered a "document component". As discussed below, the indexing and retrieval methods we used take into account a selected set of document components for generating the statistics used in the search ranking process. Because we are dealing with not only full documents, but also document components, the algorithm that we use is geared toward estimating the probability of relevance for a given document component. The complete formal description of the algorithm used can be found in [7] or in the Berkeley1 GeoCLEF notebook paper[6].

We also use a version of the Okapi BM-25 algorithm in these experiments that is based on the description of that algorithm by Robertson [10], using parameters from the TREC notebook proceedings [9]. As with the TREC3 LR algorithm, we have adapted the Okapi BM-25 algorithm to deal with document components.

The Cheshire II system also provides a number of operators to combine intermediate results of searches from different components or indexes. With these operators we have available an entire spectrum of combination methods ranging from strict Boolean operations to fuzzy Boolean and normalized score combinations for probabilistic and Boolean results. These operators are the means available for performing fusion operations between the results for different retrieval algorithms and the search results from different different components of a document. We will only describe two of these operators here, because they were the only types used in the GEOCLEF runs reported in this paper.

The MERGE_CMBZ operator is based on the "CombMNZ" fusion algorithm developed by Shaw and Fox [11] and used by Lee [8]. In our version we take the normalized scores, but then further enhance scores for components appearing in both lists (doubling them) and penalize normalized scores appearing low in a single result list, while using the unmodified normalized score for higher ranking items in a single list.

The MERGE_PIVOT operator is used primarily to adjust the probability of relevance for one search result based on matching elements in another search result. It was developed primarily to adjust the probabilities of a search result consisting of sub-elements of a document (such as titles or paragraphs) based on the probability obtained for the same search over the entire document. It is basically a weighted combination of the probabilities based on a "DocPivot" fraction, such that:

$$P_n = DocPivot * P_d + (1 - DocPivot) * P_s \tag{1}$$

where P_d represents the document-level probability of relevance, P_s represents the subelement probability, and P_n representing the resulting new probability. The "*DocPivot*" value used for all of the runs submitted was 0.64. Since this was the first year for GeoCLEF, this value was derived from experiments on 2004 data for other CLEF collections (we hope to do further testing to see if the was truly appropriate for the GeoCLEF data). This basic operator can be applied to either probabilistic results, or non-probabilistic results or both (in the latter case the scores are normalized using MINMAX normalization to range between 0 and 1).

In the following subsections we describe the specific approaches taken for our submitted runs for the GeoCLEF task. First we describe the indexing and term extraction methods used, and then the search features we used for the submitted runs.

2.2 Indexing and Term Extraction

For both the monolingual and bilingual tasks we indexed the documents using the Cheshire II system. The document index entries and queries were stemmed using the Snowball stemmer, and a new georeferencing indexing subsystem was used. This subsystem extracts proper nouns from the text being indexed and attempts to match them in a digital gazetteer. For GeoCLEF we used a gazetteer derived from the World Gazetteer (http://www.world-gazetteer.com) with 224698 entries in both English and German. The indexing subsystem provides three different index types: verified place names (an index of names which matched the gazetteer), point coordinates (latitude and longitude coordinates of the verified place name) and bounding box coordinates (bounding boxes for the matched places from the gazetteer). All three types were created, but due to time constraints we only used the verified place names in our tests. Text indexes were also created for separate XML elements (such as document titles or dates) as well as for the entire document. It is worth noting that, although the names are compared against the gazetteer, it is quite common for proper name of persons and places to be the same and this leads to potential false associations between articles mentioning persons with such name and particular places.

Table 1. Cheshire II Indexes for GeoCLEF 2005 (Berkeley1)

Name	Description	Content Tags	Used
docno	Document ID	DOCNO	no
pauthor	Author Names	BYLINE, AU	no
headline	Article Title	HEADLINE, TITLE, LEAD, LD, TI	yes
topic	Content Words	HEADLINE, TITLE, TI, LEAD	yes
		BYLINE, TEXT, LD, TX	yes
date	Date of Publication	DATE, WEEK	yes
geotext	Validated place names	TEXT, LD, TX	yes
geopoint	Validated coordinates for place names	TEXT, LD, TX	no
geobox	Validated bounding boxes for place names	TEXT, LD, TX	no

Table 1 lists the indexes created for the GeoCLEF database and the document elements from which the contents of those indexes were extracted. The "Used" column in the table indicates whether or not a particular index was used in the official Berkeley1 runs.

Because there was no explicit tagging of location-related terms in the collections used for GeoCLEF, we applied the above approach to the "TEXT", "LD", and "TX" elements of the records of the various collections. The part of news articles normally called the "dateline" indicating the location of the news story was not separately tagged in any of the GeoCLEF collections, but often appeared as the first part of the text for the story. (In addition, we discovered when writing these notes that the "TX" and "LD" were *not* included in the indexing in all cases, meaning that the SDA collection was not included in the German indexing for these indexes).

For all indexing we used English and German stoplists to exclude function words and very common words from the indexing and searching. For the runs reported here, Berkeley1 did not use any decompounding of German terms.

2.3 Berkeley1 Search Processing

For monolingual search tasks we used the topics in the appropriate language (English or German), for bilingual tasks the topics were translated from the source language to the target language using three different machine translation (MT) systems, the L&H Power Translator PC-based system, SYSTRAN (via Babelfish at Altavista), and PROMT (also via their web interface). Each of these translations were combined into a single probabilistic query. The hope was to overcome the translation errors of a single system by including alternatives.

We tried two main approaches for searching, the first used only the topic text from the title and desc elements, the second included the spatialrelation and location elements as well. In all cases the different indexes mentioned above were used, and probabilistic searches were carried out on each index, and the results combined using the CombMNZ algorithm, and by a weighted combination of partial element and full document scores. For bilingual searching we used both the Berkeley TREC3 and the Okapi BM-25 algorithm, for monolingual we used only TREC3. For one submitted run in each task we did no query expansion and did not use the location elements in the topics. For the other runs each of the place names identified in the queries were expanded when that place was the name of a region or country. For example when running search against the English databases the name "Europe" was expanded to "Albania Andorra Austria Belarus Belgium Bosnia and Herzegovina Bulgaria Croatia Cyprus Czech Republic Denmark Estonia Faroe Islands Finland France Georgia Germany Gibraltar Greece Guernsey and Alderney Hungary Iceland Ireland Isle of Man Italy Jersey Latvia Liechtenstein Lithuania Luxembourg Macedonia Malta Moldova Monaco Netherlands Norway Poland Portugal Romania Russia San Marino Serbia and Montenegro Slovakia Slovenia Spain Svalbard and Jan Mayen Sweden Switzerland Turkey Ukraine United Kingdom Vatican City", while for searches against the German databases "Europa" was expanded to "Albanien Andorra Österreich Weißrussland Belgien Bosnien und Herzegowina Bulgarien Kroatien Zypern Tschechische Republik Dänemark Estland Färöer-Inseln Finnland Frankreich Georgien Deutschland Gibraltar Griechenland Guernsey und Alderney Ungarn Island Irland Man Italien Jersey Lettland Liechtenstein Litauen Luxemburg Mazedonien Malta Moldawien Monaco Niederlande Norwegen Polen Portugal Rumänien Russland San Marino Serbien und Montenegro Slowakei Slowenien Spanien Svalbard und Jan Mayen Schweden Schweiz Türkei Ukraine Großbritannien Vatikan".

The indexes combined in searching included the headline, topic, and geotext indexes (as described in Table 1) for searches that include the location element, and the headline and topic for the searches without the locations element. For the bilingual tasks, three sub queries, one for each query translation were run and then the results were merged using the CombMNZ algorithm. For Monolingual tasks the title and topic results were combined with each other using CombMNZ and the final score combined with an expanded search for place names in the topic and geotext indexes. However, there were some errors in the scripts used to generate the queries used in the official runs. These included things such as including "Kenya" in the expansion for Europe, and including two copies of all expansion names, when a single copy should have been used. Also in some cases the wrong language form was used in expansions.

3 Berkeley2: Document Ranking, Collection and Query Processing and Translation

In all its CLEF submissions, the Berkeley2 group used a document ranking algorithm based on logistic regression first used in the TREC-2 conference[1]. The document collections for GeoCLEF consisted of standard CLEF document collections from past CLEFs covering the time periods of 1994 and 1995. The English collections are the Los Angeles Times 1994 and the Glasgow Herald 1995. The German collections are the SDA Swiss news wire (1994 and 1995), Frankfurter Rundschau and Der Spiegel. The English stopword list used consists of 662 common English words whose origin is lost in the antiquities of the early TREC conference. Berkeley2s German stopword list consists of 777 common German words developed over several CLEF evaluations. The stemmers used for GeoCLEF are the Muscat project stemmers for both English and German, also used in previous CLEF evaluations. Since Muscat is no longer open source and the English Muscat stemmer was developed by Martin Porter, very similar freely available stemmers may now be found among the SNOWBALL family: http://snowball.tartarus.org. In all official runs for GeoCLEF we utilized a blind feedback algorithm developed by Aitao Chen[1,2], adding 30 top-ranked terms from the top 20 ranked documents of an initial ranking. Thus the sequence of processing for retrieval is: query → stopword removal → (decompounding) → stemming → ranking → blind feedback. For German runs, we used a decompounding procedure developed and also described by Aitao Chen in [1,2], which has been shown to improve retrieval results. The decompounding procedure looks up document and query words in a base dictionary and splits compounds when found. We discuss the impacts of German decompounding and blind feedback in the Berkeley2 results section below.

4 Berkeley1 Results for Submitted GeoCLEF Runs

The summary results (as Mean Average Precision) for the submitted bilingual and monolingual runs for both English and German are shown in Table 2, the Recall-Precision curves for these runs are also shown in Figures 1 (for monolingual) and 2 (for bilingual). In Figures 1 and 2 the name are abbrevated to the final letters and numbers of the full name in Table 2, and those beginning with "POST" are unofficial runs described in the next section.

Table 2 indicates some rather curious results that warrant further investigation as to the cause. Notice that the result for all of the English monolingual runs exceed the results for bilingual German to English runs - this is typical for cross-langauge retrieval. However, in the case of German this expected pattern

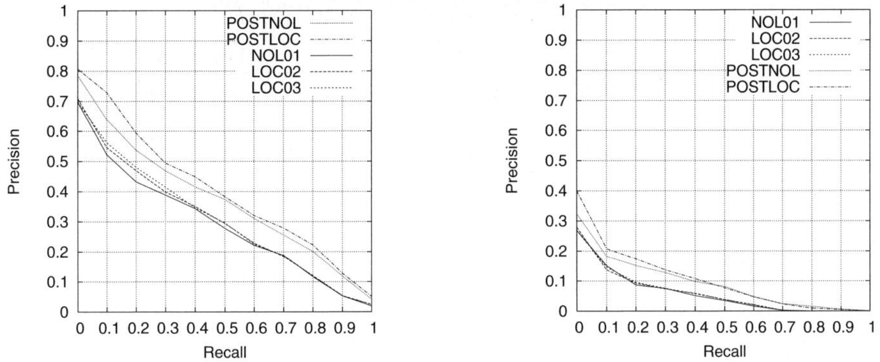

Fig. 1. Berkeley1 Monolingual Runs – English (left) and German (right)

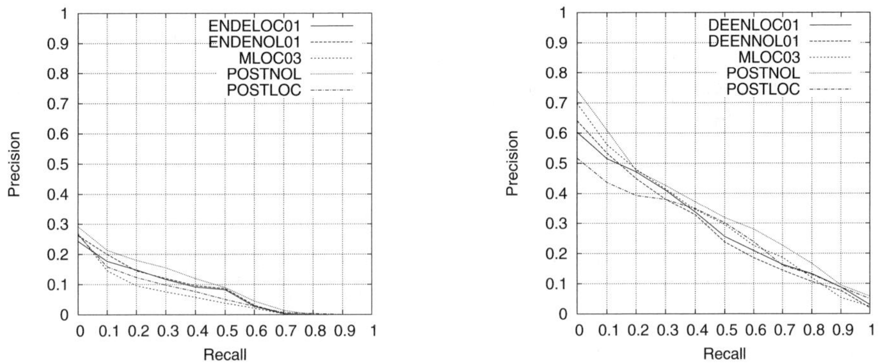

Fig. 2. Berkeley1 Bilingual Runs – English to German (left) and German to English (right)

is reversed, and the German monolingual runs *perform worse*, in terms of mean average precision (about 0.05) than either of the bilingual English to German runs (about 0.07). This is not obvious from the corresponding figures, but appears in the averages. We haven't yet determined exactly why this might be the case, but there are number possible reasons (e.g., since a combination of Okapi and Logistic Regression searches are used for the bilingual task this may be an indication that Okapi is more effective for German). Also, in the monolingual runs, both English and German, use of the location tag and expansion of the query (runs numbered LOC02 and LOC03 respectively) did better than no use of the location tag or expansion. For the bilingual runs the results are mixed, with German to English runs showing an improvement with location use and expansion (LOC01) and English to German showing the opposite. However, given the very low scores when compared to the Berkeley2 results below, we suspect that differences in stoplists, decompounding, etc. may have confused the effects.

Table 2. Berkeley1 Submitted GeoCLEF Runs

Run Name	Description	Location	MAP
BERK1BLDEENLOC01	Bilingual German⇒English	yes	0.2753
BERK1BLDEENNOL01	Bilingual German⇒English	no	0.2668
BERK1BLENDELOC01	Bilingual English⇒German	yes	0.0725
BERK1BLENDENOL01	Bilingual English⇒German	no	0.0777
BERK1MLDELOC02	Monolingual German	yes	0.0535
BERK1MLDELOC03	Monolingual German	yes	0.0533
BERK1MLDENOL01	Monolingual German	no	0.0504
BERK1MLENLOC02	Monolingual English	yes	0.2910
BERK1MLENLOC03	Monolingual English	yes	0.2924
BERK1MLENNOL01	Monolingual English	no	0.2794

4.1 Additional Runs

After the official submission we used a version of the same Logistic Regression algorithm as the Berkeley2 group (the "TREC2" algorithm), which incorporates blind feedback (which is currently lacking in the "TREC3" algorithm used in the official runs). This version of the TREC2 algorithm was implemented as another option of the Cheshire II system. The parameters used for blind feedback were 13 documents and the top-ranked 16 terms from those documents added to the original query. This is essentially an identical algorithm to that defined in [1]. The results from the bilingual and monolingual runs for both English and German using this algorithm, but with the remaining processing components the same as in the Berkeley1 official runs, are shown in Table 3, the Recall-Precision curves for these runs are also included in Figures 1 (for monolingual) and 2 (for bilingual). In Figures 1 and 2 the names abbrevated to the final letters of the full name in Table 3, prefixed by "POST". These are unofficial runs to test the difference in the algorithms in an identical runtime environment.

Table 3. Berkeley1 Additional Post-Submission GeoCLEF Runs

Run Name	Description	Location	MAP
POSTBLDEENEXP	Bilingual German⇒English	yes	0.2636
POSTBLDEENNOL	Bilingual German⇒English	no	0.3205
POSTBLENDEEXP	Bilingual English⇒German	yes	0.0626
POSTBLENDENOL	Bilingual English⇒German	no	0.0913
POSTMLDELOC	Monolingual German	yes	0.0929
POSTMLDENOL	Monolingual German	no	0.0861
POSTMLENEXP	Monolingual English	yes	0.2892
POSTMLENLOC	Monolingual English	yes	0.3879
POSTMLENNOL	Monolingual English	no	0.3615

As can be seen by comparing Table 3 with Table 2, all of the comparable runs show improvement in results with the TREC2 algorithm with blind feedback. We have compared notes with the Berkeley2 group and except for minor differences to be expected given the different indexing methods, stoplists, etc. used, the English monolingual and German⇒English results are comparable to theirs as shown in the tables below.

The queries submitted in these unofficial runs were much simpler than those used in the official runs. For monolingual retrieval only the "topic" index was used and the geotext index was not used at all, for the bilingual runs the same pattern of using multiple query translations and combining the results was used as in our official runs. This may actually be detrimental to the performance, since the expanded queries perform worse than the unexpanded queries - the opposite behaviour observed in the official runs.

In the monolingual runs there appears to be similar behavior, using the topic titles and description along with the location tag provided the best results, but expanding the locations as in the official runs (the English ML run ending in EXP) performed considerably worse than the the unexpanded runs. Also, as in the offical runs the German monolingual and English⇒German bilingual had very poor results. We believe that this indicates a significant processing problem for German (in addition to the lack of decompounding).

5 Berkeley2 Runs and Results

5.1 Monolingual Retrieval

For monolingual retrieval, we submitted one title and description run, one run with title, description and narrative, one with title, description, concept and location tag and one with title, description, concept and the manually expanded location tag.

In English monolingual, adding the geographical tags (BKGeoE1) achieved the highest result with a MAP of 0.3936, but the manual expansion strategy did not improve the average precision (BKGeoE4 0.3550). The TDN run (BKGeoE3) outperforms the TD run (BKGeoE4) by 8% and improves from 0.3528 to 0.3840.

Table 4. Berkeley2 GeoCLEF English Monolingual

Run Name	Type	MAP blind feedback (BF)	MAP no BF
BKGeoE1	TD+Concept/Locat. (CL)	0.3936 (+5.3%)	0.3737
BKGeoE2	TD	0.3528† (-0%)	0.3536
BKGeoE3	TDN	0.3840† (+3.8%)	0.3701
BKGeoE4	TD+CL manual	0.3550† (+7.6%)	0.3348

(Note that in the tables a dagger † indicates the official Berkeley2 results).

In German monolingual retrieval, 4 topics did not retrieve any relevant documents overall. Additionally, our runs failed to retrieve any relevant documents for 3 more of the remaining 21 queries. Manually adding location information lowered the average precision score considerably. The TDN run (BKGeoD3) achieved the highest MAP with 0.2042 followed by the TD run (BKGeoD2) with 0.1608. The manual expansion strategy (BKGeoD4) achieved the lowest MAP (0.1112), whereas adding the tags achieved a MAP of 0.1545. Because a significant proportion of topics retrieved very few relevant documents from the German collection, this might explain these low precision scores.

Table 5. Berkeley2 GeoCLEF German Monolingual

GeoCLEF Run Name	Type	MAP BF decomp.	MAP no BF decomp.	MAP BF no decomp	MAP no BF no decomp
BKGeoD1	TD+CL	0.1545† (+65.1%)	0.0936 (0%)	0.1547 (+65.1%)	0.0937
BKGeoD2	TD	0.1608† (+71.6%)	0.0937 (0%)	0.1613 (+72.1%)	0.0937
BKGeoD3	TDN	0.2042† (+53.5%)	0.1330 (0%)	0.2012 (+53.1%)	0.1330
BKGeoD4	TD+CL manual	0.1112 (+56.1%)	0.0711 (0%)	0.1116 (+56.7%)	0.0712

5.2 Bilingual Retrieval

For bilingual retrieval, we used the L&H Power Translator Pro to translate the topics from English to German and vice versa. In bilingual retrieval, adding the concept and location information improved the average precision score modestly. For English→German, adding the concept and location tag improved precision from 0.1685 to 0.1788, a performance that is better than the same strategy in monolingual retrieval! For German→English, adding the tags improved the average precision from 0.3586 (this TD run is even slightly better than the monolingual one) to 0.3715 in average precision.

Table 6. Berkeley2 GeoCLEF German→English Bilingual

Run Name	Type	MAP-BF	MAP-no BF
BKGeoDE1	TD	0.3586† (+8.8%)	0.3296
BKGeoDE2	TD+CL	0.3715† (+12.6%)	0.3298

Table 7. Berkeley2 GeoCLEF English → German Bilingual (with decompounding)

Run Name	Type	MAP-BF	MAP-no BF
BKGeoED1	TD	0.1685† (+52.6%)	0.1104
BKGeoED2	TD+CL	0.1788† (+57.3%)	0.1137

5.3 Impact of Blind Feedback and German Decompounding

Since our best results were considerably above an average of medians for both English and German monolingual and bilingual runs, we ran an additional set of experiments to see if we might isolate the effects of blind feedback and (for German) decompounding. What we found was that there was little effect of blind feedback on the English monolingual and German English bilingual results. Without blind feedback, English monolingual title-description (TD) run mean average precisions are virtually indistinguishable, while blind feedback title-description plus concept-location is about 5% better (0.3936 versus 0.3737). The blind feedback results for English are summarized in Tables 4 (monolingual) and 6 (bilingual German → English):

There is however, considerably greater impact of blind feedback on German monolingual and bilingual results, as Tables 5 and 7 show, on the order of 53 to 72 percent improvement.

5.4 Source of Improvement When Using Blind Feedback

To try to understand how blind feedback produced such stunning improvement in results (for both groups), we need to make a more detailed examination of improvement produced for each topic. Table 8 presents MAP of our German monolingual runs for each topic, with Median, official TD and TD without blind feedback highlighted The four queries, where query expansion through blind feedback achieved the most improvement were 10 (Hochwasser in Holland und Deutschland, BF strategy improves by 1400%), 14 (Umweltschädigende Vorfälle in der Nordsee, BF improves by 650%) and 19 (Golfturniere in Europa, BF improves by 285%) and 13 (Besuche des amerikanischen Präsidenten in Deutschland, 168%). Query 12 is an example where blind feedback has a negative effect on the average precision scores (Kathedralen in Europa, -67%).

The blind feedback algorithm adds 30 terms to the query, which are weighted half compared to the original query terms in retrieval. "Good" terms to be added are terms that are relevant to the query and add new information to the search, for example synonyms of query terms but also proper names or word variations. The most improved queries seem to add mostly proper names and word variations and very few irrelevant words that won't distort the search towards another direction.

For query 10, some of the words added by blind feedback were Hochwassergebiet (flooded area), Waal, Maas (rivers in Holland), Deich (levee) and Flut (flood) – all words that didn't occur in the title and description tags of the original query but are eminently important words for the search.

For query 12, only a few original query words (after stopword removal) were fed into the blind feedback algorithm: Kathedrale, Europa, Artikel and einzeln, of which the last two don't add relevant information to the search. Consequently, the suggested blind feedback terms don't really fit the query (e.g. Besucherinnen (female visitors), kunstvoll (artful), Aussöhnung (reconciliation), Staatsbesuch (state visit), Parade).

The more words are used to feed the blind feedback algorithm and the more distinctive they are in terms of occurrence in the collection and connectedness to a certain concept, the better the blind feedback algorithm will work. For example, the word Golfturnier doesn't occur very frequently in the collection but it always

Table 8. GeoCLEF German monolingual runs with no blind feedback comparison

GeoCLEF Topic ID	Best Overall Monoling.	Median Overall Monoling.	BKGeoD2 TD	TD decomp No BF	BKGeoD1 TD+CL	BKGeoD3 TDN	BKGeoD4 TD Manual
1‡	0.0000	0.0000	0.0000	0.0000	0.0000	0.0000	0.0000
2	0.1506	0.0018	0.008	0.0188	0.0141	0.0067	0.0000
3	0.6713	0.2336	0.2942	0.2902	0.3145	0.3579	0.0491
4	0.6756	0.0627	0.0335	0.0324	0.0626	0.6756	0.0005
5	0.5641	0.0988	0.095	0.1599	0.0988	0.4705	0.0988
6	0.3929	0.0066	0.0000	0.0000	0.0000	0.0001	0.0000
7	0.1907	0.0539	0.1033	0.0879	0.1405	0.0581	0.0005
8	0.5864	0.0003	0.0000	0.0010	0.0000	0.0005	0.0000
9	0.6273	0.5215	0.523	0.4684	0.5413	0.6273	0.5413
10	0.7936	0.0782	0.6349	0.0452	0.614	0.7936	0.6140
11	0.2342	0.0041	0.0000	0.0000	0.0000	0.0000	0.0000
12	0.2956	0.1007	0.0457	0.1387	0.0759	0.1003	0.1237
13	0.5682	0.2466	0.5682	0.3377	0.4554	0.525	0.4554
14	0.7299	0.0717	0.7299	0.1121	0.3665	0.452	0.3665
15	0.3630	0.235	0.1787	0.1345	0.2130	0.1479	0.2130
16	0.4439	0.0939	0.0651	0.0902	0.0930	0.0821	0.0930
17	0.2544	0.0421	0.0211	0.0555	0.0633	0.2499	0.0633
18	0.1111	0.0087	0.0128	0.0026	0.0139	0.0200	0.0139
19	0.6488	0.1271	0.6014	0.2108	0.6488	0.3972	0.0000
20‡	0.0000	0.0000	0.0000	0.0000	0.0000	0.0000	0.0000
21	0.1123	0.0744	0.0961	0.1324	0.1046	0.1038	0.1046
22‡	0.0000	0.0000	0.0000	0.0000	0.0000	0.0000	0.0000
23	0.1682	0.0000	0.0006	0.0055	0.0023	0.0000	0.0023
24	0.0410	0.0086	0.0086	0.0181	0.0396	0.0364	0.0396
25‡	0.0000	0.0000	0.0000	0.0000	0.0000	0.0000	0.0000
Average	0.3449	0.0828	0.1608	0.0937	0.1545	0.2042	0.1112

‡GeoCLEF topics with no relevant German documents.

co-occurs with articles that are related to golf, whereas Besucherinnen will be used in more frames (concepts) than just the European cathedrals.

The combined queries 10, 13, 14, 19 account for almost all of the improvement in the average precision score between the run without blind feedback and the run with blind feedback. This is a thought provoking fact because for the rest of the queries the impact of the blind feedback terms in precision for each query centers around zero. We have found over and over again that blind feedback improves precision, but it seems to do so for only a particular kind of query.

6 Failure Analysis

Manual expansion of general geographic regions to individual country names was a clear losing strategy. For topics 2 and 4, the German location name "Europa" was expanded using a similar list to that used by Berkeley1, which turned reasonable retrievals go to zero precision for those topics. Similarly poor results were obtained from equivalent English monolingual expansion of "Europe"or topic 3, and "Latin America" was expanded to 42 country names with equally dismal results. This does not bode well for using a geographic thesaurus to automatically obtain such expansions.

7 Discussion and Conclusions

Berkeley groups participated in the GeoCLEF track with a focus on the German and English languages for both documents and topics. Berkeley2 utilized standard information retrieval techniques of blind feedback and German complex word decompounding, while Berkeley1 used multiple algorithm fusion approaches and combinations of different document elements in searching. Query translation used commonly available machine translation software. Blind feedback was particularly impressive in improving the Berkeley2 German monolingual and bilingual English→German results and the Berkeley1 "POST" runs. The Berkeley2 venture into geographic location resolution by manual expansion of the general terms "Europe" and "Latin America" into a list of individual country names resulted in a considerably diminished performance effectiveness, which was also seen in the Berkeley1 "POST" runs. However, the message is not entirely unmixed. Expansion appeared to help in cases where fusion of multiple search elements was used. It remains for future experimentation to see whether this was an anomaly, or whether it is a useful property of the fusion algorithms. It does seem clear, however, that successful geographic expansion will only occur in the context of requiring the concept (e.g. Golf Tournaments") to also be present in the documents. This may be something that the combinations of operators and algorithms available in the Cheshire II system can test.

Analysis of these results (and cross analysis of the two groups' results) is still ongoing. There are a number of, as yet, unexplained behaviors in some of our results. We plan to continue working on the use of fusion, and hope to discover effective ways to combine highly effective algorithms, such as the TREC2 algorithm, as well as working on adding the same blind feedback capability to the TREC3 Logistic Regression algorithm.

One obvious conclusion that can be drawn is that basic TREC2 is a highly effective algorithm for the GeoCLEF tasks, and the fusion approaches tried in these tests are most definitely *not* very effective (in spite of their relatively good effectiveness in other retrieval tasks such as INEX).

Another conclusion is that, in some cases, query expansion of region names to a list of names of particular countries in that region is modestly effective (although we haven't yet been able to test for statistical significance). In other cases, however it can be quite detrimental. However we still need to determine if the problems with the expansion were due the nature of the expansion itself, or errors in how it was done.

Acknowledgements

Thanks to Aitao Chen for implementing and permitting the use of the logistic regression formula for probabilistic information retrieval as well as German decompounding and blind feedback in his MULIR retrieval system for the Berkeley2 runs.

References

1. Aitao Chen. *Cross-Language Retrieval Experiments at CLEF 2002*, pages 28–48. Springer (LNCS #2785), 2003.
2. Aitao Chen and Fredric C. Gey. Multilingual information retrieval using machine translation, relevance feedback and decompounding. *Information Retrieval*, 7:149–182, 2004.
3. William S. Cooper, Fredric C. Gey, and Daniel P. Dabney. Probabilistic retrieval based on staged logistic regression. In *15th Annual International ACM SIGIR Conference on Research and Development in Information Retrieval, Copenhagen, Denmark, June 21-24*, pages 198–210, New York, 1992. ACM.
4. Ray R. Larson. TREC interactive with Cheshire II. *Information Processing and Management*, 37:485–505, 2001.
5. Ray R. Larson. A logistic regression approach to distributed IR. In *SIGIR 2002: Proceedings of the 25th Annual International ACM SIGIR Conference on Research and Development in Information Retrieval, August 11-15, 2002, Tampere, Finland*, pages 399–400. ACM, 2002.
6. Ray R. Larson. Cheshire II at GeoCLEF: Fusion and query expansion for GIR. In *CLEF 2005 Notebook Papers*. DELOS Digital Library, 2005.
7. Ray R. Larson. A fusion approach to XML structured document retrieval. *Information Retrieval*, 8:601–629, 2005.
8. Joon Ho Lee. Analyses of multiple evidence combination. In *SIGIR '97: Proceedings of the 20th Annual International ACM SIGIR Conference on Research and Development in Information Retrieval, July 27-31, 1997, Philadelphia*, pages 267–276. ACM, 1997.
9. Stephen E. Robertson, Stephen Walker, and Micheline M. Hancock-Beauliee. OKAPI at TREC-7: ad hoc, filtering, vlc and interactive track. In *Text Retrieval Conference (TREC-7), Nov. 9-1 1998 (Notebook)*, pages 152–164, 1998.
10. Stephen E. Robertson and Steven Walker. On relevance weights with little relevance information. In *Proceedings of the 20th annual international ACM SIGIR conference on Research and development in information retrieval*, pages 16–24. ACM Press, 1997.
11. Joseph A. Shaw and Edward A. Fox. Combination of multiple searches. In *Proceedings of the 2nd Text REtrieval Conference (TREC-2), National Institute of Standards and Technology Special Publication 500-215*, pages 243–252, 1994.

Using Semantic Networks for Geographic Information Retrieval

Johannes Leveling, Sven Hartrumpf, and Dirk Veiel

Intelligent Information and Communication Systems (IICS)
University of Hagen (FernUniversität in Hagen)
58084 Hagen, Germany
{Johannes.Leveling, Sven.Hartrumpf, Dirk.Veiel}@fernuni-hagen.de

Abstract. This paper describes our work for the participation at the GeoCLEF task of CLEF 2005. We employ multilayered extended semantic networks for the representation of background knowledge, queries, and documents for geographic information retrieval (GIR). In our approach, geographic concepts from the query network are expanded with concepts which are semantically connected via topological, directional, and proximity relations. We started with an existing geographic knowledge base represented as a semantic network and expanded it with concepts automatically extracted from the GEOnet Names Server.

Several experiments for GIR on German documents have been performed: a baseline corresponding to a traditional information retrieval approach; a variant expanding thematic, temporal, and geographic descriptors from the semantic network representation of the query; and an adaptation of a question answering (QA) algorithm based on semantic networks. The second experiment is based on a representation of the natural language description of a topic as a semantic network, which is achieved by a deep linguistic analysis. The semantic network is transformed into an intermediate representation of a database query explicitly representing thematic, temporal, and local restrictions. This experiment showed the best performance with respect to mean average precision: 10.53% using the topic title and description. The third experiment, adapting a QA algorithm, uses a modified version of the QA system InSicht. The system matches deep semantic representations of queries or their equivalent or similar variants to semantic networks for document sentences.

1 Introduction

Geographic Information Retrieval (GIR) is concerned with the retrieval of documents involving the interpretation of geographic knowledge by means of topological, directional, and proximity information. Documents typically contain descriptions of events or static situations that are temporally or spatially restricted, as in *"the industrial development after World War II"* and *"the social security system outside of Scandinavia"*. Furthermore, many documents contain ambiguous geographic references. There are, for example, more than 30 cities named *"Zell"* in Germany, and any occurrence of this name can have a different

C. Peters et al. (Eds.): CLEF 2005, LNCS 4022, pp. 977–986, 2006.

Table 1. Overview of synonyms and word senses in GermaNet and GNS data for a selected subset of 169,407 geographic entities in Germany. Normalization removes name variants introduced by the transcription of German umlauts.

Characteristic	Resource		
	GermaNet	GNS (all)	GNS (normalized)
synsets total	41,777	95,993	95,993
synonyms in synsets	60,646	121,055	103,508
unique literals	52,251	94,187	80,808
synonyms per synset	1.45	1.26	1.08
word senses per literal	1.16	1.29	1.28

meaning and should be disambiguated from context. In addition, a geographic entity can be referred to with names (toponyms) in different languages or dialects, with historical names, etc., which will require normalization or translation to enable document retrieval. The latter problems are similar to the problems of polysemy and synonymy in traditional information retrieval (IR).

A traditional approach to GIR involves at least the following processing steps to identify geographic entities ([1]):

- named entity recognition (NER), including the tagging of geographic names;
- collecting and integrating information from the contexts of named entities;
- disambiguation of named entities; and
- grounding entities (i.e. connecting them to the model) and interpreting coordinates.

After identifying toponyms in queries and documents, coordinates can be assigned to them. In GIR, assigning a relevance score to a document for a given query typically involves calculating the distance between geographic entities in the query and the document and mapping it to a score.

Two major problems for GIR are the disambiguation of toponyms from semantic context and identifying spatial ambiguity (e.g. *'California'* in *'Mexico'* or in *'the USA'*). Table 1 shows a comparison of ambiguity in GermaNet ([2]) and the GEOnet Names Server data (GNS, see Sect. 2.2). Synonymy seems to be a lesser problem for German geographic names (1.08 synonyms per synset vs. 1.45 synonyms per synset in a lexical-semantic net for German), while the role of polysemy (word senses) becomes more important for GIR (1.28 vs. 1.16). Problems that are less often identified and less investigated in GIR are discussed below. Currently, there is no practical solution for these problems and their investigation is a long-term issue for GIR. We concentrate on providing a basic architecture for GIR with semantic networks, which will be refined later.

Toponyms in different languages. The translation of toponyms plays an important role even for monolingual retrieval when different and external information resources are integrated. In gazetteers, mostly English names are used.

Name variants. The same geographic object can be referenced by endonymic names, exonymic names, and historical names. An endonym is a local name for a geographic entity, e.g. *"Wien"*, *"Köln"*, and *"Milano"*. An exonym is a place name in a certain language for a geographic object that lies outside the region where this language has an official status; for example, *"Vienna"* and *"Cologne"* are the English exonyms for *"Wien"* and *"Köln"*, respectively, and *"Mailand"* is the German exonym for *"Milano"*. Examples of historical names or traditional names are *"New Amsterdam"* for *"New York"* and *"Cöllen"* for *"Köln"*. For GIR, name variants should be conflated.

Composite names. Composite names or complex named entities consist of two or more words. Frequently, appositions are considered to be a part of a name. For example, there is no need for the translation of the word *"mount"* in *"Mount Cook"*, but *"Insel"* is typically translated in the expression *"Insel Sylt"/ "island of Sylt"*. For NER, certain rules have to be established how composite names are normalized. In some composite names, two or more toponyms (geographic names) are employed in reference to a single entity, e.g. *"Frankfurt/Oder"* or *"Haren (Ems)"*. While additional toponyms in a context allow for a better disambiguation, such composite names require a normalization, too.

Semantic relations between toponyms and related concepts. In GIR, semantic relations between toponyms and related concepts are often ignored. Concepts related to a toponym such as the language, inhabitants of a place, properties (adjectives), or phrases (*"former Yugoslavia"*) are not considered in geographic tagging. For example, the toponym *"Scotland"* can be inferred for occurrences of *"Scottish"*, *"Scotsman"*, or *"Scottish districts"*.

Temporal changes in toponyms. Not all geographic concepts are static. For example, wars and treaties affect what a geographic name represents, e.g. *"the EU"* refers to a different region after its expansion. This is an indication that temporal and spatial restrictions should not be discussed separately.

Metonymic usage. Toponyms are used ambiguously. For example, *"Libya"* occurs in the news corpus as a reference to the *"Libyan government"* (as in *"Libya stated that ..."*).

2 Interpreting GIR Queries with Semantic Networks

We employ a syntactico-semantic parser (WOCADI parser – WOrd ClAss based DIsambiguating parser, [3]) to obtain the representation of queries and documents as semantic networks according to the MultiNet paradigm ([4]). This approach has been used in experiments for domain-specific IR ([5]) as well as in question answering (QA). Aside from broadening the application domain of MultiNet, its tools and applications, our work for the participation in the GeoCLEF task ([6]) serves the following purposes:

1. To identify possible improvements for WOCADI's NER component.
2. To improve the connectivity between semantic networks and large resources of structured information (e.g. databases).
3. To create a larger set of geographic background knowledge by semi-automatic and automatic knowledge extraction from geographic resources.
4. To investigate the role of semantic relations and their interpretation for GIR.

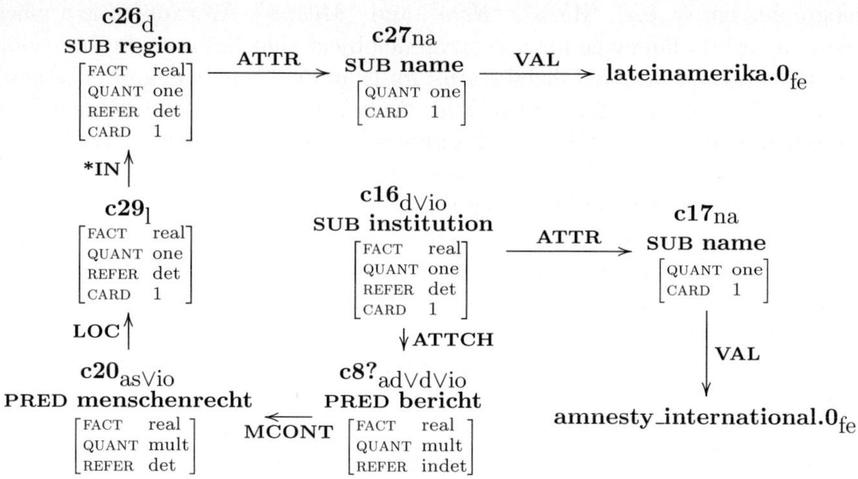

Fig. 1. Automatically generated semantic network for the description of GeoCLEF topic GC003 (*"Finde Berichte von Amnesty International bezüglich der Menschenrechte in Lateinamerika."*, *'Amnesty International reports on human rights in Latin America.'*). The relations are explained in Table 2. Nodes representing proper names bear a *.0* suffix and subordinating edges (PRED, SUB) are *folded* below the node name. The imperative verb has already been removed.

2.1 Improving Named Entity Recognition

WOCADI's NER is based on large lists of about 230,000 names including cities, countries, organizations, and products. This approach is suitable in a domain where most proper names are known in advance. In general, a method to dynamically identify proper nouns is needed. A new machine learning module that tags named entities before WOCADI parses sentences will be integrated.

2.2 Connecting Semantic Networks and Databases

Data from the GEOnet Names Server[1] (GNS[2], containing approximately 4.0 million entities with 5.5 million names world-wide and 169,407 entities for Germany) was processed to fill a gazetteer database. The GNS is a valuable resource for geographic information, but the use of this multilingual gazetteer data has proved problematic in our setup, so far.

– Some data may not be present at all (e.g. *"the Scottish Trossachs"*), so that a geographic interpretation fails for some concepts.
– Geographic names may be present in the native language, in English, or both. For some concepts, there are no native language forms (the GNS data

[1] `http://earth-info.nga.mil/gns/html/cntry_files.html`

[2] The GEOnet Names Server contains data from the National Geospatial-Intelligence Agency and the U.S. Board on Geographic Names database.

has an American English background). For example, *"The North Sea"* and *"Scotland"* are in the database, but *"Nordsee"* and *"Schottland"* are not. This means that the GNS data cannot be used for a non-English monolingual task without an additional translation phase.

– Relations or modifiers generate name variants not covered by a gazetteer (*"Süddeutschland"*/*'South(ern) Germany'*, *'the southern part of Germany'*) because they are subject to interpretation or do not have corresponding coordinates.
– The data representation may be inconsistent. For example, some streams or rivers are represented by the coordinates of a single point (e.g. *"Main"*), some are represented by the coordinates of several points (e.g. *"Alter Rhein"*).
– The gazetteer does not provide sufficient information for a successful disambiguation from context (for example, temporal information is missing).
– The ontological basis of the GNS is incomplete. For example, church (CH), religious center (CTRR), monastery (MNSTY), mission (MSSN), temple (TMPL), and mosque (MSQE) are defined (among others) in the GNS data as classes of geographic entities that refer to sacral buildings. A cathedral (GeoCLEF topic GC012) is a sacral building as well, but there is no corresponding class for cathedrals, although other types of sacral buildings are differentiated. Furthermore, no data on well-known cathedrals is provided.
– Name inflection is typically not covered in gazetteers. Many names have a special genitive form in German (and English), which the morphology component of the WOCADI parser can analyze. But there are more complicated cases, where parts of a complex name are inflected for case, e.g. the river *"(die) Schwarze Elster"* has the genitive form *"(der) Schwarzen Elster"*.

Because of these problems, we see the GNS data as a general source of information, which should be extended by domain-, language-, and application-specific knowledge. Gazetteers and derived knowledge bases share some problems. Both are always incomplete ([7] discusses problems of selecting and using gazetteers), data in both is not fine-grained or detailed enough for many tasks, and for both, entry points (valid search keys) for access must be known.

2.3 Expanding Geographic Background Knowledge

We created and maintained a large semantic network as a geographic knowledge base for expanding geographic concepts. This knowledge base was automatically extended by generating and integrating hypotheses for new geographic concepts. For all concepts from the existing semantic network ontology, hypotheses are generated for meronymy relations. A hypothetical concept is created by concatenating some prefix with regular semantics in geography with the original concept. Examples of an implied meronymy are *"Südost-"*/*'Southeast'* and *"Zentral-"*/*'Central'*. The occurrence frequency of a hypothesis is looked up in the index of base forms for the entire (annotated/tagged) news corpus. Hypothetical concepts with a frequency less than a given threshold (three occurrences) were rejected. The resulting relations were integrated into the semantic

Table 2. Some MultiNet relations for the interpretation of geographic queries

MultiNet Relation	Description
ASSOC(x, y)	association (used to link toponyms and related concepts)
ATTCH(x, y)	attachment between objects; y is attached to x
ATTR(x, y)	attribute of an object; y is an attribute of x
CIRC(x, y), CTXT(x, y)	situational circumstance (non-restrictive and restrictive)
DIRCL(x, y)	direction of events (e.g. *"the flight to Berlin"*)
EQU(x, y)	equality (used for name variants and equivalent names)
LOC(x, y)	specifying locations; x takes place at y; x is located at y
PARS(x, y)	meronymy, holonymy (PART-OF); x is part of y
PRED(x, y)	predication; every z from set x is a y
SUB(x, y)	subordination (IS-A); x is a y
SYNO(x, y)	synonyms and near-synonyms
TEMP(x, y)	temporal specification
VAL(x, y)	value specification; y is value for attribute x
*IN(x, y)	semantic function; x is contained in y
*NEAR(x, y)	semantic function; x is close to y

network containing the background knowledge. These concepts typically do not occur in gazetteers because they are vague and their interpretation depends on context.

The second approach to expanding the geographic background knowledge involved automatically extracting concepts from a database consisting of the GNS data for Germany. The GNS data shares much information with other major resources and services involving geographic information, such as the Getty Thesaurus of Geographic Names (TGN, containing about 1.1 million names) or the Alexandria Digital Library project (ADL Gazetteer, containing about 4.4 million entries). Therefore we concentrated on the GNS data.

For each GNS entry, a set of geographic codes is provided which can be interpreted to form a geographic path to the geographic object. For example, the entry for the city of *"Wien"*/*'Vienna'* contains information that the city is located in *"Amerika oder Westeuropa"*/*'America or Western Europe'*, *"Europa"*/*'Europe'*, *"Österreich"*/*'Austria'*, and in the *"Bundesland Wien"* and that *"Vienna"* is a name variant of *"Wien"*. This information is post-processed and transformed into a set of semantic relations. We extracted some 20,000 geographic relations for a subset of 27 geographic classes (out of 648 classes defined in the GNS) from the German data. Relations that can be inferred from transitivity or symmetry properties are not entered into the geographic knowledge base as they are dynamically generated in our experiments.

2.4 The Role of Semantic Relations in Geographic Queries

The MultiNet paradigm offers a rich repertoire of semantic relations and functions. Table 2 shows and briefly describes the most important relations for representing topological, directional, or proximity information. Note that the length

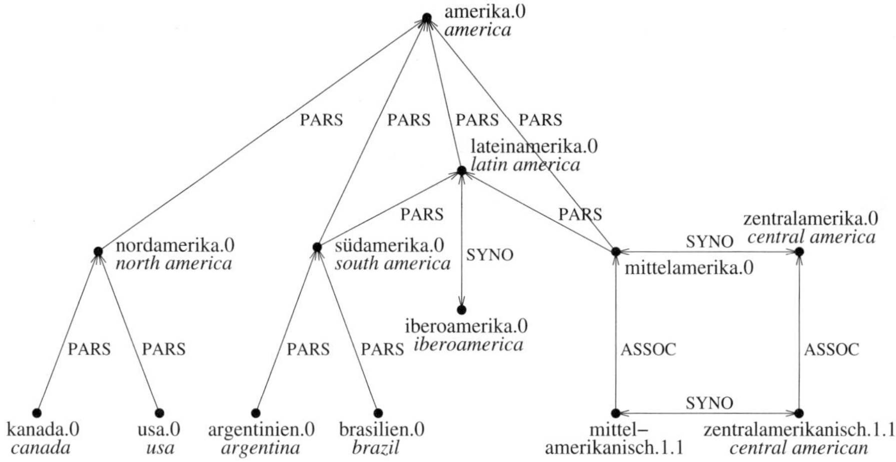

Fig. 2. Excerpt from the geographic knowledge base

of a path of relations between two related concepts may be used as an indicator of their thematic or geographic proximity. Figure 2 shows an excerpt from our geographic knowledge base. For the moment, the interpretation of the semantic functions is limited because we do not yet use the GNS coordinates.

3 Monolingual GeoCLEF Experiments

Currently, the GeoCLEF experiments follow our established setup for information retrieval tasks. The WOCADI parser is employed to analyze the newspaper and newswire articles, and concepts (or rather: lemmata) and compound constituents are extracted from the parsing results as index terms. The representations of 276,579 documents (after duplicate elimination) are indexed with the Zebra database management system ([8]), which supports a standard relevance ranking (term weighting by *tf-idf*).

Queries (topics) are analyzed with WOCADI to obtain the semantic network representation. The semantic networks are transformed into a Database Independent Query Representation (DIQR) expression. For two experiments (FUHo10tdl and FUHo14tdl), the location elements consisting of the concept (*DE-concept*), spatial relation (*DE-spatialrelation*), and place names (*DE-location*) of a topic are transformed into a corresponding DIQR expression as well. Additional concepts (including toponyms) are added to the query formulation by including semantically related concepts. This approach is described in more detail in [9]. The fifth experiment employs a modified QA approach described in Sect. 4. The experiments are characterized in the parameter columns of Table 3. It also shows the performance wrt. to mean average precision (MAP) and number of relevant and retrieved documents.

Table 3. Parameter settings, mean average precision (MAP), and the number of relevant and retrieved documents (rel_ret) for monolingual GeoCLEF experiments. (785 documents are assessed as relevant.)

Run Identifier	Parameters				Results	
	title	description	location elements	query expansion	MAP	rel_ret
FUHo10td	yes	yes	no	no	0.0779	479
FUHo10tdl	yes	yes	yes	no	0.0809	464
FUHo14td	yes	yes	no	yes	0.1053	519
FUHo14tdl	yes	yes	yes	yes	0.1022	530
FUHinstd	yes	yes	no	yes	0.0182	92

The experiments with query expansion based on additional geographic knowledge outperform the traditional IR approach wrt. MAP (FUHo14td vs. FUHo10td and FUHo14tdl vs. FUHo10tdl). The performance of the experiment employing traditional IR and the experiment with query expansion may be increased by switching to a database supporting a OKAPI/BM25 search.

4 GIR with Deep Sentence Parses

In addition to the runs described in Sect. 3, we experimented with an approach based on deep semantic analysis of documents and queries. We tried to turn the InSicht system normally used for QA ([10]) into a GIR system (here abbreviated as GIR-InSicht). To this end, the following modifications were tried: generalizing the central matching algorithm; adding geographic background knowledge; and adjusting parameters for network variation scores and limits for generating query network variants. These areas are explained in the following paragraphs.

The base system, InSicht, matches semantic networks derived from a query parse (description or title[3]) to document sentence networks one by one (whereas sentence boundaries are ignored in traditional IR). In GIR (as in IR), this approach yields high precision, but low recall because often the information contained in a query is distributed across several sentences in a document. To adjust the matching approach to such situations, the query network is split if certain graph topologies are encountered. The resulting query network parts are viewed as conjunctively connected. The query network can be split at the following semantic relations: CIRC, CTXT, LOC, TEMP (see Table 2 for definitions). For example, the LOC edge in Fig. 1 can be deleted leading to two separate semantic networks. One corresponds to *"Berichte von Amnesty International über Menschenrechte"* (*'Amnesty International reports on human rights'*) and the other to

[3] GIR-InSicht combines the results for a query from the title field and for a query from the description field. All other topic fields are ignored. The information from the attributes *DE-concept*, *DE-spatialrelation*, and *DE-location* was equally well derived from the parse result of the title or description attribute.

"Lateinamerika" (*'Latin America'*). The greatest positive impact for GeoCLEF comes from splitting at LOC edges.

The geographic knowledge base described in Sect. 3 is scanned by GIR-InSicht; relations that contain names that do not occur in the document parse results are ignored. Meronymy edges are treated like hyponymy edges so that GIR-InSicht can use all part-whole relations for *concept variations* in query networks ([10]). Without this knowledge base, recall is much lower.

Some InSicht parameters had to be adjusted in order to yield more results in GIR-InSicht and/or to keep answer time and RAM consumption acceptable even when working with large background knowledge bases like the one mentioned in Sect. 2.3. The two final steps of InSicht that come after a semantic network match has been found (answer generation and answer selection) can be skipped. Some minor adjustments further reduce run time without losing relevant documents. For example, an apposition for a named entity (like *"Hauptstadt"* (*'capital'*) for *"Sarajewo"*) leads to a new query network variant only if the combination occurs at least twice in the document collection.

We evaluated about ten different setups of GIR-InSicht on the GeoCLEF 2005 topics. The setups used different combinations of the extensions described above and other extensions like coreference resolution. The performance differences were often marginal. In some cases, this indicates that a specific extension is irrelevant for GIR; in other cases, the number of topics (23 with relevant documents) and the number of relevant documents might be too small to draw any conclusions. However, one can see considerable performance improvements for some extensions, e.g. splitting query networks at LOC edges. Larger evaluations are needed to gain more insights about which development directions are most promising for GIR-InSicht.

After the CLEF 2005 evaluation campaign, we tried to identify metonymic usage of proper names (see Sect. 1) in the documents. The parser's lexicon contains for concepts representing names their semantics and for frequent metonymies the involved *semantic facets*. For example, the name *"Libya"* refers to a state. The concept *state* has two semantic facets: an institution facet and a geographic facet. The parser identifies addressed facets by context and lexical knowledge. In the QA corpus, 5.8% of the 351,747 name occurrences (with possible metonymy) were identified as clearly referring to the institution facet, 0.6% referred to the geographic facet. For the remaining 93.6%, no decision is possible because the sentence was too vague or the parser lacks knowledge, yet. We want to employ supervised learning to decide more cases. The metonymy information will be exploited as follows. If the question addresses the geographic facet of a concept, non-geographic uses in the documents will be skipped. For the other approaches from Sect. 3, different facets of a concept will be treated as different terms.

5 Conclusion and Outlook

The MultiNet paradigm offers representational means useful for GIR. We successfully employed semantic networks to uniformly represent queries, documents, and geographic background knowledge and to connect to external resources like GNS data. Three different approaches have been investigated: a baseline corresponding to a traditional IR approach; a variant expanding thematic, temporal, and geographic descriptors from the MultiNet representation of the query; and an adaptation of InSicht, a QA algorithm based on semantic networks. The diversity of our approaches looks promising for a combined system.

We will continue research in the problem areas described in Sect. 2: improving NER, connecting semantic networks and databases, expanding geographic background knowledge, and investigating the role of semantic relations in geographic queries. In IR, there are methods that successfully treat polysemy and synonymy for terms. It remains to be analyzed whether such methods successfully treat polysemy and synonymy for toponyms in GIR, too.

References

1. Jones, C.B., Purves, R., Ruas, A., Sanderson, M., Sester, M., van Kreveld, M.J., Weibel, R.: Spatial information retrieval and geographical ontologies – an overview of the SPIRIT project. In: SIGIR 2002. (2002) 387–388
2. Kunze, C., Wagner, A.: Anwendungsperspektiven des GermaNet, eines lexikalisch-semantischen Netzes für das Deutsche. In Lemberg, I., Schröder, B., Storrer, A., eds.: Chancen und Perspektiven computergestützter Lexikographie. Volume 107 of Lexicographica Series Maior. Niemeyer, Tübingen, Germany (2001) 229–246
3. Hartrumpf, S.: Hybrid Disambiguation in Natural Language Analysis. Der Andere Verlag, Osnabrück, Germany (2003)
4. Helbig, H.: Knowledge Representation and the Semantics of Natural Language. Springer, Berlin (2006)
5. Leveling, J., Hartrumpf, S.: University of Hagen at CLEF 2004: Indexing and translating concepts for the GIRT task. In Peters, C., Clough, P., Jones, G.J.F., Gonzalo, J., Kluck, M., Magnini, B., eds.: Multilingual Information Access for Text, Speech and Images: 5th Workshop of the Cross-Language Evaluation Forum, CLEF 2004. Volume 3491 of LNCS. Springer, Berlin (2005) 271–282
6. Gey, F., Larson, R., Sanderson, M., Joho, H., Clough, P., Petras, V.: GeoCLEF: the CLEF 2005 cross-language geographic information retrieval track overview. This volume
7. Fonseca, F.T., Egenhofer, M.J., Agouris, P., Câmara, G.: Using ontologies for integrated geographic information systems. Transactions in Geographic Information Systems 6(3) (2002) 231–257
8. Hammer, S., Dickmeiss, A., Levanto, H., Taylor, M.: Zebra – User's Guide and Reference, Copenhagen. (2005)
9. Leveling, J.: University of Hagen at CLEF 2003: Natural language access to the GIRT4 data. In Peters, C., Gonzalo, J., Braschler, M., Kluck, M., eds.: Comparative Evaluation of Multilingual Information Access Systems: 4th Workshop of the Cross-Language Evaluation Forum, CLEF 2003. Volume 3237 of LNCS. Springer, Berlin (2004) 412–424
10. Hartrumpf, S.: Question answering using sentence parsing and semantic network matching. In Peters, C., Clough, P., Jones, G.J.F., Gonzalo, J., Kluck, M., Magnini, B., eds.: Multilingual Information Access for Text, Speech and Images: 5th Workshop of the Cross-Language Evaluation Forum, CLEF 2004. Volume 3491 of LNCS. Springer, Berlin (2005) 512–521

Experiments with Geo-Filtering Predicates for IR*

Jochen L. Leidner[1,2,3]

[1] Linguit GmbH, Friedensstraße 10, 76887 Bad Bergzabern, Germany
[2] University of the Saarland, FR 7.4 – Speech Signal Processing, Building C7 1, Office 0.17, 66041 Saarbrücken, Germany
[3] University of Edinburgh, School of Informatics, 2 Buccleuch Place, Edinburgh EH8 9LW, Scotland UK

Abstract. This paper describes a set of experiments for monolingual English retrieval at GEO-CLEF 2005, evaluating a technique for spatial retrieval based on named entity tagging, toponym resolution, and re-ranking by means of geographic filtering. To this end, a series of systematic experiments in the Vector Space paradigm are presented. Plain bag-of-words versus phrasal retrieval and the potential of meronymy query expansion as a recall-enhancing device are investigated, and three alternative geo-spatial filtering techniques based on spatial clipping are compared and evaluated on 25 monolingual English queries. Preliminary results show that always choosing toponym referents based on a simple "maximum population" heuristic to approximate the salience of a referent fails to outperform TF*IDF baselines with the GEO-CLEF 2005 dataset when combined with three geo-filtering predicates. Conservative geo-filtering outperforms more aggressive predicates. The evidence further seems to suggest that query expansion with WordNet meronyms is not effective in combination with the method described. A post-hoc analysis indicates that responsible factors for the low performance include sparseness of available population data, gaps in the gazetteer that associates Minimum Bounding Rectangles with geo-terms in the query, and the composition of the GEO-CLEF 2005 dataset itself.

1 Introduction

Since all human activity relates to places, a large number of information needs also contain a geographic or otherwise spatial aspect. People want to know about the *nearest* restaurant, about the outcome of the match football match *in Manchester*, or about how many died in a flood in *in Thailand*. Traditional IR however, does not accommodate this spatial aspect enough: place names or geographic expressions are merely treated as strings, just like other query terms. This paper presents a general technique to accommodate geographic space in IR, and presents an evaluation of a particular instance of it carried out within the CLEF 2005 evaluation [1].

* The author is grateful to Prof. Dr. Dietrich Klakow for discussions of the results and for hosting him in his lab during a visit in 2005. This work was supported in part by the SOCRATES program of the European Union.

C. Peters et al. (Eds.): CLEF 2005, LNCS 4022, pp. 987–996, 2006.

2 Method

This section describes the method used in this study. There are four essential processing steps. A document retrieval engine (IR) retrieves a set of documents relevant to the queries and groups them in a ranked list. A named entity tagging phase (NERC) then identifies all toponyms. Afterwards a toponym resolution (TR) module looks up all candidate referents for each toponym (i.e, the locations that the place name may be referring to) and tries to disambiguate the toponyms based on a heuristic. If successful, it also assigns the latitude/longitude of the centroid of the location to the resolved toponym. For each document-query pair a geo-filtering module (CLIP) then discards all locations outside a Minimum Bounding Rectangle (MBR) that is the denotation of the spatial expression in the query. Finally, based on a so-called geo-filtering predicate, it is decided whether or not the document under investigation is to be discarded, propagating up subsequent documents in the ranking. Below, each each phase is described in detail.

Document Retrieval (IR). The document retrieval engine provides access to the indexed GEO-CLEF collection. No stop-word filtering or stemming was used at index time, and index access is case-insensitive. The IR engine is used to retrieve the top 1,000 documents for each evaluation query from the collection using the Vector Space Model with the TF*IDF ranking function ([2] p. 78 f.)

$$score(d,q) = \sum_{\forall t in q} tf(t,d)\, idf(t)\, lengthNorm(t,d). \quad (1)$$

The *Lucene* 1.4.3 search API was used for vector space retrieval [3,2], including *Lucene*'s document analysis functionality for English text without modification (i.e., no fields, phrasal indexing or the like was used).

Table 1. List of the most frequent toponyms in the GEO-CLEF corpus. Toponyms in bold type are artifacts of the Glasgow/California bias of the corpus.

Freq. Toponym	Freq. Toponym	Freq. Toponym
18,452 Scotland	5,391 Metro	3,817 Bosnia
13,556 U.S.	4,686 Germany	3,548 France
9,013 Los Angeles	4,438 City	**3,388 Valley**
9,007 United States	4,400 London	3,273 Russia
7,893 California	**4,140 Glasgow**	3,067 New York
7,458 Japan	4,347 China	**2,964 Edinburgh**
7,294 Europe	4,235 Washington	2,919 Mexico
6,985 Orange County	4,013 England	2,782 **Southern California**
5,476 Britain	3,985 America	

Named Entity Tagging (NERC). For named entity tagging, we use a state-of-the-art Maximum Entropy classifier trained on MUC-7 data [4].[1] Tagging 1,000 retrieved document is a very expensive procedure; in a production system, this step would be carried

[1] The named entity tagger does not use location gazetteers internally and performs at an $F_\beta = 1$-score of 87.66% for locations [4].

```
Addison LOC
        USGS_PP|34.20222|-87.18139||Addison|Winston|AL|US|North America
        USGS_PP|41.71833|-72.57722||Addison|Hartford|CT|US|North America
      → USGS_PP|41.93167|-87.98889||Addison|DuPage|IL|US|North America
        USGS_PP|37.91611|-86.565||Addison|Breckinridge|KY|US|North America
        USGS_PP|44.61833|-67.74472||Addison|Washington|ME|US|North America
        USGS_PP|41.98639|-84.34722||Addison|Lenawee|MI|US|North America
        USGS_PP|42.10278|-77.23389||Addison|Steuben|NY|US|North America
        USGS_PP|38.88611|-82.14639||Addison|Gallia|OH|US|North America
        USGS_PP|39.74722|-79.33944||Addison|Somerset|PA|US|North America
        USGS_PP|35.37833|-84.52139||Addison|McMinn|TN|US|North America
        USGS_PP|32.96167|-96.82889||Addison|Dallas|TX|US|North America
        USGS_PP|37.1975|-77.50278||Addison|Dinwiddie|VA|US|North America
        USGS_PP|44.08861|-73.30306||Addison|Addison|VT|US|North America
        USGS_PP|43.42278|-88.37444||Addison|Washington|WI|US|North America
    (>) *Addison|Illinois|United States of America|us|N|37100|41.93|-88.01
        *Addison|Texas|United States of America|us|N|13800|32.96|-96.84
```

Fig. 1. Toponym resolution using the maximum-population heuristic

out at indexing time. Therefore, the retrieved documents are actually pooled across runs to speed up processing.

Toponym Resolution (TR). Complex methods have been proposed in the literature for resolving toponyms to locations [5,6,7], using graph search, statistics, spatial distance and discourse heuristics etc., but for GEO-CLEF we decided to apply a very basic technique because the task is not well understood (no comparative evaluation of the proposed methods exists to date). We use population data as a predictor for default referents ("maximum-population heuristic").

For looking up the candidate referents, we use the large-scale gazetteer described in [8] as primary gazetteer, supplemented by the *World Gazetteer*[2] for population information (as secondary gazetteer). The algorithm used to resolve toponyms to referents works as follows: first, we look up the potential referents with associated latitude/longitude from the primary gazetteer. Then we look up population information for candidate referents from the secondary gazetteer. In order to relate the population entries from the *World Gazetteer* to corresponding entries of the main gazetteer, we defined a custom equality operator ($\doteq$) between two candidate referents for a toponym T_{R_i} such that $R_1 \doteq R_2$ holds iff there is a string equality between their toponyms ($T_{R_1} = T_{R_2}$) and the latitude and longitude of the candidate referents are in the same 1-degree grid (i.e., if and only if $\lfloor R_{1_{lat}} \rfloor = \lfloor R_{2_{lat}} \rfloor \wedge \lfloor R_{1_{long}} \rfloor = \lfloor R_{2_{long}} \rfloor$). If there is no population information available, the toponym remains unresolved. If there is exactly one population entry, the toponym is resolved to that entry. If more than one candidate has population information available, the referent with the largest population is selected. Figure 1 shows the algorithm at work. In the example at the top a case is shown where only population information (prefixed by an asterisk) for one referent is available. This is used as evidence for that referent being the most salient candidate, and consequently it is selected. Note that the coordinates in the two gazetteers need to be rounded for the matching of corresponding entries to be successful. Out of the 41,360 toponym types, population information was available in the World Gazetteer for *some* (i.e., more than zero) candidate referents only for 4,085 toponyms. This means that using only the

---

[2] http://worldgazetteer.com/

population heuristics, the upper bound for system recall is $R = 9.88\%$, and for F-Score $F_{\beta=1} = 9.41\%$, assuming perfect resolution precision.

Geographic Filtering (CLIP). We use a *filtering-based approach* in which we apply traditional IR and then identify locations by means of toponym recognition and toponym resolution. We can then filter out documents or parts of documents that do not fall within our geographic area of interest. Given a polygon P described in a query, and a set of locations $L = \ell_1 \ldots \ell_N$ mentioned in a document. Be Δ_i an N-dimensional vector of geographic distances on the geoid between the N locations in a text document d (mentioned with absolute frequencies f_i) and the centroid of P. Then we can use a *filter predicate* GEO-FILTER(f,Δ) to eliminate the document if its spatial "aboutness" is not high enough:

$$\textsc{Score}'(d,P) = \begin{cases} \textsc{Score}(d) & \textsc{Geo-Filter}(f_d,\Delta_d,P) \\ 0 & \text{otherwise} \end{cases} \tag{2}$$

In filtering the decision is simply between passing through the original IR score or setting it to 0, thus effectively discarding the document from the ranking. Here are the definitions of three simple GEO-FILTER predicates:

1. ANY-INSIDE. This filter is most conservative and tries to avoid discarding true positives at the risk of under-utilizing the discriminative power of geographic space for IR. It only filters out documents that mention no location in the query polygon P:

$$\textsc{Any-Inside}(f_d,\Delta_d,P) = \begin{cases} \mathit{true} & \exists_{\ell \in d} : \ell \in P \\ \mathit{false} & \text{otherwise} \end{cases} \tag{3}$$

2. MOST-INSIDE. This filter is slightly more aggressive than ANY-INSIDE, but still allows for some noise (locations mentioned that do not fall into the geographic area of interest as described by the query polygon P). It discards all documents that mention more locations that fall outside the query polygon than inside:

$$\textsc{Most-Inside}(f_d,\Delta_d,P) = \begin{cases} \mathit{true} & |\{\ell \in d | \ell \in P\}| > |\{\ell \in d | \ell \notin P\}| \\ \mathit{false} & \text{otherwise} \end{cases} \tag{4}$$

3. ALL-INSIDE. This filter is perhaps too aggressive for most purposes; it discards all documents that mention even a single location that fall outside the query polygon P, i.e. all locations must be in the geographic space under consideration:

$$\textsc{All-Inside}(f_d,\Delta_d,P) = \begin{cases} \mathit{true} & \forall_{\ell \in d} : \ell \in P \\ \mathit{false} & \text{otherwise} \end{cases} \tag{5}$$

In practice, we use Minimal Bounding Rectangles (MBRs) to approximate the polygons described by the locations in the query, which trades runtime performance against

Table 2. Minimal bounding rectangles (MBRs) from the Alexandria and ESRI gazetteers. MBRs are given as pairs of points, each with lat/long in degrees. A dash means that no result was found or that a centroid point was available only.

Expression	Alexandria MBR	ESRI MBR
Asia	(0; 0), (90; 180)	—
Australia	(-45.73; 111.22), (-8.88; 155.72)	(-47.5; 92.2), (10.8; 179.9)
Europe	(35.0; -30.0), (70.0; 50.0)	(35.3; -11.5), (81.4; 43.2)
Latin America	—	(-55.4; -117), (32.7; -33.8)
Bosnia-Herzegovina	(42.38; 15.76), (45.45; 20.02)	—
Germany	(46.86; 5.68), (55.41; 15.68)	(47.27; 5.86), (55.057; 15.03)
Holland	(50.56; 3.54), (53.59; 7.62)	(51.29; 5.08), (51.44; 5.23)
Japan	(30.1; 128.74), (46.26; 146.46)	(24.25; 123.68), (45.49; 145.81)
Rwanda	(-3.01; 28.9), (-1.03; 31.2)	(-2.83; 28.85), (-1.05; 30.89)
UK	(49.49; -8.41), (59.07; 2.39)	(49.96; -8.17), (60.84; 1.75)
United States	(13.71; -177.1), (76.63; -61.48)	(18.93; -178.22), (71.35;-68)
California	(32.02; -124.9), (42.51; -113.61)	—
Scotland	— (56.0; -4.0)	(54.63; -8.62), (60.84; -0.76)
Siberia	— (60.0; 100.0)	—
Scottish Islands	—	—
Scottish Trossachs	— (49.63; -104.22)	—
Scottish Highlands	— (57.5; -4.5)	—
Sarajevo	— (43.86; 18.39)	(43.65; 18.18), (44.05; 18.58)
Caspian Sea	— (42.0; 50.0)	(45; 48.41), (42.40; 48.81)
North Sea	— (55.33; 3.0)	(58.04; 1.02), (58.44; 1.42)

retrieval performance. More specifically, we computed the union of the Alexandria Digital Library and ESRI gazetteers (Table 2) to look up MBRs for geographic terms in the GEO-CLEF queries.[3] In cases of multiple candidate referents (e.g. for *California*), the MBR for the largest feature type was chosen (i.e. in the case of California, the U.S. membership state interpretation). Latin America was not found in the Alexandria Gazetteer. A manual search for South America also did not retrieve the continent, but found several other hits, e.g. South America Island in Alaska. Holland was recognized by the Alexandria Gazetteer as a synonym for the Netherlands. While this corresponds to typical usage, formally speaking Holland refers to a *part* of the Netherlands. The ESRI server returned two entries for *Caspian Sea*, one as given in the table, another with MBR (41.81; 50.54), (42.21; 50.94)–since they share the same feature type they could not otherwise be distinguished. Finally, the software module CLIP performs geographic filtering of a document given an MBR, very much like the clipping operation found in typical GIS packages, albeit on unstructured documents. It would of course have been beneficial for the retrieval performance if the MBRs that were not available in the ESRI and Alexandria gazetteers had been gathered from elsewhere, as there are plenty of sources scattered across the Internet. However, then the experimental outcome would perhaps no longer reflect a typical *automatic* system.

[3] On the query side, manual disambiguation was performed.

Query Expansion with Meronyms. Query expansion is typically used as a Recall-enhancing device, because by adding terms to the original query that are related to the original terms, additional relevant documents are retrieved that would not have been covered by the original query, possibly at the expense of Precision. Here, we experimented with meronym query expansion, i.e. with geographic terms that stand in a spatial "part-of" relation (as in "Germany is part of Europe"). We used WordNet 2.0 to retrieve toponyms that stand in a meronym relationship with any geographic term from the query. The version used contains 8,636 part-of relationships linking 9,799 synsets. The choice of WordNet was motivated by the excessive size of both gazetteers used in the toponym resolution step. For each query, we transitively added all constituent geographic entities, e.g. for *California* we added *Orange County* as well as *Los Angeles*.

3 Evaluation

The GEO-CLEF 2005 evaluation was very similar to previous TREC and CLEF evaluations: for each run, *11-Point-Average Precision* against *interpolated Recall* and *R-Precision* against retrieved documents were determined. In addition, difference from median across participants for each topic were reported. Traditionally, the relevance judgments in TREC-style evaluations are binary, i.e. a document either meets the information need expressed in a TREC topic (1) or not (0). Intrinsically fuzzy queries (e.g. "*shark attacks near Australia*") introduce the problem that a strict yes/no decision might no longer be appropriate; there is no "crisp cut-off point. In the same way that the ranking has to be modified to account for geographic distance, a modification of the evaluation procedure ought to be considered. However, for GEO-CLEF 2005, binary relevance assessments were used.

Nota Bene. *For organizational reasons, this series of experiments did* not *contribute any documents to the judgment pool for the relevance assessments, which results in a negative bias of the performance results measured compared to the true performance of the experiments and other* GEO-CLEF *2005 participants.* This is because all relevant documents found by the methods described herein but not returned by any other participants will be have been wrongly assessed as "not relevant". Therefore, a discussion of the relative performance compared to other participants is not included in this paper. On the other hand, this makes the results comparable to future experiments with GEO-CLEF data outside the annual evaluation, which will of course likewise not be able to influence the pooling a posteriori.

The baseline run `LTITLE` that uses only the topic title and no spatial processing performs surprisingly well, with an Average Precision averaged over queries of 23.62% and a Precision at 10 documents of just 36%. Table 3 gives a summary of the averaged results for each run. As for the terminology, all run names start the letter `L` followed by an indicator of how the query was formed. `CONC` means using the content of the `<CONCEPT>` tag and posing a phrasal query to the IR engine, `CONCPHRSPAT` means using the content of both `<CONCEPT>` and `<SPATIAL>` tags, and `<TITLE>` uses the title tag. `PHR` refers to runs using the IR engine's phrasal query mechanism in addition to pure bag-of-terms. For these runs, queries look as follows (identifying the phrases was the only manually step):

```
(("Shark Attacks"^2.0) (("shark attack"~8)^1.5) (Shark Attacks))
```

This combined way of querying takes into account the phrase *shark attacks* (as subsequent terms in the document only) with twice the weight of the "normal" bag-of-words query (last sub-query). The middle line searches for the lemmatized words *shark* and *attack* within an 8-term window and weights this sub-query with 1.5. Runs containing ANY, MOST, or ALL as part of their name indicate that geo-filtering with the ANY-INSIDE, MOST-INSIDE or ALL-INSIDE filtering predicates, respectively, was used. Finally, WNMN as part of a run name indicates that query expansion with WordNet meronyms was applied.

Table 3. Result summary: Average Precision and R-Precision

Run	Avg. Precision	R-Precision	Run	Avg. Precision	R-Precision
LTITLE	**23.62** %	**26.21** %	LCONCPHRSPAT	**20.37** %	**24.53** %
LTITLEANY	**18.50** %	**21.08** %	LCONCPHRSPATANY	16.92 %	20.36 %
LTITLEMOST	12.64 %	16.77 %	LCONCPHRSPATMOST	11.09 %	15.51 %
LTITLEALL	8.48 %	11.97 %	LCONCPHRSPATALL	7.99 %	10.89 %
LCONCPHR	15.65 %	19.25 %	LCONCPHRWNMN	17.25 %	19.36 %
LCONCPHRANY	14.18 %	19.66 %	LCONCPHRWNMNANY	12.99 %	16.22 %
LCONCPHRMOST	9.56 %	14.46 %	LCONCPHRWNMNMOST	8.18 %	11.38 %
LCONCPHRALL	7.36 %	10.98 %	LCONCPHRWNMNALL	5.69 %	8.78 %

Applying the "maximum population" heuristic alone to achieve toponym resolution together with geo-filtering in general performed poorly and in none of the four series of experiments outperformed a baseline that applied no dedicated spatial processing. Interestingly, a plain vanilla Vector Space Model with TF-IDF and the obligatory run using title-only queries (LTITLE) performs better than the median across all participant entries for 19 out of 25 (or 76%) of the queries in GEO-CLEF 2005. For three geo-filtering predicates tested, a consistent relative pattern could be observed across all runs: The ANY-INSIDE filter almost consistently outperformed (in one case it was en par with) the MOST-INSIDE filter, which in turn always outperformed the ALL-INSIDE filter. While it was expected that MOST-INSIDE would not perform all well as the other two filter types, it is interesting that the conservative ANY-INSIDE outperformed MOST-INSIDE on average. The evidence seems to suggest further than geographic query expansion with WordNet meronyms is not effective as a recall-enhancing device, independent on whether or which geo-filter is applied afterwards: average precision at. Note however, that this is true only on average, not for all individual queries. Furthermore two queries were actually not executed by the Lucene engine because the query expansion caused the query to exceed implementation limits (too many query terms).

Regarding the *modus operandi* of GEO-CLEF, future evaluations would benefit from a separation of training/development and test set regarding the queries. Furthermore,

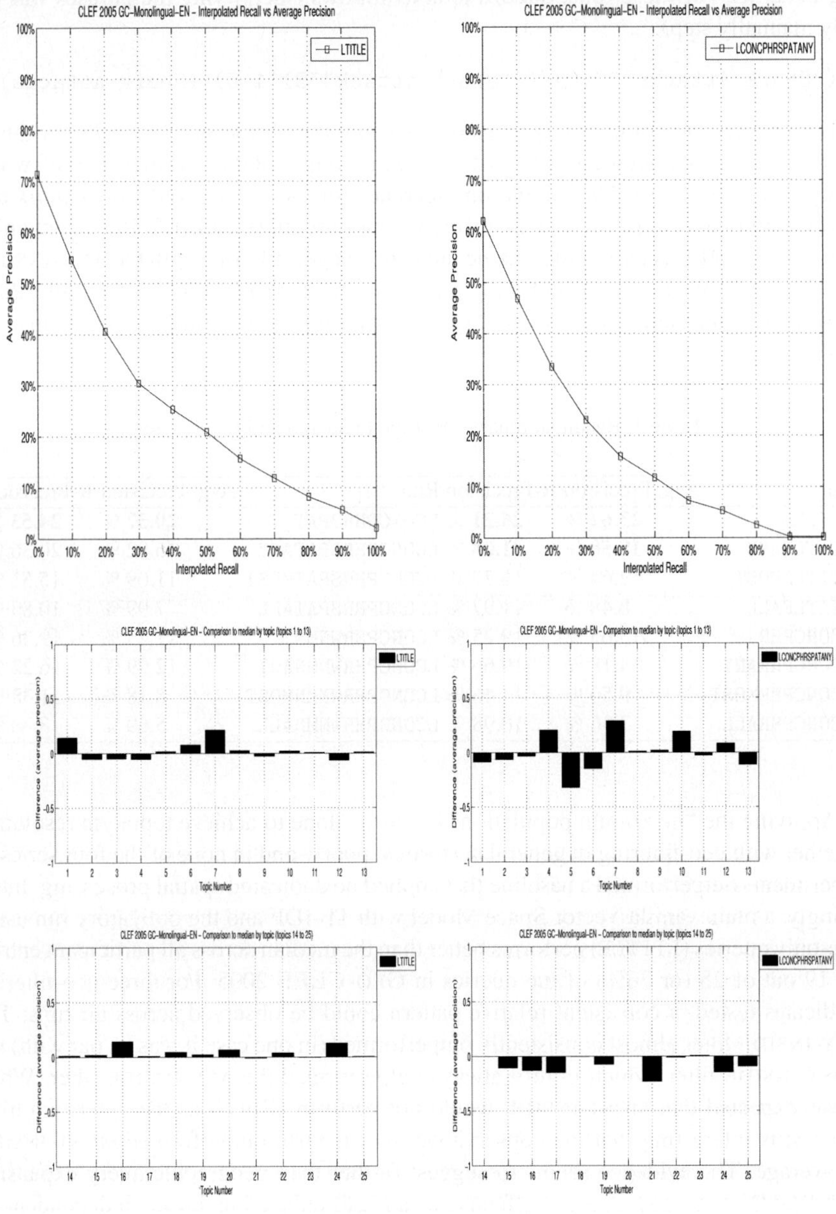

Fig. 2. Performance of the runs `LTITLE` (left) and `LCONCPHRSPATANY` (right). The first row shows mean average precision; the second row shows topic performance relative to the median across participants.

alternative relevance assessments based on geographic distance rather than binary decisions (document relevant/document not relevant) might be attempted. I propose to use *Root-Mean-Square Distance* (RMSD, Equation 6) to indicate the (geo-) distance between a query centroid q and a set of location centroids $d_1,\ldots,d_N$ in a document:

$$\mathrm{RMSD}(d,q) = \sqrt{\frac{1}{N}\sum_{i=1}^{N}(d_i - q)^2} \tag{6}$$

Such an measure could be used to compute a continuous-scale geographic relevance measure once the assessors annotated the test queries and the toponyms in the pooled result documents with their "ground truth" coordinates.

4 Conclusions and Future Work

We have described a method for geographic information retrieval based on named entity tagging to identify place names (or toponym recognition, geo-parsing), toponym resolution (or geo-coding, place name disambiguation) and geographic filtering (or clipping). First results show that a very simple method for toponym resolution based on a "maximum population" heuristic is not effective when combined with three point-in-MBR geo-filtering predicates in the setting used. We conjecture this may be due to the lack of available population data. In addition, we discovered that geographic query expansion with WordNet meronyms appears not to improve retrieval performance.

For future work, several opportunities for further study should be given consideration. The results presented here should be compared the with different, more sophisticated clipping criteria that take the amount of spatial overlap into account. For example, instead of using MBRs computed from sets of centroid points [9] proposes a *Dynamic Spatial Approximation Method (DSAM)*, which uses Voronoi approximation to compute more precise polygons from sets of points. Once polygons are available, spatial overlap metrics can be applied to improve retrieval [10]. It is vital to discover methods to determine a good balance when *weighting the spatial influence* and the term influence in the query against each other in a principled way, probably even dependent on the query type. On the query side, the specific *spatial relations* should be taking into account. However, this requires defining how users and/or CLEF assessors actually judge different relations beforehand (how near does something have to be to be considered "near"?). On the document side, *text-local relationships* from the toponym context should be taken into account. Right now, all toponyms (`LOC`) are considered equal, which does not utilize knowledge from the context of their occurrence. For instance, a document collection that has one mention of *New York* in every document footer because the news agency resides in New York can pose a problem. The *impact of the particular gazetteer* used for query expansion and toponym resolution ought to be studied with respect to the dimensions size/density (UN-LOCODE/WordNet versus NGA GeoNames) and local/global (e.g. EDINA DIGIMAP versus NGA GeoNames). Last but perhaps most importantly, more sophisticated toponym resolution strategies (e.g. [6]) should be compared against the simple population heuristic used in this study.

References

1. Gey, F., Larson, R., Sanderson, M., Joho, H., Clough, P., Petras, V.: GeoCLEF: The CLEF 2005 cross-language geographic information retrieval track overview. In: Proceedings of the Cross Language Evaluation Forum 2005. Springer Lecture Notes in Computer Science, Berlin; Heidelberg, CLEF, Springer (2006) (in this volume).
2. Gospodnetić, O., Hatcher, E.: Lucene in Action. Manning, Greenwich, CT, USA (2005)
3. Cutting, D.: Lucene. http://lucene.apache.org/ (2005) [online].
4. Curran, J.R., Clark, S.: Language independent NER using a maximum entropy tagger. In: Proceedings of the Seventh Conference on Natural Language Learning (CoNLL-03), Edmonton, Canada (2003) 164–167
5. Smith, D.A., Crane, G.: Disambiguating geographic names in a historical digital library. In: Proceedings of the 5th European Conference on Research and Advanced Technology for Digital Libraries (ECDL '01), London, UK, Springer-Verlag (2001) 127–136
6. Leidner, J.L., Sinclair, G., Webber, B.: Grounding spatial named entities for information extraction and question answering. In: Proceedings of the Workshop on the Analysis of Geographic References held at the Joint Conference for Human Language Technology and the Annual Meeting of the Noth American Chapter of the Association for Computational Linguistics 2003 (HLT/NAACL'03), Edmonton, Alberta, Canada (2003) 31–38
7. Amitay, E., Har'El, N., Sivan, R., Soffer, A.: Web-a-Where: Geotagging Web content. In Sanderson, M., Järvelin, K., Allan, J., Bruza, P., eds.: SIGIR 2004: Proceedings of the 27th Annual International ACM SIGIR Conference on Research and Development in Information Retrieval, Sheffield, UK, July 25-29, 2004, ACM (2004) 273–280
8. Leidner, J.L.: An evaluation dataset for the toponym resolution task. Computers, Environment and Urban Systems. Special Issue on Geographic Information Retrieval (2006) (in press). 30(4): 400-417
9. Alani, H., Jones, C.B., Tudhope, D.: Voronoi-based region approximation for geographical information retrieval with gazetteers. International Journal of Geographical Information Science **15**(4) (2001) 287–306
10. Larson, R.R., Frontiera, P.: Spatial ranking methods for geographic information retrieval (GIR) in digital libraries. In: Research and Advanced Technology for Digital Libraries, 8th European Conference, ECDL 2004, Bath, UK, September 12-17, 2004, Proceedings. Volume 3232 of Lecture Notes in Computer Science., Springer (2004) 45–56

The XLDB Group at GeoCLEF 2005

Nuno Cardoso, Bruno Martins, Marcirio Chaves, Leonardo Andrade, and Mário J. Silva

Grupo XLDB - Departamento de Informática
Faculdade de Ciências da Universidade de Lisboa
{ncardoso, bmartins, mchaves, leonardo, mjs} at xldb.di.fc.ul.pt

Abstract. This paper describes our participation at GeoCLEF 2005. We detail the main software components of our Geo-IR system, its adaptation for GeoCLEF and the obtained results. The software architecture includes a geographic knowledge base, a text mining tool for geo-referencing documents, and a geo-ranking component. Results show that geo-ranking is heavily dependent on the information in the knowledge base and on the ranking algorithm involved.

1 Introduction

Over the past two years, the XLDB Group developed and operated tumba!, a search engine for the Portuguese community (`http://www.tumba.pt`) [1]. We are currently extending it to handle geographic searches, under the GREASE (Geographical REAsoning for Search Engines) project.

GREASE researches methods, algorithms and software architecture for geographical information retrieval (Geo-IR) from the web [2]. Some of the specific challenges are: 1) building geographical ontologies to assist Geo-IR; 2) extracting geographical references from text; 3) assigning geographical scopes to documents; 4) ranking documents according to geographical relevance. GeoTumba, a location-aware search engine handling *concept@location* queries, is a prototype system developed in the context of GREASE.

Our participation at GeoCLEF aimed at evaluating GeoTumba. To build a system configuration that would enable us to generate the GeoCLEF runs, we made significant adaptations to GeoTumba, including using global geographic information instead of just focusing on the Portuguese territory, and replacing the geographic ranking component (still under development) by a simpler scheme.

The rest of the paper is organized as follows: Section 2 describes GeoTumba and the software configuration that was assembled for our participation at GeoCLEF. Section 3 outlines our evaluation goals and the submitted runs. Section 4 presents an analysis on the obtained results, and finally, Section 5 draws conclusions and directions for future work.

2 The Geographic IR System

We take the simplistic approach of associating each document to a single scope, or none if the assignment can not be made within a certain confidence level. This is similar to the

C. Peters et al. (Eds.): CLEF 2005, LNCS 4022, pp. 997–1006, 2006.

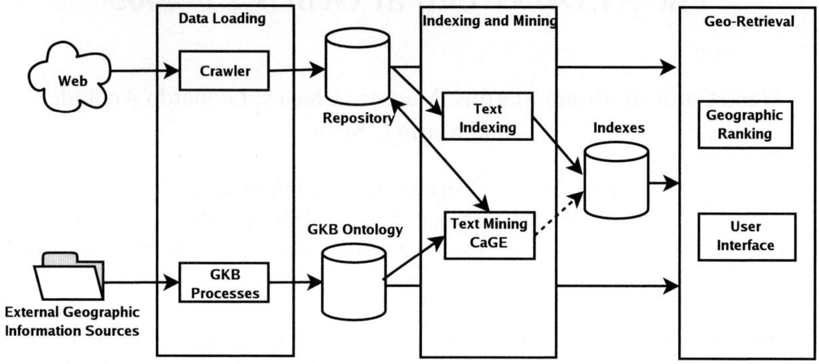

Fig. 1. The Geographic IR architecture

"one sense per discourse" assumption, taken in many recognition and disambiguation systems [3]. Figure 1 shows the architecture of the current Geo-IR system prototype. Information is processed in three phases:

Data loading: web pages are harvested into a repository by a crawling module. The geographic knowledge of GeoTumba is collected into GKB (Geographic Knowledge Base) [4]. GKB can be queried interactively to retrieve data about a geographic name or a relationship about two geographic features. It can also be used to create geographic ontologies.

Indexing and Mining: the geographic ontology is used by CaGE, a text mining module for recognizing geographical references and assigning documents with a corresponding geo-scope [5]. Once scopes are assigned to documents, we create indexes for fast retrieval. The indexing software of tumba! is being enhanced for indexing the geographic scopes information.

Geo-Retrieval: in the last phase, term indexes handle the *concept* part of the queries, while the *location* part is used as a key for fast access to documents through the scopes indexes. Result sets are generated, matching users' queries and ranked according to geographic criteria.

In the rest of this Section, we describe the main modules, GKB and CaGE, and present the software configuration that we assembled for generating the GeoCLEF submitted runs.

2.1 GKB – A Geographical Knowledge Base

GKB provides a common place for integrating data from multiple external sources under a common schema and exporting geographic knowledge for use by other components.

The geographical information in GKB includes names for places and other geographical features, information types (e.g. city, street, etc.), ontological relationships between the features, demographics data and geographic codes, such as postal codes.

We have developed two GKB instances: the first has detailed information about the main Portuguese territory; the second, holds information about the main regions,

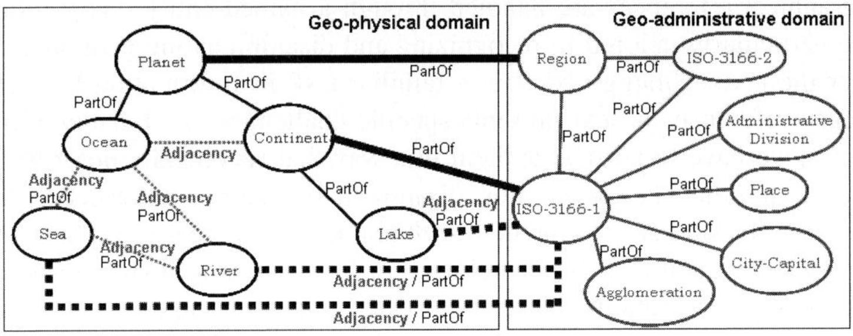

Fig. 2. Feature types and their relationships in the world ontology of GKB

countries, cities and places around the world in four different languages: Portuguese (PT), Spanish (ES), English (EN) and German (DE). While the first was created to support the GeoTumba service for Portugal, the latter is intended for validation of the GeoTumba software, through experiments with annotated multilingual corpora and Geo-IR evaluations covering other parts of the world, such as GeoCLEF. The geographic ontology of the world was built from two public information sources:

Wikipedia: on-line encyclopædia (`http://www.wikipedia.org`). We used its name definitions of countries and their capitals in the four supported languages. We also collected all the geo-physical names information from this source.

World Gazetteer: (`http://www.world-gazetteer.com`) information about the largest cities and agglomerations around the world. We selected those with population above 100,000.

We detail some statistics for the world ontology used in GeoCLEF elsewhere [4]. The majority of the relationships are of the `PartOf` type, while `Equivalence` and `Adjacency` relationships are much less frequent. For some types, the number of described features (number of Seas, Lakes and Regions) is much smaller than in reality because they were not available in the information sources.

Some features in GKB had to be added manually, as some GeoCLEF topics included place names like the North Sea, Caspian Sea and Siberia, which are not present on the GKB information sources.

2.2 CaGE – Handling Geographical References in Text

CaGE is a text mining module specifically developed to infer the geographic context from collections of documents, based on the geographic knowledge contained in a OWL ontology imported from GKB. The process of geo-referencing the textual documents is performed in two stages:

1. Identify the geographical references present in each text and weight them according to frequency.
2. Assign a corresponding geographical scope to each text, considering the geographical references, their frequency, and the relationships among them.

The geographical references are handled through a named-entity recognition (NER) procedure particularly tailored to recognizing and disambiguating geographical references over the text. Although NER is a familiar task in Information Extraction [6], handling geo-references in text presents specific challenges [7]. Besides recognizing place names, we have to normalize them in a way that specifically describes or even uniquely identifies the place in question, disambiguating them with respect to their specific type (e.g. city) and grounding them with features from the geographical ontology. CaGE follows the traditional NER architecture by combining lexical resources with shallow processing operations. It can be divided into four stages: 1) Pre-processing the documents, 2) Named-entity identification, 3) Named-entity disambiguation, and 4) Generation of feature lists [8].

After extracting geo-references, we combine the available information and disambiguate further among the different possible scopes that can be assigned to each document. Our scope assignment approach relies on a graph where the relationships between geographical concepts are specified. The geographical ontology provides the needed information. We convert it to a graph representation, weighting different semantic relationships (edges) according to their importance (i.e., equivalence relationships are more important than hierarchical relationships, which in turn are more important than adjacency relationships) and weighting different geographical concepts (nodes) according to the feature weights computed at the previous step (see Figure 3). Importance scores are then calculated for all the nodes in the graph, using a variation of the PageRank ranking algorithm [5]. After a score is computed for each feature from the ontology, we select the most probable scope for the document, by taking the highest scoring feature, or none if all features are scored below a given threshold [2].

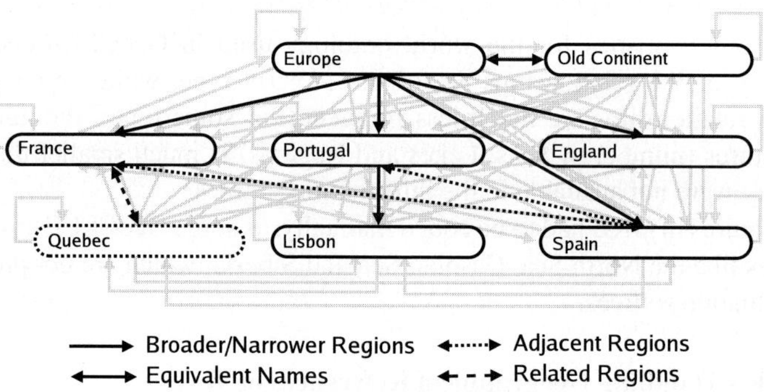

Fig. 3. Geographic concepts graph

2.3 Ranking Documents with Geo-scopes

In GeoTumba, we use geo-scopes to create new indexes supporting fast searches. The best strategies for efficiently organising this information for fast access are overviewed in [9]. We are presently pondering various similarity metrics that could be used in a global GeoTumba ranking function. As a result, we decided to participate in GeoCLEF with a system software configuration that does not use the geographic indexes, but still ranks documents according to geographic criteria, based on the assigned scopes.

2.4 Software Configuration Used to Create the GeoCLEF Runs

In our GeoCLEF experiments, we used QuerCol, a query expansion component to generate queries from the CLEF supplied topics (more details about the query generation process are presented in a separate text describing our participation in the CLEF 2005 ad hoc task [10]). The changes made to GeoTumba also include:

- Replacement of the web crawler by a custom loader already used in previous evaluations, to bring the GeoCLEF newswire text collections into the repository.
- Development of a simple alternative scope assignment algorithm, that consists in simply selecting the most frequent geographical reference as the scope of a document.
- Implementation of a geo-ranking function which does not use geographic indexes. Ranking was computed in two stages: first, we ranked documents using TF $\times$ IDF weighting. Then, we ranked the given result set with a geographic similarity function. The final ranking corresponds to the set of documents ordered by a geographic rank, followed by the non-geographic rank.

The geographic similarity metric that we used in GeoCLEF is defined on a *scopes tree* extracted from the geographic concepts graph built from the geographic ontology. In this tree, we define i) $depth(X)$ as the count of edges between node X and the root of the tree; ii) $ancestor(X,Y) = true$ if X is on the path of Y to the root node of the tree; and iii) TD, tree depth, the maximum $depth()$ of any node on the tree.

Given a query Q, a geo-scope $Scope_Q$ and a result set with documents $D_1,...,D_n$, each with a $Scope_{D_i}$ or NULL scope assigned, the geographic similarity $GS(Q,D_i)$ is obtained as follows:

$$GS(Q,D_i) = \begin{cases} 0 & if Scope_Q = Scope_{D_i} \\ depth(Scope_Q) - depth(Scope_{D_i}) & if\ ancestor(Scope_Q, Scope_{D_i}) = true \\ n \times TD + depth(Scope_{D_i}) - depth(Scope_Q) & if\ ancestor(Scope_{D_i}, Scope_Q) = true \\ 2 \times n \times TD & otherwise \end{cases}$$

The definition above means that the geographic similarity ranking function first ranks all the documents with the same scope as the query, then those with a narrower scope than the query, and then those with a wider scope. Finally, documents with NULL scopes or scopes that can not be defined as strictly narrow or wider than the scope of the query are ranked last.

3 Runs Description and Evaluation Goals

With our participation in GeoCLEF, we aimed at evaluating:

Scope ranking: measure how the ranking with the geo-scopes assigned to documents improves Geo-IR results, in comparison to including location terms in the query strings, using geographic terms as common terms, a common practice for narrowing geographic searches (e.g. '*restaurant london*') [11,12].

Scope assigning: when using geo-scopes, compare the graph-based algorithm against the simple scope assignment algorithm that selects the most frequent geographic entity in texts.

Expansion of location terms: when not using geo-scopes, measure the contribution of the expansion of geographic terms in queries to improve searches.

Topic translation: observe the performance of Portuguese to English bilingual runs. Our efforts were focused towards the English monolingual subtask. The bilingual runs obtained provide initial results on the performance of the machine translation system being developed by the Linguateca group at Braga, Portugal. There was no interest in creating runs derived from manual queries for this subtask.

We submitted a total of 14 runs (see Table 1). Below, we describe the creation procedures and observations intended for each of the submitted runs:

Table 1. The runs submitted by the XLDB group to the GeoCLEF, and their Mean Average Precision (MAP) values

Run description	Monolingual EN	Monolingual DE	Bilingual PT->EN
(Mandatory) Automatic query generation, title + description only	XLDBENAutMandTD (MAP: 0.1183)	-	XLDBPTAutMandTD (MAP: 0.0988)
(Mandatory) Automatic query generation, title + description + location	XLDBENAutMandTDL (MAP: 0.1785)	-	XLDBPTAutMandTDL (MAP: 0.1645)
Manual query generation, title + description only	XLDBENManTD (MAP: 0.0970)	XLDBDEManTD (MAP: 0.1016)	-
Manual query generation, title + description + location	XLDBENManTDL (MAP: 0.2253)	XLDBDEManTDL (MAP: 0.0717)	-
manual query, title + description run, GKB 'PageRank'-like scopes	XLDBENManTDGKBm3 (MAP: 0.1379)	XLDBDEManTDGKBm3 (MAP: 0.1123)	XLDBPTManTDGKBm3 (MAP: 0.1395)
manual query, title + description run, most frequent NE scopes	XLDBENManTDGKBm4 (MAP: 0.1111)	XLDBDEManTDGKBm4 (MAP: 0.0988)	XLDBPTManTDGKBm4 (MAP: 0.1470)

'AutMandTD and AutMandTDL': GeoCLEF required two fully automatic mandatory runs. The first should only use title and description information from the supplied topics, while the second should also use the location information. These two runs provide the evaluation baselines. The first indicates the performance of the non-geographical IR mechanisms being used, while the other provides the means to evaluate geographical IR against a simple baseline.

'ManTD': this run was generated as an intermediary step for the construction of the *ManTDL*, *TDGKBm*3 and *TDGKBm*4 runs. It provides a comparative baseline for the other submissions. We created manual queries to generate these runs, using terms from the topics's titles and descriptions, avoiding narrative terms and all related geographic terms. We did not include any location names or adjectives from the topics titles in the queries. We expanded morphologically the terms, and combined them using 'AND' and 'OR' logic operators into a single query line. As our baseline runs, the goal was to maximize recall. Precision was expected to suffer due to the lack of geographic terms on these baseline runs. These runs have a label which ends with '*ManTD*' (MANual query, Title + Description).

'ManTDL': We wanted to measure the efficiency of expanding and including geographical location terms in the query string, to restrict query scopes; hence, we created these runs by inserting the scope(s) location(s) from the topic in the manual query from the '*ManTD*' runs. When the topic location scope implicitly embraces a group of countries, we extended it to the country level. For example, in the topic with the North Sea scope, the generated query string included terms like *North, Sea, England* and *Denmark*. In the case of topics with an important spatial relation (e.g. South-West of Scotland), we expanded the scope in a similar way for each location found on the narrative, like *Ayr* and *Glasgow* on the example above (notice that this was the only information used from the narratives, regarding all query strings). These runs have a label which ends with '*ManTDL*' (MANual query, Title + Description + Location).

'TDGKBm3 and TDGKBm4': in this run, we intended to measure the efficiency of our text mining software for assigning documents with a corresponding geographical scope, as described in Section 2. Runs labeled with '*TDGKBm*3' mark the PageRank-like scope assignment, and the labels '*TDGKBm*4' mark the most frequent geographic entity as the scope's document.

We did not submit mandatory runs for the German monolingual task, because QuerCol couldn't handle the agglutinated concepts in the topic titles properly. We found no interest in submitting these runs as the German language specificities were outside the scope of our participation in GeoCLEF.

4 Results

The obtained results are presented in Figures 4 and 5.Regarding the evaluation goals presented on the previous Section, we can derive from the observation of Figures 4 and 5 the following conclusions:

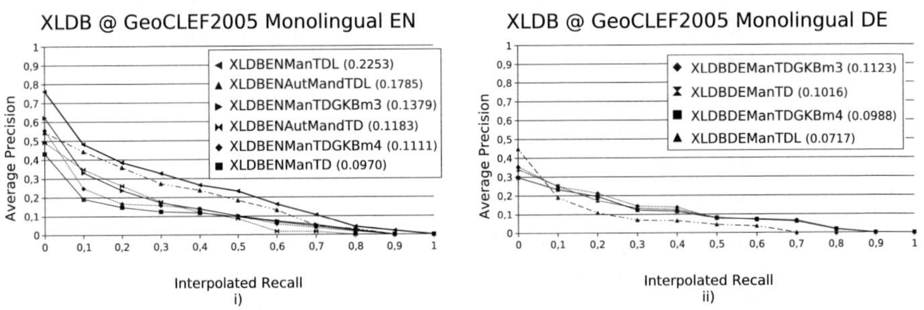

Fig. 4. Results of the XLDB group on the English monolingual subtask (i) English and ii) German) of GeoCLEF 2005. In parenthesis, the MAP values of the runs.

Scope ranking: comparing no-scope runs vs. scope-aware runs, we observe that the runs with location terms inserted in the fully automatic query (*AutMandTDL*) ended with better precision than the runs with geographic scope ranking (*TDGKBm3* and *TDGKBm4*). We didn't expect this behaviour, as our Geo-IR is able to retrieve relevant documents to a given scope without its name on the query. A more detailed

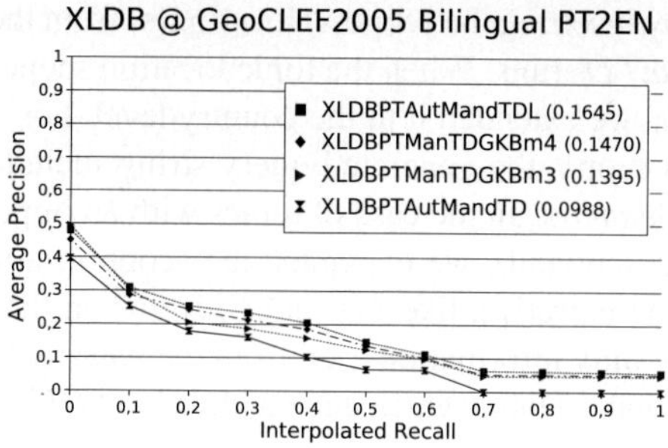

Fig. 5. Results of the XLDB group on the Portuguese to English bilingual subtask of GeoCLEF 2005. In parenthesis, the MAP values of the runs.

analysis of the qrels shows that this happened because both the geo-ranking method and the ontology data had limitations.

Scope assigning: comparing the graph-based vs. the most frequent geographical reference algorithms used to assign scopes to documents, the method based on the graph ranking algorithm (*TDGKBm3*) achieved higher precision than the alternative method of assigning the most frequent geographic reference as the document's scope (like the *TDGKBm4* runs). Analyzing the results, we can see that CaGE normally assigned the same scopes that an human would infer if he only had the same geographic knowledge passed on the world ontology.

Expansion of location terms: We can observe that the runs based on manual queries with expanded location terms (i.e. the *ManTDL* runs) obtained higher precision than the *AutMandTDL* runs. This reinforces our belief that relevant documents often do not explicitly contain the terms from the desired location. A Geo-IR system should consider the relationships between geographical concepts in order to retrieve relevant documents to a given location, even if they do not contain the location terms. However, the CaGE graph-ranking algorithm did not obtain better results than those used for generation of the runs based only on location names and standard text search (*AutMandTDL*). As scopes seemed to be correctly assigned, we suspect that the result was caused by lack of location names in the used ontology and a bad geographic ranking function.

Topic translation: The English monolingual runs exhibit better results than the bilingual runs. This results from the poor quality of the topics translation. Detailed description of these problems are included in the ad hoc participation paper [10]. This wasn't too obvious on the *ManTD* runs (they showed a similar performance), as they were created from query strings with few terms selected from the topic.

The analysis of the topic qrels shows that 61% of the relevant documents have been assigned to an unrelated or unknown scope. We realized that sub-optimal results are caused by the geographic ranking strategy adopted, and the lack of relationships in the ontology. For example, we have '*Glasgow*' as part of '*United Kingdom*', and '*United Kingdom*' as part of '*Europe*'. Yet, the record '*Scotland*' was associated to '*United Kingdom*', and thus our geo-ranking module did not have a path from '*Glasgow*' to '*Scotland*' on the scopes tree.

Further analysis also revealed that we could have profited from using the `Adjacency` relationships on the geographic similarity metric, as we couldn't associate documents with assigned scopes like *Russia* or *Azerbaijan* to regions like *Siberia* or *Caspian Sea*.

These facts had a noticeable impact on the *TDGKBm3* and *TDGKBm4* runs, meaning that we can't make an overall evaluation of our Geo-IR, compared to the *AutMandTDL* and *ManTDL* runs, at this point.

5 Conclusion

For our participation in the GeoCLEF evaluation campaign, we adapted software from a geographical web search engine currently under development at our group. Our scope assignment approach is based on a two stage process, in which geographical references in the text are recognized and a geographic scope is afterwards computed for each document. A central component of the whole process is a geographical ontology, acting as the source of geographical names and relationships.

Although our scope assignment algorithm has shown to be better than a simple baseline of selecting the scopes according to the most frequent geographical references, retrieving documents using scopes was no better than the simple inclusion of the topic locations as additional terms to a standard text search. Our evaluation of the qrels has shown that the lack of information about some of the geographic concepts or their relationship to other concepts on the built ontology was the cause for poor performance in a considerable number of topics. This shows that the success of our approach strongly depends on the amount and quality of geographic knowledge that is provided to the system. However, we suspect that if too much detailed geographic information is provided, performance would also become sub-optimal.

A similar resource to GKB is the Getty Thesaurus of Geographic Names (TGN) [13]. We believe that the number of features currently in GKB is enough to assign the geographic scope to each document. We wanted to experiment this assumption with other gazetteers, and we plan to generate runs using TGN to be compared against the results obtained with GKB.

As future work, in addition to improving the scope assignment algorithm and experimenting with more comprehensive ontologies, we plan to devise and evaluate better geographic ranking functions, capable of geographically ranking documents even in the absence of geographic knowledge about terms of the query location part or in documents, and making better use of the geographic scopes.

Acknowledgements

We thank Andreas Wichert, for the manual creation of the German queries and insight on certain aspects on diacritics expansions on German texts. Alberto Simões provided topic translations.

Thanks to all the tumba! developers and GREASE project participants. This work was financed by the Portuguese Fundação para a Ciência e Tecnologia through grant

POSI / PLP / 43931 / 2001 (Linguateca) and by grant POSI / SRI / 40193 / 2001 (GREASE). Bruno Martins is supported by FCT through grant SFRH-BD-10757-2002.

References

1. Silva, M.J.: The Case for a Portuguese Web Search Engine. In: Proceedings of ICWI-03, the 2003 IADIS International Conference on WWW/Internet, Algarve, Portugal, IADIS (2003) 411–418
2. Silva, M.J., Martins, B., Chaves, M., Afonso, A.P.: Adding Geographic Scopes to Web Resources. CEUS - Computers, Environment and Urban Systems, Elsevier Science (2005) In print.
3. Gale, W., Church, K., Yarowsky, D.: One sense per discourse. In: Proceedings of the 4th DARPA Speech and Natural Language Workshop. (1992)
4. Chaves, M.S., Silva, M.J., Martins, B.: GKB - Geographic Knowledge Base. Technical Report DI/FCUL TR 5-12, Departamento de Informática da Faculdade de Ciências da Universidade de Lisboa (2005)
5. Martins, B., Silva, M.J.: A Graph-Based Ranking Algorithm for Geo-referencing Documents. In: Proceedings of ICDM-05, the 5th IEEE International Conference on Data Mining, Texas, USA (2005)
6. Sang, T.K., F., E., De Meulder, F.: Introduction to the CoNLL-2003 shared task: Language-Independent Named Entity Recognition. In Daelemans, W., Osborne, M., eds.: Proceedings of CoNLL-2003, the 7th Conference on Natural Language Learning, Edmonton, Canada (2003) 142–147
7. Martins, B., Silva, M.J.: Challenges and Resources for Evaluating Geographical IR. In: Proceedings of GIR'05, the 2nd Workshop on Geographic Information Retrieval at CIKM 2005, Bremen, Germany (2005)
8. Martins, B., Silva, M.J.: Recognizing and Disambiguating Geographical References in Web Pages. (To Appear)
9. Martins, B., Silva, M.J., Andrade, L.: Indexing and Ranking in Geo-IR Systems. In: Proceedings of GIR'05, the 2nd Workshop on Geographic Information Retrieval at CIKM 2005, Bremen, Germany (2005)
10. Cardoso, N., Andrade, L., Simões, A., Silva, M.J.: The XLDB Group participation at CLEF 2005 ad hoc task. In Peters, C., ed.: Working Notes for the CLEF 2005 Workshop, Wien, Austria (2005)
11. Kohler, J.W.: Analysing Search Engine Queries for the Use of Geographic Terms. Master's thesis, University of Sheffield (2003)
12. Martins, B., Silva, M.J.: A Statistical Study of the WPT 03 Corpus. Technical Report DI/FCUL TR-04-1, Departamento de Informática da Faculdade de Ciências da Universidade de Lisboa (2004)
13. Getty Thesaurus of Geographic Names (TGN): (http://www.getty.edu/research/conducting_research/vocabularies/tgn/)

Portuguese at CLEF 2005

Diana Santos and Nuno Cardoso

Linguateca, Oslo node, SINTEF ICT, Norway
Linguateca, Lisbon node, DI-FCUL, Portugal
diana.santos@sintef.no, ncardoso@xldb.di.fc.ul.pt

Abstract. In this paper, we comment on the addition of Portuguese to three new tracks in CLEF 2005, namely WebCLEF, GeoCLEF and ImageCLEF, and discuss differences and new features in the adhoc IR and the QA tracks, presenting a new Brazilian collection.

1 Introduction

In order to evaluate cross-language retrieval, the obvious venue is CLEF. However, to add one more language (and/or culture) to a system or evaluation framework is not just to hire a translator and have the job done. This is one of the reasons why Linguateca has taken on the role of organising evaluation contests for systems dealing with Portuguese [1]. Another reason is that to have Portuguese as one of the languages which systems must process, query and/or retrieve within CLEF is undoubtedly beneficial to the processing of the Portuguese language in general. [2].

Our experience at CLEF 2005 reinforced what will be a recurrent idea through this paper: you have to know a language and culture well in order to organise meaningfully evaluation campaigns which include it. Just performing translation of query formulations created in another language, no matter how good, is never enough.

2 Reflections on Adding Portuguese to the CLEF Tasks

2.1 WebCLEF

WebCLEF is a striking example of where knowing the material well would be an advantage. The track could have been significantly improved if people with a working knowledge of each language (and its respective Web [3]) had been involved. The Portuguese collection included in the EuroGOV collection [4] is quite weak. Judging from the Portuguese Web crawls made by tumba! (www.tumba.pt), a Portuguese web search engine [5], we estimated that half of present-day government hosts are absent from the EuroGOV .pt set. In addition, over 70% of the crawl contained webpages from a single site (www.portaldocidadao.pt), just a hub of links to .gov.pt pages. Such an unbalanced collection made it quite difficult to come up with interesting topics that could reflect realistic scenarios of (crosslanguage or other) search in official pages.

C. Peters et al. (Eds.): CLEF 2005, LNCS 4022, pp. 1007 – 1010, 2006.

2.2 GeoCLEF

Although our participation in GeoCLEF was limited to the translation of topics (and geographical relations), we feel that our attempt to add Portuguese to this track succeeded in pointing out a few serious weaknesses in it. This mainly concerned making sense of the geographical relations. If the "relations" convey meaning there are different implications for translation than if they simply indicate prepositions. However, we could not see a way to express the distinction between "in the south of" and "south of", in the sense of a subpart of a larger region versus adjacency or simply relative location. Conversely, which fine distinctions hinged upon "in or around" versus "in and around"? In an nutshell, a clear semantics for geotopics was lacking and, thus, translation was obviously hampered. We decided to do a literal translation in most cases, but were far from happy with the resulting "Portuguese" topics.

The lack of a precise semantics for geotopics also caused doubts about scope vs content. For example, a source topic requiring documents about "Amnesty International reports on human rights in Latin America", was converted to: concept: Amnesty International Human Rights Reports, spatial relation: "in", location: "Latin America", which is altogether a different question. Of course, one may claim that the original topics were only a source of inspiration to create new geotopics, but the original user need (reports about human rights violations in Latin America) seems to make considerably more sense than the quest for arbitrary AI reports that happen to be (published?, refereed? criticized?) in Latin America.

2.3 ImageCLEF

Our task at ImageCLEF was to translate English captions into Portuguese, or provide a satisfactory description of the images in Portuguese. These are two different tasks, since what people see – and consequently take pictures of, and then describe in their own language – is extremely conditioned by culture. Most images are not self-explanatory and translation will not help if you do not know the subject, as was obvious for pictures like "golfer putting on green" or "colour pictures of woodland scenes around St Andrews". Likewise, due to the different meanings of words employed in different languages – different languages cut differently the semantic pie [8] – "people gathered at bandstand" could cover both musical events or people just gathered to take a photo, a vagueness which could not be preserved in Portuguese.

It was also hard to understand the user model of ImageCLEF: specialised librarians of St Andrews or (which) man in the street? Which makes more sense, "dog in sitting position", or "Timmy, summer holidays, 1990"? And were we justified in (inadvertently) discarding, or conveying, possibly unique presuppositions about royal visits to Scotland and monuments to Robert Burns? It obviously depends on our users.

The most interesting reflection posed by our participation in the ImageCLEF and GeoCLEF exercises is what we call the **organiser's paradox**. Considering state of the art CLIR systems, which use machine translation and bag-of-words approaches, the more idiomatic translation we provide, the more we harm recall, since the more literal the translation, the easier the system finds the relevant target information. The more natural a translation into a new language, the more understandable it is for a human but the less easy for a CLIR system (at least existing ones) to get sensible answers.

2.4 AdHoc CLEF

Given the addition of new languages with newer collections, topics for this year's adhoc track had by necessity to be more restrictive, since they would have to feature hits both in 1994-1995 and 2002 news documents. This implied, for example, that once-only events could not be selected.

This year a new Portuguese collection was added, containing the Brazilian newspaper Folha de São Paulo for 1994-1995[1]. As in 2004, we phrased some topics in the Brazilian variant of Portuguese as well as that of Portugal, in order to create a competition as variant-neutral as possible and attract broader participation [2]. We selected the topics to be conveyed in each variant randomly. The table shows how both varieties contributed in the Portuguese document pool and in the final results.

Candidates in Folha	Relevant in Folha	Candidates in Público	Relevant in Público
8213	1,035	12,326	1,869

2.5 QA@CLEF

Compared with last year's track, the changes in QA@CLEF were few [7], which may either denote that a stable setup has been found, or that the large number of languages involved (nine) actually brings some inertia and prevents change. In any case, we would like to discuss two changes in this track: (a) the increase in the amount of definition questions; and (b) the introduction of temporally restricted questions.

Definitions were unchanged from last year, although we had advocated their exclusion in [2]. There are no objective guidelines to evaluate answers of this sort of question and the process of trying to judge them consistently raised some interesting questions. For definition questions about people, we assigned a number of information pieces, and evaluated answers as incomplete ("X") if they included some of these pieces but not all. For example, if the expected correct answer was "Minister of Education of Nigeria", any of the three items (Minister, Education, Nigeria) alone would gain the system an "X". The justification for this procedure is that there could be contexts where just one of the items would satisfy the user. However, this made it no longer possible to guarantee perfect overlap (or perfect corrections given the collections) with the golden resource, since the right answers (items) could be scattered over different documents. In fact a system could get an "X", while nil stood in the golden collection, since there was no document that provided a full answer.

The temporally restricted questions (T questions) lacked a distinction between meta temporal restriction (like "temporal location" as in geoCLEF) and factual temporal restriction (inside the text), which allowed systems to answer them with no special provision. On the other hand, questions involving anaphoric reference to time, like "Which was the largest Italian party? meaning "was but no longer is" not classified as "T", were not considered temporally dependent, even though they are.

From our experience as organizers and evaluators of QA systems, we believe a real assessment of the difficulty of the questions set should be attempted. Although the decision not to provide easily identifiable nil questions was a real improvement this

[1] See the Portuguese CLEF site at http://www.linguateca.pt/CLEF/

year, we were still forced to reassess our golden answer set for three different questions for which it had been assumed that there were no answers in the collection, and for which different systems with different strategies were able to actually find a satisfactory answer. Some criteria for ranking QA pairs according to difficulty could be: (a) literal answers, (b) answers in the same sentence (or clause) but with a wording different from the question, (c) answers in separate sentences, (d) answers requiring some reasoning from a human (although not necessarily from a system).

We also suggest that more helpful than right and wrong would be to classify answers to questions as rubbish, uninformative (empty), and dangerous, as we did in [7], providing a more pragmatic view of evaluation. We also suggest that human evaluation should assess things like the following: Is the answer nonsensical so that any user can discover this at once by consulting the alleged justifying passage? Is the answer incomplete but useful? Is the answer complete and right but not supported? Is the answer wrong but (at least apparently) supported? Is the answer informative enough to lead to follow-up or reformulation questions from an interested user?

Finally, if the QA track is to develop into something that really evaluates useful systems for real users, we believe that systems must provide justification passages, in addition to the short answer, instead of just providing the whole document id.

Acknowledgements. We thank Público and Folha de São Paulo for allowing us to use their material, and respectively José Vítor Malheiros and Carlos Henrique Kauffmann for making this practically possible. We acknowledge grant POSI/PLP/43931/2001 from the Portuguese Fundação para a Ciência e Tecnologia, co-financed by POSI, and are grateful to our colleagues at Linguateca who helped with the organization and evaluation in CLEF 2005.

References

1. Santos, D. (ed.): Avaliação conjunta: un novo paradigma no processamento computacional da língua portuguesa, in print.
2. Santos, D., Rocha, P.: The Key to the First CLEF with Portuguese: Topics, Questions and Answers in CHAVE. In: C. Peters et al. (eds.) Multilingual Informa-tion Access for Text, Speech and Images. Vol. ???? LNCS, Springer (2005), 821-832.
3. Gomes, D., Silva, M.J.: Characterizing a National Community Web. ACM Transactions on Internet technology. Vol. 5(3), 2005, ACM Press, 508-531.
4. Sigurbjornsson et al.: EuroGOV: Engineering a Multilingual Web Corpus. This volume.
5. Silva, M.J.: The Case for a Portuguese Web Search Engine. Proceedings of the IADIS International Conference WWW/Internet 2003, 411-418.
6. Santos, D.: Translation-based Corpus Studies: Contrasting Portuguese and English Tense and Aspect Systems (2004). Amsterdam/NewYork, Rodopi.
7. Vallin, A. et al.: Overview of the CLEF 2005 Multilingual Question Answering Track. This volume.

Author Index

Vol. 4190: R. Larsen, M. Nielsen, J. Sporring (Eds.), Medical Image Computing and Computer-Assisted Intervention – MICCAI 2006, Part I. XXXVVIII, 949 pages. 2006.

Vol. 4189: D. Gollmann, J. Meier, A. Sabelfeld (Eds.), Computer Security – ESORICS 2006. XI, 548 pages. 2006.

Vol. 4188: P. Sojka, I. Kopeček, K. Pala (Eds.), Text, Speech and Dialogue. XIV, 721 pages. 2006. (Sublibrary LNAI).

Vol. 4187: J.J. Alferes, J. Bailey, W. May, U. Schwertel (Eds.), Principles and Practice of Semantic Web Reasoning. XI, 277 pages. 2006.

Vol. 4186: C. Jesshope, C. Egan (Eds.), Advances in Computer Systems Architecture. XIV, 605 pages. 2006.

Vol. 4185: R. Mizoguchi, Z. Shi, F. Giunchiglia (Eds.), The Semantic Web – ASWC 2006. XX, 778 pages. 2006.

Vol. 4184: M. Bravetti, M. Núñez, G. Zavattaro (Eds.), Web Services and Formal Methods. X, 289 pages. 2006.

Vol. 4183: J. Euzenat, J. Domingue (Eds.), Artificial Intelligence: Methodology, Systems, and Applications. XIII, 291 pages. 2006. (Sublibrary LNAI).

Vol. 4182: H.T. Ng, M.-K. Leong, M.-Y. Kan, D. Ji (Eds.), Information Retrieval Technology. XVI, 684 pages. 2006.

Vol. 4180: M. Kohlhase, OMDoc – An Open Markup Format for Mathematical Documents [version 1.2]. XIX, 428 pages. 2006. (Sublibrary LNAI).

Vol. 4179: J. Blanc-Talon, W. Philips, D. Popescu, P. Scheunders (Eds.), Advanced Concepts for Intelligent Vision Systems. XXIV, 1224 pages. 2006.

Vol. 4178: A. Corradini, H. Ehrig, U. Montanari, L. Ribeiro, G. Rozenberg (Eds.), Graph Transformations. XII, 473 pages. 2006.

Vol. 4177: R. Marín, E. Onaindía, A. Bugarín, J. Santos (Eds.), Current Topics in Aritficial Intelligence. XIII, 621 pages. 2006. (Sublibrary LNAI).

Vol. 4176: S.K. Katsikas, J. Lopez, M. Backes, S. Gritzalis, B. Preneel (Eds.), Information Security. XIV, 548 pages. 2006.

Vol. 4175: P. Bücher, B.M.E. Moret (Eds.), Algorithms in Bioinformatics. XII, 402 pages. 2006. (Sublibrary LNBI).

Vol. 4174: K. Franke, K.-R. Müller, B. Nickolay, R. Schäfer (Eds.), Pattern Recognition. XX, 773 pages. 2006.

Vol. 4173: S. El Yacoubi, B. Chopard, S. Bandini (Eds.), Cellular Automata. XV, 734 pages. 2006.

Vol. 4172: J. Gonzalo, C. Thanos, M. F. Verdejo, R.C. Carrasco (Eds.), Research and Advanced Technology for Digital Libraries. XVII, 569 pages. 2006.

Vol. 4169: H.L. Bodlaender, M.A. Langston (Eds.), Parameterized and Exact Computation. XI, 279 pages. 2006.

Vol. 4168: Y. Azar, T. Erlebach (Eds.), Algorithms – ESA 2006. XVIII, 843 pages. 2006.

Vol. 4167: S. Dolev (Ed.), Distributed Computing. XV, 576 pages. 2006.

Vol. 4166: J. Górski (Ed.), Computer Safety, Reliability, and Security. XIV, 440 pages. 2006.

Vol. 4165: W. Jonker, M. Petković (Eds.), Secure, Data Management. X, 185 pages. 2006.

Vol. 4163: H. Bersini, J. Carneiro (Eds.), Artificial Immune Systems. XII, 460 pages. 2006.

Vol. 4162: R. Královič, P. Urzyczyn (Eds.), Mathematical Foundations of Computer Science 2006. XV, 814 pages. 2006.

Vol. 4161: R. Harper, M. Rauterberg, M. Combetto (Eds.), Entertainment Computing - ICEC 2006. XXVII, 417 pages. 2006.

Vol. 4160: M. Fisher, W.v.d. Hoek, B. Konev, A. Lisitsa (Eds.), Logics in Artificial Intelligence. XII, 516 pages. 2006. (Sublibrary LNAI).

Vol. 4159: J. Ma, H. Jin, L.T. Yang, J.J.-P. Tsai (Eds.), Ubiquitous Intelligence and Computing. XXII, 1190 pages. 2006.

Vol. 4158: L.T. Yang, H. Jin, J. Ma, T. Ungerer (Eds.), Autonomic and Trusted Computing. XIV, 613 pages. 2006.

Vol. 4156: S. Amer-Yahia, Z. Bellahsène, E. Hunt, R. Unland, J.X. Yu (Eds.), Database and XML Technologies. IX, 123 pages. 2006.

Vol. 4155: O. Stock, M. Schaerf (Eds.), Reasoning, Action and Interaction in AI Theories and Systems. XVIII, 343 pages. 2006. (Sublibrary LNAI).

Vol. 4154: Y.A. Dimitriadis, I. Zigurs, E. Gómez-Sánchez (Eds.), Groupware: Design, Implementation, and Use. XIV, 438 pages. 2006.

Vol. 4153: N. Zheng, X. Jiang, X. Lan (Eds.), Advances in Machine Vision, Image Processing, and Pattern Analysis. XIII, 506 pages. 2006.

Vol. 4152: Y. Manolopoulos, J. Pokorný, T. Sellis (Eds.), Advances in Databases and Information Systems. XV, 448 pages. 2006.

Vol. 4151: A. Iglesias, N. Takayama (Eds.), Mathematical Software - ICMS 2006. XVII, 452 pages. 2006.

Vol. 4150: M. Dorigo, L.M. Gambardella, M. Birattari, A. Martinoli, R. Poli, T. Stützle (Eds.), Ant Colony Optimization and Swarm Intelligence. XVI, 526 pages. 2006.

Vol. 4149: M. Klusch, M. Rovatsos, T.R. Payne (Eds.), Cooperative Information Agents X. XII, 477 pages. 2006. (Sublibrary LNAI).

Vol. 4148: J. Vounckx, N. Azemard, P. Maurine (Eds.), Integrated Circuit and System Design. XVI, 677 pages. 2006.

Vol. 4147: M. Broy, I.H. Krüger, M. Meisinger (Eds.), Automotive Software – Connected Services in Mobile Networks. XIV, 155 pages. 2006.

Vol. 4146: J.C. Rajapakse, L. Wong, R. Acharya (Eds.), Pattern Recognition in Bioinformatics. XIV, 186 pages. 2006. (Sublibrary LNBI).

Vol. 4145: L. Moreau, I. Foster (Eds.), Provenance and Annotation of Data and Processes. XI, 288 pages. 2006.

Vol. 4144: T. Ball, R.B. Jones (Eds.), Computer Aided Verification. XV, 564 pages. 2006.

Lecture Notes in Computer Science

For information about Vols. 1–4143

please contact your bookseller or Springer

Vol. 4248: S. Staab, V. Svátek (Eds.), Engineering Knowledge in the Age of the Semantic Web. XIV, 400 pages. 2006. (Sublibrary LNAI).

Vol. 4241: R. Beichel, M. Sonka (Eds.), Computer Vision Approaches to Medical Image Analysis. XI, 262 pages. 2006.

Vol. 4239: H.Y. Youn, M. Kim, H. Morikawa (Eds.), Ubiquitous Computing systems. XVI, 548 pages. 2006.

Vol. 4238: Y.-T. Kim, M. Takano (Eds.), Management of Convergence Networks and Services. XVIII, 605 pages. 2006.

Vol. 4229: E. Najm, J.F. Pradat-Peyre, V.V. Donzeau-Gouge (Eds.), Formal Techniques for Networked and Distributed Systems - FORTE 2006. X, 486 pages. 2006.

Vol. 4228: D.E. Lightfoot, C.A. Szyperski (Eds.), Modular Programming Languages. X, 415 pages. 2006.

Vol. 4227: W. Nejdl, K. Tochtermann (Eds.), Innovative Approaches for Learning and Knowledge Sharing. XVII, 721 pages. 2006.

Vol. 4224: E. Corchado, H. Yin, V. Botti, C. Fyfe (Eds.), Intelligent Data Engineering and Automated Learning – IDEAL 2006. XXVII, 1447 pages. 2006.

Vol. 4223: L. Wang, L. Jiao, G. Shi, X. Li, J. Liu (Eds.), Fuzzy Systems and Knowledge Discovery. XXVIII, 1335 pages. 2006. (Sublibrary LNAI).

Vol. 4222: L. Jiao, L. Wang, X. Gao, J. Liu, F. Wu (Eds.), Advances in Natural Computation, Part II. XLII, 998 pages. 2006.

Vol. 4221: L. Jiao, L. Wang, X. Gao, J. Liu, F. Wu (Eds.), Advances in Natural Computation, Part I. XLI, 992 pages. 2006.

Vol. 4219: D. Zamboni, C. Kruegel (Eds.), Recent Advances in Intrusion Detection. XII, 331 pages. 2006.

Vol. 4217: P. Cuenca, L. Orozco-Barbosa (Eds.), Personal Wireless Communications. XV, 532 pages. 2006.

Vol. 4216: M.R. Berthold, R. Glen, I. Fischer (Eds.), Computational Life Sciences II. XIII, 269 pages. 2006. (Sublibrary LNBI).

Vol. 4213: J. Fürnkranz, T. Scheffer, M. Spiliopoulou (Eds.), Knowledge Discovery in Databases: PKDD 2006. XXII, 660 pages. 2006. (Sublibrary LNAI).

Vol. 4212: J. Fürnkranz, T. Scheffer, M. Spiliopoulou (Eds.), Machine Learning: ECML 2006. XXIII, 851 pages. 2006. (Sublibrary LNAI).

Vol. 4211: P. Vogt, Y. Sugita, E. Tuci, C. Nehaniv (Eds.), Symbol Grounding and Beyond. VIII, 237 pages. 2006. (Sublibrary LNAI).

Vol. 4209: F. Crestani, P. Ferragina, M. Sanderson (Eds.), String Processing and Information Retrieval. XIV, 367 pages. 2006.

Vol. 4208: M. Gerndt, D. Kranzlmüller (Eds.), High Performance Computing and Communications. XXII, 938 pages. 2006.

Vol. 4207: Z. Ésik (Ed.), Computer Science Logic. XII, 627 pages. 2006.

Vol. 4206: P. Dourish, A. Friday (Eds.), UbiComp 2006: Ubiquitous Computing. XIX, 526 pages. 2006.

Vol. 4205: G. Bourque, N. El-Mabrouk (Eds.), Comparative Genomics. X, 231 pages. 2006. (Sublibrary LNBI).

Vol. 4204: F. Benhamou (Ed.), Principles and Practice of Constraint Programming - CP 2006. XVIII, 774 pages. 2006.

Vol. 4203: F. Esposito, Z.W. Raś, D. Malerba, G. Semeraro (Eds.), Foundations of Intelligent Systems. XVIII, 767 pages. 2006. (Sublibrary LNAI).

Vol. 4202: E. Asarin, P. Bouyer (Eds.), Formal Modeling and Analysis of Timed Systems. XI, 369 pages. 2006.

Vol. 4201: Y. Sakakibara, S. Kobayashi, K. Sato, T. Nishino, E. Tomita (Eds.), Grammatical Inference: Algorithms and Applications. XII, 359 pages. 2006. (Sublibrary LNAI).

Vol. 4199: O. Nierstrasz, J. Whittle, D. Harel, G. Reggio (Eds.), Model Driven Engineering Languages and Systems. XVI, 798 pages. 2006.

Vol. 4197: M. Raubal, H.J. Miller, A.U. Frank, M.F. Goodchild (Eds.), Geographic, Information Science. XIII, 419 pages. 2006.

Vol. 4196: K. Fischer, I.J. Timm, E. André, N. Zhong (Eds.), Multiagent System Technologies. X, 185 pages. 2006. (Sublibrary LNAI).

Vol. 4195: D. Gaiti, G. Pujolle, E. Al-Shaer, K. Calvert, S. Dobson, G. Leduc, O. Martikainen (Eds.), Autonomic Networking. IX, 316 pages. 2006.

Vol. 4194: V.G. Ganzha, E.W. Mayr, E.V. Vorozhtsov (Eds.), Computer Algebra in Scientific Computing. XI, 313 pages. 2006.

Vol. 4193: T.P. Runarsson, H.-G. Beyer, E. Burke, J.J. Merelo-Guervós, L. D. Whitley, X. Yao (Eds.), Parallel Problem Solving from Nature - PPSN IX. XIX, 1061 pages. 2006.

Vol. 4192: B. Mohr, J.L. Träff, J. Worringen, J. Dongarra (Eds.), Recent Advances in Parallel Virtual Machine and Message Passing Interface. XVI, 414 pages. 2006.

Vol. 4191: R. Larsen, M. Nielsen, J. Sporring (Eds.), Medical Image Computing and Computer-Assisted Intervention – MICCAI 2006, Part II. XXXVIII, 981 pages. 2006.